Basic Federal Income Taxation of Individuals

Basic Federal Income Taxation of Individuals
Second Revised Edition

Richard A. Westin
Beverly Moran

Published by:

Vandeplas Publishing, LLC – March 2020

801 International Parkway, 5th Floor
Lake Mary, FL. 32746
USA

www.vandeplaspublishing.com

978-1-60042-508-0

BASIC FEDERAL INCOME TAXATION OF INDIVIDUALS

Second Revised Edition

Richard A. Westin
Beverly Moran

Table of Contents

CHAPTER 11 - TAX DEFERRED TRANSACTIONS

CHAPTER 12 - IDENTIFICATION OF THE PROPER TAXPAYER

CHAPTER 1 - INTRODUCTION AND SOME KEY CONCEPTS

A. INTRODUCTION

The subject of the course you are about to embark on is the Federal Income Taxation of individuals, meaning human beings. There will be a glimpse at the taxation of partnerships, trusts and corporations, largely for the purpose of enhancing your understanding of how individuals are taxed when they own interests in such entities. The Federal Income Tax on individuals provides the great preponderance of the federal government's revenues. The other primary sources of government revenue, aside from borrowing money and Social Security taxes, are corporate income taxes, transfer taxes imposed on gifts and the estates of decedents, and so-called excise taxes. The latter are usually in the nature of sales taxes on particular items, such as gasoline and diesel fuel, and some are just penalties under a gentler name.

The course is limited to taxation of U.S. citizens who reside in the United States, subject to some sideways glances at the implications of departing the United States or coming to it as an alien. This book is traditional in nature, and has many of the usual landmark cases on the subject. It contains numerous study problems and requires selected readings of the Internal Revenue Code and the Treasury Regulations.

B. ECONOMIC AND FISCAL IMPORTANCE OF THE FEDERAL INCOME TAX

1. Revenue

Among the several purposes served by the Federal Income Tax, the collection of revenue predominates. That has presumably been true from the earliest times; we know income taxes have been around since at least Socrates' days.[1]

1 See Plato's Republic (I.A. Richards ed., Cambridge Univ. Press 1966) at p. 26 (Thrasymachus's diatribe about the benefits of being unjust, including that, "The just man comes out worst every time in his relations with the unjust. . . . Take their doings with the government, the income tax, say. Which of them gets off best?")

You may be interested to know what revenues are produced by the Federal Income Taxes you are about to study. The Treasury reported $3.3 trillion in collections for 2016 made up of $1.79 trillion in personal income taxes and $1.1 trillion in employment taxes (primarily for Social Security). In contrast, the Treasury only raised $345.6 billion in corporate taxes, $75.8 billion in excise taxes and $22.3 billion from the Gift and Estate tax.[2]

Historically, the income tax paid by individuals is a large, but stable, fraction of gross domestic product (GDP). The Personal Income Tax and Employment Taxes (namely Social Security, Medicare and the tiny Federal Unemployment Tax) are the biggest and fastest-growing items, with the income tax on corporations trailing well behind. The U.S. does not have a national sales tax or value-added tax, although many states have sales taxes as well as income or wealth taxes, and state or local income taxes on individuals and corporations. State Income Taxes often conform rather closely to the Federal Income Tax but with lower rates (typically, 1%-10%). State and local revenues traditionally constitute about 10% of GDP.[3]

Federal Income Taxes extract huge amounts from the fruits of production in the private sector of the economy and put them at the disposal of the public sector, through the federal government. Any significant reduction in revenues from the income tax -- whether from rate changes or changes in the "tax base" -- would necessitate either a radical change in expenditures by the federal government or substantial deficit financing; no other existing federal tax can pick up much of the slack. A significant increase in income tax revenues, from rate changes or other amendments to the Internal Revenue Code, would produce a surplus, or would permit drastic reduction in other taxes and revenue sources, or a large increase in expenditures, or a reduction of the huge (over $21 trillion) federal debt.

2. Taxpayers[4]

The Federal Income Tax applies each year to all residents and citizens of the United States, and to some foreign persons as well. Not everyone files a return, however, because one need only file a return if one has more than a threshold amount of income. In 2017, for example, 138.9 million *individual* returns were filed, many of which were filed by married people who file jointly on one return, and many more persons were claimed as dependents. Corporations and some other business entities (which are legal "persons") are separate taxpayers, much like individuals.[5]

---

2 https://www.irs.gov/statistics/soi-tax-stats-gross-collections-by-type-of-tax-irs-data-book-table-6

3 www.irs.gov/uac/soi-tax-stats-gross-collections-by-type-of-tax-irs-data-book-table-6 Gross collections by type of tax 1960-2016.

4 This discussion is concerned only with those who appear to be actual taxpayers. Who actually bears the cost of an income tax is another -- and very important -- inquiry.

5 www.treasury.gov/tigta/auditreports/2018reports/201840012fr.pdf

It used to be that most of the revenue produced by the Federal Income Tax on individuals derived from taxpayers whose incomes were taxed at relatively low rates. Consequently, revenues rose and fell most when changes were made in the rates, exemptions, deductions or credits applicable to the tens of millions of taxpayers in the middle and lower income groups; much less dramatic were the revenue increases or decreases that could be affected by even the most drastic shifts in rates or other rules applicable to taxpayers with particularly high yearly incomes—there were simply too few of them. That has changed, partly because of the increasing concentration of wealth in the United States and partly because Congress has succeeded in wiping a great number of low income taxpayers off the federal income tax rolls. According to the Tax Foundation, in 2014 the bottom 50 percent of taxpayers (those with AGIs below $38,173) earned 11.27 percent of total AGI and paid approximately 2.75 percent or $38 billion in taxes. In contrast, the top 1 percent of all taxpayers (taxpayers with AGIs of $465,626 and above) earned 20.58 percent of all AGI in 2014, but paid 39.48 percent of all federal income taxes. In 2014, the top 1 percent of taxpayers accounted for more income taxes paid than the bottom 90 percent. The top 1 percent of taxpayers paid $543 billion, or 39.48 percent of all income taxes, while the bottom 90 percent paid $400 billion, or 29.12 percent of all income taxes.[6] On the other hand, the distribution of wealth in the United States is skewed in favor of high income tax earners compared to other industrialized countries, so it follows that their contribution to tax revenues would also be skewed.[7]

3. Economic, Social and Fiscal Ramifications

As well as raising revenue to finance government expenditures, the income tax serves the purposes of allocating resources, inducing or discouraging some kinds of economic and social behavior, redistributing wealth, helping to stimulate or stabilize economic growth, helping to solve specific problems (such as pollution and urban deterioration), and shaping or preserving the fundamental institutions and influences that a free market economy presupposes.

C. WHERE IS "THE TAX LAW"?

The Federal Income Tax is a creature of statute, which is found in the Internal Revenue Code, 26 U.S.C.A. §§ 1-9042.[8] The present income tax statute is the lineal descendant of the Income

6 https://taxfoundation.org/summary-latest-federal-income-tax-data-2016-update/; See also, https://www.cbo.gov/publication/53597

7 http://fortune.com/2015/09/30/america-wealth-inequality/

8 Section numbers of the Internal Revenue Code, cited in this book, correspond to sections of Title 26 U.S.C.A. Hereafter all references to tax law section numbers are made to the Internal Revenue Code of 1986, as amended, unless otherwise

Tax Act, effective as of March 1, 1913. A previous personal income tax was enacted in 1894, but the Supreme Court struck it down as violating the rule of apportionment[9], which requires that direct taxes must be apportioned among the States in proportion to population.[10] The 1913 Act followed. It depended on approval of the Sixteenth Amendment, which obliterated the apportionment requirement in February of 1913 so as to permit taxes on such items as rent, dividends and interest.

The fundamental sources of authority a person has when researching Federal Income Taxes are the following:

The Internal Revenue Code of 1986 ("the I.R.C."), as amended. This is the same as Title 26 of the United States Code, and contains the Income Tax, the Estate and Gift Tax and some other taxes. It is the primary authority and contains almost all the tax laws of the United States. The job of the courts is to interpret and apply the Internal Revenue Code and to make sure it does not breach the Constitution, using the standard tools of statutory construction. The amount of federal common law in this area is relatively small. The most persuasive interpretative materials are contemporaneous legislative histories in the form of Congressional Reports. These come from the House Committee on Ways and Means, which is the first congressional body to consider tax law changes. The House's authority flows from Article I, §7, the Origination Clause, requiring revenue bills to originate in the (populist) House of Representatives. The next set of interpretative materials will be from the Senate Finance Committee, which considers bills coming from the House, and finally, from the Joint Committee of the House and Senate that sits to reconcile the two bills. It is almost invariably the case that House and Senate bills differ at least slightly, so a reconciliation of the bills is usually essential. After the reconciliation process, Congress votes on the reconciled, final bill. There may also be floor debates on parts of tax bills, but they are fairly uncommon. It used to be that tax bills were enacted after hearings were conducted on the proposed legislation. That is much less the case today. In *Chevron USA, Inc. v. Natural Resources Defense Council,*[11] the Supreme Court held that unambiguous language of a statute displaces an inconsistent legislative intent, saying that one should analyze legislative history only if there is ambiguity in the statute.[12] This is an important restriction.

You will notice references in this book to earlier Internal Revenue Codes, such as the 1954 and 1939 versions. These are really just predecessors of the present (1986) Code, although the

---

indicated. Some Federal Income Tax provisions never make it into the Code, often because they are short-lived or are narrow special interest legislation.

9 Pollack v. Farmers' Loan & Trust Co, 157 U.S. 429, modified on rehearing, 158 U.S. 601 (1895).

10 Article I, §9, clause 4. See Chapter 2.

11 467 U.S. 837 (1984).

12 See also, Nationsbank of North Carolina, N.A. v. Variable Life Insurance Co., 513 U.S. 251 (1995), affirming the *Chevron* doctrine in a Federal Income Tax context.

numbering of the sections may change. Tax bills become law on being signed by the President, but the effective dates of different parts of a tax bill often vary greatly and are frequently retroactive. The internal revenue laws are administered by the Treasury Department.

Treasury Regulations. Treasury income tax regulations[13] are, needless to say, issued by the Department of the Treasury. They normally are ushered in only after an opportunity for public hearing and comments if the rule is "substantive", hence subject to the Administrative Procedures Act.[14] The general rule is that as long as a regulation is consistent with the Internal Revenue Code and is a reasonable interpretation of the will of Congress, or what a court imagines the will of Congress might have been, the regulation will stand. The authority for issuing the regulation may be a special grant under particular Code section, but more often is under the general grant under §7805 of the Code, which authorizes the issuance of "needful regulations." The people who draft regulations are often willing to discuss their interpretations by telephone.

In general, regulations are the second most important authority. Interpretative income tax regulations are typically cited by the number "1", followed by a decimal point, followed by the Internal Revenue Code section they interpret. An example of a citation is Reg. §1.162, which refers to the regulations interpreting §162, which governs deductions for business expenses. The regulations fall into several categories:

Procedural Regulations, which are generally preceded by the numbers "301," are of minor importance in this course; the interpretative regulations, which are most of what we will look at, perform the role of explaining and construing the Internal Revenue Code, sometimes with examples, and are rarely invalidated by the courts. Lastly, there are "legislative regulations," which are issued pursuant to broad delegations of Congressional authority to the Treasury Department and IRS and which are virtually unassailable, having the force of law. Treasury regulations appear in Title 26 of the Code of Federal Regulations. The courts generally hold the IRS to valid interpretative regulations[15], but allow them to be revoked retroactively.[16]

Revenue Rulings, Revenue Procedures and Announcements. These are interpretative pronouncements by the Internal Revenue Service (which is itself a division of the Department of the Treasury). They are entitled to only modest respect, and are often compared to nothing more than a lawyer's opinion. Typically, the IRS will issue Revenue Rulings, and Announcements to

13 They are formally known as the Treasury Administration and Procedure Regulations.

14 5 U.S.C. §§ 553(b), (c), (e). Notice and hearing is evidently not required for interpretive regulations, statements of policy, or internal rules. Nevertheless, the Treasury generally does use a notice and hearing procedure more or less whenever possible. See 26 C.F.R. 601 at §601.601(c). See, e.g., Wing v. Commissioner, 81 T.C. 17 (1983).

15 See M. Saltzman, IRS PRACTICE AND PROCEDURE ¶3.02[4][b] (1981).

16 Dixon v. United States, 381 U.S. 68 (1965), (Retroactivity to correct mistake in regulation permissible, even if taxpayer detrimentally relied).

cover important situations while awaiting the completion of regulations. The Tax Court views them as no better than an attorney's opinion. Revenue Procedures are used to explain the processes by which taxpayers are to interact with the IRS. You will see the role of the Tax Court soon.

IRS Memoranda: Memoranda prepared by the Office of the Chief Counsel of the IRS are now available to the public. They include (1) replies to requests for legal advice from the Assistant Commissioner of the Internal Revenue Service, (2) Technical Memoranda (T.M.s) prepared by the Legislation and Regulation Division of the Office of Chief Counsel with respect to proposed Treasury decisions or regulations and (3) Actions on Decisions (A.O.D.s) prepared by the Tax Litigating Division of the Chief Counsel's Office when the IRS loses a tax case. Recently, Field Service Memoranda have also been made the subject of mandatory disclosure. These are IRS working documents that provide nonbinding advice, guidance and analysis to IRS personnel to develop issues or determine hazards of litigation. None of these are authorities, but they are of great practical interest to tax experts intent on understanding the government's thinking processes.

Private Letter Rulings. These are specially-tailored letters responding to inquiries by taxpayers relating to particular transactions. Technically, one is not allowed to cite them as authority, but they are important because they reveal what the government thinks. The party requesting the ruling must generally pay a hefty fee to the IRS in order to submit the request. The ruling is binding on the IRS with respect to the taxpayer in question only, and only as to the stated facts and issue(s) ruled upon. Treasury Department pronouncements relating to tax law, including Revenue Procedures, Revenue Rulings and Treasury Decisions are first published in periodic Internal Revenue Bulletins. The Internal Revenue Bulletins are trimmed and bound at the end of the year and reissued as the Cumulative Bulletin for the year, normally in two volumes. The Senate and House Committee reports relating to revenue bills are also generally reported in this publication. Private letter rulings are not published in the Cumulative Bulletin, but are available from commercial publishers and on LEXIS and Westlaw, among other sources.

Case Law Authority. This stands roughly on the same level as regulations in importance, but of course is determinative for the parties and authoritative within the usual doctrines of precedent and *res judicata*.

D. THE TAX BASE: TAXABLE INCOME

The materials you are about to delve into are loaded with buzzwords that are probably unfamiliar to most law students, even if they have prepared a few tax returns for themselves or their relatives. Here is a simplified expression of how one arrives at an individual's Federal Income Tax liability, which ultimately involves multiplying the resulting tax base by some rate or other. [17]

Determine the taxpayer's **gross income**[18] from all sources for the year. This generally consists of cash, the fair market value of property and the fair market value of services received. Fair market value means what a willing buyer would pay a willing seller, both being reasonably informed and neither being under duress. [19]

For a taxpayer with a manufacturing, merchandising or mining business, gross income means "total sales" (the total prices paid for the goods) less the "cost of goods sold," plus any other income from investments or other operations or sources. [20] Some things that otherwise would be in gross income are **excluded** from gross income, usually by a specific statement to that effect. [21]

Subtract **deductions**. Deductions fall into two groups:

Deductions that provide **"adjustments" to gross income**, which constitute a favored class of deductions that always operate to the taxpayer's benefit. These are generally granted for costs of producing income, and are taken "above the line" of "**adjusted gross income**" on the tax return form (Form 1040, reproduced at the end of the book). Subtracting them from gross income produces "adjusted gross income."

Itemized deductions. These are less favored deductions, generally given for reasons that do not depend on their necessity to earn income. They are only useful if they exceed a certain base amount. [22] These are subtracted from adjusted gross income.

You have now arrived at the key figure **"taxable income**," which is the **"tax base"** (generally, the focal point of this course). Now you multiply taxable income by the taxpayer's applicable **tax rate**. Section 1 of the Code provides for the tax rates applicable to individuals. This creates the tentative tax bill.

17 For a guide to tax terms, see R. Westin, WG&L TAX DICTIONARY (2018 ed.).

18 I.R.C. §61(a). Henceforth in this book, section references are to the Internal Revenue Code unless otherwise indicated.

19 Reg. §20.2031-1(b).

20 See Reg. §1.61-3(a).

21 See, e.g. §§ 101-140, or possibly in §§ 71-91. Chapter 4 of the book covers the primary exclusions.

22 See §§ 63, 170, 213. You do not need to read these sections yet.

Next, subtract any **tax credits** the taxpayer is entitled to. Pay the balance to the IRS An example of a tax credit is any withholding tax on wages that an employer took out of its employee's wages and paid to the IRS as required by law. These operate as a prepayment of the employee's Federal Income Tax liability. For example, if the employee earned $10,000 of wages this year and the employer took out $3,000 of federal income taxes from her paycheck and paid the $3,000 over to the IRS and paid her a net salary of $7,000, she would be entitled to a $3,000 credit against her tentative tax bill. Notice how a tax credit provides a dollar-for-dollar reduction in tax payable. In contrast, a deduction merely reduces taxable income and consequently reduces one's taxes by an amount equal to the deduction times the otherwise applicable tax rate (always less than 100%).

The determination of taxable income can be shown by a simple example:

To illustrate: Jones is a lawyer and has consistently had gross income of $80,000, and business expenses of $20,000. She is single, has made charitable contributions of $10,000, has paid real property tax on her home and State Income Taxes of $3,000 and has made interest payments of $5,000 on her home mortgage; the last three figures are her "itemized deductions." Her statement of taxable income will be: gross income $50,000, less business deductions of $20,000, yielding adjusted gross income $30,000. From that she subtracts itemized deductions of $18,000, which yields taxable income of $42,000. She then goes to § 1 of the Code and calculates her tentative tax bill, and then offsets it by whatever credits she may be entitled to.

In tabular form, Jones' computation of taxable income would appear roughly as follows:

Gross Income	$80,000
Less: Business Deductions	(20,000)
Adjusted Gross Income	60,000
Less: Personal Deductions	(18,000)
Taxable Income	$42,000

The back of this book contains a glossary of terms that you may find useful, along with copies of the most common tax forms, the first and foremost of which is form 1040, which you might want to look at soon.

E. ANNUAL TAX PERIODS AND METHODS OF ACCOUNTING

The Federal Income Tax system is based on an annual accounting of income, "voluntarily" reported on an annual tax return. Therefore, in order to determine the income to be included in the accounting for the year one must know the period which that year encompasses. The two taxable periods used most often are the calendar year and the fiscal year. A *calendar year* is one that ends on the last day of December. A *fiscal year* is one that ends on the last day of any month except December. For example, as July 1 taxable year is a fiscal year that begins on July 1 and ends June 30 of the next calendar year. The taxpayer usually has some choice whether to use a calendar or a fiscal year. Non-business taxpayers almost invariably report on a calendar year basis.[23]

In order to ascertain what income must be included within the taxpayer's accounting period, he must use an *accounting method.*[24] There is an entire chapter devoted to the topic; this is just a thumbnail sketch. If the material does not stick, do not worry. The two most used methods are the *cash receipts and disbursements method* and the *accrual method.* Simply stated, the cash receipts and disbursements method include all income as of the date *received* and all deductions as of the date expenditures are *made.* In contrast, the *accrual method* includes all income and expenses as of the date the *right* to receive or the *obligation* to pay is unconditionally fixed. Suppose A delivers merchandise to a buyer who accepts the merchandise on December 15, and on that same day agrees to pay for it on February 1, of the following year. If A is a calendar year taxpayer reporting on an accrual basis, the amount due for the merchandise is reportable income for the first year, because A's right to the money became fixed in the first year. If A were a cash method taxpayer, he would include the income in his return for the second year, when he actually receives the payment.

F. THE GRADUATED RATE STRUCTURE

Our tax system uses what has been termed a graduated rate structure. This means that as a taxable income rises, the rate of tax on the next increment of taxable income is increased. Over the years, tax rates on a taxpayer's last dollar of income, known as *marginal* tax rates, have fluctuated considerably. They topped out at 90% after World War II, but dropped to 70% in the Kennedy era and then to 28% during the Reagan era. Massive deficits during that era made tax increases imperative, hence the present 37% top rate.

The following piece is from *Taxes in Paradise* by Professor Haight.[25] His book posits a wise king -- Helvering I (named after an early Tax Commissioner) -- who rules over the island of Paradise. Paradise is in need of revenues, which requires Helvering to communicate regularly

23 See generally §441. The taxpayer may also have a short year, which may arise in the beginning or end of an accounting by an individual taxpayer or a taxable entity, such as a newly formed corporation.

24 See generally §446.

25 Richard L. Haight, TAXES IN PARADISE: DEVELOPING BASIC INCOME TAX CONCEPTS, Fred. B. Rothman & Co., Littleton, Colo. (1990). This excerpt is from pages 9-11 of this delightful little book.

with the drafter of a new tax law, Lady Wordsmith. The subject of this excerpt is the graduated income tax structure. For those of you who feel patronized by the material, take pity on the students in your class who have no exposure to taxation and finance beyond being retail consumers.

"*+MEMORANDUM FROM THE KING+*
TO: Lady Wordsmith, Royal Drafter
RE: The Tax Rate

In our previous discussion, we talked about a 10% rate. As you recall, it was my view that all of the citizens of Paradise would pay 10% of their annual income to the Government as their income tax. I still think this is a good idea, but, on reflection, it seems to be that with a 10% rate a taxpayer earning $100,000 might not have difficulty in paying a tax of $10,000, but a person who earns only $5,000 might find it a hardship to pay a tax of $500. While I believe the 10% rate is basically sound, can we do something for our poorer citizens?

+ Helvering I+

MEMORANDUM FROM THE ROYAL DRAFTER
TO: Helvering 1, King of Paradise
RE: The Tax Rate

Your concern for the poor of Paradise is one of the reasons you are most beloved by your people.

There are at least two ways in which we might handle this situation. One method would be to subject the poorer people to a lower rate, let's say 5%. Of course, we would have to define what a poor person is. Even if we could come up with a satisfactory definition, I have a feeling that the many people who do not qualify for the lower rate (the majority of Paradisians who are not poor) might complain if the tax were not applied equally to all the citizenry.

The better solution I believe is to apply the low 5% rate to the income everyone earns, up to a specified amount (let's say $5,000), and then apply the ten percent rate to all additional income earned during the year. In that way, all citizens will benefit from the low rate, and only those citizens who can afford it will be subjected to the high rate. Here is how this "graduated" tax rate would apply:

<u>*Example 1:*</u> *Mr. Smith has $4,000 of income during the year. He pays a tax of $200, computed as follows:*
$4,000 Income
<u>*x .05*</u>
$ 200 Tax Due

Example 2: *Ms. Jones has $6,000 of income during the year. She pays a tax of $350, computed as follows:*

Step One:

$5,000	*Income (up to $5K)*
x .05	*5% Tax Rate (on income up to $5K)*
$ 250	*Tax Due (on income up to $5K)*

Step Two:

$1,000	*Income (above $5K)*
x .10	*10% Tax Rate (on income above $5K)*
$ 100	*Tax Due (on income above $5K)*

Step Three:

$ 250	*Tax-Step One (on income up to $5K)*
100	*Tax-Step Two (on income above $5K)*
$ 350	*Total Tax Due*

From these examples, it can be seen that Mr. Smith with annual income of $4,000 pays $200 in tax, and Ms. Jones with annual income of $6,000 pays $350 in tax. Both are taxed at the same rate (5%) on their income up to $5,000. Only Ms. Jones, whose income exceeded $5,000, was taxed at the high rate (10%), and the high rate applied only to that portion of her income which was above $5,000.

MEMORANDUM FROM THE KING
TO: Lady Wordsmith, Royal Drafter
RE: The Tax Rate (Memo 2)

Your solution seems indeed workable. After looking at your examples, it occurred to me that we might use your "graduated" approach as a painless method of taxing some of our wealthier citizens at a higher rate. For example, we could subject annual income above $20,000 to a tax rate of 20%. That would have no effect on the Paradisians of modest means, and it would not be particularly burdensome on the wealthy because the tax exacted will still be a relatively small portion of their total income. Do you agree?"

* * *

Take a look at §1(a)-(d) in your Code volume to see how the United States resolved the question of the appropriate level of progressivity in the Federal Income Tax, at least for the time being.

In this graduated rate system only the increased amounts of income, not the total amount, are affected by the graduated rates. The average rate is equal to the amount of tax divided by the amount of taxed income. The fact that a person may have an income which would normally subject him to a 39.6% tax rate at the top level does not mean he is paying a tax equal to 39.6% of his income. Even if it is all *taxable* income, the *average* rate may be only about 20% on taxable income of $50,000 and 27% on taxable income of $100,000 because of the graduated nature of the tax rate structure.

In addition, because of exclusions, exemptions, and special taxing provisions and other items, many individuals with high incomes pay surprisingly low *effective tax* rates, meaning the rates applicable to practical economic income, as opposed to (legalistic) taxable income. To illustrate the point, the lower rates applied to capital gains and deductions for such things as percentage depletion of oil and gas production help explain how a taxpayer with a large economic income may in fact pay less actual tax than a taxpayer with a comparatively small taxable income. This anomaly has sparked many criticisms of the present system. As a result the Code includes a "minimum tax" on a base that starts with regular taxable income and then adds back a number of deductions, exclusions and so forth.[26] Chapter 13 takes up the Alternative Minimum Tax.

From time to time other methods or rate schedules for income taxation are discussed. One favorite proposal is a *proportional* tax which would tax everyone at the same rate. Because the total tax on income of a million dollars is greater than the total tax on income of a thousand dollars, a proportional tax would achieve the objective of imposing *proportionately* (but not *progressively*) higher taxes on persons with higher incomes. Nevertheless, many people are sure that graduated rates, and a progressive tax, are the preferred method. The question of the appropriate degree of progressivity in the Federal Income Tax is highly controversial and incapable of one solution. It has the flavor of a theological question.[27]

The first important historical landmark in the field of progressive taxation is the work of Jeremy Bentham, the early 19th Century economist who sought to design a better society in which the mathematical total of individuals' satisfaction could be maximized. To this end, he used the concept of "utiles" as a uniform measure of personal satisfaction, and reasoned that as wealth grows, the additional satisfaction associated with each addition unit of wealth declines. This leads to the conclusion that progressive taxation with transfers of wealth to poorer people

26 See §§ 53 and 55 to 59.

27 Professors Blum and Kalven have written an exhaustive, brilliant and informative discussion of the *progressive* rate structure and other proposals in The Uneasy Case for Progressive Taxation. See W. Blum & H. Kalven, Univ. of Chicago Press, 1953, *passim;* 19 U. Chi. L. Rev. 417 (1952). See also, Galvin & Bittker, *The Income Tax; How Progressive Should It Be?* (American Enterprise Institute for Public Policy Research, Wash. D.C. (1969)).

increases society's aggregate satisfaction, stated in utiles.[28] You can visit Mr. Bentham in London.[29]

Bentham's writings set off a reaction that has never stopped. The principal objection to his argument seems to be that one cannot make "interpersonal comparisons" of utility; for example, it is conceivable that some poor people might value $100 less than some very rich people. True, but others dismiss this as solved by making common sense approximations rather than letting some anomalous cases destroy utility theory.[30] In fact, the concept of "utiles" is at the heart of traditional microeconomics. One has to wonder about the extent to which Americans believe that they, like Horatio Alger, will surely become rich and so want their future taxes low, and why the public discussion of progressive taxation is so inelegant.

Another line of reasoning concerns withdrawal of services (working less) as taxes rise. The arguments in this sphere seem to be self-canceling. On the one hand, high taxes should cause people to take leisure more seriously because of the declining yield from work; conversely, as taxes rise, people who have a fixed notion of what they demand from life after taxes will increase their work efforts so as to preserve their standards of living. There is precious little empirical data on these behavioral theories.[31] However, surveys of working people indicate that their willingness to supply labor is independent of income taxes.[32]

Yet another line of reasoning concerns the wasteful costs of higher taxes. The principle at work here is that as taxes rise, taxpayers spend more time and money to avoid them and government has to pay more for enforcement. This argues for a broad-based unadorned tax with a publicly acceptable rate structure.[33] Unfortunately, "public acceptability" can be influenced by demagoguery.

---

28 See Jeremy Bentham, The Philosophy of Economic Science in JEREMY BENTHAM'S ECONOMIC WRITINGS (W. Stack ed., 1952).

29 A Utilitarian to the end, he gave his body to medical science when corpses were in short supply. His skeleton is on display in the Anatomy Museum of University College in London, covered in a waxen facsimile body and fully dressed. He is known for the saying "the greatest good for the greatest number," which obscures the precision of his ideas.

30 See, e.g., Musgrave, *In Defense of an Income Concept*, 81 Harv. L. Rev. 44 (1967).

31 See B. Bittker & L. Lokken, FEDERAL TAXATION OF INCOME, ESTATES AND GIFTS, ¶ 3.2 (2018).

32 Questionnaires and statistical studies of wage earners, self-employed people, and salaried workers reported in Barlow, Brazer & Morgan, ECONOMIC BEHAVIOR OF THE AFFLUENT 129-150 (Brookings 1966); Brown & Levin, *The Economic Effects of Income Taxation of Overtime: The Results of a National Survey*, 84 Econ. J. 833 (1974) (U.K.). See further sources cited in B. Bittker & L. Lokken, FEDERAL TAXATION OF INCOME, ESTATES & GIFTS at ¶3.2.2 (2018).

33 This has been the ideology of the American Bar Association's Section of Taxation for many years. For a discussion that considers base broadening, see Graetz, *The 1982 Minimum Tax Amendments as a First Step in the Transition to a Flat Tax*, 56 S. Cal. L. Rev. 527 (1983).

G. TAX PROCEDURE AND ADMINISTRATION

The U.S. income tax system relies on having every taxpayer annually file his, her or its own annual tax return in a timely manner, with full disclosure of relevant data, submitted under oath. If the material provided by the taxpayer is incomplete, the legal view is that no return was filed and that any statute of limitations on tax liabilities with respect to the return never began to run.[34] The annual filing obligation includes mandatory reporting of all gross income, and (generally) a duty to report one's deductions.

On top of that, we have moved to a system of estimated quarterly income tax payments. Failure to keep abreast of these payments can result in expensive penalties. Curiously, there is no stated duty to pay estimated taxes, just a stiff penalty if one does not.[35] The Code bristles with penalties, on top of which taxpayers who are slow to pay their taxes (or penalties) suffer interest charges at market rates for the delay.

Individual (human) taxpayers generally *must* pay their taxes in full for the prior year no later than April 15 of the following year.[36] They have a right to delay *filing* the return itself (but not to delay paying enough tax to cover their tax obligations) for another six months by filing a Form 4868, and they may be able to obtain still another discretionary extension if the IRS grants it upon a showing of undue hardship.[37]

The administration of the federal tax system and the enforcement of taxpayer obligations is handled by the Internal Revenue Service. The IRS representative with whom a taxpayer or a practicing lawyer will most frequently meet is the Internal Revenue Agent, either in a "examination" or in connection with inquiries of various types from the offices of the Service. In recent years, many of the activities of the IRS have been decentralized so that more authority for determination and action is left with the local office of the Service. There are offices of the IRS in most cities of substantial size throughout the country.

After the taxpayer's tax return is filed at the designated IRS Service Center, it is subjected to clerical review and may be bounced back to the taxpayer for correction, which may result in a demand for more money or a refund to the taxpayer. Once the return is in the hands of the IRS, everything about the handling of the return is controlled by voluminous IRS procedures that are published in the Federal Register and reproduced in the CCH Internal Revenue Manual series. The Manual is Biblical Authority to the IRS, so wise practitioners often consult it to predict the IRS's next move. The most likely reasons to bounce back the return is a mistake in calculations

34 See B. Bittker & L. Lokken, FEDERAL TAXATION OF INCOME ESTATES AND GIFTS ¶111.1.9 (W, G&L 2018).

35 See §6654.

36 §6072(a). This is based on a duty to file not later than the 15th day of the fourth month following the end of the taxpayer›s taxable year. Virtually every human has a taxable year that ends on December 31.

37 Reg. §1.6081-1(a).

and actual or apparent understatement of income that was reported to the IRS by payors of wages, dividends and interest.

Thereafter, either nothing will happen or the taxpayer will be notified of an IRS examination by a Revenue Agent. The examination (popularly known as an "audit"), can be conducted at the IRS 's offices (known as an "office examination"), but in complex cases, the Agent will often come to the taxpayer's residence or place of business (known as a "field examination"). In general, the IRS has three years following the filing of the tax return in which to perform the audit and submit a notice of tax deficiency, a "statute of limitations".[38] Conversely, the taxpayer has only this same period to submit administrative claims for refunds or credits or redeterminations of tax. In addition, the taxpayer has only two years to file and sue after the denial of a refund claim.[39] The statutes of limitation generally run from the later of the date the tax return was actually filed, or (for most individual taxpayers) April 15 (the date the tax return was "due") if the return was filed before April 15.[40]

In certain cases the statutes of limitations can be extended, sometimes indefinitely. If the omission from reported gross income was 25% or more[41], the IRS has six years to assess the tax or file suit against the taxpayer. If no return was filed or if there was civil fraud with respect to the return, the statute of limitations <u>never</u> expires.[42] The same is true if the taxpayer filed a false or fraudulent return with the intent to evade taxes[43], or filed a return prepared by the IRS for the taxpayer[44]. Any limitations period can be extended by a voluntary written agreement between the taxpayer and the IRS[45]

If the IRS has trouble locating the taxpayer, that may be the taxpayer's problem. In many cases, the IRS need only send its mail to the taxpayer's last known address.[46] The Code generally provides that a letter's postmark date is considered its delivery date.[47] This is known as the "timely mailing is timely filing" rule.

The Revenue Agent is authorized to demand all relevant books, records and testimony, but the authority is not self-executing. If the taxpayer declines to cooperate the Agent can issue an "administrative summons" for records or testimony; if the taxpayer still balks, the Agent will

38 §6501.

39 §6532(a)

40 If the taxpayer paid late, then the IRS's audit authority extends 2 years after payment if that is longer than 3 years from filing the return.

41 §6501(e).

42 §6501(b)-(c).

43 §6501(c).

44 §6501(b)(3).

45 The IRS will provide Form 872 for this purpose.

46 See especially §6212(b).

47 §7502.

seek to enforce the summons in the local Federal District Court, where the taxpayer can raise such defenses as the irrelevance of the request, its excessively burdensome nature (hence an implied violation of procedural due process) that the information is privileged, and so forth.

If the Agent concludes that there is evidence of criminal tax wrongdoing, he is likely to contact the Criminal Investigation Division of the IRS. That is extremely serious business; prudent tax advisors will tell the client to keep mum and to appoint a competent criminal tax lawyer immediately. Each District Office of the IRS has a C.I.D. C.I.D. is an interesting division. Its personnel are known for their occasional "sting" operations and on occasion carry guns.

Once the Revenue Agent has completed the examination, he or she will issue a Revenue Agent's Report (known as a "RAR" in the trade), which contains "proposed adjustments" to the tax return. This comes wrapped in what is known as a "30 day letter," giving the taxpayer 30 days to file a Protest (basically a big letter containing the law and facts as the taxpayer sees them) with the local Appeals Division (a.k.a, the Office of Appeals) of the IRS. The Appeals Division has a capable staff that settles controversies on the basis of the "hazards of litigation," meaning the likely outcome of a lawsuit to adjudicate the particular issue. If the taxpayer does not want to bother with Appeals, there is no terrible result, but the IRS's next move will be to issue a "90 day letter," a.k.a. "statutory notice of deficiency" by registered or certified mail.[48] This is big trouble. It gives the taxpayer exactly 90 days to file a petition in the Tax Court, or become legally obligated to pay the tax, interest and penalties that the IRS demands. Unless the taxpayer files on time in the Tax Court, when the 90 days elapses, the IRS will "assess" its "deficiency," which involves formally enrolling the liability at its offices. That gives the IRS a decade to collect the unpaid deficiency.[49] In such cases, to contest liability, the taxpayer must first pay the tax and then sue for a refund in District Court or in the Federal Court of Claims. Because of the duty to pay first, tax advisors have to be extremely careful not to fumble the opportunity to litigate in the Tax Court.

If the taxpayer files in the Tax Court in the 90 day period, the price of fighting on rises sharply. Because so many taxpayers do react by filing in the Tax Court, the Tax Court's docket is vastly too large to allow more than a small fraction of the docketed cases to be litigated. Taxpayers typically hope that filing the case will result in settlement with the IRS litigating staff, which happens to be located in the local District Office of the IRS. If the case does go to trial, it is typically fairly inexpensive because the evidence gathering process is unusually informal.

If the taxpayer does choose to litigate, there is a possibility that the IRS will reimburse the taxpayer if the IRS loses. That is, a "prevailing" taxpayer can recover reasonable administrative or litigation costs, or both combined, that he incurred in connection with a Federal tax dispute, principally under the authority of §7430 of the Code. The right to a recovery is ringed with limits, namely, that the IRS's position is not "substantially justified," that the taxpayer

48 §§ 6212-6213.

49 §6502.

meet "financial eligibility" requirements (meaning a net worth of not over $2 million), show "exhaustion of administrative remedies," and that the taxpayer did not "unreasonably protract" the dispute. The taxpayers' or IRS's attorneys also may be liable for excessive litigation costs in the Tax Court. In general, there can be no recovery until after the IRS stakes out its position after the Appeals Conference. However, if the taxpayer prevails, he can collect his expenses from the date of the first letter of proposed adjustments that allows him an opportunity of administrative review in the Office of Appeals. Accountants and other non-lawyers can cash in on §7430 as well. Section 7430 is a complicated statute with a large body of case law, so what was just said is only an overview. A 1998 change to §7430 contains an intriguing rule that if the taxpayer makes a written pretrial settlement offer which the IRS rejects, the taxpayer can recover fees and expenses if the liability determined by the court is not more than what the taxpayer proposed, because the taxpayer is treated as a prevailing party who may recover under §7430.

If the taxpayer does not respond to the 90 day letter and does not pay the tax, the scene changes dramatically. The tax will become automatically due and owing, and the file will move to the IRS's Collection Division, which is a tough organization noted for its lack of sympathy for taxpayers' tales as to why they cannot pay. The Collection Division will typically begin by filing notices of liens and intentions to levy against taxpayers, and will eventually end by seizing taxpayers' assets, including assets that are exempt from creditors' claims under the Federal Bankruptcy Code. Its powers include garnishment of wages, levies of property, and super-creditor status in bankruptcy cases.[50] Although it is often an intimidating organization, it has one slightly soft touch. It will typically allow taxpayers to settle their obligations to the IRS by promising to pay off their liabilities over periods of up to 60 months, with, of course, interest charges on the deferral. Assessment and collection processes are suspended during Tax Court litigation and later judicial appeals.

A troublesome aspect of the audit process has always been the joint return filed by a husband and wife, in which they pool their income, deductions and credits into one combined tax return. Often, one spouse has little idea of what their gross income is, but might be jointly and severally liable for the taxes. As you read the following case, you might ask yourself whether the restrictions on recovering under §7430 are fair.

BURKE v. COMMISSIONER

73 T.C.M. 2291 (1997)

RUWE, J.,

[Mr. Burke was indicted in 1987 on two counts of grand larceny for embezzling more than $1.2 million in insurance premiums from U.S. Life Insurance Co. between 1985 and 1987. Pursuant to a plea agreement, Mr. Burke pled guilty to grand larceny. In March, 1991, Mr. Burke filed untimely

50 See §6301 et seq.

Federal Income Tax returns for 1985, 1986, and 1987. Mr. Burke forged his wife's signature, so that the returns looked like joint returns of a married couple in which they combined their income. Mrs. Burke was not required to file a return of her own for any of the years in issue, evidently because she had no income. She knew of her husband's financial and legal problems during the taxable years. In June of 1991, the IRS informed the couple that they were under audit. Kenneth S. Silver, the accountant for two insurance agencies owned by Mr. Burke, provided the IRS a Form 2848 (Power of Attorney and Declaration of Representative[51*]). The IRS summonsed various materials to build its case and issued the couple a 30day letter which proposed over $200,000 in taxes and penalties for 1985-1987. The 30day letter read in part as follows:

> If you do not agree and wish a conference with the Office of the Regional Director of Appeals, you must let us know within 30 days. . . . An appeals officer, who has not examined your return previously, will review your case. The appeals office is independent of the district director and resolves most disputes informally and promptly. By going to the appeals office, you may avoid court costs, resolve the matter sooner, and prevent interest from compounding. . . .

In June of 1992, Mr. Silver told the IRS that the Burkes would not be filing a protest. Neither the Burkes nor Mr. Silver ever requested an Appeals Office conference with the IRS. In June of 1993, the IRS issued a notice of deficiency and demanded payment of much larger amounts because it had discovered more problems with the old returns. By now, the case was in the hands of a tax lawyer, Michael N. Balsamo, on behalf of both petitioners. In his effort to free Mrs. Burke of liabilities, he alleged "at the time she signed the returns" she "did not know, and had no reason to know" of her husband's tax problems. At least two years later, in court, she said for the first time that she had not even signed the returns. The IRS's Criminal Investigation National Forensic Laboratory concluded that she indeed had not signed the returns. That Tax Court concluded that Mrs. Burke did not tacitly consent to the filing of joint Federal Income Tax returns and, therefore, was not jointly and severally liable for the taxes, penalties or interest in issue, but in the meantime, she had paid good money to defend herself. Next, Mrs. Burke filed a Motion for an Award of Litigation Costs under §7420.]

. . .

Discussion

Section 7430(a)(2) provides that a party that has prevailed in any court proceeding against the United States may recover reasonable litigation costs. To obtain such an award, the prevailing party must establish that: (1) She has exhausted the administrative remedies available; (2) she has "substantially prevailed" in the controversy; (3) she satisfies certain net worth requirements;

51 *[The IRS will refuse to deal with taxpayer representatives until they submit this form to the IRS. Eds.]

(4) the position of the United States in the proceeding was not substantially justified; (5) she has not unreasonably protracted the proceedings; and (6) the amount of the costs sought is reasonable. Sec. 7430(b) and (c). Petitioner bears the burden of proving that she satisfies each of these requirements. Rule 232(e).[526]

Respondent [IRS] concedes that petitioner [Mrs. Burke] has substantially prevailed and that she satisfies the net worth requirements.

Exhaustion of Administrative Remedies

The threshold requirement imposed on a taxpayer asserting a claim pursuant to section 7430 is the exhaustion of administrative remedies before suit is filed. Section 301.74301(b)(1), Proced. & Admin. Regs., provides that where an Appeals Office conference is available, administrative remedies are exhausted only if the taxpayer (1) participated in such a conference prior to filing a petition, or (2) requested an Appeals Office conference and the request was denied. *Cole v. Commissioner*, T.C. Memo. 1996375. This requirement aims "to preserve the role that the administrative appeals process plays in the resolution of tax disputes by requiring taxpayers to pursue such remedies prior to litigation." H. Rept. 97404, at 13 (1981); see also Technical Explanation of Committee Amendment, 127 Cong. Rec. sec. 15594 (daily ed. Dec. 16, 1981).

In the instant case, the following facts are not in dispute: On May 15, 1992, respondent issued to petitioners (and their representative, Mr. Silver) a 30day letter, which afforded petitioners an opportunity for an Appeals conference with respondent's Office of the Regional Director of Appeals. However, neither petitioners nor their representative requested an Appeals Office conference with respondent. Petitioner now posits several arguments in an attempt to circumvent her failure to proceed to Appeals. We shall address each one in turn.

First, petitioner argues that she did not have the opportunity to exhaust her administrative remedies, because respondent's determination in the 30day letter, which afforded petitioners the opportunity for an Appeals conference, was "entirely different" than that contained in the notice of deficiency. In the notice of deficiency, respondent determined deficiencies in petitioners' Federal income taxes that were $149,490 greater than the deficiencies determined in the 30day letter. In the notice of deficiency, respondent determined additions to tax for delinquent filing, fraud and substantial understatement as well.

Despite these additional determinations in the notice of deficiency, the fact remains that the 30day letter asserted substantial Federal income tax deficiencies and additions to tax for the years in issue against both petitioners. These deficiencies totaled $157,918, and the additions to tax for delinquent filing totaled $ 40,537. Petitioner was not required to file a Federal income tax return of her own for any year in issue. Any tax deficiencies attributable to her could only be

52 [6]In the Taxpayer Bill of Rights II, P.L.104-168 (1996), §7430(c) (4) was amended to require the Government to establish that its position was substantially justified. This amendment is effective for proceedings begun after July 30, 1996.

due to a determination by respondent that she had elected to file joint returns. Thus, when the 30day letter was sent, the central issues for petitioner Vivian Burke were whether she signed the purported joint returns, and, if not, whether she tacitly consented to their filing.

Second, petitioner maintains that even if she had availed herself of the available administrative remedies, it would have been of no consequence. In discussing the importance of the exhaustion of administrative remedies requirement, the report of the House Ways and Means Committee stated that the committee recognizes that the exhaustion of remedies requirement may be inappropriate in some cases. For example, if a notice of deficiency is issued to a taxpayer in connection with an issue which the Internal Revenue Service has identified as one which it will litigate in all cases, then it would be inappropriate to require an administrative appeal. Therefore, taxpayers are required to exhaust available administrative remedies unless the court determines that, under the circumstances of the case, such requirement is unnecessary. [H. Rept. 97404, supra at 13.]

In this case, petitioner contends that respondent's position was "set in stone," and petitioners could have agreed to respondent's proposed adjustments or else proceeded to trial. We disagree. Nothing in the record suggests that respondent would not have considered petitioner's claims had she proceeded to Appeals in 1992 and submitted relevant information regarding the joint return issue. The fact that respondent refused to concede the joint return issue after learning 2 years later that petitioner had not signed the returns does not persuade us to the contrary. By then, petitioner had affirmatively alleged in her petition that she had jointly filed the returns in question. In light of this, it was respondent's position that petitioner had consented to her husband's filing of joint returns.

Petitioner also seeks to excuse her failure to pursue administrative remedies on the grounds that she did not learn that respondent was seeking to hold her liable for deficiencies until after the issuance of the notice of deficiency. However, petitioners received notification from respondent that she would be conducting an examination of their Federal income tax returns. Petitioner signed two powers of attorney granting Mr. Silver's accounting firm the authority to represent her for purposes of respondent's audit. Moreover, through her original attorney, petitioner maintained in the petition, and until shortly before trial in this case, that the returns were jointly filed. . . .

Petitioner's reliance on our opinion in *Lomanno v. Commissioner*, T.C. Memo. 1994426, granting the taxpayer's motion for an award of attorney's fees and litigation costs, is misplaced. In *Lomanno*, we determined that the taxpayer had exhausted her administrative remedies, despite the fact that no Appeals conference was held. However, in contrast to the instant case, the taxpayer in *Lomanno* never received a 30day letter. As a result, we concluded that section 301.74301(e), Proced. & Admin. Regs., "would allow * * * [her] to be excepted from having to participate in a prepetition appeals office conference." *Lomanno v. Commissioner, supra.* In addition, we found that prior to the filing of the petition, the taxpayer's counsel had not turned his back on any opportunity that was afforded him to present evidence to support the taxpayer's position. Counsel made both written and oral requests to meet with the Commissioner's agents, although these were to no avail. On these facts, we held that the taxpayer had exhausted her *available* administrative remedies.

* * *

In contrast, the dispositive issue in petitioner's case has always been the same: whether petitioner signed the returns in issue or tacitly consented to their filing. In addition, we do not find evidence of intransigence . . . [by the IRS]. In the instant case, petitioner failed to allege that she had not filed joint returns until shortly before trial. After concluding that petitioner had not signed the returns in issue, respondent was confronted with the fact that petitioner had filed joint returns with Mr. Burke for years prior and subsequent to the years in issue and had alleged in her pleadings that the returns for the years in issue were joint returns. Had petitioner and her representatives originally come forward at the administrative Appeals conference, offered in May 1992, with the relevant facts to demonstrate that she had not filed joint returns for the years in issue, we have every reason to believe that her case could have been resolved without the need for this litigation.[53]

We hold that petitioner did not exhaust her administrative remedies, since she failed to request an Appeals office conference which was offered by respondent in the 30day letter. . . . Therefore, petitioner is not entitled to an award of reasonable litigation costs. As a result of our disposition, we express no opinion as to whether any of the remaining requirements of section 7430 have been satisfied.

An appropriate order will be issued.

H. JUDICIAL JURISDICTION AND REVIEW OF TAX CASES

The judicial system with respect to Federal Income Taxes is unique.

First, there is the Tax Court, which has its headquarters in Washington D.C., but sends judges around the country at various times of year. For example, in the case of Houston, at least one Tax Court judge appears around January of each year to hear cases. The Tax Court is an "Article I" court, not an "Article III" court, which means its judges do not have life tenure.[54] The *crucial* feature of the Tax Court is that one does not have to pay the disputed tax before obtaining the opportunity to contest the legality of the asserted tax. In other words, when a taxpayer

53 Even an Appeals conference regarding petitioner's initial position that she was an innocent spouse would have had to explore the issues of whether the 1985, 1986, and 1987 returns were joint returns, petitioner's involvement in their preparation, and her involvement in and knowledge of the underlying transactions. [Footnote No. 16 in original.]

54 See, e.g., Burns, Stix, Freeman & Co. Inc. v. Commissioner, 57 T.C. 392 (1971) (Tax Court constitutionally empowered).

has completed his or her appeals within the administrative processes of the IRS -- or just ignored the opportunity for an Appeals Conference -- he can take his case to the Tax Court and attempt to get the IRS position set aside before actually paying the money the IRS demands. The Tax Court judges are tax experts. There is no jury, and there are procedures for arbitration of factual disputes[55] as well as for mediation.[56] Appeals from the Tax Court go to the Circuit Court of Appeals for the circuit in which the Tax Court sat. For example, if one wished to appeal a Tax Court decision that was handed down in Houston, one would appeal to the Fifth Circuit. From a San Francisco decision, the case would go to the Ninth Circuit. Thereafter, as is normal, one can seek review in the Supreme Court of the United States.

Second, there are the Federal District Courts. If one is willing first to pay the tax, one goes through the following process: Pay the tax with whatever interest and penalties the IRS demands, then file a timely claim for refund with the Government, asking for the money back. Next, wait for the Government to reject the claim for refund and then file a timely lawsuit for a refund in either of two fora. The first is the local U.S. District Court. For example, in the case of Houston one would file the refund suit in the District Court for the Southern District of Texas.

The other route is to file the suit in the U.S. Court of Federal Claims. This Court is also headquartered in Washington D.C. and, like the Tax Court, operates without a jury and sends judges outside Washington, as needed. Its judges tend to be sophisticated in tax matters and at least some practitioners believe that there is a pro-taxpayer viewpoint in the Court, as opposed to what many believe to be a pro-government perspective in the Tax Court. Appeals from the District Court go to the local Circuit Court and appeals from the Claims Court must go to the Court of Appeals for the Federal Circuit. So, a well advised taxpayer will make a good "choice of forum," considering both the law that has grown up in each forum and the procedures in each forum. For example, in the District Court he has the right to trial by jury. In the U.S. Claims Court or the Tax Court the controversy will be heard without a jury. All things being equal, litigators are likely to want to go the District Court if their cases are rich with human interest, especially tragedy, because the jury is likely to sympathize with the taxpayer.

There is a little softening of the rule that one must pay the tax in full before seeking a refund. Specifically, under the *divisible tax doctrine*, a Federal tax which can be broken into smaller units (e.g., employment taxes for one employee for one payroll period) allows the taxpayer to pay one of the smaller units, seek a refund, and eventually go to a court other than the Tax Court to seek a judicial determination of the tax.[57]

The Supreme Court is rumored to have a distaste for tax cases. It takes only about ten tax cases a year and in general its decisions are quickly attacked by practitioners in a way that sometimes tends to reveal that the Supreme Court is not superbly equipped to deal with tax

55 Tax Court Rules 124. See Internal Revenue Manual 35.5.5 Arbitration and Mediation.

56 Tax Court Rule 124.

57 See Steele v. United States, 280 F.2d 89 (8th Cir. 1960); Jones v. Fox, 162 F Supp 449 (D.C. Mo. 1957).

cases. One might wonder why there is not a general court of tax appeals. In fact, this reform proposal arises from time to time but for mysterious reasons it never seems to be capable of getting out of the Senate Judiciary Committee and into receptive hands.

Notes on Authority and Tax Procedure

The usual rules of precedent apply. First, there is *stare decisis,* meaning the policy of courts to stand by judicial precedents. The typical application of this policy is that an inferior court is required to follow a decision of a superior court that may review such inferior court's decision. Thus, the United States District Court for the Middle District of North Carolina must follow the decisions of the United States Court of Appeals for the Fourth Circuit and of the United States Supreme Court. *Stare decisis* has a special application in Tax Court cases. That is because in *Golsen v. Commissioner*[58], the Tax Court held that it will follow the precedent of the Federal Circuit Court of Appeals to which the taxpayer may appeal. Thus, if a taxpayer from Texas files a suit in Tax Court, the applicable precedents under the *Golsen* rule are Fifth Circuit Court of Appeals and Supreme Court cases. Thus, Federal Circuit decisions have a *stare decisis* effect in the Tax Court as well as in the Federal District Courts within the Circuit.

Second, there is the doctrine of *res judicata* ("the matter already has been decided"), or claim preclusion, which provides that a prior adjudication on the merits of the cause of action between two parties in a court of competent jurisdiction bars further litigation of the same cause of action between the same parties in any court. This doctrine is strictly applied in tax cases. A taxpayer's income tax liability for each taxable year constitutes a single, unified cause of action. [59] Because each year is the origin of a new liability and of a separate cause of action, a court's resolution of a disputed income tax liability for any year bars any subsequent litigation regarding the liability for that year. Thus, a taxpayer raising any Federal Income Tax claims for a tax year must raise all such claims for that year or risk losing the claims not raised.

Third, the doctrine of collateral estoppel -- issue preclusion -- provides that any issue actually litigated in a prior action between two or more parties is conclusive of the same issue raised in a later action between the same parties or those in privity of interest with them. The doctrine is available in tax disputes. According to the *Sunnen* case, the doctrine

> must be confined to situations where the matter raised in the second suit is identical in all respects with that decided in the first proceeding and where the controlling facts and applicable legal rules remain unchanged.[60]

58 54 T.C. 742 (1970), affirmed Golsen v. Comm., 445 F.2d 985 (10th Cir. 1971).

59 Commissioner v. Sunnen, 333 U.S. 591 (1948).

60 Id. at 599-600.

While the basic rules of judicial authority are the same as in other courses, the remedies are sharply different. *Declaratory judgements* are virtually unavailable in federal tax litigation.[61] There are narrow exceptions such as qualification of retirement plans, tax-exempt bonds and tax-exempt organizations.[62]

In addition, there is virtually no chance for an *injunction against unlawful assessments or collection* because the so-called Anti-Injunction Act[63] prevents taxpayers from suing to restrain the assessment or collection of taxes.[64] Section 7426 provides a further exception to the anti-injunction rule for improper seizures by the IRS.

The settlement of an audit with the IRS Appeals Division may have precedential value for repetitive issues. While it is the policy of the IRS to encourage consistent treatment, the Examination Division need not follow the Appeals Settlement for later years even though the facts are the same. In practice, a Revenue Agent usually will follow the settlement in later years. On the other hand, the taxpayer and the Examination Division can enter into a settlement agreement under which the issue is stabilized for good, but it requires further administrative steps to do so.

Another problem for the country as a whole is the matter of IRS morale and skills. The following short article records an interview in 1995 with the IRS's chief of the Examination Division in the National Office of the I.R.S. in Washington. All the local and regional IRS Examination Division staff members ultimately report to this person.[65]

> Massive reorganization and training cutbacks have left the Service at a 'critical' juncture, a recently retired IRS official said April 24. John Monaco, who retired as IRS assistant commissioner (examinations) April 7, said in an interview that despite a history of resiliency, the Service 'cannot take too many more adverse changes' as it redefines itself for the 21st century, according to a transcript of the interview.
>
> The recent reorganization of several service centers forced the retooling and reassignment of some personnel to new tasks, sometimes without proper training, Monaco said. With more consolidation ahead in other areas, the Service's performance may deteriorate.
>
> 'They're not able to train people well,' said Monaco, who lamented that training is often the first program axed in a budget crisis. 'The skill level is not where it should be.' Rather than lose their

61 See 28 U.S.C. §2201.

62 See §§7428, 7476 and 7477.

63 §7421 of the Code.

64 But see, Enochs v. Williams Packing & Navigation Co., 370 U.S. 1 (1962), for a general exception where a taxpayer victory is a sure thing.

65 This Week's News: *News in Brief, Transcript of Monaco Interview on IRS's Future*, 67 Tax Notes 732 (1995).

> jobs, some people who have mastered specific tasks are being forced to learn new skills that they may find less appealing. For example, he said, a telephone operator who has been retrained for collections may end up doing a poor job but cannot be removed because 'the government doesn't fire people' as long as they are doing the bare minimum.

This impoverishment is not the fault of the IRS. It is the fault of other branches of government. To make matters worse, a large proportion of the IRS's workforce qualifies for retirement.

Problem 1-1:

Ms. Burke, an unmarried taxpayer, has come to see you about some tax issues that are troubling her and would like some answers.

1) She filed her tax return for year 1 on February 1, year 2.

    a. She asks, "when will the statute of limitations close on the return?" She assures you that it is not fraudulent and the only debatable issue is a big deduction she took and now wonders about. See §6501 and §6503(a)(1) and §6512(a).

    b. She also wonders if it is true that the IRS could force her to extend the statute of limitations and if so, what she should do. See §6501(c)(4).

2) Same as "(1)", but she willfully concealed a lot of income from the IRS. See §§ 6501(c) and 6531.

3) Same as "(1)", but she never filed her year 1 return (Form 1040). See §6501(c).

4) Instead of owing money, she forgot a big deduction and thinks she is entitled to a refund. You warn her that she will have to file an amended return the statement of procedural rules §601.105(e)(2) requires the IRS to review the entire return and perhaps bring up new weaknesses in the return, but she says she can live with that. So, she asks, what is the last day she can file for the refund? See §6511(a).

5) Some months have passed and she is in the midst of the audit. The agent has issued her a summons (1) for various documents, some of which are embarrassing and, she thinks, not pertinent to the audit and (2) to give testimony. What can be done to stop this? See §7602(a), (c).

6) You have done such a fine job that Ms. Burke has said good things about you to her volatile cousin, Larry. Recently, Larry was also notified that he was about to be audited about his business expense deductions, and he feels the Revenue Agent is insinuating that he is a liar. He is furious and says, "I am taking this to court, period!" What advice would you give him?

7) Ms. Burke is back. She says the IRS has finished the audit and she has had her Appeals Conference (she engaged someone else behind your back, namely a relative who said he would do it for free, but she thinks he did a sloppy job). The Appeals Conference went badly, and there was complete disagreement. The District Office of the IRS has sent her a 90 day letter (notice of deficiency). It is dated August 1, of this year, but she did not actually get it because she moved and it was sent to her prior address. The IRS did not know she moved and she only got the letter because her former landlord salvaged it from the trash, which he likes to go through. The letter was issued 88 days ago and postmarked as of 87 days ago.

   a. Can she safely ignore it? See §6212(b).

   b. If she wants to file in the Tax Court, by when must she file? See §6213.

8) Following up on "(7)", you researched the law and concluded that the law is favorable to your client in your Circuit, but not in the Claims Court, and that the Tax Court has not yet staked out a position on Ms. Burke's key tax issue. How would your research affect your choice of forum, and, therefore, whether to ignore the 90-day letter?

I. PRIMARY TAX POLICY CONCEPTS

It seems that Adam Smith made the first serious attempt at formulating the goals of national tax policy in THE WEALTH OF NATIONS.[66] His analysis has withstood the test of time and is still the bedrock of later analyses.[67] The following paragraphs describe the goals as Adam Smith saw them and then add a few more modern considerations.

---

66 Book V, pp. 404-end (Clarendon Press 1880).

67 See Sneed, *The Criteria of Tax Policy*, 17 Stanford Law Review 567 (1965), generally thought of among U.S. law professors as the fundamental article on the goals of fiscal policy. Sneed's article also mentions the concept that taxes be consistent with "political order," a proposition that has received minimal attention.

Revenues. The first issue is ordinarily the adequacy of the tax as a revenue source. Clearly, taxes are the foundation of government operations. The tax should also be stable as a revenue source, with no adverse impact on steady, noninflationary economic growth. The details are for economists to ponder. Most law students have formed political viewpoints, including whether the federal government is too large or too small. It is important to separate the revenue-raising process -- the subject of this course -- and the expenditure process, and to accept as a practical matter that there is a federal government with particular revenue needs. The panoramic question this course presents is how best to raise those revenues. Holding the viewpoint that any tax is a bad tax is churlish and will impede learning.

Fairness. The second issue is the perceived fairness of the tax. The simplest way of looking at taxes is to ask if the burden of the tax is offset by the benefits of the tax. For example, a garbage collection tax that is tied to the amount of garbage that a town collects from a taxpayer's home ties the benefit of the tax closely to its burden. Many would argue that such a tax is really a "fee" in the sense that it is paid for a direct government service, but it is easy to find examples that are not so directly tied. One example might be a boat use tax whose revenues are used to pay for lifesaving activities. The tax only benefits boat owners who endanger themselves. Prudent boat owners who stay close to shore are merely giving their money away. It is virtually impossible to evaluate what people would pay for the benefits they receive. For example, what would the average taxpayer pay for the assurance of a strong national defense? Is it worth more to a person with great wealth? How much more? On the other hand, unless one takes this measure into account, it seems impossible to evaluate the fairness of a tax. Economists' efforts to rise to the challenge have been heroic, but unconvincing.[68]

The subject of tax fairness also breaks down into two geometrical sounding formulations -- *vertical* equity and *horizontal* equity. Vertical equity refers to the notion of imposing proportionately or progressively higher taxes on those with greater abilities to pay, on the theory that the comparative sacrifice of paying taxes falls as discretionary income rises, because of the presumed diminishing marginal utility of money as income rises, as discussed earlier in connection with Jeremy Bentham's works. This poses the impossible question about the appropriate level of progressivity. You already observed from skimming §1 how there are five tax rates, and that those rates rise as taxable income rises. Each set of rates is popularly known as a "tax bracket". Again, whichever bracket one's last (top) dollar of income falls into is known as one's "marginal tax rate".

The lack of progressivity of sales taxes is a serious problem for the poor. For example, the U.S. tax on ozone depleting chemicals means each automobile owner, rich or poor, must pay more to replace freon in his air conditioning system. Wealthy individuals can pay several dollars more for a can of freon and never notice the cost. Poor people may find the expense so high

68 See B.Bittker & L. Lokken, FEDERAL TAXATION OF INCOME, ESTATES AND GIFTS ¶ 3.4.5 (2018).

that they give up and drive cars without air conditioning. Here, we have no vertical equity in the tax. It is absolutely insensitive to means and it results in immediate, palpable hardship, but it is consistent with economic theory about including the full cost of environmental harm in the product's price, so as to reduce production and over consumption.[69]

Horizontal equity refers to the notion that people who are in similar economic situations should pay the same amount of taxes and benefit from equivalent tax breaks. This concept is of the utmost importance in formulating tax laws and insinuates itself into much of this course.

> **To illustrate:** For many years it has been common for English employers to offer their employees the free use of a car plus a salary. English tax law exempts the free use from taxation. So, if a British employer pays Jack 20,000 pounds per year plus the use of a car, saving Jack 2,000 pounds, Jack's tax base is only 20,000 pounds. If the English employer offers Jill the same deal, but she takes 2,000 pounds in cash instead of the use of the car, her tax base is 22,000 pounds, and she will pay more taxes than Jack, even though their economic incomes are identical. This difference in tax outcomes violates horizontal equity.

Another aspect of fairness is fiscal impact, meaning the question of how much a taxpayer gets back from government compared to what she pays in.

Administrability. A tax ought to be certain, convenient and economical to collect. It may, for example, be that a tax can yield a substantial flow of revenues, but that its complexity is so great that the administrative burdens will largely offset the revenue, making the tax inefficient in a fiscal sense. The burdens may consist of the administrative costs to the government or the compliance costs to taxpayers, or both combined. It is often said that "a fair tax cannot be simple and a simple tax cannot be fair." Another aspect of administratibility is that there should be fiscal efficiency in the sense that the cost to the government of raising each dollar should be reasonable. Sometimes the concept is stated as "simplicity".

Transparency. This is a close relative of Administrability. The notion is that legal rules -- including tax rules -- should be clear ("transparent") and not, for example, only apparent to taxpayers who can afford to pay for expensive tax advice. The term is of more recent origin and is not much used in the U.S., but is common in Europe and among economists and tax policy experts generally.

---

69 There is a solution. One can provide poor people with an annual payment equal to the annual tax, thereby returning them enough money to cover the tax. This does not eliminate the appropriately high cost of the freon. However, because the compensatory payment is separated from each purchase of freon, many poor consumers will choose to use the money for other purposes that they value more highly than freon, a good thing from an environmental perspective. One alternative one might try to charge rich people more than poor people for freon, thereby distributing the suffering more equally, but that proposal is likely to be unadministerable; for one thing, a black market is likely to develop in freon.

Simplicity. A tax should be free of interpretative doubt, and have obvious meanings and purposes. In addition, it should not invite unintended behavior to defeat the tax.

Neutrality. Taxes should be compatible with a free market. A tax is "efficient" in the economic sense if, per dollar of revenue, it interferes minimally with the free-market decisions that people would make in the absence of the tax. Those decisions -- about how hard to work and how much leisure to take, how much to save and how much to consume, how much of one product to consume compared to another product, how much to spend on education, etc. -- presumably lead to an optimal allocation of resources in a perfect free market and generally should be distorted as little as possible by imposing a tax, unless the distortion or correction is desired as a matter of public policy. The concept seems obvious; in order to prevent the misallocation of resources, including the misallocation caused by tax avoidance (or compliance) practices, the tax system should not conflict with the free market system, unless the conflict is intended.

However, when speaking of taxes (or tax incentives) the subject becomes complicated. For one thing, the *lack* of a tax may imply a conflict. For example, if harmful pollution generated in the course of manufacturing a consumer good goes untaxed, then the price of the good is too low, and excessive production and consumption will occur, compared to the level of output that would occur if the item bore its full environmental cost.

Macroeconomic Considerations. A related concern is that the tax be consistent with macroeconomic (study of the overall economy) values. That body of learning generally prefers steady growth, high levels of employment and minimal inflation. A well-formed federal income tax will neither stimulate inflation nor invite a recession. Sometimes income taxes are used affirmatively to affect the overall economy, although nowadays monetary policy -- changes in interest rates dictated by the Federal Reserve Board -- are the first line of attack.

Tax Policy in Practice. A serious lack of publicly available empirical data haunts the study of all of these domestic criteria. Tax legislation tends to be born in the cauldron of political debate, influenced by the economic fashions of the day, which are often little more than clichés. Systematic follow-up studies of tax legislation may exist, but they are seldom available to the public. On top of that, in the United States at least, the Privacy Act[70] prevents government from releasing much useful data. Unfortunately, this famine of good data tends to keep political debates about tax policy on an ideological level.

This brings one to the issue of what is known in the U.S. as "targeting" of tax relief. The notion is that a reduction in a tax rate or tax base should be carefully confined to the purpose of the relief. To take a simple case, if the purpose of an income tax reduction is to stimulate consumption in order to get a national economy moving, then one should cut income taxes only

70 Privacy Act of 1974, 5 USCA §552g.

for people with low and moderate incomes. Tax cuts for wealthy people, who use most of their income for savings, are inconsistent with the policy of stimulating consumption. Conversely, if we want to stimulate savings by cutting taxes, tax cuts in the highest tax bracket will yield greater savings than cuts in lower brackets, even though doing so may result in distributive effects that make many voters uncomfortable.

Problem 1-2:

Assume that you are King Helvering I and that Paradise needs the revenues. At present, your country relies exclusively on import duties, but your finance minister has proposed that the legislature enact a bicycle tax in order to raise the necessary revenue. In light of what you have read so far, would this be a wise act of tax policy? Paradise is an island with a bustling city at its center. It has an extensive system of roads.

J. ALTERNATIVE SYSTEMS

In the early years of the American Republic, the country relied on import duties to pay for the workings of the Federal Government. Since then, import duties have become a relative drop in the bucket and income taxes on individuals have come to provide the bulk of federal revenues. The United States relies primarily on income taxes for its revenues, with little revenues from taxes on large gifts and large individual estates of decedents.

Another alternative is to shift from a system of taxing net income to taxing consumption through a national sales tax or a value added tax. There are strong political pressures in favor of such taxes, but they tend to founder on the argument that these taxes unduly burden the poor -- they are "regressive" in the language of economists. Regressive taxes are discussed later in the book.

K. THE POLITICAL IMPORTANCE OF BUDGET DEFICITS AND SURPLUSES

The United States ran up an enormous cumulative budget deficit -- over $22 trillion -- during the last 40 years. Accumulated shortfalls require the payments of massive amounts of interest to service that debt. Moreover, whatever the apparent federal revenues in any particular year, the numbers are difficult to evaluate because of questionable budgeting practices, such as characterizing deposits into the Social Security system as income. The coming problem is a tidal wave of

There is also a larger duty to the tax system itself to restrain aggressive taxpayers. One expression of the idea is as follows:

> The practitioner also owes a duty, albeit less well defined, to the tax system as a whole. The practitioner is not free to do whatever it is that the client demands, regardless of the client's willingness to incur the risk of penalty. The practitioner's duty to the system is based, in part, on a general obligation derived from the practitioner's status as a professional to encourage compliance with the law (including the tax laws).[78]

A great deal of law enforcement occurs in lawyers' offices, when lawyers advise their clients against breaking the law. That is as true in the tax field as in any other.

Problem 1-3:

The Burkes came to your law office, having learned that there is going to be an IRS examination for two tax years. They want you to represent them. Assume Mr. Burke forged tax returns for those years. Can you represent both taxpayers within the rules of professional responsibility?

N. FOREIGN INCOME AND THE GLOBAL TAX

The Federal Income Tax is global in territorial scope. It taxes all U.S. citizens and resident aliens on their worldwide income. It differs sharply from income tax laws that tax only people who reside in the country on income whose source lies within the territorial boundaries of the taxing jurisdiction[79]; such systems are common outside the U.S., and explain such phenomena as European celebrities who reside in Monte Carlo and pay no income taxes; Monte Carlo imposes no taxes[80] and the celebrities' home countries often do not tax them because their income is earned in other countries.

The Federal Income Tax is limited by certain treaties to which the U.S. is a party, mainly bilateral income tax treaties, of which there are many. In addition, the WTO imposes limits on the extent to which income taxes can impede international trade. A key example is Annex I of the WTO Subsidies Code, which prevents any member country from rebating (paying back) income taxes on exported goods.[81] An illustrative implication is that a U.S. computer maker that exports one of its computers cannot get back the income taxes it implicitly paid on the com-

78 Wolfman, Holden & Harris, STANDARDS OF TAX PRACTICE SECTION 101.2 (Little, Brown 1997).)

79 This is the so-called "territorial principle". See INTERNATIONAL TAX GLOSSARY 269 (IBFD 1988).

80 See W. Diamond, TAX HAVENS OF THE WORLD, Monaco 4.

81 See WTO Appellate Report, United States—Tax Treatment for "Foreign Sales Corporations" (Feb. 24, 2000).

puter. By contrast, it is permissible for a government to rebate retail sales taxes or value-added taxes on exports, and to levy such taxes on imports. This is one of the reasons why American industry would like to replace income taxes with sales taxes or valued-added taxes.

O. SOME RECURRENT ISSUES

Keep in mind that many tasks lie before you in the study of Federal Income Taxation. You are free to decide for yourself what emphasis to give each of them, although the instructor cannot help but have priorities of his or her own, which he or she will suggest to you both explicitly and implicitly. Tax theory and tax policy are very important. Some rules of present law must be, or inevitably will be, learned if you give this material good attention. You may even learn a little about practical compliance, forms, due dates, and so forth. No high-powered arithmetic is required, though some numbers and quantitative concepts will occasionally be used. Some procedural knowledge, some familiarity with tax administration and even a little last minute "tax scoop" should be assimilated.

Also consider the reach of income tax law in our society, not to speak of the private practice of law, as you go through this subject. How, for example, does the deduction for charitable contributions affect the allocation of resources among rich and poor? How efficiently does it provide for necessary social services to the needy? How do power relationships result?

What are the nature and origin of some of the concepts used in the tax law? For example, is marital status a tax status, a federal question or an incorporation of State law on non-tax status? Is its texture hard or soft, its outlines clear or fuzzy? How much tax planning does it invite? What alternative concepts are available?

How can the behavior or tax consequences of one taxpayer (e.g., an employer) affect the tax consequences of another person (e.g., his or her employee)?

What are the interrelationships of the rules in the law? What is the architecture of the Code (foundation, superstructure, pure ornamentation)? What are the gaps and friction points in these rules? What pressures shaped them (power politics, equity, administrative considerations, fiscal policy, economics)?

Who benefits and who loses from the present or proposed rules? How durable are they?

What do *lawyers* (as distinguished from accountants, economists, and lay persons) do with tax law?

What are the policies behind the rules? What needs revision or reform? What are the possible and proper uses of tax law in our society? How should a Federal Income Tax be integrated with, or adjusted with respect to, other taxes or considerations (such as wealth of the taxpayer)? What is the best taxpaying unit (individual, family, and so forth)? What should be included in the income tax base -- i.e., what should be taxed as income? At what rates? When?

These are some of the questions that underlie every topic, whether or not time permits them all to be raised and discussed each time. You may wish to return to them after the following materials have been started.

Problem 1-4:

Casey is a self-employed single person with no dependents. She sells tickets for salvage boat excursions, door-to-door on a commission basis. Casey picks the routes and sales procedures. Last year, she had $30,000 of net earnings from this self-employment.

Use the following sections to answer the question: income tax rates in section 1, standard deduction of section 63, social security and Medicare taxes under section 1401, and the deduction for half of Social Security and Medicare taxes under Section 164(f).

1) What is her Federal Income Tax liability for the year?

2) What is her Social Security and Medicare tax liability for the year?

3) What is her marginal Federal Income Tax rate, i.e., the tax rate on her last dollar of income?

4) What is her marginal tax rate if one includes Social Security and Medicare taxes?

5) What would be her marginal Federal Income Tax rate if she had taxable income of $1 million this year?

6) Assume Microsoft had various employee compensation plans and also hired an army of people whom they treated as independent contractors, who were cut out of the corporation's employee retirement plans. If the IRS successfully recharacterized them as employees for Federal Income Tax purposes, do you suppose Microsoft would also owe them retirement benefits? Consider how high the stakes might be if the answer is "yes".

7) Assume that Casey's twin, Marcy, has gross income of $35,000 from investments, and that Casey's gross income is a $35,000 salary, but that Casey has various expenses that are incident to earning the salary. Is horizontal equity advanced or violated if they are subject to the same tax, even though Casey may have to pay for commuting, parking, better clothes, day care, and so forth in order to earn the

salary, but Marcy does not because she can easily do her investing by calling her broker on an 800 number.

P. A LOOK AHEAD

The book is organized along the following lines:

1) *What is income? Is the particular item income or is it tax-exempt?* This occupies Chapters 2-4.

2) *What kind of income is it?* What different rates are (or should) be applied to what kinds of income? Is it unthinkable that salary income, which will terminate if the worker becomes ill, or is fired, which comes from efforts and expenditures not all of which are deductible, should be taxed at the same rate as interest or dividends received by the owner of cash or shares of stock (whether he be a wealthy man or the same wage earner)? Should source matter? Should use of the income matter? This is the subject of Chapter 8.

3) *When is it income?* When cash is received? When a contract to pay cash is received? When property appreciates in value? When a patentable idea is first written down? When non-cash property is received? When income is partially earned? When future earning power increases, as upon passing the Medical Boards (examinations)? This occupies Chapters 9, 10 and 11.

4) *Whose income is it?* Wages to the wage earner? To his or her spouse too? To his or her special friend or common-law spouse? Income on property owned jointly? Community property? Income on property received by gift? Even if the gift is made just as the income is about to be received by the donor? What if mother sells property under a contract requiring that the purchase price be paid to her son? Income on property put into a three-year revocable trust to accumulate income and pay over principal and income to the settlor's lover upon termination? This is the subject of Chapter 12.

5) *What are the answers to these same four questions on the deduction or allowance side?*

   a. What is deductible or allowable as a credit?

b. When?

c. How? In what amount? Deductible against what income?

d. By whom?

Chapters 5-7 deal with tax deductions.

6) *What is the purpose, scope and operation* of the particular Code section you are looking at? "Scope" means such things as which taxpayers are affected by the rule, whether it applies only to transactions in the United States, and so on. "Operation" refers to the mechanics of the rule. For example, does it add to the income tax base, does it only supply a definition, or does it accelerate or defer reporting income?

CHAPTER 2 - GROSS INCOME

A. INTRODUCTION

Read §61 and Reg. §1.61-1(a), 2(a) and 3(a)

The legislative history of the Sixteenth Amendment, which allows the federal government to tax "income from whatever source derived," does not offer an authoritative definition of income[82], perhaps because at the time it was not considered all that important an act.[83] That is, Congress had the power to collect so-called "indirect taxes" taxes ever since the founding of the Republic. All the Sixteenth Amendment did was to make it clearly possible to collect "direct" taxes on individuals on their income from property -- mainly rents, dividends and interest -- without the need to prorate the tax among the states in proportion to population.

Congress took the same laconic approach when, armed with the Sixteenth Amendment, it enacted the progenitor of the present-day Federal Income Tax. Section 61 of the Code has the fundamental task of defining gross income, the starting point for calculating a taxpayer's Federal Income Tax liabilities. It does so by a sweeping declaration that gross income includes all income of every sort, and then offers a nonexclusive, but impressive, list of examples. Section 61 does not actually define the term "gross income." Instead, Congress generally left the courts to breathe life into the term "income." The House Committee Report on the 1954 act did state that §61's use of the term "gross income" was meant to be the same as the constitutional meaning, which at least assured that the terms "income" in the Constitution and "gross income" in the Code overlap exactly.[84]

82 See H.R. Rep. 1337, 83d Cong., 2d. Sess. A18 (1954); see also, S. Rep. No. 1622, 83d Cong., 2d Sess. 69-169 (1954).

83 See B. Bittker & L. Lokken, FEDERAL TAXATION OF INCOME, ESTATES AND GIFTS ¶5.1(2018).

84 Arguably there is no proper definition. See Ackerman, *Taxes and the Constitution*, 99 Colum. L. Rev. 1 (1999).

1. Direct versus Indirect Taxes

The original Constitution made a sweeping income tax impossible. In contrast, there was never a constitutional problem with enacting "indirect" taxes (generally meaning consumption taxes on goods and services), but Article I, Section 9, Clause 4 contains a serious limit on poll taxes and other "direct" taxes:

> No Capitation, or other direct, Tax shall be laid, unless in Proportion to the Census or Enumeration herein before directed to be taken.

This was later read to mean that a tax on income from rents or other property was "direct" in the sense of falling on property and had to be prorated among the States in accordance with their population, a very tall order.[85] The meaning of the term "direct tax" remains controversial, perhaps because it was never clearly resolved by the Founders. According to a reliable authority on the Constitutional Convention, "Mr. King asked what was the precise meaning of direct taxation. No one answered."[86]

Some believe the Delphic language embodying the restriction on direct taxes was inserted as a move by Southern states to block Northern states from enacting laws that would tax the ownership of slaves so heavily that the institution of slavery would be abolished.[87] There being no slaves in the North, the proration would have been impossible.[88] Be that as it may, in 1913 the Sixteenth Amendment pushed all that aside with the bold declaration that,

> The Congress shall have the power to lay and collect taxes on incomes, from whatever source derived, without apportionment among the several states, and without regard to any census or enumeration.

---

85 See Pollack v. Farmer's Loan & Trust Co., 157 U.S. 429 (1895).

86 The Debates on the Adoption of the Federal Constitution in the Convention held at Philadelphia in 1787, with a Diary of the Debates of the Congress of the Confederation as reported by James Madison, revised and newly arranged by Jonathan Elliot. Complete in One Volume. Vol. V. Supplement to Elliot's Debates (Philadelphia, 1836). https://oll.libertyfund.org/titles/1909#Elliot_1314-05_4127.

87 ROBIN L. EINHORN, American Taxation, American Slavery (University of Chicago Press 2006).

88 See, e.g., Statements of James Madison and George Nicholas, Debates in the Virginia Ratification Convention (June 12 and 17, 1788) in 3 RSC-VA 1204, 1339, 1342-1343 (arguing that apportionment will prevent Congress from enacting oppressive taxes on tobacco or slaves that Northern states would escape). This is not a settled matter. For one thing, the interpretations of Madison and Nicholas may have been erroneous. Apparently Virginians were well aware of the risk of slaves being taxed under the Madison/Nicholas interpretation. See "The State Solder IV," Virginia Independent Chronicle, March 1978, in 1 RSC-VA 1339.

The Revenue Act of 1913 followed and depended on approval of the Sixteenth Amendment, which obliterated the apportionment requirement for direct taxes on income. Since passage of the 1913 income tax, the base has been clarified, and top rates have risen sharply from the original six percent to 91 percent following the Korean War and are now down to 39.6 percent.

Nowadays we tend to think of the Sixteenth Amendment as the only authority for an income tax. In fact, the Amendment merely clears the path to the taxation of income from capital in such forms as dividends, interest and rents. The authority to tax income from services is not cut off by Article I, Section 8. Objections to such taxes have to arise under more general theories, such as Due Process. The one thing Congress cannot tax is exports, but it can impose an income tax on exporters' profits.[89]

2. Intergovernmental Immunities, Indian Tribes and Exports

There is no doubt that the U.S. government can tax interest on state and local obligations[90] and state and local government employees.[91] The right of the U.S. government to tax colleges and universities on their "unrelated business income" has been upheld[92] over constitutional objections, but the federal government has not pressed its efforts to tax states and localities, so the exact boundaries of intergovernmental immunities remain to be worked out.

Indian tribes are exempt from taxation by virtue of §7871, which treats tribes as states. The exemption has expanded to include tribal corporations which has invited the growth of Indian gambling operations on a grand scale.[93] Individual tribal members, however, are generally subject to the Federal Income Tax.[94]

3. Specific Constitutional Prohibitions

Any application of the taxing power has to bend to fundamental requirements such as the right of an accused person to be offered a jury trial in criminal cases and protection from unreasonable searches and seizures. Due Process is available as a protection for taxpayers complaining of excessive taxation only if the tax is "so arbitrary . . . that it [is] not the exertion of taxation but a confiscation of property," rising to the level of a Fifth Amendment taking.[95] With the decline

89 See Article I, §9, clause 5 and WE Peck & Co. v. Lowe, 247 U.S. 165 (1918).

90 South Carolina v. Baker, 485 U.S. 505 (1988).

91 Graves v. New York ex rel. O'Keefe, 306 U.S. 466 (1939).

92 Iowa State Univ. of Science and Technology v. United States, 500 F.2d 508 (Fed. Cir. 1974).

93 See Rev. Rul. 94-16, 1994-1 CB 19, amplified in Rev. Rul. 94-65.

94 See, e.g., Squire v. Capoeman, 351 U.S. 1 (1956).

95 Brushaber v. Union Pacific RR, 240 U.S. 1 (1916).

of Substantive Due Process, this line of attack is more or less hopeless.[96] Likewise, changes in tax rates and the tax base can be retroactive, even to the year prior to the legislation, without offending Due Process, unless the changes are "so harsh and oppressive as to transgress the constitutional limitation."[97] The heart of the matter may be an unspoken judicial concern for not intruding on the workings of Congress in the governmentally crucial area of taxation, but the real world reality is that Constitutional objections to federal taxes fare poorly in the courts, despite the apparent analytical strength of the objections. This has led some practitioners to consider that there are really two Constitutions, one for taxes and one for all other matters.

C. EVOLUTION OF THE DEFINITION OF GROSS INCOME

1. From Enactment of the Sixteenth Amendment through *Glenshaw Glass*

From the outset, the courts refused to classify everything falling into a taxpayer's hands as gross income. In the course of interpreting the 1909 Corporation Excise Tax Act,[98] which was a precursor of the modern income tax, the Supreme Court refused to tax a timber company on the gross amounts it received from selling its timber lands, and insisted that the cost of the lands offset the sales proceeds, stating:

> Yet it is plain, we think, that by the true intent and meaning of the act, the entire proceeds of a mere conversion of capital assets were not to be treated as income. Whatever difficulty there may be about a precise and scientific definition of "income," it imports, as used here, something entirely distinct from principal or capital either as a subject of taxation or as a measure of the tax; conveying rather the idea of gain or increase arising from corporate activities. As was said in *Stratton's Independence v. Howbert*, 231 U.S. 399, 415: "Income may be defined as the gain derived from capital, from labor, or from both combined."[99]

That idea of that gross income must be from income, capital, or both combined was ratified in *Eisner v. Macomber*,[100] evidently the only judicial decision where imposition of the Federal

96 See B. Bittker, Constitutional *Limits on the Taxing Power of the Federal Government*, 41 Tax Lawyer 3 (1987).

97 Welch v. Henry, 305 U.S. 134, 147 (1938).

98 Doyle v. Mitchell Brothers Company, 247 U.S. 179 (1918).

99 Id. at 184.

100 252 U.S. 189 (1920). The other instance of the Supreme Court invalidating an assertion that a transaction produced gross income was in Edwards v. Cuba Railroad, 268 U.S. 628 (1925) (payments made by the Cuban government to taxpayer corporation based on miles of track laid and paid out by the taxpayer on capital items held not gross income to the corporation. The case is codified in §118 of the Code, but it might imply that certain other payments -- perhaps manpower training programs -- are nontaxable).

Income Tax was found to be unconstitutional on the ground that the taxpayer had not yet realized "income" within the meaning of the Sixteenth Amendment. The facts involved a taxpayer who challenged the constitutionality of a provision of the Revenue Act of 1916, which taxed the value of a stock dividend that was granted pro rata to all the shareholders of a corporation. The particular taxpayer owned 2,200 shares of common stock of a corporation. She received as a dividend an extra 1,100 shares of the same class of stock in the same corporation. Anyone who thinks about it for more than a moment would say that as a matter of common sense she was not wealthier as a result of the stock dividend, because every other shareholder got a proportionate increase in the amount of stock she or he held, offset by an exactly proportionate reduction in the value of each share of stock. Applying good sense, the *Macomber* case characterized the stock dividend as,

> . . . no more than a book adjustment . . . that does not affect the aggregate assets of the corporation or its outstanding liabilities; it affects only the form, not the essence, of the 'liability' acknowledged by the corporation to its own shareholders.[101]

The majority's discussion of what is gross income implied, in a cloud of words, that it would not have approved of taxing mere increases in the value of property:

> Here we have the essential matter: *not* a gain *accruing* to capital, not a *growth* or *increment* of value *in* the investment; but a gain, a profit, something of exchangeable value *proceeding* from the property, *severed from* the capital however invested or employed, and *coming in*, being "*derived*," that is, *received* or *drawn* by the recipient (the taxpayer) for his *separate* use, benefit and disposal; *that* is income derived from property. Nothing else answers the description.[102]

Eisner v. Macomber suggests that a taxpayer who finds money on the street has no gross income when she becomes entitled to keep it, because the found money was not obtained as a return on her capital, nor as a result of her labor, a short-sighted interpretation that has the potential for causing a great deal of economic gain to be exempt from the Federal Income Tax. Notice that *Eisner v. Macomber* also asserts that it is impermissible to tax annual increases in wealth unless the appreciated property is sold or otherwise "severed" from the taxpayer's capital, a crucially important concept.

Later cases watered down *Eisner v. Macomber's* restrictive definition of gross income by saying that, "any definite event could be used as the moment to account for a taxpayer's gain"[103] and that it was not always necessary to "sever capital," at least not when the gain came from

101 252 U.S. at 210.

102 252 U.S. at 206207.

103 Helvering v. Bruun, 309 U.S. 461 (1940).

canceling a taxpayer's debt.[104] It was the next case that delivered the final deadly blow to *Eisner v. Macomber*'s limit as to the source of income.

COMMISSIONER v. GLENSHAW GLASS CO.

348 U.S. 426 (1955)

Mr. Chief Justice Warren delivered the opinion of the Court.

This litigation involves two cases with independent factual backgrounds yet presenting the identical issue. The two cases were consolidated for argument before the Court of Appeals for the Third Circuit and were heard *en banc*. The common question is whether money received as exemplary damages for fraud or as the punitive twothirds portion of a trebledamage antitrust recovery must be reported by a taxpayer as gross income under § 22 (a) of the Internal Revenue Code of 1939. In a single opinion, 211 F.2d 928, the Court of Appeals affirmed the Tax Court's separate rulings in favor of the taxpayers. 18 T. C. 860; 19 T. C. 637. Because of the frequent recurrence of the question and differing interpretations by the lower courts of this Court's decisions bearing upon the problem, we granted the Commissioner of Internal Revenue's ensuing petition for certiorari. 348 U.S. 813.

The facts of the cases were largely stipulated and are not in dispute. So far as pertinent they are as follows:

> *Commissioner v. Glenshaw Glass Co.* The Glenshaw Glass Company, a Pennsylvania corporation, manufactures glass bottles and containers. It was engaged in protracted litigation with the HartfordEmpire Company, which manufactures machinery of a character used by Glenshaw. Among the claims advanced by Glenshaw were demands for exemplary damages for fraud and treble damages for injury to its business by reason of Hartford's violation of the federal antitrust laws. In December 1947, the parties concluded a settlement of all pending litigation, by which Hartford paid Glenshaw approximately $ 800,000. Through a method of allocation which was approved by the Tax Court, 18 T. C. 860, 870872, and which is no longer in issue, it was ultimately determined that, of the total settlement, $ 324,529.94, represented payment of punitive damages for fraud and antitrust violations. Glenshaw did not report this portion of the settlement as income for the tax year involved. The Commissioner determined a deficiency claiming as taxable the entire sum less only deductible legal fees. As previously noted, the Tax Court and the Court of Appeals upheld the taxpayer.
>
> [The discussion of the companion case, *Commissioner v. William Goldman Theaters, Inc.*, is omitted. Eds.]

---

104 U.S. v. Kirby Lumber Co., 284 U.S. 1 (1931), discussed later in this text.

It is conceded by the respondents that there is no constitutional barrier to the imposition of a tax on punitive damages. Our question is one of statutory construction: are these payments comprehended by § 22 (a)?

The sweeping scope of the controverted statute is readily apparent:

> "SEC. 22. GROSS INCOME[105]
>
> "(a) GENERAL DEFINITION. 'Gross income' includes gains, profits, and income derived from salaries, wages, or compensation for personal service . . . of whatever kind and in whatever form paid, or from professions, vocations, trades, businesses, commerce, or sales, or dealings in property, whether real or personal, growing out of the ownership or use of or interest in such property; also from interest, rent, dividends, securities, or the transaction of any business carried on for gain or profit, *or gains or profits and income derived from any source whatever. . . .*" (Emphasis added.)

This Court has frequently stated that this language was used by Congress to exert in this field "the full measure of its taxing power." *Helvering v. Clifford*, 309 U.S. 331, 334 . . . . Respondents contend that punitive damages, characterized as "windfalls" flowing from the culpable conduct of third parties, are not within the scope of the section. But Congress applied no limitations as to the source of taxable receipts, nor restrictive labels as to their nature and the Court has given a liberal construction to this broad phraseology in recognition of the intention of Congress to tax all gains except those specifically exempted. . . . Thus, the fortuitous gain accruing to a lessor by reason of the forfeiture of a lessee's improvements on the rented property was taxed in *Helvering v. Bruun*, 309 U.S. 461. . . . Such decisions demonstrate that we cannot but ascribe content to the catchall provision of § 22 (a), "gains or profits and income derived from any source whatever." . . .

Nor can we accept respondents' contention that a narrower reading of § 22 (a) is required by the Court's characterization of income in *Eisner v. Macomber*, 252 U.S. 189, 207, as "the gain derived from capital, from labor, or from both combined." The Court was there endeavoring to determine whether the distribution of a corporate stock dividend constituted a realized gain to the shareholder, or changed "only the form, not the essence," of his capital investment. Id., at 210. It was held that the taxpayer had "received nothing out of the company's assets for his separate use and benefit." Id., at 211. The distribution, therefore, was held not a taxable event. In that context distinguishing gain from capital the definition served a useful purpose. But it was not meant to provide a touchstone to all future gross income questions. . . .

105 This is the predecessor of §61. Eds.

Here we have instances of undeniable accessions to wealth, clearly realized, and over which the taxpayers have complete dominion. The mere fact that the payments were extracted from the wrongdoers as punishment for unlawful conduct cannot detract from their character as taxable income to the recipients. Respondents concede, as they must, that the recoveries are taxable to the extent that they compensate for damages actually incurred. It would be an anomaly that could not be justified in the absence of clear congressional intent to say that a recovery for actual damages is taxable but not the additional amount extracted as punishment for the same conduct which caused the injury. And we find no such evidence of intent to exempt these payments.

It is urged that reenactment of § 22 (a) without change since the Board of Tax Appeals held punitive damages nontaxable in *Highland Farms Corp.*, 42 B. T. A. 1314, indicates congressional satisfaction with that holding. Reenactment particularly without the slightest affirmative indication that Congress ever had the *Highland Farms* decision before it is an unreliable indicium at best. *Helvering v. Wilshire Oil Co.*, 308 U.S. 90, 100101; *Koshland v. Helvering*, 298 U.S. 441, 447. Moreover, the Commissioner promptly published his nonacquiescence in this portion of the *Highland Farms* holding and has, before and since, consistently maintained the position that these receipts are taxable. It therefore cannot be said with certitude that Congress intended to carve an exception out of § 22 (a)'s pervasive coverage. Nor does the 1954 Code's legislative history, with its reiteration of the proposition that statutory gross income is "allinclusive," give support to respondents' position. The definition of gross income has been simplified, but no effect upon its present broad scope was intended.[106] Certainly punitive damages cannot reasonably be classified as gifts, cf. *Commissioner v. Jacobson*, 336 U.S. 28, 4752, nor do they come under any other exemption provision in the Code. We would do violence to the plain meaning of the statute and restrict a clear legislative attempt to bring the taxing power to bear upon all receipts constitutionally taxable were we to say that the payments in question here are not gross income.

. . .

Reversed.

[Justice Douglas' dissent is omitted. Eds.]

106 5. In discussing §61 (a) of the 1954 Code, the House Report states:

"This section corresponds to section 22 (a) of the 1939 Code. While the language in existing section 22 (a) has been simplified, the allinclusive nature of statutory gross income has not been affected thereby. Section 61 (a) is as broad in scope as section 22 (a).

"Section 61 (a) provides that gross income includes 'all income from whatever source derived.' This definition is based upon the 16th Amendment and the word 'income' is used in its constitutional sense." H. R. Rep. No. 1337, * * * at A18. A virtually identical statement appears in S. Rep. No. 1622 * * * at 168. [Footnote No. 11 in original.]

Notes on *Glenshaw Glass* and Interpreting the Tax Code

Glenshaw Glass today. Is *Glenshaw Glass* the last word? No. The Supreme Court's attempt to define gross income in *Glenshaw Glass* was a noble effort, but does not solve every problem. It does not really tell us what the term "income" means. For example, does the term include the value of occupying one's own home? How about appreciation in marketable stock that one owns but does not sell? Neither of these is explicitly exempted by the Code. How can one reconcile those omissions in the tax system with the declaration that the term "gains or profits and income" is used by Congress "to exert in this field the full measure of its taxing power"? Likewise, the Court said that all gains are generally taxable, but stopped short of disclosing what a "gain" might be. For example, what about an award of general damages to an injured factory worker who is maimed on the job? *Glenshaw Glass* simply does not specify the answer to the question. The American Law Institute, an impressive authority, decided years ago not to recommend a more particularized or articulated legislative "definition" of "income":

> It is believed that this combination of wide inclusiveness and elasticity should be retained, and that a simple reference to "all gains, profits and income" is sufficient. It is also believed that the familiar wording should be continued to avoid generating new nebulous problems of definition.[107]

Legislative history and judicial interpretation of tax law. One of the problems one can detect in *Glenshaw Glass* is the lack of a comprehensive legislative history defining vague or ambiguous tax terms. Tax legislation is a challenging process, and is much too hurried nowadays. The Congressional Committees produce written legislative histories, but cannot do a perfect job of it, and they never describe the real (cloakroom) history of tax legislation. In fact, they sometimes just leave it to the courts to thrash out the meaning of parts of the Code. Without clear guidance from the legislature, the courts face an occasionally perplexing job trying to interpret the Code. As a result, they sometimes rely on a number of interpretative doctrines, including the re-enactment doctrine that you saw in the *Glenshaw Glass* decision.[108]

The re-enactment doctrine assumes that when a Code section is re-enacted, the judicial and administrative interpretations of the section were implicitly incorporated in the new law.[109] The problem is that the doctrine relies on the fiction that the Congress knew of all of the interpretations and actually approved of them. In fact, that almost never happens. Some courts reject the fiction and demand evidence that Congress *really* considered the interpretations, while other

107 All Federal Income Tax Statute, Vol. 1, §x115(a), at 193-194 (Feb. 1954 draft).

108 See Westin, *Dubious Interpretative Techniques for Constructing the Internal Revenue Code.* 17 Wake Forest L. Rev. 1 (1981).

109 See Griswold, *The Regulations Problem*, 54 Harv. L. Rev. 398 (1941).

courts settle for the fiction. Yet other judges presumably pick the version of the re-enactment doctrine that helps make the case come out the way they want it to.

Statutory Construction. The Internal Revenue Code is in reality just one more statute, albeit a long, sometimes intricate, and broadly applicable one, and in theory at least there are standard tools for construing statutes. (In theory, all statutes are sisters under the skin.) In American law, statutory construction, in the sense or explanation or interpretation, lacks predictability because our Courts largely use at least three different approaches to statutory construction: textualist, intentionalist and purposivist. Underneath these overarching approaches, courts may use rules for reading statutes known as Canons of Construction.

It is crucial for the lawyer working under any statute to be aware of how a court is likely to construe that statute. Few courts adhere consistently to one approach, often using two or three approaches at once to glean meaning from a statute. However, some courts are known to favor one approach over another. There is a serious problem here in that the lack of predictable rules of statutory interpretations means that judges can often predetermine the outcome of a case by choosing one interpretive methodology over the others.

Textualist Construction

The textualist approach is objective in nature and is limited to what an ordinary person could reasonably understand the text of a statute to mean at the time it was enacted.[110] Textualists will only look to legislative history to discern intent as a last resort to resolve textual ambiguity.[111] The Supreme Court's leading proponent of textualism was Justice Scalia. He summed up the concept as follows in *Green v. Bock Laundry Machine Company*:

> The meaning of terms on the statute books ought to be determined, not on the basis of which meaning can be shown to have been understood by a larger handful of the Members of Congress; but rather on the basis of which meaning is (1) most in accord with context and ordinary usage, and thus most likely to have been understood by the whole Congress which voted on the words of the statute (not to mention the citizens subject to it), and (2) most compatible with the surrounding body of law into which the provision must be integrated -- a compatibility which, by a benign fiction, we assume Congress always has in mind. I would not permit any of the historical and legislative material discussed by the Court, or all of it combined, to lead me to a result different from the one that these factors suggest.[112]

110 *See* William D. Popkin, Materials on Legislation: Political Language and the Political Process 175 (2d ed. 1997)

111 Mr. Justice Scalia was a well-known textualist. *See, e.g.* his dissent in Pauley v. Bethenergy Mines, Inc., 501 U.S. 680 (1991).

112 490 U.S. 504, 528 (1989).

Intentionalist Construction

Intentionalists are more subjective than textualists. They are quick to consider legislative history when confronted with textual ambiguity in order to ascertain legislative intent.[113]

There are at least two problems with this approach. First, if a court considers floor speeches by individual legislators, there is no guarantee that what one legislator said is what other legislators would say. Second, in broadening the judicial inquiry, courts arrogate more discretion to themselves, thereby increasing the degree of uncertainty in statutory law. A textualist would argue that intent must flow from the statute itself.

Purposivist Construction

Purposivist construction can be the most subjective of the three interpretive methods. At one extreme, its users try to discern "purpose" from an overall reading of a statute, or from legislative history, teasing out the spirit of the act. Purposivist construction may also be used objectively, deriving purpose from an explicit "purpose" section in a statute.[114] While purposivism tends to help in avoiding absurd results, its subjectivity allows for judicial discretion and may allow judicial policymaking.[115] An example is a major controversial case in which the Supreme Court held that tobacco is not a "drug" that it can regulate, even though a plain reading of the statute suggests the opposite.[116]

While the three main approaches to statutory construction fall under textualism, intentionalist, and purposivist, there are some other methods as well. For instance, "Dynamic Interpretation" would go so far as to change previously accepted interpretation of a statute to account for changes in legislative policy that seem to run against a previous interpretation or reading. While this would appear to cast much uncertainty on the law, in its defense it does lead to efficiency. Many older statutes, while largely still serving their purpose, may need some contemporary "tweaking" that a given legislature may not have the time to perform.

Canons of Statutory Construction

The canons of construction are not some formal body of rules that bind courts when interpreting statutes. They are, rather, guidelines for judges to use when faced with ambiguity. In fact, many scholars are skeptical of the canons as they are often dredged up to support strained

---

113 Chief Justice Rehnquist is a good example of an intentionalist. *See, e.g.* his dissent in United Steelworkers of Am., AFL-CIO-CLC v. Weber, 443 U.S. 193 at 254 (1979).

114 *See, e.g.* Americans with Disabilities Act of 1990, 42 U.S.C. §§21101 et seq., Purpose section (b).

115 Justice Brennan was a well-known purposivist. *See, e.g.* United Steelworkers of Am., *supra* note at 201-4.

116 Food and Drug Administration v. Brown & Williamson Tobacco Corp., 529 U.S. 120 (2000).

interpretations.[117] Nonetheless, many judges still use them and the litigator or researcher should be aware of some of the more common ones (and perhaps their paired opposites, too).

Canons can be divided under three rough rubrics. First, *textual canons* deal with dictionary usage, choice of words, grammatical construction and contextual meaning of words as they relate to the whole statute. Second, *substantive canons* are principles taken from the common law, from other statutes or from the Constitution. Third, *reference canons* direct the judge toward the correct extrinsic aids for interpreting a statute, such as the common law or legislative history.

The following is a list of just some of the major canons of construction, which are equally applicable to tax and non-tax cases, in state and federal courts:

- A thing may be within the letter of the statute and yet not within the statute, because it is not within its spirit, nor within the intention of its makers.
- Statutes in derogation of the common law are to be read narrowly.
- Remedial statutes are to be read broadly.
- Criminal statutes are to be read narrowly.
- Statutes should be read to avoid constitutional questions.
- Statutes that relate to the same subject matter (*in pari materia*) are to be construed together.
- The general language of a statute is limited by specific phrases that accompany the general language (*ejusdem generis).*
- Explicit exceptions are deemed exclusive (*expressio unius est exclusio alterius*).
- Repeals by implication are not favored.
- Words and phrases that have received judicial construction before enactment are to be understood according to that construction.
- A statute should be construed such that none of its terms is redundant.
- A statute should be read to avoid internal inconsistencies.
- Words are to be given their common meaning, unless they are technical terms or words of art.
- Titles do not control meaning.[118]
- When two provisions may apply to the same facts, the narrower provision should be applied.

117 Judge Posner has commented "for every canon one might bring to bear on a point there is an equal and opposite canon, so that the outcome of the interpretive process depends on the choice between paired opposites – a choice the canons themselves do not illuminate. (You need a canon for choosing between competing canons, and there isn't any.)" Richard A. Posner, *Statutory Interpretation – In the Classroom and in the Courtroom*, 50 U. Chi. L. Rev. 800, 806 (1983).

118 Abner J. Mikva and Eric Lane, AN INTRODUCTION TO STATUTORY INTERPRETATION AND THE TAX LEGISLATIVE PROCESS, at 24-5, Aspen, 1997.

Although scholarly attitudes to canons of construction may, at times, be scathing, at the state level they often prove to be useful because state legislative history is usually thin or nonexistent.[119]

2. Tax Concepts of Basis and Return of Capital

Article I, section nine, clause four, the Sixteenth Amendment and §61 authorize taxes on income. That implicitly does not permit taxes on *capital income* in the tax world. For example, if you lent $15 to a friend, who repaid the money, you would obviously not report the return of the $15 as income. One way to explain this is that the $15 you got back is a repayment of a loan with a "basis" of $15; that is technical tax talk that you will be familiar with later. Another explanation is to say that you are merely recovering your own capital. Section 1001(a), which defines a gain from dealing in property, confirms this thinking by only taxing receipts in excess of "basis" (your capital) as gain from selling property.

One of the most important concepts that you will leave this course with is "basis." Every item of property that falls within the contemplation of the Internal Revenue Code is assigned basis, stated as a dollar amount. The role of basis is to identify the owner's "tax investment" (or non-taxable capital) in the property in order to assure that when the property is sold or exchanged, the taxpayer will not be taxed on mere recoveries of capital.

> **To illustrate:** If you bought an automobile for $4,000 dollars and sold it six weeks later for $4,200 and knew nothing about the federal income system you would still be shocked if you were told that you had $4,200 worth of income and that you had to pay income taxes on that amount. Don't worry. You don't. The concept of basis assures that the $4,000 will not be taxed. Instead the $4,000 will be viewed as a return of your capital. What about the $200 gain? The answer is that in general if you sell a property that you bought for less than you sold it for, you have a taxable income, characterized as a "gain" under §61(a) and §1001(a).

The important point now is to recognize the role of basis as a protector against the taxation of capital. With this in mind, let us look at what has to be done when taxpayers report income from payments received in kind, followed by a sale of that property.

Let us assume that you are a dentist who is paid with a chicken for your services. Assume that your services were clearly worth $25 and that you bargained for the chicken (it is a particularly fine chicken). Reg. §1.61-2(d) makes it clear that if you are paid in kind you have to report the value of the property received as gross income. That should come as no surprise. But what if you sell the chicken? Assume that you sold it for $25, *what should be your tax basis for the*

119 For an in-depth study of the canons, Sutherland's treatise STATUTES AND STATUTORY CONSTRUCTION (Shambie Singer and Norman Singer eds., 2018) should be consulted.

chicken? Common sense tells you that it has to be $25. If you got $0 basis you would pay taxes twice on the same bird, first when it was received and later when it was sold. The practical fact would be that you would report $50 of gross income on your tax return when in fact you only got $25 in economic value; that would be a completely unfair result So exactly what part of the Code prevents this result? The answer is that you look at §1011 through §1016 for the basis rules. Section 1011 seems to be valuable only for the statement that one begins one's search at §1012. Section 1012, which you should read now, tells you that the general rule is that the basis of property is generally its "cost." Reg. §1.1012-1(a) says that, "the cost is the amount paid for such property in cash or other property."

So, what about the basis of the chicken which was paid for neither in money nor in property? Reg. §1.61-2(d)(2)(I) takes the logical position that the fair market value of the property received for services becomes its basis. Thus, you do indeed have a basis of $25 in the chicken by virtue of being taxed on $25 of income when you took the bird in exchange for your services. In a tax sense the chicken has become part of your capital, "booked" at $25 for tax purposes. Proceeds received in exchange for it cannot be taxed except to the extent those proceeds exceed $25. Otherwise, you would be taxed twice on the same income.

This may seem obvious reasoning now, but do not be fooled into thinking these doctrines were obvious at the outset. Apparently, the 1913 Congress believed that "income" was a Constitutional matter that Congress could not influence.[120] There are no Committee Reports, only materials from Congressional debates which include the following early colloquy involving how a horse bought for $900 and sold for $1,000 ought to be taxed. It should perhaps give us a sense of relief that the legislative history is as sparse as it is:

> *Mr. Cummins.* [S]uppose ten years ago I had bought a horse for $900, and this year I had sold him for $1,000, what would I do in the way of making a [tax] return? . . .
>
> *Mr. Williams* [a member of the Senate Finance Committee]. That thousand dollars is a part of the Senator's receipts for this year and being a part of his receipts, that much will go in as part of his receipts, and from it would be deducted his disbursements and his exemptions and various other things.
>
> *Mr. Cummins.* Would the price I paid for the horse originally be deducted?
>
> *Mr. Williams.* No, because it was not a part of the transactions in that year; but if the Senator turned around and bought another horse that year, it would be deducted . . . .

120 B. Bitter & L. Lokken, FEDERAL TAXATION OF INCOME, ESTATES AND GIFTS ¶5.1 (2018).

Mr. Bristow. Mr. President, I desire to ask a question, and see if I have this matter clear in my mind. As I understood the question of the Senator from Iowa, it was, if he bought a horse ten years ago for $100 --

Mr. Cummins. Nine hundred dollars.

Mr. Bristow. And sold it this year for a thousand dollars, whether or not that thousand dollars would be counted as a part of his income for this year, regardless of what he paid for the horse ten years ago. Is that correct?

Mr. Williams. No; I did not say that. It would be a part of his gross receipts for the year, of course, but it may not necessarily be a part of his net receipts, and therefore not a part of his income that is taxable.

Mr. Cummins. But I asked the Senator from Mississippi specifically whether, in the case I put, the price that was originally paid for the horse could be deducted from the price received.

Mr. Williams. The price paid ten years ago? No; of course not. How could it? When a man puts in his return for his income of the previous year in order to be taxed he puts down everything he has received and everything he has paid out, subject to the exemptions and limitations otherwise provided in the bill. Necessarily that is so. To answer the Senator, I want to read the precise language of the provision.[121]

Dazzled? You ought to be. On top of that, much of what Mr. Williams said is incorrect or at least not the way the law has turned out to be.

3. Recoveries of Capital

Now, the next question is just exactly what is "capital" that can be received as a tax-free return of capital? If a taxpayer lends a car to a friend for the afternoon and the friend returns later in the day, it is obvious that the taxpayer has no income when the car is returned, and, as you know, the same is true if the friend borrowed $10 and returned it later in the day. In both cases, the taxpayer is merely getting his property (or "capital") back. The *recovery of capital* concept is easy to grasp, but there are fact patterns where applying it can be difficult; the following case is a good example.

121 50 Cong. Rec. 3845 (1913). Reported at B. Bittker and L. Lokken, FEDERAL TAXATION OF INCOME, ESTATES AND GIFTS, ¶5.1 (2018).

CLARK v. COMMISSIONER

40 B.T.A. 333 (1939), Acq.

LEECH, J.

This is a proceeding to redetermine a deficiency in income tax for the calendar year 1934 in the amount of $10,618.87. The question presented is whether petitioner derived income by the payment to him of an amount of $19,941.10, by his tax counsel, to compensate him for a loss suffered on account of erroneous advice given him by the latter. The facts were stipulated and are so found. The stipulation, so far as material, follows:

. . .

> 3. The petitioner during the calendar year 1932, and for a considerable period prior thereto, was married and living with his wife. He was required by the Revenue Act of 1932 to file a Federal Income Tax Return of his income for the year 1932. For such year petitioner and his wife could have filed a joint return or separate returns.
>
> 4. Prior to the time that the 1932 Federal Income Tax return or returns of petitioner and/or his wife were due to be filed, petitioner retained experienced tax counsel to prepare the necessary return or returns for him and/or his wife. Such tax counsel prepared a joint return for petitioner and his wife and advised petitioner to file it instead of two separate returns. In due course it was filed with the Collector of Internal Revenue for the First District of California. . . .
>
> 5. Thereafter on or about the third day of February, 1934, a duly appointed revenue agent of the United States audited the aforesaid 1932 return and recommended an additional assessment against petitioner in the sum of $34,590.27, which was subsequently reduced to $32,820.14. This last mentioned sum was thereafter assessed against and was paid by petitioner to the Collector of Internal Revenue for the First District of California.
>
> 6. The deficiency of $32,820.14 arose from an error on the part of tax counsel who prepared petitioner's 1932 return. The error was that he improperly deducted from income the total amount of losses sustained on the sale of capital assets held for a period of more than two years instead of applying the statutory limitation required by Section 101(b) of the Revenue Act of 1932.
>
> 7. The error referred to in paragraph six above was called to the attention of the tax counsel who prepared the joint return of petitioner and his wife for the year 1932. Recomputations were then made which disclosed that if petitioner and his wife had filed separate returns for the year 1932 their combined tax liability would have been $19,941.10 less than that which was finally assessed against and paid by petitioner.

8. Thereafter, tax counsel admitted that if he had not erred in computing the tax liability shown on the joint return filed by the petitioner, he would have advised petitioner to file separate returns for himself and his wife, and accordingly tax counsel tendered to petitioner the sum of $19,941.10, which was the difference between what petitioner and his wife would have paid on their 1932 returns if separate returns had been filed and the amount which petitioner was actually required to pay on the joint return as filed. Petitioner accepted the $19,941.10.

9. In his final determination of petitioner's 1934 tax liability, the respondent included the aforesaid $19,941.10 in income.

10. Petitioner's books of account are kept on the cash receipts and disbursements basis and his tax returns are made on such basis under the community property laws of the State of California.

. . .

The theory on which the respondent included the above sum of $19,941.10 in petitioner's gross income for 1934, is that this amount constituted taxes paid for petitioner by a third party and that, consequently, petitioner was in receipt of income to that extent. The cases of *Old Colony Trust Co. v. Commissioner*, 279 U.S. 716; *United States v. Boston & Maine Railroad*, 279 U.S. 732, are cited as authority for his position. Petitioner, on the contrary, contends that this payment constituted compensation for damages or loss caused by the error of tax counsel, and that he therefore realized no income from its receipt in 1934.

We agree with petitioner. The cases cited by the respondent are not applicable here. Petitioner's taxes were not paid for him by any person as rental, compensation for services rendered, or otherwise. He paid his own taxes.

When the joint return was filed, petitioner became obligated to and did pay the taxes computed on that basis. *John D. Biggers*, 39 B.T.A. 480. In paying that obligation, he sustained a loss which was caused by the negligence of his tax counsel. The $19,941.10 was paid to petitioner, not qua taxes (cf. *T. G. Nicholson*, 38 B.T.A. 190), but as compensation to petitioner for his loss. The measure of that loss, and the compensation therefor, was the sum of money which petitioner became legally obligated to and did pay because of that negligence. The fact that such obligation was for taxes is of no moment here.

. . .

The theory of those cases is that recoupment on account of such losses is not income since it is not "derived from capital, from labor or from both combined." See *Merchants Loan & Trust Co. v. Smietanka*, 255 U.S. 509; *United States v. Safety Car Heating & Lighting Co.*, 297 U.S. 88. And the fact that the payment of the compensation for such loss was voluntary, as here, does not change its exempt status. . . . It was, in fact, compensation for a loss which impaired petitioner's capital.

. . .

Decision will be entered for the petitioner.

Notes on Return of Capital

IRS position. The IRS agrees with the *Clark* decision. It issued an "acquiescence," something it only does in Tax Court and (in the old days) Board of Tax Appeals ("B.T.A.") cases, by which it signals that although it feels it may not be legally bound, it will follow the case. [122] The Board of Tax Appeals is the predecessor of the Tax Court. The Board was not a full-fledged court, but was actually accorded more authority than the Tax Court is now in terms of respecting its analysis of tax law.

The tax law recognizes a great variety of types of "capital" that can have basis, including intangible property. For example, in *State Fish Corp. v. Commissioner*[123] the taxpayer succeeded in having damages recovered for harm to its "goodwill" freed from taxation to the extent that the recovery related to goodwill and did not exceed the taxpayer's basis for the goodwill. Goodwill generally refers to the value of a business in excess of the value of its assets, based an expectation of earnings greater than a fair return on property invested in the business or other means of production or any other positive attribute a firm acquires in the progress of its business.[124] It is usually said to depend on an expectation of continued patronage.[125] Goodwill often has to be bought and paid for, creating capital with a basis for Federal Income Tax purposes.

§104. As you will see later, there is no income tax on recoveries that compensate for physical injuries. Although the exact rationale for the exclusion is obscure, many believe the basic concept is that recoveries for personal injuries are merely recoveries of lost "human capital."[126] So far, no one has tried to provide a formula for computing the tax basis of a human being.

Inventory. The return of capital concept also appears in connection with the sale of inventory. In the case of manufacturers and others who sell inventories, not all receipts are considered gross income. Rather, these taxpayers are allowed to first recover their costs of goods sold. Once they have done that, they have their gross income figure, from which they will subtract

---

122 The acquiescence was made at 1957-1 C.B. 4.

123 48 T.C. 465 (1967), acq.

124 Rev. Rul. 59-60, 1959-1 C.B. 237, §4.02(e).

125 See, e.g., Boe v. Commissioner, 307 F.2d 339 (9th Cir. 1962).

126 See Starrels v. Commissioner, 307 F.2d 574 (9th Cir. 1962), Aff'g 34 T.C. 646 (1961). See also Solicitor's Opinion 132, 1-1 C.B. 92 (1922) for the Solicitor General's Opinion That Personal Injury Damages Just Make the Individual Whole. See Also Rev. Rul.56-518, 1956-2 C.B. 25 (same concept applied to damages on account of wartime persecution).

various other amounts, such as salaries. To take a simple example, a cigar store might have gross receipts (total sales) of $200,000 arising out of the sale of products costing $150,000. The cigar store's gross income is $50,000, not $200,000.[127]

4. Illegal Income and Selected Nontaxable Items

Income from illegal sources is taxable. At one time embezzlers were not taxed on their loot because the Supreme Court initially theorized that their victims could compel them to return the ill-gotten gains.[128] In other words, the Court likened the embezzled funds to the proceeds of a loan. Later the Supreme Court did an about face, clearing the path to taxing all illegal gains, on the theory that the, "consensual recognition of an obligation to repay" that characterizes a loan is missing when money is swiped.[129] Failing to report any income, whatever its source, is a tax crime, and often furnishes a separate basis for conviction. For example, "Big Al" Capone, the notorious 1930's Chicago mobster, eluded successful prosecution for years of murder and mayhem before he was brought down on tax charges, including failure to report income.

Problem 2-1:

1) Sitting in the bleachers, you catch a baseball hit by a famous slugger. The ball is worth $10,000. You keep it.

   a. How much income do you have?

   b. If you immediately sell the ball, how much further income should you report?

   c. Would there be any difference in result if you successfully stole the ball?

2) Assume the 16th Amendment did not exist. Which of the following would be direct taxes that would have to be apportioned?

   a. A tax on net income from cleaning services rendered after a baseball game?

   b. A tax on renting the ballpark to the baseball team?

127 Reg. §1.61-3(a).

128 Commissioner v. Wilcox, 327 U.S. 404 (1946).

129 James v. United States, 366 U.S. 213 (1961).

c. A tax on dividends paid by the incorporated owner of the ballpark to its individual shareholders?

D. ECONOMIST'S DEFINITION OF INCOME

This is the HaigSimons theoretical definition of income[130] that is much favored by economists and is often used by income tax theorists as a possible standard for reforming the income tax:

> Personal income may be defined as the algebraic sum of (1) the market value of rights exercised in consumption [for the year] and (2) the change in the value of the store of property rights between the beginning and end of the [year] in question.[131]

The words "market value of right exercised in consumption" are not a model of clarity. You can think of them as meaning "the value of your personal consumption for the year." Consumption always has a positive value, but changes in net worth (the value of one's assets minus one's liabilities) can be negative or positive. For example, if one lived on capital for a year, there would be a reduction in net worth, but it would be offset by an equal amount of personal consumption.

The economist's theoretical definition suffers from the practical problem of valuing the taxpayer's net worth every year. The U.S. income tax system avoids this problem by measuring changes in net worth only when income or losses are *realized* by means of a sale, exchange or other palpable transaction (known as a *taxable event*). Perhaps the Code could constitutionally tax all unrealized gains, but that is an issue to defer for the moment. As you will see later in the course, the Congress's pragmatic refusal to use annual appraisals to measure income flings open the door to having taxpayers decide exactly when to stage their taxable events.

A vital issue left over by the later paring back of *Eisner v. Macomber* is whether a "realization" is a constitutional requirement. Many believe it is not. For example, Professor Stanley Surrey, a pre-eminent tax scholar considered the realization requirement a rule of administrative convenience.[132] The question is still important, because if realization is not a constitutional requirement, then it would, for example, be clearly permissible to tax Mrs. Smith when Microsoft stock she bought last year for $10,000 appreciates this year to $17,500, even though she has not sold

130 Their work is in turn based on the work of von Schanz and Davidson.

131 H. Simons, PERSONAL INCOME TAXATION 50 (1938).

132 Surrey, *The Supreme Court and the Federal Income Tax: Some Implications of the Recent Decisions* 35 Ill. L. Rev. 779, 793 (1941).

it yet,[133] or to tax people who expatriate on the gains inherent in their property when they leave the country (and U.S. taxing jurisdiction) for good.[134]

E. OTHER SELECTED TYPES OF GROSS INCOME

There is no exhaustive list of items of gross income. Sometimes the question is so esoteric that courts do resort to the Haig-Simons definition.[135] Such cases are extremely rare. The rest of this chapter is given over to exploring some important, perhaps offbeat cases of gross income.

1. Treasure Trove

According to Reg. §1.61-14(a), the finder of a "treasure trove" has gross income to the extent of its value in U.S. currency, in the tax year in which it is reduced to undisputed possession under local law. For example, in a case involving the discovery of $4,467 in cash hidden in a piano bought for $15 at an auction seven years earlier, the Sixth Circuit held that the money was reduced to taxpayer's undisputed possession in the year of discovery and not in the year the taxpayer bought the piano at an auction, hence was taxable when the necessary holding period elapsed.[136]

2. Income from the Discharge of Indebtedness
Read §61(a)(12)

A taxpayer may have gross income as a result of reducing its personal liability. One can view this in the light of the Haig-Simons definition as a case where the taxpayer's liabilities decline, producing increased net worth (excess of the value of assets over liabilities). A famous early case, *United States v. Kirby Lumber Co.*[137] established the principle that if a taxpayer buys back its own debt for less than its face amount (i.e., at a discount), the taxpayer has gross income in the amount of the discount. For example, assume a company borrowed $100,000 in cash and

133 But see Baldwin Locomotive Works v. McCoach, 221 Fed. 59 (3d Cir. 1915) in which the Third Circuit held that a taxpayer who owns property that appreciates in value and who does nothing with respect to that property does not clearly realize the accession to wealth that occurs.

134 In fact, the Code taxes expatriates and departing long-term resident aliens on certain gains when they leave the U.S. §877A.

135 See Bealor v. Commissioner, 72 T.C.M. 730 (1996) and Collins v. Commissioner, 64 T.C.M. 557 (1992).

136 Cesarini v. United States., 428 F2d 812 (6th Cir. 1970), aff'g per curiam 296 F. Supp. 3 (N.D. Ohio 1969).

137 284 U.S. 1 (1931). Kirby Lumber distinguished away an older decision styled Bowers v. Kerbaugh-Empire Co. 271 U.S. 170 (1926)., which found no income where the debt cancellation occurred within the boundaries of a larger overall transaction at a loss resulting from currency fluctuations. Bowers v. KerbaughEmpire Co. is no longer a firm authority and one should assume the Supreme Court would reject the exception it stands for if the case were to come up today.

in exchange issued a note for $100,000 plus appropriate interest. If the company later bought back the note for $80,000 (ignoring interest) before having paid anything back to the lender, the Haig-Simons definition tells us the company has $20,000 of income, so the *Kirby Lumber* rule should be no surprise, given that the taxpayer enjoyed a $20,000 increase in net worth.

Kirby Lumber remains good law, but the general subject of debt cancellation income was a mass of confusion until 1980, when the area was reformed and many judge-made rules were codified. Section 108 of the Code provides some important exceptions that permit what would otherwise be income from the cancellation of debt to be excluded from gross income, but that subject is reserved for Chapter Four

Another leading case in the area is *Old Colony Trust Co. v. Commissioner*,[138] in which an employer paid an executive's income taxes for him. The executive claimed he owed nothing because he never got the money; the IRS got the money. The court held him liable for taxes on the employer's payments because the payments enriched him, whether one looked at the deal as creating cancellation of debt (to the IRS) or as a form of compensation. The court's holding is clearly right.

Consider whether the taxpayer in the next case had income from the discharge of indebtedness, or any kind of §61(a) gross income at all.

ZARIN v. COMMISSIONER

916 F.2d 110 (3d Cir. 1990)

COWEN, Circuit Judge

[Zarin was a compulsive gambler playing at an Atlantic City casino. In two years he lost about $2.5 million of his own money and about $3.5 million in chips that the casino provided to him on credit. He settled the casino debt for $0.5 million, but was in turn assessed tax on the debt cancellation of nearly $3 million.]

. . .

Agreeing with the Commissioner, the Tax Court decided, eleven judges to eight, that Zarin had indeed recognized $2,935,000 of income from the discharge of indebtedness, namely the difference between the original $3,435,000 "debt" and the $500,000 settlement. . . . Since he was in the seventy percent tax bracket, Zarin's deficiency for 1981 was calculated to be $2,047,245. With interest to April 5, 1990, Zarin allegedly owes the Internal Revenue Service $5,209,033.96 in additional taxes. Zarin appeals the order of the Tax Court.

---

138 279 U.S. 716 (1929).

II.

The sole issue before this Court is whether the Tax Court correctly held that Zarin had income from discharge of indebtedness. Section 108 and section 61(a)(12) of the Code set forth "the general rule that gross income includes income from the discharge of indebtedness." I.R.C. §108(e)(1). The Commissioner argues, and the Tax Court agreed, that pursuant to the Code, Zarin did indeed recognize income from discharge of gambling indebtedness.

Under the Commissioner's logic, Resorts advanced Zarin $3,435,000 worth of chips, chips being the functional equivalent of cash. At that time, the chips were not treated as income, since Zarin recognized an obligation of repayment. In other words, Resorts made Zarin a taxfree loan. However, a taxpayer does recognize income if a loan owed to another party is canceled, in whole or in part. I.R.C. §§61(a)(12), 108(e). The settlement between Zarin and Resorts, claims the Commissioner, fits neatly into the cancellation of indebtedness provisions in the Code. Zarin owed $3,435,000, paid $500,000, with the difference constituting income. Although initially persuasive, the Commissioner's position is nonetheless flawed for two reasons.

III.

Initially, we find that sections 108 and 61(a)(12) are inapplicable to the Zarin/Resorts transaction. Section 61 does not define indebtedness. On the other hand, section 108(d)(1), which repeats and further elaborates on the rule in section 61(a)(12), defines the term as any indebtedness "(a) for which the taxpayer is liable, or (B) subject to which the taxpayer holds property." I.R.C. §108(d)(1). In order to come within the sweep of the discharge of indebtedness rules, then, the taxpayer must satisfy one of the two prongs in the section 108(d)(1) test. Zarin satisfies neither.

Because the debt Zarin owed to Resorts was unenforceable as a matter of New Jersey state law, it is clearly not a debt "for which the taxpayer is liable." I.R.C. §108(d)(1)(A). Liability implies a legally enforceable obligation to repay, and under New Jersey law, Zarin would have no such obligation.

Moreover, Zarin did not have a debt subject to which he held property as required by section 108(d)(1)(B). Zarin's indebtedness arose out of his acquisition of gambling chips. The Tax Court held that gambling chips were not property, but rather, "A medium of exchange within the Resorts casino" and a "substitute for cash." Alternatively, the Tax Court viewed the chips as nothing more than "the opportunity to gamble and incidental services. . ." *Zarin*, 92 T.C. at 1099. We agree with the gist of these characterizations, and hold that gambling chips are merely an accounting mechanism to evidence debt.

Gaming chips in New Jersey during 1980 were regarded "solely as evidence of a debt owed to their custodian by the casino licensee and shall be considered at no time the property of anyone other than the casino licensee issuing them." N.J. Admin. Code tit. 19k, §19:461.5(d) (1990). Thus, under New Jersey state law, gambling chips were Resorts' property until transferred to `Zarin in exchange for the markers, at which point the chips became "evidence" of indebtedness (and not the property of Zarin).

Even were there no relevant legislative pronouncement on which to rely, simple common sense would lead to the conclusion that chips were not property in Zarin's hands. Zarin could not do with the chips as he pleased, nor did the chips have any independent economic value beyond the casino. The chips themselves were of little use to Zarin, other than as a means of facilitating gambling. They could not have been used outside the casino. They could have been used to purchase services and privileges within the casino, including food, drink, entertainment, and lodging, but Zarin would not have utilized them as such, since he received those services from Resorts on a complimentary basis. In short, the chips had no economic substance.

Although the Tax Court found that theoretically, Zarin could have redeemed the chips he received on credit for cash and walked out of the casino, *Zarin*, 92 T.C. at 1092, the reality of the situation was quite different. Realistically, before cashing in his chips, Zarin would have been required to pay his outstanding IOUs New Jersey state law requires casinos to "request patrons to apply any chips or plaques in their possession in reduction of personal checks or Counter Checks exchanged for purposes of gaming prior to exchanging such chips or plaques for cash or prior to departing from the casino area." N.J. Admin. Code tit. 19k, §19:451.24(s) (1979) (currently N.J. Admin. Code tit. 19k, §19:451.25(o) (1990) (as amended). Since his debt at all times equaled or exceeded the number of chips he possessed, redemption would have left Zarin with no chips, no cash, and certainly nothing which could have been characterized as property.

Not only were the chips nonproperty in Zarin's hands, but upon transfer to Zarin, the chips also ceased to be the property of Resorts. Since the chips were in the possession of another party, Resorts could no longer do with the chips as it pleased, and could no longer control the chips' use. Generally, at the time of a transfer, the party in possession of the chips can gamble with them, use them for services, cash them in, or walk out of the casino with them as an Atlantic City souvenir. The chips therefore become nothing more than an accounting mechanism, or evidence of a debt, designed to facilitate gambling in casinos where the use of actual money was forbidden. Thus, the chips which Zarin held were not property within the meaning of I.R.C. §108(d)(1)(B).

In short, because Zarin was not liable on the debt he allegedly owed Resorts, and because Zarin did not hold "property" subject to that debt, the cancellation of indebtedness provisions of the Code do not apply to the settlement between Resorts and Zarin. As such, Zarin cannot have income from the discharge of his debt.

IV.

Instead of analyzing the transaction at issue as canceled debt, we believe the proper approach is to view it as disputed debt or contested liability. Under the contested liability doctrine, if a taxpayer, in good faith, disputed the amount of a debt, a subsequent settlement of the dispute would be treated as the amount of debt cognizable for tax purposes. The excess of the original debt over the amount determined to have been due is disregarded for both loss and debt accounting purposes. Thus, if a taxpayer took out a loan for $10,000, refused in good faith to pay the full $10,000 back, and then reached an agreement with the lender that he would pay back only $7000 in full satisfaction of the debt, the transaction would be treated as if the initial loan was $7000. When the taxpayer tenders the $7000 payment, he will have been deemed to have paid the full amount of the initially disputed debt. Accordingly, there is no tax consequence to the taxpayer upon payment.

The seminal "contested liability" case is *N. Sobel, Inc. v. Commissioner*, 40 B.T.A. 1263 (1939). In *Sobel*, the taxpayer exchanged a $21,700 note for 100 shares of stock from a bank. In the following year, the taxpayer sued the bank for recission, arguing that the bank loan was violative of state law, and moreover, that the bank had failed to perform certain promises. The parties eventually settled the case in 1935, with the taxpayer agreeing to pay half of the face amount of the note. In the year of the settlement, the taxpayer claimed the amount paid as a loss. The Commissioner denied the loss because it had been sustained five years earlier, and further asserted that the taxpayer recognized income from the discharge of half of his indebtedness.

The Board of Tax Appeals held that since the loss was not fixed until the dispute was settled, the loss was recognized in 1935, the year of the settlement, and the deduction was appropriately taken in that year. Additionally, the Board held that the portion of the note forgiven by the bank "was not the occasion for a freeing of assets and that there was no gain. . ." *Id.* at 1265. Therefore, the taxpayer did not have any income from cancellation of indebtedness.

There is little difference between the present case and *Sobel.* Zarin incurred a $3,435,000 debt while gambling at Resorts, but in court, disputed liability on the basis of unenforceability. A settlement of $500,000 was eventually agreed upon. It follows from *Sobel* that the settlement served only to fix the amount of debt. No income was realized or recognized. When Zarin paid the $500,000, any tax consequence dissolved.[139]

Only one other court has addressed a case factually similar to the one before us. In *United States v. Hall*, 307 F.2d 238 (10th Cir. 1962), the taxpayer owed an unenforceable gambling debt alleged to be $225,000. Subsequently, the taxpayer and the creditor settled for $150,000. The taxpayer then transferred cattle valued at $148,110 to his creditor in satisfaction of the settlement

---

139 Had Zarin not paid the $500,000 dollar settlement, it would be likely that he would have had income from cancellation of indebtedness. The debt at that point would have been fixed, and Zarin would have been legally obligated to pay it. [Footnote No. 10 in original.]

agreement. A jury held that the parties fixed the debt at $150,000, and that the taxpayer recognized income from cancellation of indebtedness equal to the difference between the $150,000 and the $148,110 value affixed to the cattle. Arguing that the taxpayer recognized income equal to the difference between $225,000 and $148,000, the Commissioner appealed.

The Tenth Circuit rejected the idea that the taxpayer had any income from cancellation of indebtedness. Noting that the gambling debt was unenforceable, the Tenth Circuit said, "The cold fact is that taxpayer suffered a substantial loss from gambling, the amount of which was determined by the transfer." *Id.* at 241. In effect, the Court held that because the debt was unenforceable, the amount of the loss and resulting debt cognizable for tax purposes were fixed by the settlement at $148,110. Thus, the Tenth Circuit lent its endorsement to the contested liability doctrine in a factual situation strikingly similar to the one at issue.

The Commissioner argues that *Sobel* and the contested liability doctrine only apply when there is an unliquidated debt; that is, a debt for which the amount cannot be determined. See *Colonial Sav. Ass'n v. Commissioner*, 85 T.C. 855, 862863 (1985) (*Sobel* stands for the proposition that "there must be a liquidated debt"), *aff'd*, 854 F.2d 1001 (7th Cir. 1988). See also *N. Sobel, Inc. v. Commissioner*, 40 B.T.A. at 1265 (there was a dispute as to "liability and the amount" of the debt). Since Zarin contested his liability based on the unenforceability of the entire debt, and did not dispute the amount of the debt, the Commissioner would have us adopt the reasoning of the Tax Court, which found that Zarin's debt was liquidated, therefore barring the application of *Sobel* and the contested liability doctrine. *Zarin*, 92 T.C. at 1095 (Zarin's debt "was a liquidated amount" and "there is no dispute about the amount [received].").

We reject the Tax Court's rationale. When a debt is unenforceable, it follows that the amount of the debt, and not just the liability thereon, is in dispute. Although a debt may be unenforceable, there still could be some value attached to its worth. This is especially so with regards to gambling debts. In most states, gambling debts are unenforceable, and have "but slight potential . . . " *United States v. Hall*, 307 F.2d 238, 241 (10th Cir. 1962). Nevertheless, they are often collected, at least in part. For example, Resorts is not a charity; it would not have extended illegal credit to Zarin and others if it did not have some hope of collecting debts incurred pursuant to the grant of credit.

Moreover, the debt is frequently incurred to acquire gambling chips, and not money. Although casinos attach a dollar value to each chip, that value, unlike money's, is not beyond dispute, particularly given the illegality of gambling debts in the first place. This proposition is supported by the facts of the present case. Resorts gave Zarin $3.4 million dollars of chips in exchange for markers evidencing Zarin's debt. If indeed the only issue was the enforceability of the entire debt, there would have been no settlement. Zarin would have owed all or nothing. Instead, the parties attached a value to the debt considerably lower than its face value. In other words, the parties agreed that given the circumstances surrounding Zarin's gambling spree, the chips he acquired might not have been worth $3.4 million dollars, but were worth something. Such a debt cannot be called liquidated, since its exact amount was not fixed until settlement.

To summarize, the transaction between Zarin and Resorts can best be characterized as a disputed debt, or contested liability. Zarin owed an unenforceable debt of $3,435,000 to Resorts. After Zarin in good faith disputed his obligation to repay the debt, the parties settled for $500,000, which Zarin paid. That $500,000 settlement fixed the amount of loss and the amount of debt cognizable for tax purposes. Since Zarin was deemed to have owed $500,000, and since he paid Resorts $500,000, no adverse tax consequences attached to Zarin as a result.[140]

V.

In conclusion, we hold that Zarin did not have any income from cancellation of indebtedness for two reasons. First, the Code provisions covering discharge of debt are inapplicable since the definitional requirement in I.R.C. section 108(d)(1) was not met. Second, the settlement of Zarin's gambling debts was a contested liability. We reverse the decision of the Tax Court and remand with instructions to enter judgment that Zarin realized no income by reason of his settlement with Resorts.

DISSENT: Stapleton, Circuit Judge, dissenting.

I respectfully dissent because I agree with the Commissioner's appraisal of the economic realities of this matter.

Resorts sells for cash the exhilaration and the potential for profit inherent in games of chance. It does so by selling for cash chips that entitle the holder to gamble at its casino. Zarin, like thousands of others, wished to purchase what Resorts was offering in the marketplace. He chose to make this purchase on credit and executed notes evidencing his obligation to repay the funds that were advanced to him by Resorts. As in most purchase money transactions, Resorts skipped the step of giving Zarin cash that he would only return to it in order to pay for the opportunity to gamble. Resorts provided him instead with chips that entitled him to participate in Resorts' games of chance on the same basis as others who had paid cash for that privilege.[141]

---

140 The Commissioner argues in the alternative that Zarin recognized $3,435,000 of income in 1980. This claim has no merit. Recognition of income would depend upon a finding that Zarin did not have cancellation of indebtedness income solely because his debt was unenforceable. We do not so hold. Although unenforceability is a factor in our analysis, our decision ultimately hinges upon the determination that the "disputed debt" rule applied, or alternatively, that chips are not property within the meaning of I.R.C. section 108. [Footnote No. 12 in original.]

141 I view as irrelevant the facts that Resorts advanced credit to Zarin solely to enable him to patronize its casino and that the chips could not be used elsewhere or for other purposes. When one buys a sofa from the furniture store on credit, the fact that the proprietor would not have advanced the credit for a different purpose does not entitle one to a tax-free gain in the event the debt to the store is extinguished for some reason. [Footnote No. 1 in original.]

Whether viewed as a one or twostep transaction, however, Zarin received either $3.4 million in cash or an entitlement for which others would have had to pay $3.4 million.

Despite the fact that Zarin received in 1980 cash or an entitlement worth $3.4 million, he correctly reported in that year no income from his dealings with Resorts. He did so solely because he recognized, as evidenced by his notes, an offsetting obligation to repay Resorts $3.4 million in cash .... In 1981, with the delivery of Zarin's promise to pay Resorts $500,000 and the execution of a release by Resorts, Resorts surrendered its claim to repayment of the remaining $2.9 million of the money Zarin had borrowed. As of that time, Zarin's assets were freed of his potential liability for that amount and he recognized gross income in that amount. *Commissioner v. Tufts*, 461 U.S. 300 .... But see *United States v. Hall*, 307 F.2d 238 (10th Cir. 1962).[142]

The only alternatives I see to this conclusion are to hold either (1) that Zarin realized $3.4 million in income in 1980 at a time when both parties to the transaction thought there was an offsetting obligation to repay or (2) that the $3.4 million benefit sought and received by Zarin is not taxable at all. I find the latter alternative unacceptable as inconsistent with the fundamental principle of the Code that anything of commercial value received by a taxpayer is taxable unless expressly excluded from gross income.[143] ... I find the former alternative unacceptable as impracticable. In 1980, neither party was maintaining that the debt was unenforceable and, because of the settlement, its unenforceability was not even established in the litigation over the debt in 1981. It was not until 1989 in this litigation over the tax consequences of the transaction that the unenforceability was first judicially declared. Rather than require such tax litigation to resolve the correct treatment of a debt transaction, I regard it as far preferable to have the tax consequences turn on the manner in which the debt is treated by the parties. For present purposes, it will suffice to say that where something that would otherwise be includable in gross income is received on credit in a purchase money transaction, there should be no recognition of income so long as the debtor continues to recognize an obligation to repay the debt. On the other hand, income, if not earlier recognized, should be recognized when the debtor no longer recognizes an obligation to repay and the creditor has released the debt or acknowledged its unenforceability.

---

142 This is not a case in which parties agree subsequent to a purchase money transaction that the property purchased has a value less than thought at the time of the transaction. In such cases, the purchase price adjustment rule is applied and the agreed-upon value of the benefit received by the purchaser; see, e.g., Commissioner v. Sherman, 135 F.2d 68 (6th Cir. 1943(; N. Sobel, Inc. v. Commissioner, 40 B.T.A. 1263 (1939). Nor is this a case in which the taxpayer is entitled to rescind an entire transaction, thereby to restore itself to the position it occupied before receiving anything of commercial value. In this case, the illegality was in the extension of credit by Resorts and whether one views the benefit received by Zarin as cash or the opportunity to gamble, he is no longer in a position to return that benefit. [Footnote No. 2 in original.]

143 As the court's opinion correctly points out, this record will not support an exclusion under §108(a), which relates to discharge of debt in an insolvency or bankruptcy context. Section 108(e)(5) of the Code, which excludes discharged indebtedness arising from a "purchase price adjustment" is not applicable here. Among other things, §108(e)(5) necessarily applies only to a situation in which the debtor still holds the property acquired in the purchase money transaction. Equally irrelevant is §108(a)'s definition of "indebtedness" relied upon heavily by the court. Section 108(d)(1) expressly defines that term solely for the purposes of §108 and not for the purposes of §61(a)(12). [Footnote No. 3 in original.]

In this view, it makes no difference whether the extinguishment of the creditor's claim comes as a part of a compromise. Resorts settled for 14 cents on the dollar presumably because it viewed such a settlement as reflective of the odds that the debt would be held to be enforceable. While Zarin should be given credit for the fact that he had to pay 14 cents for a release, I see no reason why he should not realize gain in the same manner as he would have if Resorts had concluded on its own that the debt was legally unenforceable and had written it off as uncollectible.[144]

I would affirm the judgment of the Tax Court.

Notes on Debt Cancellation Income

Evaluating Zarin. Zarin is a provocative case. Zarin got $2,935,000 worth of gambling without paying for it, didn't he, and isn't that value therefore income to him unless expressly excluded? He, at least, placed that much value on the chips (gambling opportunities) he got, chances to win money, to "play" and feel good or adventuresome and to be treated like a "big shot," or at least an honored and welcome guest, didn't he?

Couldn't he have "sold" the chips to other customers inside the casino for cash, as a practical matter and as a legal matter? If so, doesn't that mean they were "near cash" or a "cash-equivalent," and worth their face value? Or, he could have cashed them in at once, in a moment of regret or prudence, for cash equal to the price he paid for them and their "face value," or to repay his borrowing/account, couldn't he? So aren't the chips he got, but never paid for, and used as he freely chose to do (without ultimately paying for them) the measure of his "income"?[145]

Problem 2-2:

1) Clyde, a bachelor, earned a gross salary of $600,000 last year. After deductible expenses, his taxable income was $500,000 last year; this put him in the imaginary 40% Federal Income Tax bracket, in the sense that his last dollar of additional income was taxable at a rate of 40%. His Federal Income Tax was $200,000. If during the last year Clyde's employer *had also* paid Clyde's Federal Income Tax liability of $200,000:

   a. What would have been Clyde's gross income for the year?

144 A different situation exists where there is a bona fide dispute over the amount of a debt and the dispute is compromised. Rather than require tax litigation to determine the amount of income received, the Commission treats the compromise figure as representing the amount of the obligation. I find this sensible and consistent with the pragmatic approach I would take. [Footnote No. 5 in original.]

145 But see Barton, B., *Legal and Tax Incidents of Compulsive Behavior: Lessons from Zarin*, 45 Tax Lawyer 749 (1992).

b. How much Federal Income Tax would Clyde be liable for as a result of the employer's paying the $200,000 tax?

2) Clyde has been having trouble paying off his bills. He owes the First Federal Bank $100,000, but the bank said it would settle for $80,000 if Clyde would just go away and never use the bank's services again. He agreed.

   a. How much income, if any, must Clyde report on this transaction?

   b. Is your answer consistent with the Haig-Simons definition of income?

3) Clyde borrowed $40,000 from the Friendly Bank to pay his Visa bill. To do so, he signed a promissory note in favor of the bank. Clyde does not plan to repay the bank. How much income does Clyde have as a result of getting the loan proceeds?

4) Clyde learned that the Friendly Bank sold his $40,000 debt to The Bank of Bahrain. Clyde got wind of the deal and bought the note for $38,000 from The Bank of Bahrain. He still owed $40,000 on the note. How much income, if any, does he have when he buys back the note?

3. Original Issue Discount

Interest income is obviously taxable. For one thing, §61(a)(4) says so, and for another, if that were not the rule it would be a scandal that you undoubtedly have heard of. But what is interest? According to the Supreme Court in *Deputy v. DuPont*, 308 U.S. 488 (1940), the term means "compensation for the use or forbearance of money." So interest is something like income from renting money. So far so good, but the interest payment may be concealed; for example, the parties might hide it in the form of requiring the borrower to pay back more alleged "principal" than she received.

> **To illustrate:** The Really Small Corporation issues a debt instrument with a face amount of $1,000, bearing interest at 6%, but the current rate of interest on similar debt is 7%. As a result, The Really Small Corporation can get only $860 for its debt. The $140 disparity is known as original issue discount, or OID. That discount is considered to be in the nature of interest which came into being because the debt instrument (bond) was issued at too low an interest rate to sell for the full $1,000 face amount. The Really Small Corporation will in fact have to pay the $140 shortfall for the use of the $860, so it is fair to call the shortfall interest. Original issue discount is generally taxed to the holder in little fragments every day, and increases the holder's basis in the

debt, so that if she holds the debt to maturity, its basis becomes equal to the $1,000 face amount for which it is paid off (" redeemed"), and she reports no gain on the redemption (final pay-off).

4. Purchase Price Adjustments and Bargain Purchases

One item that is not taxable is a purchase price adjustment, or rebate. For example, if a car dealer has a sticker price on a particular automobile of $15,000, but after some bargaining the dealer agrees to reduce the price by $2,000, the appropriate characterization of the transaction is the purchase of the car for $13,000, not the purchase of a $15,000, car combined with $2,000 of gross income. [146] Another instance where gross income will not be found occurs where the taxpayer obtains a bargain purchase. For example, if you bought a horse for $500 and later learned that it had excellent blood lines and could be sold as a race horse for $5,000, you would *not* have $4,500 of income on purchasing the horse, although you would have $4,500 of income under the Haig-Simons definition. Instead, the gross income would be recognized when you sold the horse, if ever, for more than your basis in it. Conversely, if you made a bad bargain your loss would also be deferred until you disposed of the property. The original case holding that a bargain purchase of property does not produce gross income appears to be *Manomet Cranberry Co. v. Commissioner.*[147] The bargain purchase doctrine reflects the realization feature of the Federal Income Tax. However, it does not extend to bargain purchases that are intended to be *compensatory*, except in specific exceptional cases which you will see in Chapter 4. If there were no general rule taxing compensatory bargain purchases, there would be a serious hole in the income tax base and a lot of tax-distorted behavior.

A troubling aspect of the Federal Income Tax base is the absence of a general *de minimis* rule with respect to gross income, with results that seem absurd on occasion. Professor Bittker, a leading authority, suggests that when Congress wrote the Code it did not intend to apply it literally to reach every form of gross income.[148] Be that as it may, the lack of *de minimis* exceptions can be distressing to the scrupulous taxpayer.

Problem 2-3:

A few months ago, you bought a painting at a local auction. You paid $100 for it and hung it on the wall. Today you noticed a diamond worth $4,000 taped to the back of the frame. Under local law, the diamond is yours. On top of that, the painting is a rare work of art worth $6,000.

146 See Rev. Rul. 76-96, 1976-1 C.B. 23.

147 1 B.T.A. 706 (1925).

148 B. Bittker & L. Lokken, FEDERAL TAXATION OF INCOME, ESTATES AND GIFTS ¶10.2.6 (1989) (in context of discussion of how intrafamily transfers, such as support payments during marriage, are not gross income despite Glenshaw Glass's sweeping language).

1) Are you taxed on the value of the diamond? See Reg. §1.61-14(a).

2) Are you taxed on the $5,900 unexpected extra value of the painting?

3) What is your basis in the diamond?

4) What is your basis in the painting?

5. Income from Bartering

What if you and a classmate swapped services? Does that mean you both have to report a taxable gain? Read on.

REV. RUL. 7924

19791 C.B. 60

. . .

FACTS

Situation 1. In return for personal legal services performed by a lawyer for a house painter, the house painter painted the lawyer's personal residence. Both the lawyer and the house painter are members of a barter club, an organization that annually furnishes its members a directory of members and the services they provide. All the members of the club are professional or trades persons. Members contact other members directly and negotiate the value of the services to be performed.

Situation 2. An individual who owned an apartment building received a work of art created by a professional artist in return for the rentfree use of an apartment for six months by the artist.

LAW

The applicable sections of the Internal Revenue Code of 1954 and the Income Tax Regulations thereunder are 61(a) and 1.612, relating to compensation for services.

Section 1.612(d)(1) of the regulations provides that if services are paid for other than in money, the fair market value of the property or services taken in payment must be included in income. If the services were rendered at a stipulated price, such price will be presumed to be the fair market value of the compensation received in the absence of evidence to the contrary.

HOLDINGS

Situation 1. The fair market value of the services received by the lawyer and the house painter and includible in their gross incomes under section 61 of the Code.

Situation 2. The fair market value of the work of art and the six months fair rental value of the apartment are includible in the gross incomes of the apartment owner and the artist under section 61 of the Code.

6. Taxation of Reimbursements

Employees and professionals expect many of their bills to be paid by others. For example, the associate at a law firm who travels on firm business would be stunned if the firm did not pay for her meals on the road. Likewise, law firms generally expect their clients to pick up the tab for a variety of expenses they incur. If the firm does not pay, we will see later that the associate will be able to reduce her tax base by claiming a tax deduction for the unreimbursed expense. Conversely, if the associate claims a deduction for the unreimbursed expense, he will be taxed on any later reimbursement, otherwise he would receive a tax windfall of claiming a deduction for money he in effect never paid (because it was reimbursed). A later chapter of the book goes into the taxation of such recoveries in detail.

If the employer maintains a scrupulous reimbursement plan, cooperative employees need not report their reimbursements as gross income, and therefore do not receive any data on their Form W2 (the employer's annual report to the IRS for the employee, declaring the employee's earnings), and the reimbursement is exempt from employment taxes. These obedient plans are referred to as "accountable plans" in Reg §1.62-2(c).

Noncompliance with the accountable plan rules can be a disaster, because payments under non-qualifying arrangements ("non-accountable plans") are taxable to the employee and may subject the employer to the duty to extract employment taxes as well as to penalties for failing to report and deposit employment taxes.[149]

What if an employer reimburses a nondeductible expense of its employee? The answer in principle has to be that the employee has gross income.

7. Frequent Flier Mileage

Airlines commonly offer "free" tickets to passengers who fly a set number of miles in a given period, and offer mileage allowances toward such tickets if the passenger uses a particular kind of credit card. In addition, if a passenger is "bumped" from a flight, the airline will often give her a "free" ticket for her trouble.

149 See Regs. §§ 1.622(c)(5), 31.3121(a)3(b)(2), 31.3306(b)2,(b)(2) and 31.3401(a)-4(b)(2).

These awards created a major ruckus some years back, because of a fear that their treatment might have violated the accountable plan rules. The details are that in 1995 the American Payroll Association, a trade association and lobbying organization, got wind of the fact that the IRS had issued a Technical Advice Memorandum ("TAM") on the subject of the taxation of frequent flier awards. The TAM was directed to an unspecified taxpayer in order to help resolve an issue that arose in an IRS audit. A TAM is a letter response from the IRS to a taxpayer and an IRS auditor, advising what the National Office thinks the law is. TAMs offer a way to get an official reading from the IRS in the midst of an audit. TAMs are not formal authority, just the IRS viewpoint. The TAM alarmed the American Payroll Association enough to provoke it to write the following open letter to then IRS Commissioner Richardson. Politically savvy Commissioners pay attention to letters from irate trade associations:

November 28, 1995
The Honorable Margaret M. Richardson
Commissioner
Internal Revenue Service, Room 3000
1111 Constitution Avenue, N.W.
Washington, D.C. 20224
Re: Taxation of All Business Air Travel to Employees Who Keep
Frequent Flyer Miles or "Denied Seating" Tickets
TAM 9547001

Dear Commissioner Richardson:

I am writing on behalf of the American Payroll Association, which as you know is a nonprofit professional association representing over 12,000 companies and individuals on issues relating to wage and employment tax withholding, reporting, and depositing, to oppose the position taken by the Internal Revenue Service in a technical advice memorandum released this week. With no advance warning or opportunity for public comment, the Service has concluded that the affected employer, which had allowed its employees to keep frequent flyer miles earned through business air travel paid for or reimbursed by the company is required to tax those employees on the value of all their business air travel. This technical advice memorandum also concludes that if the employer had allowed its employees to keep any free tickets or other compensation that they may have received if they were denied boarding on overbooked flights, such a policy would have created a second reason for taxing that employer's employees on the value of all their business air travel. The Service explains in this technical advice memorandum that, because the affected employees were allowed to keep amounts in excess of the actual cost of the business air travel (in the form of frequent flyer miles or "denied seating" tickets), this employer's business air travel reimbursement program violates the "accountable plan" rules of Code section 62(c), including specifically the "return of excess expense advance" requirement of Treas. Reg. section 1.622(f), and the "pattern of abuse" rule of Treas. Reg. section 1.622(k). (See TAM 9547001 (CC:EBEO:Br.2, Nov. 24, 1995).)

If this technical advice memorandum position were expanded to other employers, all employers that allow their employees to keep frequent flyer awards and "denied boarding tickets" would have to review old travel records, to determine the cost of each employee's business travel for all years open under the statute of limitations. The employer would then be required to pay income tax withholding, FICA taxes, and (possibly) FUTA taxes[150] on all the additional income, and to file corrected Forms 941 and Forms W2 for all affected employees. Collection of these additional payroll withholding taxes deposited on behalf of the affected employees would create a final additional administrative burden for employers.

Based on a quick survey of its member companies, the American Payroll Association believes that many employers in America operating otherwise "accountable plans" follow the practices that are prohibited by this technical advice memorandum. Some employers offer to "buy back" the frequent flyer miles, or other free tickets earned by employees, but nearly all employers allow employees to participate in frequent flyer programs and to keep their free awards, unless they choose to sell the free tickets back to the employers. Importantly, in most cases employers have no knowledge (and no way to derive knowledge) about the fact or extent of their employees, participation in frequent flyer programs, or the use by employees of free tickets awarded either under frequent flyer programs, or because of an overbooking problem.

In brief, if the position taken by the Service in this technical advice memorandum were expanded to all taxpayers, nearly every employer in America would be exposed to large potential penalties for underpayment of payroll taxes, retroactive to 1990, and a correspondingly large administrative burden for employers in calculating this tax liability and filing corrected payroll tax and information returns, because they have allowed employees to keep free airplane tickets that the employers have no way of tracking. (These frequent flyer miles could have been generated in dozens of different ways, including through personal air travel, or the increasingly prevalent use of "affinity cards" whereby credit card usage generates many different potential types of awards.) . . .

We realize that technical advice memorandums apply to (and can be relied upon) only by the taxpayer(s) to whom they are issued. However, these pronouncements are in fact used and cited by many taxpayers as an indication of the Service's position on the tax issues presented therein. Taxpayers everywhere will be justifiably concerned when news spreads about the adverse position taken by the Service in this technical advice memorandum. Taxpayers will be further

150 [FUTA refers to the Federal Unemployment Tax Act. It levies a modest tax on employers, based on employee wages, to fund unemployment benefits. §§ 3301, 3302, 3306(b)(1). The tax is imposed at a rate of 6.2% of the first $7,000 of wages. Eds.]

troubled by the fact that although the Service has indicated (in footnote 4 of TAM 9547001) that there are "several acceptable alternatives" that an employer could consider to render its plan "accountable," none of these alternatives is spelled out in the memorandum.

The American Payroll Association submits that the Service has reached an incorrect conclusion in this case, particularly in view of its long history[151] . . . of failing to announce any position whatsoever with regard to the valuation, taxability or reportability of "income" (if any) generated by frequent flyer miles or other "free ticket" bonuses . . . .

> Problem for "accountable plans." At no point during the hearings concerning the regulations and other guidance issued under Code section 62[c] did any service representative ever mention that frequent flyer programs might pose a problem that could prohibit an employer's business air travel program from qualifying as an "accountable plan." Those rules merely require employees to timely account for all their business travel expenses, and to reimburse their employers for any "amount paid" by an employer in excess of substantiated business expense. Frequent flyer bonuses or "denied seating" tickets have never before been cited by the Service as an "amount paid" by the employer that must be returned to the employer by the traveling employee . . . .

In view of this historic lack of published guidance warning employers and employees of the payroll tax consequences of participating in frequent flyer programs, the American Payroll Association urges the Service to rescind Technical Advice Memorandum 9547001, for further consideration. Such harsh payroll tax results should never be imposed on a retroactive basis, without any forewarning or opportunity for public comment. The members of the American Payroll Association, and all the other employers in America, are merely acting as agents of the Internal Revenue Service, in reporting taxable income to employees and collecting payroll tax withholding from their wages. They should not and cannot be held liable for reporting and withholding "mistakes," where the reporting and withholding instructions they have received from the Service are either significantly confusing or nonexistent. If TAM 9547001 were expanded to cover all taxpayers, additional payroll taxes and income taxes would be owed on all employerpaid business air travel, retroactive to 1990, simply because employers may have allowed employees to participate in frequent flyer programs, the tax consequences of which have been "under consideration" for ten years by the Internal Revenue Service. The resulting administrative burden imposed on employers who would have to comply with this rule is unacceptably large. The American Payroll Association objects to this or any other retroactive change in the tax laws affecting taxpayers, employers, service bureaus, and other stakeholders in the federal tax collection system. We would be pleased to meet with you to discuss our concerns in more detail.

151 [We have omitted the history, with the exception of the reference to "accountable plans". The history shows that between 1985 and 1995 The IRS indicated that it did not consider such awards taxable. Eds.]

Sincerely yours,
Carolyn M. Kelley
Director, Government Affairs
American Payroll Association
Washington, D.C.

8. "Economic Benefits"

It is possible to have gross income even though one does not receive either money, personal services or property.[152] Common examples include an employer's providing the free use of a family automobile, or free membership at a country club provided to an executive as part of her compensation package. Economic benefit cases pose difficult compliance problems for the government and are one of the slippery parts of the tax base. For example, how would you treat life insurance coverage provided to an unmarried executive who does not need or want the coverage, but just gets it? Given that she has to die for her family to get the money, should this benefit really be taxed during her life? More confusing still, where does one draw the line between economic benefits and mere incidents of the employment relationship? For example, if an employer provides fresh flowers in all its offices, should the employees be taxed?

COMMISSIONER v. DAEHLER
281 F.2d 823 (5th Cir. 1960)

WISDOM, Circuit Judge.

This Court recently held that an insurance agent's commissions on a life insurance policy purchased on his own life are compensation for services and therefore are taxable income. Commissioner v. Minzer, 5 Cir., 1960, 279 F.2d 338. The Minzer holding is in accord with Ostheimer v. United States, 3 Cir., 1959, 264 F.2d 789. The instant case raises a closely related question. Is a real estate salesman's commission on the sale of a house that the salesman bought for himself taxable income under [§61]? We think it is.

Kenneth Daehler, the taxpayer, is a real estate salesman in Fort Lauderdale, Florida, employed by Anaconda Properties, Inc. Anaconda is a registered real estate broker. Daehler's commissions are on a sliding scale of 50 to 75 per cent, depending on the volume of sales transacted. The established commission for selling vacant property in the Fort Lauderdale area is ten per cent of the selling price.

For some time Daehler had been looking for ocean front property for himself. Early in July 1952 he made a written offer of $52,500 for ten lots at Willingham Beach, outside of Fort Lauderdale. After conferring with Anaconda's sales manager as to procedure, Daehler made

152 See, e.g., Reg. §1.61-1(a).

his offer to purchase on an Anaconda form reciting that he offered $52,500 for the property. He signed as 'purchaser' and executed a check, payable to Anaconda, in the amount of $5,250, as earnest money, for submission with the offer.

Anaconda's sales manager, at Daehler's request, went to the office of the real estate broker representing the seller and stated that he had a customer who would pay $52,500 in cash. No previous offer had been made for the property, and if the owner had been released from the obligation of paying the ten per cent brokerage commission, he would have sold the property to anyone for the sum of $47,250, the net amount, exclusive of certain taxes and costs, he did receive. Later, the taxpayer substituted a check for $5,250 in favor of the seller's agent.

After the sale was consummated the two real estate brokers divided the commission. Anaconda then paid the taxpayer $1,837.50, representing seventy per cent of its check for $2,625.

A majority of the Tax Court, five judges dissenting, held that since Daehler was buying for himself he was not acting as a salesman; the $1,837.50 was not income to the taxpayer but a reduction in the purchase price. 31 T.C. 722. Similarly, in the Minzer case the Tax Court held for the taxpayer on the ground that he was a broker and not an employee. 31 T.C. 1130.

Judge Jones, speaking for the Court in Commissioner v. Minzer denied the validity of these distinctions (279 F.2d 339):

> 'It does not seem to us that the tax incidence is dependent upon the tag with which the parties label the connection between them. The agent or broker, or by whatever name he be called, is to receive or retain a percentage of the premiums on policies procured by him, called commissions, as compensation for his service to the company in obtaining the particular business for it. The service rendered to the company, for which it was required to compensate him, was no different in kind or degree where the taxpayer submitted his own application than where he submitted the application of another. In each situation there was the same obligation of the company, the obligation to pay a commission for the production of business measured by a percentage of the premiums. In each situation the result was the same to the taxpayer.'

These principles are controlling in the instant case. Like the payments to Minzer and Ostheimer, Daehler's commission was a compensatory payment for services.

Daehler performed a service for his employer in regard to real estate purchase identical with the services performed in other transactions. The services were worth 30 per cent of $2,625 to the employer. They were worth 70 per cent of $2,625 to the employee. We see no escape from the conclusion that the amount he received from his employer was compensation for the actions he performed growing out of the employer-employee relationship. Compensation for such services is taxable income of whatever kind and in whatever form it is received, short of a specific exception to the broad statutory definition of gross income.

The decision of the Tax Court is reversed with direction that a decision be entered in accordance with the Commissioner's determination that there is a deficiency in income tax for the year 1952 in the amount of $1,283.77, and that there is an addition to tax for 1952 in the amount of $1,022.23 for substantial underestimation of estimated tax for such year.

Notes and Questions on Fringe Benefits

What is going on here? Why is this not just a bargain purchase, resulting in no tax until the acquired property is disposed of? Is it that the taxpayer provided services as opposed to buying property?

Section 132 as a partial cure. Troubling cases like *Daehler* have largely been swept away by §132, whose purpose is to act as a catchall provision to take care of the miscellaneous fringe benefits that arise in employment. As such § 132 is generally limited to situations involving *employees*, as opposed to independent contractors. Section 132 exempts employees from taxation on a wide array of *de minimis* fringe benefits such as free coffee and a parking space (to the extent it is not worth over $175/month). In other respects, it formalizes some major sources of revenue loss. Chapter Four goes into §132 in some detail. Notice that the regulations under §132, selectively define people who would otherwise be independent contractors as "employees,"[153] in a generous move that is not supported by the Code, but that no one is likely to complain about. The definition does not, however, cover Daehler even if he were an employee (which he apparently was) because his discount related to land, and discounts on sales of land are not exempt. See §132(c)(4).

Effective tax rates? The taxation of people who receive nontaxable income raises the question of the *effective tax rate*, meaning the tax rate on (practical) economic income, as opposed to (legalistic) taxable income. For example, if Ms. A received $20,000 of taxable income and paid $5,000 in taxes, her effective rate would be about 25%. If, however, she also received $30,000 in nontaxable fringe benefits, her effective tax rate would be $5,000/$50,000, in other words 10%. Comparing effective tax rates is a useful way to detect violations of horizontal equity.

a. Value of Gross Income Received in the Form of Property

The general rule is that the amount of gross income received in the form of property is its *fair market value,* meaning what a willing buyer would pay a willing seller if both had a reasonable knowledge of the facts and neither was acting under duress. Although the foregoing definition is found in the estate tax regulations, it is the general meaning of this frequently used term for Federal Income Tax purposes.[154] The definition is easy to say, but often hard to apply.

153 See Reg. §1.132-1(b).

154 See, e.g., Andrews v. Commissioner, 135 F.2d 314 (2d Cir. 1943).

In selected circumstances, the taxpayer can use the value of property *to the taxpayer*, such as when a taxpayer receives a prize of a nontransferable off-season vacation cruise ticket,[155] or of a car that she sells immediately, in which case she can use the actual sale price as the amount of the prize.[156]

b. Valuation of Intangibles

Valuation of intangibles such as stock of a start-up company or the free use of a car is often quite difficult. When it can, the IRS has responded by establishing norms that it applies in particular factual settings. For example, personal travel in a company jet is valued by reference to comparable flights on commercial airliners.[157] Likewise, free use of a company-owned car is generally taxed to the employee by calculating the value of the use of the car on a cents-per-mile basis, like a car rental agreement.[158]

F. PROFESSIONAL STANDARDS OF TAX PRACTICE AND POSITIONS TAKEN ON TAX RETURNS

What is one supposed to do if one is not sure about one's legal position, but has to file a tax return? As you can tell, the tax law is full of gray areas, but there is no ambiguity about the duty to file tax returns. So, how strong must a legal position be to be put on a tax return? Imagine a client calls you and asks for advice regarding a situation that might or might not benefit from the *Clark* rule. You feel there is at least a chance the client would win if the IRS caught the issue and audited it. Assume you would like to make the client happy. How certain must you, as a lawyer, be about advising the taxpayer's position as to her tax return? The answer is that tax practitioners should neither sign returns adopting positions nor advise taxpayers to adopt tax return positions which do not have a "realistic possibility" of being sustained on the merits. This standard has been adopted by the ABA, AICPA,[159] the civil penalty provisions in the Code, and the Treasury in Circular 230, at §10.34(a)(4)(1). The IRS defines the realistic possibility standard as requiring that a reasonable and well-informed person, knowledgeable in the tax law, would,

155 Turner v. Commissioner, 13 T.C.M. 462 (1954).

156 This subject is explored in greater depth in connection with prizes and awards later in the book.

157 Reg. §1.6-21(b)(6)(ii).

158 Reg. §1.61-21(c)(1).

159 See ABA Opinion 85-352 and AICPA Statement on Standards for Tax Services.

upon analysis, conclude that the position has a greater than 50% likelihood of being sustained on its merits.[160] The ABA has not quantified the standard.[161]

There is another reason to be good. Section 6694(a) imposes a penalty of the greater of $1,000 or half the return preparer's fee on the preparer if an income tax return understates tax liability and the understatement is attributable to an unreasonable position. The penalty generally does not apply if the position (1) had "substantial authority" or (2) was adequately disclosed on the return and had a "reasonable basis, or was due to reasonable cause."[162] Finally, it can be expensive to be very bad; §6701 imposes a $1,000 penalty on any individual who assists in the preparation or presentation of any document knowing (or having reason to believe) that the document will be used for tax purposes and who knows that, if used, the document will result in the understatement of the tax liability of another person. (Incidentally, a lawyer advising a client on how to prepare a significant feature of the return is also a return preparer and is also liable for the tax return preparer penalties.) The criminal analog is §7206(2), which makes it a felony, carrying 3-year term in the Big House and fines of up to $100,000, to willfully aid in the presentation of a false or fraudulent return or document to the IRS.

A final reason to be good is that people who turn in tax cheats stand to earn a bounty. Section 7623 gives the Internal Revenue Service the discretion to grant a reward out of the proceeds collected from the wrongdoer and §7214(a) allows informers to share in fines levied on government tax personnel for various wrongdoings. The IRS is increasing its use of informants' rewards and has recently boosted the amount it pays informants to as much as 30% for highly useful information.[163]

In an important development aimed at curbing tax shelters, Circular 230 has been amended to provide that when giving written advice concerning one or more federal tax issues, a tax practitioner cannot base the advice on "unreasonable factual or legal assumptions." They also cannot unreasonably rely on representations, statements, findings or agreements of the taxpayer or any other person, fail to consider all relevant facts that the practitioner knows or should know, or take account of the "audit lottery." 31 C.F.R. §1037(a). Written advice as to tax shelters and other tax-motivated transactions must satisfy additional requirements in order to assure that the practitioner made "reasonable efforts" to the relevant facts, that the writing is well reasoned, makes sufficient disclosures adequate to apprise a reader of all important limitations and risks, and ensures that the advice cannot be misrepresented or misused by a promoter. 31 C.F.R. §10.37. Sanctions for the violator include being disbarred from representing clients before the IRS or being financially sanctioned in an amount up to the gross income derived by

160 Reg. §1.6694-2(b)(1).

161 See generally, Paul J. Sax et al., *Report of the Special Task Force on Formal Opinion 85-352,* 39 Tax Law. 635, 640 (1986).

162 §6694. There are further intricacies.

163 §7623(b)(1).

the practitioner. Lawyers that give tax opinions have to consult these rules carefully to avoid what could be very serious trouble for themselves.

G. CONSUMPTION TAXES AS ALTERNATIVES TO INCOME TAXES

Unfortunately, Americans have a notoriously low propensity to save compared to citizens of most other industrialized countries.[164] Because of our low savings rate, and a popular suspicion that the tax system only makes it worse, there is a serious interest in so-called consumption taxes[165]. Broadly speaking, a consumption tax refers to either of two things: (1) some kind of tax on sales of goods or services; or (2) a tax on "consumed income." The latter is of much greater interest to tax policy experts.

The first kind of tax is commonplace in retail sales of merchandise. You probably pay such a tax at least once a day. For people who want to get a lot more revenue out of these taxes, the confounding legislative question is how to expand the sales tax base while not imposing a crushing tax burden on low and middle income consumers.[166]

The second meaning involves redefining the tax base so as to include only consumed income. In one simplified formulation, the tax base might look like this, based on cash flows.[167]

	Receipts of all sorts, including wages, interest and dividends
+	Loan proceeds
-	Money and property the taxpayer invests during the year
	Consumption for the year (the tax base)

The tax rate would then be applied to this novel base. The rate is only a minor side show; importantly, it could be progressive. Notice how the present income tax basically just taxes the first line of this proposed formula.

The proposed formula assures that stingy people would be able to minimize their taxes by plowing their income back into investments, thereby achieving the goals of increasing national savings and productivity. Flamboyant spendthrifts would be taxed heavily.

164 Personal Savings in the United States averaged 8.82 percent from 1959 until 2018, reaching an all-time high of 17.30 percent in May of 1975 and a record low of 2.20 percent in July of 2005. https://tradingeconomics.com/united-states/personal-savings.

165 See, Andrews, *A Consumption-Type or Cash-Flow Personal Income Tax,* 87 Harv L. Rev. 1113 (974) and Warren, *Would a Consumption Tax be Fairer than an Income Tax?* 89 Yale L. J. 1081 (1980) and Graetz, *Implementing a Progressive Consumption Tax,* 92 Harv. L. Rev. 1575 (1979).

166 There are more complex variations, especially Value Added Taxes, the role of which is to identify the increase in the product's value at each level of production and to impose at tax each time the product moves along from production to final retail sale.

167 See Andrews, *A Consumption-Type or Cash-Flow Type Personal Income Tax,* 87 Harv. L. Rev. 1113 (1974).

Given that a consumption tax will tax savings once they are turned into consumption, how does this model really differ from an income tax? Or, just what is so bad about the way we presently tax savings as opposed to consumption? The following excerpt by Professor Martin Ginsburg to an assemblage of Cambridge dons provides an explanation.

> Let me state in two sentences what this is really about, and proffer a pair of simple examples to illustrate forcibly a consumption tax taxes consumption once and taxes savings once when the savings are consumed. A true income tax taxes consumption once and taxes savings twice. It is in large measure because we are uncomfortable with that perceived, systemic bias in favor of consumption and against savings that our Congress, over the decades, has converted the U.S. tax system into an extraordinarily complex hybrid.
>
> Now come the examples that quantify the precepts. Assume a simple world in which the income tax rate is 40% and the pretax yield rate on financial investments is an annual 10%. If you earn a surplus $1,000, as a good American you must promptly pay the Internal Revenue Service ("IRS") $400 for the privilege of putting $600 in the bank or investing in $600 worth of corporate shares. That yearone $400 sent to IRS is the first tax imposed on your decision to save. In year two, you receive $60 in interest or dividends on your $600 investment, but at the end of year two you must pay IRS $24, [being] 40% of the $60 earned. That $24 is the second tax imposed on your savings decision. At the end of year two, you are left in hand $636, which you may either consume or commit to further savings. Your net yeartwo return of $36 on your $600 investment reflects an aftertax rate of return of 6%. In an income tax, that is viewed as the right answer.
>
> If in the first year you had elected to consume your $600, two opera tickets and an excellent meal, you would have paid the same yearone tax of $400, but that would have been the end of it. One tax on consumption, two taxes on savings.
>
> Let me now try to expose a deeper reality about the way in which we tax the savings component of income. In my example, if we continue to tax in yearone, thus limiting my investment to an aftertax $600, but we exempt the yeartwo yield of $60 from tax, at the end of year two I will have available to consume a total of $660. The inherent rate of return is 10%, $60 on $600, and 10% is of course a pretax or taxfree rate of return.
>
> Assuming stability of tax rates over time, I can get to precisely the same $660 answer by exempting the yearone investment from tax in that year allowing me to invest in yearone a full $1,000 by awarding me a $1,000 deduction for this addition to savings and taxing me, all at once, when I later convert to consumption the investment and its accumulated yield.
>
> Let me again substitute proof for precept. In yearone I invest in full my $1,000 of surplus salary, and in yeartwo my investment earns $100, 10% on yearone's $1,000 investment. At the end of year two I withdraw from savings the entire $1,100. This obliges me to pay an immediate 40% tax of $440. I am left with $660 to consume. As we already appreciate, $660 embodies

a 10% pretax rate of return $60 on $600 and, however odd it may first appear, confirms that I have paid tax once but not twice on my savings.

It is precisely that difference, the difference between $636 and $660, and the attempt to reduce or eliminate that $24 difference, that is both central and common to the variety of socalled tax reform proposals that have sprung up in the United States during the past few years. I announce this with confidence, although I am not sure that all of the legislative sponsors have as yet figured this out.[168]

Problem 2-4:

Which of the following events are taxable, when, and in what amount?

1) Eddie Zapp is a life insurance agent. He is an independent contractor, not an employee. He buys a life insurance policy from an insurer he represents. He gets a big discount which basically allows him to buy the coverage at its cost. Is it taxable to Eddie? What if Eddie were an employee? Is it taxed? See §132(a)-(c) for who is helped by the new rules and Reg. §1.132-1(b) for selected situations in which independent contractors are treated like employees, enabling them to take advantage of some of the benefits arising under §132.

2) Your neighbor's beloved wife fell ill and died. He had a state law duty to support her. Why is this death not a taxable economic benefit to her surviving spouse?

3) Chiropractor massages Astrologer's fingers for half an hour, in exchange for which Astrologer provides helpful advice on astral signs. See Reg. §1.61-2(d)(1).

4) Assuming the Haig-Simons definition of gross income were the law, is it true that unrealized accretions in value and imputed income from the ownership of property or from rendering valuable services for oneself would be taxable?

5) Employer provides its employees with so-called group term life insurance coverage. One of the employees, retired Colonel Neville Putney, gets $100,000 worth of coverage (i.e., if he dies, the policy pays $100,000 to his relatives). If such a policy would normally cost $1,000/year, how much income does Colonel Putney have as a result of this free coverage? See §79(a). Do you think this is fair if Putney never asked for the coverage and he had no relative he would care to have benefit from the policy?

168 Professor Martin Ginsburg, *Taxing the Components of Income: A U.S. Perspective*, 86 Geo. L.J. 123, 131-2 (1997).

6) So far the IRS has not staked out a position as to airline mileage awards. Now assume for a moment that a tax professor got a $500 voucher for being "bumped" from a flight. It gives him the right to travel anywhere in a major airline's travel area and is good for a year, but it cannot be transferred. Should tax professor pay tax on the mileage award?

7) Could the Treasury Department write Regulations to exempt minor amounts of income from taxation, such as the value of unsolicited free samples of soap received in the mail? See §7805(a).

8) Under a consumption tax system, as described earlier in the chapter, what would a taxpayer's tax base be if he earned income as a factory worker, borrowed no money and made no investments during the year?

CHAPTER 3 - GAINS AND LOSSES DERIVED FROM DEALING IN PROPERTY

A. INTRODUCTION

1. Basic Concepts

Section 61(a)(3) requires taxpayers to include in gross income any gains that they generated from "dealing in property" during the taxable year, without telling us what "dealing" or "gain" mean.[169] Section 1001 fills in part of the gap by telling us that a *gain* from dealing in property means a disposition of property where the *amount realized* exceeds the *adjusted basis* of the property.[170] A *loss* arises if the adjusted basis exceeds the amount realized. At this point you should stop and read §1001(a) through (c). The remainder of this chapter is primarily devoted to defining the two key terms, amount realized and adjusted basis. First, however, we have to deal with whether the gain or loss is "realized."

2. The Realization Requirement, or "Did Anything Happen?"

The term "realization" applies in two different settings, realization of gross income and realization of gain or loss from dealing in property. An example of the former occurs when a taxpayer sitting in bleachers catches a home run ball or gets a paycheck. This chapter is concerned with realized gains or losses from dealing in property.

It is a fundamental rule of our tax system that a gain in appreciated property is taxed only when realized. Realization in this sense means "taking" or "making real" in the sense of a conversion into money or the equivalent of money, or to acquire and get hold of gain in these senses. Certainly realization occurs on a sale for cash or for other property whose value can be determined and expressed in monetary terms. Yet, as *Eisner v. Macomber*[171] shows, not every

169 See also Reg. §1.61-6.

170 §1001(a).

171 252 U.S. 189 (1920), (the facts involved a corporation that issued a stock dividend, which was held not to generate gross income to the shareholders).

change in the form of holding gain will amount to a realization. It seems there must be some transaction with respect to the property in order to "realize" the gain. So, the question arises, will any "dealing in" appreciated property constitute a realization? For example, could a disposition such as by gift, even though nothing more than gratitude or a warm feeling in the giver's heart is received in exchange, be treated as a realization of the gain? Whether or not the making of a gift could be treated as a realization of gain, the general rule of our tax system is to not tax the donor. However, there are several exceptions. For example, §84 provides that the transferor of appreciated property to a political party is taxed on the appreciation as if the taxpayer sold the property.

The realization requirement means that gains that have accrued over a period of time will be taxed only when there is a sale, or a taxable exchange, or some other palpable event that is regarded as "realization" of the gain. Similarly, losses will not be deductible during the years the property goes down in value, but only upon realization. Therefore, a taxpayer is free to choose when to realize gains and losses. As a matter of tax planning, a shrewd taxpayer may opt to realize losses early, by sale, and postpone gains by deferring sales. The appreciation or depreciation in value may occur because of profits retained by a corporation, as they were by the corporation in *Eisner v. Macomber* in years prior to the declaration and payment of the stock dividend. Or the appreciation or depreciation may simply take place because an asset that the taxpayer owns directly has risen or fallen in market value. Such an asset might be land, a painting, a diamond, whether held for personal use or for investment. Because borrowing against one's own property is not considered a form of realization, one popular way to get cash from appreciated property is to borrow against it.

The realization requirement commonly works to the advantage of taxpayers who have the ability to defer the income tax on gains. An "accretion" (or "accrual") approach to the taxation of such gains would require that the taxpayer report the gains and pay tax on them each year. This approach would impose difficult burdens of valuation, liquidity and perhaps psychic acceptance of the tax burden by taxpayers. Our system of elective deferral tends to lessen the administrative and compliance problems by imposing a tax only when the asset is disposed of. The gain or loss is then manifest and the amount can be determined with greater certainty and finality than in the case of property fluctuating in value from one year to another and not yet disposed of by the taxpayer. To tax gains on an accrual approach would probably also involve allowing accrued but unrealized losses, and there too the problems of administration and compliance would be substantial. We can use an accretion method for selected properties, such as publicly-traded stocks and bonds.

To set the stage for what is to come, consider these examples that illustrate the range of alternatives available to the legislature:

To illustrate: Suppose Taxpayer buys Blackacre for $50,000 and watches happily as it rises in value to $90,000. Should we tax her on the gain, even though she has not sold it? Perhaps, but we don't. What if she gives the property away? Should we tax her then? Same answer. What if she borrows against it? Same answer. What if she dies holding the property and it is worth $90,000? Same answer, even though basis in the property changes under the special tax rules applicable to property in a decedent's estate.[172] What if she trades it for Whiteacre, which is worth $90,000? The general answer is again no tax.[173] These are fundamental choices that Congress had to face in designing the Federal Income Tax.

Sometimes taxpayers would prefer an accrual approach because they would want to claim their transactions result in realization of *loss*in order to reduce their Federal Income Tax base. Realizing such losses for Federal Income Tax purposes without actually giving up control of the investment was a popular activity after the stock market crash in 1929. The leading case from that era is *DuPont v. Commissioner*, in which Pierre S. DuPont and his trusted business associate, John J. Raskob, concocted a plan involving millions of dollars worth of reciprocal stock sales in order to show tax losses without really disposing of the stock.[174] The IRS succeeded in knocking out the scheme as a sham.

A small body of early cases established that some corporate changes were so minor that the shareholders did not realize any gain or loss on their occurrence.

To illustrate: What if I own 10 shares of stock of X Corporation that decides to change its name, and in connection with doing so the corporation directs me to turn in my certificates for 10 shares of stock of X Corporation and get back 10 new shares of stock of Y corporation that is identical except for the name change? The answer is that there is no realization, because not enough happened to justify imposing a tax (or allowing a loss).[175] It was a "non event." Not necessarily so if X Corporation changed its place of incorporation; that can be a material change because it may have a big impact on my rights as a shareholder. If the powers described in its charter change significantly, it is realistic to say that I own stock in a truly "different company" and so there is a realization for tax purposes, even though the name, assets and liabilities of the corporation are unchanged.[176]

---

172 The estate tax is being gradually repealed, as of this writing. As that occurs, the rule that inherited property takes a fair market value at death basis will gradually be eradicated. That subject is revisited later in this book.

173 Chapter 10 discusses tax-deferred transactions, including tax-deferred exchanges of business or investment real estate.

174 37 B.T.A. 1198 (1938), aff'd 118 F.2d 544 (3d. Cir. 1941).

175 Weiss v. Stearn, 265 U.S. 242 (1924).

176 United States v. Phellis, 257 U.S. 156 (1921); Marr v. United States, 268 U.S. 536, 540542 (1925).

Normally, any exchange is considered a taxable disposition of property, but do you think the Supreme Court was right to have found a "realization" in the following case? To prepare you for the next case, imagine you went out on the town and gave your hat to the hat check counter. When you came back, you got someone else's hat by accident. It was made by the same hat maker, was the same size as your hat and was in the same condition as the hat you checked. Did that result in realization of gain or loss to you?

COTTAGE SAVINGS ASSOCIATION v. COMMISSIONER

499 U.S. 554 (1991)

Justice MARSHALL delivered the opinion of the Court.

[The taxpayer was a Savings and Loan (S&L) that held numerous low-interest mortgages that declined in value when interest rates surged in the 1970's. The taxpayer could benefit from the sale of these mortgages so as to declare the tax-deductible losses, but was deterred from doing so because it would also have to report the losses to the Federal Home Loan Bank Board (FHLBB) and risk closure. The FHLBB issued "Memorandum R-49" which stated that losses from exchanges with other lenders for "substantially identical" mortgages did not have to be reported to the FHLBB. The taxpayer engaged in such an exchange of an aggregate of such mortgages and claimed the loss deduction on its tax return. The Tax Court held the deduction was permissible, and the Court of Appeals agreed that the losses had been realized but found that the losses were not actually sustained for tax purposes in the year of the exchange. The question presented is whether the exchanged properties were "materially different," such that the loss on their exchange was "realized."]

II

Rather than assessing tax liability on the basis of annual fluctuations in the value of a taxpayer's property, the Internal Revenue Code defers the tax consequences of a gain or loss in property value until the taxpayer "realizes" the gain or loss. The realization requirement is implicit in § 1001(a) of the Code . . . which defines "the gain [or loss] from the sale or other disposition of property" as the difference between "the amount realized" from the sale or disposition of the property and its "adjusted basis." As this Court has recognized, the concept of realization is "founded on administrative convenience." *Helvering v. Horst*, 311 U.S. 112, 116 (1940). Under an appreciationbased system of taxation, taxpayers and the Commissioner would have to undertake the "cumbersome, abrasive, and unpredictable administrative task" of valuing assets on an annual basis to determine whether the assets had appreciated or depreciated in value. See B. Bitter & L. Lokken, Para 5.2, p. 516 (2d ed. 1989). In contrast, "[a] change in the form or extent of an investment is easily detected by a taxpayer or an administrative officer." R. Magill, Taxable Income 79 (rev. ed. 1945).

Section 1001(a)'s language provides a straightforward test for realization: to realize a gain or loss in the value of property, the taxpayer must engage in a "sale or other disposition of [the] property." The parties agree that the exchange of participation interests in this case cannot be characterized as a "sale" under § 1001(a); the issue before us is whether the transaction constitutes a "disposition of property." The Commissioner argues that an exchange of property can be treated as a "disposition" under § 1001(a) only if the properties exchanged are materially different. The Commissioner further submits that, because the underlying mortgages were essentially economic substitutes, the participation interests exchanged by Cottage Savings were not materially different from those received from the other S & L's. Cottage Savings, on the other hand, maintains that any exchange of property is a "disposition of property" under § 1001(a), regardless of whether the property exchanged is materially different. Alternatively, Cottage Savings contends that the participation interests exchanged were materially different because the underlying loans were secured by different properties.

We must therefore determine whether the realization principle in § 1001(a) incorporates a "material difference" requirement. If it does, we must further decide what that requirement amounts to and how it applies in this case. We consider these questions in turn.

A

Neither the language nor the history of the Code indicates whether and to what extent property exchanged must differ to count as a "disposition of property" under § 1001(a). Nonetheless, we readily agree with the Commissioner that an exchange of property gives rise to a realization event under §1001(a) only if the properties exchanged are "materially different." The Commissioner himself has by regulation construed § 1001(a) to embody a material difference requirement:

> "Except as otherwise provided . . . the gain or loss realized from the conversion of property into cash, *or from the exchange of property for other property differing materially either in kind or in extent*, is treated as income or as loss sustained." Treas. Reg. § 1.10011, 26 CFR § 1.10011 (1990) (emphasis added).

Because Congress has delegated to the Commissioner the power to promulgate "all needful rules and regulations for the enforcement of [the Internal Revenue Code]," 26 U. S. C. § 7805(a), we must defer to his regulatory interpretations of the Code so long as they are reasonable, see *National Muffler Dealers Assn., Inc. v. United States*, 440 U.S. 472, 476477 (1979).

We conclude that Treasury Regulations § 1.10011 is a reasonable interpretation of § 1001(a). Congress first employed the language that now comprises § 1001(a) of the Code in § 202(a) of the Revenue Act of 1924, ch. 234, 43 Stat. 253; that language has remained essentially unchanged through various reenactments. And since 1934, the Commissioner has construed the statutory term "disposition of property" to include a "material difference" requirement. As we have recognized, "'Treasury regulations and interpretations long continued without substantial change, applying to unamended or substantially reenacted statutes, are deemed to have received congressional approval and have the effect of law.'" *United States v. Correll*, 389 U.S. 299, 305306 (1967). . . .

Treasury Regulation § 1.0011 is also consistent with our landmark precedents on realization. In a series of early decisions involving the tax effects of property exchanges, this Court made clear that a taxpayer realizes taxable income only if the properties exchanged are "materially" or "essentially" different. See *United States v. Phellis*, 257 U.S. 156, 173 (1921); *Weiss v. Stearn*, 265 U.S. 242, 253254 (1924); *Marr v. United States*, 268 U.S. 536, 540542 (1925); . . . . Because these decisions were part of the "contemporary legal context" in which Congress enacted § 202(a) of the 1924 Act . . . and because Congress has left undisturbed through subsequent reenactments of the Code the principles of realization established in these cases, we may presume that Congress intended to codify these principles in § 1001(a) . . . . The Commissioner's construction of the statutory language to incorporate these principles certainly was reasonable.

B

Precisely what constitutes a "material difference" for purposes of § 1001(a) of the Code is a more complicated question. The Commissioner argues that properties are "materially different" only if they differ in economic substance. To determine whether the participation interests exchanged in this case were "materially different" in this sense, the Commissioner argues, we should look to the attitudes of the parties, the evaluation of the interests by the secondary mortgage market, and the views of the FHLBB. We conclude that § 1001(a) embodies a much less demanding and less complex test.

Unlike the question whether §1001(a) contains a material difference requirement, the question of what constitutes a material difference is not one on which we can defer to the Commissioner. For the Commissioner has not issued an authoritative, prelitigation interpretation of what property exchanges satisfy this requirement. Thus, to give meaning to the material difference test, we must look to the case law from which the test derives and which we believe Congress intended to codify in enacting and reenacting the language that now comprises § 1001(a). See . . . .

We start with the classic treatment of realization in *Eisner v. Macomber*, *supra* . . . . In *Macomber*, a taxpayer who owned 2,200 shares of stock in a company received another 1,100 shares from the company as part of a pro rata stock dividend meant to reflect the company's growth in value. At issue was whether the stock dividend constituted taxable income. We held that it did not, because no gain was realized. . . . We reasoned that the stock dividend merely reflected the increased worth of the taxpayer's stock . . . and that a taxpayer realizes increased worth of property only by receiving "something of exchangeable value proceeding from the property," . . . .

In three subsequent decisions *United States v. Phellis, supra*; *Weiss v. Stearn, supra*; and *Marr v. United States, supra* we refined *Macomber's* conception of realization in the context of property exchanges. In each case, the taxpayer owned stock that had appreciated in value since its acquisition. And in each case, the corporation in which the taxpayer held stock had reorganized into a new corporation, with the new corporation assuming the business of the old corporation. While the corporations in *Phellis* and *Marr* both changed from New Jersey to Delaware corporations, the original and successor corporations in *Weiss* both were incorporated in Ohio. In each case, following the reorganization, the stockholders of the old corporation received shares in the new corporation equal to their proportional interest in the old corporation.

The question in these cases was whether the taxpayers realized the accumulated gain in their shares in the old corporation when they received in return for those shares stock representing an equivalent proportional interest in the new corporations. In *Phellis* and *Marr*, we held that the transactions were realization events. We reasoned that because a company incorporated in one State has "different rights and powers" from one incorporated in a different State, the taxpayers in *Phellis* and *Marr* acquired through the transactions property that was "materially different" from what they previously had. *United States v. Phellis*, 257 U.S., at 169173; see *Marr v. United States, supra*, at 540542 (using phrase "essentially different"). In contrast, we held that no realization occurred in *Weiss*. By exchanging stock in the predecessor corporation for stock in the newly reorganized corporation, the taxpayer did not receive "a thing really different from what he therefore had." *Weiss v. Stearn, supra*, at 254. As we explained in *Marr*, our determination that the reorganized company in *Weiss* was not "really different" from its predecessor turned on the fact that both companies were incorporated in the same State. See *Marr v. United States, supra*, at 540542 (outlining distinction between these cases).

Obviously, the distinction in *Phellis* and *Marr* that made the stock in the successor corporations materially different from the stock in the predecessors was minimal. Taken together, *Phellis*, *Marr*, and *Weiss* stand for the principle that properties are "different" in the sense that is "material" to the Internal Revenue Code so long as their respective possessors enjoy legal entitlements that are different in kind or extent. Thus, separate groups of stock are not materially different if they confer "the same proportional interest of the same character in the same corporation." . . . However, they are materially different if they are issued by different corporations . . . or if they confer "different rights and powers" in the same corporation, *Marr v. United States, supra*, at 541. No more demanding a standard than this is necessary in order to satisfy the administrative purposes underlying the realization requirement in § 1001(a). . . . For, as long as the property entitlements are not identical, their exchange will allow both the Commissioner and the transacting taxpayer easily to fix the appreciated or depreciated values of the property relative to their tax bases.

In contrast, we find no support for the Commissioner's "economic substitute" conception of material difference. According to the Commissioner, differences between properties are material for purposes of the Code only when it can be said that the parties, the relevant market (in this case the secondary mortgage market), and the relevant regulatory body (in this case the FHLBB) would consider them material. Nothing in *Phellis, Weiss,* and *Marr* suggests that exchanges of properties must satisfy such a subjective test to trigger realization of a gain or loss.

Moreover, the complexity of the Commissioner's approach ill serves this goal of administrative convenience that underlies the realization requirement. In order to apply the Commissioner's test in a principled fashion, the Commissioner and the taxpayer must identify the relevant market, establish whether there is a regulatory agency whose views should be taken into account, and then assess how the relevant market participants and the agency would view the transaction. The Commissioner's failure to explain how these inquiries should be conducted further calls into question the workability of his test.

Finally, the Commissioner's test is incompatible with the structure of the Code. Section 1001(c) of Title 26 provides that a gain or loss realized under § 1001(a) "shall be recognized" unless one of the Code's nonrecognition provisions applies. One such nonrecognition provision withholds recognition of a gain or loss realized from an exchange of properties that would appear to be economic substitutes under the Commissioner's material difference test. This provision, commonly known as the "like kind" exception, withholds recognition of a gain or loss realized "on the exchange of property held for productive use in a trade or business or for investment . . . for property of like kind which is to be held either for productive use in a trade or business or for investment." . . . § 1031(a)(1). If Congress had expected that exchanges of similar properties would not count as realization events under § 1001(a), it would have had no reason to bar recognition of a gain or loss realized from these transactions.

C

Under our interpretation of § 1001(a), an exchange of property gives rise to a realization event so long as the exchanged properties are "materially different" that is, so long as they embody legally distinct entitlements. Cottage Savings' transactions at issue here easily satisfy this test. Because the participation interests exchanged by Cottage Savings and the other S & L's derived from loans that were made to different obligers and secured by different homes, the exchanged interests did embody legally distinct entitlements. Consequently, we conclude that Cottage Savings realized its losses at the point of the exchange.

The Commissioner contends that it is anomalous to treat mortgages deemed to be "substantially identical" by the FHLBB as "materially different." The anomaly, however, is merely semantic; mortgages can be substantially identical for Memorandum R49 purposes and still exhibit "differences" that are "material" for purposes of the Internal Revenue Code. Because Cottage Savings received entitlements different from those it gave up, the exchange put both Cottage Savings and the Commissioner in a position to determine the change in the value of Cottage Savings' mortgages relative to their tax bases. Thus, there is no reason not to treat the exchange of these interests as a realization event, regardless of the status of the mortgages under the criteria of Memorandum R49.

III

Although the Court of Appeals found that Cottage Savings' losses were realized, it disallowed them on the ground that they were not sustained under § 165(a) . . . . Section 165(a) states that a deduction shall be allowed for "any loss sustained during the taxable year and not compensated for by insurance or otherwise." Under the Commissioner's interpretation of § 165(a),

> "To be allowable as a deduction under section 165(a), a loss must be evidenced by closed and completed transactions, fixed by identifiable events, and, except as otherwise provided in section 165(h) and § 1.16511, relating to disaster losses, actually sustained during the taxable year. Only a bona fide loss is allowable. Substance and not mere form shall govern in determining a deductible loss." Treas. Reg. § 1.1651(b) . . . .

The Commissioner offers a minimal defense of the Court of Appeals' conclusion. The Commissioner contends that the losses were not sustained because they lacked "economic substance," by which the Commissioner seems to mean that the losses were not bona fide. We say "seems" because the Commissioner states the position in one sentence in a footnote in his brief without offering further explanation. . . .. . .

IV

For the reasons set forth above, the judgment of the Court of Appeals is reversed, and the case is remanded for further proceedings consistent with this opinion.

So ordered.

[Blackmun and White dissented on the grounds that the differences in the mortgage pools were immaterial and that no losses should be realized for tax purposes. They viewed differences as "material" only if they have "the capacity to influence a decision." Eds.]

Notes

Cottage Savings implicates the important question of how one determines whether a Treasury Regulation is valid. The case itself relied in part on the Treasury Regulations, but how does one know whether an interpretative regulation is valid? The usual judicial standard is to demand only that the regulation be a reasonable interpretation of the law. All things being equal, long-standing regulations tend to be accorded more weight than recent ones, given that taxpayer reliance on them has increased. Also, regulations that are close in time to the enactment of the law they interpret are given some preference.[177]

Numerous other transactions or events -- even "dispositions" -- do not cause realization of income or loss, including the following common transactions:

a. A gift. The donor is not taxed on unrealized appreciation when he or she gives the property to the donee. You will soon see that the donee just takes the donor's basis in the property.

b. A division of property between co-owners, such as the severance of property held as joint tenants, is not a taxable event.[178]

c. A pledge of property. This is just a security for a loan.[179]

d. Alteration of the terms of a contract.[180]

e. The grant of an option.[181]

On the other hand, some transactions are taxable events even though the reasons for taxing them are not obvious. A leading example is the modification of a debt. Bankers are known to say that debtors who get into trouble become partners, meaning that suddenly bankers develop an intimate concern for the economic health of the debtor, and often make concessions to make sure the debtor survives. These concessions can take numerous forms, including reducing the interest rate on a loan, increasing or decreasing collateral that supports the loan, or stretching the repayment period. To someone not versed in the tax law, that hardly seems like a

177 See Griswold, *A summary of the Regulations Problem*, 54 Harv. L. Rev. 398 (1941).

178 Rev. Rul. 55-77, 1955-1 C.B. 339.

179 See Helvering v. F.R. Lazarus & Co., 308 U.S. 252 (1939).

180 Commissioner v. Olmstead Life Agency, 304 F.2d 16 (8th Cir. 1962). But see Reg. § 1.1001-3(b) which makes a material modification of a debt instrument a sale or exchange as far as the creditor is concerned.

181 Koch v. Commissioner, 67 T.C. 71 (1976), acq.

disposition of the banker's debt, but as far at the Treasury Regulations are concerned, it is just that, unless the change is trivial. Reg. §1.1001-3, which is not reproduced in most companion books, is the authority for the position.[182] The practical effect is that the creditor will report the value of the new debt as the amount realized and subtract the adjusted basis of the old debt in determining the amount of gain or loss on the deemed disposition of the debt.

Even if the transaction you have under the tax microscope is a taxable event, it is not always obvious when the tax event took place. To make that determination, you need to consult the tax law and your common sense. It is an issue that comes up often in connection with sales of property. Normally, a sale occurs when title changes, but you likely recall from your real property course that it may occur earlier, when beneficial ownership changes. The tax rules are similar. The general statement is that mere passage of title is not enough to result in a completed transfer. Rather, ownership for Federal Income Tax purposes begins when the transferee taxpayer gets the benefits and burdens of ownership of the property, or title to the property, whichever occurs first. One gets the benefits of ownership if one gets the appreciation in the value of the property, and one bears the economic burden if one must bear the loss if the property loses value.[183] (It is unclear who has ownership when one becomes entitled to the benefits of ownership and the other bears the risk of loss of value.)

Problem 3-1:

1) Mary and John are both jute dealers in Dos Huevos, New Mexico. At the end of the year each one holds exactly 10 tons of jute (which is a fungible commodity) that has declined in value. By swapping titles to the jute, they think they can both realize tax losses with no change in economic position. The jute is located in adjacent warehouses in Dos Huevos. Does the plan work?

2) Mary owes John $10,000 at an interest rate of 5% payable over three years with her jute as collateral. John and she agree to replace the collateral with a mortgage on her home, which mortgage is unmarketable. What result to John, in general terms? See Reg. §1.1001-3(a)(1). It may not be in your book of Codes and Regulations, so it is reproduced below.[184] Assume, based on the foregoing footnote, that the change is a significant modification of the debt.

182 §1.1001-3(a) treats a significant modification of a debt instrument as an exchange. This includes any change of rights of the holder or issuer. §1.1001-3(e)(2) describes material modifications to include changes in interest rate of over 25 basis points (1/4 of one percent) or an over 5% change in the annual yield.

183 See, e.g., Grodt & McKay Realty, Inc. v. Commissioner, 77 T.C. 1221 (1981).

184 Here are the key words of the pertinent Regulation [Reg.§1.1001-3(b)]: "For purposes of Sec. 1.1001-1(a), a significant modification of a debt instrument, within the meaning of this section, results in an exchange of the original debt

3) Rock star David Bowie, an English pop star, set off an avalanche of activity on Wall Street when he sold bonds (for which he was personally liable), backed by his compositions and recordings. The bonds' interest rate payable to investors in the bonds depended on his success in exploiting this property (known as his "catalog" in the trade)[185]. Other musicians later joined, issuing their own "Bowie Bonds." Was he taxed on the receipt of the cash from selling the bonds? Should the fact that he used his "catalog" as security for the bonds matter?

B. REALIZATION BY SURPRISE: IMPLICIT SALES

Whenever property changes hands in exchange for consideration of any sort, the transaction may attract a Federal Income Tax.

There are a number of cases on point. For example, in *United States v. Davis* the Supreme Court considered the case of a husband who used appreciated duPont stock to discharge his marital obligations to his wife in connection with their separation agreement.[186] She accepted the stock "in full settlement of" any claims against her husband, including dower rights, testamentary rights and so forth. He claimed that the transfer was a mere nontaxable division of property. Not so, said the court. Rather it was a taxable exchange of appreciated property for the discharge of his legal obligations. He was therefore obligated to pay income taxes as if he sold the stock and gave the cash proceeds to his ex-wife. Many divorce lawyers have gotten into significant trouble as a result of overlooking the issue before §1041 was enacted. (Section 1041 treats interspousal payments and payments incident to divorce as nontaxable gifts between the spouses rather than taxable exchanges, thereby largely eliminating the *Davis* issue in practice.) Pity the poor divorce lawyer who recommended a *Davis* transaction to the like of Mr. Davis. It happened often.

What you need to recognize is that whenever appreciated (or depreciated) property is transferred be alert to the pervasive risk that the transfer is taxable. If it is not, it is only because some specific Code section exempts the gain. A gift of property is one such example. Gifts are discussed in the next chapter.

Incidentally, the *Davis* case could not be resolved without reference to state law in order to characterize the property-related transfers in the income tax dispute between Mr. Davis and the IRS. Exactly where do you find state law when you are working on a tax case that depends on state law? The general rule is that the Federal Tax Law is superimposed on state law concepts.

---

instrument for a modified instrument that differs materially either in kind or in extent. A modification that is not a significant modification is not an exchange for purposes of Sec. 1.1001-1(a). . . ."

185 See, e.g., the Scotsman [newspaper], p.10, February 4, 1998. Rod Stewart was lined up to be next, according to the article.

186 370 U.S. 65 (S. Ct. 1962).

For example, state law determines whether found property becomes the finder's, and federal law in turn taxes the finder when she has "undisputed possession" under state law.[187] So, where, exactly, do you go to find the taxpayer's property rights under state law? The federal tax answer is that if the law is found in a state statute, you use it, but if it arises from case law, only decisions of the state's highest court are deemed reliable. *Commissioner v. Estate of Bosch.*[188] Lower court rules are merely entitled to "due regard," whatever that may mean.[189] In contrast, even if a state Supreme Court case is of a non-adversarial nature, its rulings are conclusive.

> **To illustrate:** Say you had to research a situation in which a taxpayer found property and now needs to know when it is taxable. The answer under Reg. §1.61-14(a) is that such property is taxable when it is reduced to "undisputed possession" under local law. That requires you to consult local law to see if the taxpayer has gotten "undisputed possession" of the property. In order for you to ascertain local law on what "undisputed possession," is you will follow the rule of Bosch that one looks to relevant statutes and state supreme court decisions as the only controlling authorities. Assuming a state statute does not answer the questions, a relevant lower court decision under state law will carry little weight, but even a collusive case in the state Supreme Court will be of great importance as long as it is relevant.

Problem 3-2:

Harry goes to the barber, bringing with him one share of stock of Dynamic Enterprises, Inc. which he bought for $5.00. He pays the barber's bill for his haircut with that one share of the stock, now worth $15.00. There was no tip component to the payment.

1) How much (if any) income does Harry have?

2) How much income, if any, does the barber have?

3) What is the barber's basis in the stock? See Reg. §1.61-2(d)(2)(i).

C. COMPUTATION OF BASIS AND ADJUSTED BASIS

Basis is a device which assures that taxpayers will not have their capital included as gross income when they report their net income for Federal Income Tax purposes. Sections 1011

187 Reg. §1.61-14(a).

188 387 U.S. 456 (1967).

189 Id.

through 1015 provide the rules for determining initial basis in property, and §1016 forces periodic adjustments to basis. The language of §1016 is obscure but the basic notion is that one increases the basis of property when one improves it -- such as adding a swimming pool to one's backyard -- and reduces it to the extent of certain tax deductible write-offs such as depletion and depreciation. We will get into the write-offs later. The important point is that the basis of property is frequently dynamic because of these adjustments. But just how does one go about determining the initial basis? To answer that question one must study §1012 through §1015. In essence, those three provisions describe three different ways that a person can obtain basis in property.

Section 1012 contemplates cost basis, which essentially means basis acquired in a mercantile transaction. (Section 1012 has a baffling way of expressing what it intends and the regulations are not much better.) For example, if your Aunt Minnie bought a bracelet in 1933 for $100, she has a $100 basis in the bracelet.

The second way one can obtain basis appears in §1014, which contemplates inherited property. The simple statement of the rule is that inherited property takes a basis equal to its value when the owner died. For example, if your Aunt Minnie's $100 bracelet was worth $1,000 at the time of her death last year, §1014 assigns the bracelet a fresh basis of $1,000 in her estate's hands. This is done because of the administrative difficulties of trying to figure out posthumously what Minnie's cost or other basis in her various properties were.

The third way one can obtain basis appears in §1015, the basis rule for gifts. Here the essential rule is that the donee of a gift takes the same basis in property as the donor had. For example, if Minnie gave you the bracelet five years before her death, you would take a $100 (i.e., Minnie's) basis in the bracelet. There might be a slight addition to basis to account for the share of any federal gift taxes that Minnie might have to pay on the transfer.[190] The simple scenario of Minnie and her bracelet has covered all the basic rules. Minnie took a $100 cost basis when she purchased the bracelet (§1012), you would take her $100 basis in the bracelet that she gave to you (§1015) and the bracelet would take a $1,000 basis if you instead inherited it from her. There is one last little rule you need to keep in mind; if a *donee* sells the gift property at a loss, his basis in the property is the lower of the donor's basis or the value of the property when it was given to the donee. (This keeps people from shifting losses by making gifts of loss property to people who are better able to take advantage of the loss than the owner of the property.) These §1015 gift basis rules also apply, by incorporation in §1041, to sales and other transfers between spouses, and between ex-spouses incident to divorce, except there is no "lower of donee's basis or value rule" in the event of a loss.

190 §1015(d)(1).

1. Cost Basis

Read §1012

People are much more apt to buy things for cash than to exchange them "in kind." When we buy something, we know that its basis is cost, and the parties do not have any trouble determining cost; it is what the seller receives in order to part with the property, stated in dollars, i.e., it is the purchase price paid by the buyer. If the transaction is a taxable exchange of property, §1012 is useless in telling us what cost means and we have to investigate judicial and administrative rulings. The key questions are:

1. Should we use the value of what was received in the transaction for purposes of determining its cost basis, or should we instead use the value of what we gave up?

2. What do we do if we cannot honestly assign a value to one, or either, property?

For example, assume a taxpayer swapped a share of stock for an unusual flower. Assume further that the stock trades for $75 on the New York Stock Exchange (the largest U.S. exchange). What is his basis in the flower? Its value? The value of the stock? The following well-known case resolves those questions.

PHILADELPHIA PARK AMUSEMENT CO. v. UNITED STATES

126 F. Supp. 184 (Ct. Cl. 1954)

LARAMORE, Judge, delivered the opinion of the court:

The taxpayer corporation sues to recover $42,864.50, with interest thereon, representing alleged overpayment of income taxes for the calendar years 1944 and 1945. The taxpayer employed the accrual method of accounting and reported its income on a calendar year basis. The issue presented in this case is whether or not the taxpayer is entitled to include as a part of the cost of its franchise, for purposes of determining depreciation and loss due to abandonment, the undepreciated cost of a bridge exchanged for a 10-year extension of the franchise. The facts which have been stipulated by the parties may be summarized as follows: The taxpayer's predecessor was granted on July 6, 1889, by the City of Philadelphia, a franchise to construct, operate, and maintain for 50 years a passenger railway in Fairmount Park at its own cost and expense. Upon the expiration of the 50-year term the franchise was to continue indefinitely for additional successive 10-year terms unless the City gave one year's written notice of its wish to terminate it at the end of the 50-year term or the 10-year term then in duration. Upon the termination of the license the City had the right to purchase all, but not just part of, the improvements; *i. e.*, railway cars, tracks, bridges, buildings, etc., made by the licensee at the cash value at the time of purchase, or in the event the City did not desire to purchase the assets the licensee had a specified period of time within which to remove them.

Pursuant to the franchise the taxpayer's predecessor constructed the bridge in question, commonly known as Strawberry Bridge, over the Schuylkill River at a cost of $381,000. The bridge was 79½ feet wide and carried pedestrian and vehicular traffic in addition to taxpayer's streetcars. The taxpayer's principal business was the operation of an amusement park and the street railway was employed in the transportation of customers to the park. With the increase in automobile transportation the proportion of customers carried to the amusement park by the taxpayer's streetcars decreased over the years and during the latter years of its operation losses were sustained. Early in 1934 the City, in writing the taxpayer, pointed out that Strawberry Bridge was in need of extensive repairs, that it was taxpayer's obligation to make the repairs at taxpayer's expense, and threatened to close the bridge unless the repairs were made promptly. The taxpayer wrote the City explaining that its financial condition prevented the making of extensive repairs to the bridge and offered to transfer the ownership of the bridge to the City in exchange for a 10-year extension of the railway franchise. The City accepted the offer and on August 3, 1934, Strawberry Bridge was transferred to the City. The taxpayer reserved its right-of-way over the bridge for the duration of its franchise and agreed to maintain its facilities thereon. On November 14, 1934, the City amended the franchise and extended it from July 24, 1939, to July 24, 1949. The adjusted basis, *i. e.*, the undepreciated or unrecovered cost of Strawberry Bridge at the time of the exchange was $228,852.74. The taxpayer›s bookkeeper took depreciation on the bridge for the part of 1934 that taxpayer owned it and promptly wrote the asset off the books by a direct debit to surplus of $228,852.74, without reporting any gain or loss on the exchange or adding the undepreciated cost or fair market value of the bridge to the cost of the franchise. From that time until 1946 the taxpayer›s bookkeeper did not record on the taxpayer›s books or claim a deduction on its returns for the amortization of this cost. He also failed to take the undisputed deduction for the amortization of the undepreciated portion, $50,000, of the original cost of the franchise.

In 1946 the taxpayer arranged with a bus company to give passenger service to its amusement park, ceased operation of the railway, and abandoned its franchise. In its 1946 tax return the taxpayer claimed a loss due to abandonment of the railroad of $336,380.04, $74,445.89 of which was claimed to represent the undepreciated cost of the franchise. This produced a $128,897.97 net loss for the year 1946, and taxpayer claimed a net operating loss carryback to 1944 and 1945 under section 122(b) of the Code, 26 U.S.C.A. § 122(b).

On December 15, 1947, the taxpayer filed a claim for refund of 1944 taxes in the amount of $6,087.28 based on a claimed depreciation deduction of $15,218.21. This claim was founded upon the ground that the undepreciated cost of Strawberry Bridge, $228,852.74, was the cost of the 10-year extension of its franchise and, therefore, should be amortized over the remaining life of the franchise. On December 30, 1948, taxpayer filed a second claim for refund of 1944 income taxes. This claim was in the amount of $58,791.91 and was predicated on the following grounds: (1) net operating loss carryback deduction of $128,897.97 from 1946, (2) depreciation deduction of $3,816.66 as the 1944 proportion of the cost basis of taxpayer's original franchise, and (3) a repetition of the first claim for refund. On October 26, 1950, the Commissioner of Internal Revenue allowed $55,036.71 of the net operating loss carryback and $3,333.33 of the $3,816.66 claim for depreciation of the original cost of the franchise, but denied taxpayer's first claim for refund for 1944 and the repetition thereof in the second claim for a $15,218.21 depreciation deduction based upon the undepreciated cost of Strawberry Bridge. The Commissioner refunded to the taxpayer, on account of its 1944 taxes, $22,014.69 with interest thereon.

On December 30, 1948, taxpayer filed a claim for refund of income taxes for the year 1945 in the amount of $6,087.28, claiming a deduction of $3,816.66 as the depreciation deduction for the amortization of the cost of its original franchise and $15,218.21 as the depreciation deduction for the amortization of the cost of the 10-year extension of its franchise. On October 26, 1950, the Commissioner allowed $3,333.33 of the claimed deduction for the original cost of the franchise and, accordingly, refunded to taxpayer $1,282.05 with interest thereon, but denied the balance of the claim.

In its petition the taxpayer alleged that the Commissioner's rejection of all of its first claim for 1944, part of its second claim for 1944, and part of its claim for 1945 was erroneous. The defendant raised the question of statute of limitations in respect to the part of the taxpayer's claim that pertained to the allowance of a deduction for depreciation of the original cost of the franchise for the year 1944. The taxpayer claimed $3,816.16, whereas the Commissioner allowed only $3,333.33. The difference is a result of the Commissioner's amortization of the original cost of the franchise over the period beginning on the date the franchise was granted as opposed to taxpayer's desire to have it amortized over the period beginning on the date of the start of operation of the railway. This issue apparently has been abandoned by both parties inasmuch as no mention was made of it in the briefs or on oral argument. Therefore, we are only concerned with the cost basis, if any, of the 10-year extension of taxpayer's franchise and the tax consequences thereof for the years 1944, 1945, and 1946.

It is clear that the cost of this type franchise can be amortized over its life by the taking of depreciation deduction under section 23(*l*) of the Code. See Regulation 111, section 29.23(1)-3; Cleveland Railway Co. v. Commissioner, 36 B.T.A. 208, and cases cited therein. Therefore, the cost basis, if any, of the 10-year extension of the franchise should be depreciated over the remainder of the old term and over the new term. East Kauai Water Co. v. Commissioner, 11 T.C. 1014, and cases cited therein. It is also clear that when a franchise is abandoned prior to the end of its term the owner is entitled to deduct, under section 23(f)[2] of the Code, as a loss in the year of abandonment, the undepreciated cost of the franchise at that time. Elston Co., to Use and Benefit of U. S. Brewing Co. v. United States, 21 F.Supp. 267, 86 Ct.Cl. 136, and cases cited therein.

This brings us to the question of what is the cost basis of the 10-year extension of taxpayer's franchise. Although defendant contends that Strawberry Bridge was either worthless or not "exchanged" for the 10-year extension of the franchise, we believe that the bridge had some value, and that the contract under which the bridge was transferred to the City clearly indicates that the one was given in consideration of the other. The taxpayer, however, has failed to show that the exchange was one that falls within the nonrecognition provisions of section 112(b) of the Code and, therefore, it was a taxable exchange under section 112(a) of the Code.

The gain or loss, whichever the case may have been, should have been recognized, and the cost basis under section 113(a) of the Code, of the 10-year extension of the franchise was the cost to the taxpayer. The succinct statement in section 113(a) that "the basis of property shall be the cost of such property" although clear in principle, is frequently difficult in application. One view is that the cost basis of property received in a taxable exchange is the fair market value of the property *given* in the exchange.[5] The other view is that the cost basis of property received in a taxable exchange is the fair market value of the property *received* in the exchange. As will be seen from the cases and some of the Commissioner›s rulings[7] the Commissioner›s position has not been altogether consistent on this question. The view that «cost» is the fair market value of the property given is predicated on the theory that the cost to the taxpayer is the economic value relinquished. The view that «cost» is the fair market value of the property received is based upon the theory that the term «cost» is a tax concept and must be considered in the light of the designed interrelationship of sections 111, 112, 113, and 114, 26 U.S.C.A. § 114, and the prime role that the basis of property plays in determining tax liability. We believe that when the question is considered in the latter context that the cost basis of the property received in a taxable exchange is the fair market value of the property *received* in the exchange.

When property is exchanged for property in a taxable exchange the taxpayer is taxed on the difference between the adjusted basis of the property given in exchange and the fair market value of the property received in exchange. For purposes of determining gain or loss the fair market value of the property received is treated as cash and taxed accordingly. To maintain harmony with the fundamental purpose of these sections, it is necessary to consider the fair market value of the property received as the cost basis to the taxpayer. The failure to do so would result in allowing the taxpayer a stepped-up basis, without paying a tax therefor, if the fair market value of the property received is less than the fair market value of the property given, and the taxpayer would be subjected to a double tax if the fair market value of the property received is more than the fair market value of the property given. By holding that the fair market value of the property received in a taxable exchange is the cost basis, the above discrepancy is avoided and the basis of the property received will equal the adjusted basis of the property given plus any gain recognized, or that should have been recognized, or minus any loss recognized, or that should have been recognized.

Therefore, the cost basis of the 10-year extension of the franchise was its fair market value on August 3, 1934, the date of the exchange. The determination of whether the cost basis of the property received is its fair market value or the fair market value of the property given in exchange therefor, although necessary to the decision of the case, is generally not of great practical significance because the value of the two properties exchanged in an arms-length transaction are either equal in fact, or are presumed to be equal. The record in this case indicates that the 1934 exchange was an arms-length transaction and, therefore, if the value of the extended franchise cannot be determined with reasonable accuracy, it would be reasonable and fair to assume that the value of Strawberry Bridge was equal to the 10-year extension of the franchise. The fair market value of the 10-year extension of the franchise should be established but, if that value cannot be determined with reasonable certainty, the fair market value of Strawberry Bridge should be established and that will be presumed to be the value of the extended franchise. This value cannot be determined from the facts now before us since the case was prosecuted on a different theory.

The taxpayer contends that the market value of the extended franchise or Strawberry Bridge could not be ascertained and, therefore, it should be entitled to carry over the undepreciated cost basis of the bridge as the cost of the extended franchise under section 113(b) (2).[9] If the value of the extended franchise or bridge cannot be ascertained with a reasonable degree of accuracy, the taxpayer is entitled to carry over the undepreciated cost of the bridge as the cost basis of the extended franchise. Helvering v. Tex-Pen Oil Co., 300 U.S. 481, 499, 57 S.Ct. 569, 81 L.Ed. 755; Gould Securities Co. v. United States, 2 Cir., 96 F.2d 780. However, it is only in rare and extraordinary cases that the value of the property exchanged cannot be ascertained with reasonable accuracy. We are presently of the opinion that either the value of the extended franchise or the bridge can be determined with a reasonable degree of accuracy. Although the value of the extended franchise may be difficult or impossible to ascertain because of the nebulous and intangible characteristics inherent in such property, the value of the bridge is subject to more exact measurement. Consideration may be given to expert testimony on the value of comparable bridges, Strawberry Bridge›s reproduction cost and its undepreciated cost, as well as other relevant factors.

Therefore, because we deem it equitable, judgment should be suspended and the question of the value of the extended franchise on August 3, 1934, should be remanded to the Commissioner of this court for the taking of evidence and the filing of a report thereon.

The failure of taxpayer to properly record the transaction in 1934 and thereafter does not prevent the correction of the error, especially under the circumstances of this case. Countway v. Commissioner, 1 Cir. 127 F.2d 69. The taxpayer has lost not only the depreciation deductions for the years 1935 to 1944 of the cost of its original franchise, but also the benefit of the depreciation deduction for the cost of the extended franchise, even though the basis of the former was and the latter will be reduced by the amount of depreciation that should have been taken for this period. See section 113(b) (1) (B) of the Internal Revenue Code.

In the cases cited by taxpayer relating to losses claimed upon obtaining licenses and leases, or the extension or renewal thereof, the question presented was whether the amount involved was part of the cost of the license or lease and, therefore, should be capitalized and amortized over their life, or whether they were losses or expenses that should be deducted in the taxable year. In those cases either the amount in question was the actual cost, or property was not exchanged, or fair market value was not an issue. Those cases deal with different problems and are not applicable here.

We, therefore, conclude that the 1934 exchange was a taxable exchange and that the taxpayer is entitled to use as the cost basis of the 10-year extension of its franchise its fair market value on August 3, 1934, for purposes of determining depreciation and loss due to abandonment, as indicated in this opinion.

Accordingly, judgment will be suspended and the question of the value of the extended franchise on August 3, 1934, is remanded to the Commissioner of this court for the taking of evidence and the filing of a report thereon.

JONES, Chief Judge, and MADDEN, WHITAKER, and LITTLETON, Judges, concur.

. . .

Notes on the Acquisition of Basis

Philadelphia Park Amusement Company doctrine is considered good law and is of great importance in the area of determining basis in property. It is important that you understand this case well and that you understand that there is a history in the tax law of accepting valuations of property that people engaged in arm's-length haggling over the item come up with, unless there is reason to think the price was influenced by tax considerations.[191]

How does one treat the costs of getting or disposing of property? The basis of acquired property includes the incidental costs of acquiring property. People who acquire property often pay miscellaneous expenses such as brokers' commissions, accrued taxes, the cost of perfecting title to the asset, and the like. These amounts must be added to the basis of an acquired asset. This rule is implicit in §1012 and has generated numerous cases and rulings.[192] When they sell assets, the costs associated with the sale reduce the amount realized.[193]

There is also the question of when one obtains basis. In almost all cases, the taxpayer obtains basis at the time of the closing of the transaction (i.e., on getting title to the asset), on the theory

191 See, e.g., Commissioner v. Danielson, 378 F.2d 771 (3d Cir. 1967).

192 See, e.g., Helvering v. Winmill, 305 U.S. 79, 84 (1938).

193 Spreckels v. Helvering, 315 U.S. 626,630 1942); Reg. §1.263(a)-2(f).

that he incurs the cost at that time, even if he used borrowed money and actually paid the lender in the future. As we will see later, this has important implications, because it may permit the buyer to claim tax write-offs on the asset even though it may be years before the buyer fully pays for the property. The ability to use debt to multiply tax write-offs has long been exploited by crafty taxpayers. The process of using borrowed funds to buy something is often referred to as "leverage" because by borrowing money, the taxpayer "levers up" (increases) the amount he or she can buy, compared with what he could buy with just his own funds. We will look at a number of leveraged transactions later in the text.

Options. The next problems involve option contracts under which the "writer" of the option agrees to stand ready to sell her property at a fixed price (known as the "exercise price") for a certain amount of time. The person who buys the option is the "holder." Normally, the holder will pay money to the writer at the time of writing the option. Section 1234 is the controlling Code section, but it is difficult to read. The important rules are that the writer of the option does not report gross income on issuing the option, nor does the holder get any kind of deduction at that time. If the holder exercises the option, his basis in the property includes the price paid for the option plus the exercise price under the option. The writer of the option is taxed at the time of its exercise under the option. If the option is not exercised (and instead "lapses"), then the writer has a gain at that time. The option itself is often transferable and is viewed as a separate property.

Problem 3-3:

1) Adept owns a talking duck that has a unique speech impediment. Adept paid $100 for the duck. She recently accepted 100 shares of Macrosoft, Inc. stock for the duck, from Frank, a collector. The Macrosoft stock cost Frank $600 and was worth $120,000 when he transferred it to Adept. Macrosoft stock trades on the New York Stock Exchange.

    a. How much income does Adept have on selling the duck?

    b. What is Adept's basis in the Macrosoft Stock?

    c. How much gain, if any, did Frank have when he acquired the duck?

    d. What is Frank's basis in the duck?

2) Adept paid $5,000 for a one-year option to buy Grumpy's property for $100,000 (meaning the total payments would be $105,000 if Adept buys the property). See §1234(a) and (b)(1).

   a. If Adept exercises the option, what should be his basis in Grumpy's former property?

   b. If Adept sells the option for $6,000, what, if anything, is Adept's gain? See §1001(a).

   c. How would Grumpy be taxed when he gets the $5,000? When he is paid the remaining $100,000? See §1234(a).

   d. How is Grumpy taxed when Adept fails to exercise the option to buy the property and the option expires a year later?

   e. Assume that Grumpy had basis in his property of $75,000 and that in year one Adept paid Grumpy $75,000 as an option price, allowing Adept the right to buy the property on paying an extra $30,000, in year five. How would you characterize this transaction? Consider whether, if you were Adept, you would let the option lapse.

Notes on Equitable Features of Tax Procedure

The statutes of limitations in the Code can work some unreasonable results to taxpayers or the government, depending on the facts. Here are three different remedies to that problem. The first is the most important by far.

The duty of consistency. Taxpayers have a duty not to change the facts on the government. Here is the problem. The statute of limitations runs on tax liabilities for particular tax years, usually three years after of April 15 of the following year, or three years after the filing date, whichever was later.[194] For example, assume the taxpayer filed her 1995 calendar year tax return on April 12 of 1996. The statute of limitations would begin to run on April 15, 1996 and would expire with respect to her 1995 return on April 15, 1999. There is, however, no statute of limitations on "facts."

To illustrate: Suppose the taxpayer received $100 from a corporation 10 years ago and claimed at the time that it was a loan to her for tax purposes. Now she changes her position and says the

194 §6501(a).

$100 was really a taxable distribution 10 years ago, but that the statute of limitations has closed on the distribution; she says it is just tough luck for the government if for some reason the corporation fails to try to collect the $100. It won't work.

The judicially developed duty of consistency compels the taxpayer to stick by her position as to the facts over the years and not zig-zag to whatever position is the most appealing at the moment.[195] In substance, this is an application of the equitable concept of estoppel. Aside from the duty of consistency, there are at least two further ways to thwart opportunism with respect to statutes of limitations:

1) *Recoupment.* This doctrine lets the taxpayer offset a tax erroneously collected against a correct assessment, or the IRS to offset a refund claim with an otherwise time-barred deficiency.[196]

2) *Mitigation of the statute of limitations under §§ 1311-1314.* These rules prevent double inclusions of income and double deductions that might arise if the statutes of limitations were strictly applied. It allows one to reopen the year of the error and allows the item to be reapplied to the correct year.

Problem 3-4:

Sharp-eyed Allegra found a Tiffany watch on the street a few years ago. It was worth $5,000, although the owner had paid only $4,000. Allegra ran an advertisement trying to find the owner, but no one replied. A year passed and the watch became hers under applicable law in year 2, when the watch was still worth $5,000.

1) What should be her basis in the watch in year 2, as a matter of logic?

2) What if she failed to report the watch as gross income when it became hers, but now -- eight years later when she decides to sell it -- Allegra claims a $5,000 basis in it anyway?

2. Disallowance of Losses on Sales to Related Taxpayers

If a wealthy father sells his beloved daughter an investment property, it is reasonable to suspect that the father has retained at least some control over the property. Should a loss be allowed on

195 See, e.g., Beltzer v. United States, 495 F.2d 211 (8th Cir. 1974).

196 See, e.g., Rev. Rul. 71-56, 1971-1 C.B. 404.

such facts? The Congressional answer, embodied in §267(a)(1) is "no." However, §267(d) offers some relief in that if the related buyer later sells the property for a gain (i.e., more than she paid for it), then the gain is tax-exempt up to the amount of the disallowed loss.

Problem 3-5:

Read §267(a)(1), (b)(1), (c)(4) and (d). Now assume the following facts. Ernst, the father of Allegra, owns stock that has a basis of $1,500.

1) If Ernst sells it to Allegra for $1,500, although it is worth $2,000, how much gain or loss will Ernst report for Federal Income Tax purposes, and what will be Allegra's basis in the property?

2) Ernst instead sells it to her for $1,000 (its then value) and Allegra sells the stock a few years later for $1,200. What is her basis and taxable gain, if any?

3) Same as "(2)," but the resale price is instead $1,800. What is her basis and taxable gain, if any?

4) If you had the power, would you amend §267 to include a tax avoidance requirement, or would you leave it as it is, potentially disallowing losses and deductions claimed by innocent taxpayers?

3. Basis of Property Received as a Gift

Read §§ 1015(a) and 1041(a), (b) and Regs. §§ 1.1001-1(e) and 1.1015-1(a)(1), (a)(2) and -4

Section 102(a) states that the donee of property does not have any gross income on receipt of the gift. Also, the donor does not realize gain or loss on making the gift, according to *Taft v. Bowers.*[197] We will get into the definition of a gift in Chapter Four. Right now, the concern is with basis.

Until 1921 the donee's basis in a gift was its value when received. This invited wealthy families to make gifts of appreciated property to each other and then sell the property at no taxable gain. Congress ended this absurd situation by making the donee take the donor's basis.[198] The result is that if the donor would recognize gain on the sale of the property, then the donee is stuck with that same built-in gain. For example, assume your Aunt Minnie gave you a bracelet that she bought for $100. The bracelet was worth $1,000 at the time of the gift. Under §1015,

197 278 U.S.470 (1929).

198 I.R.C. § 1015(a).

your basis in the bracelet is $100 and you would have $900 taxable gain if you promptly sold it for $1,000. Likewise, if Minnie had sold the bracelet rather than giving it to you she would also have to report a $900 gain. The gift in effect shifted the income tax liability arising from a sale of the bracelet from Minnie to you. (It of course also deferred the tax.) *Taft v. Bowers* established the Constitutionality of this provision.

FARID-ES-SULTANEH v. COMMISSIONER

160 F.2d 812 (2d Cir. 1947)

CHASE, Circuit Judge.

[In connection with the impending marriage to his much younger spouse-to-be, Mr. Kresge transferred large blocks of stock of what eventually became K-Mart, in connection with which she surrendered various marital rights. Some of the stock transfers occurred before they married and some occurred after they married. She, the taxpayer, later sold 12,000 shares of Kresge stock in 1938 for $230,802.36. She claims the basis of the stock was cost, determined when received in exchange for her marital rights in the Spring of 1924, viz. $10.67 per share, as opposed to the $0.159091/share the government pressed for, on the theory that the transfer was a gift. The case raises the issue of whether stock received via an antenuptial agreement in which the recipient surrenders her inchoate marital rights is received by gift or by a taxable exchange. If the latter, she gets the high basis she claims in the stock. By the time this case was decided, the former Mrs. Kresge had married a wealthy gentleman from the Middle East.]

We find in this decision no indication . . . that the term 'gift' as used in the income tax statute should be construed to include a transfer which, if made when the gift tax were effective, would be taxable to the transferor as a gift merely because of the special provisions in the gift tax statute defining and restricting consideration for gift tax purposes. A fortiori, it would seem that limitations found in the estate tax law upon according the usual legal effect to proof that a transfer was made for a fair consideration should not be imported into the income tax law except by action of Congress.

In our opinion the income tax provisions are not to be construed as though they were in pari materia with either the estate tax law or the gift tax statutes. They are aimed at the gathering of revenue by taking for public use given percentages of what the statute fixes as net taxable income. Capital gains and losses are, to the required or permitted extent, factors in determining net taxable income. What is known as the basis for computing gain or loss on transfers of property is established by statute in those instances when the resulting gain or loss is recognized for income tax purposes and the basis for succeeding sales or exchanges will, theoretically at least, level off taxwise any hills and valleys in the consideration passing either way on previous sales or exchanges. When Congress provided that gifts should not be treated as taxable income to the donee there was, without any correlative provisions fixing the basis of the gift to the donee, a loophole which enabled the donee to make a subsequent transfer of the property and take as the basis for computing gain or loss its value when the gift was made. Thus it was possible to exclude from taxation any increment in value during the donor's holding and the donee might take advantage of any shrinkage in such increment after the acquisition by gift in computing gain or loss upon a subsequent sale or exchange. It was to close this loophole that Congress provided that the donee should take the donor's basis when property was transferred by gift. Report of Ways and Means Committee (No. 350, p.9, 67th Cong., 1st Sess.). This change in the statute affected only the statutory net taxable income. The altered statute prevented a transfer by gift from creating any change in the basis of the property in computing gain or loss on any future transfer. In any individual instance the change in the statute would but postpone taxation and presumably would have little effect on the total volume of income tax revenue derived over a long period of time and from many taxpayers. Because of this we think that a transfer which should be classed as a gift under the gift tax law is not necessarily to be treated as a gift incometaxwise. Though such a consideration as this petitioner gave for the shares of stock she acquired from Mr. Kresge might not have relieved him from liability for a gift tax, had the present gift tax then been in effect, it was nevertheless a fair consideration which prevented her taking the shares as a gift under the income tax law since it precluded the existence of a donative intent.

Although the transfers of the stock made both in December 1923, and in the following January by Mr. Kresge to this taxpayer are called a gift in the antenuptial agreement later executed and were to be for the protection of his prospective bride if he died before the marriage was consummated, the 'gift' was contingent upon his death before such marriage, an event that did not occur. Consequently, it would appear that no absolute gift was made before the antenuptial contract was executed and that she took title to the stock under its terms, viz: in consideration for her promise to marry him coupled with her promise to relinquish all rights in and to his property which she would otherwise acquire by the marriage. Her inchoate interest in the property of her affianced husband greatly exceeded the value of the stock transferred to her. It was a fair consideration under ordinary legal concepts of that term for the transfers of the stock by him. . . . She performed the contract under the terms of which the stock was transferred to her and held the shares not as a donee but as a purchaser for a fair consideration.

As the decisive issue is one of law only, the decision of the Tax Court interpreting the applicable statutory provisions has no peculiar finality and is reviewable. . . .

Decision reversed.

Notes

Taxation of property transfers in connection with antenuptial agreements. The decision in *Farid-Es-Sultaneh* focuses on Mrs. Kresge's basis in her stock, presenting the question of whether the antenuptial transfer constituted a gift, causing Mrs. Kresge to have a low basis in the stock, or if it was a bargained-for amount equal in value to the spousal rights that she abandoned. The Court did not consider the basis she had in those spousal rights, thereby leaving open the questions as to whether she should pay Federal Income Taxes computed on the difference between what she received under the antenuptial agreement and whatever basis (perhaps zero) that she had in her abandoned spousal rights.

The issue of basis in a person's antenuptial rights was resolved in a published ruling to the effect that spouses-to-be who receive property in antenuptial agreements in which they surrender marital rights have no gain or loss on the transaction, the theory being that the rights have a basis equal to their value.[199] One has to wonder if the ruling is unduly generous.

> **To illustrate:** Sirena is a beautiful, ruthless gold-digger. Five years ago she married a big executive. She got an antenuptial agreement under which she got $5 million in cash at the time of marrying the executive. Sirena soon divorced him. Next year, she married a real estate tycoon and got a horse farm worth another $5 million, deeded to her before marriage. In both cases Sirena has no taxable income and takes a fair market value basis in the property, thereby minimizing the likelihood of further taxes when she sells the horse farm. Is it likely that society would accept this outcome if it were proposed behind a "veil of ignorance"?

One needs to distinguish premarital transfers, which are generally taxable events, from interspousal transfers under §1041, which you saw earlier in connection with the *Davis* decision. The heart of §1041 is its conversion of all transfers of property between spouses, including sales and exchanges, into gifts. Because they are gifts, neither spouse will report any income and there is no change in basis in the transferred property. There is one small twist that was mentioned before; §1041 differs from §1014 in that when a spouse transfers low value, high basis property to his mate, the transferee does not have to reduce the basis in the property to its value at the time of the gift.

> **To illustrate:** If a husband buys a bracelet from his wife for $1,000 and she had a $10,000 basis in the bracelet, she is deemed to receive $1,000 from her husband as a gift and he is deemed to receive a bracelet with a basis of $10,000. If he later sells the bracelet for $1,000 he will report a $9,000 loss because his basis is $10,000. By contrast, if she gave the bracelet to her daughter,

199 See Rev. Rul. 67-221, 1967-2 C.B. 63.

who later sold it for $1,000, the first sentence of §1015(a) would prevent the daughter from reporting a loss.

The law today. Section 1041 greatly simplifies the taxation of interspousal transfers, but it can come as a shock from time to time in the case of people who are unaware of the reach of §1041. As to the stock she got before she married, §1041 would not have had any effect on Mrs. Kresge's situation if her case had come up today. However, it would affect the stock she received after she married; that stock would be treated like a gift today.

Section 1041 is of great importance with respect to divorces. The basic concept is that any transfer of property between spouses that arose as a consequence of the divorce is treated as a gift for Federal Income Tax purposes. This eliminates a treacherous area of prior law under which every item of property transferred between divorcing spouses had to be catalogued and tested to determine whether it generated a taxable gain to the person who transferred the property.

What if the donee is too polite to inquire into the donor's basis and the donor cannot be found? Most donees probably consider it bad manners to pry into the donor's basis in property received as a gift. This could have been a major problem in preparing the tax return of a donee who recently sold the property received by gift from a donor who died many years ago. If there is genuine uncertainty as to the donor's basis, the IRS is supposed to get the facts, or, failing that use the value of the property as of the date the donor got the property.[200] It has been held that if the IRS fails in this effort, there is no gain or loss when the donee sells the property.[201]

*A primer on federal estate and gift taxes.*The Code includes taxes on gratuitous transfers during life and at death. Although the taxes are being carved back, they will remain an important tax planning consideration for many years. The tax was used to provide revenue for the United States to pay for its participation in World War I. An original purpose of these taxes when they were modified during the Depression was to break up accumulations of great wealth.[202] In fact, the tax is formally justified as one imposed on the privilege of transferring wealth.[203] The base of the tax is the value of transferred property. The principal exemption from both taxes is that U.S. citizen spouses can transfer unlimited amounts of wealth between each other during life and at death, free of the federal transfer taxes.[204]

---

200 §1015(a).

201 Caldwell v. Commissioner, 234 F2d 660 (6th Cir 1956).

202 See testimony given on the estate tax before the House Ways and Means Committee between October 19 and November 3, 1925, as to proposed revenue revisions, reprinted in 7 U.S. Revenue Acts 1909-1950, at 293-510, especially the statement of Rep. Ramseyer from Iowa, who introduced an article by Andrew Carnegie to support the notion that an estate tax was an appropriate tax to impose. Id. at 398-418.

203 Knowlton v. Moore, 178 U.S. 41 (1900). The corporate income tax is justified as a tax on the privilege of doing business in corporate form, and not as an income tax. Flint v. Stone Tracy Corporation, 220 U.S. 107 (1911).

204 Bittker & Lokken, FEDERAL TAXATION OF INCOME, ESTATES AND GIFTS ¶¶ 123.9, 129.6 (2018).

The Estate Tax. The first $10 million worth of such transfers are exempt. The estate tax rate is 40 percent on amounts in excess of the exemption. Most of the taxes are collected at death by means of identifying the decedent's assets (including assets passing under will substitutes), appraising them at fair market value, subtracting various deductions, such as creditors' claims against the estate, charitable gifts under the will, and transfers to the surviving spouse and then imposing a tax on the net assets, payable by the executor out of the assets of the estate. Incidentally, a decedent's estate comes into being at the moment of death and is a separate taxpayer that files its own Federal Income Tax returns. You can detect its presence by looking at §1(e).

The Gift Tax. The tax on gifts (which generally falls only on gifts in excess of $15,000 per donee per year) is needed in order to prevent people from stripping their wealth during their lives or shortly before death, thereby avoiding the estate tax. The lifetime gift tax exemption is $5.6 million per donor. To the extent the $5.6 million gift exemption is used by the donor, it reduces the donor's $5.6 million estate tax exemption. Gift tax rates for 2018 on taxable gifts are 40%. The gift tax (but not the estate tax) increases the basis of property. However, the basis increase is limited to the gift tax attributable to the net appreciation on the gift while the donor held the property.[205]

The Generation Skipping Tax (GST). There is also a federal tax (40%), in addition to estate and gift taxes, on transfers that skip generations, *e.g.*, a gift from grandparent to grandchild. Exclusions from GST are similar (but not exactly the same) as exclusions and exemptions from gift and estate taxes. The base of the tax is the value of transferred property.

Part-gift, part-sale transactions. A sale for too low a price is likely to be a partial gift. If so, does the seller report a gain if the price is an amount greater than basis? Yes, according to Reg. §1.1001-1(e). What is the buyer's basis? The answer is that the buyer's basis is the greater of what he paid the seller/donor or the seller donor's basis in the property.[206] The former rule might have been rejected in favor of the view that the transaction was just two cross-gifts. Given the decision on reporting gain, it follows that the buyer should at least get a basis equal to what he paid, and there is also no reason to reduce basis to a figure lower than the donor's basis, given that a pure gift would have resulted in a carryover basis. Losses are not recognized in part-gift, part sale transactions.[207] This lays a trap for the unwary:

> **To illustrate**: Mom has a basis of $30 in a share of stock held for investment, which is now worth only $21. She sells the stock to her daughter for $20 intending a gift of $1. Mom cannot report a loss because of §267(a)(1) that disallows losses between related taxpayers, such as parents and children. Daughter's basis would seem to be $30. But wait! There is a trap; when the

205 §1015(d)(1)(A).

206 Reg. §1.1015-4(a).

207 Reg. §1.1015-1(e)(2), Example 4.

donee sells part-gift property, her basis is reduced, for purposes of reporting losses, to its value when it was transferred ($21). If Mom were tax-wise, she would have sold the stock and perhaps claimed a $9 tax loss. Then she could have given her daughter the $21 in cash.

Another choice as to how the law might be framed. The tax law does not have to be this way. In particular, §1011(b) uses a different approach from the previous part-gift, part-sale rule if the transaction is with a charity. This time, for Federal Income Tax purposes one presumes that the property was divided into parts, but that there was a sale of one component, in proportion to the relative amount paid for the property. For example, if Mom, above, had a basis in the Thing of $30 and it was worth $50 and she sold it to the charity for $30, then she is viewed as having sold 3/5ths of the property for cash of $30. Three-fifths of its basis is $18, so her gain would be $12. The remaining $20 is a charitable gift.

Problem 3-6:

Agatha Murchison bought a beautiful diamond bracelet for $100 in 1933. In 1997, when it was worth $1,000, she gave it to her niece, Dora. Some years later Dora sells the bracelet for the following amounts. In each of these cases how much gain or loss will Dora report on the sale for Federal Income Tax purposes?

1) $1,200

2) $90

3) Assume Agatha received the bracelet from her first husband, Harley Murchison, prior to getting married in exchange for giving up her marital rights. What would be her basis in the bracelet and how much income, if any, would she have had to report in 1933, assuming the current tax law rules applied in 1933?

The right way to approach the next problem is ask first if there is a gain under the general carryover basis rule for property acquired by gift, and if so, how much. If there is a loss under the general rule, then you should ask if there is instead a loss. If so, then you use the lower of the donor's basis or the value of the property when it was given, and then determine the amount of the loss, if any. See §1015(a). If there is a loss using this exceptional rule, then you report that loss for Federal Income Tax purposes.

Problem 3-7:

Now consider the following alternatives involving loss of value. Assume Minnie's bracelet cost $1,000 and was worth $500 at the time of Agatha's gift to Dora and that Dora later sold the bracelet for the following amounts. In each of these following cases, how much gain or loss will Dora report on the sale?

1) $1,200

2) $400

3) $750

4) Considering the practical impact of this and the prior problem, does it seem to you that taxpayers can shift the taxes associated with gains to the family and friends, but not losses? If so, why discriminate against losses, but not gains?

5) Same as "(2)," but the gift was from Agatha to her husband, Harley. See §1041(b)(2).

4. Property Acquired from a Decedent

Read §1014(a), (b)(1)(6), (e)

a. Introduction

In general, when a decedent dies the property automatically passes to an "estate" for local law purposes. Section 2031 of the Code forces the administrator or executor of the estate to compute the fair market value of all of the property in that estate. The valuation date is either the date of death, or if the executor or administrator so elects, the alternate valuation date, meaning six months after death. Section 1014 tracks §2032 by assigning the decedent's property a basis equal to fair market value, either at death or six months thereafter. However, there need not be an estate tax return for basis in the inherited property to be adjusted to its date-of death value.[208] Section 102 assures the heir that the inheritance is free of income taxes. Also, because the decedent's property gets a value-at-death basis, as long at the value remains stable, the estate or heir can promptly sell the property free of Federal Income Taxes, which makes it possible for the estate to raise cash by selling assets free of income taxes.

Section 1014 is one of the truly anomalous provisions in the Internal Revenue Code because it produces changes in basis of property without any corresponding taxable gain or loss. This

208 Reg. §1.1014-2(b)(2).

conflicts with one of the deep, but unstated, rules in the Code, namely that the basis of property does not change unless it is accompanied by a taxable event. For example, a gift of property is not a taxable event and the basis of gift property does not change when it changes owners. Conversely, when property is received in exchange for services, the property takes a fair market value basis and the service provider has income equal to the value of the property she receives. Later in the book we will review the number of "nonrecognition transactions" in which taxable gains or losses are deferred, but at the price of freezing the basis in the property that was the subject of the non-recognition transaction. Those transactions are consistent with the deep concept of only changing basis in property when a taxable event occurs.

b. Alternative Approaches

There are numerous potential legislative solutions to the anomaly of giving a decedent's property basis equal to its value at death. One solution is to give the heir the decedent's basis in the property, as if it were a gift. Former §1023 so provided, but Congress repealed it as a result of objections from practitioners who said it was impossible to gather the necessary basis information after death. Another alternative is to grant a $ zero basis to inheritances, on the theory that they passed to the heir with no income tax; or one might mimic Canada and assume that the estate sold the property (taxing the estate) and give the heir a fair market value basis in the property free of income taxes.

Another approach is to tax the heir as having income on receipt, and therefore giving her inheritance a basis equal to its value at the time of receipt.

Here is a simple example of the kind of tax planning §1014 invites.

> **To illustrate:** Some years ago your dentist was given several hundred shares of stock having an aggregate basis of $100. The stock has since increased in value to one million dollars and you have learned that your dentist died last week. During life, the dentist might have used the stock as collateral to raise money to support a pleasant lifestyle without paying taxes on receiving the loan proceeds. If your dentist's estate promptly sells the stock it will report no gain (and will pay no income tax) on the sale because the basis at death of the stock (one million dollars) will be equal to the amount realized on the sale. It can use the cash to pay off the decedent's loans, which count as liabilities of the estate and reduce the estate tax base.

Residents of community property states are especially blessed by §1014 because §1014(b)(6) treats the surviving spouse's one-half share in community (i.e., commonly-owned) property as if it were acquired from the decedent. The practical effect is that the surviving spouse will have a date-of-death value basis in his or her half of the community property.

To illustrate: Lucy and Desi have been married for some years. His separate property is worth one million dollars, her separate property is worth one million dollars and their community property is worth one million dollars. Assume that all of the property has a zero basis. When Desi died last year, his estate for federal estate purposes was $1.5 million, consisting of his million plus half of the community. Section 1014 will of course give his estate a fair market value basis ($1.5 million) in that property. The curiosity of §1014(b)(6) is that Lucy's basis in *her* half of the community property rose to $500,000 even though she obviously did not die.

c. The Enduring Life of Carryover Basis Reform

In 1976, Congress enacted §1023 of the Internal Revenue Code which would have established carryover basis rules for testamentary transfers similar to those of §1015 for *inter vivos* gifts. Section 1023 would have reversed the longstanding value-at-date-of-death basis principle, which so often exempted from Federal Income Taxation the pre-death appreciation of property in the hands of the decedent. Section 1023 turned out to be a politically unpopular reform, and was hooted down by practitioners for its undue compliance burdens and potential administrative problems, and was retroactively repealed in 1980. If one wanted a simple rule, one might assign a zero basis to inherited property (and also to gift property, so as to prevent end-runs), but there have been no public proposals along those lines as yet.

The basis rules for *inter vivos* gifts and testamentary transfers thus remain drastically different. Perhaps a rule requiring constructive realization of gain *by the decedent* at death would be an acceptable alternative to current law and prevent the complete escape from income taxation under §1014, but there is not much hope for such a change in the current political environment, in part because foes of the plan would point out that is still requires knowing the decedent's basis, the dilemma that killed §1023.

Problem 3-8:

If you were the ruler of the world, would you continue §1014 as it stands? Exclude inheritance from gross income and give beneficiaries a fair market value basis? Exclude inheritance from gross income, but give beneficiaries a $0 basis? How about repealing the estate and gift taxes, making gifts and inheritances taxable, and giving beneficiaries a fair market value basis?

Problem 3-9:

1) Suppose Father, Ernst Blofeld, is in good health and buys 10 shares of stock in one year for $1,000. In the next year when they have risen in value to $1,500 he gives them to his daughter by his first marriage, Allegra. He loves Allegra. Then, in the

next year, Allegra sells the shares for $2,100. Who is taxed on what? See §1015, §1001.

2) Some time later Ernst died in a hunting accident in Africa and the facts revealed that Ernst had willed the shares to Allegra when they were worth $1,500, and Allegra sold them the next year, as above, for $2,100? See §1014.

3) Suppose the same events, but that Ernst paid $1,000 for the stock and that Allegra sold the stock for $600. See especially Regulations §1.1014-1, -2, -5 and §1.1015-1, -4, -5.

    a. What result to Allegra if the transfer was a gift from Ernst before he left for Africa, when the stock was worth $700?

    b. What result to Allegra if the transfer was a bequest when the stock was worth $700?

4) Same as "(3)," except that the sales price was $900. If Ernst, senses doom in Africa approaching, what kinds of property should Ernst give away or sell during life and what should be kept until death and willed to Allegra?

5) Just before the unpleasantness in Africa, Ernst had contracted cancer and was given only a few years to live. Allegra gratuitously deeded him her interest in their jointly owned vacation property. Allegra's share of the property has a basis of $10,000 and a value of $100,000. What income tax planning might the family be intending to achieve by means of this transaction? What if anything, does §1014(e) do to support or thwart their plan?

6) Before his death, Ernst owned an oil painting worth $10,000 for which he had paid $40,000. He gave it to Alexis, his wife, a few years ago. What is her basis in the oil painting? See §1041.

7) What if Ernst sold the painting to Alexis for $10,000? Can he claim a loss on the sale? See §267(a)(1).

Read Reg. §1.61-6(a)

1. Apportioning Property into Spatial Components

Taxpayers often acquire large things and then sell off components. Large tracts of land sold off by developers are the most obvious example. Most people who pay a single purchase price for property may never think about what each of the components is worth at the time of the purchase. That may be a mistake.

The tax law is clear that if a taxpayer buys a parcel of land which he later subdivides and improves for resale, he must apportion the basis of the overall property among the parcels to be sold in order to determine the gain or loss upon the sale of each parcel.[209] One does the apportioning on the basis of the relative fair market value of each parcel at the time of acquisition.[210] Obviously, the parcels are unlikely to have identical per square foot values. To make it more complicated, one also has to allocate the costs of such things as legal fees, surveying costs and the like which §263 insists be added to the basis of property. In general, one apportions fees of an overall value, like legal fees to get approval to develop an entire tract, in proportion to the value of each parcel, but one apportions costs that can be tied to particular tracts (such as surveying and installing roadways) in accordance with acreage rather than value.[211]

So far, so good, but what if what one is selling is a more complex interest, such as an easement? To take a concrete example, assume a gas pipeline company approaches a rancher in order to wheedle him into allowing a pipeline to transfer high pressure liquefied gas over his property. The easement will be 60 feet wide and will allow the company free access to the pipeline. The gas company offers the rancher $60,000 for the pipeline easement. His entire acreage has a basis of $850,000. Can the rancher exclude the $60,000 and use it to reduce his basis in the land on the theory that he cannot link the amount realized to the basis of particular property that he gave up? Now, read the next case and decide for yourself if you agree with the court's outcome.

---

209 See Fasken v. Commissioner., 71 T.C. 650 (1979) and ClevelandSanduskyBrewing Corp. v. Commissioner, 30 T.C. 539 (1958).

210 Soelling v. Commissioner, 70 T.C. 1052 (1978). and Neese v. Commissioner, 12T.C.M. 1058 (1953).

211 Hannibal Mo. Land Co. v. Commissioner, 9 B.T.A. 1072 (1928), nonacq., 1928 C.B. 37.

INAJA LAND CO. v. COMMISSIONER

9 T.C. 727 (1947)

LEECH, Judge:

[The taxpayer was a fishing club that owned a large, varied tract of land along the Owens River. The City of Los Angeles greatly interfered with the flow of the water, causing a variety of damages to the taxpayer's land. After a serious dispute, the City of Los Angeles agreed to make a net payment of $48,945 to the taxpayer in order to acquire an easement to allow periodic flooding and other injuries to the land. The taxpayer did not report any gain, theorizing that it was not possible to link the payment to any particular parts of the tract.]

OPINION

The question presented is whether the net amount of $ 48,945 received by petitioner in the taxable year 1939 under a certain indenture constitutes taxable income under section 22 (a), or is chargeable to capital account. The respondent contends: (a) That the $ 50,000, less $ 1,055 expenses incurred, which petitioner received from the city of Los Angeles under the indenture of August 11, 1939, represented compensation for loss of present and future income and consideration for release of many meritorious causes of action against the city, constituting ordinary income; and, (b) since petitioner has failed to allocate such sum between taxable and nontaxable income, it has not sustained its burden of showing error. Petitioner maintains that the language of the indenture and the circumstances leading up to its execution demonstrate that the consideration was paid for the easement granted to the city of Los Angeles and the consequent damage to its property rights; that the loss of past or future profits was not considered or involved; that the character of the easement rendered it impracticable to attempt to apportion a basis to the property affected; and, since the sum received is less than the basis of the entire property, taxation should be postponed until the final disposition of the property.

The recitals in the indenture of August 11, 1939, indicate its principal purpose was to convey to the city of Los Angeles a right of way and perpetual easements to discharge water upon and flood the lands of petitioner, in connection with the water supply of the city. Among its covenants are reciprocal releases by the respective parties. The respondent relies heavily on the language of the release by petitioner as grantor, contained in paragraph (A) of the indenture, which is set forth in full in our findings of fact. We think the respondent places too much emphasis upon the release provision of the indenture. It is usual and customary in agreements of this character to incorporate a provision for the release and discharge of any possible past, present, or future claims and demands. The mutuality of the releases indicates the purpose was precautionary and protective rather than descriptive and in recognition of asserted claims and demands. Paragraph (e) of the indenture recites that "a dispute has arisen between the parties hereto wherein Grantor claims that it has been and is being damaged by reason of the discharge into said Owens River . . . of foreign waters, and that such damage will continue henceforth. . . ." The character of the damage is not specified or otherwise indicated. The record reveals, through the testimony of petitioner's officers and its attorneys who carried on the negotiations culminating in the agreement, that no claim for damages for lost profits or income was ever asserted or considered. Of primary concern was the fact that, if the city were permitted to continue interference with petitioner's rights as riparian owner, the city might acquire, by prescription or user, the right to direct foreign waters into the Owens River, flooding petitioner's lands and interfering with its fishing rights by polluting the stream. The threat of an injunction suit was to protect petitioner against the city acquiring such rights without making proper compensation therefor. The evidence does not disclose any claim for or loss of income. There is some evidence that employees of the city, from time to time, engaged in unauthorized fishing and poaching upon petitioner's lands. The remedy of the petitioner for such wrongful acts would be against the individuals and not against the municipality, since clearly such tortious acts were not within the scope of their employment. Obviously, no part of the consideration received by petitioner from the city was paid for the release of such claims and demands. The recital in the indenture that petitioner, as grantor, released the city from all claims and demands "by reason of any and all other acts of whatsoever kind or nature of said Department, its employees, officers, or agents, upon, in connection with or pertaining to Grantor's land" embraces such acts as were within the scope of their employment. The record does not disclose the existence of such acts, if there were any. No claims or demands based on acts of that character had been made. We conclude that petitioner has satisfactorily established that the $ 50,000 it received in 1939 was consideration paid by the city for a right of way and easements and for resulting damages to its property and property rights.

The respondent further contends that petitioner has failed to allocate any portion of the $50,000 to nontaxable recovery of capital. He argues that the payment was a "lump sum" settlement related to many things which were not connected with petitioner's capital, such as loss of grazing rentals, guest card fees, and loss of fish from pollution. The record establishes that the grazing rentals were constant and that the guest fees were not intended to develop a source of operating revenue, but merely to restrict the number of guests. Pollution of the stream is an injury to property. The loss of fish as a result of the pollution of the river could form no basis for a claim, since fish in their wild state belong to the sovereign. In support of his position the respondent relies upon *Raytheon Production Corporation*, 1 T. C. 952 . . . . In the *Durkee* case, the Circuit Court says:

> It is settled that since profits from business are taxable, a sum received in settlement of litigation based upon a loss of profits is likewise taxable; but where the settlement represents damages

> for lost capital rather than for lost profits the money received is a return of capital and not taxable.... [Citing many cases.] The difficulty is in determining whether the recovery is for lost profits or for lost capital. The test is as stated by this Court in Farmers' & Merchants' Bank v. Commissioner, supra ... namely, "The fund involved must be considered in the light of the claim from which it was realized and which is reflected in the petition filed."

Upon this record we have concluded that no part of the recovery was paid for loss of profits, but was paid for the conveyance of a right of way and easements, and for damages to petitioner's land and its property rights as riparian owner. Hence, the respondent's contention has no merit. Capital recoveries in excess of cost do constitute taxable income. Petitioner has made no attempt to allocate a basis to that part of the property covered by the easements. It is conceded that all of petitioner's lands were not affected by the easements conveyed. Petitioner does not contest the rule that, where property is acquired for a lump sum and subsequently disposed of a portion at a time, there must be an allocation of the cost or other basis over the several units and gain or loss computed on the disposition of each part, except where apportionment would be wholly impracticable or impossible. *Nathan Blum*, 5 T. C. 702, 709. Petitioner argues that it would be impracticable and impossible to apportion a definite basis to the easements here involved, since they could not be described by metes and bounds; that the flow of the water has changed and will change the course of the river; that the extent of the flood was and is not predictable; and that to date the city has not released the full measure of water to which it is entitled. In *Strother v. Commissioner*, 55 Fed. (2d) 626, the court says:

> ... A taxpayer ... should not be charged with gain on pure conjecture unsupported by any foundation of ascertainable fact. See *Burnet v. Logan*, 283 U.S. 404 ....

Apportionment with reasonable accuracy of the amount received not being possible, and this amount being less than petitioner's cost basis for the property, it can not be determined that petitioner has, in fact, realized gain in any amount. Applying the rule as above set out, no portion of the payment in question should be considered as income, but the full amount must be treated as a return of capital and applied in reduction of petitioner's cost basis. *Burnet v. Logan*, 283 U.S. 404.

Decision will be entered for the petitioner.

Problem 3-10:

Travis is a rancher. He bought a 500-acre spread several years ago for $500,000. He added fencing, a stock barn, a pond and a ranch house for another $400,000. This year, he plans to sell 50 acres of raw land for $110,000. Closing costs and brokers' fees are $10,000.

1) Assuming each acre of the whole ranch was worth the same as any other acre when purchased, how much gain does Travis have to report on selling the 50 acres? See Reg. §1.61-6(a).

2) Next year, an oil pipeline company offers him $25,000 to run a high pressure gas pipeline across the middle of the ranch. If the pipeline were to burst, it could severely damage the value of the entire ranch. The easement for the pipeline covers a total of 3 acres. Assume the three acres have an allocable adjusted basis of $3,000. How should Travis report the $25,000?

Notes on Unknown Basis and the Impact of Depreciation on Basis

The IRS has historically had the benefit of generally being presumed correct as to the facts it alleges in tax controversies, except in civil fraud and criminal cases. The results of that presumption could be unfair. For example, imagine that you have a client who was a refugee who recently arrived in the USA from Absurdistan, a country with no income tax, bringing with her a variety of personal effects, jewelry, and other items, many of which she has to sell quite soon. To prepare a tax return, the client is supposed to know the basis of each piece of property, but how could she know her basis if she came from a country where the concept of basis was irrelevant? If challenged on the facts by the IRS, under prior law your client would almost surely have been unable to sustain her burden of proof, given that the IRS was generally presumed correct as to facts that it alleges. All that has changed.

Who has the burden of proof of facts? The Code added §7491, in order to significantly reduce the IRS's forensic powers. It eliminates the IRS's presumption of correctness in non-fraud cases, but only when the taxpayer is in court (where only 1% of all tax disputes wind up). Nowadays, if the taxpayer introduces "credible evidence" on a factual issue and satisfies several other requirements having to do with tax records, the burden of proof on that issue shifts to the IRS. A confusing aspect of §7491 is that it only comes into play if, in the court's mind, the facts equally favor each side. Otherwise, the burden is generally on the taxpayer. See, e.g. *Bilsky v. Commissioner,* 31 T.C. 35 (1959). Notice that even though §7491 does not formally apply in the administrative process, the Appeals Division must consider "hazards of litigation" when it settles cases. That means that the Appeals Division has to take into account the role of §7491 in the process of reaching administrative settlements. Section 7491(c) also generally puts the burden of proof as to penalties on the IRS in court cases.

The important requirements for the burden of proof to shift in favor of the taxpayer concern adequate substantiation of records by the taxpayer, record keeping, and reasonably timely cooperation with the IRS's "reasonable requests" for additional information. Importantly, "cooperation" does not require the taxpayer to agree to extend the statute of limitations in favor of the

IRS, but it does require exhaustion of administrative remedies, including pursuing all appeals the IRS makes available.[212] A key limit on the new system is that an individual with net worth over $2 million and a corporation, trust, or partnership with a net worth exceeding $7 million cannot benefit from it[213].

The burden of proof shifts to the IRS with regard to any item of an individual's income that is reconstructed solely on the basis of statistical information on other taxpayers, a slap at the unbridled use of technology. As to penalties the IRS seeks to impose on individuals, it now has burden of "production"; that is, it must present some evidence that the proposed penalty is appropriate. If the government does meet its burden, however, taxpayers are required to establish defenses, such as "reasonable cause" for their actions.[214]

These rules do not solve the problem of the immigrant and his or her basis. The situation has the potential for great unfairness and invites false statements about basis. Canada has stepped up to the problem by providing for "landed basis"; property is given a basis equal to its value when the immigrant arrived ("landed") in Canada.[215]

2. Apportionment of Property by Relative Usage

The previous section involved apportioning property into lesser-included physical components. This section involves apportioning them by usage. For example, if a salesman owns a fancy car which he drives partly for personal purposes and partly for his sales business, the tax law lets him claim tax deductions only with respect to the business use. The logical way to do so is by keeping a logbook in which he records his relative mileage between those two uses. This being tax law, things are of course not always so easy.

Even if you have correctly identified the initial basis of property used for mixed purposes, that basis may not be stable. A primary reason for changing basis is depreciation. In order to understand the next case, all you need to know is that depreciation refers to currently deducting from gross income the predicted decline in value of a long-term asset of a type that wears out. Sections 167 and 168 of the Code are the core provisions. There is no need to read them now. To take a simple example, under §168, one writes off the cost of a light truck used for business purposes over five years.

> **To illustrate:** If the local pizza company bought a delivery van for $20,000, it would claim an average deduction of $4,000 ($20,000 divided by 5 years) each year for the deemed loss in value

---

212 § 7430(b) and SUMMARY OF THE CONFERENCE AGREEMENT ON H.R. 2676, IRS Restructuring Act of 1998 (June 24, 1998), Joint Comm. Print 50-98R.

213 Section 7491(a)(2)(C) and 28 U.S.C. 2412(d)(2)(B).

214 §7491(c).

215 §128.1(1)(b), Canada Income Tax Act.

of the truck. That $4,000 would offset the pizza company's gross income in determining its annual income tax liability. At the end of the five years the truck would have an adjusted basis of zero.

SHARP v. UNITED STATES

199 F. Supp. 743 (D.C. Del. 1961)

LAYTON, District Judge.

[In 1946, Hugh and Bayard Sharp, who were brothers and business partners, bought a Beechcraft airplane for $45,875 and paid $8,398.50 to improve it, producing a total basis of $54,273,50. They claimed depreciation of $13,777.93 in proportion to business use, which was 26.346% of total use. They later sold the plane for $35,380. They claim the right approach is to consider that they simply sold a plane with an adjusted basis of $40,495.58:

Amount realized	$35,380.00
Adjusted Basis	(40,495.58)
Loss	5,115.58

The IRS advanced a more refined theory, which in effect found an almost fully depreciated "business plane" and a high basis "personal plane":

"Business plane":

Amount realized	$9,321.21	(.26346 x $35,380)
Adjusted basis	(520.98)[216]	
Gain	8,800.23	

"Personal plane":

Amount realized	$26,058.79	(.73653 x $35,380)
Adjusted basis	(39,974.60)	(no depreciation)
Loss	(13,915.81)	

Using the latter analysis, the IRS found a taxable gain on the "business plane" and a nondeductible personal consumption loss on the "personal plane." Incidentally, the normal way to apportion the usage of an airplane is by relative flying hours, since airplanes do not contain odometers.]

. . .

216 Proportionate initial basis, .26346 x $54,273.5 = $14,298.90, less depreciation of $13,777.93 = $520.97

Counsel for the government have said this is the first challenge by a taxpayer to Rev. Rul. 286, 19532 Cum. Bull. 20, and that if the position argued for by the taxpayers be sustained, it would 'produce serious and far reaching inequities in the administration of the internal revenue laws.'

While research has disclosed no decided case in which an allocation has been made in accordance with percentages of past business and personal use of property, taxpayers are clearly in error if it is their contention that courts will not regard a thing, normally accepted as an entity, as divisible for tax purposes. There are numerous decisions in which the sale proceeds from an orange grove, for instance, have been allocated between the trees (capital gain) and the unharvested crop (income), or where the proceeds from the sale of an interest in a partnership have been allocated between the earned but uncollected fees, or income producing property (income), and the other assets of the business (capital gain). A different sort of allocation was ordered in a leading Third Circuit case, Paul v. Commissioner. In Paul, taxpayer, who was in the business of holding rental property for investment purposes, bought a partially completed apartment building in May, which he sold more than six months later, in November. The issue was whether the taxpayer could treat the entire gain or any part thereof as long term capital gain, under Section 117(j) of the Internal Revenue Code of 1939. The Court held that a portion of the gain must be allocated to the part of the building erected more than six months before the sale and given long term treatment. The remainder of the proceeds allocable to the construction between May and November was taxed as short term gain.

The closest analogy to the case at bar is the sale of depreciable and nondepreciable property as a unit the sale of a building and land together, for instance. In United States v. Koshland [298 U.S. 441, 443-46 (1936)] a hotel caught fire and was destroyed. At issue in the case was the amount of the casualty loss deduction permissible under the circumstances. However, in the course of its opinion, the Court discussed the allocation problem directly, noting that the hotel was depreciable whereas the land on which it stood was not.

> '. . . The result is that there is no single 'adjusted basis' for the land and building as a unit. The depreciation allowed or allowable on the building reduces the basis of the building only. No depreciation is allowed on the land, and the original basis of the land therefore remains unaffected. The adjusted basis of the building and the basis of the land cannot be combined into a single 'adjusted basis' for the property as a whole, for to do so would in effect be reducing the basis of the whole by depreciation allowed or allowable only as against the building, a part.
>
> 'Thus, for tax purposes, upon a sale of the property as a whole the selling price must be allocated between the land and building and the gain or loss separately determined upon each, by reference to the adjusted basis of each.'

This principle has been recognized in other cases without discussion. The taxpayers point out that an airplane is not capable of separation into business and personal uses in the same way that a hotel is separable from the land on which it stands, or in the same way that the unharvested crop may be separated from the trees of the grove, or the accounts receivable from the other partnership assets. There were not two airplanes, say the taxpayers a business airplane and a personal airplane there was one airplane. There were not two sales; there was but one sale, one adjusted basis and one selling price. Any division or allocation, therefore, involves resorting to fiction, which is anathema to the tax law.

The taxpayers' argument against allocation in this case has superficial appeal. The whole idea of allocation is lacking in explicit authority from the literal words of the relevant sections in the Code. Since the situation here is not covered literally by the Statute, perhaps any interstices in statutory coverage should be filled by Congress not the Court. But this argument ignores the basic fact that no tax statute can encompass every situation which may arise. The Statute is phrased in general terms leaving it to the Commissioner by regulation or ruling and the Courts by interpretation to solve problems arising under unusual and novel facts. Merely because Congress did not specifically provide for the facts presented here does not mean it intended to exempt profits arising from the sale of property used both for business and pleasure. The taxpayers' argument also overlooks the fact that allocation has long been accepted by the courts in other cases. In dealing with another allocation problem, the Third Circuit Court of Appeals has said:

> 'The federal revenue laws are to be construed in the light of their general purpose 'so as to give a uniform application to a nationwide scheme of taxation.' Burnet v. Harmel, 1932 . . . .

But if taxpayers' theory prevails, there will be lack of uniformity in tax treatment between those who use property partially for business and pleasure on the one hand, and those who use property exclusively for business on the other. To use round figures, if property used exclusively for business has an adjusted basis of $500 ($14,000 cost less $13,500 depreciation) and it is sold for $9,000, nobody will deny that a taxable gain of $8,500 has been realized. Now, suppose that a larger piece of property is used only 1/4 for business purposes and 3/4 for pleasure, but that the adjusted basis of the business part is the same as in the first example, namely $500, and that depreciation figures and cost of the business part are also the same. Taxes levied on the business segment of the larger property should not be different from taxes levied on the other property used exclusively for business. To put it another way, taxpayers having two business properties with the same cost and depreciation should pay the same taxes, if the properties are sold for the same price. The fact that one of the properties was also used for pleasure should make no difference.

Under the government's allocation theory, uniformity is achieved; under the taxpayers', it is not. If the government's theory involves, as the taxpayers suggest, 'dividing' the plane up, it can only be replied that this is precisely what was done in calculating the depreciation deduction to which the taxpayers acquiesced. There is no greater peculiarity in doing the same thing when computing gain or loss on a sale. The depreciable business use and nondepreciable personal use of the airplane are not essentially different from the depreciable hotel and nondepreciable land discussed in the Koshland case, supra.

The fairness of the government's theory can be seen more easily using a different analysis. This different analysis involves allocation of loss instead of sale proceeds and cost basis. Continuing the use of round numbers, the $20,000 loss on the sale of the airplane (cost of $55,000 less sale proceeds of $35,000) can be allocated 3/4 to the personal use and 1/4 to the business use. If the property had not been depreciable, but used in the same fashion, it would seem proper that the taxpayer should be allowed to deduct $ 5,000 as a business loss no more, no less. Since depreciation deductions were taken in our case with respect to the business use of the airplane of about $13,500, and whereas the actual loss on this part of the plane's use was only $5,000, it would appear that taxpayer has received fortuitously the benefit of depreciation deductions equal to the difference between $13,500 and $5,000, or $8,500. Even though all depreciation was allowed or allowable, it is the government's position that the 'excessive' depreciation should be taxed. This Court agrees.

Application of the rationale and certain of the language of Paul v. Commissioner to the instant case compels the following conclusion. Allocation of the proceeds from the sale of this plane in accordance with its percentages of business and personal use is 'practical and fair.' This Court believes that Rev. Rul. 286, 19532 Cum.Bull. 20,[217] as applied here, represents a reasonable exercise by the Commissioner of his rule making power. There is no reason to make this an 'all or nothing proposition.' It is realistic to recognize that there are 'gradations' between the percentage of business and personal use of a piece of property. It is concluded here that it is 'proper that those gradations have tax significance.'

The taxpayers' motion for summary judgment is denied and the government's is granted. Let an order be submitted in conformity herewith.

---

217 The relevant portion of Rev. Rul. 286, 19532 Cum.Bull. 20, reads as follows:

"Only that part of a loss resulting from the sale of property used for both personal and incomeproducing purposes that can be allocated to the incomeproducing portion of the property constitutes a loss within the meaning of § 23(e) of the Internal Revenue Code (26 U.S.C.A. (I.R.C.1939), § 23(e)). In determining the gain or loss on the sale, there must be an actual allocation of the amounts which represent cost, selling price, depreciation allowed or allowable, and selling expenses to the respective portions of property in the same manner as if there were two separate transactions." [Footnote No. 7 in original.]

Read §1001(b) and Reg. §1.1001-1(a), -2(b)

1. General Rules

Probably 99% of all commercial transactions are just cash sales. In such cases, the amount realized is the sales price. There are also some exceptional situations. The first involves the taxable exchange of property where it is hard to appraise the value of the property received. In that case, the amount realized and the initial basis are the fair market value of the property surrendered, as was seen in the *Philadelphia Park*[218] case. Another possibility is that the payment was made in services. For example, a dentist might provide $1,000 of orthodontic services in exchange for a bracelet. In such case the person who transferred the bracelet to the dentist is deemed to have received $1,000 worth of services (the patient's amount realized[219]) in exchange for the bracelet, and, of course, the dentist has $1,000 of gross income from services. If the bracelet has a basis of $100, then we should know by now that the patient who transferred the bracelet would have a $900 gain on the transaction. The easy way to think of this is via an imaginary additional step in which the patient who transferred the property in exchange for services first *sold* the property for its fair market value to a stranger, and then took the cash proceeds and used the cash to buy the services. The *Davis* case illustrated that concept. Another good example is from Revenue Ruling 83-75[220] where a trustee distributed appreciated securities to a beneficiary of the trust to satisfy a beneficiary's right to receive a specified dollar amount from the trust. The IRS ruled the transfer was an "exchange" of the securities, resulting in taxable gain to the trust. The outcome is reasonable if one considers the practical equivalent, namely the trust's selling the securities to a stranger for cash, followed by the trust's paying that cash to the beneficiary. The cash sale would surely be taxable; it is best as a matter of policy to tax the more subtle, but functionally identical transaction involving the distribution the same way as the direct sale for cash, otherwise the tax law would invite needless complication.

2. Role of Debt

Debt is part of American culture; rarely does an American buy a house for cash. Instead she provides a cash down payment and borrows the rest from a financial institution, or from the seller.

218 Philadelphia Park Amusement Co. v. United States, 126 F. Supp. 184 (Ct. Cl. 1954)

219 Riley v. Commissioner, 37 T.C. 932 (1962), affirmed 328 F.2d 428 (CA5 1964).

220 19831 C.B. 114

To illustrate: The Cranes have spotted the house of their dreams in the suburbs. The purchase price is $100,000, but they have only $20,000 in cash. They get a loan from the Friendly Bank, which agrees to lend them $80,000, but demands a security interest in the home, with the result that if they default on their payments, the bank can foreclose, forcing a public sale of the house, with the bank taking the first $80,000 of the sales proceeds (or a smaller amount to the extent the Cranes have paid down some of the debt). Assuming they go through with the deal, the Cranes' basis in the home is $100,000. The loan will call for equal payments from the Cranes every month over a fixed period of time, such as 30 years. In addition to getting a security interest, the bank is almost sure to demand that the Cranes be personally responsible for the debt. That way, if they default and the foreclosure sale yields less than the outstanding debt on the house, the bank can hold them personally liable for the balance. Importantly, if the loan from the Friendly Bank is "assumable," then if someone buys the house from the Cranes, that person can step into their shoes and take over the debt. Banks rarely allow assumable mortgages, because the new borrower may have a mediocre credit rating.

Variation one: The Cranes agree to pay the seller $20,000 down and get title to the house, but will give the seller a security interest in the house until the Cranes make the last payment on the $80,000 "purchase money debt" (also known as "seller financing"). Their basis in the house the day they take the title is again $100,000, the purchase price.

Variation two: The Cranes sell their home, on which there is still a mortgage of $80,000 in favor of the Friendly Bank. The buyers like the rate of interest on the loan, so they assume the Cranes' loan and step into their shoes. The assumption frees the Cranes from their personal liability. In such a case, the debt the buyers assume is part of the Cranes' amount realized under §1001(b).

Variation three: The Friendly Bank is so confident about the future of real estate in the Crane's neighborhood that it lends the $80,000, but with no personal liability, just a security interest in their home. The Cranes provide the usual $20,000 down payment, and the bank pays the seller the necessary $80,000, but this time the Cranes have no personal liability on the debt. If they default, the bank can foreclose, but it cannot recover against the Crane's for unpaid principal on the debt. The kind of credit the Cranes got in this case is known as "nonrecourse debt" because the bank has no personal recourse against the debtors, just a security interest in the property.

In general, nonrecourse debt is found only in the real estate industry and nowadays is much rarer than it was in the past when real estate prices seemed to be capable of rising without limit. Whether the debt is recourse or nonrecourse, the debt service (which in U.S. banking practice usually consists of level monthly payments) normally consist of both repayments of principal plus current interest. In the early years, the proportion of interest is much greater than the proportion of principal that is repaid; but toward the end of the term of the mortgage, that pattern reverses itself and almost all of the debt service payments to the bank consist of repayments of principal. Sometimes, a persuasive borrower can get the lender to provide a "balloon" debt, meaning that only interest is payable on the debt until well into the future, at which time the borrower makes a large ("balloon") payment of principal.

The next case is the bedrock decision as to the effect of nonrecourse debt on the basis of property and the amount realized when the property is disposed of. It is not an easy read.

CRANE v. COMMISSIONER

331 U.S. 1 (1947)

MR. CHIEF JUSTICE VINSON delivered the opinion of the Court.

[The taxpayer, Beulah Crane, inherited a lot and building with a fair market value of $262,042.50, subject to a mortgage for $255,000 and interest in default. Soon after her inheritance, she entered into an agreement with the lender (mortgagee) to continue to operate the property and remit the net rents to the mortgagee. She followed this plan and took deductions for taxes, operating expenses, and depreciation for seven years. She then sold the land and building for $3,000 with the mortgage thereon and reported a gain of $1,250. She argued that the property she had acquired and sold was the equity. There was zero equity when the property came to her and the gain then was the amount realized of $3,000, less $500 expenses of sale, minus her basis in the equity of zero, for a gain of $2,500; which she then halved (under prior law rules relating to capital gains) to report $1,250 as taxable "on the assumption that the entire property was a 'capital asset'." The fair market value of the property exceeded the amount of the nonrecourse mortgage. The core question is how to compute the gain or loss when the taxpayer acquires property with a mortgage and sells it subject to the same. Is the gain computed based on equity or on a gross basis that includes the debt, as the IRS argues?]

. . .

The 1938 Act, § 111 (a), defines the gain from "the sale or other disposition of property" as "the excess of the amount realized therefrom over the adjusted basis provided in section 113 (b) . . . ." It proceeds, § 111 (b), to define "the amount realized from the sale or other disposition of property" as "the sum of any money received plus the fair market value of the property (other than money) received." Further, in § 113 (b), the "adjusted basis for determining the gain or loss from the sale or other disposition of property" is declared to be "the basis determined under subsection (a), adjusted . . . [(1) (B)] . . . for exhaustion, wear and tear, obsolescence, amortization . . . to the extent allowed (but not less than the amount allowable) . . . ." The basis under subsection (a) "if the property was acquired by . . . devise . . . or by the decedent's estate from the decedent," § 113 (a) (5), is "the fair market value of such property at the time of such acquisition."

Logically, the first step under this scheme is to determine the unadjusted basis of the property, under § 113 (a) (5), and the dispute in this case is as to the construction to be given the term "property." If "property," as used in that provision, means the same thing as "equity," it would necessarily follow that the basis of petitioner's property was zero, as she contends. If, on the contrary, it means the land and building themselves, or the owner's legal rights in them, undiminished by the mortgage, the basis was $ 262,042.50.

We think that the reasons for favoring one of the latter constructions are of overwhelming weight. In the first place, the words of statutes including revenue acts should be interpreted where possible in their ordinary, everyday senses. The only relevant definitions of "property" to be found in the principal standard dictionaries are the two favored by the Commissioner, i. e., either that "property" is the physical thing which is a subject of ownership, or that it is the aggregate of the owner's rights to control and dispose of that thing. "Equity" is not given as a synonym, nor do either of the foregoing definitions suggest that it could be correctly so used. Indeed, "equity" is defined as "the value of a property . . . above the total of the liens. . . ." The contradistinction could hardly be more pointed. Strong countervailing considerations would be required to support a contention that Congress, in using the word "property," meant "equity," or that we should impute to it the intent to convey that meaning.

In the second place, the Commissioner's position has the approval of the administrative construction of § 113 (a) (5). With respect to the valuation of property under that section, Reg. 101, Art. 113 (a) (5)1, promulgated under the 1938 Act, provided that "the value of property as of the date of the death of the decedent as appraised for the purpose of the Federal estate tax . . . shall be deemed to be its fair market value . . . ." The land and building here involved were so appraised in 1932, and their appraised value $ 262,042.50 was reported by petitioner as part of the gross estate. This was in accordance with the estate tax law and regulations, which had always required that the value of decedent's property, undiminished by liens, be so appraised and returned, and that mortgages be separately deducted in computing the net estate. As the quoted provision of the Regulations has been in effect since 1918, and as the relevant statutory provision has been repeatedly reenacted since then in substantially the same form, the former may itself now be considered to have the force of law.

Moreover, in the many instances in other parts of the Act in which Congress has used the word "property," or expressed the idea of "property" or "equity," we find no instances of a misuse of either word or of confusion of the ideas. In some parts of the Act other than the gain and loss sections, we find "property" where it is unmistakably used in its ordinary sense. On the other hand, where either Congress or the Treasury intended to convey the meaning of "equity," it did so by the use of appropriate language.

A further reason why the word "property" in § 113 (a) should not be construed to mean "equity" is the bearing such construction would have on the allowance of deductions for depreciation and on the collateral adjustments of basis.

Section 23 (l) permits deduction from gross income of "A reasonable allowance for the exhaustion, wear and tear of property . . . ." Sections 23 (n) and 114 (a) declare that the "basis upon which exhaustion, wear and tear . . . are to be allowed" is the basis "provided in section 113 (b) for the purpose of determining the gain upon the sale" of the property, which is the § 113 (a) basis "adjusted . . . for exhaustion, wear and tear . . . to the extent allowed (but not less than the amount allowable). . . ."

Under these provisions, if the mortgagor's equity were the § 113 (a) basis, it would also be the original basis from which depreciation allowances are deducted. If it is, and if the amount of the annual allowances were to be computed on that value, as would then seem to be required, they will represent only a fraction of the cost of the corresponding physical exhaustion, and any recoupment by the mortgagor of the remainder of that cost can be effected only by the reduction of his taxable gain in the year of sale. If, however, the amount of the annual allowances were to be computed on the value of the property, and then deducted from an equity basis, we would in some instances have to accept deductions from a minus basis or deny deductions altogether. The Commissioner also argues that taking the mortgagor's equity as the § 113 (a) basis would require the basis to be changed with each payment on the mortgage, and that the attendant problem of repeatedly recomputing basis and annual allowances would be a tremendous accounting burden on both the Commissioner and the taxpayer. Moreover, the mortgagor would acquire control over the timing of his depreciation allowances.

Thus it appears that the applicable provisions of the Act expressly preclude an equity basis, and the use of it is contrary to certain implicit principles of income tax depreciation, and entails very great administrative difficulties. It may be added that the Treasury has never furnished a guide through the maze of problems that arise in connection with depreciating an equity basis, but, on the contrary, has consistently permitted the amount of depreciation allowances to be computed on the full value of the property, and subtracted from it as a basis. Surely, Congress' longcontinued acceptance of this situation gives it full legislative endorsement.

We conclude that the proper basis under § 113 (a) (5) is the value of the property, undiminished by mortgages thereon, and that the correct basis here was $ 262,042.50. The next step is to ascertain what adjustments are required under § 113 (b). As the depreciation rate was stipulated, the only question at this point is whether the Commissioner was warranted in making any depreciation adjustments whatsoever.

Section 113 (b) (1) (B) provides that "proper adjustment in respect of the property *shall in all cases be made* . . . for exhaustion, wear and tear . . . to the extent allowed (but not less than the amount allowable) . . . ." (Italics supplied.) The Tax Court found on adequate evidence that the apartment house was property of a kind subject to physical exhaustion, that it was used in taxpayer's trade or business, and consequently that the taxpayer would have been entitled to a depreciation allowance under § 23 (1), except that, in the opinion of that Court, the basis of the property was zero, and it was thought that depreciation could not be taken on a zero basis. As we have just decided that the correct basis of the property was not zero, but $ 262,042.50, we avoid this difficulty, and conclude that an adjustment should be made as the Commissioner determined.

Petitioner urges to the contrary that she was not entitled to depreciation deductions, whatever the basis of the property, because the law allows them only to one who actually bears the capital loss, and here the loss was not hers but the mortgagee's. We do not see, however, that she has established her factual premise. There was no finding of the Tax Court to that effect, nor to the effect that the value of the property was ever less than the amount of the lien. Nor was there evidence in the record, or any indication that petitioner could produce evidence, that this was so. The facts that the value of the property was only equal to the lien in 1932 and that during the next six and onehalf years the physical condition of the building deteriorated and the amount of the lien increased, are entirely inconclusive, particularly in the light of the buyer's willingness in 1938 to take subject to the increased lien and pay a substantial amount of cash to boot. Whatever may be the rule as to allowing depreciation to a mortgagor on property in his possession which is subject to an unassumed mortgage and clearly worth less than the lien, we are not faced with that problem and see no reason to decide it now.

At last we come to the problem of determining the "amount realized" on the 1938 sale. Section 111 (b), it will be recalled, defines the "amount realized" from "the sale . . . of property" as "the sum of any money received plus the fair market value of the property (other than money) received," and § 111 (a) defines the gain on "the sale . . . of property" as the excess of the amount realized over the basis. Quite obviously, the word "property," used here with reference t a sale, must mean "property" in the same ordinary sense intended by the use of the word with reference to acquisition and depreciation in § 113, both for certain of the reasons stated heretofore in discussing its meaning in § 113, and also because the functional relation of the two sections requires that the word mean the same in one section that it does in the other. If the "property" to be valued on the date of acquisition is the property free of liens, the "property" to be priced on a subsequent sale must be the same thing.

Starting from this point, we could not accept petitioner's contention that the $ 2,500 net cash was all she realized on the sale except on the absurdity that she sold a quarterofAmillion dollar property for roughly one per cent of its value, and took a 99 per cent loss. Actually, petitioner does not urge this. She argues, conversely, that because only $ 2,500 was realized on the sale, the "property" sold must have been the equity only, and that consequently we are forced to accept her contention as to the meaning of "property" in § 113. We adhere, however, to what we have already said on the meaning of "property," and we find that the absurdity is avoided by our conclusion that the amount of the mortgage is properly included in the "amount realized" on the sale.

Petitioner concedes that if she had been personally liable on the mortgage and the purchaser had either paid or assumed it, the amount so paid or assumed would be considered a part of the "amount realized" within the meaning of § 111 (b). The cases so deciding have already repudiated the notion that there must be an actual receipt by the seller himself of "money" or "other property," in their narrowest senses. It was thought to be decisive that one section of the Act must be construed so as not to defeat the intention of another or to frustrate the Act as a whole, and that the taxpayer was the "beneficiary" of the payment in "as real and substantial [a sense] as if the money had been paid it and then paid over by it to its creditors."

Both these points apply to this case. The first has been mentioned already. As for the second, we think that a mortgagor, not personally liable on the debt, who sells the property subject to the mortgage and for additional consideration, realizes a benefit in the amount of the mortgage as well as the boot.[221] If a purchaser pays boot, it is immaterial as to our problem whether the mortgagor is also to receive money from the purchaser to discharge the mortgage prior to sale, or whether he is merely to transfer subject to the mortgage it may make a difference to the purchaser and to the mortgagee, but not to the mortgagor. Or put in another way, we are no more concerned with whether the mortgagor is, strictly speaking, a debtor on the mortgage, than we are with whether the benefit to him is, strictly speaking, a receipt of money or property. We are rather concerned with the reality that an owner of property, mortgaged at a figure less than that at which the property will sell, must and will treat the conditions of the mortgage exactly as if they were his personal obligations. If he transfers subject to the mortgage, the benefit to him is as real and substantial as if the mortgage were discharged, or as if a personal debt in an equal amount had been assumed by another.

Therefore we conclude that the Commissioner was right in determining that petitioner realized $ 257,500 on the sale of this property.

The Tax Court's contrary determinations, that "property," as used in § 113 (a) and related sections, means "equity," and that the amount of a mortgage subject to which property is sold is not the measure of a benefit realized, within the meaning of § 111 (b), announced rules of general applicability on clearcut questions of law. The Circuit Court of Appeals therefore had jurisdiction to review them.

Petitioner contends that the result we have reached taxes her on what is not income within the meaning of the Sixteenth Amendment. If this is because only the direct receipt of cash is thought to be income in the constitutional sense, her contention is wholly without merit. If it

---

221 [This is the famous 'footnote 37' in the case proper and is referred to by number in the tax literature and the Tufts case that follows. Eds.]

"Obviously, if the value of the property is less than the amount of the mortgage, a mortgagor who is not personally liable cannot realize a benefit equal to the mortgage. Consequently, a different problem might be encountered where a mortgagor abandoned the property or transferred it subject to the mortgage without receiving boot.That is not this case."

is because the entire transaction is thought to have been "by all dictates of common sense . . . a ruinous disaster," as it was termed in her brief, we disagree with her premise. She was entitled to depreciation deductions for a period of nearly seven years, and she actually took them in almost the allowable amount. The crux of this case, really, is whether the law permits her to exclude allowable deductions from consideration in computing gain. We have already showed that, if it does, the taxpayer can enjoy a double deduction, in effect, on the same loss of assets. The Sixteenth Amendment does not require that result any more than does the Act itself.

Affirmed.

[Justice Jackson's dissent is omitted. Eds.]

Notes

What exactly is Beulah Crane's position? Crane is a puzzling case to many readers because it seems that Mrs. Crane was speaking out of both sides of her mouth in that she claimed that all she should be taxed on was her "equity" in the property, but at the same time she claimed depreciation deductions that greatly exceeded her "equity." What was really going on? The answer is that the *Crane* case has a lot to do with statutes of limitations. Beulah Crane was cashing in on the rule that, in general, after three years following the later of April 15 or the actual filing date, the IRS loses its ability to assess deficiencies and the taxpayer loses the right to seek tax refunds with respect to that year. Beulah Crane claimed depreciation on the property, using a (large) fair market value at death basis as the starting point for her computation. Later, she repudiated the idea that she inherited the gross property, and claimed that all she got was the (small) "equity," meaning the gross value of the property minus its encumbrances. She did not assign the equity the negative basis required to reconcile her two positions. (The courts are staunchly opposed to finding negative basis.) Because the statute of limitations had closed on prior years in which she had claimed depreciation, she could not go back and correct the "error" of using the wrong basis. Nowadays, the duty of consistency would presumably preclude her from taking inconsistent positions.

*Now for more general concepts.*Debt that is included in the basis of property consists *only* of acquisition indebtedness, meaning debt the taxpayer incurred to finance the acquisition of the property (such as a mortgage from a bank or the seller's extension of credit to the buyer) plus debt that encumbered the property when the taxpayer acquired the property. If the owner later pays down the debt, that payment does not increase her basis in the property.

To illustrate: Buyer paid $20 in cash and borrowed $80 from the Friendly Bank to buy Whiteacre. Buyer's basis in Whiteacre is $100. If Whiteacre were also encumbered by a $50 nonrecourse debt that continues to burden the property after its purchase, then Whiteacre's basis is instead $150. If Buyer later uses Whiteacre as collateral for a further $5 debt, that debt will have no impact on his basis in Whiteacre because it is not acquisition indebtedness. However, if Buyer happened to use the $5 to build an irrigation system on the property, that improvement would increase Buyer's total basis in Whiteacre by $5. By contrast, when a taxpayer sells encumbered property, he includes in his amount realized all debt that the buyer assumes or (in the case of nonrecourse debt) that encumbers the property at the time of the transfer.

Second, the disposition itself need not be a sale to be taxable. Cases following *Crane* established that a foreclosure of property is treated as taxable sale by the owner[222] and that even an *abandonment* of a property subject to a nonrecourse debt is a taxed like a sale and results in mandatory inclusion of the debt in the abandoning taxpayer's amount realized.[223]

To illustrate: A bought Blackacre for $20 cash and an $80 nonrecourse debt. When Blackacre has a basis of $50, but the debt is still $80, A abandons Blackacre. A has a $30 gain.

What about the unusual case where the debt is with recourse but the buyer does not assume the debt? The Regulations under §1001 contemplate two traditional transactions, one where the loan is nonrecourse and the buyer takes the property with the debt attached, and the other where the buyer goes to the lender and works out an assumption of the old loan (really, a novation of the loan agreement). There is another deal you need to consider. The buyer might take a deed to the property, with the property left subject to a recourse debt that the seller remains responsible for. In commercial dealings, the buyer will often give the seller a "wrap-around loan" based on an unassumed recourse loan. Here is how it often looks.

To illustrate: Seller owns the Baltic Hotel, which has a basis and value of $100. Seller owes the Friendly Bank $60 under a "recourse" loan used to finance the purchase of the Baltic Hotel five years ago. The loan is at a particularly favorable rate of interest. Buyer offers seller $25 in cash plus a $75 second "wrap-around mortgage," pursuant to which Seller promises to service the underlying "wrapped" $60 debt. Buyer will have a basis of $100 in the Baltic Hotel. Seller should be viewed as having sold the hotel and reporting an amount realized of $100, consisting of the $25 plus the $75 "wrapper." Buyer will be entitled to interest expense deductions with respect to the $75 purchase money debt, because it is Buyer's personal responsibility.[224] Seller will report the interest income on the $75 debt, but will claim interest expense deductions for servicing the continuing $60 debt. This can be an excellent way to keep from losing a good loan when property is sold, but it is hard on the seller, who presumably would rather have as much cash as

222 Helvering v. Hammel, 311 U.S. 504 (1941).

223 Middleton v. Commissioner, 77 T.C. 310 (1981).

224 See Stonecrest Corp. v. Commissioner, 24 TC 659 (1955).

possible at the time of the closing and run. NB: because Seller remains liable on the $60 debt, the $60 is not part of Seller's amount realized.[225]

This analysis is supported by *Aizawa v. Commissioner.*[226] The facts involved property that was subject to recourse debt, on which there was a foreclosure. The court ruled that there was no cancellation of debt income to the extent the foreclosure transfer did not discharge the debt when the property was sold in foreclosure.[227] Thus, only the proceeds of the foreclosure sale constituted an "amount realized." The taxpayer still owed the remaining unpaid balance of the debt.

In fact, the next case addresses footnote 37 of *Crane.*[228] It is an extremely important case because at the time it was decided many areas of the U.S. were overbuilt and in trouble. Numerous projects were financed by nonrecourse debt, and investors were allowing the lenders to take back the properties, and then taking the position that the particular property was worth less than the debt, and that footnote 37 of *Crane* let them to reduce the amount realized on disposition to the value of the property, even though that value was less than the amount of the nonrecourse debt.

COMMISSIONER v. TUFTS

461 U.S. 300 (1983)

JUSTICE BLACKMUN delivered the opinion of the Court.

[A builder and his wholly-owned corporation formed a partnership which took out a nonrecourse loan for $1,851,500 to construct an apartment complex. Other partners were admitted; the sum of their capital contributions was $44,212. The partners claimed a total of $439,972 in ordinary losses and depreciation deductions, making their adjusted bases $1,455,740. The property was then sold for its sale expenses, subject to the mortgage. The value of the property at that time was only $1,400,000. Each partner claimed a loss, based on his or her share of the $55,740 loss (being adjusted basis minus fair market value). The IRS claimed the amount realized

---

225 The Regulations treat Seller has having a $15 gain in the year of sale. Reg. Section 15a.453-1(b)(3)(ii). The Tax Court held the regulation invalid in Professional Equities, Inc. v. CIR, 89 TC 165 (1987)and the IRS has acquiesced. The situation is more complicated than the example indicated because the Regulation and case implicate timing issues arising out of the installment sale method under § 453, which is considered later in the book.

226 99 T.C. 197 (1992), aff'd 29 F.3d 630 (9th Cir.1994); see also Stonecrest Corp. v. Commissioner, 24 TC 659 (1955) ((non acq.) (property is "taken subject to" mortgage "only where the payments [by the buyer] on the mortgage are to be made to the mortgagee and not to the seller").

227 99 T.C. 197 (1992), aff'd without pub. opinion, 29 F3d. 630 (9th Cir. 1994).

228 The famous footnote 37 in Crane v. Commissioner stated:

"Obviously, if the value of the property is less than the amount of the mortgage, a mortgagor who is not personally liable cannot realize a benefit equal to the mortgage. Consequently, a different problem might be encountered where a mortgagor abandoned the property or transferred it subject to the mortgage without receiving boot. That is not this case."

The Tufts case that follows raises exactly this question.

included the full amount of the nonrecourse debt. The partners claimed that footnote 37 of the *Crane* case limited their amount realized to the property's value.]

. . .

II

Under § 1001(a), the gain or loss from a sale or other disposition of property is defined as the difference between "the amount realized" on the disposition and the property's adjusted basis. Subsection (b) of § 1001 defines "amount realized": "The amount realized from the sale or other disposition of property shall be the sum of any money received plus the fair market value of the property (other than money) received." At issue is the application of the latter provision to the disposition of property encumbered by a nonrecourse mortgage of an amount in excess of the property's fair market value.

A

In *Crane v. Commissioner*, supra, this Court took the first and controlling step toward the resolution of this issue. Beulah B. Crane was the sole beneficiary under the will of her deceased husband. At his death in January 1932, he owned an apartment building that was then mortgaged for an amount which proved to be equal to its fair market value, as determined for federal estate tax purposes. The widow, of course, was not personally liable on the mortgage. She operated the building for nearly seven years, hoping to turn it into a profitable venture; during that period, she claimed income tax deductions for depreciation, property taxes, interest, and operating expenses, but did not make payments upon the mortgage principal. In computing her basis for the depreciation deductions, she included the full amount of the mortgage debt. In November 1938, with her hopes unfulfilled and the mortgagee threatening foreclosure, Mrs. Crane sold the building. The purchaser took the property subject to the mortgage and paid Crane $ 3,000; of that amount, $ 500 went for the expenses of the sale.

Crane reported a gain of $ 2,500 on the transaction. She reasoned that her basis in the property was zero (despite her earlier depreciation deductions based on including the amount of the mortgage) and that the amount she realized from the sale was simply the cash she received. The Commissioner disputed this claim. He asserted that Crane's basis in the property, under [the current version is §1014], was the property's fair market value at the time of her husband's death, adjusted for depreciation in the interim, and that the amount realized was the net cash received plus the amount of the outstanding mortgage assumed by the purchaser.

In upholding the Commissioner's interpretation of [§1014] the Court observed that to regard merely the taxpayer's equity in the property as her basis would lead to depreciation deductions less than the actual physical deterioration of the property, and would require the basis to be recomputed with each payment on the mortgage. . . . The Court rejected Crane's claim that any loss due to depreciation belonged to the mortgagee. The effect of the Court's ruling was that the taxpayer's basis was the value of the property undiminished by the mortgage. *Id.*, at 11.

. . .

Crane, however, insisted that the nonrecourse nature of the mortgage required different treatment. The Court, for two reasons, disagreed. First, excluding the nonrecourse debt from the amount realized would result in the same absurdity and frustration of the Code. *Id.*, at 1314. Second, the Court concluded that Crane obtained an economic benefit from the purchaser's assumption of the mortgage identical to the benefit conferred by the cancellation of personal debt. Because the value of the property in that case exceeded the amount of the mortgage, it was in Crane's economic interest to treat the mortgage as a personal obligation; only by so doing could she realize upon sale the appreciation in her equity represented by the $ 2,500 boot. The purchaser's assumption of the liability thus resulted in a taxable economic benefit to her, just as if she had been given, in addition to the boot, a sum of cash sufficient to satisfy the mortgage.[229]

In a footnote, pertinent to the present case, the Court observed:

> "Obviously, if the value of the property is less than the amount of the mortgage, a mortgagor who is not personally liable cannot realize a benefit equal to the mortgage. Consequently, a different problem might be encountered where a mortgagor abandoned the property or transferred it subject to the mortgage without receiving boot. That is not this case." *Id.*, at 14, n. 37.

B

This case presents that unresolved issue. We are disinclined to overrule *Crane*, and we conclude that the same rule applies when the unpaid amount of the nonrecourse mortgage exceeds the value of the property transferred. *Crane* ultimately does not rest on its limited theory of economic benefit; instead, we read *Crane* to have approved the Commissioner's decision to treat a nonrecourse mortgage in this context as a true loan. This approval underlies *Crane's* holdings that the amount of the nonrecourse liability is to be included in calculating both the basis and the amount realized on disposition. That the amount of the loan exceeds the fair market value of the property thus becomes irrelevant.

229 Crane also argued that even if the statute required the inclusion of the amount of the nonrecourse debt, that amount was not Sixteenth Amendment income because the overall transaction had been "by all dictates of common sense . . . a ruinous disaster." Brief for Petitioner in Crane v. Commissioner, O. T. 1946, No. 68, p. 51. The Court noted, however, that Crane had been entitled to and actually took depreciation deductions for nearly seven years. To allow her to exclude sums on which those deductions were based from the calculation of her taxable gain would permit her "A double deduction . . . on the same loss of assets." The Sixteenth Amendment, it was said, did not require that result. 331 U.S., at 1516. [Footnote No. 4 in original.]

When a taxpayer receives a loan, he incurs an obligation to repay that loan at some future date. Because of this obligation, the loan proceeds do not qualify as income to the taxpayer. When he fulfills the obligation, the repayment of the loan likewise has no effect on his tax liability.

Another consequence to the taxpayer from this obligation occurs when the taxpayer applies the loan proceeds to the purchase price of property used to secure the loan. Because of the obligation to repay, the taxpayer is entitled to include the amount of the loan in computing his basis in the property; the loan, under § 1012, is part of the taxpayer's cost of the property. Although a different approach might have been taken with respect to a nonrecourse mortgage loan,[230] the Commissioner has chosen to accord it the same treatment he gives to a recourse mortgage loan. The Court approved that choice in *Crane*, and the respondents do not challenge it here. The choice and its resultant benefits to the taxpayer are predicated on the assumption that the mortgage will be repaid in full.

When encumbered property is sold or otherwise disposed of and the purchaser assumes the mortgage, the associated extinguishment of the mortgagor's obligation to repay is accounted for in the computation of the amount realized. See *United States v. Hendler*, 303 U.S. 564, 566567 (1938). Because no difference between recourse and nonrecourse obligations is recognized in calculating basis,[231] Crane teaches that the Commissioner may ignore the nonrecourse nature of the obligation in determining the amount realized upon disposition of the encumbered property. He thus may include in the amount realized the amount of the nonrecourse mortgage assumed by

---

230 The Commissioner might have adopted the theory, implicit in Crane's contentions, that a nonrecourse mortgage is not true debt, but, instead, is a form of joint investment by the mortgagor and the mortgagee. On this approach, nonrecourse debt would be considered a contingent liability, under which the mortgagor's payments on the debt gradually increase his interest in the property while decreasing that of the mortgagee. Note, Federal Income Tax Treatment of Nonrecourse Debt, 82 Colum. L. Rev. 1498, 1514 (1982); Lurie, Mortgagor's Gain on Mortgaging Property for More than Cost Without Personal Liability, 6 Tax L. Rev. 319, 323 (1951); cf. Brief for Respondents 16 (nonrecourse debt resembles preferred stock). Because the taxpayer's investment in the property would not include the nonrecourse debt, the taxpayer would not be permitted to include that debt in basis. Note, 82 Colum. L. Rev., at 1515; cf. Gibson Products Co. v. United States, 637 F.2d 1041, 10471048 (CA5 1981) (contingent nature of obligation prevents inclusion in basis of oil and gas leases of nonrecourse debt secured by leases, drilling equipment, and percentage of future production).

We express no view as to whether such an approach would be consistent with the statutory structure and, if so, and Crane were not on the books, whether that approach would be preferred over Crane's analysis. We note only that the Crane Court's resolution of the basis issue presumed that when property is purchased with proceeds from a nonrecourse mortgage, the purchaser becomes the sole owner of the property. 331 U.S., at 6. Under the Crane approach, the mortgagee is entitled to no portion of the basis. Id., at 10, n. 28. The nonrecourse mortgage is part of the mortgagor's investment in the property, and does not constitute a coinvestment by the mortgagee. But see Note, 82 Colum. L. Rev., at 1513 (treating nonrecourse mortgage as coinvestment by mortgagee and critically concluding that Crane departed from traditional analysis that basis is taxpayer's investment in property). [Footnote No. 5 in original.]

231 The Commissioner's choice in Crane "laid the foundation stone of most tax shelters," Bittker, Tax Shelters, Nonrecourse Debt, and the Crane Case, 33 Tax L. Rev. 277, 283 (1978), by permitting taxpayers who bear no risk to take deductions on depreciable property. Congress recently has acted to curb this avoidance device by forbidding a taxpayer to take depreciation deductions in excess of amounts he has at risk in the investment. Pub. L. 94455, § 204(a), 90 Stat. 1531 (1976), 26 U. S. C. § 465; Pub. L. 95600, §§ 201204, 92 Stat. 28142817 (1978), 26 U. S. C. § 465(a) (1976 ed., Supp. V). Real estate investments, however, are exempt from this prohibition. §465(c)(3)(D) (1976 ed., Supp. V). Although this congressional action may foreshadow a day when nonrecourse and recourse debts will be treated differently, neither Congress nor the Commissioner has sought to alter Crane's rule of including nonrecourse liability in both basis and the amount realized. [Footnote No. 7 in original.]

the purchaser. The rationale for this treatment is that the original inclusion of the amount of the mortgage in basis rested on the assumption that the mortgagor incurred an obligation to repay. Moreover, this treatment balances the fact that the mortgagor originally received the proceeds of the nonrecourse loan taxfree on the same assumption. Unless the outstanding amount of the mortgage is deemed to be realized, the mortgagor effectively will have received untaxed income at the time the loan was extended and will have received an unwarranted increase in the basis of his property. The Commissioner's interpretation of § 1001(b) in this fashion cannot be said to be unreasonable.

C

The Commissioner in fact has applied this rule even when the fair market value of the property falls below the amount of the nonrecourse obligation. Treas. Reg. § 1.10012(b), . . .[232] Rev. Rul. 76111, 19761 Cum. Bull. 214. Because the theory on which the rule is based applies equally in this situation. . . . we have no reason, after *Crane*, to question this treatment.

Respondents received a mortgage loan with the concomitant obligation to repay by the year 2012. The only difference between that mortgage and one on which the borrower is personally liable is that the mortgagee's remedy is limited to foreclosing on the securing property. This difference does not alter the nature of the obligation; its only effect is to shift from the borrower to the lender any potential loss caused by devaluation of the property. If the fair market value of the property falls below the amount of the outstanding obligation, the mortgagee's ability to protect its interests is impaired, for the mortgagor is free to abandon the property to the mortgagee and be relieved of his obligation.

This, however, does not erase the fact that the mortgagor received the loan proceeds taxfree and included them in his basis on the understanding that he had an obligation to repay the full amount. . . . When the obligation is canceled, the mortgagor is relieved of his responsibility to repay the sum he originally received and thus realizes value to that extent within the meaning of § 1001(b). From the mortgagor's point of view, when his obligation is assumed by a third party who purchases the encumbered property, it is as if the mortgagor first had been paid with cash borrowed by the third party from the mortgagee on a nonrecourse basis, and then had used the cash to satisfy his obligation to the mortgagee.

Moreover, this approach avoids the absurdity the Court recognized in Crane. Because of the remedy accompanying the mortgage in the nonrecourse situation, the depreciation in the fair market value of the property is relevant economically only to the mortgagee, who by lending on a nonrecourse basis remains at risk. To permit the taxpayer to limit his realization to the fair

232 The regulation was promulgated while this case was pending before the Court of Appeals for the Fifth Circuit. T. D. 7741, 45 Fed. Reg. 81744, 19811 Cum. Bull. 430 (1980). It merely formalized the Commissioner's prior interpretation, however. [Footnote No. 9 in original.]

market value of the property would be to recognize a tax loss for which he has suffered no corresponding economic loss. Such a result would be to construe "one section of the Act . . . so as . . . to defeat the intention of another or to frustrate the Act as a whole." . . .

In the specific circumstances of *Crane*, the economic benefit theory did support the Commissioner's treatment of the nonrecourse mortgage as a personal obligation. The footnote in *Crane* acknowledged the limitations of that theory when applied to a different set of facts. *Crane* also stands for the broader proposition, however, that a nonrecourse loan should be treated as a true loan. We therefore hold that a taxpayer must account for the proceeds of obligations he has received taxfree and included in basis. Nothing in either § 1001(b) or in the Court's prior decisions requires the Commissioner to permit a taxpayer to treat a sale of encumbered property asymmetrically, by including the proceeds of the nonrecourse obligation in basis but not accounting for the proceeds upon transfer of the encumbered property. . . .

. . .

IV

When a taxpayer sells or disposes of property encumbered by a nonrecourse obligation, the Commissioner properly requires him to include among the assets realized the outstanding amount of the obligation. The fair market value of the property is irrelevant to this calculation. We find this interpretation to be consistent with *Crane v. Commissioner*, 331 U.S. 1 (1947), and to implement the statutory mandate in a reasonable manner. . . .

The judgment of the Court of Appeals is therefore reversed.

It is so ordered.

JUSTICE O'CONNOR, concurring.

I concur in the opinion of the Court, accepting the view of the Commissioner. I do not, however, endorse the Commissioner's view. Indeed, were we writing on a slate clean except for the decision in *Crane v. Commissioner*, 331 U.S. 1 (1947), I would take quite a different approach that urged upon us by Professor Barnett as *amicus*.

Crane established that a taxpayer could treat property as entirely his own, in spite of the "coinvestment" provided by his mortgagee in the form of a nonrecourse loan. That is, the full basis of the property, with all its tax consequences, belongs to the mortgagor. That rule alone, though, does not in any way tie nonrecourse debt to the cost of property or to the proceeds upon disposition. I see no reason to treat the purchase, ownership, and eventual disposition of property differently because the taxpayer also takes out a mortgage, an independent transaction. In this case, the taxpayer purchased property, using nonrecourse financing, and sold it after it declined in value to a buyer who assumed the mortgage. There is no economic difference between the events in this case and a case in which the taxpayer buys property with cash; later obtains a nonrecourse loan by pledging the property as security; still later, using cash on hand, buys off the mortgage for the market value of the devalued property; and finally sells the property to a third party for its market value.

The logical way to treat both this case and the hypothesized case is to separate the two aspects of these events and to consider, first, the ownership and sale of the property, and, second, the arrangement and retirement of the loan. Under *Crane*, the fair market value of the property on the date of acquisition the purchase price represents the taxpayer's basis in the property, and the fair market value on the date of disposition represents the proceeds on sale. The benefit received by the taxpayer in return for the property is the cancellation of a mortgage that is worth no more than the fair market value of the property, for that is all the mortgagee can expect to collect on the mortgage. His gain or loss on the disposition of the property equals the difference between the proceeds and the cost of acquisition. Thus, the taxation of the transaction *in property* reflects the economic fate of the *property*. If the property has declined in value, as was the case here, the taxpayer recognizes a loss on the disposition of the property. The new purchaser then takes as his basis the fair market value as of the date of the sale. See, e. g., *United States v. Davis*, 370 U.S. 65, 72 (1962) . . . .

In the separate borrowing transaction, the taxpayer acquires cash from the mortgagee. He need not recognize income at that time, of course, because he also incurs an obligation to repay the money. Later, though, when he is able to satisfy the debt by surrendering property that is worth less than the face amount of the debt, we have a classic situation of cancellation of indebtedness, requiring the taxpayer to recognize income in the amount of the difference between the proceeds of the loan and the amount for which he is able to satisfy his creditor. . . . § 61(a)(12). The taxation of the financing transaction then reflects the economic fate of the loan.

The reason that separation of the two aspects of the events in this case is important is, of course, that the Code treats different sorts of income differently. A gain on the sale of the property may qualify for capital gains treatment, §§ 1202, 1221 (1976 ed. and Supp. V), while the cancellation of indebtedness is ordinary income, but income that the taxpayer may be able to defer. §§ 108, 1017 . . . . Not only does Professor Barnett's theory permit us to accord appropriate treatment to each of the two types of income or loss present in these sorts of transactions, it also restores continuity to the system by making the taxpayerseller's proceeds on the disposition of property equal to the purchaser's basis in the property. Further, and most important, it allows us to tax the events in this case in the same way that we tax the economically identical hypothesized transaction.

Persuaded though I am by the logical coherence and internal consistency of this approach, I agree with the Court's decision not to adopt it judicially. We do not write on a slate marked only by Crane. The Commissioner's longstanding position, Rev. Rul. 76111, 19761 Cum. Bull. 214, is now reflected in the regulations. Treas. Reg. § 1.10012 . . . . In the light of the numerous cases in the lower courts including the amount of the unrepaid proceeds of the mortgage in the proceeds on sale or disposition . . . it is difficult to conclude that the Commissioner's interpretation of the statute exceeds the bounds of his discretion. As the Court's opinion demonstrates, his interpretation is defensible. One can reasonably read § 1001(b)'s reference to "the amount realized *from* the sale or other disposition of property" (emphasis added) to permit the Commissioner to collapse the two aspects of the transaction. As long as his view is a reasonable reading of § 1001(b), we should defer to the regulations promulgated by the agency charged with interpretation of the statute. . . . Accordingly, I concur.

Notes

Dissonance is the treatment of recourse and nonrecourse debt. The regulations under §1001 do what Justice O'Connor (concurring) wanted done with respect to recourse debt, but the regulations do not follow her lead with respect to nonrecourse debt. In other words, a disposition of property that is encumbered by a nonrecourse debt is treated as a simple sale or exchange, with the nonrecourse debt merely being part of amount realized. By contrast, if the foreclosure is of property that is subject to a *recourse* debt, the transaction is broken into two parts, namely:

1. An imaginary transaction in which the owner sells the property for its then value to an outsider for cash; immediately followed by

2. A transaction in which the recipient of the imaginary cash (now stripped of the property) pays that cash from "1" above to the lender. To the extent the lender accepts less than the amount of the debt, the debt so released is ordinary income under §§ 61(a)(12) and 108(a).

If it helps, one can think of step "1" as a "property" transaction and step "2" as a "bank" transaction. Because the second step results in cancellation of indebtedness *income* (under §61(a)(12)), the debtor may be able to take advantage of a special relief provision (§108) which allows taxpayers to exclude from gross income certain cancellation of indebtedness income. Such an exclusion is not available for *gains* from dealing in property (which arise under §1001). This means that being released from a nonrecourse debt can create a *gain* that cannot be exempted from gross income under §108, whereas if the debt is with recourse, the release from the debt may be tax-exempt. We will explore this possibilityin Chapter Four.The difference in the rules plays out in strange ways in the real world. For one thing, borrowers who have property subject to nonrecourse debts sometimes negotiate with lenders who plan to release them from the debt to make the debt recourse and *then* release the debt, so that they can exploit §108 in order to avoid reporting what would otherwise be a taxable gain under §1001. Justice O'Connor's preference for treating recourse and nonrecourse debt the same way makes sense in light of this distortion.

What if a donee pays the donor's gift taxes on a major gift? The answer is that the result can be a taxable gain to the donor. In *Diedrich v. Commissioner*[233] the Supreme Court considered the case of the donor who gave away property whose basis was lower than the gift tax imposed on the donor upon making the gift. The donee agreed to pay the tax as a condition to receiving the gift. The result, in the Court's view, was a taxable gain to the donor, on the theory that the donee's payment of the gift tax constituted an "amount realized" to the donor. Other possible outcomes were that there were simply two nontaxable gifts, (one from A to B of the gift tax payment and the other from B to A of the property). Another possible analysis was that the donee's payment constituted an indirect debt cancellation and was ordinary income to the donor. It seems that the majority was impressed with the fact that the tax issue arose in connection with a disposition of property, and they were therefore attracted to §1001 gain or loss theories (like a moth to a flame?).

Problem 3-11:

You have decided to buy the old Frimler Hotel in downtown Buffalo. It is worth $1 million dollars, but it is encumbered by an $800,000 mortgage. You plan to operate the hotel and to correctly claim depreciation deductions of $100,000 per year:

1) You buy the hotel for $200,000 cash plus the assumption of the debt:
   What is its adjusted basis to you?

2) Same as "(1)," but the debt is nonrecourse: What is its adjusted basis to you?

3) You claim depreciation deductions of $100,000 per year over the following 3 years, meaning that you claim a $100,000/year deduction for the erosion the property's value. You adjust the basis of the property under §1016 as a result of each such deduction.
   What is its adjusted basis? *From now on, use this figure as the Frimler's adjusted basis.*

4) Same as "(3)," but you pay down $200,000 of the mortgage debt (so it is now $600,000): What is its adjusted basis?
   Until otherwise directed, assume that "4" is the fact pattern and the Frimler is worth $1 million and the mortgage debt is $600,000. Assume that the next day a buyer appears ready to make the following offers.

233 457 U.S. 191 (1982).

5) Buyer will pay cash of $400,000 and will assume the recourse debt:
   If he does so, the amount realized will be?
   The adjusted basis is?
   Gain or loss would be?
   (See Reg. §1.1001-2(b), Example 1.)
   Why is $400,000 the right amount of cash?

6) This time, the debt is nonrecourse. Buyer will pay cash of $400,000 and will take the Frimler, "subject to" the nonrecourse debt:
   The amount realized is?
   The adjusted basis is?
   Gain or loss is?
   (See Reg. §1.1001-2(b), Example 2.)

7) Same as "(6)," but the Frimler is worth only $400,000, so buyer will pay no cash:
   The amount realized is?
   The adjusted basis is?
   Gain or loss is?

8) Same as "(7)," but you abandon the Frimler:
   The amount realized is?
   The adjusted basis is?
   Gain or loss is?

9) Same as "(8)," but the debt is recourse:
   The amount realized is?
   The adjusted basis is?
   Gain or loss is?
   Some years later you default and the statute of limitations runs against the lender.
   What result?

10) This time the Frimler is worth $400,000; the debt is nonrecourse (this time $800,000, as under problem 2, above) and you transfer the Frimler to the lender who accepts the property in full satisfaction of the $800,000 debt:
   The amount realized is?
   The adjusted basis is?
   Gain or loss is?

11) Same as "(10)," but assume the hints in *Crane* footnote 37 control the result:

The amount realized is?

The adjusted basis is?

Gain or loss is?

12) Same as "(10)," but the debt is recourse and you transfer the Frimler (value $400,000) to the lender, which releases you from the $800,000 debt. See Reg. §1.1001-2(b), Example (8):

The amount realized is?

The adjusted basis is?

Gain or loss is?

The amount of the debt is?

The fair market value of the property is?

§61(a)(12) income is?

CHAPTER 4 - EXCLUSIONS FROM GROSS INCOME

Chapters Two and Three covered the concept of "gross income," and emphasized the broad embrace of §61(a), with a view to identifying what goes into the Federal Income Tax base. This Chapter generally covers items that are gross income unless specifically excluded. Chapter 4 only covers the major exclusions. The end of Chapter 4 contains a list of relatively offbeat exclusions that are not usually covered in an introductory tax course.

A. IMPUTED INCOME

Imputed income means the dollar value of goods and services that are produced and consumed within the family unit, plus the dollar value of using property which the taxpayer or family member owns. Common examples of imputed income on a significant scale are crops consumed by farmers, the savings that tax professionals enjoy when they prepare their own tax returns, and the rental value of occupying one's own home. Likewise, if one mows one's own lawn one has avoided the cost of hiring a person to mow the lawn and has imputed income.

At an abstract level it might be appropriate to include this imputed income in the tax base because it represents a form of consumption or relief from expenditure that ought to be taxed, but such a tax invites unusually difficult questions of line-drawing. For example, is it true that sitting in one's chaise lounge and *not* mowing one's lawn is also a form of imputed income (leisure), at least in a middle-class neighborhood?

There is an enormous volume of what might otherwise be taxable gross income that is never reached because it hides under the umbrella term "imputed income." For example, the value of uncompensated household services is said to constitute 26% of the Gross National Product.[234] It is likely that if any Congress were to make a serious attempt to tax this form of income there would be a rapid change in the membership of the legislature. Nevertheless, as a result of its scale, the question of taxing imputed income is unlikely to leave quietly, at least in law school classrooms.

234 See B. Bittker & L. Lokken, FEDERAL TAXATION OF INCOME, ESTATES & GIFTS ¶ 5.3.2. (2018). (The authors report that the estimates run as high as 48 percent.)

Only one Supreme Court case has addressed the issue, declaring *in dictum* that an insurance company could not be taxed on the value of occupying its own quarters.[235] There are a number of reasons to think that the Treasury Department's willingness to leave its hands off imputed income will not change. For one thing, the record-keeping requirements for computing such income are extremely complicated. For another, it is not at all clear that Congress, in enacting the Federal Income Tax, ever intended to reach so far into family and personal affairs.

Another aspect of the issue is that, if one did tax people on their imputed income from services, then the question would arise as to their claim to "imputed costs" as tax deductions. For example, if a person spends lots of money (non-deductible, as we will see later) to get a professional education to qualify as a doctor or a lawyer, should he or she be entitled to gradually deduct that education from the savings of fees when the doctor fixes his own, or his child's, broken leg or when the lawyer handles her own litigation or estate planning and is taxed on the imputed income arising from the savings?

Not every country is as relaxed about the issue as the United States. For example, England taxed the value of occupying one's own home until 1963.[236] France has an interesting alternative tax system which allows the government to impose income taxes based on estimated income based on "exterior signs of wealth" (racehorses, yachts, servants, and so forth) if that tax yields significantly more than the income tax.[237] One of the items subject to tax is the value of occupying one's residence (chateau?).

Now consider the following fact pattern, which you ought to find at least somewhat troubling:

> **To illustrate:** William Wealthy owns his own home, which cost him $500,000. The rental value of Wealthy's home is $50,000 per year. Next door to him is Andy Achiever who has no capital but plenty of energy. He pays $50,000 in rent for an identical house. Andy Achiever is not entitled to a tax deduction for renting the house, because that expense is considered a personal consumption item. Therefore, Achiever, who is in the 40% bracket, must earn about $83,400 in order to generate the after-tax $50,000 needed to pay his rent. By contrast, Wealthy need do nothing. For good measure, include in the picture Mrs. Sandy Saver (also a renter) who has $500,000 in the bank and is able to earn 10% interest on her money. She will earn $50,000 per year also, but that $50,000 will be whittled down by taxes, let us say to $35,000. Is there something wrong with this picture, as a matter of tax policy or of tax planning? If so, what should be done about it?

---

235 Helvering v. Independent Life Ins. Co., 292 U.S. 371 (S. Ct. 1934).

236 See Hellmuth, Homeowner Preferences, in COMPREHENSIVE INCOME TAXATION 170 (J. Pechman ed. 1977). Wisconsin did the same for several years. See Haig, The Concept of Income -- Economic and Legal Aspects, in THE FEDERAL INCOME TAX 14-15 (R. Haig, ed., 1921). Other countries that have taxed imputed income from owner-occupied housing include Germany and Australia. H.C. Simons, PERSONAL INCOME TAXATION, 112-119 (1938).

237 See Campbell, Philippart, Delsouiller & Bonnet, Business Operations in France, 961 Tax. Mgt. Portfolio (1992) at A82 et seq.

Expenses that one incurs in generating nontaxable income are nondeductible under §§ 262 and 265. That should not be a surprise.

> **To illustrate:** You are a farmer. You harvest 10% of your crop for your personal consumption, solely to save money. Ten percent of your crop expenses are nondeductible because they are costs incurred to generate nontaxable imputed income.[238]

B. GIFTS

Read §102 and Reg. §1.102-1(a)-(c)

1. Background

It has long been the law that gifts are not taxable. Does that mean that compensatory payments can be labeled "gift," thereby freeing the transferee from taxes? Absolutely not. What you are about to read includes a perfect example of the pervasive doctrine that in Federal Income Tax matters, substance must prevail over form.

Letter to the King[239]

Respected Sir:

I hope that you and your family are enjoying good health.

I am writing over a concern that I have regarding the new income tax. As you know, Paradisians are very generous people and are constantly bestowing gifts on one another. My neighbor said he thought that the person receiving the gift would have to pay income tax. He also thought that, when relatives receive property as a bequest or inheritance from a deceased Paradisian, they, too, would have to pay an income tax. If this is true, I think it would make a great many people unhappy and would discourage such generosity in the future. Does your income tax apply to gifts, bequests, and the like?

I eagerly await your reply with respect.

Bill Barney

MEMORANDUM FROM THE ROYAL DRAFTER
TO: Helvering I, King of Paradise

238 In case of doubt, see Nowland v. Commissioner, 244 F.2d 450 (4th Cir. 1957)

239 From TAXES IN PARADISE by Professor Richard L. Haight.

RE: Scope of Gross Income

While the concept of gross income is an all-inclusive one—broad enough to include gifts, bequests, devises, and inheritances within its scope—there may be good reason why, as a matter of policy, we might not want to tax certain items. Therefore, we could put into the Paradise Tax Code specific provisions which exclude those items from gross income. I suspect you believe that receipts in the nature of gifts should not fall within the purview of the gross income concept. Toward this end, I will draft a Code section which says that gross income does not include gifts, bequests, devises, and inheritances. I am sure Mr. Barney and his neighbor will be grateful.

I imagine that, as the drafting process progresses, we may find other items which, from the standpoint of public policy, we will want to exclude from gross income. Therefore, even though the receipt of such an item by a citizen will enhance the recipient's economic status, it will not result in the payment of income tax.

Lady W.

MEMORANDUM FROM THE KING
TO: Lady Wordsmith, Royal Drafter
RE: Scope of Gross Income (Memo 2)

I think we have created a monster. Please see Mr. Barney's letter, enclosed.

Helvering

Letter to the King

Respected Sir:

Thank you for your prompt response to my letter inquiring about the taxability of gifts. My wife and I were most pleased to see that gifts will not be subject to the income tax. As a consequence to your decision, I have decided that I will no longer receive any salary from my employer. Instead, I will arrange for him to make weekly gifts to me of the amount that used to be my weekly salary. In that way, I will not have to pay any income tax at all. This new income tax is not going to turn out to be so bad after all.

My appreciation to you with respect.

Bill Barney

MEMORANDUM FROM THE ROYAL DRAFTER
TO: Helvering I, King of Paradise
RE: Scope of Gross Income (Memo 2)

I suspect that this will not be the first time that one of our citizens attempts to avoid the application of the income tax by casting a transaction in a more favorable light. It would seem to me that, in determining whether the income tax is applicable, the true nature of the transaction should control—not the manner in which the taxpayer structures the transaction or the labels which the taxpayer applies to it. Taxation should be based on the realities of the situation; the substance of the transaction, not its form, should determine the tax result.

If we apply this principle, then an attempt by someone like Mr. Barney to label his salary as a gift will fail. The reality of the situation is that Mr. Barney is performing services for his employer and is receiving money from his employer as compensation for those services. That is what is clearly intended by the parties to the transaction; the payment to Mr. Barney is not a disinterested act of generosity on the part of the employer. One can label the weekly payment to Mr. Barney a "gift" or anything else, but casting the transaction in that light does not alter the substance of what is actually occurring: the payment of money for services rendered. The payment is, therefore, gross income.

Lady W

2. Federal Income Tax Definition of a "Gift"

The correspondence between King Helvering and Lady Wordsmith points out the problem that a tax law has to rely on substance; only true gifts can be excluded from gross income. But what is a true gift? Whose motives count in that determination? What follows is the bedrock case in the area.

COMMISSIONER v. DUBERSTEIN

363 U.S. 278 (1960)

MR. JUSTICE BRENNAN delivered the opinion of the Court.

Th[is case concerns] . . . the provision of the Internal Revenue Code which excludes from the gross income of an income taxpayer "the value of property acquired by gift."[240] [It] pose[s] the frequently recurrent question whether a specific transfer to a taxpayer in fact amounted to a "gift" to him within the meaning of the statute. The importance to decision of the facts of the cases requires that we state them in some detail.

No. 376, *Commissioner v. Duberstein*. The taxpayer, Duberstein,[241] was president of the Duberstein Iron & Metal Company, a corporation with headquarters in Dayton, Ohio. For some years the taxpayer's company had done business with Mohawk Metal Corporation, whose

240 The operative provision in the cases at bar is §22 (b)(3) of the 1939 Internal Revenue Code. The corresponding provision of the present Code is §102 (a). [Footnote No. 1 in original.]

241 In both cases the husband will be referred to as the taxpayer, although his wife joined with him in joint tax returns. [Footnote No. 2 in original.]

headquarters were in New York City. The president of Mohawk was one Berman. The taxpayer and Berman had generally used the telephone to transact their companies' business with each other, which consisted of buying and selling metals. The taxpayer testified, without elaboration, that he knew Berman "personally" and had known him for about seven years. From time to time in their telephone conversations, Berman would ask Duberstein whether the latter knew of potential customers for some of Mohawk's products in which Duberstein's company itself was not interested. Duberstein provided the names of potential customers for these items.

One day in 1951 Berman telephoned Duberstein and said that the information Duberstein had given him had proved so helpful that he wanted to give the latter a present. Duberstein stated that Berman owed him nothing. Berman said that he had a Cadillac as a gift for Duberstein, and that the latter should send to New York for it; Berman insisted that Duberstein accept the car, and the latter finally did so, protesting however that he had not intended to be compensated for the information. At the time Duberstein already had a Cadillac and an Oldsmobile, and felt that he did not need another car. Duberstein testified that he did not think Berman would have sent him the Cadillac if he had not furnished him with information about the customers. It appeared that Mohawk later deducted the value of the Cadillac as a business expense on its corporate income tax return.

Duberstein did not include the value of the Cadillac in gross income for 1951, deeming it a gift. The Commissioner asserted a deficiency for the car's value against him, and in proceedings to review the deficiency the Tax Court affirmed the Commissioner's determination. It said that "The record is significantly barren of evidence revealing any intention on the part of the payor to make a gift. . . . The only justifiable inference is that the automobile was intended by the payer to be remuneration for services rendered to it by Duberstein." The Court of Appeals for the Sixth Circuit reversed. 265 F.2d 28.

. . .

The Commissioner asserted a deficiency against the taxpayer after the latter had failed to include the payments in question in gross income. After payment of the deficiency and administrative rejection of a refund claim, the taxpayer sued the United States for a refund in the District Court for the Eastern District of New York. . . .

The exclusion of property acquired by gift from gross income under the federal income tax laws was made in the first income tax statute[242] passed under the authority of the Sixteenth Amendment, and has been a feature of the income tax statutes ever since. The meaning of the term "gift" as applied to particular transfers has always been a matter of contention.[243] Specific and illuminating legislative history on the point does not appear to exist. Analogies and

242 §II.B., c. 16, 38 Stat. 167. [Footnote No. 4 in original.]

243 The first case of the Board of Tax Appeals officially reported in fact deals with the problem. Parrott v. Commissioner, 1 B. T. A. 1. [Footnote No. 5 in original.]

inferences drawn from other revenue provisions, such as the estate and gift taxes, are dubious. See *Lockard v. Commissioner*, 166 F.2d 409. The meaning of the statutory term has been shaped largely by the decisional law. With this, we turn to the contentions made by the Government in these cases.

First. The Government suggests that we promulgate a new "test" in this area to serve as a standard to be applied by the lower courts and by the Tax Court in dealing with the numerous cases that arise.[244] We reject this invitation. We are of the opinion that the governing principles are necessarily general and have already been spelled out in the opinions of this Court, and that the problem is one which, under the present statutory framework, does not lend itself to any more definitive statement that would produce a talisman for the solution of concrete cases. The cases at bar are fair examples of the settings in which the problem usually arises. They present situations in which payments have been made in a context with business overtones an employer making a payment to a retiring employee; a businessman giving something of value to another businessman who has been of advantage to him in his business. In this context, we review the law as established by the prior cases here.

The course of decision here makes it plain that the statute does not use the term "gift" in the commonlaw sense, but in a more colloquial sense. This Court has indicated that a voluntary executed transfer of his property by one to another, without any consideration or compensation therefor, though a commonlaw gift, is not necessarily a "gift" within the meaning of the statute. For the Court has shown that the mere absence of a legal or moral obligation to make such a payment does not establish that it is a gift. *Old Colony Trust Co. v. Commissioner*, 279 U.S. 716, 730 and, importantly, if the payment proceeds primarily from "the constraining force of any moral or legal duty," or from "the incentive of anticipated benefit" of an economic nature, *Bogardus v. Commissioner*, 302 U.S. 34, 41, it is not a gift. And, conversely, "where the payment is in return for services rendered, it is irrelevant that the donor derives no economic benefit from it." *Robertson v. United States*, 343 U.S. 711, 714.[245] A gift in the statutory sense, on the other hand, proceeds from a "detached and disinterested generosity," *Commissioner v. LoBue*, 351 U.S. 243, 246; "out of affection, respect, admiration, charity or like impulses." *Robertson v. United States, supra*, at 714 and in this regard, the most critical consideration, as the Court was agreed in the leading case here, is the transferor's "intention." *Bogardus v. Commissioner*, 302 U.S. 34, 43. "What controls is the intention with which payment, however voluntary, has been made." *Id.*, at 45 (dissenting opinion).

The Government says that this "intention" of the transferor cannot mean what the cases on the commonlaw concept of gift call "donative intent." With that we are in agreement, for our

244 The Government's proposed test is stated: "Gifts should be defined as transfers of property made for personal as distinguished from business reasons." [Footnote No. 6 in original.]

245 The cases including "tips" in gross income are classic examples of this. See, e. g., Roberts v. Commissioner, 176 F.2d 221. [Footnote No. 7 in original.]

decisions fully support this. Moreover, the *Bogardus* case itself makes it plain that the donor's characterization of his action is not determinative that there must be an objective inquiry as to whether what is called a gift amounts to it in reality. 302 U.S., at 40. It scarcely needs adding that the parties' expectations or hopes as to the tax treatment of their conduct in themselves have nothing to do with the matter.

It is suggested that the *Bogardus* criterion would be more apt if rephrased in terms of "motive" rather than "intention." We must confess to some skepticism as to whether such a verbal mutation would be of any practical consequence. We take it that the proper criterion, established by decision here, is one that inquires what the basic reason for his conduct was in fact the dominant reason that explains his action in making the transfer. Further than that we do not think it profitable to go.

Second. The Government's proposed "test," while apparently simple and precise in its formulation, depends frankly on a set of "principles" or "presumptions" derived from the decided cases, and concededly subject to various exceptions; and it involves various corollaries, which add to its detail. Were we to promulgate this test as a matter of law, and accept with it its various presuppositions and stated consequences, we would be passing far beyond the requirements of the cases before us, and would be painting on a large canvas with indeed a broad brush. The Government derives its test from such propositions as the following: That payments by an employer to an employee, even though voluntary, ought, by and large, to be taxable; that the concept of a gift is inconsistent with a payment's being a deductible business expense; that a gift involves "personal" elements; that a business corporation cannot properly make a gift of its assets. The Government admits that there are exceptions and qualifications to these propositions. We think, to the extent they are correct, that those propositions are not principles of law but rather maxims of experience that the tribunals which have tried the facts of cases in this area have enunciated in explaining their factual determinations. Some of them simply represent truisms: it doubtless is, statistically speaking, the exceptional payment by an employer to an employee that amounts to a gift. Others are overstatements of possible evidentiary inferences relevant to a factual determination on the totality of circumstances in the case: it is doubtless relevant to the overall inference that the transferor treats a payment as a business deduction, or that the transferor is a corporate entity. But these inferences cannot be stated in absolute terms. Neither factor is a shibboleth. The taxing statute does not make nondeductibility by the transferor a condition on the "gift" exclusion; nor does it draw any distinction, in terms, between transfers by corporations and individuals, as to the availability of the "gift" exclusion to the transferee. The conclusion whether a transfer amounts to a "gift" is one that must be reached on consideration of all the factors.

Specifically, the trier of fact must be careful not to allow trial of the issue whether the receipt of a specific payment is a gift to turn into a trial of the tax liability, or of the propriety, as a matter of fiduciary or corporate law, attaching to the conduct of someone else. The major corollary to the Government's suggested "test" is that, as an ordinary matter, a payment by a corporation cannot be a gift, and, more specifically, there can be no such thing as a "gift" made by a corporation which would allow it to take a deduction for an ordinary and necessary business expense. As we have said, we find no basis for such a conclusion in the statute; and if it were applied as a determinative rule of "law," it would force the tribunals trying tax cases involving the donee's liability into elaborate inquiries into the local law of corporations or into the peripheral deductibility of payments as business expenses. The former issue might make the tax tribunals the most frequent investigators of an important and difficult issue of the laws of the several States, and the latter inquiry would summon one difficult and delicate problem of federal tax law as an aid to the solution of another. Or perhaps there would be required a trial of the vexed issue whether there was a "constructive" distribution of corporate property, for income tax purposes, to the corporate agents who had sponsored the transfer. These considerations, also, reinforce us in our conclusion that while the principles urged by the Government may, in nonabsolute form as crystallizations of experience, prove persuasive to the trier of facts in a particular case, neither they, nor any more detailed statement than has been made, can be laid down as a matter of law.

Third. Decision of the issue presented in these cases must be based ultimately on the application of the factfinding tribunal's experience with the mainsprings of human conduct to the totality of the facts of each case. The nontechnical nature of the statutory standard, the close relationship of it to the data of practical human experience, and the multiplicity of relevant factual elements, with their various combinations, creating the necessity of ascribing the proper force to each, confirm us in our conclusion that primary weight in this area must be given to the conclusions of the trier of fact. . . .

This conclusion may not satisfy an academic desire for tidiness, symmetry and precision in this area, any more than a system based on the determinations of various factfinders ordinarily does. But we see it as implicit in the present statutory treatment of the exclusion for gifts, and in the variety of forums in which federal income tax cases can be tried. If there is fear of undue uncertainty or overmuch litigation, Congress may make more precise its treatment of the matter by singling out certain factors and making them determinative of the matter, as it has done in one field of the "gift" exclusion's former application, that of prizes and awards.[246] Doubtless diversity of result will tend to be lessened somewhat since federal income tax decisions, even those in tribunals of first instance turning on issues of fact, tend to be reported, and since there may be a natural tendency of professional triers of fact to follow one another's determinations,

246 Section 74, which is a provision new with the 1954 Code. Previously, there had been holdings that such receipts as the "Pot O' Gold" radio giveaway, Washburn v. Commissioner, 5 T. C. 1333, and the Ross Essay Prize, McDermott v. Commissioner, 80 U. S. App. D. C. 176, 150 F.2d 585, were "gifts." Congress intended to obviate such rulings. S. Rep. No. 1622, 83d Cong., 2d Sess., p. 178. We imply no approval of those holdings under the general standard of the "gift" exclusion. Cf. Robertson v. United States, supra. [Footnote No. 12 in original.]

even as to factual matters. But the question here remains basically one of fact, for determination on a casebycase basis.

. . .

Fourth. A majority of the Court is in accord with the principles just outlined and, applying them to the *Duberstein* case, we are in agreement, on the evidence we have set forth, that it cannot be said that the conclusion of the Tax Court was "clearly erroneous." It seems to us plain that as trier of the facts it was warranted in concluding that despite the characterization of the transfer of the Cadillac by the parties and the absence of any obligation, even of a moral nature, to make it, it was at bottom a recompense for Duberstein's past services, or an inducement for him to be of further service in the future. . . .

. . .

It is so ordered.

[The concurring and dissenting opinions are omitted. Eds.]

Notes

Should gifts of appreciated property trigger taxable gain? For example, suppose Father buys ten shares of stock in one year for $1,000. In the next year when they have risen in value to $1,500, he gives them to his son. How about taxing Father in that year on income by reason of that gift? The answer is that the Code does not tax Father, but the Constitution does not preclude the son from being taxed, and the Constitution almost surely does not preclude taxing Father on the built-in gain on the transfer, although there is no authority precisely on point. Be all that as it may, the practical black letter rule is that there is no income tax at the time of the gift, but that someone will pay a tax when the gift is sold, which is accomplished by giving the donee the donor's basis.

It does not have to be this way. Section 84 offers the alternative model of constructive realization of taxable gain by the donor upon giving appreciated property to a political organization. Section 84 cuts a path, conceptually, to taxing the gain inherent in property given from one person to another, but of course the tax implies that there should be a change in the basis of property to its value at the time of the transfer.

Tax deductions for gifts. Duberstein opens the door to letting a donor claim tax deductions for gifts of valuable property that the donee can exclude under §102. Congress all but shut that door when it enacted §274(b), which limits the deduction for most business-related gifts to $25. The $25 limit has been in the Code for many years, and has not been increased for inflation. Is it an adequate remedy for the fiscal problem that a transaction can be a nondeductible gift to the donee and deductible by the donor? You should briefly read §274(b).

Now that only $25 of business-related gifts can be deducted, revenue losses from these asymmetrical transactions are not a serious threat. However, if the donor is a tax-exempt organization which cannot benefit from tax deductions, such as a church, the loss of the deduction neutralizes the financial damage to the Treasury. That was the situation in the *Stanton* case[247] that was decided as a companion case to *Duberstein.* There, the Supreme Court was unable to determine whether a retiring employee of a real estate subsidiary of a church who received a $20,000 "gratuity" from the church on his departure was the fortunate recipient of a nontaxable gift. As it happened, the taxpayer won on remand.[248]

Gifts to employees. Apparently dissatisfied by merely cutting back tax deductions under §274(b), Congress struck again by cutting back the tax-exemption for gifts by enacting §102(c), which you should read. Note how §102(c) does not overlap with §274(b) because §274(b) only applies if the transfer is a tax-free gift for Federal Income Tax purposes. What impact does §102(c) have on gifts to employees who are related to the taxpayer? The general answer is that they cannot be excluded, but there is some daylight here, because Prop. Reg. §1.102-1(f)(2) provides:

> (2) EMPLOYER/EMPLOYEE TRANSFERS. For purposes of section 102(c), extraordinary transfers to the natural objects of an employer's bounty will not be considered transfers to or for the benefit of, an employee if the employee can show that the transfer was not made in recognition of the employee's employment. Accordingly, section 102(c) shall not apply to amounts transferred between related parties (e.g., father and son) if the purpose of the transfer can be substantially attributed to the familial relationship of the parties and not to the circumstances of their employment.[249]

An alternative way to make a nontaxable transfer to an employee is to make an "employee achievement award." This is discussed later in the chapter under the heading "Prizes and Awards." The benefit of this pathway is that it expands the dollar amount of nontaxable transfers that can be made to employees and the dollar amounts of such transfers that an employer can deduct.

The differing definitions of a gift. By now you have probably noticed that a gift for common law purposes is not the same thing as a gift for Federal Income Tax purposes, or as it turns out, a gift for federal estate and gift tax purposes (where it basically means any transfer to the extent not paid for in full). This led one judge to suggest that lawyers need to keep in mind at least

247 Stanton v. United States, 268 F.2d 727 (2d Cir. 1961), vacated and remanded, 363 U.S. 278 (1960).

248 Stanton v. United States, 186 F. Supp. 393 (EDNY 1960), aff'd's per curiam, 287 F.2d 876, 877 (2d Cir. 1961).

249 The receipt could be excluded if the motivation for the transfer is extraneous to the employment relationship. HR Rep No 426, 99th Cong., 2(d) Sess. 106 n 5 (1986). See also Prop. Reg. §1.102-1(f)(2).

three different kinds of gifts, which he referred to as "gifts" (income tax), "gafts" (gift tax) and "gefts" (estate tax).[250] That does not even mention common law gifts.

3. Policy Option: Taxation of Gifts and Bequests as Income

Powerful arguments can be made that gifts and bequests should be included in income. These arguments include some that are concerned with correcting the base of the income tax. Gifts and bequests are an important form of accretion to a person's ability to pay tax, as well as to consume or to invest. Omitting such items from the tax base makes the income tax less fair, when measured against an accretion version of income or an ability to pay standard. Also, the redistributive effect of the income tax might be greater if gifts and bequests were included in income. Some authors have supported inclusion of gifts and bequests in income in general or in connection with eliminating transfer taxes.[251] The following excerpt crystallizes the discussion.[252]

> An elegantly simple and economically attractive alternative to the present mode of taxing bequests and gifts would be to stop applying special transfer taxes to either transferors or transferees and merely tax the latter as having received income. Technically, at the federal level, this proposal consists of repealing Internal Revenue Code § 102, which excludes property acquired by gift, bequest, devise, or inheritance from the income tax law's definition of income and also repealing the Federal Estate and Gift Tax laws.
>
> One goal of such a change would be simplification of the law. In its basic form, the proposal would add nothing to existing law on the books; in fact, it would repeal many sections of the Internal Revenue Code. Some amendment in the income tax law probably would be necessary, however, to deal with particular problems to which reference will be made subsequently. (Moreover, some theorists would even insist on a new deduction for the donor if the donee is to be taxed on a gift as income; others would vehemently disagree.)

The simplicity gains of this proposal would be substantial, because the federal transfer taxes are immensely complex and entail a great deal of compliance and administration costs, and extensive legal efforts to avoid paying the tax. In addition, the taxes are in some respects unfair. They can often be avoided, but only with the use of techniques that require tax planning advice,

250 Opinion of Judge Jerome Frank in Commissioner v. Estate of Beck, 129 F.2d 243 (2d Cir. 1942).

251 See Dodge, *Beyond Estate and Gift Tax Reform: Including Gifts and Bequests in Income*, 91 Harv.L.Rev. 1177, 1179, Note 11 (1978); McNulty, J.K., *A Transfer Tax Alternative: Inclusion Under The Income Tax*, 26 Tax Notes 24 (1976).

252 It is taken from McNulty, "Fundamental Alternatives to Present Transfer Tax Systems," which is Ch. 6 of *Death, Taxes and Family Property*, pp. 95-99 (Halbach, ed.), West Publishing Co. (1977).

and in some instances, enough wealth to let the taxpayer implement the tax planning technique that relieves the burden.

The present law follows neither of these approaches and instead excludes the gift from the base of the *donee*, but leaves it in the income tax base of the *donor*, by not allowing any deduction for the gift. If the family unit were taken as the taxable unit, then gifts within a family would be treated differently. Perhaps one should ignore gifts within the family, but use when a person left the family group as an occasion to tax the recipient and possibly to allow a deduction to the donor. This was the approach taken by Canada's Carter Commission.[253]

Consider also whether the inclusion of gifts and bequests in gross income would require special income-averaging rules, because the receipt of an unusually large, once-in-a-lifetime bequest or gift is something that the present annual system, with its progressive rates in the lower brackets, is not well suited to tax. Consider also whether some form of minimal exemption should be retained, even if §102 were repealed in general, so that small birthday, Christmas and other gifts did not have to be recorded and reported for income tax purposes.

The recipient of property cannot always be sure whether a receipt is a gift or taxable income. If the facts are bad enough, failure to report the income may cross the line into criminal behavior. There is certainly no shortage of tax crimes; the Code bristles with criminal tax liabilities, but the primary crime is tax evasion, the elements of which are: a substantial tax due and owing; an affirmative attempt to evade or defeat the tax; and, willfulness on the taxpayer's part.[254] Other principal crimes include failure to account for and pay over a tax,[255] and failure to file (assuming there was a duty to file[256]) and the filing of a false return.[257] These also require "willfulness" on the taxpayer's part. That term generally means a voluntary, intentional violation of a known legal duty. Sometimes the tax law is so complicated that it is impossible to say the taxpayer willfully avoided taxes. For example, where a donor (seller) of especially rare blood did not report the proceeds of the blood sales, the court concluded that it was unclear whether the sales generated taxable income, and sprung the taxpayer from criminal liability.[258]

Once one has committed a tax crime, there is no going back by filing an amended return confessing to the wrongdoing. What is done is done.[259]

253 See 3 Royal Commission on Taxation Report, 465-519 (1966) (Canada).

254 §7201. This one draws five years and $100,000 for individuals.

255 §7202, also five years and $10,000.

256 §7203, punishable by one year plus $25,000.

257 Section 7206(1). There are numerous other tax crimes.

258 The law has since concluded that such sales are taxable. United States v. Garber, 607 F.2d 92 (5th Cir. 1979).

259 Badaracco v. Commissioner, 464 U.S. 386 (1984) (in addition to not purifying a fraudulent return, filing an honest amended return does not start the three year statute running).

If you like salacious fact patterns, the next case was made for you. It explores the difficult question of how to tax income earned for companionship and what the government must show to make a criminal tax evasion case stick.

UNITED STATES v. LYNNETTE HARRIS and LEIGH ANN CONLEY

942 F.2d 1125 (7th Cir. 1991)

ESCHBACH, Senior Circuit Judge:

David Kritzik, now deceased, was a wealthy widower partial to the company of young women. Two of these women were Leigh Ann Conley and Lynnette Harris, twin sisters. Directly or indirectly, Kritzik gave Conley and Harris each more than half a million dollars over the course of several years. For our purposes, either Kritzik had to pay gift tax on this money or Harris and Conley had to pay income tax. The United States alleges that, beyond reasonable doubt, the obligation was Harris and Conley's. In separate criminal trials, Harris and Conley were convicted of willfully evading their income tax obligations regarding the money,[260] and they now appeal.

Under *Commissioner v. Duberstein*, 363 U.S. 278 . . . (1960), the donor's intent is the "critical consideration" in distinguishing between gifts and income. We reverse Conley's conviction and remand with instructions to dismiss the indictment against her because the government failed to present sufficient evidence of Kritzik's intent regarding the money he gave her. We also reverse Harris' conviction. The district court excluded as hearsay letters in which Kritzik wrote that he loved Harris and enjoyed giving things to her. These letters were central to Harris' defense that she believed in good faith that the money she received was a nontaxable gift, and they were not hearsay for this purpose.

We do not remand Harris' case for retrial, however, because Harris had no fair warning that her conduct might subject her to criminal tax liability. Neither the tax Code, the Treasury Regulations, or Supreme Court or appellate cases provide a clear answer to whether Harris owed any taxes or not. The closest authority lies in a series of Tax Court decisionsbut these cases favor Harris' position that the money she received was not income to her. Under this state of the law, Harris could not have formed a "willful" intent to violate the statutes at issue. For this reason, we remand with instructions that the indictment against Harris be dismissed. The same conclusion applies to Conley, and provides an alternative basis for reversing her conviction and remanding with instructions to dismiss the indictment.

260 Harris was sentenced to ten months in prison, to be followed by two months in a halfway house and two years of supervised release. She was also fined $12,500.00 and ordered to pay a $150.00 special assessment. Conley was sentenced to five months in prison, followed by five months in a halfway house and one year supervised release. She was also fined $10,000.00 and ordered to pay a $ 100.00 assessment. [Footnote No. 1 in original.]

Insufficiency of the Evidence as to Conley

Conley was convicted on each of four counts for violating 7203, which provides,

> Any person . . . required . . . to make a [tax] return . . . who willfully fails to . . . make such return . . . shall, in addition to other penalties provided by law, be guilty of a misdemeanor. . . .

Conley was "required . . . to make a return" only if the money that she received from Kritzik was income to her rather than a gift. Assuming that the money was income, she acted "willfully," and so is subject to criminal prosecution, only if she knew of her duty to pay taxes and "voluntarily and intentionally violated that duty." *Cheek v. United States*, 498 U.S. 192(1991). The government met its burden of proof if the jury could have found these elements beyond a reasonable doubt, viewing the evidence in the light most favorable to the government. . . .

The government's evidence was insufficient to show either that the money Conley received was income or that she acted in knowing disregard of her obligations. "Gross income" for tax purposes does not include gifts, which are taxable to the donor rather than the recipient. . . . In *Commissioner v. Duberstein*, 363 U.S. 278, 285 (1960), the Supreme Court stated that in distinguishing between income and gifts the "critical consideration . . . is the transferor's intention." A transfer of property is a gift if the transferor acted out of a "detached and disinterested generosity, . . . out of affection, respect, admiration, charity, or like impulses." *Id.* By contrast, a transfer of property is income if it is the result of "the constraining force of any moral or legal duty, constitutes a reward for services rendered, or proceeds from the incentive of anticipated benefit of an economic nature."

Regarding the "critical consideration" of the donor's intent, the only direct evidence that the government presented was Kritzik's gift tax returns. On those returns, Kritzik identified gifts to Conley of $ 24,000, $ 30,000, and $ 36,000 for the years 19846, respectively, substantially less than the total amount of money that Kritzik transferred to Conley. This leaves the question whether Kritzik's other payments were taxable income to Conley or whether Kritzik just underreported his gifts. The gift tax returns raise the question, they do not resolve it.

This failure to show Kritzik's intent is fatal to the government's case. Without establishing Kritzik's intent, the government cannot establish that Conley had any obligation to pay income taxes. Further, Conley could not have "willfully" failed to pay her taxes unless she knew of Kritzik's intent. Even if Kritzik's gift tax returns proved anything, the government presented no evidence that Conley knew the amounts that Kritzik had listed on those returns. Absent proof of Kritzik's intent, and Conley's knowledge of that intent, the government has no case.

The government's remaining evidence consisted of a bank card that Conley signed listing Kritzik in a space marked "employer" and testimony regarding the form of the payments that Conley received. The bank card is no evidence of Kritzik's intent and even as to Conley is open to conflicting interpretationsshe contends that she listed Kritzik as a reference and no more. As to the form of the payments, the government showed that Conley would pick up a regular check at Kritzik's office every week to ten days, either from Kritzik personally or, when he was not in, from his secretary. According to the government, this form of payment is that of an employee picking up regular wages, but it could just as easily be that of a dependent picking up regular support checks.

We will "not permit a verdict based solely upon the piling of inference upon inference." *United States v. Balzano*, 916 F.2d 1273, 1284 (7th Cir. 1990). In this regard, we emphasize the indirect, inconclusive nature of the evidence in establishing Kritzik's intent. We further emphasize that the gift tax returns and the bank card speak for themselvesthe jury heard no testimony that would enable them to make a credibility determination based on information that is unavailable to the Court. Similarly, the fact that Conley received checks at fairly regular intervals was not in dispute, and the presentation of that evidence through the testimony of Kritzik's former secretary could not have provided the jury with additional insight. *Cf. United States v. DeCorte*, 851 F.2d 948 (7th Cir. 1988) (suggesting that a challenge to the sufficiency of the evidence rests on "firmer legal ground" when no credibility determinations are at issue).

This Court's decision in *United States v. Delay*, 440 F.2d 566 (7th Cir. 1971) provides a close analogy. In *Delay*, the government sought to prove that the defendant had knowingly participated in the sale of stolen cars. The main evidence was the defendant's endorsement on the checks that were payment for the sales at issue. With certain vague testimony, this endorsement would have supported the inference that the defendant knowingly participated in the sales. But this evidence was also consistent with the contrary inference. *Id.*, p. 568. This Court reversed because "where the evidence as to an element of a crime is equally consistent with a theory of innocence as a theory of guilt, that evidence necessarily fails to establish guilt beyond a reasonable doubt." *Id.*

Similarly, in the present case, the bare facts of Kritzik's gift tax return, the bank card, and the form of the payments are as consistent with an inference of innocence as one of guilt. The evidence does not support a finding of guilt beyond a reasonable doubt, and we reverse Conley's conviction and remand with instructions to dismiss the indictment against her.

The Admissibility of Kritzik's Letters

[Harris was convicted of two counts of willfully failing to file federal income tax returns under 26 U.S.C. §7203 (the same offense for which Conley was convicted) and two counts of willful tax evasion under 26 U.S.C. §7201. The trial court refused to allow in as evidence letters from Kritzik indicating that he loved Harris. The appellate court found that in doing so the lower court violated her right to a fair trial and reversed the conviction.]

The Tax Treatment of Payments to Mistresses

Our conclusion that Harris should have been allowed to present the letters at issue as evidence would ordinarily lead us to remand her case for retrial. We further conclude, however, that current law on the tax treatment of payments to mistresses provided Harris no fair warning that her conduct was criminal. Indeed, current authorities favor Harris' position that the money she received from Kritzik was a gift. We emphasize that we do not necessarily agree with these authorities, and that the government is free to urge departure from them in a noncriminal context. But new points of tax law may not be the basis of criminal convictions. For this reason, we remand with instructions that the indictment against Harris be dismissed. Although we discuss only Harris' case in this section, the same reasoning applies to Conley and provides an alternative basis for dismissal of the indictment against her.

Again, the definitive statement of the distinction between gifts and income is in the Supreme Court's *Duberstein* decision, which applies and interprets the definition of income contained in 26 U.S.C. §§ 61. But as the Supreme Court described, the *Duberstein* principles are "necessarily general." It stated, "'One struggles in vain for any verbal formula that will supply a ready touchstone. The standard set up . . . is not a rule of law; it is rather a way of life. Life in all its fullness must supply the answer to the riddle.'" *Id.* . . .

Duberstein was a civil case, and its approach is appropriate for civil cases. But criminal prosecutions are a different story. These must rest on a violation of a clear rule of law, not on conflict with a "way of life." If "defendants [in a tax case] . . . could not have ascertained the legal standards applicable to their conduct, criminal proceedings may not be used to define and punish an alleged failure to conform to those standards." *United States v. Mallas*, 762 F.2d 361, 361 (4th Cir. 1985). This rule is based on the Constitution's requirement of due process and its prohibition on ex post facto laws; the government must provide reasonable notice of what conduct is subject to criminal punishment. . . . The rule is also statutory in tax cases, because only "willful" violations are subject to criminal punishment. . . . In the tax area, "willful" wrongdoing means the "voluntary, intentional violation of a known"and therefore knowable"legal duty." . . . If the obligation to pay a tax is sufficiently in doubt, willfulness is impossible as a matter of law, and the "defendant's actual intent is irrelevant." . . .

We do not doubt that *Duberstein's* principles, though general, provide a clear answer to many cases involving the gift versus income distinction and can be the basis for civil as well as criminal prosecutions in such cases. We are equally certain, however, that *Duberstein* provides no ready answer to the taxability of transfers of money to a mistress in the context of a long term relationship. The motivations of the parties in such cases will always be mixed. The relationship would not be long term were it not for some respect or affection. Yet, it may be equally clear that the relationship would not continue were it not for financial support or payments.

[The court went on to say that there was little authority as to how transfers made by people like Kritzik are taxed, and to a series of pre-Duberstein cases which suggest that if a transferee/lover is not paid for specific acts of sex, then the transfers are generally nontaxable as gifts. In turn the Court concluded that the current state of the pertinent law was muddled enough that Harris could not fairly be on notice that she had to report the swag from Kritzik as income or be criminally liable from not doing so.]

In short, criminal prosecutions are no place for the government to try out "pioneering interpretations of tax law." . . . The United States has not shown us, and we have not found, a single case finding tax liability for payments that a mistress received from her lover, absent proof of specific payments for specific sex acts. Even when such specific proof is present, the cases have not applied penalties for civil fraud, much less criminal sanctions. The broad principles contained in *Duberstein* do not fill this gap. Before she met Kritzik, Harris starred as a sorceress in an action/adventure film. She would have had to be a real life sorceress to predict her tax obligations under the current state of the law.[261]

Conclusion

For the reasons stated, we REVERSE Harris and Conley's convictions and remand with instructions to DISMISS the indictments against them.

[The concurring opinion of Judge Flaum is omitted. Eds.]

Notes

Afterword. Mr. Kritzik's money seemed to create nothing but sorrow. He died in 1989, two years after his relationship with the twins ended. Ms. Conley was later reported to have been audited by the IRS civilly in an effort to collect income taxes on what the IRS continued to insist were taxable receipts, not gifts. Her reported reaction was one of stunned disbelief.[262] Later, she filed for bankruptcy, reporting assets of about $75,000 and liabilities, mainly Federal Income Taxes, of more than 10 times that amount.[263] Around the time that the twins were tried, David Kritzik submitted evidence that what the twins got from him were not gifts at all. A suspicious press article suggested that his real concern was that if what he paid did constitute gifts for Federal Income Tax purposes, they would surely be gifts for federal gift tax purposes, and yet he had

261 Harris and Conley have already served most of the sentences under the convictions that we now reverse. This is an injustice, and requires at least a brief explanation. To be released pending appeal of a criminal conviction, a defendant must show "by clear and convincing evidence that the person is not likely to flee or pose a danger to the safety of any other person" and "that the appeal is not for the purpose of delay and raises a substantial question of law or fact likely to result in reversal or an order for a new trial." 18 U.S.C. §3143(b). [Footnote No. 7 in original.]

262 Milwaukee Journal, B1, June 15, 1994.

263 Chicago Tribune, April 30, 1992.

only reported a fraction of those amounts on his gift tax returns.[264] His will left nothing to either twin, which triggered more litigation, including a claim by Conley that he promised $5 million for her services.[265] Kritzik's cousin had reportedly said appalling things about her, poisoning Kritzik against leaving her anything.[266]

Nontax crimes. On top of the specific tax crimes, Title 18 of the U.S. Code creates liability for such things as fraudulent claims against the government, obstruction of justice, perjury, RICO activities, conspiracy and money laundering, all of which might be present in a tax evasion scheme. As you might imagine, criminal tax charges are often attached to cases that primarily involve non-tax crimes, such as racketeering and drug charges. Incidentally, if you were wondering whether to be criminally liable for failure to report anddescribe the *source* ofill-gotten gains violates the Constitutional rights of Due Process or the protection against self-incrimination afforded by the Fifth Amendment, it does not. For example, in *United States v. Jacobsen*[267] a loan shark who misidentified the source of his income was found guilty of making a false tax return under §7206(1), a crime that can draw a $100,000 fine and three years in prison, along with paying the government's costs of the prosecution. One can file a return on which one explicitly defends an omission to ascribe a source to the income on Fifth Amendment grounds, but that of course invites an audit. Obviously, under-reporting one's income can be a crime, as in *United States v. Greenberg.*[268]

Again, filing a fraudulent return means there is no going back. One cannot purge a fraudulent return by filing an honest amended return. Now remember how under §6501(c)(1) filing a fraudulent return means that the statute of limitations never begins to run in a civil fraud case. Can one start the usual three-year period running if one files an honest amended return? No, again; so the statute runs forever on civil frauds.[269]

Criminal tax cases are complicated and should be handled only by criminal tax experts. A criminal tax investigation usually arises when a Revenue Agent discovers evidence of serious wrongdoing, and refers the matter to the (sometimes gun-toting) Criminal Investigation Division ("CID") of the District Office of the IRS that is handling the audit. As the case develops into a full-scale prosecution, the Justice Department takes over, including acting as the trial attorney for the government. Recent law graduates can handle many civil tax controversies, but criminal controversies are a specialized area and should be approached with care, employing an expert co-counsel. ABA Model Rule 1.1, which requires lawyers to provide competent representation, demands such collaboration to avoid an ethics claim and malpractice risks.

264 Milwaukee Journal, 14, June 5, 1994.

265 Milwaukee Journal, B7, June 6, 1990.

266 Wisconsin State Journal, Metro p. 15, Jan 9, 1992.

267 547 F.2d 21 (2d Cir. 1976).

268 735 F.2d 29 (2d Cir. 1984).

269 Badaracco v. Commissioner, 464 U.S. 386 (1984).

Professional responsibility aspects of advising the potential criminal. A.B.A Model Rule 1.2(d) states that a lawyer must not counsel or assist a client to engage in conduct that the lawyer knows is criminal or fraudulent. The lawyer may discuss the legal consequences of any proposed course of conduct with a client and can counsel a client with respect to the validity, scope, meaning, or application of the law. If the client uses advice obtained from a professional in the course of action that is criminal or fraudulent, that does not make the lawyer a party to the wrongdoing. If the client is not interested in committing a crime, but nevertheless pushes the lawyer in the direction of breaking the rules of professional responsibility, Rule 1.16(a) requires the lawyer to withdraw from representation if called upon to act in violation of the rules of professional conduct.

Rule 1.6 bars a lawyer from disclosing a client's wrongdoing, but at the same time the lawyer must not further the purpose, for example, by suggesting how the wrongdoing might be covered up.[270]

Professional Responsibility and the Limited Duty of Candor to the IRS. Model Rule 3.3(a) of the A.B.A. Rules of Professional Conduct demands that lawyers not knowingly omit to state a material fact to *a tribunal* when disclosure is necessary to avoid assisting a criminal or fraudulent act by the client. Because the duty of disclosure often conflicts with the duty to maintain the client's confidences, the lawyer should first try to persuade the client that disclosure to the tribunal is necessary, but if she fails, then the general rule in civil cases is that the lawyer must not reveal the existence of her client's deception.

The A.B.A does not consider the IRS a "tribunal" that is entitled to benefit from the disclosure rules of Rule 3.3(a). However, A.B.A Formal Opinion 314 concerning practice before the IRS, states that the lawyer must not mislead the IRS deliberately, either by misstatements or by letting the client mislead the IRS. The lawyer may, however, stress the strong points of the client's case and need not reveal weakness in that case to the IRS. If a client has made misstatements to the IRS, then the lawyer must advise the client to correct them, and, if the client refuses, the lawyer may have a duty to withdraw. Even then, the lawyer must maintain the confidences of the client.

Notes on the "tax gap" and noncompliance. Noncompliance with the tax laws is something the IRS has worked hard to try to measure. It estimated that in 2008-2010 the revenues that should have been collected but were not (the estimated net "tax gap") was around $406 billion, $319 billion from the individual tax, $44 billion from the corporate tax, $91 billion from the employment tax, and $4 billion from the gift and estate tax.[271] Compliance is higher when amounts are subject to information reporting and even higher when also subject to withholding. Misreporting of income subject to substantial information reporting and withholding is 1 percent; of income

270 Comment to Rule 1.2(d).

271 Federal Tax Compliance Research: Tax Gap Estimates for Tax Years 2008–2010. https://www.irs.gov/pub/irs-soi/p1415.pdf.

subject to substantial information reporting but not withholding, is 7 percent; and of income subject to little or no information reporting, 63 percent.[272] Noncompliance tends to be more serious in larger cities, especially, New York and Los Angeles.[273] Cheating is also more likely to occur among the young than among older taxpayers[274] and among people who think they will have to reach into their pockets and pay taxes at the end of the year, as opposed to people who expect refunds.[275] Perhaps most interestingly, the problem is much more serious at the high end of the socio-economic scale than one might expect:

> What detail there is on composition is thoughtprovoking. . . . [T]he overwhelming share of currently detected or imputed noncompliance is attributable to property and entrepreneurial incomes. This contradicts the widespread impression that noncompliance is largely the province of busboys, cabbies, field hands, and street vendors. In fact our image of tax cheaters should be decidedly more "white middle class." Or at least we should distinguish sharply between the most numerous types of evaders and those who may account for the largest share of evasion.[276]

C. GOVERNMENT AND DONATIVE TRANSFERS

A loose form of the concept of a gift as embodied in *Duberstein* has been applied by the IRS to exclude strike benefits and welfare payments that are based on need from gross income.[277] On the other side of the coin, all unemployment benefits are now taxable.[278] The general exemption of government benefits creates a serious problem in that people who move off welfare not only pay taxes on their earnings, including Social Security taxes, but also lose various nontaxable benefits, such as subsidized housing, Medicaid, and food stamps. Losing these benefits creates a major disincentive to enter the job market.[279] The shift from unemployment to employment may also require buying nondeductible child-care services, or commuting or workplace clothing with after-tax dollars, as opposed to providing those services on a non-taxed basis pursuant to the imputed income doctrine.

---

272 Id.

273 See St. Louis Dispatch IRS Audits Distributed Unevenly, p. 8C, April 13, 1997.

274 Klepper & Nagin, Tax Compliance and Perceptions of Risks and Detection and Criminal Prosecution, 23 Law & Society Rev. 210 (1989).

275 Casey & Scholz, Beyond Deterrence: Behavioral Decision Theory and Tax Compliance, 25 Law & Society Rev. 210 (1989).

276 Henry, *Noncompliance with U.S. Tax Law Evidence on Size, Growth, and Composition*, 37 Tax Law. 1, 53 (1983).

277 See, e.g., Rev. Rul. 76-144, 1976-1 C.B. 17; and see United States v. Kaiser, 363 U.S. 299 (1960) (decided the same day as Duberstein, above). See also Rev. Rul. 61-136, 1961-2 C.B. 20 (disbursements in the interest of general welfare, including such items as disaster relief and aid to low-income families or persons who are disabled are excluded from gross income).

278 §85(a).

279 See, e.g., Steuerle, Combined Tax Rates and AFDC Recipients, 69 Tax Notes 4 (October 23,1995).

An interesting and important area of study has recently opened up on the subject of how the tax system helps keep people on welfare. Welfare recipients who choose to enter the job force and who earn 200% of minimum wage would face a tax rate as high as 129% (defining taxes as actual taxes plus lost benefits).[280] The earned income tax credit[281] is inadequate to cope with this barrier, especially for single people who get at most a bit over $300 from the credit to reportedly "solve" the problem.

Problem 4-1:

1) Does the Constitution prevent the taxation of gifts?

2) Would the Constitution prevent the taxation of gifts in the absence the 16th Amendment?

3) There are several children under ten years of age in a family. Each whine persistently about getting his or her allowance and its inadequacy compared to those of other neighborhood children. Are the cash allowances, given by the beleaguered parents to the children each week, taxable to the children?

4) Dad, a luggage maker, gave each of his four children a leather suitcase at Christmas. One of the children was an employee of the father. Would that child be obligated to report the luggage as taxable income? See §102(c) and consider the Proposed Regulations mentioned earlier in this chapter.

5) Gamblers often get superstitious and give the croupier or dealer at a casino a gratuity known as a "toke," or a share of their winnings, to help their luck. Is a toke taxable?[282]

6) The Mountain Commune operates along the usual lines, bound by ties of common values and a desire for cosmic harmony. Each member contributes according to ability and motivation, and receives according to need. Is each member taxable on the benefits of membership? How are the benefits measured?

---

280 Gene Steuerle, Giving Jobs to Welfare Recipients: The Tax Rates They Face, TAX NOTES 10/30/95. The article shows, for example, that an unmarried welfare recipient with two children is better off working 20 hours per week (netting $18,122) and preserving welfare benefits, than working full time at 250% of minimum wage (netting $17,725). The Social Security tax is generally much more burdensome than the income tax in this situation.

281 §32(a).

282 See Olk v. U.S., 536 F,.2d 876 (9th Cir., 1976), cert. den., 429 U.S. 920(1976).

7) The Good Samaritan Hospital has a free clinic for the poor, funded by a "poor tax" paid by the rich, who despise the tax. Are patients in the free clinic taxable on medical services they receive?

Problem 4-2:

How would you respond as a lawyer if Ms. Harris (of the case with her name that you recently read) said that she planned not to report the money Kritzik gave her and asked how she could get away with it?

D. PRIZES AND AWARDS

Read§74

1. Introduction

If a taxpayer receives money or property as a prize or award, has he received "income"? At one time, many people might have answered that question in the negative, because "income" seemed to be restricted to periodic or recurrent receipts or those that resulted from the devotion of labor or capital to the production of gain. Under more recent and expansive interpretations of the term "income" however, one would expect the answer to be affirmative, at least under the current interpretation of "income" as it appears in the Sixteenth Amendment and in §61(a) of the Code.

Even if a prize or award is income in the sense of the Constitution and §61(a), it may not be includible in "gross income" because of statutory exclusions enacted by Congress. The present law is in §74, which contains rules of inclusion and exclusion.

Before enactment of §74, winners of prizes and awards often sought to exclude their receipts from gross income on the ground that the prize was a "gift" under §102 an exclusion for which was found in the Code. For example, in *Washburn v. Commissioner*[283], it was held that a payment of $900 received by the taxpayer from the "Pot O' Gold" program on the radio was an outright gift, and not income. The facts show that the taxpayer was merely sitting at home, answered the ringing phone and then heard congratulations on her winning of the $900 cash, which was confirmed by a telegram received within a half hour. The telegram was accompanied by a draft for $900, which the taxpayer deposited the following day. The taxpayer later was asked if she would care to appear on the "Tums" program; she replied in the negative and never had any other connection with the "Pot O' Gold" program or with the company that manufactures "Tums."

283 5 T.C. 1333 (1945).

She had never bought or used the product, nor had she given a testimonial about it. She never authorized anyone to announce that she had received the money. She was selected by spinning a wheel bearing some numbers and then dialing those numbers on the telephone. The court decided that the gift had none of the "earmarks of income," it was neither a gain from capital, nor from labor, nor from both combined. It came without expectation or effort, was not the result of a wager and involved no subsequent obligation or service on her part. The *Washburn* decision may help explain the fact that §74 begins with the rule that *includes* amounts received as prizes and awards in gross income. The rule of inclusion is then followed with a rule of exception for certain described prizes and awards if received under specified conditions.

It is now clear that a prize or award must be included unless it fits the exclusion in §74(b) or (c) or unless the prize or award is a scholarship grant excluded from gross income by §117, in which event the rules of §117 prevail.

2. Valuation of Prizes

The Regulations, at §1.74-1(a)(2) assert that prizes are included in income at their "fair market value." That does not settle the question whether the value is the retail value, or the often substantially lower amount that the taxpayer could obtain by selling the property, or some other amount. The IRS insists that retail value is the measure, but the courts have on occasion used a lower amount, sometimes on the grounds that the taxpayers would not have paid the full retail price for the property awarded to them. Particularly if the property is not transferable, or if other restrictions are placed on the use of the property, there may be a justification for valuing the property by emphasizing the taxpayer recipient's perspective. For example, in *Turner v. Commissioner*[284] the taxpayer won an unwanted prize of a ticket to Venezuela, subject to restrictions on use and transfer. The court valued it at its worth to the taxpayer. *McCoy v. Commissioner*[285] stands for the proposition that one may use the resale value of a transferable prize to determine how much to include in gross income, but unless one disposes of the prize promptly, the decline in value will be attributed to personal use of the prize. That seems a sensible solution.

Problem 4-3:

Grandfather gives one of his children a prize of a share of stock worth $25 for having the cleanest teeth in the family for the year. The stock cost him $10.

1) Does the lucky winner have gross income (i.e., does §102 or §74 apply)?

284 13 T.C.M. 462 (1954).

285 38 T.C. 841 (1962), acq.

2) Does Grandfather have gross income?

Problem 4-4:

Professor Miles Fonebone has devoted his entire life to working on the private habits of spiders, for which he recently received a $250,000 Nobel Prize. His research indicates a chance to cure cancer. His younger brother, Willie, is a night watchman in a beer factory who received a $1,000 Tiffany clock for his flawless 5-year record of arriving sober and on time for work.

1) Must Miles pay taxes on the Nobel Prize?

2) Can Willie exclude the clock? See §§ 74 and 274(j). If so, are there any special conditions for the exclusion?

3) As matter of policy, can you defend the different results as between the two Fonebones in "(1)" and "(2)"?

4) Professor Fonebone also won a prize of seven colorful plastic dwarves for the lawn (he was surprised when they arrived because he did nothing to enter any contest; he just won). Their retail value was $259.95, but he found them unappealing and threw them into the basement on the theory that he might give them to someone with very bad taste. Ten years later, when he was in the process of moving, he noticed the dwarves, which are now collector's items worth $1,000. What result on receiving them? On finding them a decade later?

E. PROPERTY ACQUIRED BY INHERITANCE

Reread §102

1. Background

One of the enduring features of the Internal Revenue Code is that it has consistently excluded from gross income the value of property acquired by bequest (a transfer of personal property under a will), devise (a transfer of real property under a will) or inheritance (a transfer of property by reason of death in the absence of a will). For simplicity, "inheritance" is used henceforth to cover all three. Unfortunately, there was never a formal Congressional explanation of the exclusion, which now appears in §102, and the problem of defining the concepts of inheritances for Federal Income Tax purposes has been thrown to the courts rather than to the Treasury Department.

The term "inheritance" raises many issues. For example, in some states a putative heir who gets a favorable settlement of a will contest may formally have only a contractual right, not an inheritance, whereas other states might recognize the putative heir's settlement as a transfer under its inheritance laws. Should the same transfer be taxed differently under federal law just because of a variation in state law? *Lyeth v. Hoey*[286] furnished the answer. It involved an alleged heir who obtained a settlement with the estate in the Massachusetts court by virtue of his relation to the decedent, but the settlement was only a contract interest in Massachusetts, which furnished the IRS with a theory for refusing to treat what the taxpayer received as a non-taxable inheritance.

The Supreme Court disagreed with the IRS and established several important points in *Lyeth.* First, it defined an inheritance as any "acquisition [of property] in the devolution of a decedent's estate" under a will or intestacy, as a result of one's status as an heir or legatee, or even as a putative heir or legatee. It does not matter how the particular state characterizes the claimant's share. State law establishes the claim, but federal law characterizes the claim for Federal Income Tax purposes, the normal analysis under the federal tax laws.[287] One obvious limit on the definition of an inheritance in *Lyeth* is that a devolution does not include a payment that is belated compensation for services rendered or property sold to the decedent. For example, a payment for legal services cannot be rendered nontaxable by having it paid by a "bequest" in the client's will.[288] This is hard to administer in the cases of domestic servants and trusted advisors who may gradually become more like family members than employees.

Another important aspect of *Lyeth v. Hoey* is its refusal to distinguish between amounts received as negotiated settlements between disputants and judicial awards. The practical result is to prevent a great deal of money from being wasted on litigation the results of which might be identical to the final outcome of private negotiation. It is, therefore, clear that the exclusion for inheritances is available even if the claimant never proved that she was a legitimate heir, and even though the matter was settled rather than litigated. It has even been held that a settlement award paid to a putative child could be excluded from gross income even though the claimant agreed to allow the probate decree finding against the relationship.[289] By contrast, *Lyeth* was an easier case because the status as an heir of the decedent was admitted.

A troubling aspect of the exclusion for inheritances is that it is difficult to determine what motivated a dead person to make a transfer. As a consequence, the exclusion for inheritances is phrased in a negative way when applied to run of the mill cases, namely that a transfer under

286 305 U.S. 188 (1938)

287 See Commissioner v. Estate of Bosch, 387 U.S. 456 (1967).

288 See Lyeth v. Hoey, 305 U.S. 188 (1938).

289 Parker v. United States, 573 F.2d 42 (Ct. Cl. 1978).

a will or in a will contest is generally excluded from taxation as an inheritance unless it can be shown that it has a compensatory feature. By contrast, in order to have a nontaxable gift, one must show that the donor had a specific, generous state of mind. Notice that §102(c)(1) prevents a person acting as an employee from excluding what might otherwise be a nontaxable inheritance. The following example is from material in the St. Louis PostDispatch:[290]

> A lawsuit underscores just how tricky the rules can be. It took only a couple of weeks after Byrnece Green met wealthy Boston businessman Maxwell Richmond for them to fall in love and become engaged. But 10 months later, Maxwell begged Byrnece to end the engagement because he had "a mental problem about marriage." His solution: sidestep the legal ceremony and just live together. In return for doing that, he promised to leave her "everything."
>
> The arrangement was a good deal for Maxwell, as Byrnece was both loyal to the nth degree and savvy. Besides holding down a job as a stockbroker, she did a daily market report on a Boston radio station owned by Maxwell and advised him on his business affairs and investments. Those chores were just for starters. Byrnece also monitored Maxwell's diet, cared for him during illnesses, and accompanied him on business trips and to social engagements.
>
> While she never saw his will, Maxwell assured his inamorata that it provided for her. They were inseparable for nine years, until Maxwell's death. That was when Byrnece first became aware of a will in which Mr. Right left his entire $ 7 million dollar estate to his brother and sister.
>
> Byrnece's understandable response was to sue Maxwell's estate for the value of services she rendered to him in reliance on his promise. After a jury trial and appeal, she settled with the estate for $ 900,000.
>
> She attached a note to her 1040, explaining that the $ 900,000 was a nontaxable gift or bequest from Maxwell, as all that she had performed were "wifely services." The reply from the IRS came in the form of a bill for taxes, an assessment upheld by the Tax Court and, on appeal, the Second Circuit.
>
> Said the Tax Court: "The taxability of the proceeds of a lawsuit depends . . . upon the nature of the claim." Byrnece based her claim on the value of her services. Hence, the $900,000 clearly was taxable income.

290 September 9, 1995, "Gifts usually not taxable, but IRS will try anyway," by Julian Block of the Tribune Media Services Inc.

Problem 4-5:

If Byrnece had been married, she would presumably have been entitled to a widow's elective share of Maxwell's estate, and that amount would presumably have been tax-exempt. Why, then, should being married matter to the tax result? How would you change the rules, if at all?

Problem 4-6:

Edward Klopman is the grandson of Cyrus Klopman, who discovered the legendary Klopman Diamond. Cyrus is fabulously wealthy. Edward knows he has been named as a one-third heir to Cyrus' estate. Suppose Edward sells his interest under the will to Expectancies, Inc., a New York corporation that specializes in buying and selling future interests, for $2 million.

1) Can Edward exclude the $2 million under §102(a)?

2) How should Expectancies, Inc. treat the amount that it receives when Cyrus dies? Should it be entitled to an offset of some sort?

Problem 4-7:

1) Cyrus also provided that his investment adviser, Harry, would receive $100,000 in cash. Harry has served faithfully for many years, but there are over $100,000 of fees outstanding from Harry and unpaid by Cyrus, which Harry would never press. What result to Harry? Would it matter if the estate paid Harry's $100,000 alleged inheritance and left his bill as a liability of the estate?

2) Does it seem likely to you that if society acted behind a "veil of ignorance" that it would have enacted the §102 exclusion for inheritances?

2. The Problem of Distinguishing Income from Property

It is common for people to allow one party to receive income from property for life with the purpose of passing it to another person at death. For example, assume that a father arranged for his son to receive the income from a rental property for the son's life with the balance to the son's wife at the time of the son's death. Could the son make the claim that instead of receiving rental income from property he had a property interest, namely a non-taxable life estate manifested in the form of annual cash proceeds? Section 102(b)(2) makes it clear that the son's argument will fail because the code treats the rent as a bequest of "income from property."[291] He will also be entitled to no basis or deduction for the decline in value of his interest, so the full amount of the rents he receives will be income.[292] The person who receives the remainder will get the full measure of basis.[293] If however, the remainderman and life income beneficiary sell the entire interest to a third person, the sellers will each get a prorated share of the basis in the entire property.[294]

3. Income in Respect of a Decedent

Section 691 provides special rules for the income taxation of "income in respect of a decedent." The term "income in respect of a decedent" is not defined in the statute but it basically means income earned, but not taxed before the decedent passed away. An example is a claim for wages that had been earned but not paid before the death of the decedent and which the decedent had not taken into income because it was not yet received or accrued. Under §691, the estate must report income from an item such as a claim for wages, if it collects the wages. If the estate instead distributes the claim, uncollected, to a legatee, then legatee must report the wages when he or she collects them. Thus, §691 makes an exception to the usual rules that inherited property takes a basis equal to fair market value at the date of death. It also creates an exception to §102's exclusion from income for property acquired by bequest, devise or inheritance. In other words, some property inherited from a decedent will give rise to taxable income when collected by the recipient, and those items do not take on a new basis at the time of the decedent's death.

Before enactment of §691 in 1942, such items were included in the final income tax return of the decedent. The effect was to stack many such items up in the final return even though they might be collected only gradually. While §691 preserves the taxable status of income in respect of the decedent, it now taxes IRD when collected at the rates applicable to the person who collects it (the estate or distributee), and not in the decedent's last income tax return. Section 691 then grants the person who paid income taxes on the I.R.D. an income tax deduction for the Federal Estate Tax that the estate paid on the item. So, the recipient of the claim has taxable income on collecting the claim, but can deduct the estate tax attributable to inclusion of that claim in the decedent's estate.[295]

To illustrate: Minnie's estate consists, among other things, of assets worth $800,000 and $1,000 of unpaid salary income. The executor who has to prepare the Federal Estate Tax return correctly

291 See also Irwin v. Gavit, 268 U.S. 161 (1925); Reg. §1.102-1(b).

292 See §273.

293 See Reg. §1.1014-4(a).

294 See §1001(e)(3).

295 See also §1014(c).

reports her gross estate at $801,000, and pays an estate tax of $95,000. Assume the estate tax would have been $94,600 in the absence of the salary paid to the estate and that Minnie's friend, Doris, gets the right to Minnie's paycheck as her sole inheritance. Doris has to report the check as $1,000 of income. Because the receipt of the paycheck attracted an extra $400 of estate taxes, Doris can claim an income tax deduction of $400, so the net effect of getting the paycheck is to increase her Federal Income Tax base by $600.

4. The Short, Unhappy Life of Carryover Basis Reform

As part of the Tax Reform Act of 1976, Congress enacted §1023 of the Internal Revenue Code which established carryover basis rules for testamentary transfers similar to those of §1015 presently applicable to *inter vivos* gifts. Section 1023 would have reversed the longstanding value-at-date-of-death basis principle, which so often exempted from Federal Income Taxation the pre-death appreciation of property in the hands of the decedent. Section 1023 turned out to be a politically unpopular reform. It was hooted down by practitioners for its undue compliance burdens and potential administrative problems, and was retroactively repealed in 1980. If one wanted a simple rule, one might assign a zero basis to inherited property (and also to gift property, so as to prevent end-runs), but there have been no public proposals along those lines as of yet.

The basis rules for *inter vivos* gifts and testamentary transfers thus remain drastically different. Perhaps a rule requiring constructive realization of gain *by the decedent* at death would be an acceptable alternative to current law and prevent the complete escape from income taxation under §1014, but there are currently no proposals for such a change in the taxation of inheritances.

Problem 4-8:

If you were the ruler of the world, would you continue §1014 as it stands? Exclude inheritances from gross income and give them a fair market value basis? Exclude them but give them a carryover basis? A $0 basis? How about repealing the estate and gift taxes and making gifts and inheritances taxable as income to the recipient and giving them a fair market value basis?

Problem 4-9:

The same Cyrus Klopman left a life estate to his son, Edward, and the remainder to Carole Klopman, his niece. On Cyrus's death his estate was worth $100 million, after estate taxes. Edward's life estate is worth $97 million and Carole's remainder is currently worth $3 million, although it will become more valuable as time passes.

1) What basis will Edward be entitled to in the life estate if he sells his life estate? See §§ 102(b)(2), 273 and 1001(e).

2) What is the result to Edward if he and Carole together immediately sell the entire interest for $100 million, of which $97 million goes to Edward?

3) Carole also inherited Cyrus's last rent check from his tenant for $38,000, covering a period prior to his death. Must Carole report the check as gross income or can she exclude it as an inheritance?

F. SCHOLARSHIPS, FELLOWSHIPS, STUDENT LOAN CANCELLATIONS AND SELECTED EDUCATIONAL INCENTIVES

Read §117(a), (b), and (c)

1. Background

In the abstract, Congress might have chosen to exclude scholarships entirely using a gift or nontaxable family support model; alternatively, it might have chosen to tax scholarships in full using a "prize or award" model. In fact, §117 reflects a middle path, lying somewhere between §102 with its blanket prohibition on taxing gifts and §74, with its almost universal taxation of prizes and awards.

Section 117 broadly exempts scholarships for degree candidates, but it was sharply narrowed in 1986 by excluding non-degree candidates. Moreover, even degree candidates can only exclude amounts covering tuition, fees and expenses for their course work. This means that if and to the extent one uses scholarship funds for living expenses, one has gross income. In all cases, to the extent a scholarship is granted in exchange for personal services, that scholarship becomes gross income. Section 117(c) makes it absolutely clear that service providers such as research assistants and graduate students who perform teaching services in partial payment of their tuition are subject to income taxes on that compensation. Although most college and graduate students have such low incomes that the failure to exclude paid living expenses from gross income is not likely to hurt, it still invites some distorted behavior. For example, sensible universities now structure their work-study programs so that the compensation earned by work-study students is applied to room rather than tuition reduction.

Discussions of scholarships tend to overlook the reality that scholarships are often only the tip of the iceberg of assistance to students. Universities typically operate in part on funds from the state and federal governments and they have lasting endowments from donors that carry large parts of most universities' budgets. These other educational subsidies that reduce tuition costs are generally ignored in the debates over §117.

Now, what about that great oxymoron, the "athletic scholarship"?

REV. RUL. 77-263

19772 C.B. 47

. . .

Advice has been requested whether, under the circumstances described below, the value of scholarships awarded by a university to students who expect to participate in the university's intercollegiate athletic program is excludable from their gross incomes under section 117 of the Internal Revenue Code of 1954.

A university that participates in an intercollegiate athletic program as a member of a collegiate athletic association provides scholarships to certain incoming freshmen who expect to participate in the university's athletic program. The awarding of such scholarships is controlled by rules established by the association governing the conduct of intercollegiate athletics, the manner in which scholarships are awarded, and the value of the scholarships. These rules include the following requirements: To be eligible to participate in intercollegiate athletics and to be eligible for an athletic scholarship, a student must be accepted at the university according to the admissions requirements applicable to all students at the university and must be a fulltime student. The athletic scholarships are awarded by the agency of the university that is responsible for awarding scholarships to students in general. Once an athletic scholarship is awarded for a given academic year, it cannot be terminated in the event the student cannot participate in the athletic program, either because of injury or the student's unilateral decision not to participate, and the student is not required to engage in any other activities in lieu of participation in a sport.

Under the association's rules, the amount of a scholarship may not exceed the expenses for tuition and fees, room and board (or commuting and lunches), and books and supplies necessary for the student's studies. The amount of the scholarship is required to be reduced by the amount of any other scholarship or grant awarded the student and by the amount of wages from any employment of the student during the school year. If the amount awarded the student by the university exceeds the amount of the commonly accepted educational expenses, it is not considered a scholarship by the association but is pay for participation in intercollegiate athletics and disqualifies the student from further participation in intercollegiate athletics.

The university requires that all prospective students demonstrate academic ability; however, once a student has been admitted to the university, no minimum grade average is required for the student to obtain or retain either an academic or an athletic scholarship. Generally, the university's requirements for granting financial aid are academic ability and financial need. However, a student's financial need is not considered in awarding an athletic scholarship.

The association requires an incoming freshman to have a specified minimum high school grade average. Further, to be eligible to have an athletic scholarship renewed for succeeding years, the association requires the student to achieve a specified minimum grade average at the end of each enrollment year.

Section 61 of the Code and the Income Tax Regulations thereunder provide that, except as otherwise provided by law, gross income means all income from whatever source derived including, but not limited to, compensation for services, including fees, commissions, and similar items.

Section 117(a) of the Code provides, subject to certain limitations and qualifications, that gross income of an individual does not include amounts received as a scholarship at an educational institution or as a fellowship grant.

Section 1.1173(a) of the regulations provides that a scholarship generally means an amount paid or allowed to, or for the benefit of, a student, whether an undergraduate or a graduate, to aid such individual in pursuing the individual's studies. . . .

Section [117(c)] of the Code provides that, in the case of an individual who is a candidate for a degree at an educational institution, the exclusion provided by section 117(a) shall not apply to that portion of any amount received that represents payments for teaching, research or other services in the nature of parttime employment required as a condition to receiving the scholarship or fellowship grant. . . .

Section 1.1174(c) of the regulations provides, in part, that amounts paid or allowed to, or on behalf of, an individual to enable the individual to pursue studies or research are considered to be amounts received as a scholarship or fellowship grant for the purpose of section 117 of the Code if the primary purpose of the studies or research is to further the education and training of the recipient in the recipient's individual capacity and the amount provided by the grantor for such purpose does not represent compensation or payment for services. However, any amount paid or allowed to, or on behalf of, an individual to enable the individual to pursue studies or research is not considered to be an amount received as a scholarship or fellowship grant for the purposes of section 117 if such amount represents compensation for past, present, or future employment services or for services that are subject to the direction or supervision of the grantor, or if such studies or research are primarily for the benefit of the grantor. Any of these conditions will negate the existence of a scholarship or fellowship grant as defined in the regulations. ["Fellowships" paid to post-graduates who are not enrolled in courses can no longer be excluded. Eds.]

In *Bingler v. Johnson*, 394 U.S. 741 (1969), 19692 C.B. 17, the Supreme Court of the United States held that the definitions supplied in section 1.1174(c) of the regulations are proper, comporting as they do with the ordinary understanding of "scholarships" and "fellowships" as relatively disinterested, "nostrings" educational grants, with no requirement of any substantial quid pro quo from the recipients, and that the thrust of the provision dealing with compensation is that bargainedfor payments, given only as the quo in return for the quid of services rendered, whether past, present, or future, should not be excludable from income as "scholarship" funds.

. . .

In the instant case, the university requires no particular activity of any of its scholarship recipients. Although students who receive athletic scholarships do so because of their special abilities in a particular sport and are expected to participate in the sport, the scholarship is not canceled in the event the student cannot participate and the student is not required to engage in any other activities in lieu of participating in the sport.

Accordingly, in the instant case, the athletic scholarships are awarded by the university primarily to aid the recipients in pursuing their studies, and therefore, the value of the scholarships is excludable from the recipients' gross incomes under section 117 of the Code.

2. Compensatory Scholarships

There is no exclusion for scholarship money that compensates students for services even if it is not the university that benefits from the services. In *Bingler v. Johnson*[296] -- mentioned in the ruling you just read -- the Supreme Court held that scholarship-type payments received by employees of Westinghouse Electric Corporation from their employer were not eligible for exclusion under §117. More specifically, in *Bingler*, the Supreme Court validated what is now Reg. §1.117-6, which provides that amounts representing compensation for past, present or future employment services, and amounts paid to an individual to enable him to pursue studies or research primarily for the benefit of the grantor are not excludable as scholarships. Even if part of the scholarship is not taxable, the Regulations state that a scholarship or fellowship grant that exceeds the limitations on the exclusion in §117 must be included in the gross income of the recipient notwithstanding the exclusion for gifts by §102 and the exclusion for certain prizes and awards in §74(b).[297] The facts of *Bingler* showed the corporate payor was not altruistic. The facts were that, under company rules, a participant in the Westinghouse doctoral program, after completing course work at local universities with up to eight hours of released time from his 40-hour work week, was eligible for an educational leave of absence. The participant had to submit a proposed dissertation topic for approval by Westinghouse and the Atomic Energy Commission; if the topic was approved and the leave of absence granted, then the employee received a "stipend" based on a percentage (70%90%) of salary. Moreover, the employee retained seniority status and received all employee benefits, and was required to

---

296 394 U.S. 741 (1969).

297 See Reg. 1.1171(a).

submit progress reports to Westinghouse. Finally, the employee receiving a leave of absence had to agree to return to Westinghouse for a minimum period of two years after completion of his leave of absence. Viewing all of these facts, the Supreme Court held that the payments received by the employees were taxable compensation; "Westinghouse unquestionable extracted a *quid pro quo* for its grants."

G. EMPLOYER-PROVIDED EDUCATIONAL ASSISTANCE PLANS

Read §127(a), (b)(1) and (3)

1. The Section 127 Exclusion

Section 127 offers a tax exclusion to beneficiaries of employer-provided permanent, written, stringently nondiscriminatory educational assistance programs operating for the exclusive benefit of employees and not in lieu of compensation. Limited amounts of such benefits provided under such plans (paid directly or reimbursed) are excludable from employees' gross income, and should generally be deductible by a business employer.[298] Excess amounts might be working condition fringes that can be excluded from gross income under §132. Permissible payments or reimbursements may be made for tuition, fees, books, supplies, and equipment related to the course or courses, even if not job-related, but not sports, games, or hobbies. Law students can cash in on this. The maximum annual exclusion is now $5,250 per employee per calendar year.[299]

Notions of symmetry, fairness and economic neutrality suggest that an exclusion should be allowed if a deduction had been granted to the employee, and vice-versa. Section 127 is an anomaly in the sense that it produces a fringe benefit that cannot be deducted if paid directly (say because the course was an art history course taken by a tax lawyer), but can be excluded if paid by the employer. This asymmetry is in fact a fairly common feature of fringe benefits in employment, such as free-parking for commuters, employee discounts and free vacation travel for airlines employees, none of which are deductible if paid by the employee but all of which are excludable if employer-provided.

---

298 §§ 127(b), 162.

299 The requirements for qualification of an educational assistance plan are contained in §127(b): (1) the employer must have a separate written plan for the exclusive benefit of its employees to provide them with educational assistance; (2) the plan may not discriminate in favor of officers, owners, or highly compensated employees or their dependents; (3) the plan may not provide more than 5% of the annual educational assistance amounts paid to or incurred on behalf of shareholders or owners (or their families) of more than 5% of the stock or capital or profit interests of the employer; (4) eligible employees may not choose between educational assistance or other compensation or benefits; and (5) the plan provides for reasonable notification of the availability and terms of the program to eligible employees.

2. Miscellaneous Educational Incentives

A variety of modest tax breaks for education were granted or modified by the Small Business Job Protection Act of 1996 (§529) and the Taxpayer Relief Act of 1997 (§530). Their high points are: contributions are treated as gifts of present interests, income earned by investment of contributed funds are tax exempt and distributions from the plans for qualified educational expenses are tax exempt.

Section 529 plans were only for higher education expenses including room and board for students who are at least one-half time. Starting in 2018, taxpayers can use §529 plans for elementary or secondary public, private, or religious school tuition up to a $10,000 limit per tax year.[300] Section 529 also allows contributions to a state-sponsored tax-exempt fund that pays out in the form of prepaid tuition of a designated beneficiary.

Section 530 lets contributors gift up to $2,000 per beneficiary per year, but the deduction phases out in an income range starting at $95,000 and ending at $110,000 for single taxpayers ($190,000 ending at $220,000 for a joint return). The funds put in the account must be used for education tuition, fees and books for elementary, secondary or higher education and room and board. The program can be for a part-time student. These are known as Coverdell Educational Assistance Plans after the name of the Congressman who lobbied for them.

Loan Forgiveness in Exchange for Services: There is an attractive loan forgiveness program for students under §108(f). That subsection offers an exclusion from gross income if a student loan is discharged because the student works for a certain period of time in a certain profession or for any of a broad class of employers. The exclusion seems mainly to be used to encourage people in the medical or teaching professions to work in areas where they are greatly needed. Numerous law schools have instituted loan repayment assistance programs intended to encourage law graduates to work in public interest areas such as legal aid.[301] The taxability of loan cancellations under such programs was unclear,[302] until 1998 when Congress clarified that such cancellations are tax-exempt.

For discharges of indebtedness after Dec. 31, 2017 and before Jan. 1, 2026, the Tax Cuts and Jobs Act excludes discharge of indebtedness income of certain student loans that are discharged on account of the student's death or total and permanent disability.[303]

300 §529(c)(7).

301 See Beck, *Loan Repayment Assistance Programs for PublicInterest Lawyers: Why Does Everyone Think They Are Taxable?* 40 N.Y.L. Sch. L. Rev. 251 (1996) (reports that as of the fall of 1994 49 law schools had such programs; six states had such programs funded by state bar foundations, state interest on lawyers' trust accounts programs, or direct state legislative funding).

302 Id.

303 §108(f), as amended by the Tax Cuts and Jobs Act of 2018.

In addition, there is a Lifetime Learning Credit and a Hope Credit. They are discussed later in the book in connection with deductions for educational expenses.

Problem 4-10:

Which of the following amounts is potentially tax-exempt as a scholarship under §117?

1) A waiver of one-half of tuition and all lab fees.

2) A college scholarship of $20,000, which covers tuition ($17,000) and room rent ($3,000).

3) Same as "a," but it is a graduate program and all graduate instructors must teach one course to get the scholarship. See §117(c) and Prop. Reg. §1.117-6(d)(1), (2) and (d)(5), Example (5).

4) A football scholarship for four years, conditioned on playing football every year for the college from July 1 to the end of the season. If the student drops football, he loses the scholarship.

5) Law student's government educational loans are canceled in exchange for a three-year stint as a poverty law intern.

6) A secretary who works for your university takes tuition-free college courses. All university employees have the same rights to take such courses under a written university policy. See §117(d).

7) The Frimler Hotel Corporation offers to pay half the tuition of any employee as long as the course is relevant to Frimler's business.

8) Review the following situation and consider whether the tax rules should be changed:

Joque is on a full scholarship to Big U. The scholarship covers all his expenses, including room and board. Nerd also has a full scholarship and has gotten high academic honors all his life. Joy is a B student who gets no scholarship and pays her way through school by being a dishwasher in the student cafeteria, where she sometimes sees Joque and Nerd dining. Tuition at Big U is

$10,000 per year and room and board cost $5,000. What is wrong with this picture from a tax perspective?

H. FRINGE BENEFITS IN EMPLOYMENT

1. Background

The Code contains an array of benefits in employment that have the common feature of being excluded from the income of the employee or (in some cases) independent contractor.

The nature of this course makes it impossible to do much more than survey this topic, starting with a few of the major exclusions from gross income and then scanning the hodgepodge of miscellaneous provisions.

2. Economic Inefficiency and "Dead-Weight Loss"

When some "compensation" or economic benefits provided to employees or other workers can be excluded from gross income, but cash wages or other forms of compensation cannot be excluded, the difference in tax treatment may change the preferences of individuals or groups, such as labor unions, as to the kind of compensation they seek. The result may be that workers get a form of (tax-free) benefit when they really would rather have cash or some other taxable benefit if it were not for the difference in tax treatment. If the employer's costs for the two forms are the same and if both are deductible (or not) by the employer, the employees' preferences may be determinative, yet they may be worse off than if they could have chosen among various benefits all of which were taxable or all of which were tax-free. They may be worse off by more than just the amount of revenue collected by the government or the amount of revenue lost by the government in granting the tax exclusion.

> **To illustrate:** Suppose an employer can offer either a $100 per month pay raise in cash or $100 (cost to the employer) of a tax-exempt benefit, such as meals on the premises that will be excludable under §119, which is analyzed later in the book One employee might be indifferent between the two in a world with no income tax, or prefer the cash somewhat, and yet be influenced to choose the free meals costing $100, even if they are only worth $80 to the employee, if there is a 30% income tax in effect. (After a 30% tax, the $100 of cash wages yield only $70 to the employees, whereas the $80 worth of meals aren't taxed and yield an $80 after-tax benefit. It is only the after-tax return that the employee wisely compares in making his choice.) An employee whose bargaining unit chooses the meals over the cash in the foregoing example, but who doesn't

> eat lunch, or can't eat or doesn't like the food offered, but who has no individual choice in the matter, will be badly affected. He or she would have preferred the cash and the choice of buying the meals on the premises or using the cash for other purposes. But even the gastronome who thinks the meals are not very good, and worth only $75 (even though costing the employer $100) probably will choose them rather than the $70 of after-tax cash. So the employer is spending $100 but the employee is getting only $75 in value, a $25 "deadweight loss" to the economy, and the government gets no revenue if the employer chooses the tax-free benefit over cash wages. The result is sub-optimal, since it causes a misallocation of resources in the economy in the form of excessive production and consumption of meals on the premises, compared to what the allocation would have been in the absence of this element of the tax law.[304] A less technical way to think of the subject is that the revenue leakage that resulted from allowing the meals exclusion was poorly managed in that it added unjustifiably little to the national welfare.

Consider this efficiency point as you review the excludable benefits, such as group-term life insurance purchased for employees (§79), reimbursement for moving expenses (§82), contributions by employers to accident and health plans (§106), amounts received under accident and health plans (§105), educational assistance programs (§127), meals and lodging (§119), dependent care assistance programs (§129) and the items covered by §132. It cannot be wise tax policy for Congress to bias choices of compensation (and jobs) by excluding these items from the tax base, but including taxable compensation in cash or in kind in other forms (payment or benefits paid in soybeans, flowers, reductions in mortgage indebtedness, and so forth). Some may be more socially desirable than others to encourage or subsidize, but the economic biases and dead weight losses are real costs as are the tax revenues lost by the exclusions from tax.

I. BOARD AND LODGING EXCLUSION

Read §119

1. Background

It is easy to understand that if one taxed a sailor on the value of occupying his cabin while on the high seas, the result would be further bargaining between the sailor and the shipping line, as well as administrative headaches in valuing the cabin, all in exchange for precious little

304 "Efficiency" in its most formal economic sense is an element of classical microeconomics. The concept is elegant and esoteric, and beyond the scope of this course.

revenue. Likewise, it seems preposterous to tax a G.I. on the value of occupying a pup tent while on patrol.[305]

On the other hand, §119, which codifies prior law, is generous -- perhaps lavish -- in that it covers employees, their spouses and dependents, and -- partly because it has no dollar ceiling -- invites overreaching where the employer and employee are closely related. The temptation to overdo it arises because the provision of the housing is deductible by the employer, but is not taxed to the employee. So a hotel manager or a college president or a logger living on the premises of the employer, along with their families, may receive very substantial economic benefits in the form of gratuitous housing, tax-free. The temptations of abusing §119 are enhanced by §119(a)(1), which renders meals on the business premises for the convenience of the employer excludable from gross income, and which again extends to the employee's spouse and dependents.

Section 119 depends on the existence of an *employer* who provides meals or lodging, but if one is self-employed, there is obviously no employer. Can taxpayers somehow create an employer? The answer is "yes" and the usual choice is a corporation[306]. For example, a self-employed rancher might form a new corporation to which he transfers the ranch's assets. Now he can hire himself as the president and, as president, hire the ranch hands on behalf of the corporation. It is a fair criticism of §119 to say that it needlessly encourages the incorporation of ranches and the like in order to create an "employer" so that the owners of the ranch corporation can claim an exclusion for their meals and lodging, while at the same time allowing the corporation a tax deduction for providing those same meals and lodgings to the ranch hands and also to the family of the boss/owner.

The meals and lodging need not be thrust on the employee to be tax-free. In *Coyner v. Bingler*[307] a caretaker whose *only* compensation for extra duties was employer-provided housing was allowed to exclude the value of the housing from gross income. This invites economic waste. For example, an employee who is about to go to work for a hotel might negotiate to live in a lavish suite instead of accepting a larger amount of cash compensation and living elsewhere. The economy as a whole is not served by the result because it encourages transactions that occur only because of the tax system, and are unintended by Congress.

305 Reg. §1.119-1(b).

306 See, e.g., J. Grant Farms, Inc. v. Commissioner, 49 T.C.M. 1197 (1985) (farmer who incorporated entitled, along with family, to treat incorporated farm as principal place of business, permitting §119 exclusion).

307 344 F.2d 736 (1965).

PETERSON v. COMMISSIONER

25 T.C.M. 1002 (1966)

[The Petersons owned two corporations. One was Farms, which bred cockerels, and the other was Sales, which sold the young animals. The Petersons also owned the land on which the corporations operated. The couple lived in the nearby town of Decatur, Georgia, but in 1956 decided to move out of town to the farm. Decatur had poor lodging for visitors. The Petersons arranged for Farms' to rent the land from them for 25 years. Farms built the house, and it was agreed that Farms could remove it at the end of the lease, provided there would be "no substantial damage to the land". The Petersons arranged that the land would pass to their daughter, Debra, who would get title at age 21. The corporate minutes showed that Mr. Peterson, the controlling shareholder, was hired as President and made to live in the house as a condition of employment, in order to entertain business visitors. The employment contract and lodging arrangement were entered into after construction of their new home began, seemingly as a tax-driven afterthought. The new home had two guest bedrooms, but otherwise just seemed to be a spacious ranch style house. It was located across from an airport used solely by the business of Farms. Peterson was intimately involved with the breeding and selection processes. The court accepted that 25% of the home was used for business purposes and that there was no suitable local accommodation for guests in Decatur. The Petersons kept good records of the number of visits and overnight visitors. The rental value of the premises occupied by the Petersons was $400/month, a finding of the court, being somewhere between the high IRS figure and the low taxpayer figure.]

KERN, Judge:

The principal question presented for our [decision is]: (1) Whether the whole or any part of the value of the food and lodging furnished petitioners Lloyd E. and Lorrayne Peterson is excludable from their gross income under section 119 of the 1954 Code. . . .

Section 119 of the 1954 Code has two tests for determining whether the value of meals furnished to an employee is excludable from gross income. They are that the meals be furnished on the business premises of the employer and that they be furnished for the convenience of the employer. See section 1.1191(a), Income Tax Regs. The statute and regulations add a third test in the case of lodging furnished by the employer that the employee be required to accept the lodging as a condition of employment. See section 1.1191(b), Income Tax Regs.

Petitioners argue that the instant cases come within all of the tests of both the statute and regulations. They urge that the house was constructed in the heart of the property of Farms and that it was adjacent to the location of Lloyd E. Peterson's work. They point out that the board of directors of Farms had determined that a facility of this type was necessary in order to entertain business prospects because of the lack of overnight accommodations in the area. Moreover, they contend that petitioner's supervision of the cockerel pedigree work required that he closely observe the bird selection process during 'all hours of the day and night during the selection period' and that his residence 'in the business guest house' was prescribed by the board of directors of Farms 'as a condition of [Lloyd Peterson's] employment.' In support of their position petitioners cite William I. Olkjer, 32 T.C. 464, and Arthur Benaglia, 36 B.T.A. 838.

Respondent contends that the record establishes that the services performed by petitioner were of a supervisory nature which could be adequately performed even if he had not lived on the business premises of Farms. Moreover, he urges that the resolutions of the board of directors of Farms with regard to the house and Lloyd Peterson's residing therein as a condition of his employment do not constitute proof of the fact that the Petersons were required to live in the guest house as a condition of Peterson's employment, because the board of directors was completely dominated by Peterson on account of his controlling stock interest. . . .

Our findings have set out the nature of petitioner Lloyd E. Peterson's work for Peterson Farms, Inc. His own testimony established that he supervised the entire operation of the business, and that he paid especial attention to the breeding process and the selection of birds. He made every individual decision with regard to the breeding process.

Although it is clear from the record that the facility in question was on the 'business premises' of the employer, Farms, we are of the opinion that the petitioners have not established that they were either required to live upon the premises as a condition of their employment, or that the housing in question was furnished for the convenience of the employer. An examination of petitioner's duties reveals that, notwithstanding his constant attention to the various aspects of the business of Peterson Farms, Inc., he was not required to be present at all times of the day and night. Rather, his responsibilities were of a supervisory nature and could be properly performed without living on the business premises of the employer.

The instant cases are unlike either that of William I. Olkjer, supra, or Arthur Benaglia, supra. In Olkjer the taxpayer employee was working in an area where the only living facilities available were at the job site. If the housing and meals were not provided by the employer, no work could have been accomplished by the employee. In the Benaglia case the taxpayer was a manager in full charge of several hotels. We found that "[his] duty was continuous and required his presence at a moment's call." See Arthur Benaglia, supra at 839.

In the instant cases we are not persuaded by the record before us that petitioners have successfully borne their burden of proving that the meals and lodging furnished to the Petersons by Farms were 'for the convenience of the employer' or that Lloyd E. Peterson was 'required to accept such lodging on the business premises of his employer as a condition of his employment.' The Petersons maintained a home in the town of Decatur prior to 1957. There is no evidence with regard to the distance between this home and the business premises of Farms and its predecessor corporation or with regard to any inconvenience suffered by his employer by reason of the Petersons' residence in Decatur. There is no evidence as to any material change in the character of the business of Farms in 1957 and subsequent years, and no evidence that a suitable residence could not be found in Decatur. In 1955 the Petersons themselves first formed the intention of constructing a residence on their property adjacent to the business premises of their wholly owned corporation. Construction of the residence was practically completed before any corporate resolution was adopted which purported to require Peterson to accept lodging on the business premises of Farms as a condition to his employment as president. At that time he owned all but two shares of the stock of Farms, and his wife and mother owned those two shares. On the record before us we are unable to accept 'the bona fides of the employer's demand' that Peterson occupy lodging on Farms' premises as a condition of his employment as president. See Mary B. Heyward, supra at 744.

We therefore conclude that neither Lloyd nor Lorrayne Peterson lived in the house for the convenience of the employer nor as a condition of employment within the meaning of section 119.

Although the house was partially used on frequent occasions for entertainment of customers, this fact did not require that the Petersons reside in it. . . . Whether adequate facilities for the entertainment of clients existed in the area is not a factor in considering the question of the necessity for the Petersons to occupy the house.

We conclude that the fair market value of the meals and lodging is includible in the gross income of the Petersons for the years 1958, 1959, and 1960.

Our findings contain the schedule in which respondent has determined the additional amounts to be included in the Petersons' gross income for the years in question. Respondent's determination with regard to the fair market value of the rent for such a house indicates that he believes that the rental value was approximately $817.86 per month for 1958, $867.74 per month for 1959, and $873.82 per month for 1960. Petitioners argue that the fair rental value of the house did not exceed $300 per month.

The record contains the testimony of only one expert witness on this subject, a real estate man in the area. He testified that there was little rental activity in Decatur and its environs. His only knowledge with regard to rentals in the vicinity of Decatur concerned a house worth $28,000, which was rented for $125 per month.

Upon the record before us and using our best judgment, we have concluded that the fair market rental value of the house was not less than $400 per month.

Respondent has also included in the Petersons' gross income other cash expenses made by the corporation relating to the upkeep of the house. These expenses consist of repairs, maintenance, household supplies, special food for guests, and utilities, etc. Respondent has allowed a portion of the expenses for each year as pertaining to the operation of the house as a business guest house and has included only the balance in the gross income of the Petersons.

Petitioners have failed to prove that respondent's allowances did not fairly approximate the ordinary and necessary expenses of the house which related to the conduct of the business of

Peterson Farms, Inc. Therefore, we decline to disapprove his determinations with regard to this issue.

. . .

Decisions will be entered under Rule 50.

Notes on the Lodging Exclusion

Qualifying under §119 involves meeting a set of cumulative tests, a key element of which is that the meals or lodging be accepted as a "condition of employment." Being required to accept lodging really means that the lodging is necessary in order for the employee to do her job.[308]

Another piece of key terminology that has gradually been sorted out are the words "business premises," which have come to mean a place where the business of the employer is performed, such as leased range land where ranching is done, or areas along the highway that state troopers patrol.[309] In the case of a domestic servant it has even been held that an employer's business premises include the employer's residence.[310] In the case of a military person, it includes his tent and barracks.[311]

Section 119 does not allow taxpayers to exclude cash given in lieu of meals.[312] Groceries are a bit closer to meals than simple cash. The authorities are mixed as to whether an employee can exclude the value of employer-provided groceries.[313]

2. Parsonage Allowances

There is a parallel housing exclusion for the clergy. Section §107 allows "ministers of the gospel" to exclude from gross income the rental value of a residence which they are provided as part of their compensation or cash housing allowances to the extent the cash is used to rent a residence. By the way, a "minister of the gospel" is not limited to Christians. It includes clergy of all faiths. In a particularly gaudy era of tax avoidance, taxpayers subscribed to "mail order ministries," contributed their homes to their "churches" and, as part of the scheme, lived in their "parsonages" tax-free, or at least so they claimed, under §107. That practice has apparently ended.

308 Reg. §1.119-1(b).

309 See Reg. §1.119-1(c)(1).

310 Dole v. Commissioner, 43 T.C. 697 (1965), acq., aff'd per curiam, 351 F.2d 308 (1st Cir.1965).

311 Reg. §1.61-2(b)(2).

312 Kowalski v. Commissioner, 434 U.S. 77 (1977).

313 Jacob v. United States, 493 F.2d 1294 (3d Cir. 1974). held that groceries furnished on the premises to the director a of mental institution who was on permanent call were also excludable "meals" where the groceries were turned into meals. By contrast, Tougher v. Commissioner, 441 F.2d 1148 (9th Cir. 1971), (hewing close to the letter of the law, held that groceries are not "meals," and are therefore taxable).

Problem 4-11:

Elvira is a college student who has worked out a deal with the Suburbanites, who have two young children, and need a helper on call. The agreement provides that Elvira can live in their garage apartment for free, provided she does ten hours a week of child care and house cleaning. The apartment would normally rent for $300 per month.

1) Does Elvira have income, as a result of the arrangement? See Reg. §1.119-1(a).

2) Do the Suburbanites?

3) What difference, if any, in "(1)" would it make if the Suburbanites did not need Elvira to be "on call" to help the family?

4) As part of the bargaining under "(1)," Elvira is offered $1,000 per year or free dinners. Can she exclude the dinners from gross income?

5) But for the job, Elvira would need $6,000/year to pay her rent. Her parents offer her a choice of receiving a gift of $100,000 and using it to pay for her rent. Assume her parents pay for the utilities in both cases and that:

    a. She can earn 7% per year simple interest on the $100,000 and that she is in the 20% tax bracket, or

    b. She could instead use the $100,000 to buy a home that would be as good as the place she rents.

    What is your advice as to which she should do, considering only financial and tax issues?

J. OTHER EMPLOYEE FRINGE BENEFITS

Scan §132

1. Background and Legislative History of §132

For many years there was doubt about the excludability of a long list of fringe benefits in employment, such as an employee's right to a large discount when he buys a television from the store that employs him. Other questions surround such things as free parking, trips on company airplanes and so forth. In 1984 the Congress sewed up most of these loose ends by enacting §132 which provides rules under which taxpayers can exclude six categories of fringe benefits. The following excerpt has been heavily edited.

Joint Committee on Taxation JCS-41-84

General Explanation of the Revenue Provisions of the Deficit Reduction Act of 1984 (H.R. 4170, 98th Congress, P.L. 98-369 starting at page 838)

a. Present Law

General rules

The Internal Revenue Code defines gross income for purposes of the Federal income tax as including "all income from whatever source derived," and specifies that it includes "compensation for services" (sec. 61). Treasury regulations provide that gross income includes compensation for services paid other than in money (Reg. sec. 1.611(a)). Further, the U.S. Supreme Court has stated that Code section 61 "is broad enough to include in taxable income any economic or financial benefit conferred on the employee as compensation, whatever the form or mode by which it is effected."

. . .

Certain employee benefits, such as health plan benefits, are excluded by statute from gross income and wages. Nontaxable benefits offered under a plan which offers a choice between taxable and nontaxable benefits (a "cafeteria plan") may be excluded from gross income if certain conditions are met (sec. 125).[314]

. . .

b. Reasons for Change

In providing statutory rules for exclusion of certain fringe benefits for income and payroll tax purposes, the committee has attempted to strike a balance between two competing objectives.

First, the committee is aware that in many industries, employees may receive, either free or at a discount, goods and services which the employer sells to the general public. In many cases, these practices are long established, and have been treated by employers, employees, and the IRS as not giving rise to taxable income. Although employees may receive an economic benefit from the availability of these free or discounted goods or services, employers often have valid

314 The subject of "cafeteria plans" is deferred to Chapter 9 of the book, involving tax accounting. Eds.

business reasons, other than simply providing compensation, for encouraging employees to avail themselves of the products which they sell to the public. For example, a retail clothing business will want its salespersons to wear, they deal with customers, the clothing which it seeks to sell to the public. In addition, the fact that the selection of goods and services usually available from a particular employer usually is restricted makes it appropriate to provide a limited exclusion, when such discounts are generally made available to employees, for the income employees realize from obtaining free or reducedcost goods or services. The committee believes, therefore, that many present practices under which employers may provide to a broad group of employees, either free or at a discount, the products and services which the employer sells or provides to the public do not serve merely to replace cash compensation. These reasons support the committee's decision to codify the ability of employers to continue these practices without imposition of income or payroll taxes.

The second objective of the committee's bill is to set forth clear boundaries for the provision of taxfree benefits. Because of the moratorium on the issuance of fringe benefit regulations, the Treasury Department has been precluded from clarifying the tax treatment of many of the forms of noncash compensation commonly in use. As a result, the administrators of the tax law have not had clear guidelines in this area, and hence taxpayers in identical situations have been treated differently. The inequities, confusion, and administrative difficulties for businesses, employees, and the IRS resulting from this situation have increased substantially in recent years. The committee believes that it is unacceptable to allow these conditions - which have existed since 1978 - to continue any longer.

In addition, the committee is concerned that without any welldefined limits on the ability of employers to compensate their employees taxfree by using a medium other than cash, new practices will emerge that could shrink the income tax base significantly, and further shift a disproportionate tax burden to those individuals whose compensation is in the form of cash. A shrinkage of the base of the Social Security payroll tax could also pose a threat to the viability of the Social Security system above and beyond the adverse projections which the Congress recently addressed in the Social Security Amendments of 1983. Finally, an unrestrained expansion of noncash compensation would increase inequities among employees in different types of businesses, and among employers as well.

The nondiscrimination rule is an important common thread among the types of fringe benefits which are excluded under the bill from income and employment taxes. Under the bill, most fringe benefits may be made available taxfree to officers, owners, or highly compensated employees only if the benefits are also provided on substantially equal terms to other employees. The committee believes that it would be fundamentally unfair to provide taxfree treatment for economic benefits that are furnished only to highly paid executives. Further, where benefits are limited to the highly paid, it is more likely that the benefit is being provided so that those who control the business can receive compensation in a nontaxable form; in that situation, the reasons stated above for allowing taxfree treatment would not be applicable. Also, if highly paid executives could receive free from taxation economic benefits that are denied to lowerpaid employees, while the latter are compensated only in fully taxable cash, the committee is concerned that this situation would exacerbate problems of noncompliance among taxpayers. . . .

. . .

c. Explanation of Provisions

1. Overview

. . .

[Under the bill, t]he excluded fringe benefits are those benefits that qualify under one of the following five categories as defined in the bill: (1) a noadditionalcost service, (2) a qualified employee discount, (3) a working condition fringe, (4) a de minimis fringe, and (5) a qualified tuition reduction. Special rules apply with respect to certain parking or eating facilities provided to employees, onpremises athletic facilities, and demonstration use of an employerprovided car by auto salespersons. . . .

. . .

Any fringe benefit that does not qualify for exclusion under the bill (for example, free or discounted goods or services which are limited to corporate officers) and that is not excluded under another statutory fringe benefit provision of the Code is taxable to the recipient under Code sections 61 and 83, and is includible in wages for employment tax purposes, at the excess of its fair market value over any amount paid by the employee for the benefit.

. . .

2. NoAdditionalCost Service . . .

General Rule

. . .

To qualify under this exclusion, the employer must incur no substantial additional cost in providing the services to the employee, computed without regard to any amounts paid by the employee for the service. For this purpose, the term cost includes any revenue forgone because the service is furnished to the employee rather than to a nonemployee. In addition, the service provided to the employee must be of the type which the employer offers for sale to nonemployee customers in the ordinary course of the line of business of the employer in which the employee is performing services.

. . .

3. **Qualified Employee Discount . . .**

General Rule

Under the bill, certain employee discounts allowed from the selling price of qualified goods or services of the employer are excluded for income and employment tax purposes, but only if the discounts are available to employees on a nondiscriminatory basis (see description below of the nondiscrimination rules of the bill). The exclusion applies whether the qualified employee discount is provided through a reduction in price or through a cash rebate from a third party.

The exclusion is not available for discounts on any personal property (tangible or intangible) of a kind commonly held for investment or for discounts on any real property. . . . This limitation is provided because the committee does not believe that favorable tax treatment should be provided when noncash compensation is provided in the form of property which the employee could typically sell at close to the same price at which the employer sells the property to its nonemployee customers. . . .

. . .

In the case of merchandise, the excludable amount of the discount may not exceed the selling price of the merchandise, multiplied by the employer's gross profit percentage.

For this purpose, the employer's gross profit percentage for a period means the excess of the aggregate sales price for the period of merchandise sold by the employer in the relevant line of business over the aggregate cost of such merchandise to the employer, then divided by the aggregate sales price.

. . .

4. **Working Condition Fringe . . .**

General Rule

Under the bill, the fair market value of any property or services provided to an employee of the employer is excluded for income and employment tax purposes to the extent that the costs of the property or services would be deductible as ordinary and necessary business expenses (under Code secs. 162 or 167) if the employee had paid for such property or services. The nondiscrimination rules . . . do not apply as a condition for exclusion as a working condition fringe, except for employee parking (as described below).

Examples

By way of illustration, the value of use by an employee of a company car or airplane of business purposes is excluded as a working condition fringe. (However, use of a company car or plane for personal purposes is not excludable. Merely incidental personal use of a company car, such as a small detour for a personal errand, might qualify for exclusion as a de minimis fringe.) As another example, assume the employer subscribes to business periodicals for an employee (e.g., a brokerage house buys a financial publication for its brokers). In that case, the fair market value of the subscriptions is an excluded working condition fringe, since the expense could have been deducted as a business expense if the employee had directly paid for the subscription.

. . .

5. De Minimis Fringe . . .

General Rule

Under the bill, if the fair market value of any property or a service that otherwise would be a fringe benefit includible in gross income is so small that accounting for the property or service would be unreasonable or administratively impracticable, the value is excluded for income and employment tax purposes. The nondiscrimination rules applicable to certain other provisions of the bill do not apply as a condition for exclusion of property or a service as a de minimis fringe, except for subsidized eating facilities . . . .

. . .

6. Qualified Tuition Reductions . . .

The bill adds a new provision to Code section 117 (relating to scholarship and fellowship grants) to exclude, for income and employment tax purposes, the amount of qualified tuition reductions, including cash grants for tuition, provided to an employee of an educational institution (as defined in Code sec. 170(b)(1)(a)(ii)). This new provision supersedes, as of the effective date of the provision, the existing regulation relating to tuition remission (Reg. sec. 1.1173(a), last sentence). To qualify for the exclusion, the tuition reductions must be made available to employees on a nondiscriminatory basis (see description below of the nondiscrimination rules of the bill).

. . .

7. **Athletic Facilities . . .**

In general, the fair market value of any onpremises athletic facility provided and operated by an employer for its employees, where substantially all the use of the facility is by employees of the employer (or their spouses or dependent children), is excluded under the bill for income and employment tax purposes. . . .

. . .

2. Selected Details

As you can see, all of these benefits are ringed with limitations. Many exclusions are unavailable if they discriminate in favor of highly compensated employees. However, even in these cases, the rank and file employees will not lose the exclusion, just the top ranks do.

Benefits that an employer provides in the form of cash or a cash equivalent (e.g., through a gift certificate or credit card) generally do not qualify as an excludable de minimis fringe, even if the cash is meant to be used for property or services which would be a de minimis fringe benefit if provided in kind.[315] An exception applies to cash for occasional meals and local transportation necessitated by overtime work.[316] Another exception to the no-cash-or-cash-equivalent rule is cash the employer provided for local transportation required by unusual circumstances with respect to the employee and the lack of safety or other available means of transportation.[317] Such benefits are de minimis fringe benefits only to the extent that the transportation cost exceeds $1.50 per oneway commute; the first $1.50 is not excludable as a de minimis fringe. "Unusual circumstances" are determined with respect to the particular employee. A temporary change in schedule from the day shift to the night shift would be unusual; a permanent change would no longer be unusual. Safety concerns refer to crime in the area and time of day. For example, if an associate is temporarily working especially late and it would be unsafe to wait for a midnight bus in a dangerous area of town, the law firm/employer's payment of cab fare (in excess of $1.50 per oneway commute) would be a nontaxable de minimis fringe benefit.

Section 132 was supposed to wrap up loose ends and not induce changes in behavior. In fact, there is evidence that §132 did alter behavior. For example, there is anecdotal evidence that the clarification that free parking provided by the employer is not taxable has induced large law firms to pay for their associates' parking out of cash the associates would otherwise be paid in the form of higher salaries. This was not done before for anyone under the partner level. By taking the money out of what would otherwise be paid in cash, the law firms often also reduce

315 Reg. §1.1326(c).

316 Reg. §1.1326(d)(2)(i) (not applicable where the cash is calculated on the basis of the amount of overtime).

317 Reg. 1.1326(d)(2)(iii)(A).

their Social Security contributions, actually saving them money. Congress did not intend such outcomes when it enacted §132. Unintended consequences are regular features of tax legislation.

Problem 4-12:

Which of the following fringe benefits can these employees receive tax-free?

1) Barnacle Bill is a sailor for Klopman Lines. He gets the following fringe benefits:

   a. Free passage anywhere on Klopman Lines ships, as long as it is not in a cabin otherwise occupied by a customer. See §132(a)(1)

   b. Free passage on Klopman Lines private jet, which the company uses to ferry its executives to business meeting0073. He can go on the jet as long as there is space. See §132(b)(1) and Reg. 1.132-4.

2) His mother, Marge, works for Marcy's Department Store. She gets the following fringe benefits:

   a. A discount of 20% in the department store. The average mark-up on goods in the store is 22%. See §132(a)(2).

   b. Free parking in the parking lot the store owns. She would otherwise have to pay $175/month for the parking. See §132(f).

   c. Free coffee and pretzels on her breaks.

   d. Recently, the company has offered free bus passes to and from work. They are worth $55/month. See §132(f).

Read §103

1. Introduction

Interest income that private taxpayers earn on federal debt obligations is taxed, because interest received is "gross income" and there is no statutory exclusion for such income. By contrast, the Federal Income Tax does not reach most interest on state and local obligations, the theory being that doing so might impose an unreasonable burden on the ability of state and local government to borrow money. This was originally thought a Constitutional requirement, but the intergovernmental tax immunity doctrine is in retreat, and, at this point, many categories of special state and local obligations do produce interest that is subject to Federal Income Taxation.[318] Nevertheless, general purpose state bond interest remains tax-exempt, and the appetite for tax-exempt obligations in the market has proven insatiable. These securities are popular investments with wealthy taxpayers seeking tax-exempt income. Note that §103 is not limited to interest on bonds.[319]

It is instructive to compare the effective yield of a tax-exempt bond with the yield on a taxable bond. Here is a prototypical schedule of the benefits of investing in tax-free bonds. The table shows, at various tax brackets, the percentage yield one would have to get from a taxable bond to equal the return from tax-exempt municipal debt.[320]

Equivalent Taxable Yield Table				
	After-Tax Yield			
Income Tax Bracket	**2%**	**4%**	**6%**	**8%**
15%	2.3%	4.71%	7.06%	9.3%
28%	2.9%	5.56%	8.33%	11%
31%	2.9%	5.8%	8.7%	12%
36%	3.290%	6.2%	9.4%	12.5%
39.6%	3.3%	6.62%	9.93%	13.2%

318 See Powell, *the Waning of Intergovernmental Immunities*, 58 Harv. L. Rev. 633 (1945).

319 Bittker & Lokken, FEDERAL TAXATION OF INCOME, ESTATES AND GIFTS ¶15.1 (2018).

320 A huge share of tax-free debt is issued by municipalities. Their debts are often referred to as "muni bonds" or tax free "muni's."

For example, looking at the second column, a 39.6% bracket taxpayer would consider a 4% tax-free yield as attractive as a 6.62% taxable yield, all other things being equal. So, faced with putting her money in a bank account that offered a to pay $6.62/year on each $100 she invested, she would consider it no better than an investment in a tax-free municipal bond costing $100 and offering a $4/year yield, all other things being equal.

From the table above, it appears that a taxpayer in the 28% marginal tax bracket will prefer a state or municipal bond paying 8% tax-exempt interest to a 9% taxable private sector bond of equal risk and duration. If he invests $1,000 in the 9% bond and pays 28% in tax out of each $90 of interest it pays him, he will have to pay tax of $25.20 ($90 x 28%), leaving $64.80 after tax, whereas if he buys the municipal bond for $1,000, the bond will produce $80 after-tax interest, making it a more profitable investment of his $1,000.

If tax-exempt obligations are pegged to attract investors in brackets lower than the top bracket, such as the 28% bracket, then top income-tax bracket investors will receive an economic windfall, which is referred to by some as the "trickle up effect".[321] It is apparently a common occurrence.

Section 103 is loaded with policy issues and questionable outcomes. For one thing, the benefits of §103 are obviously "income-variant." One way of viewing this result is to see that a bond offering a 6% tax-free return gives a 50% marginal bracket taxpayer the equivalent of 12% pre-tax return, while it gives a 20% marginal bracket taxpayer the equivalent of a 7.5% pre-tax return. The exclusion also can be seen as an inefficient federal subsidy or grant of benefits to the states and municipalities that issue these bonds. The inefficiency consists of the windfalls to high-bracket investors. The effect is a dead weight loss. That is, it would be cheaper collectively if the federal government repealed the exclusion of §103 and states therefore had to pay higher (i.e. "market") interest rates on their borrowing. Federal Income Tax revenues would then rise because of the tax on the higher interest, enabling the federal government to pay cash grants to the States in amounts equal to the higher interest costs they bore after repeal of the §103 exclusion. The states would be in the same cost situation as before, and the federal government would be better off with no windfall gains (i.e. revenue losses) to the top bracket investors. A possible alternative would be to make interest on such debt taxable and at the same time offer a tax credit to each municipal bond investor, rather than an *exemption*, to avoid the income-variant feature of §103. Another alternative is revenue sharing as a substitute for §103.

The exclusion of interest on state and local bond debt is regarded by tax expenditure analysts as a prime example of what a "tax expenditure" is, namely a hole in an otherwise comprehensive, coherent tax base.[322]

---

321 See B. Bittker & L. Lokken, FEDERAL TAXATION OF INCOME, ESTATES AND GIFTS ¶15.1.1 (2018).

322 The excerpt is from *Tax Expenditures, Compendium of Background Material on Individual Provisions*, Committee on the Budget of the United States Senate, March 17, 1976, 94th Congress, 2nd Session, pp. 151-153. For other references, see Surrey, *Tax Incentives as a Device For Implementing Government Policy: A Comparison with Direct Government Expenditures*, 83 Harv. L. Rev. 705 (1970); Surrey, *Federal Income Tax Reform: The Varied Approaches Necessary to Replace*

"IMPACT"

> Because the interest is exempt from tax, the interest rate on State and local government obligations is lower than the rate on comparable taxable bonds. In effect, the Federal Government subsidizes States and localities by paying part of their interest cost. For example, if the market rate on tax exempt bonds is 7% when the taxable rate is 10%, there is a three percentage point subsidy to State and local subsidy to State and local governments.
>
> Tax exempt bonds are viewed by some persons as a particularly attractive form of indirect Federal aid because it operates automatically without Federal regulation.
>
> The tax-exempt bond provision is estimated to cost the Treasury approximately $1 to deliver $.75 in aid to municipal governments through this means. It is estimated that in fiscal year 1976, $4.8 billion in Federal revenue was foregone to save State and local governments about $3.6 billion in interest costs. The estimated difference of $1.2 billion is tax relief to investors.
>
> Commercial banks and high-income individuals are the major buyers of tax exempt bonds. Of the $207 billion in outstanding municipal debt (more than double the $93 billion in 1964), about 50% is held by commercial banks and 30% by individuals. One study indicated that the tax exemption reduced the tax rate of commercial banks by an average of 19 percentage points . . . .

Even though the federal government generally does not tax state and local bond interest (and the states generally do not tax interest on federal debt), the exemption is not required by the Constitution. Over the years, Congress has gradually tightened the noose on the exemption, especially when it is used to finance taxable activities, such as building a new factory leased by the state to private businesses lured to the state by promises of easyrental expenses, thanks to the federal tax subsidy implicit in financing the factory with tax-exempt bonds. Under current law, that kind of financing is generally no longer tax-exempt under the so-called "private activity bond" rules.[323]

Problem 4-13:

Imagine you are a financial planner who recently landed Cyrus Klopman as a client. Assume Cyrus is in the imaginary 40% Federal Income Tax bracket. You also represent Bob Busted, who is in the imaginary 20% Federal Income Tax bracket. Assume that the general interest rate

---

Tax Expenditures with Direct Governmental Assistance, 84 Harv. L. Rev. 352(1970). See also Rolph and Break, PUBLIC FINANCE, 118121, 562701 (Ronald Press, 1961).

323 See §141(a).

for a safe taxable investment lasting 10 years is 10%. Assume also that you can find Busted or Cyrus a 10-year bond that pays tax-free interest at 6.66%, with the same level of safety as the 10% investment.

1) Should Busted buy the tax-exempt bond, all other things being equal?

2) Would Klopman consider the tax-exempt bond a good deal? Why?

3) Is the result anomalous? If the top interest rate on tax-exempt bonds in this scenario were 6%, would you be less troubled? Why?

4) Now imagine that Klopman can borrow money at 10%, deducting the interest costs. Would you advise him to do so if he can borrow money at 10% and earn tax-exempt income at 6.66%? Keep in mind that each time he pays $100 in tax-deductible interest, he will save $40 in Federal Income Taxes.

5) Does §265(a)(2) block the ploy you just considered in "(4)"?

6) Is there a tax policy problem if indeed the general rate of interest on taxable debt is 10%, but top-bracket taxpayers can purchase debt yielding 6.6% with the same risk and maturity dates?

2. Discounts and Premiums

Now comes a difficult problem and concept for which you will need to know some financial terms of art. First, when the debtor pays off the debt at the end of the debt's term the debtor is said to "redeem" the debt "at maturity". Sometimes, the debtor will want to redeem the debt early, say because interest rates generally have dropped, making it advantageous to buy back the old debt and issue new debt paying a lower interest rate. Second, when a financial instrument sells for more than its face amount (the amount payable when it is redeemed at the end of its life) it is said to sell for a "premium" over its face amount. If it sells for an amount less than its face amount, it is said to sell "at a discount". A third term is the "accrual" of interest; this refers to the fact that interest on a bond or other debt grows every day, but the interest is only paid at intervals. Between the payments, there is said to be "accrued but unpaid interest".

Discounts or premiums crop up because interest rates changed since the debt was issued. For example, assume a bond paying 6% interest was issued for $1,000 in cash some years ago. Its value would drop if interest rates rose to 8%. Perhaps its market price would decline to $860. If the owner sells the bond to someone else for $860, the tax law generally defers the extra

$140 that the new owner will get until the bond is redeemed.[324] This $140 is known as "market discount" because it occurred "in the market" after the bond was issued. By contrast, if the $860 existed on the day the bond was issued, then the $140 disparity is so-called "original issue discount," also known as "OID" in the trade. That discount is considered interest; it exists solely because the bond was issued at too low an interest rate to sell for the full $1,000 face amount, and it is in substance a partial substitute for an appropriate explicit interest rate. The issuer will in fact have to pay the $140 shortfall for the use of the $860, so it is fair to call the shortfall interest.

OID is taxed to the holder in daily fragments. Each daily payment of income increases the holder's basis in the bond, so that if she holds it to maturity, its basis will equal the $1,000 face amount for which it is eventually redeemed, and she will report no gain on the redemption. Now, what happens if she bought nontaxable bonds, as opposed to taxable bonds? Should OID on a tax exempt bond also be tax-exempt?

Here is an example of how all these elements are sorted out, based on Revenue Ruling 80-143:[325]

To illustrate: Your client acquired a 20-year, 6-percent municipal bond with a face amount of $1,000 for a price of $800 on the date of issue, January 2, 2009. The $200 discount ($1,000 less $800) was original issue discount. At the time the bond was issued, the issuer had no intention of redeeming the bond before maturity. On January 2, 2019, the issuer redeemed the bond for its face amount of $1,000 plus accrued annual interest of $60 consisting of:

1. $60 of earned but unpaid actual interest
2. $800 return of capital
3. $100 of accumulated OID
4. $100 redemption premium paid for the privilege of forcing the bond's early retirement

Under Revenue Ruling 80-143, each component is taxed separately.

1. The $60 of earned but unpaid actual interest is exempt under §103(a)(1) which provides that gross income does not include interest on an obligation of a state or political subdivision of a state.

324 §1271(a)(1)(A).

325 1980-1 C.B. 19.

2. The $100 of accumulated OID is also exempt under §103(a)(1) and United States v. Midland-Ross Corporation, 381 U.S. 54 (1965).

3. The $800 return of capital is return of capital based on the purchase price of $800. It is not taxed.

4. The $100 redemption premium paid for the privilege of forcing the bond's early retirement is not interest income and so is not excludable from the gross income of the taxpayer under the provisions of section §103(a)(1). The $100 redemption premium is gain from a sale or exchange.

3. Computing Original Issue Discount and Bond Premium

Under §1288, the original issue discount on a tax-exempt obligation accrues (is 'earned') on a daily basis, just as with taxable debt. The practical way to look at the calculation is that the interest rate is fixed, but that it is applied to an ever-rising indebtedness figure, with the result that each annual accrual is larger than the previous one. The trouble with using an equal annual accrual is that it is out of step with the marketplace, which for good reasons assumes a compounding effect that results in a rising accrual. Many technically-based tax avoidance schemes in the past depended on this rarified difference, so the tax law switched to the more complex compounding approach.

Each time that §1288 produces a deemed amount of nontaxable interest, that interest is added to the basis of the obligation. That correspondingly reduces any gain (or increases any loss) that the owner will realize on selling the bond. This basis increase prevents any gain from arising at the time of redeeming the tax exempt bond.

Taxpayers who buy bonds often confront the reverse of bond discount, namely "bond premium". The tax law favors them in that they are generally allowed to deduct part of the premium each year as a reduction of their interest income.

To illustrate: Assume that the exempt bond was issued for $110, which is $10 over its face amount. When it matures, the obligor -- say the City of Oz -- will redeem the bond for $100. The $10 here is "original issue premium." Should the buyer be entitled to deduct the $10 gradually (known as "amortizing" the premium) over time or not at all? Section 171(a) says that the holder of a *taxable* bond can claim a current amortization deduction. (Section 171(e) requires the deduction to offset interest income.) This makes sense because the buyer paid an extra amount that he will not receive back when the bond is redeemed. One might treat the extra $10 as a loss on retirement of the debt, but that is the only fair alternative. The dark shadow of §265 disallows the $10 tax deduction if the security generates tax-exempt interest. §1016(a)(5) insists on amortization (reduction) of the premium over time, but it is not deductible. As a result, when the debt is redeemed, there will be no premium, and therefore there is no loss left to claim. This is the mirror image of how people who hold tax-free debt with original issue discount are taxed.

The attractions of tax-exempt financing have led to some fiscally necessary paring back of the kinds of bonds that can qualify. For example, many bonds are issued by state and local governments in order to support businesses that they are trying to attract. These bonds are known as "private activity bonds" in the Code and in general they produce taxable interest income.[326] This is a complex area controlled by §§ 141150 technicalities that lie well beyond the scope of this course.

Another troubling subject is "arbitrage bonds". These are bonds that otherwise produce tax-exempt interest, except for the fact that the issuer uses the proceeds to invest in higher-yield financial instruments.[327] Arbitrage bonds are considered an abuse of the exclusion in §103(a) and therefore the interest they generate is taxable.

On a happier note, §135 offers moderate and low income parents of children who are college-bound an exclusion for interest received when they cash in certain U.S. savings bonds. The exclusion phases out as the parents' "modified adjusted gross income" rises from $40,000 to $60,0000n a joint return, adjusted for inflation.[328]

The $60,000 and $40,000 figures, adjusted for inflation, are:

	Joint Returns		Other Taxpayers	
Year	Phaseout Threshold	Phaseout Completed	Phaseout Threshold	Phaseout Completed
2018	$119,550	$149,550	$79,700	$94,700
2016	$116,300	$146,300	$77,550	$92,550
2015	$115,750	$145,750	$77,200	$92,200
2014	$113,950	$143,950	$76,000	$91,000
2013	$112,500	$142,050	$74,700	$89,700
2012	$109,250	$139,250	$72,850	$87,850
2011	$106,650	$136,650	$71,100	$86,100
2010	$105,100	$135,100	$70,100	$85,100
2009	$104,900	134,900	$69,950	$84,950[1]

326 §103(b)(1) and §141.

327 See §103(b)(2); §148(a)(1).

328 The phase-out range rises over time.

Problem 4-14:

Plutocrat is a cash method, calendar year taxpayer. This year he had the following items:

Interest on Vermont Bond	1,000
Interest on U.S. Treasury Note	800
Gain on sale of Utah Bonds	5,000
Tax refund from U.S.	970
Interest on the tax refund from U.S.	65

Annual share of original issue discount on 10 year bonds:	
Issued by state of Vermont	14
Issued by General Electric Co.	16
Redemption premium on Vermont bond	10
Earned but unpaid interest on IBM bond for which buyer paid	3

In addition, he sold a tract of land to the City of Flyneck, N.J., with a provision in the contract of sale that he be paid 10% interest on the unpaid purchase price.

Which of these items is taxable or deductible? Assume none of the bonds is a "private activity bond" or an "arbitrage bond."

L. LESSEE IMPROVEMENTS ON LESSOR'S PROPERTY

Read §§ 109 and 1019

Years ago, the Supreme Court ruled that a building constructed by a tenant produced income to the lessor to the extent of the value of the building when the lessor regained possession of the property at the end of the lease term, or when the tenant abandoned the premises, whichever happened first.[329] Sections 109 and 1019 were enacted to modify that precedent. Now let us consider a few concrete cases of §§ 109 and 1019 in action:

> **To illustrate:** Imagine that you are the owner of a shopping mall that is falling apart. You induce a retail merchant to be a tenant in the mall if it will make major improvements of a specified sort to the premises it occupies. Do you have income from this arrangement? The answer is "clearly yes". Section 109 offers you no protection. What is the impact on your basis in the mall?

329 Helvering v. Bruun, 309 U.S. 461 (1940). See also McBride v. Commissioner, TC Memo 1987-94 (landlord has income where tenant pays reduced rent and tenant reciprocates by making capital improvements for landlord).

The answer is that it is increased at once under §1019. This prevents an inappropriate second tax if you sell the premises.

Now consider the opposite case.

To illustrate: You own a building in the same mall, which is presently being used as a restaurant. The restaurant is about to quit its lease and you are looking for a new tenant. You have had some discussions with a pet shop owner who says she would like to rent the space, but that major improvements will be required, including soundproofing, installation of six interior kennels and the like. Do you have income when she voluntarily makes these improvements? No. What is the impact of the improvements on your basis in the property? The answer is that the tenant gets the basis in the improvements; you do not add them to your gross income or to basis.

Now, think back to the *Peterson* decision involving the taxpayers who formed a corporation that built them a home as to which they sought a §119 exclusion of the value of the lodging. Recall how the Petersons bought the farm and rented the property on which the home was built to their corporation. Presumably, the plan was to treat the construction of the home as a §109 "lessee's improvement" by the corporation. When the lease term ended, the home was for all practical purposes the Petersons'. Should they have income at that point? The court did not pay attention to the issue because the IRS presumably did not raise it. Here is the key part of the court's description of the facts:

On July 21, 1956, according to its minutes, the board of directors of Peterson Produce Company discussed the possibility of constructing quarters to be used for accommodating business visitors. This was after the construction of the residence in question had commenced. The president, Lloyd E. Peterson, was asked to have a longterm lease prepared covering the property upon which the residence was being constructed. Pursuant to this request, Peterson rented the land which he and his wife owned and upon which the new house was being constructed to the Peterson Produce Company on August 21, 1956, for a term of 25 years at a rent of $444.31 per month. The lease provided, inter alia, as follows:

It is mutually agreed that the improvements which have been previously constructed and placed on the property by Lessors [the Petersons] and other improvements which may be constructed and placed on the property of Lessors by Lessee [Peterson Produce Company] hereafter shall remain the property of Lessee and may be removed by Lessee at the end of the term hereof or any extensions or renewals hereof, provided that said improvements can be removed without substantial damage to the land.[330]

330 Peterson v. Commissioner, 25 T.C.M. 1002, 1007 (1956).

On April 1, 1959, Peterson and his wife transferred the land to an irrevocable trust for the benefit of their daughter Debra. Title to the land was to pass to her when she reached the age of 21.

Problem 4-15:

So, what are the odds that the controlled corporation/"lessee" will remove the large, sturdy home at the end of the term? Are the Petersons slyly rewarding themselves with a new tax-free home which they are giving to Debra when they will likely be in a nursing home? If you were a Revenue Agent, how would you address this situation?

Problem 4-16:

Landlord owns a property that she leases to Student.

1) The lease provides that Student must install a new bathroom, costing $1,000 (which $1,000 student pays) and worth $1,500 in lieu of paying rent. At the end of the lease two years later, Student leaves and the bathroom is worth $1,300. What is the tax impact to Landlord? To Student? Make sure you consider basis effects, if any, in each case.

2) There is no such condition, but Student installs such a bathroom on his own because he can't stand the old one. What is the tax impact to Landlord? To Student?

M. CHILD AND DEPENDENT CARE ASSISTANCE

Skim §129

This provision recognizes the reality that more and more women enter the marketplace, but lack proper day care to facilitate making a living. Some of the high points that you ought to note are the following:

a) An exclusion is available to employees, partners or the proprietor of a business under § 129(e)(3)-(4). There is no need to manufacture an "employer" in order to get this exclusion. This is an enlightened feature of §129.

b) The plan must be available to all workers with qualifying dependents or must be extended to classes of employees who are defined in such a way that there is no discrimination in favor of the highly compensated. §129(d)(3). The concept of being highly compensated is defined in dollar terms and there are exclusions for groups that are often excluded elsewhere in the Code, such as people under age 21 and unionized employees whose bargaining agent has negotiated with the employer about dependent care assistance. §129(d)(9).

c) There is a $5,000 annual ceiling on the §129 exclusion. The ceiling is designed to create rough equivalence with the complementary dependent care credit found in §21 that workers can claim if they pay for day care services.

d) Child care services paid for by an employer but provided by a member of the employee's family are not exempt from tax. §129(c)(2).

e) There needs to be a written plan which is legally enforceable. §129(d)(1).

N. RECOVERIES FOR PERSONAL INJURIES AND SICKNESS

Read §104(a)(2)

1. Background

Section 104 contains a number of exclusions from gross income, the most important of which is §104(a)(2), for recoveries for physical personal injuries and sickness, including wrongful death. Section 104(a)(2) represents an extremely significant exclusion from gross income, largely because of the occasionally immense amounts of wealth changing hands via personal injury litigation.

The history of §104(a)(2) is a curious one. Its fountain head is the antique *Eisner v. Macomber* theory that income resulted from labor, capital or both combined and that as a consequence it is impossible for personal injury awards to be taxed, and that it was therefore not even necessary to have a statutory exclusion, although one has been in the Code since 1918. Later, the *Glenshaw Glass* decision made any accession to wealth a potential candidate for classification as gross income. Section 104(a)(2), in turn prevents *Glenshaw Glass* from including many personal injury awards in gross income.

Running parallel to §104 is a general rule that the taxability of damage awards turns on the theory for claiming damages. For example, if the claim is that the taxpayer lost business income, then the award is taxable, since the business income would have been taxable. *Raytheon Prod. Corp. v. Commissioner*[331] is the leading authority. Likewise, if the taxpayer's claim was that the

331 144 F.2d 110 (1st Cir. 1944), cert. denied, 323 U.S. 779 (1944).

defendant had destroyed her property, the plaintiff can exclude the recovery as a return of capital, up to her basis in the destroyed property. If the recovery exceeded the property's basis, the excess would be a gain from the disposition of property.[332]

Now the questions are which particular types of awards for what types of damages can be excluded under §104(a)(2)? The best starting point is to say that one must inspect each award and, ask "in lieu of what were the damages received?" For example, if the recovery is paid to compensate for lost capital, then the award is generally a non-taxable return of capital. If it was paid to compensate for lost profits, it is taxable as business income, and so forth. This straightforward analysis is not enough if the recovery is for a personal injury, because only some personal injury recoveries are nontaxable. The following pages devote a lot of space to the subject of personal injuries.

As a result of an important change in the law, nontaxable personal injury recoveries are limited to those for physical injuries. Recoveries for libel, slander and other nonphysical torts are no longer tax-exempt. This is clear from the last sentence of §104(a) which explicitly says that damages can be excluded only if they arise in connection with a *physical* tort.

By contrast to compensatory damages, punitive or exemplary damages are always taxable according to a recent Supreme Court decision, on the theory that they are not recoveries, but a punishment and a windfall or gain to the recipient.[333] That doctrine has since been codified in §104(a)(2)'s parenthetical language.

2. Legislative History

The concept of not taxing recoveries for personal injuries has been with us since the Revenue Act of 1918, when it was apparently the prevailing view that tort recoveries and insurance reimbursements were not the kind of "gains or profits and income" that fell within the Constitutional definition of gross income.[334] The Constitutional doubts have since dissolved in favor of a more expansive definition of gross income, but the statutory exemption has remained, perhaps because taxing people who have been seriously injured would seem cruel.

The following House Report explains the important aspects of the recent legislative changes that have narrowed §104(a)(2)'s exclusion.

332 Id.

333 O'Gilvie v. Commissioner, 519 U.S. 79, 117 S. Ct. 452 (1996), and Commissioner v Glenshaw Glass Co., 348 U.S. 426 (1955).

334 See Revenue Act of 1918, §213(b)(6) and B. Bittker & L. Lokken, FEDERAL TAXATION OF INCOME, ESTATES AND GIFTS ¶ 13.1.1 (2018).

HOUSE WAYS AND MEANS COMMITTEE REPORT

Report on the Small Business Job Protection Act of 1996, (H.R. 3448) 104th Congress, 2d Session 300-302 (1996).

Modify exclusion for personal injury or sickness damages.

. . .

Include in income all punitive damages. -- The bill provides that the exclusion from gross income does not apply to any punitive damages received on account of personal injury or sickness whether or not related to a physical injury or physical sickness. Under the bill, present law [which renders wrongful death awards tax exempt] continues to apply to punitive damages received in a wrongful death action if the applicable State law (as in effect on September 13, 1995 without regard to subsequent modification) provides only punitive damages may be awarded in a wrongful death action . . . .

Include in income damage recoveries for nonphysical injuries. -- The bill provides that the exclusion from gross income only applies to damages received on account of a personal physical injury or physical sickness. If an action has its origin in a physical injury or physical sickness, then all damages (other than punitive damages) that flow therefrom are treated as payments received on account of physical injury or physical sickness whether or not the recipient of the damages is the injured party. For example, damages (other than punitive damages) received by an individual on account of a claim for loss of consortium due to the physical injury or physical sickness of such individual's spouse are excludable from gross income. In addition, damages (other than punitive damages) received on account of a claim of wrongful death continue to be excludable from taxable income as under present law.

The bill also specifically provides that emotional distress is not considered a physical injury or physical sickness.

Thus, the exclusion for gross income does not apply to any damages received (other than for medical expenses as discussed below) based on a claim of employment discrimination or injury to reputation accompanied by a claim of emotional distress. Because all damages received on account of physical injury or physical sickness are excludable from gross income, the exclusion from gross income applies to any damages received based on a claim of emotional distress that is attributable to a physical injury or physical sickness. In addition, the exclusion from gross income specifically applies to the amount of damages received that is not in excess of the amount paid for medical care attributable to emotional distress.

. . .

Note

The legislative history explains *why* Congress insisted on physical injuries and why it withdrew the protection of §104 from purely nonphysical torts. Perhaps it considered that too many lawsuits were being filed with an extra personal injury claim thrown in for good measure to create a loophole for not taxing some or all of the ultimate award. By insisting on the presence of a physical injury, far-fetched claims of emotional distress are now cut off, along with genuine claims that may result from real agony.

3. The Core Concepts

First, as to medical expenses of a tort victim, you will notice that §104 contains an important exception with respect to medical expense deductions. Section 213 allows taxpayers to deduct their extraordinary medical expenses. In essence, §104 states that if and to the extent the taxpayer has *already* obtained a medical expense deduction, any recovery of those medical expenses is taxable. Were it not for this principle, the taxpayer would enjoy the best of all possible worlds, namely a tax deduction under §213 paid for with funds that are non-taxable under §104, the combination of which would result in a raid on the Treasury.

> **To illustrate:** Tort Victim was run over by a reckless driver in year 1. In year 1, Tort Victim paid $10,000 in medical expenses as a result of the injury, which he deducted in computing his Federal Income Tax liability. Those were the only medical expenses he incurred in connection with the injury. In year 3, he received a $90,000 award, of which $10,000 was allocable to medical expenses. In year three Tort Victim must include $10,000 in income. See Reg. §1.213-1(g).

If the victim receives the reimbursement in the same year as she incurs the medical expense, the §104 exclusion of the reimbursement applies, but §213 denies the medical expense deduction, because §213(a) disallows any medical expense deduction if it is "compensated for by insurance or otherwise".

Most awards consist of a number of different items, such as a physical injury recovery, pre-judgment interest, injury to property and so forth. It is necessary to allocate any award, whether received by settlement or by a court decree, among the theories of actions claimed by the taxpayer.[335] As a result, there is a tendency for plaintiffs' lawyers to include a physical injury claim whenever possible and to then allocate as much of the award as possible to that claim in order to prevent the award from being taxable to the victim.

Part of the good news for tort victims is that the recovery may be partly based on lost income and still be excluded from gross income. This is true even though the general rule is

335 See, e.g.,Seay v. Commissioner,58 T.C. 32 (1972).

that a damage award received for lost profits is taxable, just as the profits would have been had they been earned. This means that personal injury awards can be based in part on lost earnings and still be tax-exempt.[336] Thus, it is no disadvantage -- in spite of the *Raytheon* doctrine -- for a plaintiff's lawyer to introduce evidence about an auto accident victim's lost salary as a result of being injured, because the jury will simply include this consideration in its determination of the amount of compensatory personal injury damages to which the tort victim is entitled.

Liquidated damages are generally treated as taxable income and not a recovery of capital.[337] Taxpayers are entitled to exclude damages to lost business goodwill, on the theory that they constitute recoveries of capital up to basis.[338] To the extent the award exceeds basis, the excess will generally be taxed as a capital gain.

Tort victims often enter into a "structured settlement" payable in installments. The benefit is that the payor can defer the payments to some extent and the payee can receive what boils down to nontaxable interest in exchange for permitting the deferral.[339]

> **To illustrate:** Tortfeasor has settled a deductible personal injury claim for $1million, but Victim has not yet been paid. Tortfeasor offers to pay $100,000 per year for ten years plus what is in substance interest. The market rate of interest is 8%, the tax-exempt rate is 5% and Victim will settle for 6% that is in substance interest on the taxable deferral of the $1 million payment. This is a good deal from both parties' perspective. The Tortfeasor pays less than the market rate of interest for the privilege of deferring payment. Victim may earn a better than average tax-exempt rate of interest on the deferral, and will be assured of tax-exempt treatment for the disguised interest thanks to §104(a)(2).[340]

Note Well: the parties must call the payments compensation for personal injuries; if and to the extent they make the mistake of identifying a payment as consisting of interest income, that part will be taxable.[341]

Allocating awards to plaintiffs among the various components is a tricky business. The tortfeasor rarely cares what the amounts are allocated to because the odds are the payments will be fully deductible (because they arise in a business) or entirely nondeductible; the tortfeasor usually just wants to pay as little as possible. The victim wants to get as much as possible after taxes.

---

336 Rev. Rul. 85-97, 1985-2 C.B. 50.

337 See, e.g., Smith v. Commissioner, 50 T.C. 273 (1968), affirmed 418 F.2d 573 (CA9 1969).

338 Raytheon Prod. Corp. v. Commissioner, 144 F.2d 110 (lst Cir. 1944).

339 Section 130 facilities these transactions, but is not of direct interest to the tort victim or her lawyer.

340 See Rev Rul. 79-220, 1979-2 CB 74 (Victim not taxed on annuity payments, despite implicit interest component); Rev Rul. 79-313, 1979-2 CB 75 (5% escalator exempt); PLR 9032036 (May 16, 1990) (earnings on agent orange fund). But see, Pagliarulo v Commissioner, 68 TCM 917 (1994) (interest on workers' compensation award is taxable).

341 See, e.g., Kovacs v. Commissioner, 100 T.C. 124 (1993) (stated interest on a personal injury award held taxable).

Parties to a lawsuit know that, in general, the more likely it is that the plaintiff will receive tax-exempt income, the less the plaintiff will demand by way of relief. Assuming the plaintiff alleges a variety of causes of action and several forms of damages, and the parties settle the case, how does one tell what the plaintiff-taxpayer was *really* compensated for? Obviously, the lawyers for the parties can write up the settlement documents more or less any way they wish, but the IRS is not bound by their private writings. The complaint filed with the court may contain some sort of allocation. If so, the IRS is likely to be impressed, but not overwhelmed. Rev. Rul. 8598 indicates that the IRS will look to the complaint as the most persuasive evidence of how to characterize an amount recovered in settlement of a lawsuit. The IRS will not always use the complaint as the best authority, and the Tax Court has accepted the refusal because it knows the parties' allocations are suspect, since they are often the result of tax planning against the IRS.[342] However, if the bargaining involves real adversarial interests, the allocation is much more likely to be accepted.[343] The allocation is also more credible if the judge in the case reviews the allocation and formally approves of it.[344]

How about the plaintiff's right to deduct the costs of obtaining a tort recovery? The answer depends on what was recovered. Expenses that are allocable to earning a tax-exempt litigation recovery are nondeductible because of §265(a)(1). If the award is partly taxable and partly nontaxable, then the expenses must be apportioned between the two. The general rule is simply to prorate the expenses (including legal fees) in proportion to relative amounts received.[345] If the settlement agreement or verdict does not apportion the recovery between taxable and nontaxable components, the allocation of receipts and disbursements should generally be made in the same ratio as the plaintiff's complaint sought exempt and taxable damages.[346] One has to wonder if this does anything other than invite exaggerated claims with respect to the exempt components.

In recent years a fight has broken out between the IRS and the plaintiffs' bar over contingent fees. Basically, the IRS claims the client must include the full recovery in income (to the extent the recovery is taxable) and then find a basis for deducting the associated contingent fees. The attorneys' position is that the contingent fees belong to the lawyers.[347]

---

342 See Bresler v. Commissioner, 65 T.C. 182 (1975), acq., 19762 C.B. 1, where the court said that "the allocation in the complaint, by itself, is insufficient to determine how the settlement should be allocated."

343 See, e.g., McKay v. Commissioner, 102 T.C. 465 (1994), vacated and remanded 84 F.3d 433 (CA5 1996).

344 See Robinson v. Commissioner, 102 T.C. 116 (1994).

345 See Rev. Rul. 85-98, 1985-2 CB 51.

346 Id.

347 Raymond v. United States, 355 F. 3d 107 (2d Cir. 2004) (portion of award for contingent attorney's fees not excluded from injured plaintiff's income)

4. Physical Injuries, Allocations of Recoveries and Related Expenses

The following case deals with income and expense allocation issues of interest to tort claimants and is fairly typical.

DELANEY v. COMMISSIONER

70 T.C.M. 353 (1995), aff'd 99 F.3d 20 (CA1 1995)

WELLS, Judge.

[Mr. Delaney, a tort victim, fell off a roof and obtained a judgment. He was initially awarded $287,000 of which 39% was prejudgment interest. After appeal there was a settlement and Mr. Delaney agreed to reduce the award to $250,000. The settlement was unallocated and Mr. Delaney reported no income from it, and stipulated that there was no interest. The IRS asserted that 39% is taxable ($97,561). Delaney claimed no deduction for legal fees on his tax return. The IRS was prepared to allow a deduction of 39% of legal fees.]

. . .

OPINION

We must decide whether a portion of the $250,000 settlement proceeds constitutes taxable interest. Petitioners contend that the entire $250,000 is excludable from gross income as damages from tort like personal injuries pursuant to section 104(a)(2). Respondent concedes that the portion of the settlement proceeds attributable to petitioner's tort claim is excludable under section 104(a)(2) as damages received on account of personal injuries. Respondent, however, contends that the settlement agreement does not contain any specific allocations regarding interest. Additionally, respondent contends that because the original judgment included statutory prejudgment interest in the amount of $112,000, the portion of the proceeds received in lieu of such interest is not excludable under section 104(a)(2). Respondent's determination in the notice of deficiency is presumptively correct, and petitioners have the burden of proving that no part of the amounts received constituted interest. . . .

Section 61 defines gross income to include "all income from whatever source derived." Section 61(a)(4) specifically provides that gross income includes "interest." Section 104(a)(2) provides for the exclusion of "the amount of any damages received (whether by suit or agreement and whether as lump sums or as periodic payments) on account of personal injuries". The regulations broadly interpret this language as encompassing damages received "through prosecution of a legal suit or action based upon tort or tort type rights, or through a settlement agreement in lieu of such prosecution." Sec. 1.1041(c), Income Tax Regs. Statutory interest imposed on tort judgments, however, must be included in gross income under section 61(a)(4) even under circumstances in which the underlying damages are excludable under section 104(a)(2). *Robinson v. Commissioner*, 102 T.C. 116, 126 (1994) . . . .

We have often been asked to decide the proper allocation of the proceeds of a settlement agreement in the context of section 104(a)(2). . . . In cases involving a settlement agreement which contains an express allocation, such allocation is generally the most important factor in deciding whether a payment was made on account of a tortious personal injury for purposes of exclusion under section 104(a)(2). It is well settled that express allocations in a settlement agreement will be respected to the extent that the agreement is entered into by the parties at arm's length and in good faith . . . .

In cases involving a civil damage action which has been settled, in order to characterize settlement proceeds as income which is taxable under section 61 or as income which is excluded from taxation under section 104(a)(2), we must ascertain "in lieu of *what* were damages awarded" or paid. . . .

If no lawsuit was instituted by the taxpayer, then we must consider any relevant documents, letters, and testimony. e.g., *Fitts v. Commissioner*, T.C. Memo. 199452, affd. 53 F.3d 335 (8th Cir. 1995). If a lawsuit was filed but not settled, or if a lawsuit was settled but no express allocations were made in the settlement agreement, we must consider the pleadings, jury awards, or any court orders or judgments. *McKay v. Commissioner*, supra at 483 . . . . If a taxpayer's claims were settled and express allocations are contained in the settlement agreement, we must carefully consider such allocations. See *Byrne v. Commissioner*, 90 T.C. 1000, 1007 (1988) . . . . As we stated above, however, we are not required to respect the express allocations unless they were negotiated at arm's length between adverse parties.

Petitioners contend that the instant case is indistinguishable from *McShane v. Commissioner*, T.C. Memo. 1987151, in which we held that none of the settlement proceeds received by the taxpayers were includible in gross income as interest, taking into account express language in a settlement agreement. Respondent contends that the instant case is distinguishable from *McShane* because petitioner's "Settlement Agreement and Joint Tortfeasor Release" did not contain express language as to the allocation of the settlement proceeds. Respondent also contends that the language found in the stipulation is ambiguous.

In *McShane*, the taxpayers were seriously injured by a gas explosion and a fire occurring in a railroad yard. Subsequently, the taxpayers initiated negligence actions, and the jury awarded the taxpayers compensatory damages totaling $1,275,000. Additionally, each taxpayer was entitled to statutory interest under State law. While the case was on appeal, the taxpayers and the defendants settled the lawsuit. As part of the written settlement agreements, the taxpayers agreed to accept lumpsum payments in settlement of the negligence suit. At the insistence of one of the defendants, the settlement agreements further provided that the proceeds were to be paid "without costs and interest." In negotiating the settlement amounts, the parties never addressed the tax consequences of settling the case without interest, but instead considered their respective risks in continuing the appeal.

In *McShane*, we were required to decide whether any portion of the settlement proceeds received by each taxpayer was includible in income as interest. After a careful review of the record, we concluded that none of the settlement proceeds were attributable to interest. Our decision was based on the express language in the settlement agreements that payments were made "without costs and interest" as well as other evidence in the record which established that the inclusion of the language in the settlement agreements was the result of bona fide arm'slength negotiations.

In the instant case, in contrast to *McShane*, the jury verdict identified statutory interest as a specific component of the sum awarded to petitioner. The jury awarded petitioner $287,000, which consisted of $175,000 in tort damages and $112,000 in statutory prejudgment interest. The parties later settled for $250,000. Although the stipulation expressly provided that the settlement amount did not include interest, the record in the instant case, unlike *McShane*, is devoid of evidence that such provision of the stipulation was the product of arm'slength negotiations between the parties. The only evidence in the record is that the parties did not discuss the tax implications of such aspect of the stipulation. Accordingly, we conclude that petitioners have failed to establish that there was no interest component to the settlement. . . .

Petitioners also contend that we are conclusively bound as to the characterization of the settlement proceeds by *Factory Mut. Liab. Ins. Co. of America v. Cooper*, 262 A.2d 370 (R.I. 1970). In Factory Mutual, the Supreme Court of Rhode Island was called upon to analyze the plaintiff insurance company's liability to persons (the defendants) for injuries caused by the insured party in an automobile accident. The defendants had appealed judgments entered by the trial court. The narrow issue raised by the appeal was whether the plaintiff was obligated to pay, in excess of its policy limit, interest added to the verdicts in accordance with the mandate in R.I. Gen. Laws sec. 92110. The court held that the plaintiff was not liable for such payment in excess of the policy limit. In so holding, the court construed the word "damages" as used in the insurance policy to include prejudgment statutory interest. Consequently, the plaintiff was liable for prejudgment interest included in the verdicts up to the policy limit.

. . .

In the notice of deficiency, respondent allowed petitioners a deduction under sections 212(1) and 265 for legal fees allocable to the interest portion of the settlement proceeds. Petitioners have failed to make any arguments or to offer any evidence with respect to the deductibility of their attorney's fees.

Section 212(1) permits a deduction of all ordinary and necessary expenses paid for the production or collection of income. Section 265, however, disallows deductions for amounts which are allocable to taxexempt income. Consequently, only the attorney's fees attributable to interest are deductible. In *Church v. Commissioner*, 80 T.C. 1104 (1983), we used the following formula to calculate the correct deduction:

$$\frac{\text{Total attorney's fees} \times \text{Nonexempt income}}{\text{Total award}} = \text{Deductible expenses}$$

In the instant case, respondent utilized the *Church* formula in the notice of deficiency.

Because we have held that a portion of the settlement proceeds is interest and is includible in income, we sustain respondent's determination with respect to the deductibility of attorney's fees. . . .

To reflect the foregoing, *Decision will be entered for respondent.*

Problem 4-17:

Eleanor Higby was a watchmaker in Anytown. Over the past several months, she noticed a strange smell in her store, which turned out to be a leaking gas main. The leaking gas exploded one morning while she was in the store, permanently injuring her hands. She sued the Gas Company and recovered various amounts. Determine which are taxable:

1) Assume Eleanor was wrongfully imprisoned by the State for 20 years for arson. When she got out, she successfully sued the State for $5 million for her unlawful confinement. Can she exclude the recovery from gross income?

2) Assume that Eleanor was not in the building at the time of the explosion, and that she sued for $400,000 of lost profits.
For the rest of the problem, assume Eleanor was in the building at the time of the explosion.

3) $1 million for pain and suffering as a result of being injured in the explosion;

4) $40,000 for lost consortium, shared equally with her husband;

5) $200,000 punitive damages;

6) $400,000 for lost income from her activities as a watchmaker;

7) $35,000 for destruction of the building. She has an adjusted basis in the building of $32,000;

8) $150,000 for lost goodwill, in which she had a basis of $0; and

9) $25,000 medical that she incurred, paid and deducted from her income taxes several years ago (under §213). Incidentally, according to the IRS, damage awards are allocated first to recoveries of previously deducted medical expenses. Rev. Rul. 75230, 19751 C.B. 93.

10) It cost her $100,000 in attorneys' fees to obtain the amounts in "(1)" through "(9)" To what extent are they deductible? See §265(a)(1) and Reg. §1.2121(e).

11) What if instead Mrs. Higby had sued for $3 million in punitive damages and $1 million in compensatory damages, but the parties settled for the above amounts? Would the allocation in c-e stand, or would some other allocation be used?

12) Assume Mrs. Higby was killed in the blast and her estate got a wrongful death recovery. Is the recovery excludable? What must the estate show to get the exclusion?

13) Assume that a competitor claimed the explosion occurred because Mrs. Higby was an alcoholic and left the gas on because she was intoxicated. Assume further that Mrs. Higby brought a personal injury suit against the competitor for slander for $3 million and won. Under the fees agreement, her attorney got 33% of the recovery. In your view, as a matter of first impression, should she report the recovery and then claim a deduction for the $1 million? What would the IRS position be, and why would it pose a tax problem for her?

5. Damages and Reimbursement for Medical Expenses

Sections 104 through 106 of the Code contain a confounding set of interrelated rules on the allimportant subject of the taxation of accident and health coverage. In the real world, many employers reimburse their employees' medical expenses or else they buy such coverage from a commercial insurance company.

The easiest rule appears in section 106. It promises that employees will not be taxed when the employer *contributes* money to its accident or health plan, or when it purchases such coverage for its employees. One then turns to §105. Section 105 begins with a bark, but almost never bites; although §105(a) asserts that employer-financed sickness benefits are taxable, it quickly backs off. The first retreat appears in §105(b), which assures that their employers' reimbursements for medical care of the taxpayer, as well as his or her spouse and dependents, are excluded from the employee's gross income, unless they relate to payments that the employee previously deducted as medical expenses. The latter provision is needed to prevent double-dipping by taxpayers. As far as employerpaid medical insurance coverage goes, §105(e) contains a benign parallel tax exemption for employerpaid insurance premiums which the employer pays directly to the medical provider. When the statutory smoked clears, one recognizes that employer-provided medical coverage is a godsend compared to going without such coverage and claiming personal medical expense deductions. This is because the medical expense deduction is unavailable except to the extent medical expenditures exceed 10% of adjusted gross income, i.e. are catastrophic. The book covers this in some detail later on. Personal injuries or sickness payments received under accident or health insurance are generally taxed.

Wage continuation (disability) plans, (applying when an employee becomes sick or injured) are excludable from gross income if they are made in light of the "permanent loss or loss of use of a member or function of the body or permanent disfigurement and are made without regard to the length of time the employee is absent from work" -- not exactly generous.[348] On the other hand, if the taxpayer herself paid for the disability insurance, there is no tax (and no tax deduction) for her payment of premiums, regardless of whether the absence from work is based on loss of bodily function; personal injury or sickness is enough.See §104(a)(3). If the wage continuation payments arise out of an occupational injury or sickness as worker's compensation, Reg. §1.104-1(b) renders them tax-free. See §104(a)(1).

Problem 4-18:

On the first day of what was supposed to be a twoweek vacation, Harold Hatman was involved in a serious automobile accident which required his immediate hospitalization. His child, Sonny, also suffered minor injuries. That year, Harold received the following payments under a health and accident policy, half the monthly premiums of which were paid by Harold, the other half by his employer:

1) $12,000 as a payment of his hospital and medical expenses. See §§ 104(a)(3) and 105(b).

2) $225 for Sonny's medical expenses; and

3) $700 per week for ten weeks out of work (during which his $800 weekly salary was discontinued). See §105(c).

348 See §105(c).

Read §72(a)-(c)(1)

1. Commercial Annuities

An annuity contract is one under which a person purchases the right to future payments of money, often annually, or at other regular intervals. The usual seller of an annuity is a life insurance company or sometimes a bank or charity. The typical use of an annuity is to provide the purchaser with a predictable stream of cash during retirement. Variable annuities are a popular investment. The basic idea is that the premiums paid for the annuity flow into mutual fund shares. If the mutual funds perform well, the customers may enjoy a large flow of post-retirement annuity payments. These are becoming popular investments for pension plans.

The annuity may run for a set number of years or it may track the lifetime of the annuitant, or even someone else's life. In fact, actuaries can do more tricks with annuities than a monkey on a 90-foot vine, so the discussion that follows is limited to the most basic types of annuities. When the annuitant buys a so-called "life annuity" she is gambling that she will live longer than the actuaries at the life insurance company believe. If she is correct in her guess, she will continue to be paid past the actuaries' morbid expectation as to when she will die, but if she dies before that date, then the insurance company reaps the gruesome benefit of her early death.

Because annuities pay out later than the date when the purchaser of the annuity transfers the money to the insurance company, it is only natural that the insurance company will have to pay the purchaser somewhat more than the amount the annuitant paid, so the question becomes how can one tell whether the annuitant was paid a return of her capital first or something in the nature of interest? One might treat the payments to the annuitant as capital until the owner gets back her investment, or income first, or some kind of proration between income and a return of capital applied to each payment. For the answer one must refer to §72, which calls for prorating each annuity receipt into a mix of income and a nontaxable return of capital.

By the way, a simple way to approach annuity calculations is to use this formula to determine how much of each payment to the annuitant is taxable. Once you have computed the ratio, you apply it to all payments received under the annuity, subject to some exceptions you will see shortly.

$$\text{Exclusion ratio} = \frac{\text{Taxpayer's investment in the contract}}{\text{Expected return from annuity}}$$

The following is a basic example of how an annuity operates.[349]

349 The example is from B. Bittker & L. Lokken FEDERAL TAXATION OF INCOME, ESTATES AND GIFTS.¶ 12.3.1 (2018).

To illustrate: A 56-year-old woman pays $1,500,000 to a life insurance company in a lump sum in exchange for an annuity contract which promises to pay her $100,000 per year starting at age 65, and ending with her death. There is no refund if she dies before receiving back the $1,500,000 that she paid. Assume that the company bases its payments on mortality tables produced by its actuaries, which tables indicate that the average 65 year-old woman will live 20 more years. If the taxpayer lives exactly those 20 years, she will receive a total of $2,000,000 and the annuity will operate like a savings account that also pays interest. If she lives beyond age 85, thenshe will enjoy a so-called "mortality gain" because she will continue to be paid until she dies, but if she lives a shorter time than that,she will suffer a "mortality loss."

This poses the key question of what to do about taxing mortality gains and losses on annuity contracts. There are in theory several possibilities, which the following problem will reveal. To solve the problem, you will want to have the following annuity tables found in the Regulations. Notice how in the old days (Table I, applicable before July of 1986) the Regulations distinguished between the sexes, but that they are now "unisex" (Table V). Both Tables tell one how long a taxpayer is expected to live as of a certain age. For example, under Table I, a 62 year-old male and a 67 year-old female were both expected to live 16.9 more years. The mortality assumption allows one to compute the expected return under a life annuity -- one that stops at the annuitant's death. By contrast, under the current unisex tables, a 64 year-old male or female are both expected to live 20.8 years.[350]

Recently, variable annuities have caught on. They differ only in that the total amount that the insurance company pays out depends on the performance of the underlying fund, such as investments in mutual funds.

2. Private Annuities

Imagine an elderly parent who owns a farm that the parent can no longer operate. The parent wants the child to take over the farm, but the parent also needs cash to meet his or her needs. One solution is to sell the farm to the child using a private annuity; the heart of the deal is that the child buys the farm with periodic payments that end when the parent dies. Each payment is broken into components for Federal Income Tax purposes, namely a return of capital, a gain (or loss) and income comparable to interest for the deferral in payment that the child enjoys. Rev. Rul. 6974, 19691 C.B. 43 sets forth the procedure for making the calculations. In general, it seems private annuities are more discussed than used and that they are an estate planning device to strip the estate of assets at death. They do not seem to be used for income tax planning purposes.

---

350 Reg. §72-9 Tables.

Problem 4-19:

Barton Bean recently bought a single-premium annuity on his life for $50,000 in cash. Barton's actuarially-determined life expectancy is ten years. The contract promises to pay $8,000 per year of Barton's life. The annuity begins to pay out immediately.

The next step is to apply the exclusion ratio to each payment under the annuity to determine the nontaxable component of each payment.

For problems 1-3, use the old rules table (sex dependent).

1) How much income must Barton report in the first year of the contract -- that is, the first year the annuity begins to pay out? See §72. Notice how the answer relates to the familiar concept of a nontaxable return of capital.

2) If Barton is still alive in 15 years, how much income must Barton report that year?

3) If Barton dies a year after the annuity begins to pay out, is anyone entitled to a deduction?

For problems 4)-6), use the new rules table (unisex).

4) Barton is a 65 year-old male. He buys a life annuity for $100,000. It pays $8,000/year, starting immediately. How much of that $8,000 can he exclude from gross income in the first few years?

5) In your view, would it be better to ignore the effects of early deaths (and therefore disallow a deduction to the annuitant's estate) and to allow the exclusion to continue if the annuitant outlives his life expectancy?

6) If Barton is a male, is he worse or better off than his female counterparts when he goes to buy an annuity?

Read §101(a)

1. Background

These coming paragraphs are from "Life 202, what you never learned in college". A life insurance contract is in essence another gamble between the insurer and the consumer. The consumer ("insured") is gambling that he or she will not live as long as the insurance company expects. If the consumer is correct, the early death is a bittersweet triumph of financial planning. If the consumer outlives the life insurance company's expectations, the insurance company is the financial victor.

Life insurance contracts fall into two basic categories. The first category is the so-called term policy, which provides pure insurance coverage. Because the probability of an individual's death rises with each passing year, term insurance for any particular amount of coverage becomes more expensive with the passage of time. This fact has led to the development of a second kind of insurance, namely whole life insurance. This form of insurance is in effect a combination of a term policy plus a savings account held by the insurer which grows over time, filling the gap in coverage that would otherwise not be available from a term policy because of the rising mortality risk as the insured ages. There is a considerable suspicion as to whether this so-called inside build-up should be entitled to grow on a nontaxable basis (as it essentially does) and then be treated as nontaxable life insurance when it is paid out at death (as it is) or whether life insurance arrangements ought to be taxed more aggressively. Tax-free inside build-up is reported as a major component of the tax expenditure budget.[351] The Canadian tax law includes build-up in a life insurance policy in gross income as the cash value grows.

Life insurance is usually sold on the basis of fixed prices for fixed amounts of coverage, but it is becoming more common for consumers to buy variable life insurance coverage. Variable life insurance arrangements can be hard to distinguish from the purchase of a diversified stock market investment plus life insurance. Congress reacted to the risk of abuse by enacting §7702 which contains complex rules designed to confine the benefits of §101 to honest life insurance without eliminating reasonable variable life insurance policies.[352] Even if a contract does meet

351 Analytical Perspectives, Budget of the United States Government, Fiscal Year 2019 Chapter 13 tax expenditures (2/12/2018).

352 In recent years, insurance companies began marketing flexible premium life insurance contracts, known as "universal life" or "adjustable life" insurance policies. These contracts are similar to whole life policies, but the policyholder is permitted to change the amount and timing of the premiums and the size of the death benefit automatically as his or her needs change. A policyholder may also invest a sizeable cash fund without a related increase in the amount of insurance protection, thereby acquiring an interest in a cash fund that acts as a savings vehicle (apart from the insurance protection). Because such flexible premium contracts can be so used as a vehicle for tax-favored investment, alternative tests which such policies must meet in order to be treated as life insurance for tax purposes were added, as §7702, §101(f), §817(h).

the definition of a life insurance contract, there can be further trouble if the insured made especially heavy premium prepayments in the early years of the policy. The policy may be classified as a "modified endowment contract," the burden of which is that money taken out of the policy, even a loan or proceeds of pledging the policy, is taxed as ordinary income to the extent that untaxed income has built up inside the policy.[353] There are lots of extra complications to the taxation of life insurance, but they are beyond the scope of this course.

As far as the insured is concerned, the purchase of life insurance is like the purchase of any other consumer good. The taxpayer does not report any gross income from the death proceeds and does not get a deduction for the acquisition of the policy. The theory, which is not well-explained, is that the death proceeds are comparable to a nontaxable bequest.[354] If a business takes out a policy on a key employee and holds the policy as the beneficiary, there is no income tax on the employer or on the business when the insured dies,[355] but the employer cannot deduct the premiums; that restriction is to prevent deductions from earning tax-exempt income.[356]

Although proceeds of a life insurance policy received by a beneficiary are tax-exempt, this is not true where there is a "transfer for a valuable consideration,'' under §101(a)(2). In such cases the tax-exempt amount is limited to the amount of the consideration the transferee paid for the policy. There are two exceptions to the transfer for value rule. These exceptions apply: (a) if the transferee takes the transferor's basis, even in part; or, (b) the transfer is to the insured or to an entity in which the insured has an important stake.[357]

> **To illustrate:** Mr. Bigly used to run his own unincorporated consulting company, but recently he decided to go into partnership with Ms. Sensible. As part of their partnership agreement, he promised to transfer his whole life insurance policy to the new partnership, naming the partnership as the beneficiary in the event of his death. The partnership will pay the premiums, not him. The partnership will get the same basis in the policy as he had in it, thanks to §723 of the Code. His transfer of the policy is exempt from the transfer for value rule for two reasons: (a) the partnership took his basis in the policy and (b) he is a partner in the partnership that got the policy. As a result, when he dies the partnership will not be taxed on the death proceeds.

Life insurance is an integral part of the planning for large estates, because it permits the insured to pass the policy to another person -- typically a trust -- that will obtain the death proceeds outside the estate, thereby allowing wealth to pass to the beneficiaries of the policy without a federal income gift or estate tax.

353 See §7702A and 72(v).

354 See §102(a).

355 §101(a)(1).

356 §264(a)(1).

357 §101(a)(2)(A)-(B).

One might wonder if a respectable argument can be made, that the "mortality gain" in life insurance, which is the excess of the proceeds of the policy over the amount of premiums paid in, is not income because the proceeds are replacement of human capital. At an earlier time, the Supreme Court indicated that it would not assume that Congress meant to tax life insurance proceeds, because of doubts about whether such proceeds would ordinarily be thought of as income,[358] but the Ninth Circuit rejected the theory that the Constitution prevented the taxation of death benefits paid out under a life insurance policy,[359] and since that time it has been generally accepted that the only restriction on taxing death benefits is based on legislative action. Interestingly, there is no legislative history in connection with the enactment of §101. Might it have been an "inside job" by the life insurance industry? If so, it has been well buried.

Another explanation of the exclusion for death benefits is that the premiums are treated like personal consumption expenditures as opposed to investment. The payor cannot deduct the premiums,[360] since they are paid in order to earn tax-free income, and there is no income if the taxpayer gets more than he had a right to expect actuarially. There is no deduction and no income if the taxpayer's beneficiaries benefit from the insured's early death. The reasoning can be expressed as a question: if a consumer buys a washing machine that provides benefits equal to 10 times its cost, we do not tax the machine's services, so why should we tax a good life insurance investment?[361] The trouble with the argument is that the death proceeds on a whole life policy in fact contain a return on investment in the form of the build-up in value of the invested funds. That is not true of pure "term" insurance, however.

Problem 4-20:

Colonel Neville Putney, aged 35, married and with two young children, buys $300,000 of life insurance in the form of three $100,000 face value policies. He is the owner (that is he can cancel them, change beneficiaries, and so forth) but he names his wife as primary beneficiary and his children as contingent beneficiaries, to receive the proceeds if his wife is not living at his death. The annual premium is $6,000 and a cash surrender value builds up each year, meaning Neville can borrow against the policy to the extent of the increased cash value, but the amount payable on his death will decline equally. At age 38, Neville is killed by a drunk driver and his wife receives the $300,000. He did not borrow against the cash surrender value.

1) What tax consequences to the wife under §101?

358 See United States v. Supplee-Biddle Hardware Co., 265 U.S. 189 (1924).

359 James F. Waters, Inc. v. Commissioner, 160 F2d 596 (9th Cir. 1947), Cert. denied 332 U.S. 767 (1947).

360 §264(a)(1).

361 See B. Bittker and L. Lokken, FEDERAL TAXATION OF INCOME, ESTATES AND GIFTS, ¶12.1.2 (2018).

2) Do you agree with this result as a matter of tax policy?

3) Assume that instead of $300,000 of coverage that he bought himself, his employer bought him $50,000 of group term life insurance that qualifies under §79. Can Neville's beneficiary still exclude the death proceeds?

4) If instead Neville bought a 5-year term policy for $20,000 and lived past the 5-year period, can he claim a loss on the now worthless purchase?

5) Denise is doing well as a lawyer, but recently she decided to take a job as Vice President and General Counsel of Swindler Enterprises, Inc. She holds a life insurance policy on her life with a face amount of $100,000. Annual premiums are $6,000. She transfers the policy to Swindler Enterprises, Inc. which names itself as beneficiary. Can Swindler Enterprises deduct the premium it paid to carry the policy? See §264.

6) She sells the policy to Stranger for $8,000 at a time when her basis in the contract is $5,000. If Denise dies, Stranger will receive $100,000. After Stranger paid five years worth of premiums, Denise dies and Stranger collects $100,000.

   a. What result to Denise on selling the policy?

   b. What result to Stranger on receiving the proceeds? See §101(a)(2).

   c. Instead, she transfers the policy to Swindler Enterprises, Inc., in exchange for stock in a transaction in which Swindler Enterprises takes a basis in the policy equal to Denise's basis in the policy and thereafter the corporation pays the premiums. She dies five years later. What result to Swindler Enterprises on receiving the death proceeds? See §101(a)(2)

Problem 4-21:

In your view, which has the more sophisticated approach to dealing with investment income and mortality gains and losses, the annuity rules or the insurance rules? Why?

Scan §121

The home has always occupied a special place in the heart of Congress. Taxpayers love their homes, and Congress is correspondingly wary of taxing the gains their constituents realize when they sell those homes.

Under new §121,[362] a married couple who file a joint return can permanently exclude from gross income up to $500,000 in gain from the sale or exchange of their principal residence. The figure is $250,000 for single taxpayers. There is no reinvestment requirement; this lets people get out of the real estate market completely, with nontaxable cash. Taxpayers can claim the §121 exclusion only once every two years.§121(b)(3). You might wonder what a principal residence is. The answer is found at Reg. §1.121-1(b)(1)&(2).

Under §121 the taxpayer must have owned and used the property as a principal residence for at least two out of the five years before the sale or exchange.[363] There is a hardship exception; if, because of health reasons, job relocation or some other major unforeseen event, the taxpayer does not fully meet the twoyearsoutoffive ownership and use tests, the exclusion is still is available for part of the gain, prorating the statutory exemption $500,000/$250,000 to the period of ownership.§121(c)(1).

To illustrate: In year one, the DeSotos (a married couple) buy a new home for $300,000. It is their first home. Eighteen months later they move to a different city to take new jobs and sell the new home for $380,000, for a gain of $80,000. The DeSotos failed the two-year test and prima facie cannot exclude the entire $80,000 gain under §121(a). However, under §121(c), they can exclude 18/24 (75 percent) x $500,000 (i.e., $375,000) because they moved for "hardship" and they owned and used the home as a principal residence 75 percent (18 months) of the necessary two years (24 months). The special rule means they can exclude the full $80,000 gain.

If business or investment property is obtained in § 1031 like-kind exchange and then converted to use as a principal residence, § 121 does not apply if the home is transferred within 5 years of the like-kind exchange. This test must be met along with the two-of-five-years requirement found in §121(a).

Gains realized by spouses, surviving spouses, and divorced persons can often be excluded even though they fail to personally meet the ownership and use requirement. 121(d)(3)(A) Beginning in 2019, a taxpayer can count the time that a former spouse used the home as a principal residence in her own 2 year calculation. Id.

362 Former §121 provided limited relief for people over age 55. It is gone.

363 If the taxpayers are filing jointly, only one need meet the ownership requirement. §121(b)(2)(A).

Observe how for the rich, the \$500,000/ two-year exclusion may invite selling the home once it approaches the \$500,000-of-gain threshold and buying another home -- surely an example of deadweight loss and a godsend to the real estate brokerage industry.

Problem 4-22:

Harold is a semi-retired businessman who made a lot of money in the advertising business in New York. In year 0 he married Edna and they lived in his expensive home on the south shore of Long Island. The house cost him \$400,000 and is now worth \$1 million. After living on Long Island for five years, Edna insisted on moving to New York City, so Harold and Edna bought a furnished condo in Manhattan, in year 6, moving there September 1, year 6, but returning to the Long Island house from Friday to Monday. Now Harold and Edna have decided to sell the Long Island house and use the proceeds of the sale to buy a house in Maine. It is now September 1 of year 8 and Harold and Edna want your advice. Since acquiring the New York City condominium, they have claimed the Long Island house as their residence when filing tax returns and claim a reduced local tax rate on the theory that it is their home. They vote in New York City, licensed their car in New York City, and rent their condo for about six weeks every summer to make some extra money. The market for the Long Island home is good, and they have rejected a few offers they consider too low. They hope to make a good profit on selling the Long Island home and are waiting for a good offer, but they have not listed it for sale. The market is good enough that one just has to put the word out that one's house is for sale and potential buyers tend to appear.

1) Can Harold and Edna sell the Long Island house and claim the §121 exclusion? If so, can they exclude the full gain?

2) How long do they have to sell the Long Island house?

R. TAXATION OF SOCIAL SECURITY BENEFITS

Scan §86

Social Security taxes have generally been presented to the public as amounts contributed to a national trust fund for each payor's retirement. If that is right, then one would think that Social Security checks that retirees receive would be nontaxable returns of the capital they had contributed (plus some accrued interest or earnings[364]). Section 86 in fact renders a large measure of such benefits taxable. The taxable portion rises with the taxpayer's prosperity. The

364 In fact, the amounts paid out to the Social Security retiree can very considerably exceed the amounts paid in.

details are intricate and likely not worth the trouble of examining in detail. The basic approach to taxing Social Security benefits is to group taxpayers into tax return filing categories, such as "married filing a joint return," on the basis of which they are assigned a dollar-denominated "base amount". If their "modified adjusted gross income" plus half their Social Security income exceeds their "base amount," then one-half of that excess creates exposure to income taxation of Social Security receipts; the taxable amount cannot exceed 85% of the taxpayer's Social Security receipts. Modified adjusted gross income consists of adjusted gross income (a term defined in §62) plus certain classes of nontaxable income, such as tax-exempt interest. These amounts are added back into gross income because they represent economic income that the taxpayer can use for his or her support. The base amounts are fairly low -- for example $34,000 in the case of a married couple filing jointly in 1994 and thereafter[365] -- so the chances of being nicked by §86 are good.

To illustrate: Mr. Labor is single and retired. He has modified adjusted gross income of $50,000 per year and he receives $10,000 in Social Security retirement benefits. Because Mr. Labor's modified A.G.I. plus half of his Social Security receipts together ($55,000) exceed his $34,000 base amount by $21,000, this year, he must include 85% of his $10,000 of Social Security benefits in gross income. This complicated formula yields a simple fact; he has an extra $8,500 of gross income.

Problem 4-23:

Former President Ronald Reagan was fond of saying that the taxation of Social Security benefits was a form of double taxation, once to earn the money that went into the Social Security trust fund, and then again when it was received after retirement. However, the employer paid half the amount contributed to the fund; if the payor was self-employed, she could deduct under §164(f) half of the amount she paid to the fund.

1) Does that make the former President wrong? Is there a double tax on Social Security?

2) How about the fact that there may also have been an income tax on the money that was subject to the Social Security tax?

3) Given that the Social Security trust fund runs close to "empty," is it time to stop having a separate Social Security tax and just put Social Security into the general federal budget, thereby reducing the tax disincentive for going to work?

---

365 1994 is a base year. The base amounts are not increased by inflation after 1994.

4) Should former workers be entitled to recover all their nondeductible Social Security contributions tax-free before they suffer any income tax on Social Security receipts?

S. DISCHARGE OF INDEBTEDNESS INCOME AND ITS AVOIDANCE FOR TAX PURPOSES

§61(a)(12) and §108(a)

1. Background

Borrowers often manage to escape their obligation to repay their debts. To take a simple example, you might borrow $100, and issue an IOU for that amount. You have no income when you borrow the money because the assumption is that you will pay the $100 back. If your creditor allowed you to repay a mere $80, and released you from the remaining $20 of the debt, your net worth has increased by $20 and by this point in the course you would surely sense that you have gross income of $20. If instead you bought back the IOU for $80 the next day, you would clearly also expect to have $20 of income.[366] Section 61(a)(12) confirms your intuition. The Code even dictates the same result if a close relative bought the debt from the creditor at that price. §108(e)(4)(A).

Congress has devised a number of important exceptions that allow cancellation of debt income to escape taxation, and those exceptions are the focus of what follows. Before proceeding, one needs to master the concepts of "net worth" and "net operating loss".

Net worth. When an individual goes to a bank to borrow money, the bank will look at two basic questions. One is whether the individual has a positive flow of cash that is sufficient to pay the debt service (principal plus interest) required by the loan, and the other is the extent to which the individual has a positive net worth. In making the appraisal of net worth, the bank will compare the value of the borrower's total assets against the total face amount of the borrower's liabilities. If the value of the assets exceeds the total liabilities, then the individual is said to have a positive net worth to that extent. In §108 of the Code, the term "solvency" is used to mean positive net worth.[367] You saw the net worth concept before in connection with the Haig-Simons definition of gross income.

Net operating loss. The excess of business expenses over business income produces a so-called net operating loss ("NOL"), which is defined in §172. The NOL first offsets income from

366 See United States v. Kirby Lumber Co., 284 U.S. 1 (1931).

367 Unfortunately, the term "insolvency" is confusing because it has two inconsistent meanings: (1) negative net worth (i.e., liabilities more than assets, called insolvency in the "equity sense") and (2) inability to pay debts as they fall due, called insolvency in the "bankruptcy sense."

other sources (such as investment income or wages). If the NOL for the year exceeds the taxpayer's other income for the year, she can elect to carry forward the NOL against income earned in future years. If there is still an NOL after completing that exercise, then what is left of the NOL is carried over again to the next year. The concept is that the NOL carryforward operates as a crude income-averaging device. The important thing to recognize is that unused NOLS are valuable assets in their own way. Sometimes they are the only real value or "asset" that a business corporation has after a brush with financial death.

To illustrate: If Optimist had gross receipts in her business of $100 and costs of $160, the result would be an NOL of $60. She can use the NOL against her other income. Assuming she had income from other sources of $15, she could offset all her income for the year, but that still leaves over $45. What does she do with that? The answer is that she must simply use that against income in future years.

Disputed debts. Recall the *Zarin* case from Chapter Two in which a compulsive gambler was held not to have cancellation of debt income upon payment of debt.

Discharge of a debt that lacked consideration. A common law exception does not treat the discharge of a debt as cancellation of indebtedness income if the debtor received nothing of value when the indebtedness was incurred.[368]

Spurious debt cancellation. You need to be able to separate debt cancellations which are taxable as such, from "spurious" debt cancellations, where the cancellation is just a medium for a different transaction. For example, if you ran a restaurant and you owed a customer $100 which you borrowed from him, you and the customer might agree that the customer would get back the $100 in the form of meals. That is not a debt cancellation; it is repayment of the debt in kind. Section 108 is not implicated, but the debtor will have to report the $100 worth of meals as income because the debt was paid for, however circuitously.

Amount realized distinguished. You also need to distinguish debt cancellation from the "amount realized" in connection with a property transfer of the type you saw in *Tufts* and *Crane.* The amount realized arises as a feature of a property transfer; debt cancellation is best viewed as an independent transaction with respect to a financial obligation.

To illustrate: Seller owns a building with a basis of $100, a gross value of perhaps $160 and subject to a nonrecourse debt of $100. Seller sells the property for $60. The $100 debt is part of her §1001 amount realized. If she abandons the property, her amount realized is $100 and her gain is $0, being the nonrecourse debt less her adjusted basis in the property. If the property's basis were only $40, *Tufts* dictates a $60 gain. If, at a time when the property was worth $40, the debt

368 *Commissioner v. Rail Joint Co.*, 61 F. 2d 751 (2d. Cir. 1932) and *Fashion Park, Inc. v. Commissioner*, 21 T.C. 600 (1954).

were a personal liability and the bank released her from the $60 balance of the debt, her cancellation of indebtedness income would be $60.

The creditor's side. The Regulations treat a material change in terms of a debt as a taxable exchange of the old debt for a new debt. So, for example, if a bank lent a debtor $100 and renegotiated the terms of the debt so that it was worth only $80, then the bank would report a $20 loss for Federal Income Tax purposes. Reg. §1.1001-3. Generally, lenders may be pleased with the result because it gives them a chance to report a tax loss on a debt that has already lost value, which the renegotiation may help establish.

2. Bankruptcy Tax Act of 1980

The following legislative history covers the high points of the 1980 reforms.[369]

Present Law

In General

Under present law, income is realized when indebtedness is forgiven or in other ways canceled (sec. 61(a)(12) of the Internal Revenue Code). For example, if a corporation has issued a $ 1,000 bond at par which it later repurchases for only $ 900, thereby increasing its net worth by $ 100, the corporation realizes $ 100 of income in the year of repurchase (United States v. Kirby Lumber Co., 284 U.S. 1 (1931)).

There are several exceptions to the general rule of income realization. Under a judicially developed "insolvency exception," no income arises from discharge of indebtedness if the debtor is insolvent both before and after the transaction; and if the transaction leaves the debtor with assets whose value exceeds remaining liabilities, income is realized only to the extent of the excess. . . . Further, cancellation of a previously accrued and deducted expense does not give rise to income if the deduction did not result in a reduction of tax (Code sec. 111). A debt cancellation which constitutes a gift or bequest is not treated as income to the donee debtor (Code sec. 102).

. . .

369 S. Rep. No. 96-1035, 96th Cong., 2nd Sess. (1980).

Reasons for Change

Overview

In P.L. 95598, Congress repealed provisions of the Bankruptcy Act governing Federal Income Tax treatment of debt discharge in bankruptcy, effective for cases instituted on or after October 1, 1979. The committee's bill provides tax rules in the Internal Revenue Code applicable to debt discharge in the case of bankrupt or insolvent debtors, and makes related changes to existing Code provisions applicable to debt discharge in the case of solvent debtors outside bankruptcy.

. . .

Explanation of Provisions

Debt Discharge in Bankruptcy

In General

Under the bill, no amount is to be included in income for Federal income tax purposes by reason of a discharge of indebtedness in a bankruptcy case. Instead, the amount of discharged debt which is excluded from gross income by virtue of the bill's provisions (the "debt discharge amount") is to be applied to reduce certain tax attributes.

Unless the taxpayer elects first to reduce basis in depreciable assets (or in real property held primarily for sale to customers in the ordinary course of a trade or business), the debt discharge amount is applied to reduce the taxpayer's tax attributes in the following order:

1) Net operating losses and carryovers;

2) Carryovers of the investment tax credit (other than the ESOP credit), the WIN credit, the new jobs credit, and the credit for alcohol used as a fuel;

3) Capital losses and carryovers;

4) The basis of the taxpayer's assets (both depreciable and nondepreciable); and

5) Carryovers of the foreign tax credit.

. . .

After reduction of the attributes specified in categories (1), (2), and (3) above, any remaining debt discharge amount is applied to reduce asset basis, but not below the amount of the taxpayer's remaining undischarged liabilities. (Thus, a sale of all the taxpayer's assets immediately after the discharge generally will not result in income tax liability unless the sale proceeds and cash on hand exceed the amount needed to pay off the remaining liabilities.) Any amount of debt discharge which remains after such reduction in asset basis, including any debt discharge amount which remains unapplied solely by virtue of the limitation just described with respect to undischarged liabilities, is applied to reduce carryovers of the foreign tax credit.

Any amount of debt discharge which is left after attribute reduction under these rules is disregarded, i.e., does not result in income or have other tax consequences.

. ..

Debt Discharge Outside Bankruptcy - Insolvent Debtors

The bill provides that if a discharge of indebtedness occurs when the taxpayer is insolvent (but is not in a bankruptcy case), the amount of debt discharge is excluded from gross income up to the amount by which the taxpayer is insolvent. The excluded amount is applied to reduce tax attributes in the same manner as if the discharge had occurred in a bankruptcy case. Any balance of the debt discharged which is not excluded from gross income (because it exceeds the insolvency amount) is treated in the same manner as debt cancellation in the case of a wholly solvent taxpayer.

. . .

Certain Reductions as Purchase Price Adjustments [§108(e)(5)]

The bill provides that if the seller of specific property reduces the debt of the purchaser which arose out of the purchase, and the reduction to the purchaser does not occur in a bankruptcy case or when the purchaser is insolvent, then the reduction to the purchaser of the purchasemoney is to be treated (for both the seller and the buyer) as a purchase price adjustment on that property. This rule applies only if but for this provision the amount of the reduction would be treated as income from discharge of indebtedness.

This provision is intended to eliminate disagreements between the Internal Revenue Service and the debtor as to whether, in a particular case to which the provision applies, the debt reduction should be treated as discharge income or a true price adjustment. If the debt has been transferred by the seller to a third party whether or not related to the seller), or if the property has been transferred by the buyer to a third party (whether or not related to the buyer), this provision does not apply to determine whether a reduction in the amount of purchase money debt should be treated as discharge income or a true price adjustment. Also, this provision does not apply where the debt is reduced because of factors not involving direct agreements between the buyer and the seller, such as the running of the statute of limitations on enforcement of the obligation.

. . .

Debt Acquired by Related Party

The bill provides that, for purposes of determining income of the debtor from discharge of indebtedness, an outstanding debt acquired from an unrelated party by a party related to the debtor is treated as having been acquired by the debtor to the extent provided in regulations issued by the Treasury Department.

For purposes of this rule, a person is treated as related to the debtor if the person is (1) a member of a controlled group of corporations; (2) a trade or business treated as under common control with respect to the debtor; (3) either a partner in a partnership treated as controlled by the debtor or a controlled partnership with respect to the debtor; or (4) a member of the debtor's family or other person bearing a relationship to the debtor specified in Code section 267(b). The definition of "family" for this purpose also includes a spouse of the debtor's child or grandchild.

. . .

3. The Mechanics of §108

First, let's look at the insolvency exclusion, which assures an exemption from taxation to the extent the taxpayer was not rendered solvent by the discharge of a debt. "Solvency" in the context of §108 means having assets that are worth at least the face amount of the taxpayer's debts, measured immediately before the discharge occurs. §108(d)(3). For example, if one's debts were $120 and one's assets were worth $130, one would be solvent to the extent of $10. Section 108 appears to include all of the taxpayer's assets (including assets exempt under the Bankruptcy Code). However, most practitioners exclude these so-called exempt assets, relying on older authority that was not explicitly codified in §108.[370] The exemptions can include such major assets as pension monies.[371] Because the Supreme Court treats discharge of, or relief from, a nonrecourse debt as part of amount realized, there is no doubt that one includes nonrecourse debts when measuring one's liabilities.[372] However, it is illogical to include debt which is secured by an exempt asset, so such debt does not count when computing solvency.

Reduction of tax attributes lies at the heart of §108. The terminology here is strange and deserves an introduction. Every taxpayer has "tax attributes," such as property having some

---

370 See, e.g., Cole v. Commissioner, 42 B.T.A. 1110 (1940) (non acq.).

371 SeePatterson v Shumate, 504 U.S. 753 (1992).

372 See generally §108(d)(1).

basis or other, or a net operating loss from a business, or a tax credit that will be claimed on a tax return. As you read above, in exchange for not taxing gross income from discharges in bankruptcy or insolvency, the excluded amount must generally be applied to reduce certain specified tax attributes.[373] Where the bankruptcy and insolvency rules overlap, the bankruptcy rules take precedence.[374] The term *bankruptcy* is limited to a proceeding under (U.S.C.) Title 11 and does not include proceedings such as foreclosure, receivership, and the like in federal or state courts.[375] A taxpayer need not be insolvent in order to go into bankruptcy and enjoy the benefits of §108. There are those who believe that many financially troubled taxpayers file bankruptcy primarily for tax reasons.

As the legislative history points out, there is a steep price to be paid for using the umbrella of §108; the taxpayer must surrender "tax attributes" as a sort of tribute paid to the Treasury, in an amount equal to the income that §108 excluded. As you saw in the legislative history, the taxpayer must reduce the following attributes in the following prescribed order. It differs slightly from what you saw in the legislative history because the Code has since been amended:

1. Net operating losses and carryovers; then
2. Carryovers of general business credits; then
3. Minimum tax credits; then
4. Capital loss carryovers; then,
5. The basis of debtor's assets (both depreciable and nondepreciable); then
6. Carryovers of the passive activity losses and credits; then finally
7. Foreign and Possessions Tax Credits.

The taxpayer has one important option; §108(b)(5) lets him elect to reduce his basis in property first, leap-frogging the attributes listed before it. From the taxpayer's point of view, net operating losses are generally better than depreciation deductions from a timing point of view, because they are available in full at once, whereas depreciation deductions flow to the taxpayer more slowly. Depreciation deductions are dealt with in detail later in the book.

373 §108(b).

374 §108(a)(2)(A).

375 §108(d)(2).

The upshot is that §108(a) generally *defers* but does not *eliminate* discharge of indebtedness income and in general bankruptcy is better for taxpayers. This is because the insolvency exclusion is limited to the amount of predischarge insolvency, whereas the bankruptcy exemption is indifferent to the extent, if any, to which the taxpayer was insolvent before the discharge.[376] Whether the bankruptcy or insolvency exception applies, if the taxpayer runs out of tax attributes, there is no punishment. The cancellation of debt income is still forgiven permanently.

One computes the taxpayer's income for the year before one computes attribute reduction.[377] This can be disadvantageous, because if there is income for the year (independent of cancellation of debt income), it first reduces net operating losses carried forward from prior years. Once one has computed taxable income for the year (aside from cancellation of debt income), one then determines the amount of the exclusion, and then reduces tax attributes to the extent there are any.

> **To illustrate:** Harry Hapless has a $100 discharge in bankruptcy and a NOL carryover from a prior year of $75, and taxable income (ignoring the NOL and the discharge of debt) of $50. Hapless must first reduce the NOL carryover from $75 to $25 (which becomes the revised NOL carryover). The full $100 is excluded from gross income under §108(a)(1)(A). Unless he elects to reduce basis first, he must reduce the $25 NOL carryover to $0, then reduce other tax attributes (if any) in the prescribed order.

Again, most taxpayers like Mr. Hapless want to preserve NOLs rather than basis in depreciable property, because they expect to make money in the future, and the NOLs can offset future income at once, whereas depreciation is only available over time. In such a case the taxpayer will elect §108(b)(5).

Impact on the creditor

The lender will normally have a bad debt deduction when the loan goes sour. Bad debt deductions are covered in a later chapter.

Problem 4-24:

Dan Debtor has non-exempt assets with a gross fair market value of $500,000 (all in cash) and a single debt of $610,000. He has a current net operating loss (NOL) of $50,000. None of the assets is exempt from creditors under the bankruptcy laws. He is not in bankruptcy. As a result of negotiations with the creditor, the creditor forgives the entire debt for $490,000 in cash.

376 §108(a)(3).

377 §108(b)(4)(A).

1) How much cancellation of indebtedness income does Dan have?

2) Must Dan reduce the NOL as a result of "(1)"?

3) What would be the difference if Dan had no cash or other assets?

4) Same as "(1)". Would there be any difference in result if the same debt were discharged in bankruptcy?

5) Same as "(1)," but Dan's pre-discharge assets were worth $700,000. Now does it matter if the discharge is in bankruptcy, compared to not being in bankruptcy?

6) What if the creditor got exasperated and canceled the entire $610,000 for free?

7) Dan's creditor, Ivana Tinkle, died recently. In her will, Ivana directed her executor not to press her claim against Dan, who still owes her $9,000 from many years ago. Because the executor stayed his hand, the statute of limitations against Dan expired on the $9,000 claim. Does Dan have gross income as a result of the directive in the will?

8) Assuming Dan lives in a state where a debtor's personal residence is exempt from creditors and that he has time to plan his debt readjustment, would you recommend that:

   a. Dan's mother buys one of his debts from a bank; the loan has a balance of $5,000, but his mother is pretty sure she can talk the bank into selling it to her for $4,500? See §108(e)(4)(B) especially.

   b. Dan shifts his wealth into assets that are exempt from the reach of creditors?

9) After all these terrible events, the IRS audited Dan and found him liable for $10,000 in unpaid past taxes. He failed to respond to the 90 day letter he got, and it is now a year later. Dan is in the collection division, where, with your help he has gotten the division to reduce his tax liability by $4,000. Is that $4,000 taxable to Dan?

Problem 4-25:

The Friendly Appliance Company recently sold Mr. Charlie Consumer a 92inch diameter television set for use in his basement. The price was $6,999. He still owes $5,000 under the store's "layaway plan". The Friendly Appliance Company recently realized that they charged him more than they might have, so when he returned a few weeks later to object to the price, they agreed to reduce the price by $1,000. The reason was to retain him as a customer and to prevent him from spreading the word that Friendly Appliance was a rip-off establishment.

1) Does Charlie have gross income, or does he perhaps just have a "lemon" on his hands?

2) Assuming Charlie bought the TV set for use in his business so that the interest charges on the layaway plan were deductible, would the store's decision to free him from a part of his interest obligation be nontaxable? See §108(e)(2).

3) If the appliance company sold the debt to a bank, and the bank agreed to the purchase price adjustment in "(1)," would the result be any different? See §108(e)(5).

T. CAPITALIZATION OF TAX BENEFITS

Tax benefits or burdens can find their way into prices. For example, a tax-exempt bond commands a higher price than a taxable one, all other things being equal. The table on page ___ gives concrete illustrations. For example, if the tax exemption in §103 were repealed, the value of tax-exempt bonds might collapse. Congress tends to anticipate these collapses and buffer the shock with such measures as "grandfather" rules and phase-ins. Even changes in tax rates can influence the value of property. For example, if top tax rates rose, the after-tax value of municipal bonds would also rise.

Problem 4-26:

Let us assume that Congress changes the law and taxes the value of occupying one's own home. Clearly, this will have an adverse impact on the value of owner-occupied housing. It is not hard to think of hardship cases. For example, imagine a retired person who lives on a small pension in her own home. If she is taxed on the value of occupying the home, she will have to enter the marketplace to raise the cash to pay the tax. Is it reasonable to force such a person into the marketplace, or is it, in the popular mind at least, an unreasonable incursion on personal liberty?

So, should taxpayers be entitled to a deduction for the loss in value as a result of withdrawing the exemptions for imputed income, without the need to sell the home? At least one economist thinks they should.[378]

1) Does anyone really rely on the stability of the tax laws? Should they? Wouldn't such a rule stymie tax legislation?

2) Assuming there was a consensus that people should be compensated for this type of loss, does that mean that if a change in the law showered a taxpayer with gold, (say by driving up the value of municipal bonds he owns) that he should be taxed immediately on the windfall?

U. ADVANCED APPLICATIONS

The Internal Revenue Code has an array of other forms of tax-free income. Here is a partial list of some others not covered in this Chapter. They are beyond the scope of the course.

a) Reimbursements of moving expenses. §82

b) Combat zone payment to members of the armed forces. §112.

c) Income earned by States and lesser subdivisions. §115.

d) Contributions to the capital of a corporation, §118.

e) Certain retirement pay for members of the armed forces. §122.

f) Exemption for reimbursed costs of victims of casualties. §123. Only amounts in excess of normal living expenses can be excluded, which prevents an exclusion for payments that cover normal personal consumption.

g) Certain cost sharing payments, §126.

h) Certain foster care payments, §131.

378 See Feldstein, Compensation in Tax Reform, 29 Nat'l Tax J. 123 (1976); Feldstein, Martin, On the Theory of Tax Reform, Harvard University, Institute of Economic Research (1975).

i) Certain military benefits, §134.

j) Energy conservation subsidies provided to customers for purchase or installation of energy conservation measures. §136.

k) Adoption assistance programs, §137.

l) Disaster relief payments, §139.

m) An exclusion of some income earned overseas, based on the need for international competitiveness. §911. The maximum exclusion in the year 2018 was $103,900, and it gradually rises in years after. There is also an associated exclusion for certain foreign housing costs. §911(c), Rev. Proc. 2018-18.

n) Political funds are not taxed to the candidate if used for expenses of the campaign, but are taxed if the politician diverts such funds for his own personal use. Compare Rev. Proc. 6819, 19681 C.B. 810 with Rev. Rul. 71449, 19712 C.B. 77.

CHAPTER 5 - BUSINESS AND PROFIT-SEEKING DEDUCTIONS AND CREDITS

A. INTRODUCTION

So far you have been looking at what goes into the Federal Income Tax base of an individual. This has included a review of the concept of gross income, a study of items that are explicitly excluded from gross income and a survey of items that are partially included and partially excluded. Now you are going to look at specific costs and expenditures that a taxpayer can subtract from gross income to bring down his or her tax base, and as a result bring down his or her tax bill at the end of the year.

These subject merges uncomfortably with Constitutional considerations. The Sixteenth Amendment permits a tax on *income*, but it fails to distinguish between gross income and net income. We have already concluded that the taxation of capital or a "return of capital" is presumptively impermissible under the Constitution, but the question of what can be subtracted in determining the tax base is not so clear. Costs of producing income must be allowed as deductions if the law is to tax only "gain" or "profit." Most such costs are allowed as deductions, under §§ 162, 212 and 168 and elsewhere. In contrast, the general perspective is that every other expenditure is presumptively a cost of personal consumption, and it is classified -- at least mentally -- under §262. This approach tends to lead to a sloppy cliché that tax deductions are a matter of "legislative grace" and that the taxpayer has to scramble to prove Congress intended to allow any particular deduction. This judicial attitude is pervasive.

Although business and nonbusiness deductions are spread out in the Code, they converge neatly in §§62 and 63. At this point, set aside the text and scan the following Code provisions: §61 (which defines "Gross Income"); then §62 (which defines an interim tax base peculiar to individuals known as "Adjusted Gross Income"); and then §63 (which defines "Taxable Income"). Now if you jump to §1 you will see that the federal tax rates are imposed on "Taxable Income," the product of §63.

You will come to see that §62 provides a list of expenditures that have the magical quality of being deductible *per se*. They are said to be deductible "above the line," the line being "Adjusted Gross Income" on Form 1040, the annual Federal Income Tax return for individuals. They appear at the bottom of the facing page of Form 1040. By contrast, the deductions alluded to in §63 -- which are in fact drawn in from all over the Code -- are not *per se* available, because they face various thresholds and ceilings.

Take a look at the top of the second page of Form 1040 where you can detect their presence. Clearly, it is a strong theme in Congress that business-related deductions are necessary and good deductions, but that most non-business deductions are suspect. To put it another way, most business expense deductions are favored in that they are used as adjustments to gross income under §62, as opposed to being (flimsy) "Itemized Deductions." In general, Congress has enacted an ever-growing list of choke points on itemized tax deductions, some of which are highly technical in nature and generally arise more out of revenue needs than out of tax policy considerations.

This chapter partly focuses on deductions that arise in a trade or business, and hence are deductible under §162. In fact, many of the same deductions, such as for legal expenses or bank service charges, are also available under §212 to profit-seeking investors and others who pay them as a cost of producing income, even though the taxpayers are not technically "engaged in a trade or business" as that phrase is defined and used in §162. Therefore, they are also covered in this Chapter. In terms of tax forms, individuals' business expense deductions appear on Schedule C to Form 1040. Depreciation expenses are summarized on Schedule C, and are further detailed on yet other Federal Tax Form. The ultimate number -- income or loss from the business -- flows through as a positive or negative net income figure on the facing page of the Form 1040. A glance at Schedule C will make the rest of what is to come less intimidating. Each business' income or loss is computed separately, with the result that each generates a separate Schedule C.

Section 162 is the most important of all business tax deductions. It has to be parsed carefully, piece-by-piece. It is now time to begin that process.

B. WHAT ARE DEDUCTIBLE BUSINESS EXPENSES OR EXPENSES ARISING IN PROFIT-SEEKING ACTIVITIES?

Read §162(a) and §262

1. Introduction

Among the following cases are some involving a taxpayer's attempt to deduct an expense or other cost that was eventually denied by the courts, despite the existence of a relationship between the expense and the trade, business, or other profit-seeking activity. The important task is not to understand the detailed law in each subject matter area involved, but to pursue an understanding of which economic policy, or internal logic or tax law imperative led the court in each case to deny the deduction. The implication of denying the deduction is that the expenditure is treated as personal consumption. One of the deep themes of the tax law is that personal consumption should be paid for with after-tax money.

C. CLOTHING AND PERSONAL GROOMING

Arguably, an actor who gets an especially elegant haircut should be able to deduct the cost of the extra amount he paid over the cost of a normal haircut. Likewise, a lawyer who buys a bottle of Lavoris to conceal his halitosis might claim it was an ordinary and necessary expense of gaining and keeping clients. Taxpayers have fared poorly with these kinds of arguments. The following excerpt is from *Drake v. Commissioner*[379], a case in which an enlisted man in the military sought to deduct the cost of his mandatory haircuts and of cleaning his fatigue uniform. He won on the fatigues, but his claim to deductions for his haircuts fell on deaf ears:

> Expenses for personal grooming are inherently personal in nature; e.g., in *Sparkman v. Commissioner*... the cost of dentures used to aid an actor's enunciation was not deductible, and in *Paul Bakewell, Jr.*, ... the cost of a hearing aid used by a lawyer both in his trade or business and for personal purposes was not deductible as a business expense. The fact that the Army may have required such grooming does not make the expenses therefor any less personal. The evidence showed that the Army's requirement was directed toward the maintenance by the petitioner of a high standard of personal appearance and not toward the accomplishment of the duties of his employment. In setting standards for personal grooming, the Army is not unique. Many employers, expressly or otherwise, establish standards to which their employees are expected to conform. Men are to be clean shaven and are often required to wear suits, ties, and clean shirts, and women are expected to be dressed attractively. To conform to these requirements, employees must make expenditures which would not be required if they were at home or not on the job. Nevertheless, such expenditures for general personal grooming are inherently personal in nature and cannot be considered as business expenses.[380]

In considering the following case, look for the court's attempt to draw a line between expenses that are deductible costs of producing income and nondeductible expenses that are costs of living (or "living it up"); if one could deduct personal consumption the income tax would be a tax on saved income (i.e., savings).

---

379 52 TC 842 (1969), acq.

380 Id at 844.

PEVSNER v. COMMISSIONER OF INTERNAL REVENUE

628 F.2d 467 (5th Cir. 1980)

Johnson, J.

OPINION

This is an appeal by the Commissioner of Internal Revenue from a decision of the United States Tax Court. The Tax Court upheld taxpayer's business expense deduction for clothing expenditures in the amount of $ 1,621.91 for the taxable year 1975. We reverse.

Since June 1973 Sandra J. Pevsner, taxpayer, has been employed as the manager of the Sakowitz Yves St. Laurent Rive Gauche Boutique located in Dallas, Texas. The boutique sells only women's clothes and accessories designed by Yves St. Laurent (YSL), one of the leading designers of women's apparel. Although the clothing is ready to wear, it is highly fashionable and expensively priced. Some customers of the boutique purchase and wear the YSL apparel for their daily activities and spend as much as $ 20,000 per year for such apparel.

As manager of the boutique, the taxpayer is expected by her employer to wear YSL clothes while at work. In her appearance, she is expected to project the image of an exclusive lifestyle and to demonstrate to her customers that she is aware of the YSL current fashion trends as well as trends generally. Because the boutique sells YSL clothes exclusively, taxpayer must be able, when a customer compliments her on her clothes, to say that they are designed by YSL. In addition to wearing YSL apparel while at the boutique, she wears them while commuting to and from work, to fashion shows sponsored by the boutique, and to business luncheons at which she represents the boutique. During 1975, the taxpayer bought, at an employee's discount, the following items: four blouses, three skirts, one pair of slacks, one trench coat, two sweaters, one jacket, one tunic, five scarves, six belts, two pairs of shoes and four necklaces. The total cost of this apparel was $ 1,381.91. In addition, the sum of $ 240 was expended for maintenance of these items.

Although the clothing and accessories purchased by the taxpayer were the type used for general purposes by the regular customers of the boutique, the taxpayer is not a normal purchaser of these clothes. The taxpayer and her husband, who is partially disabled because of a severe heart attack suffered in 1971, lead a simple life and their social activities are very limited and informal. Although taxpayer's employer has no objection to her wearing the apparel away from work, taxpayer stated that she did not wear the clothes during offwork hours because she felt that they were too expensive for her simple everyday lifestyle. Another reason why she did not wear the YSL clothes apart from work was to make them last longer. Taxpayer did admit at trial, however, that a number of the articles were things she could have worn off the job and in which she would have looked "nice."

On her joint federal income tax return for 1975, taxpayer deducted $ 990 as an ordinary and necessary business expense with respect to her purchase of the YSL clothing and accessories. However, in the Tax Court, taxpayer claimed a deduction for the full $ 1381.91 cost of the apparel and for the $ 240 cost of maintaining the apparel. The Tax Court allowed the taxpayer to deduct both expenses in the total amount of $ 1621.91. The Tax Court reasoned that the apparel was not suitable to the private lifestyle maintained by the taxpayer. This appeal by the Commissioner followed.

The principal issue on appeal is whether the taxpayer is entitled to deduct as an ordinary and necessary business expense the cost of purchasing and maintaining the YSL clothes and accessories worn by the taxpayer in her employment as the manager of the boutique. This determination requires an examination of the relationship between Section 162(a) of the Internal Revenue Code of 1954, which allows a deduction for ordinary and necessary expenses incurred in the conduct of a trade or business, and Section 262 of the Code, which bars a deduction for all "personal, living, or family expenses." Although many expenses are helpful or essential to one's business activities such as commuting expenses and the cost of meals while at work these expenditures are considered inherently personal and are disallowed under Section 262. . . .

The generally accepted rule governing the deductibility of clothing expenses is that the cost of clothing is deductible as a business expense only if: (1) the clothing is of a type specifically required as a condition of employment, (2) it is not adaptable to general usage as ordinary clothing, and (3) it is not so worn. Donnelly v. Commissioner, 262 F.2d 411, 412 (2d Cir. 1959).[381]

In the present case, the Commissioner stipulated that the taxpayer was required by her employer to wear YSL clothing and that she did not wear such apparel apart from work. The Commissioner maintained, however, that a deduction should be denied because the YSL clothes and accessories purchased by the taxpayer were adaptable for general usage as ordinary clothing and she was not prohibited from using them as such. The Tax Court, in rejecting the Commissioner's argument for the application of an objective test, recognized that the test for deductibility was whether the clothing was "suitable for general or personal wear" but determined that the matter of suitability was to be judged subjectively, in light of the taxpayer's lifestyle. Although the court recognized that the YSL apparel "might be used by some members of society for general purposes," it felt that because the "wearing of YSL apparel outside work would be inconsistent with . . . (taxpayer's) lifestyle," sufficient reason was shown for allowing a deduction for the clothing expenditures.

In reaching its decision, the Tax Court relied heavily upon Yeomans v. Commissioner, 30 T.C. 757 (1958). In Yeomans, the taxpayer was employed as fashion coordinator for a shoe manufacturing company. Her employment necessitated her attendance at meetings of fashion experts

381 When the taxpayer is prohibited from wearing the clothing away from work a deduction is normally allowed. See Harsaghy v. Commissioner, 2 T.C. 484 (1943). However, in the present case no such restriction was placed upon the taxpayer's use of the clothing. [Footnote No. 3 in original.]

and at fashion shows sponsored by her employer. On these occasions, she was expected to wear clothing that was new, highly styled, and such as "might be sought after and worn for personal use by women who make it a practice to dress according to the most advanced or extreme fashions." 30 T.C. at 768. However, for her personal wear, Ms. Yeomans preferred a plainer and more conservative style of dress. As a consequence, some of the items she purchased were not suitable for her private and personal wear and were not so worn. The Tax Court allowed a deduction for the cost of the items that were not suitable for her personal wear. Although the basis for the decision in Yeomans is not clearly stated, the Tax Court in the case sub judice determined that

> (a) careful reading of Yeomans shows that, without a doubt, the Court based its decision on a determination of Ms. Yeomans' lifestyle and that the clothes were not suitable for her use in such lifestyle. Furthermore, the Court recognized that the clothes Ms. Yeomans purchased were suitable for wear by women who customarily wore such highly styled apparel, but such fact did not cause the court to decide the issue against her. Thus, Yeomans clearly decides the issue before us in favor of the petitioner.

Notwithstanding the Tax Court's decision in Yeomans, the Circuits that have addressed the issue have taken an objective, rather than subjective, approach. Stiner v. United States, 524 F.2d 640, 641 (10th Cir. 1975); Donnelly v. Commissioner, 262 F.2d 411, 412 (2d Cir. 1959). An objective approach was also taken by the Tax Court in Drill v. Commissioner, 8 T.C. 902 (1947). Under an objective test, no reference is made to the individual taxpayer's lifestyle or personal taste. Instead, adaptability for personal or general use depends upon what is generally accepted for ordinary street wear.

The principal argument in support of an objective test is, of course, administrative necessity. The Commissioner argues that, as a practical matter, it is virtually impossible to determine at what point either price or style makes clothing inconsistent with or inappropriate to a taxpayer's lifestyle. Moreover, the Commissioner argues that the price one pays and the styles one selects are inherently personal choices governed by taste, fashion, and other unmeasurable values. Indeed, the Tax Court has rejected the argument that a taxpayer's personal taste can dictate whether clothing is appropriate for general use. See Drill v. Commissioner, 8 T.C. 902 (1947). An objective test, although not perfect, provides a practical administrative approach that allows a taxpayer or revenue agent to look only to objective facts in determining whether clothing required as a condition of employment is adaptable to general use as ordinary street wear. Conversely, the Tax Court's reliance on subjective factors provides no concrete guidelines in determining the deductibility of clothing purchased as a condition of employment.

In addition to achieving a practical administrative result, an objective test also tends to promote substantial fairness among the greatest number of taxpayers. As the Commissioner suggests, it apparently would be the Tax Court's position that two similarly situated YSL boutique managers with identical wardrobes would be subject to disparate tax consequences depending upon the particular manager's lifestyle and "socioeconomic level." This result, however, is not consonant with a reasonable interpretation of Sections 162 and 262.

For the reasons stated above, the decision of the Tax Court upholding the deduction for taxpayer's purchase of YSL clothing is reversed. Consequently, the portion of the Tax Court's decision upholding the deduction for maintenance costs for the clothing is also

REVERSED.

Problem 5-1:

1) Vincent Pugugli, a former boxer, has taken a job as a clown. Can he deduct the cost of the clown suit?

2) He quit. Now he works as a bartender at The Fishnet Café where he enjoys conversing with the clientele. His employer requires him to wear a tuxedo, which he would not be caught dead in on the street. Can he deduct the cost of the tuxedo?[382]

3) What if he in fact uses the tuxedo around town as regular garb?

4) How about "scrubs" worn around town by a physician?

D. CHILD-CARE EXPENSES

This old fossil of a case involved a mother who took a job outside the home, incurring various child care expenses. She met with a hostile reception. How would you have decided this case if you were Judge Opper?

SMITH v. COMMISSIONER

40 B.T.A. 1038 (1939), aff'd without opinion, 113 F.2d 114

OPPER, J.

[The Commissioner] determined a deficiency . . . in petitioners' 1937 income tax. This was due to the disallowance of a deduction claimed by petitioners, who are husband and wife, for

382 We are indebted to Professors Gunn and Ward for inspiring this question from their casebook, FEDERAL INCOME TAXATION (4th Ed.).

sums spent by the wife in employing nursemaids to care for petitioners' young child, the wife, as well as the husband, being employed. . . .

Petitioners would have us apply the "but for" test. They propose that but for the nurses, the wife could not leave her child; but for the freedom so secured, she could not pursue her gainful labors, and but for them, there would be no income and no tax. This thought evokes an array of interesting possibilities. The fee to the doctor, but for whose healing service, the earner of the family income could not leave his sickbed; the cost of the laborer's raiment, for how can the world proceed about its business unclothed; the very home which gives us shelter and rest and the food which provides energy, might all by an extension of the same proposition be construed as necessary to the operation of business and to the creation of income. Yet these are the very essence of those "personal" expenses the deductibility of which is expressly denied. [§262.]

We are told that the working wife is a new phenomenon. This is relied on to account for the apparent inconsistency that the expenses in issue are now a commonplace, yet have not been the subject of legislation, ruling, or adjudicated controversy. But if that is true, it becomes all the more necessary to apply accepted principles to the novel facts. We are not prepared to say that the care of children, like similar aspects of family and household life, is other than a personal concern. The wife's services as custodian of the home and protector of its children are ordinarily rendered without monetary compensation. There results no taxable income from the performance of this service and the correlative expenditure is personal and not susceptible of deduction. . . . Here the wife has chosen to employ others to discharge her domestic function and the services she performs are rendered outside the home. They are a source of actual income and taxable as such. But that does not deprive the same work performed by others of its personal character . . . .

We are not unmindful that, as petitioners suggest, certain disbursements normally personal may become deductible by reason of their intimate connection with an occupation carried on for profit. In this category fall entertainment, . . . traveling expenses,. . . and the cost of an actor's wardrobe . . . . The line is not always an easy on to draw nor the test simple to apply. But we think its principle is clear. It may for practical purposes be said to constitute a distinction between those activities which, as a matter of common acceptance and universal experience, are "ordinary" or usual as the direct accompaniment of business pursuits, on the one hand; and those which, though they may in some indirect and tenuous degree relate to the circumstances of a profitable occupation, are nevertheless personal in their nature, of a character applicable to human beings generally, and which exist on that plane regardless of the occupation, though not necessarily of the station in life, of the individuals concerned. . . .

In the latter category, we think fall payments made to servants or others occupied in looking to the personal wants of their employers. . . . And we include in this group, nursemaids retained to care for infant children.

Decision will be entered for the respondent.

Notes and Questions on Child Care Expenses

Exactly why were the expenses in *Smith* not deductible? Answer in terms of policy as well as in terms of statutory language. Since the time of the *Smith* decision Congress has added a number of provisions to try to let working parents combine their roles with less "frictional" cost. The key provisions are §24, which provides a $2000 nonrefundable Child Tax Credit for qualifying-child dependents with an additional $500 credit for non-qualifying-child dependents.383 For tax years 2018 to 2025 the credit is refundable to the extent of 15% of the taxpayer's earned income in excess of $2,500. The refundable portion cannot exceed an inflation-adjusted amount ($1,400 for 2018 and 2019). In addition, §21 provides a 20% credit (sometimes rising to 35%) against "employment-related expenses" for household services and the care of "qualifying individuals." The credit is limited to $3,000 of expenses if the taxpayer's household includes only one qualifying individual or $6,000 if it includes two or more, is not refundable, and cannot be carried forward. The $3,000 and $6,000 caps are further reduced if the taxpayer receives excluded income from an employer sponsored dependent care assistance program under §129.

E. WHAT IS A "TRADE OR BUSINESS?"

Curiously, the Code and Regulations do not contain a definition of this central term[384]. The crucial features of a trade or business are activities that are regularly and continuously undertaken for a bona-fide profit (even if unreasonable, such as trying to invent an anti-gravity machine), other than the activities of an investor trading in securities. The activities can be for only part of the year, as in the case of a ski instructor. The Code expressly includes performance of the functions of a public office as a trade or business.[385]

There is a refined difference between a "trade" and a "business," although the concepts have become merged in the minds of tax experts. The term "trade" implies skilled employment and specialization, such as that of a lawyer, doctor or cobbler. By contrast, a "business" implies a non-professional or non-artisanal activity such as selling merchandise. The informal antonym to a "trade or business" is an "investment". In general, most tax people would tell you that the taxpayer must interact with the public in order to be engaged in a trade or business, but a relatively recent Supreme Court case holding that a full-time race track gambler was in a trade or business

383 The $2,000 credit applies for tax years 2017 through 2025. Pub. L. No. 115-97, § 11022, 131 Stat. 2195 (2017). The $500 credit is limited to the tax years 2018 through 2025. §24(h)(4)(A).

384 See Orbach & White, *How To Establish Existence Of a Trade or Business In Light of Recent Conflicting Decisions,* 13 Tax For Lawyers 38 (July-August 1984).

385 §7701(a)(26).

has thrown the general requirement that one deal with the public into serious doubt.[386] A more graphic example of someone engaged in business was supplied by a taxpayer who characterized himself as an "unemployed part-time salesman," but was in fact engaged in street-hustling, panhandling, pimping, and gambling. The IRS wanted his Social Security Self-Employment Taxes.[387] The case provided a synopsis of what it means to be engaged in a trade or business for Social Security Tax purposes, which is the same as for Federal Income Tax purposes:

> To be engaged in a trade or business within the meaning of section 1402(a), an individual must be involved in an activity with continuity and regularity, and the primary purpose for engaging in the activity must be for income or profit. Commissioner v. Groetzinger, 480 U.S. 23, 35 (1987). A sporadic activity, a hobby, or an amusement diversion does not qualify. Commissioner v. Groetzinger, supra at 35. Whether an individual is carrying on a trade or business requires an examination of the facts involved in each case. Higgins v. Commissioner, 312 U.S. 212, 217 (1941).
>
> . . .
>
> . . .
>
> After a review of the record, we find that petitioner was engaged in the trade or business of streethustling during the years in issue. Petitioner was engaged in streethustling with continuity and regularity, and with the primary objective of earning an income or profit. Further, petitioner's activities were regular, frequent, and substantial. They were not sporadic, nor do we believe that they were a hobby or an amusement diversion of petitioner.[388]

To be engaged in a trade or business, a person need not own the business or be self-employed; an employee is viewed as engaged in a trade or business of whatever the occupation involves—rendering,janitorial, farming or legal services, for example.[389] But that still leaves open the question of which, if any, of an employee's expenses, related to his employment and the production of income, can be deducted. Remember *Pevsner*, above. The distinction between a peaceful trade or business and a time-consuming investment can become foggy at times, a problem that is explored next in connection with deductions allowed under §212, having to do with investment-related expenses.

386 Commissioner v. Groetzinger, 480 U.S. 23 (1987).

387 Basada v. Commissioner, 75 T.C.M. 2159 (1998).

388 Id. at 2160.

389 See §62(a)(2), which allows deductions associated with the business of being an employee, for confirmation.

In the following case, note carefully the distinction between the expenses that were held to be deductible and those that were held not to be deductible, and see if you can locate an analysis as to what legal standard distinguishes the two. It is important to keep in mind that at the time this case was decided, the forerunner of §162 had been enacted, but the forerunner of present §212 was not yet part of the law.

HIGGINS v. COMMISSIONER

312 U.S. 212 (1941)

Mr. Justice REED delivered the opinion of the Court.

Petitioner, the taxpayer, with extensive investments in real estate, bonds and stocks, devoted a considerable portion of his time to the oversight of his interests and hired others to assist him in offices rented for that purpose. For the tax years in question, 1932 and 1933, he claimed the salaries and expenses incident to looking after his properties were deductible under §23(a) of the Revenue Act of 1932 [now §162]. The Commissioner refused the deductions. The applicable phrases are: "In computing net income there shall be allowed as deductions: (a) *Expenses.* --Allthe ordinary and necessary expenses paid or incurred during the taxable year in carrying on any trade or business . . ." There is no dispute over whether the claimed deductions are ordinary and necessary expenses. As the Commissioner also conceded before the Board of Tax Appeals that the real estate activities of the petitioner in renting buildings constituted a business, the Board allowed such portions of the claimed deductions as were fairly allocable to the handling of the real estate. The same officers and staffs handled both real estate and security matters. After this adjustment there remained for the year 1932 over twenty and for the 1933 over sixteen thousand dollars expended for managing the stocks and bonds.

Petitioner's financial affairs were conducted through his New York office pursuant to his personal detailed instructions. His residence was in Paris, France, where he had a second office. By cable, telephone and mail, petitioner kept a watchful eye over his securities. While he sought permanent investments, changes, redemptions, maturities and accumulations caused limited shifting in his portfolio. These were made under his own orders. The offices kept records, received securities, interest and dividend checks, made deposits, forwarded weekly and annual reports and undertook generally the care of the investments as instructed by the owner. Purchases were made by a financial institution. Petitioner did not participate directly or indirectly in the management of the corporations in which he held stock or bonds. The method of handling his affairs under examination had been employed by petitioner for more than thirty years. No objection to the deductions had previously been made by the Government.

The Board of Tax Appeals held that these activities did not constitute carrying on a business and that the expenses were capable of apportionment between the real estate and the investments. The Circuit Court of Appeals affirmed, and we granted certiorari, because of conflict.

Petitioner urges that the "elements of continuity, constant repetition, regularity and extent'" differentiate his activities from the occasional like actions of the small investor. His activity is and the occasional action is not "carrying on business." On the other hand, the respondent urges that mere "personal investment activities never constitute carrying on a trade or business, no matter how much of one's time or of one's employees' time they may occupy."

. . .

Petitioner relies strongly on the definition of business in Flint v. Stone Tracy Company:

> "Business' is a very comprehensive term and embraces everything about which a person can be employed." This definition was given in considering whether certain corporations came under the Corporation Tax law which levies a tax on corporations engaged in business. The immediate issue was whether corporations engaged principally in the "holding and management of real estate" were subject to the act. A definition given for such an issue is not controlling in this dissimilar inquiry.

To determine whether the activities of a taxpayer are 'carrying on a business' requires an examination of the facts in each case. As the Circuit Court of Appeals observed, all expenses of every business transaction are not deductible. Only those are deductible which relate to carrying on a business. The Bureau of Internal Revenue has this duty of determining what is carrying on a business, subject to reexamination of the facts by the Board of Tax Appeals and ultimately to review on the law by the courts on which jurisdiction is conferred. The Commissioner and the Board appraised the evidence here as insufficient to establish petitioner's activities as those of carrying on a business. The petitioner merely kept records and collected interest and dividends from his securities, through managerial attention for his investments. No matter how large the estate or how continuous or extended the work required may be, such facts are not sufficient as a matter of law to permit the courts to reverse the decision of the Board. Its conclusion is adequately supported by this record, and rests upon a conception of carrying on business similar to that expressed by this Court for an antecedent section.

The petitioner makes the point that his activities in managing his estate, both realty and personalty, were a unified business. Since it was admittedly a business in so far as the realty is concerned, he urges there is no statutory authority to sever expenses allocable to the securities. But we see no reason why expenses not attributable, as we have just held these are not, to carrying on business cannot be apportioned. It is not unusual to allocate expenses paid for services partly personal and partly business.

Affirmed.

Notes on the Aftermath of *Higgins*

The *Higgins* decision created an anomaly in that the Court allowed Higgins to deduct his losses with respect to dispositions of property (now §165) and the expenses borne in his real estate business (now §162), but not his securities-related expenses. Congress reacted to that anomaly by promptly enacting the predecessors of §212(1) and (2), which fill the gap left by §162 by allowing investors to deduct their investment-related expenses, thereby taxing both investors and business people on net income. Section 212 covers individuals, estates, and trusts, leaving the deduction of investment expenses by corporations in a state of unexplored doubt. Presumably corporations would assert that §162 allows them to deduct the costs of managing assets they hold for investment and their right to deduct expenses in connection with determining their taxes, something individuals can deduct under §212(3).

The relevance to an individual taxpayer of the distinction in *Higgins* between a trade or business and other profit seeking activities remains important after the enactment of §212. For example, it bears on whether Mr. Higgins would be accorded capital gain or ordinary income (or deduction) treatment on the sale of stocks and bonds at a loss, discussed in Chapter Eight. It also affects whether he is entitled to a bad debt deduction under §166, discussed in Chapter Six. On top of that, §62 prefers business-related deductions over investment-related deductions in computing adjusted gross income.

The same person can run several businesses. A full-time law professor is a law school employee, but he might also be an author and the proprietor of a corner cigar store. He will have to sort out the income and deductions associated with each activity. His income as an employee will go on the facing page of his Form 1040 under the heading "wages, salaries, tips, etc."; his income from the business of being an author and the business of running a cigar store will each be reported on two separate Schedule C's, which he will attach to his annual Form 1040. His status as a law professor is nevertheless a business in a curious form, namely the "business of being an employee." One can detect this concept in §62. It is a good idea to scan Schedule C to Form 1040 if you have not done so already, to see how a sole proprietorship reports its profits or losses.

G. THE OPERATION OF §212

Read §212 and Reg. §1.212-1

Before we look at the details, let's look at the big picture. Are §212 deductions really appropriate? To answer the question, consider how America taxes a nonresident alien's income from U.S. sources. Whereas U.S. citizens and aliens who reside permanently in the United States are taxed on worldwide *net income* from their *investments and businesses*, nonresident aliens pay a flat 30% tax on *gross investment income* from U.S. sources, with no deductions.[390] In contrast, nonresident aliens pay income taxes on net income from *businesses* they operate in the United States, at normal graduated §1 rates.

> **To illustrate:** Lord Nubble lives in Islandia, but he buys and sells shares on the American stock markets (which makes him an investor, not a businessman). Recently, he earned $20,000 in taxable dividend income from the U.S., but he had to pay his American lawyer $18,000 to get the money. His U.S. income tax base on the dividend income is nevertheless $20,000, taxable at 30%. So he owes $6,000 in taxes, even though his economic income is only $2,000. By contrast, if the interest were earned as a businessman, thanks to his §162 deductions, Lord Nubble's tax base would be only $2,000, which would be taxable at graduated rates under §1.

Does this example make you question talk of flat rates on gross income without deductions? Presumably, we allow this shocking taxation of nonresident aliens, since they are not entitled to the protections against governmental confiscation of private property.

Now, back to American investors. As you know, the *Higgins* decision led to enactment of §212's predecessor which let investors deduct their gain-seeking expenses like parallel §162 expenses. The classic examples of §212 deductions for an investor are the costs of caring for an investment portfolio of stocks and bonds, including the costs of maintaining a bank safety-deposit box in which one holds stock certificates, or the costs of maintaining a real estate investment, such as underdeveloped land, or a rental unit or two whose operation does not constitute a "trade or business." One important aspect of §212 is that as §162 changes (legislatively or by Regulations), so generally do the Regulations under §212, but the amendments to the §212 regulations tend to be slow in coming. This is not surprising since the Treasury Department is sometimes decades behind on its regulations projects because of the constant flow of tax legislation.

390 §871. The 30% rate is frequently reduced by bilateral tax treaties. (Because of the hardship of being taxed on gross income can cause, the Code grants a special election that allows nonresident aliens to be taxed on their net investment income from real estate operations in the U.S. §871(d)(1).

Sections 162 and 212 are only available to taxpayers who genuinely intend to make a profit. A leading example in the area is *Dreicer v. Commissioner*.[391] The facts involved a taxpayer who traveled extensively, allegedly in order to gather materials for a book, and styled himself a writer-lecturer, although no one paid for his lectures. It was all too much for the court, which concluded that the taxpayer's, "activity of traveling around the world allegedly to obtain material for a manuscript was an 'activity . . . not engaged in for profit' . . . since he did not have a bona fide expectation of profit."[392] Here is the appellate court's explanation of the facts:

> Dreicer, a citizen of the United States, maintains his residence in the Canary Islands, Spain, and engages heavily in global travel. He derives a substantial income as beneficiary of a family trust, and in the early 1950's, Dreicer began to focus his professional attention on the fields of tourism and dining. In 1955, he published The Diner's Companion, a compilation of his opinions on dining and on various restaurants throughout the world, but the book was a commercial failure. Undaunted, Dreicer conceived the idea of some day writing another book, this one to enshrine his reminiscence on a life dedicated to epicurism and travel. In preparation for this sybaritic swan song, he spent the next twenty years traveling about the world, staying in some of the finest hotels and dining in some of the best restaurants. The material he gathered was also to be utilized in lectures before travel organizations and public appearances on radio and television. By the mid-1970s, Dreicer had completed a rough draft of the second book -parts of which originally had appeared in The Diner's Companion -and titled it My 27 Year Search for the Perfect Steak-Still Looking. Two publishing houses to which he submitted the manuscript, however, returned it, and seemingly he abandoned all hope of publishing.[393]

The primary purpose of the activity has to be profit-making in order for it to be a business; it seems that having a subjective intention to make an economic profit (ignoring tax savings) is evidently good enough, even if the prospect of a profit is objectively hopeless.

Some activities, such as collecting and trading postage stamps, begin as hobbies, grow into investments and emerge as businesses, and then drop back to one of the lower levels as the taxpayer tires of the activity. The Code will tax the profits along the way, and will grant more generous deductions as the activity grows into a serious effort to make money. At the bottom level, §183 will only allow a hobbyist deductions only up to gross income from the hobby. (A later part of this chapter takes up §183 in detail.) Once the hobby grows into an investment, §212 will step in with fairly generous deductions, and when the investment grows into a business, §162 will displace §212, and the expenses it generates will become above-the-line deductions

391 39 T.C.M. 233 (1979), rev'd and remanded, 665 F.2d 1292 (D.C. Cir. 1981).

392 Id. at 79-1542. See also, Reg. §1.212-1(c) (activity must be primarily to earn income if it is to be de deductible as investment expense).

393 665 F.2d 1292 at 81-5885 (D.C. Cir. 1981).

in computing adjusted gross income, as opposed to "mere" itemized deductions. The next case poses the question whether a particular activity was in fact a hobby or an investment for Federal Income Tax purposes.

WRIGHTSMAN v. UNITED STATES

428 F.2d 1316 (Claims Ct. 1970)

LARAMORE, Judge.

[The Wrightsmans were wealthy art collectors. Mr. Wrightsman had retired from an oil company of which he was an executive and around the time of the litigation had amassed an art collection worth over $16 million. The art was bought shrewdly and appreciated greatly. He began it as a hobby in 1947 and later bought as an appreciator and investor (including a view that art works are a hedge against inflation). He and Mrs. Wrightsman are art experts with excellent records. Their files followed them from home to home (New York and Palm Beach) each year. They maintained extensive excellent catalogs in binders (26 of them) and care for the works with great attention. Many were on their walls in their New York apartment, evidently because that was a good climate-controlled location. They spent only a small part of the year in New York. Their lives revolved around collecting art. They claimed deductible expenses for maintaining the art, insurance -- about $26,000 over two years for insurance, maintenance, subscription services, shipping, as well as travel and entertainment that directly related to their art. They also claimed a tax loss on the disposition of one work. The IRS position was that only physically segregated art should produce deductions. If you visit the Metropolitan Museum of Art in New York, you will notice that a modest part of the building houses the Wrightsman Collection -- presumably it came from the taxpayers in the instant case.]

. . .

Plaintiffs assert that the facts and circumstances in evidence, with which they say their personal declarations of purpose and intent are in complete accord, clearly establish the deductibility of the incurred expenses as primarily investmentmotivated. Defendant responds that because of the nature of the properties involved, plaintiffs are entitled to deduct the subject expenses only by showing a physical segregation of the works of art which precludes personal pleasure; a showing which, defendant contends, plaintiffs have failed to make. In the alternative, defendant opposes any recovery here on the ground that plaintiffs have not shown any action on their part inconsistent with the holding of their collection for pleasure, and have thereby failed to satisfy their burden of proof that the pertinent expenses were incurred primarily for an investment purpose. Although we hold that plaintiffs are not entitled to recover, neither of the alternative theories advanced by defendant constitutes, in our view, the proper application of the apposite legal standard upon which we premise our holding.

Section 212 provides, in parts pertinent to this suit:

> In the case of an individual, there shall be allowed as a deduction all the ordinary and necessary expenses paid or incurred during the taxable year
>
> 1) for the production or collection of income;
>
> 2) for the management, conservation, or maintenance of property held for the production of income; or
>
> . . .

Treasury Regulations . . . section 1.2121(c) imparts, moreover, with respect to the deductible investment expensenondeductible personal expense dichotomy and the apposite standard for proper classification:

> Expenses of carrying on transactions which . . . are not carried on for the production or collection of income or for the management, conservation, or maintenance of property held for the production of income, but which are carried on *primarily* as a sport, hobby, or recreation are not allowable as nontrade or nonbusiness expenses. The question whether or not a transaction is carried on *primarily* for the production of income or for the management, conservation, or maintenance of property held for the production or collection of income, rather than *primarily* as a sport, hobby, or recreation, is *not to be determined solely from the intention of the taxpayer but rather from all the circumstances of the case.* [Emphasis supplied.]

It is clear from the above that the burden of proof which plaintiffs must satisfy if they are to prevail is that as a factual matter, from an objective view of the operative circumstances in suit, they acquired and held works of art during the years here involved primarily for investment, rather than for personal use and enjoyment. Plaintiffs must establish that their investment purpose for acquiring and holding works of art was "principal," or "of first importance." *See, Malat v. Riddell*, 383 U.S. 569, 572 (1966). And, they must establish this notwithstanding the pleasure-giving quality commonly recognized as inherent in art objects.

The perplexing nature of the issue in suit apparently has caused defendant to seek a narrow rule possessing ease of application and certainty of result. We are unaware of any authority, however, for the interpretations which defendant places upon the applicable legal standard. Those cases cited by defendant with respect to its physical segregationpleasure preclusion standard do not, in our view, support the interpretation urged. *See, R. Foster Reynolds*, 4 T.C.M. 837 (1945) . . . . Neither do they support defendant's alternative position which turns upon whether there was action on the part of the Wrightsmans inconsistent with the holding of their art collection for pleasure. We prefer to resolve the instant controversy by the more conventional application of the legal standard involved, namely, an analysis of the particular facts and circumstances, and a determination as to plaintiffs' primary purpose therefrom. a careful review of the entire record with this conventional approach in mind indicates, we think, that plaintiffs have failed to sustain their burden.

Plaintiffs have carefully marshaled a broad array of evidence in support of their declared investment purpose. In this regard, we have no reason to doubt that Mr. Wrightsman was wary of the more traditional forms of investment, or that he recognized an investmentaspect incident to the acquisition and retention of works of art. Indeed, the greatly increased current value of the Wrightsman collection would seem, at least in retrospect, to confirm the financial wisdom of plaintiffs' purchases. Nor do we doubt that meticulous bookkeeping detail was observed by plaintiffs with respect to the purchase, care, and maintenance of their collection, or that the Wrightsmans devoted considerable time and effort to their collection activities. We fully appreciate, moreover, that because of plaintiffs' mode of living, much of their time was spent away from their residences wherein the majority of their works of art were maintained. It is our judgment, however, that this evidence, when viewed in proper relationship to the additional evidence below, relegates investment intent to a position of something less than primary among plaintiffs' purposes for acquiring and holding works of art.

It may fairly be said, and the record so indicates, that plaintiffs' personal lives revolve around their art collection and related collecting activities. The Wrightsmans, without any prior formal education with respect to works of art, have since the late 1940's consistently and diligently pursued course of selfeducation in that field, visiting major museums and art dealer establishments in the United States and overseas, studying works of art themselves, reviewing auction catalogues and price lists, and engaging in discussions with recognized art experts, such as collectors, museum curators, dealers and others knowledgeable in the world art community. They have reviewed all of the leading art periodicals, and engaged in extensive reading in their chosen field of 18th century French art and related areas. They have acquired a substantial art library, and Jayne has engaged in extensive research, while Charles has concentrated on the restoration and conservation of art objects and the conditions of the art market. Jayne has educated herself in the use of the French language, to be qualified to engage in discussions and reading of materials in that language concerning 18th century French furniture and works of art. Whether in Palm Beach, New York, or abroad, the major portion of the Wrightsmans' daytoday activities throughout each year is devoted to studying works of art. And, the Wrightsmans' social life in Palm Beach, New York, or abroad involves principally people knowledgeable and interested in the field of art.

As to the place and manner in which the Wrightsmans have held their collection, the record reveals that, except for occasional displays of items at other locations, plaintiffs have kept their works of art in their New York apartment, their Palm Beach home, and in the Metropolitan

Museum on loan for display by that institution. As of March 31, 1967, about 77.8 percent of such objects (on an insurance evaluation basis) was in the New York apartment, about 17.7 percent in the Palm Beach home, and about 4.5 percent in the Metropolitan Museum. The works of art are on display, or in use as in the case of such items as French period furniture, in the New York apartment and the Palm Beach home, except that a small amount of furniture is stored in one room at Palm Beach.

Plaintiffs have provided air conditioning and humidity controls, considered necessary for the preservation of works of art, similar to those employed in the Metropolitan Museum. In this respect, the New York apartment is better equipped, accounting for the concentration of works of art there. Such apartment occupies the entire third floor of the building. Storage facilities for works of art have not been readily available to provide the required atmospheric controls especially needed for paintings and furniture.

The record also reveals extensive personal use by the Wrightsmans of various parts of their collection. 18th century oriental wallpaper had been installed by the previous owner on the walls of plaintiffs' Palm Beach residence which had been acquired as a completely furnished home. 18th century French parquet flooring has been installed by plaintiffs in their Palm Beach home, and in their New York apartment. Plaintiffs' paintings are never stored but, instead, a limited number are hung on the walls of their Palm Beach home, with most of them on the walls of their New York apartment. Mr. Wrightsman's bedroom in their apartment is furnished with 18th century French furniture and fixtures, and his bedroom in their Palm Beach home contains a French commode. Mrs. Wrightsman's bedroom in their apartment is furnished completely with Louis XV matching furniture and fixtures. Plaintiffs' apartment also has other rooms which contain other works of art from their collection in the form of matching furniture and furnishings.

In sum, what we wish to make clear from the foregoing is that we recognize as established an investment purpose for plaintiffs' collection. To be sure, many of the abovedetailed facts and circumstances are entirely consistent with investment intent. On balance, however, the evidence does not establish investment as the most prominent purpose for plaintiffs' acquiring and holding works of art. The complete record does establish, to the contrary, personal pleasure or satisfaction as plaintiffs' primary purpose.

Plaintiffs place much reliance upon *George F. Tyler, supra*, wherein a loss sustained on the sale of part of a stamp collection was held deductible under section 23 of the 1939 Internal Revenue Code as having been incurred in a transaction entered into for profit. The precise factual issue before the court was whether the stamp collection was held primarily for profit or primarily as a hobby. In finding the former purpose to be primary, the Tax Court emphasized that the taxpayer from the outset undertook stamp collecting as an investment; that he consummated all purchases through a professional philatelist, who stressed the investment feature of stamps; that he purchased stamps only upon the philatelist's recommendation; that he exhibited scant interest in or knowledge of stamps; and that he participated little in those activities generally associated with stamp hobbyists. Thus it was found that although the collection and possession of stamps afforded the taxpayer some pleasure, such activities were undertaken primarily for profit.

The great disparity in facts and circumstances between *Tyler* and the instant case compels the conclusion, we think, that the *Tyler* decision in no sense advances plaintiffs' current cause. The actual importance of the *Tyler* case, for our purposes, lies in the standard there applied:

> . . . The difficulty, then reduces itself to the task of ascertaining whether petitioner has sustained his burden of proving that the desire to make a financial profit was the most important motive which led him to acquire the components of his collections. [6 T.C.M. at 280]

The Tax Court determined, in the factual context of the *Tyler* case, that the taxpayer *had* sustained his burden of proof. We hold, in the factual context of the case before us, that the instant plaintiffs *have not.*

Also easily distinguished from the case at hand are *Juliet P. Hamilton, supra*, and *R. Foster Reynolds, supra*, to which we are referred by defendant. The *Hamilton* case involved the denial of a deduction for a loss sustained on the sale of a single painting which the taxpayer had acquired by specific bequest from her deceased father. Prior to its sale, the painting had been kept by the taxpayer in her home, except that, on several occasions, without profit to the taxpayer, the painting was placed on exhibition for inspection by art students and lovers of art. While in the taxpayer's home, the painting was sometimes made available, by special arrangement, for free inspection, 25 B.T.A. at 1718. The *Reynolds* case, on the other hand, involved the allowance of a deduction for a loss sustained on the sale of certain jewelry which the taxpayer had acquired by inheritance from his deceased aunt. The jewelry, which was sold for the taxpayer by Cartier, Inc., of New York had been kept in a safe deposit box and at no time had been used by the taxpayer or any member of his family. 4 T.C.M. at 838. We have no quarrel with the rule or reason of the *Hamilton* and *Reynolds* cases. We feel constrained to point out, however, that the rather conspicuous absence of any investmenttype activity in the former or personal use in the latter serves to emphasize the appreciably more complex nature of the present controversy.

While the cases cited by the parties afford only minimal guidance for the resolution of the issue in suit, they do affirm as proper the analysis undertaken herein. That is to say, where the issue in question turns upon a taxpayer's state of mind, courts can best treat with such an issue through traditional principles of inferencedrawing from an objective view of surrounding facts and circumstances, necessarily on a casebycase basis. . . .

. . . [W]e hold that plaintiffs have failed to sustain their burden of proving the primacy of their investment purpose. Plaintiffs are, therefore, not entitled to recover in this action, and their petition is dismissed.

Collins, Judge, dissenting:

I cannot agree with the court's conclusion in this case, and reluctantly I must dissent. At the outset, it should be stated that I regard this as a very difficult and a very close case. Very simply stated, my disagreement with the majority is that I feel that plaintiffs have sustained their burden of proof in showing that they acquired and held works of art primarily for investment rather than for personal enjoyment.

The majority have cited a number of facts and circumstances which they claim support their position that plaintiffs were engaged in the collection of art primarily for personal pleasure. As I view these same facts and circumstances, they could just as easily support a position favoring investment intent. Consequently, I feel that the factors relied upon by the court could be applied with equal weight to either side. If these facts were the only points to consider, I would have to agree with the majority since I would conclude that this would not be sufficient to satisfy plaintiffs' burden of proof.

However, there are a few other factors mentioned by the court which point directly to an investment intent. These include plaintiffs' desire to find an investment which would act as a hedge against inflation, plaintiffs' meticulous bookkeeping system, and the fact that they spent so little time at their homes where the large majority of their works of art were kept. (They spend 30 days a year in their New York apartment where 77.8 percent of their art objects are located.) These factors are the ones which, to me, tip the scales in favor of an investment intent.

I am further influenced by the fact that Commissioner Hogenson[394], who conducted the trial and heard the testimony of all the witnesses, found that plaintiffs had met their burden of proof and were engaged in the collection of art primarily for investment purposes. I feel that, in a case which is as close and as difficult as this one, some weight should definitely be attached to this advantage of the commissioner to observe demeanor and judge credibility.

I conclude, therefore, that the weight of the evidence presented is in favor of showing that plaintiffs were engaged in the collection and maintenance of art objects primarily for investment reasons rather than for their own personal pleasure and enjoyment. I would adopt the commissioner's findings of fact (which has been substantially done by the court) and his recommended opinion.

Problem 5-2:

Which of the following are likely deductible under §212?

1) $250 paid to rent a safe deposit box to hold common stocks purchased with the hope that they will appreciate.

394 [A "Commissioner" of the Claims Court is comparable to a trial judge. Eds.]

2) $200 paid to a part-time typist to prepare a schedule of income and expenses for the month, summarizing the taxpayer's investment results.

3) $450 paid as a commission on the purchase of stock held for investment.

4) $100 paid to hold tax-exempt municipal bonds.

5) $100 that an investor pays a lawyer to help collect an overdue bill from a stockbroker.

6) Client pays a real estate broker $100 to list her personal residence for rent during the summer season.

7) Are any §212 expenses adjustments to gross income under §62? Recall that adjustments to gross income under §62 are more favorable than itemized deductions because they are sure to reduce one's income tax base. Read §62.

8) What about §162 expenses? Are they always adjustments to gross income? Peruse §62, which lists the adjustments to gross income.

H. WHAT ARE THE STANDARDS AND BOUNDARIES OF §212 EXPENSE DEDUCTIONS?

Read Reg. §1.212-1(a)(1), (b) and (d)

SURASKY v. UNITED STATES

325 F.2d 191 (5th Cir. 1963)

Before TUTTLE, Chief Judge, and JONES and BELL, Circuit Judges.

TUTTLE, Chief Judge.

[Surasky joined a group of financiers who had a plan to invest in Montgomery Ward, a national retailer, with a view to improving the company and making a profit on a later sale of their stock. Surasky invested a lot of money at the time ($296,000) and ultimately made a profit of about $51,000. In that connection, he contributed $17,000 to a shareholders' committee to force changes on the company. He deducted the contribution, sought a refund and was denied it. He disputed the denial of the refund in the District Court and lost.]

Trying the case without a jury, the trial court based its legal conclusion that the expenditures were not deductible on the following summarization of the facts:

"To summarize the facts, the plaintiff herein contributed $ 17,000 to a committee which was to use the money to solicit proxies from other shareholders of a large, publiclyheld corporation, in the hope that the committee would be able to seat a sufficient number of its candidates on the board of directors so that new management policies could be carried out which might result in larger profits and larger dividends to the shareholders.

"The plaintiff had clear title to his Ward stock and was receiving dividend income therefrom. It was certainly most speculative whether his contribution to the Wolfson Committee would touch off a series of events culminating in the production of increased income to the plaintiff. Furthermore, the plaintiff was not a candidate for the board of directors nor does the record reflect that he anticipated obtaining a position in Ward's management. . . .

"The Court specifically finds lacking the necessary proximate relationship between the expenditure and the production of income or the management of income producing property. At the time the plaintiff contributed his funds to the committee, it was pure speculation whether he would derive any monetary reward therefrom. At the time the expenditure was made, the Court could certainly not find that it was necessary, nor was it even ordinary, within the common meaning of that word.

"The Court is not unmindful of the fact that the plaintiff, at the time he contributed the $ 17,000 to the committee, did so with hopes of realizing a profit and that, as a matter of fact, the dividends on his stock increased following the election of three of the Wolfson Committee's candidates. However, it is necessary to view the instant transaction as of the time it occurred, without the benefit of hindsight. The record is completely devoid of any evidence of a direct proximate relationship between the plaintiff's expenditure and the increased dividends; the latter could have been caused by any one of a myriad of factors. As for the plaintiff's desire to make a profit, there are any number of transactions entered into by the parties with a profit motive which are not accorded preferential tax treatment. The Treasury cannot be expected to underwrite all profit seeking speculations."

The appellant here urges that in its stressing of the "speculative" nature of the expenditure and the court's apparent reliance on the theory that for an expense, to be deductible under subparagraph 2 of Section 212, i.e., "for the management, conservation, or maintenance of property held for the production of income," there must be some threat of the loss of the property by the taxpayer, the court has imposed too rigid a requirement. We agree.

There is one thing both parties here agree upon, that is, that it was to change the result of the distinction between "business" and "personal" expenses that Section 212 was added to the Internal Revenue Code in 1942. The United States, in its brief, cites the decision by the Supreme Court in McDonald v. Commissioner, 323 U.S. 57, 61, . . . as authority for the following statement: "In order to correct the inequity of making nontrade or nonbusiness income taxable, but not allowing nontrade or nonbusiness expenses to be deducted, Congress allowed a deduction in the new subsection (a) (2) for 'all the ordinary and necessary expenses paid or incurred' (1) 'for the production or collection of income' or (2) 'for the management, conservation, or maintenance of property held for the production or collection of income.' "

The parties also agree that in construing the language of Section 212, it is to be taken in pari materia with Section 162 so far as relates to the language "ordinary and necessary business expenses."

From the manner in which the trial court stressed the terms "speculative" and "speculation" it is apparent that the court may have been too greatly persuaded by the language of the income tax regulations declaring, in Section 1.2121(d), that "expenses to be deductible under Section 212, must be 'ordinary and necessary'. Thus, such expenses must be reasonable in amount and must bear a reasonable and proximate relation to the production or collection taxable income or to the management, conservation, or maintenance of property held for the production of income." While we do not determine that this regulation is not warranted by the section of the statute with which we are involved, we think that it has been construed by the trial court to require much too difficult a showing of proximate cause in the commonlaw tort concept than is required by the statute.

It will be noted that nothing in the statute expressly requires a showing of a "proximate relation to the production or collection of taxable income." None of the cases cited to us by the United States contain such language. We think Congress had in mind allowing deduction of expenses genuinely incurred in the exercise of reasonable business judgment in an effort to produce income that may fall far short of satisfying the common law definition of proximate cause. Thus, we think the use of the term "speculative" is not an apt expression that would describe the determining factor in deciding this issue.

This Court has held in Harris & Co. v. Lucas, Commissioner, 5th Cir., 48 F.2d 187,

> "It is evident that the words 'ordinary' and 'necessary' in the statute are not used conjunctively, and are not to be construed as requiring that an expense of a business to be deductible must be both ordinary and necessary in a narrow, technical sense. On the contrary, it is clear that Congress intended the statute to be broadly construed to facilitate business generally, so that any necessary expense, not actually a capital investment, incurred in good faith in a particular business, is to be considered an ordinary expense of that business. This in effect is the construction given the statute by the Treasury Department and the courts. . . ." 48 F.2d 187, 188.

. . .

In dealing with the "necessary" part of the formula, the Supreme Court has indicated in Welch v. Helvering, 290 U.S. 111, at page 1, 54 S.Ct. 8, at page 9, 78 L.Ed. 212, that this requirement may be satisfied if the expenditures "were appropriate and helpful", saying as to the taxpayer, Welch, "He certainly thought they were, and we should be slow to override his judgment."

Then, dealing with the question of what expenses are "ordinary" the Supreme Court in the same opinion said, "Here, indeed, as so often in other branches of the law, the decisive distinctions are those of degree and not of kind. One struggles in vain for any verbal formula that will supply a ready touchstone. The standard set up by the statute is not a rule of law; it is rather a way of life. Life in all its fullness must supply the answer to the riddle."

Here, it seems incontestable that the payments made by the taxpayer were made with the anticipation that profit to the taxpayer would result. It may have been a long chance that Mr. Surasky was taking. However, he testified he knew Mr. Wolfson well enough to know his ability and believed that there was reasonable likelihood of success. This testimony is undisputed. In point of fact, the activity resulting from the expenditures by the taxpayer and his associates did produce direct and tangible results in that three nominees of the Committee were elected to the Board of Directors, the President, who had been severely criticized by the Committee was caused to resign as was the Chairman of the Board, and many other actions which parallel those sought for by the Committee were undertaken by the corporation. Profits were increased; dividends were increased; the stock enhanced in value. We think that for a trial court to conclude that there was not sufficient connection between the expenditure to assist the Committee in its activities and the achievement of so many of its objectives was too remote to meet the test of what is reasonable and ordinary in this particular type of investor activity is to apply too rigid a standard in the application of a remedial statute.

While there are differences in the facts, as there must always be in different cases, we think that the Tax Court decision in Allegheny Corporation, 28 T.C. 298, acq. 19572 C.B. 3, points the direction in which the statute should be applied. The expenditures there sought to be deducted were for proxy solicitation and other committee activities in a railroad reorganization. To be sure, the proposal that was fought successfully in that case would have resulted in diluting the taxpayer's common stock possibly to the vanishing point. However, we think it immaterial whether the expenditure is directed towards an effort to prevent the loss or dilution of an equity interest or to cause an enhancement or increase of the equity value, as was the undoubted purpose in the case before us. The Tax Court there said, 28 T.C. page 304, "We think it is clear that the expenditures in question were made for no other purpose than to protect petitioner's business." . . .

. . .

The judgment is reversed and the case is remanded to the trial court for the entry of a judgment in favor of the appellant, taxpayer.

Problem 5-3:

Client owns ½ of 1% of the stock of X Corporation. She pays lawyer $200 to make a preliminary investigation of allegations that company officials had taken bribes, believing that, if it is true, something must be done about it. Assume variously that the corporation is a small local bank or Microsoft.

LOWRY v. UNITED STATES

384 F. Supp. 257 (D.C. N.H. 1974)

Bownes, District Judge.

Plaintiffs bring this action to recover federal income taxes and interest, in the amount of $1,072, which they allege were erroneously or illegally assessed and collected. Jurisdiction is based on 28 U.S.C. § 1346(a)(1).

The issue is whether plaintiffs, who ceased to use their summer house as residential property in 1967 and immediately offered it for sale without attempting to rent the property, converted it into "income producing property," thereby entitling them to deduct the maintenance expenses incurred after it was put on the market and prior to its sale in 1973. The Internal Revenue Service allowed plaintiffs to take maintenance deductions in the tax years 1968 and 1969. They disallowed similar maintenance deductions in the tax year 1970. The only year in issue is 1970.[395]

Plaintiffs are husband and wife domiciled in Peterborough, New Hampshire. (Since Edward G. Lowry, Jr., is the principal party in this case, he alone will hereinafter be referred to as plaintiff.) Plaintiff filed a joint federal income tax return for 1970 with the District Director of Internal Revenue in Portsmouth, New Hampshire. On his 1970 income tax return, plaintiff deducted expenditures made for the care and maintenance of his former summer residence. He based these deductions upon the premise that the summer residence was no longer personal property, but was property "held for the production of income." Int. Rev. Code of 1954 § 212. The Internal Revenue Service disagreed with plaintiff and disallowed the deduction basing its decision on Internal Revenue Code of 1954 § 262 which provides:

> Except as otherwise expressly provided in this chapter, no deductions shall be allowed for personal, living, or family expenses.

395 Plaintiff, due to his own mistake, failed to take the allowable depreciation deductions and that matter is not before this court.

On November 27, 1971, plaintiff paid the disputed $1,072 under written protest.

The property in question is plaintiff's former summer residence on Martha's Vineyard (hereinafter referred to as Vineyard property). The Vineyard property is part of a cooperative community known as Seven Gates Farm Corporation.

Seven Gates was formed in 1921 by five persons, one of whom was plaintiff's father. Upon forming the corporation, plaintiff's father acquired the Vineyard property. In 1942, plaintiff acquired "title" to the property by gift from his father.

Legal title to the Vineyard property is held by Seven Gates. In 1970, plaintiff had a lease for the Vineyard property and was a 3% stockholder in the corporation. The leasing arrangement treated plaintiff as the de facto owner of the property. It ran for the life of the corporation with the proviso that, upon dissolution of the corporation, it would automatically be converted into a fee title. No stockholderlessee, however, could sell his stock and lease without the prior consent of 75% of the stockholderlessees. Each lease further provided that a rental for a year or less required the prior consent of the Committee on Admissions and that a lease for more than a year required the prior consent of 75% of the other stockholderlessees.

In 1966, plaintiff owned three residential properties: he maintained his legal residence in Maryland; he had a winter residence in Florida; and the Vineyard property. During 1966, plaintiff sold his Maryland home and purchased a house in Peterborough, New Hampshire. Because the Peterborough house did "all the things that the house in Martha's Vineyard did," plaintiff decided, in 1967, to sell the Vineyard property and put a sales price on it of $150,000. From 1921 through 1967, plaintiff had spent nearly all of his summers at the Vineyard property.

After it was put on the market, the house was never again used as residential property. Each spring plaintiff went to Martha's Vineyard, opened the house, put up curtains, pruned the shrubbery, generally cleaned and spruced up the property, and then left. This took two or three days and plaintiff occupied the house during this period. Each fall plaintiff returned and closed the house for the winter. The closing also took two to three days and plaintiff stayed in the house. The only other time that plaintiff occupied the property was once a year, when the corporation had its annual meeting of stockholders. As evidence of his intent to treat the Vineyard property as a business asset, plaintiff testified that in 1971 his daughter, after returning from abroad, requested the use of the property plaintiff refused, stating that the property was a business proposition. As a fatherly gesture, however, he rented a summer home in Maine for her use.

Plaintiff made no attempt to rent the house for the following reasons: He believed that it would be easier to sell a clean empty house than one occupied by tenants; the house being suitable for summer occupancy only, would have had to have been rented completely equipped, which would have required the plaintiff to purchase linen, silver, blankets, and recreational equipment at a cost which would not have been justified by any possible rental; rental prices bore no reasonable relation to the value of the property and the expected sales price; and rental was complicated by the restrictive provisions of the corporation's bylaws.

In 1968, a prospective purchaser offered to buy the property for $150,000. Plaintiff, however, could not obtain the necessary 75% approval of the stockholders of Seven Gates and the sale was not completed. In 1973, plaintiff received a cash offer of $150,000 for the property and the sale was closed in September of 1973. Plaintiff's 1973 tax return showed a net longterm capital gain of $100,536.50, as a result of the sale.

RULINGS OF LAW

The tax issue in this case is: When and how does residential property become converted into income producing property?

The Tax Court, in attempting to establish a clear guideline in a murky area, created a simple test: The taxpayer had to make a bona fide offer to rent in order to convert residential property into "income producing property." The Tax Court's *sine qua non* was a product of administrative reality. There are three basic reasons why the Government established a rental prerequisite. First, it stemmed from a fear that taxpayers would countermand the listing for sale after taking a series of deductions and reoccupy the house on a personal basis. Mary Laughlin Robinson, 2 T.C. 305, 309 (1943). Second, the rental requisite provided a clear and convenient administrative test. Warren Leslie, Sr., 6 T.C. 488, 494 (1946). Third, the rental requirement found some implied support in Treas. Reg. § 1.2121(h) (1954), which provides:

> Ordinary and necessary expenses paid or incurred in connection with the management, conservation, or maintenance of property held for use as a residence by the taxpayer are not deductible. However, ordinary and necessary expenses paid or incurred in connection with the management, conservation, or maintenance of property held by the taxpayer as rental property are deductible even though such property was formerly held by the taxpayer for use as a home.

In Hulet P. Smith, 1967 T.C. Memo (1967), aff'd 397 F.2d 804 (9th Cir. 1968), the Tax Court abandoned the rental test and held that an offer for sale plus an abandonment transformed the property into an investment asset. The Court of Appeals, in affirming, circumspectly stated:

> The Government makes a strong case for reversal. See Recent Developments, Hulet P. Smith, 66 Mich. L. Rev. 562 (1968). Unusual circumstances are present, however, and we are not persuaded that the Tax Court's factual finding and its consequent conclusions are clearly wrong. *Smith, supra*, 397 F.2d 804.

In a subsequent decision, the Tax Court was presented with a fact pattern which was similar to the one presented in *Smith* and came to the opposite conclusion. Frank A. Newcombe, 54 T.C. 1298 (1970). The court stated that *Smith* was "of little precedential value." *Id.* at 03.

In *Newcombe* the taxpayers moved out of their personal residence and immediately offered it for sale. At no time was the property offered for rent. The taxpayers argued that, under the *Smith* doctrine, the property was being held for the production of income. The Government contended that the *Smith* case was erroneous and that property can only be converted into income producing property use when there has been a bona fide offer to rent.

In rejecting both parties' positions, the court stated:

> We do not share the penchant for polarization which the arguments of the parties reflect. Rather, we believe that a variety of factors must be weighed.... *Newcombe, supra*, 54 T.C. at 129900.

The *Newcombe* court found that "[the] key question, in cases of the type involved herein, is the purpose or intention of the taxpayer in light of all the facts and circumstances." *Id.* at 03. The critical inquiry is, therefore, whether the taxpayer had or intended an "expectation of profit." To aid in its inquiry, the court took into account the following considerations: length of time the taxpayer occupied his former residence prior to abandonment; the availability of the house for the taxpayer's personal use while it was unoccupied; the recreational character of the property; attempts to rent the property; and, whether the offer to sell was an attempt to realize postconversion appreciation. The court explained its final criterion as follows:

> The placing of property on the market for immediate sale, at or shortly after the time of its abandonment as a residence, will ordinarily be strong evidence that a taxpayer is not holding the property for post conversion appreciation in value. Under such circumstances, only a most exceptional situation will permit a finding that the statutory requirement has been satisfied. *On the other hand, if a taxpayer believes that the value of the property may appreciate and decides to hold it for some period in order to realize upon such anticipated appreciation, as well as an excess over his investment, it can be said that the property is being "held for the production of income." Id.* at 0203 (emphasis added).

I rule that the Vineyard property was converted into income producing property in 1967 and that plaintiff was entitled to deduct his maintenance expenses. In ruling in plaintiff's favor, I adopt the approach taken by the *Newcombe* court and do not regard renting as the "litmus test" for conversion.

Administrative difficulty in determining when personal property is transformed into investment property should not create a rigid and inflexible barrier to the benefits of conversion. Plaintiff gave sound and substantial business reasons for his failure to rent. I also note that the rental rule does not provide an elixir to administrative ills, for it must be determined that the offer to rent is bona fide and not a sham. Paul H. Stutz, 1965 PH Tax Ct. Mem. ¶ 65,166; S. Wise, 1945 PH Tax Ct. Mem. ¶ 45,298. Finally, I do not believe that Treas. Reg. § 1.2121(h) (1954) commands a rental offer as a prerequisite to converting a prior residence into income producing property. I find the language contained therein, with regard to renting, to be illustrative and not an explicit statement of law.

In fact, another regulation provides that: "[the] term 'income' for the purpose of section 212 . . . is not confined to recurring income but applies as well to gains from the disposition of property." Treas. Reg. § 1.2121(b) (1954). The regulation further provides that the maintenance expenses of property held for investment are deductible; even if the property is not producing income, there is no likelihood of current income, and there is no likelihood of gain upon the sale of the property.

The determination of whether plaintiff's prior residence has been converted into income producing property is made by examining the taxpayer's purpose in light of all the facts and circumstances. Treas. Reg. § 1.2121(c)(1954). I find that the facts and circumstances presented clearly indicate that plaintiff intended to benefit from postabandonment appreciation.

I take judicial notice that the price for recreational property on Martha's Vineyard and everywhere else in New England has skyrocketed in the past decade. Plaintiff has had wide exposure to financial and real estate transactions. He was thoroughly exposed to the real estate world from 1934 to 1943. During that period, he liquidated about 15,000 properties in about 1,200 communities located in thirtysix states. He was specifically aware of Martha's Vineyard land values, having spent nearly all of his summers there. Plaintiff also testified that he was aware, during the latter half of the 1960's, of changing economic conditions. As administrator of a large New York insurance company, he saw increasing cash flow and rising prosperity. He testified that, as a result of this exposure, he came to the conclusion, during the latter part of 1967, that we were in the beginning of an inflationary trend and that the value of land would appreciate markedly. Although the 1967 market value of the Vineyard property was $50,000, plaintiff's business acumen and experience suggested that he could obtain his list price of $150,000 if he kept the property visible and in good condition and waited for the anticipated real estate boom coupled with the anticipated inflation. After a period of five and onehalf years, plaintiff did, in fact, sell the property in September of 1973, for his original list price. A capital gain of $100,536.50 appeared on his 1973 income tax return as a consequence of the sale.

The fact that plaintiff immediately listed the property does not negate his contention that he intended to capitalize on postabandonment appreciation in land values. By an immediate listing, plaintiff made the property a visible commodity on a demanding market. He patiently waited until the economic forces pushed the market value of his property up to his list price.

Based on all the facts and circumstances, I find that plaintiff had a reasonable "expectation of profit" and that the Vineyard property was held as income producing property during 1967. Accordingly, I rule that plaintiff was entitled to deduct the property's maintenance expenses incurred during 1970.

Judgment for the plaintiffs.

SO ORDERED.

Notes and Questions

In your opinion, why did Lowry win his case for deductions under §212, while the Wrightsmans, lost?

Deductible maintenance expenses versus losses on the disposition of property: Mr. Lowry got deductions for maintenance under §212, not losses on disposing of property under §165(a) and (c)(3), which you should read. Here is a summary of a leading Tax Court case that dealt with both §212 investment-related deductions and §165(c) loss on the disposition of property.

> **To illustrate:** August Horrmann inherited the family residence on Howard Avenue, Staten Island, on his mother's death in February 1940. He redecorated and moved into the family residence and sold his own home. The newly acquired home was found to be unsuitable, so he abandoned it as a residence in October 1942. After making several unsuccessful attempts to rent or to sell the property it was finally sold in June 1945, at a loss. The Tax Court held that in 1942, the property was held for the production of income and so Mr. Horrmann was entitled to deductions for depreciation, and maintenance and conservation expenses, during 1943, 1944, and 1945. The §165 loss incurred upon the sale of the property in 1945 was not deductible as the loss was not incurred in any transaction entered into for profit. In the court's words:
>
> We have held that an actual rental of the property is not always essential to a conversion [so as to make it a property acquired in a "transaction entered into for profit" under §165(c)(3)], *Estate of Maria Assmann*, 16 T. C. 632, but that case is not controlling here for the taxpayer there abandoned the residence only a few days after it was inherited, and then later demolished the residence. In *Mary E. Crawford*, 16 T. C. 678, which involved only the question of whether the loss was a [§165(c)(3)] loss the owner-taxpayer had also demolished the residence. While we held in both cases that such action constituted an appropriation or conversion [under § 165(c)(3)], in both cases the facts indicate that from the moment the properties were inherited the taxpayers did not intend to continue to occupy the property as their personal residence.
>
> Here the situation is different. The petitioners in the instant case soon after the death of petitioner's mother took immediate and decisive action, fixing the character of the property in their hands as residential. The surrounding circumstances point to this conclusion; their expenditure of approximately $ 9,000 in redecorating the house in preparation for their use of it as a home; their moving into the property within nine months after they acquired it; the sale of their former residence at Ocean Terrace shortly after they had moved into the Howard Avenue property; and finally, their occupancy of the Howard Avenue property for a period of about two years as a

home and residence. They could hardly have gone further more decisively to fix the character of this property, originally neutral in their hands, as personal residential property.[396]

Mandatory basis adjustments: Section 167, which you will study later, lets taxpayers claim periodic deductions against income for the presumed decline in values of their business or investment properties with the passage of time. These depreciation deductions reduce the basis of property, thanks to §1016. Assume for a minute that Lowry ultimately sold the Vineyard property at a loss. Could Lowry have gotten indirectly via depreciation deductions what he could not get under §165(c)(3) if he sold the property at a loss? The answer is "largely no," because Reg. §1.165-9(b)(2) forces taxpayers like Lowry who convert property whose value has fallen below its adjusted basis to a gain-seeking use to reduce its basis down to value at the time of the conversion so as to prevent what was lost via consumption from being deducted as depreciation, or as a property loss.

To illustrate: Lowry bought his property for $100. When the property was worth $95, Lowry converted it to rental use in order to realize a gain on its post-conversion value (thereby qualifying it as property held for the production of income, so as to qualify for maintenance and depreciation deductions). Under Reg. §1.165-9(b)(2), his depreciation is founded on an adjusted basis of $95 its value when converted to gain-seeking use. If he later claimed $1 of depreciation deductions and sold it for $91, he would be allowed a $3 loss (i.e., $91 amount realized minus $94 adjusted basis). The decline in value from $100 to $95 is treated as personal consumption for which no tax benefit is available.

Lowry did not claim depreciation deductions, but perhaps he should have.[397] The "allowed or allowable" rule of §1016 seemingly required him to reduce his basis in the property by depreciation from the time of conversion, regardless of whether he actually claimed depreciation deductions on his tax return. The reason he could claim depreciation deductions is that the house was "held for the production of income" under §167 in the sense of being held for post-conversion appreciation. On the other hand, under the law at the time, he had to base his claim to depreciation deductions on the excess of his present basis over the value of the property when its useful life in his hands was projected to end (known as its "salvage value"). Because he expected a profit, it makes sense that he would not have claimed depreciation and that the government would not have imposed it on him. After all, his position all along was that his "salvage value" exceeded his investment in the property.

396 Horrmann v. Commissioner, 17 T.C. 903 (1951).

397 At the time, he would have claimed the deduction under § 167(a)(2) which grants the deduction with respect to property "held for the production of income."

Problem 5-4:

The Hapless family bought their New Jersey home 12 years ago for $120,000. They have not improved it. They were recently hired by an employer in California. They left New Jersey a few months ago and found the sale of the house is not going well. In fact, it is just sitting there empty. Assume the house was worth $110,000 when they put it on the market.

1) They would like to know if they can deduct the maintenance costs of the house.

2) Under §212, they also wonder if they can claim a deductible loss if they sell their former home for only $100,000. See Reg. §1.165-9(b) as to the loss issue.

3) Assuming the property was worth $140,000 when they left and they were holding it to benefit from post-conversion appreciation, must they claim depreciation deductions with respect to the home? See §§ 167(a) and 1016 (a)(2).

I. SECTION 183: RESTRICTIONS ON LOSSES IN CONNECTION WITH HOBBIES

Read §183(a)-(d). Skim §183(e).

Wrightsman raises a difficult problem: exactly how does one inquire into taxpayer motives given the constraints of Due Process? One can see from the case that operating losses generated by business and investment activities can offset gains realized from more mundane activities, even if the taxpayer enjoys the business or investment activities. Naturally, this attractive combination of business and pleasure leads to abuses, hence the need for the limitations found in §183. Although §183's primary purpose is to deny deductions with respect to activities that are not sincerely engaged in for a profit, it also provides helpful Regulations containing nine factors that offer objective standards to use in the hunt for the presence of a genuine intent to make a profit. The main issue to be resolved is just what does "engaged into for profit" mean. To best understand this question, it is helpful to look at the proposition in this light; is the taxpayer considering engaging in the activity as a profitable trade, business, or investment, or is the taxpayer engaging in the activity for primarily personal reasons? The former would support a tax deduction, while the latter would not.

The crucial phrase in §183 -- "activity not engaged in for profit" -- has been defined as any activity that is neither a trade or business, nor an activity that involves the production or collection of income, nor any activity dealing with the management of property held for the production of income. As one can plainly see, this definition is circular because, if the activity *is* engaged in primarily or exclusively as a trade, business, or investment it cannot be engaged in other than for a subjectively intended profit.

For tax purposes, most Circuits consider that an activity is "engaged in for profit" if the taxpayer has a *primary purpose* and *intention* of making a profit. In a fight with the IRS, the objective facts of the taxpayer's situation are more important than subjective intent, since the government is not free to inject taxpayers with truth serum. Section 183(c)'s circularity demands clarifying regulations in order for it to make sense. Reg. §1.183-2(b) fills the gap with the nine unranked factors that one must consider in order to decide whether the activity is conducted for a profit. Note the serious problem that if one does not meet the requirements of §183, then disallowed deductions are lost forever, not just deferred, because they are considered mere personal consumption. You should now read Reg. §1.183-2(a) and (b), if you have not done so already, to identify the Big Nine factors used to search for a genuine intent to make a profit.[398]

As a simplifying measure, §183 includes a safe harbor rule that activities are *presumed* to be engaged in for profit if gross income from the activity is greater than the expenses attributable to the activity during 3 of the 5 previous years (2 out of 7 for horses). Canny taxpayers may be able to manipulate the timing of the activity's income and deductions to satisfy these tests.

Section 183 offers an interesting amnesty. It says that taxpayers may deduct the expenses associated with their hobbies, but only to the extent the income from the activity exceeds allocable expenses that are deductible without regard to motive (such as casualty losses).

To illustrate: Mrs. Bassett runs a dog breeding operation out of her home, strictly for fun. Her gross income from the activity is $1,000 per year. Her state income taxes allocable to dog breeding amount to $600 (and are deductible in all events up to $10,000) and her hobby-related expenses are $1,100 (for expenses such as pet food). How much of the $1,100 is deductible? The answer is $400, computed as follows:

Gross income from dog breeding activity	$1,000
Otherwise deductible amounts[399]	(600)
Limit on hobby-related deductions	400
Other deductions -- tentative	(1,100)
Balance	(700)

The practical result is that she cannot deduct the remaining $700 against other income, such as her salary or investments because of her lack of profit intent. They are treated as mere personal

398 See the discussion of this pointy the majority and minority in Groetzinger v. Commissioner, 87 T.C. 533 (1986). Reg. §1.183-2(a). See Blum, *Motive, Intent and Purpose in Federal Income Taxation*, 34 U. Chi. L.R. 485, 498 (1967); Marxer, *Symposium: Section 183 of the Internal Revenue Code: The Need for Statutory Reform*, 62 Ind. L.J. 425 (1987).

399 These consist of a ratable share of state and local real estate taxes and part of the mortgage interest expenses. A later chapter explores these subjects in detail.

consumption and are gone forever from an income tax point of view. They would be deductible if her dog breeding were an "actively entered into for profit."

Advising taxpayers on §183 is an ethically challenging activity. Sometimes, the advice "goes public" as in the case of the following excerpt:

> (1) keep good financial records that are used throughout the year for decision making and planning purposes. Make certain that expenses related to the land can be separated if necessary.
>
> (2) Before and throughout the years of operation consult a number of experts. Obtain written advice and follow it. This should also include information about available markets.
>
> (3) Devote considerable time to the activity, especially to managerial and financial duties.
>
> (4) Avoid swimming pools, tennis courts, etc., on the property. Keeping them separate from farm operations does not remove their potential damages.
>
> (5) Hire qualified personnel to do the things you cannot do competently.
>
> (6) Testify in court. Appear forthright, honest, and knowledgeable about the operation and about the type of activity in general.
>
> Some extras that should help:
>
> (1) have a profit plan in writing and update it periodically.
>
> (2) Keep nonfinancial records on the animals, crops, etc.
>
> (3) Document extraordinary events that affect the operation.
>
> (4) Advertise frequently in the manner appropriate to the activity.
>
> (5) Select and use a business name. Register it when appropriate.
>
> (6) Implement some costcutting measure when possible.
>
> (7) Periodically, obtain information about fair market values for all assets used in the business.

Warnings to the taxpayer are:

(1) anyone converting from a hobby must be considerably more conscientious than anyone else.

(2) Do not continue unsuccessful methods.

(3) Be careful about using the farm facilities for socializing or attending functions related to the activity that cannot be justified as good for business.

(4) Be careful about arranging transactions to insure profits occur. This may be held against you.

(5) An expert witness may damage your case. While this may be personally and financially objectionable to the owner, it may be the only action that will convince the court that a profit motive did exist.[400]

Problem 5-5:

Dr. Henry Carry is a rich orthodontist. Eighteen years ago, he purchased a 100-acre apple orchard. The orchard had a small house on it, into which Henry moved the man he hired as the farm manager, Alfred. Henry then built a four bedroom house and a swimming pool. He spent nearly every weekend there after at the farm. Nearly every weekend he and his wife had two or more guests. However, Dr. Carry spent part of every Saturday morning while at the farm discussing matters relating to the farm with Alfred. From January 8 years ago to January of last year the gross receipts from the farm amounted to $80,000/year and the expenses, including $20,000 per year for the main house, averaged $120,000 per year. This year, Alfred decided to change the crop and as a result there was no gross income this year and the expenses were $105,000. Dr. Carry deducted the excess of expense over gross income each year as a loss under §172. In answering these questions, make sure to identify the extent to which Dr. Carry can claim deductions relating to farm operations even if he is only engaged in a hobby.

1) Is his farming activity presumptively engaged in for a profit? See §183(d) and the permanent Regulations.

2) Was Dr. Carry right to report his farm results for the past eight years as he did?

3) What about the present year?

---

400 Burns & Groomer, *Effects of Section 183 on the Business/Hobby Controversy*, 58 TAXES 195, 206 (1980).

4) Can he properly claim that his farm losses should be allowed because, in fact, the value of the farm land has been steadily rising? Assume his guaranteed-deductible local taxes and interest on the farm land are $25,000/year. See Reg. §1.183-1(d) and -2(b)(4).

5) Now assume Dr. Carry quits being a dentist, moves to the farm, fires Alfred and takes over the operation on a full-time basis. If the farm still runs at a loss, can Dr. Carry deduct those losses?

J. WHAT DOES "CARRYING ON" A TRADE OR BUSINESS MEAN?

On a close reading of §162, one can see that even if expenses are "ordinary and necessary," one can only deduct them if they were incurred while one was *carrying on* a trade or business. By contrast, the expenses of acquiring a business or investigating an unrelated business do not qualify. The meaning of the term "carrying on" was explored in the famous Tax Court case that is excerpted from next.

FRANK v. COMMISSIONER

20 T.C. 511 (1953)

VAN FOSSAN, Judge.

[Morton Frank returned from the Navy and traveled the country looking for a newspaper plant to purchase in order to earn a living.]

OPINION

The only question presented is whether the petitioners may deduct $ 5,965 in the determination of their net income for the year 1946 as ordinary and necessary business expenses or as losses. The petitioners base their claim for deductions upon section [§162] of the Internal Revenue Code. The evidence reasonably establishes that the petitioners expended the amount of expenses stated in our Findings of Fact during the taxable year in traveling, telephone, telegraph, and legal expenses in the search for and investigation of newspaper and radio properties. This total amount was spent by the petitioners in their travels through various states in an endeavor to find a business which they could purchase and operate. These expenses do not include amounts spent while living in Phoenix, Arizona.

The travel expenses and legal fees spent in searching for a newspaper business with a view to purchasing the same cannot be deducted under the provisions of section 23 (a) (1), Internal Revenue Code. The petitioners were not engaged in any trade or business at the time the expenses were incurred. The trips made by the taxpayers from Phoenix, Arizona, were not related to the conduct of the business that they were then engaged in but were preparatory to locating a business venture of their own. The expenses of investigating and looking for a new business and trips preparatory to entering a business are not deductible as an ordinary and necessary business expense incurred in carrying on a trade or business. *George C. Westervelt*, 8 T. C. 1248. The word "pursuit" in the statutory phrase "in pursuit of a trade or business" is not used in the sense of "searching for" or "following after," but in the sense of "in connection with" or "in the course of" a trade or business. It presupposes an existing business with which petitioner is connected. The fact that petitioners had no established home during the period of their travels further complicates the question and alone may be fatal to petitioners' case. If they had no home, how could they have expenses "away from home"? The issue whether all or part of the expenses so incurred were capital expenditures is not raised or argued and we do not pass judgment on such question.

...

We conclude that the petitioners may not deduct the expenses claimed for 1946 under the applicable provisions of the Internal Revenue Code.

Decision will be entered for the respondent.

K. LOSSES AT THE "TRANSACTIONAL STAGE"

Frank is good law, but other rules now relax its grip. One is §195 that allows tax-deductible 180-month amortization of investigatory and start-up costs if the taxpayer acquires a business.[401] Another is the rule that once an investigation has ripened into negotiations to acquire a business, the taxpayer can deduct as a loss under §165 the costs that led to the negotiations -- as well as the cost of the negotiations -- if the deal falls apart. The following ruling provides an illustration of the latter concept. The concept behind applying §165 here is that the taxpayer has developed an intangible property interest in the deal which he can deduct if it collapses.

REV. RUL. 77-254

1977-2 C.B. 63

...

Advice has been requested whether, under the circumstances described below, a deduction in accordance with section 165(c)(2) of the Internal Revenue Code of 1954 is allowable to a taxpayer for a loss that was not compensated for by insurance or otherwise.

401 Rev. Rul. 99-23, 1990-1 C.B. 998 (all investigatory expenses in connection with a general search are deductible if taxpayer acquires a business), clarified by Announcement 99-89, 1999-2 CB 408.

An individual taxpayer began to search for a business to purchase. The individual placed advertisements in several newspapers and traveled to various locations throughout the country to investigate various businesses that the individual learned were for sale. The individual commissioned audits to evaluate the potential of several of these businesses. Eventually, the individual decided to purchase a specific business and incurred expenses in an attempt to purchase this business. For example, the individual retained a law firm to draft the documents necessary for the purchase. Because of certain disagreements between the individual and the owner of the business that developed after this decision was made, the individual abandoned all attempts to acquire the business.

Section 165(a) of the Code allows as a deduction any loss sustained during the taxable year that is not compensated for by insurance or otherwise. Section 165(c) provides that, in the case of individuals, the deduction is limited to (1) losses incurred in a trade or business, (2) losses incurred in any transaction entered into for profit, though not connected with a trade or business, and (3) losses of property not connected with a trade or business, if such losses arise from fire, storm, shipwreck or other casualty, or from theft.

Rev. Rul. 57-418, 1957-2 C.B. 143, holds that losses incurred in the search for a business or investment are deductible only when the activities are more than investigatory and the taxpayer has actually entered a transaction for profit and the project is later abandoned.

In *Seed v. Commissioner*, 52 T.C. 880 1969), *acq.*, 1970-2 C.B. xxi, the United States Tax Court allowed a deduction for expenses incurred by a taxpayer during an unsuccessful attempt to secure a charter to operate a savings and loan association. The court found that the taxpayer's extensive activities in the venture qualified as a transaction entered into for profit. Following the decision in *Seed* the court has continued to find that a taxpayer has entered a transaction for profit in cases in which the facts indicate that the taxpayer has gone beyond a general search and focused on the acquisition of a specific business or investment. *See Price v. Commissioner*, T.C. Memo. 1971- 323; *Domenie v. Commissioner*, T.C. Memo. 1975-94

In view of the decision in *Seed*, Rev. Rul. 57-418 is amplified to provide that a taxpayer will be considered to have entered a transaction for profit if, based on all the facts and circumstances, the taxpayer has gone beyond a general investigatory search for a new business or investment to focus on the acquisition to a specific business or investment.

Expenses incurred in the course of a general search for or preliminary investigation of a business or investment include those expenses related to the decisions *whether* to enter a transaction and *which* transaction to enter. Such expenses are personal and are not deductible under section 165 of the Code. Once the taxpayer has focused on the acquisition of a specific business or investment, expenses that are related to an attempt to acquire such business or investment are capital in nature or investment are capital in nature and, to the extent that the expenses are allocable to an asset the cost of which is amortizable or depreciable, may be amortized as part of the asset's cost if the attempted acquisition is successful. If the attempted acquisition fails, the amount capitalized is deductible in accordance with section 165(c)(2). The taxpayer need not actually enter the business or purchase the investment in order to obtain the deduction.

Accordingly, in the present case, the individual may deduct as losses incurred in a transaction entered into for profit the expenses incurred in the unsuccessful attempt to acquire a specific business. Thus, the individual's expenses in retaining a law firm to draft the purchase documents and any other expenses incurred in the attempt to complete the purchase of the business are deductible. The expenses for advertisements, travel to search for a new business, and the cost of audits that were designed to help the individual decide whether to attempt an acquisition were investigatory expenses and are not deductible.

. . .

Business Start-ups and Expansions

Section 195. In 1980 Congress enacted §195 in an attempt to reduce the kind of difficulties that taxpayers like Morton Frank confronted in the course of investigating and starting new businesses. Section 195 offers a middle ground between the taxpayer's desire for an immediate 100 percent deduction and the Treasury's Department's justifiable argument that if the taxpayer ultimately winds up with a business, then all the outlays associated with searching for the business should be capitalized into the business (i.e., frozen and made part of the basis of the business) as a part of the cost of its acquisition.

Section 195 covers a business the taxpayer acquires or the taxpayer starts from the ground up. Its approach is to identify "start-up expenditures," shunt them in to a separate account established solely for tax purposes, and allow the taxpayer to "amortize" (deduct against gross income in equal periodic amounts) those expenses over a not-less-than 180 month period beginning when the trade or business opens its door for business, with the possibility of deducting all the expenditures in the years the business begins business; the problems that follows handle the details.

The term "start-up expenditures" covers both the cost of investigation and the cost of starting up the business, but it excludes acquisition costs (such as legal fees paid in connection with buying a company), the costs of getting financing for the business, and "hard costs," such as the price of building a factory, that would have to be capitalized if the business were under way when the cost was incurred. This latter restriction performs the necessary function of preventing taxpayers from rapidly deducting capital expenses, while allowing deductions for expenses that would have been deductible if the taxpayer merely expanded its ongoing activities. (The last rule is consistent with the general rule that if the taxpayer is already in a particular industry, then the cost of seeking to expand within that industry is considered a mere "intramural expansion," the expenses of which are deductible under §162.) Morton Frank's problem was that he was not already in the media business. If he were already in the media business, and his search was for a way to expand the business, then there is authority that the investigatory expenses would have been deductible, unless the expenses resulted in acquiring a new entity (such as a corporation that owns a radio station).[402]

If the taxpayer does not choose to take advantage of the options available to her under §195, then she must capitalize her start-up expenses. Because one can never tell how long a business will last, and hence what the useful life of these expenditures might be, it is extremely unlikely that the taxpayer will otherwise be able to write off any of those expenditures until she either sells the business or the business fails (in which case she can claim a §165 loss for the capitalized expenditures). Unsuccessful "extramural" searches mean §195 never applies and the expenditures cannot be deducted because, as in the *Frank* case, they fall into the "personal consumption" category.

Job Searches. Employment agency expenses are a familiar application of §162. The IRS acknowledges that an employee can deduct the expense of seeking employment in the same trade or business, even if the attempt to obtain the job ends in failure.[403] This concession does not cover the taxpayer's first job or a job in a new trade or business, nor, according to the IRS, does it include a situation where the taxpayer obtained a job after an extensive bout of unemployment. This produces some odd results for people seeking public office. Apparently, the general rule is that one can never deduct the cost of seeking public election because one is no longer in the trade or business after one's term ends, and if one was not elected before, then one is entering a new trade or business. This is the way the Supreme Court put it in the case of a judge who sought to deduct re-election expenses; he did not incur the expenses while carrying on the business of being a judge, but rather he incurred them "in trying to be a judge."[404]

Problem 5-6:

Borton Mank, who is freshly out of the Navy and owns no business, comes to your law office to explain that he wants to buy a website business that accepts Euros, and wonders what will happen from a tax point of view if the following events occur:

1) He finds such a company for sale after paying $23,000 of search costs and he acquires the company, paying $2,000 in brokerage fees to buy the business.

402 See, e.g., York v. Commissioner, 261 F.2d 421 (4th Cir. 1958). But see, Central Texas S&L v. United States, 731 F.2d 1181 (5th Cir. 1984) (S&L's new branch capitalized under §263).

403 Rev. Rul. 77-16, 1977-1 C.B. 37.

404 McDonald v. United States, 323 U.S. 57 (1944). But see Rev. Rul. 71-470, 1971-2 C.B. 121 ruling that a judge was entitled to deduct the expenses he incurred in resisting a recall procedure that would have resulted in his removal from office. To put it another way, but for the expenditures he would have ceased carrying on the business of being a judge.

a. Can he elect to write off some or all of the $25,000 under §195, and if so, how much each year?

b. What if the business fails 40 months after starting up? What can he write off, if anything?

c. How would he treat the $23,000 search costs if he does not make the §195 election?

2) Same, but Borton instead incurs $23,000 in search costs and $1,000 in legal fees, but the deal falls apart after he enters into negotiations to buy the business. What can he deduct, if anything?

3) Same as "(1)," but he never even gets to into negotiations. He just gives up

4) Some years later, never having found the right business, Borton goes to law school and pays an employment agency a fee to get him his first job as a lawyer.

   a. Is the fee deductible as a business expense?

   b. What if he were a lawyer who lost his job in a law firm and paid an employment agency to help him find another job as a lawyer?

5) Borton wants to know if he can make an unenforceable offer so as to draw the sellers into negotiations, which he would then quit, but as to which he would claim a Rev. Rul. 77-254 deduction on his tax return for his expenses leading up to the negotiations. What do you advise him?

L. WHAT ARE "ORDINARY AND NECESSARY" EXPENSES?

Read §162(a) and Reg. §1.162-1

The Congress tends to be in a hurry when it comes to the fine points of tax legislation. Sometimes it is even in a hurry when it comes to constructing basic definitions; think back to how the Supreme Court was forced to define the term "gift" in *Duberstein.* Likewise, Congress failed to defined the crucial words "ordinary and necessary" in the predecessor to §162(a). The Supreme Court did provide important guidance in *Welch v. Helvering,*the next case, in which the taxpayer-salesman voluntarily paid many of the debts of a bankrupt former employer in order to improve his standing in his industry.

WELCH v. HELVERING

290 U.S. 111 (1933)

MR. JUSTICE CARDOZO delivered the opinion of the Court.

The question to be determined is whether payments by a taxpayer, who is in business as a commission agent, are allowable deductions in the computation of his income if made to the creditors of a bankrupt corporation in an endeavor to strengthen his own standing and credit.

In 1922 petitioner was the secretary of the E. L. Welch Company, a Minnesota corporation, engaged in the grain business. The company was adjudged an involuntary bankrupt, and had a discharge from its debts. Thereafter the petitioner made a contract with the Kellogg Company to purchase grain for it on a commission. In order to reestablish his relations with customers whom he had known when acting for the Welch Company and to solidify his credit and standing, he decided to pay the debts of the Welch business so far as he was able. In fulfillment of that resolve, he made payments of substantial amounts during five successive years. In 1924, the commissions were $ 18,028.20; the payments $ 3,975.97; in 1923, the commissions $ 31,377.07; the payments $ 11,968.20; in 1926, the commissions $ 20,925.25, the payments $ 12,815.72; in 1927, the commissions $ 22,119.61, the payments $ 7,379.72; and in 1928, the commissions $ 26,177.56, the payments $ 11,068.25. The Commissioner ruled that these payments were not deductible from income as ordinary and necessary expenses, but were rather in the nature of capital expenditures, an outlay for the development of reputation and good will. The Board of Tax Appeals sustained the action of the Commissioner (25 B.T.A. 117), and the Court of Appeals for the Eighth Circuit affirmed. 63 F.2d 976. The case is here on certiorari.

> "In computing net income there shall be allowed as deductions . . . all the ordinary and necessary expenses paid or incurred during the taxable year in carrying on any trade or business." Revenue Act of 1924, c. 234 . . . .

We may assume that the payments to creditors of the Welch Company were necessary for the development of the petitioner's business, at least in the sense that they were appropriate and helpful. *McCulloch v. Maryland*, 4 Wheat. 316. He certainly thought they were, and we should be slow to override his judgment. But the problem is not solved when the payments are characterized as necessary. Many necessary payments are charges upon capital. There is need to determine whether they are both necessary and ordinary. Now, what is ordinary, though there must always be a strain of constancy within it, is none the less a variable affected by time and place and circumstance. Ordinary in this context does not mean that the payments must be habitual or normal in the sense that the same taxpayer will have to make them often. a lawsuit affecting the safety of a business may happen once in a lifetime. The counsel fees may be so heavy that repetition is unlikely. None the less, the expense is an ordinary one because we know from experience that payments for such a purpose, whether the amount is large or small, are the common and accepted means of defense against attack. Cf. *Kornhauser v. United States*, 276 U.S. 145. The situation is unique in the life of the individual affected, but not in the life of the group, the community, of which he is a part. At such times there are norms of conduct that help to stabilize our judgment, and make it certain and objective. The instance is not erratic, but is brought within a known type.

The line of demarcation is now visible between the case that is here and the one supposed for illustration. We try to classify this act as ordinary or the opposite, and the norms of conduct fail us. No longer can we have recourse to any fund of business experience, to any known business practice. Men do at times pay the debts of others without legal obligation or the lighter obligation imposed by the usages of trade or by neighborly amenities, but they do not do so ordinarily, not even though the result might be to heighten their reputation for generosity and opulence. Indeed, if language is to be read in its natural and common meaning . . . we should have to say that payment in such circumstances, instead of being ordinary is in a high degree extraordinary. There is nothing ordinary in the stimulus evoking it, and none in the response. Here, indeed, as so often in other branches of the law, the decisive distinctions are those of degree and not of kind. One struggles in vain for any verbal formula that will supply a ready touchstone. The standard set up by the statute is not a rule of law; it is rather a way of life. Life in all its fullness must supply the answer to the riddle.

The Commissioner of Internal Revenue resorted to that standard in assessing the petitioner's income, and found that the payments in controversy came closer to capital outlays than to ordinary and necessary expenses in the operation of a business. His ruling has the support of a presumption of correctness, and the petitioner has the burden of proving it to be wrong. *Wickwire v. Reinecke*, 275 U.S. 101 . . . . Unless we can say from facts within our knowledge that these are ordinary and necessary expenses according to the ways of conduct and the forms of speech prevailing in the business world, the tax must be confirmed. But nothing told us by this record or within the sphere of our judicial notice permits us to give that extension to what is ordinary and necessary. Indeed, to do so would open the door to many bizarre analogies. One man has a family name that is clouded by thefts committed by an ancestor. To add to his own standing he repays the stolen money, wiping off, it may be, his income for the year. The payments figure in his tax return as ordinary expenses. Another man conceives the notion that he will be able to practice his vocation with greater ease and profit if he has an opportunity to enrich his culture. Forthwith the price of his education becomes an expense of the business, reducing the income subject to taxation. There is little difference between these expenses and those in controversy here. Reputation and learning are akin to capital assets, like the good will of an old partnership. Cf. *Colony Coal & Coke Corp. v. Commissioner*, 52 F.2d 923. For many, they are the only tools with which to hew a pathway to success. The money spent in acquiring them is well and wisely spent. It is not an ordinary expense of the operation of a business.

Many cases in the federal courts deal with phases of the problem presented in the case at bar. To attempt to harmonize them would be a futile task. They involve the appreciation of particular situations, at times with borderline conclusions. . . .

The decree should be

Affirmed.

Notes on the term "Ordinary and Necessary"

Policy considerations. One deep theory for *Welch* is that taxpayers should always, as a general matter, use only after-tax dollars for their personal consumption. Another is that taxpayers should never be allowed to deduct gain-seeking expenses that are paid now, but that benefit future periods. Those deep preferences manifest themselves in §§262 and 263. They lie at the heart of this Chapter. The concept of "ordinariness" is now generally codified in §263, which requires taxpayers to capitalize (turn into basis of an asset, as opposed to currently deduct) expenditures that produce lasting value. The Supreme Court's decision in *Commissioner v. Tellier*[405] puts it this way:

> The principal function of the term "ordinary" in §162(a) is to clarify the distinction, often difficult, between expenses that are currently deductible and those that are in the nature of capital expenditures, which, if deductible at all, must be amortized over the useful life of the asset.

Notice how the court hedged by using the words "principal function." That implies that there is always a risk that the IRS will attack the taxpayer's expenditure as personal consumption using the alternative definition of "ordinary", meaning "not strange." For example, if the expenditure had only a slight benefit from the point of view of furthering his business career, but had a significant impact on improving his reputation on his block, it is likely that a present day Mr. Welch would not be entitled to deduct his expenditures because they were "not necessary." Alternatively, they might be attacked as too enduring to write off under the usual meaning of "ordinary."

Jenkins v. Commissioner[406] is a useful counterpoint to *Welch* with respect to the alternative meaning of "ordinary." The facts involved a highly successful country singer known as Conway Twitty. Conway Twitty had long used a unique logo in connection with his work as an enter-

405 383 U.S. 687, 689-690 (1966).

406 47 T.C.M. 238 (1983).

tainer and in connection with his stage name. It consisted of an image of a small yellow bird (the Twitty Bird) strumming a guitar. Twitty earned his living from live performances and from song writing and record royalties, including from contracts with major record distributors. Twitty began a restaurant enterprise known as "Twitty Burger, Inc." The restaurant enterprise failed and caused his co-investors to lose their investments. The taxpayer repaid the investors out of his own pocket, and claimed a business expense deduction as a country music performer for doing so. His theory was that he had a particular reputation to maintain. The Tax Court allowed Conway his deduction, reasoning that country music singers are "different" in that their reputations for honest dealings are crucial to preserving their careers. In Jenkins' case, he had a lot to lose because he had a highly successful career that demonstrably stood to be harmed by not repaying his investors. Had the deal worked out, the product would have been "Twitty Burgers" (naturally).

Capital expenditures. An example of a typical capital expenditure occurs if a doctor adds a new wing to his medical building which will enhance his income for years to come. No one would consider that the new wing was an expense that he should be entitled to write off this year against his Federal Income Tax base. It is obviously an improvement that adds value to his building. The general rule is that anything one makes or acquires that will last substantially beyond the taxable year constitutes capital expenditure.[407] This is subject to the so-called "small hand tools" exception, which allows people to deduct small items such as hammers and pens even though they may last well into the following year.[408] As always, there are exceptions. Take a brief look at §§ 263(a)(1)(A)-(G), which lists items that are in substance improvements that Congress allows taxpayers to treat as ordinary current deductions.

Costs of generating tax-exempt income. There is no deduction for generating tax-exempt income. For example, if you were a farmer and raised crops that cost you $10,000 in potential tax deductions and ate 10% of the crop, your deduction would drop to $9,000. See § 265(a)(1).

Mexican Law on Business Deductions. Not every country is as tolerant of business-related deductions as the United States. In Mexico, for example, an expenditure must be "strictly indispensable" to be deductible.[409] There must be moments when every student of the Code (but few taxpayers) would appreciate the simplicity of that rule.

Problem 5-7:

Investment advisors typically charge an annual fee for their services, based on the amount of money of the client that they manage. The Tax Court has ruled[410] that annual fees paid to

407 See Reg. §1.263(a)-2.

408 See, e.g., §1.162-3 (Materials and supplies), §1.162-12 (Expenses of farmers).

409

410 Dolin v. Commissioner, 54 TCM 1448 (1988); see also Reg. Sec. 1.67-1T(a)(1)(ii).

investment advisors to make recommendations as to which stocks to buy and which to sell can be deducted, as opposed to being capitalized into the cost of the stocks. Do you agree with the ruling? Why or why not?

Problem 5-8:

Joan Bronson operated a grocery store in San Francisco. Although she had been in business at the same location for many years and had a large regular group of customers, she became worried when the chain supermarkets started using cash prize contests. She decided that she would not try to compete in this way, but instead she sent a letter to each of her regular customers, inviting them to a cocktail party. During that year she had two cocktail parties, one in the store itself, and one at her home, in each case with regular customers. The total cost was $1,000. During that same year Bronson's gross receipts declined about 10 percent. She had not previously spent any money on advertising or on entertainment. Is the $1,000 deductible?[411] Do not be alarmed if there is no obvious answer. This problem is designed to provoke thought and does not lend itself to a clear-cut answer.

M. DEDUCTIONS FOR LEGAL EXPENSES

One can generally deduct legal fees incurred in a trade or business or as an investor under §§162 and 212, respectively. However, as in all other areas, if the fees and costs are associated with the acquisition or improvement of a property with a useful life that continues well past the end of the year, the expenses must be capitalized, studying the issue of deduction prospectively.[412] Litigation fees, however, are evaluated using a retrospective test, which is described very soon.

A personal litigation cost, such as the cost of suing a merchant who sold you a defective home refrigerator, is treated as nondeductible consumption expenditures. Often the hard part is determining whether an expenditure is personal or gain-seeking. For example, should a husband be entitled to deduct legal fees paid to protect his source of his livelihood -- say his car dealership -- from becoming his wife's property in a bitter divorce suit?[413]

411 See Reg. §1.162-20(a)(2) and Sanitary Farms Dairy, Inc v. Commissioner,., 25 T.C. 463 (1955), Acq. 1956-2 C.B. 8 holding that the cost of a big game hunt in Africa was deductible as an ordinary and necessary expense of a dairy business in Erie, Pennsylvania because the dairy had in large measure become a museum containing stuffed wild animals and the trip had great publicity value. And see Sullivan v. Commissioner, 43 T.C.M. 880 (1982) in which a gas station owner was allowed a $162 deduction for beer served to customers to boost sales.

412 Reg. §1.263(a)-1.

413 See generally Barton, *Tax Aspects of Divorce and Property Settlement Agreements -- The Davis, Gilmore and Patrick Cases*, U.So.Cal.1964 Tax Inst. 421; Barton, *Current Tax Problems in Marriage and Divorce*, U.So.Cal.1967 Tax Inst. 609.

UNITED STATES v. GILMORE

372 U.S. 39 (1963), 83 S. Ct. 623

MR. JUSTICE HARLAN delivered the opinion of the Court.

[The taxpayer was the owner of the controlling stock interests in three automobile franchises. He had spent $32,537.15 in 1953 and $8,074.21 in 1954 on litigation expenses for a divorce from his wife. His wife had filed for divorce and tried to get the stock interests. He counterclaimed and sought to defeat his wife's claim for two reasons: first, to protect the stock interests which ensured his livelihood through corporate positions with the dealerships; second, to defeat her claim for divorce because it alleged marital infidelity which, if believed, might lead to cancellation of the franchises. He won the counterclaim and defeated his wife's original divorce claim. He tried to deduct the litigation expenses as expenditures to "conserve" property held for the production of income. The Court of Claims allocated 80% of his expenses to the business side of the litigation. The government disagreed with the legal standard the Court of Claims applied, and appealed.]

. . .

. . . In so holding the Court of Claims stated:

> "Of course it is true that in every divorce case a certain amount of the legal expenses are incurred for the purpose of obtaining the divorce and a certain amount are incurred in an effort to conserve the estate and are not necessarily deductible under section 23 (a)(2), but when the facts of a particular case clearly indicate [as here] that the property, around which the controversy evolves, is held for the production of income and without this property the litigant might be denied not only the property itself but the means of earning a livelihood, then it must come under the provisions of section 23 (a)(2) . . . . The only question then is the allocation of the expenses to this phase of the proceedings." 290 F.2d, at 947.

The Government does not question the amount or formula for the expense allocation made by the Court of Claims. Its sole contention here is that the court below misconceived the test governing §23 (a)(2) deductions, in that the deductibility of these expenses turns, so it is argued, not upon the *consequences* to respondent of a failure to defeat his wife's community property claims but upon the *origin* and *nature* of the claims themselves. So viewing Dixie Gilmore's claims, whether relating to the existence or division of community property, it is contended that the expense of resisting them must be deemed nondeductible "personal" or "family" expense under §24 (a)(1), not deductible expense under §23 (a)(2). For reasons given hereafter we think the Government's position is sound and that it must be sustained.

I.

For income tax purposes Congress has seen fit to regard an individual as having two personalities: "one is [as] a seeker after profit who can deduct the expenses incurred in that search; the other is [as] a creature satisfying his needs as a human and those of his family but who cannot deduct such consumption and related expenditures." The Government regards § 23 (a)(2) as embodying a category of the expenses embraced in the first of these roles.

Initially, it may be observed that the wording of § 23 (a)(2) more readily fits the Government's view of the provision than that of the Court of Claims. For in context "conservation of property" seems to refer to operations performed with respect to the property itself, such as safeguarding or upkeep, rather than to a taxpayer's retention of ownership in it. But more illuminating than the mere language of § 23 (a)(2) is the history of the provision.

Prior to 1942 § 23 allowed deductions only for expenses incurred "in carrying on any trade or business," the deduction presently authorized by § 23 (a)(1). In *Higgins v. Commissioner*, 312 U.S. 212, this Court gave that provision a narrow construction, holding that the activities of an individual in supervising his own securities investments did not constitute the "carrying on of a trade or business," and hence that expenses incurred in connection with such activities were not tax deductible. Similar results were reached in *United States v. Pyne*, 3 U.S. 127, and *City Bank Co. v. Helvering*, 3 U.S. 121. The Revenue Act of 1942 (56 Stat. 798, § 121), by adding what is now § 23 (a)(2), sought to remedy the inequity inherent in the disallowance of expense deductions in respect of such profitseeking activities, the income from which was nonetheless taxable.

As noted in *McDonald v. Commissioner*, 323 U.S. 57, 62, the purpose of the 1942 amendment was merely to enlarge "the category of incomes with reference to which expenses were deductible." And committee reports make clear that deductions under the new section were subject to the same limitations and restrictions that are applicable to those allowable under § 23 (a)(1). Further, this Court has said that § 23 (a)(2) "is comparable and *in pari materia* with § 23 (a)(1)," providing for a class of deductions "coextensive with the business deductions allowed by § 23 (a)(1), except for" the requirement that the incomeproducing activity qualify as a trade or business. *Trust of Bingham v. Commissioner*, 325 U.S. 365, 373, 374.

A basic restriction upon the availability of a § 23 (a)(1) [now §162(a)] deduction is that the expense item involved must be one that has a business origin. That restriction not only inheres in the language of § 23 (a)(1) itself, confining such deductions to "expenses . . . incurred . . . in carrying on any trade or business," but also follows from § 24 (a)(1), expressly rendering nondeductible "in any case . . . personal, living, or family expenses." See note 9, *supra*. In light of what has already been said with respect to the advent and thrust of § 23 (a)(2), it is clear that the "personal . . . or family expenses" restriction of § 24 (a)(1) must impose the same limitation upon the reach of § 23 (a)(2) in other words that the only kind of expenses deductible under § 23 (a)(2) are those that relate to a "business," that is, profitseeking, purpose. The pivotal issue in this case then becomes: was this part of respondent's litigation costs a "business" rather than a "personal" or "family" expense?

The answer to this question has already been indicated in prior cases. In *Lykes v. United States*, 343 U.S. 118, the Court rejected the contention that legal expenses incurred in contesting the assessment of a gift tax liability were deductible. The taxpayer argued that if he had been required to pay the original deficiency he would have been forced to liquidate his stockholdings, which were his main source of income, and that his legal expenses were therefore incurred in the "conservation" of incomeproducing property and hence deductible under § 23 (a)(2). The Court first noted that the "deductibility [of the expenses] turns wholly upon the nature of the activities to which they relate" (343 U.S., at 123), and then stated:

> "Legal expenses do not become deductible merely because they are paid for services which relieve a taxpayer of liability. That argument would carry us too far. It would mean that the expense of defending almost any claim would be deductible by a taxpayer on the ground that such defense was made to help him keep clear of liens whatever incomeproducing property he might have. For example, it suggests that the expense of defending an action based upon personal injuries caused by a taxpayer's negligence while driving an automobile for pleasure should be deductible. Section 23 (a)(2) never has been so interpreted by us. . . .
>
> "While the threatened deficiency assessment . . . added urgency to petitioner's resistance of it, neither its size nor its urgency determined its character. It related to the tax payable on petitioner's gifts . . . . The expense of contesting the amount of the deficiency was thus at all times attributable to the gifts, as such, and accordingly was not deductible.
>
> "If, as suggested, the relative size of each claim, in proportion to the incomeproducing resources of a defendant, were to be a touchstone of the deductibility of the expense of resisting the claim, substantial uncertainty and inequity would inhere in the rule. . . . It is not a ground for . . . [deduction] that the claim, if justified, will consume incomeproducing property of the defendant." 343 U.S., at 125126.

In *Kornhauser v. United States*, 276 U.S. 145, this Court considered the deductibility of legal expenses incurred by a taxpayer in defending against a claim by a former business partner that fees paid to the taxpayer were for services rendered during the existence of the partnership. In holding that these expenses were deductible even though the taxpayer was no longer a partner at the time of suit, the Court formulated the rule that "where a suit or action against a taxpayer is directly connected with, or . . . proximately resulted from, his business, the expense incurred is a business expense . . . ." 276 U.S., at 153. Similarly, in a case involving an expense incurred in satisfying an obligation (though not a litigation expense), it was said that "it is the origin of the liability out of which the expense accrues" or "the kind of transaction out of which the obligation arose . . . which [is] crucial and controlling." *Deputy v. du Pont, 308 U.S. 488, 494, 496.*

The principle we derive from these cases is that the characterization, as "business" or "personal," of the litigation costs of resisting a claim depends on whether or not the claim *arises in connection with* the taxpayer's profitseeking activities. It does not depend on the consequences that might result to a taxpayer's incomeproducing property from a failure to defeat the claim, for, as *Lykes* teaches, that "would carry us too far" and would not be compatible with the basic lines of expense deductibility drawn by Congress. Moreover, such a rule would lead to capricious results. If two taxpayers are each sued for an automobile accident while driving for pleasure, deductibility of their litigation costs would turn on the mere circumstance of the character of the assets each happened to possess, that is, whether the judgments against them stood to be satisfied out of income or non incomeproducing property. We should be slow to attribute to Congress a purpose producing such unequal treatment among taxpayers, resting on no rational foundation.

Confirmation of these conclusions is found in the incongruities that would follow from acceptance of the Court of Claims' reasoning in this case. Had this respondent taxpayer conducted his automobiledealer business as a sole proprietorship, rather than in corporate form, and claimed a deduction under § 23 (a)(1), the potential impact of his wife's claims would have been no different than in the present situation. Yet it cannot well be supposed that § 23 (a)(1) would have afforded him a deduction, since his expenditures, made in connection with a marital litigation, could hardly be deemed "expenses . . . incurred . . . in carrying on any trade or business." Thus, under the Court of Claims' view expenses may be even less deductible if the taxpayer is carrying on a trade or business instead of some other incomeproducing activity. But it was manifestly Congress' purpose with respect to deductibility to place all incomeproducing activities on an equal footing, and it would surely be a surprising result were it now to turn out that a change designed to achieve equality of treatment in fact had served only to reverse the inequality of treatment.

For these reasons, we resolve the conflict among the lower courts on the question before us . . . in favor of the view that the origin and character of the claim with respect to which an expense was incurred, rather than its potential consequences upon the fortunes of the taxpayer, is the controlling basic test of whether the expense was "business" or "personal" and hence whether it is deductible or not under § 23 (a)(2). We find the reasoning underlying the cases taking the "consequences" view unpersuasive.

Baer v. Commissioner, 196 F.2d 646, upon which the Court of Claims relied in the present case, is the leading authority on that side of the question. There the Court of Appeals for the Eighth Circuit allowed a § 23 (a)(2) expense deduction to a taxpayer husband with respect to attorney's fees paid in a divorce proceeding in connection with an alimony settlement which had the effect of preserving intact for the husband his controlling stock interest in a corporation, his principal source of livelihood. The court reasoned that since the evidence showed that the taxpayer was relatively unconcerned about the divorce itself "the controversy did not go to the question of . . . [his] liability [for alimony] but to the manner in which . . . [that liability] might be met . . . without greatly disturbing his financial structure"; therefore the legal services were "for the purpose of conserving and maintaining" his incomeproducing property. 196 F.2d, at 649650, 651.

It is difficult to perceive any significant difference between the "question of liability" and "the manner" of its discharge, for in both instances the husband's purpose is to avoid losing valuable property. Indeed most of the cases which have followed *Baer* have placed little reliance on that distinction, and have tended to confine the deduction to situations where the wife's alimony claims, if successful, might have completely destroyed the husband's capacity to earn a living. Such may be the situation where loss of control of a particular corporation is threatened, in contrast to instances where the impact of a wife's support claims is only upon diversified holdings of incomeproducing securities. But that rationale too is unsatisfactory. For diversified security holdings are no less "property held for the production of income" than a large block of stock in a single company. And as was pointed out in *Lykes, supra*, at 126, if the relative impact of a claim on the incomeproducing resources of a taxpayer were to determine deductibility, substantial "uncertainty and inequity would inhere in the rule."

We turn then to the determinative question in this case: did the wife's claims respecting respondent's stockholdings arise in connection with his profitseeking activities?

II.

In classifying respondent's legal expenses the court below did not distinguish between those relating to the claims of the wife with respect to the *existence* of community property and those involving the *division* of any such property. *Supra*, pp. 4142. Nor is such a breakdown necessary for a disposition of the present case. It is enough to say that in both aspects the wife's claims stemmed entirely from the marital relationship, and not, under any tenable view of things, from incomeproducing activity. This is obviously so as regards the claim to more than an equal division of any community property found to exist. For any such right depended entirely on the wife's making good her charges of marital infidelity on the part of the husband. The same conclusion is no less true respecting the claim relating to the existence of community property. For no such property could have existed but for the marriage relationship. Thus none of respondent's expenditures in resisting these claims can be deemed "business" expenses, and they are therefore not deductible under § 23 (a)(2).

In view of this conclusion it is unnecessary to consider the further question suggested by the Government: whether that portion of respondent's payments attributable to litigating the issue of the existence of community property was a capital expenditure or a personal expense. In neither event would these payments be deductible from gross income.

The judgment of the Court of Claims is reversed and the case is remanded to that court for further proceedings consistent with this opinion. It is so ordered.

Judgment of Court of Claims reversed and case remanded.

MR. JUSTICE BLACK and MR. JUSTICE DOUGLAS believe that the Court reverses this case because of an unjustifiably narrow interpretation of the 1942 amendment to § 23 of the Internal Revenue Code and would accordingly affirm the judgment of the Court of Claims.

Notes on Litigation Expenses

The questionable deduction for the costs of enforcing alimony payments. Until 2018, attorney's fees paid by an ex-wife to collect alimony are deductible according to Reg. §1.2621(b)(7).[414] The deduction for qualified alimony and separate maintenance payments by the payor and the inclusion of the payments in gross income by the payee, as well as the special rules for alimony trusts, are generally repealed after 2018; but only for divorce or separation instruments executed after December 31, 2018 or executed before January 1, 2019, and modified after 2018 when the modification expressly applies the repeal of the qualified alimony and separate maintenance rules.Would a deduction not conflict with the origin of the claim doctrine? How can the Regulation be reconciled with *Gilmore?*

Gilmore II. The *Gilmore* decision you just read was followed by a later decision, known as "Gilmore II," in which the court held that Mr. Gilmore's expenditures to defend his ownership interest in stock could be capitalized into the stock.[415] As a result, Mr. Gilmore salvaged a tax benefit from his expenditures by assuring himself of a smaller taxable gain (or larger loss) if and when he eventually sold the stock. That is a lot better from his perspective than seeing those expenditures classified as nondeductible personal consumption.

Capitalizing litigation expenses. In *Woodward v. Commissioner*[416] the Court held that expenses of litigation relating to appraisal of minority shares were not deductible but must instead be capitalized, affirming the Gilmore II doctrine.[417] This time, the origin of the claim underlying the legal fees was found to be "capital" and profit-seeking, not personal in nature, because it involved determining the price of a capital asset -- stock -- to be sold. The decision ultimately did yield a tax benefit because it was added to the basis of the stock.

Deduction for tax advice. In addition to deducting legal fees under §212(1) and (2), there is §212(3), the darling of tax lawyers and tax accountants. It lets individual taxpayers deduct fees and expenses incurred "in connection with the determination, collection, or refund of any tax." Incidentally, notice how §212(3) conflicts with the caption to §212, which suggests it only covers

414 See also Wild v. Commissioner, 42 T.C. 706 (1964), (such expenses held deductible).

415 Gilmore v. U.S., 245 F. Supp. 383 (N.D.Cal.S.D.1965) ("Gilmore II").

416 397 U.S. 572 (1970).

417 See Gilmore v. U.S., 245 F. Supp. 383 (N.D.Cal.S.D.1965) ("Gilmore II").

gain-seeking expenses. The caption is wrong; one can deduct tax assistance even if the tax relates solely to personal consumption. Captions do not count in interpreting the Code.[418]

Apportioning litigation expenses. So far, we have looked at legal expenses as being either entirely deductible or entirely nondeductible. In some cases, apportionment of legal costs is required, say where the fees are partly for deductible tax advice and partly for purely divorce-related expenses. Even if the legal fees are entirely business-related, an allocation may have to be made between fees that must be capitalized (such as those incurred in defense of title to property) and those that may be deducted currently.[419] This makes it tempting, but obviously improper, for a lawyer to misallocate an invoice for legal services as tax advice.[420]

A selective deduction for particular recoveries. Section 62(a)(20) grants an above-the-line deduction for attorneys fees and related costs that plaintiffs incur in connection with certain listed discrimination actions (e.g., the Age Discrimination in Employment Act, and the Americans with Disabilities Act), certain claims against the government, and certain actions brought under the Medicare Secondary Payer statute.

There is now a general "tax advice" privilege. Score one for the accountants. Section 7525 extends the attorneyclient privilege of confidentiality to "tax advice" furnished to a taxpayer by any "federally authorized tax practitioner" meaning a lawyer, CPA, Enrolled Agent or Enrolled Actuary. "Tax advice" means any advice given "with respect to a matter which is within the scope of the individual's authority to practice" under 31 U.S.C. §330, meaning his or her right to make presentations before the IRS. It does not authorize accountants to practice law.

The privilege may only be asserted in any "noncriminal tax matter before the Service" and in any "noncriminal tax proceeding in federal court with respect to such matter," brought by or against the U.S. The privilege may be asserted, "to the extent the communication would be considered a privileged communication if it were between a taxpayer and an attorney." The new privilege does not apply to any written communications made between a corporation or its representative and a federally authorized tax practitioner (meaning a C.P.A., enrolled agent, or enrolled actuary) in connection with the promotion of the corporation's participation in any tax shelter. The §7525 privilege also does not protect communications with nonlawyers if the inquiry comes from another agency, such as the Securities & Exchange Commission.

In addition, the privilege for communications with an accountant comes into being if the accountant is retained by the client's lawyer for purposes of providing assistance to the lawyer.[421] The accountant must be retained to advise the lawyer, as distinguished from the law-

418 §7806(b).

419 See, e.g., Eisler v. Commissioner, 59 T.C. 634 (1973) (fees to defend business reputation involving both allegations of negligence and claims to property). Acq. 1973-2.

420 It would presumably be both "disreputable conduct" under the Circular 230 as well as a deceptive practice under Model Rule 8.4.

421 United States v. Kovel, 296 F.2d 918, (2d Cir. 1961).

yer's client while hiding behind a false cloak of lawyer-client privilege;[422] this rule discourages taxpayers from opportunistically appointing a lawyer to appoint an accountant who does the real tax work. Preparing a tax return is generally not subject to attorney-client privilege because it is perceived as clerical in nature[423] and so cannot be protected by §7525 or by regular attorney-client privilege.

Problem 5-9:

Which of the following expenses paid by a client to a lawyer are likely to be deductible under the authority of §212?

1) Client, going through a divorce, pays lawyer $100 for tax advice incident to the divorce.

2) Client, going through a divorce, pays $100 for legal advice on how to obtain a fair share of the community property of the spouses.

3) Client, owner of an automobile dealership, pays lawyer $1,000 to defend against loss of the automobile dealership in a divorce proceeding.

4) Client, a member of a shareholder group, pays lawyer her $1,000 share of a collective legal fee to sue in Delaware Chancery Court to establish fair value for stock which she declined to dispose of as part of a merger arrangement and is exercising her legal right to sell the stock at its fair market value.

5) Homeowner pays lawyer $100 to contest this year's property tax assessment by the county.

6) Ex-spouse pays lawyer $1,000 to collect unpaid taxable alimony. See Reg. §1.262-1(b)(7)

7) Wife pays $1,000 to collect nontaxable child support. See §265(a).

8) Judge pays lawyer $100 to defend him against reckless driving charge. If the judge loses, he may lose his job.

---

422 United States v. Adlman, 68 F.3d 1495, (2d Cir. 1995).

423 See Graves, *Attorney-Client Privilege in Preparation of Income Tax Returns: What Every Attorney-Preparer Should Know*, 42 Tax Lawyer 577 (1989).

Read lightly §162(c), (e) and (f)

A current expense incurred to generate taxable income may be disallowed as being in violation of public policy. There is a long history of Supreme Court decisions along this line. The standard developed by the Court is that a deduction must be disallowed if its allowance "would frustrate sharply defined national or state policies proscribing particular kinds of conduct."[424]

The Supreme Court refused to apply the public policy doctrine with respect to paying the costs of mounting a legal defense in *Commissioner v. Tellier*[425]. The case involved a securities dealer charged with violating federal securities laws, resulting in a fine and imprisonment. The Court reasoned that the expenses grew out of the dealer's business, under the origin of the claim test, and noted the IRS concession that they were appropriate and helpful (albeit once in a lifetime), and they were ordinary, there being no capital asset involved. The Court stressed that the income tax is a tax on net income, citing the words of Senator Williams (below) and framed the issue in terms of whether hiring a lawyer results in an immediate and sharp frustration of a declared public policy. Having framed the issue, it was easier for the Court to conclude that the public policy limitation did not apply. After all, Tellier was merely exercising his Constitutional rights. The words of Senator Williams in a key 1913 Floor Debate are worth quoting:

> [T]he object of this bill is to tax a man's net income; that is to say, what he has at the end of the year after deducting from his receipts his expenditures or losses. It is not to reform men's moral characters; that is not the object of the bill at all. The tax is not levied for the purpose of restraining people from betting on horse races or upon "futures," but the tax is framed for the purpose of making a man pay upon his net income, his actual profit during the year. The law does not care where he got it from, so far as the tax is concerned, although the law may very properly care in another way.[426]

Since 1969, particular subsections of §162 have largely pre-empted the field of moral restrictions on deductions, but the express restrictions in §162 (which are largely restated in the §212

424 Tank Truck Rentals v. Commissioner, 356 U.S. 30, 33 (1958) (disallowance of deduction for fines imposed on trucking company that chose to violate Pennsylvania maximum weight limits). See generally Comment, *The Tax Treatment of Illegal Payments after Alex v. Commissioner*, 79 Colum. L. Rev. 589 (1979); Note, *Business Expenses, Disallowance and Public Policy: Some Problems of Sanctioning With the Internal Revenue Code*, 72 Yale L.J. 108 (1962).

425 383 U.S. 687 (1966).

426 50 Cong. Rec. 3849. Floor colloquies are sometimes fabricated by special interest groups with the collaboration of the speakers. See, e.g., Stratton, *Accountant-Client Privilege: Unclear from the Start*, 98 Tax Notes Today 128-2 (July 6, 1998) (reports that large accounting firms were "scripting a colloquy to be held between key Senators" with respect to a bill of importance to the accounting profession).

regulations[427]) do not apply to other Code sections such as §§165 (property losses) or 166 (bad debts). Accordingly, the judicially constructed public policy limitation on deductions remains vibrant outside §162 and §212.

MAZZEI v. COMMISSIONER

61 T.C. 497 (1974)

Quealy, J.

Respondent determined a deficiency in income tax against petitioners for the taxable year 1965 in the amount of $7,676.86. As a result of certain concessions by the parties, the sole question presented for decision is whether the petitioners are entitled to deduct a loss in the taxable year 1965 on account of being defrauded in a scheme to reproduce United States currency. Petitioners claim the deduction under section 165(c)(2) or section 165(c)(3).

FINDINGS OF FACT

Some of the facts have been stipulated, and such facts and stipulated exhibits attached thereto are incorporated herein by this reference.

Petitioners Raymond Mazzei and Elizabeth D. Mazzei are husband and wife. Their residence at the time they filed their petition herein was Hopewell, Va. Petitioners filed their joint Federal income tax return for the calendar year 1965 with the Internal Revenue Service Center in Philadelphia, Pa. As Elizabeth D. Mazzei is a party herein solely because she filed a joint income tax return with her husband, Raymond Mazzei will hereinafter be referred to as petitioner.

During the year at issue, and for some time prior thereto, petitioner operated a sheet metal company in Hopewell, Va., in partnership with his brother. Vernon Blick was an employee of the company in 1965 and had been an employee for 4 or 5 years.

In March 1965, Blick was told by a man named Cousins of a scheme for reproducing money. Blick accompanied Cousins to a hotel in Washington, D.C., where Cousins introduced Blick to two other men named Collins and Joe. At that time, Collins and Joe showed Blick a black box which they asserted was capable of reproducing money. The black box was approximately 15 inches long, 8 or 10 inches wide, and 6 inches deep, about the size of a shoebox. It was made of metal and had a handle on it.

Blick gave Collins a $10 bill which Collins took and placed between two pieces of white paper of about the same size. Collins put the money and the paper into the box and connected the box to an electric outlet. The black box began a buzzing sound which continued for about 10

427 Reg. §1.212-1(p) adopts many of the public policy restrictions that appear in §162, trying bring the two Code sections into harmony. Unfortunately, the §212 regulations never quite manage to catch up because the Treasury Department is swamped by the need to issue new ones.

minutes. Then Collins reached into the box and pulled out Blick's $10 bill and what appeared to be a new $10 bill. Collins then told Blick that they could not reproduce any more money at that time because they did not have enough of the type of paper required. In addition, Collins indicated that they would rather not use small denomination bills, but instead they wanted larger denominations such as $100 bills. Blick then returned to Hopewell.

Blick having told Cousins about petitioner, Cousins requested Blick to have petitioner meet with Cousins. In April or May of 1965, Blick recounted the events of the demonstration to petitioner. Thereafter, petitioner and Blick went to see Cousins in Hopewell and discussed a "deal" to reproduce money with Cousins, Collins, and Joe in Washington, D.C., and New York City. Petitioner was to provide money which Cousins, Collins, and Joe would reproduce and then return to petitioner.

After his first meeting with Cousins, petitioner was contacted several times concerning further arrangements for reproducing money.

In May 1965, Cousins took petitioner and Blick to New York City. Petitioner carried $10,000 in cash with him at Cousins' request. They went to a hotel in Brooklyn where Cousins telephoned Collins and Joe who then came over with the black box. Petitioner gave Collins a $100 bill in order to demonstrate the reproduction box. Collins went through the "reproduction" process and returned to petitioner his bill and a new $100 bill. Petitioner requested that they reproduce more money, but was told that there was not enough of the right kind of paper, which was supposed to be a special type used by the Federal Government and obtained through a "friend" in Washington, D.C. Cousins then took petitioner and Blick back to Hopewell that afternoon.

Petitioner continued to inquire of Cousins about reproducing more money but again was told that the difficulty in obtaining the right kind of reproducing paper was holding things up. However, petitioner did give $700 to Cousins who supposedly went to New York and reproduced it. Cousins returned petitioner's $700 plus $300 more, supposedly reproduced. Once again, Cousins said that the reason he did not reproduce more was because of the lack of sufficient paper.

Approximately a week later, Joe telephoned petitioner from New York and stated that they would be ready in a few days to proceed with the deal. Joe requested petitioner to obtain $20,000 in large denominations, preferably $100 bills.

On June 1, 1965, petitioner cashed a check for $20,000 on his company's account at a local bank, taking the proceeds in $100 bills. Blick obtained $5,000, borrowed from petitioner's brother, also through a check on the company account. Several days later, Joe called petitioner, confirmed that petitioner had acquired the cash and requested petitioner and Blick to meet him in New York.

On June 3, 1965, petitioner and Blick flew to New York City with the money. Once in New York, petitioner and Blick went to a designated hotel to meet Cousins, Collins, and Joe. Joe came by the hotel and met petitioner, confirming that petitioner and Blick had the money. The three then went outside where Collins was waiting with a taxicab. They proceeded to an apartment in Brooklyn, stopping on the way for Collins or Joe to purchase some liquor.

Once at the apartment, petitioner and Blick were again shown the black box. Collins then asked petitioner for the money. Petitioner handed Collins a packet of money containing $5,000. Collins removed the wrapper and placed the money into a pan of water. Collins then removed the money from the water and placed each $100 bill between two pieces of white paper which he then set aside. Collins continued the process until he finished with the series of bills in the $5,000 packet. Petitioner then handed Collins another $5,000 packet, and Collins repeated the same process. This continued until petitioner had given Collins the entire $20,000. Petitioner then informed Collins that Blick had $5,000, which Blick then gave to petitioner who in turn gave it to Collins.

Collins then informed petitioner and Blick that the black box was broken and would not work. Collins told them that they would have to use an oven, apparently to complete the reproduction process. Collins then turned on an ordinary electric oven which was in the apartment and put all of the money in the oven. At this point, two armed men broke into the room impersonating law enforcement officers making a counterfeiting raid. Petitioner and Blick were held at gunpoint while one of the men placed handcuffs on Joe. The two men representing themselves to be officers then removed the money from the oven. As the two intruders proceeded to the door of the apartment, petitioner broke away and ran up the street to seek the assistance of a police officer whom he saw. Petitioner reported the incident to the police officer, who told petitioner to wait until a squad car could arrive.

Meanwhile, Blick, who had remained with Collins, Joe, and the two intruders, requested them to return the money. Blick was told he would be shot if he attempted to retrieve the money. Then Collins, Joe, and the two intruders went out of the apartment, got into a taxicab and left with the money.

Petitioner returned with the police and found Blick alone. The black box was examined and found to be nothing more than a tin box with a buzzer. It could not have reproduced any money. Petitioner and Blick accompanied the police to the police station and filed a report of the incident. The next day, petitioner and Blick returned to Hopewell and reported the incident to the police there. The incident was also discussed with the Federal Bureau of Investigation.

On his Federal income tax return for the calendar year 1965, petitioner claimed a theft loss in the amount of $20,000 and took a deduction therefor in the amount of $19,900.

In his statutory notice of deficiency, respondent disallowed the deduction for the loss under section 165(c) (2) or (3) on the grounds of lack of adequate substantiation of the loss and, further, that allowance of the deduction would be contrary to public policy.

OPINION

Petitioner contends that the fact that he incurred a loss is substantiated by the evidence and that such loss is deductible under section 165(c)(2) or section 165(c)(3). Respondent contends initially that petitioner has failed to prove that a loss was in fact suffered, and, further, that even if a loss were proven in fact, a deduction for such loss would not be allowed under section 165(c)(2) or section 165(c)(3) on the grounds that allowance of such a deduction would be contrary to public policy. As our findings of fact indicate, the Court is convinced that petitioner, in fact, incurred a loss in the sum of $20,000, as the result of being defrauded. However, the deductibility of such loss is precluded by our decision in *Luther M. Richey, Jr.*, 33 T.C. 272 (1959).

In the *Richey* case, the taxpayer became involved with two other men in a scheme to counterfeit United States currency. The taxpayer observed a reproduction process involving the bleaching out of $1 bills and the transferring of the excess ink from $100 bills onto the bleached-out bills. Upon observing this demonstration, the taxpayer became convinced that the process could reproduce money. When the taxpayer later met with the other men in a hotel room to carry out the scheme, the taxpayer turned over to one of the other men $15,000 which was to be used in the duplication process. Before the process was completed, one of the other men to whom the taxpayer had given the $15,000 left the room under the pretext of going to get something and never returned. The taxpayer later discovered that his money was gone and was not able to recover it. We disallowed the taxpayer's claimed loss deduction under section 165(c)(2) and section 165(c)(3), on the grounds that to allow the loss deduction would constitute an immediate and severe frustration of the clearly defined policy against counterfeiting obligations of the United States as enunciated by title 18, U.S.C., sec. 471.This Court said:

> The record establishes that petitioner's conduct constituted an attempt to counterfeit, an actual start in the counterfeiting activity, and overt acts looking to consummation of the counterfeiting scheme. Petitioner actively participated in the venture. He withdrew money from the bank and changed it into high denomination bills with the full knowledge and intention that the money would be used to duplicate other bills. He was physically present at the place of alteration, and assisted in the process by washing the bills and otherwise aiding Randall and Johnson in their chores. He was part and parcel of the attempt to duplicate the money. Petitioner's actions are no less a violation of public policy because there was another scheme involved, namely, that of swindling the petitioner. From the facts, we hold that to allow the loss deduction in the instant case would constitute a severe and immediate frustration of the clearly defined policy against counterfeiting obligations of the United States. . . .

Petitioner would distinguish the *Richey* case on the grounds that there the taxpayer was involved in an actual scheme to duplicate money where the process was actually begun, only to have the taxpayer swindled when his cohorts made off with his money, whereas in the instant case there never was any real plan to counterfeit money, it being impossible to duplicate currency with the black box. Petitioner contends that, from the inception, the only actual illegal scheme was the scheme to relieve petitioner of his money, and petitioner was a victim and not a perpetrator of the scheme.

In our opinion, the fact that the petitioner was victimized in what he thought was a plan or conspiracy to produce counterfeit currency does not make his participation in what he considered to be a criminal act any less violative of a clearly declared public policy. Not only was the result sought by the petitioner contrary to such policy, but the conspiracy itself constituted a violation of law. The petitioner conspired with his covictim to commit a criminal act, namely, the counterfeiting of United States currency and his theft loss was directly related to that act. If there was a transaction entered into for profit, as petitioner argues, it was a conspiracy to counterfeit.

While it is also recognized that the Supreme Court in *Commissioner v. Tellier*, 383 U.S. 687 (1966), may have redefined the criteria for the disallowance on grounds of public policy of an otherwise deductible business expense under section 162(a), we do not have that type of case. The loss claimed by the petitioner here had a direct relationship to the purported illegal act which the petitioner conspired to commit. Compare *Commissioner v. Heininger*, 320 U.S. 467 (1943).

We also do not feel constrained to follow *Edwards v. Bromberg*, 232 F. 2d 107 (C.A. 5, 1956), wherein the court allowed a deduction for a loss incurred by the taxpayer when money, which he thought was being bet on a "fixed" race, was stolen from him. The taxpayer never intended to participate in "fixing" the race.

The ultimate question for decision in this case is whether considerations of public policy should enter into the allowance of a theft loss under section 165(c)(3) where there is a "theft" -- and the loss by the petitioner of his money would certainly qualify as such -- the statute imposes no limitation on the deductibility of the loss. Neverthless, in *Luther M. Richey, Jr.*, supra, this Court held that the deduction of an admitted theft was properly disallowed on grounds of public policy in a factual situation which we find indistinguishable. We would follow that case.

Decision will be entered for the respondent.

Featherston, J., dissenting: I have joined in Judge Sterrett's dissenting opinion, but I add that I do not think the facts show that petitioner was a party to any conspiracy to counterfeit United States currency. He and his covictim knew they could not counterfeit currency. The other parties pretended that they could and would use their black box for currency reproduction purposes, but they knew the box could not be so used. Thus, there was no conspiratorial agreement between petitioner and anyone who actually intended to do any counterfeiting. The whole scheme was designed to defraud petitioner of his money, and that is what happened. His intentions may have been evil, but that is no ground for denying him a tax deduction. In my opinion, the case is controlled by *Edwards v. Bromberg*, 232 F. 2d 107, 111 (C.A. 5, 1956), now deeply imbedded in the tax law and heavily reinforced by the subsequent Supreme Court decisions cited in Judge Sterrett's dissent. I do not think the Court should decline to follow that precedent.

[Judge Sterrett's dissent, as well as 2 concurring opinions are omitted. Eds.]

Notes on the Public Policy Limitation

What is "public policy"? Not every public policy is agreed upon. For example, is there really a public policy against private small-scale use of marijuana? Against logging ancient forests? Against shooting coyotes? Even if these examples do not move you, there have to be some cases of public policies that are either unsettled or on the way in or out.

Getting around the limit. One way to beat the public policy limitation is to build the expense into the cost of the property one sells and assert that one is not claiming a deduction. The leading example is *Max Sobel Wholesale Liquors v. Commissioner.*[428] The taxpayer was a liquor dealer that paid kickbacks to buyers. It did so by secretly transferring extra bottles of liquor to them. The transfers violated the applicable liquor price law, a serious problem under §162(c). The court held that the taxpayer could nevertheless add the cost of the extra bottles to its cost of goods sold that it reported as part of its inventory accounting practices. As a result, the deduction was placed outside §162's specific prohibitions and reduced the taxpayer's income by increasing the cost of its sales. In the words of the worldly philosopher, Yogi Berra, "It ain't over 'till it's over."

Does the limit result in the unconstitutional taxation of gross income? The Constitution casts a shadow over the public policy limitation. Here is the issue: if an expense incurred to produce income from property is not tax deductible, for public policy reasons, the result is a tax on something more than income within the meaning of the Sixteenth Amendment. Yet only income, in the sense of gain or profit or net income can be taxed by the income tax, unless one interprets the term "income" in the Sixteenth Amendment to mean something more than gross revenues. Remember that this limit does not apply to indirect taxes because the Article I, §8 tax power authorizes "indirect taxes."The Sixteenth Amendment was imposed to permit a direct tax without apportionment on income so the limit is a mild one.

Problem 5-10:

Which of the following is nondeductible under §162? Assume each is appropriate and helpful to the business that made the payment.

1) A bribe paid to a Federal Judge? See §162(c).

428 630 F.2d 670 (9th Cir. 1980).

2) Interest charged for slow payment of a state law fine? See §162(f).

3) Treble damages paid under the criminal anti-trust laws? See §162(g).

4) A fee paid to a lobbyist by a business in order for her to testify in the U.S. Congress on a pending bill that could cost the business a lot of money if enacted? See §162(e).

5) A physician's payment of a kickback to a druggist for encouraging the druggist to direct potential patients her way? Assume it does not violate Medicaid or Medicare rules, but that the state the taxpayer resides in hates commercial kickbacks and vigorously enforces it laws against them. See §162(c)(2).

6) A speeding ticket paid to the State of Louisiana by a trucker in a hurry to get to the destination?

7) A $500,000 legal fee that a drug dealer pays to defend himself against having his business shut down? See §280E.

8) A businessman pays $10,000 to a law firm to defend him in a securities suit brought by the SEC. He is charged with violating the anti-insider trading rules of §16(b) of the Securities Act of 1934. If the charges stick, he may lose his job.

9) A bribe paid to a port employee in Rio de Janeiro to clear a ship for docking. The vessel was legally qualified to enter, but everyone knew a "gift" of this sort was expected or there could be trouble. Incidentally, the Foreign Corrupt Practices Act does not prohibit traditional "grease" payments of this sort. See §162(c)(1).

10) Amounts paid by an oil company to clean up a massive Alaskan oil spill caused by a drunken captain whom the company should have fired years ago.

11) How about depreciation claimed (under §§ 167 and 168) on a pipeline used by an manufacturer to illegally pump away a hideous toxic waste?

12) A company has had collection problems lately. To remedy the situation, it has paid Vincent Pugugli, a retired boxer with a terrifying way about him, to visit and reason with recalcitrant debtors, day or night, and encourage them to pay in full, promptly. He plans to visit your home soon.

CHAPTER 6 - SELECTED OTHER DEDUCTIONS FOR GAIN-SEEKING EXPENDITURES

A. INTRODUCTION

This chapter continues the study of tax deductions granted for costs or expenses of producing income, either in a trade or business or investment or other activity. This extends the subject of Chapter Five, but only as to some specific applications, such as travel expenses, meals, entertainment and certain taxoriented investments (a.k.a., tax shelters). This entails going into the basic rules allowing the tax benefit as well as rules designed to block wrongful or excessive use of one or more tax benefits. We will see a few rules that are designed to encourage or subsidize certain activities, as well. All these allowances arise (supposedly, at least) in connection with gainseeking activities of the taxpayer. They are deductible predominantly because they represent costs of producing income. These are traditional topics taught in every law school.

B. TRAVEL EXPENSES: TESTS OF DEDUCTIBILITY

Read Reg. §1.1622(a)(b) and 274(h), (k) and (n)

1. Background

Business travel is a fact of modern life. Companies cannot live without it, but travel can be abused because it often has a pleasure element, and the expenses are often not duplicative. For example, a wealthy art dealer travels from Pennsylvania to Paris on board a luxury liner. He rents an automobile on the French coast and drives peacefully to his luxury hotel in Paris. A week later, and a few pounds heavier, he re-embarks for the United States, carrying two valuable art works he purchased at a shrewd price that he will sell back in his gallery that he runs as a sole proprietorship. After a week of leisurely sea travel on his return voyage, he is back in Philadelphia refreshed and beginning his diet. On the other side of the country his counterpart has been struggling to hold together his dilapidated automobile that he has driven from Los

Angeles to Seattle and back after purchasing a load of secondrate amphibians that he plans to sell in his Los Angeles pet store. He arrives in worse health than he left in. Both individuals will be required to file a Federal Income Tax return and both will use Schedule C on which they will report the results of their unincorporated businesses. Both will claim travel expense deductions. When the tax returns arrive at the local Service Center for processing, clerical personnel at the IRS will have absolutely no notion of the extent to which these taxpayers incurred pleasure or pain in their businessrelated travel. That will be up to an Examining Agent from the IRS, should either of these taxpayers be audited -- an unlikely event these days, given that only about 0.5% of all individual income tax returns are examined in any given year.[429] Even then, both taxpayers will have compelling stories about the business necessities and the tribulations that surrounded their travel.

Congress has struggled with this dilemma for years, little aided by the Supreme Court. The result is a complicated lexicon of tax terms that one must master in order to be qualified to discuss the subject of business or investment-related travel with anything approaching technical skill.

There are two primary kinds of Code sections at work here. One kind consists of sections such as §§ 162, 165, 167, and 212, which grant the deduction and the other kind is exemplified by §§ 183, 274, and 280A, which attempt to winnow down the claims of overreaching taxpayers. Their purpose is to take an axe to expenditures that are especially likely to be consumption in reality, as opposed to business necessities, sometimes without regard to motive.

Some key terms. "Transportation costs" refer to the cost of moving oneself. These costs can range anywhere from a taxi cab across town to a seat on a flight to China. "Travel" is the status of "being away from home." Unless one walks, one must incur transportation expenses in order to be away from home. When one achieves the status of being engaged in "travel" in the pursuit of business (or investment) then the expenses so incurred become "travel expenses." These include the cost of transportation as well as cost at the venue, such as meals, lodging, telephone calls, baggage claim charges, baggage handling charges, dry cleaning, and laundry.[430] This raises the question of how one manages to be "away from home."

The general answer is that one is "away from home" only if one's sojourn requires "sleep or rest." In our example involving the diverse business people, there was no doubt that they had to be away from home, but questions can become much closer than that. For example, take the case of the salesman who drives from New York to Boston and back in one day. That is a possible, although arduous trip. Assuming the individual set out at 7:00 in the morning and got back at 3:00 the following morning, was he away from home? The law has been interpreted to mean he is "away from home" if he gone so long that it is necessary to get some substantial sleep or

429 https:/www.irs.gov/statistics/enforcement-examinations.

430 See Rev. Rul. 63-145, 1963-2 C.B. 86 (laundry and local transport); Rev. Rul. 75-432, 1975-2 C.B. 60 (trips home on weekend can be deducted up to amount taxpayer would have spent on food at temporary job site).

rest.[431] If there is no need for sleep or rest, then he was not a "away from home," which means he was never in "travel status" which means he cannot claim travel expense deductions (other than transportation costs). The distance traveled is irrelevant;[432] it is the need for sleep or rest that counts. It looks bad for our East Coast salesman. He can deduct his transportation expenses (such as auto mileage or air fare), but -- because we cannot be sure if he satisfied the "sleep or rest" test -- perhaps not his travel expenses (such as meals and rental of a shower). The chances are that the courts would declare that he did not have to sleep, but if the traffic returning from Boston were intolerably bad and he was becoming dangerously drowsy and he chose to pull off the road and sleep in the car for five hours the outcome should differ.

On the flip side, if the taxpayer is away long enough, she develops a new home and therefore cannot be "away from home." Under the last sentence of §162(a), the longest one can be temporarily absent from home in "travel status" is one year. See Rev. Rul. 93-86, 1993-2 C.B. 1, which applies the one-year rule by asking if the employment is realistically expected to last, and does last, for not over a year. If it originally expected to last not over a year, but is extended to beyond a year, expenses up to the day the expectation changed are deductible. Conversely, if the trip is expected to last over a year, but does not in fact last that long, none of the expenses are deductible.

Although the cost of traveling between an individual's residence and work location is almost always a nondeductible personal commuting expense rather than a deductible business expense, an employer may deduct qualified transportation fringe benefits that are excludable from the employee's income §132(a)(5). A qualified transportation fringe is (a) transportation in a commuter highway vehicle between the employee's residence and workplace; (b) a transit pass; (c) qualified parking; or (d) a qualified bicycle commuting reimbursement. For 2017, the employee's exclusion is limited to $255 per month for aggregated highway vehicle transport and transit passes, or for qualified parking benefits ($260 per month for 2018) (Rev. Proc. 2016-55 and Rev. Proc. 2017-58). The maximum exclusion for bicycle commuting reimbursements is $20 per month (§132(f)). Transportation fringes can defray an employee's commuting expenses and increase the employer's deductible business expenses, without increasing the employee's income.

Under the Tax Cuts and Jobs Act of 2017, the exclusion from gross income and wages for qualified bicycle commuting reimbursements is suspended for tax years beginning after December 31, 2017, and before January 1, 2026. Further, although employer-provided qualified transportation fringe benefits remain tax-free for employees, they are no longer deductible for employers.

Now, remembering that one has to be "away from home," what does "home" mean?

---

431 United State v. Correll, 389 U.S. 299 (1967).

432 Rev. Rul. 75170, 19751 C.B. 60.

COMMISSIONER v. FLOWERS

326 U.S. 465 (1946)

MR. JUSTICE MURPHY delivered the opinion of the Court.

This case presents a problem as to the meaning and application of the provision of §23(a)(1)(A) [now §162] of the Internal Revenue Code allowing a deduction for income tax purposes of "traveling expenses (including the entire amount expended for meals and lodging) while away from home in the pursuit of a trade or business."

[Flowers, a lawyer, resided in Jackson, Mississippi where he had practiced law privately for 24 years. Then he was made general solicitor of a railroad whose main office was in Mobile, Alabama. It was agreed that Flowers could continue to live in Jackson on the condition that he pay his traveling expenses to and living expenses in Mobile, which was his principal place of business.]

. . .

During 1939 he spent 203 days in Jackson and 66 in Mobile, making 33 trips between the two cities. During 1940 he spent 168 days in Jackson and 102 in Mobile, making 40 trips between the two cities. The railroad paid all of his traveling expenses when he went on business trips to points other than Jackson or Mobile. But it paid none of his expenses in traveling between these two points or while he was at either of them.

The taxpayer deducted $900 in his 1939 income tax return and $1,620 in his 1940 return as traveling expenses incurred in making trips from Jackson to Mobile and as expenditures for meals and hotel accommodations while in Mobile. The Commissioner disallowed the deductions, which action was sustained by the Tax Court. But the Fifth Circuit Court of Appeals reversed the Tax Court's judgment, 148 F.2d 163, and we granted certiorari because of a conflict between the decision below and that reached by the Fourth Circuit Court of Appeals in *Barnhill v. Commissioner*, 148 F.2d 913.

The portion of [§162] authorizing the deduction of "traveling expenses (including the entire amount expended for meals and lodging) while away from home in the pursuit of a trade or business" is one of the specific examples given by Congress in that section of "ordinary and necessary expenses paid or incurred during the taxable year in carrying on any trade or business." It is to be contrasted with the provision of §24(a)(1) of the Internal Revenue Code disallowing any deductions for "personal, living, or family expenses." And it is to be read in light of the interpretation given it by §19.23(a)-2 of Treasury Regulations 103, promulgated under the Internal Revenue Code. This interpretation, which is precisely the same as that given to identical traveling expense deductions authorized by prior and successive Revenue Acts, is deemed to possess implied legislative approval and to have the effect of law. *Helvering v. Winmill*, 305 U.S. 79; *Boehm v. Commissioner*, 326 U.S. 287. In pertinent part, this interpretation states that "Traveling expenses, as ordinarily understood, include railroad fares and meals and lodging. If the trip is undertaken for other than business purposes, the railroad fares are personal expenses and the meals and lodging are living expenses. If the trip is solely on business, the reasonable and necessary traveling expenses, including railroad fares, meals, and lodging, are business expenses. . . . Only such expenses as are reasonable and necessary in the conduct of the business and directly attributable to it may be deducted. . . . Commuters' fares are not considered as business expenses and are not deductible."

Three conditions must thus be satisfied before a traveling expense deduction may be made under [the predecessor of §162]:

1) The expense must be a reasonable and necessary traveling expense, as that term is generally understood. This includes such items as transportation fares and food and lodging expenses incurred while traveling.

2) The expense must be incurred "while away from home."

3) The expense must be incurred in pursuit of business. This means that there must be a direct connection between the expenditure and the carrying on of the trade or business of the taxpayer or of his employer. Moreover, such an expenditure must be necessary or appropriate to the development and pursuit of the business or trade.

Whether particular expenditures fulfill these three conditions so as to entitle a taxpayer to a deduction is purely a question of fact in most instances. See *Commissioner v. Heininger*, 320 U.S. 467, 475. And the Tax Court's inferences and conclusions on such a factual matter, under established principles, should not be disturbed by an appellate court. . . .

In this instance, the Tax Court without detailed elaboration concluded that "The situation presented in this proceeding is, in principle, no different from that in which a taxpayer's place of employment is in one city and for reasons satisfactory to himself he resides in another." It accordingly disallowed the deductions on the ground that they represent living and personal expenses rather than traveling expenses incurred while away from home in the pursuit of business. . . .

. . .

. . . Failure to satisfy any one of the three conditions destroys the traveling expense deduction.

Turning our attention to the third condition, this case is disposed of quickly. There is no claim that the Tax Court misconstrued this condition or used improper standards in applying it. And it is readily apparent from the facts that its inferences were supported by evidence and that its conclusion that the expenditures in issue were non-deductible living and personal expenses was fully justified.

The facts demonstrate clearly that the expenses were not incurred in the pursuit of the business of the taxpayer's employer, the railroad. Jackson was his regular home. Had his post of duty been in that city the cost of maintaining his home there and of commuting or driving to work concededly would be non-deductible living and personal expenses lacking the necessary direct relation to the prosecution of the business. The character of such expenses is unaltered by the circumstance that the taxpayer's post of duty was in Mobile, thereby increasing the cost of transportation, food and lodging. Whether he maintained one abode or two, whether he traveled three blocks or 300 miles to work, the nature of these expenditures remained the same.

The added costs in issue, moreover, were as unnecessary and inappropriate to the development of the railroad's business as were his personal and living costs in Jackson. They were incurred solely as the result of the taxpayer's desire to maintain a home in Jackson while working in Mobile, a factor irrelevant to the maintenance and prosecution of the railroad's legal business. The railroad did not require him to travel on business from Jackson to Mobile or to maintain living quarters in both cities. Nor did it compel him, save in one instance, to perform tasks for it in Jackson. It simply asked him to be at his principal post in Mobile as business demanded and as his personal convenience was served, allowing him to divide his business time between Mobile and Jackson as he saw fit. Except for the federal court litigation, all of the taxpayer's work in Jackson would normally have been performed in the headquarters at Mobile. The fact that he traveled frequently between the two cities and incurred extra living expenses in Mobile, while doing much of his work in Jackson, was occasioned solely by his personal propensities. The railroad gained nothing from this arrangement except the personal satisfaction of the taxpayer.

Travel expenses in pursuit of business within the meaning of [§162] could arise only when the railroad's business forced the taxpayer to travel and to live temporarily at some place other than Mobile, thereby advancing the interests of the railroad. Business trips are to be identified in relation to business demands and the traveler's business headquarters. The exigencies of business rather than the personal conveniences and necessities of the traveler must be the motivating factors. Such was not the case here.

. . .

[The dissenting opinion of MR. JUSTICE RUTLEDGE is omitted. Eds.]

Notes

Exactly why were the expenditures in *Flowers* not deductible? What is the answer in terms of policy as well as in terms of statutory language?

What if one has to pay a premium for the commute? In the leading *Fausner* decision[433] a pilot who used his own car to get to his place of employment (an airport) because he had to carry his two flight and overnight bags was not allowed to deduct the cost of driving his car to and from the airport, the theory being that he would otherwise have used his car anyway, with or without the bags. In *Fausner* the Supreme Court disallowed any deduction for travel by car, but acknowledged that he should be allowed to deduct the excess cost of bringing bulky objects to work (apparently even if he used a different mode of transport). The IRS later narrowed *Fausner* to the excess cost of using the *same means* of transportation (e.g., the extra costs of operating a truck with tools in it versus the same truck without the tools).[434]

2. Business Expenses and Reimbursements

If Flowers had been reimbursed the railroad expenses, could he have excluded the reimbursement? In the analogous case of *Commissioner v. Starr*,[435] the court held that money received by an employee from his employer to reimburse him for temporary living expenses when he was transferred to a new post of duty was includable as income and not deductible as moving expenses,[436] because he could not have deducted them if he paid them out of his own pocket. The moral is that if you could not have deducted an expense, you should not be able to avoid being taxed when an employer reimburses you for the expense. On the other hand, the symmetry falls apart at times. For example, an employee may be able to exclude the value of employer-provided meals under §119 even if she could not have deducted them if she paid for the meals herself. Also, under the "accountable plan" rules that you saw earlier, employees who live on expense accounts have to report their expenses and reimbursements scrupulously to the employer. If they fail to, they have to report all the reimbursements in income and report as deductions the expenditures for which they got reimbursed. This is discussed below in connection with meal and entertainment costs. Independent contractors are relatively liberated; they can short-cut the system by excluding reimbursements from gross income, provided that what they were reimbursed would have been deductible if there had been no reimbursement.[437]

REV. RUL. 99-7

19995 I.R.B. 4

433 Fausner v. Commissioner, 413 U.S. 838 (1973), citing Rev. Rul. 63-100, 1960-1 C.B. 34 with favor. The latter allowed a musician to deduct automobile costs to carry bulky instrument to place of work.

434 Rev Rul. 75-380, 1975-2 C.B. 59.

435 399 F.2d 675 (10th Cir.1968).

436 Section 217 allows an adjustment to gross income for moving a significant distance in connection with a job. This deduction is suspended for years 2018 through 2025. I.R.C. §217(K).

437 See, e.g., Rev. Rul. 80-99, 1980-1 C.B. 10.

ISSUE

Under what circumstances are daily transportation expenses incurred by a taxpayer in going between the taxpayer's residence and a work location deductible under § 162(a) of the Internal Revenue Code?

LAW AND ANALYSIS

Section 162(a) allows a deduction for all the ordinary and necessary expenses paid or incurred during the taxable year in carrying on any trade or business. Section 262, however, provides that no deduction is allowed for personal, living, or family expenses.

A taxpayer's costs of commuting between the taxpayer's residence and the taxpayer's place of business or employment generally are nondeductible personal expenses under §§ 1.1622(e) and 1.2621(b)(5) of the Income Tax Regulations. However, the costs of going between one business location and another business location generally are deductible under § 162(a). Rev. Rul. 55109, 19551 C.B. 261.

Section 280A(c)(1)(A) (as amended by § 932 of the Taxpayer Relief Act of 1997, Pub. L. No. 10534, 111 Stat. 881, effective for taxable years beginning after December 31, 1998) provides, in part, that a taxpayer may deduct expenses for the business use of the portion of the taxpayer's personal residence that is exclusively used on a regular basis as the principal place of business for any trade or business of the taxpayer. (In the case of an employee, however, such expenses are deductible only if the exclusive and regular use of the portion of the residence is for the convenience of the employer.) In *Curphey v. Commissioner*, 73 T.C. 766 (1980), the Tax Court held that daily transportation expenses incurred in going between an office in a taxpayer's residence and other work locations were deductible where the home office was the taxpayer's principal place of business within the meaning of § 280A(c)(1)(A) for the trade or business conducted by the taxpayer at those other work locations. The court stated that "we see no reason why the rule that local transportation expenses incurred in travel between one business location and another are deductible should not be equally applicable *where the taxpayer's principal place of business with respect to the activities involved is his residence*." 73 T.C. at 777778 (emphasis in original). Implicit in the court's analysis in Curphey is that the deductibility of daily transportation expenses is determined on a businessbybusiness basis.

Rev. Rul. 190, 19532 C.B. 303, provides a limited exception to the general rule that the expenses of going between a taxpayer's residence and a work location are nondeductible commuting expenses. Rev. Rul. 190 deals with a taxpayer who lives and ordinarily works in a particular metropolitan area but who is not regularly employed at any specific work location. In such a case, the general rule is that daily transportation expenses are not deductible when paid or incurred by the taxpayer in going between the taxpayer's residence and a *temporary* work site *inside* that metropolitan area because that area is considered the taxpayer's regular place of business. However, Rev. Rul. 190 holds that daily transportation expenses are deductible business expenses when paid or incurred in going between the taxpayer's residence and a *temporary* work site *outside* that metropolitan area.

Rev. Rul. 9023, 19901 C.B. 28, distinguishes Rev. Rul. 190 and holds, in part, that, for a taxpayer who has one or more regular places of business, daily transportation expenses paid or incurred in going between the taxpayer's residence and temporary work locations are deductible business expenses under § 162(a), regardless of the distance.

. . .

If an office in the taxpayer's residence satisfies the principal place of business requirements of §280A(c)(1)(A), then the residence is considered a business location for purposes of Rev. Rul. 9023 or Rev. Rul. 9447. In these circumstances, the daily transportation expenses incurred in going between the residence and other work locations in the same trade or business are ordinary and necessary business expenses (deductible under § 162(a)). *See Curphey*; *see alsoWisconsin Psychiatric Services v. Commissioner*, 76 T.C. 839 (1981). In contrast, if an office in the taxpayer's residence does not satisfy the principal place of business requirements of §280A(c)(1)(A), then the business activity there (if any) is not sufficient to overcome the inherently personal nature of the residence and the daily transportation expenses incurred in going between the residence and regular work locations. In these circumstances, the residence is not considered a business location for purposes of Rev. Rul. 9023 or Rev. Rul. 9447, and the daily transportation expenses incurred in going between the residence and regular work locations are personal expenses (nondeductible under §§ 1.1622(e) and 1.2621(b)(5)). . . .

For purposes of determining the deductibility of travel away from home expenses under §162(a)(2), Rev. Rul. 9386 defines "home" as the "taxpayer's regular or principal (if more than one regular) place of business." . . .

HOLDING

In general, daily transportation expenses incurred in going between a taxpayer's residence and a work location are nondeductible commuting expenses. However, such expenses are deductible under the circumstances described in paragraph (1), (2), or (3) below.

1) A taxpayer may deduct daily transportation expenses incurred in going between the taxpayer's residence and a *temporary* work location *outside* the metropolitan area where the taxpayer lives and normally works. However, unless paragraph (2) or (3) below applies, daily transportation expenses incurred in going between the

taxpayer's residence and a *temporary* work location *within* that metropolitan area are nondeductible commuting expenses.

2) If a taxpayer has one or more regular work locations away from the taxpayer's residence, the taxpayer may deduct daily transportation expenses incurred in going between the taxpayer's residence and a *temporary* work location in the same trade or business, regardless of the distance. (The Service will continue not to follow the *Walker* decision [which allowed a logger to deduct the cost of driving to logging sites, on the theory that his home was his business headquarters. Eds.].)

3) If a taxpayer's residence is the taxpayer's principal place of business within the meaning of § 280A(c)(1)(A), the taxpayer may deduct daily transportation expenses incurred in going between the residence and another work location in the same trade or business, regardless of whether her work location is regular or *temporary and regardless* of the distance.

For purposes of paragraphs (1), (2), and (3), the following rules apply in determining whether a work location is *temporary.* If employment at a work location is realistically expected to last (and does in fact last) for 1 year or less, the employment is *temporary* in the absence of facts and circumstances indicating otherwise. If employment at a work location is realistically expected to last for more than 1 year or there is no realistic expectation that the employment will last for 1 year or less, the employment is *not temporary,* regardless of whether it actually exceeds 1 year. If employment at a work location initially is realistically expected to last for 1 year or less, but at some later date the employment is realistically expected to exceed 1 year, that employment will be treated as temporary (in the absence of facts and circumstances indicating otherwise) until the date that the taxpayer's realistic expectation changes, and will be treated as *not temporary* after that date.

The determination that a taxpayer's residence is the taxpayer's principal place of business within the meaning of §280A(c)(1)(A) is not necessarily determinative of whether the residence is the taxpayer's tax home for other purposes, including the travelawayfromhome deduction under §162(a)(2).

. . .

Problem 61:

Edwina Klopman, the self-employed San Francisco lawyer, owns a touring motorcycle which she commutes to work on. She calculates the cost of commuting at $1 each way. Recently, she has had to do a good deal of litigation and finds the motorcycle too small. It cost her, by her calculation, an extra five cents each way to go by motorcycle because of the extra weight of the documents. After a week or so of struggling with her motorcycle, she decided she needed to take a cab each way at a cost of $5 each way. She has no office at home and her full-time occupation is being a litigator operating out of her own downtown office in San Francisco.

1) What can she deduct if she used her motorcycle before she carried the bulky materials?

2) What can she deduct if she uses her motorcycle for carrying bulky materials?

3) What can she deduct as cab fare?

4) What if she goes to and from court (from her office) using her motorcycle or cab? Can she deduct those costs?

5) Instead, Edwina is a professor of tax law at your law school. She has published several books in the tax field. She works on books at home because the law school is a distracting environment. She has a separate office at home which she uses exclusively for her writing projects. Can she deduct the cost of her transportation from the office at home to the law school and back again? Make sure to consider the *Curphey* case that is described in the ruling. Use the alternative assumptions:

    a. Her office at home is the principal office where she does her writing;

    b. Writing is expected of law professors and she is therefore doing law school work at home when she writes at home. Read the pertinent parts of §280A in connection with answering the question.

3. So Where is "Home"?

The Supreme Court has declined to define the term "tax home" in a practical way, but there seems to be no escaping that the term either means the taxpayer's residence (if any) or the town in which her business or employer has its headquarters. The IRS in Rev. Rul. 75-432, 1975-2 CB 60 says that the general rule is that the term means business headquarters, but the "regular place of abode" is used if there is no business headquarters. Taxpayers who are temporarily away from their "tax homes" are considered to be away from home, as long as they have to be away "overnight." The Circuits have been left to puzzle out their own rules as to what the term "home" means. Whatever "home" means, every taxpayer has a home, right?

HENDERSON v. COMMISSIONER

143 F.3d 497 (9th Cir. 1998), cert. denied 1998.

[The taxpayer, James Henderson, was a lighting technician for Walt Disney's World on Ice during 1990. While traveling around the country, he left many of his belongings, such as his dog and his car, at his parents' home in Idaho. He worked on three tours in 1990. Henderson returned to Idaho between the tours, hoping he would be rehired for the next tour. When in Idaho, he stayed with his parents at no charge, although he did do some work around the house. He received a $30 per diem allowance while he was on tour. He claimed over $ 14,000 for travel expenses on his 1990 tax return, on the theory that his employment was only temporary and that his tax home was in Idaho with his parents. The IRS, with the Tax Court's approval, disallowed the deductions on the theory that Henderson was a tax turtle with no home to be away from.]

WIGGINS, Circuit Judge:

. . .

[T]he Supreme Court has held that the taxpayer's expenses must (1) be reasonable and necessary expenses, (2) be incurred while away from home, and (3) be incurred while in the pursuit of a trade or business. *Flowers v. Commissioner*, 326 U.S. 465, 470 (1946).

The first and third criteria are not at issue. The subject of this appeal is whether the expenses Henderson claims as deductions were incurred while "away from home." If Henderson establishes that his home was Boise, his reasonable traveling expenses on the Disney tours are deductible. The Tax Court concluded that Boise was not Henderson's tax home because his choice to live there had nothing to do with the needs of his work; thus, the Tax Court held that Henderson could not claim the deduction for traveling expenses incurred while away from Boise. It held that Henderson had no tax home because he continuously traveled for work. We agree.

Henderson builds a strong case that he treated Boise as his home in the usual sense of the word, but "for purposes of [section] 162, 'home' does not have its usual and ordinary meaning." *Putnam v. United States*, 32 F.3d 911, 917 (5th Cir. 1994) ("In fact, 'home' in the usual case means 'work.' "). We have held that the term "home" means "the taxpayer's abode at his or her principal place of employment." *Folkman v. United States*, 615 F.2d 493, 495 (9th Cir. 1980); *see also Coombs v. Commissioner*, 608 F.2d 1269, 1275 (9th Cir. 1979) (stating that "tax home" is generally, but not always, exact locale of principal place of employment). If a taxpayer has no regular or principal place of business, he may be able to claim his place of abode as his tax home. See *Holdreith v. Commissioner*, 57 T.C.M. (CCH) 1383 (1989).

A taxpayer may have no tax home, however, if he continuously travels and thus does not duplicate substantial, continuous living expenses for a permanent home maintained for some business reason. *James v. United States*, 308 F.2d 204, 207 (9th Cir. 1962).... Clearly, if a taxpayer has no "home" for tax purposes, then he cannot deduct under section 162(a)(2) for expenses incurred "away from home." This is for good reason. In *James*, we examined the statutory precursor to the present version of section 162(a) and explained that the deduction was designed to mitigate the burden on taxpayers who travel on business. 308 F.2d at 207. The burden exists "only when the taxpayer has a 'home,' the maintenance of which involves substantial continuing expenses which will be duplicated by the expenditures which the taxpayer must make when required to travel elsewhere for business purposes." *Id.*; *see also Andrews*, 931 F.2d at 135 (emphasizing that the deduction's purpose was to mitigate duplicative expenses); *Hantzis*, 638 F.2d at 253. Thus, a taxpayer only has a tax home and can claim a deduction for being away from that home when it appears that he or she incurs substantial, continuous living expenses at a permanent place of residence. *James*, 308 F.2d at 207 08.

Revenue Ruling 73-539, 1973-2 C.B. 37, outlines three factors to consider in determining whether a taxpayer has a tax home or is an itinerant. Essentially, they are (i) the business connection to the locale of the claimed home; (ii) the duplicative nature of the taxpayer's living expenses while traveling and at the claimed home; and (iii) personal attachments to the claimed home. While subjective intent can be considered in determining whether he has a tax home, objective financial criteria are usually more significant. *Barone*, 85 T.C. at 465.

The location of Henderson's tax home is a determination of fact reviewed for clear error. *Frank v. United States*, 577 F.2d 93, 97 (9th Cir. 1978). Similarly, we believe the determination of whether a taxpayer has a tax home or is an itinerant depends on the facts of each case and should be reviewed for clear error. Considering these factors, the Tax Court did not clearly err when it concluded that Henderson is an itinerant taxpayer.

First, Henderson had virtually no business reason for his tax home to be in any location he constantly traveled in 1990 as part of his work with the World on Ice tours. His personal choice to return to Boise was not dictated by business reasons. Except for brief intervals, he was employed for the tours. He worked only one night in Boise. While he testified he looked for other work in Boise between tours, he also testified that at the end of each tour he would have a contract talk with the company manager about the next tour. The Tax Court determined that Henderson merely returned to Boise during his "idle time" between tours. While his reasons for returning may be entirely understandable, we cannot say the Tax Court clearly erred in concluding they were personal, not business, reasons. His minimal employment efforts in Boise do not change this analysis.

The importance of the business reason for residing in a certain place is illustrated in *Hantzis*. In that case, the First Circuit disallowed the "away from home" deduction for a law student from Boston who took a summer job in New York. The court held that she did not have a tax home in Boston, even though her husband lived in Boston and she lived there during the school year, because she had no business reason to maintain a home in Boston during the summer while she worked in New York. The court explained why the deduction did not apply in those circumstances:

> Only a taxpayer who lives one place, works another and has business ties to both is in the ambiguous situation that the temporary employment doctrine is designed to resolve.... [A] taxpayer who pursues temporary employment away from the location of his usual residence, but has no business connection with that location, is not "away from home" for purposes of section 162(a)(2).

Hantzis, 638 F.2d at 255.

Second, Henderson did not have substantial, continuing living expenses in Boise that were duplicated by his expenses on the road. The evidence showed that he lived with his parents when he stayed in Boise. The Tax Court found that he paid no rent and had no ownership interest in his parents' home. His financial contributions in Boise were limited. He contributed some labor to maintenance and improvement of the home while he was there, and he paid about $ 500 for supplies. While his parents may have expended money that benefitted Henderson as well i.e., maintaining a mortgage, paying utilities, and so forth this is not a substantial living expense incurred by Henderson. Further, any minor expense he may have incurred while living with his parents was not continuing during the periods while he traveled on tour. That is, there is no evidence he had any expenses in Boise while he traveled on the Disney tours.

The fact that Henderson may have incurred higher expenses while traveling with Disney than he would have if he had obtained a fulltime job in Boise is not dispositive. The issue presented is whether his claimed expenses were incurred while he was away from his tax home. To assume that Henderson is entitled to the deduction simply because Henderson incurred higher expenses than he would have had he worked in Boise ignores the important question of whether Boise was his tax home at all. Only if Boise is his tax home can Henderson claim deductions for expenses incurred while away from Boise.

Because these two factors weigh against finding that he had a tax home in Boise, the Tax Court did not clearly err when it discounted his evidence on the third factor: personal attachment to Boise. Henderson cites cases, *e.g. Horton v. Commissioner*, 86 T.C. 589, 593 (1986), which hold that a taxpayer may treat a personal residence as his tax home even if it is not the same as the place of his temporary employment with a certain employer. This principle does not help Henderson, however, because he cannot establish any (non*de minimis*) business connection to Boise to justify the position that it was his permanent tax home. *See Hantzis*, 638 F.2d at 25455. Thus, travel away from Boise while on tour with Disney was not travel "away from home" as that term is understood for income tax purposes.

AFFIRMED.

[In his dissent, Judge Alex Kozinski considered that the "work is home" rule is inapplicable when the taxpayer's work itself has no fixed location, as in Henderson's case. He could not have avoided incurring travel expenses by moving his home closer to work. That his parents did not charge him room and board,

> is of no consequence. Neither the Code nor common experience requires that a taxpayer pay for his home, else all minors and many inlaws would be deemed homeless. . . . What matters is that, by going on the road in pursuit of his job, Henderson had to pay for food and lodging that he would not have had to buy had he stayed home.

The judge also chided the government." Leave it to the IRS to turn a family reunion into a taxable event."]

Foreign and Domestic Travel Expenses

Is it not true that even a homeless taxpayer will likely spend extra money because motels and restaurant meals normally cost more than basic rent and home cooking?

Transportation expenses within the United States are 100% deductible if the primary reason for the travel is business.[438] *Domestic* travel need only be primarily for business or investment purposes in order for all the transportation costs to and from the destination to be deductible, although expenses on the ground must be apportioned between gain-seeking and non-gain-seeking components. Because overseas business travel is often used as a jumping off point for vacations, Congress has retaliated by enacting §274(c) which pares back deductions for *foreign* travel as a business expense. The core of the restriction is that if and to the extent the traveler spends days on the ground not involved in business, then the deduction for the transportation, such as an airline ticket to Greece to attend a business meeting, is carved back proportionately. In fact, §274(c) is riddled with exceptions, some of which appear to engulf the rule, including a blanket exemption for trips not over a week. Scan §274(c) and ask yourself the following question: to what extent can the imaginary art dealer from Philadelphia described at the beginning of this Chapter, deduct the cost of going to and from Paris by air?

How about his delightful trip on that luxury liner? Paragraph 274(m)(1) limits the deductible portion of transportation on an ocean liner to twice the highest per diem allowance for meals and lodging granted to federal employees. This limit does not apply to cruise ships on which conventions or seminars are held, but the latter expenditures are deductible (up to $2,000 per year) only if a series of restrictions are satisfied, including that the ship stop only at U.S. and certain Possessions destinations.

---

438 Reg. §1.1622(b).

To illustrate: Consider the Philadelphia art dealer. Assume for convenience that twice the daily maximum government per diem is $223 and that our art dealer spent ten days on board the ship and paid $4,460 for the tickets. He can deduct the luxury liner tickets only up to $2,230. The remaining $2,230 is deemed to have been paid for nondeductible consumption.

The expenses of bringing spouses or other companions are generally nondeductible, except in the case where the companion is an employee traveling for bona fide business reasons.[439] What if the art dealer were accompanied by his spouse, who was fluent in French and socially gracious? Could he deduct the cost of her travel? The answer is "yes", but only if his companion or wife is an employee who could have deducted the expenses if she or he had incurred them personally.

There is a soft spot in the rules in that one need not *proportionately* reduce one's transportation expense deductions merely because one brought a spouse or companion along on an otherwise deductible business trip. The denial of deductions only extends of the *extra* expenses one incurs because of bringing along a companion.[440] Hotels know it, and often advertise rates at conventions that are no higher for customers who bring along their spouses.

Problem 6-2:

Edwina Klopman is a self-employed litigator in San Francisco.

1) What, if anything, can she deduct if she flies to San Diego for an extended litigation? Assume she is self-employed and she stays, as she expected:

    a. Nine months?

    b. Thirteen months?

    c. Does the 50% limit on deductions for meals in travel status apply to either of these cases? See §274(n)

2) Next year, Edwina marries the charming Alphonse l'Enfant, who has many connections, and with whom she files a joint return. She invites him to accompany her to an ABA convention, for business reasons.

    a. What does she have to show in order to deduct the expense of his travel?

439 §274(m)(3).

440 See Rev. Rul. 56-168, 1956-1 C.B. 93.

b. Would it matter if they were not married? See §274(m).

3) Later, Edwina takes a one week Caribbean cruise aboard the SS Love Boat where she studies recent developments at seminars in her area of the law. They would certainly be deductible if she bought the same educational services in San Francisco. The Love Boat flies the Panama flag on a week long cruises from Miami to the US Virgin Islands and back. To what extent can she deduct the costs of the cruise, including the airfare to get to the port of embarkation? See §274(h) and Reg. §1.162-2(a).

4) Many years have passed. Edwina travels by car from San Francisco to Detroit for another ABA meeting. She has packed her spouse and six children into the car. Can she deduct the cost of gas, tolls and the like for going to Detroit and back? See Reg. §1.162-2(b). What about the meals and hotel costs assuming all the kids sleep on the floor at no extra cost?

5) Same as "(4)", but the trip is to attend a seminar in investing in commodities? See §274(h)(7).

6) Next year, Edwina travels to Bali from San Francisco. She spends half her time working on important depositions for her law firm, and the next week on vacation at the lovely beaches. How much of her $1,000 airline ticket to and from Bali can she deduct? See §274(c).

C. ENTERTAINMENT AND MEALS

Read §274(a)(1)(A), (B) and (n)

1. Entertainment expenses before 2018

Before the Tax Cuts and Jobs Act of 2017, expenses for entertainment, or for a facility used in connection with entertainment, were generally deductible only to the extent that they were either:

(1) directly related to the active conduct of the taxpayer's trade or business, or

(2) associated with the active conduct of the taxpayer's trade or business, and the expense item directly precedes or follows a substantial and bona fide business discussion (Code Sec. 274(a)(1)).

Under the pre 2018 rules, entertainment includes any activity of a type that is generally considered to constitute entertainment and may include expenses that satisfy personal or family needs, such as food and beverages, a hotel room, or a car (Reg. §1.274-2(b)). When the IRC disallowed entertainment expense deductions for any portion of a facility, that portion is treated as used for personal, living and family purposes rather than as an asset used in a trade or business (Code Sec. 274(g)). Deductions for tickets to entertainment and sporting events are subject to two additional rules. First, an expense for seats in a skybox or other luxury box that is leased for more than one event is limited to the sum of the face value of non-luxury box seat tickets for the events. Second, the expense that is taken into account for a ticket to an entertainment event or facility cannot exceed the face value of the ticket (so, for instance, additional payments to scalpers or other resellers are not taken into account). However, this limit does not apply to tickets to a charitable sporting event. A charitable sporting event is one that benefits a Section 501(c)(3) tax-exempt organization, and for which volunteers perform substantially all of the work (Code Sec. 274(l)).

Section 274 generally limits the deduction for entertainment to 50 percent of the expense, but there are several exceptions, including:

(a) certain entertainment expenses for goods, services, and facilities that are treated as compensation to an employee-recipient;

(b) expenses for recreational, social, or similar activities and related facilities primarily for the benefit of employees who are not highly compensated employees;

(c) expenses for entertainment available to the general public; and

(d) entertainment expenses for goods, services, and facilities that are includible in the gross income of a non-employee recipient as compensation for services rendered or as a prize or award (Code Sec. 274(e) and (n)).

Entertainment expense deductions must satisfy strict substantiation requirements. The taxpayer must show (a) the amount of the expense; (b) the time and place of the entertainment; (c) the business purpose of the expense, and (d) the business relationship with the persons entertained (Code Sec. 274(d)).

2. Starting in 2018

Entertainment expenses, including expenses for a facility used in connection with entertainment that are paid or incurred after 2017 are generally not deductible under the 2017 Tax Cuts and Jobs Act.

Because it eliminated directly-related and associated-with entertainment expense deductions under §274, Congress also eliminated the following related provisions:

(1) The rules that treated a club as an entertainment facility unless it was used primarily to further, and was directly related to the active conduct of, the taxpayer's trade or business (Code Sec. 274(a)(2)(C), as stricken by the 2017 Tax Cuts Act); and

(2) the limit on deductions for tickets to entertainment and sporting events, including the special rules for seats in skyboxes and the special exception for charitable sporting events (Code Sec. 274(l)(1)(B), as stricken by the 2017 Tax Cuts Act);

(3) the 50-percent limit on entertainment expense deductions (Code Sec. 274(n)(1)(B), as stricken by the 2017 Tax Cuts Act).

Some entertainment expenses remain fully deductible, including:

(1) Certain entertainment expenses for goods, services, and facilities that are treated as compensation to an employee-recipient;

(2) Expenses for recreational, social, or similar activities and related facilities primarily for the benefit of employees who are not highly compensated employees;

(3) Expenses for entertainment sold to customers; and

(4) Entertainment expenses for goods, services, and facilities that are includible in the gross income of a non-employee recipient as compensation for services rendered or as a prize or award (§ 274(e) and (n)(2)(A)).

These deductions must satisfy strict substantiation requirements; however, the taxpayer will not have to substantiate the time and place of the entertainment (§ 274(d), as amended by the 2017 Tax Cuts Act).

3. Meals

Although taxpayers may deduct ordinary and necessary business expenses paid for services rendered §162(a)(1), there are special requirements and limits to deductions for employer-provided meals §274. Indeed, business expense deductions for some employer-provided meal expenses disappear after 2025.

Some business meals are deducted as entertainment expenses under §274. Entertainment expenses are only allowed to the extent that: (1) they are directly related to the active conduct of the taxpayer's trade or business, or (2) they are associated with the active conduct of the taxpayer's trade or business, and the expense item directly precedes or follows a substantial and bona fide business discussion §274(a)(1). Even then, the deduction is limited to 50 percent of the expense. §274(e) and (n) and the taxpayer must show (a) the amount of the expense; (b) the time and place of the entertainment; (c) the business purpose of the expense, and (d) the business relationship with the persons entertained §274(d).

Sometimes, an employer may deduct expenses for meals it provides to employees, and the employees may exclude the value of the meals from gross income. For instance, if an employer provides meals to employees and their spouses and dependents for the employer's convenience and on the employer's business premises, the value of the meals is excludable from the employee's income §119(a). The employer can claim a business expense deduction, but it is subject to the general rule that limits deductions for food and beverages to 50 percent of the expense §274(n); IRS Chief Counsel Advice 201151020).

In contrast, employees may exclude and employers may deduct, the full cost of de minimis fringe meals because they are exempt from the 50-percent limit that applies to most meal expenses §274(n)(2)(B). An employer operated employee cafeteria is a de minimis fringe benefit if (a) the facility is located at or near the employer's business premises, and (b) revenue derived from the facility normally equals or exceeds its direct operating costs. §132(e).

Under the Tax Cuts and Jobs Act of 2017, no deduction is allowed after December 31, 2025, for: (a) meals that are excludable from an employee's income under §119(a) or food, beverage, and facility expenses for meals that are de minimis fringe benefit under §132(e). (§274(o), as added by the 2017 Tax Cuts Act). Because the employer's deduction for meal expenses is eliminated only for expenses described in §119(a) or §132(e), an employer may continue to deduct 50 percent of its expenses for food, beverages, and related facilities that are furnished on its business premises primarily for its employees, such as in a typical company cafeteria or executive dining room. §274(e)(1), Reg. §1.274-2(f)(2)(ii)).

The basis for the public's suspicion of the expense-account existence was well put in the following Life Magazine article in 1953:

> In cities like New York, Washington and Chicago it is safe to say that at any given moment well over half of the people in the best hotels, in the best nightclubs and the best restaurants are charging the bill as an expense account item to their companies, which in turn are charging it to the government in the form of a tax deduction.[441]

Congress retaliated with the crude rule that meals are now at most halfdeductible, even when taken while traveling.[442] Employers typically reimburse their employees' meals if the meals have a business nexus. Reg. §1.16217 says that if the employer has an "accountable plan," under which the employee carefully reports the expenditures to her employer, the employee need not report the reimbursement in income as long as reimbursements equal expenses for the year.[443] (If the reimbursement is for meals and entertainment, the employer can only deduct one-half of the reimbursement[444].) If she does not report the expense to her employer, she may be entitled to deduct her expense as an unreimbursed employee expense, but there will likely be trouble because §62 turns unreimbursed employee expenses into socalled "itemized deductions." Itemized deductions are subject to a variety of cutbacks that you will see later. As a result of all this, employees have a strong practical reason to press their employers to establish "accountable plans."

There is a fairly long list of common-sense exceptions to the §274 limits for such cases as meals and entertainment that occur at company picnics or where the public pays for admission.[445]

MOSS v. COMMISSIONER

758 F.2d 211 (7th Cir. 1985), cert. denied 1985.

POSNER, Circuit Judge

The taxpayers, a lawyer named Moss and his wife, appeal from a decision of the Tax Court disallowing federal income tax deductions of a little more than $1,000 in each of two years, representing Moss's share of his law firm's lunch expense at the Café Angelo in Chicago. 80 T.C. 10. . . .

Moss was a partner in a small trial firm specializing in defense work, mostly for one insurance company. Each of the firm's lawyers carried a tremendous litigation caseload, averaging more than 300 cases, and spent most of every working day in courts in Chicago and its suburbs. The members of the firm met for lunch daily at the Café Angelo near their office. At lunch the lawyers would discuss their cases with the head of the firm, whose approval was required

441 See for example Lucas v Commissioner 79 T.C. 1 (1982).

442 See for example Lucas v Commissioner 79 T.C. 1 (1982).

443 See for example Lucas v Commissioner 79 T.C. 1 (1982).

444 See for example Lucas v Commissioner 79 T.C. 1 (1982).

445 See for example Lucas v Commissioner 79 T.C. 1 (1982).

for most settlements, and they would decide which lawyer would meet which court call that afternoon or the next morning. Lunchtime was chosen for the daily meeting because the courts were in recess then. The alternatives were to meet at 7:00 a.m. or 6:00 p.m., and these were less convenient times. There is no suggestion that the lawyers dawdled over lunch, or that the Café Angelo is luxurious.

The framework of statutes and regulations for deciding this case is simple, but not clear. Section 262 of the Internal Revenue Code (Title 26) disallows, "except as otherwise expressly provided in this chapter," the deduction of "personal, family, or living expenses." Section 119 excludes from income the value of meals provided by an employer to his employees for his convenience, but only if they are provided on the employer's premises; and section 162(a) allows the deduction of "all the ordinary and necessary expenses paid or incurred during the taxable year in carrying on any trade or business, including -- . . . (2) traveling expenses (including amounts expended for meals . . .) while away from home . . . ." Since Moss was not an employee but a partner in a partnership not taxed as an entity, since the meals were not served on the employer's premises, and since he was not away from home (that is, on an overnight trip away from his place of work, see *United States v. Correll*, 38 U.S. 299, 19 L. Ed. 2d 537, 88 S. Ct. 445 (1967)), neither section 119 nor section 162(a)(2) applies to this case. The Internal Revenue Service concedes, however, that meals are deductible under section 162(a) when they are ordinary and necessary business expenses (provided the expense is substantiated with adequate records, see section 274(d)) even if they are not within the express permission of any other provision and even though the expense of commuting to and from work, a traveling expense but not one incurred away from home, is not deductible. Treasury Regulations on Income Tax §1.2621(b)(5) . . . .

The problem is that many expenses are simultaneously business expenses in the sense that they conduce to the production of business income and personal expenses in the sense that they raise personal welfare. This is plain enough with regard to lunch; most people would eat lunch even if they didn't work. Commuting may seem a pure business expense, but is not; it reflects the choice of where to live, as well as where to work. Read literally, section 262 would make irrelevant whether a business expense is also a personal expense; so long as it is ordinary and necessary in the taxpayer's business, thus bringing section 162(a) into play, an expense is (the statute seems to say) deductible from his income tax. But the statute has not been read literally. There is a natural reluctance, most clearly manifested in the regulation disallowing deduction of the expense of commuting, to lighten the tax burden of people who have the good fortune to interweave work with consumption. To allow a deduction for commuting would confer a windfall on people who live in the suburbs and commute to work in the cities; to allow a deduction for all businessrelated meals would confer a windfall on people who can arrange their work schedules so they do some of their work at lunch.

Although an argument can thus be made for disallowing any deduction for business meals, on the theory that people have to eat whether they work or not, the result would be excessive taxation of people who spend more money on business meals because they are business meals than they would spend on their meals if they were not working. Suppose a theatrical agent takes his clients out to lunch at the expensive restaurants that the clients demand. Of course he can deduct the expense of their meals, from which he derives no pleasure or sustenance, but can he also deduct the expense of his own? He can, because he cannot eat more cheaply; he cannot munch surreptitiously on a peanut butter and jelly sandwich brought from home while his client is wolfing down tournedos Rossini followed by souffle au grand marnier. No doubt our theatrical agent, unless concerned for his longevity, derives personal utility from his fancy meal, but probably less than the price of the meal. He would not pay for it if it were not for the business benefit; he would get more value from using the same money to buy something else; hence the meal confers on him less utility than the cash equivalent would. The law could require him to pay tax on the fair value of the meal to him; this would be (were it not for costs of administration) the economically correct solution. But the government does not attempt this difficult measurement; it once did, but gave up the attempt as not worth the cost, see *United States v. Correll, supra*, 389 U.S. at 301. The taxpayer is permitted to deduct the whole price, provided the expense is "different from or in excess of that which would have been made for the taxpayer's personal purposes." *Sutter v. Commissioner*, 21 T.C. 170, 1 (1953).

Because the law allows this generous deduction, which tempts people to have more (and costlier) business meals than are necessary, the Internal Revenue Service has every right to insist that the meal be shown to be a real business necessity. This condition is most easily satisfied when a client or customer or supplier or other outsider to the business is a guest. Even if Sydney Smith was wrong that "soup and fish explain half the emotions of life," it is undeniable that eating together fosters camaraderie and makes business dealings friendlier and easier. It thus reduces the costs of transacting business, for these costs include the frictions and the failures of communication that are produced by suspicion and mutual misunderstanding, by differences in tastes and manners, and by lack of rapport. A meeting with a client or customer in an office is therefore not a perfect substitute for a lunch with him in a restaurant. But it is different when all the participants in the meal are coworkers, as essentially was the case here (clients occasionally were invited to the firm's daily luncheon, but Moss has made no attempt to identify the occasions). They know each other well already; they don't need the social lubrication that a meal with an outsider provides at least don't need it daily. If a large firm had a monthly lunch to allow partners to get to know associates, the expense of the meal might well be necessary, and would be allowed by the Internal Revenue Service. See *Wells v. Commissioner*, T.C. Memo 1977419 . . . aff'd without opinion, 626 F.2d 868 (9th Cir. 1980). But Moss's firm never had more than eight lawyers (partners and associates), and did not need a daily lunch to cement relationships among them.

It is all a matter of degree and circumstance (the expense of a testimonial dinner, for example, would be deductible on a moralebuilding rationale); and particularly of frequency. Daily for a full year is too often, perhaps even for entertainment of clients, as implied by *Hankenson v. Commissioner*, T.C. Memo 1984200, (1984), where the Tax Court held nondeductible the cost of lunches consumed three or four days a week, 52 weeks a year, by a doctor who entertained other doctors who he hoped would refer patients to him, and other medical personnel.

We may assume it was necessary for Moss's firm to meet daily to coordinate the work of the firm, and also, as the Tax Court found, that lunch was the most convenient time. But it does not follow that the expense of the lunch was a necessary business expense. The members of the firm had to eat somewhere, and the Café Angelo was both convenient and not too expensive. They do not claim to have incurred a greater daily lunch expense than they would have incurred if there had been no lunch meetings. Although it saved time to combine lunch with work, the meal itself was not an organic part of the meeting, as in the examples we gave earlier where the business objective, to be fully achieved, required sharing a meal.

The case might be different if the location of the courts required the firm's members to eat each day either in a disagreeable restaurant, so that they derived less value from the meal than it cost them to buy it, cf. *Sibla v. Commissioner*, 611 F.2d 1260, 1262 (9th Cir. 1980); or in a restaurant too expensive for their personal tastes, so that, again, they would have gotten less value than the cash equivalent. But so far as appears, they picked the restaurant they liked most. Although it must be pretty monotonous to eat lunch the same place every working day of the year, not all the lawyers attended all the lunch meetings and there was nothing to stop the firm from meeting occasionally at another restaurant proximate to their office in downtown Chicago; there are hundreds.

An argument can be made that the price of lunch at the Café Angelo included rental of the space that the lawyers used for what was a meeting as well as a meal. There was evidence that the firm's conference room was otherwise occupied throughout the working day, so as a matter of logic Moss might be able to claim a part of the price of lunch as an ordinary and necessary expense for work space. But this is cutting things awfully fine; in any event Moss made no effort to apportion his lunch expense in this way.

AFFIRMED.

Some Questions and a Note on the Failure to Claim Reimbursements

Varying the Factors of Moss. What if the facts of *Moss* differed only in that the meetings were in the firm's conference room and the food was pizza? What if the facts of *Moss* were the same, but the meeting only took place once a week? What if a different client was always invited to the luncheon?

Reimbursements. It is common for employees to incur expenses on behalf of their employers and then to demand reimbursements. What if the employee decided not to bother submitting a voucher to his employer and instead decided to claim the deduction on his own? Should the taxpayer be entitled to pick and choose whether to bother being reimbursed? The answer is that sometimes the failure to claim a reimbursement is viewed as making the expenditure not "necessary" and therefore incapable of supporting a tax deduction for unreimbursed employee expenses.[446] The Treasury Department has a legitimate reason to be concerned:

> **To illustrate:** Mr. Big owns all of BigCo., Inc., which is a 21% bracket taxpayer. Mr. Big is in the 37% bracket. If he fails to make BigCo. reimburse a $1,000 business related Hertz rental car expense, he might deduct the $1,000 and claim a $370 personal tax saving, as opposed to $210 of taxes that BigCo. would save if it reimbursed him. If the rates were reversed, Mr. Big would do better to have the corporation reimburse the expense and claim the deduction.

Income to the Guest? Curiously, there seems to be no general authority with respect to the guest's right to exclude the value of meals and entertainment. It is apparently just assumed. In some cases, the guest may be able to exclude the meal or entertainment as a fringe benefit under §132(a).

D. SUBSTANTIATION OF SELECTED BUSINESS DEDUCTIONS

Read §274(d)

In general, taxpayers are entitled to estimate their expenses, although it is much better if they have precise substantiating evidence of all their deductions, in case of a tax audit. The origin of the right to estimate one's expenses is a holding by Judge Learned Hand that the flamboyant Broadway showman, George M. Cohan, was allowed to estimate his then huge outlays of about $55,000 over three years in the 1920's.[447] However, this generous attitude is reversed in the case of the short list of deductions that are unpopular with Congress, namely those for travel, business gifts, entertainment and business meals, exactly what Cohan got away with. Nowadays, the taxpayer is obligated to maintain reasonable records showing the date, amount, and business purpose of the expenditure. The problem with respect to claiming deductions for meals, travel, business gifts, and entertainment is that when one fails to maintain these records, then in principle one is not allowed any deduction. This provision in fact comes roaring in like a lion but departs more like a lamb in that the taxpayer is allowed to use certain corroborative evidence if she did not maintain contemporaneous records.[448] Still, prudent taxpayers keep contemporaneous logs rather than risk losing fights with the IRS.

---

446 See for example Lucas v Commissioner 79 T.C. 1 (1982).

447 Cohan v. Commissioner, 39 F.2d 540 (2d Cir. 1930), rev'g 11 B.T.A. 743 (1928).

448 See Reg. §1.2745T(c)(1).

Problem 6-3:

Mr. Pleasure is a prosperous self-employed salesman. Today was especially busy.

1) First, he paid a scalper $100 for two $20 tickets to an afternoon baseball game.

    a. He took a customer to the game to get to know him and to do a little talking about his competitors' products and to compare the prices of some of his products. Can Mr. Pleasure deduct the cost of the tickets when he takes a customer to the ball game? See Reg. §1.274-2(d)(7)(ii).

    b. Would the result differ if the conversations took place just after the game at a quiet bar?

    c. Assuming the tickets are otherwise deductible, how much can he deduct? See §274(l)

2) Mr. Pleasure gave his favorite customer a TV set costing $250. It was a gift; he loves the customer. Can he deduct it? See §274(b). What if it did not qualify as a gift, i.e. was partly to get more business?

3) Mr. Pleasure made reservations for two for his best customer (whom he planned to make a big sales pitch to) at the best restaurant in town. Mr. Pleasure paid for the meal in advance, but was unable to attend because a sales opportunity came up. He told the client, "Forget me. I'm not coming. Just go with your spouse. It's on me." Can he deduct it? See §274(k). What if he sent one of his employees to make the same pitch at the meal?

4) Mr. Pleasure made reservations at the best restaurant in town and this time he was present and closed a big sale at dinner. The customer's wife was also present and participated actively in the business discussion, and Mr. Pleasure ate seemingly endless amounts of truffles, costing in total $1,322. Assuming a non-lavish meal under the circumstances would cost $100, how much can Mr. Pleasure deduct for his meal? Can he deduct the cost of the customer's spouse's meal?

5) Think back to problem 5-8 involving Mrs. Bronson, who entertained customers of her grocery store to improve their relations with her store. Would it be a "directly

related" entertainment expense that she could deduct? Take a look at Reg. §1.274-2(c)(4). Could it be "associated with" entertainment?

6) You are employed by a business as a lawyer. The business sends you to a nearby city to meet with a state government agency that is menacing the business. You take an assistant state commissioner to lunch and discuss the company's legal issues in a way that is helpful to the company. It costs $20.00. The state employee pays for her own meal. You seek reimbursement of the meal, which you get.

   a. If you have an accountable plan, must you report the income? How much can your employer deduct? §1.274-5T(f)(2).

   b. Assume the same facts as "a)", except you are self-employed. You paid the $20 bill in cash and paid a $3.00 cash tip and all you got as evidence was a check from the waiter for $20.00, which you kept. What should you note on the check (assuming that keeping receipts is your only form of record keeping) in order to comply with the requirement that meal, business gift, and entertainment expenses be adequately substantiated? See §274(d).

E. MOVING EXPENSE DEDUCTIONS

Until the Tax Cuts and Jobs Act of 2017, an employee could exclude qualified moving expense reimbursements as gross income. Qualified moving expense reimbursements are direct or indirect payments from an employer for moving expenses that would be deductible under §217 if directly paid or incurred by the employee §132(g) but do not include amounts actually deducted by the employee in a prior year.

The Tax Cuts and Jobs Act of 2017 suspends the exclusion for qualified moving expense reimbursements for tax years 2018 through 2025. §132(g), as amended by the Tax Cuts and Jobs Act (P.L. 115-97)). Members of the U.S. Armed Forces on active duty who move pursuant to a military order and incident to a permanent change of station may still take the exclusion. §132(g)(2), as amended by the Tax Cuts and Jobs Act of 2017.

Read Reg. §1.1627(a)(b)

Corporations are not entitled to deduct dividends that they pay, but dividends are nevertheless taxable to shareholderrecipients under §301. The prototypical excessive compensation case involves a parent who is the president of a familyowned corporation, and takes out a particularity large amount of compensation (counting deferred compensation such as future pension benefits and fringe benefits) which the corporation seeks to deduct in full under §162(a)(1). As a result, owner-employees of corporations have an incentive to mischaracterize what are really distributions of profits as bonuses, rental payments and the like. If the officer is also a shareholder, the IRS is likely to argue that excessive part of the payment is in substance a (nondeductible) dividend to the employee. If the parent is not a shareholder, then the IRS can simply argue that the payment is superfluous and, to that extent, nondeductible. Congress has a legitimate stake in trying to stop the deception. This inability to deduct dividends has driven many taxpayers away from doing business in the corporate form in favor of partnerships and other forms of business organization that cause the owner alone to be taxed on the entity's profits.

Note Well: Under current law most dividends are taxable at rates of not over 20%, so the IRS's interest in reasonable compensation cases with respect to shareholder-employees has declined.

The following case involves an allegation of excessive compensation paid to an employee of a partnership. Most cases involve a payee who is an owner of the enterprise. As you read the case, you might wonder if the Revenue Agent and the supervisor(s) who reviewed his proposed adjustments went too far.

PATTON v. COMMISSIONER OF INTERNAL REVENUE

168 F.2d 28 (6th Cir. 1948)

Before HICKS, McALLISTER and MILLER, Circuit Judges.

HICKS, Circuit Judge

[Father and son owned and operated a machine shop as partners. Initially they hired a bookkeeper, Kirk, who had only two years of high school commercial training, at a salary of under $2,000 per year. The company thrived because in 1941 GM contracted with the partnership. The taxpayers then agreed with Kirk to pay him an annual salary of 10% of the partnership's net sales. This resulted in Kirk receiving $46,000 in 1943, this amount which the partnership deducted. The IRS claims that his reasonable salary was $13,000. Kirk was unrelated to the Pattons.]

...

The case strips to one question: whether, as determined by the Commissioner, $13,000.00 was reasonable compensation to Kirk for 1943. We are dealing with a pure question of fact. Wilmington Co. v. Helvering, 316 U.S. 164, 62 S.Ct. 984, 986, 86 L.Ed. 1352. In the Wilmington case, supra, the court said: 'It is the function of the Board, not the Circuit Court of Appeals, to weigh the evidence, to draw inferences from the facts, and to choose between conflicting inferences. The court may not substitute its view of the facts for that of the Board. Where the findings of the Board are supported by substantial evidence they are conclusive.'

In the proceedings before the Tax Court the presumption is that the Commissioner was right and petitioners have the burden of proving that his determination was wrong. We think that the findings of the Tax Court are supported by substantial evidence and an affirmance must result. There is no hard and fast rule by which reasonableness of compensation may be determined by the Tax Court. Every case must stand or fall upon its own peculiar facts and circumstances. Among other factors to be considered by the Court are: The nature of the services to be performed, the responsibilities they entail, the time required of the employee in the discharge of his duties, his capabilities and training, and the amount of compensation paid in proportion to net profits. An exclusive function of the Tax Court is the determination of the weight and credibility to be given to the witnesses.

We think that petitioners have failed to carry the burden, which the law imposes upon them, to make out their case by clear and convincing evidence. Atlas Plaster & Fuel Co. v. Comm'r, 6 Cir., 55 F.2d 802, 803 . . . . Probably one of the most important factors in determining the reasonableness of compensation is the amount paid to similar employees by similar concerns engaged in similar industries. The petitioners introduced no evidence upon this subject. Moreover, it occurs to us that the books of the partnership kept by Kirk would have disclosed to a great extent the nature and volume of his work and his capabilities to perform it, but neither the books nor any verified entries therefrom were introduced by petitioners. There is of course a presumption that as between the parties to the contract the compensation agreed to be paid was reasonable. But, as between petitioners and the Commissioner, such a presumption is not controlling in a controversy of this nature before the Tax Court. Botany Worsted Mills v. United States, 278 U.S. 282, 292, 49 S.Ct. 129, L.Ed. 379.

Affirmed.

McALLISTER, Circuit Judge (dissenting).

According to Section [162] of the Internal Revenue Code, to which reference has been made, petitioners are entitled to a deduction in their taxes for all 'the ordinary and necessary expenses paid or incurred during the taxable year in carrying on' their business, 'including a reasonable allowance for salaries or other compensation for personal services actually rendered.' The issue is whether the compensation which was paid to Kirk, in accordance with his contract of employment, was a reasonable allowance. As is said in the prevailing opinion, there is a presumption that, as between the parties to the contract, the compensation agreed to be paid was reasonable. But it is declared that as between petitioners herein and the Commissioner, such a presumption is not controlling a controversy of this nature before the Tax Court, and Botany Worsted Mills v. United States, 278 U.S. 282, 292, 49 S.Ct. 129, 133, L.Ed. 379, is cited as authority to sustain this conclusion.

. . .

In United States v. Philadelphia Knitting Mills Co., 3 Cir., 2 F. 657, 658, the court said: "As the board of directors is charged with the duty and clothed with the discretion of fixing the salaries of the corporation's officers, the Government has no right (until expressly granted by statute) to inquire into and determine whether the amounts thereof are proper, that is, whether they are too much or too little. But, while the amount of salary fixed by a board of directors is presumptively valid, it is not conclusively so, because the Government may inquire whether the amount paid is salary or something else. Admittedly the Government has a right to collect taxes on net income of corporation based on profits after all ordinary and necessary expenses, including salaries, are paid. It has a right, therefore, to attack the action of a board of directors and show by evidence, not that a given salary is too much, but that, in the circumstances, the whole or some part of it is not salary at all but is profits diverted to a stockholding officer under the guise of salary and as such is subject to taxation."

. . .

In all of these cases, the amounts were paid to officers who were really the beneficial owners of the corporation and who controlled its action in contracting for and paying them the unusually high salaries based upon net profits. The reasons the courts have held such salaries were not deductible as 'ordinary and necessary expenses,' were because they were not, in fact, compensation, but merely a distribution of profits; that such profits, divided on the basis of stock holdings, were not payments of compensation; that the claimed salaries were not salaries at all, but profits diverted to stock holding officers under the guise of salaries; and that a distribution of profits 'under the guise of salaries' to officers who held the stock of a company and controlled its affairs, is not an ordinary and necessary expense, within the meaning of the statute.

In this case, Kirk was not an owner or part owner of the company, directly or indirectly. His contract of employment, providing for a salary, based on profits, was not a distribution of profits under the guise of a salary. There is no question that the contract of employment was bona fide. As was said in United States v. Philadelphia Knitting Mills Co., supra, the Government has no right to inquire into and determine whether the amount of the salary was proper, or whether it was too much or too little, but only 'whether the amount paid is salary or something else.'

It is impossible to escape the conclusion that the Commissioner based his disallowance on the ground that the amount of compensation provided by the contract eventually turned out to be too high, merely because the profits during the years in question were so great. No such arbitrary determinations are valid, either in administrative decisions or in court adjudications. The decision that the amount provided by the contract of employment was too high was, as has been stated by the courts, no business or concern of the Government. The decisive question is whether the amount paid to Kirk was salary or a distribution of profits paid under the guise of salary. It was not a distribution of profits, for Kirk has no interest in the company.

It is admitted in this case that the amount paid to Kirk was salary, and there is nothing in the case to overcome the presumption that such compensation was reasonable. In my opinion, the partners were entitled to deduct the payment of such salary as an ordinary and necessary expense incurred during the taxable year, and the decision of the Tax Court to the contrary should be reversed.

Notes on Compensation Expense Deductions

The strange legislative history of the reasonable compensation limit. The legislative history of the "reasonable compensation" limit is curious, to put it mildly. Specifically, during the First World War there was an excess profits tax which could be reduced by the generous grant of an allowance for unpaid salaries (a "reasonable allowance" in the Code's words).[449] The IRS and the courts have turned that into a limiting rule that only a *reasonable* salary is "allowed" as a deduction. So what was originally a shield for taxpayers almost imperceptibly evolved into a sword in the IRS's hands.

Special relaxation for "free-bargains." Reg. §1.1627(b) in effect says that a compensation package that was struck at arm'slength in the past, and which provides for contingent income, based on how the business performs after the employee is hired will stand up even if it is unreasonably high compared to what would have resulted if the compensation had been negotiated on a fixed dollar basis. However, the courts will not uphold a bargain in favor of employees who can browbeat their employers. For example, consider how a deal in which a casino hired a new operator for 10% of the entity's profits might result in huge profits to the new operator; as long as the original bargain was at arm's-length and was not influenced by outside factors (such as the new operator being the oppressive father of a weakling son who owned the casino),[450] the later massive compensation will stand as "reasonable compensation."

The weak limit on mega-compensation for top executives. Executive compensation in publicly-held corporations has become extraordinary. For example, according to one survey of 1995 compensation, CEO compensation at 30 major U.S. companies soared to 212 times what the average U.S. worker earned, up from a multiple of 44 in 1965. Subsection 162(m) limits deductions for

449 See Griswold, *New Light on "A Reasonable Allowance for Salaries,"* 59 Harv. L. Rev. 286 (1945).

450 See, e.g., Harold's Club v. Commissioner, 340 F.2d 861 (9th Cir. 1965) (dominating father's contingent compensation paid by son's company held excessive; no free bargain).

compensation paid to executives of publiclyheld corporations to $1 million per year, but the exceptions greatly erode the rule. The vital exception is for adequately disclosed "performance-based compensation," the levels of which are set by a compensation committee with at least two outside directors, meaning directors who are not employed by the same company as the executive in question. Some impressive skeptics believe that the idea of an independent director is a naive corporate law concept,[451] which suggests the idea that there is an objective check on excessive contingent compensation is believed only by the gullible.

Golden parachutes. Another recent compensation-related novelty is the so-called "golden parachute" payment. Section 280G, which you are not expected to read, disallows deductions for socalled "excess parachute payments," which are in essence payments to corporate employees or independent contractors working for the corporation and who are highly compensated, which amounts are paid by virtue of a takeover of the company. The legislative purpose behind §280G is to take away some of the tax benefits of golden parachute payments. The problem that Congress perceived was that corporations were arranging compensation packages that were contingent upon the corporation's takeover, and that these packages were so lavish that they actually encouraged such takeovers because they tended to neutralize the resistance of the target company's management. There seems to be no empirical evidence as to whether withdrawing this tax deduction has made a bit of difference.

Before 2018: A publicly held corporation may not deduct more than $1 million a year paid to a covered employee 162(m)(1)). The $1 million cap is further reduced by excess parachute payments that are not deductible by the corporation (§162(m)(4)(F)).

Generally, "covered employees" include the chief operating officer (CEO) of the corporation and the four most highly compensated employees of the corporation other than the CEO, whose compensation is required to be reported to the shareholders by the Securities and Exchange Commission (SEC) under the Securities Exchange Act of 1934 (§162(m)(3); Notice 2007-49). This includes the principal executive officer (PEO), the principal financial officer (PFO), and the three most highly compensated officers other than the PEO or PFO must disclose their compensation.

Compensation subject to the deduction limit generally includes the taxable wages paid to the employee for services performed (§162(m)(4); Reg. §1.162-27).

Types of compensation that are not taken into account in determining whether compensation exceeds the $1 million limit include:

- Specified commissions, compensation based on performance goals, income payable under a written binding contract that was in effect on February 17, 1993, and

- Compensation paid before a corporation became publicly held.

451 See, e.g., R. Clark, CORPORATE LAW p. 182-183 (Little Brown, 1986).

Payments excluded from the definition of compensation include: (1) payments to a tax-favored retirement plan (including salary reduction contributions), and (2) amounts that are excludable from the executive's gross income (such as employer-provided health benefits and miscellaneous fringe benefits).

After the Tax Cuts and Jobs Act of 2017: The definition of covered employee is expanded to include both the principal executive officer and the principal financial officer, as well as the other three most highly compensated employees. Employees who are covered employees after December 31, 2016, remain covered employees for all future tax years.

Covered employee. A covered employee is any employee of the corporation who:

- is the principal executive officer (PEO) of the corporation (or an individual acting in such capacity) at any time during the tax year;
- is the principal financial officer (PFO) of the corporation (or an individual acting in such capacity) at any time during the tax year;
- is among the three highest compensated officers for the tax year (other than the PEO or the PFO); or
- was a covered employee of the corporation (or any predecessor) for any prior tax year beginning on or after January 1, 2017 (§162(m)(3), as amended by the Tax Cuts and Jobs Act (P.L. 115-97)).

Compensation.

- The exclusions from the limitation for commission-based and performance-based compensation have been repealed.
- The exceptions for commissions and performance-based compensation are repealed (§162(m)(4), as amended by the 2017 Tax Cuts Act).
- Applicable employee compensation (remuneration) for tax years beginning after 2017, includes any cash and noncash benefits paid for services, including commissions and performance-based compensation, but does not include:
    - income from specified employee trusts, annuity plans, or pensions;
    - any benefit that is reasonably anticipated to be tax free under the Code;

- income payable under a written binding contract which was in effect on February 17, 1993; and
- compensation paid before a corporation became publicly held (§162(m)(4), as amended by the 2017 Tax Cuts Act).

A transition rule applies to compensation provided pursuant to a written binding contract which was in effect on November 2, 2017, and that is not modified in any material respect on or after such date (Act Sec. 13601(e)(2) of the 2017 Tax Cuts Act). Compensation paid pursuant to a plan qualifies for this exception provided that the right to participate in the plan is part of a written binding contract with the covered employee in effect on November 2, 2017. The fact that a plan was in existence on November 2, 2017 is not by itself sufficient to qualify the plan for the exception for binding written contracts (Conference Report on H.R. 1, Tax Cuts and Jobs Act (H. Rept. 115-466)).

Golden parachutes before 2018: Generally, for-profit employers are allowed a deduction for reasonable compensation expenses under §162(a). In some cases, however, compensation in excess of specific levels is not deductible. A publicly held corporation cannot deduct compensation to a covered employee to the extent the compensation exceeds $1 million per tax year (§162(m)). The $1 million threshold is reduced (but not below zero) by excess parachute payments that are not deductible under the golden parachute provisions of §280G. These deduction limits generally do not affect tax-exempt organizations.

A payment in the nature of compensation made to or for the benefit of a disqualified individual is a parachute payment if:

- it is contingent on a change in the ownership or effective control of the corporation or the ownership of a substantial portion of the assets of a corporation, and its present value equals or exceeds 300 percent of the individual's average annual compensation for the last five years (a "change-in-control parachute payment"), or

- it is made under an agreement that violates securities laws (a "securities violation parachute payment").

Certain amounts are not considered parachute payments, including payments under a qualified retirement plan, a simplified employee pension plan, or a simple retirement account.

For this purpose, disqualified individuals (also called "covered employees") are employees, independent contractors, and other persons who perform personal services for a corporation and who are officers, shareholders or highly compensated individuals are subject to the golden parachute provisions. Disqualified individuals also include personal service corporations and similar entities (§280G(c)).

Negative tax consequences are imposed only on excess parachute payments.

An excess parachute payment is the portion of any parachute payment that exceeds the base amount, which is the recipient's average annual compensation over the five years before the change in ownership, reduced, in the case of a change-in-control parachute payment, by the excess of the amount of the payment determined to be reasonable compensation for services performed before the date of the change over average compensation. The excess amount is determined separately for each parachute payment received.

Golden parachutes after the Tax Cuts and Jobs Act of 2017: There is an excise tax on remuneration of highly-compensated exempt organization executives.—A tax-exempt organization will be liable within a tax year for a 21 percent excise tax (equal to the maximum corporate tax rate on income) on the sum of:

- "remuneration" paid to a "covered employee" in excess of $1 million (not including any excess parachute payment) by an "applicable tax-exempt organization", and

- any excess parachute payments paid to a covered employee by that tax-exempt organization (§4960, as added by the Tax Cuts and Jobs Act of 2017 (P.L. 115-97)).

An exempt organization can be liable for this excise tax even when a covered employee's remuneration is less than $1 million if there is an excess parachute payment. For purposes of this excise tax, there is a new definition for parachute payments that is limited to the payment of compensation to a covered employee when such payment is contingent on:

- the employee's separation from employment with the tax-exempt employer, and

- the aggregate present value of the compensation payments being equal or in excess of an amount equal to three times the base amount (§4960(c)(5)(B), as added by the 2017 Tax Cuts Act).

The base amount is determined under §280G(b)(3). However, certain payments are excluded from calculating the aggregate present value, including:

- payments under qualified plans, as described in §280G(b)(6));

- payments made to or under a tax-deferred annuity contract as described in §403(b), or
- the deferred compensation plan of a government employer as described in §457(b);
- payments to a doctor, nurse, or veterinarian for the performance of medical or veterinarian professional services; and
- payments to an individual who is not a highly compensated employee as defined in §414(q) (§4960(c)(5)(C), as added by the 2017 Tax Cuts Act).

An "applicable tax-exempt organization" is one that is exempt from taxation under §501(a), a farmers' cooperative under §521(b)(1), a political organization described in §527(e)(1), or an organization that has income excluded from taxation under §115(1) (§4960(c)(1), as added by the 2017 Tax Cuts Act).

Problem 6-4

1) Alice is a covered employee hired by XYZ Corporation on October 2, 2017. One of the terms of her written employment contract is that she is eligible to participate in the company's deferred compensation plan. The written plan provides for participation after six months of employment, amounts payable under the plan are not subject to discretion, and the corporation does not have the right to amend materially the plan or terminate the plan except on a prospective basis. Do payments to Alice under the plan meet the binding contract exception even though she was not actually a participant in the plan on November 2, 2017?

G. TRADE OR BUSINESS INTEREST

Read §163(a) and (h)(2)

1. Background and Introduction

People pay interest for the right to use other people's money. It is similar to renting a piece of business hardware. Until fairly recently, the U.S. tax system had a warm place in its heart for interest expense deductions of any kind.

Until recently, the deduction for interest paid by a business remains the most secure of the interest expense deductions. Examples of business interest are accounts payable to suppliers of business inventory, or to banks that lend money to finance working capital needed to keep the business going. One of the interesting features of interest expenses is that, in general, one need not capitalize them even though they are associated with the purchase of properties with long life-spans.

Business interest deductions before 2018: Interest and other borrowing expenses incurred in a trade or business were generally deductible from gross income before 2018 under §163. When a debt instrument had original issue discount (OID), the taxpayer included the OID as interest over the life of the obligation.

Several pre-2018 limitations on the deduction of interest continue under the new Tax Cuts and Jobs Act of 2017 including limits on:

- Tax-exempt interest,
- interest from obligations not in registered form,
- interest paid in connection with insurance contracts, and
- interest paid on an original issue discount (OID) high-yield obligation.

Sometimes taxpayers must capitalize interest that is allocable to the production of property.

Taxpayer other than corporations may not deduct more business interest in a given tax year than their investment income (§163(d)). The taxpayer carries forward any excess investment interest expense indefinitely until net investment income is recognized.

Business interest deductions after the Tax Cuts and Jobs Act of 2017:

After 2017, business interest deductions are limited regardless of the form the taxpayer's business (i.e., corporation, partnership, sole proprietorship, etc.) although there is an exception for a small business with average gross receipts of $25 million or less.

Taxpayers carry forward any disallowed interest subject to certain restrictions for partnerships and S corporations.

Limitation on business interest. The deduction for business interest is limited to the sum of the taxpayer's:

- business interest income for the tax year;
- 30 percent of adjusted taxable income for the year, including any increases in adjusted taxable income as a result of a distributive share in a partnership or S corporation but not below zero; and
- floor plan financing interest the tax year (§163(j)(1), as added by the 2017 Tax Cuts Act).

Business interest. Business interest means any interest paid or accrued on debt properly allocable to a trade or business of the taxpayer (§163(j)(5), as added by the 2017 Tax Cuts Act). Business interest does not include investment interest.

Business interest income is the amount of interest includible in the taxpayer's gross income for the tax year that is properly allocable to a trade or business (§163(j)(6), as added by the 2017 Tax Cuts Act). It does not include any investment income.

Investment interest is interest allocable to property that produces interest, dividends, annuities, royalties, gains, or losses not derived in the ordinary course of a trade or business. It also includes interest in a trade or business activity that is not a passive activity and in which the taxpayer does not materially participate. However, **investment expenses** are determined after application of the two-percent-over adjusted gross income (AGI) limitation on miscellaneous itemized deductions.

Investment income is the gross income derived from property held for investment or from its disposition including interest received, annuities, dividends, royalties, and short-term gain on the disposition of property and capital gain. Investment income also includes qualified dividend income but only to the extent that the taxpayer elects to treat it as investment income. §163(d)

Adjusted taxable income is the taxpayer's regular taxable income computed without regard to:

- any item of income, gain, deduction, or loss that is not properly allocable to a trade or business;
- any business interest or business interest income;
- the amount of any net operating loss (NOL) deduction;

- the 20-percent deduction for qualified business income of a passthrough entity under §199A and
- in tax years beginning before January 1, 2022, an allowable deduction for depreciation, amortization, or depletion (§163(j)(8), as added by the 2017 Tax Cuts Act).

Floor plan financing indebtedness is interest paid or accrued on debt use to finance the acquisition of motor vehicles held for sale or lease to retail customers and secured by the inventory (§163(j)(9), as added by the 2017 Tax Cuts Act).

Trade or business for purposes of calculating the business interest deduction limitation does not include the performance of services as an employee (§163(j)(7)(A)(i), as added by the 2017 Tax Cuts Act). Thus, wages of an employee are not included as part of the taxpayer's adjusted taxable income.

A taxpayer may also elect to exclude from the limitation any real property trade or business as defined under the passive activity rules (§163(j)(7)(A)(ii) and (B), as added by the 2017 Tax Cuts Act).

An electing real property trade or business is any real estate development, redevelopment, construction, reconstruction, acquisition, conversion, rental, operation, management, leasing, or brokerage trade or business. The election keeps interest expenses paid or accrued in the electing real property trade or business out of the definition of business interest and so out of the limitation on business interest deductions.

The limitation on the deduction of business interest applies after the application of other limitations on interest and after the capitalization rules (House Committee Report for the Tax Cuts and Jobs Act (P.L. 115-97) (H.R. Rep. No. 115-409).

H. DEPRECIATION

Read §§ 167(a) and 168(a)(c)

1. Background

You are now about to embark upon one of the more arcane mysteries in the Internal Revenue Code, namely the twin concepts of amortization of intangible property and its cousin, the depreciation of tangible property. First, a little definitional work. "Amortization" means writing off intangible property (such as secret processes, franchises, patents and so forth) over a number of years, normally in equal annual amounts. A good example is a commission that a tenant pays in order to obtain a business lease. Such a commission would be deducted in equal annual measures over the term of the lease. Section 167 is the bedrock authority for amortization deductions, but other speciallytailored Code sections describe parallel but unique deductions. An example you saw before of an amortization deduction appears in §195, which allows taxpayers who begin businesses to deduct startup costs in equal amounts over as few as 60 months, beginning when the business opens its door to the public.

"Depreciation" refers to writing off (deducting the cost of) tangible property, with no implication that the writeoff is expected to be in equal measures over time. "Cost recovery" is a fancy reference to depreciation of tangible property under a specific Code section, namely §168. Section 168 was enacted in 1981 to simplify the depreciation processes and to accelerate the allowances as an incentive for capital investments. It instituted what is known as the accelerated cost recovery system (a.k.a., "ACRS"), whose earmarks are short statutory depreciation periods (known as "useful lives" or "recovery periods"), along with an amazing, irrebuttable presumption that the property is worthless when its statutory life ends. In most cases these writeoffs are faster in the early years of the property's use than in later years. "Straightline depreciation" (or "straightline cost recovery") refers to the writing off of tangible property in equal amounts over time, such as 10% per year. "Accelerated depreciation" refers to writing property off at a more rapid than average rate early in the life of the property and at a correspondingly slower rate in the twilight years of the property. ACRS covers only hardware, and never intangibles. The Regulations contain precise descriptions of the basic depreciation methods.[452]

The hub for depreciation and amortization deductions is in §167(a). Make sure to read it. As you can see, it covers both business property and property held for the production of income (such as a rental property held for investment). Section 168 supplements §167 by providing systematic pigeonholes for tangible property and associated life spans and methods of depreciation, such as accelerated or straightline.

Before going further, one needs to get a grasp on what this is all about. Why depreciation? Well, what are the choices? Take the case of an owner of a small factory who buys a new injection molding machine. The price of the machine is a cost of producing income. Assume that the machine is likely to last five years after which the factory owner will discard it. Should the owner be entitled to write the entire cost off right now? When the property is discarded? Or perhaps it would be better to write it off in gradual stages over the five year life span? Congress opted for the last approach and in doing so it satisfied accountants' preference for matching income and deductions so as to produce a realistic, steady picture of income over time. For example, if the tax law allowed a full write-off of the cost of the machine in the year the taxpayer bought it, the

452 See Reg. §1.167(a)-1, 1.167(b)1-(straight line), 1.167(b)-2 (declining balance method) and 1.167(b)-3 (sum-of-the-years'-digits method).

likely outcome would be an unrealistically low statement of taxable income in the first year and correspondingly overstated income in the subsequent years. After all, the machine has not lost all its value when placed in service, so a complete, immediate write-off in the first year would distort the picture by producing an unreasonably pessimistic statement of the factory owner's initial income and net worth. Now compare the buyer of a machine with a five year life to a person who rents such a machine from someone else for five years. You know that the rental expenses are deductible under §162(a). The depreciation deduction parallels the rental expense deduction. At the end of the period the owner of the machine and the person who rented it will both have a worthless object -- a piece of scrap or the memory of a lease.

One of the mysteries in this realm is the role of inflation. What does one do if there is terrible inflation and the factory equipment actually rises in dollar value, even though it is losing value compared to new replacement machines? The basic response from Congress is to ignore the problem. Supporters of rapid depreciation like to point out generous depreciation deductions have the salutary effect of offsetting the ravages of inflation.

The Code contains a number of special opportunities to claim an extraordinary amount of depreciation in early years, such as for certain recycling equipment and equipment used for disaster relief.

2. Depreciable Assets

So what costs can one amortize or depreciate? Read Reg. §1.167(a)(b), then the following controversial case, not only for its issues but also for the background information and explanation of depreciation doctrines in general.

SIMON v. COMMISSIONER

103 T.C 247 (1994)

LARO, Judge:

[Plaintiffs, both professional musicians, claimed deductions under the accelerated cost recovery system (§168) on two 19thcentury violin bows that they routinely used in their trade or business of being fulltime professional violinists. The IRS disallowed these deductions, asserting that the bows were depreciable under ACRS only if the taxpayers could prove the useful life of each bow under the law that applied before ACRS. The IRS also argued that the useful lives of the bows were indeterminable because the bows were treasured works of art that appreciate in value and for which it is impossible to determine "useful lives" in the business.]

OPINION

. . .

Taxpayers have long been allowed asset depreciation deductions in order to allow them to allocate their expense of using an incomeproducing asset to the periods that are benefitted by that asset. The primary purpose of allocating depreciation to more than 1 year is to provide a more meaningful matching of the cost of an incomeproducing asset with the income resulting therefrom; this meaningful match, in turn, bolsters the accounting integrity for tax purposes of the taxpayer's periodic income statements. *Hertz Corp. v. United States*, 364 U.S. 122, 126 (1960); .... Such a system of accounting for depreciation for Federal income tax purposes has been recognized with the approval of the Supreme Court for over 65 years; as the Court observed in 1927: "The theory underlying this allowance for depreciation is that by using up the plant, a gradual sale is made of it." *United States v. Ludey*, 274 U.S. 295, 301 (1927) .... In this sense, an allocation of depreciation to a given year represents that year's reduction of the underlying asset through wear and tear. *United States v. Ludey, supra* at 300301. Depreciation allocations also represent a return to the taxpayer of his or her investment in the incomeproducing property over the years in which depreciation is allowed....

Prior to the Economic Recovery Tax Act of 1981 (ERTA), Pub. L. 9734, 95 Stat. 172, personal property was depreciated pursuant to section 167 of the Internal Revenue Code of 1954 (1954 Code). Section 167(a) provided:

> SEC. 167(a). General Rule. There shall be allowed as a depreciation deduction a reasonable allowance for the exhaustion, wear and tear (including a reasonable allowance for obsolescence)
>
> (1) of property used in the trade or business, or
>
> (2) of property held for the production of income.

The regulations under this section expanded on the text of section 167 by providing that personal property was only depreciable before ERTA if the taxpayer established the useful life of the property. See sec. 1.167(a)1(A) and (b), Income Tax Regs.

The "useful life" of property under preERTA law was the period over which the asset could reasonably be expected to be useful to the taxpayer in his or her trade or business, or in the production of his or her income.... This useful life period was not always the physical life or maximum useful life inherent in the asset.... sec.1.167(a)1(b), Income Tax Regs. A primary factor to consider in determining an asset's useful life was any "wear and tear and decay or decline from natural causes" that was inflicted upon the asset. Sec. 1.167(a)1(b), Income Tax Regs.

Before ERTA, the primary method that was utilized to ascertain the useful life for personal property was the asset depreciation range (ADR) system. Under the ADR system, which was generally effective for assets placed in service after 1970 and before 1981, property was grouped into broad classes of industry assets, and each class was assigned a guideline life. See, e.g., sec. 1.167(a)11, Income Tax Regs.; Rev. Proc. 8335, 19831 C.B. 745, superseded by Rev. Proc. 8756, 19872 C.B. 674; see also ERTA sec. 209(a), 95 Stat. 226. A range of years, i.e., the ADR, was then provided for each class of personal property; the ADR extended from 20 percent below to 20 percent above the guideline class life. For each asset account in the class, the taxpayer selected either a class life or an ADR that was utilized as the useful life for computing depreciation. See, e.g., sec. 1.167(a)11(A), Income Tax Regs.; Rev. Proc. 8335, *supra.* If an asset was not eligible for ADR treatment, or if the taxpayer did not elect to use the ADR system, the useful life of that asset was generally determined based on either the particular facts and circumstances that applied thereto, or by agreement between the taxpayer and the Commissioner. . . . sec. 1.167(a)1(b), Income Tax Regs. See generally Staff of Joint Comm. on Taxation, General Explanation of the Economic Recovery Tax Act of 1981, at 67 (J. Comm. Print 1981) (hereinafter referred to as the 1981 Bluebook[453]).

In enacting ERTA, the Congress found that the preERTA rules for determining depreciation allowances were unnecessarily complicated and did not generate the investment incentive that was critical for economic expansion. The Congress believed that the high inflation rates prevailing at that time undervalued the true worth of depreciation deductions and, hence, discouraged investment and economic competition. The Congress also believed that the determination of useful lives was "complex" and "inherently uncertain," and "frequently [resulted] in unproductive disagreements between taxpayers and the Internal Revenue Service." S. Rept. 97144, at 47 (1981), 19812 C.B. 412, 425. See generally 1981 Bluebook, at 75. Accordingly, the Congress decided that a new capital cost recovery system would have to be structured which, among other things, lessened the importance of the concept of useful life for depreciation purposes. S. Rept. 97144, *supra* at 47, 19812 C.B. at 425. See generally 1981 Bluebook, at 75. This new system is ACRS. ACRS is mandatory and applies to most tangible depreciable assets placed in service after 1980 and before 1987. . . .

. . .

Thus, through ERTA, the Congress minimized the importance of useful life by: (1) reducing the number of periods of years over which a taxpayer could depreciate his or her property from the multitudinous farreaching periods of time listed for the ADR system to the four short periods of time listed in ERTA (i.e., the 3year, 5year, 10year, and 15year ACRS periods), and (2) basing depreciation on an arbitrary statutory period of years that was unrelated to, and shorter than, an asset's estimated useful life. This minimization of the useful life concept through a deemed useful life was in spirit with the two main issues that ERTA was designed to address, namely: (1) Alleviating the income tax problems that resulted mainly from complex depreciation computations and useful life litigation, and (2) responding to economic policy concerns that the pre-ERTA depreciation systems spread the depreciation deductions over such a long period of time

453 The Staff of the Joint Committee on Taxation often produces a useful technical explanation of new laws, often under a blue cover. These are well-written and useful, but they are not formal legislative history. Eds.]

that investment in incomeproducing assets was discouraged through the income tax system. S. Rept. 97144, supra at 47, 19812 C.B. at 425. See generally 1981 Bluebook, at 75.

[The initial IRS position was] that a taxpayer generally could not deduct depreciation on expensive works of art and curios that he purchased as office furniture. See A.R.R. 4530, II2 C.B. 145 (1923). This position was superseded by a similar position that was reflected in Rev. Rul. 68232, 19681 C.B. 79. That ruling states:

> A valuable and treasured art piece does not have a determinable useful life. While the actual physical condition of the property may influence the value placed on the object, it will not ordinarily limit or determine the useful life. Accordingly, depreciation of works of art *generally* is not allowable. [Emphasis added.]
>
> . . .

We agree with petitioners that they may depreciate the Tourte bows under ACRS. ERTA was enacted partially to address and eliminate the issue that we are faced with today, namely, a disagreement between taxpayers and the Commissioner over the useful lives of assets that were used in taxpayers' trades or businesses. With this "elimination of disagreements" purpose in mind, the Congress defined five broad classes of "recovery property," and provided the periods of years over which taxpayers could recover their costs of this "recovery property." Two of these classes, the 3year and 5yearclasses, applied only to personal property; the 3year class included certain shortlived assets such as automobiles and lightduty trucks, and the 5year class included all other tangible personal property that was not within the 3year class. H. Conf. Rept. 97215, at 206208 (1981), 19812 C.B. 481, 487488. Thus, under section 168 as added to the 1954 Code by ERTA, personal property that is "recovery property" must be either 3year or 5yearclass property. Sec. 168(c)(2) as added to the 1954 Code by ERTA ("Each item of recovery property shall be assigned to one of the following classes of property"). Although "3year property" requires a taxpayer to determine whether the property had a class life under ADR of 4 years or less, the term "5year property" is appropriately designed to include all other section 1245 class property.

Inasmuch as section 168(a) allows a taxpayer to amortize depreciation with respect to "recovery property," petitioners may deduct depreciation on the Tourte bows if the bows fall within the meaning of that term. The term "recovery property" is defined broadly under ERTA to mean tangible property of a character subject to the allowance for depreciation and placed in service after 1980. Accordingly, property is "recovery property" if it is: (1) tangible, (2) placed in service after 1980, (3) of a character subject to the allowance for depreciation, and (4) used in the trade or business, or held for the production of income. Sec. 168(c)(1) . . . .

The Tourte bows fit snugly within the definition of recovery property. First, it is indisputable that the Tourte bows are tangible property, and that they were placed in service after 1980. Thus, the first two prerequisites for ACRS depreciation are met. Second, petitioners regularly used the Tourte bows in their trade or business as professional violinists during the year in issue. Accordingly, we conclude that petitioners have also met this prerequisite for depreciating the Tourte bows.

The last prerequisite for depreciating personal property under section 168 is that the property must be "of a character subject to the allowance for depreciation." The term "of a character subject to the allowance for depreciation" is undefined in the 1954 Code. Comparing the language that the Congress used in section 167(a) of the 1954 Code immediately before its amendment by ERTA, *supra* p. 254, with the language that it used in section 168(a) and (c)(1) as added to the 1954 Code by ERTA, *supra* pp. 255257, we believe that the Congress used the term "depreciation" in section 168(c)(1) to refer to the term "exhaustion, wear and tear (including a reasonable allowance for obsolescence)" that is contained in section 167(a). See *Noyce v. Commissioner*, supra at 689. Accordingly, we conclude that the term "of a character subject to the allowance for depreciation" means that property must suffer exhaustion, wear and tear, or obsolescence in order to be depreciated. Accordingly, petitioners will meet the final requirement under section 168 if the Tourte bows are subject to exhaustion, wear and tear, or obsolescence.

We are convinced that petitioners' frequent use of the Tourte bows subjected them to substantial wear and tear during the year in issue. Petitioners actively played their violins using the Tourte bows, and this active use resulted in substantial wear and tear to the bows. Indeed, respondent's expert witness even acknowledged at trial that the Tourte bows suffered wear and tear stemming from petitioners' business; the witness testified that the Tourte bows had eroded since he had examined them 3 years before, and that wood had come off them. Thus, we conclude that petitioners have satisfied the final prerequisite for depreciating personal property under section 168, and, accordingly, hold that petitioners may depreciate the Tourte bows during the year in issue. Allowing petitioners to depreciate the Tourte bows comports with the text of section 168, and enables them to match their costs for the Tourte bows with the income generated therefrom. Refusing to allow petitioners to deduct depreciation on the Tourte bows, on the other hand, would contradict section 168 and vitiate the accounting principle that allows taxpayers to write off incomeproducing assets against the income produced by those assets.

With respect to respondent's arguments in support of a contrary holding, we believe that respondent places too much reliance on the fact that the Tourte bows are old and have appreciated in value since petitioners acquired them. Indeed, respondent believes that this appreciation, in and of itself, serves to prevent petitioners from claiming any depreciation on the Tourte bows. We disagree; section 168 does not support her proposition that a taxpayer may not depreciate a business asset due to its age, or due to the fact that the asset may have appreciated in value over time. *Noyce v. Commissioner, supra* at 675, 691 (taxpayer allowed to deduct depreciation under section 168 on an airplane that had appreciated in economic value). Respondent incorrectly mixes two wellestablished, independent concepts of tax accounting, namely, accounting for the physical depreciation of an asset and accounting for changes in the asset's value on account of price fluctuations in the market. . . . Moreover, we find merit in petitioners' claim that they should be able to depreciate an asset that receives substantial wear and tear through frequent use in their trade or business. Simply stated, the concept of depreciation is appropriately designed to allow taxpayers to recover the cost or other basis of a business asset through annual depreciation deductions.

We also reject respondent's contention that the Tourte bows are nondepreciable because they have value as collectibles independent of their use in playing musical instruments, and that this value prolongs the Tourte bows' useful life forever. First, it is firmly established that the term "useful life" under preERTA law refers to the period of time in which a particular asset is useful to the taxpayer in his or her trade or business. . . . Thus, the fact that an asset such as the Tourte bows may outlive a taxpayer is not dispositive of the issue of whether that asset has a useful life for depreciation purposes under preERTA law. Second, the same argument concerning a separate, nonbusiness value can be made of many other assets. Such types of assets could include, for example, automobiles, patented property, highly sophisticated machinery, and real property. For the Court to delve into the determination of whether a particular asset has a separate, nonbusiness value would make the concept of depreciation a subjective issue and would be contrary to the Congress' intent to simplify the concept and computation of depreciation.

With respect to respondent's contention that petitioners must prove a definite useful life of the Tourte bows, we acknowledge that the concept of useful life was critical under preERTA law. Indeed, the concept of useful life was necessary and indispensable to the computation of depreciation because taxpayers were required to recover their investments in personal property over the estimated useful life of the property. Sec. 1.167(a)1(A), Income Tax Regs. However, the Congress enacted ERTA, in part, to avoid constant disagreements over the useful lives of assets, to shorten the writeoff periods for assets, and to encourage investment by providing for accelerated cost recovery through the tax law. S. Rept. 97144, at 47 (1981), 19812 C.B. 412, 425. See generally 1981 Bluebook, at 75. To these ends, the Congress created two short periods of years over which taxpayers would depreciate tangible personal property used in trade or business; the 3year and 5year recovery periods, respectively, are the *deemed useful life* of personal property. After the taxpayer has written off his or her asset over this 3year or 5year period, the taxpayer's basis in that asset will be zero; thus, the taxpayer will need to purchase a new asset in order to receive a future tax deduction with respect thereto. Respondent's argument that a taxpayer must first prove the useful life of personal property before he or she may depreciate it over the 3year or 5year period would bring the Court back to preERTA law and reintroduce the disagreements that the Congress intended to eliminate by its enactment of ERTA. This the Court will not do.

. . .

We sustained respondent's determination that the taxpayer was not entitled to deductions on the painting under ACRS. In so doing, we rejected the taxpayer's argument that the concept of useful life was eliminated with the enactment of ACRS, and accepted respondent's argument that a taxpayer must prove a determinable useful life. Our holding there, however, is distinguishable from the case at hand; unlike the Tourte bows, the painting in *Clinger* was not an asset that suffered substantial wear and tear through its regular, active, and physical use in the taxpayer's trade or business. To the extent, however, that respondent relies on a broad reading of *Clinger* to support her proposition that petitioners must prove the useful life of the Tourte bows in order to depreciate them, respondent misconstrues our holding in *Clinger*. In *Clinger*, the Court merely held that ACRS required that the taxpayer had to prove a determinable useful life of her passive business asset that suffered no discernible wear and tear. Determinable means "that can be determined." Webster's New World Dictionary 375 (3d coll. ed. 1988). Accordingly, once a taxpayer establishes that an asset is subject to exhaustion, wear and tear, or obsolescence, we can determine whether its useful life is 3 year or 5 year class property under ACRS. As coherently and succinctly stated by this Court in a Court reviewed opinion:

> Availability of deductions for depreciation on tangible property in this case is dependent solely upon compliance with section 168, which has only two requirements for deduction of depreciation. First, the asset (tangible) must be of a type which is subject to wear and tear, decay, decline, or exhaustion. . . . Second, the property must be used in the taxpayer's trade or business or held for the production of income. . . . The language of the section is unequivocal. [*Noyce v. Commissioner*, 97 T.C. at 689.]
>
> . . .

The record in the instant case . . . is replete with evidence showing clearly that the Tourte bows suffered substantial wear and tear while petitioners used them in their trade or business. Accordingly, unlike the taxpayer in *Browning*, petitioners have met their burden of proving wear and tear to their business asset. To state the obvious, violin bows are subject to wear and tear when in use by a professional violinist. Indeed, as stated by Publilius Syrus circa 42 B.C.: "The bow too tensely strung is easily broken." Bartlett, Familiar Quotations 1103 (12th ed. 1951).

We have considered all other arguments made by respondent and find them to be without merit.

To reflect concessions by the parties,

Decision will be entered under Rule 155.

[The concurring and dissenting opinions are omitted. Eds.]

Post-Simon Authority and the Concept of Salvage Value

Presumably, *Simon* means that a valuable Persian carpet used in a law firm's reception area can be depreciated, but an equally valuable tapestry on the wall (and out of the sunlight) cannot be. Shortly after the *Simon* decision, the Tax Court stuck to its guns and held that Ferrari automobiles held strictly for show or exhibition could be depreciated because of their obsolescence, even though there was no wear and tear from actual driving.[454] Apparently, an older Ferrari just does not turn heads like a new one.

Under prior law, depreciation deductions were generally calculated on the basis of the difference between the original basis of the property and its salvage value.

> **To illustrate:** Imagine the Simons bought a Tourte bow for $1,000 for use in their trade of being musicians. The Simons expected to use the bow for 10 years, after which they would expect to sell it for $1,100, its "salvage value" at the end of its useful economic life, at which time it would be too fragile to use regularly. The Simons could not, under prior law, claim any depreciation deduction, because under prior law only the initial basis minus salvage value was depreciatiable. Here, the expected depreciation is "negative."

The accelerated cost recovery system's amazing assumption of a zero salvage value was the vital change in the law for the Simons. Under prior law, their depreciation deductions would have been exactly $0. Now it is $1,000.

3. Mechanics of Computing Depreciation

Read §168(a)(d)(3) and (g)

Law students are not expected to become experts in depreciation and amortization deductions. They are supposed to understand the fundamental principles of the modified accelerated cost recovery system ("MACRS") reflected in §168. The starting point is §167(a), which tells you which properties can be depreciated or amortized, namely properties that wears out or become obsolete. Assuming the property satisfies §167(a), the next stop is §168(a) -- covering tangible property which tells you that you are dealing with a troika of factors:

1. *The recovery period*, begin with §168(e) which classifies property as 3-year property, 5-year property, 7-year property, 10-year property, 15-year property, or 20-year

454 Selig v. Commissioner, T.C. Memo. 1995519 (sole proprietor could depreciate exotic neverdriven show cars on the ground that they would become technologically obsolete even though he could not prove a useful life for the cars; obsolescence arises from fact that people will no longer pay to stare at a $ 290,000 Ferrari Testarossa after Ferrari has come out with a newer, more advanced model).

property. This is each property's "class life."[455] Section 168(c) assigns a "recovery property" for each class life. For example, §168(e)(3(b)(i)) gives automobiles a class life of 3 years and §168(c) gives property with a 3 year class life a 3 year recover period.

2. *The depreciation rate*is controlled by §168(b). For example, for 3 year property, §168(b)(1) calls for a 200% declining balance method. That is an accelerated method, providing more generous deductions in early years than in later years.

3. *The applicable recovery (depreciation) method*, which is straightline (equal amounts in each period of time) for real estate and accelerated (greater in earlier than in later years) for tangible personal property, unless the owner elects straightline.

4. The *applicable convention,* defined in §168(d), which refers to a legally created supposition that personal property is placed in service (and therefore can begin to be written off) at a particular time of year, no matter when it was actually placed in service. The usual assumption is that the taxpayer placed property in service July 1st (i.e., at the middle of the year). §168(d)(1).
   If you think about General Motors, you can quickly see the convenience in making this assumption. Can you also see that General Motors might be tempted to acquire an excessive amount of property at the end of the year and then claim the benefit of the full half year of depreciation deductions? Section 168(d)(3) cuts off the scheme by in effect saying that, if the taxpayer places over 40% of its depreciable property in service the last quarter of its tax year, then all the property placed in service in the last quarter will be written off for a mere one half of one quarter of the year. Real estate is presumed placed in service in mid-month.[456]

5. *Basis for depreciation. No salvage value.* §168(d)(4) treats the salvage value of property as zero, meaning thatCongress presumes that at the end of the recovery period the property is absolutely worthless. That is even true for property a US taxpayer places in service overseas. Zero salvage value is unrealistic but extremely convenient

Section 168 is full of other twists and turns, one of the most important of which is found in §168(g)(2) which compels the use of longer lives and straightline depreciation; it is known as the Alternative Depreciation System, or "ADS."

455 The rest of §168(e) consists of sui generis items, including properties that are not written off over time.

456 §168(d)(2).

A leading example arises when the subject is property located overseas, or is leased to an exempt organization (such as a charity). An example of the former might be a General Motors factory located in Taiwan.

Taxpayers can always elect to use the ADS system if they wish to.

a. Impact of Depreciation on Basis

Section 1016 requires constant adjustments to basis. For example, the addition of a longterm improvement such as a new roof is written off at the same rate as the apartment building it is installed on, but is separately accounted for because commingling the improvement with the building would result in accelerating the write-off of the roof.[457] At the same time, the taxpayer must reduce basis by depreciation that the taxpayer claims on the property (known as depreciation "allowed") as well as depreciation the taxpayer could have claimed, but did not (known as "allowable depreciation").[458] While forcing taxpayers to reduce the basis of property by depreciation they *could have* claimed this might seem a highhanded act of government, being a kind of expropriation of basis, consider the wholesale tax avoidance that would occur if each taxpayer could pick and choose the years in which he decided to claim his depreciation deductions.

If the taxpayer inadvertently failed to claim depreciation, she may be able to amend her return and claim a tax refund, if she takes action in time. Otherwise, she may be able to change her method of accounting for depreciation. A special procedure allows taxpayers to change their method of accounting to claim allowable depreciation deductions that were not claimed in prior years, even if the years are closed.[459] This is an unusual provision, because normally taxpayers must apply for IRS permission to change accounting methods, and the grant of permission is generally contingent on making complicated adjustments under §481 to smooth out the effects of the change of method.[460] The requirement that one apply for the change even applies if the taxpayer has been using an incorrect method and just wants to change to a proper method.

b. "Bonus Depreciation" under §168(k) and "Bonus Expensing" under §179

Read: §§ 168(k) & 179(a)-(d)

Bonus Depreciation §168(k)

Taxpayers may claim a 100% bonus depreciation allowance under §168(k) for eligible property acquired and placed in service after Sept. 27, 2017, and before Jan. 1, 2023. The 100% rate is

457 See IRS Pub. 946 (2017).

458 Reg. §1.167(a)10(a).

459 Rev. Proc. 97-37, 1997-2 C.B. 455.

460 See §446(e).

scheduled to "phase down," to 80% in 2023, 60% in 2024, 40% in 2025, 20% in 2026, and 0% for property acquired and placed in service in 2027 and thereafter. Before 2018, the bonus depreciation rate was 50%.

Bonus depreciation applies to new or used qualified property. Before 2018, bonus depreciation was only for new property.

In general, qualified property is property that is eligible for depreciation under MACRS with recovery periods of 20 or fewer years, off-the-shelf computer software, and "qualified improvement property."[461] Nonresidential realty improvements, which have recovery periods of greater than 20 years under MACRS, are only eligible for § 179 expensing. Qualified real property acquired by purchase for use in the active conduct of a trade business is also eligible for Code § 179 expensing. (§179(d)(1).[462]

A company that invests in assets that are eligible for both §179 bonus expensing and §168(k) bonus depreciation must recover its cost in a prescribed order. The §179 expensing allowance is taken first, lowering the company's basis in the asset by that amount. The taxpayer then may apply the bonus depreciation allowance to any remaining basis amount, further reducing the company's basis in the property. Finally, the taxpayer may claim a depreciation allowance under MACRS for any remaining basis, using the double declining balance method.

Bonus Expensing§179

Section 179 lets taxpayers elect to deduct all or part of the cost of any "section 179 property" that the taxpayer places the property in service during the taxable year. This is not duplicative; it displaces regular depreciation deductions. Section 179 only applies to property once, in the year that the taxpayer places the property in service. §179(a) Property is placed in service when it is *available* for its assigned use.[463]

Section 179 depreciation is convenient for small businesses and the IRS because of its simplicity; but it is only available for up to $1 million of property placed in service per year. §179(b)(1) Large taxpayers cannot use §179 because the $1 million ceiling declines as the taxpayer's section 179 property placed in service for the year exceeds $2,500,000 (adjusted for inflation). §179(b)(2).

The deduction cannot exceed the taxpayer's taxable income (calculated before the §179 deduction) derived from the active conduct of a trade or business. §179(b)(3)

461 Under a Tax Cuts and Jobs Act drafting error, "qualified improvement property" inadvertently became ineligible for bonus depreciation and is, unless Congress alters the language, treated as 39-year nonresidential real property. For property placed acquired and placed in service after Sept. 27, 2017, the TCJA generally excludes public utility property from the definition of qualified property.

462 Effective for property placed in service in tax years beginning after Dec. 31, 2017, qualified real property consists of two categories: (1) qualified improvement property; and (2) a grab bag of specific property improvements.

463 Rev. Rul. 76-238, 1976-1 C.B. 55.

Qualifying §179 property is tangible personal property purchased for use in the active conduct of a trade or business. If the section 179 property ceases to be used predominately in the business before its recovery period expires, the taxpayer has to include part of the §179 deduction in income in the year of the conversion.§179(d)(10); Reg. §1.179-1(e).

Section 179 also reaches qualified real property. The Tax Cuts and Jobs Act of 2017 changed the definition of qualified real property eligible for expensing.

Prior to 2018, qualified real property generally consists of qualified leasehold improvements as defined in § 168(e)(6), qualified restaurant property as defined in § 168(e)(7), and qualified retail improvement property as defined in § 168(e)(8) (§ 179(f)(2)). These types of property are depreciable under MACRS over 15-years using the straight-line method.

Starting in 2018, qualified real property includes improvements to the interior of any nonresidential real property ("qualified improvement property"), as well as roofs, heating, ventilation, and air-conditioning property, fire protection and alarm systems, and security systems installed on such property.

Problem 6-5:

In Year 10, Taxpayer A buys $2,000 of equipment that is 5-year MACRS property. This is its sole machinery/equipment purchase for the year. The equipment is eligible for Code § 179 expensing and is qualified property eligible for 100% bonus depreciation. Before taking depreciation into account, A has $2,000 of taxable income and a $800 NOL that expires in Year 10. Should Taxpayer A elect bonus depreciation under §168(k) or §179 bonus expensing?

c. Specific Applications

The following are the basic methods under §168, concisely defined in the Regulations:[464]

Straight-Line Method. This method produces an equal deduction in each period. For example, in the case of real estate §168 assumes that the asset declines equally every month.

To use a simplified example of the straight-line method, assume a building has a 4 year recovery period and costs $48,000. (In fact, the recovery period is much longer under §168.)

Basis: $48,000

Period: 48 months

Result: the writeoff amounts to $1,000 per month. (It is actually $500 per month in the first month for a building because it is deemed placed in service in the middle of the month, whatever the actual facts.)

464 See Regs. §1.167(b)1, (b)2 and (b)3.

Double DecliningBalance Method. This method results in greater deductions in the early life of the property than in its later years. For example, assume that a Thing which is not real estate has a basis of $48,000 and a recovery period under ACRS of 4 years. (The following illustration ignores the mid-year convention relating to when most personal property is deemed to be placed in service.)

This time one divides remaining basis in the Thing by the recovery period and then doubles the deduction. In our case, $48,000/4 years = $12,000, which, when doubled equals $24,000 for the first year.

Next year, one divides the remaining basis in the Thing (now $24,000) by 4 years for $6,000, then doubles it to $12,000. The process repeats itself until basis is exhausted.

Section 168 generally uses the double decliningbalance method, either using 200% (doubledeclining balance), as above, or using a more modest 150% rate. In most cases, there is a later switch to straightline, when a straight line deduction becomes larger than the declining balance deduction.

Sum-of-the-YearsDigits Method. This method accelerates depreciation even more. For example, assume a Thing has a basis of $48,000, and a recovery period of four years. The sum of the years' digits equals: 4 + 3 + 2 + 1 or 10. So, in the first year 4/10ths or 40 percent ($19,200) of the Thing's basis is written off; in year two, 3/10ths or 30 percent ($14,400) is deductible; in year three, 2/10ths or 20 percent ($9,600) and in the last year 1/10 or 10 percent ($4,800), for a grand total of 100 percent.

Income Forecast Method. Certain artistic properties, such as movies, can be written off in proportion to the anticipated net income that the property is expected to earn.[465] This ties to §168(f) (3) and (4) and no doubt produces a good deal of audit activity because it requires speculating about future income flows. It appears to be a favorite in Hollywood.

The rates of depreciation or cost recovery under some of the methods described above can be compared by using the following chart, which assumes a 10year useful life for some particular kinds of property under §167, "depreciation," using a midyear convention, and still shorter periods under the Accelerated Cost Recovery System of §168. The first year amount is small because of the half-year convention. In all cases, the assumption under §168 is that the property has no salvage value when its recovery period ends.

465 See, e.g., Rev. Rul. 79285, 19792 C.B. 91.

	STRAIGHT-LINE		DOUBLE DECLINING BALANCE		SUM OF THE YEAR'S DIGITS		POST-1986 A.C.R.S. (7 yr. property)	
Year	Annual Deduction	Cumulative Cost Recovered	Annual Deduction	Cumulative Cost Recovered	Annual Deduction	Cumulative Cost Recovered	Annual Deduction	Cumulative Cost Recovered
1	$ 5	$ 5	$ 10	$ 10	$ 9	$ 9	$ 14.29	$ 14.29
2	10	15	18	28	17	26	24.49	38.78
3	10	25	14.4	42.4	15.5	41.5	17.49	56.27
4	10	35	11.52	53.92	14	55.5	12.49	68.76
5	10	45	9.22	63.14	12	67.5	8.93	77.69
6	10	55	7.37	70.51	10	77.5	8.93	86.61
7	10	65	6.55	77.06	8	85.5	8.92	95.54
8	10	75	6.55	83.61	6	91.5	4.46	100
9	10	85	6.55	90.71	4.5	96		
10	10	95	6.55	96.72	3	99		
11	5	100	3.29	100	1	100		

Writing off Goodwill and Advertising

Goodwill has a variety of meanings. The principal one is the expectation of earnings greater than a fair return on property invested in the business or other means of production, or any other positive attribute a firm acquires in the progress of its business.[466] For example, the Rolls Royce Company's name and reputation has a major value, as a result of which the company can be sold for much more than the value of its tangible assets. Until recently, the view has been that goodwill potentially lasts forever, so it still cannot be amortized. Now, §197 permits taxpayers to amortize *purchased* goodwill over 15 years. Selfcreated goodwill still cannot be written off at all for Federal Income Tax purposes. Section 197 also allows 15 year amortization deductions for a long list of other purchased intangibles used for business or investment purposes, including many forms of intellectual property.[467] It arrived just in time to prevent a great deal of exasperating tax litigation.

Advertising enjoys special tax relief. The rules requiring taxpayers to capitalize assets with long, useful lives does not apply to advertising, even advertising designed to create long-term goodwill in the public's mind toward the taxpayer's business.[468] It is hard to reconcile this with the rule against the general nondeductibility of self-created goodwill. On the other hand, this simple pro-taxpayer rule avoids a lot of squabbles over the "useful life" of an ad campaign. The IRS remains on patrol, however, and has urged that there are cases where one must capitalize some advertising, citing the case where it prevailed in forcing capitalization of a power company's advertising at the grass roots level to overcome public resistance to its effort to get a license to build a nuclear power plant.[469]

Listed Property

Congress has identified a variety of properties that it felt were being abused in the sense of being subject to depreciation deductions even though they were likely to be overused for personal purposes. Examples include cars, cell phones and computers. The basic penalty is accelerated depreciation on such property is allowed only if every year the property is at least 50 percent

---

466 Rev. Rul. 5960, 19591 C.B. 237.

467 These include going concern value (meaning the value of a company attributable to the fact that it does not collapse when the owner changes), certain specified types of intangible property that generally relate to workforce in place, information base, know-how, customers, suppliers, or the like; a license, permit, or other right granted by a governmental unit or any agency or instrumentality thereof; a covenant not to compete entered into in connection with the direct or indirect acquisition of an interest in a trade or business; and a franchise, trademark, or trade name. See Alabama Coca-Cola Bottling Co. v. Commissioner, 28 T.C.M. 635 (1969).

468 See Rev. Rul. 92-80, 1992-2 C.B. 57 (INDOPCO v. Commissioner, 503 U.S. 79 (1992), does not affect the treatment of advertising costs even though such expenses may benefit future periods).

469 Rev. Rul. 92-80, 1992-2 C.B. 57, citing Cleveland Electric Illuminating Company v. United States, 7 Cl. Ct 220 (1985). To the extent advertising money goes into hardware such as a billboard, depreciation deductions are of course not available.

used for business. If business use ever drops below 50%, the amount by which any depreciation deductions (including considered bonus expensing under §179) exceeds the amount that would have been claimed under the alternative depreciation system (which uses straight-line depreciation) is taxed ("recaptured") as ordinary income and added to the basis of the property. From then on, only straight-line depreciation can be used. §280F. Naturally, to the extent the property is used for personal purposes (such as playing a computer game), the depreciation allocable to that personal use is disallowed and does not create recapture potential.

Problem 6-6:

Classify the following properties. That is, state the applicable recovery period and applicable method under §168 for the following property:

1) A bond held for investment

2) An apartment building held as an investment.

3) An office building and the land on which is sits, owned by an investor. Treat each of the two items separately.

4) An automobile purchased for use in a taxicab business. It is available to drivers, but because of a recent citywide health craze, the cab has not yet been used.

5) An office building located in Paris and owned by a Delaware corporation. How about the Parthenon in Athens, bought by a hotel conglomerate as a curiosity for its guests?

6) A lawyer buys a new computer system which cost $14,000. Can he write the entire amount off in the year of the purchase? Does it matter if the lawyer's practice yields only a modest income? See §179(a)(b)(3) and (d)(1)(3).

7) A forensic orthodontist buys a brand new Mercedes Benz automobile which he uses exclusively for business purposes. How much can he write off in the third year of ownership? See §280F(a) and (d).

8) Referring to the facts of "(7)" above, assume the car was used 100% for business in years 13 and then in year 4 it was used 45% for business.

a. How much recapture is there under §280F(b) in year 4?

b. What is the impact of the recapture on the basis of the car? See Reg. §1.280F-3T(d)(1).

9) An architect buys a cellular telephone and a computer for use at home and in her car, but she finds that her children enjoy using them and she generously permits them to do so.

a. Is this going to create a tax problem for her, and if so, what is the problem? See §280F(b)(1)(3) and (d)(4)(5).

b. Would it make any difference if the computers were in an office that qualified under §280F(d)(4)(B)?

c. What is the write-off period for purchased computer software? See §167(f)(1).

10) The taxpayer is a mining company which installs rails and cars in its mine. The cars are sturdy but the manufacturer of the car has assured the mining company that each car has a lifetime capacity to carry 10,000 tons of material out of the mine, after which it is a worthless derelict. The mine operates irregularly and the accountants for the mining company insist that depreciation be based on the proportionate part of 10,000 tons of materials in the ground that each car carries out of the mine each year (a.k.a., the unit-of-production method). Is it permissible to do so? See §168(f).

11) The taxpayer is a film distributor that purchased the rights to a blockbuster of a movie and has acquired certain videocassette rights that relate to a different asset. In the abstract, how should they be written off? See §168(f)(3), (4).

12) A new third floor, placed on top of a two story apartment complex? See §168(i)(6).

Read §§ 611(a) and 613(a)

You have already studied depreciation and amortization. Now you will get a glimpse at depletion. Depletion is the write-off for the exhaustion of natural resources. The general rule is that taxpayers *must* claim a depletion deduction equal to the greater of: (1) a percentage of the proceeds of the year's sale of natural resources (known as percentage depletion), or; (2) a portion of the basis of the minerals, oil or gas, prorated to the amount of those natural resources extracted during the year (known as "cost depletion" and resembling depreciation). Cost depletion under §612 is allowed for all exhaustable material resources. Percentage depletion under §§613 and 613A is allowed for most hard minerals and, sometimes, for oil and gas.

No depletion is allowed for inexhaustible resources.[470] Timber qualifies for cost depletion only, but §636 makes it possible for timber owners and people who cut timber under a contract to get a capital gain result on their timber harvesting.

The following Private Letter Ruling involves the availability of cost depletion for water extracted from the enormous but slow-moving Ogallala Aquifer that underlies a large part of the United States.

PRIVATE LETTER RULING 8226022

March 30, 1982

ISSUE

Whether a cost depletion deduction is allowable for groundwater extracted from the Ogallala Formation (Ogallala Aquifer) under the facts described below?

FACTS

Taxpayer A owns y acres of farm property in State S and extracts groundwater for irrigation-farming from the Ogallala Formation underlying its property.

A claimed a deduction of x dollars for cost depletion of groundwater. That deduction was computed in accordance with Rev. Proc. 6611, 19661 C.B. 624, on a decline in the water table in the saturated thickness of the Ogallala Formation by d feet as compared to a total saturated thickness, at the time of purchase of the land, of e feet.

470 See, e.g., Rev. Rul. 65-7, 1965-1 C.B. 254 (saline content of Great Salt Lake is effectively inexhaustible because of replenishment).

LAW AND ANALYSIS

Section 611 of the Internal Revenue Code provides that in the case of mines, oil and gas wells, other natural deposits, and timber there shall be allowed as a deduction in computing taxable income a reasonable allowance for depletion and for depreciation of improvements, according to the peculiar conditions in each case; such reasonable allowance in all cases to be made under regulations prescribed by the Secretary.

Section 612 of the Code provides that the basis for cost depletion shall be the adjusted basis provided in section 1011. Section 1011 states that the adjusted basis shall be the basis under section 1012, which is cost, adjusted as provided in section 1016.

Section 1016(a)(2) of the Code provides, in part, that the adjustments to basis shall be made in respect to any period since February 28, 1913, for depletion to the extent of the amount allowed as deductions, but not less than the amount allowable.

The Court in United States v. Shurbet et ux., 347 F.2d 103 (5th Cir. 1965) . . . held that, in the case of farmers who obtain water for irrigation purposes from the Ogallala Formation under the High Plains of Texas, a deduction for cost depletion was allowable and shall be allowed during years in which there is a decrease in the groundwater level under their properties.

In Revenue Ruling 65296, 19652 C.B. 181, the Internal Revenue Service announced that it will follow the decision of the United States Court of Appeals for the Fifth Circuit in Shurbet and will allow cost depletion to taxpayers in the Southern High Plains under facts similar to those in the Shurbet case.

Revenue Procedure 6611, C.B. 19661 624, was issued to furnish guidelines for taxpayers entitled to cost depletion deductions for the exhaustion of their capital investment in groundwater. Section 3.02 of that Procedure states that taxpayers claiming cost depletion deductions must establish to the satisfaction of the district director both the amount of water present at acquisition and their cost basis of the water.

Prior to the decision by the Court in Shurbet, a deduction was not allowed for the depletion of groundwater. The position of the Service was based on the contention that, as a matter of law, water is not a "natural deposit" as that term is used in section 611 of the Code. However, the Court in Shurbet found that cost depletion was allowable under the "peculiar conditions of the Southern High Plains." Rev. Rul. 65296 restricted that holding to the facts similar to those in that case and only to taxpayers in the Southern High Plains.

The availability of groundwater has been the subject of extensive studies which indicate that groundwater in areas of the Ogallala Formation, other than in the Southern High Plains, is being similarly depleted. Where it can be demonstrated that the groundwater is being depleted and that the rate of recharge is so low that once it is exhausted the groundwater would be lost to the taxpayer and immediately succeeding generations, cost depletion may be allowed to taxpayers under facts similar to these in the Shurbet case. Whether the facts in the instant case are similar to the Shurbet case is a factual determination within the purview of your office.

Rev. Proc. 6611 provides guidelines to taxpayers entitled to cost depletion deductions for the exhaustion of their capital investment in groundwater and may be used by taxpayers in areas of the Ogallala Formation other than the Southern High Plains. When a taxpayer claims cost depletion on ground water the cost basis of the property, the amount of water present at the time of acquisition of the property, and the net decline in the water table must be established to the satisfaction of the district director. The amount of cost depletion is a factual determination. This factual determination is also within the purview of your office.

Cost depletion will be allowed to a taxpayer under facts similar to those in the Shurbet case where it can be demonstrated that the groundwater is being depleted and that the rate of recharge is so low that once extracted the groundwater is lost to a taxpayer and immediately succeeding generations.

. . .

1. Policy Questions

The *Shurbet* decision found as a fact that the Ogallala Aquifer (which overlays a vast area of the central United States) takes thousands of years to replenish itself. Is there something wrong with a tax law that grants a current tax deduction for effectively destroying part of the Nation? Can one defend it by saying -- as many economists do -- that the depletion of the aquifer is offset by other capital created elsewhere in the economy? Should we disallow the deduction and instead make the taxpayer wait to realize the loss in value when the exhausted property is sold? Or, should we allow the deduction as a cost of producing income that is taxable, to treat the taxpayer fairly, and tax only its *net* income. If one did not allow a depletion deduction or a deduction for a loss on the sale of the depleted property, there might be constitutional problem of taxing capital, but likely not given Congress's willingness to deny deductions on various grounds. Certainly, tax logic does not demand a current deduction; a loss deduction (or reduced gain) when the property is sold is good enough. So, disallowing depletion deductions would result in deferring a deduction to later rather than sooner, not "now or never."

2. Percentage Depletion §613

The private letter ruling you just read involved cost depletion. Cost depletion under §612 allows the taxpayer to deduct its basis in the natural resources in proportion to the rate at which the resource is exhausted. What irks tax policy thinkers about depletion is not so much what gets depleted for Federal Income Tax purposes, but how depletionoccurs.[471] Here is the problem. Both cost depletion and percentage depletion deductions reduce one's basis in the oil, gas or mineral property. However, percentage depletion deductions are calculated based on a percentage of the taxpayer's gross income from the property and are not limited by the taxpayer's adjusted basis. Instead, percentage depletion continues for as long as production continues, even after prior deductions exceed the taxpayer's entire investment.

Under § 613(a), if both cost and percentage depletion apply to a particular natural resource, the larger deduction for the particular year is "allowable," and the taxpayer's basis is reduced accordingly. Once basis drops to zero, cost depletion terminates, but percentage depletion continues.

There are four basic steps in computing percentage depletion:

1) determination of whether the mineral qualifies for percentage depletion §613(b)

2) if the mineral qualifies for percentage depletion, what is the appropriate percentage, (this varies from 5 to 22 percent depending on the mineral)§613(b)

3) application of the percentage rate to the taxpayer's "gross income from the property"§613(a)

4) application of a limit of 50 percent of the taxpayer's "taxable income from the property" (100 percent for oil and gas).§613(a)

Section 613A imposes an additional threshold step for oil and gas—whether or not the taxpayer is eligible for percentage depletion.In general, oil and gas must use cost depletion unless the taxpayer meets a complex exception under§ 613A(c).

Section 613A(c) allows 15 percent depletion for oil and gas. Certain marginal properties can increase the deduction by one percentage point for each whole dollar by which the price for crude oil is below $20.The allowance is subject to strict limitations. For example, only domestic crude oil and natural gas qualifies and the allowance is only permitted for up to 1,000 barrels of oil per day or 6 million cubic feet of natural gas per day. Because the allowance is tied to production quantities, a "lease bonus, advance royalty, or other amount payable without regard to production from property" cannot be depleted under this rule.

471 Sources include Gadda, *Taxation as a Tool of Natural Resource Management: Oil as a Case Study*, 1 Ecol.L.Q. 749 (1971); Due, *The Developing Economies, Tax and Property Payments by the Petroleum Industry, and The United States Income Tax*, 10 Nat. Res. J. 10 (1970); Mead, *The System of Government Subsidies To The Oil Industry*, 10 Nat. Res. J. 113 (1970); Comment, *The Impact of the Income Tax Laws on the Energy Crisis: Oil and Congress Don't Mix*, 64 Calif. L. Rev. 1040 (1976).

Percentage depletion does have one indisputable merit; it does not require determining the amount of "recoverable reserves" in the ground, as does cost depletion. Because recoverable reserves call for both a physical measure and an evaluation of how much the taxpayer can be expected to extract in light of market conditions, there is a perpetual, expensive disagreement between the IRS and taxpayers on this factual issue. Needless to say, it is impossible to fix the exactly correct number.

You might also scan §613, which defines the term "mining." The term is significant in determining gross income from the property, the base on which percentage depletion is claimed. In the case of a so-called integrated miner, such as a company that mines iron and converts it into steel, the exact definition is vital because those companies can apply percentage depletion to the (ever larger) value of the product when mining treatment ends.

> **To illustrate:** X Corp. mines and processes the mineral garnet. Garnet qualifies for a 14% depletion rate. (Garnet is commonly used on nail files.) If "mining" of garnet ends at the mine mouth and the company's yearly production of garnet is worth $1,000 at the mouth, then X Corp. gets a $140 percentage depletion deduction. Assume instead that "mining" treatment ends after the garnet has been heated, crushed and rolled, at which point annual production is worth $8,000. In that case, X Corp.'s percentage depletion deduction is $1,120.

As a result of lobbying pressure, the definition of "mining" has become progressively more expansive and improbable.[472] As Professor Bittker put it:

> If a latter-day Michelangelo purchased a marble quarry to ensure a supply of suitable stone, he would no doubt seek to apply the 14 percent depletion rate for marble to the value of the stone after "treatment" by his mallet and chisel rather than to its value at the quarry.[473]

3. The Future and Environmental Taxes

As Yogi Berra has pointed out, "The future is not what it used to be." Industrial pollution is now a global problem, ozone depletion continues to haunt us, and topsoil is being lost at a great rate, to name just some of the issues. Taxes may play a useful remedial role, if they were ever to be unleashed in a serious way.

The idea of the environmental tax probably originates with the English scholar Arthur Pigou, who provided us a classic study[474] of smoke from factories that soiled laundered clothes hung outside to dry in the air. In particular, a 1918 study done in the industrial city of Manchester

472 See B. Bittker, FEDERAL TAXATION OF INCOME, ESTATES, AND GIFTS ¶ 24.3.4 (2019).

473 Id.

474 Arthur C. Pigou, ECONOMICS OF WELFARE (Boutledge 2017).

compared the cost of household washing in that city as opposed to the nearby but much cleaner town of Harrogate. (These kinds of damaging activities are known as "negative externalities" among current economists.[475]) The Manchester Air Pollution Advisory Board determined that:

> The total loss for the whole city, taking the extra cost of fuel and washing materials alone, disregarding the extra labor involved, and assuming no greater loss for middleclass than for workingclass households (a considerable understatement), works out at over 290,000 Pounds a year for a population of three quarters of a million.

This memorable example has led to the concept of a "Pigouvian tax," meaning a tax that forces actors to bear the cost of their actions. In the case of Manchester in 1918, the tax would have amounted to at least 290,000 Pounds, and would have been imposed on the offending manufacturers. The effects of such taxes are generally to encourage changed technology, to force reductions in offending output, to build funds to remedy the problem, or put the actor out of business. The trouble is that environmental costs can rarely be calculated with such certainty. On the other hand, should one do nothing or impose an imperfect tax? One can leave the solution to environmental regulators, but that attracts the objection of business that regulators impose "one size fits all" solutions that prevent business enterprises from coming up with practical, specially-tailored solutions on a case by case basis.

Pigou's work has led to theorizing that the appropriate solution to the excessive consumption and production that arises as a result of not including the expropriation of clean air and other common resources invites systematic taxation of production that drives up the price of offending goods and services to the "correct" level. The absence of such taxes leads to "market failure" because it results in a theoretically incorrect amount of production and consumption.[476] Remedial taxes to cure market failure are extremely rare, but they remain as a beacon for environmental policy. The United States has actually moved backward in this field, at least in the federal sphere. Congress has repealed the former broad-based environmental tax,[477] and collection of the Superfund taxes on chemicals[478] and petroleum[479] that were designed to fund hazardous waste clean-ups. The U.S. still has a significant tax on ozone depleting substances.[480] The "gas

475 There can also be positive externalities, as when someone places flowers in the windows, beautifying the neighborhood for everyone.

476 Three Nobel Prizes in economics have been given for studies of market failure: Arrow (1972), DeBreu (1983), and Tirole (2014).

477 Former §59A. It was imposed at a low rate on modified taxable income.

478 §4662(a)(1).

479 §4611.

480 §§ 4681(b), 4682.

guzzler" tax on inefficient passenger vehicles[481] also remains, but it seems to have had no practical impact and it does not reach many of the very large passenger vehicles at all.[482] The Federal Excise Tax on gasoline is under 20 cents per gallon,[483] compared to multi-dollar per gallon taxes imposed by European governments. There is, however, an excise tax on the extraction of coal ranging from 55 cents to $1.10 per ton,[484] the purpose of which is to defray the costs of a federal fund to assist coal miners suffering from black lung disease.

Clearly, there is plenty of room for improvement in the environmental tax area, but Congress has shown little stomach for a fight, despite the tax system's conflicts with current environmental norms.

Problem 6-7:

Carl Coalman purchased a mine recently for $1,000. It contains 1,000 tons of coal. Each ton is worth $9 at the surface. This year, he mined 500 tons and sold them for $4,500 (his "gross income from the property"). Ignore the taxable income from the property limit of §613(a).

1) What is his cost depletion for the year?

2) What is his percentage depletion? See §613(b).

3) Can he elect to report the smaller number? See Reg. §1.611-1(a)

4) Can he use percentage depletion in the following year?

5) Is there a problem of intergenerational equity in allowing a depletion deduction for the exhaustion of natural resources?

481 §4064(a).

482 See Code section 4064.

483 §4081(a)(2)(A).

484 §4121(b).

J. RENTAL EXPENSE DEDUCTIONS AND THE PROBLEMS OF SUBSTANCE VERSUS FORM

Read §§ 162(a)(3), and 263.

Businesses commonly rent real estate and personal property, such as factory sites and manufacturing equipment, from owners of the property. It is obviously necessary to allow a tax deduction for these expenditures, but from time to time, taxpayers find ways to push the limits. As you read the next case, which involves a dispute as to the whether a purported lease of a sprinkler system was in substance a sale, try to identify the key factors that led to the tax law conclusion.

> **To illustrate:** Taiwan Shipyards builds supertankers. In most cases, it sells its ships outright to its customers, but in many cases, the customers prefer to rent the vessels for five years, with an option to renew the lease for another five years, and a further option to buy the tanker at the end of the 10th year for a stated price. In the usual case, the shipping line that rents the tanker reports the deal as producing a stream of deductible rental expenses. Other shipping lines engaged in the same business might take the position for financial and tax purposes that they are really buying the vessel, because they know they will exercise the option to buy after the decade of renting has passed. Those taxpayers will claim depreciation deductions on their vessel and will presumably claim that the rental payments are in substance a combination of deductible interest and nondeductible principal paid to Taiwan Shipyards. Who is right? How can you tell? Read on.

ESTATE OF STARR v. COMMISSIONER

274 F.2d 294 (9th Cir. 1959)

CHAMBERS, Circuit Judge

Yesterday's equities in personal property seem to have become today's leases. This has been generated not a little by the circumstance that one who leases as a lessee usually has less trouble with the federal tax collector. At least taxpayers think so.

But the lease still can go too far and get one into tax trouble. While according to state law the instrument will probably be taken (with the consequent legal incidents) by the name the parties give it, the internal revenue service is not always bound and can often recast it according to what the service may consider the practical realities. . . . The principal case concerns a fire sprinkler system installed at the taxpayer's plant at Monrovia, California, where Delano T. Starr, now deceased, did business as the Gross Manufacturing Company. The 'lessor' was 'Automatic' Sprinklers of the Pacific, Inc., a California corporation. The instrument entitled 'Lease Form of Contract' (hereafter 'contract') is just about perfectly couched in terms of a lease for five years with annual rentals of $ 1,240. But it is the last paragraph thereof, providing for nominal rental for five years, that has caused the trouble. It reads as follows:

> '28. At the termination of the period of this lease, if Lessee has faithfully performed all of the terms and conditions required of it under this lease, it shall have the privilege of renewing this lease for an additional period of five years at a rental of $ 32.00 per year. If Lessee does not elect to renew this lease, then the Lessor is hereby granted the period of six months in which to remove the system from the premises of the Lessee.'

Obviously, one renewal for a period of five years is provided at $ 32 per year, if Starr so desired. Note, though, that the paragraph is silent as to status of the system beginning with the eleventh year. Likewise the whole contract is similarly silent.

The Tax Court sustained the commissioner of internal revenue, holding that the five payments of $ 1,240, or the total of $ 6,200, were capital expenditures and not pure deductible rental. Depreciation of $ 269.60 was allowed for each year. Generally, we agree.

Taxpayers took the deduction as a rental expense under trade or business pursuant to Section [162] of the Internal Revenue Code, as amended by Section 121(a) of the Revenue Act of 1942.

The law in this field for this circuit is established in . . . Robinson v. Elliot, 9 Cir., 262 F.2d 383. There we held that for tax purposes form can be disregarded for substance and, where the foreordained practical effect of the rent is to produce title eventually, the rental agreement can be treated as a sale.

In this, Starr's case, we do have the troublesome circumstance that the contract does not by its terms ever pass title to the system to the 'lessee.' Most sprinkler systems have to be tailormade for a specific piece of property and, if removal is required, the salvageable value is negligible. Also, it stretches credulity to believe that the 'lessor' ever intended to or would 'come after' the system. And the 'lessee' would be an exceedingly careless businessman who would enter into such contract with the practical possibility that the 'lessor' would reclaim the installation. He could have believed only that he was getting the system for the rental money. And we think the commissioner was entitled to take into consideration the practical effect rather than the legal, especially when there was a record that on other such installations the 'lessor', after the term of the lease was over, had not reclaimed from those who had met their agreed payments. It is obvious that the nominal rental payments after five years of $ 32 per year were just a service charge for inspection.

Recently the Court of Appeals for the Eighth Circuit has decided Western Contracting Corporation v. Commissioner, 1959, 271 F.2d 694, reversing the Tax Court in its determination that the commissioner could convert leases of contractor's equipment into installment purchases of heavy equipment. The taxpayer believes that case strongly supports him here. We think not.

There are a number of facts there which make a difference. For example, in the contracts of Western there is no evidence that the payments on the substituted basis of rent would produce for the 'lessor' the equivalent of his normal sales price plus interest. There was no right to acquire for a nominal amount at the end of the term as in Oesterreich and the value to the 'lessor' in the personalty had not been exhausted as in Starr's case. And there was no basis for inferring that Western would just keep the equipment for what it had paid. It appears that Western paid substantial amounts to acquire the equipment at the end of the term. There was just one compelling circumstance against Western in its case: What it had paid as 'rent' was apparently always taken into full account in computing the end purchase price. But on the other hand, there was almost a certainty that the 'lessor' would come after his property if the purchase was not eventually made for a substantial amount. This was not even much of a possibility in Oesterreich and not a probability in Starr's case.

In Wilshire Holding Corporation v. Commissioner, 9 Cir., 262 F.2d 51, we referred the case back to the Tax Court to consider interest as a deductible item for the lessee. We think it is clearly called for here. Two yardsticks are present. The first is found in that the normal selling price of the system was $ 4,960 while the total rental payments for five years were $ 6,200. The difference could be regarded as interest for the five years on an amortized basis. The second measure is in clause 16 (loss by fire), where the figure of six per cent per annum discount is used. An allowance might be made on either basis, division of the difference (for the five years) between 'rental payments' and 'normal purchase price' of $ 1,240, or six per cent per annum on the normal purchase price of $ 4,960, converting the annual payments into amortization. We do not believe that the 'lessee' should suffer the pains of a loss for what really was paid for the use of another's money, even though for tax purposes his lease collapses.

We do not criticize the Commissioner. It is his duty to collect the revenue and it is a tough one. If he resolves all questions in favor of the taxpayers, we soon would have little revenue. However, we do suggest that after he has made allowance for depreciation, which he concedes, and an allowance for interest, the attack on many of the 'leases' may not be worth while in terms of revenue.

Decision reversed for proceedings consistent herewith.

Notes on Transactions Subject to Multiple Characterizations

Substance over form. The case you just saw involves distinguishing a lease from a sale. Why does the taxpayer care? The primary tax reason has to do with timing. Rental expenses are deductible in full at once but debt service payments on an installment purchase are only deductible to the extent of the interest. On the other hand, a buyer can claim depreciation deductions on the purchased hardware, but the permissible depreciation schedule may be slow and paltry.

At a more complicated level, a property owner may purport to sell its property to a bank and then rent it back from the bank. The question presented in such cases is whether the "real deal" is in fact a mortgage. The decisive question will typically be whether the seller/lessee can buy back the property for a low price in the future. If so, the courts are apt to reason that the taxpayer will *necessarily* buy back the property because the cheap price creates an "economic compulsion" to do so. That in turn suggests that the "real deal" is some kind of financing arrangement, and not a sale plus a leaseback to the seller. Other significant objective factors are whether the payments the seller/lessee makes are similar in amount and timing to debt service payments on a loan, and whether the alleged buyer (bank) was exposed to any serious risk of loss if, for example, the property lost value. The rules in the area are still not fully stabilized.[485]

The accounting profession has developed its own rules for when a transaction is a lease or a sale. The standards generally track the judicial standards, but are more formalized.

Tax-planning with gifts and lease-backs. Another fairly common tax trick is the gift and leaseback in which a parent gives business or investment property to a trust and then rents the property back from the trust, claiming a rental expense deduction. The practice has generally succeeded, but the Fifth Circuit has held out against it, refusing to allow a rental expense deduction, theorizing that the rental expense is not "necessary" because the whole arrangement was launched with a gift, and "gifts are not necessary."[486] The Second Circuit rejects the Fifth Circuit's position and allows the parent/tenant a rental expense deduction.[487] The transaction is most likely to hold up for Federal Income Tax purposes if the donee/title holder is an independent entity that the taxpayer/donor does not control. If the donee/title holder is a spouse, for example, the transaction is likely to fail on the theory that the transfer is a sham.[488]

Taxpayer's Right to Disavow Form. In *Starr's Estate* the taxpayers were straining to uphold the form of the transaction that they adopted. What if instead it was the taxpayer who was straining to recharacterize the transaction as a sale in substance? Should taxpayers be allowed to disavow the forms they selected? To put it another way, can taxpayers cut their way out of the red tape they create, or are they stuck with it? The indisputable Professors Bittker and Lokken[489] offer that the courts generally do allow taxpayers to disavow the form of their transaction, under step-transaction principles or substance over form principles. To add to the confusion,

485 See generally, Frank Lyon Co. v. United States, 435 U.S. 561 (1978) (sale and leaseback upheld; not a financing transactions); S. Randleman, Sales and Leasebacks, 34-4th Tax Mgt. Portfolio (BNA). These portfolios are found in many law libraries and are good source of close, technical analyses.

486 Mathews v. Commissioner, 520 F.2d 323 (5th Cir. 1975), rehearing denied 11-21-75.

487 Rosenfeld v. Commissioner, 706 F.2d 1277 (2d Cir., 1983) (rent deductions allowed).

488 See, White v. Fitzpatrick, 193 F.2d 398 (2d Cir. 1951).

489 B. Bittker & L. Lokken, FEDERAL TAXATION OF INCOME ESTATE AND GIFTS at ¶ 4.4.6 (2019).

consistency of tax treatment as between the parties to a transaction (say parties to a gift and leaseback) is not automatic, and it may at times be necessary to use *ad hoc* approaches, such as consolidating cases in the Tax Court, to assure consistency of treatment.[490] In any case, the IRS resists the notion that there is any such right on the part of taxpayers to deny the "forms" they conjure up.[491]

Problem 6-8:

Your client, a manufacturer, has been approached by a banker who proposes that the bank buy your client's factory, and rent it back to the client for 25 years. At the end of the 25 years, your client will have an option to buy the property back for $1. The client will be responsible for maintaining and insuring the property.

1) What advice do you give him as to what the alternative characterization of the transaction might be?

2) Do you need more information? If so, what information would be relevant?

Problem 6-9:

A dentist, Dr. Ow, sells the building which for many years housed his office and facilities to a trustee for his minor children, Mindy and Sam, and rents it back from the trust for a fair market rental. The sale price is appropriate and the trustee is unrelated to Dr. Ow. He plans to deduct the rent paid to the trust. The trust will use part of the rental income to pay off the debt incurred to buy the building, and can depreciate the building (its cost basis to the trust) and pay income taxes, presumably at rates lower than their parents', on the profits if and when they roll in. The trustee is Slime, Dr. Ow's tame accountant.

1) What is the overall tax benefit to Dr. Ow? What tax benefits do the kids get?

2) Will this stand up for Federal Income Tax purposes? Should it?

3) Suppose he gives the children the building and rents it back, as above?

490 Id.

491 See, e.g., J. Bruce Donaldson, *When Substance-Over-Form Argument is Available to the Taxpayer,* 48 Marq. l. Rev. 41 (1964-65) and Robert T. *Smith, Substance and Form: A Taxpayer's Right to Assert the Priority of Substance,* 44 Tax Law. 137 (1990).

Read Reg. §1.1624

One persistent source of audit activity involves determining whether a taxpayer's expenditure is for a "repair" or an "improvement." For example, filling a few holes on a parking lot is a repair; but replacing the entire surface is an improvement. The next two cases explore the distinction between a repair and an improvement.

MIDLAND EMPIRE PACKING CO. v. COMMISSIONER

14 T.C. 635 (1950)

ARUNDELL, Judge:

[The taxpayer owned a meat-packing plant. It relined the basement with concrete and installed a concrete floor, where it stored and cured meats, in order to keep out recent oil infiltration that was hurting business. Inspectors had threatened to close down the plant if it did not keep out the oil. The repair cost to the taxpayer was $4,868. The question presented was whether the payment to modify the basement was deductible as a repair, or had to be capitalized.]

. . .

OPINION

The issue in this case is whether an expenditure for a concrete lining in petitioner's basement to oil proof it against an oil nuisance created by a neighboring refinery is deductible as an ordinary and necessary expense under section [162] of the Internal Revenue Code, on the theory it was an expenditure for a repair, or, in the alternative, whether the expenditure may be treated as the measure of the loss sustained during the taxable year and not compensated for by insurance or otherwise . . . .

The respondent has contended, in part, that the expenditure is for a capital improvement and should be recovered through depreciation charges and is, therefore, not deductible as an ordinary and necessary business expense or as a loss.

It is none too easy to determine on which side of the line certain expenditures fall so that they may be accorded their proper treatment for tax purposes. Treasury Regulations 111, from which we quote in the margin, is helpful in distinguishing between an expenditure to be classed as a repair and one to be treated as a capital outlay. In *Illinois Merchants Trust Co., Executor*, 4 B. T. A. 103, at page 106, we discussed this subject in some detail and in our opinion said:

> It will be noted that the first sentence of the article . . . relates to repairs, while the second sentence deals in effect with replacements. In determining whether an expenditure is a capital one or is chargeable against operating income, it is necessary to bear in mind the purpose for which the expenditure was made. To repair is to restore to a sound state or to mend, while a replacement connotes a substitution. A repair is an expenditure for the purpose of keeping the property in an ordinarily efficient operating condition. It does not add to the value of the property, nor does it appreciably prolong its life. It merely keeps the property in an operating condition over its probable useful life for the uses for which it was acquired. Expenditures for that purpose are distinguishable from those for replacements, alterations, improvements, or additions which prolong the life of the property, increase its value, or make it adaptable to a different use. The one is a maintenance charge, while the others are additions to capital investment which should not be applied against current earnings.

It will be seen from our findings of fact that for some 25 years prior to the taxable year petitioner had used the basement rooms of its plant as a place for the curing of hams and bacon and for the storage of meat and hides. The basement had been entirely satisfactory for this purpose over the entire period in spite of the fact that there was some seepage of water into the rooms from time to time. In the taxable year it was found that not only water, but oil, was seeping through the concrete walls of the basement of the packing plant and, while the water would soon drain out, the oil would not, and there was left on the basement floor a thick scum of oil which gave off a strong odor that permeated the air of the entire plant, and the fumes from the oil created a fire hazard. It appears that the oil which came from a nearby refinery had also gotten into the water wells which served to furnish water for petitioner's plant, and as a result of this whole condition the Federal meat inspectors advised petitioner that it must discontinue the use of the water from the wells and oil proof the basement, or else shut down its plant.

To meet this situation, petitioner during the taxable year undertook steps to oil proof the basement by adding a concrete lining to the walls from the floor to a height of about four feet and also added concrete to the floor of the basement. It is the cost of this work which it seeks to deduct as a repair. The basement was not enlarged by this work, nor did the oil proofing serve to make it more desirable for the purpose for which it had been used through the years prior to the time that the oil nuisance had occurred. The evidence is that the expenditure did not add to the value or prolong the expected life of the property over what they were before the event occurred which made the repairs necessary. It is true that after the work was done the seepage of water, as well as oil, was stopped, but, as already stated, the presence of the water had never been found objectionable. The repairs merely served to keep the property in an operating condition over its probable useful life for the purpose for which it was used.

While it is conceded on brief that the expenditure was "necessary," respondent contends that the encroachment of the oil nuisance on petitioner's property was not an "ordinary" expense in petitioner's particular business. But the fact that petitioner had not theretofore been called upon to make a similar expenditure to prevent damage and disaster to its property does not remove that expense from the classification of "ordinary" for, as stated in *Welch v. Helvering*, 290 U.S. 111, "ordinary in this context does not mean that the payments must be habitual or normal in the sense that the same taxpayer will have to make them often. . . . the expense is an ordinary one because we know from experience that payments for such a purpose, whether the amount is large or small, are the common and accepted means of defense against attack. Cf. *Kornhauser v. United States*, 276 U.S. 145. The situation is unique in the life of the individual affected, but not in the life of the group, the community, of which he is a part." Steps to protect a business building from the seepage of oil from a nearby refinery, which had been erected long subsequent to the time petitioner started to operate its plant, would seem to us to be a normal thing to do, and in certain sections of the country it must be a common experience to protect one's property from the seepage of oil. Expenditures to accomplish this result are likewise normal.

In *American Bemberg Corporation*, 10 T. C. 361, we allowed as deductions, on the ground that they were ordinary and necessary expenses, extensive expenditures made to prevent disaster, although the repairs were of a type which had never been needed before and were unlikely to recur. In that case the taxpayer, to stop caveins of soil which were threatening destruction of its manufacturing plant, hired an engineering firm which drilled to the bedrock and injected grout to fill the cavities where practicable, and made incidental replacements and repairs, including tightening of the fluid carriers. In two successive years the taxpayer expended $ 4,316.76 and $ 199,154.33, respectively, for such drilling and grouting and $ 153,474.20 and $ 79,687.29, respectively, for capital replacements. We found that the cost (other than replacement) of this program did not make good the depreciation previously allowed, and stated in our opinion:

> In connection with the purpose of the work, the Proctor program was intended to avert a plantwide disaster and avoid forced abandonment of the plant. The purpose was not to improve, better, extend, or increase the original plant, nor to prolong its original useful life. Its continued operation was endangered; the purpose of the expenditures was to enable petitioner to continue the plant in operation not on any new or better scale, but on the same scale and, so far as possible, as efficiently as it had operated before. The purpose was not to rebuild or replace the plant in whole or in part, but to keep the same plant as it was and where it was.

The petitioner here made the repairs in question in order that it might continue to operate its plant. Not only was there danger of fire from the oil and fumes, but the presence of the oil led the Federal meat inspectors to declare the basement an unsuitable place for the purpose for which it had been used for a quarter of a century. After the expenditures were made, the plant did not operate on a changed or larger scale, nor was it thereafter suitable for new or additional uses. The expenditure served only to permit petitioner to continue the use of the plant, and particularly the basement for its normal operations.

In our opinion, the expenditure of $ 4,868.81 for lining the basement walls and floor was essentially a repair and, as such, it is deductible as an ordinary and necessary business expense. This holding makes unnecessary a consideration of petitioner's alternative contention that the expenditure is deductible as a business loss, nor need we heed the respondent's argument that any loss suffered was compensated for by "insurance or otherwise."

Decision will be entered under Rule 50.

Question

What were the key facts in *Midland Empire* and how do you compare them with the key facts in the next case?

MT. MORRIS DRIVEIN THEATRE CO. v. COMMISSIONER

25 T.C. 272 (1955)

KERN, Judge

[The taxpayer built an openair theater on sloping land that was formerly covered with vegetation, without including in the construction any drainage system. In 1950 it spent $ 8,224 to construct a drainage system extending into and over adjacent land belonging to another in compromise of a pending lawsuit against it based upon allegations that petitioner's use of its own property had caused accelerated and concentrated drainage onto the adjacent land.]

OPINION.

When petitioner purchased, in 1947, the land which it intended to use for a drivein theater, its president was thoroughly familiar with the topography of this land which was such that when the covering vegetation was removed and graveled ramps were constructed and used by its patrons, the flow of natural precipitation on the lands of abutting property owners would be materially accelerated. Some provision should have been made to solve this drainage problem in order to avoid annoyance and harassment to its neighbors. If petitioner had included in its original construction plans an expenditure for a proper drainage system no one could doubt that such an expenditure would have been capital in nature.

Within a year after petitioner had finished its inadequate construction of the drivein theater, the need of a proper drainage system was forcibly called to its attention by one of the neighboring property owners, and under the threat of a lawsuit filed approximately a year after the theater was constructed, the drainage system was built by petitioner who now seeks to deduct its cost as an ordinary and necessary business expense, or as a loss.

We agree with respondent that the cost to petitioner of acquiring and constructing a drainage system in connection with its drivein theater was a capital expenditure.

Here was no sudden catastrophic loss caused by a "physical fault" undetected by the taxpayer in spite of due precautions taken by it at the time of its original construction work as in *American Bemberg Corporation*, 10 T. C. 361; no unforeseeable external factor as in *Midland Empire Packing Co.*, 14 T. C. 635; and no change in the cultivation of farm property caused by improvements in technique and made many years after the property in question was put to productive use as in *J. H. Collingwood*, 20 T. C. 937. In the instant case it was obvious at the time when the drivein theater was constructed, that a drainage system would be required to properly dispose of the natural precipitation normally to be expected, and that until this was accomplished, petitioner's capital investment was incomplete. In addition, it should be emphasized that here there was no mere restoration or rearrangement of the original capital asset, but there was the acquisition and construction of a capital asset which petitioner had not previously had, namely, a new drainage system.

That this drainage system was acquired and constructed and that payments therefor were made in compromise of a lawsuit is not determinative of whether such payments were ordinary and necessary business expenses or capital expenditures. "The decisive test is still the character of the transaction which gives rise to the payment." *HalesMullaly v. Commissioner*, 131 F. 2d 509, 511, 512.

In our opinion the character of the transaction in the instant case indicates that the transaction was a capital expenditure.

Decision will be entered for the respondent.

[The concurring and dissenting opinions are omitted. Eds.]

Notes on Repairs and Improvements

Why the repair versus improvement distinction is so important. This is a key subject to business taxpayers, because claiming a current tax deduction for a repair means an immediate tax saving, compared to a deferred saving if the expenditures produce a long-term improvement. If the expenditure merely restores the property to its normal operating efficiency, the deduction is assured, but if the taxpayer delays repairing a major asset and waits for it to deteriorate severely, the correction of the problem is likely to be viewed as made in connection with a general plan of rehabilitation whose entire cost has to be capitalized because, to paraphrase Reg. §1.1624, the expenditure is in the nature of a replacement which appreciably prolongs the life of the property; in contrast, a regular repair program can mean fully usable current deductions. Once a major overhaul is undertaken, associated disbursements, such as painting that could otherwise be deducted currently, must also be capitalized as incidental to a general reconditioning.[492]

Capitalizing depreciation on assets used to self-produce property. Capitalization of expenses is a controversial area even though it generally results only in timing differences. Those differences can represent a great deal of tax revenues accelerated through immediate deduction or deferred through capitalization. The details as to what must be capitalized are ornate when it comes to construction projects because the taxpayer must include what seem to be current expenses in the cost of self-constructed assets:

> **To illustrate**: Idaho Power Company built a new dam for its own use. The dam will produce electric power that Idaho Power Company will sell to the public. Among the economic costs of building the dam is the wear and tear on heavy equipment that Idaho Power Company owns and used to build the dam. Idaho Power Company sought to deduct depreciation on the heavy equipment, which amounted to $1 million. The Supreme Court held that Idaho Power must capitalize the $1 million into its basis in the dam because the depreciation is just another cost of obtaining a long term asset -- the dam. In addition, if this were not the law, then companies like Idaho Power would have an unfair advantage over smaller companies that must hire others to build dams for them and who must capitalize the costs of hiring those contractors. Those contractors would, in a world of rational bargaining, include the wear and tear on the builder's equipment as part of the purchase price of the dam. Later, §263A of the Code codified the result in the Idaho Power case.[493] As a practical matter, Idaho Power will get the benefit of depreciation of its heavy equipment via enhanced depreciation of the dam, or via the enlarged basis at the time of sale of the dam, or both combined, but not via current depreciation of the construction equipment.

Capitalization is even required if the taxpayer does not create a separate asset. In *INDOPCO*, the Supreme Court ruled that expenditures that benefit future periods must be capitalized even though the expenditures do not create an independent asset that can be separately disposed of.[494] The taxpayer was a target company in a merger. Its expenditures consisted of proxy expenses, SEC fees, investment bankers' fees, and the like. The Court's view was that because the merger would benefit the taxpayer well beyond the current year and would result in changing the taxpayer's internal structure, the expenditures had to be capitalized even though no

---

492 Compare Bank of Houston v. Commissioner, 19 T.C.M. 589 (1960) (capitalize if part of overhaul) with Kurtz v. Commissioner, 8 BTA 679 (1927) (otherwise deduct cost of paint).

493 418 U.S. 1 (1974). In fact, it was not clear exactly what was being built in Idaho power. It might have included dams. The court just referred to "Capital Facilities."

494 INDOPCO, Inc. v. Commissioner, 503 U.S 79 (1992).

asset was acquired. Thus, the mere durability of the value of the expenditure may be enough to force its capitalization into an independent intangible asset. The IRS has been quick to ratify *INDOPCO*, and in fact has issued a number of rulings relaxing *INDOPCO*'s powerful grip. For example, it has ruled that severance pay to workers who are fired in corporate "down-sizings" need not be capitalized because the severance payments related to past performance.[495] The exact scope of *INDOPCO* remains to be worked out.

Problem 6-10:

Swindler Enterprises operates a theater that has been running for many years. The projector is a wreck and asphalt shingles have fallen off the exterior walls here and there. The theatre has seats made with flammable plastic stuffing. The local fire code exempts theaters, but recent tort cases in other parts of the country have led the company's lawyers to recommend replacing the seats with nonflammable ones that will not last any longer than the old ones. In fact, they will give out about the same time the old ones would have. Over the objection of its tightfisted founder, Mr. Swindler, the lawyers won the day. Can the company deduct the cost of:

1) Replacing the projector?

2) Replacing the shingles?

3) Installing new seats?

4) Swindler is considering entirely rehabilitating the theater. In that connection, he used his own mechanical scraper to refurbish the hall. He used the scraper the whole year of the refurbishing process. How should he treat the annual depreciation on the scraper, which amounted to $100?

L. TAX SHELTERS, TAX-DRIVEN INVESTMENTS AND THE TAX LAW'S RESPONSES

The term "tax shelter" does not have a specific meaning, but in the minds of tax practitioners it generally means an investment that a taxpayer bought in order to show tax losses that the taxpayer will use to offset income from other sources. The usual features of a tax shelter are:

495 Rev. Rul. 94-77, 1994-2 C.B. 19.

Deferral - meaning the taxpayer's income tax burden is put off into future years thanks to investing in the tax shelter;

Conversion - meaning the taxpayer tries to get 100% deductible expenses (even losses from dealing in property) from carrying the investment, and then turn those deductions into favorably taxed capital gains when exiting from the shelter; and

Leverage - meaning the taxpayer uses other peoples' money to increase the amount invested, thereby maximizing the "shelter."

One of the reasons this three-part strategy used to work so well is that it was remarkably easy to go into a "trade or business" for Federal Income Tax purposes, thereby producing net operating losses under §172 that could offset income from other sources such as salary or investments.[496] All that is required is regular and continuous *bona fide* efforts at making a profit.[497] A business normally involves offering goods and services to the public, but not always.[498] As an illustration, consider the case of one Mrs. Gilford, an owner of eight New York rental properties. Her only link with the properties was that she hired a managing agent for the apartment buildings. Nevertheless, the Second Circuit declared that she was in the real estate business because the activities of her agents were imputed to her.[499] Likewise, the business activities of partnerships have long been attributed to their limited partners. This attribution of businesses' losses to partners in the business was dear to the tax shelter industry.

This liberal willingness to find taxpayers engaged in business led to abuse. The primary area of Congressional concern prior to 1986 was the syndicated tax shelter investment almost always in the form of a limited partnership that was peddled to the public for its tax benefits. The investments themselves were often of a poor quality, and many investors were victimized by unscrupulous promoters who disappeared when the going got tough.

Section 183 -- the hobby loss rules -- applies to tax losses, eliminating them if there is no genuine profit-seeking intent on the taxpayer's part. The IRS's mixed success in using the essentially subjunctive and therefore somewhat weak §183 as a sword to fight tax shelters required the enactment of more powerful measures, especially §469, the so-called passive loss rules, and §465 (the at-risk rules).

---

496 By contrast, investment expenses may be deductible, but they are deductible under Schedule A and are subject to numerous limitations (e.g., §§ 67 and 68 and 163(d)).

497 Many courts considered that there have to be dealings with the public in order to have a trade or business. The notion that dealing with the public is an element of a trade or business arose from interpretations of the case of Higgins v Commissioner, 312 U.S. 212, reh'g denied, 312 U.S. 714 (1941).

498 United States v. Groetzinger, 480 U.S. 23, 33 (1987) (the goods and services test is from a concurring opinion in Deputy v. DuPont, 308 U.S. 488, 499 (1940)).

499 Gilford v. Commissioner, 201 F.2d 735 (2d. Cir. 1953).

Organizers of tax shelters generally found it easy to get "tax leverage" at low risk. The *Crane* case, which appears much earlier in the book, was a bedrock decision on which the "tax shelter" industry was founded. The concept behind the tax shelter was to offer the public opportunities to buy interests in partnerships which were sold either through clubby, private placements or through public offerings registered with the SEC. The core of the typical deal was that the investor/partner contributed a modest amount of cash, with the promoters of the partnership finding lenders to the partnership to provide the balance of the money needed to acquire the subject of the deal, very often an apartment building. The typical investor never visited the property. The property would generally produce just enough cash rental income to offset the cash expenses for carrying the building, namely interest, local taxes, insurance costs and maintenance costs. In addition, the tax laws generously allowed depreciation deductions that exaggerated the decline in value of the property because of wear and tear and obsolescence.

> **To illustrate**: Dr. Fonebone, alarmed at the prospect of paying "too much" in income taxes, asks his financial adviser to find a good do-it-yourself tax shelter. The financial advisor comes back with a proposal for an investment along the following lines; Fonebone will invest $10,000 of his own money in an advanced medical device and will borrow another $90,000 on a nonrecourse basis to finance the purchase, thereby getting a $100,000 basis in the device. Suppose that the revenues from renting the device will amount to $25,000 per year.

As to costs, assume the following:

1. Interest - $9,000 per year on a loan at 10% (deductible under §163):
   cash.. $9,000

2. Depreciation - if cost recovery on the asset could be taken over a five year period (§§ 167,168):
   noncash.. $20,000

3. Property and other taxes of $2,500 per year, deductible under §164:
   cash.. $2,500

4. Principal payments on debt of $3,500 per year
   cash.. $3,500

5. Annual maintenance expenses, deductible under §212:
   cash.. $10,000
   TOTAL.. **$45,000**

Notice how the *cash outlay* each year will be $25,000. Although the total annual tax outlaysare $45,000, $20,000 of that amount is a cost in the form of deductible depreciation, which does not require an out-of-pocket expenditure each year. Of the cash outlay of $25,000 per year, $3,500 is the principal payment on the loan and operates as forced savings by the doctor. The overall cash outlay of $25,000 equals the rental income of $25,000 (cash flow receipts). The total amounts that are deductible aggregate $21,500 ($9,000 interest, plus $2,500 in taxes, plus $10,000 annual maintenance). These deductible amounts plus the deductible depreciation, total $41,500. So this year, the investment provides a tax shelter of $16,500, namely the excess of the total deductible amount each year ($41,500) minus the gross income generated by the property, namely $25,000. The income from the property covers the cash outflow in full, some of that cash outflow even provides a form of saving. In addition, the investment generates $16,500 of excess deductions which can be taken on the owner's individual tax return and can shelter investment or personal service income tax rates at least as high as 37%.

This is the essence of a tax shelter -- deductions or other allowances from the activity not only cover income from that activity but also shelter income from other sources. While the figures and legal rules in this example are streamlined and oversimplified for illustration, their lack of realism does not detract from the utility of the example.

Having seen the advantages of the tax shelter in providing deductions in excess of income, it is then useful to compare what happens after a tax shelter reaches the "cross-over point' and becomes a "negative tax shelter." To illustrate this, imagine the investment described above has been held for five years and that at the end of that time the cash outlay is still $25,000 per year and the rental income still amounts to $25,000. However, at this point and for succeeding years the deductions that can be taken will amount to only $21,500 each year for interest, taxes and maintenance. Depreciation can no longer be taken because the property will have no basis because $20,000 of depreciation will have been taken in each of the five prior years, adjusting the cost basis of the property downwards by $100,000, under §1016, to an adjusted basis of $0.

Now the investment continues to generate includable income that exceeds deductible expenses by $3,500. That is to say, the rental income is $25,000 and the deductible expenses amount to $21,500. Thus, the investment has begun to generate taxable income, hence income taxes. Even though it is still true that the rental income of $25,000 covers the amount of expenses that have to be paid each year, and therefore there is no out-of-pocket cost to Dr. Fonebone for those expenses, there will be an out-of pocket cost to him in order to pay the income tax on the $3,500 of positive income now generated by the investment.

It is at this point, when the shelter has reached the "cross-over point" and has begun to generate taxable income, that the owner of the property may wish to "get out of" the investment. That is easier said than done.

Let us suppose that the investment has been a fortunate one and that the value of the property is still $100,000, even though it is five years older. This means that if the taxpayer sells it for that $100,000 there will be significant Federal Income Tax consequences. The adjusted basis having been reduced to $0, so the entire $100,000 will be taxable as gain, perhaps producing a tax of $37,000, which will exceed the cash remaining after the balance of the debt is paid off. The gain will arise even if the property is abandoned or given away because the nonrecourse debt will count as an amount realized. Later in the book we will look at the use of trusts as a possible way out of this dilemma.

1. Judicial Limits on the Use of Leverage to Create Depreciable Basis

From time to time the courts have knocked down tax shelter schemes by finding the debt used to purchase property is illusory.

a. Specious Debt

ESTATE OF FRANKLIN v. COMMISSIONER
544 F.2d 1045 (9th Cir. 1976)

SNEED, Circuit Judge:

[The facts involve an alleged sale-leaseback. The taxpayer was a member of a tax driven limited partnership that "purchased" a motel from the Romneys for $1,224,000 to be paid over 10 years at an annual interest rate of 7.5%. There was an initial payment of $75,000 as prepaid interest, then monthly installments of interest and principal of $9,045.36 for ten years, and then finally a balloon payment of the $975,000 balance. The obligation was nonrecourse. The only risk then was a foreclosure and loss of the investment in the property. The partnership never took possession of the motel. The Romneys were able to increase the mortgages which they were responsible for and make capital improvements. The Tax Court held that the partnership merely acquired an option to buy the property and disallowed the taxpayer's share of deductions associated with allegedly owning a share of the motel as a partner.]

. . .

In holding that the transaction between Associates and the Romneys more nearly resembled an option than a sale, the Tax Court emphasized that Associates had the power at the end of ten years to walk away from the transaction and merely lose its $75,000 "prepaid interest payment." It also pointed out that a deed was never recorded and that the "benefits and burdens of ownership" appeared to remain with the Romneys. Thus, the sale was combined with a leaseback in which no cash would pass; the Romneys remained responsible under the mortgages, which they could increase; and the Romneys could make capital improvements. The Tax Court further justified its "option" characterization by reference to the nonrecourse nature of the purchase money debt and the nice balance between the rental and purchase money payments.

Our emphasis is different from that of the Tax Court. We believe the characteristics set out above can exist in a situation in which the sale imposes upon the purchaser a genuine indebtedness within the meaning of section 163(a), Internal Revenue Code of 1954, which will support both interest and depreciation deductions. They substantially so existed in *Hudspeth v. Commissioner*, 509 F.2d 1224 (9th Cir. 1975) in which parents entered into saleleaseback transactions with their children. The children paid for the property by executing nonnegotiable notes and mortgages equal to the fair market value of the property; state law proscribed deficiency judgments in case of default, limiting the parents' remedy to foreclosure of the property. The children had no funds with which to make mortgage payments; instead, the payments were offset in part by the rental payments, with the difference met by gifts from the parents to their children. Despite these characteristics this court held that there was a bona fide indebtedness on which the children, to the extent of the rental payments, could base interest deductions. . . .

In none of these cases, however, did the taxpayer fail to demonstrate that the purchase price was at least approximately equivalent to the fair market value of the property. Just such a failure occurred here. The Tax Court explicitly found that on the basis of the facts before it the value of the property could not be estimated. 64 T.C. at 767768.[500] In our view this defect in the taxpayer's proof is fatal.

Reason supports our perception. An acquisition such as that of Associates if at a price approximately equal to the fair market value of the property under ordinary circumstances would rather quickly yield an equity in the property which the purchaser could not prudently abandon. This is the stuff of substance. It meshes with the form of the transaction and constitutes a sale.

No such meshing occurs when the purchase price exceeds a demonstrably reasonable estimate of the fair market value. Payments on the principal of the purchase price yield no equity so long as the unpaid balance of the purchase price exceeds the then existing fair market value. Under these circumstances the purchaser by abandoning the transaction can lose no more than a mere chance to acquire an equity in the future should the value of the acquired property increase. While this chance undoubtedly influenced the Tax Court's determination that the transaction before us constitutes an option, we need only point out that its existence fails to supply the substance necessary to justify treating the transaction as a sale *ab initio*. It is not necessary to the disposition of this case to decide the tax consequences of a transaction such as that before us if in a subsequent year the fair market value of the property increases to an extent that permits the purchaser to acquire an equity.

500 Given that it was the appellants' burden to present evidence showing that the purchase price did not exceed the fair market value and that he had a fair opportunity to do so, we see no reason to remand this case for further proceedings. [Footnote No. 4 in original.]

Authority also supports our perception. It is fundamental that "depreciation is not predicated upon ownership of property *but rather upon an investment in property. Gladding Dry Goods Co.*, 2 BTA 336 (1925)." . . . No such investment exists when payments of the purchase price in accordance with the design of the parties yield no equity to the purchaser. . . . In the transaction before us and during the taxable years in question the purchase price payments by Associates have not been shown to constitute an *investment in the property.* Depreciation was properly disallowed. Only the Romneys had an investment in the property.

Authority also supports disallowance of the interest deductions. This is said even though it has long been recognized that the absence of personal liability for the purchase money debt secured by a mortgage on the acquired property does not deprive the debt of its character as a bona fide debt obligation able to support an interest deduction. *Mayerson, supra* at 352. However, this is no longer true when it appears that the debt has economic significance only if the property substantially appreciates in value prior to the date at which a very large portion of the purchase price is to be discharged. Under these circumstances the purchaser has not secured "the use or forbearance of money." *SeeNorton v. Commissioner*, 474 F.2d 608, 610 (9th Cir. 19). Nor has the seller advanced money or forborne its use. *SeeBornstein v. Commissioner*, 334 F.2d 779, 780 (1st Cir. 1964); . . . . Prior to the date at which the balloon payment on the purchase price is required, and assuming no substantial increase in the fair market value of the property, the absence of personal liability on the debt reduces the transaction in economic terms to a mere chance that a genuine debt obligation may arise. This is not enough to justify an interest deduction. To justify the deduction the debt must exist; potential existence will not do. For debt to exist, the purchaser, in the absence of personal liability, must confront a situation in which it is presently reasonable from an economic point of view for him to make a capital investment in the amount of the unpaid purchase price. . . . Associates, during the taxable years in question, confronted no such situation. *Compare Crane v. Commissioner*, 331 U.S. 1, 1112, . . . (1947).

Our focus on the relationship of the fair market value of the property to the unpaid purchase price should not be read as premised upon the belief that a sale is not a sale if the purchaser pays too much. Bad bargains from the buyer's point of view as well as sensible bargains from buyer's, but exceptionally good from the seller's point of view do not thereby cease to be sales. . . . We intend our holding and explanation thereof to be understood as limited to transactions substantially similar to that now before us.

AFFIRMED.

Notes

Is there civil fraud here? The taxpayers in *Estate of Franklin* were taking an aggressive tax position, likely based on the advice of expensive tax professionals. The Revenue Agent examining the case might well conclude that the facts justified imposing the §6663 civil fraud penalty of

75% of the underpayment of income taxes that their scheme caused. The general standard for finding civil fraud is bad faith and an attempt to evade tax. *Ehlers v. Vinal,* 382 F.2d 58 (8th Cir. 1967). The burden on the government is to show such fraud by "clear and convincing evidence," whereas criminal fraud must be shown "beyond a reasonable doubt." Could the IRS make a civil fraud charge stick in *Estate of Franklin*?

The "whipsaw" problem. Taxpayers will often take contradictory positions with respect to the same transaction. For example, a payor might claim her payment to her stockbroker was a deductible bonus for doing a great job, but the stockbroker might claim that the payment was a tax-free gift.

If the IRS is lucky, it can audit taxpayers who are in reverse forensic positions and use the arguments of one to attack the other. For example, the Romneys and the Franklins might both have claimed to own the building, a "whipsaw" against the government, resulting in duplicated depreciation deductions. On the other hand, the IRS could retaliate by first auditing both groups and claiming neither owned the property. The Franklin group would assert they really did own the building, as would the Romneys. That would smoke out the taxpayer with the more persuasive claim to ownership of the motel.

Who really wins from the whipsaw possibility? Aggressive taxpayers who are emboldened by low audit rates? An overbearing government? Is it enough that revenues tend to balance out over a large number of audits? What happens as the number of audits declines? To meet this problem, Congress occasionally requires consistent treatment by the parties. A good example is the requirement that the buyer and seller of a business report the gain or loss on the sale of a business on a single IRS Form that they complete together to met their obligations under §1060. That subject is reserved for later in the book.

b. Sham Transactions, Lack of Economic Substance and Purposive Economic Activity Doctrines

The interest expense deduction has proven to be a fertile garden in which tax law doctrines of more general application have flourished. The bluntest is the sham transactions doctrine. The idea here is that if the transaction is bogus, it will be disregarded.

To illustrate: If X purports to sell a house to Y, but has a secret option to buy it back from Y for $1 anytime, the sale is a sham. We know X will buy it back unless X and Y are related parties. If they are related, then the transfer looks like a gift by a suspicious donor. Either way, it is not a genuine sale. Those are easy cases, and can lead to criminal fraud convictions.[501]

501 See, e.g., United States v. Clardy, 612 F.2d 1139 (9th Cir 1980).

A more sophisticated kind of tax avoidance activity involves transactions that are not misrepresented, but are driven by tax minimization to the point where one can fairly say they lack commercial *economic substance* and can therefore be denied the tax benefits they seek. The leading case is *Knetch v. United States*,[502] in which the IRS successfully managed to disallow a taxpayer all his interest expense deductions arising out of contrived dealings in which there was no beneficial result other than tax deductions. The scheme involved borrowing money to buy annuities that would produce a smaller profit than the interest expense deductions. The deal would never have been profitable. It would never be done in a taxfree system. There was no risk of loss from external circumstances, unless perhaps the insurance company that issued the annuities were to fail. The basic outofpocket cost was interest paid of about $440,000 versus increases in cash value of the annuity of only $310,000 (resulting in a cash drain of $130,000). The reason for the deal was that, because the taxpayer was in the 90% bracket at the time of taking the deductions, he would reduce his taxes by about $396,000 (i.e., 90% of $440,000), which was more than the cash drain of $130,000 and the increases in the cash value of the annuities would not be taxable to him until withdrawn. The income from the annuity would come later with favorable tax treatment, the description of which would only create confusion here. In essence, the Supreme Court imperiously declared in *Knetch* that the lack of non-tax profit-making purpose and the relationship between the loans and growth of the cash values meant there was no "debt" for purposes of §163. (Unfortunately, the Supreme Court muddied the water by adding that the deal was a "sham".)

GOLDSTEIN v. COMMISSIONER

364 F.2d 734 (2d Cir. 1966), cert. denied 1967

Waterman, Moore and Friendly, Circuit Judges

WATERMAN, Circuit Judge:

[Mrs. Tillie Goldstein won about $140,000 from the Irish Sweepstakes and worked out a tax avoidance plan with her son, Bernard, a C.P.A. She borrowed $950,000 from two banks in order to finance the purchase of $1 million of U.S. government securities, which she pledged to secure the loans. She claimed an interest prepayment deduction of $81,000 on taking out the loans. She hoped for a favorably taxed capital gain on disposing of the securities she bought. The tax burden of the capital gains would have been much smaller than the taxes saved by the interest expense deduction she expected. The interest she paid exceeded the interest she received on the securities and on top of that she paid hefty fees to her advisors. She planned to recover her out-of-pocket costs from tax savings. The Tax Court found the loans were "shams" that created "no genuine indebtedness" and denied her claims for interest expense deductions.]

502 364 U.S. 361 (1960).

. . .

In our view, however, the facts of the two loan arrangements now before us fail in several significant respects to establish that these transactions were clearly shams. We agree with the dissent below that the record indicates these loan arrangements were ". . . regular and, moreover, indistinguishable from any other legitimate loan transaction contracted for the purchase of Government securities." 44 T.C. at 301 (Fay, J., dissenting). In the first place, the Jersey City Bank and the Royal State Bank were independent financial institutions; it cannot be said that their sole function was to finance transactions such as those before us. Compare Lynch v. Commissioner of Internal Revenue, 2 F.2d 867 (2 Cir. 1959). . . . Second, the two loan transactions here did not within a few days return all the parties to the position from which they had started. *Ibid.* Here the Royal State Bank loan remained outstanding, and, significantly, that Bank retained the Treasury obligations pledged as security until June 10, 1960, at which time petitioner instructed the bank to sell the notes, apply the proceeds to the loan, and credit any remaining balance to her account. The facts relating to the Jersey City Bank loan are slightly different: this loan was closed in June 1959 when the brokerage house of Gruntal & Co. was substituted for the Jersey City Bank as creditor. Gruntal received and retained the 1962 Treasury 1 ½'s originally pledged as security for the loan until December 1, 1959 when, pursuant to instructions from petitioner and her advisors, these notes were sold, and $500,000 face amount of United States Treasury 2 1/2% bonds were purchased to replace them as security. Petitioner's account with Gruntal was not finally closed until June 13, 1960 when the last of these substituted bonds were sold, the petitioner's note was marked fully paid, and the balance was credited to petitioner. Third, the independent financial institutions from which petitioner borrowed the funds she needed to acquire the Treasury obligations possessed significant control over the future of their respective loan arrangements: for example, the petitioner's promissory note to the Jersey City Bank explicitly gave either party the right to accelerate the maturity of the note after 30 days, and it was the Jersey City Bank's utilization of this clause that necessitated recourse to Gruntal; the Royal State Bank had the right at any time to demand that petitioner increase her collateral or liquidate the loan, and on several occasions it made such a demand. Fourth, the notes signed by petitioner in favor of both banks were signed with recourse. If either of the independent lending institutions here involved had lost money on these transactions because of the depreciation of the collateral pledged to secure the loans we are certain that, upon petitioner's default of payment, they would have without hesitation proceeded against petitioner to recover their losses. Compare Lynch v. Commissioner of Internal Revenue, supra (nonrecourse notes). See also Jockmus v. United States, 335 F.2d 23 (2 Cir. 1964). Moreover, all things being equal, the banks' chances of judgments in their favor would have been excellent. In view of this combination of facts we think it was error for the Tax Court to conclude that these two transactions were "shams" which created no genuine indebtedness. Were this the only ground on which the decision reached below could be supported we would be compelled to reverse.

. . . We think the interest of candor is better served if the "sham" and "absence of indebtedness" rationales are reserved for cases like Lynch v. Commissioner of Internal Revenue, supra, and Goldstein v. Commissioner of Internal Revenue, supra. Different considerations govern decision as to whether interest payments are deductible by a taxpayer who borrows money from an independent lending institution, executes a promissory note with recourse, and purchases Treasury obligations that are then in fact pledged with the lender as security for the loan for a significant period of time, unless it can be concluded from other facts (not present in this case) that the transaction is simply a sham.

One ground advanced by the Tax Court seems capable of reasoned development to support the result reached in this case by that court. The Tax Court found as an ultimate fact that petitioner's purpose in entering into the Jersey City Bank and Royal State Bank transactions "was not to derive any economic gain or to improve here [sic] beneficial interest; but was *solely* an attempt to obtain an interest deduction as an offset to her sweepstake winnings." 44 T.C. at 295 (emphasis added). . . . [P]etitioner and her financial advisors . . . estimated that the transactions would produce an economic loss in excess of $18,500 inasmuch as petitioner was out of pocket the 4% interest she had prepaid and could expect to receive 1 1/2% interest on the Treasury obligations she had just purchased plus a modest capital gain when the obligations were sold. . . . [I]f the plan was successful this economic loss would be more than offset by the substantial reduction in petitioner's 1958 income tax liability due to the large deduction for interest "paid or accrued" taken in that year. . . . In fact, petitioner sustained a $25,091.01 economic loss on these transactions for some of the Treasury obligations were ultimately sold for less than the price that had been originally anticipated by petitioner's advisors.

. . .

In holding that petitioner's "sole" purpose in entering into the Jersey City Bank and Royal State Bank transactions was to obtain an interest deduction, the Tax Court rejected this explanation of her purpose in entering into these transactions. For several reasons we hold that this rejection was proper. First, petitioner's evidence tending to establish that she anticipated an economic profit on these transactions due to a rising market for Treasury obligations is flatly contradicted by the computations made by Bernard contemporaneously with the commencement of these transactions and introduced by the Commissioner at trial. These computations almost conclusively establish that petitioner and her advisors from the outset anticipated an economic loss. . . .

For all of the above reasons the Tax Court was justified in concluding that petitioner entered into the Jersey City Bank and Royal State Bank transactions without any realistic expectation of economic profit and "solely" in order to secure a large interest deduction in 1958 which could be deducted from her sweepstakes winnings in that year. This conclusion points the way to affirmance in the present case.

We hold, for reasons set forth hereinafter, that Section 163(a) of the 1954 Internal Revenue Code does not permit a deduction for interest paid or accrued in loan arrangements, like those now before us, that can not with reason be said to have purpose, substance, or utility apart from their anticipated tax consequences. See Knetsch v. United States, 364 U.S. 361 . . . . Although it is by no means certain that Congress constitutionally could tax gross income, see Surrey & Warren, Federal Income Taxation 22829 (1960 ed.), it is frequently stated that deductions from "gross income" are a matter of "legislative grace." E. g., Deputy v. DuPont, 308 U.S. 488, 493, 60 S. Ct. 363, 84 L. Ed. 416 (1940). There is at least this much truth in this oftrepeated maxim: a close question whether a particular Code provision authorizes the deduction of a certain item is best resolved by reference to the underlying Congressional purpose of the deduction provision in question.

Admittedly, the underlying purpose of Section 163(a) permitting the deduction of "all interest paid or accrued within the taxable year on indebtedness" is difficult to articulate because this provision is extremely broad: there is no requirement that deductible interest serve a business purpose, that it be ordinary and necessary, or even that it be reasonable. 4 Mertens, Law of Federal Income Taxation §26.01 (1960 ed.). Nevertheless, it is fair to say that Section 163(a) is not entirely unlimited in its application and that such limits as there are stem from the Section's underlying notion that if an individual or corporation desires to engage in purposive activity, there is no reason why a taxpayer who borrows for that purpose should fare worse from an income tax standpoint than one who finances the venture with capital that otherwise would have been yielding income.

In order fully to implement this Congressional policy of encouraging purposive activity to be financed through borrowing, Section 163(a) should be construed to permit the deductibility of interest when a taxpayer has borrowed funds and incurred an obligation to pay interest in order to engage in what with reason can be termed purposive activity, even though he decided to borrow in order to gain an interest deduction rather than to finance the activity in some other way. In other words, the interest deduction should be permitted whenever it can be said that the taxpayer's desire to secure an interest deduction is only one of mixed motives that prompts the taxpayer to borrow funds; or, put a third way, the deduction is proper if there is some substance to the loan arrangement beyond the taxpayer's desire to secure the deduction. . . .

In many instances transactions that lack all substance, utility, and purpose, and which can only be explained on the ground the taxpayer sought an interest deduction in order to reduce his taxes, will also be so transparently arranged that they can candidly be labeled "shams." In those instances both the rationale of the decision we announce today, and that of [prior cases] are available as grounds for disallowing the deduction. The present case makes plain, however, that these rationales are distinct from each other, and that a court need not always first label a loan transaction a "sham" in order to deny a deduction for interest paid in connection with the loan.

... Section 163(a) does not "intend" that taxpayers should be permitted deductions for interest paid on debts that were entered into solely in order to obtain a deduction. It follows therefore from the foregoing, and from the Tax Court's finding as a matter of "ultimate" fact that petitioner entered into the Jersey City Bank and Royal State Bank transactions without any expectation of profit and without any other purpose except to obtain an interest deduction, and that the Tax Court's disallowance of the deductions in this case must be affirmed.

Notes on Vulnerable Transactions

A brief lexicon of tax law doctrines used to attack vulnerable transactions. So what was the exact problem in *Goldstein*? A lack of economic substance? A faulty taxpayer purpose or motive? Was it a sham transaction?

One must make an effort, roughly at least, to sort out the doctrines from the most serious cases (i.e., jailable offenses) to the least disturbing:

a) Tax crimes: require the element of willfulness: Examples are concealment of income or deliberately misstated sources of income. This is tax evasion, sometimes distinguished from tax avoidance (by legitimate planning). The crime is often based on the fact that tax returns are submitted under penalties of perjury.

b) Shams: the forms selected are so badly misrepresented (bogus) that they should be ignored. Another way to view sham transactions is as transactions that, if contrived more carefully, would have been denounced by a less abrasive doctrine, such as being one whose substance fell short of its form. For example, if parents purported to sell property to their children, but never bothered with any paperwork and the children never in fact paid, the children's claim to a basis in property established by a sale would collapse under judicial scrutiny as a mere sham. If, on the other hand, the parents documented the transaction with sales contracts and notes, but only took half-hearted steps to collect from the children because they were too genteel, a court would be more likely to say that the transaction failed on substance over form grounds (and was a gift for Federal Income Tax purposes), rather than that it was a (disreputable) sham. As the fact patterns move towards the middle ground between "shams" and more dignified criticism, it can be impossible to tell which tool a court will use to penetrate the transaction. The major practical difference if that if the transaction is found to be a sham, the civil penalties are apt to be stiffer. In addition, the statute of limitations might never end, because a sham may well entail a civil fraud as to which there is no statute of limitations.

c) *Substance over form doctrine:* on analysis the form was not badly misrepresented, but does not reflect realty; the substance is something different. The tax law analysis must, therefore, be of the substance of the transaction, i.e., the "real" deal. The doctrine does not depend on the taxpayer's intent; sometimes the taxpayer may be innocent of any tax planning scheme. Indeed, she may never even have considered the tax implications of the deal. For example, a sale and leaseback transaction may be intended as such, but be condemned as a mere mortgage to the taxpayer's surprise, at least if the taxpayer is unsophisticated in financial matters. Conversely, if the form is carefully structured so that its form and structure are the same, a transaction that is otherwise open to debate as to its true character will normally be respected, despite a tax avoidance motive. Conversely, there are times when form is completely controlling. For example, the Code is riddled with accounting elections, such as the choice of taxable year for a regular corporation, whose implementation depends exclusively on compliance with strict legal requirements.

d) *Steptransactions doctrine*: multiple steps are integrated and the intervening steps are ignored. The transaction is then characterized by reference to the first and last steps only. Unfortunately, there is no single method by which to collapse the steps. Instead, there are the following inconsistent approaches:

1. Integrate the steps only if there is a preexisting binding commitment to take each step, all known to the taxpayer; or
2. Integrate the steps only if they are logically interdependent, meaning that one would not undertake one step unless one knew one was going to undertake the next step and so forth all along the chain of anticipated steps; or
3. Integrate the steps only if the taxpayer intended that the various steps occur.

To illustrate: Unhealthy, the parent of Robust, is dying. Robust has a painting with a basis of $100 and a value of $1,000 that she gives to Unhealthy. Unhealthy has no practical use for it. Unhealthy dies 15 months later and, as expected, wills the painting back to Robust. Robust claims a $1,000 basis in the painting under §1014 (fair market value at death) and soon sells it for no gain or loss.

This transaction has no binding commitments, but, on these bare facts, it looks like there was a plan to get a basis step-up in the property. Robust would not have made the gift but for the expectation of Unhealthy's death, resulting basis step-up, and her expectation of inheriting the property. Here the "intention test" and the "interdependent steps" test both yield the same result, namely that the several transfers should be disregarded and only the first and last elements should be studied. Through that lens, nothing happened. Robust never relinquished the property. Section 1014(e) imposes the same result if Unhealthy received the property within a year of death and willed it to Robust. Beyond that period, the step transaction doctrine might be invoked to defeat the plan.

Judges can select whichever formulation they prefer, or use all three. The right approach, to prevent chaos, ought to be to apply all three tests. A lawyer advising a client on a proposed transaction would be imprudent not to do the same as part of the tax analysis of the transaction.[503]

e) *Purposive economic activity*: the notion is that the tax benefit depends on the taxpayer's action being within the implied intention of the Congress. *Goldstein* is the leading example. Borrowing that is part of a program whose sole purpose is to defer or reduce taxes is not within Congress' plan for interest expenses and should not be allowed to produce tax deductions. If the same issue arises in a business setting, the courts are apt to use the term "business purpose" in place of "purposive economic activity."[504]

f) *Economic substance*: This is the hardest nut to crack. Perhaps the best statement is that the doctrine insists that transactions that claim to be gain-seeking in character have meaningful economic consequences, aside from tax benefits.[505] In its simplest form, this means the taxpayer changed her economic position in some meaningful way.[506] The *Goldstein* case could have been decided on the ground that it lacked economic substance, but it was instead formally decided on the narrower grounds of "purposive economic activity." Notice how close the two doctrines are; the lack of meaningful tax-independent consequences greatly influenced the court to apply the purposive economic effect doctrine.

Attempts to describe these doctrines with scientific accuracy have so far failed, partly because courts have confused the subject by combining their thoughts, as when the Supreme Court in *Knetch* announced that the taxpayer's scheme was a "sham" without significant economic

503 See generally Chirelstein & Lopata, *Recent Developments in the Step Transaction Doctrine*, 60 Taxes 970 (1982).

504 See Gregory v. Helvering, 293 U.S. 465 (1935), which seems to be the fountainhead of this branch of reasoning. See Bittker, *Pervasive Judicial Doctrines in the Construction of the Internal Revenue Code*, 21 How. L. J. 693, 715 (1978).

505 See Hariton, *Sorting Out the Tangle of Economic Substance*, 52 Tax Lawyer 235, 235-236 (1999).

506 According to the author, the taxpayer can stave off the doctrine if the taxpayer can show either: (1) the transaction is not primarily tax motivated or (2) the taxpayer's economic position was materially changed -- apparently in terms of risk or profit potential -- as a result of the transaction or (3) the tax results are reasonable or justified. Id. at 268-270.

results because, "there was nothing of substance [that the taxpayer could realize] beyond a tax deduction." What this really indicates is a pervasive judicial mood of skepticism when evaluating any tax-motivated transaction. Yet, taxpayers are endlessly optimistic, putting the tax lawyer in the difficult position of rejecting bad plans without losing the client. A leading tax scholar of the past summarized the situation this way:

> Above all things, a tax attorney must be an indefatigable skeptic; he must discount everything he hears and reads. The market place abounds with unsound avoidance schemes which will not stand the test of objective analysis and litigation. The escaped tax, a favorite topic of conversation at the best clubs and the most sumptuous pleasure resorts, expands with repetition into fantastic legends. But clients want opinions with happy endings, and he smiles best who smiles last. It is wiser to state misgivings at the beginning than have to acknowledge them ungracefully at the end. The tax adviser has, therefore, to spend a large part of his time advising against schemes of this character. I sometimes think that the most important word in his vocabulary is "No".[507]

2. Statutory Limits on the Use of Leverage: Section 465, the "At-Risk" Rules

Read §465(a)(1)(2), (b)(1)(2)

There are several statutory restrictions on the use of leverage. A primary one is §465, which restricts losses that arise from the use of nonrecourse debt. The gist of the rule is that taxpayers cannot claim tax losses except to the extent that their own capital is jeopardized. The provision is of limited importance nowadays because nonrecourse debt is almost impossible to arrange, but the one industry that can still attract nonrecourse debt is the real estate industry, and §465(b)(6) exempts "the activity of holding real property" from the at-risk rules, opening the door to the use of nonrecourse debt where it is the most available. The atrisk rules were of tremendous significance to the tax shelter industry, but §465 has less significance now that banks have been chastened by recent financial disasters.

The principal target of the atrisk rules is the nonrecourse loan. Additional targets are loans subject to stoploss agreements and other guarantees against risk. The atrisk rules apply on an activitybyactivity basis. As a result, positive amounts at risk in one activity (such as leasing trucks) cannot be used to salvage losses from an activity (say an oil and gas project) with an inadequate amount at risk.

The Code tests amounts at risk as of the end of the taxpayer's taxable year, but the proposed regulations rightly undercut this rule by ignoring yearend additions if they lack economic normality.[508] The following items are considered to be at risk:

---

507 Paul, *The Lawyer as Tax Adviser*, 25 Rocky Mntn. Law Rev. 412, 416 (1953).

508 Prop. Reg. §1.4654(a). The regulations have been in proposed form for an exceptionally long time.

1. Cash and the adjusted basis of property contributed to the activity.
2. Borrowings for use in the activity which are subject to personal liability.
3. Borrowings secured by pledged property, other than property contributed to the activity, up to fair market value. There is a special limit here; if the pledged property which is not used in the suspect activity is directly or indirectly financed by property contributed to the activity, then such pledged property cannot be used to test borrowings secured by pledged property outside the activity.[509]

> **To illustrate:** Mrs. Partner contributes a car with an adjusted basis of $5,000 to a partnership. She also contributes $5,000 in cash obtained from a loan which was secured by pledging her ring. Both items count as being at risk. If, however, the ring had been financed by using the car as collateral, the $5,000 cash borrowing is not treated as being at risk.

Losses denied as a result of the atrisk rules are suspended and are available in future years to offset future income or may be claimed for income tax purposes if and to the extent that the taxpayer adds amounts at risk in later years.[510] That makes §465 a deferral provision, not a disallowance, a vital distinction in the tax laws.

> **To illustrate:** Mr. Lilliput, a maker of miniature toys, contributes cash of $50 from his savings account and acquires $50 worth of tools which he uses in his business, a sole proprietorship. He also borrows $10 on a nonrecourse basis from a local bank. These are the only funds used in the business. The business loses $60 in the first year. Because he has only $50 at risk, he can claim only $50 of losses. If, instead, he contributed an extra $10 from his savings account at yearend, he could claim a full $60 loss, assuming the year-end contribution was genuine.[511] Alternatively, if he did not contribute the extra $10, but the business earned $10 in the next year, that $10 profit would be offset (and rendered nontaxable) by his $10 of suspended losses that are carried over to year 2.

Recapture. In order to prevent crafty taxpayers from claiming losses and then withdrawing property, or converting debt from recourse to nonrecourse status without adverse tax consequences, §465(e) provides that when the amount at risk drops below zero, the excess must be taken into income if the sum of the losses previously claimed exceeds the amounts currently

509 §465(b)(2).

510 §465(a).

511 See Prop. Reg. §1.465–4(a).

at risk. This recapture in turn creates a disallowed loss which can be salvaged through future income or future at-risk amounts transferred to the activity.

Problem 6-11:

J.R. Klopman borrows $100,000 to buy a diesel-powered auto compactor for $40,000 and $60,000 for working capital, all with personal liability. The compacting business loses $50,000 in year 1.

1) Does §465 restrict the loss?

2) What if the $100,000 loan were nonrecourse?

3) What if the $100,000 loan were nonrecourse but secured by his home worth $500,000 and otherwise debt-free?

4) Same as "(1)," but at the beginning of next year J.R. renegotiates the debt so that it is changed to nonrecourse debt. What result, if any, to J.R.?

5) Assume that instead of buying a compactor, JR bought a Boston apartment building from an unrelated party, paying an unrelated broker a commission for finding him the property. He rents the building to students, having financed the purchase by taking out a loan from the Friendly Bank, which provided the debt with no personal liability. JR has no ownership interest in the bank.

    a. Would §465 limit his losses?

    b. What if there was personal liability, but the bank was owned by the J.R. and had a 30% share of the building? See §465(b)(3).

6) Same as "(2)". What if the borrower was Exxon Corporation and the numbers were in the billions of dollars?

3. Tax Return Preparation Liabilities and Taxpayer Penalties

There are many situations in which the tax law is either unclear or hard to apply to a given situation, and yet tax returns *must* get filed. Assume for a moment that you are asked to advise on whether a particularly aggressive tax position can be taken on the return. If you recommend taking the aggressive position, you expose the client to possible tax deficiencies, penalties, interest and the fees and expenses of cleaning up the situation with the IRS. You are exposed to malpractice liability if you are wrong, and yet you also have a duty to work diligently for the client. What follows is a survey of leading trouble spots for the client and the tax practitioner who advises on the preparation of a Federal Income Tax return that has significant errors.

First, how do the taxpayer and the tax return preparer share liability for defective returns? The lawyer who prepares the return, or even who provides advice on how to fill in an important line on a return, becomes a "tax return preparer" under §7701(a)(36)(A).[512] Subsection 6694(b) imposes a $5000 fraud or reckless disregard civil tax penalty, on "return preparers" and §7407 authorizes civil actions to enjoin wrongful tax return preparation activities, and §6694(a) imposes a $1000 "unrealistic position civil tax penalty." That is not the end of it by any means.[513] For one thing, you have to keep especially mum because §7216 imposes criminal sanctions for divulging tax return information. The return preparer penalties can head off aggressive tax planning:

> **To illustrate:** Flim-Flam, a lawyer, advises Gullible to invest in a especially aggressive tax shelter. Gullible asks her tax return preparer if the investment makes sense. The preparer is likely to say that he would not be willing to sign her tax return if that particular item were to make its way onto the return. Thus warned, Gullible would likely shy away from the investment.

The problem of preparing a questionable return is worsened by §6662 -- the accuracy-related penalty -- which imposes a major 20% penalty on a tax underpayment that is due to any of the following acts, although the taxpayer's disclosure of the specific tax issue can sometimes fend off a §6662 penalty, if there is a "reasonable basis" for the taxpayer's position.[514] It is the most common of the penalties (which collectively seem endless), so it is described in detail below.

1. *Negligence.* Negligence occurs if a tax return position does not have a reasonable basis or if the taxpayer fails to make a reasonable attempt to comply with the tax law, or if the taxpayer does not keep adequate books and records to substantiate items on the return.[515] One can sometimes "abate" -- meaning reduce or eliminate -- tax penalties by showing good faith reliance on the advice of a tax professional.[516]

---

512 An item at issue is considered insubstantial (unimportant) if it concerns gross income, deductions, or amounts on which a credit is based, of: (1) less than $10,000; or (2) less than $400,000 and also less than 20 percent of adjusted gross income (gross income for taxpayers who are not individuals) reported on the return or refund claim. Reg. §301.7701-15(b)(3)(ii)(A).

513 See, e.g., §§ 6060, 6107, 6695 (associated penalties).

514 Reg. §1.66621.

515 Reg. §1.66623(b)(1).

516 Chamberlain v. Commissioner, 66 F.3d 729, (5th Cir. 1995).

The advisor has to be reasonably confident of her tax position. For example, if she says there is a "plausible argument" that a regulation was invalid, and the taxpayers are sophisticated businessmen who deliberately ignored the regulation and made no disclosure on their returns, the defense collapses.[517] In cases where a disclosure can have a defensive effect, one has to put it front and center in the sense that one file the disclosure on IRS Form 8275, which has a chilling effect compared, for example, to slipping a few well-chosen words onto the bottom of a tax form. Disclosure is ineffective as a defense against the negligence or valuation misstatement components of the accuracy penalty.[518]

2. *Disregard of rules or regulations.* "Disregard" includes careless, reckless, or intentional disregard of the Code, Regulations, Revenue Rulings, or Notices. A position contrary to a Revenue Ruling or Notice does not disregard the Ruling or Notice if the position has a "realistic possibility of being sustained on its merits." The courts generally consider Rulings and Notices no more authoritative than a lawyer's opinion. A penalty based on disregard of the rules can be avoided by disclosure if the taxpayer maintains and substantiates adequate books and records. If a regulation is disregarded, however, disclosure will not avoid the penalty unless the taxpayer engaged in a sincere challenge to the validity of the regulation.[519]

3. *Substantial understatement of income tax.* Another basis for imposing the 20% "accuracy-related penalty" is a "substantial understatement" of Federal Income Tax, something that occurs if an income tax underpayment exceeds the greater of 10% of the tax due or $5,000 and the position giving rise to the underpayment lacks "substantial authority."[520] So what is "substantial authority?" That is not so easy. There is substantial authority if the weight of authorities supporting the position is substantial compared to authorities supporting a contrary position.[521] That means there may be substantial authority for more than one position. Essentially all governmentissued materials count, but privatelyissued material such as treatises, legal periodicals, and opinions of tax professionals do not count, an insular point of view. If there is no authority, then substantial authority may rest on a wellreasoned construction of the tax law. If the substantial understatement arises because of

517 Cramer v. Commissioner, 64 F.3d 1406, (9th Cir. 1995), cert. denied 1995.

518 Reg. §§ 1.66621, 1.66627(b).

519 Reg. §1.66623(c)(1).

520 Section 6662(d)(1).

521 Reg. §1.66624(d)(2).

a "tax shelter," tighter rules apply;[522] disclosure in such a case cannot avoid the penalty.

4. *Valuation misstatement.* There are major valuation misstatement penalties (ranging from 20% up to 40% of the underpayment of tax) that apply where income, pension, and estate or gift tax valuations exceed or fall below stated threshold limits.[523] The valuation misstatement component cannot be avoided by disclosure.[524]

In all cases, one can avoid the accuracy penalty if one can show there was reasonable cause for the underpayment and that the taxpayer acted in good faith.[525] Most civil tax penalties have a "reasonable cause" exception. The tougher penalty is for civil fraud under §6663, which imposes a whopping 75% penalty for a tax underpayment that is due to fraud.

M. LIMITATIONS ON BUSINESS LOSS DEDUCTIONS: THE PASSIVE LOSS RULES

Read in the following sequence §§ 469(a)(1), (d)(1), (c)(1)(2) and (7), then (h)(1)2, (b), (e)(1), then (g).

In numerous industrialized countries taxpayers cannot offset income from one source with losses from different sources. Countries with this rule are said to have a "scheduler system," in the sense that income and deductions fall onto different groupings ("schedules") that are quarantined from each other. To cite one example, in Sweden losses from running a business cannot offset income from other sources, such as salary. Instead, business losses are carried forward indefinitely, and can offset business income in later years.[526] Until recently, the United States took a much more relaxed view. Outside of the division between capital gains and ordinary income, the IRS basically allowed taxpayers to accumulate all their income and losses into a single net number. This relaxed attitude spawned considerable abuse of the income tax system and finally gave rise to §469, a rule that bears some resemblance to Sweden's.

Section 469 contains what has come to be known as the passive loss rules. It is the stake in the heart of the publicly syndicated tax shelter sold to individuals. It operates by deferring

522 Reg. §1.66624(g). For this purpose, a tax shelter includes any plan whose principal purpose is to avoid Federal Income Tax. Reg. §1.66624(g)(2), (3).

523 Section 6662(e), (f), and (g).

524 Reg. §1.66625(a).

525 §6664(c)(1); Reg. §1.66644(a).

526 H. Ault, COMPARATIVE INCOME TAXATION, 3d ed. (2010).

operating losses from rental activities and half-hearted business. It applies after the hobby loss rules and the at-risk rules (§§ 183 and 465).[527]

Section 469 counteracts two problems. One is that business activities of a partnership are imputed to their partners under §702 of the Code. The other is the generosity with which the case law treats a real estate owner as being engaged in business, thereby lavishing business expense deductions on such people. Think back to Mrs. Gilford, who owned shares of several Manhattan buildings used for stores and apartments. Apparently, her only business contact with her "rental business" was to appoint an agent to rent out the properties, collect the money and do the other things real estate lessors do.[528]Nevertheless, she was held to be in the real estate business. The passive loss rules retaliate by making rental activities of individuals *per se* "passive." The term "rental activity" is defined to mean an activity where the payments are principally for the use of tangible property, as opposed to services.[529] Rewriting a lease as a "service contract" will not do the trick; substance, not form, is in the driver's seat.[530]

> **To illustrate:** Entrepreneur owns a skybox at the local professional football stadium arena that she actively rents out at a loss. Might she be able to deduct those losses? Assume that anyone who has the right to use the skybox automatically gets tickets to the football games. Reg. §1.469-1T(e)(3)(i) defines a rental activity as one that primarily earns its income from renting tangible property (as opposed to, for example, rendering services). This is likely not a rental activity because the users mainly pay for the right to see baseball games, an entertainment service.

The key effect of §469 is to invent a new category of activity whose losses are "corralled" together, away from income of other types. The new category is the "passive activity," defined in §469(c)(1) as any trade or business activity in which the individual taxpayer does not "materially participate," including *all* rental activities (so much for Mrs. Gilford[531]) and activities attributed to investor limited partners in business partnerships.[532] "Material participation" means "regular, continuous and substantial" involvement in the business. This sorts out the investors from the real doers, and ties up investors' losses in §469's cobweb of limiting rules. In all cases, the activities of agents are generally not imputed to their principals. This keeps the taxpayer

527 See "IRS Releases MSSP Audit Guide for Passive Activity Losses," 96 Tax Notes 110-27 (June 3, 1996).

528 Gilford v. Commissioner, 201 F.2d 735 (2d Cir. 1953).

529 §469(j)(8).

530 Reg. §1.469-1T(e)(3)(i)(B).

531 There is an exception, seen later for people who have less than stellar adjusted gross incomes who can deduct up to $25,000 of loses for rental properties they actively manage, but it seems Mrs. Gilford would not have qualified. She was too rich and too passive. There is a further exception for real estate professionals. They devote substantial time to supervising the real estate business.

532 §469(c)(2).

from sitting back and letting someone else do the work and claiming tax losses based on the sweat off other peoples' brows.[533]

If the taxpayer has several "passive activities" (say an apartment building which she personally rents, plus an ownership interest in a publicly syndicated tax shelter), then she can offset the profits from one passive activity against the losses of the other.[534] If the taxpayer's passive activity losses ("PALs") more than offset the profits from other passive activities, the net amount is put in suspense by §469(a) and is carried forward under §469(b) to later years, when they are subject to the same limits as before.[535]

So what do we have now? The visual answer is that all income is broken up into four columns, with §469 losses cordoned off:

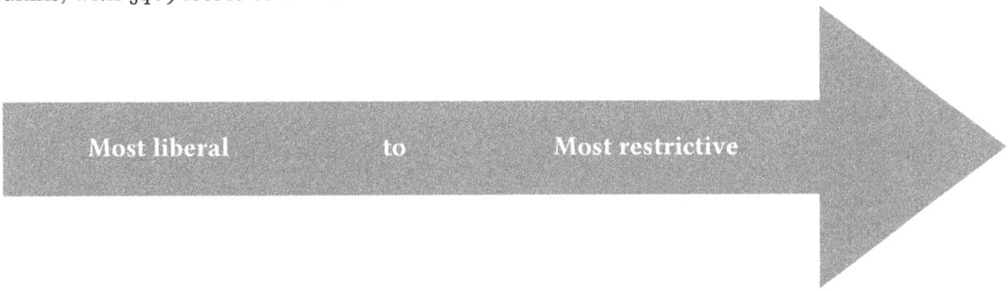

Ordinary losses §165	**Portfolio losses §469(e)**	**Capital losses§1211**	**Passive losses §469**
Ordinary losses can offset:	Portfolio losses can offset:	Capital losses can offset:	Passive losses can offset:
Ordinary income	Ordinary income	Ordinary income but only up to $3,000	
		Passive income if the passive income is also a capital gain	Passive income
Portfolio income	Portfolio income	Portfolio income up to $3,000	
Capital gains	Capital gains	Capital gains	

533 See General Explanation of the Tax Reform Act of 1986 as prepared by the Staff of the Joint Committee on Taxation (May 4, 1987), www.jct.gov/jvc_10_87.pdf.

534 See §469(d)(1).

535 §469(b).

Ordinary income §61	Portfolio income §469(e)	Capital gains §165	Passive income §469
Ordinary income can absorb:	Portfolio income can absorb:	Capital gains can offset:	Passive income can offset:
Ordinary losses	Ordinary losses	Ordinary losses	Ordinary losses
			Passive losses
Portfolio losses	Portfolio losses	Portfolio losses	Portfolio losses
Capital losses, only up to $3,000	Capital losses, only up to $3,000	Capital losses	Capital losses, only up to $3,000

Overall, §469 seems to have done its job. Tax shelters are no longer hawked to the public, subject to some exceptions, most notably:

1) Oil and gas investments that do not protect the investor from operating risks; and

2) Investments purchased by widelyheld business corporations -- by far the more exploited exception (perhaps this is more of a "truckhole" than an exception).

Another exception operates along industry (i.e., special interest) lines; §469(c)(7) exempts real estate professionals such as real estate agents and brokers from §469 in the sense of declaring that their real estate rental activities are not *presumed* to be inactive. This is craven special interest legislation.

The passive activity loss system is not confiscatory. It is essentially a timing limit. One arrives at this inference by inspection of the key rule that taxpayers can deduct all their suspended losses when they dispose of their investments in a passive activity to unrelated persons in fully taxable transactions.[536] If the disposition yields a gain, the gain first offsets the suspended passive losses, and then the remainder of the suspended losses are available to offset regular income.[537] On the other hand, taxpayers cannot use their pure investment income (such as interest) to offset their passive losses, because otherwise §469 would be easily avoided by wealthy taxpayers who could reshuffle their investments to cancel their passive activity losses with investment income. This restriction appears in §469(e)(1), which hauls out income from "portfolio" investments (a.k.a., "portfolio income") from the definition of passive income. However, if one can find a former tax shelter that now operates at a profit, that income may be quite handy indeed for offsetting one's passive losses from other sources. Such an asset is popularly known as a "passive income generator", or "P.I.G."

536 §469(g).

537 §469(g)(1)(A).

To illustrate: Dr. DeSoto, a dentist, invested in a real estate tax shelter some years ago. All he really knows about it is that long ago he sent a check for $20,000 to a stock brokerage firm and that he was promised that he would get to deduct $10,000 per year of depreciation on an apartment building for about 10 years, after which the building (located far away) would be sold at a gain. Recently, he has learned that §469 may be a problem. Dr. DeSoto's net income from his orthodontic practice is $150,000 per year. He also has $5,000 per year of income from cash dividends on stocks he invested in. Because of §469 he is faced with the following problems:

1. The $10,000 per year loss is suspended. Only if and to the extent he has "passive business income" or net rental income from other passive activities or rental properties ("passive income generators") or disposes of the entire shelter in a taxable transaction, can he deduct and use the $10,000 loss.

2. The $5,000 of investment income will not be offset by the passive activity loss because it is "portfolio" income.

3. He can carry forward the suspended $10,000 passive activity loss indefinitely. Because the loss is from rental property, no matter how much he participates, he cannot make the loss from the partnership "active" so as to allow the losses. He will pine for a "passive income generator" to absorb his deferred passive losses.[538]

Members of the middle class who own rental property that they operate as a sideline business enjoy special tax relief. If they own at least 10% of the interests in a rental real estate activity in which they "actively participate," §469 lets them offset up to $25,000 of such losses against investment or service income. Active participation is a good deal less strenuous than "material participation."

The technical reason why only the middle class enjoys this benefit is that §469(i)(3) phases out the $25,000 exemption by half of the taxpayer's adjusted gross income in excess of $100,000. Thus, the phaseout starts at $100,000 and creeps upward until, at AGI of $150,000, the $25,000 exception evaporates completely.

A few other high points:

1. Section 469 also applies to passively created tax credits, except for certain low-income housing credits; and

2. The activities of spouses are attributed to each other, a pro-taxpayer rule.

538 His best bets will be to invest in a profitable S corporation or a real estate partnership that generates a profit from its rental income.

Beyond these basic rules lies a thicket of definitions and selective relaxations of the rules, all of which are beyond the scope of this book.

Problem 6-12:

Alice Friendly is a lawyer who resides in Florida and is who unmarried. At the end of the dock is her 30-foot sloop, the SS Friendly, which she busily rents out on a weekly basis. People who rent the boat take it out alone. Her annual gross income from the charters is $5,000 and her expenses are as follows:

Insurance	$ 500.00
Maintenance	800.00
Fuel	100.00
Depreciation	6,000.00
Total expenses	$7,400.00

1) Assuming she has a *bona fide* profit intent, and that she materially participates in the business, to what extent can she deduct her losses? $2,400? Something else?

2) Same as "(1)", but she also has a limited partnership interest[539] in which she is passive. It generates $1,000 of profits this year. What impact, if any, do the passive profits have on her losses in "(1)"?

3) Assume she owns the limited partnership interest described in "(2)," but in year two, her boat operation nets her $2,000 and her partnership continues to generate $1,000 of profit. How much income or loss will the combined activities cause to be reported on her tax return? See §469(f)(1) and (3).

4) Assume the same facts as in "(1)" alone, but at the very beginning of year two she sells the boat for a $1,000 gain to an unrelated person. What will be the impact of the sale in year two? See §469(g).

5) Assume the same facts as in "(1)" alone except that the property is a condominium unit in her home town that she actively manages and that her adjusted gross income is $125,000. Is there any difference in result? See §469(i).

539 Section 469(i)(7) renders limited partners per se passive, but allows room in the regulations for exceptions. Reg. §1.469-5T(e)(2) contains the point of entry to the exceptions, cross-referencing Reg. §1.469-5T(a)(1), (5) and (6).

6) Assume the same facts as in "(1)" alone except that she dies at the very beginning of year two. Assume the boat's value at the time of her death was $1,000 greater than its basis in her hands. See §469(g)(2).

7) Assume the same facts as in "(1)" alone except that the boat operation has its own checking account that pays interest and that the interest on the account is $100 in the first year. Can she offset the passive loss with the interest from the bank account? See §469(e)(1)(A)(i).

N. FINANCIAL ANALYSIS

You are now far enough along in the course to put what you have learned about income taxation into an advanced framework by integrating the materials to date with the tools of finance taught in business schools. This information is presented as part of a tax course, but it applies across the board in business settings. The objective of the material is to show how financial people decide whether or not to recommend an investment. Obviously, there are many other reasons to make an investment aside from the pure financial return, but the financial return is often the key factor, and the impact of taxes is a key component of financial return.

It used to be that business people often evaluated their investments on the basis of the "payback period," meaning the amount of time it takes to get back one's investment the shorter the better. Things have changed markedly since then, and lawyers are often among the last to catch up, given that they frequently come from backgrounds in the arts and humanities and may get cold sweats when numbers are presented to them. This is unfortunate, and the next few pages will try to do something about the problem, using straightforward language. These "time value of money" concepts you are about to see are important in the tax area for two reasons:

1. Congress now understands that tax law has to keep up with the increasingly sophisticated technology of tax avoidance by enacting appropriately advanced legislation; and

2. Business and professional people use these tools in their daily lives and expect their lawyers -- even litigators settling a complex case -- to be able to keep up.

To today's financial wizards, the payback period is an antique. Today's focus is on compounding and discounting cash receipts and disbursements in current and future years. The wizards are right that without such analysis, one cannot rationally evaluate investment opportunities, including those designed purely to minimize taxes. Indeed, without a "time value of money" analysis, one often cannot even rank alternative opportunities. On the other hand, quantitative techniques are imperfect and incomplete tools. For one thing, they call for an estimate, inherently impossible, of a theoretical alternative investment opportunity (often referred to as an "external rate of return"), stated as an after-tax percentage rate of return. Estimates are only estimates. Second, they fail to account for such factors as risk and the taxpayer's liquidity needs.

Compounding of interest. The most important idea is the simplest: a dollar today is worth more than a dollar tomorrow.As a result, people charge money for the use of money. There are a variety of ways to state the interest charge the borrower pays, the most important aspect of which is whether the interest is "compounded," meaning that there is interest on the unpaid amount, plus further interest on the unpaid interest, et cetera ad nauseam. The practical effect of compounding is that interest is applied to an ever-increasing principal. If the debt obligation does call for compounding of interest, then the second key aspect is whether the compounding period is performed annually or more often. More frequent compounding at any stated rate of interest earns the lender more money than mere annual compounding. One of the simplest forms of frequent compounding is semi-annual (twice per year) compounding. Of course, the higher the rate and the longer the investment period, the larger the returns. Albert Einstein was reportedly startled by the power of compounding. One version of his remark is, "Compound interest is the eighth wonder of the world."[540]

Here is a fairly easy way to understand how to compute semi-annual compounding using symbols. Take the principal you own (P), divide it in two and apply the interest rate (I) to it. That tells you what you are entitled to at the middle of the year (P/2 x I). At the end of the year apply the interest rate (I) to half of [(P/2 x I) + P/2]. That tells you how much interest you are entitled to for the second half of the year. The sum of these two numbers is the interest for the year. It will always be higher than mere annual compounding at the same rate of annual interest.

This exercise is useful because the Code dictates the use of semi-annual compounding for various purposes. One has to wonder why, in such an imperfect world, the IRS insists on semi-annual compounding, but we have to live with it.

Here is a semi-annual compound interest table for 5 percent interest and 10 percent interest for 10 years. "0" means the moment the loan was made and "1" is exactly one year later. For example, at the moment the loan is made ("0" under "Date"), the debtor owes the creditor no interest, only the principal. At the end of the first year, using 5% compounded semi-annually, the debtor owes the creditor the principal plus 5.062% of the principal (the interest).

For example, $10,000 compounded semi-annually at 10% yields roughly $26,533 in 10 years in a world without taxes. Now, look at the table to understand the basic concept of compounding, if it was not clear to you already.

540 "Managing bonds in today's rate environment," Pensions and Investments (Crain Comm. April 18, 1984), p.28.

Discounting. Discounting is compounding in reverse. It refers to reducing future amounts, be they receipts or disbursements, by some rate of interest in order to determine the value (or cost) of a receipt (or disbursement) in today's dollars. Without discounting, the economic fact of "futurity" is hopelessly obscured. By way of illustration, $26,533 in hand in 10 years discounted at a semi-annual compound rate of 10% equates to $10,000 now, in a world without taxes. The higher the assumed rate of interest, the less a dollar received in the future is worth. You can tell it from looking at the table under the 10% column. By contrast, if the discount rate were 5%, then $16,386.20 received 10 years from now would be $10,000 today.

Table	**Semi-annual Compound Interest**	
Year	5%	10%
0	1	1
.5	1.025	1.05
1	1.05062	1.1025
1.5	1.07689	1.15763
2	1.10381	1.21551
2.5	1.13141	1.27628
3	1.15969	1.3401
3.5	1.18869	1.4071
4	1.2184	1.47746
4.5	1.24886	1.55133
5	1.28008	1.62889
5.5	1.31209	1.71034
6	1.34489	1.79586
6.5	1.37851	1.88565
7	1.41297	1.87993
7.5	1.4483	2.07893
8	1.48451	2.18287
8.5	1.52162	2.29202
9	1.55966	2.40662
9.5	1.59865	2.52695
10	1.63862	2.6533

Now for some applications. Assume you live in Paradise and everyone agrees that the right and honorable rate of interest is 5% compounded semi-annually. Paradise is a land of conformists.

A simple inference from inspecting the tables is that if someone in Paradise borrows $1,000 from you now and promises to pay you the right rate of interest a year later, you know you ought to receive exactly $1,050.62 a year later. Conversely, if The Bank of Paradise made a special offer to its depositors to pay $1,103.81 in two years per $1,000 deposited today, you would know that the offer was reasonable, because it was the right and honorable 5% compounded semi-annually.

The concept of "present value." The value of a dollar tomorrow stated in today's dollars is the "present value" of the future dollar. For example, the present value of $1,484.51 payable 8 years from now in Paradise is $1,000 at the discount rate of 5%, compounded semi-annually. The term "present value" is synonymous with the term "discounted present value." Again, discounting (reducing future amounts to today's values) is the reverse of compounding, which builds today's dollars into future dollars.

Problem 6-13:

1) You operate in an environment in which you can earn 5% compounded semi-annually after taxes and no more. If someone promised you $1,638.62 at the end of 10 years, what would you pay today for that promise, assuming you knew you could trust the promisor?

2) Assume instead you had cash of $1,000 and that you were offered $1,344.89 payable at the end of year 6 to lend it.

   a. Would you agree to the deal?

   b. What would you agree to if you had other investment opportunities that paid 10% compounded semi-annually?

3) You have a chance to defer $163,862 of income taxes for 10 years. You operate in an environment in which you can earn 5% compounded semi-annually after taxes. What is the present value (really meaning cost in today's dollars) of the deferred tax bill? Would you be willing to pay a large fee to a tax professional who could tell you how to defer the tax? Give a dollar amount and explain why.

Application of Compounding, Discounting and "Present Values" to Financial Decision-Making

Nowadays, financial decision-making generally relies on stripping transactions down to their "cash flows" over the period of the investment. To take a simple example, if you bought a piece of raw land today for $60 and expected to sell it for $100 in six years, you would have only two cash flow events -- the purchase and the sale.

Once the cash flows have been established, one discounts them all into the present, but by what interest factor? *The answer is the rate of return after tax that the tax payer thinks she can safely make on an after-tax basis.*

External Rate of Return

Selecting an assumed interest rate (known as an "external rate of return") is nettlesome, because inflation and general rates of interest are impossible to fix. Nonetheless, there are only a few basic choices. One is simply to select the rate of interest available on highly rated taxfree municipal bonds. While this may be appropriate for a highbracket taxpayer, the lowerbracket taxpayer should consider instead the rate available on an aftertax basis from a taxable investment (e.g., money market funds or bonds with a high rating issued for a term equal to the term of the proposed investment). When evaluating an investment it is important to use an aftertax external rate of return, something done from here on.

> **To illustrate:** Raymond Renovator is in the 25% marginal tax bracket. He has an interesting investment opportunity which will provide a taxfavored investment return for four years. Ray believes he can safely earn 13.33% in taxable fouryear bonds; hence, he might use an after-tax external rate of return of 10% (i.e., 75% of 13.33%) in evaluating the investment.

The application of an aftertax net present value analysis tells an investor whether the proposed use of funds is financially sensible. This involves estimating the period over which the investment will take place (e.g., five years) and determining what the aftertax cash receipts and disbursements, including the original investment, will be in each such year.

Next, each such aftertax item of inflow or disbursement is discounted to the present by the external rate of return. If the result is positive, then the proposal is prima facie worthwhile because it exceeds the external rate return by which the cash flows were discounted.

> **To illustrate:** The same Raymond Renovator has prospered. He is now in the 40% bracket. A promoter has offered him a chance to invest $12,000 at the beginning of the year in a residential housing partnership. Assume losses from the partnership are legally deductible. He will pay and

receive nothing further for the next four years, but will get depreciation deductions of $3,000 per year at the end of years 1 through 4, which will result in a tax saving of $1,200 per year (i.e., $3,000 times 40%). At the end of year 4, the property will be sold for its purchase price, as a result of which Renovator will receive cash of $12,000 and will pay a $3,000 tax (i.e., $12,000 capital gain times 25% tax rate),[541] so his *net* receipt at the end of year four on the sale will be $9,000 (i.e. $12,000 cash minus $3,000 tax). Assume Renovator has the same aftertax external rate of 10%. He evaluates the project as follows (the amounts in brackets are disbursements; the others are receipts in cash or in the form of taxes saved):

Year	Action	After-tax Cash Flow (ATCF)	Discounted ATCF at 10%
one	Investment	($12,000)	($12,000)
one	Tax Benefit	$1200	$1,080
two	Tax Benefit	$1200	$972
three	Tax Benefit	$1200	$875
four	Tax Benefit	$1200	$787
Subtotal of Tax Benefit		$4800	$3714
four	Net proceeds from sale	$9000	$5,905
Subtotal of tax benefits and sales proceeds		$13,800	$9619
Net after taking account of the original $12,000 investment		$1800	($2,381)

Conclusion: The first column shows there is a profit of $1,800 from the deal, but that is an almost worthless observation. The second column shows the aftertax net present value of the deal is negative. Renovator should avoid the investment. If it is zero he would be indifferent to the project; if it is over zero he should take it seriously, and rank it against other projects that he has the chance to invest in.

Internal Rate of Return

Consideration of Renovator's opportunity leads to the next topic, the internal rate of return. This tool enables taxpayers to rank alternative investments. The net aftertax discounting

541 The 25% tax rate is correctly based on the assumption that the full gain is based on prior depreciation. A later Chapter takes up the details of capital gains taxes.

technique merely enables taxpayers to determine whether an investment is acceptable in light of a hypothesized baseline, the external rate of return. The internal rate of return analysis is much the same as for discounting; cash flows must first be established on a periodbyperiod basis. The next step is to infer an aftertax rate of return that gives the overall investment a $0 discounted cash flow value. That discovered rate is the internal rate of return.

> **To illustrate:** Returning to Renovator's case, what aftertax compound rate of return will equate the positive cash flows following the investment with the original $12,000 investment (the negative cash flow)? In other words, what is the discount rate that makes the net present value of all the cash flows equal zero? The answer is somewhat over 3%. For Renovator, it is a rotten internal rate of return and therefore a rotten project.

Knowing the internal rate of return, taxpayers can rank projects offering equal risk but different returns.[542] This procedure can apply to tax driven investments because tax savings and tax costs are part of cash flow. Carefully honed discounted net cash flow and internal rate of return analyses offer objective measures of just how valuable those tax impacts can be.

O. DEDUCTIONS FOR EXPENDITURES FOR EDUCATION

Read Reg. §1.1625(a)(c), but not the examples.

1. Deductions under Section §162

The rules in this area are fairly simple, but they raise a difficult tax policy question about what one is supposed to do about longterm investments in human capital. In general, the Code takes a grudging view of educational expense deductions, generally treating them as personal expenses designed to improve the person as a whole rather than as a currently deductible business expense. The deep issue in the area is whether the tax system is too stingy with respect to allowing deductions for educational expenses that are really a cost of producing future income, such as the cost of getting a law or medical degree.

How about the educational expense of investors? Educational costs incurred by an investor should also be deductible under §212, but §274(h)(7) carves back the deduction by saying:

542 Unfortunately, there are difficulties with the internal rate of return analysis. For one thing, negative future cash flows cannot be accounted for except by reintroducing rate assumptions. The easiest solution is to factor out negative cash flows by discounting them to a present value and adding them to the initial cost of the investment.

To illustrate: If Renovator expected to invest $10,000 now, and to have positive cash flows in all years other than the third year, in which he expected a $1,000 negative cash flow, he would increase his investment by $1,000 discounted at his compounded external rate (10%), which would have the effect of increasing his initial investment by about $751. He would then be free to perform the analysis needed to generate the internal rate of return.

No deduction shall be allowed under section 212 for expenses allocable to a convention, seminar, or similar meeting.

So much for deducting an investment seminar at a ski resort.

2. Maintaining Skills or New Trade or Business?

Educational expenses that the taxpayer incurs in order to sharpen or maintain skills needed for work are deductible, but if they qualify the taxpayer for a new trade or business, Reg. §1.162-5 renders them nondeductible. This barrier applies to expenses incurred to meet minimum educational expenses required to gain an entry-level position (such as requiring a substitute teacher to get a teaching certificate in order to get a full-time position) or that qualifies the taxpayer for a new trade or business (such as a law degree). The former limit is often a problem for temporary or provisional employees who are forced to continue their education in order to be permanently employed.

What, then, is a new trade or business? Few people have exactly the same job for life. At what point is a change of job description a new line of business, so that expenses for training in that new line are nondeductible? Reg. §1.1625(b)(3)(i)(ii) offers some guidance. In addition, there is a patchwork of cases. Here are some examples of where a deduction was allowed:

1. Lawyer already practicing tax law gets an LLM in tax.[543]

2. Lawyer gets a general LLM.[544]

3. Adult education discussion leader gets M.A. in Psychology.[545]

4. Assistant District Attorney takes Spanish lessons to be able to interview Spanish-speaking witnesses and victims.[546]

5. A teacher trains to be a guidance counselor or principal. Reg. §1.162-5(b)(3)(c)-(d). That this generous position shows a preference for the teaching profession was the

543 Compare Cobb v. Commissioner, 35 T.C.M. 1480 (1976) (educational expense deduction allowed for getting tax LLM) with Wassenaar v. Commissioner, 72 T.C. 1195 (1979) (law graduate not yet in practice; deduction denied). See also Johnson v. United States, 332 F. Supp. 906 E.D. La.1971), Adamson v. Commissioner, 32 T.C.M. 484 (1973) and. PLR 9112003 .

544 Ruehmann v. Commissioner, 30 T.C.M. 675 (1971).

545 Schwerm v. Commissioner, 51 T.C.M. 270 (1986).

546 Kosmal v. Commissioner, 39 T.C.M. 651 (1979), affirmed 670 F.2d 842 (CA9 1982).

basis for an unsuccessful Constitutional objection by an accountant who was denied deductions for getting a law degree.[547]

Conversely, in *Robinson v. Commissioner,* 78 T.C. 550 (1982) a licensed practical nurse working in Minnesota who had only one year of training, was held to have gone into a new "trade or business" when she became a registered nurse, following three more years of training. The reasoning was that she had greater responsibilities as a result of the hospital's rules and Minnesota law, including her new rights to supervise licensed practical nurses, exercise greater medical judgment, and take verbal drug orders from doctors. Her educational achievement led to a denial of her claims to deductions for educational expenses incurred in those extra three years of study. It was a fairly close case that used a traditional analysis of authority and responsibilities before and after the education to evaluate whether she entered a new trade or business. The ax has also fallen on an intern pharmacist[548] who became a registered pharmacist and a teacher of disabled children who became a social worker,[549] to name just a few.

You might want to pay special attention to the next case, because one of these days it is likely to affect you.

SHARON v. COMMISSIONER

66.T.C. 515 (1976)

SIMPSON, Judge.

[Joel A. Sharon graduated from Brandeis in 1961 and then Columbia Law School, from which he graduated in 1964. He took his first job with a New York law firm and in 1967 went to work for the IRS in California, where he was under various restrictions that limited his ability to practice law. Later, he was admitted to the California bar. He sought to deduct various items:

$ 11,125 to obtain a college degree;

$ 6,910 to obtain a law school degree;

$ 175.20 to take the New York bar review courses;

$ 25 to take the New York State bar examination;

$ 230 to take a California bar review course;

$ 571 to take the California bar examination;

$ 11 for the privilege of practicing before two Federal courts in California; and

$ 313.35 in obtaining a license to practice before the U.S. Supreme Court.]

547 See Taubman . Commissioner, 60 T.C. 814 (1973).

548 Antozoulatos v. Commissioner, T.C. Memo. 1975-327.

549 Burnstein v. Commissioner, 66 TC 492 (1976).

OPINION

. . .

2. Amortization of License to Practice Law in New York

The next issue to be decided is whether the petitioner may amortize the cost of obtaining his license to practice law in New York. The petitioner contends that he is entitled under section 167 to amortize the cost of such license over the period from the date of his admission to the bar to the date on which he reaches age 65, when he expects to retire. In his cost basis of this "intangible asset," he included the costs of obtaining his college degree ($ 11,125), obtaining his law degree ($ 6,910), a bar review course and related materials ($ 175.20), and the New York State bar examination fee ($ 25). As justification for including these education expenses in the cost of his license, he points out that, in order to take the New York bar examination, he was required to have graduated from college and an accredited law school.

The petitioners rely upon section 1.167(a)3 of the Income Tax Regulations, which provides in part:

> If an intangible asset is known from experience or other factors to be of use in the business or in the production of income for only a limited period, the length of which can be estimated with reasonable accuracy, such an intangible asset may be the subject of a depreciation allowance. . . .

There is no merit in the petitioner's claim to an amortization deduction for the cost of his education and related expenses in qualifying himself for the legal profession. His college and law school expenses provided him with a general education which will be beneficial to him in a wide variety of ways. See James A. Carroll, 51 T.C. 213, 216 (1968). The costs and responsibility for obtaining such education are personal. Section 1.2621(b)(9) of the Income Tax Regulations provides that expenditures for education are deductible only if they qualify under section 162 and section 1.1625 of the regulations. In the words of section 1.1625(b), all costs of "minimum educational requirements for qualification in . . . employment" are "personal expenditures or constitute an inseparable aggregate of personal and capital expenditures." There is no "rational" or workable basis for any allocation of this inseparable aggregate between the nondeductible personal component and a deductible component of the total expense. Fausner v. Commissioner, 413 U.S. 838, 839 (19). Such expenses are not made any less personal or any more separable from the aggregate by attempting to capitalize them for amortization purposes. David N. Bodley, 56 T.C. 1357, 1362 (1971); . . . . Since the inseparable aggregate includes personal expenditures, the preeminence of section 262 over section 167 precludes any amortization deduction. . . . The same reasoning applies to the costs of review courses and related expenses taken to qualify for the practice of a profession. William D. Glenn, 62 T.C. 270, 274276 (1974).

In his brief, the petitioner attempts to distinguish our opinion in Denman by asserting that he is not attempting to capitalize his educational costs, but rather, the cost of his license to practice law. Despite the label which the petitioner would apply to such costs, they nonetheless constitute the costs of his education, which are personal and nondeductible. Moreover, in his petition, he alleged that the capital asset he was seeking to amortize was his education.

There remains the $ 25 fee paid for the petitioner's license to practice in New York. This was not an educational expense but was a fee paid for the privilege of practicing law in New York, a nontransferable license which has value beyond the taxable years, and such fee is a capital expenditure. Cf. Arthur E. Ryman, Jr., 51 T.C. 799 (1969); Glenn L. Heigerick, 45 T.C. 475 (1966); S.M. Howard, 39 T.C. 833 (1963); O.D. 452, 2 C.B. 157 (1920). The Commissioner has limited his argument to the educational expenses and apparently concedes that the fee may be amortized. Since the amount of the fee is small, the petitioner might, ordinarily, be allowed to elect to deduct the full amount of the fee in the year of payment, despite its capital nature. Cf. sec. 1.16212(a), Income Tax Regs., with respect to the treatment of inexpensive tools. However, since the fee was paid prior to the years in issue, we cannot allow a current deduction in this case. Therefore, in view of the Commissioner's concession and our conclusion with respect to the third and fourth issues, a proportionate part of such fee may be added to the amounts to be amortized in accordance with our resolution of the third issue.

3. License to Practice Law in California

The next issue to be decided is whether the petitioner may deduct or amortize the expenses he incurred in gaining admission to practice before the State and Federal courts of California. The Commissioner disallowed the amounts paid in 1969 to take the attorney's bar examination in California and the amounts paid for admission to the bar of the U.S. District Court for the Northern District of California and for admission to the U.S. Court of Appeals for the Ninth Circuit. He determined that such expenses were capital expenditures. In his brief, the petitioner argues for a current deduction only if the costs of his license to practice in California are not amortizable.

It is clear that the petitioner may not deduct under section 162(a) the fees paid to take the California attorney's bar examination and to gain admission to practice before two Federal courts in California. In Arthur E. Ryman, Jr., supra, an associate professor of law sought to deduct as an ordinary business expense the cost of his admission to the bar of the State in which he resided. We held that since the taxpayer could reasonably expect the useful life of his license to extend beyond 1 year, the cost of such license was a capital expenditure and not a currently deductible business expense. Unlike the small fee paid to New York, the aggregate amount of such payments in 1969 is too large to disregard their capital nature and allow the petitioners to deduct them currently.

In connection with his alternative claim that he be allowed to amortize the costs of acquiring his license to practice law in California, the petitioner asserts that such costs total $ 801. Such amount includes the cost of a California bar review course, registration fees, and other items specified in our Findings of Fact. However, the petitioner is in error in including the cost of his bar review course, $ 230, in the capital cost of his license to practice in California.

It is clear that the amount the petitioner paid for the bar review course was an expenditure "made by an individual for education" within the meaning of section 1.1625(a) of the Income Tax Regulations. See William D. Glenn, 62 T.C. 270, 2274 (1974); sec. 1.1625(b)(2)(iii), example (3), Income Tax Regs. Although the petitioner was authorized to practice law in some jurisdictions when he took the California bar review course, such course was nevertheless educational in the same sense as the first bar review course. The deductibility of such educational expenses is governed by the rules of section 1.1625 of the regulations. The evidence indicates that the petitioner took the California bar examination twice, the latter time in early 1969, so that the payment for the California bar review course must have been made in a year prior to 1969. Thus, even if such payment is otherwise deductible, it may not be deducted in 1969.

Nor may the petitioner treat the payment for the California bar review course as a part of the costs of acquiring his license to practice in California. Educational expenses which are incurred to meet the minimum educational requirements for qualification in a taxpayer's trade or business or which qualify him for a new trade or business are "personal expenditures or constitute an inseparable aggregate of personal and capital expenditures." Sec. 1.1625(b), Income Tax Regs. We find that the bar review course helped to qualify the petitioner for a new trade or business so that its costs are personal expenses.

We have previously adopted a "common sense approach" in determining whether an educational expenditure qualifies a taxpayer for a "new trade or business." Kenneth C. Davis, 65 T.C. 1014, 1019 (1976). . . . If the education qualifies the taxpayer to perform significantly different tasks and activities than he could perform prior to the education, then the education qualifies him for a new trade or business. William D. Glenn, supra; Ronald F. Weiszmann, supra. Thus, we have held that a professor of social work is in a different trade or business than a social caseworker. Kenneth C. Davis, supra. a licensed public accountant is in a different trade or business than a certified public accountant. William D. Glenn, supra. a registered pharmacist is in a different trade or business than an intern pharmacist, even though an intern performs many of the same tasks as a registered pharmacist, but under supervision. Gary Antzoulatos, T.C. Memo. 1975327.

Before taking the bar review course and passing the attorney's bar examination, the petitioner was an attorney licensed to practice law in New York. As an attorney for the Regional Counsel, he could represent the Commissioner in this Court. However, he could not appear in either the State courts of California, the Federal District Courts located there, nor otherwise act as an attorney outside the scope of his employment with the IRS. . . . If he had done so, he would have been guilty of a misdemeanor. Cal. Bus. & Prof. Code sec. 6126 (West 1974). Yet, after receiving his license to practice law in California, he became a member of the State bar with all its accompanying privileges and obligations. He could appear and represent clients in all the courts of California. By comparing the tasks and activities that the petitioner was qualified to perform prior to receiving his license to practice in California with the tasks and activities he was able to perform after receiving such license, it is clear that he has qualified for a new trade or business. Consequently, the expenses of his bar review course were personal and are not includable in the cost of his license to practice law in California.

It is true that even before he became a member of the bar of California, the petitioner was engaged in the business of practicing law. . . . However, in applying the provisions of section 1.1625 of the regulations to determine whether educational expenses are personal or business in nature, it is not enough to find that the petitioner was already engaged in some business we must ascertain the particular business in which he was previously engaged and whether the education qualified him to engage in a different business. Before taking the bar review course and becoming a member of the bar of California, the petitioner could not generally engage in the practice of law in that State, but the bar review course helped to qualify him to engage in such business.

The Commissioner does not argue that the capital expenditures incurred in obtaining his license to practice law in California may not be amortized. In a series of cases, the courts have held that the fees paid by physicians to acquire hospital privileges are not current business expenses but are capital expenditures amortizable over the doctor's life expectancy. Walters v. Commissioner, 383 F.2d 922, 924 (6th Cir. 1967) . . . . We hold that the petitioner may treat the costs of acquiring his license to practice in California in a similar manner. Such costs include:

Registration fee	$20
General bar exam fee	150
Attorney's bar exam	375
Admittance fee	26
U.S. District Court fee	6
U.S. Court of Appeals	5
Total	582

Although the petitioner testified that he would retire at age 65 if he were financially able to do so, such testimony is not sufficient to establish the shorter useful life for which he argues.

We are aware that the petitioner's business as an employee of the Office of Regional Counsel did not require him to become a member of the California bar, and it may be argued that, within the meaning of section 167(a)(1), this intangible asset was not "used" in the petitioner's business during 1969 and 1970. However, the record does demonstrate that membership in the California bar was of some assistance to the petitioner in those years. Furthermore, when an attorney commences the practice of law, it is impossible to anticipate where his work will take him. He cannot with certainty establish what work he will receive and what bar memberships will be useful to him. Once he launches into the practice of law, he must decide what bars to join, and so long as there is some rational connection between his present or prospective work and those that he joins, we think that the expenses of joining them should be accepted as an appropriate cost of acquiring the necessary licenses to practice his profession. Since in 1969 and 1970, the petitioner was working in California, he had reason to anticipate that he might eventually leave the Government and enter into the private practice of law in that State; thus, when that possibility is considered together with the immediate benefit to be derived from membership in the California bar, there was ample reason for him to join such bar at that time. For these reasons, we are satisfied that in 1969 and 1970, the petitioner did make use of the tangible asset constituting the privilege of practicing law in California.

4. Supreme Court Admission

The fourth issue to be decided is whether the petitioner may either deduct amortize the cost of gaining admission to practice before the U.S. Supreme Court. The petitioner deducted the travel costs he incurred in 1970 in traveling to Washington, D.C., to be personally present for the Supreme Court admission, as required by that Court's rules. The Commissioner disallowed the deduction and argued in his brief that such expenditures were capital in nature since the petitioner acquired an asset with a useful life beyond 1 year.

In his brief, the petitioner concedes that he may not deduct the costs he incurred if we find that his license to practice before the Supreme Court is an intangible asset with a useful life of more than 1 year. For the same reasons that we have concluded that the petitioner's New York and California licenses were intangible assets with a useful life of more than 1 year, we also hold that his Supreme Court license is an intangible asset with a useful life exceeding 1 year. Thus, the petitioner may not deduct under section 162 the cost of obtaining such license.

In order for such license to be amortizable pursuant to section 167, the petitioner must show that it was property used in his trade or business. There is little evidence concerning the petitioner's "use" in 1970 of his license to practice before the Supreme Court. However, he did testify that the admission to various bars was a factor used in evaluating attorneys for promotion by his employer, and the Commissioner never disputed such testimony. Furthermore, it is altogether appropriate for any attorneyatlaw to become a member of the bar of the Supreme Court whenever it is convenient for him to do so. No one can know when the membership in such bar may be useful to him in the practice of law it may bring tangible benefits today, tomorrow, or never; yet, if one holds himself out to practice law, there is ample reason for him to acquire membership in the bar of the Supreme Court. Under these circumstances, we find that the intangible asset acquired by becoming a member of such bar was used by the petitioner in 1970 and hold that he may amortize the costs of acquiring such asset over his life expectancy.

. . .

To reflect the foregoing,

Decisions will be entered under Rule 155.

[Scott, J. dissented on the ground that one should not amortize the $571, $11 or $313.35 because there was no showing of a reasonable useful life. Sterrett, J. agreed. Irwin, J. said that (as to the $25, $571 and $313.25), becoming a California lawyer is not a new trade or business because the types of tasks and activities do not change. The partial dissent of Dawson, C.J. is omitted. Eds.]

Notes on Human Capital, New Job Descriptions and the New Education Credits

Is Congress too cheap about letting people deduct the costs of improving their job skills? Most people would likely agree that educational expenses up through high school, and perhaps even college expenses, are generally not sufficiently focused on the production of income to justify their deductibility, but, on the other hand, at least some law students would agree that there is little pleasure to be derived from the law school experience and that the reason for attending is primarily economic. Nevertheless, nothing in the Code or Regulations lets law students write off their education, either at once or over their anticipated "useful lives" as lawyers. By contrast, if a business person who was not previously engaged in the same line of business goes out and buys a business, §195 allows him to amortize his startup expenses over the first 60 months of the business, and to depreciate business hardware over unrealistically short recovery periods. Why not allow law students a similar 60 months amortization deduction?[550]

On the other hand, once one has engaged in a trade say as a lawyer the cost of subsequent education in order to maintain one's skills is deductible. There is an analogy here between deductible repairs paid to keep an asset in operating condition and keeping a human being abreast of developments in her field. The difference is the inability to depreciate the cost of developing the humans. (We know humans do expire, so there definitely is a limited "useful life," as with a business machine.)

550 See McNulty, J., *Tax Policy and Tuition Credit Legislation Federal Income Tax Allowances For The Personal Costs of Higher Education*, 61 Calif. L. Rev. 1 (1973).

Tax Credits for Education Expenses

The Lifetime Learning Credit and the HOPE Credit help to tilt the balance in favor of human capital. The following excerpt[551] describes new tax credits for education, enacted in 1997 and found in §25A. Each of these credits begins to phase out for 2019 at modified adjusted gross income of $80,000 ($160,000 on a joint return) for the HOPE credit and $58,000 for individuals and $116,000 for joint returns in the Lifetime Learning Credit.

For a taxable year, a taxpayer may elect with respect to an eligible student, the HOPE credit, the 20percent Lifetime Learning credit, or the exclusion from gross income for certain distributions from an education IRA.

The Lifetime Learning Credit

The Lifetime Learning Credit is coordinated with the so-called HOPE Credit. However, the Lifetime Learning Credit is available for graduate courses (including law school) and to part-time students. Nevertheless, the two credits are mutually exclusive in a given year, and the lifetime credit is nonrefundable, meaning that, if the credit exceeds one's personal income tax liability for the year, the excess is lost and not merely deferred. The following summaries are from a Congressional Report on the 1997 Bill.[552]

> Lifetime Learning credit. The bill provides that individual taxpayers are allowed to claim a nonrefundable Lifetime Learning credit against Federal income taxes equal to 20 percent of qualified tuition and fees paid during the taxable year on behalf of the taxpayer, the taxpayer's spouse, and any dependent. The student must be enrolled at an eligible educational institution but need not be enrolled on at least a halftime basis. Instead, the student is eligible for the Lifetime Learning credit so long as he or she is taking undergraduate or graduatelevel classes to acquire or improve job skills (assuming that the other requirements for the credit are satisfied) . . . . (the maximum credit per taxpayer return is $2,000).
>
> The Lifetime Learning credit is computed on a pertaxpayer return basis (i.e., the credit does not vary based on the number of students in a taxpayer's family). However, in contrast to the HOPE credit, the Lifetime Learning credit may be claimed for an unlimited number of taxable years. If a parent claims a child as a dependent, then only the parent may claim the Lifetime Learning credit with respect to such child, and any qualified tuition and fees paid by the child are deemed to be paid by the parent.

551 Summary of Revenue Provisions of H.R. 2014 ("Taxpayer Relief Act of 1997")(JCX 97), August 1, 1997, Joint Committee on Taxation Staff Summary, p.4.

552 *Id.*

The HOPE Credit:

Individual taxpayers are allowed to claim a non-refundable HOPE credit against Federal Income Taxes for qualified tuition and fees paid during the year on behalf of a student (i.e., the taxpayer, the taxpayer's spouse, or a dependent) who is enrolled in a postsecondary degree or certificate program at an eligible institution on at least a halftime basis. The credit rate for 2019 is 100 percent on the first $2,000 of qualified tuition and fees and books and 25 percent on the next $2,000 of qualified tuition and fees for a maximum credit of $2,500. The HOPE credit is available only for the first four years of a student's postsecondary education. The Hope Credit is also known as the American Opportunity Tax Credit

The HOPE credit is computed on a perstudent basis (i.e., a HOPE credit may be computed separately for each eligible student in a taxpayer's family). If a parent claims a child as a dependent, then only the parent may claim the HOPE credit with respect to such child, and any qualified expenses paid by the child are deemed to be paid by the parent.Phase out of the credit begins at $80,000 ($160,000 on a joint return).The Hope credit is allowed against the alternative minimum tax.

Summary of Education Tax Incentives		2019	2018	2017
Hope Credit maximum credit (per student)		$2,500	$2,500	$2,500
Lifetime Learning Credit maximum credit (per return)		$2,000	$2,000	$2,000
Education credit phase-out begins at AGI of:				
Married filing joint	Hope Credit	$160,000	$160,000	$160,000
	Lifetime Learning	$116,000	$114,000	$112,000
Single, Head of Household, or Qualifying Widow	Hope Credit	$80,000	$80,000	$80,000
	Lifetime Learning	$58,000	$57,000	$56,000
Married filing separately		Not Allowed	Not Allowed	Not Allowed

Student loan interest deduction limit		$2,500	$2,500	$2,500
Student loan interest deduction phase out begins at AGI of:				
	Married filing Joint	$140,000	$135,000	$135,000
	Single, Head of Household or Qualifying Widower	$70,000	$65,000	$65,000
	Married filing separately	Not Allowed	Not Allowed	Not Allowed
Savings bonds income exclusion phase-out begins at AGI of:				
	Married filing Joint	$121,600	$119,300	$117,250
	Single, Head of Household or Qualifying Widower	$81,100	$79,550	$78,150
	Married filing separately	Not Allowed	Not Allowed	Not Allowed
Source		Rev. Proc. 2018-57	Rev. Proc. 2018-18	Rev. Proc. 2016-55

Problem 6-14:

1) Monica is a teacher in Phoenix. She goes to Dallas to attend a convention on teaching methods. For the trip to Dallas, she pays these expenses: airline tickets,

$550; meals, $220; hotel room, $260; and cab fares, $50 in town to visit friends and $40 to travel to and from the airport. What can she deduct?

2) What conditions would a law student have to have met in order to qualify for the Lifetime Learning Credit? See §25A.

3) What is the maximum Lifetime Learning Credit worth this year?

4) If the law student were a dependent and her parents paid her tuition, could they claim the HOPE credit? See §25A.

5) Which of the following expenditures are deductible?

   a. Portia is a lawyer who attends a three-hour seminar in her city in her area of law in order to stay current. See Reg. §1.162-5(c).

   b. Madeline is a high school teacher of geography. She travels for three weeks in Antarctica in order to be a better geography teacher. See §274(m)(2).

   c. Madeline instead travels to Paris to attend a week-long seminar on Antarctic geography. See Reg. §1.162-5(c)(1).

   d. Carlos was hired as a law professor before he got his JD degree. His continued employment depended on getting the degree, which he did within a year. See Reg. §1.162-5(b)(2).

   e. Some years later Madeline finds herself under a legal obligation to get 6 hours of continuing education, which she does, in order to retain her job. The new level of skill was devised as a result of a recent study that showed teachers in her state were often incompetent.

   f. Buzz, a rising young executive, got an MBA over three years of evening classes in order to sharpen needed skills on the job. Assume his job description did not change afterward, and his job was not contingent upon his receiving the MBA.

   g. Edwina got an LLM in tax. She is a litigator who is tired of the long hours and wants a more normal life and intellectual stimulation in the tax department.

h. Paris is a CPA who is about to get his JD degree. He wants to get better at tax law, but will never practice law. See Reg. §1.162-5(b)(3).

i. Madeline is told she will have to teach physics, requiring her to learn a new subject. See Reg. §1.162-5(b)(3)(i).

P. LOSSES ON TRANSACTIONS ENTERED INTO FOR PROFIT

Read §165(a)(f)

If you bought some stock on a tip from a friend, and then sold it at a loss, you would presume that you would be entitled to some sort of tax benefit, particularly, if you had made gains on some other investments and had to pay taxes on those gains. Section 165 secures the loss deduction. According to §165(c)(2) you can claim the loss if you acquired the stock with a view to making a profit. In turn, §165(f) warns that if it was a capital asset, then §§ 12111212 will impose some disagreeable limits. All loss deductions are limited to basis (not value), according to §165(b). This implies that §165 relates to losses with respect to dealing in money or property.

That term "losses" can be confusing because the tax law uses the same term to describe two distinctly different situations. One, under §165, involves the disposition of *property* for less than its basis. Section 1001 defines the amount of the loss, and §165 determines whether it can reduce one's tax base, or is treated as mere personal consumption. The other kind of loss involves an operating deficit, in which a business or investment has negative income (more expenses then income). In order for a taxpayer to get the benefit of a §165 loss, she must show that the loss with respect to the property was "closed and completed" by means of a transaction such as a sale or exchange, a fire, theft or government condemnation. As you have already seen, in our system mere declines in value do not produce deductible losses. Rather, each loss must be "realized" in some concrete way, as demanded by Reg. §1.165-l (b) and (d).[553]

Section 165(c)(2) speaks of allowing losses on the disposition of property acquired in a "transaction entered into for profit." What does that mean? The answer is that it means acquiring property with a view to making a profit, either by renting it to others or selling it. For example, if an investor buys stock for $1,000 and sells it for $750, the $250 loss is deductible under §165(c)(2) as being in a loss in a transaction entered into for a profit. The more difficult cases involve transactions in which the taxpayer claims that property acquired for personal use was *converted* to a gainseeking use, thereby justifying a loss when she sells it. Now read Reg. §1.1659(b), relating

553 See, e.g., Horrrmann v. Commissioner, 17 T.C. 903 (1951) (person who inherited property and put it up for sale at once was allowed maintenance deductions as investment expenses but no deduction for a loss on its sale for lack of a conversion of the property into a transaction entered into for a profit).

to conversions of homes from personal residences to rental properties. The obvious question is whether the regulation should apply to other property as well, say an automobile?

1. Impact on Basis on Conversion of Depreciable Property from Personal to Gain-Seeking Use

The following case poses the question of whether one must reduce the basis of property that one converts from personal to business use. In particular, should the taxpayer reduce basis by its decline in value while it was used for personal purposes? Read on.

AU v. COMMISSIONER

40 T.C. 264 (1963), affirmed 330 F.2d 1008 (CA. 9, 1964)

OPPER, Judge

[Mr. Au, an accountant, claimed that his car, which he purchased for $2,500 in 1950, should get a basis of the same amount when he converted it to business use in 1957. The IRS asserted it should only get a basis equal to value at conversion, a much lower figure. The debate over basis could influence his claims to depreciation deductions for the car. That depended on whether he had to use the original cost of the car or its value when it was converted to business use as the base on which he claimed depreciation.]

. . .

In 1957, when petitioner converted the automobile to business use, it had been operated for about 25,000 miles and was in good condition. In 1957, Plymouth automobiles of the model and type herein involved were being offered for sale in the Honolulu area, and could be purchased in good condition for less than $ 650. The Official Guide used in the Hawaii area representing the average of used car prices reflected the average retail price of 1950 Plymouth automobiles at less than $ 650.

The fair market value of the 1950 Plymouth automobile was not in excess of $ 650 when it was converted to business use in 1957.

OPINION

. . .

"Respondent's computation of depreciation on the basis of fair market value at the time of [conversion to business use] must, we think, be approved, not because the acquisition is significant, but because that happens also to be the time of conversion." *Ralph Perkins*, 41 B.T.A. 1225, 1227 (1940), affirmed per curiam 125 F. 2d 150 (C.A. 6, 1942).

Depreciation is a fact and must be taken into account even where there is no provision for its deduction as in the case of properties devoted to personal use. *Helvering v. Owens*, 305 U.S. 468 (1939). Petitioner's automobile, which, according to his theory, was used only for personal purposes before its contribution to the putative partnership, had no depreciation basis prior to that time. In *Ralph Perkins, supra*, where donated property was simultaneously converted to business use, we said: "Even though the conversion took place at the moment of acquisition . . . it was nevertheless a conversion, since the property had no depreciation base before." *Ralph Perkins, supra* at 1227. See *Robert H. Montgomery*, 37 B.T.A. 232 (1938). The basis for depreciation, whether of petitioner or of the partnership, is computed upon conversion value, just as it would be if there had been no transfer to the partnership. See *Charles J. Thatcher*, 24 B.T.A. 10, 12 (1931).

While the terms of the applicable provision of the 1954 Code vary somewhat from those of its predecessor, it is clear that Congress intended no change in this respect[.]

. . .

It seems to us to follow that respondent was correct in attributing as its basis the fair market value of the automobile at the time of its conversion to business use, whether as a contribution to the partnership or as the continuing individual property of petitioner.

We find no adequate evidence of fair market value sufficient to overcome the presumption of correctness of respondent's determination. The only witness on the subject was petitioner's brother, whose qualifications as an expert in the valuation of secondhand automobiles are questionable, to say the least. We have accordingly found as a fact that the fair market value of the automobile on the date of its conversion was the amount determined by respondent.

Decision will be entered for the respondent.

Notes

Normally, personal use property declines in value, but not always. For example, assume the taxpayer bought a particularly fine object, such as a uniquely reliable washing machine, and that after using it for 1,000 loads of laundry it was still worth the original $1,000 that its owner paid for it. If the owner then sells it for $1,000 there is no gain, unless the law makes one reduce the basis of personal consumption property. Must one? The simple answer is "no," the tax law does not allow depreciation deductions nor demand that basis be reduced merely by the passage of time or amount of use. The important tax policy problem occurs with respect to such things as jewelry and art which are in fact likely to appreciate in value but suffer no basis reduction associated with the (non-taxable) consumption usage.[554]

---

554 See Mark Kelman, *Time Preference and Tax Equity*, 35 Stan. L.R. 649 (1983).

Problem 6-15:

Ignore the passive loss and hobby loss rule, and assume the conversion results in operating the property as a business.

1) Suppose Harold owned a personal residence that he converted into rental property. The house was bought for $200,000 and he owned it and lived in it for two years. Then, when it was worth $160,000, he moved, rented it out and held it for income production only. He sold it five years later for $80,000. (Ignore depreciation deductions.) Can Harold deduct $120,000? $80,000? Something else? See Reg. §1.165-9(b).

2) Same as "(1)," but what would be the gain or loss on sale for $80,000 if depreciation deductions of $20,000 per year were allowed or allowable during the 5-year rental period? See §165(b) and Reg. §1.1659(b). For basis adjustments, see §1016. As to the depreciation question, see Reg. §1.167a10.

3) Assume Harold bought the home as a personal residence for $200,000 and after two years converted it to income producing property when the house was worth $240,000.

    a. Now, if after five years, the depreciation deductions totaling $50,000, Harold sells it for $170,000, will he have any deductible loss?

    b. Same, but instead Harold sells it, after five years, for $120,000. Any deductible loss? How much?

    c. Same as "(1)," but instead Harold sells it for $250,000 after five years. What result?

2. Retirements of Business Assets

According to Rev. Rul. 69-487, the retirement of an automobile from business to personal use is not a disposition for purposes of realization of gain or of §1245 recapture (a topic we will take up later).[555] Further, according to the Regulations[556] the retirement of an asset from business use,

555 1969-2 C.B. 165. It also does not cause §1245 or §1250 recapture of depreciation as ordinary income, a topic taken up in Chapter 8.

556 Reg. §1.167(a)8(a)(3)(4).

(where the asset is not sold or exchanged), will generate no gain; but a loss can be recognized in some limited instances. Prop. Reg. §1.1686(a) similarly prevents the recognition of gain on the retirement of §168 property, but symmetrically prevents the recognition of losses when such property is converted to personal use. A serious risk associated with converting property to personal use is that if the property is "listed property," then it is subject to §280F(b)(2) recapture when business use falls to or below 50%. Would it be good tax planning for a lawyer to buy a Persian carpet for her office, and bring it home for use in her den a few years later, assuming the carpet is not an item of listed property? For a caution, see Reg. §1.179-1(e)(1), the first sentence of which provides:

> IN GENERAL. If a taxpayer's section 179 property is not used predominantly in a trade or business of the taxpayer at any time before the end of the property's recovery period, the taxpayer must recapture in the taxable year in which the section 179 property is not used predominantly in a trade or business any benefit derived from expensing such property. . . . The benefit derived from expensing the property is equal to the excess of the amount expensed under this section over the total amount that would have been allowable for prior taxable years and the taxable year of recapture as a deduction under section 168 (had section 179 not been elected) for the portion of the cost of the property to which the expensing relates (regardless of whether such excess reduced the taxpayer's tax liability).

Q. LIMITATION ON DEDUCTIONS FOR PROPERTY "USED AS A RESIDENCE" -- HOME OFFICES AND OTHER BUSINESS USES

Read §280A(a), (b), (c)(1), (c)(5), (d)(1)(2) and (e)

The §183 hobby loss rules have proven difficult to administer because they relies on the taxpayer's subjective intent and an unreliable multifactor analysis to infer intent that may even invite lying. To combat these weaknesses, Congress added an objective provision for dwelling units.

1. General Rules

Thanks to §280A, a dwelling unit "used as a residence" by the taxpayer will never generate operating loss deductions for the taxpayer. A "dwelling unit" is any habitable structure. This could be anything from a small boat or trailer with cooking and sleeping facilities to a multimillion dollar mansion. Generally, "used as a residence," means the taxpayer, or family members,[557] use the dwelling unit at least 15 days out of the year for personal purposes. However, if the taxpayer

557 See §280A(d)(2)(A) and 267(c)(4).

uses his residence for business purposes he may be eligible for some important deductions with respect to the business portion of the home, provided he adequately quarantines it from personal use.

2. Businesses Operated Out of the Home

Logically, it should not matter whether a taxpayer uses a portion of her residence for engaging in business, or rents space from a landlord for the same purpose. To a certain extent, the Code adopts this view by allowing some deductions to those engaged in either situation. By contrast, the cost of renting a downtown office is surely deductible under §162. As far as offices at home go, §280A lists certain narrow instances when space in a taxpayer's home will generate maintenance and depreciation deductions. The most notable of these circumstances follow:

1. If the home office is the taxpayer's principal place of a particular business.

2. If the home office is used to meet and deal with patients, clients, or customers in the normal course of business; merely receiving numerous phone calls at home does not constitute "meeting and dealing" with clients.

3. If the taxpayer's home office is located in a structure that is separate and distinct from the home. An example is a detached closedin garage converted to, and used as, an office.

4. If the taxpayer uses his home office for storing items that will be sold at wholesale or retail; for this exception to apply the home office must be the sole location of the taxpayer's business.

5. If the taxpayer uses part of his home for day care purposes; this allowance includes areas used for preparing food for the children, such as the kitchen.[558]

There is an equity problem with respect to §280A in that people who for some narrow reason cannot qualify for a home office deduction are at a disadvantage compared to people whose employers provide them with offices.

> **To illustrate:** Dr. Fonebone (the professor's sister) has a medical practice on the ground floor of her home. She uses a ground floor back office in her home to do her paperwork, and she also uses it for some administration of her investments. The back office is "used as a residence"

558 Rev. Rul. 92-3, 1992-1 C.B. 141.

because it is not used exclusively for business purposes. Assume her competitor, Dr. Peabody, has an employer that provides him with an office in the medical office tower where he works. Dr. Peabody will not have to report the availability of the office as gross income because §132(a)(3) and (d) make it a working condition fringe benefit meaning one the cost of which the recipient could deduct if the recipient had to pay for it even if he uses it occasionally for managing investments. By contrast, Dr. Fonebone, who must conduct the same functions out of her home for lack of employerprovided facilities, may be unable to deduct those same expenses unless she lies about the minor investment use of the office.

3. Section 280A's Bite: Deferral of Deductions

Perhaps it is not as bad as it seems. After all, Congress has a legitimate stake in not subsidizing personal consumption and has the authority to put sharp limits on the availability of suspicious tax deductions. Demanding that a home office be 100% dedicated to business use is not absurd. Assuming the taxpayer meets the conditions for claiming home office deductions, §280A(c)(5) simply defers her office-related deductions if they exceeded gross income from the business (minus deductions not dependent on business use). If she moved into a new apartment with an office in which she regularly met with patients, and did her investment accounting in a comfortable den, she could use any deferred deductions against business income attributable to the new, qualifying home office.

Problem 6-16:

Professor Fonebone, a night owl by nature, writes books at home and at work. He also sometimes acts as a consultant to law firms and acts as a paid expert witness. He does some of his writing and consulting at home and some at the law school. His writings produce $1,000/year in royalties. He has a segregated home office, which he has to use at night because the law school offices close at 8:00PM. He uses it solely for his writing and consulting. Consider the benefit of the office, if it works:

1) Will he be able to claim a larger amount of real estate taxes and mortgage interest expense as a business expense deduction?[559]

2) Will Fonebone be able to claim depreciation deductions for the home office part of the residence? See §280A(c)(4)(C) and Form 8829 at the end of the book.

---

559 Form 8829 provides clear guidance as to how to perform the allocations, but leaves the question of exactly how one attributes income to an office up to the taxpayer to determine. There is a copy of the form at the back of the book.

3) Does the answer to "2" depend on how much money Fonebone makes at home? §280A(c)(5)

4) Assume that Professor Fonebone quits teaching and writing books and goes to work for a law firm. The firm expects him to work at home.

   a. Can he get a deduction for his office at home?

   b. Should the firm insist that he work at home after hours in order to enhance the likelihood of getting a home office deduction?

5) Assume he leaves home in the summer for two weeks and rents his home out for two weeks. Can he exclude the income? See §280A(g).

6) Same as "5." but he rents it for 21 days? Can he report an operating loss for the rental period for Federal Income Tax purposes? See §280A(a), (b) and (d).

R. DEDUCTIONS FOR BAD DEBT LOSSES

Read §166

1. Introduction

A fable: you lend someone $100. That person does not repay you. You have to address three questions. Was there a debt? If not, there will be no bad debt deduction. Is it a bad debt? If not, there is no bad debt deduction. Was it a business bad debt? If so, you are in luck, as opposed to its being a mere non-business bad debt. (There is more on that later on in the book.) So, there are three key questions: Debt? Bad debt? Business bad debt?

All bad debts are broken down into two headings: "business bad debts" and "nonbusiness bad debts." Business bad debts are fairly appealing because their loss can be deducted even if they are only partially worthless and when they are deducted they produce ordinary loss deductions. By contrast, nonbusiness bad debts are deductible, but are treated as shortterm capital losses[560] which, as you will see later, are less beneficial than ordinary losses. The theory for imposing the unfavorable capital loss rules is apparently that so many non-business bad debts are likely to be

560 §166(d).

gifts or other personal, non-gain-seeking transactions that a mechanical rule to reduce the tax benefit from the "loss" was thought necessary.[561]

One type of business debt is one that is created or acquired in the course of business, such as a retail store that sells to customers on credit, even if the debt is no longer owned by the business. Another type is a debt that might have been created outside the business, but went bad in the hands of the business.[562]

> **To illustrate:** In 1974 Dizzy had $4,200 on deposit at the Friendly Bank. An employee of the bank embezzled $400,000, including Dizzy's money, causing the bank to becomes insolvent and taken over by the FDIC. In 1975 Dizzy demanded her money, but got only $2,200. In 1976, the FDIC said there was an expectation that the losses would be paid in full to depositors, including Dizzy. Unsatisfied by the assurance, Dizzy reported a theft loss of $2,000 in 1976. Wrong! It is not a theft because the taking was from the bank, not Dizzy. The bank merely owes Dizzy the money. Moreover, if there is a loss (which is not yet really established), it is not a business bad debt because: (1) it was not created or incurred in the course of Dizzy's business; and, (2) the debt was not acquired by Dizzy's business. As a result, it is a non-business debt. Dizzy cannot claim a loss because its worthlessness was not established in 1976, given that the FDIC might cause Dizzy to be repaid in full.[563]

Notice the problems for Dizzy: being a non-business bad debt, it cannot be deducted unless it is entirely worthless, and even if it is a bad debt, it only produces a capital loss, which results in serious restrictions. (The restrictions are dealt with in Chapter Eight.) So, Dizzy would almost always prefer treatment as a business bad debt loss because it is ordinary in nature (not capital) and can be deducted even if it is only partially worthless.

There is another problem. If the debt is evidenced by a security, such as a publicly traded bond, then §165(g) generally treats its worthlessness as a capital loss, the theory being that absent this rule taxpayers looking at a security (bond, stock, rights to subscribe for stock, debentures and so forth) whose value is declining would likely hang onto it until it becomes worthless so as to get a bad debt loss, rather than sell it at a capital loss.[564] This special rule equates the treatment of people who sell capital assets that have declined in value with people who let them lapse into worthlessness.

561 See B. Bittker & L. Lokken, FEDERAL TAXATION OF INCOME, ESTATES & GIFTS ¶33.6 (2019).

562 §166(d).

563 See Rev. Rul. 77-383, 1977-2 C.B. 66 from which the illustration was drawn.

564 The technical explanation of this oddity is that §1222, which defines a capital loss, requires a "sale or exchange." Because worthlessness is not a sale or exchange, the loss cannot be a capital loss. See also §166(e) which denies a bad debt loss for debts evidenced by "securities."

2. The Unique Problem of Lawyer's Advances

Bad debt issues have plagued plaintiffs' lawyers working under contingent fee arrangements. Their clients often do not have the money to cover even the costs of the case, so the lawyer will advance the money on the understanding that if the plaintiff prevails the lawyer will get the case costs back before the client gets his or her share of the recovery. The IRS has generally asserted that such an advance creates a loan, not a business expense deduction. Before you read the next case, review the first sentence of Reg. §1.1661(c).

3. Is there a Debt?

BURNETT v. COMMISSIONER

356 F.2d 755 (5th Cir. 1966), cert. denied (CA5 1966)

MOORE, Circuit Judge:

[Burnett was a successful plaintiffs' lawyer in Odessa, Texas who chose his contingent fee cases carefully. If he accepted a contingent fee case, he advanced a variety of costs, but on the understanding that he would be repaid "off the top" if the case was a winner. He claimed deductions for the advances when he paid them. It was clear that he would not be repaid unless the client got a victory.]

. . .

The initial issue raised on appeal is whether the Tax Court's treatment of the disbursements as advances virtually certain of repayment rather than as business expenses, despite the fact that they were not made as formal loans for which the clients were personally liable, is supported by substantial record evidence. At the outset, we reject as without merit the contention that the Tax Court committed reversible error by refusing to hear the testimony of a Certified Public Accountant to the effect that it was proper accounting for petitioner to record the disbursements as expenses on his books. Whether the expenditures were properly characterized as expenses from the standpoint of sound accounting principles has no significant bearing on the issue presented here. The authorities are clear that labels or book entries given to expenditures do not control their deductibility as expenses. The true character of expenditures, which "depends upon the 'special facts' of each case," Dixie Mach. Welding & Metal Works, Inc. v. United States, 315 F.2d 439, 445 (5th Cir. 1963), determines their income tax consequences. . . .

To be deductible under Section 162(a), an expenditure must constitute an expense of carrying on a trade or business, as distinguished from some other type of expenditure made in connection with the taxpayer's business. . . . ([L]oans are to be distinguished from expenses) . . . . Moreover, it is well settled that an expenditure for which there is an unconditional right of reimbursement is not deductible as a business expense . . . since "such expenditures are in the nature of loans or advancements. . . . And, this principle has been relied upon to disallow claimed deductions for business expenses based on advances made by attorneys to, or on behalf of, their clients. Henry F. Cochrane, 23 B.T.A. 202 (1931) (attorney had absolute right to reimbursement); see Reginald G. Hearn, 36 T.C. 672 (1961) (record does not disclose whether clients' obligation to reimburse was absolute or conditional).

Petitioner argues, however, that the fact that the recovery of the disbursements involved here was conditional, i. e., if, when, and to the extent that a client's case was successfully concluded, renders the above principles inapposite and justifies treating the disbursements as business expenses which, if deemed ordinary and necessary would be deductible under Section 162(a). It is contended that no debt or loan can arise in the absence of an unconditional obligation to repay the money expended and that, therefore, there was no justification for the Tax Court's holding that petitioner's contingent disbursements constituted advances to clients, notwithstanding that they were made with the obvious expectation of reimbursement, and that a substantial portion of them were actually repaid.

It is essential to point out initially that the cases relied on by petitioner for the proposition that indebtedness requires an unconditional obligation to repay are not controlling here, for none of them deal with the question of what constitutes an expense for purposes of Section 162(a). Rather, they deal with the question of what constitutes a debt for purposes of Section 166 of the Internal Revenue Code of 1954, 26 U.S.C.A. §166 (deductions for bad debts), see Zimmerman v. United States, 318 F.2d 611 (9th Cir. 1963) . . . . The technical definition of indebtedness employed in the application of such provisions of the tax law, which deal in terms with indebtedness, cannot properly be invoked in this proceeding where the deductibility of an expenditure as a business expense under Section 162(a) is at issue. Here there is no occasion to define the expenditures precisely, and it is enough to determine negatively that they were not expenses of petitioner's business when made. . . .

We find that the record amply supports the Tax Court's conclusion that petitioner's expenditures constituted advances to his clients which were virtually certain to be repaid and, consequently, were not deductible as business expenses. Petitioner's contention that contingency of recovery, in and of itself, is sufficient reason for permitting the disbursements to be deducted fails to recognize that the question of whether an expenditure constitutes an expense within the meaning of Section 162(a) must be determined by examining the circumstances and conditions under which it was made. Here there was a close correlation between the conditions of reimbursement and the primary criterion employed by petitioner to select clients to receive financial assistance, e. g., although reimbursement was tied to the recovery of a client's claim, assistance was granted only to those whose claims would in all probability be successfully concluded. Moreover, petitioner experienced a high rate of return on the advances, evidenced by the fact that during the fiveyear period ending in 1961 in which petitioner's conditional advances were made, only $4,417 out of approximately $290,000 of them became worthless. These factors clearly indicate that the advances were intended to, and did, operate as loans, i. e., advances virtually certain of repayment, to petitioner's clients. Under the circumstances, we agree with the Government that the Tax Court's decision in *Reginald G. Hearn*, supra, where it was determined that advancements by an attorney to his clients are not deductible as business expenses under Section 162(a), is highly persuasive. While the record in *Reginald G. Hearn* does not disclose whether the advances there were conditional, as petitioner's were here, the court's decision was greatly influenced by the fact that the taxpayer recovered a substantial portion of the advances ($3,018.49 out of a total of $3,639.94) shortly after they had been paid out. Id. at 674. Similarly, petitioner's recovery experience as of the close of 1961 he had recovered 96% of the disbursements made in 1957; 83% of those made in 1958; 88% of those made in 1959; 75% of those made in 1960; and 34% of those made in 1961 militates in favor of treating his disbursements to clients as nondeductible advances.

In sum, the disbursements here were made only with the expectation that they would be substantially repaid, as evidenced by petitioner's high degree of selectivity in approving clients for financial aid (disbursements were to only 450 out of 2,200 clients represented by petitioner during the fiveyear period from 1957 to 1961). Moreover, there is nothing in the record to show that petitioner's rate of recovery under the contingent arrangement for repayment was any less that if his clients had assumed personal liability for repayment. Thus, the Tax Court properly characterized the disbursements as advancements virtually certain to be repaid, rather than deductible business expenses.

. . .

Question

Consider for yourself if you can square the court's treatment of Mr. Burnett's advances with Reg. §1.1661(c). If not, how would you treat the advances?

4. Is there a Bad Debt and When?

The following is a mock tax shelter, affectionately known to some practitioners as "the Herbie shelter." It goes like this. Bob and Herbie are friends. Bob wants to make a gift to Herbie, but he is cheap, so he lends Herbie the money instead. Herbie predictably defaults. This seems like a stupid scheme because Herbie's cancellation of debt income should match Bob's deduction. Maybe not. Herbie may be insolvent, so he may have no taxable income and Bob may claim a bad debt loss deduction. If the tax scheme fails it will presumably be because the transaction is in substance a gift from Bob, and (if caught) Bob will likely pay interest and penalties to the IRS. Because of the risk of encouraging "Herbie shelters", the IRS and the courts take an understandably skeptical view of claims of bad debt losses in dealings between friends or family members.

The timing of bad debt losses poses serious problems. Taxpayers are obligated to determine the year in which a debt became worthless and the amount of the loss. They are supposed to finger an "identifiable event" that signals this worthlessness.[565] For example, how would you treat a filing of a bankruptcy action by a debtor? Would you consider that it is necessarily conclusive that the debt you hold is worthless? The answer is that there is no answer because you would need to know how the debt would fare in bankruptcy.

The difficulty of determining exactly when a debt went bad is a troubling subject. The IRS is free to come in and simply declare, "you claimed the debt in year 3, but you were wrong; it was not bad in year 3, but in some other year." If the IRS is right, then you lose, but the debt may still be bad. Let's say you conclude the debt really became worthless in year 2, but it is closed by the usual threeyear statute of limitations. It looks bad. But wait a minute! Paragraph 6511(d)(1) declares that there is actually a sevenyear statute. That may leave time to file a refund claim for year 2.

5. Is it a Business Bad Debt?

Read Reg. §1.1665(a), (b)

The next problem is how to characterize the debt as business versus non-business. The following bedrock case involves a common fact pattern of an entrepreneur who invests in his employer to support his investment.

WHIPPLE v. COMMISSIONER

373 U.S. 193 (1963)

MR. JUSTICE WHITE delivered the opinion of the Court.

[The taxpayer was an original incorporator in seven corporations in 1949 and 1950. In 1951 and 1952, he formed eight new corporations, one of which was the Mission Orange Bottling Co. of Lubbock, Texas ("Mission"). In 1951 he obtained a franchise from a drink company (Mission Dry) and the assets of a bottling business. He sold the bottling equipment to Mission and bought land on which he built a new bottling plant which he leased to Mission and lent a net amount of $56,975 to Mission up until the end of 1953. He kept 80% of the stock in "Mission." He deducted the $56,975 as a business bad debt expense in 1953 when the loan went sour, which the IRS rejected on the theory that it was a non-business bad debt.]

565 Reg. §1.166-2(d)(1); Rev. Rul. 84-95, 1984-2 C.B. 53.

I.

The concept of engaging in a trade or business as distinguished from other activities pursued for profit is not new to the tax laws. As early as 1916, Congress, by providing for the deduction of losses incurred in a trade or business separately from those sustained in other transactions entered into for profit, §5, Revenue Act of 1916, c. 463, 39 Stat. 756, distinguished the broad range of income or profit producing activities from those satisfying the narrow category of trade or business. This pattern has been followed elsewhere in the Code. See, e. g., §23 (a)(1) and (2) (ordinary and necessary expenses); §23 (e)(1) and (2) (losses); §23 (l)(1) and (2) (depreciation); § 122 (d) (5) (net operating loss deduction). It is not surprising, therefore, that we approach the problem of applying that term here with much writing upon the slate.

In *Burnet v. Clark*, 287 U.S. 410 (1932), the longtime president and principal stockholder of a corporation in the dredging business endorsed for the company which he was forced to pay. These amounts were deductible by him in the current year under the then existing law, but to carry over the loss to later years it was necessary for it to have resulted from the operation of a trade or business regularly carried on by the taxpayer. The Board of Tax Appeals denied the carryover but the Court of Appeals for the District of Columbia held otherwise on the grounds that the taxpayer devoted all of his time and energies to carrying on the business of dredging and that he was compelled by circumstances to endorse the company's notes in order to supply it with operating funds. This Court in turn reversed and reinstated the judgment of the Board of Tax Appeals, since "the respondent was employed as an officer of the corporation; the business which he conducted for it was not his own. . . . The unfortunate endorsements were no part of his ordinary business, but occasional transactions intended to preserve the value of his investment in capital shares. . . . A corporation and its stockholders are generally to be treated as separate entities." . . .

A few years later, the same problem arose in another context. A taxpayer with large and diversified investment holdings, including a substantial but not controlling interest in the du Pont Company, obtained a block of stock of that corporation for distribution to its officers in order to increase their management efficiency. The taxpayer, as a result, became obligated to refund the annual dividends and taxes thereon and these amounts he sought to deduct as ordinary and necessary expenses paid or incurred in the carrying on of a trade or business pursuant to § 23 (a) of the Revenue Act of 1928. The Court, *Deputy v. du Pont*, 308 U.S. 488 (1940), assuming *arguendo* that the taxpayer's activities in investing and managing his estate were a trade or business, nevertheless denied the deduction because the transactions "had their origin in an effort by that company to increase the efficiency of its management" and "arose out of transactions which were intended to preserve his investment in the corporation . . . . The well established decisions of this Court do not permit any such blending of the corporation's business with the business of its stockholders." 308 U.S., at 494. . . .

The question assumed in *du Pont* was squarely up for decision in *Higgins v. Commissioner*, 312 U.S. 212 (1941). Here the taxpayer devoted his time and energies to managing a sizable portfolio of securities and sought to deduct his expenses incident thereto as incurred in a trade or business under §23 (a). The Board of Tax Appeals, the Court of Appeals for the Second Circuit and this Court held that the evidence was insufficient to establish taxpayer's activities as those of carrying on a trade or business. "The petitioner merely kept records and collected interest and dividends from his securities, through managerial attention for his investments. No matter how large the estate or how continuous or extended the work required may be, such facts are not sufficient as a matter of law to permit the courts to reverse the decision of the Board." 312 U.S., at 218.

Such was the state of the cases in this Court when Congress, in 1942, amended the Internal Revenue Code in respects crucial to this case. In response to the *Higgins* case and to give relief to Higginstype taxpayers, see H. R. Rep. No. 2333, 77th Cong., 2d Sess. 46, §23 (a) was amended not by disturbing the Court's definition of "trade or business" but by following the pattern that had been established since 1916 of "[enlarging] the category of incomes with reference to which expenses were deductible," *McDonald v. Commissioner*, 323 U.S. 57, 62; *United States v. Gilmore*, 372 U.S. 39, 45, to include expenses incurred in the production of income.

At the same time, to remedy what it deemed the abuses of permitting any worthless debt to be fully deducted, as was the case prior to this time, see H. R. Rep. No. 2333, 77th Cong., 2d Sess. 45, Congress restricted the full deduction under [§162] to bad debts incurred in the taxpayer's trade or business and provided that "nonbusiness" bad debts were to be deducted as shortterm capital losses. Congress deliberately used the words "trade or business," terminology familiar to the tax laws, and the respective committees made it clear that the test of whether a debt is incurred in a trade or business "is substantially the same as that which is made for the purpose of ascertaining whether a loss from the type of transaction covered by section 23 (e) is 'incurred in trade or business' under paragraph (1) of that section." H. R. Rep. No. 2333, 77th Cong., 2d Sess. 7677; S. Rep. No. 1631, 77th Cong., 2d Sess. 90. Section [162] of course, was a successor to the old §5 of the Revenue Act of 1916 under which it had long been the rule to distinguish between activities in a trade or business and those undertaken for profit. The upshot was that Congress broadened [§162] to reach income producing activities not amounting to a trade or business and conversely narrowed [§162] to exclude bad debts arising from these same sources.

The 1942 amendment of [§162], therefore, as the Court has already noted, *Putnam v. Commissioner*, 352 U.S. 82, 9092, was intended to accomplish far more than to deny full deductibility to the worthless debts of family and friends. It was designed to make full deductibility of a bad debt turn upon its proximate connection with activities which the tax laws recognized as a trade or business, a concept which falls far short of reaching every income or profit making activity.

II.

Petitioner, therefore, must demonstrate that he is engaged in a trade or business, and lying at the heart of his claim is the issue upon which the lower courts have divided and which brought the case here: That where a taxpayer furnishes regular services to one or many corporations, an independent trade or business of the taxpayer has been shown. But against the background of the 1942 amendments and the decisions of this Court in the *Dalton, Burnet, duPont* and *Higgins* cases, petitioner's claim must be rejected.

Devoting one's time and energies to the affairs of a corporation is not of itself, and without more, a trade or business of the person so engaged. Though such activities may produce income, profit or gain in the form of dividends or enhancement in the value of an investment, this return is distinctive to the process of investing and is generated by the successful operation of the corporation's business as distinguished from the trade or business of the taxpayer himself. When the only return is that of an investor, the taxpayer has not satisfied his burden of demonstrating that he is engaged in a trade or business since investing is not a trade or business and the return to the taxpayer, though substantially the product of his services, legally arises not from his own trade or business but from that of the corporation. Even if the taxpayer demonstrates an independent trade or business of his own, care must be taken to distinguish bad debt losses arising from his own business and those actually arising from activities peculiar to an investor concerned with, and participating in, the conduct of the corporate business.

If fulltime service to one corporation does not alone amount to a trade or business, which it does not, it is difficult to understand how the same service to many corporations would suffice. To be sure, the presence of more than one corporation might lend support to a finding that the taxpayer was engaged in a regular course of promoting corporations for a fee or commission, see Ballantine, Corporations (rev. ed. 1946), 102, or for a profit on their sale, see *Giblin v. Commissioner*, 227 F.2d 692 (C. A. 5th Cir.), but in such cases there is compensation other than the normal investor's return, income received directly for his own services rather than indirectly through the corporate enterprise, and the principles of *Burnet, Dalton, duPont* and *Higgins* are therefore not offended. On the other hand, since the Tax Court found, and the petitioner does not dispute, that there was no intention here of developing the corporations as going businesses for sale to customers in the ordinary course, the case before us inexorably rests upon the claim that one who actively engages in serving his own corporations for the purpose of creating future income through those enterprises is in a trade or business. That argument is untenable in light of *Burnet, Dalton, duPont* and *Higgins*, and we reject it. Absent substantial additional evidence, furnishing management and other services to corporations for a reward not different from that flowing to an investor in those corporations is not a trade or business under [§162]. We are, therefore, fully in agreement with this aspect of the decision below.

III.

With respect to the other claims by petitioner, we are unwilling to disturb the determinations of the Tax Court, affirmed by the Court of Appeals, that petitioner was not engaged in the business of money lending, of financing corporations, of bottling soft drinks or of any combination of these since we cannot say they are clearly erroneous. See *Commissioner v. Duberstein*, 363 U.S. 278, 289291. Nor need we consider or deal with those cases which hold that working as a corporate executive for a salary may be a trade or business. *E. g., Trent v. Commissioner*, 291 F.2d 669 (C. A. 2d Cir.). Petitioner made no such claim in either the Tax Court or the Court of Appeals and, in any event, the contention would be groundless on this record since it was not shown that he has collected a salary from Mission Orange or that he was owed one. Moreover, there is no proof (which might be difficult to furnish where the taxpayer is the sole or dominant stockholder) that the loan was necessary to keep his job or was otherwise proximately related to maintaining his trade or business as an employee. Compare *Trent v. Commissioner*, supra.

We are more concerned, however, with the evidence as to petitioner's position as the owner and lessor of the real estate and bottling plant in which Mission Orange did business. The United States does not dispute the fact that in this regard petitioner was engaged in a trade or business but argues that the loss from the worthless debt was not proximately related to petitioner's real estate business. While the Tax Court and the Court of Appeals dealt separately with assertions relating to other phases of petitioner's case, we do not find that either court disposed of the possibility that the loan to Mission Orange, a tenant of petitioner, was incurred in petitioner's business of being a landlord. We take no position whatsoever on the merits of this matter but remand the case for further proceedings in the Tax Court.

Vacated and remanded.

MR. JUSTICE DOUGLAS dissents.

Notes on Bad Debt Losses

"Dual capacity taxpayers." Taxpayers are often both investors in a business enterprise and (dually) employees. When such people lend money to the employer-entity (or they guarantee debts of the entity) and the debtor fails to pay, they often assert that their debt is a business bad debt under §166(a), claiming that they made the loan to protect their salaries. The leading decision in the area is *Generes v. United States,*[566] which sorts business debts from non-business debts held by an investor-employee on the basis of whether the "dominant motivation" for the loan was to preserve his salary. The facts of *Generes* involved a taxpayer who spent most of his time as the president of an S&L where he earned $19,000 per year. He had invested $38,000 in

566 405 U.S. 93 (1972).

a construction company with his soninlaw as a 50% owner, out of which the taxpayer drew an annual salary of $12,000. In 1958 he signed a blanket indemnity agreement with a surety company on the company's construction contacts. In 1962, he paid $162,000 to the surety on the corporation's collapse. Generes claimed a business bad debt deduction, swearing he signed the indemnity contract to protect his job and salary. The Supreme Court determined that because Generes's "dominant motivation" for extending credit was not to protect his job (which was secure at the S&L) the debt was a non-business debt, and its worthlessness gave rise to a mere shortterm capital loss, deductible under §166(d). The subtle difference between "dominant" and "significant" has meant far fewer dual status taxpayers have been able to claim bad debt losses on loans to their employers.

There are several other viable theories for getting a business bad debt loss. The other theories are that: (1) the taxpayer is in the business of lending money; (2) the taxpayer is a venture capitalist who lends money to startup companies in order to get them underway and then profits as an equity investor; or, (3) the loan was made to protect a business relationship (e.g., as a paid consultant to the borrower).[567]

The important concept of subornation. In order to deal with the next question, you may need a refresher about subrogation. If you borrow $100 from the bank and a friend of yours guarantees the debt, the guarantor must pay if you fail to. Your friend (the guarantor) has paid the bank, the guarantor can sue you as if it were the bank, provided the guarantor has a "right of subrogation." The Treasury Regulations prohibit guarantors from claiming a bad debt loss until they have actually paid the other person's debt *and* have concluded that subrogation (if any) efforts are no longer fruitful.[568] The next problem illustrates the primary rules.

Problem 6-17:

For years Fred has been the short order cook down at Barney's Fishnet Café, a sole proprietorship. He was not obligated to lend the money in order to work there, but he lent $5,000 to the business at the manager's request. The restaurant went broke a year later and did not, and will not, pay back the money.

1) How should he report the loss on his tax return? See Reg. §1.166-5. If so, it is an ordinary or capital loss?

2) What if the manager insisted on the loan as a condition for Fred to keep his job? What kind of loss, if any, can Fred claim?

567 See Adelson v. United States, 737 F.2d 1569 (Fed. Cir. 1984).

568 Reg. §1.166-9.

3) Same as "(2)," but rather than lending money directly, he personally guaranteed a loan that the tavern got from a local bank and defaulted on, leaving Fred to pay off the debt via his guarantee. See Reg. §1.1669.

4) It is next year, and things are going even worse for Fred. How should he treat each of the following losses:

   a. A $200 loss on bonds of a publicly-traded company. The company defaulted on the bonds. See §165(g).

   b. $400 he lent to you so you could take a vacation. You will never repay him.

S. BUSINESS-RELATED TAX CREDITS

Scan §38

Business tax credits offer a special incentive in order to achieve some particular economic objective, whereas personal tax credits generally try to achieve special policy goals (such as education), or equity goals (such as making sure that people who have already been subject to withholding taxes on income they earned as employees do not pay again, but can instead use the taxes already paid as credits to offset their personal tax liabilities).[569] Credits are politically popular in comparison to tax deductions because they are not affected by tax rates; for example, a $10 tax credit is worth as much to a person in poverty as to a billionaire, provided it is refundable (available even if you lack taxes to apply the credit against). Section 38 is the central switchboard for business tax credits. Your quick scan may have revealed some basic themes:

1. The §38 credits are either designed to stimulate particular employment (e.g, the §38(b)(2) targeted jobs credit for the needy and the §38(b)(10) Indian Employment Credit) or to stimulate preferred investments (e.g., the §38(b)(1) investment credit for rehabilitation of historic buildings). These credits often provide the equivalent of a cash down payment that allows the taxpayer to borrow the rest of the money needed to undertake the project.

2. Other credits provide humanitarian assistance, such as a subsidy for retrofitting buildings to assist the disabled found in §38(b)(7), or the §38(b)(9) credit for hiring

569 See §31(a)(1).

people who work in impoverished neighborhoods, or the §42 low-income housing credit.

3. Some meet industrial needs, such as the §41 research and development tax credit for increasing R&D expenditures.

4. Other credits include the credit for foreign income taxes paid in order to relieve international double taxation of income (§27) and a credit for the portion of an employer's Social Security taxes paid with respect to employee cash tips (§45B).

Under the general business credit, eligible employers get a 12.5 percent credit against wages they pay to qualifying employees during Family and Medical Leave Act (FMLA) leave but only if the employer pays 50 percent or more of the normal wage rate. The credit is only available for wages paid in tax years beginning after December 31, 2017, and before January 1, 2020.

The FMLA credit is only available with respect to wages paid in tax years beginning in 2018. The credit terminates after 2019 and therefore may not be claimed to wages paid in tax years beginning after 2019 (§45S(i), as added by the Tax Cuts Act and Jobs Act of 2017).

The nature of a basic income tax course makes it unrealistic to investigate these credits closely, but they are definitely important. They represent a major leakage of Federal Income Tax revenues, and they are of intense interest to their beneficiaries.

CHAPTER 7 - DEDUCTIONS AND OTHER ALLOWANCES THAT ARE NOT DEPENDENT ON PROFIT-SEEKING

A. INTRODUCTION

Most expenditures incurred to turn a profit are deductible as business or investment expenses, and virtually all others are rendered nondeductible as "consumption." The statutory foundation for the disallowance of personal consumption is §262, which declares that "no deduction shall be allowed for personal, living or family expenses." The Supreme Court elaborated on this point in *United States v. Gilmore*, when it said,

> Congress has seen fit to regard an individual as having two personalities, . . . a seeker after profit who can deduct the expenses incurred in that search [and] a creature satisfying his needs as a human and those of his family, but who cannot deduct such consumption and related expenditures.[570]

This observation has led many tax experts to consider that in substance the Code consists of a tax on income that is saved or consumed. They are right, except that the Code also grants deductions for a number of expenditures, costs or losses that are for consumption. The important question in each case is why Congress grants such exceptional allowances.

The principal exceptions to the general denial of deductions for personal consumption are those for home mortgage interest, state and local taxes, charitable contributions, casualty losses, non-business bad debts and catastrophic medical expenses, all of which make their appearances in this chapter. These expenses and losses are often referred to as "itemized deductions" and are allowed -- as you will come to see -- only if the taxpayer elects to forego the socalled "standard deduction." Non-business bad debts are an exception; they are treated as short-term capital losses and are combined with the taxpayer's other capital transactions, if any, for the year.

It is most important to keep in mind that deductions for personal living and family expenses will generally not be allowed and can be taken only when specifically authorized by the Code or the Regulations. Unlike income, which is presumptively taxable unless specifically excluded

570 372 U.S. 39, 44 (1963).

or falling within one of the historic "uncodified exclusions," deductions are presumptively not allowed. Therefore, it is necessary to find express authority to support an argument for allowance in the form of a deduction for any expenditures, and especially for those that would otherwise fall within the prohibition of §262.

1. Deductions Unique to Individuals

Among taxpayers, only human beings can have medical expenses and moving expenses in the sense of changing residences in order to change jobs. Only individuals grapple with the tax concept of adjusted gross income. All of these issues will soon become familiar to you, if they are not already.

2. Summary of How a Federal Income Tax Bill is Computed for Individuals

The following reading offers a capsule summary of the relationship of gross income to adjusted gross income, statutory rates, marginal rates, and effective rates.

Individual Income Tax Rates and Other Key Elements of the Federal Individual Income Tax: 1988 to 2019 Tax Years

Gary Guenther
Analyst in Public Finance

Updated February 8, 2019

Congressional Research Service
www.crs.gov
RL34498

Statutory individual income tax rates are the tax rates that apply by law to various amounts of taxable income. Statutory rates form the basis of marginal effective and average effective tax rates, which most economists believe have a greater impact on the economic behavior of companies and individuals than do statutory rates. Marginal effective rates capture the net effect of special tax provisions on statutory rates. They differ from average effective rates, which measure someone's overall income tax burden.

***

Ordinary income is taxed at seven statutory individual income tax rates, from 2018 to 2026: 10%, 12%, 22%, 24%, 32%, 35%, and 37%. (Starting in 2026, these rates will revert to their levels in 2017.) Income from long-term capital gains and dividends is taxed at 0% for single filers with capital gains below $39,375 (below $78,750 for joint filers), 15% for single filers with capital gains between $39,375 and $434,550 (between $78,750 and $488,850 for joint filers), and 20% for single filers with capital gains above $434,550 (above $488,850 for joint filers). Since 2013, a 3.8% tax has been imposed on the lesser of net investment income received by individuals, estates, or trusts, or the amount of their modified adjusted gross incomes above $250,000 for joint filers and $125,000 for single filers. In addition, the individual alternative minimum tax (AMT), which functions like a separate income tax in that its rate structure is narrower and tax base broader than those of the regular income tax, applies to income above exemption amounts in 2019 of $111,700 for joint filers and $71,700 for single filers; the AMT taxes income at two rates: 26% and 28%.

Tax rates and the income brackets to which they apply are not the only elements of the individual income tax that determine the tax liabilities of taxpayers. Personal exemptions, exclusions, deductions, credits, and certain other elements have an effect as well. Some of these elements are indexed for inflation. Congress added annual indexation to the individual income tax in 1981, using the Consumer Price Index for All Urban Consumers. Such a mechanism helps prevent tax increases and unintended shifts in the distribution of the tax burden that are driven by inflation alone. The indexed elements are tax rate brackets, personal exemptions and their phaseout threshold, standard deductions, the itemized deduction limitation threshold, and the exemption amounts for the AMT. Starting in 2018, these items are indexed for inflation with the Chained Consumer Price Index for All Urban Consumers.

***

Three Commonly Used Concepts of Tax Rates and How They Differ

In analyzing the effects of U.S. individual income tax rates, it is important to be clear about which rates are being discussed. Among tax analysts, the three most widely used measures are statutory rates (STRs), marginal effective rates (MERs), and average effective rates (AERs). Each has its own applications. Those interested in how individual income taxes affect the economic behavior of households should have a clear understanding of the ways in which the three rates differ and the implications of these differences for the economic analysis of income taxes.

STRs are the rates prescribed by law that apply to specified ranges of taxable income. For any individual, the applicable rate depends on her/his taxable income. Since the federal income tax is progressive in nature, taxpayers with relatively low taxable incomes face lower STRs than do taxpayers with relatively high taxable incomes.

Effective rates, by contrast, whether marginal or average, measure how STRs are affected by tax provisions that modify someone's taxable income or tax liability. A taxpayer's MER shows the percentage of an additional dollar of income that is taxed, while her/his AER indicates how much of her/his total income is taxed. In general, someone's average tax rate is lower than her/his marginal tax rate.

***

Most economists believe that taxpayers change their economic behavior in response to MERs, not to statutory rates. Drawing on a standard model of consumer behavior, they argue that a person's MER influences important decisions concerning whether and how much to work, how much to spend, and how much to save. For example, someone's MER may help determine whether he takes on an overtime shift, bargains for wages and benefits, takes a second job, or even enters the labor force. The idea that MERs help shape an individual's economic behavior can be extended to an entire tax system, including federal payroll and excise taxes and state and local taxes.

***

Major Legislation Affecting Individual Statutory Rates Since 1986

The current income tax is largely a product of the Tax Reform Act of 1986 (TRA86; P.L. 99-514). Among other things, the act reduced the individual tax rate structure to two statutory rates: 15% and 28%. TRA86 also imposed a 5% surcharge on the taxable income of certain upper-income households, effectively adding a third marginal tax rate of 33%.

Since the enactment of TRA86, several other major changes in the federal individual income tax rate structure have been made.

The Omnibus Budget Reconciliation Act of 1990 (OBRA90; P.L. 101-508) eliminated the 5% surcharge and replaced it with a statutory rate of 31%. In addition, OBRA90 imposed a limit on the amount of itemized deductions upper-income households could claim and accelerated the phase-out of personal exemptions for upper-income households. These provisions had the effect of raising effective tax rates above statutory tax rates for affected taxpayers.

The Omnibus Budget Reconciliation Act of 1993 (OBRA93; P.L. 103-66) added two new statutory rates at the upper end of the income scale: 36% and 39.6%. It also delayed the indexation of the two new tax brackets for one year and permanently extended the limitation on itemized deductions and the accelerated phase-out of the personal exemption from OBRA90.

Eight years later, the Economic Growth and Tax Relief Reconciliation Act of 2001 (EGTRRA; P.L. 107-16) added a new 10% statutory rate. It also included a phased-in reduction in the top four statutory rates to 25%, 28%, 33%, and 35%. Several other provisions of the act modified the tax brackets and limitations on personal exemptions and deductions for higher-income taxpayers.

The Jobs and Growth Tax Relief Reconciliation Act of 2003 (JGTRRA; P.L. 108-27), the Working Families Tax Relief Act of 2004 (WFTRA; P.L. 108-311), and the Tax Increase Prevention and Reconciliation Act of 2005 (TIPRA; P.L. 109-222) collectively accelerated and extended the tax rate reductions enacted under EGTRRA through 2010.

Under a last-minute agreement between President Obama and congressional leaders from both parties, Congress extended the Bush-era individual income tax cuts through 2012 under the Tax Relief, Unemployment Insurance Reauthorization, and Job Creation Act of 2010 (TRUC; P.L. 111-312).

Facing the unwanted prospect of an across-the-board increase in all STRs, the 112th Congress permanently extended (through the American Taxpayer Relief Act of 2012 [ATRA; P.L. 112-240]) each of the Bush-era STRs, with one exception: the top rate increased from 35% to 39.6%.

Six years passed before Congress made another significant change in individual income tax rates. Through P.L. 115-97, often referred to as the Tax Cuts and Jobs Act, Congress temporarily reduced five of the seven individual income tax rates under prior law. For tax years beginning after December 31, 2017, and before January 1, 2026, individual income tax rates are 10%, 12%, 22%, 24%, 32%, 35%, and 37%; they are set to return to the levels that applied in 2017, for tax years beginning on or after January 1, 2026.

***

Tax Cuts and Jobs Act of 2017 P.L. 115-97

Individual marginal income tax rates did not change after ATRA until the enactment of P.L. 115-97 in December 2017.

The act made significant changes to a number of individual income tax provisions, including individual tax rates and the standard deduction. For tax years beginning in 2018 and ending before 2027, the individual income tax rate structure consists of seven brackets: 10%, 12%, 22%, 24%, 32%, 35%, and 37%. (The rates are scheduled to revert to their levels in 2017 starting in 2026.)

For individuals receiving income from pass-through businesses (i.e., partnerships, S corporations, and sole proprietorships), the current rates can be adjusted downward as a result of a new deduction under Section 199A; the deduction is equal to up to 20% of a noncorporate business owner's qualified income from a qualified trade or business.

The 2017 tax revision also made the following changes in these key elements of the individual income tax for the 2018 to 2025 tax years:

- It terminated the personal exemption (which was $4,050 in 2017).

- It increased the standard deduction (which is indexed for inflation using the chained consumer price index for urban consumers) for non-itemizers to $24,000 for joint filers and $18,000 for head-of-household filers, and $12,000 for single filers, from 2018 to 2025.

- It eliminated the deduction for miscellaneous expenses from 2018 through 2025.

- It suspended the overall limit on itemized deductions for certain high-income taxpayers.

B. STANDARD DEDUCTION

Read §63(a)-(e)

1. Introduction

This complicated-seeming provision is an alternative to itemized deductions. See page 2 of Schedule A to Form 1040 where you can see the election to claim itemized deductions. The underlying theories for it are:

1. That everyone has a certain amount of itemized expenses that they cannot account for;

2. The deduction helps to prevent taxing people into poverty; and

3. It greatly reduces the work of taxpayers and the IRS.[571]

Here is a simple example of how it works.

> **To illustrate**: Assume Dr. Peabody has adjusted gross income of $94,000 and in the particular year his standard deduction, under §63 is $24,000. His itemized deductions consist of a charitable contribution of $2,000 and home mortgage interest expenses of $4,000. Because his itemized deductions of $6,000 are less than his standard deduction ($24,000), he will elect to claim his standard deduction, thereby reducing his Federal Income Tax base by $24,000 rather than the $6,000 from his itemized deductions.

571 See B. Bittker & L. Lokken, FEDERAL TAXATION OF INCOME, ESTATES AND GIFTS at ¶30.5 (2019)

The amount of the standard deduction can have an enormous impact on the number of people who have to prepare more than the simplest tax return. For example, in 1977 the New York Times reported that President Carter's proposal to increase the standard deduction caused a stock analyst to change his recommendation on H&R Block stock from "buy" to "neutral," such was the analyst's fear of a drop-off in H&R Block tax return preparation business.[572]

An interesting recent change in the standard deduction is Congress' refusal -- found in §63(c)(5) -- to extend it in full to dependents. The refusal takes the form of granting a dependent a standard deduction limited to $500 (adjusted for inflation) or $250 plus earned income, whichever is greater (but not more that the normal standard deduction). This in effect punishes lazy rich kids. This is all part of a campaign to limit shifting income to children and letting them take advantage of the "tax shield" offered by the standard deduction.

Problem 7-1:

Your child lives with you. You provide him with support worth $10,000. Around April 15 he tells you that he received $2,000 of earned income last year and he has $5,000 of interest income.

1) Assuming he is entitled to a standard deduction, how large is it?

2) Must he file a tax return? See §6012(a)(1)(A)(i).

3) What was his taxable income last year if he had no deductible expenses last year? Make sure to consider his basic standard deduction and his personal exemption. See §63(a)-(c).

4) Assuming he were your dependent, could he claim a full standard deduction? What would be the amount? See §63(c)(5).

    a. What would be the amount of his personal exemption?

2. Child Tax Credit - §24

An individual may claim the child tax credit of up to $1,000 for each qualifying child he or she supports during the tax year (§ 24). The definition of qualifying child for this purpose is the same as that for claiming a dependency exemption, except that the child must not have attained the age of 17 by the end of the year and must be a U.S. citizen, national, or resident. §152.

572 NY Times, Feb. 10, 1977, at 58, col. 3, reported in B. Bittker & L. Lokken, FEDERAL TAXATION OF INCOME, ESTATES AND GIFTS, ¶ 30.5 (2019).

The child tax credit is generally a nonrefundable personal credit allowed against both the taxpayer's regular tax liability and alternative minimum tax (AMT) liability (§ 26). A portion of the credit is refundable to the extent it exceeds the taxpayer's tax liability. This is referred to as the additional child tax credit (ACTC) and is equal to the lesser of the unclaimed portion of the nonrefundable credit amount (i.e., up to $1,000 per child) or 15 percent of the taxpayer's earned income in excess of $3,000 (§ 24(d)).

The child tax credit phases out once the taxpayer's modified adjusted gross income (MAGI) exceeds $110,000 if married filing jointly, $75,000 if filing as single, and $55,000 if married filing separately (§24(b)).

The child tax credit is temporarily expanded after 2017 by increasing the credit amount for each qualifying child to $2,000, increasing the phase-out threshold to $400,000 if married filing jointly ($200,000 for other taxpayers), and providing a $500 nonrefundable credit for each dependent who is not a qualifying child. The refundable portion of the credit (additional child tax credit) is limited to $1,400 per qualifying child, but is indexed for inflation and the earned income threshold is reduced to $2,500. A taxpayer must include a qualifying child's Social Security number on his or her return to receive the nonrefundable or refundable portion of the credit with respect to the child.

C. THE EARNED INCOME TAX CREDIT (EITC), THE WELFARE TO WORK CREDIT, AND THE WORK OPPORTUNITY CREDIT

Earned Income Tax Credit. The "tax shield" offered by the standard deduction does not protect low income taxpayers from income and Social Security taxes, and it encourages tax evasion by dealing in unreported cash. The Earned Income Tax Credit (EITC) is a novel provision that was enacted to encourage the working poor to move into the job market free of unreasonable or discouraging tax burdens. The credit appears in §32 and is often referred to as a "negative income tax," because the amount of the credit the taxpayer receives varies inversely with the amount of that taxpayer's income. The EITC is available to married taxpayers with children, surviving spouses, heads of households with children, and to some childless people.

The heart of the EITC is a tax credit equal to a percentage of earned income for the taxable year. A unique aspect of the EITC is that the IRS grants a cash refund to the taxpayer to the extent that the EITC exceeds the taxpayer's tax liability, making it a so-called "refundable tax credit." A taxpayer with two qualifying children receives a 40% credit for each dollar of earned income up to a dollar ceiling, resulting in a maximum credit of $6,330 (adjusted for inflation) (34% if there is only one child, and 7.65% with no qualifying children). Those figures are for 2018, and rise with inflation. The amounts remain constant until either earned income or AGI exceeds certain threshold amounts, at which point the credit gradually phases out.

One convenient feature of the EITC is that the credit can be received in advance throughout the year, instead of in a lump sum. To name but a few inadequacies of the credit, it is unavailable to childless people under age 25 or over 64.

Work Opportunity Credit. Section 38(a) provides for a general business credit made up of the current year's credit plus carry forwards and carry backs. Section 38(b) defines the current year's general business credit as the sum of a variety of credits. Within the current year's general business credit, §38(b)(2) covers the work opportunity credit which is defined by §51(a). Employers who hire members of certain targeted groups receive a credit against income taxes of up to $24,000 of first-year wages. The credit requires employment before 2020. §51(c)(4).

The maximum credits per year are as follows:

1. $6,000 for each new hire;
2. $12,000 for each new hired veteran described in §51(d)(3)(A)(ii)(I)
3. $24,000 for each new veteran hired described in §51(d)(3)(A)(ii)(II); and
4. $14,000 for each new qualified veteran under §51(d)(3)(A)(iv)

The fast food industry and other service industries guard the credit fiercely, but it does not necessarily add to employment, although it likely helps keep down the price of fast food.[573]

D. CHARITABLE CONTRIBUTIONS

Read §170(a)(1), (c) and (e)

Private charity is part of our way of life, and it is definitely helped along by the tax Code. Charities offer an alternative to government transfers and invite creativity in the arts, education, medicine and the delivery of help to the poor. The deduction itself is a product of World War I, and was enacted out of a fear that with rising war taxes, charitable giving to hospitals, colleges and other charities might decline sharply.[574] Another explicit justification for the deduction is that charitable giving replaces government expenditures.[575] The tax rules pose some serious questions. For example, how does §170 "fit in" as a Code section? Is it an exception to §262, which disallows deductions for personal consumption? Should §170 be repealed in favor of having the federal government give direct aid? If so, how could the federal government

573 See *Labor Department Study Shows Targeted Jobs Tax Credit Harms Job Seekers*, 86 Tax Notes Today 50-5 (1986).

574 See Remarks of Senator Hollis, 55 Cong. Rec. 6728 (1917), reported in B. Bittker & L. Lokken, FEDERAL TAXATION OF INCOME, ESTATES AND GIFTS ¶ 35.1.1 (2019).

575 See H.R. Rep. No. 1860, 75th Cong., 3d Sess. (1938), reprinted in 1939-1 (part 2) C.B. 728, 742.

give to churches, and would it ever give to controversial donees such as a cutting edge dance group?

Most of one's charitable giving attracts a tax deduction, but not all, because many gifts need to thread their way through a maze of requirements if they are to be deducted. As you will come to see, the magic of charitable giving is the chance to get a charitable contribution deduction for the value of a donation, not just its basis.

> **To illustrate:** Joan Generous, a taxpayer in the 40% bracket, gives $100,000 in cash to her alma mater, an art school. She will probably be able to claim a $100,000 tax deduction, saving her $40,000 in Federal Income Taxes. If, however, she gives away a painting she shrewdly bought at a flea market many years ago for $10, and which is now worth $100,000, she gets the same $100,000 deduction. If the law taxed her on the art work as if she sold it first and gave away the $100,000 of cash, the deal would be much less attractive to her. For most people, this kind of opportunity is the holy grail of tax planning with respect to charitable contributions. One cannot get rich by making deductible charitable contributions, but with some planning, the pain can be minimized, and for many people a big gift brings the psychic rewards -- beyond a comforting feeling of having done good -- of being known as a philanthropist, or being invited to and seen at charitable events.

The charitable sector is enormous. One source estimates that it controls over two trillion dollars.[576] On the other hand people seem to be getting less generous, and many charities are on the ropes.[577]

Section 170 is the heart of the charitable contribution area. The other important provision is §501, which exempts a long list of organizations from taxation on (1) the donations they receive, (2) income from related activities, and in some cases (3) from taxes on their investment income.

From the donor's tax planning perspective, the most important single fact is that one can deduct the value of one's contribution in property, not just the basis of the property.[578] However, this only applies to so-called capital assets that have been held for the necessary long-term holding period, which is presently not less than a year and a day.[579] As a result, it is generally possible to claim a full fair market value deduction for donations of assets held for over a year. The book

576 https://philanthropynewyork.org/sites/default/files/resources/The%20Nonprofit%20Sector%20in%20the%20United%20States%20Size%20and%20Scope.PDF.

577 https://philanthropynewyork.org/sites/default/files/resources/The%20Nonprofit%20Sector%20in%20the%20United%20States%20Size%20and%20Scope.PDF.

578 Reg. §1.170-1(c).

579 §§ 170(e)(1)(A) and 1222(3).

considers the definition of a capital asset in detail later on. For the time being it is enough to know that assets held for investment will almost invariably qualify as capital assets.[580]

Now for some details. Taxpayers who itemize their deductions can deduct their charitable contributions in amounts totaling up to their annual adjusted gross income, depending on the kind of property they contribute and the nature of the donee organization (especially whether it is a public charity or a private foundation). Amounts in excess of the ceilings can be carried forward for up to five years. The amount of the contribution of property is generally its fair market value, but in some cases the amount is reduced.

1. Nature of a Charitable Contribution

A charitable contribution is deductible only if it is made in cash or property (but not services) and meets these tests:

1. The gift must be "to" or "for the use of" the charity.[581] "For the use of" has come to mean "in trust for";[582]

2. The contribution has to be paid within the taxable year; pledging is not good enough;[583]

3. The contribution must be within the applicable percentage (50%, 30% or 20%) ceilings; and,

4. The gift/contribution must be substantiated.[584]

From 2018 to 2025, the 50% limit under 170(b) for cash contributions to all public charities and a few private foundations goes up to 60%.

There is no deduction for contributions of services or the use of property, except that the taxpayer can deduct the cost of using his car in connection with helping a charity.[585] The standard mileage rate is higher than for medical and moving expenses, but lower than for business

580 See Chapter 8.

581 §170(c).

582 Rockefeller v. Commissioner, 676 F.2d 35, 40-41 (2d Cir. 1982).

583 §170(a). There is an exception for certain accrual method corporations. We need not be concerned with it.

584 See Reg. §1.170A-1(h)(6).

585 For example, for 2019, taxpayers could deduct 14 cents/mile for charitable use of the car. 170(i)). The IRS periodically increases standard mileage allowances for automobile usage to account for inflation.

use of one's car.[586] Unreimbursed expenses incurred for a charity's benefit are generally also deductible.[587]

> **To illustrate**: If a lawyer stays away from her private office on Thursdays and goes to do free legal work for a charitable organization, or if someone else goes to the Red Cross on Thursdays and rolls bandages, there is no taxation of income, imputed or otherwise, to either donor. However, if the lawyer and bandage roller had instead plied their trades for ordinary legal fees and wages for rolling bandages, and then had contributed an amount of money equal to the fees or wages they earned every Thursday to the charity, they would clearly get a charitable contribution deduction for the cash contributions. By denying a deduction for free services, the unpaid service provider and the person who earns and pays over his earned income are placed in similar after-tax positions. This has to be the right result.

2. Qualifying Charities

Scan §170(c)

To qualify as such, a charitable organization must either have received a letter from the IRS granting it an exemption from taxation, conditioned on good behavior,[588]or the taxpayer must be able to show that the entity qualifies *per se* despite the absence of such a letter. The obvious case of the latter is a local government or a church; for good Constitutional reasons, churches are not required to obtain such letters, although some churches fall short of any credible standard and are rightly treated as bogus. In fact, during one of the gaudier eras in tax history, unscrupulous promoters offered "mail order ministries" behind which the founders sought to hide their income from personal services. The promoters from the "parent church" charged healthy fees, and offered the new convert's "church" an opportunity to affiliate with an "established" parent church. The taxpayer would transfer all his property and future income to the alleged local church and would take a vow of poverty, while characterizing his housing expenses disbursed by the church to the "convert" as a tax-exempt parsonage allowance under §107.

Section 501(c)(3) contains the true charities. The Regulations[589] require their charters to limit their purposes to one or more "exempt purposes." A "charitable purpose" (the second exempt purpose in §501(c)(3)) includes[590]: relief of the poor and distressed or the underprivileged;

586 For example, it is 58 cents/mile for business use of one's car (Notice 2019-2), 14 cents/mile for charitable use (170(i)), and 20 cents/mile for medical and deductible moving use (Notice 2019-2).

587 See, e.g., Louis v. Commissioner, 25 T.C.M. 1966 (phone calls).

588 One uses Form 1023 to seek the exemption, which is provided in the form a of "determination letter." Once granted, the exemption is retroactive.

589 Reg. §1.501(c)(3)-1(b)(1).

590 Reg. §1.501(c)(3)-1(d)(2).

advancement of religion; advancement of education or science; erection or maintenance of public buildings, monuments or works; lessening of the burdens of government; and promotion of social welfare by organizations designed to accomplish any of the above purposes, or to lessen neighborhood tensions; to eliminate prejudice and discrimination; to defend human and civil rights secured by law; or to combat community deterioration and juvenile delinquency.

The cases go further than the Code suggests. As a leading example, it has been held that a entity formed to accumulate funds to construct the headquarters for the Kentucky Bar Association was a charity because of the various benefits of the Bar Association, including a client security fund, a forum for inquiring in to claims of unethical conduct and unauthorized practice of law and fee arbitration plans benefitted the public so much more than the local bar.[591]

A major area of concern has been restricting racial discrimination by exempt organization. The IRS guidelines on racial preference relating to schools provides, among other things, that the selection of students for a religious school can prefer students of a given religion if membership in the denomination is open to all on a racially nondiscriminatory basis.[592] This concept logically goes beyond schools. On the other hand, a school that practices racial discrimination in its admission policies, even if based on religious doctrines, stands to lose its tax exemption, according to the Supreme Court in *Bob Jones University v. United States.*[593]

Lobbying by charities is a problem. The general resolution is to threaten them with disqualification if they engage in political lobbying, but to leave some slack for doing so, provided they pay a penalty, phrased as an excise tax on excessive lobbying expenditures.[594] Charities that participate in political campaigns, as opposed to lobbying, face the loss of their tax exemption.[595] There is no slack here.

Finally, charities that regularly engage in trades or business that are substantially unrelated to the exempt organization's "exempt purpose" are taxable on their profits under §511. This keeps charities from having an unfair competitive advantage.

> **To illustrate**: The University Bookstore regularly operates a book business, but it is related to the university's exempt function (teaching students). If instead the university ran a public racetrack, the racetrack's profits would be subject to income taxation.

591 Kentucky Bar Foundation v. CIR, 78 T.C. 921 (1982).

592 Rev. Proc. 75-50. §3.01-.02.

593 461 U.S. 574 (1983).

594 §4911.

595 Reg. §1.170A-1(h)(5).

3. The Effect of Personal Benefit from the Contribution

There needs to be donative intent, but it need not rise to the level of a gift in the *Duberstein* sense.[596] The transfer must merely be of money or property, and if there is consideration, then the donor must reduce his deduction by the value of what he received back, such as a coffee mug from a PBS station, or college football tickets at the 50 yard line.[597] The question of whether there is a personal benefit can become complicated. For one thing, the benefit may be mingled with religion. For example, a parishioner might pay an additional amount to get a more comfortable pew in a church. In a recent controversial case, the Supreme Court ruled that scientologists who get psychological assistance in at least partial exchange for their contributions are not able to deduct the full value of their contributions because they were strictly for a *quid pro quo* and lacked any donative intent.[598]

If one cannot separate out a *quid pro quo,* and if the primary reason for the contribution is to benefit one's self, then no charitable contribution deduction is allowed.[599] The charitable contribution deduction is nonexclusive, so sometimes the contribution may also be deductible as business expenses under §162.[600] That may make the personal benefit issue more smoke than fire.

> **To illustrate:** The Bigly Corporation makes computer chips. It makes a $100,000 payment to Smart University, with directions that the money be used to furnish a lab that specializes in advanced chip engineering. Bigly Corporation anticipates that it will be the first in line to get access to the chips, which promises to make Bigly Corporation ever bigger. (As it turned out, everything went according to plan.) The $100,000 is not deductible as a charitable contribution. It was given primarily to benefit Bigly Corporation and cannot be broken into deductible and nondeductible parts. Bigly would be better off claiming a business expense deduction for the payments to the university.

The following matrix of annual charitable contribution limitations, as percentage of contribution and amount, may be helpful to you. The important issue is whether the donor can deduct the value or only the basis of appreciated property she gives. The percentage limits may just

---

596 See Rev. Rul. 71112, 19711 93.

597 See Rev. Rul. 67246, 19672 C.B. 104; Rev. Proc. 90-12, 1990-1 C.B. 471.

598 Hernandez v. Commissioner, 490 U.S. 680 (1989). Curiously, after achieving this major litigating success, the IRS backed down administratively and in Rev. Rul. 93-73, 1973-2 C.B. 75 "obsoleted" Rev. Rul. 78-189, 1978-1 C.B. 68 (no §170 deductions for payments to Scientology), impliedly allowing the deductions knocked out in Hernandez. One author questions whether the IRS has such authority. Eaton, *Can the IRS overrule the Supreme Court?* 45 Emory L.J. 987 (1996). A letter to the IRS indicates the IRS and Scientology entered into a settlement that now allows deductions for Scientology "audit." See 95 Tax Notes Today 223-28 (Oct. 31, 1995) (arguing that this opens the door to allowing deductions for tuition payments for religious studies at Yeshiva Day Schools because the payments are for intangible religious benefits).

599 §6115.

600 Reg. §1.162-15(b).

represent deferral, not forfeiture, of tax deductions. That is, because the limits are annual, and the balance is carried forward to future years, only an exceptionally large contribution (compared to income) is likely to be forfeited. In fact, for some taxpayers the limits may be a blessing in disguise because the limits keeps from eroding the taxpayer's income to the point that they offset low-bracket income.

4. Gifts of Tangible Personal Property, Gifts to Certain Private Foundations, and Gifts of Short-Term Capital Gain Property

Tangible Personal Property. One can deduct the value of a gift of appreciated tangible personal property, such as a sculpture, if the gift relates to the donee's exempt function (such as an art museum). Otherwise, §170(e)(1)(B)(i) cuts the gift down to its basis. If the donee is a "private foundation," the news is even worse because the annual limit on charitable contributions shrinks to 20% of modified adjusted gross income. If the §501(c)(3) charity does not get broad public financial support,[601] then it is a "private foundation" and is subject to special scrutiny, restrictions and excise taxes, largely to make sure it is not "milked" by insiders. The reason for creating this special, disadvantageous category is that Congress was concerned that private foundations were being run as little kingdoms that were in need of policing.[602] Governments, churches and a short list of charities are never private foundations.

Gifts to Private Foundations. Gifts to private foundations get badly trimmed. In general, one can only deduct the *basis* of appreciated property given to a typical private foundation.[603] The most important exception is for donations of publicly traded stock in limited amounts.[604] (There are also exceptions to this rule for gifts of appreciated personal property that go to certain favored species of private foundations.[605])

> **To illustrate:** Marge establishes a charity. The charity falls under §501(c)(3). Because she contributes almost all of its capital, the charity is a private foundation. If she gives the foundation 100 shares of appreciated Dell Computer Co. stock (which is publicly traded) and 100 shares of a Marge Enterprises, Inc, a privately-held company, both held for at least a year, she can deduct not more than the basis of the Marge Enterprises stock, but she can deduct the value of the Dell stock because it is publicly traded.

---

601 This basically means a §501(c)(3) organization as to which not over a third of its support normally comes from the public. See §509.

602 See Hearings Before the House Ways and Means Committee, 91st Cong., 2d Sess. (1969).

603 §170(e)(1)(B)(ii).

604 §170(e)(5)(C) (the limit is 10% of the stock of the company, given by the donor and relatives). Such stock is known as "qualified appreciated stock."

605 See §170(b)(1)(E) (private operating foundations, foundations that disgorge their contributions, and certain pooled income funds that disgorge their income).

Gifts of Short-Term Capital Gain Property. You will see later that most assets are capital assets and that if they are held for over a year and a day they qualify for favorable long-term capital gains treatment when they are sold. The Code denies deductions beyond basis for gifts of assets which do not qualify for long-term capital gains if sold.

> **To illustrate**: Kindly runs a cigar store which he has owned for years. He has some old cigars from 1982 and some stock of a dot.com company that cost him $30 and is now worth $100. He has held the stock eight months. He gives his church the stock and all his cigars, which cost $40 and are also worth $100. The cigars are inventory and as such cannot be capital assets. Kindly's charitable contribution deduction is limited to $70, not $200, because -- tracking the Code -- neither the stock nor the cigars would have generated long-term capital gains if they had been sold rather than donated.

5. Contributions of Partial Interests in Property

There are imaginative ways to use charitable contributions through gifts of partial interests in property. For example, §170(h) allows people to give away conservation contributions consisting of either (1) remainder interests (2) perpetual restrictions on use that can be made of the property (such as a facade easement on a historic building or antidevelopment easements on open space) (3) the donor's whole interest, except for retained interests in subsurface minerals, or (4) an undivided interest in the property. The donation must advance a real conservation or historic purpose in perpetuity.

6. Percentage Limits on Charitable Contributions

The charitable contribution rules include confusing percentage limits on charitable contribution deductions. They are of interest to philanthropists, and make handy elements of exam questions. The limits are based on a modified form of adjusted gross income (AGI) for the year, known as the "contribution base," consisting of AGI less net operating loss carry backs to the taxable year.[606] The limits are generally only deferral provisions in that disallowed amounts are carried forward up to five future years and are subjected to the same treatment in those later years.

606 §170(b)(1)(F).

DONEE

PROPERTY	"§170(b)(1)(A)" charity	Private foundation	"Good" private foundation or government unit	Authority
Cash	50% [30% if given in trust]	30%[20% if in trust]	50%[30% if in trust]	§170(b)
Long-term capital gain marketable stock	30% of value, unless taxpayer elects to use 50% of basis	20% of value	30% of value unless taxpayer elects to use 50% of basis	§170(b), (e)(1) and (5)
Long-term capital gain property, but not listed below	30% of value unless taxpayer elects to use 50% of basis	20%/basis	30%/value	§170(b)
Ordinary income property	30% of basis	20% of basis	30% of basis	§170(e)(1)
Tangible personal property -- related use	30% of value	20% of basis	30% of value	§170(e)(1)
Tangible personal property -- unrelated use	30% of basis	20% of basis	30% of basis	§170(e)(1)

Percentage limit for cash charitable contributions by individuals temporarily increased.—

For tax years 2018 through 2025, the Tax Cuts and Jobs Act of 2017 temporarily increases the 50 percent of modified adjusted gross income limit for an individual taxpayer's cash charitable contributions to public charities, private operating private foundations, and governmental units to 60 percent. §170(b)(1)(G)(ii), as added by the Tax Cuts Act and Jobs Act of 2017.

7. Substantiation

Section 170(a)(1) denies *any* deduction for donated property if the taxpayer fails to substantiate it as required under the Regulations. This means that the donor must get a rigorous appraisal (known as a "qualified appraisal" by a "qualified appraiser") which she attaches to her tax return for the year of the gift if she claims the property (aside from publicly traded securities, such as IBM stock) is worth over $5,000.[607] If the gift is merely over $250, the charity must give the donor a detailed statement (not an appraisal) describing the donation, by the time she files

607 Reg. §1.170A-13(c). One is expected to use Form 8283.

her return.[608] Section 6115(a) requires modest reporting where the charity receives over $75 in value in connection with a quid pro quo charitable donation. Notice that charitable contribution deductions are allowed only in the year they are made, so pledges are not good enough. Only payment counts.

The following cases show why we need substantiation rules.

PASQUALINI v. COMMISSIONER OF INTERNAL REVENUE
103 T.C. 1 (1994)

COLVIN, Judge.

Petitioners in these consolidated cases claimed charitable contributions deductions for the donation of a total of 180,000 Christmas cards to Catholic Charities. Respondent disallowed the deductions and determined income tax deficiencies, with additions to tax and increased interest.

. . .

. . .

Another issue for decision, whether, if petitioners had sold the Christmas cards, the gain would have been ordinary income and reduced petitioners' charitable contribution deductions pursuant to section 170(e)(1)(A), will be decided by separate opinion.

There are two groups of petitioners: (a) Clients of the accounting firm of Albano, Leaf, Saltzman, Pfeil, Maeder & Co. (the Albano, Leaf firm), and (b) accountants employed by the Albano, Leaf firm. Petitioners . . . were clients of the Albano, Leaf firm. Petitioners . . . and Albano were accountants employed by the Albano, Leaf firm. . . .

. . .

FINDINGS OF FACT

Some of the facts have been stipulated and are so found. . . .

. . .

2. The Customs Service Auction of Christmas Cards

On December 8, 1981, Adler [one of the taxpayers] went to a U.S. Customs Service (Customs Service) auction preview at the World Trade Center in New York City to buy medical equipment. While there, he saw Christmas cards with gold medallions among the property to be auctioned

608 §170(f)(8). The key component is a good faith estimate of the value of the contribution. The receipt must be obtained by the due date for filing (including extensions) or the actual filing date, whichever is earlier. For charitable contributions of property in excess of $500, the taxpayer must maintain further records regarding the manner of acquisition of the property and the date such property was acquired. Reg. §1.170A-13(b)(3)(i)(A). Form 8283.

2 days later. There were 10 lots of 18,000 cards each, for a total of 180,000 cards. The Customs Service auction catalogue stated that the cards were valued for import duty purposes at $ 10.50 each, for a total of $ 1,890,000.

Adler immediately contacted Saltzman to ask whether the cards could be purchased and donated to obtain tax benefits. Saltzman said yes, if they found a charitable donee to use the cards in its normal operations. Adler contacted a friend of his, Hy Frankel (Frankel), who occasionally did work for Catholic Charities, Diocese of Brooklyn (Catholic Charities). Frankel said that Catholic Charities might be interested in the cards.

Saltzman contacted Leonard Gubar, an attorney at Spengler, Carlson, Guber, Brodsky & Rosenthal (Spengler, Carlson), a law firm which specialized in tax matters. Saltzman described the proposed transaction and made an appointment for Adler and him to meet the next day with Gubar and Len Schneidman, another Spengler, Carlson tax partner. Schneidman briefly researched the deductibility of the cards. Gubar and Schneidman gave Saltzman and Adler the impression that they believed the proposed acquisition and donation of the cards was a sound arrangement, and that it was reasonable for petitioners to use the Customs Service value for charitable contributions purposes because the Customs Service is a branch of the Treasury Department.

Gubar told Saltzman that Spengler, Carlson wanted to buy two or three lots of the cards for their clients. Saltzman let them buy only one lot because he wanted to make the others available to his firm and its clients.

Saltzman and one of his partners, Peter Albano, contacted clients to recommend that they buy and donate the cards. They concentrated primarily on people who could invest money on short notice and who had participated in the medical goods contribution arrangement. Saltzman told the clients that Spengler, Carlson believed that the donation arrangement was sound and that they wanted to participate in it. Saltzman told petitioners the IRS might challenge the value of the Christmas cards when they bought them. The Albano, Leaf firm did not receive compensation from its clients for arranging the Christmas cards donation.

On December 10, 1981, Adler, Saltzman, and Emil Solimine (Solimine) purchased the 180,000 Christmas cards for $ 30,000 at the Customs Service auction. After the auction, Solimine insured the cards at their Customs Service value ($ 1,890,000). Adler paid for the cards to be delivered and stored in a warehouse, where they remained until they were delivered to Catholic Charities. The cards were packed in large crates which were about 5 feet high and 5 feet across and weighed about 600 pounds.

Petitioners have not dealt with Christmas cards or any similar property in any trade or business.

3. The Christmas Cards

Each of the Christmas cards contained one of a series of six medallions embossed on gold foil which depicted a common Biblical scene related to Christmas (e.g., the Nativity). The Christmas cards were essentially identical; only the medallion and the text describing the scene on the medallion varied. The cards stated that the medallions were replicas of a gold medal created by Norman Sillman, "one of the World's renowned sculptors." The record contains samples of four of the six different cards and medallions. Four of the scenes were The Annunciation, The Manger Scene, The Three Wise Men, and the Departure To Egypt.

Each Christmas card was inside a folder (the outer folder). The outer folder bore the following legend on the inside left page:

> The Order of The Holy Cross of Jerusalem
>
> Apostolic Mission to the Children of Central and South America 60 East 94th Street, New York, N.Y. 10028. Telephone 3480948
>
> The Story of Christmas in Medallic Art
>
> On the back of each card was a Maltese cross type seal, followed by these words:
>
> Lorenzo Michel de Valitch, Titular Bishop of Ephesus, Grand Chancellor
>
>> A donation has become available through your purchase of this card replica and is gratefully acknowledged.
>>
>> The welfare of children is the concern of all. Please contact us for further information. All contributions are taxexempt under Certificate of the U.S. Treasury Department M69E00 573.

Each card contained the words "A Merry Christmas and a Prosperous New Year" on the outside front cover. On the middle of the left inside page were the words "wish you." "Wish you" is printed on the wrong side of the page on each card; it should have been printed on the outside front cover.

On the inside right page of each card was a small gold foil medallion and a Biblical quotation. The card with the Departure To Egypt medallion bears a Biblical quotation from St. Matthew 2:13/14, which refers to King "Herold." This is a misspelling of King "Herod." The card with the Three Wise Men medallion did not capitalize "Bethlehem" and "I."

The printing on the sample cards in the record is in red ink and is of poor quality. Some of the cards have small red spots resulting from the cards having been stacked before the ink was dry. The imprinting of the text is uneven. In some places the ink is splashed on the page.

The medallions are round, paper thin, and about 113/16 inches in diameter. The medallions are under a plastic acetate film that is attached at the top and fastened to the right inside page of the card. The medallions are easily removed from under the acetate cover.

The words "Embossed on 23 carat gold" appear on each card on the right inside page below the medallion. However, the medallions are not 23 carat gold. The middle of the medallion is paper, the front is gold foil, and the back is an aluminum and copper foil. An independent testing service assayed the contents of the gold medallions. The medallions weigh .371 grams each. Of this amount, only .439% (less than ½ of 1 percent) or 1.62 mg is gold. The workmanship is of average quality. On December 31, 1982, the price of gold was $449.90 per troy ounce.

4. Donation of the Cards to Catholic Charities

After the auction, Frankel referred Adler to Thomas DeStefano (DeStefano), the Executive Director of Catholic Charities. Catholic Charities is a tax exempt under section 501(c)(3). Adler sent DeStefano one of the cards which petitioners intended to donate. Adler did not send DeStefano an outer folder, which referred to the Order of the Holy Cross of Jerusalem. DeStefano told Frankel that Catholic Charities could use the cards to distribute to its parishes. Shortly after the auction, Catholic Charities agreed to accept the cards.

Petitioners held the cards for more than 1 year. Around December 27, 1982, petitioners donated the cards to Catholic Charities. The cards were insured, shipped, stored, and donated in bulk. . . .

In December 1982, Adler gave DeStefano a list of donors and the number and Customs Service value of the cards donated by each. DeStefano accepted the donation and sent acknowledgment letters to the donors.

Adler arranged storage until Catholic Charities could use the cards. In the spring of 1983, DeStefano arranged for the crates containing the cards to be stored at the St. Anthony's Hospital building (St. Anthony's) in New York City. St. Anthony's was a former hospital that various organizations affiliated with the Catholic Church used as a storage facility. The cards were stored at St. Anthony's for several years. The cards were later misplaced or discarded during renovations at St. Anthony's. This was discovered in 1989.

5. Petitioners' 1982 Tax Returns and Investigation of the Cards' Fair Market Value

Shortly after the auction, Saltzman suggested that Adler contact the Customs Service to obtain the work papers used to value the cards. Adler wrote to the Customs Service to request this information. In May 1982, Adler received a letter from Alice Wong, Director of the Merchandise Control Unit of the Customs Service, which included a worksheet showing the value which appeared in the December 1981 auction catalogue ($ 1,890,000) and an excerpt from 19 C.F.R. sec. 127.23 (1993) which establishes the procedure for appraising unclaimed merchandise by the Customs Service. Adler received the worksheet before petitioners filed their Federal income tax returns for tax year 1982.

Saltzman did not do any legal research regarding whether petitioners could use the Customs Service value for charitable deduction purposes before the auction or before they filed their 1982 returns. Petitioners did not know the expertise of the Customs Service employee who completed the worksheet, learn how the Customs Service chose the value, or order an appraisal of the cards before they filed their returns.

. . .

6. Valuation of the Cards by the Customs Service

The Customs Service sold the Christmas cards because an import duty of $ 78,246 had not been paid. The Customs Service valued the cards for import duty purposes at $ 7 foreign value and $ 10.50 domestic value per card. Foreign value is the price or value of the item in the foreign country from which it was imported under 19 U.S.C. sec. 1677b (1988). The Customs Service estimates the domestic value of unclaimed merchandise that is to be sold at auction based on the foreign value plus other costs incident to the landing of the merchandise in the United States and the importer's wholesale markup.

The Customs Service valuation process may be based on an invoice from the foreign exporter stating the transaction value, i.e., the price paid or payable, for the goods under 19 U.S.C. sec. 1401a(b)(1) (1988). However, there is often no invoice for unclaimed merchandise. Absent an invoice, the value may be based on the opinion of a Customs Service national import specialist. See 19 U.S.C. sec. 1401a(f)(1) (1988).

Evelyn Booker (Booker) was the Customs Service commodity specialist who completed part of the Customs Service appraisal form and selected the $ 10.50 value for the Christmas cards. She specialized in textile valuation and had no expertise in valuing greeting cards. Her worksheet for the Customs Service valuation contains no analysis. . .

OPINION

1. Value of the Christmas Cards

a. Fair Market Value

The first issue for decision is the fair market value of the Christmas cards for which petitioners claimed charitable contribution deductions totaling $ 1,890,000.

Section 170(a)(1) allows a deduction for any charitable contribution made within the taxable year. The taxpayer bears the burden of proving he is entitled to deductions. . . . In general, the amount of a charitable contribution made in property other than money is the fair market value of the property at the time of the contribution. Sec. 1.170A1(c)(1), Income Tax Regs. Fair market value is the price at which the property would change hands between a willing buyer and a willing seller, neither being under any compulsion to buy or sell and both having a reasonable knowledge of the facts. *United States v. Cartwright*, 411 U.S. 546, 550551 (1973); sec. 1.170A1(c)(2), Income Tax Regs.

Fair market value is a question of fact [and] . . . . a question of judgment rather than mathematics. . . . Valuation is an approximation derived from all the evidence. . . .

b. The Customs Service Valuation

[The court did not address the contention that the Customs Service, as another arm of the Treasury Department, spoke for the Department as a whole, including the IRS.]

. . .

Here, the Customs Service value is not persuasive evidence of the value of the Christmas cards. As in Brittingham, we have no explanation of how the Customs Service selected the value for the cards. The Customs Service employee who set the value specialized in textiles and had not previously handled greeting cards or other similar property. As discussed below, expert opinion in the record was helpful to us in deciding the value of the cards. Thus, we are not convinced that the Customs Service value was indicative of an arm'slength price for the cards and we do not rely on it in deciding the value of the cards.

c. The Appropriate Market

Section 20.20311(b), Estate Tax Regs., provides that the fair market value of property is based on the market where the property is most commonly sold to the public. Petitioner contends that the appropriate market to consider here is the retail market. We disagree.

The determination of the proper market is a factual question. . . . We believe that the cards could not be sold to a retail customer in the condition they were donated, i.e., without envelopes, in large bales, in the outer folders which named The Order of the Holy Cross of Jerusalem, and some with printing flaws. We conclude that wholesale is the appropriate market because a wholesale price (unlike a retail price) would properly recognize that significant effort would be required to prepare the cards for retail sale (e.g., remove the outer folder, provide an envelope for each card, box loose cards, and eliminate cards with printing flaws) to a retail customer. . . .

[The discussion of the clashing testimony of the government's and the taxpayers' expert witnesses is omitted. Eds.]

. . .

Taking into account the entire record, we find that the Departure To Egypt cards have zero value because of the misspelling of King Herod and that the value of the Three Wise Men cards was 25 cents per card because of the failure to capitalize "Bethlehem" and "I." We hold that the fair market value of the remaining 120,000 cards was 50 cents per card.

[The court went on to uphold penalties for negligence against the clients and the professional involved. The clients were held liable for negligence penalties, on the basis of the following reasoning.]

. . .

Petitionerclients knew they paid $ 30,000 for the cards, but that the Customs Service valued them for $ 1,890,000. They should have known that deducting 63 times the cost of the cards was too good to be true. *LaVerne v. Commissioner*, 94 T.C. 637, 652653 (1990). . . (11:1 writeoff "should have raised serious questions in the minds of ordinarily prudent investors"); *Weitz v. Commissioner*, T.C. Memo. 198999 (deduction of medical goods for 10 times auction price was "too good to be true"). When a transaction involves tax benefits even less fantastic than the 63to1 writeoff here, blind reliance on professional advisers is not in keeping with the standard of the ordinarily prudent person. . . .

Petitionerclients' reliance on their accountants and lawyers regarding the value of the cards was not reasonable because neither the accountants nor the lawyers were experts in valuing Christmas cards and neither investigated the appropriateness of using, or the legitimacy of, the Customs Service valuation of the cards. . . .

. . .

Decisions will be entered under Rule 155.

Notes on Charitable Contributions and Misvaluations

The taxpayers in *Pasqualini* carefully aged the cards so that they would be held for over a year. That would make them assets held for the necessary amount of time in order to qualify as *long-term* capital assets, if they were capital assets. Assuming they were capital assets, then §170(e)(1)(A) would not have been a problem. The taxpayers won this point. As a result they got a $67,500 deduction. Remember that the cards cost them only $30,000.

Charitable contributions depend on valuations. The higher the value of the gift, the more taxes one saves. Congress has strewn specific penalties in the path of misvaluations. As you know already, §6662 imposes a 20%/40% accuracyrelated penalty on, among other things, substantial valuation overstatements and understatements. For example, if a taxpayer in the 30% bracket under-reported $100 of income as a result of an exaggerated charitable contribution deduction, then the underpayment of tax would be $30 and the 20% accuracy-related penalty would be $6.

8. Income-Variant Effect

The tax planning potential of donations of property to charity has attracted the attention of ingenious tax advisors. While no one seems to have figured out how to get a greater tax benefit than the value of the contributed property, it is clear that the higher the tax bracket the donor is in, the less it hurts to give. The following condensed table shows how much a donor can give to a qualified charity while reducing net worth by only $1,000 (depending on her tax bracket). The differences depend on the taxpayer's marginal rate.

Marginal Rate	Gross Contribution	Reduction of Net Worth After Taxes
15%	$1,176	$1,000
28%	1,388	1,000
36%	1,563	1,000
39%	1,639	1,000
50%	2,000	1,000

Note the relative advantages to a very highbracket taxpayer of giving appreciated property, rather than cash, to charities. If she wished to make a contribution of $1,000, and if she had stock that had appreciated by a factor of 10, she would have to sell a great deal more than $1,000 worth of stock to have $1,000 left, after taxes, to contribute in cash to the charity (and get a corresponding $1,000 charitable contribution deduction). But by giving stock, she can still get $1,000 into her favorite charity's hands (and get the same $1,000 deduction) by giving it $1,000 worth of stock (which cost her only $100). If Congress is troubled by the income-variant effect, it is free to repeal §170 and replace it with an income-neutral tax credit.

Problem 7-2:

Which of the following qualify as deductible charitable contributions, and in what amount?

1) In 1998 the twisted "Unabomber," Ted Kaczynski, was captured as a result of information provided to the authorities by this brother, David Kaczynski. David received a $1 million reward, which he pledged to give the families of his brother's victims:

    a. Is David taxed on the $1 million?

    b. Can David deduct the gifts to the victims as a charitable contribution?

2) Mr. Y works hard to set up an auction for a local charity. He would normally earn $50 per hour, but he instead generously dedicated his time to the charity. See Reg. §1.170A1(g).

3) How would Mr. Y treat $50 of unreimbursed telephone calls made for the benefit of the charity? How about 167 miles of travel for the benefit of the charity at 14 cents/mile (the 2013 allowance)? See Reg. §1.170A-1(g) and §170(i).

4) George Generous paid $100 to his local Public Television Broadcasting station. He loves their programs.

5) George Generous paid $100 for a "designated donor" ticket to the Benefit Ball for the Home for the Unpleasant, a §501(c)(3) organization which has received an exemption letter from the IRS. The normal price for a ticket to the ball would be $30.

6) George also made a gift of a modern sculpture to a local hospital, which it stored away for eventual sale. See §170(e)(1)(B). It cost him $1,000 in 1965 and was worth $42,000 when donated.

7) Mrs. Van Gelt owns a valuable island off the coast of Maine, on which she has a summer house. She will give away all but one acre to the Nature Conservancy, a public charity, by means of a perpetual easement that prevents development of the

encumbered land. She wants no one to set foot on that part of the island aside from herself and her relatives. Before the gift, the entire island is worth $1,000,000, of which $150,000 is from the value of the acre Mrs. Van Gelt will keep (combined with the house on this acre). After the gift, the acre she kept and the house are worth a combined $500,000. In effect, the value of the acre with the house on it increased in value by $350,000 because of the gift. How much can Mrs. Van Gelt deduct under §170? See §170(h) and Reg. §1.170A-14(h)(3)(i).

8) Harry Klopman had modified AGI of $2 million this year. He makes a gift of $2 million this year to the following alternative donees, both of which have received exemption letters from the IRS. How much of the $2 million is deductible this year? If there is a limit on this year's deduction, how is the excess treated?

   a. Old Ivy, his alma mater, a well-known university.

   b. The Society For The Preservation of Water. Harry started the foundation. The $2 million is its first contribution, and there is not likely to be more money for it from the public.

9) Professor Fonebone, a calendar year taxpayer who filed his Federal Income Tax return on April 15, gave the local Maritime Academy (a school under §501(c)(3)) an old boat of his, as to which he claimed a $300 deduction. Can he claim the deduction if the Academy gave him a "§170(f)(8) statement" on June 1?

10) The first time Harold's daughter got married it killed him that he had to pay so much for the wedding, even including $42,000 for flowers for the ceremony and reception, so the second time she got married he got the florist to send the flowers to the local publicly-supported charity hospital for the patients right after the wedding. The flowers cost him $40,000 this time. The florist gave him a receipt on which it wrote that it was sure the flowers were worth $35,000 by the time the hospital got them. That was true. The patients and staff loved the flowers and were very happy. The flowers lasted about three more days.

    a. Can Harold deduct the $35,000? See §170(a) and (e).
    Harold was so pleased with the deduction he claimed for the flowers that he began his own flower garden. He would grow the flowers all summer and then he would cut them and give them to the hospital. It cost him about $200 to grow them, but they were worth $10,000.

b. How much can Harold deduct? See §170(e)(1)(A).

c. Harold gave 100 shares of GM stock to his college. It has a basis of $100 and had value of $200. He has owned the stock for many years. How much can he deduct?

d. What if his basis had instead been $350 and the value of the stock was only $100? See Reg. §1.170A-1(c).

e. In the case of "4)," would he be better off to sell the stock and give the cash proceeds to the college? What would your advice be?

f. What can he deduct if he gave the same stock (basis $100, value $200) to the Friends of Cats Foundation, which, because he is its only contributor, is a private foundation? See §170(e)(5).

11) Dr. Ahmed is a kindly physician who has prospered in the United States, even though he arrived from his native Pakistan only 25 years ago as a college student. He wishes to organize a charity which will "provide support for needy Muslims," the exact language of the charter in the not-for-profit organization he recently formed under state law. He now wishes to proceed with getting it §501(c)(3) status.

a. Must it apply for §501(c)(3) status, or is such status automatic?

b. Is there a problem with the purposes of the entity that will cause it not to achieve §501(c)(3) status?

12) Should college varsity athletic programs be taxable on the theory that they produce unrelated business taxable income under §511?

Read §213(a)-(d)(4), (d)(9)-(10)

1. Introduction and Background

In 1942 Congress enacted the predecessor of §213 so as to allow a deduction for medical expenses paid during the year, but the deduction was and still is limited to "extraordinary" medical expenses. The deduction was justified as a tax incentive for good health and as provision for relieving hardship, "in consideration of the heavy tax burden" borne by people during WWII and in light of "the desirability of maintaining the present high level of public health and morale."[609] From the outset, payments for illegal surgical procedures or operations have been nondeductible, a limitation that proved to be of special significance in those years and states where abortions were illegal. Now, cosmetic surgery is nondeductible. §213(d)(9).

The current deduction for medical expenses is fairly broad in that it covers the taxpayer and their dependents and a broad range of expenses, such as prescribed medicines. However, the 10% of adjusted gross income (AGI) floor puts the whole system onto a disaster model for most people.[610] As a result, it is fair to say the deduction does not support discretionary personal consumption because the expenditures are so likely to be involuntary.

> **To illustrate:** A taxpayer with adjusted gross income of $100,000 who pays a $15,000 medical bill in this year can deduct at most $5,000 because of the 10% of AGI floor (i.e., $10,000).

The most important tax policy question is, should only extraordinary expenses be deductible? If so, then a threshold makes some sense, but the selection of the level is necessarily arbitrary. Arguably, the standard deduction includes some medical expense, justifying a threshold, at least in part. At a cruder level, thresholds offer a subtle way of repealing tax deductions without the political heat associated with doing so.

The relative unavailability of the deduction means that the practical question for today's taxpayers is how to get employer-paid medical coverage.

Medical expenditures are deductible only if they are not reimbursed -- through insurance, damages from a tortfeasor, an employer's plan, or otherwise. Sections 104 and 105 assure that medical expense reimbursements are untaxed unless the taxpayer previously claimed a medical

---

609 S. Rep. No. 1631, 77th Cong., 2d Sess. 6 (1942).

610 **Medical expense deduction AGI threshold temporarily reduced.** The threshold to claim an itemized deduction for unreimbursed expenses paid for the medical care of the taxpayer or the taxpayer's spouse or dependents is reduced to 7.5 percent of adjusted gross income (AGI) for 2017 and 2018. §213(f) as amended by the Tax Cuts and Jobs Act of 2017. The reduced threshold applies for both regular tax and alternative minimum tax purposes §56(b)(1)(B) as amended by the Tax Cuts and Jobs Act of 2017.

expense deduction for the reimbursement. (If the employer bought health insurance for its employees, §106 shields the employees from being taxed when the employer pays the health insurance premiums.) Amounts received for physical injury damages, or that are otherwise not reimbursements for medical expenses, are tax-free and can be spent on deductible medical care.

Notice that payments for medical insurance coverage are also deductible if the policy covers medical care, prescription drugs, ambulance hire or other items that fall within the meaning of "medical care" under §213(d). It is even possible for a taxpayer who is under age 65 to claim current deductions for future medical care as long as the premiums are payable on a level basis over a substantial period of time.[611] The premiums are lumped together with other medical expenses for the year and are subject to the 10.0% of AGI floor.[612]

Even though capital expenditures generally are not currently deductible for Federal Income Tax purposes,[613] an expenditure that otherwise qualifies as a medical expense under §213 is not disqualified merely because it is a capital expenditure, as long as its primary purpose is the medical care of the taxpayer, a spouse, or dependent. So, a capital expenditure that is related only to the sick person and is not related to permanent improvement or betterment of other property (such as a swimming pool in the backyard of a luxury home) is deductible if it otherwise qualifies as an expenditure for medical care. For example, an expenditure for eyeglasses, artificial teeth or limbs, a wheelchair, or a seeing-eye dog are deductible.

A capital expenditure that does permanently improve property and that would not ordinarily be for the purpose of medical care, may still qualify for the medical expense deduction to the extent that the expenditure exceeds the increase in value of the related property, provided that the particular expenditure is directly related to medical care. For example, a taxpayer who has to install an elevator in his residence because he is afflicted with heart disease, and is advised by his physician not to climb stairs, may deduct the cost of the elevator minus the increase in the value of his residence that results from adding the elevator. If the value of the residence did not increase, the entire cost of installing the elevator may qualify for the medical expense deduction.[614]

To illustrate: One taxpayer, Bonnie Ferris, had a medical problem which prompted her doctor to recommend that the family install an indoor swimming pool. The home was a luxury residence and the Ferrises built a magnificent pool costing $194,000 of which they claimed $127,000 as medical care expense, being the cost of the pool that did not increase the property's value from adding the pool. The Commissioner contended that an adequate pool would have cost $70,000 and would have increased the property value by $31,000 and thus only $39,000 was a

611 See §213(d)(7).

612 7.5% for 2017 and 2018.

613 See §263.

614 See generally Reg. §1.2131(e)(1)(iii).

medical expense. The court agreed with the IRS, reasoning that the premium that the Ferrises paid was driven by personal aesthetic motivations, not the need for medical care, and fell outside §213.[615]

Few taxpayers realize that cost of transportation "primarily for and essential to" medical care can be deducted as medical expenses.[616] One can use a standard mileage rate in lieu of demonstrated actual costs.[617] Lodging expenses while away from home can be included in medical expense if incurred as an essential element of medical care by a physician at a licensed hospital or other medical facility. Reg. §1.213-1(e). Meals are not deducted and the lodging deduction is capped at $50 per day. In addition, the House Committee Report on the Tax Reform Act of 1984 says the lodging expense of someone necessarily accompanying the patient (e.g., a parent with an ill child) is also deductible, up to $50 per day.[618] As inflation rises, it seems smaller and smaller.

COMMISSIONER v. BILDER

369 U.S. 499 (1962)

MR. JUSTICE HARLAN delivered the opinion of the Court.

This case concerns the deductibility as an expense for "medical care," under §213 of the Internal Revenue Code of 1954, 26 U.S.C.A. §213, of rent paid by a taxpayer for an apartment in Florida, where he was ordered by his physician, as part of a regimen of medical treatment, to spend the winter months.

The taxpayer, now deceased, was an attorney practicing law in Newark, New Jersey. In December 1953, when he was 43 years of age and had suffered four heart attacks during the previous eight years, he was advised by a heart specialist to spend the winter season in a warm climate. The taxpayer, his wife, and his threeyearold daughter proceeded immediately to Fort Lauderdale, Florida, where they resided for the ensuing three months in an apartment rented for $1,500. Two months of the succeeding winter were also spent in Fort Lauderdale in an apartment rented for $829.

. . .

We consider the Commissioner's position unassailable in the light of the congressional purpose explicitly revealed in the House and Senate Committee Reports on the bill. These reports, anticipating the precise situation now before us, state:

615 See Ferris v. Commissioner, 582 F.2d 1112 (7th Cir. 1978).

616 See Reg. §1.2131(e)(1)(iv).

617 Elwood v. Commissioner, 72 T.C. 264 (1979) and, see §213(d)(2).

618 See §213(d)(2).

"Subsection (e) defines medical care to mean amounts paid for the diagnosis, cure, mitigation, treatment, or prevention of diseases or for the purpose of affecting any structure or function of the body (including amounts paid for accident or health insurance), or for transportation primarily for and essential to medical care. The deduction permitted for "transportation primarily for and essential to medical care" *clarifies existing law* in that it *specifically excludes deduction of any meals and lodging while away from home receiving medical treatment.* For example, if a doctor prescribes that a patient must go to Florida in order to alleviate specific chronic ailments and to escape unfavorable climatic conditions which have proven injurious to the health of the taxpayer, and the travel is prescribed for reasons other than the general improvement of a patient's health, the cost of the patient's transportation to Florida would be deductible *but not his living expenses while there.* However, if a doctor prescribed an appendectomy and the taxpayer chose to go to Florida for the operation not even his transportation costs would be deductible. The subsection is not intended otherwise to *change* the existing definitions of medical care, to deny the cost of ordinary ambulance transportation nor to deny the cost of food or lodging provided as part of a hospital bill." H.R.Rep. No. 1337, 83d Cong., 2d Sess., A60 (1954); S.Rep. No. 1622, 83d Cong., 2d Sess. 219220 (1954). (Emphasis supplied.)

Since under the predecessor statute, as it had been construed, expenses for meals and lodging were deductible as expenses for "medical care," it may well be true that the Committee Reports spoke in part inartistically when they referred to subsection (e) as a mere clarification of "existing law," although it will be noted that the report also referred to what was being done as a *pro tanto* "change" in "the existing definitions of medical care." Yet Congress' purpose to exclude such expenses as medical deductions under the new bill is unmistakable in these authoritative pronouncements . . . .

. . . . The Committee Reports foreclose any reading of that provision which would permit this taxpayer to take the rental payments for his Florida apartment as "medical care" deductions.

. . .

2. Deductions of Medical Expenses Outside §213

If §213 were repealed, would that end the deductibility of all medical expenses? The answer is "no," because §213 does not claim to monopolize the area. Occasionally, medical expenses do qualify as business expenses under §162, but if the medical expense has a general or personal value, §262 makes it unlikely to be allowed as a business expense deduction. An example is an actress who seeks to deduct the cost of dentures to correct a speech impediment. Eliminating the impediment helps her career, but it also offers satisfaction off the job.

REV. RUL. 75-316

19752 C.B. 54

. . .

The Internal Revenue Service has been asked whether amounts paid by blind individuals for the services of readers, under the circumstances described below, may be deducted as business expenses under section 162 of the Internal Revenue Code of 1954 rather than as medical expenses under section 213.

Many blind individuals employed in professional or semiprofessional positions require the services of fulltime or parttime readers in order to perform their business duties satisfactorily. The cost of the readers is generally paid by the blind individuals and not by their employers and the blind individuals are not entitled to reimbursement of such expenses by their employers. The services provided by the readers relate solely to the professional or semiprofessional work performed by their blind clients. The readers may render their services during regular working hours and at their blind clients' places of employment, or outside of regular working hours and away from such places of employment.

Section 262 of the Code provides that, except as otherwise expressly provided, no deduction shall be allowed for personal, living, or family expenses.

Section 213(a) of the Code expressly allows a deduction, subject to certain limitations not relevant here, for expenses paid during the taxable year, not compensated for by insurance or otherwise, for the medical care of the taxpayer, his spouse, and his dependents. Section 213(e) provides, in part, that the term "medical care" includes amounts paid for the diagnosis, cure, mitigation, treatment, or prevention of disease or for the purpose of affecting any structure or function of the body.

Section 162(a) of the Code provides, in part, that there shall be allowed as a deduction all the ordinary and necessary expenses paid or incurred during the taxable year in carrying on a trade or business. The performance of services as an employee constitutes the carrying on of a trade or business. However, employee business expenses are deductible only as itemized deductions in computing taxable income unless they are . . . . (2) covered by a reimbursement or other expense allowance arrangement by the employer, or (3) transportation costs . . . .

Section 1.162l(a) of the Income Tax Regulations provides, in part, that a taxpayer's ordinary and necessary expenses for labor directly connected with or pertaining to the taxpayer's trade or business are deductible under section 162 of the Code.

The fact that a particular expense may under certain circumstances be a nondeductible personal expense does not preclude the deduction of such an expense as an ordinary and necessary business expense under other circumstances. See Rev. Rul. 70474, 19702 C.B. 34, which provides that the acquisition and maintenance costs of work uniforms of police officers, firemen, letter carriers, nurses, bus drivers, and railway men, which are required as a condition of employment and are not adaptable for general wear, are deductible business expenses under section 162 of the Code. Generally, the cost of clothing used by a taxpayer in connection with his work is a nondeductible personal expense under section 262 of the Code. See *Donnelly v. Commissioner*, 262 F.2d 411 (2d Cir. 1959), aff'g 28 T.C. 1278 (1957).

As with the deductibility of a taxpayer's expenses for work clothing under section 162 of the Code, the deductibility under that section of the expenses of blind professionals and semiprofessional for readers required by them to satisfactorily perform their work depends upon the particular facts and circumstances.

Where it is questionable whether an expense is deductible as a business expense rather than as a medical expense, such expense may be deducted as a business expense under section 162 of the Code if all three of the following elements are present: (1) the nature of the taxpayer's work clearly requires that he incur a particular expense to satisfactorily perform such work, (2) the goods or services purchased by such expense are clearly not required or used, other than incidentally, in the conduct of the individual's personal activities, and (3) the Code and regulations are otherwise silent as to the treatment of such expense.

In the instant case, the readers' services are required and used solely in the conduct of the work of the blind individuals. Accordingly, the expenses incurred by a blind individual in these circumstances for readers' services may be deducted as business expenses under section 162 of the Code, provided the blind individual itemizes his deductions.

Compare Rev. Rul. 75317, page 57, this Bulletin, which holds, under one set of facts stated therein, that the amounts paid by an invalid taxpayer for the meals and lodging expenses of a neighbor who accompanied him on business trips to assist him with his wheelchair, his luggage, the driving, the daily removal and replacement of prostheses, and the daily administration of his medication (such services being required and used by the taxpayer in his personal activities as well as incidentally in his business activities) are in the nature of payments for nursing services, which amounts are deductible as medical expenses under section 213 but are not deductible as business expenses under section 162.

The question whether a particular expense is a deductible business expense rather than a deductible medical expense is discussed in Rev. Rul. 57461, 19572 C.B. 116 (dealing with the maintenance expenses incurred by a blind individual for his seeingeye dog used in the conduct of his business), Rev. Rul. 58382, 19582 C.B. 59 (dealing, in part, with expenses of an airline flight agent for medical treatment required to maintain the physical fitness necessary to retain his position), and Rev. Rul. 7145, 19711 C.B. 51 (dealing with the expenses of a professional singer for required treatments of his throat by a medical specialist). Rev. Rul. 57461, Rev. Rul. 58382, and Rev. Rul. 7145 are distinguishable from the instant case since the stated facts in each of those rulings are such that the taxpayers there clearly incurred expenses for medical care used in the conduct of both their business and their personal activities, and thus such expenses may be deducted only under section 213 of the Code.

Policy Issues and Distortions

Before 2007, self-employed individuals could not deduct 100% of their health insurance and long-term care insurance although employees could exclude 100% of their employer paid their health insurance and long-term care insurance. The excerpt below explains the thinking and the rules.

House Ways and Means Committee Report on the Taxpayer Relief Act of 1998, HRRepNo 105-739, 105th Congress HR 4579, Congress (United States)

Reasons for Change

The Committee believes it appropriate to increase the deduction for health insurance expenses of self-employed individuals in order to reduce the disparity of treatment between such expenses and employer-provided health insurance and to help make health insurance more affordable for self-employed individuals.

Present Law

Under present law, self-employed individuals are entitled to deduct a portion of the amount paid for health insurance, including (within certain limits) long-term care insurance, for the self-employed individual and the individual's spouse and dependents. ...

Under present law, employees can exclude from income 100 percent of employer-provided health insurance.

Reasons for Change

The Committee believes it appropriate to increase the deduction for health insurance expenses of self-employed individuals in order to reduce the disparity of treatment between such expenses and employer-provided health insurance and to help make health insurance more affordable for self-employed individuals.

Explanation of Provision

The provision increases the deduction for health insurance of self-employed individuals to 100 percent....

Bunching Medical Deductions

The 10% threshold for medical expense deductions (7.5% for 2017 and 2018) creates an incentive for taxpayers to postpone payment of medical expenses in an attempt to "bunch" a sufficient amount into one taxable year in order to exceed the 10% floor on deductible medical payments. This violates the tax policy preference for neutrality within the marketplace. The statutory language cannot be entirely mechanical, however, and a prepayment of a medical bill may be disallowed on the ground that, if it is paid before the care has been tendered or a duty to pay has arisen, then it is not a payment of a medical expense, but is instead a mere nondeductible deposit. Another occasional tactic for married people is to file separate returns, so as to reduce the AGI of the payor spouse who may need major medical care, thereby making the 10% of AGI floor less of a problem.

Health Savings Accounts

Congress added health savings accounts (HSAs) to the tax mix in 2003. These are investment funds that are combined with high deductible health plans (HDHPs). See §223.An HDHP is generally an employer-provided health plan that offers no benefits each year unless and until medical expenses of the employee exceed a deductible amount, which must be not less than $1,000 for self-only coverage or $2,000 for family coverage. Someone who is covered by an HDHP can set up an HSA, to which he or she makes annual contributions equal to the lesser of the HDHP deductible or a statutory ceiling, which is $2,250 for a person with self-only coverage under an HDHP or $4,500 for family coverage. (All the dollar figures are inflation-adjusted). The employee can deduct his or her contributions to the HSA, and employer contributions to the employee's HSA are excluded from the employee's gross income. In addition, HSAs are tax-exempt, and distributions from them used to pay qualified medical expenses are excluded from gross income. Self-employed people can also benefit from HSAs. There are other tax incentives in this area, but the HSA is the most notable in recent years.

Problem 7-3:

Mork and Mindy are married and have adjusted gross income of $60,000. This year Mindy had an emergency appendectomy for which she paid $5,000. Mindy thinks the insurance company will probably pay $4,000 of those expenses but so far the insurer is indecisive and payment this year is unlikely.

1) Assuming the $5,000 qualified as a medical expense, can any deductions be claimed this year for an appendectomy?

2) What is the impact of the uncertain reimbursement?

3) What result if the insurance company reimburses half the $5,000 in the following year? See Reg. §1.213-1(g)(1).

4) Assume the same facts as in "1)." Is there any difference in result if the person who suffered the medical problem were Mork and Mindy's child?

5) Mork's problem is that he has an enormous nose, resulting from an untruthful nature. It has reached two feet in length and breathing has become difficult. Can he deduct the proposed surgery to shorten his nose?

6) Same as "(5)," but Mork is a diamond cutter and his nose is interfering more and more with his job. Has he any other justifiable basis for a deduction aside from §213?

7) At his doctor's insistence, Mork bought a $6,000 air conditioning unit that added $4,500 to the value of his home. The unit allows him to breathe safely. What is the maximum medical expense deduction he can claim for the unit? See Reg. §1.213-1(e)(1)(iii).

F. THEFT AND CASUALTY LOSSES

1. Introduction and Background

Before the Tax Cuts and Jobs Act of 2017, individuals could claim certain personal casualty losses, not compensated by insurance or otherwise, as itemized deductions including losses arising from fire, storm, shipwreck, other casualty, or theft. There were two limitations to qualify for a deduction: (1) a loss had to exceed $100, and (2) aggregate losses the individual could deduct had to exceed 10% of adjusted gross income.

For tax years 2018 through 2025, the personal casualty and theft loss deduction is no longer available, except for casualty losses incurred in a federally declared disaster and casualty losses that offset casualty gains. The casualty loss deduction helped to lessen the financial impact of casualty and theft losses on individuals. Now that the deduction is generally not available – except in the case of afederally declared disaster or as an offset to casualty gains – insurance becomes increasingly important.

Read §163(a) and (h)(1)(3)(C)

1. Introduction and Background

Debt is part of the American way of life. Americans are used to being in debt and to the way debt is calculated. When the repayment period is open-ended, as in the case of credit card debt, the borrower owes a fixed amount of interest on the debt for the period that the debt was outstanding, and can pay off the interest or the principal as she prefers.

> **To illustrate:** Nancy owes $10,000 on a revolving business loan from a bank that charges her 18% interest. Of the $10,000, the overdue principal is $6,000 and the overdue interest is $4,000. If the bank does not object, she could send the bank a check for $4,000, allocating it all to interest and get a $4,000 business interest expense deduction.

If the repayment period is fixed, the US practice is to call for an equal periodic payment, and to pre-calculate the specific amount to interest and principal and interest that is paid in each installment. For example, the typical home mortgage loan constitutes threequarters or more of the purchase price of a home and a great deal of the loan remains outstanding for many years. Of each equal monthly payment by a homeowner in the early years of the loan, a high proportion will go for interest and only a small part to reduce the principal on the loan. In later years that same flat monthly payment will consist of a larger share for principal and an equally smaller share for interest. This industry practice may unintentionally invite taxpayers to refinance their mortgages, even if there is no interest rate change, so as to increase the part of the monthly debt service that is apportioned to interest charges.

We all have an instinctive idea about what constitutes interest, but taxpayers are creative and not every question on the subject yields an intuitively comfortable answer, as the following case shows.

DORZBACK v. COLLISON
195 F.2d 69 (3d Cir.1952)

MARIS, Circuit Judge.

[Wife made a subordinated loan to her husband of $8,500 in exchange for 25% of the net profits of a retail business, after paying Husband a $4,000 salary. The result was an enormous profit ($8,000/yr.) for Wife. The IRS disallowed the interest to the extent it exceeded 5% interest.]

...

The . . . question to be determined is whether the taxpayer was entitled to deduct the payments made under the 1943 agreement "in lieu of interest" as interest payments under Section 23(b). The defendant contends that the payments of 25% of net profits, which amounted almost to the amount of the principal in 1943 and 1944 and in 1945 were greater than the actual indebtedness, could not be considered to be interest under that section. . . . Deputy v. Du Pont, 1940, 308 U.S. 488, 498. The word must be given the "usual, ordinary and everyday meaning of the term." Old Colony R. Co. v. Commissioner, 1932, 284 U.S. 552, 561. In the Old Colony case the Supreme Court said [284 U.S. at page 560]: 'And as respects 'interest,' the usual import of the term is the amount which one has contracted to pay for the use of borrowed money. He who pays and he who receives payment of the stipulated amount conceives that the whole is interest.'

. . .

. . . . In Kena, Inc., v. Commissioner, . . . the Board of Tax Appeals said:

. . .

'It is not essential that interest be computed at a stated rate, but only that a sum definitely ascertainable shall be paid for the use of borrowed money, pursuant to the agreement of the lender and borrower.' Generally speaking, payments made for the use of money "in lieu of interest" are deductible as interest under Section 23(b).

Throughout the ages lenders have exacted all they could from borrowers for the use of money. How much has been exacted has depended upon the desperation of the borrower and the exigency of the moment. There is no requirement in Section 23(b) that deductible interest be ordinary and necessary or even that it be reasonable, 4 Mertens, Law of Federal Income Taxation §26.01. Hence the phrase "all interest paid" contained in that section must be taken in its plain and literal meaning to include whatever sums the taxpayer has actually had to pay for the use of money which he has borrowed. Arthur R. Jones Syndicate v. Commissioner of Internal Revenue, 7 Cir., 1927, 23 F.2d 833. We conclude that the district judge did not err in holding that the payments made by the taxpayer to his wife in 1943, 1944 and 1945 were interest paid on indebtedness and deductible under Section 23(b) of the Internal Revenue Code.

The judgment of the district court will be affirmed.

Why does it Matter?

The wife in *Dorzback* might as well have been a business partner with her husband. She just got a share of the profits as interest income, not a share of profits as a partner. Either way, she had more income and her husband reported correspondingly less income. If the couple filed a joint return, their loan deal would have had no tax impact because all their income and deductions would be combined, but it likely had a major tax impact at the time because in the years 1943-1944 couples in noncommunity property states could not file joint returns.

Problem 7-4:

Rock star David Bowie sold bonds backed by his compositions and recordings by issuing bonds whose yield depended on the success in exploiting those properties (known as his "catalog" in the trade).[619] What was Bowie up to with his "Bowie Bonds" from a Federal Income Tax point of view with respect to interest income or expenses, assuming he is liable for Federal Income Taxes on his earnings?

2. Original Issue Discount: Debts for Cash

This is mainly a refresher. Original issue discount (OID) *income* is the excess of the stated redemption price at maturity of a debt instrument over its issue price (what the issuer sold the debt for).[620] You can generally assume that any longterm instrument that pays little interest prior to maturity was issued at a discount. The most extreme such instrument is the zero coupon bond, meaning a bond paying no explicit interest and sold for less than the face amount of the debt (the amount due when the debt is paid off).

> **To illustrate**: In 1997 Mrs. Gasgoigne bought a 10year 7 percent bond issued by Huge Motor Corporation, with a stated redemption price at maturity of $1,000. The bond was issued for $950 because Huge Motors miscalculated the market's appetite for its terms.[621] The OID is $50. If Mrs. Gasgoigne holds the bond to maturity, she will have to report the $50 in annual installments averaging $5.00 of OID income per year over the 10-year life of the bond. (Her bond is not a zerocoupon bond because it does pay actual interest in addition to having OID.) Obviously, she would much rather defer any tax on the discount until the bond is paid in full. Instead, she must report OID on a "compounded" basis, starting at less than $5/year and gradually reporting more than $5/year by the time it matures. This complication is appropriate because it reflects the way financial wizards value such bonds.

Taxpayers can disregard the discount and treat it as zero if it is less than onefourth of 1% (.0025) of the stated redemption price multiplied by the number of full years from the date of original

619 Bowie sets ball rolling. (1998, Feb 17). *The Globe and Mail (1936-Current)* Retrieved from http://login.proxy.library.vanderbilt.edu/login?url=https://search-proquest-com.proxy.library.vanderbilt.edu/docview/1146287394?accountid=14816.

620 §1273(a)(1).

621 A common reason for a discount is that the interest rate it pays is too low, say only 6% in an environment where 7% would be normal.

issue to maturity.[622] (Using the figures in the illustration that works out to a $25 discount, so if the bond had initially sold for $975.01 or more, then the OID would be ignored for Federal Income Tax purposes.) This is just a *de minimis* rule designed to eliminate trivial cases. Also, the OID provisions generally do not apply to shortterm obligations, meaning those with a fixed maturity date of one year or less from the date of issue.[623]

What about Mrs. Gasgoigne's basis in the debt? The answer is that it rises as she reports OID. If that were not true, she would be taxed both when the OID arose (and was taxed) and when the debt was sold, which would result in unacceptable double taxation. Note that the basis rises daily, creating a dailychanging "adjusted issue price."[624]

Now for the new part. What about the issuer (Huge Motors) and its right to claim a deduction for its ultimate obligation to pay the discount on the debt? Should it be entitled to a parallel deduction for interest deemed paid at the same time as Mrs. Gasgoigne is taxed on OID income? The answer is again "yes," given that the borrower has to pay back more than it received from the lender.[625] Economically, the excess has to be an interest expense. Later in the book you will see how the OID rules apply to sales of property with payments deferred over time, where the seller understates the interest rate on the unpaid amounts, and calculations as to how one derives the periodic amount of inferred OID.

3. The Tightened Noose on Interest Expense Deductions - §163(h)

The deduction for interest expenses results in a great deal of interest paid for consumption items, especially housing, being deducted, even though our income tax system is based on the concept of preventing deductions for consumption from reducing one's income tax base. It is easier to see why interest paid to finance business or investment activities should be deductible. After all, §§ 162 and 212 would presumably allow such deductions if §163 were not in the Code.

Before 1986 taxpayers could deduct all interest, including such things as interest on credit cards used to finance personal consumption. The 1986 Act changed that by adding §163(h), which in general renders interest expenses on debt used to finance personal consumption nondeductible. The provision has a roundabout quality because if defines nondeductible ("personal") interest as interest *other than* business interest, investment interest, passive activity interest, interest on certain deferred payments of estate taxes, and "qualified residence interest." The most important interest expense deduction for most individual taxpayers is qualified residence interest.

The rules for the home mortgage interest deduction were changed for tax years starting in 2018 as described below.

622 §12(a)(2).

623 §1272(a)(C).

624 §1272(a)(4).

625 §163(e)(1).

Conference Report on H.R. 1, Tax Cuts and Jobs Act (H. Rept. 115-466)

Present Law

As a general matter, personal interest is not deductible. Qualified residence interest is not treated as personal interest and is allowed as an itemized deduction, subject to limitations. Qualified residence interest means interest paid or accrued during the taxable year on either acquisition indebtedness or home equity indebtedness. A qualified residence means the taxpayer's principal residence and one other residence of the taxpayer selected to be a qualified residence. A qualified residence can be a house, condominium, cooperative, mobile home, house trailer, or boat.

Acquisition indebtedness

Acquisition indebtedness is indebtedness that is incurred in acquiring, constructing, or substantially improving a qualified residence of the taxpayer and which secures the residence. The maximum amount treated as acquisition indebtedness is $1 million ($500,000 in the case of a married person filing a separate return).

Acquisition indebtedness also includes indebtedness from the refinancing of other acquisition indebtedness but only to the extent of the amount (and term) of the refinanced indebtedness. Thus, for example, if the taxpayer incurs $200,000 of acquisition indebtedness to acquire a principal residence and pays down the debt to $150,000, the taxpayer's acquisition indebtedness with respect to the residence cannot thereafter be increased above $150,000 (except by indebtedness incurred to substantially improve the residence).

Interest on acquisition indebtedness is allowable in computing alternative minimum taxable income. However, in the case of a second residence, the acquisition indebtedness may only be incurred with respect to a house, apartment, condominium, or a mobile home that is not used on a transient basis.

Home equity indebtedness

Home equity indebtedness is indebtedness (other than acquisition indebtedness) secured by a qualified residence.

The amount of home equity indebtedness may not exceed $100,000 ($50,000 in the case of a married individual filing a separate return) and may not exceed the fair market value of the residence reduced by the acquisition indebtedness.

Interest on home equity indebtedness is not deductible in computing alternative minimum taxable income.

Interest on qualifying home equity indebtedness is deductible, regardless of how the proceeds of the indebtedness are used. For example, personal expenditures may include health costs and education expenses for the taxpayer's family members or any other personal expenses such as vacations, furniture, or automobiles. A taxpayer and a mortgage company can contract for the home equity indebtedness loan proceeds to be transferred to the taxpayer in a lump sum payment (e.g., a traditional mortgage), a series of payments (*e.g.*, a reverse mortgage), or the lender may extend the borrower a line of credit up to a fixed limit over the term of the loan (e.g., a home equity line of credit).

Thus, the aggregate limitation on the total amount of a taxpayer's acquisition indebtedness and home equity indebtedness with respect to a taxpayer's principal residence and a second residence that may give rise to deductible interest is $1,100,000 ($550,000, for married persons filing a separate return).

***

Conference Agreement

The conference agreement provides that, in the case of taxable years beginning after December 31, 2017, and beginning before January 1, 2026, a taxpayer may treat no more than $750,000 as acquisition indebtedness ($375,000 in the case of married taxpayers filing separately). In the case of acquisition indebtedness incurred before December 15, 2017, this limitation is $1,000,000 ($500,000 in the case of married taxpayers filing separately). For taxable years beginning after December 31, 2025, a taxpayer may treat up to $1,000,000 ($500,000 in the case of married taxpayers filing separately) of indebtedness as acquisition indebtedness, regardless of when the indebtedness was incurred.

Additionally, the conference agreement suspends the deduction for interest on home equity indebtedness. Thus, for taxable years beginning after December 31, 2017, a taxpayer may not claim a deduction for interest on home equity indebtedness. The suspension ends for taxable years beginning after December 31, 2025.

Effective Date

The provision is effective for taxable years beginning after December 31, 2017.

4. Linking Debt to Use

Reg. §1.1638T requires borrowers to characterize their interest expenses by tracing the use of the loan proceeds to see how the funds were used. Once that is done, they can describe the interest expenses as associated with a business, an investment, personal consumption, and so forth. The regulations demand careful record keeping for deposits, expenditures, and repayments of loan proceeds.[626]

> **To illustrate:** If a taxpayer incurs a debt of $50,000, and uses $30,000 of the proceeds to buy investments, and the remaining $20,000 to buy an automobile for personal use, threefifths of the interest on the debt is prorated as deductible as investment expense, and twofifths is prorated as nondeductible personal interest.

There are some modifications to the tracing rules. The important one for our purposes is in Reg. §1.1638T(m)(3), which says "qualified residence indebtedness" is deductible regardless of how it is allocated under the regulations. This opens the door to rendering "home equity indebtedness," based on such things as credit card debt, deductible, as long as the home secures the debt and the debt itself is not more than the taxpayer's equity in the house (meaning its value minus debt that encumbers it).

> **To illustrate**: Lenny paid off the $100,000 mortgage on his $150,000 home years ago. As a result, he has "equity" of $150,000 in his home. Lenny now borrows $30,000 from a local car dealer, using his home as collateral, in order to buy a new car. The debt is qualified residence interest, even though the proceeds of the loan were not used for any application having to do with the home.[627]In particular, it is a home equity loan; it is not acquisition indebtedness because that debt was paid off in the past and therefore cannot be refinanced.

First, an observation: if a home is used to secure a business debt, the debt can produce business interest expense deductions. But what if a business property supports a loan made to acquire a home?

PRIVATE RULING 9418001

November 5, 1993

Control Number: TR.3221693. . . .

626 Reg. §1.1638T(c)(4) provides ordering rules where borrowed and other funds are commingled in one account. Reg. §1.1638T(d) provides another set of ordering rules to accord priority among the kinds of expenditures considered liquidated when a multi-purpose loan is paid off.

627 See Reg. §1.1638T(m)(3).

ISSUE

May interest be treated as qualified residence interest under section 163(h)(3)(A) of the Internal Revenue Code if the related debt is allocable under section 1.1638T(c)(1) of the temporary Income Tax Regulations to the purchase of a residence, but the debt is not secured by the residence?

CONCLUSION

No. Interest may not be treated as qualified residence interest under section 163(h)(3)(A) if the debt is not secured by the residence.

FACTS

The taxpayers incurred debt, the proceeds of which were allocated, within the meaning of section 1.1638T(c)(1), to purchase their principal residence. The debt was secured by commercial rental property which was owned 50% by the taxpayers and 50% by another person. The debt was not secured by the taxpayers' residence.

LAW

Section 163(h)(1) states that, in the case of a taxpayer other than a corporation, no deduction shall be allowed for personal interest paid or accrued during the taxable year.

Section 163(h)(2) states that personal interest is any interest other than (A) interest paid or accrued on indebtedness properly allocable to a trade or business, (B) any investment interest, (C) any interest taken into account under section 469, (D) any qualified residence interest, and (E) certain interest payable under section 6601.

Section 163(h)(3)(A) defines "qualified residence interest," in part, as any interest which is paid or accrued during the taxable year on acquisition indebtedness with respect to any qualified residence of the taxpayer.

Section 163(h)(3)(B)(i) defines "acquisition indebtedness" as any indebtedness which (I) is incurred in acquiring, constructing, or substantially improving any qualified residence of the taxpayer, and (ii) is secured by such a residence.

Section 1.1638T relates to allocation of debt and interest expense. Section 1.1638T(a)(3) provides that in general, interest expense on a debt is allocated in the same manner as the debt to which such interest expense relates is allocated. Debt is allocated by tracing disbursements of the debt proceeds to specific expenditures.

Section 1.1638T(c)(1) states:

> Debt is allocated to expenditures in accordance with the use of the debt proceeds and, except as provided in paragraph (m) of this section, interest expense accruing on a debt during any period is allocated to expenditures in the same manner as the debt is allocated from time to time during such period. Except as provided in paragraph (m) of this section, debt proceeds and related interest expense are allocated solely by reference to the use of such proceeds, and the allocation is not affected by the use of an interest in any property to secure repayment of such debt or interest.

Section 1638T(m) provides for coordination with other provisions. Section 1.1638T(m)(1)(i) states that "all debt is allocated among expenditures pursuant to the rules in this section, without regard to any limitations on the deductibility of interest expense on such debt."

Section 1.1638T(m)(2) provides generally that any limitation on the deductibility of an item applies without regard to the manner in which debt is allocated under section 1.1638T.

Section 1.1638T(m)(3) states that "qualified residence interest . . . is allowable as a deduction without regard to the manner in which such interest expense is allocated under the rules of this section."

Notice 8874, 19882 C.B. 385, provides that debt may be treated as incurred in acquiring a residence to the extent that the proceeds of the debt are used, within the meaning of section 1.1638T, to acquire the residence. It also states, however, that "even though debt may be incurred in acquiring, constructing or substantially improving a qualified residence, the debt will not qualify as acquisition indebtedness until the debt is secured by the qualified residence."

ANALYSIS

The taxpayers argue that under section 1.1638T the debt used to purchase their residence, and the related interest, are to be allocated to the residence, notwithstanding that the debt is secured only by their commercial property. They argue that, since the allocation of the interest expense is not affected by the security for the debt under section 1.1638T, it follows that the fact that the debt is not secured by their residence has no bearing on the deductibility of the interest expense under section 163(h)(3).

We agree that the debt and the related interest expense are allocated to the residence under section 1.1638T, even though the debt is secured by other commercial property. However, the allocation of interest under section 1.1638T does not determine the deductibility of the interest expense as qualified residence interest under section 163(h)(3). Section 163(h)(3)(A) clearly requires acquisition indebtedness to be secured by the residence. Notice 8874 also requires the debt to be secured by the residence. These requirements are not contradicted by the interest allocation rules under section 1.1638T.

Since the interest is not qualified residence interest, it is personal interest under section 163(h)(2), and is not permitted as a deduction under section 163(h)(1), subject to the phasein period provided in section 163(h)(5).

Notes on Allocations

Just how does one allocate (attribute) one thing to another? Linking expenses to income is sometimes easy and sometimes all but impossible, but the Code and Regulations often call for it. For example, a large appliance manufacturing company might want to calculate how much of its president's salary is allocable to each refrigerator (as opposed to each toaster, or TV or dishwasher) the company manufactures. The company's cost accountants could use any one or a mass of factors, but none would be satisfying. For example, they could allocate his salary to refrigerator sales as a percentage of net income, or gross sales attributable to refrigerators, or time he spent worrying about refrigerators, to name a few.

Broadly speaking, there are several choices as to how to allocate one item to another. One is by *tracing*; for example, as you know, the general rule for allocating interest expense deductions is to trace the borrowed money to its final destination (say to buying a family car) and then determining whether the expense is deductible (no, in the case of the car, *unless* the source of the loan was home equity indebtedness). Another approach is "*stacking*" expenses so that they first go to one application until exhausted, then to another, and so forth. Another way is *prorating* them equally or proportionately to their separate uses; that might be a reasonable way to tie a corporate president's salary to the flow of various manufactured products. The Code and Regulations are often silent as to which methodology to use, and often cop out by saying things along the line of "use a reasonable method."

Problem 7-5:

Mary bought her tiny Silicon Valley home two years ago for $700,000. In order to purchase it she borrowed $500,000 at 10% interest from the Friendly Bank, secured by a mortgage on the home.

1) How much of Mary's debt will produce deductible interest?

2) Two years later Mary borrowed another $600,000 at 9% interest from her employer at a time when her home was worth $1.1 million dollars. This second loan was secured by a second mortgage on the home and was used to finance the purchase of her favorite toy, a huge sailboat. How much of the latter debt produces interest that can be deducted as qualified residence interest?

3) Mary's brother, Bob, who used to live in a motel, bought a new boat for $1.1 million. The boat company gave him a $1.1 million loan to do so, secured by the boat. Now he lives on the boat as his home. How much of the debt can qualify for interest expense deductions? Read §163(h)(3)(B)-(C) carefully in answering the question. The boat is his only residence.

4) In cases "(1)" and "(2)" does it make any difference if Mary is married?

5. Tax Expenditures from Personal Residence Interest Deductions, Equity and Efficiency

Deductions for personal expenses related to personal residences are disturbing from a tax policy perspective. One way to look at the area is in light of the so-called "tax expenditure budget." What follows is a famous illustration and explanation of the concept.

The Tax Expenditure Budget

The Federal Income tax system consists really of two parts: one part comprises the structural provisions necessary to implement the income tax on individual and corporate net income; the second part comprises a system of tax expenditures under which governmental financial assistance programs are carried out through special tax provisions rather than through direct government expenditures. The second system is simply grafted on to the structure of the income tax proper; it has no basic relation to that structure and is not necessary to its operation.

Instead, the system of tax expenditures provides a vast subsidy apparatus that uses the mechanics of the income tax as a method of paying the subsidies. The special provisions under which this subsidy apparatus functions take a variety of forms, covering exclusions from income, exemptions, deductions, credits against tax, preferential rates of tax, and deferrals of tax.The Tax Expenditure budget . . . identifies and qualifies the existing expenditures. This Tax Expenditure Budget is essentially an enumeration of the present "tax incentives" or "tax subsidies" contained in our income tax system. . . .

The Tax Expenditure Budget enables us to look at the income tax provisions reflected in that Budget in a new light. Once these tax provisions are seen not as inherent parts of an income tax structure but as carrying our programs of financial assistance for particular groups and activities, a number of questions immediately come into focus. Once we see that we are not evaluating technical tax provisions but rather expenditure programs, we are able to ask the traditional questions and use the analytical tools that make up the intellectual apparatus of expenditure experts.

We thus can put the basic question of whether we desire to provide that financial assistance at all, and if so in what amount, a stock question any budget expert would normally ask of any item in the regular Budget. We can inquire whether the program is working well, how its benefits compare with its costs, is it accomplishing its objectives indeed, what are its objectives: Who is actually being assisted by the program and is that assistance too much or too little? Again, these are stock questions directed by any budget expert at existing programs. They all equally must be asked of the items and programs in the Tax Expenditure Budget . . . .

The translation and consequent restatement of a tax expenditure program in direct expenditure terms generally show an upsidedown result utterly at variance with usual expenditure policies. Thus, if cast in direct expenditure language, the present assistance for owneroccupied home under the tax deductions for mortgage interest and property taxes would look as follows, envisioned as a HUD program:

> For a married couple with more than 200,000 in income, HUD would, for each $100 of mortgage interest on the couple's home pay $70 to the bank holding the mortgage, leaving the couple to pay $30. It would also pay a similar portion of the couple's property tax to the State or city levying the tax.
>
> For a married couple with income of $10,000, HUD would pay the bank on the couple's mortgage $19 per each $100 interest unit, with the couple paying $81. It would also pay a similar portion of the couple's property tax to the State or city levying the tax.
>
> For a married couple too poor to pay an income tax, HUD would pay nothing to the bank, leaving the couple to pay the entire interest cost the couple would also have to pay the entire property tax.

One can assume that no HUD Secretary would ever have presented to Congress a direct housing program with this upsidedown effect.[628]

Note

Law professors rarely have major impacts on the federal budget process, but Professor Stanley Surrey, the author of what you just read, did. His Tax Expenditure Budget is now a formal part of every annual federal budget. It is prepared by the Treasury Department, which converts tax expenditure holes in an otherwise comprehensive revenue base into imaginary subsidies in order to assist the analysis of tax policy. It has to be every industry's nightmare to appear as a contributor to that budget.

628 Excerpts from Hearings Before the Subcommittee on Priorities and Economy in Government of the Joint Economic Committee, 92d Cong., 1st Sess. 49-51 (1972).

At the back of the book you will find a table of tax expenditures. It is a kind of public rogues gallery, but it does not include gifts and inheritances and it has been greatly pared down in the editing of this book to limit it to the tax expenditures you are likely to be at least somewhat familiar with.

The public is not about the give up the home mortgage interest or local real estate tax deductions. One politically feasible way out might be to replace the deduction with a credit to neutralize its inverted effect. Another is to withdraw the deductions in exchange for lower tax rates; the ABA has been pressing this kind of program for years. That is, the general ideology of the ABA Tax Section has been to try to broaden the tax base by eliminating special exceptions, while at the same time reducing tax rates.

In addition, it is widely believed that lowering tax rates will result in less tax evasion and less resources wasted in the economically sterile activity of structuring tax dodges. Microeconomists would probably say that greed is infinite and that if taxpayers can dodge taxes by paying less than the tax savings for tax shelters or other avoidance schemes, they will do it, and that rate cuts have only a modest effect on tax avoidance.

6. Business versus Investment Interest

Taxpayers have traditionally used debt to buy investment assets, deducting the interest to carry the investment, hoping that the sale of the asset will yield a favorably taxed capital gain. Assuming it works, the result for them is at least partial conversion of fully deductible expenses into capital gains. The Congressional retaliation is §163(d), which limits the deductibility of interest payments denominated in the Code as "investment interest," as defined in §163(d)(3)(D). The bite of §163(d) is that it forces the taxpayer to defer interest expenses on their investments.

There are several limitations on the deduction of interest including tax-exempt interest, interest from obligations not in registered form, interest paid in connection with insurance contracts, and interest paid on original issue discount (OID) high-yield obligation. If a debt instrument has original issue discount (OID), the insurer deducts the OID over the life of the obligation on a yield to maturity basis. Sometimes, taxpayers must capitalize Interest allocable to the production of property. The discussion below concerns limitations on business interest and limitations on investment interest.

Limits on business interest

The Tax Cuts and Jobs Act of 2017 limits deductions of business interest for all taxpayers to the sum of the taxpayer's:

1. Business interest income,

2. floor plan financing, and

3. 30% of adjusted taxable income.

The limitation does not apply to investment interest. §163(j)(5) There is an exception to the limitation for a small business with average gross receipts of $25 million or less. Any interest not deductible generally is carried forward indefinitely subject to certain restrictions for partnerships and S corporations.

The practical effect of the rule is to limit the deduction of net interest expenses to 30 percent of the taxpayer's adjusted taxable income.

Business interest means any interest paid or accrued on debt properly allocable to a trade or business of the taxpayer. § 163(j)(5), as added by the Tax Cuts and Jobs Act of 2017. Business interest does not include investment interest.

Business interest income is the amount of the taxpayer's gross income that is properly allocable to a trade or business. § 163(j)(6), as added by the Tax Cuts and Jobs Act of 2017. Business interest income not include investment income.

A **trade or business** for purposes of calculating the business interest deduction limitation does not include the performance of services as an employee §163(j)(7)(A)(i), as added by the Tax Cuts and Jobs Act of 2017. Thus, wages of an employee are not included as part of the taxpayer's adjusted taxable income.

Adjusted taxable income. The adjusted taxable income of a taxpayer for purposes of the limitation is the taxpayer's regular taxable income computed without regard to:

1. any item of income, gain, deduction, or loss that is not properly allocable to a trade or business;

2. any business interest or business interest income;

3. the amount of any net operating loss (NOL) deduction;

4. the 20-percent deduction for qualified business income of a passthrough entity under § 199A and

5. in tax years beginning before January 1, 2022, an allowable deduction for depreciation, amortization, or depletion (§ 163(j)(8), as added by the Tax Cuts and Jobs Act of 2017).

Floor plan financing interest is interest paid or accrued on debt use to finance the acquisition of motor vehicles held for sale or lease to retail customers and secured by the inventory §163(j)(9), as added by the Tax Cuts and Jobs Act of 2017). A motor vehicle for this purpose includes any self-propelled vehicle designed for transporting people or property on a public street, highway, or road, as well as a boat, and farm machinery or equipment.

A taxpayer may also elect to exclude from the limitation any real property trade or business as defined under the passive activity rules § 163(j)(7)(A)(ii) and (B), as added by the Tax Cuts and Jobs Act of 2017. **An electing real property trade or business** is any real estate development, redevelopment, construction, reconstruction, acquisition, conversion, rental, operation, management, leasing, or brokerage trade or business. Thus, interest expenses paid or accrued in the electing real property trade or business is not business interest subject to the limitation. The election is made at a time and manner as provided by the IRS. Once made, the election is irrevocable.

If a taxpayer elects to exclude a real property trade or business from the business interest limitation, then the business must use the alternative depreciation system (ADS) for certain property §163(j)(10)(A) and §168(g)(1)(F), as added by the Tax Cuts and Jobs Act of 2017.

Limits on investment interest

Individual taxpayers may deduct "investment interest" up to the taxpayer's net investment income. The taxpayer carries forward any disallowed investment interest to the next taxable year. Investment expense deductions are determined after application of the two-percent-over adjusted gross income (AGI) limitation on miscellaneous itemized deductions.

Investment income is the gross income derived from property held for investment or from its disposition including interest received, annuities, dividends, royalties, and short-term gain on the disposition of property. § 163(d). Investment income includes capital gain and qualified dividend income only to the extent that the taxpayer elects to treat those amounts as investment income. It also includes interest in a trade or business activity that is not a passive activity and in which the taxpayer does not materially participate.

Investment interest is interest properly allocable to property held for investment.§163(d)(5). Investment interest does not include qualified residence interest or interest taken into account under section 469 in computing income or loss from a passive activity.

In addition, §264(a)(2) and (a)(3) deny deductions for interest expenses incurred in order to purchase single premium life and annuity contracts or for purchasing such contracts if the purchase is systematically financed by increases in the policy's cash value.[629] This is another aspect of the campaign to prevent taxpayers from deducting the costs of generating tax-exempt income.

Problem 7-6:

On January 1 of year 1, Sarah had outstanding acquisition indebtedness of $50,000 secured by her principal residence. This was her only debt secured by any qualified residence. On that date, Sarah took out another mortgage on her principal residence in the amount of $300,000. Of the proceeds of this debt, she used $50,000 to pay off the original acquisition indebtedness; $150,000 to buy stocks and bonds for investment; and $100,000 for personal expenditures.

1) How much of the debt, after these transactions, will produce qualified residence interest for Sarah? See §163(h)(3)(B) and Reg. §1.163-8T(m)(3).

2) Assume Sarah used the $150,000 borrowing from "(1)" to buy Beanie Babies Corp. stock. She paid $150,000 for the stock and now wants to deduct the interest, which amounts to $10,000 this year. The stock paid a $1,000 dividend and has doubled in value by year-end. How much of the $10,000 interest can Sarah deduct, assuming it is the only investment income for the year?

3) She also had a $3,000 long-term capital gain this year. Can Sarah include some or all of the capital gain in her net investment income so as to increase her annual investment interest expense deduction? See §163(d)(4), (5).

7. **Points**

Read §461(g)

"Points" are a percentage of a loan, charged by the lender and paid at the time the loan closes. Each "point" equals one percent of the loan, so for example three "points" on a $100,000 loan equals $3,000. A bank's typical mortgage loan summary might be:

Amount:	$100,000
Security:	Residence at 222 Orphanage Blvd., Billboard City, USA
Term:	30 years

629 See Knetch v. United States, 364 U.S. 361 (1960), above.

Rate:	7.5%, Fixed
Monthly payment:	Fixed
Prepayment:	No penalty
Points:	Three, due at closing

Why points? Sometimes points are an incentive to encourage bankers to make the loan, sometimes they offset some feature of the loan that is disadvantageous to the bank, and sometimes, they are really for services the bank provides, such as appraising the property. The general rule for Federal Income Tax purposes is that as long as the points are not demonstrably tied to a service, then they are deemed to be interest charges, and they are generally viewed as prepaid interest.[630] As such, the prepaid interest has to be written off over the life of the loan. If the borrower prepays the loan, perhaps as a result of selling the home or refinancing it, the deferred deductions are correspondingly accelerated and can produce tax deductions for the borrower.[631] No other treatment makes sense, given that there is no longer a loan by which to measure the amortization rate for the points.

There is an exception which permits such prepaid interest to be deducted immediately if the payments meet the tests of §461(g). The benefits of §461(g) are limited by the terms of that subsection. As a result, points paid to refinance a home are not currently deductible, except to the extent that the loan is used to improve the home, nor can one deduct points with respect to obtaining home equity loans.

Section 461(g)(2) assures that the benefit of §461(g) applies only to the payment of "points" on a home mortgage and then only to the extent that the payment is representative of the business practice of the community. It is supposed to be implemented by regulations, but they have never appeared. It seems clear that they are not needed. To the extent points are paid for services in connection with buying or improving a principal residence, they are simply nondeductible.

What about capitalizing interest that is not prepaid, but relates to acquiring long-term assets? For years, nothing in the Code or case law required taxpayers to capitalize interest, but that has gradually changed. First, under §266, taxpayers can elect to capitalize certain interest, taxes and other carrying charges -- unappetizing to most taxpayers. Second, and far more importantly, §263A forces the capitalization of interest attributable to producing inventory or long-term property, such as construction projects a business taxpayer has underway. The origin of §263A was the need to generate offsetting revenues to make the 1985 tax legislation "revenue neutral." Section 263A is commonly known as the "uniform capitalization rules" or "UNICAP rules." It is exceptionally complicated and does not apply to a taxpayer who builds his own home. It may be an example of a provision that is conceptually accurate, but may in some cases result in a contempt for the tax system that threatens the income tax's general acceptance.

630 See Rev. Rul. 69-582, 1969-2 C.B. 2.

631 See, e.g., Rev. Rul. 57-198, 1957-1 C.B. 94 (deduction of prepayment penalties allowed).

Problem 7-7:

The following is a basic example of tax planning. Assume Fairlee Friendly will be going to college next fall. Not long ago, the Friendlys had Mr. Swindler over for dinner. He mentioned that he bought a condominium for his son, Wiley, who is also at college. He refused to explain the details. Sensing Swindler had discovered yet another way to beat taxes, the Friendlys ask your advice as to the wisdom of doing the same thing. They tell you that they are in the 40% bracket (and always will be) and that Fairlee would have to pay $400 per month to rent an apartment or dorm for 9 months per year. Utilities are free in both cases. The Friendlys are confident that they can get their bank to lend all the money needed to buy Fairlee a condominium unit in an apartment building on a "balloon note" basis, meaning they would pay interest only (i.e., no principal) at a rate of 10% simple interest per year, and the principal would be due in full in 20 years. If they buy the unit, it cannot be sublet to others. They are sure they can sell the unit any time for the same price they paid for it. The condominium unit would cost $40,000, so annual interest would be $4,000 and local taxes are and will remain $1,000. Both are deductible. Assume that insurance and utilities cost nothing whether they own the unit or rent one for Fairlee. Ignore the effects of §§ 67 and 68, if any.

1) Should they buy the apartment for Fairlee's use?

2) Would you change your conclusion in "(1)" if utilities and insurance averaged $200/ month if they bought the unit (but not if they rented it), whether or not Fairlee was in the unit?

3) Same as "(1)," but the interest and taxes are nondeductible.

4) Same as "(1)," but the Friendlys are also taxed on the imputed value to Fairlee of occupying the condominium unit that they may buy.

5) Can they claim a deduction for "points" paid in connection with financing the purchase of the unit?

Read §164(a), (b)(1)(3), (c), (d) and (f)

1. Purpose

For Federal Income Tax purposes, a "tax" is a charge imposed by a government that is not in exchange for a particular service, nor a disguised sanction. For example, the price of admission to a national park is obviously not a tax, but is instead a "user charge" of some sort. Likewise, fees for a "local benefit assessment," such as for sidewalk improvements that run past a homeowner's house, are not local property estate taxes.[632]

The important tax deduction in terms of the income taxation of individuals is for state income taxes and local property taxes. The local property tax deduction is designed to soften the blow of double taxation, but it is not secured by the Constitution, and it is generally conceded that the deduction is a courtesy.[633] The big missing element in §164 is a deduction for state or local *sales* taxes. Under §164 individuals can deduct either state and local income taxes or sales tax. The deduction works best in a state with no income tax.The deduction does not eliminate the burden of state or local taxes. For example, if a taxpayer in the 40% bracket earned $100 of gross revenues and her only deduction was a $20 local income tax, her Federal Income Tax liability would be $32 (i.e., 40% of $80), and her total tax burden would be $52 (i.e., $32 to the federal government plus $20 to the locality) out of $100, or 52%. If instead she got a federal tax *credit* for her local income taxes, she would reduce her Federal Income Tax liability from $40 (40% of $100) by $20. As a result she would pay only $20 in federal taxes and $20 in local taxes, resulting in a tax rate of only 40%. This is how the foreign tax credit works for U.S. businesses and investors that pay foreign income taxes.[634] One has to wonder why taxpayers do not get the same benefit when they pay state income taxes. The likely answer is that the foreign tax credit promotes international competitiveness, a consideration that justifies the large revenue losses associated with that credit.

The most debatable aspect of the deduction for state and local taxes is that homeowners can deduct local property taxes, thereby getting a deduction for a cost of personal consumption. It is unpopular with tax theorists.[635] Section 216 extends this questionable tax benefit to owners of condos and cooperatives in the interest of economic neutrality.

632 §164(c)(1). The Code deals with this case by in effect acknowledging that the payment is a "tax" but disallowing the deduction.

633 See Powell, *Waning of the Intergovernmental Immunities Doctrine*, 58 Harv. L. Rev. 757 (1945).

634 §901 902. Section 904 assures that the credit operates only as a down payment against U.S. taxes on foreign source income, and not as a subsidy for operating overseas.

635 See, e.g., Kahn, *Personal Deductions in the Federal Income Tax*, 92108 (Princeton Univ. Press 1960).

Perhaps a justification can be found if one thinks of taxable income as a measure of the taxpayer's ability to pay a tax and as a figure to be arrived at after involuntary payments such as state and local taxes. In earlier days of very high Federal Income Tax rates, the deduction for state taxes reduced the risk of exposing taxpayers to an aggregate rate equal to or exceeding one hundred percent of income. Top federal rates went to 90% at the margin in the 1950's and 1960's. With the present top rate of 37%, this theory has largely fallen by the wayside. In general, why allow a deduction for taxes not attributable to business income, or any income? The subject invites provocative policy questions. For example, why allow a deduction for taxes paid on a personal owneroccupied residence, when the (imputed) income from occupying the home goes untaxed? Does the deduction discriminate unfortunately between the home owner and the one who rents a home? Or does the rental price paid by the latter reflect the lower cost to the landlord resulting from the deduction he takes for the taxes he pays? Is the §164 deduction defensible as a federal subsidy to state and local governments? If so, one might wonder if it is a hidden rebate of federal taxes without federal control or conditions? Also the deductibility of some state taxes but not others may well affect state tax policy choices.

2. Operation of §164

Section 164(a) lets taxpayers deduct six specific taxes, even though there is no gain-seeking component to the payment. However, §164 is nonexclusive. Amounts that qualify as business or investment expenses may be deductible under §§ 162 and 212, free of the restrictions of §164.

Only the person on whom the taxes are imposed can claim the deduction.[636] For example, where the tax is imposed on property, the owner of the property (or the person who has a beneficial interest in the property) can take the deduction for taxes he paid.

Co-owners of property are generally only allowed to deduct their proportionate share of the taxes, but if a co-owner pays all (or a disproportionate share) of taxes on co-owned property to avoid personal liability or to preserve his or her interest in the property, that co-owner is entitled to a deduction for the full amount of the payment.[637]

Local governments determine and assess real estate taxes as of a particular date, such as June 30, of each year. If the property changes hands during the year, taxes are inevitably accounted for by the parties. Section 164(d) provides the rules for determining how the deduction is shared, using a daily proration method.

State, local, and foreign taxes directly attributable to a trade or business, or imposed on property held for the production of income are deductible either as ordinary and necessary business expenses or investment expenses. This includes income taxes, property taxes, sales taxes, and employment taxes.

636 Reg. §1.1641(a).

637 See, e.g., Powell v. Commissioner, T.C. Memo. 1967-32.

In general, taxpayers may not deduct most types of federal taxes, estate and inheritance taxes, and real estate taxes imposed on another taxpayer. However, a self-employed individual may deduct 50 percent of his or her federal self-employment taxes as an above-the-line deduction in computing adjusted gross income (AGI).

Taxpayers must capitalize taxes that are otherwise deductible as business or income-producing expenses paid or accrued in connection with the acquisition or disposition of property.

Taxes paid or accrued by an individual that are not directly connected with a trade or business, or with property held for the production of income, may only be deducted as itemized deductions on Schedule A of Form 1040. This includes: (1) state, local, and foreign income taxes; (2) state and local sales taxes in lieu of deducting state and local income taxes; (3) state, local, and foreign real property taxes; (4) state and local personal property taxes; and (5) federal and state generation-skipping transfer (GST) taxes imposed on income distributions (§ 164).

A taxpayer whose adjusted gross income (AGI) exceeds a threshold normally must reduce the amount of itemize deductions claimed on his or her federal income tax return. However, the phase-out for itemized deductions is temporarily repealed for tax years 2018 to 2025.

The itemized deduction for state, local, and foreign property taxes, and state and local income taxes and general sales taxes paid or accrued during the tax year is limited for tax years 2018 through 2025. An individual cannot deduct foreign real property taxes at all, but may still claim an itemized deduction of up to $10,000 ($5,000 for married taxpayer filing a separate return) for state and local property taxes, income taxes, and general sales taxes paid or accrued in the tax year. A taxpayer may still claim an itemized deduction for foreign income taxes subject to the $10,000/$5,000 limit. However, no deduction is available for foreign real property taxes for tax years 2018 through 2025. § 164(b)(6), as amended by the Tax Cuts and Jobs Act of 2017.

For purposes of applying the dollar limit, an individual cannot claim an itemized deduction in 2017 on a prepayment of income tax for a future tax year in order to avoid the dollar limit for tax years 2018 through 2025 (Conference Report on H.R. 1, Tax Cuts and Jobs Act (H. Rept. 115-466). The prepayment restriction specifically applies to state or local income taxes; it does not refer to state and local property taxes.

Problem 7-8:

Which of the following are deductible and under what Code section?

1) A special state tax on new automobiles purchased at a car dealership.

2) An assessment by a town, denominated as a tax by the City Council, to pay for sewer repairs, including the homeowner's share of the cost.

3) A foreign tax on luxury goods, assessed on their value on January 1 of each year.

4) Local unemployment taxes paid by an employer out of withholdings on its employees' wages.

5) A self-employed person's Social Security taxes. See §164(f).

6) A business employer's share of Social Security taxes.

7) A local gasoline tax paid by a consumer. Would the result differ if the taxpayer were a cab company?

8) Federal Income Taxes. See §275(a)(1).

9) Domestic or foreign inheritance taxes. See §275(a)(3).

10) Assume for a moment you were a legislator in the capitol of Texas. Texas has a major sales tax, but no personal income tax. Would you favor replacing the sales tax with an income tax? What are the considerations? Also, does §164 grant Texas residents a special tax benefit? Do not expect to see the word "Texas."

11) Mrs. Powell and her daughter own a condominium as joint tenants (with joint and several liability for real estate taxes). Mrs. Powell pays the real estate taxes for the year. Should Mrs. Powell be able to deduct them in full?

12) Assume for a moment that real estate tax deductions were repealed. How would the price of personal residences be affected?

I. DEDUCTIBLE CONTRIBUTIONS TO SELECTED TAX-DEFERRED COMPENSATION PLANS

Section 219 allows people with modest earned income without employer provided pension plan to contribute up to $5,000 per year to individual retirement accounts ("IRAs") and to deduct their contributions when made, even after year-end. Banks, insurers or brokerage firms typically manage the accounts. They have become a major constituency pushing for broadening the availability of these accounts. Money earned in the IRA is not taxed until paid out. All payouts from deductible contributions are 100% ordinary income. Children who mow lawns for a "living" can take advantage of this, along with the working poor and the struggling middle class. In some further instances, individuals can make nondeductible contributions to an IRA, in which event earnings that build up within the plan enjoy deferral from tax until withdrawal and, on withdrawal, only the accumulated earnings, but not the amounts originally contributed, are taxed. There is also an option to make nondeductible contributions to an IRA for one's spouse.

Sections 401 and 404 allow self-employed people to contribute and deduct up to the lesser of $40,000 (inflation-adjusted) or 20% of their earned income to an individually tailored pension plan. These "Keogh plans" have the usual feature of allowing funds to grow tax free until distributed, at which point they are fully taxed to the recipient. Keoghs and IRAs are unique in that one can deduct contributions made after the close of the prior year. Self-employed lawyers are a classic example of contributors to Keogh plans.

Another popular plan arises under §401(k). It lets employees elect to defer some of their wages, with the usual tax-deferred inside build-up, and allows the employer to make matching contributions. The employees are not taxed on the employer's contributions, but everything that comes of the plan out is fully taxed when received. This is only a deduction as to the employee in the rough sense of being the equivalent of letting the employee take her salary in full and deduct some of it by putting it into a §401(k) plan.

Some other "personal allowances" include an experimental provision for tax advantaged "medical savings accounts" increasing the deductible medical expense categories, and "Roth IRAs" under §408A. Roth IRAs are amazing accounts that operate as islands of nontaxation. One cannot deduct the up to $5,000/year that one puts in, but everything one pulls out is nontaxable. They are not available for the very prosperous because they phase out at moderate levels of AGI.

Congress's allowance of deductions for contributions to these plans is best explained as a way to help insure personal financial security after retirement, but there is no dollar limit on how large the funds can become, so at least arguably the tax benefits for these and other pension plans ought to be capped at some reasonable level.

J. CHIPPING AWAY AT ITEMIZED DEDUCTIONS - SECTIONS 67 AND 68

Up to now, the book has described taxpayers as being in some particular Federal Income Tax bracket or other, and has generally described the top rate as 37%. Based on what you are about to see, it is obvious that there are many cases where one cannot easily tell what a taxpayer's marginal income tax bracket is. Probably the only way to do it without going insane is to buy a tax return preparation program, input the taxpayer's tax return information, and then add or subtract a hundred dollars of income and see how much the taxpayer's Federal Income Tax liability rises or falls. For example, if it rises forty-three dollars, then the taxpayer is in the 43% bracket, at the margin. Tax return preparation programs are quite easy to use.

1. Section 67 - The First Phase-Out

Read §67

A taxpayer's effective tax rate is a function of all the rates applied to the taxpayer's taxable income. To the extent that the taxpayer is able to reduce taxable income by deductions, the taxpayer's effective rate will fall. In order to prevent taxpayers from reducing their taxable income by too much, Congress enacted two means of limiting itemized deductions through §67 and §68.

Section 67 limits the amount of miscellaneous itemized deductions that taxpayers can take.

The term "miscellaneous itemized deductions" includes all deductions other than (1) deductions allowed in determining AGI under § 62; (2) deductions for interest, taxes, casualty and wagering losses, charitable gifts, and medical expenses; and (3) a variety of less common deductions. §67(b)

The principal types of miscellaneous itemized deductions are:

(1) Non-business investment expenses (including costs of investment advice, subscriptions to investment periodicals, and safe deposit boxes);

(2) Expenses incurred in determining or contesting taxes (including return preparation costs);

(3) Expenses of an activity not carried on for profit allowable under § 183 which allows expenses related to hobbies to the extent of gross income from the hobby; and

(4) Employee business expenses that are not deductible under § 62 in determining AGI.

Until the Tax Cuts and Jobs Act of 2017, taxpayers were limited in their ability to deduct miscellaneous itemized deductions to those that exceeded 2 percent of their adjusted gross income (AGI). §67(a)

For tax years 2018 through 2025, the IRC completely disallows "miscellaneous itemized deductions."

2. Section 68 - The Next Phase-Out

Until the Tax Cuts and Jobs Act of In 2017, high-income taxpayers faced limits on their ability to take all their itemized deductions. For example, in 2017, married taxpayers who filed joint began to lose their ability to take itemized deductions when their adjusted gross income exceeded $313,800 ($287,650 for heads of households, $261,500 for other unmarried taxpayers and $156,900 for married taxpayers who filed separate returns). Rev. Proc. 2016-55, I.R.B. 2016-45, 707.

For tax years beginning in 2018, the adjusted gross income thresholds do not apply. Rev. Proc. 2018-18, I.R.B. 2018-10, 392, modifying and superseding in part Rev. Proc. 2017-58, I.R.B. 2017-45, 489.

Problem 7-9:

Patience, a corporate employee, has been ill during the year and has paid $1,000 for medical insurance, $2,000 in hospital bills, $500 for prescription drugs, $400 for over-the-counter medications, and $3,000 to doctors for medical care. Use the uninflated figures that appear in your book of Code and Regulations to work the following problem.

1) Assuming her AGI is $20,000, what is Patience's medical expense deduction for the year?

2) Would §67 reduce the deduction?

3) Would §68 reduce the deduction?

Problem 7-10:

Wanda, who is single, was formerly married to the heartless socialite Caldwell Murchfield. Caldwell is years behind on his alimony payments. Wanda sued him about five years ago, and has finally gotten a taxable recovery of $15,000, which is peanuts compared to the $70,000 legal fee she incurred in getting the money. She paid the $70,000 this year and has no other deductions of any sort. She has regular salary of $40,000 per year. Assume, correctly, that her legal fee is deductible under §212 as an itemized deduction and that her AGI is $125,000 (which includes the $15,000 recovery). Again, do not bother with any inflation adjustments if your Code volume does not have the inflation-adjusted figures.

1) What is her regular taxable income? Consider the impact of impact of §§ 67 and 68, applying §67 first, then §68. Also, take into account the possibility that she may have to reduce her personal exemptions.

The Federal Income Tax evidences Congress' frequent attempts to encourage or subsidize socially desirable activity,[638] or to extend aid to persons or families in difficulty, or to enhance the fairness of the tax and budget systems by extending tax relief or even cash payments (e.g., refundable tax credits) to some taxpayers (or even to persons who are not obliged to pay any tax).

Many of these attempts take the form of tax credits, refundable or nonrefundable, and can be found clustered in §§2150 of the Code. Once they are enacted, there is generally little empirical reporting on their success or failure, at least not to the public. Some credits are given for straightforward corrective reasons: the §31 credit for tax withheld on wages (and hence prepaid); the §33 credit for tax withheld at source on nonresident aliens and foreign corporations and the §37 credit for overpayment of taxes. Others are aimed at preserving the environment or to direct capital toward developing better sources of energy, such as the §48 energy credit.

Sometimes the allowance is designed to encourage socially desirable activity, employment or investment, as with the credit for qualified electric vehicles (§30), for economic activity in Puerto Rico (§30A), or for alcohol used as fuel -- an enormous subsidy largely reaped by the Archer Daniels Midland Company (§40). These energy-related tax credits have been multiplying rapidly in recent years.

There is also a credit for expenditures to provide better access to buildings for disabled individuals (§44), for up to $10,000 for adoption expenses (§23), and a credit, in §22, to help the elderly or permanently totally disabled. Originally it was designed to reduce the tax difference between retired persons who received (then) tax-exempt Social Security pension payments and those who received fully taxable payments from their own retirement savings, company pensions or annuities. Now the credit applies to lowincome taxpayers with respect to income from any source. It, too, phases out as their incomes rise.

Finally, §§ 90019012 contains a checkoff system for contributions to political campaigns. It does not decrease taxes; it just funds political campaigns.

638 Some say that this year's tax loophole is the last Administration's tax incentive.

CHAPTER 8 - CHARACTERIZATION OF GAINS AND LOSS

A. INTRODUCTION

So far, we have seen how to calculate gains and losses with respect to the disposition of property. Now we are going to characterize losses. Characterization of losses is an issue of intense interest to individual taxpayers, for the following reasons:

1. A "net capital gain" is taxable at a rate not more than 28% (and generally not more than 20%), compared to a top rate of 39.6% for ordinary income.[639]

2. A capital loss standing alone has less value than an ordinary loss. This is because only $3,000 per year of net capital losses can offset ordinary income. A capital loss offsets capital gains, which, if not offset, might be taxed at a relatively low rate.[640]

3. Some ordinary losses on the disposition of property have the advantage of being fully deductible against ordinary income. In the case of individuals, §165(c) restricts this benefit to assets used in a trade or business, or purchased with a view to generating a profit from their resale or rent, or victimized by casualty or theft, or a business bad debt loss.

These disparities between capital gains and ordinary income are of immense practical importance to taxpayers and occupy a great deal of the time and attention of tax professionals. In this setting, the tax advisors' goals are to produce favorably taxed long-term capital gains, or, if there are losses, ordinary losses. The booby prizes are ordinary income and capital losses. Back in the 1980's when the top individual income tax rate and the top capital gains rate were both 28%, there was no pressure to bother trying to generate capital gains. Now that we have significant difference between ordinary income and long-term capital gains rates, tax advisors

639 See §1(h).

640 §1211(b). The rate remains 28 percent for long-term gains from sales of art works and other collectibles.

are back in business, straining to replace ordinary income with capital gains, a fundamentally sterile activity.

Congress has complicated the rules. It used to be that the taxpayer could simply isolate his or her net capital gain and then prevent that gain from being taxed at rates in excess of 28%. Things are no longer so simple.

For tax years beginning in 2019, net capital gains and qualified dividends are taxed as follows:

- 0 percent if taxable income is less than $78,750 if married filing jointly or surviving spouse, less than $52,750 if head of household, less than $39,375 if single or married filing separately, and $2,650 for an estates or trust;
- 15 percent if taxable income is less than $488,850 if married filing jointly or surviving spouse, less than $461,700 if head of household, less than $434,550 for 2019 if single, less than $244,425 if married filing separately, and less than $12,950 for 2019 for an estate or trust;
- 20 percent if taxable income is at least $488,850 for 2019 if married filing jointly or surviving spouse, at least $461,700 if head of household, at least $434,550 if single, at least $244,425 if married filing separately, and at least $12,950 for an estate or trust.

There are other rates for specialized types of gains.

Do not worry about the different rates for the different properties for the time being. Concentrate on the general rule of §1(h) that capital assets owned for more than one year generally qualify for a top tax rate of not over 23.8% when they are disposed of.[641] This is not a separate tax rate, but a ceiling on the otherwise applicable Federal Income Tax rate.[642]

B. THE CAPITAL GAINS PREFERENCE: THE PURPOSES AND IDEOLOGIES

There are some subjects that simply cannot be resolved by science or logic. One of them is the eternal question of the right level of progression in the income tax rates applicable to individuals and another, which we will look at now, is the question of the extent, if any, to which income

641 (a) The Patient Protection and Affordable Care Act, starting in 2013, imposes an additional 3.8 percent surtax on the lesser of:

-net investment income,

-the excess of the taxpayer's modified AGI over $200,000 (single filers) or $250, 000 (joint filers.)

This threshold is based on adjusted gross income, rather than, as with the above rates, taxable income, so it's conceivable that taxpayers in the lower marginal tax brackets could still be subject to the surtax if their AGI is over the threshold but they have lots of itemized deductions. If a taxpayer is in the 32 percent, 35 percent or 37 percent bracket, he or she will be definitely subject to the surtax, so it is included in the rate shown for those brackets.

642 See Congressional Budget Office, How Capital Gains Affect Revenues: The Historical Evidence 30-1 (March 1998) (half the capital gains are enjoyed by the top 1% by adjusted gross income of the population).

from the disposition of assets held for a long time should be entitled to special treatment. What follows is a summary of the principal arguments and considerations.

People who would like to see capital gains taxed favorably assert that the present tax system discriminates against capital and income earned from capital because, in order to produce capital, one must first earn income, pay tax on that income, and then, after one invests what is left over, the income that the investment throws off is also taxed. This is said to favor consumers over people who save and invest, the theory being that, if a consumer spends all of her income, then she is taxed only once, whereas, if a comparable but thrifty taxpayer saves or invests his earnings, then he pays taxes twice, once on the earnings that he invests and then on the investment income from the investment. Here is an example, one you saw before:

> **To illustrate:** Assume a simple world in which the income tax rate is 40% and the pretax yield rate on financial investments is an annual 10%. If you earn a surplus $1,000, as a good American you must promptly pay the Internal Revenue Service ("IRS") $400 for the privilege of putting $600 in the bank or investing in $600 worth of corporate shares. That year one $400 sent to IRS is the first tax imposed on your decision to save. In year two, you receive $60 in interest on your $600 investment, but at the end of year two you must pay IRS $24, 40% of the $60 earned. That $24 is the second tax imposed on your savings decision. At the end of year two, you are left in hand $636, which you may either consume or commit to further savings. Your net year two return of $36 on your $600 investment reflects an after-tax rate of return of 6%. In a world with an income tax, that is viewed as the right answer. (Note that if the $60 of earnings were in the form of qualified dividends, those dividends would generally be taxed at a maximum tax rate of only 20%.)
>
> If in the first year you had elected to consume your $600 on two opera tickets and an excellent meal, you would have paid the same year one tax of $ 400, but that would have been the end of it. One tax on consumption, twotaxes on savings. The argument is, in essence, that this bias against capital investment deserves a remedy, capital gain treatment. Congress has granted the remedy, but it has not tried to reverse the preference in cases where the taxpayer sells capital assets and uses the proceeds for personal consumption. Perhaps it should.

An aside: the bias against savings does not necessarily justify the great disparity between 37% taxation and 23.8% based on a year-and-a-day deadline. The disparity calls for a more refined correction, if any.

Another argument for favoring long-term capital gains is that if such gains are not more gently taxed, people will live in such dread of a heavy capital gains tax that they will refrain from selling their appreciated assets. This is known as the "lock-in effect." It results especially if the asset has appreciated gradually over many years, but is taxed in one year by the rule of realization. Such an effect would, the argument goes, cause a general loss of liquidity in the economy and in the lives of the owners of such assets, which would be economically inefficient. Moreover, potential buyers who might have been able to obtain such assets will be precluded from doing so. This problem would not exist if we used an "accretion" system of taxation under which unrealized gains and losses were accounted for annually. An important counter-argument made against the lock-in argument is that the people who enjoy capital gains are the wealthy, and they reside permanently in the top bracket. As a result, accelerating capital gains into any particular year will not drive up their tax rates.

A variant of the "lock-in" argument is that a big sale in one year could throw a person into a particularly high bracket, because of the "bunching" effect of the gain. This should be remedied by averaging the income over many years, which we do by crudely granting a lower rate on long-term capital gains. However, the holding period for generating a favorably taxed long-term capital gain is in fact fairly short; a year and a day make a gain a long-term gain that qualifies for a top tax rate of 23.8%.[643] This leads to the more sophisticated argument that the basis of capital assets should simply be indexed for inflation[644], and only the sales proceeds that exceeded the inflation-adjusted basis should be taxed at regular rates. That eliminates the unfairness of taxing people on gains that are caused by inflation. It seems that France uses a realization system (as does the U.S.), but makes generous use of inflation adjustments.[645]

Other countries have taken disparate measures with respect to capital gains. For example, in Germany all gains with respect to land and buildings are fully taxable for the first two years, on the theory that they are merely gains from (immoral?) speculation, and they are fully exempt thereafter.[646] Gains on sales of securities and other assets held by private investors are generally tax-free.[647]

643 See §1222(3).

644 For example, England has indexed capital gains since 1982. H. Ault, COMPARATIVE INCOME TAXATION p. 200 (Kluwer Law Int'l '(1997).

645 H. Ault, COMPARATIVE INCOME TAXATION, p. 41 and 193 (Kluwer Law Int'l 1997).

646 H. Ault, COMPARATIVE INCOME TAXATION, p. 197 (Kluwer Law Int'l 1997).

647 Id.

Read §1222 and skim §1(h)

1. Basic Operations

The computation of net capital gain can be confusing because of the welter of terms one has to master. Perhaps the simplest way of thinking of the process is the following. First, assume the taxpayer has four boxes, one marked "long-term capital gains," another marked "long-term capital losses," another marked "short-term capital gains," and a final box marked "short-term capital losses." Now imagine that each time the taxpayer sells a capital asset she puts a report in the appropriate box, depending on whether the result was a gain or a loss and whether the asset she sold had a long-term or a short-term holding period. A short-term holding period is -- no surprise -- a holding period of one year or less.

At the end of the year, the taxpayer goes through a multi-step process. First, she sums the results in each box and gets a net figure, which will either be zero, positive or negative for the box. (We will ignore zero results from now on, because they are trivial cases.) Second, she combines long-term gains and the long-term losses, which will yield a net long-term figure. Third, she goes to the short-term boxes, combines the results and comes up with the net short-term result.

If she has a net long-term capital gain and a short-term capital gain, she keeps them separate and the net long-term gain is her *net capital gain* (the prize); likewise, if both net results are negative, she keeps both sets separate. If she has a net long-term capital gain and a net short-term capital loss she offsets them. If the net figure is still positive (i.e., a net long-term capital gain), then that figure is her "net capital gain." Finally, if the result from the long boxes was a capital gain, but the short-term capital losses overwhelm that gain, then she will have a net *short*-term capital loss for the year.[648]

Any free-standing short-term capital gain that is left over is taxed as ordinary income. Any capital loss carry forward from a prior year preserves its character as long- or short-term capital loss, and will offset any capital gains of the current year plus $3,000 of ordinary income.[649]

From the taxpayer's point of view, the first prize is to obtain a net capital gain for the year. The consolation prize is a capital loss that can be used to offset up to $3,000 of ordinary income for the year. The $3,000 offset against ordinary income only occurs if there is a deductible capital loss left over after offsetting capital gains.[650] The $3,000 is a modest figure to begin with, and is not inflation adjusted, an unhappy fact as far as investors with big losses are concerned.

648 These steps are necessary because of the operational terms used in the Code (e.g., §1(h)) and their definitions in §1222.

649 See §1212(a)(1)(C).

650 See §1211(b).

Problem 8-1:

William Welloff, a single individual, has a long-term capital gain of $30,000 from the sale of some stock and a $10,000 long-term capital loss from the sale of a bond and a short-term capital loss of $6,000 from the sale of some land. He has held the long-term assets for three years.

1) Does Welloff have a net capital gain? If so, what is the amount of the net capital gain and, assuming he is otherwise in the 33% Federal Income Tax bracket, what will be the tax imposed on Welloff's net capital gain, if any?

2) If Welloff were single and had taxable "ordinary" income of $15,000 aside from these capital gain and capital loss transactions, what tax rate would apply to his net capital gain? See §1(h)(1)(B). What if he had $29,950 of ordinary income?

2. Computation of Capital Losses

Read §1211(b) and §1212(b)(1)

a. Introduction

When dealing with losses, one must never overlook the possibility that the loss is incapable of being included in this or the previous computation. That can occur if the loss is disallowed because it was neither of property that was acquired for use in a trade or business, nor incurred in a transaction entered into for a profit, nor wiped out as a casualty loss or bad debt loss.[651] This topic is discussed a few pages later. Losses that fall outside this charmed circle are deemed personal "consumption" and are tough luck for the taxpayer. To take a simple example, a home lawnmower sold by the homeowner at a loss is outside the charmed circle.

Notice how lopsided this arrangement is. For example, if a taxpayer bought an exceptionally fine lawnmower which doubled in value, gain on its sale is taxable, whereas, if it lost half of its value, there is no tax benefit available in the form of a loss deduction for that financial misfortune. What reason can you give for the denial of a personal loss deduction, but taxation of the personal gain, and for having a system with both rules? Social Darwinism? An obsessive desire to prevent tax benefits from anything that seems like personal consumption? Something else?

b. Application

Assuming that the loss falls within the charmed circle of §165(c), one must begin dealing with some limitations. The first is that capital losses *must* be applied first against capital gains, if

651 See §165(c).

any.[652] Thereafter, up to $3,000 ($1,500 if the taxpayer is married and files a separate return) of such net losses can be used to offset other taxable income. Whatever capital losses are not absorbed by the $3,000 allowance can be carried forward into future years when they will receive the same treatment as they did in the present year.[653] This is fine for the small investor, but for the investor who incurs a large loss, the $3,000 cap can mean a deduction will be allowed each year for what is almost only a trivial amount of total loss. They can be carried forward for the rest of the taxpayer's life, but they expire at death.

There is a good reason for first netting capital losses against capital gains, namely to block taxpayers from creating a net tax loss from a transaction that produces no economic gain or loss during the tax year.

> **To illustrate:** If a stock market investor in the 37% marginal tax bracket generated a long-term capital gain of $1,000 and a short-term loss of $1,000, he could claim the capital gain attracted a tax of only $238 (23.8% of $1,000), but that the deductible short-term loss should generate a tax reduction of up to $370 (37% of $1,000), by offsetting ordinary income. By mandatorily combining them, the Code prevents this kind of opportunism.

Likewise, the $3,000 cap limits the strategy of selectively selling only loss assets in a particular tax year. On given facts, assuming a taxpayer's net long-term capital loss is large enough, an unlimited capital loss deduction could completely offset his ordinary income from other sources, such as salary or interest. In contrast to capital losses, we still allow taxpayers unlimited deductions for the cost of producing business income

You might want to scan Schedule D to the Form 1040 at the back of the book. It lays out the calculations.

Problem 8-2:

Investor is unmarried and has net income of $500,000. During the current year he incurred the following capital gains and losses:

Long-term capital gain:	$1300
Long-term capital loss:	$2500
Short-term capital gain:	$1600
Short-term capital loss:	$1200

652 §1211(b).

653 §1212. Incidentally, if both long and short-term capital losses carry forward, one uses up the short-term losses first. One can glean this from reviewing §1212(b) very, very thoughtfully.

1) What is the impact of these transactions on Investor's Federal Income Tax base?

2) What would be the impact on Investor if he *only* had *each* transaction, and not the other three? Describe the results one-by-one.

3) What would be the result if he incurred the following capital gains and losses from his stock market investments:

Long-term capital gain:	$2500
Long-term capital loss:	$1300
Short-term capital gain:	$1200
Short-term capital loss:	$1600

4) Same as "(1)," but Investor, who is unmarried, has $200,000 of ordinary income from other sources and has the following capital gains and losses this year:

Long-term capital gain:	$13,000
Long-term capital loss:	$25,000
Short-term capital gain:	$16,000
Short-term capital loss:	$12,000

5) Imagine two taxpayers, Wealth (who was born rich) and Hardworking (who was born poor). Each earns $1 million per year, Wealthy from capital gains taxable at not over 20% and Hardworking as a professional, taxed at 37%. If the "theory of the veils" were applied to legislation proposing such an outcome, do you think it would be accepted?

Problem 8-3:

Mac Walton, a 75 year-old retiree, traveled abroad for a year, leaving his $800,000 fortune in capital assets in the hands of a go-go stock broker who lost the entire amount by speculative transactions. What tax benefit, if any, can Mac get from the loss caused by the broker's mismanagement? Assuming there is a benefit, how long will it take him to realize the full benefit assuming he cannot generate capital gains? See §1211(b).

Mac's situation brings up a reminder under §165(h)(2). If a taxpayer suffers casualties or thefts to property held for personal use that collectively produce a gain -- perhaps because of insurance recoveries -- then *each* transaction is treated as a capital transaction; but if they sum to a loss, then *each* is treated as an ordinary transaction; this can yield a net casualty loss which cannot be deducted. If the personal casualty gains exceed personal casualty losses, then *each* such gain and loss goes into the capital gains calculation (Schedule D of the Federal Income Tax return) and may wind up being favorably taxed.[654] Chapter 7 discusses this in detail.

c. When are Losses on the Disposition of Property Allowed?

You need to review §165(a)-(c), because it is one of the most important components of the Code. Notice how §165(a) and (b) limit all losses for the year to the basis of the property. Subsection 165(c) tells us that in the case of *individuals* there are only three ways to get a tax loss from dealing in property:

1. Incur the loss in a trade or business;

2. Incur the loss in a transaction entered into for a profit (but not in a business); or

3. Incur the loss in a theft, fire, storm, shipwreck, or other casualty from a disaster that occurred in a federally declared disaster zone, even though the property was neither used in a business nor acquired in a transaction entered into for a profit.

So under what part of §165 would a business corporation claim a loss on disposing of its property?

We have already covered casualties in Chapter 7 and what constitutes a trade or business in Chapter 5, but this latest term, "transaction entered into for a profit" is a fresh mystery. Just what does the term mean? The answer is that it refers to the acquisition or change in use of property with a sincere view to a subsequent profit from its use or resale. The taxpayer's subjective intent is what counts. Some examples of transactions entered into for a profit include:

1. Buying bonds to get a stream of interest:
2. Buying a condo to rent out at a profit:
3. Converting a home to rental use;[655] and
4. Selling a property acquired by gift or inheritance, if the recipient did not use it for personal purposes and quickly put the property to a profit-making use.[656]

654 §165(h)(3) and (c)(3).

655 Reg. §1.165-9(b)(1).

656 See, e.g., Campbell v. Commissioner, 5 T.C. 272 (1945).

A transaction entered into with a hope for tax losses alone does not qualify, as you may recall from *Knetsch v. United States*[657] earlier in the book.

If the property has a dual use one apportions the property into imaginary parts that do and do not qualify under §165(c). For example, if a doctor buys a car partly to make house calls and partly for personal use, the trade-related portion of the car may qualify for a §165(c) deductible loss treatment when it is sold. The *Sharp* "divided aircraft" case that you saw in Chapter 3 was your first glimpse of this possibility.

If the entire property was bought with mixed purposes but a single use, then the primary purpose of the acquisition must have been to make a profit from sale or use of the property.[658] For example, if you bought a home partly to have a place to reside and partly as an investment you hoped would appreciate in value, you could claim a loss on the sale of the home only if the investment purpose was the principal one for buying the home. You should expect a chilly reception from the IRS.

The Regulations say that the taxpayer's loss on property that has been converted from personal use to a business use is to be measured by the difference between the amount realized and the lower of the cost of the property or its value when converted, minus depreciation for the subsequent period of business use. This result applies so that a decline in value attributable to the period of personal use is not deductible.[659] You saw this before, too.

Problem 8-4:

Gyro Klopman always swam against the stream. He spends his days chanting and wandering in the woods. Recently, a psychic strongly encouraged him to purchase oil company stocks to get in tune with modern life by cultivating his greed. He followed her advice, but the stocks fell out of favor because of the global warming problem, and so he sold them at a $1,000 loss, his only capital loss for the year.

1) Can he claim the loss on his tax return?

2) What if he inherited the property from Cyrus, who held them for investment, and Gyro promptly sold them?

657 348 F.2d 932 (Ct. Cl. 1965), cert. den., 383 U.S. 957 (1966).

658 Helvering v. National Grocery Co., 304 U.S. 282, 289 n5. (1938).

659 See Reg. §1.165-9(c), Examples (1) and (2). For a suggestion that depreciation should always be computed and subtracted from the taxpayer's basis so as, for example, to increase gain on the sale of a personal residence. See Epstein, Consumption and Loss of Personal Property Under the Internal Revenue Code, 23 Stan. L. Rev. 454 (1971).

d. The Complications under the 1997 and 1998 Acts

Now we need to look at losses under the amendments to the Code that fragment capital gains into the various subclasses. The following excerpt was issued by the IRS in anticipation of a Technical Corrections Act that was pending at the time. (New tax laws frequently contain errors and omissions that need prompt correction by means of a Technical Amendments Act; the 1997 Act was no exception.) The particular problem was that Congress forgot to tell taxpayers the order in which losses offset gains. The following notice, based on then pending 1998 legislation, answered some, but not all, of the questions. The IRS conclusions definitely favor taxpayers, not the Treasury.

The 1998 Act adopted the concepts in the Notice, including the loss absorption rules you are about to read. Basically, it resolved every dilemma in favor of the taxpayer. The basic rule is that one now determines the net result in each category. One then offsets the highest taxed gain (say collectibles) with the unused losses, in the most taxpayer-friendly order.

NOTICE 97-59

1997-45 I.R.B. 7

. . .

BACKGROUND

. . .

The definitions of net capital gain, net longterm capital gain or loss, and net shortterm capital gain or loss were not changed by the 1997 Act. However, under new section 1(h), if a noncorporate taxpayer has a net capital gain, the taxpayer's long term capital gains and losses are separated into three tax rate groups.

(1) *The 28percent group.* The 28percent group consists of the following:

. . .

(c) [C]apital gains and losses from collectibles (including works of art, rugs, antiques, metals, gems, stamps, coins, and alcoholic beverages) held for more than one year, regardless of the date taken into account.
This group also includes longterm capital loss carryovers. . . .

(2) *The 25percent group.* The 25percent group consists of unrecaptured section 1250 gain (there are no losses in this group). Unrecaptured section 1250 gain is longterm capital gain, not otherwise

recaptured as ordinary income, attributable to prior depreciation of real property and which is from property held for more than one year . . . .

[**To illustrate:** Mrs. Gasgoigne bought a building for investment for $100 and claimed depreciation deductions of $40, leaving her with an adjusted basis of $60. She later sold the building for $75. The full $15 gain is founded on depreciation. This capital gain is taxable at rates not over 25%.]

(3) *The 20percent group.* The 20percent group (10 percent in the case of gain that would otherwise be taxed at 15 percent) consists of longterm capital gains and losses that are not in the 28percent or 25percent group. . . .

New section 1(h) also applies to gains and losses that are characterized as capital under section 1231,[660] which covers certain transactions including sales of depreciable property or real property used in a trade or business. These gains and losses are included in the appropriate rate group, depending on the holding period and disposition date of the particular asset.

NETTING GAINS AND LOSSES

Within each group, gains and losses are netted to arrive at a net gain or loss. Taking into account the pending legislation, the following additional netting and ordering rules apply:

(1) *Short-term capital gains and losses.* As under prior law, shortterm capital losses (including shortterm capital loss carryovers) are applied first to reduce shortterm capital gains, if any, otherwise taxable at ordinary income rates. a net short term capital loss is then applied to reduce any net longterm gain from the 28percent group, then to reduce gain from the 25percent group, and finally to reduce net gain from the 20percent group.

(2) *Long-term capital gains and losses.* A net loss from the 28 percent group (including longterm capital loss carryovers) is used first to reduce gain from the 25percent group, then to reduce net gain from the 20percent group. A net loss from the 20percent group [the 2009 15% group] is used first to reduce net gain from the 28percent group, then to reduce gain from the 25percent group.

Any resulting net capital gain that is attributable to a particular rate group is taxed at that group's marginal tax rate.

660 You will see §1231 later. Eds.

COORDINATION WITH OTHER PROVISIONS[661]

The pending legislation coordinates the multiple rates of new § 1(h) with certain other provisions of the Code. Accordingly, the following rules apply:

> (1) *Holding Periods.* Under prior law, certain inherited property, if disposed of within one year after the decedent's death, was deemed to have been held for more than one year under section 1223(11) or (12). Such property, if disposed of within [12] months after the decedent's death, is now deemed to have been held for more than [12] months. A similar rule applies for certain patents described in section 1235(a). Gain or loss from a section 1256 contract, to the extent that it is treated as longterm capital gain or loss under section 1256(a)(3), is now treated as attributable to property held for more than [12] months. Rules similar to those of section 1233(b) and (d) (involving short sales of substantially identical property) and section 1092(f).
>
> . . .

Problem 8-5:

1) Angelica sold the following three items, each of which had been held for well over a year. Assume she is in the top Federal Income Tax bracket. How does she offset the gains and losses from these transactions?

    a. An artwork she collected and hung in her bedroom, costing $2,000 and sold for $4,000 (taxable at not over 28%).

    b. Stock of a corporation, costing $5,000 and sold for $2,000 (taxable at not over 15%).

    c. Real estate, the gain on which was from depreciation (taxable at not over 25%). The gain was $3,000.

2) Consult §1223(1), (2) and (11) and answers the following short problems.

    a. Yesterday, donee received a gift of property which donor has held for two years. What is donee's holding period? See also §1015.

    b. Decedent died three weeks ago. What is the estate's holding period for the decedent's property? See also §1014.

661 These provisions are unfamiliar at this point in the course. Do not worry about them yet. Eds.

Scan §1221(a)

Section 1221(a), defining a "capital asset," is straightforward. It says that all items of "property" are capital assets except for the properties listed in the paragraphs that follow §1231(a).

1. The Exceptions to Capital Asset Treatment

The next part of the book focuses on the most commonly encountered exceptions on the "bad list" and points out that there is also a Federal common law exception for property that is in substance just a substitute for ordinary income. The first exception is for inventory, stock in trade and "dealer property."

a. Dealer Property Exception

Reread §1221(a)(1)

On the face of it, §1221(a)(1) looks like a simple provision. Inventory and stock in trade is reasonably easy to spot. More or less everyone knows what inventory is. Stock in trade is generally synonymous with inventory. Property "held . . . primarily for sale to customers in the ordinary course of . . . business" seems to be just a second cousin to inventory. In fact, however, that last category, known as "dealer property," has proven to be immensely troublesome.

The worst problem for taxpayers is that if appreciated property is dealer property, then all the gain is ordinary, not just the gain following the time when it was first held for sale, even though much of the gain accrued over the years prior to the decision to sell it. This all or nothing outcome is sometimes called a "cliff effect" among tax types. The next, well-known, case explores what the word "primarily" means in the context of §1221(1) and is the only Supreme Court foray into the area.

MALAT v. RIDDELL

383 U.S. 569 (S. Ct. 1966)

PER CURIAM

Petitioner was a participant in a joint venture which acquired a 45acre parcel of land, the intended use for which is somewhat in dispute. Petitioner contends that the venturers' intention was to develop and operate an apartment project on the land; the respondent's position is that there was a "dual purpose" of developing the property for rental purposes or selling, whichever proved to be the more profitable. In any event, difficulties in obtaining the necessary financing were encountered, and the interior lots of the tract were subdivided and sold. The profit from those sales was reported and taxed as ordinary income.

The joint venturers continued to explore the possibility of commercially developing the remaining exterior parcels. Additional frustrations in the form of zoning restrictions were encountered. These difficulties persuaded petitioner and another of the joint venturers of the desirability of terminating the venture; accordingly, they sold out their interests in the remaining property. Petitioner contends that he is entitled to treat the profits from this last sale as capital gains; the respondent takes the position that this was "property held by the taxpayer primarily for sale to customers in the ordinary course of his trade or business,"[662] and thus subject to taxation as ordinary income.

The District Court made the following finding:

> "The members of [the joint venture], as of the date the 44.901 acres were acquired, intended either to sell the property or develop it for rental, depending upon which course appeared to be most profitable. The venturers realized that they had made a good purchase pricewise and, if they were unable to obtain acceptable construction financing or rezoning . . . which would be prerequisite to commercial development, they would sell the property in bulk so they wouldn't get hurt. The purpose of either selling or developing the property continued during the period in which [the joint venture] held the property."

The District Court ruled that petitioner had failed to establish that the property was not held *primarily* for sale to customers in the ordinary course of business, and thus rejected petitioner's claim to capital gain treatment for the profits derived from the property's resale. The Court of Appeals affirmed . . . . We granted certiorari . . . to resolve a conflict among the courts of appeals[663] with regard to the meaning of the term "primarily" as it is used in § 1221 (1) of the Internal Revenue Code of 1954.

The statute denies capital gain treatment to profits reaped from the sale of "property held by the taxpayer primarily for sale to customers in the ordinary course of his trade or business." (Emphasis added.) The respondent urges upon us a construction of "primarily" as meaning that a purpose may be "primary" if it is a "substantial" one.

As we have often said, "the words of statutes including revenue acts should be interpreted where possible in their ordinary, everyday senses." . . . Departure from a literal reading of statutory language may, on occasion, be indicated by relevant internal evidence of the statute itself and necessary in order to effect the legislative purpose. . . . But this is not such an occasion. The

662 Internal Revenue Code of 1954, § 1221 (1), 26 U. S. C. § 1221 (1). [Footnote No. 2 in original.]

663 Compare Rollingwood Corp. v. Commissioner, 190 F.2d 263, 266 (C. A. 9th Cir.); American Can Co. v. Commissioner, 317 F.2d 604, 605 (C. A. 2d Cir.), with United States v. Bennett, 186 F.2d 407, 410411 (C. A. 5th Cir.); Municipal Bond Corp. v. Commissioner, 341 F.2d 683, 688689 (C. A. 8th Cir.). Cf. Recordak Corp. v. United States, 163 Ct. Cl. 294, 300301, 325 F.2d 460, 463464. [Footnote No. 3 in original.]

purpose of the statutory provision with which we deal is to differentiate between the "profits and losses arising from the everyday operation of a business" on the one hand . . . and "the realization of appreciation in value accrued over a substantial period of time" on the other. . . . A literal reading of the statute is consistent with this legislative purpose. We hold that, as used in § 1221 (1), "primarily" means "of first importance" or "principally."

Since the courts below applied an incorrect legal standard, we do not consider whether the result would be supportable on the facts of this case had the correct one been applied. We believe, moreover, that the appropriate disposition is to remand the case to the District Court for fresh factfindings, addressed to the statute as we have now construed it.

Vacated and remanded.

. . .

Notes on Dealer Property and the Business versus Investment Distinction

Dealer property. After *Malat v. Riddell*, the population of properties qualifying for capital asset treatment increased in comparison to the population that would have qualified if the Supreme Court had come out the other way. That helps if one invested shrewdly in such property. The flip side is that the decision hurts taxpayers who show losses, because they *want* to show *ordinarylosses* unfettered by the $3,000 per year limit applicable to *capital* losses. Do you suppose that this is a heads-I-win, tails-you-lose situation in which taxpayers are apt to call their gains capital and their losses ordinary? Does the IRS have much to lose by taking a reverse forensic position?

The biggest dealer property issue involves real estate. The underlying problem is the cliff effect; if property is declared "dealer property" then *all* the gain is taxed as ordinary income, even though much of the gain accrued over many years. Taxpayers have on occasion managed to avoid the problem by selling appreciated property to related entities at a capital gain, and then having the related entity sell the property as dealer property at little or no gain. This culls out the long-term gain, which can be favorably taxed, from the current gain attributable to improving the property.

> **To illustrate:** A partnership acquired vacant land for investment. A corporation owned by the partnership is in business to develop and sell real estate. The partnership sold the land to the corporation, reporting a long-term capital gain. The IRS asserted the gain was ordinary because the partnership was in the business of selling land, based on the activities of the corporation and their relationship. The Tax Court agreed with the IRS, but the Fifth Circuit reversed, saying that the business of a corporation ordinarily is not attributable to its shareholders, and concluded that the partnership was not directly in the business of selling land, given its modest sales. Also, there was no evidence that the corporation ever acted as agent for the partnership, or that it

could bind the partnership. Moreover, the sales price was reasonable, so the activities of the corporation were not attributed to the partners and they were able to walk away with a long-term capital gain.[664]

People involved with stocks and bonds get quite different treatment. If they are "traders," meaning people who buy and sell for their own account with some frequency, they are never exposed to §1221(a)(1) and all their gains and losses are capital transactions.[665] This exclusion was deliberate; during the Depression investors lost huge sums which they sought to wring ordinary losses by claiming trader status. In 1934 Congress modified the predecessor of §1221(a)(1) to add the words "to customers" to put an end to such claims.[666] By contrast, "dealers" in securities, meaning people who sell stocks and bonds to a clientele as 'market makers', are subject to ordinary income and loss treatment. Because dealers can sometimes buy as investors or traders, §1236 grants them until the end of the day of the purchase to identify securities they bought for investment. If they fail to do so, they are stuck with an ordinary income or loss result (not bad if there is a loss).

One area the IRS will not rule on is the "inherently factual" matter. As a result, there is no hope of getting an IRS private letter ruling on characterizing property, because the issue of trader versus dealer status is considered "inherently factual." This is referred to as a so-called "no ruling" area (of which there are many).

Business versus investment revisited. You need to be sure you have a good grip on these concepts:

"Investment activity" involves gain-seeking but falls short of a trade or business because it is less intensive and more concerned with deploying capital and waiting for profits to roll in. Investment activities generate §§212 expenses and §§167-168 depreciation deductions.

"Trade or business activity" involves regular activity sincerely designed to make a profit, and in some circumstances may not even require interacting with the public as long as the activity is the source of the taxpayer's livelihood.[667] A trade or business may be part-time or even seasonal. The existence of a trade or business sets the stage for deductions under §162, §§167-168, and

664 Bramblett v. Commissioner, 960 F.2d 526 (5th Cir., 1992), rev'g TCM 1990 296.

665 See, e.g. Reinach v. Commissioner 373 F.2d 900 (2d Cir. 1967), cert. denied (1967).

666 H.R. Conf. Rep. No. 1385, d Cong., 2d Sess. p.22.

667 See Commissioner v. Groetzinger, 480 U.S. 23 (1987) (full-time gambler held engaged in business even though he did not hold himself out to the public as offering goods or services; it suffices to be involved in a for profit activity on a regular basis and were the source of his livelihood). Up until then, most tax practitioners believed there had to be interaction with the public, based on a common interpretation of the decision in Higgns v. Commissioner, 312 U.S. 212 (1941) that you saw earlier in the book. Groetzinger makes it harder to draw the line between investors and business people and raises the question of whether there is any difference between betting on horses and betting on such things as commodities futures.

attracts many specialized provisions, such as elective five-year amortization of research and development expenditures under §174 and of start-up expenses under §195. In addition, it attracts §1231, producing a lavish tax result for owners of property used in the business. Section 1231 is dealt with later in this Chapter.

(i) The Dealer Property "Factor" Analysis

The question of whether an item constitutes inventory under §1221(a)(1) is rarely a difficult question, and the area is simplified by a rule that real estate is not inventory (although it can be "dealer property").[668]

By contrast, determining whether a particular asset is so-called dealer property, as in *Malat. v. Riddell*, can be exasperating. The classic example involves the farmer who has owned his land for many years and decides to sell it off in pieces. Whether his sales produce ordinary income or capital gains is a difficult, ticklish inquiry, which has to be undertaken sale-by-sale. As the case law in this area has grown, it more and more resembles a viper's tangle than a road map. You will see a commonly used list of unranked factors for identifying dealer property in the following Private Letter Ruling.

PRIVATE LETTER RULING 8140015

June 30, 1981

Issue:

Whether the sale of scrap silver by an Indian Jewelry manufacturer, under the circumstances described below, results in capital gain or ordinary income.

Facts:

Corp X purchases flat rolled silver and forwards it to Indian craftsmen who use such silver to manufacture Indian jewelry. The craftsmen subsequently return the finished product to Corp X along with any remaining scrap silver. Corp X represents that it segregates the reusable scrap for use in its operations and stores the unusable scrap in boxes in a vault. Such unusable scrap is not subsequently used in the manufacture of Corp X's finished products. Corp X has accumulated this scrap silver since 1972, the year of incorporation. From 19721979, Corp X did not sell or advertise for sale any of the scrap silver, except for a sale amounting to approximately $11x which was, as stated by Corp X, an isolated instance since the buyer was a close acquaintance

---

668 Miller, W.C.& A.N., Development Co. v. Commissioner, 81 T.C. 619 (1983).

of Corp X's president. Corp X represents that it refused other frequent offers from potential outside buyers to purchase the scrap silver.

Up until October 1978 Corp X classified the scrap silver as inventory on its balance sheet. At that time, the scrap was formally classified as an investment. Corp X states that this reclassification reflected what had always been its intention with respect to the unusable scrap silver.

In 1979 and 1980, Corp X sold scrap silver worth $261x and $1,300x, respectively. The silver was sold because of Corp X's net operating loss and the need for funds. Approximately nine months prior to the sale in 1979, Corp X converted its scrap silver into silver bars. Silver in this form would not be used by Corp X in its ordinary course of business.

Law:

Section 1221(1) of the Code provides that the term "capital asset" means property held by the taxpayer (whether or not connected with his trade or business), but does not include stock in trade of the taxpayer or other property of a kind which would properly be included in the inventory of the taxpayer if on hand at the close of the taxable year, or property held by the taxpayer primarily for sale to customers in the ordinary course of his trade or business.

Rev. Rul. 579, 19571 C.B. 265, holds that income from the sale of tree stumps from land held by an investment company which is not in the timber or stump business, either as a buyer, seller or processor, is taxable as a capital gain where the land was acquired in a cutover state as a real estate investment and the stumps were sold in one lot. The ruling states: "Whether property is held for sale to customers in the ordinary course of a taxpayer's trade or business is a question of fact to be determined in the light of all the circumstances of each particular case."

Rev. Rul. 57565, 19572 C.B. 546, describes a situation where the taxpayer bought a 300acre tract of undeveloped land. He established a nursery on a 50acre parcel of the land, held a 45acre wooded section for speculation, subdivided 140 acres into lots for sale, and held the remaining 65 acres of unimproved land as an investment. The ruling held that the subsequent sale of the 65 acres of unimproved land constitutes the sale of a capital asset within the meaning of section 1221 of the Code because the taxpayer is not in the business of selling real estate as to that tract of land.

Rev. Rul. 7894, 19781 C.B. 58, holds that a prominent business motive for the purchase of stock cannot preclude the stock from capital gain or loss treatment, so long as there was a substantial investment motive for acquiring or holding the stock.

Rationale:

The income from the sale of Corp X's scrap silver will be classified as ordinary income, and not as capital gain from the sale of a capital asset, as defined in section 1221(1), if the scrap silver was (1) stock in trade or other property of a kind which would be properly included in inventory, and (2) property held primarily for sale to customers in the ordinary course of the taxpayer's trade or business.

In determining whether the scrap silver was stock in trade or other property of a kind which would be properly included in inventory, reference is made to section 1.4711 of the Income Tax Regulations which defines "inventory" as including "all finished or partly finished goods and, in the case of raw materials and supplies, only those which have been acquired for sale or which will physically become a part of merchandise intended for sale. Therefore, to be properly included in inventory, the unused scrap silver would have to be classified as a raw material which had been acquired for sale. Corp X represents that the acquisition of the flat rolled silver for use in producing the Indian jewelry unavoidably entailed the acquisition of unusable scrap silver which was consistently held as an investment. It cannot be concluded that the scrap silver was acquired for sale, especially since, from 19721979, Corp X did not sell or advertise for sale any of the scrap silver except for one isolated instance of a small sale amounting to $11x. Although the scrap silver probably could have been converted into flat rolled silver for manufacturing purposes, this does not mean that it should be classified as inventory. . . .

An asset does not become an inventory item simply because it has been classified as such on the books. As stated by the Tax Court in Pontchartrain Park Homes, Inc. v. Commissioner, T.C.M. 196392, affirmed 349 F. 2d 416 (5th Cir. 1965),

> "the fact that petitioners actually carried the unimproved portions of the 211 acres on its books in an inventory account is not at all conclusive of the true character of such property."
>
> . . .

In this case, the mere fact that the scrap silver was classified as inventory until 1978, at which time was reclassified as an investment, does not mean that it must be treated as inventory for the purpose of applying section 1221(1) of the Code. Since Corp X did not acquire the scrap silver for sale, it should not be treated as stock in trade or other property of a kind which would be properly included in inventory. The result may have been different if Corp X had sold scrap silver on a regular basis.

The determination of whether property is held primarily for sale to customers in the ordinary course of the taxpayer's trade or business, within the meaning of section 1221(1) of the Code, depends on the facts and circumstances of each case. Factors to consider include:

1. The purpose for which the property was initially acquired;
2. The purpose for which the property was subsequently held;
3. The extent to which improvements, if any, were made to the property by the taxpayer;

4. The frequency, number, and continuity of sales;
5. The extent and nature of the transactions involved;
6. The ordinary business of the taxpayer;
7. The extent of advertising, promotion, or other active efforts used in soliciting buyers for the sale of the property;
8. The purpose for which the property was held at the time of the sale.

Rev. Rul. 579, cited above, recognizes a difference between a sale of tree stumps in one lot by a taxpayer who is not in the timber or stump business, either as a buyer, seller, or processor (therefore, capital gain) and a sale of tree stumps as a byproduct by timber operators after the merchantable standing timber has been cut and removed, in which case the stumps are considered to be property held by the taxpayer for sale to customers in the ordinary course of his trade or business (therefore, ordinary income). Similarly, in Rev. Rul. 57565, cited above, it was held that a taxpayer who sells the unsubdivided part of a tract of land, a part of which has been subdivided into lots for sale, is not in the business of selling real estate as to the unsubdivided part and the sale thereof constitutes the sale of a capital asset. Applying the rationale of these two revenue rulings to the case at hand, it can be concluded that if Corp X is not in the business of selling scrap silver, then the income resulting from an isolated sale of scrap silver will result in capital gain.

Property may be held for more than one purpose, but to be treated as "property held by the taxpayer primarily for sale to customers in the ordinary course of his trade or business," within the meaning of section 1221(1) of the Code, it must be held "primarily" for that purpose. In Malat v. Riddell . . . the Supreme Court held that the purpose of section 1221(1) is to differentiate between the "profits and losses arising from the everyday operations of a business" on the one hand and "the realization of appreciation in value accrued over a substantial period of time" on the other. The court held that, as used in section 1221(1), "primarily" means "of first importance" or "principally." The fact that there is always an intent to sell the property in the future does not mean that it is held primarily for sale. . . .

Applying the factors described above to the case at hand, we feel that the sales of scrap silver were of an isolated nature. Substantial sales of scrap silver were made in 1979 and 1980, and these were the only sales since 1972 except for one nominal transaction. Corp X's sales of scrap silver were entirely different from its principal trade or business, which is the sale of Indian jewelry. The transactions were of an unusual nature. From 19721979, Corp X did not advertise for sale any of the scrap silver. We conclude that the gain from Corp X's sale of scrap silver represents the realization of appreciation in value accrued over a substantial period of time, the scrap silver should be classified as a capital asset and any gain realized from these sales should be classified as capital gain.

Conclusion:

The sale of scrap silver by an Indian jewelry manufacturer, under the circumstances described above, results in capital gain.

. . .

Note

There seems to be no escape from the multi-factor analysis described in the Ruling. It does seem that factor "4" involving the "frequency, number and continuity of sales" is the pre-eminent factor.

(ii) Modest Relief from Dealer Property Status under Section 1237

Congress has intervened to assist the amateur real estate developer. This relief provision is important to landowners who choose to subdivide and move on. Read §1237(a) and (b)(3), then try your hand at the following problem. Make sure to recognize how limited a "safe harbor" §1237 offers.

Problem 8-6:

1) An Illinois real estate dealer in land owns a lot in Florida. His notion is that he will retire there unless someone offers him a good price. Yesterday, a nearby dealer offered him a particularly good price for the lot, and the Illinois dealer accepted the offer. Is this a sale of a capital asset?

2) After decades of doing nothing but prune farming, Mr. Brown subdivided and is now selling off his farm land as 50 building lots of two acres each. Brown had been farming the land for 18 years, and he installed culverts, roads, electricity and sewage lines to facilitate lot sales. Sales have been about 10 per year, and quite lucrative. He has done the selling himself, attracting business by word of mouth and a sign along his road. He does the paperwork and telephoning about the sales from his den at home.

   a. Do any of his development activities fall within the safe harbor of §1237?

   b. Can you be sure how his sales are characterized? Consider the factors in Technical Advice Memorandum 8140015.

c. Assuming a particular lot sale was considered a sale of dealer property, must he report some part of the gain on each lot as ordinary income or all of it?

d. If his profits are taxed as ordinary income, what can he do in terms of limiting his development activities to improve his chances of getting a capital gains result?

e. What if he sold the land in a single sale to a corporation owned by his uncle who developed the property?

3) Professor Fonebone teaches at your law school. You probably did not know that boring old Fonebone has a second life as a maker of clocks of a type that certain collectors crave. During almost every vacation Fonebone goes to a cabin in the woods of New England and diligently works on them, one at a time, with great care. Fonebone sells one or two of these works every year, and has quite a reputation in the field. The clocks sometimes take years to sell and sometimes sell right away. In several cases, Fonebone has managed to sell his clocks in the same summer during which they were being made. What is the character of the income generated by the sales of the clocks? Recall that a business can be part-time or seasonal, and might last only one season as long as it was undertaken regularly during that season. See the first three sentences of Reg. §1.471-1, which explain what kind of things have to go into inventory.

4) In the *Pasqualini* decision that you read earlier, the donated Christmas cards were held to be capital assets in the hands of the taxpayer who bought the cards and gave them to charity. Is that correct, in your view? Recall that a capital asset held for over a year and given to an appropriate charity (including a church) is deductible to the extent of its value, not its basis.

b. Section 1231 Assets

Read §1221(a)(2)

This category basically consists of assets used in a business and held for over a year. They are discussed below. They are squeezed out of §1221, which initially looks bad for them. In fact they enjoy especially hallowed status, not an adverse one. That subject is taken up later in the book.

c. Copyrights and Like Property

Art works and copyrights were made notorious after World War II when President Eisenhower and others wrote their autobiographies, aged the manuscripts for the necessary long-term holding period and then sold them to publishers as alleged capital assets.[669] Section 1221(a)(3) put an end to that just in the nick of time; it was made famous by President Nixon, who gave away certain memorabilia by means of a backdated transfer to the National Archives, contrived to avoid the effective date of §1221(a)(3). His tax problem was that if §1221(a)(3)[670] applied to his transfer, then his charitable contribution would be whittled down from its value to its basis.[671]

Section 1221(a)(3) has moved closer to center stage as time passes. The practical effect of a federal copyright is to grant the author or transferee a form of monopoly over the use of the property for a statutory period. The IRS agrees that such fragmentation of a copyright produces numerous lesser "properties" for Federal Income Tax purposes, such as the right to turn a book into a play or a movie.[672]

There are two basic models of how to exploit intellectual property, namely by sale or by license. Sorting out sales and licenses is important for tax reasons. For example:

1. If the transfer is a license, the licensor has the right to depreciate the asset.
2. If the property is a capital asset, the seller may benefit from long-term capital gains treatment.
3. If the property is licensed for business use, the licensee can deduct the royalty payments.

You know already that a copyright interest held by the creator (other than a musical composition) is not a capital asset, but it can easily become one if it is bought by someone else. How can one tell if the property was sold (so that it might be resold for a capital gain) or merely licensed? The answer is that one has to make a realistic evaluation of the rights transferred to see if the transferee got all the substantial rights to the property. For example, in *Conde Nast Publications Inc. v. United States*[673] the Court of Appeals for the Second Circuit held that the terms of a 1961 transfer of a trademark and trade name gave rise to a sale rather than a license, because the

---

669 See New Yorker Magazine, October 30, 1948, at 15-16.

670 See B. Bittker & L. Lokken, FEDERAL TAXATION OF INCOME, ESTATE AND GIFTS ¶47.4 (2019). His action precipitated a Congressional inquiry that might have led to his impeachment. See House Comm. on the Judiciary, Impeachment of Richard M. Nixon, President of the United States, H. Rep. No. 93-1305, 93 Cong., 2d Sess. 221-223 (1974).

671 See §170(e)(1)(A).

672 Rev. Rul. 60-226, 1960-1 C.B. 26.

673 575 F.2d 400 (2d Cir. 1978).

transferor retained no significant rights or interests in the asset transferred, or control of the business in the hands of the transferee. The transferor's retention of the right to inspect for quality control, and its right to terminate the agreement under certain specified circumstances, were held to be no more than legitimate steps to protect the value of the property which was to be the source of the payments to the transferor.

The following case involves a transaction that was found to be a sale. The issue was whether the property interest was a capital asset in the transferor's hands.

STERN v. UNITED STATES

164 F. Supp. 847 (E.D. La. 1958), affirmed 262 F.2d 957 (CA5 1959), cert. denied 1959

WRIGHT, J.

This case concerns ' Francis, ' the talking mule. Francis is a product of World War II. It was created by a lonely second lieutenant in the Pacific theater of operations who sometimes wondered whether there was anything in the Army lower than a second lieutenant. Francis convinced him there was. Now, seven motion pictures later, that second lieutenant, the taxpayer here, is claiming that the income from 'Francis' is entitled to capital gains treatment under the Internal Revenue laws.

In 1933, . . . David Stern, III, was employed as a dramatic critic for the Philadelphia Record, a newspaper owned by his father. Beginning four months later, he became successively comptroller of the Record, classified advertising salesman, assistant classified manager, classified manager, promotion manager, and general manager. During the time that Stern was learning the business, he continued to serve the Record as part-time dramatic critic. In 1938 he became publisher of the Courier-Post newspapers in Camden, New Jersey. Throughout the prewar years, when Stern was a newspaper business executive, his hobby was writing. He wrote some stories and articles in his spare time, but he was unable to sell any of them.

In the spring of 1943, Stern enlisted as a private in the United States Army. He was later commissioned as a second lieutenant, and subsequently became co-officer in charge of the Central Pacific Edition of Stars and Stripes. While in the Pacific, Stern wrote some imaginary dialogue between a second lieutenant and an old Army mule, some of which he sold to Esquire for approximately $200. He also wrote several short stories while in the Army which he sold to magazines for $50 to $250.

After his release from the Army in 1946, Stern returned to Camden as publisher of the Courier-Post newspapers. In 1947 Stern's connection with the Courier-Post newspapers was terminated. He immediately entered negotiations to purchase a newspaper. While so doing and at the suggestion of a book publisher, he rewrote in book form all of the episodes about the talking mule, Francis. During this period he also wrote a sequel to 'Francis' called 'Francis Goes to Washington.' It, too, was published by Farrar-Strauss, publisher of 'Francis.' In July 1949 Stern completed negotiations for the purchase of The New Orleans Item and took over the controlling interest and active management of the newspaper as its publisher. Since that date, he has devoted virtually his full time to the newspaper business as publisher.

On June 2, 1950 Stern sold to Universal Pictures Co., Inc., all of his 'right, title and interest . . . in and to . . . that certain character known as 'Francis' conceived and created by' him, together with all of his rights to the two novels mentioned above and all of his rights to any contracts with respect to the properties conveyed. In consideration of this transfer, Universal agreed to pay him $50,000 plus 5% of the net profits from photoplays based on the character Francis, and 75% of all sums received by Universal under contracts for the use of licensing of the property. Payment of the $50,000 entitled Universal to a 'commitment period' of two years within which to make a motion picture. Thereafter, and following release of each picture, Universal was entitled to additional commitment periods by paying a similar fixed consideration of $50,000 as to each picture or period. The contract further provided that 'if purchaser shall elect not to pay fixed consideration with respect to any next succeeding commitment period . . . the property shall revert to the seller,' all rights in motion pictures produced to remain in Universal. Under this agreement, Universal produced six additional motion pictures in which the character Francis was used. Stern prepared the screen play for the first of these pictures but has had no connection whatever with the writing or production of subsequent pictures except occasionally and incidentally as a consultant. The novel, 'Francis Goes to Washington,' was not used for screen material.

Plaintiffs have reported as ordinary income for tax purposes all amounts received by them from the sale of the motion picture and publishing rights to the novel 'Francis,' for preparing a short screen treatment of the book, 'Rhubarb,' and income received under the agreement for writing screen plays. Only those amounts received from Universal for the character Francis have been treated by plaintiffs as capital gains, accrued during the years received. For the year 1950, the Internal Revenue Service originally accepted plaintiffs' treatment of this income as capital gains from the sale of the character Francis. In considering subsequent years, the Appellate Division of the Internal Revenue reopened the return for the year 1950 and ruled that income from the character Francis was not subject to capital gains treatment for the reason that the contract with Universal was not a sale of the character Francis, that if it were, Francis was property held by the taxpayer primarily for sale to customers in the ordinary course of his business and, further, under the provision of Section 210(a) of the Revenue Act of 1950, amending the provisions of [now §1221(a)(3)] the character Francis was similar to a copyright, a literary or artistic composition and, therefore, not a capital asset.

Taxpayer has paid the Government the asserted deficiencies in income taxes for the years 1950-53 resulting from the Commissioner's refusal to recognize his treatment of amounts received from Universal Pictures Company pursuant to the contract in suit as a long-term capital gain. Timely claims for refund have been filed and disallowed, after which disallowance this suit was instituted. Taxpayer's position here is the same as it has been since the filing of his original income tax returns. He states that his contract with Universal Pictures Company was a sale of the capital asset, Francis, not in the ordinary course of his business, and, consequently, he is entitled to capital gains treatment of the income received from that sale. The Government here takes the same position taken by the Appellate Division of Internal Revenue Service as well as the Commissioner in his disallowance of the claim for refund.

The question as to whether the taxpayer's contract with Universal Pictures is a sale will be considered first because if it is not a sale, it will be unnecessary to consider the other objections to capital gains treatment of the income made by the Government. It will be noted in the contract that Stern sold all of his interest in the books 'Francis,' and 'Francis Goes to Washington,' the character Francis, and all rights and pending contracts concerning them. The agreement makes reference to 'the full and complete ownership in the property sold, transferred and granted to (Universal) hereunder.' It declares that Stern 'hereby sells, transfers and conveys . . . all right, title and interest' in the property to Universal and guarantees 'the full benefit of (Universal's) full and complete ownership in the property.' Obviously, the draftsmen of this contract intended that it be a sale and called it such. Apparently they were familiar also with the one case, Cory v. Commissioner of Internal Revenue, 2 Cir., 230 F.2d 941, which the Government cites as authority for its contention that this agreement is not a sale, because the language of the agreement leaves no doubt that Stern transferred his entire bundle of rights in all the Francis properties, together with rights of future exploitation, to Universal Pictures. Thus this agreement is different from the agreement under consideration in Cory v. Commissioner, supra, because there the agreement provided for 'a transfer of a part of the cluster of rights' inhering in the taxpayer. Cory v. Commissioner, supra, at page 944.[674]

The Government's suggestion, without citation of authority, that the contract in suit is not a sale because it provided for contingent payments of indeterminate sums similar to royalties, and because the property reverted back to Stern if the fixed consideration for any period is not paid, cannot convert this contract of sale into a licensing agreement. Perhaps a sale which provides for contingent payments of indeterminate sums and reversion does violence to the doctrinaire concepts of what a sale should be. But the tax cases interpreting Section [1221] of the Code have so long and so consistently held such contracts to be sales that the Internal Revenue Service itself in a recent ruling is now indicating its acquiescence in this classification.

The Government next contends that if the contract in suit is a sale, then the income therefrom is still not entitled to capital gains treatment because it was a sale of 'property held by the taxpayer primarily for sale to customers in the ordinary course of his trade or business.' .

---

674 The full text, pertinent here, from Cory v. Commissioner, supra at page 944, reads:

'We do not now decide that a transfer by a citizen of but a part of the bundle for a definite sum, or a transfer of the whole for an indeterminate sum, is a sale for purposes of Section 117.5[now 1221]. We do hold that when, as here, the transfer is both (1) a transfer of a part of the cluster of rights and (2) for an amount wholly indeterminable at the time of the transfer, no such sale occurs.' [Footnote No. 2 in original.]

. . The resolution of this question depends on appraisal of the total factual situation. Smith v. Commissioner of Internal Revenue, 5 Cir., 232 F.2d 142; Consolidated Naval Stores Company v. Fahs, 5 Cir., 227 F.2d 923. Unquestionably . . . a taxpayer may have more than one business. Snell v. Commissioner of Internal Revenue, 5 Cir., 97 F.2d 891. Before any business can come within Section [1221(a)(1)], however, it must be an 'occupational undertaking which required the habitual devotion of time, attention or effort with substantial regularity.' Thomas v. Commissioner of Internal Revenue, 5 Cir., 254 F.2d 233, 237. The criteria in making this determination are fully set forth in opinions by the Fifth Circuit so it would serve no useful purpose to repeat them here. Those cases do show that a court should not be quick to put a man in business . . . simply because he has been successful in earning extra income through a hobby or some other endeavor which takes relatively small part of his time.

Here the taxpayer is a newspaper publisher and has been, with the exclusion of the war years, actively directing newspapers since 1938. Virtually his entire time has been given to that endeavor. As a hobby he has written a few short stories, some of which have been productive of small amounts of income. On two occasions he has written screen plays. He has created the character Francis and written two novels about it. This literary work has taken relatively little of his time. It was more or less a relaxation from his principal employment. Under the circumstances, it can hardly be said that the taxpayer created 'Francis' to hold as 'property held by the taxpayer primarily for sale to customers in the ordinary course of his trade or business.' . . .

The Government makes much of the fact that in one of the schedules attached to taxpayer's return, he professes to be a writer. Even if the taxpayer were responsible for this statement, his literary license in this regard should not be allowed to affect the tax treatment accorded his income. Actually, the indication of Stern as a writer was the work of the accountant who prepared the return. It is further noted that the schedule on which the profession appears relates to income and expenses attendant his writing. On the first page of each return in the space provided for 'Occupation,' the word 'Publisher' appears.

Finally, and unfortunately for the taxpayer, the Government's position on the 1950 amendment to the 1939 Code is well taken. That amendment excludes from capital gains treatment income from the sale of 'a copyright; a literary, musical, or artistic composition; or similar property' held by 'a taxpayer, whose personal efforts created such property.' The purpose of this amendment is obvious. It is intended to deny capital gains treatment to income from the sale, by their creator, of literary, musical, or artistic compositions, or similar property. Prior to 1950, various rulings of the Internal Revenue Service had approved capital gains treatment of various literary, musical and artistic compositions, including books and radio programs. Congress determined to eliminate such treatment for such compositions. Hence the amendment.

The taxpayer contends that the character 'Francis' is not covered by the amendment, that it is not subject to copyright, that it is not a literary, musical or artistic composition or similar property. He argues that he has paid his taxes at the regular rates on all his income from his writings. He states that the character 'Francis' is an 'intellectual conception' and that as such the income from the sale thereof is entitled to capital gains treatment.

The taxpayer cites several cases in support of his position that the character Francis is not subject to being copyrighted. And he spends much time in his brief arguing that the Internal Revenue Service itself has limited the words of the statute 'or similar property' to property capable of being copyrighted. It is not necessary for this Court to appraise the taxpayer's citations, his argument on this point, or the counter citations and argument of the Government. It is this Court's view that the character Francis, irrespective of its susceptibility to copyright, is 'a literary composition' and as such the income from the sale thereof is not entitled to capital gains treatment. The taxpayer concedes, as he must, that the novel, 'Francis,' in which the character Francis is the leading figure, is a literary composition, but he argues that Francis, the principal characterization in the book, is not. In this he is mistaken. The character Francis gets its definition and its delineation from the book. The literary description in the book composes the character. How can it be said that the book is a literary composition yet the main character delineated therein is not? A slice of the loaf is still bread. It would be absurd to attribute to Congress the intention, under the 1950 amendment, of covering whole literary compositions but not parts thereof, particularly in view of the catchall, 'or similar property,' which appears at the end of the amendment.

Without the literary description of Francis, his mannerisms and his manifestations, Francis would cease to exist. In any event, an amorphous Francis could hardly be called 'property held by the taxpayer,' the sale of which is entitled to capital gains treatment. . . . If Francis is, as taxpayer suggests, an 'intellectual conception,' sans form and substance, existing in the mind alone, it is incapable of ownership and, therefore, of being 'property held by the taxpayer.' . . . If Francis has sufficient form and substance to be considered property capable of ownership, this is so because of its literary composition. Compare Warner Bros. Pictures v. Columbia Broadcasting System, 9 Cir., 216 F.2d 945.

The taxpayer is entitled to capital gains treatment on the income from the contract in suit for the year 1950 because the 1950 amendment to the Code does not apply to income received during that year. As to subsequent years, however, capital gains treatment of the income from the contract must be denied as proscribed by that amendment.

Judgment accordingly.

Problem 8-7:

1) Do you agree that the transaction involving Francis was a sale?

2) What might have made it a license?

3) Was Francis "primarily" held for sale?

4) If not, was the government wasting its time with the argument?

5) Remember that the *Stern* case was decided eight years before *Malat v. Riddell.* If Stern purported to sell the movie rights to Francis forever, would that be a sale for Federal Income Tax purposes?

d. Accounts Receivable

Business receivables are generally obvious; someone who sells beans over the counter or repairs used cars simply must not be allowed to turn so-far-untaxed rights to future payments for these goods or services into capital gains. Section 1221(4) assures the right result.

> **To illustrate:** Dr. Peabody is a cash method physician who has fallen on hard times. To raise cash, he sells his $1,000 face value accounts receivable (owed by his patients) to a bank for $800. The $800 is ordinary income, just as if the patients had paid $800 for his services in a timely manner. He is not entitled to a bad debt loss on the $200 shortfall because he never got basis in the accounts receivable from the patients.

e. U.S. Government Publications

Section 1221(a)(5), covering government publications, reverses an earlier IRS ruling granted to a Congressman who gave copies of the Congressional Record to charity and got a deduction for the value of the copies; the ruling implied that the copies were capital assets.[675]

> **To illustrate**: Former President Clinton got free copies of numerous federal reports while President. If and when he sells them, he must report ordinary gain on the transaction. He almost surely will have excluded them as a de minimis fringe benefit under §132 and will, therefore, have no basis in them.

f. Commodities Derivatives

This specialized provision prevents commodities dealers from claiming capital gains on "derivatives" unless they are clearly identified as investments.[676]

---

675 PLR 7502120610A 02/12/1975.

676 §1221(a)(6).

g. Section 1221(a)(7) and the Corn Products Doctrine Exception

In *Corn Products Refining Co. v. Commissioner*,[677] the Supreme Court in effect created yet another exception in §1221; assets that are integrally related to the daily operations of the business, namely hedging against the risk of adverse price movements in the commodity the taxpayer relied on for its business. The doctrine's scope expanded and became unclear with the passage of time, but it was pruned back to the roots in *Arkansas Best Corp. v. Commissioner*.[678] Now the doctrine means that assets acquired as part of a day-to-day business hedging function are not capital assets because they are tantamount to a form of inventory. The Code has been amended to add §1221(a)(7) to codify *Arkansas Best*.

h. Supplies Used in a Business

This provision (§1221(a)(8)) seems self-explanatory.

i. The "Substitutes for Ordinary Income" Exception

The next case you are going to read is of great importance. Not only does it in effect judicially legislate "§1221(a)(9)," but it also shows how willing the courts are to look through the form in which transactions are structured to get at their substance for tax purposes.

HORT v. COMMISSIONER
313 U.S. 28 (S. Ct. 1941)

MR. JUSTICE MURPHY delivered the opinion of the Court.

We must determine whether the amount petitioner received as consideration for cancellation of a lease of realty in New York City was ordinary gross income as defined in [§61 (a)] . . . and whether, in any event, petitioner sustained a loss through cancellation of the lease which is recognized in [§165].

Petitioner acquired the property, a lot and tenstory office building, by devise from his father in 1928. At the time he became owner, the premises were leased to a firm which had sublet the main floor to the Irving Trust Co. In 1927, five years before the head lease expired, the Irving Trust Co. and petitioner's father executed a contract in which the latter agreed to lease the main floor and basement to the former for a term of fifteen years at an annual rental of $ 25,000, the term to commence at the expiration of the head lease.

---

677 350 U.S. 46 (1955).

678 485 U.S. 212 (1988).

In 1933, the Irving Trust Co. found it unprofitable to maintain a branch in petitioner's building. After some negotiations, petitioner and the Trust Co. agreed to cancel the lease in consideration of a payment to petitioner of $ 140,000. Petitioner did not include this amount in gross income in his income tax return for 1933. On the contrary, he reported a loss of $ 21,494.75 on the theory that the amount he received as consideration for the cancellation was $ 21,494.75 less than the difference between the present value of the unmatured rental payments and the fair rental value of the main floor and basement for the unexpired term of the lease. He did not deduct this figure, however, because he reported other losses in excess of gross income.

The Commissioner included the entire $ 140,000 in gross income, disallowed the asserted loss, made certain other adjustments not material here, and assessed a deficiency. The Board of Tax Appeals affirmed. 39 B. T. A. 922. The Circuit Court of Appeals affirmed per curiam on the authority of *Warren Service Corp. v. Commissioner*, 110 F.2d 723. 112 F.2d 167. Because of conflict with *Commissioner v. Langwell Real Estate Corp.*, 47 F.2d 841, we granted certiorari limited to the question whether, "in computing net gain or loss for income tax purposes, a taxpayer [can] offset the value of the lease canceled against the consideration received by him for the cancellation." 311 U.S. 641, 61 S.Ct. 174.

Petitioner apparently contends that the amount received for cancellation of the lease was capital rather than ordinary income and that it was therefore subject to [the code sections] which govern capital gains [treatment]. Further, he argues that even if that amount must be reported as ordinary gross income he sustained a loss which [§165] authorizes him to deduct. We cannot agree.

The amount received by petitioner for cancellation of the lease must be included in his gross income in its entirety. Section [61 (a)] . . . expressly defines gross income to include "gains, profits, and income derived from . . . rent, . . . or gains or profits and income derived from any source whatever." Plainly this definition reached the rent paid prior to cancellation just as it would have embraced subsequent payments if the lease had never been canceled. It would have included a prepayment of the discounted value of unmatured rental payments whether received at the inception of the lease or at any time thereafter. Similarly, it would have extended to the proceeds of a suit to recover damages had the Irving Trust Co. breached the lease instead of concluding a settlement. . . . That the amount petitioner received resulted from negotiations ending in cancellation of the lease rather than from a suit to enforce it cannot alter the fact that basically the payment was merely a substitute for the rent reserved in the lease. So far as the application of [§ 61(a)] is concerned, it is immaterial that petitioner chose to accept an amount less than the strict present value of the unmatured rental payments rather than to engage in litigation, possibly uncertain and expensive.

The consideration received for cancellation of the lease was not a return of capital. We assume that the lease was "property," whatever that signifies abstractly. Presumably the bond in *Helvering v. Horst*, 311 U.S. 112, and the lease in *Helvering v. Bruun*, 309 U.S. 461, were also "property," but the interest coupon in *Horst* and the building in *Bruun* nevertheless were held to constitute items of gross income. Simply because the lease was "property" the amount received for its cancellation was not a return of capital, quite apart from the fact that "property" and "capital" are not necessarily synonymous in the Revenue Act of 1932 or in common usage. Where, as in this case, the disputed amount was essentially a substitute for rental payments which § 61 (a) expressly characterizes as gross income, it must be regarded as ordinary income, and it is immaterial that for some purposes the contract creating the right to such payments may be treated as "property" or "capital."

For the same reasons, that amount was not a return of capital because petitioner acquired the lease as an incident of the realty devised to him by his father. Theoretically, it might have been possible in such a case to value realty and lease separately and to label each a capital asset. . . . But that would not have converted into capital the amount petitioner received from the Trust Co., [the tax law] . . . would have required him to include in gross income the rent derived from the property, and that section, like [§61 (a)], does not distinguish rental payments and a payment which is clearly a substitute for rental payments.

We conclude that petitioner must report as gross income the entire amount received for cancellation of the lease, without regard to the claimed disparity between that amount and the difference between the present value of the unmatured rental payments and the fair rental value of the property for the unexpired period of the lease. The cancellation of the lease involved nothing more than relinquishment of the right to future rental payments in return for a present substitute payment and possession of the leased premises. Undoubtedly it diminished the amount of gross income petitioner expected to realize, but to that extent he was relieved of the duty to pay income tax. Nothing in §[165(c)] indicates that Congress intended to allow petitioner to reduce ordinary income actually received and reported by the amount of income he failed to realize. . . . We may assume that petitioner was injured insofar as the cancellation of the lease affected the value of the realty. But that would become a deductible loss only when its extent had been fixed by a closed transaction. . . .

The judgment of the Circuit Court of Appeals is

Affirmed.

Notes on the Acceleration of Income

Acceleration as a tax planning strategy. Imagine you have a charitable contribution carry forward of $100 that is about to expire and that you expect a dividend on some stock next year of $105. You might sell the future dividend for (say) $100. The tax cost would be $0, because any gain is offset by the deduction you were going to lose anyway. You avoid tax on the dividend.

Doctrinal confusion. It is hard to disagree that if someone sells some future income, the result should be ordinary income and not capital gain. However, income and property are not always easily separated. For example, if you owned an apartment building that commanded $2,000/month in rents, the building might be worth $200,000 to an investor who viewed the investment as an alternative to buying a bond. If there were a severe housing shortage and new zoning restrictions, the rents might double, and if you sold the building to the same investor for $400,000 you would be entitled to report the result as a capital gain. Many would defend the result by saying that capital gains result from the operation of market forces; in fact, you can also fairly say that what you were really selling was an enhanced flow of income.

Stock options compared. A sale of the lease by the *tenant* can qualify for capital gains treatment. For example, assume the (tenant) Irving Trust Company in the *Hort* case had sold its rights under the lease in a hot real estate market. In that transaction, the tenant is just cashing in on favorable market forces. There is no reason to punish the Irving Trust Company under the *Hort* theory, because it did not accelerate income. Any easy way to explain the difference is that, in such a case, the taxpayer-tenant sold its *entire* interest in the property at a price reflecting the play of market forces (as opposed to just selling a stream of rents), and is therefore entitled to treat the lease as property that may be capable of achieving capital asset status.[679]

The taxation of compensatory stock options makes a striking contrast. Here is the issue. Corporate directors are generally supposed to maximize the value of the corporation's stock. To do so, they hire executives and pay them well, including with compensatory stock options. If the officers do their jobs, the company prospers and the value of the stock rises and the executives' options rise in value, sometimes dramatically. If the executives have already been taxed on the value of the options when they received them, the executives report no income when they exercise them and buy the stock. When they later sell the stock obtained from the exercise of the options, they can sell the stock and enjoy a general top rate of 23.8% provided they held the stock for at least a year and a day. The point here is that this substitution of capital gains in place of ordinary income from compensation for services is an anomaly. (To the extent the options rose as a result of market forces and not the company's management, those gains should qualify for capital gains.) Perhaps one day Congress will choose to tax gains on such options as income from services. Do not hold your breath waiting.

2. Identifying "Property"

As you know, § 1221 defines a capital asset as any item of "property" that does not fit into a list of exceptions, but what does "property" mean for this purpose? That is not an easy question.

---

679 See, e.g., Commissioner v. Golonsky, 200 F.2d 72 (3d Cir. 1952) (tenant who gives up his lease in exchange for payment from landlord has capital gain result). The case law on the subject is buttressed by §1241, which provides that in many instances a payment to a tenant in cancellation of a lease will be treated as an amount paid in exchange for the lease, implicating capital gain treatment.

The deepest analysis appears in *Commissioner v. Ferrer*,[680] an actor (Jose Ferrer) entered into a deal with the author of a book on the life of the French painter Talouse Lautrec. The deal allowed Ferrer (1) to turn the book into a play and (2) veto film and radio versions of the play as long as it was running successfully and (3) a percentage of income from a movie version of the play. Later, the deal was canceled and Ferrer wound up taking the leading role in the movie. He was well-compensated when his contract with the author was canceled. The Second Circuit studied each of the three rights and found the first two comparable to a tenant's rights in a lease to use to the property and to block rentals to competitors. The third right was considered comparable to a landlord's right to be paid prepaid rent, the sale of which merely accelerates ordinary income (not "property"). The court emphasized the presence of equitable protection of each right in evaluating whether it rose to the level of being "property" for purposes of §1221. The greater the equitable protection, the more likely the item is property.

Other cases struggling with the problem of sorting property from income have looked to such questions as:

1. Whether the gain or loss with respect to the right was the result of the play of appreciation over a number of years, which is a favorable factor in terms of finding property.[681]
2. Whether there is separate investment that is somehow transferred, as opposed to merely transferring the right to use a property (such as where the government merely appropriates a factory to meet war time needs and pays the owner for its use).[682]
3. Whether the payment is in substance a payment in lieu of personal service income.[683]

FOOTE v. COMMISSIONER

81 T.C. 930 (1983), aff'd in unpublished opinion, 751 F.2d 1257 (1985)

DRENNEN, Judge.

. . .

680 304 F.2d 125 (2d Cir. 1962).

681 *Commissioner v. Gillette MotorTransport*, 364 US 130 (1960).

682 Id.

683 See, e.g., *Holt v. Commissioner*, 303 F. 2d 687 (9th Cir. 1962) (payments to cancel contract with film producer working on a fee-plus-percentage-of-revenues basis).

In 1968, petitioner accepted a position as an associate professor of management science at the Southern Methodist University School of Business Administration (university). In 1971 he was promoted to the rank of assistant professor.

In 1972, the university officially recognized petitioner's tenure. Normally, a professor is accorded the status of tenure only by a process of review after the individual has taught for a period of 6 years. Petitioner, however, received tenure by the less common procedure called de facto tenure, whereby a faculty member is deemed to have received tenure if he has taught for more than 6 years without the university's taking the necessary administrative steps to review his performance. Petitioner's de facto tenure arose unintentionally and without the knowledge of the university, due to the fact that under guidelines followed by the university, petitioner's prior teaching experience at another university counted towards his tenure at SMU.

Contrary to general understanding, tenure is not "granted" by the university. Rather, it is a status that arises as a result of a faculty member's service to the university; it is then recognized by the university. Tenure is essentially an assurance of lifetime employment with the university. A tenured professor at SMU can be dismissed only on the grounds of moral turpitude or gross incompetence. Tenure generally allows a professor more freedom to engage in scholarly activities such as research and writing, as well as activities outside of the university, such as consulting and other professional work, than would a nontenured professor be permitted. Tenure cannot be purchased, and a tenured faculty member cannot sell his tenure to another person

While tenure may be viewed as an informal employment contract with the university, it does not guarantee any specific salary. Petitioner entered into annual employment contracts with the university that specified his salary.

During his employment with the university, petitioner taught courses and engaged in other academic activities in a normal manner. However, during 1975 and 1976, some students and faculty members expressed concerns about his work, and friction apparently developed between petitioner and the administration. Petitioner was inclined to devote more time to his outside business activities than to his teaching and other university responsibilities. He described himself as "not a team player."

In January 1977, petitioner and the university entered into an agreement whereby petitioner resigned his tenured appointment in exchange for a sum of $45,640, to be paid him by the university in monthly installments throughout 1977 and 1978. Under the agreement, petitioner had no further obligations to the university, and he ceased teaching at that time.

During 1977 and 1978, petitioner realized net losses from consulting of $ 4,435 and $ 1,700, respectively.

Pursuant to the agreement, petitioner received monthly payments of $ 1,901.67 from the university. Petitioner reported these payments as long-term capital gain on his income tax returns for those years.

. . .

OPINION

The primary issue is whether petitioner is allowed to treat the payments received from the university pursuant to his resignation of his tenured appointment as assistant or associate professor as long-term capital gain, rather than ordinary income. Petitioner contends that his tenure was a capital asset, which he "sold" to the university. Respondent contends that the transaction cannot be viewed as the sale or exchange of a capital asset within the meaning of sections 1221 and 1222, but rather represents a termination of petitioner's rights under an employment agreement, the payment for which is ordinary income.

Petitioner cites no authority supporting his position, but presents us with a comprehensive discussion of why tenure, from the viewpoint of economics, constitutes an intangible capital asset. His argument, briefly stated, is that tenure affords a faculty member the freedom and opportunity to use the benefits of his university affiliation to generate income from activities such as consulting, speaking, and writing. The university affiliation provides resources such as contacts, prestige, visibility, and marketing channels for business activities. Because tenure assures job security, the faculty member is free to devote most of his time and energy to such personal business pursuits, contrary to the wishes of the university. Petitioner asserts that the aggressive exploitation of the business potential of tenure can produce income and capital appreciation far in excess of a teaching salary. Furthermore, he argues, as tenure is exploited in this fashion, its value increases, as does the university's incentive to disassociate itself from a tenured professor by "purchasing" his tenure.

Thus, according to petitioner's economic thesis, the agreement in question constitutes a sale of an intangible capital asset, his tenure, the consideration for which primarily reflects the capital asset value of the tenure, rather than the value of the right to receive future salary, and hence is properly taxable as capital gain.

While we find petitioner's argument to be ingenious and well presented, we are not so free to approach the question unencumbered by statute and case law. In order to entitle himself to preferential capital gain treatment, petitioner must demonstrate that the gain was produced by the (1) "sale or exchange" of (2) a "capital asset." Secs. 1221 and 1222. We think it is clear, from the extensive case law interpreting the capital gains provisions, that petitioner does not satisfy either of these requirements, and we therefore must find for the respondent.

"Capital asset" is defined in section 1221. Generally, it is property held by the taxpayer (whether or not connected with his trade or business), but does not include stock in trade or property held primarily for sale to customers in the ordinary course of his trade or business, or depreciable property used in his trade, or certain other specified types of property.

It is well established that a taxpayer does not bring himself within the capital gains provisions merely by showing that a contract constitutes "property," that he held a contract, and that his contract does not fall within a specified exclusion of section 1221. . . . Generally, the consideration received for the transfer or termination of a contract right to receive income for the performance of personal services is taxable as ordinary income. . . .

The central theme of the many cases denying capital gains treatment on the termination of such contract rights is that the payment received is essentially a substitute for ordinary income which would have been earned in the future. See *Kingsbury v. Commissioner, supra* at 1082-1083, and *Commissioner v. P. G. Lake, Inc.*, 356 U.S. 260, 266 (1958). Despite petitioner's effort to imbue his tenure with the attributes of a capital asset, we think his rights were not substantially different than the rights under any long-term employment or agency agreement.

It is clear from petitioner's own testimony that petitioner's tenure put him in a position to earn additional income. Not only could he continue to earn his salary with a minimum amount of teaching, but he was put in a position to earn fees from consulting, writing, research, and other activities performed for additional monetary considerations. All of such income would have been taxable as ordinary income. What petitioner gave up through the resignation of his tenured position was the opportunity to receive future ordinary income. What he received was not paid for any increase in the value of his tenure over a long period of time, which is the basis for the favored tax treatment given capital gains. *Commissioner v. P. G. Lake, Inc.*, supra. As one court stated: "The nature of the right to receive future income as ordinary income does not change into capital gain by the mere receipt of a lump sum in lieu of such future payments." *Holt v. Commissioner*, 303 F.2d 687, 691 (9th Cir.1962), affg. 35 T.C. 588 (1961). We conclude that petitioner's tenure did not qualify as a capital asset.

Even were we to accept the proposition that tenure has significant value independent of its assurance of future salary, petitioner has not executed a "sale or exchange" for the purposes of the capital gains provisions. The agreement in question simply terminated petitioner's rights; his tenure did not pass to the university, but was extinguished. Tenure is a personal right. It cannot be transferred to, or utilized by, another. As explained by Professor John Stieber in his testimony (transcript at 34), tenure is not granted by the university, it is recognized by the university. Under these circumstances, there is no "sale or exchange." . . . While there has been some uncertainty among the courts as to whether the release of various rights and obligations constituted a sale or exchange, as witness the preceding and other cases, we think it is clear in this case that there was no sale or exchange. The agreement simply terminated petitioner's tenure and released the university of its obligations. Petitioner's tenure rights "were not transferred to the promisor; they merely came to an end and vanished." . . .

. . .

Decision will be entered for the respondent.

Notes

In *North Dakota State University v. United States*[684], the Eight Circuit was faced with two groups of university employees each of who was paid a lump-sum to terminate employment with the university, administrators and professors, including tenured professors. The university treated the tenured professors specially in that the university's documentation showed that the professors had 'sold' their rights under the tenure system. The IRS demanded FICA taxes from both groups on theory that both classes of payments constituted 'wages.' It lost only as to the professors because of the court's finding that their payments were more for yielding up their rights than compensation for services. That saved the university the cost of contributing its employer's share of FICA taxes

3. Sale or Exchange

Read §1222(2), (4), (6) and (10)

On a plain reading of §1222, there has to be a "sale or exchange" in order for there to be a capital gain or loss. In turn, acute tax planners noticed that if the taxpayer owned a capital asset that had lost value, its sale would result in an undesirable long-term capital loss, but an "other disposition," such as an abandonment, would result in no "sale or exchange," hence no capital loss under §1222. This inspired aggressive tax planners to suggest that taxpayers caught in this jam abandon their properties and claim ordinary losses, as opposed to being entangled in the restrictions on the deductibility of capital losses.[685]

If one wished to press this argument one would almost surely cite the case of *Hudson v. Commissioner*.[686] The facts involved a woman who sued a Mr. Howard and got a judgment of $75,000. When she died, the judgment was still not paid. A Mr. Hudson bought the judgment from her estate for $11,000. A few years later, Howard paid Hudson $21,000 to settle the claim. Hudson asserted that his $10,000 profit was a capital gain because he sold the claim back to Howard. The IRS and the Tax Court saw it another way; they pointed out that *after* the transaction there was no "property" because it was eliminated by legal merger when it went back to Howard. As a result, there was no sale or exchange and, therefore, the $10,000 was ordinary income. That case helped set the stage for crafty taxpayers to invent ways to turn undesirable capital losses into more appetizing ordinary losses by disposing of property with no "sale or exchange." Reform-minded judges gradually rejected the "no sale means no capital loss" theory and equated sales with "other dispositions."[687]

---

684 255 F.3d 599 (CA 8 2001).

685 See §1222(1)-(4), (9) and (10).

686 20 T.C. 734 (1953), affirmed 216 F.2d 748 (CA 6 1954).

687 See, e.g., Yarbro v. Commissioner, 737 F.2d 479 (5th Cir. 1984), cert. denied 1985.

Section 1271(a) has since been amended to reverse the *Hudson* doctrine. Now, money a debt-holder receives on the retirement of a debt issued by a natural person is treated as received on the sale or exchange of the obligation.[688] Before amendments, debts issued by individuals were not covered. As a result of the changes to §1271(a), the creditor gets capital -- not ordinary -- gain or loss arises when an individual debtor pays off his debt, provided the obligation is a capital asset in the hands of the holder of the debt. Mr. Hudson would have done much better today.

Learned commentators have shown that the use of the narrow term "sale or exchange" in §1222 instead of the more sweeping term "sale or other disposition" used in §1001(c) was the work of hasty drafting.[689] Congress eventually stepped in and put an end to the problem; the Taxpayer Relief Act of 1997 added §1234A to the Code, under which gain or loss attributable to the cancellation, lapse, expiration, or other termination of any right or obligation with respect to property that is a capital asset in the hands of the holder is a capital gain or loss. Examples given in the Conference Report include a landlord's payment to induce a tenant to give up her lease and leave and a buyer's forfeiture of a down payment under a contract to buy stock. The seller, like the tenant, gets a capital gain result as long as the property is a capital asset in his or her hands. Presumably, §1234A includes the case where an owner abandons property, but the language could be clearer. One has to wonder why Congress did not simply amend §1222 to substitute "sale or other disposition" where "sale or exchange" appears. Be that as it may, §1234A seems to have put an end to the "sale or exchange" versus "sale or other disposition" controversy. In short, now even an "other disposition" can create a capital gain or loss.

Problem 8-8:

Several taxpayers received payments from the sales of the following items under the following circumstances. Which dispositions were of capital assets?

1) Stock bought by an investor to be held in his portfolio.

2) Nails sold off the shelf by hardware store owner.

3) An account receivable, sold by an orthodontist who generated the receivable. Assume the face amount of the receivable is $10,000 and it is sold for $7,500. Also assume that the orthodontist is on the cash method, meaning he does not report income until he is paid, and the notes are not income when he receives them.

688 §1271(b), as amended.

689 See B. Bittker & L. Lokken, FEDERAL TAXATION OF INCOME, ESTATES AND GIFTS ¶ 48.1.1 (2019).

4) Government memoranda held by a United States President, including some that he prepared, sold to a collector.

5) A manuscript of a book, sold by the author's donee.

6) The name and likeness of Scrooge McDuck, sold by Disney to a German conglomerate.

7) Goodwill (basically meaning the premium a buyer of a company is willing to pay because of the good name and reputation of the business).

8) A parking lot owned and used by a movie theater for its customers. The theater has owned the lot for over a year. See §§ 1221(2) and 1231(b)(1).

9) Same as "8," but the theater has not owned the lot for over a year.

10) A 19th Century work of art, received by a dentist as payment for a root canal operation.

11) After hearing repeated disgusting stories about the cockroaches in his ice machine, Taco Bell headquarters terminated Fred's Taco Bell franchise and paid him $100,000. See §1241.

12) How would you tax these transactions? Assume Landlord is in a booming part of town and has a building that is subject to long-term leases:

   a. He sells the leases for $1 million, being their discounted present value.

   b. He sells the building at a profit of $600,000, reflecting the increased value of the rental stream arising from the local boom.

   c. His major commercial tenant assigns its lease, which it has held for many years, to a replacement tenant, receiving $50,000 on the spot from the new tenant for doing so. His old tenant is freed of its obligations and the new one steps into its shoes and pays Landlord the rent directly.

   d. Tenant pays Landlord $5,000 to break the lease and leave the property.

13) Law Professor sells his copyright to a casebook on Federal Income Taxation to Sam Student for $1,000.

14) Sam Student later sells the copyright to Huge Publishers, Inc. at a small gain. What result to Sam?

15) Inventor Gyro Klopman licenses all his rights to his patent for his invention (the Klopman Sipiromometer) to General Electric, Inc. for worldwide use for the term of the patent.[690]

   a. Is this a capital gain? See §1235.

   b. What if the patent license only covered the U.S. west of the Mississippi?

16) Senator Ernie Harbaugh gave his entire collection of *The Congressional Record* that he got for free over 40 years, to the library of Old Ivy, the college from which he barely graduated. The memoranda have a $0 basis and are worth $650,000. Is he stuck with a $0 tax deduction? See §170(e).

17) Investor paid $800 for a $1,000 face amount bond issued (without OID) by Defeated Railway, Inc. ("DRI"). The bond was issued in 1952. (Recall that a discount on market discount bonds issued on or before July 18, 1984 is not subject to tax reform rules that convert the discount into ordinary income.) DRI repurchased the bond for $1,000 this year and retired it for good.

   a. How is Investor treated? See §1271(a)(1).

   b. What if the bond were instead a promissory note issued last year by Mr. Borton Mank? See §1271(b).

---

690 Reg. 1.1235-2(b) contains the primary definition of "all substantial right to a patent, namely:

"(1) The term All substantial rights to a patent means all rights (whether or not then held by the grantor) which are of value at the time the rights to the patent (or an undivided interest therein) are transferred. The term all substantial rights to a patent does not include a grant of rights to a patent:

(i) Which is limited geographically within the country; (ii) Which is limited in duration by the terms of the agreement to a period less than the remaining life of the patent; (iii) Which grants rights to the grantee, in fields of use within trades or industries, which are less than all the rights covered by the patent, which exist and have value at the time of the grant; or (iv) Which grants to the grantee less than all the claims or inventions covered by the patent which exist and have value at the time of the grant."

18) Buzz recently got a job with InterCookie.Com in Duluth. The company moved him to Tulsa a month ago. He paid $10,000 as a deposit on a new home in Tulsa to Mrs. Gasgoigne, who has owned the home for many years. Suddenly, Buzz was informed he was going to have to move to San Diego. He abandoned the deposit. How is Mrs. Gasgoigne taxed? See §1234A.

E. HOLDING PERIODS AND RATES

Read §1223

F. THE SECTION 1231 ASSET EXCEPTION

Read §1231(a)(1)-(4) and (b)

1. Introduction

Section 1231 is perhaps the most conspicuously pro-taxpayer provision in the Code. It provides that property used in a business is eliminated from the capital asset category under § 1221(a)(2) and is picked up by § 1231 if it was held for over a year. The practical effect of §1231 is that, if in any particular year the aggregate transactions in section 1231 assets yield a net gain, then *each* such transaction is treated as one involving a long-term capital asset (which guarantees a net capital gain from this grouping). If, on the other hand, the net result of all the transactions in section 1231 assets for the year is a loss, then each transaction is considered to involve a non-capital asset, and therefore produce an overall ordinary loss. It can hardly get better than that from the taxpayer's point of view.

The assets eligible for this treatment include depreciable property (such as machinery and equipment) or land, but in all cases the property must have been used in or "in connection with" the trade or business, and must neither be includable in inventory nor be held primarily for sale to customers in the ordinary course of business. The property must have been held for over a year, otherwise it will simply produce ordinary gain or loss when sold.[691] Also included in §1231 are certain special assets including interests in timber, coal, domestic iron ore, certain livestock and certain unharvested crops.

We will get into the details later, but the immediate question is why there is such an astonishingly pro-taxpayer rule? The answer is that §1231 was enacted during World War II to address some problems unique to war-time, especially that, in the early days of that war, many shipping

691 See §1231(b)(1).

companies whose vessels had risen sharply in value realized involuntary profits when a ship insured under a war risk policy was destroyed by Nazi submarines or was requisitioned for military use. The same problem arose with involuntary profits on the condemnation of factories and equipment by the U.S. for the war program. Less fortunate taxpayers suffered sudden involuntary losses due to wartime reallocations and price changes, or the loss of uninsured property destroyed in war, or losses due to sales forced by being drafted into military service.

There was already in place a predecessor of current §1033, which allows proceeds of involuntary conversions to be ploughed back into similar property, thereby avoiding a current tax, but it was not good enough because of a shortage of replacement property during WWII. Section 1231 was enacted to overcome that problem. Needless to say, although §1231 has outlived the circumstances that produced it, it has not been repealed, although its edges have been nibbled slightly since the end of World War II.

The following sorry tale of §1231 shows how its mandatory character can operate as a trap for the unwary.

WASNOK v. COMMISSIONER

30 T.C.M. 39 (1971)

SACKS, Judge.

Memorandum Findings of Fact and Opinion

SACKS, Commissioner: Respondent determined deficiencies in the income tax of petitioners for the taxable years and in the amounts set forth below:

Petitioner	Year	Amount
Stephen P. Wasnok	1967	$ 195.70
Mary Alice Wasnok	1967	158.66
Stephen P. and Mary Alice Wasnok	1968	54.46

The sole issue for decision is whether petitioners' disposition of certain real property at a loss constitutes an ordinary loss fully deductible in 1965, the year in which the loss was sustained, or a capital loss, deductible as a loss carryover in 1967 and 1968.

Findings of Fact

Most of the facts have been stipulated by the parties. Their stipulation, together with attached exhibits, is incorporated herein by this reference.

Stephen P. and Mary Alice Wasnok, sometimes hereinafter referred to as petitioners or as Stephen and Mary, are husband and wife who resided in Fullerton, California at the time of the filing of their petition herein. Their separate income tax returns for the taxable year 1967 and their joint income tax return for the taxable year 1968 were filed with the district director of internal revenue, Los Angeles, California.

In 1960 petitioners were residing in Cincinnati, Ohio. Sometime during that year they purchased a home there located at 5654 Sagecrest Drive, hereinafter referred to as the Sagecrest property. a substantial portion of the purchase price of this property was borrowed on a promissory note secured by a first mortgage on the property from Spring Grove Avenue Loan and Deposit Company (hereinafter referred to as Spring Grove Loan Co.).

Early in 1961 petitioners decided to move to California. They listed the Sagecrest property with its builder for sale, but without result since the market at the time was extremely poor. Finally, on June 15, 1961 petitioners leased the property for a monthly rental of $225.00 and thereafter departed for California.

Between June 15, 1961 and May 7, 1965 petitioners leased the Sagecrest property to various tenants at an average rental of $200.00 per month. Such tenants were located by advertising the property for rent in Cincinnati newspapers and by referrals from former neighbors. During this period petitioners on two occasions listed the property for sale with brokers, in each case, however, for only a ninety day period of time. Neither listing generated an offer for more than the amount due on the mortgage.

By 1965 petitioners found themselves unable to continue payments due on their note on the Sagecrest property to Spring Grove Loan Co. Spring Grove thereafter notified petitioners that they would either have to deed the property back or the company would have to institute foreclosure proceedings. On May 7, 1965 petitioners executed a deed conveying their interest in the Sagecrest property to Spring Grove Loan Co. in satisfaction of the then balance due on their note in the amount of $24,421.04.

For the taxable years 1961 through 1964 petitioners filed federal income tax returns reporting thereon rental income and claiming various expenses, including depreciation, on the Sagecrest property. Their return for 1961 was examined by the Internal Revenue Service and the cost basis of the land and improvements was agreed upon in the amount of $32,729.70. Total depreciation on the improvements claimed and allowed for the taxable years 1961 through 1964 was $4,697.42.

Petitioners did not file federal income tax returns for the taxable years 1965 and 1966 on the premise that no returns were required because no tax appeared to be due.

For 1965, however, petitioners had gross income in the amount of $5,603.21 and for 1966, in the amount of $3,180.00.

On their separate returns for the taxable year 1967, petitioners for the first time each claimed a capital loss carryforward deduction in the amount of $1,000.00 which was predicated upon their disposition in 1965 of the Sagecrest property to Spring Grove Loan Co. Thereafter, on their joint return for 1968, petitioners claimed a further capital loss carryforward deduction of $389.00, computed as follows:

Cost of Sagecrest property	$32,729.70
Less: depreciation taken	4,697.42
Adjusted basis	$28,032.28
Sale on May 7, 1965	24,421.04
Capital Loss	$ 3,611.24
Claimed in 1967 (separate return)	2,000.00
Sub-total	$ 1,611.24
Claimed in 1968	$ 389.00
Balance to carryover	$ 1,222.24

In his notices of deficiency, respondent disallowed to petitioners the claimed capital loss carryover deductions for the taxable years 1967 and 1968 on the ground that the loss involved was an ordinary loss deductible in the year sustained (1965) rather than a capital loss subject to the carryover provisions of the Internal Revenue Code of 1954.

Petitioners' disposition of the Sagecrest property at a loss constitutes an ordinary loss fully deductible in 1965, the year in which the loss was sustained and not a capital loss.

Opinion

It is petitioners' position herein that the Sagecrest property was a capital asset in their hands, and that its disposition at a loss resulted in a capital loss which they properly deferred deducting on their returns until 1967 and 1968 when they had sufficient income to file returns.

Respondent contends that the property in question was not a capital asset in petitioners' hands, but an asset of the type described in section 1231 of the Code losses upon the disposition of which are ordinary in nature and required to be deducted, to the extent that there is gross income, in the year in which sustained. Since petitioners' gross income in 1965 was more than sufficient to absorb the loss in that year, no deduction of any kind is allowable in the years here at issue.

Section 1221 of the Code defines the term "capital asset" as any property held by the taxpayer, excluding however, "property used in his trade or business, of a character which is subject to the allowance for depreciation . . . or real property used in his trade or business." With respect to "property used in the trade or business" of a taxpayer, section 1231 provides that while net gains on sales or exchanges of such property shall be treated as capital gains, net losses are not to be treated as capital losses, but as ordinary losses.

The evidence presented to the Court is not complex. Simply stated, it shows that when petitioners moved from Ohio to California in 1961 they could not sell their residence in Ohio and therefore rented it to various tenants until May, 1965, when it was deeded back to the mortgagee because petitioners could no longer make the mortgage payments and did not desire the mortgagee to foreclose. It further shows that during the period 1961 through 1964 petitioners received rents of about two hundred dollars per month except for brief periods when the property was vacant. Their return for 1961 was examined by respondent and the tax basis for the property agreed upon. Depreciation was claimed on the improvements during the period 1961 to 1964 and, after reducing basis by the amount of depreciation claimed, the difference between the adjusted basis and mortgage balance produced a loss of $3,611.24.

In our view petitioners' activity in renting out the Sagecrest property for a fairly continuous period of four years between 1961 and 1965, at a substantial rental, together with the concurrent claiming on their income tax returns for these years of the expenses incurred in such rental activity, including depreciation, establishes the use of such property in a "trade or business." Leland Hazard, 7 T.C. 372 (1946).

We therefore find that the property in question was not a capital asset in petitioners' hands at the time of its disposition, but an asset of the kind described in section 1231. The loss sustained on the disposition of such an asset is an ordinary loss. Since such loss was sustained in 1965, when petitioners had gross income sufficient to entirely absorb it, no loss is allowable to petitioners in either 1967 or 1968.

Reviewed and adopted as the report of the Small Tax Case Division.

Decision will be entered for respondent.

Small Tax Court Cases

How can people of modest means, like the Wasnoks, litigate a Tax Court case? The answer is, anyone can litigate a case involving not over $50,000 in the Tax Court in a simplified proceeding,[692] and one can always litigate *pro se*. The drawback (or advantage) is that small tax cases cannot be reviewed or used as precedent.

692 §7463.

2. Computations under §1231

Section 1231 does not apply to all business-related property. For one thing, it does not apply if the property was not held for at least a year; in those instances the property sale will simply produce ordinary gains and losses.

The calculations call for identifying all the transactions in §1231 assets for the year, lumping them together into the §1231 computation (sometimes referred to as the "hotchpot") and examining it to see if there is a net gain or a net loss.

If there is a net gain, then all the gains and losses are treated as capital gains and losses; if there is a net loss, they are all treated as ordinary assets.[693] It gets even better because of the so-called "firepot" of §1231(a)(4), which calls for a separate preliminary netting for certain involuntary conversions of business properties and capital assets.[694] The notion is that if the combined results produced a net gain, then those transactions are added to the other §1231 transactions. If there is a net loss, they are removed from §1231, which has the effect of protecting the losses from being swamped by §1231 gains.

A common gimmick in the past was to hold off on realizing any gains on §1231 property in some years, so that all the realized transactions produced only losses, deductible against ordinary income without the $3,000 limit. Then, in later years, the taxpayer would sell off the gain properties and report only a gain, taxable at long-term capital gains rates. That pattern optimized the power of §1231. To take the fun out of the practice, §1231(c) now converts later gains into ordinary gains to the extent of ordinary §1231 losses in the past five years.

Problem 8-9:

Portia Klopman is a self-employed lawyer in Billboard City. She has had an unusual year and now has to decide how to handle the following items, all of which were held over a year. How should she treat these items on her tax return?

1) Theft of her personal car which had a value and basis of $1,000. She was reimbursed with $1,100 of casualty insurance.

2) The State condemned her office building which had a basis of $100,000, and paid her $97,000. She held it as an investment.

693 §1231(a)(1), (2), (3).

694 These consist of the usual casualties with respect to either (1) trade or business property or (2) capital assets held in connection with a trade or business use or acquired in a transaction entered into for a profit.

3) She sold her actively-managed apartment units, having a value of $60,000 and a basis of $50,000.

4) She sold stock of a publicly traded corporation that she owned for 15 months and which had a basis of $20,000 and a value of $22,000.

5) What would be the tax effect, if any, on the prior losses if on top of her other troubles her uninsured factory burned down, assuming the factory had a basis and value of $100,000?

6) Assume she is in the 37% bracket, that she bought the building in 2007 and sold it in 2019. What will be the top rate on the sale, assuming it was the only asset she sells in 2019?

7) She decided to hire a timber cutting company to cut and sell her standing timber at a price of 45 cents per board foot. She has held the timber land for years. There will be a nice profit in it for her.

8) Same as "(7)", but the subject of the deal is some coal underlying land in Eastern Kentucky that she bought in 2007.

G. CORRELATION WITH PRIOR TRANSACTIONS

The general rule is that each taxable year stands on its own feet, but there is some slippage in this generalization for instances where a transaction today is clearly linked to a transaction in the past. A leading example is *Merchants National Bank v. Commissioner*,[695] in which a bank first wrote off loans it made as fully-deductible business bad debts, and later -- after the loans developed some value -- sold the loans and claimed a capital gain. The Court in effect swept aside the taxpayer's treatment as too opportunistic, saying that Congress never intended such lavishly pro-taxpayer results and confirmed that the sale of the loans generated ordinary gains, not capital gains. The converse question is, can an earlier capital gain or loss transaction make a later, connected transaction also capital? The following, case answers that question, in principle.

695 199 F.2d 657 (5th Cir. 1952)

ARROWSMITH v. COMMISSIONER

344 U.S. 6 (S. Ct. 1952)

MR. JUSTICE BLACK delivered the opinion of the Court.

This is an income tax controversy growing out of the following facts as shown by findings of the Tax Court. In 1937 two taxpayers, petitioners here, decided to liquidate and divide the proceeds of a corporation in which they had equal stock ownership. Partial distributions made in 1937, 1938, and 1939 were followed by a final one in 1940. Petitioners reported the profits obtained from this transaction, classifying them as capital gains. They thereby paid less income tax than would have been required had the income been attributed to ordinary business transactions for profit. About the propriety of these 19371940 returns, there is no dispute. But in 1944 a judgment was rendered against the old corporation and against Frederick R. Bauer, individually. The two taxpayers were required to and did pay the judgment for the corporation, of whose assets they were transferees. . . . Classifying the loss as an ordinary business one, each took a tax deduction for 100% of the amount paid. Treatment of the loss as a capital one would have allowed deduction of a much smaller amount. . . . The Commissioner viewed the 1944 payment as part of the original liquidation transaction requiring classification as a capital loss, just as the taxpayers had treated the original dividends as capital gains. Disagreeing with the Commissioner the Tax Court classified the 1944 payment as an ordinary business loss. 15 T. C. 876. Disagreeing with the Tax Court the Court of Appeals reversed, treating the loss as "capital." 193 F.2d 4. This latter holding conflicts with the Third Circuit's holding in *Commissioner v. Switlik*, 184 F.2d 299. Because of this conflict, we granted certiorari. 343 U.S. 976.

I. R. C., § 23 (g) treats losses from sales or exchanges of capital assets as "capital losses" and I. R. C., § 115(c) requires that liquidation distributions be treated as exchanges. The losses here fall squarely within the definition of "capital losses" contained in these sections. Taxpayers were required to pay the judgment because of liability imposed on them as transferees of liquidation distribution assets. And it is plain that their liability as transferees was not based on any ordinary business transaction of theirs apart from the liquidation proceedings. It is not even denied that had this judgment been paid after liquidation, but during the year 1940, the losses would have been properly treated as capital ones. For payment during 1940 would simply have reduced the amount of capital gains taxpayers received during that year.

It is contended, however, that this payment which would have been a capital transaction in 1940 was transformed into an ordinary business transaction in 1944 because of the wellestablished principle that each taxable year is a separate unit for tax accounting purposes. *United States v. Lewis*, 340 U.S. 590; *North American Oil v. Burnet*, 286 U.S. 417. But this principle is not breached by considering all the 19371944 liquidation transaction events in order properly to classify the nature of the 1944 loss for tax purposes. Such an examination is not an attempt to reopen and readjust the 1937 to 1940 tax returns, an action that would be inconsistent with the annual tax accounting principle.

. . .

Affirmed

MR. JUSTICE DOUGLAS, dissenting.

I agree with MR. JUSTICE JACKSON that these losses should be treated as ordinary, not capital, losses. There were no capital transactions in the year in which the losses were suffered. Those transactions occurred and were accounted for in earlier years in accord with the established principle that each year is a separate unit for tax accounting purposes. See *United States v. Lewis*, 340 U.S. 590. I have not felt, as my dissent in the Lewis case indicates, that the law made that an inexorable principle. But if it is the law, we should require observance of it not merely by taxpayers but by the Government as well. We should force each year to stand on its own footing, whoever may gain or lose from it in a particular case. We impeach that principle when we treat this year's losses as if they diminished last year's gains.

MR. JUSTICE JACKSON, whom MR. JUSTICE FRANKFURTER joins, dissenting.

This problem arises only because the judgment was rendered in a taxable year subsequent to the liquidation.

Had the liability of the transferorcorporation been reduced to judgment during the taxable year in which liquidation occurred, or prior thereto, this problem, under the tax laws, would not arise. The amount of the judgment rendered against the corporation would have decreased the amount it had available for distribution, which would have reduced the liquidating dividends proportionately and diminished the capital gains taxes assessed against the stockholders. Probably it would also have decreased the corporation's own taxable income.

Congress might have allowed, under such circumstances, tax returns of the prior year to be reopened or readjusted so as to give the same tax results as would have obtained had the liability become known prior to liquidation. Such a solution is foreclosed to us and the alternatives left are to regard the judgment liability fastened by operation of law on the transferee as an ordinary loss for the year of adjudication or to regard it as a capital loss for such year.

This Court simplifies the choice to one of reading the English language, and declares that the losses here come "squarely within" the definition of capital losses contained within two sections of the Internal Revenue Code. What seems so clear to this Court was not seen at all by the Tax Court, in this case or in earlier consideration of the same issue; nor was it grasped by the Court of Appeals for the Third Circuit. *Commissioner v. Switlik*, 184 F.2d 299 (1950).

I find little aid in the choice of alternatives from arguments based on equities. One enables the taxpayer to deduct the amount of the judgment against his ordinary income which might be taxed as high as 87%, while if the liability had been assessed against the corporation prior to liquidation it would have reduced his capital gain which was taxable at only 25% (now 26%). The consequence may readily be characterized as a windfall (regarding a windfall as anything that is left to a taxpayer after the collector has finished with him).

On the other hand, adoption of the contrary alternative may penalize the taxpayer because of two factors: (1) since capital losses are deductible only against capital gains, plus $ 1,000, a taxpayer having no net capital gains in the ensuing five years would have no opportunity to deduct anything beyond $ 5,000; and (2) had the liability been discharged by the corporation, a portion of it would probably in effect have been paid by the Government, since the corporation could have taken it as a deduction, while here the total liability comes out of the pockets of the stockholders.

Solicitude for the revenues is a plausible but treacherous basis upon which to decide a particular tax case. A victory may have implications which in future cases will cost the Treasury more than a defeat. This might be such a case, for anything I know. Suppose that subsequent to liquidation it is found that a corporation has undisclosed claims instead of liabilities and that under applicable state law they may be prosecuted for the benefit of the stockholders. The logic of the Court's decision here, if adhered to, would result in a lesser return to the Government than if the recoveries were considered ordinary income. Would it be so clear that this is a capital loss if the shoe were on the other foot?

Where the statute is so indecisive and the importance of a particular holding lies in its rational and harmonious relation to the general scheme of the tax law, I think great deference is due the twiceexpressed judgment of the Tax Court. . . . I still think the Tax Court is a more competent and steady influence toward a systematic body of tax law than our sporadic omnipotence in a field beset with invisible boomerangs. . . .

Notes

So how does one tell whether a prior year's transaction is sufficiently linked to a later year's transaction to cause the tax character of the earlier transaction to supply the tax character of the later transaction? Here are a few cases that suggest where the line might be drawn:

a) In *Clay v. Commissioner*,[696] the court held that a seller's payment of liabilities under an indemnification agreement on the sale of a business produced capital losses, tied back to the sale of the business.

696 42 T.C.M. 456.

b) In *Commissioner v. Adam,* and *Meldrum & Anderson Co.,*[697] a shareholder deducted capital loss on the worthlessness of his bank stock. Additional payments which he was later required to make under his statutory liability were held capital losses, because they tied to the prior transaction.

c) In *Slater v. Commissioner,*[698] the taxpayer transferred to his former employer rights in stock that he had bought from the employer at a bargain price. The taxpayer had been taxed on the bargain element as ordinary income. Nevertheless, the loss on the later sale was a capital loss because it was unrelated to the circumstances under which he acquired the stock. The two events could not be integrated because the stock was received as an employee, but it was thereafter held as an investment.

Problem 8-10:

1) Executive made a small killing when he bought and, four months later, sold some stock in the corporation that employs him. Next year, a shareholder pointed out that he violated the federal insider trading rules and, preferring not to fight the issue, he correctly repaid the profits to the company. How should he treat the repayment?[699]

2) The Friendly Bank lent a business customer $100,000 last year. The customer defaulted on the loan and the bank deducted a $100,000 bad debt loss. Next year, the debtor started a dot.com company, took it public and paid off the loan. How should the Friendly Bank treat the repayment of the loan?

H. SALE OF DEPRECIABLE PROPERTY BETWEEN RELATED TAXPAYERS

Read §1239(a)

This one is easy. Section 1239 blocks off the following kind of transaction:

> **To illustrate**: Clara owns an apartment building with a basis of $100,000 and a value of $1 million. She does not own the land, so the whole building is depreciable. She sells the building to her wholly-owned corporation for $1 million. The corporation claims a $1 million basis in the property and claims depreciation deductions.

---

697 215 F.2d 163 (2d Cir. 1954), cert. denied, 348 U.S. 913 (1955).

698 64 T.C. 571 (1975).

699 See Cumming v. Commissioner, 506 F.2d 449 (2d Cir. 1974) for an analogous situation.

Section 1239 does not touch the corporation, but it does turn Clara's $900,000 gain into ordinary income. This punishment applies if the transferee is related to the transferor and then only as to depreciable property, both of which tests are met in this example. Relatives for this purpose include controlled corporations and partnerships, but not, for example, children.[700]

I. DEPRECIATION RECAPTURE

Read §1245(a)-(b)(3) and §1250(a)(1)(a), (b)(1), (c), and (d)(1)-(3)

1. Section 1245 Recapture

a. Introduction

Section 1245 treats gain based on depreciation previously claimed as ordinary income, on the theory that the income should have the same character as the deduction.

> **To illustrate:** You bought a truck to use in your trade or business six years ago for $50,000. You claimed $50,000 of depreciation deductions, which offset your ordinary income. When the truck has a basis of $0, you sell it for $10,000 and correctly report a $10,000 gain. Prima facie it appears to be a §1231 gain, but §1245 converts it into ordinary income. Section 1245 keeps you from claiming depreciation deductions that save you 37 cents on the dollar while only reporting 23.8 cents of tax on the dollar when the truck is sold.
>
> Note well: *all §1245 does is recharacterize gain based on prior depreciation as ordinary income.* It cannot affect a loss and it cannot affect a gain that is not based on prior depreciation, nor does it affect the amount of the gain.

Now let's put the issue into a more complex setting. Imagine that you are able to walk through an invisible door into the past, which took you to 1960 where you entered a room containing a cigar-smoking tax shelter promoter and some investors who are desperate to reduce their income taxes. The tax shelter promoter is attempting to earn a commission by promoting the sale of a deal, the essence of which is that investors will buy depreciable property for $1 million, all of which is borrowed from a bank as a loan. The subject of the deal is a passenger aircraft, which will be chartered out to a major airline. The airline's rental payments will be big enough to cover the interest due the lender. (The airline will care for and insure the aircraft.) Thereafter,

700 The rules of affinity are not exactly the same as under §267, relating, inter alia, to losses on transactions with related parties. The Code is often inconsistent in its affinity rules.

using prevailing tax depreciation practices, the investors will claim the fastest available depreciation method on the aircraft.

One investor in the audience, Irv, becomes excited and announces that he will buy the aircraft tax shelter deal all by himself. Now let us look at what will happen to Irv from a tax perspective simplifying it a bit by using the current depreciation rates so that the aircraft is written down to zero in five years. Assume that his income tax rate at the time was 70%. That means Irv saves $700,000 in income taxes via the depreciation deductions.

When the aircraft is sold it will still be worth a fair amount of money. Let us imagine that everyone correctly assumes it will be worth $700,000 dollars when the lease ends and Irv sells the aircraft. As a consequence, the whole $700,000 dollar gain (i.e., amount realized of $700,000 minus adjusted basis of $0) on the sale of the airplane will be taxed, but back in those days it was taxed at long-term capital gains rates, say not over 20%. This means that Irv will have to pay $140,000 in taxes on the sale of the plane for $700,000.

Finally, the bank will want its $1,000,000 back. Irv will have to repay the bank.

Here is the cash impact on Irv in the year of sale of the plane:

Cash proceeds from sale of plane:	$ 700,000
Federal Income Tax on gain on sale of plane (20% of $700,000):	(140,000)
Amount due bank:	(1,000,000)
Net cash inflow/outflow in year of sale:	(440,000)

This $440,000 outflow in the last year is *less* than the taxes saved in the years before the plane was sold (namely $700,000). The net cash gain over the life of the deal is $260,000 on Irv's investment in the deal, i.e. $700,000 minus $440,000. This may seem too much like taking candy from a baby, and the example is exaggerated, but it illustrates the essence of the early tax shelter deals, with their lavish opportunities to convert ordinary deductions based on depreciation into later long-term capital gains.

Congress enacted §1245 in 1962 to retaliate against the practice. What §1245 does is to assure that the illustrative $700,000 dollar gain will be fully taxed as ordinary income, not capital gain. As a result, today's tax shelter investor will have no net tax benefit from the *conversion* effects of the transaction. He may still benefit from the opportunity to *defer* the income tax. The deferral benefit itself may be magnified by his ability to *leverage* the entire transaction, but deferral and leverage are separate considerations.

Again, the only gains that are converted into ordinary income ("recaptured as ordinary income" in tax lingo) under current §1245 are gains based on depreciation; so if Irv's zero basis aircraft were instead sold for $1,200,000 (which would be a fully taxable gain) then only $1,000,000 of that gain would be "recaptured" as ordinary income. The remaining $200,000 would be §1231 gain. You can also see that, in general, any non-sale/non-exchange disposition of property results in recapture because of the insertion of "fair-market-value" in lieu of "amount realized" in §1245(a).

REV. RUL. 69-487

1969-2 C.B. 165

. . .

An individual taxpayer operating a business as a sole proprietorship converted to personal use an automobile that had been used solely for business purposes. At that time, the fair market value of the automobile was substantially higher than its adjusted basis.

Held, for the purposes of section 1245 of the Internal Revenue Code of 1954, the conversion to personal use is not a "disposition" of the automobile. Accordingly, there is no gain to be recognized by the taxpayer upon the conversion to personal use. However, the provisions of section 1245 of the Code would apply to any disposition of the automobile by the taxpayer at a later date.

b. Recapture of Unclaimed Depreciation?

Chapter 5 discussed the "allowed or allowable" rule, under which allowable depreciation reduces basis even if the taxpayer did not bother to claim the deduction on her tax return.[701] This can work a hardship in connection with sales of property, because not only can there be a gain based on depreciation the taxpayer actually deducted, but there might even be depreciation recapture to the extent the depreciation not claimed might have been ordinary income on the sale of the property, because of §1245 or §1250. Both §1245 and §1250 prevent this potentially confiscatory result by imposing depreciation recapture only on depreciation that was actually *allowed*, provided the taxpayer can prove he took less than the amount allowable.[702] There is still taxable gain on such amounts, but it is not recaptured as ordinary income.

Problem 8-11:

Industrious buys a new button smashing machine for her laundromat. The machine costs $5,000 and will be written off electively on the alternative depreciation system with the result that Industrious claims only straight-line depreciation. When the machine has a basis of $3,000, Industrious sells it for the following amounts. Describe how each sale will be treated with respect to whether it results in ordinary income or some other form of gain and its amount. In connection with answering these problems state in each case the "recomputed basis" of the machine under §1245 and whether §1221 or §1231 applies.

701 See §1016(a)(2).

702 §§ 1245(a)(2)(B) and 1250(b)(3).

1) Industrious sells it for $2,000.

2) Industrious sells it for $5,000.

3) Industrious sells it for $6,000.

4) How much capital gain, if any, is there in "(3)," assuming this is Industrious's only property transaction for the year?

Problem 8-12:

Portia Klopman, the Billboard City lawyer, bought a Oriental rug and a tapestry for her office some years back. They cost her $500 each. After taking the appropriate depreciation deductions such that they now have a $0 basis, she decided to take them home.

1) What is the income tax result to Portia, if any, of taking home the rug and tapestry?

2) What is the result if she sells them for $500 each?

3) Describe the implications with respect to her basis in the property if she dies some years later and still owns the rug and tapestry.

2. Section 1250 Recapture

Section 1245 basically refers to tangible and intangible personal property of a depreciable nature along with certain specialized properties which may be real estate locally, but are classified as personal property by the Code, such as industrial research facilities. By contrast, its analog, §1250 -- which also turns capital gains into ordinary income -- applies to real estate, but which is or has been property of a character subject to depreciation but is not local law real estate that the Code classifies as §1245 (personal) property.[703] Naturally, this only covers improvements to property and improvements to real estate. Land is not depreciable.

a. Pre-1997 Act Law

Until 1997, when the law changed, §1250 only applied to so-called *additional depreciation*, meaning depreciation *in excess of* what would have claimed if straight-line depreciation had been used. Because §168 now forces real estate into straight-line depreciation, §1250 became a

703 §1250(c).

paper tiger as to new property and became applicable only to older property (meaning property placed in service in or before 1986) or to property disposed of within a year and a day. Section 1250 became less and less important even as to those older properties because the amount that was recaptured was only the excess of accelerated over straight-line depreciation. The reason is that as property ages, the accelerated depreciation component becomes ever smaller and eventually the two depreciation amounts converge.

b. Post-1997 Act Law

Section 1250 still causes only the excess over straight-line, to be taxed at as ordinary income. The important change is that the *remaining* gain that is attributable to depreciation (up to original basis) is taxed at not over 25%, as opposed to the 20% top rate that applies to most capital assets. §1(h)(1)(E). This is the work of §1(h), not §1250. Here is an example of the new law in action applied to an older property. It is difficult, but worth the trouble.

To illustrate: Dr. Peabody acquired an apartment building in 1984 for $500,000 and sells it in late 2009 for $800,000. The property was depreciated on an accelerated method, but by now the total depreciation Dr. Peabody claimed ($410,000) is only $5,000 more than he would have obtained if he had used the straight-line method from the outset. The property's adjusted basis has declined to a mere $90,000 (so the gain is $710,000). The tax on this sale (ignoring other factors such as §1231, and assuming he is in the 35% tax bracket) is $148,000 computed as follows:

Gain	Tax Rate	Tax
Sales proceeds	$800,000	
Adjusted basis	(90,000)	
Total gain	710,000	
Less: Ordinary depreciation recapture*	(5,000) x 35%	= $1,750
Additional gain due to depreciation**	(405,000) x 25%	= 101,250
Remaining gain***	300,000 x 15%	= 45,000
Total tax		$148,000

* Excess of accelerated over straight-line depreciation. §1250. This can only apply to older properties.

** Total depreciation, $410,000, less $5,000.[704] §§ 168 and 1(h).

*** $800,000 sale price minus original $500,000 purchase price. §1(h). In 2019, this rate is 20% not the 15% shown in the illustration.

704 See Jackel, *The Taxpayer Relief Act of 1997*, reported in 98 Tax Notes 21-66 (1997).

Problem 8-13:

Quite a number of years ago (before the Code dictated only straight-line depreciation for real estate), Merchant had a warehouse built on her land for $30,000. Merchant is in the 35% Federal Income Tax Bracket. She held it for many years and took a total of $10,000 of depreciation on the warehouse over that period, using an accelerated method of depreciation. Her basis is now $20,000, but would have been $25,000 had she used the straight-line method.

1) What result under §1250 if Merchant sells the warehouse (her only sale for the year) for the following amounts:

   a. $27,000

   b. $32,000

   c. $22,000

   d. $18,000

2) What would the result be if the property were personal property, rather than real property? Can you justify the difference? Which system is better from a tax policy standpoint?

c. Practical Impact of the 1997 Act

The 1997 Congress did not intend to repeal §1250. Nevertheless, because real estate placed in service since 1986 has all been written off on the straight-line method, the population of real estate which can attract ordinary income tax under §1250 has disappeared. On the other hand, the 1997 Act's 25% rate of tax on the straight-line component is an important new calculation.

3. Relationship of §1231 to the Recapture Provisions

Depreciation recapture prevents capital gain or §1231 treatment on that part of an asset's basis that has been depreciated by taxing the depreciation as ordinary income when the owner sells the property. This conversion affects §1231 computations, because one must strip out the §§ 1245 or 1250 ordinary income component before one applies §1231 and then go back to the §1231 "hotchpot." Gain in excess of depreciation recapture remains eligible for §1231 treatment, and goes into the §1231 hotchpot. The practical effect is generally to produce some ordinary income (mainly under §1245) and to increase the likelihood of finding an excess of §1231 losses over §1231 gains. This approach has to be used as to each item of §1231 property separately. Thereafter, one combines the unrecaptured gain and losses on the §1231 properties.Reg. §1.1245-6(a); 1.1250-1(c)(1).

4. Combining Gains, Losses and Depreciation Recapture after the 1997 Act

What follows is an example that combines many of the rules described up to this point.

To illustrate: In 2009 Joe Gasgoigne, a 35% bracket taxpayer, sold his collector automobile, some jewels, some real estate and some stock, as follows:

Property	Basis	Price	Holding Period	Gain/Loss	Tax Rate if Gain
Metzo Combusto Automobile	$10,000	$13,000	36 months	$3,000	28%
Big Jewel	$10,000	$5,000	13 months	($5,000)	28%
Stock	$20,000	$23,000	100 months	$3,000	15% (20% in 2019)
Real Estate	$30,000	$35,000	48 months	$5,000	25%
Computer	$0	$2,000	48 months	$2,000	35%

Assume all the gain on the real estate is unrecaptured §1250 gain because the property was bought for $35,000 after 1986, written off to $30,000, and then sold for the original purchase price.

Step 1: The Code requires one first to combine the collectibles consisting of the car and jewel.[705]

Step 2: Then one uses the losses from the top category ($2,000 loss on sale of collectibles) to offset gains in the highest taxed category first (namely, $5,000 -- unrecaptured §1250 gains, taxable at 25%.[706]

Assume the computer was bought for $5,000 and was used in the business and completely written off and is therefore subject to 100% depreciation recapture under §1245. It will be a "stand alone" amount, taxable as ordinary income and is unaffected by the capital loss provisions. The upshot is:

705 §1(h)(4)-(6).

706 §1(h)(1).

Step 1	Collectibles gain or loss:	$ 0[707]
Step 2	Unrecaptured §1250 gain:	3000[708]
	Tax at 25%:	750
	Stock sale gain:	3000
	Tax at 15% (20% in 2019):	450
	Computer gain:	2000
	Tax at 35%:	700
	Total tax	**$ 1,900**

5. Limits on Recapture Provisions

There are various exceptions to §1245 and §1250 treatment. Even though §1245 and §1250 begin with the pugnacious declaration that they apply "notwithstanding any other provision of this subtitle," both §1245(b) and §1250 contain a variety of exceptions for dispositions that are otherwise nontaxable, such as gifts, inheritances, the formation of corporations, contribution of assets to partnerships and like-kind exchanges of business or investment property. That does not put an end to depreciation recapture. Instead the Code hands the hot potato of future depreciation recapture over to the donee in the case of a gift and by other appropriate means in the case of the other transactions.

J. SALE OF A SOLE PROPRIETORSHIP

The sale of an incorporated business can be easily achieved by selling its stock. The sale of a proprietorship, meaning an unincorporated business that has one individual owner, is more complicated because gain or loss has to be calculated for each asset. In contrast, when one sells an incorporated business, one simply sells the stock which is normally a capital asset in the seller's hands. By the way, if instead of selling their stock in an incorporated business, the directors might instead order the corporation to sell its assets. In that case, the corporation will have to report gains and losses asset-by-asset, just like a sole proprietor.

707 Jewel and car, which offset each other.

708 $5,000 gain on building, less $2,000 less from the jewelry that was not absorbed by the car offset each other.

WILLIAMS v. McGOWAN

152 F.2d 570 (2d Cir. 1945)

L. HAND, Judge.

This is an appeal from a judgment dismissing the complaint in an action by a taxpayer to recover income taxes paid for the year 1940. . . .

Williams, the taxpayer, and one, Reynolds, had for many years been engaged in the hardware business in the City of Corning, new York. On the 20th of January, 1926, they formed a partnership, of which Williams was entitled to twothirds of the profits, and Reynolds, onethird. They agreed that on February 1, 1925, the capital invested in the business had been $ 118,082.05, of which Reynolds had a credit of $ 29,029.03, and Williams, the balance $ 89,053.02. At the end of every business year, on February 1st, Reynolds was to pay to Williams, interest upon the amount of the difference between his share of the capital and onethird of the total as shown by the inventory; and upon withdrawal of one party the other was to have the privilege of buying the other's interest as it appeared on the books. The business was carried on through the firm's fiscal year, ending January 31, 1940, in accordance with this agreement, and thereafter until Reynolds' death on July 18th of that year. Williams settled with Reynolds' executrix on September 6th in an agreement by which he promised to pay her $ 12,187.90, and to assume all liabilities of the business; and he did pay her $ 2,187.98 in cash at once, and $ 10,000 on the 10th of the following October. On September 17th of the same year, Williams sold the business as a whole to the Corning Building Company for $ 63,926.28 its agreed value as of February 1, 1940 'plus an amount to be computed by multiplying the gross sales of the business from the first day of February, 1940 to the 28th day of September, 1940,' by an agreed fraction. This value was made up of cash of about $ 8100, receivables of about $ 7000, fixtures of about $ 800, and a merchandise inventory of about $ 49,000, less some $ 1000 for bills payable. To this was added about $ 6,000 credited to Williams for profits under the language just quoted, making a total of nearly $ 70,000. Upon this sale Williams suffered a loss upon his original twothirds of the business but he made a small gain upon the onethird which he had bought from Reynolds' executrix; and in his income tax return he entered both as items of 'ordinary income,' and not as transactions in 'capital assets.' This the Commissioner disallowed and recomputed the tax accordingly; Williams paid the deficiency and sued to recover it in this action. The only question is whether the business was 'capital assets' . . . .

It has been held that a partner's interest in a going firm is for tax purposes to be regarded as a 'capital asset.' . . . We too accepted the doctrine in McClellan v. Commissioner, 2 Cir., 117 F.2d 988, although we had held the opposite in Helvering v. Smith, 2 Cir., 90 F.2d 590, 591, where the partnership articles had provided that a retiring partner should receive as his share only his percentage of the sums 'actually collected' and 'of all earnings . . . for services performed.' Such a payment, we thought, was income; and we expressly repudiated the notion that the Uniform

Partnership Act had, generally speaking, changed the firm into a juristic entity. See also Doyle v. Commissioner, 4 Cir., 102 F.2d 86. If a partner's interest in a going firm is 'capital assets' perhaps a dead partner's interest is the same. New York Partnership Law Secs. 61, 62(4), Consol. Laws N.Y. c. 39. We need not say. When Williams bought out Reynolds' interest, he became the sole owner of the business, the firm had ended upon any theory, and the situation for tax purposes was no other than if Reynolds had never been a partner at all, except that to the extent of onethird of the 'amount realized' on Williams' sale to the Corning Company, his 'basis' was different. The judge thought that, because upon that sale both parties fixed the price at the liquidation value of the business while Reynolds was alive, 'plus' its estimated earnings thereafter, it was as though Williams had sold his interest in the firm during its existence. But the method by which the parties agreed upon the price was irrelevant to the computation of Williams' income. The Treasury, if that served its interest, need not heed any fiction which the parties found it convenient to adopt; nor need Williams do the same in his dealings with the Treasury. We have to decide only whether upon the sale of a going business it is to be comminuted into its fragments, and these are to be separately matched against the definitions [in §1221] or whether the whole business is to be treated as if it were a single piece of property.

Our law has been sparing in the creation of juristic entities; it has never, for example, taken over the Roman 'universitas facti';[709] and indeed for many years it fumbled uncertainly with the concept of a corporation.[710] One might have supposed that partnership would have been an especially promising field in which to raise up an entity, particularly since merchants have always kept their accounts upon that basis. Yet there too our law resisted at the price of great continuing confusion; and, even when it might be thought that a statute admitted, if it did not demand, recognition of the firm as an entity, the old concepts prevailed. Francis v. McNeal, 228 U.S. 695 .... And so, even though we might agree that under the influence of the Uniform Partnership Act a partner's interest in the firm should be treated as indivisible, and for that reason a 'capital asset' within Sec. 117(a)(1), we should be chary about extending further so exotic a jural concept. Be that as it may, in this instance the section itself furnishes the answer. It starts in the broadest way by declaring that all 'property' is 'capital assets,' and then makes three exceptions. The first is 'stock in trade ... or other property of a kind which would properly be included in the inventory'; next comes 'property held ... primarily for sale to customers'; and finally, property 'used in the trade or business of a character which is subject to ... allowance for depreciation.' In the face of this language, although it may be true that a 'stock in trade,' taken by itself, should be treated as a 'universitas facti,' by no possibility can a whole business be so treated; and the same

709 "Universitas facti" means: a number of things of the same kind which are regarded as a whole; e.g. a herd, a stock of wares. Mackeldey, ROMAN LAW Sec. 162. [Footnote No. 1 in original.]

710 To the "church" modern law owes its conception of a juristic person, and the clear line that it draws between 'the corporation aggregate' and the sum of its members. Pollack & Maitland, Vol. 1, 489. [Footnote No. 2 in original.]

is true as to any property within the other exceptions. Congress plainly did mean to comminute the elements of a business; plainly it did not regard the whole as 'capital assets.'

As has already appeared, Williams transferred to the Corning Company 'cash,' 'receivables,' 'fixtures' and a 'merchandise inventory.' 'Fixtures' are not capital because they are subject to a depreciation allowance; the inventory, as we have just seen, is expressly excluded. So far as appears, no allowance was made for 'goodwill'; but, even if there had been, we held in Haberle Crystal Springs Brewing Company v. Clarke, Collector, 2 Cir., 30 F.2d 219, that 'goodwill' was a depreciable intangible. It is true that the Supreme Court reversed that judgment . . . but it based its decision only upon the fact that there could be no allowance for the depreciation of 'goodwill' in a brewery, a business condemned by the Eighteenth Amendment. There can of course be no gain or loss in the transfer of cash; and, although Williams does appear to have made a gain of $ 1072.71 upon the 'receivables,' the point has not been argued that they are not subject to a depreciation allowance. That we leave open for decision by the district court, if the parties cannot agree. The gain or loss upon every other item should be computed as an item in ordinary income.

Judgment reversed.

[Judge Frank dissented in part, proposing that Congress intended that a sale of a sole proprietorship be treated as a sale of a single entity, not each of its parts.]

Notes on Sales of Businesses

Going concern value is the premium a business commands because of the fact that it can continue despite a change of ownership. Goodwill is the premium a company is worth over the value of its assets plus its going concern value. Section 1060 directly affects these intangibles.

Section 1060 applies to sales of trade or business assets when sold en masse. Its significance is that it demands the use of a "residual method" of allocating the purchase price to nondepreciable goodwill and going concern value. The practical effect is to attribute the purchase price first to highly saleable assets, then to various other assets in declining order of marketability, all the rest to intellectual property, then finally to goodwill and going concern value.

The result is that if a buyer purchases a business with bright prospects and pays a premium for the company, the premium will be allocated to goodwill and going concern value, under §1060, and are written off over 15 years under §197(a).

> **To illustrate**: A buys B's business for $100,000. The business has cash of $10,000 and physical assets worth $30,000. Under §1060, a will assign a basis of $10,000 to the cash, $30,000 to the hardware and $60,000 to goodwill and going concern value.

The parties must jointly report their respective allocations of purchase price, thus assisting the IRS in identifying inconsistent positions for audit. If the seller also promises not to compete with the buyer, payments allocable to that promise are ordinary income to the recipient but the payor has to capitalize them and write them off over 15 years under §197(a).

The sale of a partnership interest is somewhat simpler because is usually treated as the sale of an entity, but it is not as simple as sale of stock. The details are beyond the scope of this course.

The tax rules for the sale of corporate stock are easy. Taxpayers can freely convert their proprietorships and partnerships into corporations on a tax-deferred basis.[711] If they later sell the stock, the transaction is much easier than selling the assets because the latter usually require complicated conveyances.

Problem 8-14:

Mr. Swindler has decided to close his calendar year, accrual-method amusement park, following a flood of threatening letters from enraged parents of young children. He has run the business for years as a sole proprietorship. He has agreed to sell it lock, stock and barrel to Lance Klopman for $200,000 in cash plus Lance's assumption of a note payable from Mr. Swindler to the Friendly Bank in the amount of $800,000. The assets of the business are as follows:

Asset	Value	Adjusted Basis
Inventory (popcorn, unused tickets, etc.)	$32,000	$10,000
Unimproved parking lot and park land	180,000	400,000
Machines & equipment	60,000	200,000
High-speed tot-spinner ride: "Mega Drum 2000"	40,000	10,000
$10,000 loan note due from uncle Benny Swindler, written off as a business bad debt long ago	5,000	0
Accounts receivable	8,000	9,000
Storage building	15,000	13,000
Goodwill and going concern value	[for you to determine]	0

1) What are the amounts and characters of the gains or losses from the sale? If any of the gains are capital gains, what is the top rate at which they are taxable?

711 See, especially, §§ 351 (corporations) and 721 (partnerships).

2) Can Lance's buyer write off the goodwill and going concern value, if any? If so, over how many years? Scan §197(a)-(d).

3) Let us say that they agreed that he would give his covenant not to compete under which he was paid $660,000 in installments over three years, and would sell all the assets for only $340,000. What would the difference in result, if any, as to himself and Lance from the result in "2)"? See § 197(d)(1)(E) and (f)(3).

4) Section 351 of the Code allows him to incorporate the business on a tax-free basis, taking back stock, which would be a capital asset in his hands. Would it be a good strategy for Swindler to do so, and wait a while before selling the stock? Take a look at §1202(i) for an anti-Swindler rule, if Swindler wants a top effective tax rate of 14% under §1202.

K. ADVANCED APPLICATIONS

The capital gain or loss provisions offer Congress a unique opportunity for legislative tinkering. In viewing what has gone before, you can see that, in the mind of the taxpayer, for Federal Income Tax purposes a long-term capital gain is a relatively good thing, an ordinary loss is a good thing (compared to a capital loss). In contrast, a capital loss is a relatively bad thing and ordinary income is comparatively horrible. By legislatively declaring that certain transactions automatically fall into one of those categories, Congress can reward, encourage and relieve or punish transactions as it sees fit. There is an extravagant list of transactions that Congress has tinkered with this way and there is not time enough in a basic Federal Income Tax course to dwell on each of them. Instead, prepare yourself for a list of some of the most significant manipulations, many of which you already saw:

a) When a taxpayer turns in a bond or other debt obligation to any creditor, §1271(a)(1) generally declares the transaction an exchange. Before it was amended, debts issued by individuals were not covered. As you saw, the addition of §1271(b) eliminates the problem that appears in the *Hudson* case and opens the door to a capital gain for the holder of a debt bought at a discount from anyone.[712] That is, capital gain or loss can even arise on the retirement of a debt instrument issued by a natural person if, depending on the facts, the obligation is a capital asset in the debt holder's hands.

712 This applies to debt obligations issued or purchased after June 8, 1997. §1271(b)(1)(A).

b) When a landlord cancels a lease or a distributor suffers the cancellation of a lease or distribution agreement, §1241 steps into the breach and declares that the transaction is a sale or exchange as to the tenant or franchisee (such as someone who paid to be a Burger King franchisee and is later paid to close the franchise by Burger King). As a result, the lessee or distributor can enjoy the benefit of a capital gain, but runs the risk of suffering a "mere" capital loss. You saw this in problem 8-8.

c) If the taxpayer disposes of a franchise, trademark or trade name and retains any significant right or interest in that intangible property, §1253 declares the result is *not* a sale or exchange of a capital asset. So, if Burger King ran a hamburger joint and transferred the operation to someone else, Burger King would have ordinary income on the transfer of the trademark because Burger King retained significant rights in the Burger King trademark. The same is true if the disposition is contingent upon earnings from the trademark. This can be helpful for purposes of showing an ordinary loss on the termination of a franchise, but on the whole this provision operates to the detriment of taxpayers by producing ordinary income even if the taxpayer disposes of a partial interest in the franchise or mark in exchange for a fixed payment.

d) If a security which is a capital asset becomes worthless during the year, §165(g)(1) views it as having been sold or exchanged on the last day of the taxable year. This produces a capital loss and is generally unfavorable to taxpayers. You saw this in Chapter 6.

e) When an option lapses in the hands of the person who holds it, it is treated as if he had sold the underlying property, after holding it as long as he held the option. §1234.

f) If a taxpayer has entered into one of several complex financial transactions in order to defer the recognition of a gain in a way that shuts off chances of further gain or loss, the deferred gains may be mandatorily recognized under §1259. The approach is to "deem" the taxpayer to have sold the gain position (referred to in the Code as an "appreciated financial position"). An example of how this might apply runs as follows:

To illustrate: Shrewd bought 100 shares of Folly.Com stock last year for $1,000. The shares are now worth $80,000. Last week he entered into a "short sale" of a different 100 share block of Folly. Com stock, basically meaning that he stands to profit if that new block declines in value.

That means he has locked in his gain in Folly.Com because, if the original block rises in value, he loses an equal amount on the short sale, but, if the price of Folly.Com stock drops, he will pick up an identical amount of gain from the short position. Section 1259(c)(1) causes Shrewd to report the $79,000 gain when he enters into the short sale.

This affects the timing, but not the character, of the gain. There has been a great increase in complex financial transactions in recent decades. They have often taken the form of dividing a financial instrument into parts and disposing of them separately. These are often known as "derivatives."

g) Under §1256(a) (the "mark-to-market system") Congress has *invented* a set of deemed sales of commodities contracts and taxes them. The provision is indifferent to motives. The essence of the rule is that if the taxpayer holds certain kinds of commodities investments at year-end, then he is deemed to sell them at year-end. Period.

Might this violate the rule of *Glenshaw Glass* that defines income in terms of realization? The present answer, which you might not agree with, is "no." In *Murphy v. United States,*[713] the Ninth Circuit rejected the taxpayer's argument that the §1256 marktomarket regime was unconstitutional because it taxes unrealized gains. The claim was dismissed on the ground that Congress did not act arbitrarily or confiscatorily when it decided that "the gains inherent in [futures contracts] are properly treated as constructively received" because taxpayer Murphy could have gotten cash for his commodities positions any time he wanted to."

The Court declined to address the broader issue of whether Congress could tax the gains inherent in all capital assets prior to realization or constructive receipt. Instead, the Court accepted the Government's constructive receipt rationale because the taxpayer was allowed to draw against the daily gains in his account even without disposition of the futures contracts themselves. The fact that the investment that produced the economic gains remained at risk (which the court noted is likewise true of loaned or deposited funds) was viewed as inconsequential.

h) In 1993, Congress adopted a similar marktomarket regime (§475) for determining taxable income of certain securities dealers. Enactment of §475 did not cause an extended debate regarding the constitutionality of the regime. The system has at least one foreign analog. France applies a mark-to-market system to foreign currencies held at year end and it treats transfers of property by gift or as a result

713 992 F.2d 929 (9th Cir. 1993).

of death as realizations.[714] It is conceivable that the Federal Income Tax might move in favor of forcing taxpayers to mark all their liquid assets "to market" every year, expanding the invasion of the accretion system of taxation with respect to financial assets. The camel's nose is certainly under the tent flap in the form of §1256 and §475. For example, you know that §166(d) has for many years treated a nonbusiness bad debt as if it were a short-term capital loss, so the idea of deemed sales for purposes of characterizing gain is not shocking. The difference is that this time there is no visible taxable event.

714 See H. Ault COMPARATIVE INCOME TAXATION, p. 193. See Evans, *The Evolution of Federal Income Tax Accounting a Growing Trend Towards MarktoMarket?* 67 Taxes 824, 833 (1989).

CHAPTER 9 - TAX ACCOUNTING

A. INTRODUCTION

The subject of the book so far has been the tax base and tax rates. In other words, we have generally been looking at whether something goes into gross income, or is a deduction that reduces gross income. Now we are going to look at *when* the item increases or reduces the base. Identifying the right year in which to report a taxable event, such as an item of gross income or a deduction, depends on two factors.

The first factor is the taxpayer's taxable year. Most people simply report the income they got during the calendar year, which runs from the 1st of January to the end of December, using a tax return generally filed not later than April 15.

The second factor is the taxpayer's method of accounting for the item. In most cases, individual taxpayers simply use the cash receipts and disbursements method, reporting income when it is received and deductions when they are paid. In some cases, the tax law will dictate the use of a unique method.

B. TAXABLE YEAR

Read §441(a)-(b), (f)

We are used to the idea of reporting our Federal Income Taxes on an annual basis, but that is not the only way to do it. For example, Congress could amend the Code to provide that each tax return would cover two calendar years. This would require the IRS to evaluate only half the usual number of tax returns per year. In the U.S., taxpayers using the calendar year as their tax year must file an annual Federal Income Tax return not later than the 15th of the fourth month following the close of their taxable year, i.e., April 15. An automatic extension of time, not to exceed six months, is allowed. However, any tax liability is due by April 15.[715] The paperwork can wait, but not the money. Payments delayed after April 15 attract late payment penalties.

715 §§ 6072 and 6651(a).

What is a taxable year? According to the Code, it is the period -- normally 12 months -- regularly used by the taxpayer in computing his income and keeping his books.[716] Again, for most taxpayers it is the calendar year. To be sure, there is an opportunity to select a different year, although virtually no *individual* taxpayer takes advantage of this opportunity because the election is made thoughtlessly in the first return, usually as a teenager, when tax accounting is at the very bottom of human consciousness. The other years are:

a) A fiscal year, which begins on the first day of a given month and ends at the end of the preceding month of the next calendar year. For example, someone whose fiscal year runs from July 1 to June 30 of the following year is said to be "on a June 30 fiscal year."

b) A so-called 52-53 week year, a specialized period used for merchants to accommodate the need to calculate their inventory. IRC §441(f).

c) A short taxable year. Tax years are often shorter than a whole year. For example, if two individuals formed a calendar year partnership on October 10, the first year of the partnership would consist of the October 10-December 31 period.[717] On a more somber note, if a calendar year taxpayer dies on August 3 of this year, Reg. §1.451-1(b)(1) creates a short year ending at death, and his estate will have a short tax year that begins on August 4 and ends on December 31.

Taxpayers are obligated to use the same taxable year as their financial reporting year, or the calendar year if the taxpayer does not maintain books.[718] In most cases, §442 prevents the taxpayer from changing its taxable year without the IRS's consent. In such cases, §481 contains directives to eliminate duplications and omissions and to phase in the change in over several years.

In the past, taxpayers could often delay actually paying their income taxes until April 15th of the following year. Nowadays, employers are obligated to withhold income taxes out of their employees' paychecks and pay over the withholdings to the government. IRC §3402. Even if taxpayers have income other than wages and salaries, they are under a practical obligation to make estimated tax payments over the course of the year, paying once in each calendar quarter, or suffer significant nondeductible penalties for delaying their payments. IRC §6654. In a sense, the estimated tax system results in the mandatory filing of five returns--four imaginary estimated tax returns and (for most people) one real return by April 15 of the following year. Section 6654 imposes the penalty for underpayment of estimated taxes. Employees who do not have outside

716 §441(a)-(c).

717 See Reg. §1.441-1(b)(1).

718 Reg. §1.441-1(b)(1)(iv).

income and whose income is subject to adequate withholdings by their employers need not make estimated tax payments; their employers have taken care of the problem for them.

One thing the Congress strongly discourages is what an early Supreme Court case, *Burnet v. Sanford & Brooks Co.*,[719] referred to as "transactional accounting" under which taxes are deferred until a multi-year transaction is completed. The Supreme Court has repudiated the argument that taxing incomplete transactions as we do (rather than using a transactional approach) might violate the Constitution, reasoning in part that transactional accounting is impossibly sophisticated.[720] Congress's typical response to the hardships of a rigorous annual accounting has been to enact narrow relief provisions, such as the equitable taxation of annuities and installment sales.[721]

Here is an example of how transactional accounting can differ from annual accounting:

To illustrate: The Enormous Corporation of Newport News builds aircraft carriers. It takes three years to build a single ship. Assume the following income and payments occurred, the effect of which was a negative cash flow in years 1 and 2 and a positive cash flow in year 3.

Year 1: Income: $0	Expenses: $5 million
Year 2: Income: $0	Expenses: $5 million
Year 3: Income: $16 million	Expenses: $2 million
Total: $16 million	Total: $12 million

If only the overall profit or loss of $4 million were taxed using transactional accounting, one would report nothing in years 1 and 2, and a $4 million profit in year 3. The polar alternative would be to report losses of $5 million in year 1 and in year 2, and a $14 million profit in year 3. That would be the outcome under strict annual accounting. Certain small contractors are allowed to wait until their construction contracts are completed until they report the profit or loss on the contract,[722] but most taxpayers, such as the Enormous Corporations, prorate their profits over the life of the contract using the percentage of completion method of accounting.

719 282 U.S. 359 (1931).

720 Id. at 365.

721 The installment sale method is authorized by §453 and is discussed later in the Chapter.

722 See §460(e)(1), covering taxpayers with average annual gross receipts of under $25 million and certain residential construction contracts. Homebuilders seem to be the primary beneficiaries.

Read §446(a)-(c)

Methods of accounting are "conventions" (methodologies) used to pigeonhole income and deduction into particular taxable years. Read that again; it is that straightforward. Methods of accounting themselves are broken into two fundamental categories:

1. Overall methods of accounting; and

2. Methods of accounting that relate to a particular item of income or deduction.

Taxpayers are allowed to use an overall method and specific methods at the same time, but they are not allowed to synthesize permissible methods into a hybrid method. The overall methods are the *cash receipts and disbursements method* and the *accrual method.* We will look at each of them in some detail. A typical example of a specific method of accounting is the installment sale method, which is used to spread gains from the sale of specific properties where payments are deferred over several years. For example, a taxpayer on the cash method might use the installment method to report the gain on the sale of a tract of land while using the cash method for all other purposes.

Taxpayers can change a method of accounting, but the IRS generally requires a substantial reason for the change and conditions the change on phasing in the impact of the change over several years under §481. A change of method means a change in either the taxpayer's overall method or a change in the time for reporting of any item of income or expense.[723] Even if the taxpayer has been using an erroneous accounting method, the taxpayer generally has to get the IRS to approve the change to a correct method.[724] For example, depreciation deductions involve *when* one adjusts the basis of property, hence it is a method of accounting for an item of expense, and requires IRS consent to change. Now think back to the rule that one must reduce the basis of depreciable property by the greater of the amount allowed or allowable. The IRS position is that a taxpayer who has been claiming less depreciation than she is entitled to has indeed adopted a method of accounting which requires the consent of the IRS to change, even though it is an incorrect method. In such cases, the IRS will grant an automatic consent to change to a proper method, and waive its usual user fee for the requested consent, provided the taxpayer follows the IRS's procedure.[725] Other automatic consents are also available.[726]

723 Reg. §1.446-1(e)(2).

724 IRC §446(e). Any methodology that affects the timing of income or deduction is a method. Reg. §1.446-1(e)(2)(ii)(a).

725 Rev. Proc. 99-49, 1999-52 I.R.B.725.

726 Publication 538 www.irs.gov/pub

> **To illustrate:** Lance bought a drill press three years ago. Assume Lance was allowed to write off the cost of the drill press using the 200% declining balance method over 7 years. Instead, he thoughtlessly wrote off the property under the straight-line method over a period of ten years. Assume that the allowable depreciation using 100% declining balance depreciation was $5,000 but that using the erroneous method it was $3,000. Under the usual rule, Lance must seek IRS approval to switch to the (correct) 200% method (even though his present method is erroneous) because the different depreciation methods are *timing* issues. However, in this instance, the approval is automatic, so he can shift to the 200% method.[727]

Section 446(a) directs taxpayers to use their financial (i.e., non tax) method of accounting in preparing their Federal returns. Reg. §1.446-1(a)(4) goes on to say that they must:

> [M]aintain such accounting records as will enable him to file a correct return.. Accounting records include . . . regular books of account and such other records and data as may be necessary to support the entries on his books of account and on his return, as for example, a reconciliation of any differences between such books and his return.

In practice, most individuals get by with their Form W-2s (annual reports of wages and salaries provided by the employer) and Form 1099s (reports of payors of interest, dividends and the like) and their checkbooks, credit card receipts, bills and rudimentary files.

If the taxpayer has more than one business that she runs as a sole proprietorship, she will file a separate Schedule C for each of them, and can select a different method of accounting for each business.[728] However, she can only use her own regular tax year for an unincorporated business.[729] If she uses an overall method of accounting for the business's financial records (such as the accrual method) she must use that same method in preparing her tax return, but she can use a different method (such as the cash method) for Federal Income Tax purposes outside that business.[730]

Tax accounting rules often differ sharply from financial accounting rules. This is largely because the two systems have different objectives. The purpose of financial accounting is to provide creditors, shareholders, partners and other persons with a conservative picture of the business's financial position and income, stated on a consistent basis from year to year, matching income and expenses to the extent possible so that income is reported on a relatively level basis.

727 Bloomberg Tax Portfolio, No. 530, DEPRECIATION: GENERAL CONCEPTS; NON-ACRS RULES, § XIV-A for a discussion of this intricate subject. It does suggest that in a case such as Lance's, he might get back the $2,000 of lost basis via a §481 adjustment.

728 IRC §446(d). See Instructions for Form 1040, Schedule C.

729 But, c.f., Vance v. Commissioner, 56 T.C.M. 1408 (1989).

730 §446(d).

To do so, the accounting profession relies on its own unique rules. Tax accounting is subordinated to the larger purposes of the income tax, namely the "equitable collection of revenue"[731] in which conservatism and matching are at most secondary considerations. In addition, the rules of tax accounting tend to have an ad hoc character because they are often Congressional reactions to particular tax abuses that the IRS unearths or to demands from special interest groups for helpful legislation.

1. Cash Method

Read IRC §451(a) and Reg. §§ 1.451-1(a), 1.446-1(c)(1)(i) and 1.461-1(a)

This is the method of choice (or default) for virtually all individuals, and is unwittingly chosen by virtually everyone on filing his or her first income tax return. In addition, many entities are entitled to use the cash method, although several Code sections, especially 448, deny the use of the cash method to taxpayers who are likely to abuse it. The first subject in the readings that follow is the treatment of receipts of cash and cash-like items.

2. Receipts under the Cash Method

The general rule is that one reports cash or a "cash equivalent," and the value of property received as income in the year actually or constructively received.[732] (We will see what "constructively" means soon.) For example, a taxpayer who receives a share of stock in compensation for her services must include its fair market value in income for the year of receipt, not when the stock is converted into cash by a sale. Likewise, a negotiable note is generally taxable when received from the obligor.

In addition to cash, cash equivalents (such as checks), negotiable notes,[733] services received, and property, cash method taxpayers must also report "economic benefits" as income when they are conferred on the taxpayer. For example, a cash method taxpayer is taxed when his employer supplies him with the free use of an automobile, or other benefits as compensation, even though the employee cannot sell the benefit to a third party.

Not every form of income fits neatly into the cash method. Some forms of income are taxable even though they are not literally "received," such as cancellation of indebtedness income and income that arises when restrictions on certain restricted property (discussed below) lapse. While these cases are hard to reconcile with cash method accounting, there is no reasonable alternative to their current inclusion in gross income.

731 See, Thor Power Tool v. Commissioner, 439 US 522, 542-544 (1979).

732 Reg. §1.446-1(c)(1)(i).

733 See, e.g., Barnsley v. Commissioner, 31 TC 1260 (1959).

a. Actual Receipts

The following materials deal with how one reports the receipt of checks, a form of actual receipt.

In the earlier well-known case of *Lavery v. Commissioner*[734] the court was faced with the basic question of whether one should treat a check received late in the year, but in time to be cashed as taxable. The court held the check was a taxable receipt, based on the language of the Regulations. *Lavery* did not reach the harder question of whether a check received at the end of the year after banking hours is subject to taxation. That was left to the following decision.

KAHLER v. COMMISSIONER
18 T.C. 31 (1952)

RICE, Judge.

[The Findings of Fact are omitted.]

OPINION.

The sole issue is when did the petitioner realize the income represented by the commission check delivered December 31, 1946. Was it in 1946, as determined by respondent, or in 1947, as claimed by petitioner? This, in turn, is based on the question whether the receipt of a check by a cash basis taxpayer after banking hours on the last day of the taxable period constitutes a realization of income.

In his brief, petitioner argues that "the mere receipt of a check does not give rise to income within the taxable year of receipt unless the check is received in sufficient time before the end of the taxable year so the check may be converted into cash within the taxable year." In support of such result, petitioner relies upon *L. M. Fischer*, 14 T. C. 792 (1950); *Urban A. Lavery*, 5 T. C. 1283 (1945), affd. (C. A. 7, 1946) 158 F. 2d 859 . . . .

In the *Fischer* case, we held that a check delivered to the taxpayer on December 31, 1942, which was not deposited until 1943, was not income in 1942 but in 1943, since the check was subject to a substantial restriction. At the time of delivery of such check, there was an oral agreement made between the drawer and the taxpayer that the latter would hold the check for a few days before he cashed it since the drawer was short of money in the bank. Such a situation is completely distinguishable from that in the instant case.

The *Lavery* and *Ostenberg* cases both decided that checks delivered to the taxpayers were income in the year of delivery. In the *Lavery* case delivery was on December 30, and in the *Ostenberg* case delivery was on December 31. Petitioner relies on the dicta appearing in these

734 158 F.2d 859 (7th Cir. 1946).

cases to the effect that the result might have been different had the petitioner in either case been able to show that he could not have cashed the check in the year drawn. We fail to see where there should be any difference in result just because it might be impossible to cash a check in the year in which drawn, where delivery actually took place in such year. Respondent's regulations provide that all items of gross income shall be included in the taxable year in which received by the taxpayer, and that where services are paid for other than by money, the amount to be included as income is the fair market value of the thing taken in payment.[735]

Analogous cases to the instant case are those which were concerned with the proper year in which deductions might be taken where a check was drawn and delivered in one year and cashed in a subsequent year. Under the negotiable instruments law, payment by check is a conditional payment subject to the condition that it will be honored upon presentation; and once such presentation is made and the check is honored, the date of payment relates back to the time of delivery. See *Estelle Broussard*, 16 T. C. 23 (1951); *Estate of Modie J. Spiegel*, 12 T. C. 524 (1949); and cases cited therein. In the *Spiegel* case we said, at page 529:

> It would seem to us unfortunate for the Tax Court to fail to recognize what has so frequently been suggested, that as a practical matter, in everyday personal and commercial usage, the transfer of funds by check is an accepted procedure. The parties almost without exception think and deal in terms of payment except in the unusual circumstance, not involved here, that the check is dishonored upon presentation, or that it was delivered in the first place subject to some condition or infirmity which intervenes between delivery and presentation.

Under such circumstances, we feel that it is immaterial that delivery of a check is made too late in the taxable year for the check to be cashed in that year. The petitioner realized income upon receipt of the commission check on December 31, 1946.

Decision will be entered for the respondent.

[The concurring opinion of Judge Murdock is omitted. Eds.]

Notes on the Cash Method of Accounting

Kahler is consistent with the general rule that cash-method taxpayers are taxed when they receive cash, property or services.[736] Cash equivalents are items of property that are nearly as liquid as cash. Examples include checks and promissory notes, provided they are not subject to substantial restrictions or dishonored. We will see more about how notes are taxed later.

735 Treasury Regulations 111 §29.22 (a)3, and §29.412.[Footnote No. 2 in original.]

736 Reg. §1.446-1(c)(1)(i).

The forfeiture of alternative rights may justify not reporting income. For example, suppose a cash-method taxpayer might be able to get her hands on money or property only by forfeiting some other valuable right. In such cases, she is "subject to a substantial limitation or restriction."[737] For example, she would not be taxed on severance pay that is available only on termination of employment, at least not until she terminates her job, because quitting her job would be such a high price to pay in exchange for getting severance benefits.

Section 83 of the Code superimposes special rules on situations in which employees or independent contractors get property in exchange for their services. The basic rule appears in §83(a), taxing recipients when the transfer, meaning change of beneficial interest in the property, occurs. For this purpose, property excludes "mere unfunded, unsecured promises to pay money in the future"; if it did include such promises, it would pretty well end cash method accounting as far as written promises are concerned.[738] An obligation is "unfunded" if there is no actual trust agreement or other deposit with a third party to provide the resources for the payment. It is "unsecured" if the taxpayer is not a special creditor, meaning someone with a security interest, such as a lien or mortgage. We will return to this subject soon. (The antonym of a special creditor is a "general creditor".)

Security deposits held by landlords and others are completely different. They are treated like loans from tenant to landlord and are not taxable to the landlord until forfeited and applied against unpaid rents or damage to the property.[739] If, however, the money is provided as advance rent it is currently taxable.[740]

b. Constructive Receipt

Read Reg. §1.451-2(a) and IRC §267(a)(2)

Taxpayers cannot simply turn their back on income by such measures as waiting to cash their checks, not bothering to collect their interest on their bank accounts, or failing to submit their matured but uncashed bond coupons until they feel like it. The Regulations prevent such tricks by taxing people on what they "constructively" receive as well as what they actually receive.[741] In the interest of fairness, the taxation of constructive receipts is also restrained by the "substantial restrictions and limitation" principle. So, for example, while the constructive receipt doctrine generally taxes one on interest that accumulates in a savings account, that is not true if the withdrawal results in one's surrender of three months' worth of interest in order to make

737 See Reg. §1.451-2(a).

738 Reg. §1.83-3(e).

739 Clinton Hotel Realty Corp. v. Commissioner, 128 F.2d 968 (5th Cir. 1942).

740 See, e.g., Andantech L.L.C. v. CIR, 331 F.3d 972 (CADC 2003).

741 Reg. §§ 1.446-1(c)(1)(i) and 1.451-2(a).

the withdrawal.[742] On the other hand, inconsequential restrictions are ignored. An example of an inconsequential restriction might be a bank's requirement that a customer fill out one of the bank's forms in order to make a large withdrawal by certified check.

Before you read the next case, study §267(a)(2).

FETZER REFRIGERATOR CO. v. UNITED STATES

437 F.2d 577 (6th Cir. 1971)

PECK, Circuit Judge.

The sole issue presented on this appeal is whether, for purposes of §267(a)(2) of the Internal Revenue Code of 1954 the controlling shareholder of the taxpayer corporations "constructively received" certain accrued rents, where he had the authority as controlling shareholder and officer to draw checks upon the bank accounts of the corporations and the amounts in question had been accrued as payable on the books of the corporations at the time they became due.

For the years 1960 and 1962-64, Clifford L. Fetzer and his wife leased some parcels of real property to the two corporations. Mr. Fetzer was the president and 92 percent shareholder of the Fetzer Refrigerator Co. and secretary-treasurer and 50 percent shareholder of the Louisville Cooler Mfg. Co. The terms of the leases called for the Fetzers to receive each year as rent, the greater amount of a fixed monthly sum payable in advance, or 1 percent of gross sales. At the end of each calendar year, the accountant for the two corporations computed the amount of rents owing to the Fetzers, and recorded the unpaid rents by "debiting rent and crediting accrued expenses." The accrued account consisted mainly of the rents payable to the Fetzers, but it also included accrued rents due on other property and equipment.

Each of the companies was incorporated in Kentucky and reported its income on a calendar year basis, using the accrual method of accounting. The Fetzers used the cash method of accounting for receipts and disbursements in respect of items of gross income. Accordingly, the corporations deducted the full amount of the rent expenses for each year in which they became due, without regard to whether actual payment was made. The Fetzers, however, did not report the accrued rents as income until the year following the year in which the corporations claimed their deductions. The Commissioner disallowed the deductions for rent expenses for each of the above years and assessed deficiencies against each corporation.

The corporations brought a suit in the District Court seeking a refund of the respective taxes and interest totaling $13,293.05. After submitting their pleadings and affidavits, both sides moved for a summary judgment. The corporations' motion was granted and the Commissioner did not appeal concerning the rents accrued during 1964 because the corporations had given a note to the Fetzers for that year. The Commissioner agreed that the holding of this court in

742 Reg. §1.451-2(a)(2). Do not think you have discovered a tax loophole by simplying waiting a long time; if the restriction last for over a year, the OID rules, discussed below, apply, and tax the interest as it accumulates.

Musselman Hub-Brake Co. v. Commissioner of Internal Revenue, 139 F.2d 65 (6th Cir. 1943), requires that taxpayers be allowed to deduct rent expenses in such circumstances. As a result, this appeal is concerned with only the three years 1960, 1962 and 1963.

The Commissioner relies on the provisions of §267(a)(2) of the Code, which if they have application to the taxpayers herein, require that the subject deductions be disallowed. A consideration of the background of that section may therefore be helpful. This Court, speaking through Judge Hamilton, described the occasion for the passage of the predecessor section of §267(a)(2), *supra*, in Musselman Hub-Brake Co. v. Commissioner of Internal Revenue, *supra*, as follows (p. 66):

> "The Joint Committee on tax evasion and avoidance of the 75th Congress found that many corporations credited on their books to their controlling stockholder incurred business expenses and accrued interest and deducted them from gross income without the stockholder including such items in his gross income for the current year, and that the corporation paid the credits to the stockholder in a subsequent year when his net income was low, which resulted in the stockholder shifting his taxable income from a high to a low bracket.
>
> "The committee also found that some debtors kept their accounts on an accrual basis and the creditor reported his income on a cash basis which resulted in the debtor taking the deduction in one taxable year and the creditor reporting the income in another. The committee found too that in some cases corporations made credits on their books to their controlling stockholder of items deductible from gross income and such credits were subsequently extinguished with the result that they were at no time reported by the stockholder." (Citations omitted.)

In order for §267(a)(2) to apply, each of its requirements must first be satisfied. ... Such satisfaction as to only one requirement is in dispute. Paraphrased, this requirement provides that the amounts involved be includable in the gross income of the person to whom the payment is to be made within the taxable year of the taxpayer or two and one-half months after the close thereof. Int. Rev. Code of 1954, §267(a)(2)(A). To determine whether the amounts are includable in the gross income of such person, the Regulations for §267 refer to the rules of constructive receipt which are found in the Regulations under §451 of the Code. Treas. Reg. §1.267(a)-1(b)1(iii) (1958).

Regulations Section 1.451-2(a) gives the following definition of constructive receipt of income:

> "... Income although not actually reduced to a taxpayer's possession is constructively received by him in the taxable year during which it is credited to his account, set apart for him, or otherwise made available so that he may draw upon it at any time, or *so that he could have drawn upon it during the taxable year if notice of intention to withdraw had been given* ...." (Emphasis Supplied.)

As has been pointed out in Hyland v. Commissioner of Internal Revenue, 175 F.2d 422 (2d Cir. 1949), "constructive receipt of income by a taxpayer on the cash receipts basis is a creature of the Regulations; they prescribe the conditions which make the doctrine applicable." 175 F.2d at 423. Thus, our purpose here is to determine whether the facts of this case permit a finding of constructive receipt within the language of § 1.451-2(a) above.

In Ross v. Commissioner of Internal Revenue, 169 F.2d 483 (1st Cir. 1948), Justice Frankfurter described the coverage of the doctrine of constructive receipt of income in the following manner: "The doctrine of constructive receipt treats as taxable income which is *unqualifiedly subject to the demand of a taxpayer* on the cash receipts and disbursements method of accounting, whether or not such income has actually been received in cash. . . . ." (Emphasis supplied.) There was no evidence presented in this case to negate the conclusion that the rents due Mr. Fetzer were subject to his unqualified demand. . . . Nothing herein indicates that any limitations had been placed upon Mr. Fetzer's right to withdraw the funds at any time after the rents became due. The Commissioner did not deny that the taxpayer corporations had the ability to pay Mr. Fetzer during 1960, 1962 and 1963. Although Mr. Fetzer never physically received the amounts due him, he did possess the power and the right to receive the payments. Under these circumstances, it is clear that Mr. Fetzer "could have drawn upon [the rent due] during the taxable year if notice of intention to withdraw had been given." Treas. Reg. § 1.451 -2(a).

Consistent with this reasoning, many of the cases involving § 267(a)(2) in which no constructive receipt was found, turned on the fact that the shareholder's failure to receive the income was not the result of his own choice. . . . Where limitations were placed on the shareholder's right to receive payments, the courts have been reluctant to find constructive receipt, even though the controlling shareholder possessed the power to extract the payments prior to the time he was to be paid. . . . At the other end of the spectrum are cases such as Musselman Hub-Brake Co. v. Commissioner of Internal Revenue, *supra*, in which constructive receipt was found because the shareholder had control over the payment of the funds of the corporation and held notes with a readily realizable value of par executed by the corporation. Indeed, as has been hereinabove pointed out, in the present case the Commissioner conceded that because the corporations gave the Fetzers a note for the 1964 accrued rent, constructive receipt by them had occurred. However, such clear evidence of the obligation as such notes has not generally been required, and constructive receipt has been found where the controlling shareholder had the right to make payment and the amounts due him were credited on the books of the corporation without any restrictions placed on his right to receive the payments. *E. g.*, Platt Trailer Co., 23 T.C. 1065 (1955). In one case, the tax court found that constructive receipt was present although the corporation did not have sufficient cash on hand to pay the amounts when due, but could have borrowed the funds necessary to make the payments. Ohio Battery & Ignition Co., 5 T.C. 283 (1945). In our view, the facts of the present case fall within the realm of these latter cases.

The Commissioner urges, however, that for the accrued rents to be constructively received, they must have been set aside in a separate account for the Fetzers. We disagree. The accountant for the two corporations stated in his affidavit that the accounts in question consisted primarily of the accrued rents due the Fetzers. In small family-owned corporations, there is not the same need for multiplicity of accounts as might be required for a large corporation with many officers and shareholders. *See* O. H. Kruse Grain & Milling at 423.

While not rising to the dignity of a model of precision, the book entries reflecting the accrual of the amounts in question are capable of no interpretation other than the implementation of an intent to so earmark the sums in question. This conclusiveness, in our view, satisfies the requirement of the Regulations. This conclusion is not inconsistent with the contrary result reached in Hyland v. Commissioner of Internal Revenue, *supra,* since the record therein failed to establish the power of the controlling shareholder to draw upon the corporation's depository.

Affirmed.

Question

How does §267(a)(2) differ from the same Code section discussed in *Fetzer*?

c. Cafeteria Plans and the "Mailbox Rule"

Section 125 of the Code provides an important limit on the constructive receipt doctrine as applied to employees. In essence, it says that if an employee is offered a series of benefits, some of which are taxable and some of which are excludable, the employee is not taxed just because of the right to select among two or more benefits, including cash. These are known as "cafeteria plans" because the employee can select from a "menu" of benefits. But for §125, the mere opportunity to select a benefit (including the cash) could give rise to constructive receipt and attract a tax, even though the employee in fact rejected everything on the menu.

Estate of Witt v. Fahs[743] held that a person who made a charitable contribution was entitled to deduct for the payment, mailed near year end, because the Post Office was found to be the agent of both the payor and the recipient. The case justifies taxpayers' actions in putting year-end checks into the mail so as to get a deduction when the letter falls into the box. The Regulations say -- without analysis -- that dividends payable on December 31 are not constructively received in December if the corporation customarily pays the dividends by checks that arrive in January, with no reference to *Witt v. Fahs.*[744] There is a similar ruling as to year-end paychecks customarily mailed out at year-end, subject to a warning that if the mailing was timed with tax avoidance

743 160 F. Supp. 521 (S.D. Fla 1956).

744 Reg. §1.451-2(b).

in mind, the recipients are taxed when the checks are mailed.[745] It is not clear if this ruling is limited to the context of payrolls or if it has a broader meaning. Nothing in the ruling explicitly so limits it.

In Rev. Rul. 80-335,[746] the IRS ruled that where a taxpayer (whose name is "A" in the ruling) used his bank's "pay by phone" facility, the date of A's payment was the date that the bank paid on behalf of A (who was treated as the bank's principal). Rev. Rul. 80-335 shored up the *Witt v. Fahs* doctrine:

> If a taxpayer, who uses the cash receipts and disbursements method of accounting, mails checks to creditors, the taxpayer is entitled to allowable deductions therefor on the day the checks are placed in the mail, provided the checks are subsequently paid by the bank. Estate of Witt v. Fahs, 160 F. Supp. 521 (S.D. Fla. 1956).
>
> If the taxpayer, who uses the cash receipts and disbursements method of accounting, authorizes payment by the taxpayer's agent, payment occurs on the date the agent, on behalf of the taxpayer, delivers a check to the payee. See Commissioner v. Bradley, 56 F.2d 728 (6th Cir. 1932). In the present case M is acting as the agent of A, and therefore, if M mails checks to A's creditors, transfers funds to creditors' accounts, or actually delivers checks to creditors, the payments are made on the date of the mailings, transfers, or deliveries, as the case may be.

Notice the difference in the agency theory here; whereas the Post Office is the agent of the payor *and* payee in *Witt v. Fahs*, in Rev. Rul. 80-335 the payee is not taxed until delivery, suggesting that the Post Office is only the payor's agent.

Problem 9-1:

Lucky Pierre, a cash method, calendar-year taxpayer, went to the racetrack on December 30th of year 1. He bet $10 on Deductible to win in the 8th race. Deductible came in second and Pierre left the track not knowing that the first place horse had been disqualified and Deductible declared the winner, paying 30 to 1. By then, the track had closed. Lucky Pierre read this news in the paper the next morning, but the track was not open on the 31st and he had to wait until January 2 of year 2, to go to the track and collect his winnings.

1) Assuming Deductible had simply come in first, in what year would Lucky have income?

---

745 Rev. Rul. 73-99, 1973-1 CB 412.

746 1980-2 CB 170.

2) Now assume the facts given in the problem. If the winnings are income, in what year do they fall?

3) What if Pierre had torn up the ticket and had to file an affidavit that day at the track to collect and he had the time to do so?

4) What if there was no way to collect after he had torn up the ticket?

Problem 9-2:

Mrs. Gasgoine, a cash-method calendar-year taxpayer, owns an apartment building with a store on the first floor. Last year, she received the following amounts from operating the units. Which should be included in gross income?

1) Current rents	$20,000
2) Prepaid rents for next year	8,000
3) Security deposits held by her	9,000
4) Security deposit held in escrow for store as tenant	6,000
5) Receipts paid by tenant to break lease	3,000
6) Rent in the mail to her on December 31 of last year but not yet received	1,000
7) Check issued for late rent issued by former tenant, held by clerk in the same city in its hotel lobby late in day on December 31, but inconvenient to collect	2,500

d. Deferral of Income by Contract

Imagine a rock band that is about to become very rich, but whose career is likely to be short, perhaps only a few years. If the band can spread its earnings over the next 10 years the total tax bill may be much smaller than if the earnings are taxed at the height of the band's success. This is a natural result of the progressive income tax.

It used to be that taxpayers who were thrown into high tax brackets could engage in "income averaging" (as if the income were earned over several years) to soften the blow, but that relief provision is long gone, along with the high rates that justified the relief provision. As a result, tax planners whose clients enjoy sudden good fortune often tell their clients to defer some of their income into future years when client's tax rate is likely to be lower.

The following early case deals with the question of whether compensation that is deferred by contract is taxable under the constructive receipt or economic benefit doctrines. Mr. Welch, the former president of G.E. received a 14% interest rate on his multi-million dollar deferrals. That interest income is also tax-deferred until it is paid.[747]

SPROULL v. COMMISSIONER

16 T.C. 244 (1951), affirmed 194 F.2d 541 (1952)

TIETJENS, Judge.

[Sproull was the president of Brainard Steel Company, which had seen hard times in the past. When times got better (1945) the directors voted him a $11,500 bonus, payable in 1946 and 1947. The money was put in trust for him in 1945 and duly paid out in 1946 and 1947. The IRS asserted that Sproull should have paid taxes on the $11,500 in 1945, either under the constructive receipt doctrine or the economic benefit doctrine.]

OPINION.

The Commissioner included in petitioner's 1945 taxable income as bonus income the sum of $10,500 paid by Brainard Steel Corporation to the Union Savings And Trust Company of Warren, Ohio, trustee under the agreement of December 26, 1945.

Petitioner contends the respondent taxed him in the wrong year and that instead of being taxable on the full $10,500 in 1945 he was properly taxable in 1946 and 1947 on the amounts paid him by the trustee in those years.

Neither the stipulated facts nor the oral testimony establish whether petitioner made his returns on a cash basis. However, since that is the most common method of reporting income and since the trial apparently proceeded on that basis we assume the cash method was used.

Superficially the issue looks simple. Petitioner actually received no cash until the years 1946 and 1947. Why, then, should he be taxed in 1945? And what was the basis for respondent's action in so doing?

A possible basis is the application of the doctrine of constructive receipt and petitioner in his main argument assumes that to be the fact. He sets out to demonstrate the doctrine's in applicability, pointing out (1) that although the sum was fixed and paid by his employer as

747 David Cay Johnson, Teamsters Are Challenging G.E. Chief's Compensation, New York Times, March 3, 1997, page D2.

compensation for services, he actually received no part of the money in 1945; (2) that he could not have reduced any part of the money to possession in that year because of the time limitations on payment to him set in the trust instrument, and (3) that he had no control of the corporate action in establishing the trust, nor was such action taken at his suggestion or pursuant to his direction.

This Court has rather fully discussed the doctrine of constructive receipt in *Richard R. Deupree*, 1 T. C. 113, and *J. D. Amend*, 13 T. C. 178. Although it be conceded that if we apply the tests described in those cases to the situation here we must agree with petitioner's argument that this is not a true case for application of the doctrine, agreeing with petitioner on that point does not dispose of the case. Respondent argues that if constructive receipt does not apply, then the doctrine of cash equivalent does. He cites the broad language of § 22 (a) of the Internal Revenue Code which reads, in part, as follows:

SEC. 22. GROSS INCOME.

(a) General Definition. "Gross Income" includes gains, profits, and income derived from salaries, wages, or compensation for personal service (including personal service as an officer or employee of a State, or any political subdivision thereof, or any agency or instrumentality of any one or more of the foregoing), of whatever kind and in whatever form paid, or from professions, vocations, trades, businesses, commerce, ...

Reliance is placed on *Renton K. Brodie*, 1 T. C. 275, and J. H. McEwen, 6 T. C. 1018. We paraphrase the language used in Brodie, supra. Even if the doctrine of constructive receipt as it is commonly understood cannot here be correctly applied, it is undoubtedly true that the amount which the Commissioner has included in petitioner's income for 1945 was used in that year for his benefit, albeit not at his direction, in setting up the trust of which petitioner, or, in the event of his death then his estate, was the sole beneficiary and that the whole arrangement was part of a plan for his additional remuneration.

The question then becomes, as in *McEwen, supra*, was "any economic or financial benefit conferred on the employee as compensation" in the taxable year. If so, it was taxable to him in that year. This question we must answer in the affirmative. The employer's part of the transaction terminated in 1945. It was then that the amount of the compensation was fixed at $10,500 and irrevocably paid out for petitioner's sole benefit. While this factor alone is not controlling, it does serve to distinguish this case from those in which the exact amount of compensation is subject to some future contingency or subject to the possibility of return to the employer. . . .

It is true, as petitioner argues in trying to pull free from *Brodie* and *McEwen, supra*, that the arrangement gave petitioner only an equitable interest in the trust fund and that he had no vested interest in an annuity contract delivered into his possession as in *Brodie, supra*. But, that does not determine the issue whether the establishment of a trust such as was here established does not itself constitute taxable income to petitioner. This is especially true when it is considered that one of the arguments of petitioner in *Brodie, supra,* was that the annuity had no cash value and could not be assigned. Yet we held the amount expended for the annuity in *Brodie* taxable in the year expended. We think the case at hand is a stronger one for taxability than *Brodie.* Here, we think it must be held that the expenditure of the $10,500 in setting up the trust conferred an economic or financial benefit on petitioner properly taxable to him in 1945. The fund was ascertained and paid over by petitioner's employer for his benefit in that year. Petitioner had to do nothing further to earn it or establish his rights therein. The only duties of the trustee were to hold, invest, accumulate, and very shortly pay over the fund and its increase to petitioner or his estate in the event of his prior death. No one else had any interest in or control over the monies. The trust agreement contained no restriction whatever on petitioner's right to assign or otherwise dispose of the interest thus created in him. On the facts here there is no doubt that such an interest had a value equivalent to the amount paid over for his benefit, and that this beneficial interest could have been assigned or otherwise alienated requires the citation of only the most general authority. See Bogert, Trusts and Trustees, § 188. Respondent contends that the circumstances of the creation of this interest in petitioner was tantamount to paying over to him the cash in 1945.

Of course, petitioner argues that *Brodie* and *McEwen, supra,* are distinguishable on their facts. They involved annuity contracts purchased with funds furnished by petitioners' employers, in *Brodie* without the petitioner's direction or control but on his signing a written application, and in *McEwen* pursuant to a contract of employment to which petitioner was party. We think those differences are not significant here in view of petitioner's acquisition of a vested valuable interest in the trust fund here in question in the taxable year under consideration.

Decision will be entered for the respondent.

Problem 9-3:

Exactly what was the economic benefit to Mr. Sproull?

The following ruling is the fountainhead of learning on the deferral of income by contract. It relies on the *Sproull* case, as you will see.

REV. RUL. 60-31

19601 C.B. 174

. . .

Advice has been requested regarding the taxable year of inclusion in gross income of a taxpayer, using the cash receipts and disbursements method of accounting, of compensation for services received under the circumstances described below.

(1) On January 1, 1958, the taxpayer and corporation X executed an employment contract under which the taxpayer is to be employed by the corporation in an executive capacity for a period of five years. Under the contract, the taxpayer is entitled to a stated annual salary and to additional compensation of 10 x dollars for each year. The additional compensation will be credited to a bookkeeping reserve account and will be deferred, accumulated, and paid in annual installments equal to onefifth of the amount in the reserve as of the close of the year immediately preceding the year of first payment. The payments are to begin only upon (a) termination of the taxpayer's employment by the corporation; (b) the taxpayer's becoming a parttime employee of the corporation; or (c) the taxpayer's becoming partially or totally incapacitated. Under the terms of the agreement, corporation X is under a merely contractual obligation to make the payments when due, and the parties did not intend that the amounts in the reserve be held by the corporation in trust for the taxpayer.

The contract further provides that if the taxpayer should fail or refuse to perform his duties, the corporation will be relieved of any obligation to make further credits to the reserve (but not of the obligation to distribute amounts previously contributed); but, if the taxpayer should become incapacitated from performing his duties, then credits to the reserve will continue for one year from the date of the incapacity, but not beyond the expiration of the fiveyear term of the contract. There is no specific provision in the contract for forfeiture by the taxpayer of his right to distribution from the reserve; and, in the event he should die prior to his receipt in full of the balance in the account, the remaining balance is distributable to his personal representative at the rate of onefifth per year for five years, beginning three months after his death.

(2) The taxpayer is an officer and director of corporation A, which has a plan for making future payments of additional compensation for current services to certain officers and key employees designated by its board of directors. This plan provides that a percentage of the annual net earnings (before Federal income taxes) in excess of 4,000x dollars is to be designated for division among the participants in proportion to their respective salaries. This amount is not currently paid to the participants; but, the corporation has set up on its books a separate account for each participant and each year it credits thereto the dollar amount of his participation for the year, reduced by a proportionate part of the corporation's income taxes attributable to the additional compensation. Each account is also credited with the net amount, if any, realized from investing any portion of the amount in the account.

Distributions are to be made from these accounts annually beginning when the employee (1) reaches age 60, (2) is no longer employed by the company, including cessation of employment due to death, or (3) becomes totally disabled to perform his duties, whichever occurs first. The annual distribution will equal a stated percentage of the balance in the employee's account at the close of the year immediately preceding the year of first payment, and disHtributions will continue until the account is exhausted. However, the corporation's liability to make these distributions is contingent upon the employee's (1) refraining from engaging in any business competitive to that of the corporation, (2) making himself available to the corporation for consultation and advice after retirement or termination of his services, unless disabled, and (3) retaining unencumbered any interest or benefit under the plan. In the event of his death, either before or after the beginning of payments, amounts in an employee's account are distributable in installments computed in the same way to his designated beneficiaries or heirsatlaw. Under the terms of the compensation plan, corporation A is under a merely contractual obligation to make the payments when due, and the parties did not intend that the amounts in each account be held by the corporation in trust for the participants.

(3) On October 1, 1957, the taxpayer, an author, and corporation Y, a publisher, executed an agreement under which the taxpayer granted to the publisher the exclusive right to print, publish and sell a book he had written. This agreement provides that the publisher will (1) pay the author specified royalties based on the actual cash received from the sale of the published work, (2) render semiannual statements of the sales, and (3) at the time of rendering each statement make settlement for the amount due. On the same day, another agreement was signed by the same parties, mutually agreeing that, in consideration of, and notwithstanding any contrary provisions contained in the first contract, the publisher shall not pay the taxpayer more than 100x dollars in any one calendar year. Under this supplemental contract, sums in excess of 100x dollars accruing in any one calendar year are to be carried over by the publisher into succeeding accounting periods; and the publisher shall not be required either to pay interest to the taxpayer on any such excess sums or to segregate any such sums in any manner.

(4) In June 1957, the taxpayer, a football player, entered into a twoyear standard player's contract with a football club in which he agreed to play football and engage in activities related to football during the twoyear term only for the club. In addition to a specified salary for the twoyear term, it was mutually agreed that as an inducement for signing the contract the taxpayer would be paid a bonus of 150x dollars. The taxpayer could have demanded and received payment of this bonus at the time of signing the contract, but at his suggestion there was added to the standard contract form a paragraph providing substantially as follows:

> The player shall receive the sum of 150 x dollars upon signing of this contract, contingent upon the payment of this 150 x dollars to an escrow agent designated by him. The escrow agreement shall be subject to approval by the legal representatives of the player, the Club, and the escrow agent.

Pursuant to this added provision, an escrow agreement was executed on June 25, 1957, in which the club agreed to pay 150 x dollars on that date to the Y bank, as escrow agent; and the escrow agent agreed to pay this amount, plus interest, to the taxpayer in installments over a period of five years. The escrow agreement also provides that the account established by the escrow agent is to bear the taxpayer's name; that payments from such account may be made only in accordance with the terms of the agreement; that the agreement is binding upon the parties thereto and their successors or assigns; and that in the event of the taxpayer's death during the escrow period the balance due will become part of his estate.

(5) The taxpayer, a boxer, entered into an agreement with a boxing club to fight a particular opponent at a specified time and place. The place of the fight agreed to was decided upon because of the insistence of the taxpayer that it be held there. The agreement was on the standard form of contract required by the state athletic commission and provided, in part, that for his performance taxpayer was to receive 16x percent of the gross receipts derived from the match. Simultaneously, the same parties executed a separate agreement providing for payment of the taxpayer's share of the receipts from the match as follows: 25 percent thereof not later than two weeks after the bout, and 25 percent thereof during each of the three years following the year of the bout in equal semiannual installments. Such deferments are not customary in prize fighting contracts, and the supplemental agreement was executed at the demand of the taxpayer. Upon the taxpayer's insistence, the agreements also provided than any telecast of the fight must receive his prior consent and that he was to approve or disapprove all proposed sales of radio and motion picture rights.. . .

Section 1.4511(a) of the Income Tax Regulations provides in part as follows:

> Gains, profits, and income are to be included in gross income for the taxable year in which they are actually or constructively received by the taxpayer unless includible for a different year in accordance with the taxpayer's method of accounting. . . .

And, with respect to the cash receipts and disbursements method of accounting, §1.4461(c)(1)(i) provides in part:

> Generally, under the cash receipts and disbursements method in the computation of taxable income, all items which constitute gross income (whether in the form of cash, property, or services) are to be included for the taxable year in which actually or constructively received. . . .

As previously stated, the individual concerned in each of the situations described above, employs the cash receipts and disbursements method of accounting. Under that method, as indicated by the abovequoted provisions of the regulations, he is required to include the compensation concerned in gross income only for the taxable year in which it is actually or constructively received. Consequently, the question for resolution is whether in each of the situations described the income in question was constructively received in a taxable year prior to the taxable year of actual receipt.

A mere promise to pay, not represented by notes or secured in any way, is not regarded as a receipt of income within the intendment of the cash receipts and disbursements method.

[Citations omitted] Also *C. Florian Zittel v. Commissioner*, 12 B.T.A. 675, in which, holding a salary to be taxable when received, the Board said: "Taxpayers on a receipts and disbursements basis are required to report only income actually received no matter how binding any contracts they may have to receive more."

This should not be construed to mean that under the cash receipts and disbursements method income may be taxed only when realized in cash. For, under that method a taxpayer is required to include in income that which is received in cash or cash equivalent. *W.P. Henritze v. Commissioner*, 41 B.T.A. 505. And, as stated in the abovequoted provisions of the regulations, the "receipt" contemplated by the cash method may be actual or constructive.

With respect to the constructive receipt of income, §1.451-2(a) of the Income Tax Regulations (which accords with prior regulations extending back to, and including, Article 53 of Regulations 45 under (the Revenue Act of 1918) provides, in part, as follows:

> Income although not actually reduced to a taxpayer's position is constructively received by him in the taxable year during which it is credited to his account or set apart for him so that he may draw upon it at any time. However, income is not constructively received if the taxpayer's control of its receipt is subject to substantial limitations or restrictions. Thus, if a corporation credits its employees with bonus stock, but the stock is not available to such employees until some future date, the mere crediting on the books of the corporation does not constitute receipt.[748]

Thus, under the doctrine of constructive receipt, a taxpayer may not deliberately turn his back upon income and thereby select the year for which he will report it. . . . Nor may a taxpayer, by a private agreement, postpone receipt of income from one taxable year to another. . . .

However, the statute cannot be administered by speculating whether the payor would have been willing to agree to an earlier payment. See, for example, *J.D. Amend, et ux., v. Commissioner*, 13 T.C. 178. . ., in which the court, citing a number of authorities for its holding, stated:

> It is clear that the doctrine of constructive receipt is to be sparingly used; that amounts due from a corporation but unpaid, are not to be included in the income of an individual reporting his income on a cash receipts basis unless it appears that the money was available to him, that the corporation was able and ready to pay him, that his right to receive was not restricted, and that his failure to receive resulted from exercise of his own choice.

Consequently, it seems clear that in each case involving a deferral of compensation a determination of whether the doctrine of constructive receipt is applicable must be made upon the basis of the specific factual situation involved.

---

748 [A forfeiture of three months' interest on a time deposit of one year or less is a "substantial limitation or restriction" which will prevent constructive receipt. Reg. §1.4512(a)(2). Eds.]

Applying the foregoing criteria to the situations described above, the following conclusions have been reached:

(1) The additional compensation to be received by the taxpayer under the employment contract concerned will be includible in his gross income only in the taxable years in which the taxpayer actually receives installment payments in cash or other property previously credited to his account. To hold otherwise would be contrary to the provisions of the regulations and the court decisions mentioned above.

(2) For the reasons in (1) above, it is held that the taxpayer here involved also will be required to include the deferred compensation concerned in his gross income only in the taxable years in which the taxpayer actually receives installment payments in cash or other property previously credited to his account.

In arriving at this conclusion and the conclusion reached in case "(1)," consideration has been given to §1.402(b)1 of the Income Tax Regulations and to Revenue Ruling 5737, C.B. 19571, 18, as modified by Revenue Ruling 57528, C.B. 19572, 263. Section 1.402(b)1(a)(1) provides in part, with an exception not here relevant, that any contribution made by an employer on behalf of an employee to a trust during a taxable year of the employer which ends within or with a taxable year of the trust for which the trust is not exempt under §501(a) of the Code, shall be included in income of the employee for his taxable year during which the contribution is made if his interest in the contribution is nonforfeitable at the time the contribution is made. Revenue Ruling 5737, as modified by Revenue Ruling 57528, held, *inter alia*, that certain contributions conveying fully vested and nonforfeitable interests made by an employer into separate independently controlled trusts for the purpose of furnishing unemployment and other benefits to its eligible employees constituted additional compensation to the employees includible, under §402(b) of the Code and §1.402(b)1(a) of the regulations, in their income for the taxable year in which such contributions were made. These Revenue Rulings are distinguishable from cases "(1)" and "(2)" in that, under all the facts and circumstances of these cases, no trusts for the benefit of the taxpayers were created and no contributions are to be made thereto. Consequently, §402(b) of the Code and §1.402(b)1(a)(1) of the regulations are inapplicable.

(3) Here the principal agreement provided that the royalties were payable substantially as earned, and this agreement was supplemented by a further concurrent agreement which made the royalties payable over a period of years. This supplemental agreement, however, was made before the royalties were earned; in fact, it was made on the same day as the principal agreement and the two agreements were a part of the same transaction. Thus, for all practical purposes, the arrangement from the beginning is similar to that in (1) above. Therefore, it is also held that the

author concerned will be required to include the royalties in his gross income only in the taxable years in which they are actually received in cash or other property.

(4) In arriving at a determination as to the includibility of the 150x dollars concerned in the gross income of the football player, under the circumstances described, in addition to the authorities cited above, consideration also has been given to Revenue Ruling 55727, C.B. 19552, 25, and to the decision in *E.T. Sproull v. Commissioner*, 16 T.C. 244.

In Revenue Ruling 55727, the taxpayer, a professional baseball player, entered into a contract in 1953 in which he agreed to render services for a baseball club and to refrain from playing baseball for any other club during the term of the contract. In addition to specified compensation, the contract provided for a bonus to the player or his estate, payable onehalf in January 1954 and onehalf in January 1955, whether or not he was able to render services. The primary question was whether the bonus was capital gain or ordinary income; and, in holding that the bonus payments constituted ordinary income, it was stated that they were taxable for the year in which received by the player. However, under the facts set forth in Revenue Ruling 55727 there was no arrangement, as here, for placing the amount of the bonus in escrow. Consequently, the instant situation is distinguishable from that considered in Revenue Ruling 55727.In *E.T.Sproull v. Commissioner*, 16 T.C. 244, affirmed, 194 Fed. (2d) 541, the petitioner's employer in 1945 transferred for the petitioner the amount of $10,500. The trustee was directed to pay out of principal to the petitioner the sum of $5,250 in 1946 and the balance, including income, in 1947. In the event of the petitioner's prior death, the amounts were to be paid to his administrator, executor, or heirs. The petitioner contended that the Commissioner erred in including the sum of $10,500 in his taxable income for 1945. In this connection, the court stated:

> . . . it is undoubtedly true that the amount which the Commissioner has included in petitioner's income for 1945 was used in that year for his benefit. . . in setting up the trust of which petitioner, or, in the event of his death then his estate, was the sole beneficiary. . . .
>
> The question then becomes. . . was "any economic or financial benefit conferred on the employee as compensation" in the taxable year. If so, it was taxable to him in that year. This question we must answer in the affirmative. The employer's part of the transaction terminated in 1945. It was then that the amount of the compensation was fixed at $10,500 and irrevocably paid out for petitioner's sole benefit. . . .

Applying the principles stated in the *Sproull* decision to the facts here, it is concluded that the 150x- dollar bonus is includible in the gross income of the football player concerned in 1957, the year in which the club unconditionally paid such amount to the escrow agent.

> (5) In this case, the taxpayer and the boxing club, as well as the opponent whom taxpayer had agreed to meet, are each acting in his or its own right, the proposed match is a joint venture by all of these participants, and the taxpayer is not an employee of the boxing club. The taxpayer's share of the gross receipts from the match belong to him and never belonged to the boxing club. Thus, the taxpayer acquired all of the benefits of his share of the receipts except the right of immediate physical possession; and, although the club retained physical possession, it was by virtue of an arrangement with the taxpayer who, in substance and effect, authorized the boxing club to take possession and hold for him. The receipts, therefore, were income to the taxpayer at the time they were paid to and retained by the boxing club by his agreement and, in substance, at his direction, and are includible in his gross income in the taxable year in which so paid to the club. See the Sproull case, supra, and Lucas v. Guy C. Earl, 281 U.S. 111.

As previously stated, in each case involving a deferral of compensation, a determination of whether the doctrine of constructive receipt is applicable must be made upon the basis of the specific factual situation involved.

Consistent with the foregoing, the nonacquiescence published in C.B. 1952- 2, 5, with respect to the decision in Commissioner v. James F. Oates, 18 T.C. 570, affirmed, 207 Fed. (2d) 711, has been withdrawn and acquiescence substituted therefor at page 5 of this Bulletin.

With respect to deductions for payments made by an employer under a deferred compensation plan, see §404(a)(5) of the 1954 Code and §1.404(a)12 of the Income Tax Regulations.

In the application of those sections to unfunded plans, no deduction is allowable for any compensation paid or accrued by an employer on account of any employee under such a plan except in the year when paid and then only to the extent allowable under §404(a). Thus, under an unfunded plan, if compensation is paid by an employer directly to a former employee, such amounts are deductible under §404(a)(5) when *actually paid in cash or other property to the employee*, provided that such amounts meet the requirements of §162 or §212.

. . .

More on Nonqualified Deferred Compensation

So far the income tax planning strategies we have seen are income-leveling, income-splitting with low bracket taxpayers, conversion, deferral and leverage. Deferred compensation practices are normally an effort at the tax strategy of tax-rate leveling, based on the belief that one is apt to have less income, and therefore be in a lower tax bracket, after one retires. The strategy is less reliable these days, now that top rates are at low levels compared to the past. Despite that, deferring income remains a common tax-planning strategy for taxpayers and a nemesis for the Treasury Department.

One need not stop at just one deferral of income. Taxpayers can contractually defer payments to dates later than when the payor originally contracted to defer payment; but to be effective for Federal Income Tax purposes, the new contract must be formed before the due date for payment under the first contract. (Absent a specific agreement, state law generally requires payment for goods or services within a reasonable time after performance.) Otherwise, the taxpayer has constructive receipt when the payment is proffered with no further deferral.

> **To illustrate:** Mr. Oates was a life insurance agent who sold a large number of policies. The contract between Oates and the insurance company provided for initial premiums paid to Oates as well as "renewal premiums" payable after the customers renewed a contract that would otherwise expire. Oates entered into a contract to defer payment of the initial premiums. Before the renewal premiums were due (but long after he had performed the services that gave him the right to payment), Oates and the company agreed to a new contract further deferring receipt of the renewal commissions. The deferral worked for Federal Income Tax purposes. Oates was not taxed until he had actual receipt of the payments due under the second contract, in accordance with that second contract.[749]

Offers made in the course of bargaining are not taxed. You can see from the football player case in the Revenue Ruling that one can defer income that the opposing party is willing to pay now (in the player's case, it was a bonus), but rejects in the course of bargaining over the final compensation contract. The IRS could not possibly administer any other rule.

It is now time to go back to §83 and "restricted property." Section 83(a) of the Code was enacted after Rev. Rul. 60-31. As you know, it provides that people who receive property in exchange for services are taxed when the property is theirs, but it contains a big limitation, namely that there is no current tax *if* the property is non-transferable *and* subject to a substantial risk of forfeiture for some good reason, such as going to work for a competitor, where that is a meaningful possibility. However, the moment the property becomes transferable *or* nonforfeitable, the restriction is said to "lapse," and the full value of the property at that later date is taxable to the service provider, minus whatever she paid for the property.

> **To illustrate:** Zip.com, Inc. recently hired Silvia, a dynamic young executive, to come to work for them. As part of the bargaining, Zip.com agreed to transfer 1,000 shares of its stock to Silvia; but the stock certificates bear a legend that says "these shares are nontransferable and forfeitable in accordance with a contract between Silvia and Zip.com." The contract says that the stock will

749 Commissioner v. Oates, 207 F.2d 711 (1953). See also Veit v. Commissioner, 8 T.C. 809 (1947) where an executive deferred a bonus that was already earned, but not yet payable to him, in connection with renewing his employment contract. He was held entitled to defer the tax until the deferred payment date.

not be transferable for 10 years and that Silvia will forfeit the stock if she goes to work for any other Internet-related company in the next 10 years.

There is an important detail. Section 83(b) lets her elect to accelerate the taxation of the value of the restricted property, such as stock, that she received to the day she received the property. That means she pays ordinary income tax on the bargain element (in Sylvia's case the value of the 1000 shares) when she gets the restricted property. This is not as suicidal as it sounds, because if she does so, any subsequent gain will be taxable as a capital gain when she sells the stock. The risk to her of a §83(b) election is that if she forfeits the stock, she gets no basis (and therefore no tax deduction) beyond whatever she paid for the stock, even though she was taxed on the bargain element of her stock purchase by virtue of her election.[750] If she does not forfeit the stock, Reg. §1.83-2(a) gives her a basis in the property equal to its value when she makes the election, plus what she paid for the stock, if anything.

Section 83 and Revenue Ruling 60-31 both provide that if the promise of payment is supported by an escrow of money, then the future recipient of the money is taxed now under §83. The theories vary; the ruling taxes the escrow as an "economic benefit," whereas Reg. §1.83-3(e) taxes it as property. Providing for possible forfeiture of escrowed funds is the way to prevent escrow funds from being currently taxed.

So far, we have looked at the payee's side. What about the payor's deduction? The answer is that the payor cannot claim a deduction unless and until the payee reports gross income from the property.[751]

Problem 9-4:

Which of the following amounts of income are deferred, and if so, until when? Assume that the taxpayers are on the cash method and use the calendar year.

1) Boxer agrees in advance of fight that he will be paid the prize money in equal installments in the next three years.

2) Same, but the money is placed in an escrow account for his benefit.

3) Same as "(2)," but the money in the escrow account is subject to forfeiture if the boxer, who is in top form, engages in another boxing match in the next three years.

750 See §83(b)(1), last sentence.

751 §§ 83(h) and 404 (similar rule for amounts paid from trusts used to fund pension and similar plans).

4) Congregation, wishing its 45-year old Rabbi a secure future, promises to pay him $30,000 per year for the rest of his life, starting at age 65. Congregation buys an annuity in its own name to fund the obligation, and retains the annuity contract.

5) Lawyer's new client, Start-up Co., issues its lawyer 10 shares of stock as compensation. The stock is not restricted.

6) The stock described in "(5)" is nontransferable but not forfeitable.

7) The stock described in "(5)" is nontransferable and is forfeitable.

8) Assume "(7)" to be the case, would you advise the lawyer to make the §83(b) election? What are the considerations for the lawyer?

9) An artist feels a sudden inspiration and paints a good painting, demonstrably worth $5,000. Can she make the §83(b) election as to the art work?

10) Telemarketer is entitled to commissions that she has earned in the sense of having provided the necessary services. Before the commissions are due, she contracts to defer them yet again.

11) You represent Buzz, a successful executive used to making $500,000 per year. He has been offered $1 million as a signing bonus to be president of Grabber Industries, Inc. Would you advise him to defer the bonus? If so, how can he get some reasonable assurance that he will be paid the deferred bonus without paying a current tax?

More on Nonqualified Stock Options and §83

Sometimes §83 works in two steps, starting with the grant of an option to buy property, followed by a bargain purchase of the property itself, which can also be taxed or deferred under §83. There are also specialized "qualified stock options," not discussed here.

The basic rule for options received as compensation for services is that they are tax deferred unless they have a readily ascertainable fair market value.[752] The regulations on what makes an option transferable are so narrow that it is rare for a option to have a readily ascertainable value, even if the stock that the option covers is traded on a stock market. Assuming the option has no readily ascertainable value, the recipient defers including the value of the option in income until

752 §83(e)(3) and Reg. §1.83-7(b).

she buys the stock. At that point, the bargain inherent in the deal is taxable, unless the stock is "restricted." If the stock is restricted, there will be no tax until one of the restrictions lapse.

> **To illustrate:** Buzz, the rising executive, recently went to work for Cell Computers, Inc. ("CCI"). CCI stock trades at $10/share on the New York Stock Exchange. There are also CCI options that trade on the stock exchange, but they all expire 6 months or less after their issue dates. As part of the bargaining, CCI granted Buzz the right to buy 1 million shares of CCI for $8/share. The options will remain outstanding for two years, which means they have an unascertainable value[753] because the time that the options are outstanding is so long that they are unlike the 6-month options traded on the stock market. As a result, Buzz reports no income when he gets the options.[754] A year later, when CCI stock is selling for $25/share, Buzz exercises the option, paying $8/share for the CCI stock. At that point, he bagged a $17/share profit. Unless the CCI stock he buys is "restricted," he will have to report $17/share of ordinary income from compensation. That may be a good idea if he expects the stock to rise, because once this bargain element is taxed, the CCI stock is a capital asset (with a $25/share basis) when he sells the stock at favorable long-term capital gains rates. Assuming the stock is "restricted" and that the restrictions lapse when the stock is worth $30/share, the result is a $22/share gain (i.e., $30 minus $8 cost), all of which is ordinary income from compensation. At that point the stock gets a $30 basis.

Getting options as part of a compensation package is often crucial to the bargaining over executive compensation. The employer will generally want the option deal to be taxable to the executive as early as possible so that it can claim the deduction. Under §83(h),there is no deduction unless and until the recipient has taxable income.

Deferral of Qualified Deferred Compensation

"Qualified" deferred compensation plans offer the deluxe form of deferred compensation, but they are exceptionally complicated because, in order to pass muster, they must meet both the requirements of §§ 401-418E of the Code as well as companion rules policed by the Labor Department pursuant to the Employee Retirement Income Security Act of 1974 (known as "ERISA). "ERISA lawyers" are viewed as super specialists. Qualified plans offer the benefits of:

a) Current income tax deductions for employer contributions;

b) Employees exclude the contributions until they are paid out, even though their rights may have vested under their plan; and

753 Reg. §1.83-7(b)(2).

754 See Commissioner v. LoBue, 351 U.S. 243 (1956).

c) The investment income of the plan is tax-free until paid out.[755]

3. Payments under the Cash Method

Read Reg. §1.461-1(a)

a. Actual Payments

Payments under the cash method are generally considered made when they are delivered to the payee. Posting a payment by mail counts as a delivery. For example, a charitable contribution in the form of a check is made in the taxable year in which the check is mailed, provided the check is honored and paid and there are no restrictions as to time and manner of its payment.[756] Some deductions are available to cash method taxpayers even thought there is no apparent current expenditure; examples include depreciation and bad debts.

Now what about the real currency -- credit cards? Stores often issue credit cards to their customers. When the customer makes a purchase, the store tenders the merchandise and the customer owes the store the money. The store later mails the customer a bill. Should these be treated differently from bank credit cards like Visa and MasterCard where the taxpayer incurs a debt to a third party (bank) in order to finance the purchase? Is it really any different from just promising to pay a merchant? When is payment delivered?

REV. RUL. 78-39

19781 C.B.

. . .

Advice has been requested whether the use of a credit card to pay an expense for medical care is "payment" sufficient to support a deduction of the amount of the charge as an expense for medical care "paid during the taxable year," for the year the credit card charge was made, under §213 of the Internal Revenue Code of 1954.

An individual (cardholder), who files tax returns on a calendar year basis, uses credit cards issued by a bank to purchase goods and services. The contract between the cardholder and the bank includes a provision that the cardholder agrees to pay the bank the total amount on the charge statement used to document each purchase. The bank provides blank charge statements (drafts) to participating vendors from whom the cardholder may make purchases by use of the bank credit card.

November 15, 1976, the cardholder used the bank credit card to pay a hospital $500 for medical services rendered to the cardholder. The bank billed the cardholder for this charge in

755 §§ 401(a) and 501(a).

756 Rev. Rul. 54-465, 1954-2 C.B. 93; Estate of Modie J. Spiegel v. Commissioner, 12 T.C. 524 (1949), acq.

December 1976, but the cardholder made no payment until January 1977. The cardholder paid the full amount of the indebtedness to the bank during the course of calendar year 1977.

The specific question presented is whether the $500 payment to the hospital by the use of a bank credit card is includible in the medical expense deductions claimed on the cardholder's 1976 tax return.

Section 213(a) of the Code allows as a deduction expenses paid during the taxable year, not compensated for by insurance or otherwise, for medical care of the taxpayer, the taxpayer's spouse, or dependent, subject to certain limitations.

Section 1.2131 (a)(1) of the Income Tax Regulations provides, in pertinent part, that a deduction is allowable only to individuals and only with respect to medical expenses actually paid during the taxable year, regardless of when the incident or event that occasioned the expense occurred and regardless of the method of accounting employed by the taxpayer in making income tax returns. Thus, if the medical expenses are incurred but not paid during the taxable year, no deduction for such expenses shall be allowed for such year.

In the instant case, when the cardholder used the bank credit card to pay the hospital for the medical expenses, the cardholder became indebted to a third party (the bank) in such a way that the cardholder could not prevent the hospital from receiving payment. The credit card draft received by the hospital from the cardholder could be deposited in the bank and credited to the hospital's account as if it were a check.

Since the cardholder's use of the bank credit card created the cardholder's own debt to a third party, the use of the bank credit card to pay a hospital for medical services is equivalent to use of borrowed funds to pay a medical expense. The general rule is that when a deductible payment is made with borrowed money, the deduction is not postponed until the year in which the borrowed money is repaid. Such expenses must be deducted in the year they are paid and not when the loans are repaid. *William J. Granan*, 55 T.C. 753 (1971).

Accordingly, the $500 payment made by bank credit card to the hospital is includible in the medical expense deductions claimed on the cardholder's 1976 tax return.

Notes on Unpaid Amounts

If a cash method taxpayer lends $100, it creates a basis in the debt of $100. If it is not repaid, the lender can claim a bad debt deduction. If, however, the taxpayer does not advance money, but only services, in exchange for a debt (such as a promissory note), there is no basis in the debt because no capital in the sense of after-tax dollars were invested in the debt. That means a cash-method taxpayer gets no basis in receivables from services because he has not been taxed on them, and so -- for lack of basis -- a cash method taxpayer cannot claim a bad-debt loss on unpaid service-based receivables.[757]

757 Raich v. Commissioner, 46 T.C. 604 (1966).

To illustrate: Portia Klopman, a cash method lawyer, charges a client $150 for services rendered. Because she is on the cash method, she does not report any income unless and until she is paid. If she is not paid, and the law allowed her to claim a $150 bad debt deduction, the result would be a tax subsidy to her because she would report a deduction, but no offsetting $150 of income, even though no money or property changed hands in the transaction. The income tax laws prevent this result by assigning zero basis to her debt.

Accrual-method taxpayers do get a basis in their accounts receivable arising from their services. Their basis is equal to the amount they include in income.

ALSOP v. COMMISSIONER

290 F.2d 726 (2d Cir.1961)

FRIENDLY, Circuit Judge.

[The taxpayer was a cash method author whose literary agent, Rowe Wright, intercepted and embezzled royalties aggregating about $57,000 for petitioner's account from various foreign publishers. Alsop discovered the crime in 1952, fired Wright, and got a roughly $47,000 judgment against Wright in 1952 and a second judgment for about $10,000 in 1953. In 1952, Alsop deducted the unpaid 1952 judgment as a "Loss due to embezzlement and defalcation of funds by agent," which caused a net loss for the year. In his 1953 return, as amended, Alsop deducted the unpaid 1953 judgment, as well as a net operating loss carryover from 1952. In the amended return for 1954, Alsop claimed a further deduction of the net operating loss carryover. Alsop recovered about $11,000 in 1954, but did not include this as 1954 income. The IRS disallowed the embezzlement losses and the resulting NOLs and claimed that the 1954 recovery was taxable. The Tax Court agreed with the IRS as to the losses and uncollected judgments on the theory that Alsop had no basis in the embezzled and uncollected funds.]

. . .

. . . Petitioner was on a cash receipts and disbursements basis. Section 23(e) can hardly be read as permitting a deduction for the deprivation of income taxpayer has not received. . . .

Normally, indeed, "receipt of income by an agent is equivalent to receipt by the principal and such income is either actually or constructively received by him," 2 Mertens, Law of Federal Income Taxation (1955), p. 19 . . . . But this rule can hardly apply where the agent of a cash basis taxpayer spirits away income of whose receipt the taxpayer never knew. Cf. Stoumen v. C.I.R., 3 Cir., 1953, 208 F.2d 903, 906 . . . . What Rowe Wright did was to transform taxpayer's accounts receivable from the publishers into a claim in tort against the agent. That this was an economic loss to taxpayer is undeniable; but it was not the kind of loss that would appear in a cash receipts and disbursements system of income accounting.

. . .

With respect to the [approximately $11,000] recovered in 1954, taxpayer's argument is that this represented income of the years when the royalties were received and is excluded from 1954 income under §111 of the 1954 Code, 26 U.S.C.A. §111, providing that "Gross income does not include income attributable to the recovery during the taxable year of a bad debt, prior tax, or delinquency amount, to the extent of the amount of the recovery exclusion with respect to such debt, tax or amount" since, if the embezzlement losses are disallowed, the recovery would come within the definition of "recovery exclusion" in paragraph (b)(4). If the first step in taxpayer's argument were correct, the second would follow; but it is not. These payments constitute 1954 income not because they are attributable to a "recovery" but because they became income to this cash basis taxpayer in 1954 for the first time.

Affirmed.

b. Constructive Payment Doctrine?

There is no "constructive payment" doctrine. The rationale is that a deduction would be a matter of legislative grace, and Congress has not seen fit to enact a constructive deduction.[758]

4. Deductibility of Prepayments under the Cash or Accrual Method

Read §§ 263(a) and 461(g)

You can conceptually assign expenditures to three categories. Number one is §262, which renders many expenditures mere nondeductible consumption. The remaining expenditures generally offset one's tax base. The next slice cuts perpendicular to the first one; §263 declares that expenditures that result in "permanent improvements and betterments" cannot be immediately deducted, leaving the rest as "current" expenditures -- those that can be deducted immediately.

Capitalized expenditures create new assets or are added to the basis of existing assets. A simple example is the purchase of an apartment building held for rental income. Clearly, one cannot deduct the building's cost against one's taxes when one buys it, as one capitalizes purchase price along with major improvements to the building.

Notice how the imaginary grid renders only one third of the items currently deductible. Sections 262 and 263 affect both cash and accrual-method taxpayers. Capitalized expenditures increase one's basis in property, and may decrease gain (or increase loss) on the sale of the property.

If one is a cash-method taxpayer who spends money that benefits future periods, one must spread out the prepayment to match the time it relates to.

---

758 Vander Poel Francis & Co., Inc. v. Commissioner, 8 T.C.407 (1947).

To illustrate: Mrs. Gasgoine buys a two-year casualty insurance policy to cover risks associated with owning an apartment building run as a business. Section 263 forces her to capitalize the portion of the payment attributable to the following year, whatever the proration might turn out to be. The remaining portion, consisting of this year's premium, is a currently deductible business expense deduction. The capitalized expenditures for the insurance become deductible in future years in proportion to the life of the policy.[759]

If the IRC did not defer deductions this way, taxpayers would regularly distort their income by prepaying interest, business rental costs and the like.

To illustrate: If a business tenant paid for the last three months of this year plus the next two years at the time of signing a business lease, he can deduct 3/27ths of the rent this year, and 12/27ths of the prepayment in each of the next two years.[760] If the tenant could instead deduct the full cost of the lease on prepayment, the tenant's business would appear to have made an unduly small amount of money this year and an unduly large amount of money in next two years. Neither financial nor tax accounting allow this result.

There is a little slack for *de minimis* prepayments. The Regulations require capitalization of expenses that create an asset with a useful life extending *substantially* beyond the end of the current tax year.[761] In *Zaninovitch v. Commissioner*[762] the Ninth Circuit case held, in applying Reg. §1.461-1(a)(1) to prepaid rent, that the useful life of an asset extends substantially beyond the end of the current year only if, at the time of its acquisition, the asset has a useful life exceeding one year.

To illustrate: XYZ a cash basis, calendar year partnership that had made a December payment of rent covering the 12-month period ending with the next November, was allowed to deduct the payment in full for the year in which it was made. The rationale for allowing the deduction is that the asset (prepaid rent) did not have a value lasting over a year (but instead only 11 months). The Supreme Court seemingly approved of *Zaninovitch* in another case, opening up a small can of legal worms.[763]

759 See Commissioner v. Boyleston Market Ass'n, 131 F.2d 966 (1st Cir. 1942).

760 See Reg. §1.461-1(a)(1).

761 Id.

762 616 F.2d 429 (9th Cir. 1980), rev'g., 69 T.C. 605 (1978).

763 See Hillsboro National Bank v. Commissioner, 460 U.S. 370 (1983).

Despite the Ninth's Circuit's questionable decision, the majority view is that rental and interest expenses are deductible with the passage of time, and that prepayments are not immediately deductible.[764]

Notice that the converse of the anti-prepayment rule does not apply; taxpayers can put off paying their deductible expenses and then pay them in full in a high income year, assuming they deal with obligees who are willing to tolerate such shenanigans. For example, one might manage to stave off a bank from collecting interest this year in order to move the payment (and deduction) into next year. This might be a clever strategy if one expected a sharp rise in one's income next year. So, the cash method, as supplemented by §263, does not defer receipts of prepaid income, but it does defer prepaid deductions.

a. Prepaid and Capitalized Interest of a Cash-Method Taxpayer

A cash method taxpayer has no basis in a promissory note she draws up; it is just a piece of paper. As a result, if she gives her promissory note to pay an interest obligation, it has been held that the giving of the note did not constitute a "payment" of interest as required by §163(a).[765] That is not surprising.

What if a cash method taxpayer borrows money from the lender to make the payment of "points" on a mortgage from the same lender? The judicial answer is that the taxpayer literally and legally did not "make a payment" and so is not entitled to a tax deduction, and therefore could only claim the deduction for the points over the life of his loan.[766]

Whatever its wisdom, the case law has massed in favor of the Commissioner. For example, *Battlestein v. Commissioner*[767] ruled that the taxpayer was not entitled to deduct points that he borrowed from the creditor, commingled with other money at the same bank and paid out of the account. Evidently, the case would come out the other way if the taxpayer borrowed the money for the points from a bank across the street. That suggests the right tax planning strategy for such taxpayers is to borrow from the bank across the street. If so, is there something wrong with this picture? Is the conclusion that a cash method taxpayer with good credit is entitled to an immediate deduction if he borrows from Peter to pay Paul, but he postpones the deduction if he borrows from Paul to pay Paul?

Capitalization of interest was greatly broadened by §269A, enacted as part of the Tax Reform Act of 1982. It requires many merchants, manufacturers and contractors to capitalize indirect expenses, including interest, real estate taxes, and overhead, into their outputs. The details are

764 See Reg. §1.461-4(e); Rev. Rul. 83-84, 1983-1 C.B. 97; H. Rpt. No. 97-760, 97th Cong. 2d Sess., 553 (1982) (interest) and Rev. Rul. 60-122, 1960-1 C.B. 50 (rent).

765 See, e.g., Don E. Williams Co. v. Commissioner, 429 U.S. 569 (1977).

766 See especially Cathcart v. Commissioner, 36 T.C.M. 1321 (1977)

767 631 F.2d 1182 (5th Cir. 1980), cert. denied (1981).

dizzying. It may be appropriate from an accounting viewpoint to capitalize such interest, but the price in complexity seems excessive to many.

Incidentally, the federal government has several computers with national econometric models which can be used to predict the impact of even minute changes in the tax law, using a base of over 100 million tax returns.[768] One wonders if the very existence of these tools encourages complicated tinkering with the tax law, as, for example, §269A.

b. Prepaid Expenses of Cash-Method Farmers

Farmers have interesting opportunities to avoid income taxes by claiming current deductions for planting crops or fattening animals and deferring the income into the following year. For example, if Farmer Fred planted corn in May and harvested it in September, he might wait until January to actually sell his corn. That means he got a big deduction for seeds, planting and harvesting in the present year, which he can use to offset his income from other sources. Next year, he will report the income from selling the corn, but he will also have offsetting deductions for planting and harvesting the next crop. He will hope for a profit in the second year, but if he stays at it, he will push forward the day of reckoning for the first year's tax bonanza for a long time by staying on this tax accounting treadmill. If he is energetic, he may be able to expand his farm operations little by little, generating some further current taxable income while increasing his wealth.

In the bad old days various tax shelters were built on this simple model. A fairly extreme example was the cattle feeding shelter in which investors made year-end purchases of feed to fatten up Western cattle in Mid-Western feedlots. The cattle would be sold in the following year and the investor would show a modest cash profit, approximately equal to the cash he put into the deal. In the meantime, like Farmer Fred, the investor captured a tax bonanza in the first year. If the taxpayers were troubled by the prospect of paying taxes in the second year, they would invest in a similar deal in the second year, putting off their tax problem once again. Tax shelter promoters, like drug dealers, could profit handsomely by addicting the public into repetitive purchases. The Tax Reform Act of 1986 generally took people off the tax shelter treadmill by reducing top tax rates (the carrot) and by enacting §469, which suspends losses for passive investors (the stick).

Section 464 now prohibits members of "farming syndicates" from using the cash-method with respect to seed, feed and the like. Genuine farmers are not affected. Also, §448 prohibits tax shelters from using the cash method, largely overlapping §464. The following Revenue Ruling is germane to the topic.

768 See Written Testimony of the Staff of the Joint Committee on Taxation Regarding the Revenue Estimating Process, January 5, 1995, at pp. 4-8.

REV. RUL. 79-229

19792 C.B. 210

ISSUE

In which year may a person engaged in the business of raising or feeding livestock and using the cash receipts and disbursements method of accounting deduct amounts paid for livestock feed to be consumed in a subsequent year?

LAW AND ANALYSIS

Generally, amounts paid by persons engaged in the business of raising or feeding livestock, who are on the cash receipts and disbursements method of accounting, for feed to be consumed by their livestock in the taxable year of payment or in a subsequent taxable year are ordinary and necessary business expenses within the meaning of section 162 of the Code. See section 1.16212 of the Income Tax Regulations. However, three tests must be met before such a person may deduct in the year of payment the cost of feed to be consumed by the person's own livestock in the subsequent taxable year. *First,* the expenditure for the feed must be a payment for the purchase of feed rather than a deposit; *second,* the prepayment must be made for a business purpose and not merely for tax avoidance; and *third,* the deduction of such costs in the taxable year of prepayment must not result in a material distortion of income. The purchase of a commodity future contract, however, is considered to be the purchase of a right to acquire the specific commodity rather than a purchase of the commodity itself, see *Modesto Dry Yard, Inc. v. Commissioner,* 14 T.C. 374 (1950), acq., 19502 C.B. 3, and accordingly, is excluded from the coverage of this Revenue Ruling.

Whether a particular expenditure is a deposit or a payment depends on the facts and circumstances of each case. When it can be shown that the expenditure is not refundable and is made pursuant to an enforceable sales contract, it will not be considered a deposit. The following factors, although not all inclusive, are indicative of a deposit rather than a payment: the absence of specific quantity terms; the right to a refund of any unapplied payment credit at the termination of the contract, see *Lillie v. Commissioner,* 45 T.C. 54 (1965), aff'd per curiam, 370 F.2d 562 (9th Cir. 1966); the treatment of the expenditure as a deposit by the seller; and the right to substitute other goods or products for the feed ingredients specified in the contract. However, a provision permitting substitution of ingredients for the purpose of varying the particular feed mix to accommodate the current diet requirements of the livestock for which the feed was purchased will not be considered indicative of a deposit. The fact that adjustment is made to the contract price to reflect market value at the date of delivery, is not, standing alone, conclusive of a deposit.

The second test requires that the prepayment must be made for a valid business purpose and not merely for tax avoidance.

Generally, the factor that distinguishes the earlier court decisions allowing a deduction for prepaid feed costs from those disallowing the deduction is the acquisition of, or the reasonable expectation by the taxpayer of receiving, some business benefit as a result of the prepayment. . . . Examples of business benefits include, but are not limited to: fixing maximum prices and securing an assured feed supply or securing preferential treatment in anticipation of a feed shortage. Whether the prepayment was a condition normally imposed by the seller as an independent arm's length transaction and whether such condition was otherwise meaningful should also be taken into account in determining whether there was a business purpose for the prepayment.

However, in each of the above cases in which a business purpose was found, the taxpayers were traditional farmers and had a significant capital investment in agricultural assets in addition to the feed and animals involved. For this reason, the courts concluded that a business purpose existed when the entire farming business was benefitted.

When the transaction in question is carried out in the context of closely held investor oriented groups, which are usually formed to take advantage of syndicated tax shelter schemes, there is little if any capital investment in assets other than the feed. Generally, the "prepaid" feed is pledged as security to purchase the cattle to be fed. Consequently, the Service will look carefully at the substantive purpose behind such transactions to determine the motives behind them. A motive based on the Federal income tax advantages of prepayment of feed costs and the consequent deferral of resulting income is not a valid business purpose.

The business practice of prepayment does not necessarily refute the existence of a primary tax avoidance purpose or a material distortion.

In addition, the fact that the first two tests are satisfied does not automatically mean that the expenditure will be deductible in the year paid. A deferral of the deduction may be necessary to clearly reflect the taxpayer's income. The legitimate use of the cash or accrual methods of accounting does not encompass certain tax shelter techniques, and thus, the presence of such techniques supports the exercise of the Service's broad administrative authority to disallow such practices through the timing discretion provided in sections 446(b), 451, and 461 of the Code.

Section 461 of the Code and the regulations thereunder control the time for the allowance of deductions and provide, in part, that the amount of any allowable deduction shall be taken for the taxable year that is proper under the method of accounting used in computing taxable income. The timing authority in section 461 of the Code is therefore subject to the clear reflection of income requirement contained in section 446(b). . . .

Section 446(b) of the Code provides, in part, that if the method of accounting used by the taxpayer does not clearly reflect income, the computation of taxable income shall be made under such method, as, in the opinion of the Secretary, does clearly reflect income.

Furthermore, section 1.4611(a)(1) of the regulations provides that an expenditure resulting in the creation of an asset having a useful life extending substantially beyond the close of the taxable year may not be deductible, or may be deductible only in part, for the taxable year in which made. Thus, although a taxpayer using the cash receipts and disbursements method of accounting generally can deduct expenses in the year paid. The taxpayer cannot do so if the allowance of a deduction in that year will produce a material distortion of income. . . . This rule applies equally to persons engaged in the business of farming. *Clement v. United States*, 580 F.2d 422 (Ct. Cl. 1978).

Some of the factors to be considered in determining whether the deduction results in a material distortion of income include, but are not limited to: the useful life of resulting assets during and beyond the taxable year paid, Rev. Rul. 68643, 19682 C.B. 76 (the relationship of the amount of the prepaid expenditure in question to the projected magnitude of the business in a subsequent year should therefore be considered, see *Cole*); the materiality of the expenditure in relation to the taxpayer's income for the year, *Clement*; the purpose for paying in advance, *Baird v. Commissioner*, 68 T.C. 115 (1978); the customary, legitimate business practice of the taxpayer in conducting livestock operations; the amount of the expenditure in relation to past purchases, and the time of the year the expenditure was made; whether the taxes paid by a taxpayer consistently deducting prepaid feed costs over a period of years are reasonably comparable to the taxes that would have been paid had the same taxpayer consistently not paid in advance.

HOLDING

Unless a taxpayer meets all of the three tests described above, amounts paid for feed to be consumed by livestock in a subsequent taxable year will not be deductible in the taxable year paid. *See also* section 447 of the Code which requires certain corporations engaged in farming to compute the taxable income therefrom on an accrual method of accounting. *See also* section 464 for additional limitations on deductions in the case of farming syndicates.[769]

. . .

Deposits

The ruling's statement that a deposit is not deductible because it is not a payment is correct. The hallmark of a deposit is the holder's contingent duty to repay it, which makes it comparable to a loan. A typical example of a nontaxable deposit is money customers pay in connection with

769 [See §464(d), limiting deductions for prepaid seed and feed to 50% of total farm expenses. Eds.]

getting an account with a utility company, paid by customers to comfort the utility company that its exposure to nonpayment of its utility bills is at limited.[770]

Notes

The ruling has found a place in the heart of the judiciary. In *Keller v. Commissioner*[771] the Tax Courtand the Eighth Circuit both applied the three-pronged test of the Ruling to prepayments for the soft costs of drilling an oil well. That means Revenue Rulings 79-229 has a broad but uncertain scope.

Problem 9-5:

Dr. Peabody and Patient are on the cash method of accounting and both use the calendar year. Assume the costs of Peabody's services are deductible by patient. What result to each if:

1) Peabody performs a root canal operation on Patient in November and Patient pays him cash in November.

2) Same as "(1)" but the payment is in the form of a negotiable note issued by Patient.

3) Same as "(1)" but Patient pays in January.

4) Peabody purchases three years worth of dental malpractice insurance in November of this year.

5) Now read Reg. §1.461-1(a)(1). Can you reconcile it with the result in *Zaninovitch*?

6) Peabody performs the root canal operation, but Patient never pays. Can Peabody claim a bad-debt deduction?

7) Same as "(1)" except that Patient, while in Peabody's office and holding his checkbook, offers to pay Peabody in November, but Peabody tells him to keep the money and pay him in January of next year.

---

770 See Commissioner v. Indianapolis Power & Light Co., 493 U.S. 203 (1990), aff'g 857 F.2d 1162 (7th Cir. 1988). holding that deposits by high credit risk customer were not taxable.

771 725 F2d 1173, (1984), aff'g 79 TC 7 (1982). The costs at issue are known as "intangible drilling and development costs" and are described in §263(c).

8) Same as "(7)," but the contract calls for payment in January of next year.

9) Peabody has subscribed to a Visa card service that he uses for billing his patients. The service requires him to get receipts from embossing forms with the Visa card, then taking the embossed, signed forms to the bank, which pays him 97% of their face amounts. What if in November Patient signs the embossed form, but Peabody does not bring the forms to the bank until next year and Patient does not pay the card bill for November until February of the following year?

10) Peabody mails out a check in payment for disposable syringes and pain killers on December 31. The payee corporation receives the check, which clears in due course, in January of the following year. It so happens that Patient sold the goods to Peabody. Peabody customarily makes these year-end payments.

11) Peabody recently had to borrow $100,000 to get a mortgage from the Friendly Bank to buy his home. The mortgage required him to pay two "points" ($2,000). The bank provided him with a gross amount of $102,000, but withheld $2,000. Assuming the points are normal in his vicinity, can he claim them as an itemized deduction on his tax return? (Do not consider the bank's side of the deal.)

5. Income on the Accrual Method

Read §446(c)(2) and Reg. §1.451-1(a) and 1.461-1(a)(2) and scan §448(a)-(c)

a. General Rules

The accrual method is the other overall method of accounting almost invariably used by larger businesses. The accrual method must be used by regular business corporations (known as "C corporations" in tax jargon because they are subject to Subchapter C of the Code).[772] Section 448 also imposes the accrual method on partnerships that have a C corporation as a partner and on any tax shelter (a very broadly defined term). Section 448(b) lets off farmers and most incorporated professional practices. The accrual method is imposed on all taxpayers for whom inventories are a material income-producing factor, but only as to the purchases and sale of their inventories.[773]

Taxpayers who use an accrual method of accounting must report items of gross income when (a) all the events have occurred which fix the right to receive such income, (b) the amount thereof can be determined with reasonable accuracy, *and* (c) the income is reasonably

772 §448(a)(1).

773 Reg. §1.446-1(c)(2)(i).

collectible.[774] Like cash-method taxpayers, if their expenses create an asset whose life lasts substantially beyond the close of the taxable year, those expenses must be capitalized.

It is important to recognize that a true accrual method does not depend upon the flow of cash, which is ignored, but instead depends upon the totality of events which, once they occur, trigger a finding of income. It is even a bit more confusing than that, because the system does not contemplate a present legal liability, only the coalescing of events that create the right to be paid.

> **To illustrate:** A solvent friend promises to pay you $1,000 if the sun rises tomorrow, but his payment will not be due until a year later. You must accrue the income at sunrise tomorrow if you are an accrual-method taxpayer, because the sunrise was the event that established the right to payment your friend is solvent, and the amount owed you is clear. If your friend fails to pay you a year later, you can then presumably claim a bad debt deduction under §166.

You must also recognize that there is more than one accrual method. In fact, accrual methods tend to be highly individualistic. For example, if you are in the business of manufacturing and selling ties by the box load, your internal accounting practices -- which dictates your application of the accrual method for tax purposes -- may report the sales income at any number of specific points in time such as:

1. When the customer puts in the order for a box of ties;
2. When the customer submits a signed order form of your making;
3. When you ship the ties; or
4. When you deliver the ties.

There are other possibilities as well. The important point is that the taxpayer should have a systematic accrual policy for financial reporting purposes and then use that policy for tax purposes on a consistent basis over the years. Accountants insist on using accounting methods consistently from year to year in order to accurately report income over the years. The Congress has legislated the same result by demanding that changes in methods of accounting be approved by the IRS in advance.

It is possible to use one financial reporting system for non-tax purposes and another for tax purposes but this requires maintaining yet another set of books in order to reconcile the two different systems.[775] Most taxpayers prefer to avoid that headache.

Accrual accounting does not exist solely to confound law students. It meets with greater approval from accountants because it tends to match income and deductions better than the

774 Reg. §1.451-1(a) and 1.461-1(c)(2).

775 Rev. Rul. 68-35, 1968-1 C.B. 190.

cash method, thereby showing a smoother and more realistic flow of net income and solvency over time.

So, can you remember any of this? Perhaps a strangely evocative passage from the following case would help:

KNIGHT-RIDDER NEWSPAPERS, INC. v. UNITED STATES

743 F.2d 781, 787-88 (5th Cir. 1984)

. . .

The initial issue in this case concerns the authority of the Commissioner to force a taxpayer to change accounting methods [under §446(b)], in particular to change from the cash to accrual method. These are the two most common accounting methods and could be said to emblemize the polar nature of the human spirit. The cash method simple, plodding, elemental stands firmly in the physical realm. It responds only through the physical senses, recognizing only the tangible flow of currency. Money is income when this raw beast actually feels the coins in its primal paw; expenditures are made only when the beast can see that it has given the coins away.

The accrual method, however, moves in a more ethereal, mystical realm. The visionary prophet, it recognizes the impact of the future on the present, and with grave foreboding or ecstatic anticipation, announces the world to be. When it becomes sure enough of its prophecies, it actually conducts life as if the new age has already come to pass. Transactions producing income or deductions spring to life in the eyes of the seer though nary a dollar has moved.

The Internal Revenue Code, the ultimate arbiter, stands to the side, shifting its eyes uneasily from the one being to the other. The Code is possessed of great wisdom and tolerance. It knows that man must generally choose his own way. Therefore, it leaves to the taxpayer the original choice of which accounting method to use. Section 446(c) specifically authorizes both the cash and accrual methods. . . .

Yet the Code also understands that either extreme possesses inherent weaknesses and can become blinded to reality. Thus the Code and subsequent Treasury Regulations empower the Secretary of the Treasury and the Commissioner of Internal Revenue to cure the blindness. Section 446(b) of the Code provides that if

> the method used does not clearly reflect income, the computation of taxable income shall be made under such method as, in the opinion of the secretary, does clearly reflect income.

. . .

b. Accrued Income as an Asset

When a taxpayer accrues an item of income, it has an "account receivable," which is an asset, whose basis is the amount of accrued income.[776] The accrual may turn out to have been a mistake because the obligor may never pay the taxpayer, or only pay in part. Default in payment results in a bad debt, which may, depending on the facts, be deductible as a business bad debt.

> **To illustrate:** Portia Klopman, the accrual method lawyer, charges a client $150 for services rendered. Because she is on the accrual method, she reports income of $150 and gets a $150 basis in the debt. If she is not paid, §166 allows her to claim a $150 bad debt deduction (or even less, since §166 authorizes partial losses for business debts) when some identifiable event occurs fixing the loss. There is no tax subsidy to her because, combining the results over the years, she will report a $150 deduction, and an offsetting $150 of income, even though no money or property changed hands in the transaction. If she did not get a deduction, it would be unfair because she would be taxed on income she demonstrably would never receive. Contrast this to the *Alsop* case where the cash method taxpayer reported no income from a promise of payment and was allowed no deduction when the promise of payment failed to materialize.[777]

Section 448(d)(5) helps out taxpayers dealing with payors who are chronic deadbeats. It provides that even if the taxpayer has otherwise earned the money under accrual concepts, it can avoid the accrual if experience indicates that the fee will probably not be paid. There is no need for such a provision for cash-method taxpayers.

Incidentally, whenever you find yourself dealing with an income tax question, whether in life or on law examinations, you should *always* first ask the following questions:

1. What is the taxpayer's taxable year? and,

2. What is the taxpayer's method of accounting?

c. Long-Term Contracts Regarding Interest and Rents

Does the accrual method, applied strictly, mean accrual-method lenders and landlords must accrue the full amount of the income under their loans and leases when their borrowers or tenants sign their leases, given that "all the events fixing the right to be paid" have seemingly occurred? The result would be preposterous if you considered a tenant that signed a 20-year lease on a prime Rockefeller Center property. The answer is that the courts and the IRS long ago

776 See, e.g., P.L.R. 9534023 (May 31, 1995); Scott v. Commissioner, 74 T.C. Memo 1157 (1997).

777 Alsop v. CIR, 290 F.2d 726 (CA2d 1961).

came to the rescue. These outcomes are consistent with accountants' preference for matching income and expenses, even if they do seem out of step with strict accrual accounting:

1. A landlord who signs a multi-year leasemust report rental income as time passes, as it provides the space;[778] and,

2. A lender defers reporting interest income until it is earned, which occurs continuously over time.[779]

6. The Dilemma of Early Receipts under the Accrual Method

In a pure accrual system a prepaid receipt is not income because it has not yet been earned. Nevertheless, government litigators have enjoyed great success in taxing such receipts and have thereby substantially accelerated revenues for the federal government. One needs to carefully sort out the theory under which advanced payments have been taxed. The case you are about to read established the first major incursion on pure accrual accounting, namely the *claim-of-right* doctrine. Even though it is an old case, it remains good law.

a. Claim-of-Right Doctrine Exception to Strict Accrual of Income

As you read this case, see if you can detect what accounting method the taxpayer used.

NORTH AMERICAN OIL CONSOLIDATED v. BURNET
286 U.S. 417 (S. Ct. 1932)

MR. JUSTICE BRANDEIS delivered the opinion of the Court.

The question for decision is whether the sum of $171,979.22 received by the North American Oil Consolidated in 1917, was taxable to it as income of that year.

The money was paid to the company under the following circumstances. Among many properties operated by it in 1916 was a section of oil land, the legal title to which stood in the name of the United States. Prior to that year, the Government, claiming also the beneficial ownership, had instituted a suit to oust the company from possession; and on February 2, 1916, it secured the appointment of a receiver to operate the property, or supervise its operations, and to hold the net income thereof. The money paid to the company in 1917 represented the net profits which had been earned from that property in 1916 during the receivership. The money was paid to the receiver as earned. After entry by the District Court in 1917 of the final decree dismissing

778 C.f., Rod Realty Co. v. Commissioner, 26 T.C.M. 243 (1967).

779 See, e.g. Rev. Rul. 83-84, 1983-1 CB 97.

the bill, the money was paid, in that year, by the receiver to the company. *United States v. North American Oil Consolidated*, 242 Fed. 723. The Government took an appeal (without supersedes) to the Circuit Court of Appeals. In 1920, that Court affirmed the decree. 264 Fed. 336. In 1922, a further appeal to this Court was dismissed by stipulation. 258 U.S. 633.

The income earned from the property in 1916 had been entered on the books of the company as its income. It had not been included in its original return of income for 1916; but it was included in an amended return for that year which was filed in 1918. Upon auditing the company's income and profits tax returns for 1917, the Commissioner of Internal Revenue determined a deficiency based on other items. The company appealed to the Board of Tax Appeals. There, in 1927 the Commissioner prayed that the deficiency already claimed should be increased so as to include a tax on the amount paid by the receiver to the company in 1917. The Board held that the profits were taxable to the receiver as income of 1916; and hence made no finding whether the company's accounts were kept on the cash receipts and disbursements basis or on the accrual basis. 12 B. T. A. 68. The Circuit Court of Appeals held that the profits were taxable to the company as income of 1917, regardless of whether the company's returns were made on the cash or on the accrual basis.... This Court granted a writ of certiorari....

It is conceded that the net profits earned by the property during the receivership constituted income. The company contends that they should have been reported by the receiver for taxation in 1916; that if not returnable by him, they should have been returned by the company for 1916, because they constitute income of the company accrued in that year; and that if not taxable as income of the company for 1916, they were taxable to it as income for 1922, since the litigation was not finally terminated in its favor until 1922.

First. The income earned in 1916 and impounded by the receiver in that year was not taxable to him, because he was the receiver of only a part of the properties operated by the company. Under §13 (c) of the Revenue Act of 1916, receivers who "are operating the property or business of corporations" were obliged to make returns "of net income as and for such corporations," and "any income tax due" was to be "assessed and collected in the same manner as if assessed directly against the organization of whose business or properties they have custody and control." The phraseology of this section was adopted without change in the Revenue Act of 1918, 40 Stat. 1057, 1081, c. 18, §239. The regulations of the Treasury Department have consistently construed these statutes as applying only to receivers in charge of the entire property or business of a corporation; and in all other cases have required the corporations themselves to report their income. Treas. Regs. 33, arts. 26, 209; Treas. Regs. 45, arts. 424, 622. That construction is clearly correct. The language of the section contemplates a substitution of the receiver for the corporation; and there can be such substitution only when the receiver is in complete control of the properties and business of the corporation. Moreover, there is no provision for the consolidation of the return of a receiver of part of a corporation's property or business with the return of the corporation itself. It may not be assumed that Congress intended to require the filing of two separate returns for the same year, each covering only a part of the corporate income, without making provision for consolidation so that the tax could be based upon the income as a whole.

Second. The net profits were not taxable to the company as income of 1916. For the company was not required in 1916 to report as income an amount which it might never receive. See *Burnet v. Logan*, 283 U.S. 404, 413. . . . There was no constructive receipt of the profits by the company in that year, because at no time during the year was there a right in the company to demand that the receiver pay over the money. Throughout 1916 it was uncertain who would be declared entitled to the profits. It was not until 1917, when the District Court entered a final decree vacating the receivership and dismissing the bill, that the company became entitled to receive the money. Nor is it material, for the purposes of this case, whether the company's return was filed on the cash receipts and disbursements basis, or on the accrual basis. In neither event was it taxable in 1916 on account of income which it had not yet received and which it might never receive.

Third. The net profits earned by the property in 1916 were not income of the year 1922 the year in which the litigation with the Government was finally terminated. They became income of the company in 1917, when it first became entitled to them and when it actually received them. If a taxpayer receives earnings under a claim of right and without restriction as to its disposition, he has received income which he is required to return, even though it may still be claimed that he is not entitled to retain the money, and even though he may still be adjudged liable to restore its equivalent. See *Board v. Commissioner*, 51 F.2d , 75, 76. Compare *United States v. S. S. White Dental Mfg. Co.*, 274 U.S. 398, 403. If in 1922 the Government had prevailed, and the company had been obliged to refund the profits received in 1917, it would have been entitled to a deduction from the profits of 1922, not from those of any earlier year. Compare *Lucas v. American Code Co., supra.*

Affirmed.

Problem 9-6:

1) What was the right accrual date? Could the taxpayer have accrued the $171,979.22 in 1922? In 1916? In 1917? If the taxpayer were on the cash method, when would it have had income on the facts of *North American Oil*?

2) Assume for a moment that North American Oil Consolidated later had to pay back some of the money that it got from the receiver, something the Supreme Court recognized as a possibility. Should North American Oil be entitled to deduct the repayment?

b. The §446(b) Power and Prepayments

Read §446(b)

Accrual method taxpayers often receive advance payments for goods, services, memberships, or subscriptions. Because the accrual method is indifferent to when cash is received or paid, you might rightly assume that an accrual taxpayer would ignore these receipts and disbursements. Nevertheless, the IRS has had great success in applying §446(b) to accrual method taxpayers, arguing that not reporting the income represents a distortion of income. Three major U.S. Supreme Court decisions (*Automobile Club of Michigan v. Commissioner*, 353 U.S. 180 (1957); *American Automobile Association v. United States*, 367 U.S. 687 (1961),[780] and *Schlude v. Commissioner*, 372 U.S. 128 (1963)) have warmly accepted the IRS's efforts to apply the §446(b) power in such cases. Legally, the Supreme Court's conclusion in each case was that the IRS did not abuse its discretion by behaving "arbitrarily and capriciously" in forcing current tax reporting of prepaid receipts. Realistically, it has changed the law to mean that in all but extreme cases, the accrual method taxpayer who obtains prepaid receipts might as well just give up and report the income now, because the taxpayer is virtually certain to lose if the issue is audited. Accountants would consider the Supreme Court's conclusions a major incursion on their profession's standards.

To illustrate: In *Schlude v. Commissioner* an accrual-method taxpayer that offered Arthur Murray Dance Studio dancing lessons, had to report the entire prepayment income under dance contracts when received. The contracts called for a fixed number of lessons, scheduled over a fixed period of time, with no make-up sessions for missed lessons, and no refunds for cancellations. The taxpayer claimed that the income was not earned until the lessons were given. The Supreme Court held that because as the lessons were "on demand," it is inappropriate to defer reporting the prepaid receipts. The taxpayer could not accelerate future expenses to track the accelerated income, so the matching of income and deductions was worsened, not improved, by the IRS's victory.

8. Successful Deferral of Prepaid Receipts by Accrual-Method Taxpayer

The IRS's troika of successes in the Supreme Court in the automobile and dance club cases does not mean that the taxpayer always loses when the IRS brandishes the §446(b) weapon; but, taxpayer success is definitely the exception. If the matching of expenses and income can be clearly demonstrated, and is not polluted by the claim that the clientele can get their services "on demand," the taxpayer may be able to overcome a §446(b) attack:

780 Nevertheless, the automobile clubs got their revenge by lobbying for and getting §456, which gives them by special interest legislation what they were denied in litigation.

To illustrate: In *Artnell Co. v. Commissioner*[781] the Chicago White Sox, an accrual method taxpayer, sold baseball tickets early in the baseball season, giving each customer a right to attend a set number of games, with adjusted dates in the case games were rained out. The White Sox tax year ended May 31, well after the ticket sales occurred. The IRS asserted that the ticket sales income should have been reported before May 31. The IRS was held to have abused its discretion because, unlike the "on demand cases," there was no uncertainty as to when the services would be performed. Matching the ticket sales to when the games were played was a proper way to match income and expenses, which resulted in a better reflection of income than the IRS's.

Not long after its triumphs in the courts, the IRS retreated as to prepayments for services. In Rev. Proc. 71-21,[782] the IRS generously allowed accrual-method taxpayers who receive prepayments in one taxable year for services to be performed before the end of the next taxable year to include the payments in gross income as earned, rather than as received. Receipts under a contract for the sale of services extending over more than two years cannot be deferred at all.[783] Would the Revenue Procedure have eliminated the controversy in *Artnell* if it had been in place at the time?

The IRS also retreated as to advance payments for goods and certain long-term contracts. The main feature of Reg. §1.451-5 is that it lets a merchant defer tax on the advance payment until the merchandise is delivered. If the sale is of inventory, the taxpayer must report the profit on the sale not later than the second tax year after the year in which the advanced payments are received. This is a generous provision for merchants and manufacturers and without it, the IRS victories in the automobile cases would generally preclude any opportunity to defer receipts from long- term sales of goods and other long-term contracts.

To illustrate: An accrual method merchant who sells a $25 gift certificate that can be redeemed for inventory at his store is allowed to defer the $25 advance payment until the certificate is redeemed.[784] He has to report the payment in income not later than the second year following the sale of the certificate, or else the full $25 is income at the time of receipt.

At a deeper level, should the law require matching the acceleration of income with acceleration of deductions? If taxpayers have to report cash prepayments as current income, does this mean they ought to be able to accelerate their associated deductions? Maybe, but you need to know that is generally not the law despite the distorted picture of income that results from only accelerating prepaid receipts.

781 400 F. 2d 981 (7th Cir. 1968), reversing and remanding 48 T.C. 411 (1967).

782 1971-2 C.B. 549.

783 Rev. Rul. 72-207, C.B. 1972-1 CB 126.

784 Reg. §1.451-5(a)(2).

Given that accountants seem to be better at measuring income than Congress, does this mean we should follow the accounting profession's definitions of net income? The answer is almost surely no. For one thing, accounting "conservatism" in finding income tends to understate economic income. For another, the industry pressure on the accounting profession could cause it to buckle under its clients' demands for ever more "conservative" definitions of net income.

a. Deductions on the Accrual Method

Read §461(a) and (h)

Applying the accrual method of accounting to deductions is different from applying it to income. As on the income side, one must meet an "all events test," the "reasonably ascertainable amount" test, and a softened "reasonable collectibility" test in order to accrue a deduction.[785] The courts have not entirely agreed with how to apply the all-events test to deductions associated with future payments. Early cases allowed deductions only when the taxpayer performed the activities it was called on to perform,[786] but later more liberal cases allowed deductions when the taxpayer had committed to perform, even though performance might be deferred. That opened up opportunities for taxpayers to raid the Treasury.

> **To illustrate:** Swindletop Oil begins drilling on a certain property in 2017, at which time it knows that under State law it must remove the equipment, plug the well and clean up the area, at an anticipated cost of $500,000. It *will* pay Clean-Up, Inc. to do the work, and it contracts for the work in 2017, when it starts drilling, so as to lock in the clean-up price. It can deduct the $500,000 in 2017, under the more modern liberal interpretation of the all events test.[787] This liberal result is now foreclosed by §461(h).

Nowadays, there is also a fourth test, namely the so-called economic performance requirement of §461(h), the effect of which is to defer deductions until performance under a contract occurs. The requirement applies only to deductions, not income:

785 Even if the taxpayer is financially weak, the test is met. See, e.g. Zimmerman Steel Co. v. Commissioner, 130 F.2d 1011 (8th Cir. 1942), reversing and remanding 45 BTA 1041 (1941). Even going into bankruptcy does not necessarily prevent accruing a deduction if the bankruptcy court might direct the debtor to make the payment. Id. In Cohen v. Commissioner, 21 T.C. 855 (1954), acq. 1954-2 C.B. 4. it was said that denial of the deduction occurs only where it can ''categorically'' be said at the time of accrual that payment will not take place. See generally Diamond and Salles, U.S. Income Tax Portfolio 570-4th, Accounting Methods General Principles.

786 See, e.g., Spencer, White & Prentis v. Commissioner, 144 F.2d 45 (2d Cir. 1944).

787 See, e.g., Harrold v. Commissioner, 192 F.2d 1002 (4th Cir. 1951), reversing 16 TC 134 (miner's right to accrue deduction at time of stripping land for later closing of the site).

a) If a taxpayer must pay someone else to perform services, then "economic performance" occurs when the services are performed. (This would doom Swindletop's current deduction.)

b) If the taxpayer must pay for property, then "economic performance" occurs when the property is provided, for example, when the taxpayer takes delivery of deductible cleaning supplies.

c) If the taxpayer must pay for the use of property, "economic performance" occurs as the property is used, for example, as the lessor provides the taxpayer a rented automobile.

d) If the taxpayer has a Worker's Compensation Act or tort liability judgment, then "economic performance" occurs as payment is made to the victim.

e) If the taxpayer must provide services or property to another person, then "economic performance" occurs as the taxpayer provides the services or property.

So, why did Congress tack on the economic performance test? The answer is that it was worried that taxpayers were cunningly manufacturing accrued deductions long before the actual economic event took place, thereby taking advantage of the time value of money associated with premature reductions in tax liability; one might call it borrowing from the government at no interest.[788]

b. Section 267 Limit on Accrued Expenses Payable to Related Cash Method Payees and Related Associated Provisions

If a payee is on the cash method and the payor is on the accrual method, there is a chance for real tax abuse, because the payor may accrue a deduction that his related cash-method payee may not in fact receive for years. If the taxpayers are unrelated, they may conspire to cash in on the potential bonanza. If they are related, it is even more likely that they will abuse this unintended opportunity. To staunch the potential flow of revenue losses, §267(a)(2) defers accrued deductions to a related taxpayer until the cash-method payee gets paid. The related taxpayers for purposes of this section include family members,[789] majority shareholders and their corporations, multiple controlled corporations that are under the taxpayer's common control, trusts

788 See Staff of Joint Comm. on Tax'n, 98th Cong., 2d Sess., General Explanation of the Revenue Provisions of the Deficit Reduction Act of 1984, PL 98-369, 258-263 (Comm. Print 1984), discussing new §461(h).

789 §267(b)(1).

and their grantors and beneficiaries, and controlled charitable organizations. Section 267(c) sets forth rules of constructive or "deemed" ownership pursuant to which individuals, various of their relatives, corporations, partnerships, trusts, and estates are considered to own corporate stock for purposes of determining whether taxpayers are considered sufficiently related to justify the intervention of §267(a)(2).

Some other Code sections will not let the payor claim a deduction until the payee reports income. For example, §83(h) keeps a payor from deducting a payment of property in exchange for services until the worker reports the service income.

Problem 9-7:

Dr. Peabody owns 100% the stock of Family Corporation. Family Corporation uses an accrual method of accounting. One of the executives of the corporation is his daughter, Regina. Regina is paid a salary of $20,000 a year, and at the end of the year the corporation declares an $80,000 bonus payable to Regina on January 2nd of the following year. Both Regina and the corporation use the calendar year to compute their taxes. Regina uses the cash method of accounting.

1) Does the economic performance limitation bar the year-end accrual? Why or why not?

2) What is the impact of §267(a)(2) on the transaction? Consider both the tax effect at the time the bonus is declared and when the bonus is paid.

3) Assume that Regina is in town on December 31 of year one and that morning is told she can come around any time to pick up the check (which is dated December 30), but she does not bother to. What result to Family Corporation? Does this change the result in "(2)"?

4) Family Corporation receives cash this year for services to be performed next year. Must it report the cash as income?

5) You bet $10 that the sun will not rise tomorrow, promising to pay 10 years from tomorrow if it does. When can you claim the deduction for $10 (assuming it is deductible)? See Reg. §1.461-4(g).

c. Restricting Premature Accruals Using §446(b)

The government can use §446(b) to put a stop to accrual method taxpayers' effort to claim current deductions under contracts calling for extremely deferred cash payments. The leading case seems to be *Mooney Aircraft, Inc. v. United States*[790] in which accrual method aircraft dealers gave away $1,000 "Mooney bonds" that were payable when a Mooney airplane was permanently retired from service, typically after about 20 years. The dealers claimed a $1,000 deduction in the year of the sale, even though payment would have to wait about two decades on the average for the aircraft to retire. The IRS asserted the result was a distortion of income. The court upheld the IRS's application of the §446(b) power to defer the deductions in a notably cryptic opinion. More recently, the following case reignited excitement about accrual method taxpayers' claims to current deductions for greatly deferred payments of cash.

FORD MOTOR CO. v. **COMMISSIONER**
102 T.C. 87 (1994)

WELLS, Judge.

[In 1980, Ford Motor Co. entered into about 20 "structured settlements" of personal injury and wrongful death claims, with Ford agreeing to pay the claimants their recoveries in fixed amounts periodically for up to fiftyeight years. In total, Ford agreed to pay about $24.5 million to the claimants. Ford bought annuity contracts from insurance companies for premiums totaling about $4.5 million to fund the $24.5 million of liabilities. Ford owned the annuities and remained liable to the claimants for the full amount of the payments, but the contracts sufficed to discharge Ford's liabilities to its tort victims. Ford asserted that the "all events" test had been met and deducted the entire $24.5 million obligation at once. The IRS argued that Ford's accrual method of accounting did not clearly reflect income as required by §446(b) and sought to allow it only a deduction for the $4.5 million it paid.]

. . .

The issue of whether the taxpayer's method of accounting clearly reflects income is a question of fact to be determined on a casebycase basis. . . . *In Capitol Fed. Sav. & Loan Association v. Commissioner, supra* at 213, we stated:

> In reviewing the Commissioner's actions, however, we do not substitute our judgment for the Commissioner's, nor do we permit taxpayers to carry their burden of proof by a mere preponderance of the evidence. Taxpayers are required to clearly show that the Commissioner's action was arbitrary, capricious, or without sound basis in fact. [Citations omitted.]

790 420 F.2d 400 (5th Cir. 1969).

In reviewing the Commissioner's determination that the taxpayer's method of accounting does not clearly reflect income, the function of a court is to determine whether there is any adequate basis in law for the Commissioner's conclusion. . . . Consequently, for petitioner to prevail, it must prove that respondent's disallowance of petitioner's deductions beyond the amounts petitioner paid to purchase the annuity contracts is arbitrary and capricious and without sound basis in fact or law.

. . .

Petitioner's position is grounded upon three principal arguments: (1) That expenses which satisfy the "all events" test[791] cannot be disallowed under section 446(b) even if the accrual would not result in a clear reflection of income; (2) that respondent's position is a veiled attempt by respondent to apply post1984 law to the instant case; and (3) that deferral of petitioner's deduction will result in a mismatching of its income and expenses. We will address each of petitioner's arguments in turn.

Petitioner's first argument is that respondent's determination is an abuse of discretion because the obligations which gave rise to the deduction satisfy the all events test and consequently cannot be disallowed on the theory that the deductions do not clearly reflect income. We disagree. Based upon our analysis below, we hold that satisfaction of the all events tests for accrual does not necessarily preclude respondent's use of section 446(b) to determine that the accrual does not clearly reflect income. As stated above, the parties presented extensive arguments concerning whether the obligations in question meet the all events test. We, however, do not address those arguments, and, for the purpose of our discussion below, we assume that the all events test has been satisfied.

Petitioner relies heavily on *United States v. Hughes Properties, Inc.*, 476 U.S. 593 (1986). Petitioner contends that *Hughes Properties* stands for the proposition that an accrual basis taxpayer may deduct an expense that satisfies the all events test in the year of accrual, regardless of the time of payment. We find *Hughes Properties* to be distinguishable. *Hughes Properties* involved an accrual basis taxpayer which owned a gambling casino in Nevada. The casino had several special slot machines that provided for "progressive" jackpots; i.e., the jackpots increased over time based on the amount of machine usage, until either the jackpots were won or maximum figures were reached. Each progressive slot machine had a "payoff indicator" that showed casino customers the current level of the jackpot. At the end of each taxable year, the taxpayer calculated the sum of the payoff indicator amounts for all progressive slot machines. From that figure, the taxpayer subtracted the equivalent figure that had been computed at the end of the prior

791 Sec. 1.4461(c)(1)(ii), Income Tax Regs., as in effect for 1980, provides that under an accrual method "deductions are allowable for the taxable year in which all the events have occurred which establish the fact of the liability giving rise to such deduction and the amount thereof can be determined with reasonable accuracy." [Footnote No. 9 in original.]

year. The taxpayer accrued the increase in the future payoff liability as a deductible ordinary business expense.

The Commissioner disallowed the deduction on the ground that the all events test had not been satisfied because the liability was not fixed. Prior to addressing the issue of whether the taxpayer satisfied the all events test, the Supreme Court stated:

> The major responsibility of the Internal Revenue Service is to protect the public fisc. Therefore, although section 446(c)(2) permits a taxpayer to use an accrual method for tax purposes if he uses that method to keep his books, section 446(b) specifically provides that if the taxpayer's method of accounting "does not clearly reflect income," the Commissioner may impose a method that "does clearly reflect income." Thus, the "Commissioner has broad powers in determining whether accounting methods used by a taxpayer clearly reflect income." . . .

The Supreme Court then rejected the Commissioner's assertion that the liability in question was too contingent to meet the all events test. In the context of dismissing the Government's fear of the potential for manipulation, the Court stated:

> None of the components that make up this parade of horribles, of course, took place here. Nothing in this record even intimates that . . . [the taxpayer] used its progressive machines for taxavoidance purposes. Its income from these machines was less than 1 percent of its gross revenue during the tax years in question. . . . [The taxpayer's] revenue from progressive slot machines depends on inducing gamblers to play the machines, and, if it sets unreasonably high odds, customers will refuse to play and will gamble elsewhere. Thus, respondent's economic selfinterest will keep it from setting odds likely to defer payoffs too far into the future. Nor, with Nevada's strictly imposed controls, was any abuse of the kind hypothesized by the Government likely to happen. *In any event, the Commissioner's ability, under section 446(b) of the Code, to correct any such abuse is the complete practical answer to the Government's concern. . . .*

The Supreme Court's statement that the "complete practical answer" to correct abuses of the accrual method of accounting lies in the Commissioner's broad authority under section 446(b) indicates to us that, had the obligation which the taxpayer sought to accrue in *Hughes Properties* extended over 58 years, the Commissioner's time value of money concerns would not have been dismissed by the Court. The length of the payout in the instant case causes a gross distortion of petitioner's true economic obligations to the tort claimants.

Unlike the situation in *Hughes Properties*,[792] in the instant case, the significant length of time for the payout is the cause of the distortion. Moreover, petitioner's selfinterest is furthered by

792 The average deferral of the jackpots in Hughes Properties was only 4 ½ months. See United States v. Hughes Properties, Inc., 476 U.S. 593, 596 n.1 (1986). [Footnote No. 10 in original.]

deferring the payout period. Additionally, the instant case does not involve a State law or regulation that specifically limits the ability of petitioner to extend the payments over long periods of time.

. . .

In the instant case, we think that the statute itself provides clear guidance on the issue of whether the clear reflection standard is subordinate to the all events test. Section 446 provides in relevant part:

> SEC 446(a). General Rule. Taxable income shall be computed under the method of accounting on the basis of which the taxpayer regularly computes his income in keeping his books.
>
> (b) Exceptions. If . . . the method used does not clearly reflect income, the computation of taxable income shall be made under such method as, in the opinion of the Secretary, does clearly reflect income.
>
> (c) Permissible Methods. *Subject to the provisions of subsections (a) and (b)*, a taxpayer may compute taxable income under any of the following methods of accounting
>
> > (1) the cash receipts and disbursements method;
> >
> > (2) *an* accrual method;
>
> . . .

The provisions of section 446 make it clear that a taxpayer's ability to use one or more of the methods of accounting listed in section 446(c) is contingent upon the satisfaction of subsections (a) and (b). The statute does not limit the Commissioner's discretion under section 446(b) by the taxpayer's mere compliance with the methods of accounting generally permitted under section 446(c). To the contrary, section 446 provides that the use of an accounting method is conditioned upon the method clearly reflecting income "in the opinion of the Secretary." In short, the statute clearly provides that the taxpayers may use an accrual method so long as it clearly reflects income.

Moreover, the regulations under section 446 comport with our interpretation of the statute. Section 1.4461(a)(2), Income Tax Regs., states:

> It is recognized that no uniform method of accounting can be prescribed for all taxpayers. Each taxpayer shall adopt such forms and systems as are, in his judgment, best suited to his needs. However, no method of accounting is acceptable unless, in the opinion of the Commissioner,

> it clearly reflects income. A method of accounting which reflects the consistent application of generally accepted accounting principles[793] in a particular trade or business in accordance with accepted conditions or practices in that trade or business *will ordinarily* be regarded as clearly reflecting income.... [Emphasis supplied.]

The regulations under section 446 simply state that the consistent application of accounting methods permitted under section 446(c) will generally be regarded as clearly reflecting income and that no method of accounting is acceptable unless it passes the Commissioner's scrutiny for the clear reflection of income. *Thor Power Tool Co. v. Commissioner*, 439 U.S. at 603. Neither section 446 nor the regulations provide that the satisfaction of the tests for accrual will alone be dispositive of the issue of whether the taxpayer's method of accounting clearly reflects income.

Such an interpretation would be at odds with the Supreme Court's statement in *United States v. Hughes Properties, Inc.*, 476 U.S. 593 (1986), regarding the Commissioner's authority to curb abuses under section 446(b). It would also be inconsistent with our many cases holding that the Commissioner has the authority under section 446(b) to require a taxpayer to report specific items of income or expense on the basis of a method of accounting other than the one being used by the taxpayer, when the taxpayer's method does not clearly reflect income. Frequently, we have allowed the Commissioner to require taxpayers who utilize the cash method of accounting to accrue specific items of income and expense....

...

Finally, we address petitioner's last principal argument. Petitioner argues that respondent's position mismatches income and expense. We do not agree. We have concluded above that petitioner's method does not clearly reflect income. A corollary to the proposition that petitioner's method must clearly reflect income is that the method which the Commissioner seeks to apply to the taxpayer must also clearly reflect income. Section 446(b) states:

> If no method of accounting has been regularly used by the taxpayer, or if the method used does not clearly reflect income, the computation of taxable income shall be made under such method as, in the opinion of the Secretary, *does clearly reflect income.* [Emphasis supplied.]

Courts will not approve the Commissioner's change of a taxpayer's method from an incorrect method to another incorrect method....

793 As noted above, for financial reporting purposes, petitioner deducted the cost of the annuities. Although there is nothing in the record indicating whether petitioner complied with generally accepted accounting principles for financial reporting purposes, we think that the fact that petitioner's securities are publicly traded makes it highly likely that petitioner's financial reports complied with generally accepted accounting principles. 15 U.S.C.A. §78n(a) (West 1981). [Footnote No. 13 in original.]

In the instant case, we think that the method of accounting petitioner used for financial reporting purposes resulted in a better matching of its income and expenses than the method used for tax purposes.[794] Although a basic principle of financial accounting is the matching of income with related expenses, the principal purpose of tax accounting is the accurate reflection of the taxpayer's income, a concept which does not necessarily correlate with the goal of financial accounting. . . . In the instant case, for financial reporting purposes, petitioner expensed only the costs of the annuities it purchased, which were not exceeded by the present value of the deferred payments it was obligated to make.[795] As we see it, the true economic costs of petitioner's losses to the tort claimants are the amounts it paid for the annuities. With regard to settlements for which petitioner did not purchase annuities,[796] the present value of the obligations is the true economic cost of petitioner's loss. Consequently, the accrual method of accounting which petitioner used for financial reporting purposes resulted in the proper matching of income and expense and clearly reflects petitioner's income. Accordingly, we sustain respondent's determination.

Finally, we want to make clear that the mere fact that a deduction which accrues prior to the time payment is made (the timing factor) does not, by itself, cause the accrual to run afoul of the clear reflection of income requirement. Inherent in the use of an accrual method is the fact that a deduction may be allowed in advance of payment. Our holding in the instant case is not intended to draw a bright line that can be applied mechanically in other circumstances. We decide only the ultimate question of fact in the instant case; namely, whether, for tax purposes, petitioner's method of accounting for its obligations under the structured settlements clearly reflects income. We hold that it does not and that the Government did not abuse its discretion in making that determination.

To reflect the foregoing,

Decision will be entered under Rule 155.

[The dissent is omitted. Eds.]

794 We have held that the Commissioner has the authority under 446(a) to require a taxpayer to report income on the basis of the same accounting method used for bookkeeping purposes. *Mifflin v. Commissioner*, 24 T.C. 973 (1955); see also *Yates v. United States*, 205 F. Supp. 738 (E.D. Ky. 1962). [Footnote No. 17 in original.]

795 In other years, with regard to settlements for which petitioner did not purchase annuity contracts, it expensed the present value of the future payments. [Footnote No. 18 in original.]

796 As noted above, during 1980, the year in issue, all of the structured settlements into which petitioners entered were funded by annuities.

Notes

The IRS's attempts to invoke §446(b) to override narrow, specific accounting methods have not fared well. For example, in *Hallmark Cards, Inc. v. Commissioner*,[797] also an "allevents test" case, the Tax Court held that the IRS does not have the authority under §446(b) to reject a method of accounting that is specifically authorized by the Code or regulations, if it was consistently applied by the taxpayer.[798] In *Williams v. Commissioner*,the Tax Court held that §446(b) could not be used to disallow excessive interest accruals mandated by §483 and Reg. §1.4832(a)(1)(i) for lack of any intention in the Regulation to let §446(b) override §483.[799]

Returning to the case, Ford's literal-minded application of the accrual method suggested a tax bonanza because it would have been able to deduct the full dollar amount of its future payments, even though the real cost of the future payments was much smaller. Make sure you understand the deal from Ford's perspective. You can assume that Ford paid income taxes at a rate of at least 35%, with the result that the tax benefits of the current deduction (i.e., 35% of the accrued $24.5 million deduction) well exceeded the $4.5 million of current cash costs of paying for the human tragedies. The case invites the question of whether accrual method taxpayers should perhaps be made to discount (reduce) their future payments if they can currently deduct them.

On a more global scale, might it be better to use general discounting principles to handle long-term deferrals of income and deductions? For example, one might allow Ford to deduct the obligation to the tort victim when it was incurred, but discount it to take account of the fact that Ford's actual payments would occur in the future. Or is it perhaps better to leave the area alone on the theory that the remedy is too complex to fix? Be that as it may, the problem of accrual method taxpayers' claims to exaggerated current deductions has been largely eliminated by §461(h), the economic performance requirement, which defers accrued deductions until the performance associated with the accrual has occurred.

Section 461(h) has also eliminated what was known as general reserve accounting. General reserve accounting permitted a taxpayer on the accrual method to claim a current deduction for anticipated future expenses and then reverse the deduction in later years, in effect deferring income in a two-step dance.

> **To illustrate:** A dealer sold used cars and knew from experience that in the first year following the sale the average cost to the dealer of repairing the car would be $100. Before enactment of §461(h), for Federal Income Tax purposes the dealer could sell the car for the stated sale price,

797 90 T.C. 26 (1988).

798 See also RLC Industries and Subsidiaries Co. v. Commissioner, 98 T.C. 457 (1992); Estate of Ratliff v. Commissioner, 101 T.C. 276 (1993).

799 94 T.C. 464 (1990), affirmed, 1 F.3d 502 (7th Cir. 1993).

but deduct as an addition to a $100 reserve for expenses that he was sure (based on experience) to have to pay under the warranty. Next year, he reversed the $100 addition to the reserve and reported that $100 in income. The dealer would also claim a current deduction for the *actual* expenses of repairing each car that the dealer sold. The outcome was reasonable from a financial reporting point of view.

Congress did not care for the deferral effect of general reserve accounting and eliminated it by enacting §461(h), subject to exceptions for selected industries, such as certain reserves for anticipated bad debts allowed to certain banks and savings and loan associations. Those exceptions appear in other specific Code sections.

The accrual method is not just for accrual method taxpayers. The Code forces cash method taxpayers onto the accrual method for certain transactions. You have already seen how the OID rules generally put the borrower and lender on the accrual method with respect to reporting original issue discount. There is more. Section 467, enacted in 1987: (1) requires some landlords and tenants to go onto the accrual method of accounting for rental income and deductions, and (2) a separate provision requires a level accrual of rents under some tax-avoidance motivated leases where the lease contract calls for increasing rents. The evil Congress was worried about with respect to "(1)," was the accrual-method tenant who rents from a cash-method landlord, under a lease calling for deferred payments of rent. Here is an example of the pre-reform scheme and how Congress addressed it:

To illustrate: A real estate lease calls for Accrual Method Tenant to pay $100,000/year in rent, but provides that only $60,000 is due now and $40,000 is due two years later. Tenant could deduct $100,000 now, but Cash Method Landlord would report only $60,000 of income now and $40,000 in two years. Section 467(a) in effect puts Landlord on the accrual method and §467(b)(1) reduces Tenant's deduction for the future $40,000 payment to its discounted present value. Assuming that the discounted deduction is $35,000, when the full $40,000 is paid, the parties report the $5,000 discount as interest.

The rent-leveling provision (item "(2)") is even more elaborate and reverses the increasing rents with complicated discounting rules that level the accrual of rental income and expenses to constant annual amounts.[800]

Provisions like §467 are no fun, but they exist for a reason. They are there because tax advisors, aided by computer-generated spreadsheets, have been able to invent complicated schemes that depend on deferring taxes by mismatching payments and deductions, frequently offering

800 §467(b)(2). Section 467(a) is not a universal rule; it only applies if the aggregate rents exceed $250,000 and the rent-leveling rules have various fair exceptions, such as rents tied to the tenant's profits, general price levels or reasonable rent holidays to account for hard times in the rental area.

the payee a premium for going along with the game, paying for its participation with the government's money.

Not every country is as patient with this kind of technical game playing. In Mexico, tax planning is a crime. In Australia the Taxation Office has the right to void tax driven schemes and restructure them as if they had taken place in a world without taxes.[801] Is this the best way to go? Are we too suspicious of government ever to allow such a rule? Does *not* enacting such a rule mean the well-heeled who can afford cutting-edge tax advice will always have an advantage over the common citizen?

There are special rules for funds that manage money contributed to pay for mass tort claims. An accrual method taxpayer can claim a current deduction for any actual payment to a *designated settlement fund* (DSF) or *qualified settlement fund* (QSF) under §468B. This softens the blow of §461(h)'s rule that accrual method taxpayers can only deduct payments to tort victims as the victim is paid. Today Ford, for example, could deduct a payment of money to a DSF to extinguish its liability to a class of its victims, with payouts to the victims over time. This relaxes the grip of the economic performance requirement for tort claims by allowing a full deduction for cash paid to the fund, even if the ultimate payment to the victims is deferred into a future year. A drawback of a DSF is that it is a taxable entity, although its tax base does not include its biggest source, namely payments from tortfeasors. The DSF's cousin, the QSF, works similarly, but is looser than the DSF in that it need not entirely extinguish the transferor's liability, and it need not be set up by a court. These funds are the creatures of §468B and the related Treasury regulations. Wise tort lawyers ought to understand this area well.

> **To illustrate:** Diabolical Cigarettes, Inc. ("DCI") is an accrual-method calendar year corporation. It made and sold cigarettes between years 1-10. In year 15 it was sued by cancer victims. DCI settled the lawsuit permanently by contributing $50 million to a judicially-approved settlement fund to pay smokers $2 million/year for 25 years, plus interest on the fund. DCI deducts this liability when it pays in the $50 million. Normally, §461(h) would limit the deduction to the annual payments to the cancer victims. The interest the $50 million fund earns is subject to income taxation.

Problem 9-8:

Garfield ("Grubby") Peabody, CPA, and Client are on the calendar year and (suspend your disbelief) use the accrual method. Assume Peabody's accounting services produce deductible tax return preparation expenses under §212(3) for his clients. As to Client, recall §461(f). What result in terms of income and deductions to each if:

---

801 See Hugh J. Ault and Brian J. Arnold, COMPARATIVE INCOME TAXATION, A STRUCTURAL ANALYSIS 3rd Edition 22-24 (Kluwer Law Int'l 2010). The text oversimplifies Professor Ault's description.

1) Peabody prepares Client's tax return in November and bills Client in November. Client pays a week later, as required under their contract.

2) Same as "(1)," but Client pays next year.

3) Peabody and Client contract to have the work performed in January of the following year.

   a. Client pays this year, as required under Peabody's contract. Pay particular attention as to whether as an Examining Agent of the IRS you might be able to force Peabody to report income this year. First answer without regard to Rev. Proc. 71-21, 1971-2 C.B. 549, then consider the impact of the Rev. Proc. on your analysis.

   b. Client pays in January of the next year after the services are performed, as required under Peabody's contract.

4) Same as "(1)," but Client defaults in payment by December, and it is clear that he will never pay. Would the result be any different if Peabody were on the cash method of accounting?

5) Client receives tax services this year and, although furious about his filthy-looking tax return with its illegible calculations, and threatening to sue, he pays Peabody this year. Does Peabody have income this year? Does Client have a deduction? See §461(f).

6) Peabody contracts to get three years' worth of professional malpractice insurance on January 1 of this year. He pays the full $15,000 for the three years' coverage on January 1 of this year. The insurance company is on the accrual method. How much can he deduct? How much income does the insurance company have? Consider accrual method accounting, the claim of right doctrine, and the §446(b) power.

7) Every January Peabody has "Roach Busters" come through his office and eradicate insects in his office as required by contract. He pays Roach Busters $100 for next January's service this November. Can he deduct the cost of the service in the year of payment, i.e. this year? See §461(h)(3).

Problem 9-9:

Which of the following expenses can an accrual-method taxpayer deduct in the current year?

1) Swindletop Oil Corporation is a calendar year, accrual-method taxpayer. It contracts with Petro Cleano ("PC") to drill for oil and operate the oil field. On October 1 of year one Swindletop installs a platform and starts drilling. Under the contract, PC must remove the well equipment when it abandons the well or ends the lease (which cannot exceed 10 years), whichever happens first. In year 7, Swindletop abandons the lease and pays PC $100,000 to remove the platform, which it promptly does. When can Swindeltop claim the deduction? See Reg. §1.461-4(d)(7), Ex. (1).

2) Bank charges interest to a customer who has filed voluntary bankruptcy under Chapter 11 (reorganization in bankruptcy), when the debt is secured and the customer is still operating a business, although the business is financially distressed. Can customer confidently deduct the interest it owes the bank?

Problem 9-10:

In your opinion, does the cash or accrual method of accounting more closely reflect the Haig-Simons definition of income?

9. Sales for Deferred Payments

Small purchases are usually paid for in cash on the spot or else deferred until the end of the month, after the merchant or other seller mails out a bill, perhaps along with an interest charge for the deferral of the payment. These transactions are easily accounted for on the basis of either cash or accrual accounting practices. When the dollars become larger, however, financial embarrassment may set in. The buyer may not have the cash needed to pay for the entire transaction at the time of the purchase. In such cases, the buyer will either borrow from a third party, such as a bank, or else the seller will agree to defer the receipt of the payments that are due, but often with the requirement that the buyer provide some collateral and some interest charges accompanying the deferral. If the financing is done by a bank, the seller will typically be paid in full at the closing, and, once again, there is no question about how the seller reports the sale because there are no deferrals. The seller simply walks away with all of the money she is entitled to at the closing and reports the gain or loss that year. Those deals are easy.

The subject of this part of the Chapter is how one reports transactions in which the seller finances the sale, with the buyer paying for the property over several years. The answer will often depend in part on whether the taxpayer is on the cash or accrual method. The important practical implication of the deferral as far as the buyer is concerned is that interest payments will have to be paid along with payments of principal and those interest payments may or may not be deductible, generally depending on whether they are paid in connection with a business, an investment, or merely finance personal consumption. Incidentally, the buyer will always obtain basis in the purchased property at the time of the closing. For example, if you buy a home for $100,000 with the seller financing $90,000 of the price, you still get an immediate $100,000 basis. The hard part is how to treat the seller, especially how one ought to treat the obligation the seller receives from the buyer at the time of the closing. That will be considered later in the Chapter.

Now, let us look at the three fundamental ways that the courts and Congress have chosen to treat sellers on their profitable sales for deferred payments:

1. Defer any gain until the seller has been paid an amount at least equal to basis and treat any subsequent payments as 100% taxable gain (the "open-transaction" method). The *Clark* case in Chapter 3 was your first exposure to this approach.

2. Treat the obligation that the seller receives as fully taxable on the spot and report the face amount or the value of the promise as part of the amount realized (the "closed-transaction" method).

3. Tax each payment that the seller receives as if it were in the nature of an annuity, consisting partly of a return of capital and partly of gain (the "installment sale method").

The remainder of this Chapter studies these three outcomes in the order just presented and then looks briefly at the question of imputing interest on sales for deferred payments. Until then, assume the seller adds a separate appropriate amount of interest for the privilege of not paying in full right away.

a. Open Transaction Method

The following case is the bedrock decision with respect to the open transaction doctrine. Although the doctrine has been greatly whittled down, it is still viable in exceptional circumstances. Taxpayers who dispose of appreciated property generally adore the open transaction method because it defers gains until they receive payments equal to their basis in the property. After that, the balance is pure gain.

BURNET v. LOGAN

283 U.S. 404 (S. Ct. 1931)

MR. JUSTICE McREYNOLDS delivered the opinion of the Court.

[In 1916 taxpayer sold stock of Andrews & Hitchcock (A&H) to Youngstown Sheet & Tube for cash plus 12% royalty from the Mahoning mine. The royalty-based part of the purchase price arose because A&H owned 12% of Mahoning Ore & Steel (MOS), an operating company which was the lessee of the Mahoning mine. The lease had no maximum or minimum tonnage mined obligations, nor any definite payments, which made the value of the lease to MOS uncertain, and therefore made it virtually impossible to tell what would ultimately be paid for the stock when the stock was sold. The taxpayer's mother's estate valued the stock at $277,000.]

The Circuit Court of Appeals held that, in the circumstances, it was impossible to determine with fair certainty the market value of the agreement by the Youngstown Company to pay 60 cents per ton. Also, that respondent was entitled to the return of her capital the value of 250 shares on March 1, 1913, and the assessed value of the interest derived from her mother before she could be charged with any taxable income. As this had not in fact been returned, there was no taxable income.

We agree with the result reached by the Circuit Court of Appeals.

The 1916 transaction was a sale of stock not an exchange of property. We are not dealing with royalties or deductions from gross income because of depletion of mining property. Nor does the situation demand that an effort be made to place according to the best available data some approximate value upon the contract for future payments. This probably was necessary in order to assess the mother's estate. As annual payments on account of extracted ore come in they can be readily apportioned first as return of capital and later as profit. The liability for income tax ultimately can be fairly determined without resort to mere estimates, assumptions and speculation. When the profit, if any, is actually realized, the taxpayer will be required to respond. The consideration for the sale was $2,200,000.00 in cash and the promise of future money payments wholly contingent upon facts and circumstances not possible to foretell with anything like fair certainty. The promise was in no proper sense equivalent to cash. It had no ascertainable fair market value. The transaction was not a closed one. Respondent might never recoup her capital investment from payments only conditionally promised. Prior to 1921 all receipts from the sale of her shares amounted to less than their value on March 1, 1913. She properly demanded the return of her capital investment before assessment of any taxable profit based on conjecture.

"In order to determine whether there has been gain or loss, and the amount of the gain, if any, we must withdraw from the gross proceeds an amount sufficient to restore the capital value that existed at the commencement of the period under consideration." *Doyle v. Mitchell Bros. Co.*, 247 U.S. 179, 184, 185. Rev. Act 1916, §2, 39 Stat. 757, 758; Rev. Act 1918, c. 18, 40 Stat. 1057. Ordinarily, at least, a taxpayer may not deduct from gross receipts a supposed loss which in fact is represented by his outstanding note. *Eckert v. Commissioner of Internal Revenue*, *ante*, p. 140. And, conversely, a promise to pay indeterminate sums of money is not necessarily taxable income. "Generally speaking, the income tax law is concerned only with realized losses, as with realized gains." *Lucas v. American Code Co.*, 280 U.S. 445, 449.

From her mother's estate Mrs. Logan obtained the right to share in possible proceeds of a contract thereafter to pay indefinite sums. The value of this was assumed to be $277,164.50 and its transfer was so taxed. Some valuation speculative or otherwise was necessary in order to close the estate. It may never yield as much, it may yield more. If a sum equal to the value thus ascertained had been invested in an annuity contract, payments thereunder would have been free from income tax until the owner had recouped his capital investment. We think a like rule should be applied here. . . .

The judgments below are

Affirmed.

Notes on Electing Out of the Installment Method

Most sales for deferred payments automatically get installment sales treatment, although the taxpayer is free to "elect out" under §453(d).

The Regulations under §453 relating to installment sales aggressively move in on transactions in which the taxpayer elects out of the installment sales method in order to use the open transaction method. Temp. Reg. §15A.453-1(d)(2)(iii) states that if the taxpayer elects out of the installment method and claims that *Burnet v. Logan* applies because the obligation the seller receives cannot be valued, then the taxpayer still has to report at least the fair market value of the property that was sold as the amount realized in the year of sale, even though the cash received in the transaction may not be enough to pay the related taxes. The Regulations do leave the door open just a crack, and acknowledge that it might be possible that neither the property that was sold nor the obligation received is capable of valuation, so that the open transaction method is available.

There are significant risks associated with electing out of installment sale treatment under §453(d) and using the open transaction theory. The risk is that if the transaction turns out (say under IRS audit) to have been "closed," then the taxpayer's worst fears will be realized; he must realize the entire gain in the year of sale, yet cash received that year may not be enough to pay the related taxes. He will be stuck procedurally because once an election out of §453 is made, it can be revoked only with the government's consent.[802] On top of that, notifying the

802 §453(d)(3).

IRS of the election out may in itself be an "audit flag," inviting an IRS examination, resulting in disallowance of open transaction treatment.

The mechanics of electing out vary with the taxpayer's method of accounting. If the seller is on the cash method and elects out under §453(d), he reports the *value* of the note or other obligation as the amount realized in the year of sale; an accrual method seller who elects out reports the *face amount* of the obligation.[803]

Assume that a cash-method taxpayer, who has properly elected out of the installment sale method, sells property whose value is unascertainable for a note; and that note has an ascertainable value. The taxpayer must report the note's value as her amount realized in the year of the sale.

Here is what happened under prior law if there was a discount because the note was worth less than its face amount:

> **To illustrate:** Steve Fish, a cash-method taxpayer, received a promissory note relating to the sale of a capital asset, not on the installment method, for $20,000 from John Pollo. Steve received no cash, just the note. If Steve were to sell the note immediately, it would only be worth $18,000. In the year of sale, Steve had to include $18,000 in his gross income. If Steve kept the note, he will eventually collect the $20,000 amount realized. The $2,000 discount constitutes "collection gain" and, under prior law it was ratably reported as ordinary income as it was received.[804] The theory for giving the $2,000 ordinary gain treatment was that it was not received from a sale or exchange, since the discount was considered to have been received in connection with extinguishing a debt.

Under current law, for debt obligations issued or bought after June 8, 1997, money received in retirement of a debt obligation issued by an individual is treated as received on the sale or exchange of the obligation. As a consequence, capital gain or loss will arise on the retirement of a debt instrument that a natural person issued, provided the obligation is a capital asset in his or her hands. §1271(b).

> **To illustrate:** In the example, the $2,000 discount would be a gain from disposing of a capital asset because a sale of the debt would have produced a capital gain to Steve. The capital gain would arise as the note was paid off.

803 §15A.453-1(d)(2)(i) (consistent with case law). There is no separate form for the election.

804 Shapfa Realty Corp. v. Commissioner, 8 B.T.A. 283 (1927).

b. Closed Transaction

To understand this case, imagine you sold something on a deferred payment basis, and got back a note from the buyer and elected out of the installment method. What would you have to report your tax return as your amount realized in the year of the sale if the transaction was not "open"?

WARREN JONES COMPANY v. COMMISSIONER

524 F.2d 788 (9th Cir. 1975), reversing 60 TC 663

ELY, Circuit Judge.

During its taxable year ending on October 31, 1968, the Warren Jones Company, a cash basis taxpayer, sold an apartment building for $153,000. In return, the taxpayer received a cash down payment of $20,000 and the buyer's promise in a standard form real estate contract, to pay $133,000, plus interest, over the following fifteen years. The Tax Court held, with three judges dissenting, that the fair market value of the real estate contract did not constitute an "amount realized" by the taxpayer in the taxable year of sale under section 1001(b) of the Internal Revenue Code. . . .

I. Background

On May 27, 1968, the taxpayer, a family-held corporation chartered by the State of Washington, entered into a real estate contract for the sale of one of its Seattle apartment buildings, the Wallingford Court Apartments, to Bernard and Jo Ann Storey for $153,000. When the sale closed on June 15, 1968, the Storeys paid $20,000 in cash and took possession of the apartments. The Storeys were then obligated by the contract to pay the taxpayer $1,000 per month, plus 8 percent interest on the declining balance, for a period of fifteen years. The balance due at the end of fifteen years is to be payable in a lump sum. The contract was the only evidence of the Storeys' indebtedness, since no notes or other such instruments passed between the parties. Upon receipt of the full purchase price, the taxpayer is obligated by the contract to deed the Wallingford Apartments to the Storeys.

The Tax Court found, as facts, that the transaction between the taxpayer and the Storeys was a completed sale in the taxable year ending on October 31, 1968, and that in that year, the Storeys were solvent obligors. The court also found that real estate contracts such as that between the taxpayer and the Storeys were regularly bought and sold in the Seattle area. The court concluded, from the testimony before it, that in the taxable year of sale, the taxpayer could have sold its contract, which had a face value of $133,000, to a savings and loan association or a similar institutional buyer for approximately $117,980. The court found, however, that in accordance with prevailing business practices, any potential buyer for the contract would likely have required the taxpayer to deposit $41,000 of the proceeds from the sale of the contract in a savings account, assigned to the buyer, for the purpose of securing the first $41,000 of the Storeys' payments. Consequently, the court found that in the taxable year of sale, the contract had a fair market value of only $76,980 (the contract's selling price minus the amount deposited in the assigned savings account.)

On the sale's closing date, the taxpayer had an adjusted basis of $61,913 in the Wallingford Apartments. In determining the amount it had realized from the sale, the taxpayer added only the $20,000 down payment and the portion of the $4,000 in monthly payments it had received that was allocable to principal. Consequently, on its federal income tax return for the taxable year ending October 31, 1968, the taxpayer reported no gain from the apartment sale. The taxpayer's return explained that the corporation reported on the cash basis and that under the Tax Court's holding in *Nina J. Ennis*, 17 T.C. 465 (1951), it was not required to report gain on the sale until it had recovered its basis. The return also stated, however, that in the event the taxpayer was required to report gain in the taxable year of the sale, it elected to do so on the installment basis (I.R.C. § 453).

The Commissioner disagreed with the taxpayer's assertion that it had realized no gain on the sale, but he conceded that the sale qualified as an installment sale. Consequently, the Commissioner recalculated the taxpayer's gain in accordance with section 453 and notified the taxpayer that it had recognized an additional $12,098 in long term capital gain. The taxpayer then petitioned the Tax Court for a redetermination of its liability.

Section 1001 provides, in pertinent part, as follows:

> (a) COMPUTATION OF GAIN OR LOSS. - The gain from the sale or other disposition of property shall be the excess of the amount realized therefrom over the adjusted basis....
>
> (b) AMOUNT REALIZED. - The amount realized from the sale or other disposition of property shall be the sum of any money received plus the fair market value of the property (other than money) received.

The question presented is whether section 1001(b) requires the taxpayer to include the fair market value of its real estate contract with the Storeys in determining the "amount realized" during the taxable year of the sale.

Holding that fair market value of the contract was not includable in the amount realized from the sale, the Tax Court majority relied on the doctrine of "cash equivalency." Under that doctrine, the cash basis taxpayer must report income received in the form of property only if the property is the "equivalent of cash." . . .

The Tax Court majority adopted the following as its definition of the phrase, "equivalent of cash":

> . . . if the promise to pay of a solvent obligor is unconditional and assignable, not subject to set-offs, and is of a kind that is frequently transferred to lenders or investors at a discount not substantially greater than the generally prevailing premium for the use of money, such promise is the equivalent of cash. . . .

. . . . Applying the quoted definition, the Tax Court held that the taxpayer's contract, which had a face value of $133,000, was not the "equivalent of cash" since it had a fair market value of only $76,980. Had the taxpayer sold the contract, the discount from the face value, approximately 42 percent, would have been "substantially greater than the generally prevailing premium for the use of money."

The Tax Court observed that requiring the taxpayer to realize the fair market value of the contract in the year of the sale could subject the taxpayer to substantial hardships. The taxpayer would be taxed in the initial year on a substantial portion of its gain from the sale of the property, even though it had received, in cash, only a small fraction of the purchase price. To raise funds to pay its taxes, the taxpayer might be forced to sell the contract at the contract's fair market value, even though such a sale might not otherwise be necessary or advantageous. Most importantly in the Tax Court's view, if the taxpayer were required to realize the fair market value of the contract in the year of the sale, the sale transaction would be closed for tax purposes in that year; hence, the taxpayer's capital gain on the transaction would be permanently limited to the difference between its adjusted basis and the contract's fair market value plus the cash payments received in the year of sale. If the taxpayer did retain the contract, so as to collect its face value, the amounts received in excess of the contract's fair market value would constitute ordinary income. The Tax Court also noted that requiring the cash basis taxpayer to realize the fair market value of the real estate contract would tend to obscure the differences between the cash and accrual methods of reporting.

The Commissioner does not dispute the Tax Court's conclusion that the taxpayer's contract with the Storeys had a fair market value of $76,980, or any other of the court's findings of fact. Rather, the Commissioner contends that since, as found by the Tax Court, the contract had a fair market value, section 1001(b) requires the taxpayer to include the amount of that fair market value in determining the amount realized.

The taxpayer contends that the basic question before us is one of fact. We disagree. The question is essentially one of statutory construction and it therefore presents an issue of law.

II. Statutory Analysis

The first statutory predecessor of section 1001(b) was section 202(b) of the Revenue Act of February 24, 1919, which stated:

> When property is exchanged for other property, the property received in exchange shall for the purpose of determining gain or loss be treated as the equivalent of cash to the amount of its fair market value, if any. . . .

Ch. 18, § 202(b), 40 Stat. 1060. We have no doubt that under that statute, the taxpayer would have been required to include the fair market value of its real estate contract as an amount realized during the taxable year of sale.

Only three years later, however, in the Revenue Act of November 23, 1921, Congress replaced the language of the statute enacted in 1919 with the following:

> On an exchange of property, real, personal, or mixed, for any other such property, no gain or loss shall be recognized unless the property received in exchange has a readily realizable market value. . . .

Ch. 136, § 202(c), 42 Stat. 230. The original statute had created "a presumption in favor of taxation." H.R. Rep. No. 350, 67th Cong., 1st Sess. (1921), reproduced at 1939-1 Cum. Bull. (Part 2) 168, 175. In the 1921 Act, Congress doubtless intended a policy more favorable to the taxpayer. Interpreting the 1921 statute, the Treasury Regulations provided that

> property has a readily realizable market value if it can be readily converted into an amount of cash or its equivalent substantially equal to the fair value of the property.

Treas. Reg. 62, Art. 1564 (1922 ed.). The law established in 1921 appears to have been substantially in accord with the position taken in this case by the Tax Court majority.

Notwithstanding the foregoing, in the Revenue Act of 1924, ch. 234, §202(c), 43 Stat. 256, Congress again changed the law, replacing the 1921 statute with the language that now appears in §1001(b) of the current Code. Of the 1921 statute, and its requirement of a "readily realizable market value," the Senate Finance Committee wrote in 1924:

> The question whether, in a given case, the property received in exchange has a readily realizable market value is a most difficult one, and the rulings on this question in given cases have been far from satisfactory. . . . The provision can not be applied with accuracy or consistency.S. Rep. No.

398, 68th Cong., 1st Sess. (1924), reproduced at 1939-1 Cum. Bull. (Part 2) 266, 275. See also H.R. Rep. No. 179, 68th Cong., 1st Sess. (1924), reproduced at 1939-1 Cum. Bull. (Part 2) 241, 251.

Under the 1924 statute, "where income is realized in the form of property, the measure of the income is the fair market value of the property at the date of its receipt." H.R. Rep. No. 179, *supra*, 1939-1 Cum. Bull. (Part 2) at 250; S. Rep. No. 398, *supra*, 1939-1 Cum. Bull. (Part 2) at 275.

There is no indication whatsoever that Congress intended to retain the "readily realizable market value" test from the 1921 statute as an unstated element of the 1924 Act. Indeed, as noted above, Congress sharply criticized that test. We cannot avoid the conclusion that in 1924 Congress intended to establish the more definite rule for which the Commissioner here contends and that consequently, if the fair market value of property received in an exchange can be ascertained, that fair market value must be reported as an amount realized.

Congress clearly understood that the 1924 statute might subject some taxpayers to the hardships discussed by the Tax Court majority. In the Revenue Act of 1926, ch. 27, §212(d), 44 Stat. 23, Congress enacted the installment basis for reporting gain that is now reflected in section 453 of the current Code. Under §453, a taxpayer who sells real property and receives payments in the year of sale totaling less than 30 percent of the selling price may elect to report as taxable income in any given year only

> that proportion of the installment payments actually received in that year which the gross profit (realized or to be realized when payment is completed) bears to the total contract price. . . .

By providing the installment basis, Congress intended ". . . to relieve taxpayers who adopted it from having to pay an income tax in the year of sale based on the full amount of anticipated profits when in fact they had received in cash only a small portion of the sales price." *Commissioner v. South Texas Lumber Co.*, 333 U.S. 496, 503, 92 L. Ed. 831, 68 S. Ct. 695 (1948). For sales that qualify, the installment basis also eliminates the other potential disadvantages to which the Tax Court referred. Since taxation in the year of the sale is based on the value of the payments actually received, the taxpayer should not be required to sell his obligation in order to meet his tax liabilities. Furthermore, the installment basis does not change the character of the gain received. If gain on an exchange would otherwise be capital, it remains capital under section 453. Finally, the installment basis treats cash and accrual basis taxpayers equally.

We view section 453 as persuasive evidence in support of the interpretation of section 1001(b) for which the Commissioner contends. The installment basis is Congress's method of providing relief from the rigors of section 1001(b). In its report on the Revenue Act of 1926, the Senate Finance Committee expressly noted that in sales or exchanges not qualifying for the installment basis, "deferred-payment contracts"

> ... are to be regarded as the equivalent of cash if such obligations have a fair market value. In consequence, that portion of the initial payment and of the fair market value of such obligations which represents profit is to be returned as income as of the taxable year of the sale. S. Rep. No. 52, 69th Cong., 1st Sess. (1926), reproduced at 1939-1 Cum. Bull. (Part 2) 332, 347.

On this appeal, however, the taxpayer has made another argument with respect to section 453. It contends that subsection (b)(3), added to section 453 in 1969, may be read as Congress's definition of the phrase "equivalent of cash." As noted above, taxpayers who sell property and receive "payments" in the year of sale that exceed 30 percent of the selling price may not report on the installment basis. Under section 453(b)(2)(A)(ii), "evidences of indebtedness of the purchaser" are not to be considered as "payments" in the year of sale in determining whether the payments constitute 30 percent of the selling price. Section 453(b)(3), added by the Tax Reform Act of 1969, provides that

> ... a bond or other evidence of indebtedness which is payable on demand, or which is issued by a corporation or a government or a political subdivision thereof (A) with interest coupons attached or in registered form (other than one in registered form which the taxpayer establishes will not be readily tradable in an established securities market), or (B) in any other form designed to render such bond or other evidence of indebtedness readily tradable in an established securities market, shall not be treated as an evidence of indebtedness of the purchaser.

In the taxpayer's view, property received in a sale or exchange should not be considered the equivalent of cash under section 1001(b) unless the property is of the types described in section 453(b)(3).

Congress added section 453(b)(3) to the Code for the purpose of excluding from the installment basis those taxpayers who sell property and receive more than 30 percent of the selling price in the form of highly liquid instruments of debt. Congress concluded that such taxpayers, like taxpayers receiving cash, would not suffer the hardships that the installment basis was designed to alleviate. *See* H.R. Rep. No. 413, 91st Cong., 1st Sess. 107-08 (1969) (1969-3 Cum. Bull. 200, 267) U.S. Code. Cong. & Admin.News 1969. We find no indication that Congress intended that section 453(b)(3) should be given a broader application. If we were to adopt the taxpayer's argument, we would substantially nullify section 453 with respect to cash basis taxpayers receiving deferred payment obligations other than those described in section 453(b)(3). Such taxpayers, not required to include the fair market value of their obligations in determining the amount realized under section 1001(b), would rarely, if ever, elect to report on the installment basis. In the light of the other legislative history of section 453, hitherto discussed, it is clear to us that Congress, in 1969, did not contemplate, or intend, such a result.

III. Case Law

The prior decisions of our own court support the conclusion we have reached. On several occasions, we have held that if the fair market value of a deferred payment obligation received in a sale or other exchange can be ascertained, that fair market value must be included as an amount realized under §1001(b). Most recently, in *In re Steen*, 509 F.2d 1398, 1404-05 (9th Cir. 1975), we held that the fair market value of an installment payment contract received in exchange for shares of stock was ascertainable and that, consequently, that fair market value was an amount realized in the year of the sale. In *Heller Trust v. Commissioner*, 382 F.2d 675, 681 (9th Cir. 1967), our court affirmed a Tax Court decision requiring a taxpayer to include the fair market value of real estate contracts as an amount realized in the year of a sale, even though the fair market value of the contracts there involved was only 50 percent of their face value. See also *Clodfelter v. Commissioner*, 426 F.2d 1391 (9th Cir. 1970); *Tombari v. Commissioner*, 299 F.2d 889, 892-93 (9th Cir. 1962); *Gersten v. Commissioner*, 267 F.2d 195 (9th Cir. 1959).

There are, of course, "rare and extraordinary" situations in which it is impossible to ascertain the fair market value of a deferred payment obligation in the year of sale. See Treas. Reg. §1.1001-1(a). The total amount payable under an obligation may be so speculative, or the right to receive any payments at all so contingent, that the fair market value of the obligation cannot be fixed. See *Burnet v. Logan*, 283 U.S. 404, 75 L. Ed. 1143, 51 S. Ct. 550 (1931); *In re Steen*, 509 F.2d 1398, 1403-04 (9th Cir. 1975) (right to payment depended on favorable judicial decision on novel question of state law); *Westover v. Smith*, 173 F.2d 90 (9th Cir. 1949). If an obligation is not marketable, it may be impossible to establish its fair market value. See *Willhoit v. Commissioner*, 308 F.2d 259 (9th Cir. 1962) (uncontradicted testimony that there was no market for high risk contracts); *Phillips v. Frank*, 295 F.2d 629 (9th Cir. 1961) (uncontradicted testimony that highly speculative contracts could not have been sold in the year of sale). But see *United States v. Davis*, 370 U.S. 65, 71-74, 8 L. Ed. 2d 335, 82 S. Ct. 1190 (1962) (wife's release of her marital rights in a property settlement agreement held to have a fair market value equal to the value of property that her husband transferred to her in exchange); *Gersten v. Commissioner*, *supra* at 197 ("It is not necessary to find any actual sales of like articles to establish a fair market value.")

The Tax Court found, as a fact, that the taxpayer's real estate contract with the Storeys had a fair market value of $76,980 in the taxable year of sale. Consequently, the taxpayer must include $76,980 in determining the amount realized under §1001 (b). As previously noted, however, the Commissioner has conceded that the taxpayer is eligible to report on the installment basis and has calculated the taxpayer's deficiency accordingly.

The decision of the Tax Court is reversed, and on remand, the Tax Court will enter judgment for the Commissioner.

REVERSED and remanded, with directions.

The Different Theories for Taxing Written Promises

In contrast to *Warren Jones*, the Fifth Circuit in *Cowden v. Commissioner*,[805] applied tax accounting principles and ruled that a written obligation is taxable only if it is a "cash equivalent," and that it is a cash equivalent only if it is assignable and trades at not more than a modest discount. In that decision, on facts conceptually similar to *Warren Jones*'s, the court held that as long as the property received has a fair market value and there actually is a market for such property in that area, the cash-method taxpayer must report that value as an amount realized when received. *Warren Jones* depends on §1001 (amount realized in connection with property transactions) as the basis for the decision, whereas *Cowden* relied on cash equivalency, which is a tax accounting concept. One has to wonder how the courts can get so far apart over basic issues. Notice how Reg. §15A.453-1(d)(2)(i) adopts the *Warren Jones* property-oriented rule that cash method sellers who elect out of the installment method must be taxed on t least the value of the property they sold if the sold property is capable of valuation. Is this overreaching in the sense that Congress did not amend §451 (which contains the general rule for the taxable year of inclusion of income) so the Treasury Department has no authority under §453 to regulate how one is taxed under §1001 on electing out?[806] Could *Warren Jones* doom cash-method accounting in the sense of turning almost any promise into taxable property?

10. Sales on the Installment Method

Read §453(a)-(c), (i) and Reg. §15A.453-1(a)-(b)(2)

The installment method is of the utmost importance to taxpayers engaged in sales of large properties. It is a separate method of tax accounting applied on a sale-by-sale basis. Thus, for example, a cash method farmer is free to use the installment method when he or she sells a barn for a note. If it were not for the installment sale method, the seller would generally have to report the purchase price in the year of the sale, as we saw above. The purpose of installment sales treatment is to let the seller match receipts of cash with his tax liabilities by prorating the tax to the payments received. In effect, installment sales treatment assures that the taxpayer will always have at least enough cash to pay the tax that is due on the associated payment. If it were not for this relief provision, the seller might not be able to meet its Federal Income Tax obligations. Consistent with the theory, §453's scope is limited to spreading gains, never losses. Also, it is unavailable for sales of inventory, most dealer property, and publicly traded stock.[807]

805 289 F.2d 20 (5th Cir. 1961).

806 See Goldberg, *Open Transaction Treatment of Deferred Payment Sales After the Installment Sales Act of 1980*, 34Tax Lawyer 605 (1981).

807 See §453(b), (k).

The operative heart of §453 is §453(c). It is one of those Code sections that can be reduced to a formula. Once the formula is revealed, the installment sale method seems much less mysterious. The purpose of the formula is to identify the portion of each current payment, aside from interest, which is treated as producing a taxable gain in the year in which it is received. The approach is to multiply every cash payment received by a fraction. The fraction is:

$$\frac{\text{Gross Profit}}{\text{Total Contract Price}}$$

"Total contract price" means the selling price of the property. The term "selling price" means the gross sales price -- ignoring debt encumbering the property, interest and selling expenses. The term "gross profit" is the selling price of the property minus its adjusted basis.[808]

To illustrate: Imagine that you owned a car which had a basis of $1,000 and that you agreed to sell it to a friend of yours for $3,000, but the friend could only pay one-half today and the remaining one-half next year. How much of each of these payments will be taxable and how much would be treated as a return of capital? Applying the formula you would determine that the installment gain fraction was:

$$\frac{\text{Gross Profit}}{\text{Total Contract Price}} \qquad \frac{\$2{,}000}{\$3{,}000}$$

In other words 2/3rds of any payment is taxable, so of this year's $1,500 payment, $1,000 is taxable as a gain and $500 is a nontaxable return of capital. As a consequence of not electing out of the installment sale method you have in effect elected into it, and as a result, you will report a $1,000 gain this year and a $1,000 gain next year, correctly reporting a $2,000 profit over the two-year span.

Reg. §15A.453-1(b)(2) covers the situation in which property is subject to an encumbrance.

To illustrate: If you sold the same car as above, but it was subject to "qualifying indebtedness" of $1,000 (which the buyer either assumed or to which the property would remain subject after the sale) you must only get $2,000 (not $3,000) in cash. The Regulations force you to reduce the total contract price from $3,000 to $2,000 and every penny of cash paid is taxable. (To put it another way, the gross profit ratio is 100%). You ought to see that it is a logical result because it does not result in over-taxation or under-taxation of your economic gain, which is $2,000, all of which you will get in cash.

808 See Reg. §15A.453-1(b)(2).

Reread Reg. §15A.453-1(b)(2)(iv) for the definition of the term "qualifying indebtedness." Now what if the qualifying indebtedness exceeds the taxpayer's basis in the property? The answer is that the excess is treated as a cash payment in the year of the sale, because the seller and her property are no longer subject to, or the primary obligors on, the debt.[809]

> **To illustrate:** Tracking the running example, one could change the facts to make the indebtedness $1,500. In that case, there would be a deemed payment of $500 of cash in the year of sale arising out of the debt in excess of basis. We also know that the buyer would only pay $1,500 in cash for the car because she valued it only at $3,000. This time the gross profit divided by the total contract price is again 100%, so all of the cash will be taxed when received. That means that if the buyer paid $750 in cash this year and $750 in cash next year all of that cash should be taxed. Once again, the system makes sense because it would impose a tax on a total of $2,000 of gain, (i.e., $500 (deemed cash gain in first year) + $750 (actual cash gain in first year) + $750 (actual cash gain in second year) which is the true economic gain.

The character and holding period of the gain arising from an installment sale is determined by the character of the property on the day it is sold.[810] This makes it possible to have installment sales of assets that produce short-term capital gain, even though the payments are made over decades, as well as sales that are simply of noncapital assets; however, many noncapital assets (such as inventory) are specifically excluded from installment sale treatment.

Now for another significant restriction, namely §453(i). This is a potentially devastating rule, because it means that the entire amount of any taxable depreciation recapture must be reported in the year of sale, even though the taxpayer is otherwise reporting the transaction on the installment method. The result may be a larger tax than the cash available from the sale. To the extent that any gain remains after reporting the ordinary income arising from depreciation recapture, that remaining gain can be reported under §453. The calculation is a bit knotty, but it is logical.

> **To illustrate:** Mr. X, a stranger, sells depreciated property in which he has an adjusted basis of $20 to a buyer for $100, payable in 10 annual installments of $10 starting in the year *after* the sale. Mr. X has taken $30 in depreciation deductions, all of which constitute recapture income. He must recognize the $30 recapture income in the year of sale, even though he was paid nothing that year. His gross profit percentage for each $10 payment received after the year of sale is 50% ($20 basis + $30 recapture income added to basis = $50, divided by the total contract price of $100). This means he correctly reports a total profit of $80, of which $30 is in year one and the rest over the life of the contract, just as if he had sold the property for $100 of cash in year one.

---

809 See Reg. §15A.453-1(b)(3)(i).

810 See, e.g., Picchione v. Commissioner, 440 F.2d 170 (1st Cir. 1971), cert. denied (1971).

> The nasty part is that recapture income comes so fast, instead of being prorated. The rule exists to put an end to tax avoidance practice, but it seems like overkill.

Note

Sweden recognizes the policy problem that postponing tax on sales for deferred payments instantly creates depreciable basis for the buyer, and counters by taxing gain immediately if the property is a depreciable capital asset. Japan puts almost all transactions on the accrual method, thereby forcing immediate taxation of sales for deferred payments, evidently with no discount for the fact that the payments are deferred. There are numerous other approaches.[811]

Problem 9-11:

Clara sold one-tenth of an acre of land held for investment to her son, a third-year law student. He could not pay the purchase price of $50,000 at one time, so Clara (who had a basis of $1,000 in the land, which she had held for 40 years) accepted a down payment of $2,000 in August of the year of sale (Year 1), plus payments of $2,000 to be made annually beginning in Year 2 and in each of the next 23 years. If the sale goes according to plan, how will Clara be taxed, in dollars, assuming she does not make the §453(d) election, in this and later years?

Contingent Payment Sales

Sometimes, one just cannot settle on a price. Here is one way bargaining between the shrewd and not-so-shrewd may go:

> Buyer: [Planning to trap Seller] "So, what are the prospects for the company you want to sell me?"
>
> Seller: [Being naive and thinking he is safe "puffing" the company's prospects] "I figure sales will double every three years, and profits will triple every four years."
>
> Buyer: "OK, let's set the sales price at $100,000 plus three times the profits in year six." [More than the asking price, if what seller claims is true, but less than the asking price if Seller is exaggerating.]
>
> Seller: [Sheepishly] "Okay."

811 See H. J. Ault, COMPARATIVE INCOME TAXATION 3rd ed. pp. 258-260 (Kluwer 2010).

After the seller gets over being trapped so easily into fixing a risky purchase price, the parties will settle on a contingent sales price, meaning a price that cannot be determined at the end of the year of sale.[812] Bowing to the need to accommodate the installment sales method to the reality that contingent sales price contracts do occur, §453(j)(2) and Reg. §15A.453-1(c)(1) lay out some helpful, if arbitrary, rules. The core idea is to break contingent price sales into three groups, and treat each group differently:

1. Those with a contract having a maximum stated selling price, such as "not over $325,000";

2. Those with no maximum selling price, but having a determinable sales period, such as "payable for 25 years"; and,

3. Those with neither a maximum price nor a maximum period; one has to inspect these with care and first make sure they are not really licenses or rentals.

Now the rules for each type:

1. If there is a maximum stated price, then all contingencies are resolved in favor of maximizing the price.[813] This means one assumes the maximum price *is* the sales price. If this turns out to be wrong, and the taxpayer's profit is overstated, then the taxpayer claims a remedial loss in the final year. This is pretty complicated and a fairly harsh result for the taxpayer.

2. If there is only a maximum period, then Reg. §15A.453-1(c)(3)(i) generally requires the taxpayer to divide his basis in the property sold by the maximum period (say 25 years) and then apply that identical amount of basis against all receipts to determine his gain for each year. This can result in overstated income if in some years the taxpayer receives less cash than the basis allocated to the year. Instead of being allowed a current loss, the regulations defer all losses until the last possible year.

3. Where there is no maximum price or term, the general rule is to take the taxpayer's basis, divide it by (a completely arbitrary) 15 years, and offset each payment by one-15th of basis for 15 years to determine his gain for each year. Thereafter, the result

812 Reg. §15A.453-1(c)(1).

813 Reg. §15A.453-1(c)(2)(i)(A).

may be pure gain. Again, any potential losses are pushed forward to the last year of the transaction.[814]

Now, turn to the Regulations and work the following problem. It is really just a matter of "plugging in the numbers" to calculate the result.

Problem 9-12:

Dr. Hu is a cash-method calendar-year engineer who owns all the stock of Embigulator, Inc. a company that claims to be able to make things bigger by means of its novel invention, the Embigulator. The company has highly uncertain prospects. Dr. Hu has a $100 basis in the stock. Dr. Hu sells all the stock of Embigulator, Inc. to Grabber International Corp. for 20% of the earnings of Embigulator, Inc. for the next 25 years. She in fact got $15/year for the next 25 years.

1) What result to Dr. Hu each year?

2) What if she were on the accrual method? Any difference in result?

3) Assume there is no 25-year limit, but that the maximum stated sales price is $300. What result if after 20 years of paying $15/year Grabber International Corp. rightly stops paying Dr. Hu?

4) Assume there is no stated maximum period or sales price, and Grabber International Corp. pays $15 per year like clockwork. Assuming it is really a sale, how is Dr. Hu taxed?

5) Dr. Hu owns and operates a mine with a basis of $1,000. She sells the mine to Centrifugal Mining Co. for $500 down and 10% of the output. Assume that Dr. Hu is on the cash method of accounting and she elects out of §453 and assume neither the mine nor the obligation can be valued, but that it is a real sale, not a license.

    a. What does she report on her return at the end of year one?

    b. If in year two the mine opens and has $4,000 of output, what result?

    c. If in year three the mine has $2,000 of output, what result?

814 Reg. §15A-453-1(c)(4).

6) Same as "(5)", except that this time she sells her mine for $2,000 down and a note with a face amount of $48,000 issued from Centrifugal Mining, payable in ten years.

   a. What result in the year of sale if she is an accrual method taxpayer and elects out of §453?

   b. What result in the year of sale if the note is only worth $35,000? See Reg. §15A.453-1(d)(2)(i). Assume that Dr. Hu is on the cash method.[815]

a. First Abuse: Second Disposition of Property Sold on the Installment Method

The installment method gives the buyer a cost basis in the property when it is bought. That is consistent with the general rules for creating cost basis. The trouble is, it can lead to abuse because the buyer may get a major increase in basis compared to the seller's basis, and can sell the purchased property at once with no gain. That is not a big deal if the buyer and seller are unrelated; but if they are related, there is a chance to put tax-free money in the buyer's hands while deferring income to the seller.

Here is an example.

> **To illustrate:** Texans, W.B. Rushing and his partner, Max Tidmore, sold appreciated corporate stock to trusts they formed for their children. Assume the stock had a basis of $40 to Rushing and Tidmore and was worth $100. The trustee was the Lubbock Citizens Bank, which Rushing and Tidmore did not control. Next year, the trusts sold the stock claiming a full cost $100 basis against the sale's price. The IRS sought to deny Rushing and Tidmore the benefit of installment sales treatment, claiming they rather than the trust were the sellers and just turned over the sales proceeds to the trusts. No, said the Fifth Circuit, Rushing and Tidmore were engaged in legitimate tax planning and the sales to the trusts were genuine. It was not long until the case became a blueprint for a new tax-avoidance practice, the "Rushing Trust."

Now take a look at §453(e) and see if it changes the result in *Rushing*.

Problem 9-13:

Refer back to Problem 9-9, and assume the following:

815 My thanks to Messrs. Freeland, Lathrope, Lind and Stephens, FUNDAMENTALS OF FEDERAL INCOME TAXATION, 17th Ed. (Fndn. Press 2010), for inspiring this problem set.

After making the payment in Year 2 in December, Clara's son sold the property to a stranger for $35,000. How does Clara report the income from the sale in year 1 and year 2 under the installment sale method? Assume there was tax avoidance intent.

b. Second Abuse: Disposition of the Installment Obligation

Read §453B(a)-(b)

The principle underlying the installment sale is that the seller has a tax timing problem that Congress sought to resolve, namely that the seller is exposed to the risk of holding installment paper and owing a tax without the necessary cash to pay the tax. If the seller in fact sells, exchanges or otherwise dumps the installment obligation, Congress takes the view that need for relief has ended and generally seeks to tax the seller on the deferred gain. The key concept is that the taxpayer must report as the amount realized whatever he got for the installment obligation (or its fair market value if it was transferred away in a non-taxable exchange) minus its remaining unrecovered basis. The basis in the obligation is the excess of its value over the amount of gain that would have been recognized if it were satisfied in full. In other words, it is the return of capital component if the obligation were paid in full. There is no change in the *character* of the gain resulting from the taxable disposition of the installment obligations. There are relief provisions for transfers resulting from death, between spouses, or incident to divorce, among others, but not for gifts.[816]

Problem 9-14:

Refer back to Problem 9-11 and assume that in Year 2, before Clara received any further payments, Clara sold the notes for $45,000 in cash.

1) What is her realized gain in Year 1?

2) What is her basis in the notes at the beginning of Year 2?

3) What is her recognized gain in Year 2?

4) If Clara dies at the beginning of Year 2, owning the notes, and they pass to her estate, do the notes get a full step-up in basis or do they produce gain to the person who inherits them? See §§ 691(a)(4)(A) and §691(c).

816 §453B(c), (g).

5) How would Clara be taxed if her son paid her only $2,000 per year for 15 years, and never made any payments after paying a total of $30,000, completed in year 15? (The balance then became uncollectible because of her son's financial troubles and later flight to Turkestan.) See §453B(f).

c. Third Abuse: Pledge of Installment Obligations

Read §453A(d)

Again, Congress was concerned that certain taxpayers might be stuck in the position of having more taxes than they have cash to pay when they engage in sales for deferred payments. However, in the real world, it is often possible to bring an installment obligation to a bank and to borrow against it. In such cases the need for relief is at least partially eliminated by the taxpayer's own actions. What would be the impact of §453A(d) if the following were to occur?

Problem 9-15:

You agree to sell your car, which has a basis of $1,000, to a friend who agrees to pay $2,000, of which $1,000 will be paid now and $1,000 next year, plus an appropriate rate of interest. After receiving $1,000 of payments, you take the installment note to the bank and grant the bank a security interest in the note. In exchange, you borrow $800 on the strength of the security interest.

1) What is the Federal Income Tax effect of this transaction?

2) What, if anything, should happen to you for tax purposes in year two when your friend in fact pays you the $1,000 and you repay the bank the remaining $1,000?

d. Fourth Abuse: Overuse of the Installment Sale Method

Read §453A(a)-(c)

Section 453A was enacted in response to the Treasury Department's view that the installment method was causing an excessive deferral of taxes.[817]

Section 453A tacks an interest charge onto the tax deferral associated with sales of property on the installment method, but only if the taxpayer had at least $5 million worth of outstanding installment obligations at year-end, and then only if the item was sold for over $150,000. Interest is based on the rate imposed on underpayments of tax.[818] There are various exceptions,

817 See, *ABA Committee Advises Treasury on Formulating Forthcoming Nondealer Regulations*, 91 Tax Notes 115-121 (1991).

818 §453A(a)-(c).

especially for sales of personal use property and farm property.[819] As a practical matter, §453A all but robs "Fortune 500" corporations of the opportunity to use the installment sale method.

11. Variations on the Installment Sale Method

Estate planners use variants of the installment sale method to minimize their clients' estates. The planner's goal is to have the obligation that the estate owner holds expire at the estate owner's death. By doing so, the property is exempt from estate taxes. Two leading techniques are:

1. The private annuity. This is an annuity contract issued by a buyer of property. It provides for payments as long as the seller is alive. Each payment is prorated into a return of capital, gain and an interest component.[820] When the seller dies, the annuity expires and is not in his estate, thereby saving estate taxes. The regulations under §72 may kill the practice off.[821]

2. The self-canceling installment obligation ("SCIN"). This is an installment obligation that expires on the seller's death.

The details of these powerful planning concepts are for the course in estate planning.

12. Inventory Accounting

Merchants and manufacturers are not expected to account for each separate item of inventory they sell, because the task of tracing each item, its cost and its sale price, would be overwhelming. Instead, we have so-called inventory accounting as a crude surrogate.

Now, imagine for a moment you run a country store and that you bought no inventory this year. Assuming you started the year with $50,000 of inventory and were left with $10,000 of year-end inventory, you would know that the cost of the inventory you sold was $40,000. (The $40,000 is your "cost of goods sold.") You would compare it to your sales and that would give you your gross inventory profit or loss. You could then deduct further items such as rents and salaries to calculate the net profit or loss from your store for the year.

You can't keep this up for long, or you will have nothing to sell, so you will also buy inventory and pay for related freight costs. You can now understand why cost of goods sold is calculated as follows:

---

819 §453A(b)(3).

820 See Rev. Rul. 69-74, 1969-1 C.B. 43.

821 Reg. §1.72-6(e) and 1.1001-1(j).

	Beginning inventory
+	Purchases and freight costs
-	Closing inventory
	Cost of goods sold

There are various complicating factors. One is that one has to make an assumption about how the year-end inventory was valued. Do we assume the closing inventory is left over after selling the most recently purchased inventory (this is the last-in-first-out method, aka LIFO) or vice-versa (first-in-first-out, aka FIFO)? Also, so-called "full absorption" inventory forces taxpayers to include various kinds of overhead (such as salaries) in each unit of manufactured inventory such as the worker's wages.[822] Another issue is how one appraises the year-end inventory; the general rule is that one uses the lower of its cost or market value.[823] Inventory accounting is definitely not a subject for Tax I.Fortunately, we now have sophisticated software that allows small merchants to use "point of sale" inventory accounting.

Problem 9-16:

The Beenie Baby Store buys dolls wholesale from the National Beenie Baby Corporation and sells them at retail. This year the Beenie Baby Store had opening inventory (This is the same as closing inventory for the prior year)of $110,000, and closing inventory of $97,000. In addition, it bought $236,000 worth of dolls, including freight and got $399,000 in sales revenues.

1) What was its cost of goods sold?

2) What was its gross profit or loss on sales of dolls?

3) Can it use the cash method to account for purchases and sales of the dolls? See Reg. §1.446-1(c)(2)(i).

Notice how if a merchant removed some dolls for personal consumption, he could probably get away with concealing his misdeed. The result would be a tax deduction (via apparently increased cost of goods sold) for untaxed personal consumption.[824] According to one commentator, if taxpayers would stop cheating on their inventories the national debt would be paid off quickly.[825] Taxpayers are entitled to reduce the value of closing inventory to accommodate

822 See Reg. §1.471-11(a) and §263A.

823 Reg. §1.471-2(c).

824 §471.

825 See Skinner, *Inventory Valuation Problems*, 50 TAXES 748(1972).

the problem of "shrinkage" (damage to goods, shoplifting, etc.).[826] The trouble is, they may be shoplifting from themselves.

13. Debt Instruments Issued for Property

a. Background -- Compounding and Discounting

For a refresher on how compounding and discounting interest works, refer back to the discussion beginning in Chapter 6 subchapter N (Financial Analysis).

b. Imputed Interest under §483

So far, we have assumed that the seller charges a reasonable amount of interest to account for the deferral in payment. What if there is no separate interest charge, but the sales price of a capital asset is raised to compensate the seller for the deferral in payment? If the parties can get away with it, the result would be an enlarged capital gain to the seller and a higher cost basis for the buyer. Congress caught on to this in 1964 and enacted §483 which converts some part of the alleged purchase price into interest. This stowaway interest is often referred to as "unstated interest." When unstated interest is discovered, it reduces the sales price of the property and replaces it with identical amounts of " unstated interest." This unstated interest is reported only as actual payments are made, unlike the case for OID, where the imputation occurs with the passage of time. Section 483 is simpler than its relatives, §§ 1274 and 1274A, so the materials begin with §483.

Section 483 only applies to deferred-payment transactions if specific conditions are met, the most important of which are that the sales price be over $3,000 and that there be at least one payment scheduled more than a year from the sale date.

Section 483 works by comparing the interest rate that was actually charged to an external standard for determining what should have been charged at a minimum, and declares the shortfall unstated interest. That shortfall reduces the amount realized and increases the unstated interest component by the same amount.

So how can one tell if there is unstated interest? The answer is that unstated interest exists when the stated interest in a transaction is less than the Applicable Federal Rate ("AFR"). The calculation requires three steps.

First, determine the applicable AFR. To do so, you must determine whether the transaction is a short-term, mid-term, or long-term transaction and check the relevant Internal Revenue Bulletin for the AFR for that term. Short-term means the term of the contract is 3 years or less. Mid-term mean the term exceeds 3 years but is less than 9 years. Long-term means the term

826 See §471(b).

exceeds 9 years.[827] To find the answer, you go to the tax library and look up the AFR for the month of the transaction, as set forth in an Internal Revenue Bulletin. Assume for illustrative purposes that the term is four years, so it is a medium-term loan, and that the AFR is 5 percent, compounded semi-annually.

Second, determine if there is unstated interest. Unstated interest, if any equals:

A. The sum of alleged principal payments, minus

B. The amount of these payments plus any stated interest,[828] discounted by the AFR, calculated semiannually.[829]

Present value is the principal amount, reduced by the erosion in value caused by the passage of time. Think of it this way: $1,000 loaned today will be worth more in the future because the interest is added to it. So if the interest rate is 10%, $1,000 today is worth $1,100 in one year at simple interest. Conversely, money received now for a debt to be paid in the future is reduced. If someone has agreed to pay you $1,100 in a year and the applicable interest rate is 10%, that money is only worth $1,000 now in a world without taxes.

So, if the sum of all payments was $10,000 and the amount of these payments plus any stated interest discounted by the AFR was $8,400, you would conclude that there was $1,600 of unstated interest. Once unstated interest is unmasked, the amount realized on the sale and the buyer's cost basis of the property that was sold must be reduced by that unstated interest. One must complete the next step to time the imputed interest income.

Third, stated and unstated interest must be apportioned among the payments. Stated and unstated interest are spread over the instrument's term by §1271(a). This calls for determining the amount of unstated interest paid semiannually by multiplying the present value of the payments by the AFR, and then subtracting any stated interest for that period. The illustration will expand on this.

To illustrate: Clara sells her car to her son for the strange sum of $3,154.43. Both are cash-method, calendar- year taxpayers. Clara's basis in the car is $2,000. Her son must pay $1,000 down, $1,050.62 a year later and another $1,103.81 in year 3. The contract does not call for interest payments.

The contract is signed on July 1, 2018 with the down payment due immediately. The next payment is due on July 1, 2019. Determine the amount, if any, of unstated interest.

827 §1274(d)(1)(A).

828 §483(b).

829 §1274(b)(2).

1) Determine the AFR:

Assume that the Internal Revenue Bulletin lists the AFR as 5 percent, compounded semi-annually.

2) Isolate the unstated interest:

	Sum of the alleged principal payments	*$3,154.43*
Minus discounted present value of $3,154.43:		
	$1,000 this year [down payment]	
+	1,000 next year [present value of the $1,050.62]	
+	1,000 two years later [present value of the $1,103.81]	
	Total actual principle payments equal $3,000	(3,000.00)
Answer: unstated interest		*$ 154.43*

3) Allocate the unstated interest to each payment:

	Down payment	$0
	First installment	$1,050.62
-	Its present value @ 5% compounded semiannually is	(1,000.00)
Interest apportioned to first installment		*$ 50.62*
	Second installment:	$1,103.81
-	Its present value @ 5% compounded semiannually is	(1,000.00)
Interest apportioned to second installment:		*$ 103.81*

Because the taxpayers are both on the cash method, Clara cannot report interest income and her son cannot report interest expense until actual payments are made; the interest is buried in the actual payments.

Accrual method taxpayers will report the income or expense as it accrues, regardless of when payments are made.

We now know that the gross-profit percentage is $1,000/3,000 = 33%. Thus, the gain on the car sale is really $1,000, not $1,154.43. The $154.43 is taxed as interest.

In daily life, §483 is the most likely tool for imputing interest to deferred payment sales. The next subject is the more elegant system of §1274, which generally involves larger sales and usually compels the buyer and seller to use the accrual method to expose and report the interest income.

c. Section 1274 and 1274A: Debts Issued for Property under the OID Rules

The OID rules are broader and more powerful than §483, but they serve the same basic function of smoking out stowaway interest. The rules are too intricate for a survey course, so what follows is a high-altitude view of the subject.

OID arises where a debt instrument is issued for cash at a price lower than its face amount. The difference is treated as interest and accrues on a daily basis to the buyer of the debt, and may be deducted by the issuer as the debt accrues, a tidily symmetrical result. This kind of OID is fairly easy to detect and deal with. It is controlled by §1272, which you have already seen. This is a fast review:

> **To illustrate:** Grabber International, Inc. publicly issues a 20 year bond with a face amount of $1,000,000 (known as the "redemption price at maturity"). The public only paid $800,000 for the bond. That means that the "issue price" for the bond only added up to $800,000.[830] As a result, there is $200,000 of OID.
>
> As time passes, the holders of the bonds will gradually report the $200,000 as income, and will increase their bases in their bonds every day,[831] as the OID accrues.
>
> Grabber International will claim symmetrical interest expense deductions under §163(e). The interest so discovered will be reported on a compound method of the type you saw above.[832]
>
> The legislative alternative would be to treat the $200,000 as a capital gain and allow it to be taxed at low rates creating a huge loophole in the tax laws.

The subject of this section is sales of property, so we need to contemplate debt instruments issued for property. This time the dominant authority is §1274, which generally steps in when the debt instrument has a term of over six months and the sum of all the payments of interest and principal under the debt exceed $250,000.[833] OID computations are more complicated if debt is issued for property than when issued for cash because with property the "issue price" is not clear. It must be inferred. By contrast, if the property buyer (issuer) got cash, we would

830 See §1273(a)-(b).

831 This increase results in a new, higher "adjusted issue price" of the debt every day. Prospective additions of OID are calculated once every six months, resulting in a gradually-rising level of daily interest and additions to basis.

832 The method has various impressive names: the "economic accrual method" or "constant yield to maturity method" (meaning a constant rate of interest applied to an increasing base that accounts for prior accumulated interest).

833 §1274(c)(3)(C).

know the exact issue price. Determining the OID calls for an easy subtraction, as you saw in the illustration. The only hard part is timing.

If the buyer transferred property in exchange for the debt, the issue price ought to be the value of the property when it was transferred. If the property is publicly traded -- say IBM stock -- finding a value is easy. In these easy cases, one just adapts the usual OID rules, pretending the value of the publicly-traded property was the "issue price" in cash. The other cases -- where the property does not have a readily ascertainable value -- are not so easy. Congress might have required appraisals of such property, but instead it enacted §1274, which generally ignores the problem of appraising the value of the property received and instead discounts the actual payments under the debt instrument and derives their value in today's dollars. Here is an example that ought to seem familiar:[834]

> **To illustrate:** Seller conveys a Big Thing to Buyer for $3,154,430 payable: $1 million down on January 1 of year one plus a note for $2,154,430 bearing no interest, of which $1,050,620 is in year 2, and another $1,103,810 is due in year 3. Assume the applicable short-term AFR for January of year one to be 5% compounded semi-annually,which freezes the unstated interest rate for the life of the contract. One then grabs one's imaginary hand calculator and discounts each of the deferred payments, using semi-annual compounding. Conclusion: the discounted present value of the two payments is $2 million and the OID is $154,430.
>
> The OID hidden in the deal is $154,430, determined as follows:
>
> | | |
> |---|---|
> | Nominal payment of principal | $2,154,430 |
> | Less present value of nominal payments | (2,000,000) |
> | Unmasked OID | $ 154,430 |
>
> As usual, Buyer will take a basis that is pared down by the OID; in this case, basis will be $3 million -- because it is the "real" purchase price of the Big Thing. That will also be Buyer's amount realized. Buyer will report interest expense of $154,430 and Seller will report $154,430 of interest income in addition to gain.

Now we know the OID, but we do not know how much has to be reported during the two-year period. The answer is to start by taking the discounted present value of the future payments ($2 million) and multiplying them by the OID rate, compounded semi-annually.

> **To illustrate:** Take the discounted present value of the future payments ($2 million) and multiply it by 5%, compounded semi-annually. The product of $2 million at 5 percent is $100,000.

834 The example is from B. Bittker & L. Lokken, FEDERAL TAXATION OF INCOME, ESTATES AND GIFTS ¶ 54.3 (2019).

Now divide that $100,000 by two to satisfy the law's requirement of *semi-annual* compounding; the solution is $50,000. This is the amount accrued by mid-year.

Now add that amount to the original debt ($2,000,000 + $50,000 = $2,050,000). Now multiply $2,050,000 by the 5% AFR. This time the product is $51,250. That means the sum of all OID for the first year is $101,250 (i.e., $50,000 + $51,250). This is what Seller must report as income and what Buyer can likely claim an interest expense deduction for in Year 2. Seller increases its basis in the debt every day as the interest income accrues, in order to prevent double taxation as the debt matures and is paid off.

The remaining interest of $53,180 will arise in year 3, based on the unpaid balance of $1,101,250.[835]

These examples have been extreme in that the contracts called for no stated interest. They would have been more complicated if there had been some stated interest and some unstated interest; but the basic procedures are the same.

Problem 9-17:

Seller sells a Very Big Thing for $2,653,300 when the long-term AFR is 10%, compounded semi-annually. The money is due in full in 10 years and there is no stated interest. Use the compounding table a few pages back for help.

1) How much of the "sales price" is really interest?

2) When is the interest reported? Year 1? Year 10? Some in each year?

3) If Seller has a $100,000 basis in the Very Big Thing, what is her gain or loss on the sale?

4) Can she report the gain on the installment method?

5) When does she report the gain?

6) Assuming Buyer can deduct the interest, if any, when does buyer deduct it? All in year 1? Year 10? Over the years?

7) How much interest, if any, can Buyer deduct in total?

835 Those who wish to work out the answer will find a rounding error of about $2,600.

8) If Seller does report interest periodically, will it be reported in equal amounts each year? If not, will the interest be larger or smaller per period over time?

9) What will be Seller's basis in the debt at the end of year 10?

10) If the Very Big Thing were Seller's home, what would be the difference in tax treatment to the parties? See §1274(c).

D. ADVANCED APPLICATIONS

There is a long list of specialized timing rules that there is no time to study in detail. These include:

1) Small commercial banks can generally deduct estimated bad-debt losses on the basis of their experience. Commercial banks with over $500 million in assets can deduct bad debts only as they arise.[836]

2) Publishers of periodicals can claim current tax deductions for expenditures to increase their subscribers, even though the expenditure should otherwise be capitalized.[837]

3) Mining companies can deduct exploration costs under §617 and mine development costs under §616, even though they would normally be capitalized.

4) People who drill for oil can deduct the soft costs (labor, fuels, etc, known as "intangible drilling and development costs") of drilling a well currently, even though they would normally be capitalized.[838]

5) Taxpayers can deduct up to $15,000 of costs for removing architectural and transportation barriers that interfere with the mobility of people with disabilities, even though such costs would normally be capitalized.[839]

---

836 §585(c).

837 §173.

838 §263(c).

839 §190.

6) The long-term contract method of accounting is commonly used for large projects and military procurement. The system calls for determining how much of the contract was completed each year and allocating income to the year in accordance with portion of estimated costs that were actually incurred during the year.[840] If it is not a long-term contract, then one prorates income to the percentage of the contract completed in the year.

7) Nuclear power facilities' owners can make current contributions to trust funds used to hold money in anticipation of shutting down the "nuke." There is no deduction except to the extent the taxpayer puts in money.[841]

8) Owners of mines and solid waste sites can deduct accruals made to fund future cleanups and mine closings. The system is at once elegant and shady. It is elegant in that the accruals use a "sinking fund" approach under which each subsequent year's deduction is slightly larger than the prior year's, to accommodate the investment return on the prior year's contribution. It is shady in that no cash need in fact be contributed so there is a risk that no actual payment will ever be made. For example, a mine owner might go bankrupt, leaving the public in the lurch.[842]

840 §460.

841 §468A(a).

842 §468.

CHAPTER 10 - INTEGRITY OF THE TAXABLE YEAR

A. INTRODUCTION

If you were designing a tax system, you would probably want to make sure that your tax administrators could file away taxpayers' annual returns with confidence that they would only be reopened under unusual circumstances. At the same time, you would see that some transactions, such as building an aircraft carrier, cannot be completed in a single year, and that trying to calculate annual profits or losses in such circumstances is not realistic and that, with the benefit of hindsight, the earlier years' tax results could be quite wrong because of their speculative foundation.

There are various ways to resolve these multi-year problems. Solutions fall into various categories:

a) Statutes of limitations on audits and refunds -- putting an end to changes in earlier years' tax liabilities;

b) Special treatment of long-term contracts, in which profits are determined annually by prorating projected profits to the current year;

c) Allowing business losses and losses on sales of capital assets to be preserved by spreading them into other years, rather than obliterating them as if they were mere personal consumption. This is performed by the net operating loss rules of §172 and the capital loss carryover rules of §1212.

d) Some way of handling situations where the taxpayer returns amounts that she over or under reported in a now closed tax year (handled by §1341); and,

e) Some way of dealing with situations where the taxpayer receives back something that she deducted in a now closed tax year (handled by §111).

The rest of this Chapter is primarily concerned with the last two items: first §1341, then §111 and a few words about long-term contracts.

B. RESTORATION OF PREVIOUSLY TAXED ITEMS

Read §1341(a), (b)(1)-(2)

1. Restorations under the Case Law

The following case shows the ancestry of §1341. The dissent by Justice Douglas is especially important.

UNITED STATES v. LEWIS
340 U.S. 590, 71 S. Ct. 522 (1951).

MR. JUSTICE BLACK delivered the opinion of the Court.

Respondent Lewis brought this action in the Court of Claims seeking a refund of an alleged overpayment of his 1944 income tax. The facts found by the Court of Claims are: In his 1944 income tax return, respondent reported about $ 22,000 which he had received that year as an employee's bonus. As a result of subsequent litigation in a state court, however, it was decided that respondent's bonus had been improperly computed; under compulsion of the state court's judgment he returned approximately $ 11,000 to his employer. Until payment of the judgment in 1946, respondent had at all times claimed and used the full $ 22,000 unconditionally as his own, in the good faith though "mistaken" belief that he was entitled to the whole bonus.

On the foregoing facts the Government's position is that respondent's 1944 tax should not be recomputed, but that respondent should have deducted the $ 11,000 as a loss in his 1946 tax return. See G. C. M. 160, XV1 Cum. Bull. 179 (1936). The Court of Claims, however, relying on its own case, *Greenwald v. United States*, 102 Ct. Cl. 272, 57 F.Supp. 569, held that the excess bonus received "under a mistake of fact" was not income in 1944 and ordered a refund based on a recalculation of that year's tax. . . ."

In the *North American Oil* case we said: "If a taxpayer receives earnings under a claim of right and without restriction as to its disposition, he has received income which he is required to return, even though it may still be claimed that he is not entitled to retain the money, and even though he may still be adjudged liable to restore its equivalent." . . . Nothing in this language permits an exception merely because a taxpayer is "mistaken" as to the validity of his claim. Nor has the "claim of right" doctrine been impaired, as the Court of Claims stated, by *Freuler v. Helvering*, 291 U.S. 35, or *Commissioner v. Wilcox*, 327 U.S. 404. The *Freuler* case involved an entirely different section of the Internal Revenue Code, and its holding is inapplicable here. . . . And in *Commissioner v. Wilcox, supra*, we held that receipts from embezzlement did not constitute income, distinguishing *North American Oil* on the ground that an embezzler asserts no "bona fide legal or equitable claim." . . .

Income taxes must be paid on income received (or accrued) during an annual accounting period. . . . The "claim of right" interpretation of the tax laws has long been used to give finality to that period, and is now deeply rooted in the federal tax system. . . . We see no reason why the Court should depart from this wellsettled interpretation merely because it results in an advantage or disadvantage to a taxpayer.

Reversed.

MR. JUSTICE DOUGLAS, dissenting.

The question in this case is not whether the bonus had to be included in 1944 income for purposes of the tax. Plainly it should have been because the taxpayer claimed it as of right. Some years later, however, it was judicially determined that he had no claim to the bonus. The question is whether he may then get back the tax which he paid on the money.

Many inequities are inherent in the income tax. We multiply them needlessly by nice distinctions which have no place in the practical administration of the law. If the refund were allowed, the integrity of the taxable year would not be violated. The tax would be paid when due; but the Government would not be permitted to maintain the unconscionable position that it can keep the tax after it is shown that payment was made on money which was not income to the taxpayer.

Notes on *Lewis*

The last line of the case hints at something the majority did not state, namely that taxpayer Lewis reported $11,000 of gross income in 1944, but the deductible 1946 repayment did him no tax good, suggesting that he had little or no income in 1946.

The term "integrity of the taxable year" is often used as a shorthand expression for the concept that transactions in subsequent years cannot be the basis for adjusting the tax calculated for a prior year. The concept is well-established, and it haunts the Code.[843] Preserving the "integrity" of the prior year calls for changing the results in the current year only. In *Lewis* it called for not tampering with 1944.

843 See, e.g., Bainbridge v. United States, 107 F.Supp. 377 (N.D.N.Y. 1952).

2. Restoration under §1341

Read §1341(a)

Congress did not take the *Lewis* case sitting down. It responded by enacting §1341, a mandatory relief provision. When it applies, §1341 gives the taxpayer who restores an amount previously reported as gross income *the better of* a current deduction (as in *Lewis*), or a current tax credit equal to the prior year's Federal Income Tax burden caused by reporting the amount that the taxpayer eventually repaid. This generally puts taxpayers in a no-lose position, unless for example their tax rates are relatively stable in the year of overpayment and the year of restoration, in which case their only loss is of interest not received on the prior overpayment.

> **To illustrate:** Mr. Lyman, a single taxpayer, has gross income of $50,000 in year 1. His taxable income in year 1 was $34,100, on which he paid a tax of $7,507. Part of his income consisted of a $3,001 bonus, which was taxed at an imaginary top marginal rate of 34 per cent, producing a tax of $1,020.
>
> In year 10, Mr. Lyman earned the same amount of income and was in the 28 per cent bracket. In that year, he had to give back the $3,001 bonus.
>
> As a result of the payback, §1341 directs him to reduce his year 10 income by 34 per cent of $3,001, viz. $1,020. (He is not allowed to deduct the $3,001 in year 10, because that would yield a smaller tax saving (only 28% x $3,001) than the $1,020 credit.
>
> Ignoring the time value of money on the $1,020, Mr. Lyman gets a full reimbursement of the overpayment. If, by contrast, he were in a higher bracket in year 10 than in year 1, he would actually make money on the combined transaction (disregarding interest) because the tax burden on the extra income in the year of receipt would be less than the tax benefit of the deduction in the later year. Note that because of §1341(a)(3), if the restoration were $3,000 or less he would at most be entitled to a deduction. That gives §1341 an elitist touch.

Section 1341 is not an example of impressively thoughtful drafting. Because it unnecessarily incorporates the claim of right doctrine in its caption ("Computation of Tax Where Taxpayer Restores Substantial Amount Held Under Claim of Right"), its application has been erratic.

Relief under §1341 is available only if all following conditions are met:

1. An item was properly included in gross income for a prior taxable year (or years) because it *appeared* that the taxpayer had an unrestricted right to that item. This implication that the claim to the income has to be fragile from the outset has

created all sorts of trouble. For example, if the receipt was illegal, there could be no "claim of right."[844] The IRS has ruled,[845] with mixed judicial support,[846] that corporate expense reimbursement agreements that apply when excessive compensation has to be repaid to the employer, cannot qualify for §1341 treatment if the repayment is stimulated by an *intervening cause,* namely an IRS audit. In such cases, however, §162 can provide the employee who is forced to restore the excessive part of his compensation a separate basis for deduction,[847] which is generally fine with the taxpayer as long as the taxpayer's marginal tax rate did not decline between the year of the inclusion and the year of the restoration. In any case, it is clear that the duty to repay must not arise out of a reimbursement agreement executed after the intervening event occurs.[848]

To illustrate: Buzz, a young dot.com executive, was promised a salary of $450,000/year by Grabber.Com. As part of his employment contract, Buzz promised to repay any part of the $450,000 that the IRS determined was excessive. A few years later, there was an audit and the IRS asserted that Buzz's salary in a particular year was $100,000 too high, and so Buzz repaid $100,000 to Grabber.Com. Buzz's repayment is the result of an "intervening cause" (the tax audit) and does not qualify for §1341 treatment according to the IRS. Buzz may be able to deduct the $100,000 under §162.

2. A deduction is allowable for the taxable year because it was *established* after the close of such prior taxable year that the taxpayer did not have an unrestricted right to some or all of that item. This has created another bevy of troubles; taxpayers who cannot establish the duty to repay, even though it makes perfect sense to repay, lose.[849]

3. The amount of the repayment exceeds $3,000.

---

844 Rev. Ruls. 65-254, 1965-2 C.B. 50 and 69-115, 1969-1 C.B. 50.

845 Rev. Ruls. 67-437 1967-2 C.B. 296 and 69-115, 1969-1 CB 50.

846 Van Cleave v United States, 718 F.2d 193 (6th Cir. 1983), reversing 82-1 USTC 9116 (1981) (§1341 applicable where duty to repay was triggered by audit).

847 Pike v Commissioner, 44 T.C. 787 (1965).

848 Blanton v. Commissioner, 46 T.C. 527 (1966), affd per curiam, 379 F.2d 558 (5th Cir. 1967).

849 See, e.g., Hope v. Commissioner, 471 F.2d 738 (3d. Cir. 1973, aff'g 55 T.C. 1020 (1971), cert. den. 414 U.S. 824 (1973) (§1341 held unavailable to taxpayer/seller who rescinded contract because of alleged fraud; he repaid voluntarily) and Pike v Commissioner, 44 TC 787 (1965) (lawyer's repayment of profits, not proven to be illegal, in order to protect reputation held voluntary, hence outside §1341).

4) The amount repaid is otherwise deductible. This means that the restoration must be deductible under some other Code provision, such as §162(a) or §212, if §1341 is to apply.

5) The inclusions and restorations are not for inventory or dealer property.[850]

The requirement that the receipt has to be vulnerable to being forfeited when it is received (even though it was correctly included in gross income) arose out of a literal-minded view of the claim of right doctrine used in the *Lewis* case and imprudently incorporated into §1341. The doctrine was for a time considered a shield to the taxation of illegal gains. Because such loot was received under no claim of right, cash method taxpayers were not subject to taxation on money they received but might have to return because, the theory went, they had no "claim of right" to it.[851] The concept that income from criminal activity is not taxable was killed off in *James v. United States*,[852] relying largely on the *Glenshaw Glass* definition of gross income ("accession to wealth, clearly realized, and over which the taxpayers have complete dominion"), but lives on pointlessly in §1341. Nowadays, the claim of right doctrine is not needed in order to tax cash method taxpayers on amounts they may have to return. The claim of right doctrine that you saw in *North American Oil Consolidated*[853] is only of real interest these days to accrual method taxpayers. As a result, there would be less confusion and more equity if the Code just said that the taxpayer had to report the amount he initially received as gross income, but Congress has not bothered to address this anomaly. There seems to be no constituency for these kinds of modest improvements to the Code.

Problem 10-1:

Orville Lampwick was a pitcher for the Flyneck (N.J.) Sultans. Lampwick's contract guaranteed him $10,000 for every no-hitter he pitched. On August 10 of year one, Lampwick pitched a perfect no-hitter in an 8-inning game that was shortened by extreme air pollution. Lampwick was paid the $10,000 the next day. He was in the 28% tax bracket in year one and in the 35% bracket in year two. The Commissioner's rulings in his league are absolute.

1) In year two the League Commissioner correctly ruled that it was improper for a pitcher to be attributed a no-hitter unless he pitched a full nine innings. Under great

850 §1341(b)(2).

851 Commissioner v Wilcox, 327 U.S. 404 (1946).

852 366 U.S. 213 (1961), reversing 273 F.2d 5 (CA7 1959).

853 See Chapter Nine.

pressure from the Commissioner (who rightly threatened to kick Lampwick out of the League), Lampwick repaid the money to the Sultans.

a. Can Orville amend his year one return to reduce his income by $10,000?

b. Must he use §1341 to report the repayment?

c. Assuming §1341 applies, what exactly (in dollars) will Lampwick report in the way of tax relief in year two?

d. Same as "3)", but he was in the 28% tax bracket in year two and in the 35% bracket in year one.

2) Same as "(1)", but Lampwick's contract called for being paid a measly $2,000 for pitching a no-hitter. What form of relief is he entitled to, if any?

3) Same as "(1)", but the Commissioner changed the rules in year two, retroactive to January 1 of year one. What form of relief is Lampwick entitled to, if any?

C. RECOVERIES AND THE TAX BENEFIT RULE UNDER THE CASE LAW

Read §111

We are now looking at the reverse of restorations -- "recoveries." Recoveries involve a deduction in a prior year followed by a receipt in a later year. Recoveries are deeply affected by the so-called "tax benefit rule." The so-called tax benefit rule has an *inclusionary* feature and an *exclusionary* feature. The exclusionary feature limits the taxation of the reversal of a prior year's deduction, where the original deduction was of little or no tax value. Section 111 handles such cases. The inclusionary feature forces taxpayers to include in income certain amounts that they previously deducted. The *Alice Phelan Sullivan Corp* case, which follows, exemplifies that situation.

1. Actual Recoveries under the Case Law

The following case reviews an equitable rule that evolved in the Court of Claims and which the Court of Claims later repudiated in light of the enactment of §111. To prepare for the case, consider the following imaginary facts:

To illustrate: George Generous gives an art work with a basis and value of $10,000 to the Museum of Art at a time when he was in the 15% bracket. He correctly deducted the full $10,000, but because he was in such a low tax bracket he saved only $1,500 in Federal Income Taxes. A few years later, when he was in the 40% bracket, the charity surprised him by returning his art work (still worth $10,000) for some reason. The return cost him $4,000 in taxes. This is not a happy outcome. Can §111 help alleviate the harshness of rate changes? No. On a plain reading, §111 will do George no good, because he deducted the $10,000 in full. At best, §111 can offer an exclusion if and to the extent that the prior deduction was not allowed in full. Can the courts modify §111 to take inter-year tax rates into account so that Generous's tax bill in the year of the recovery is not more than $1,500? Or are they stuck with §111's mechanical "pure exclusion" approach"? Keep reading.

ALICE PHELAN SULLIVAN CORP. v. UNITED STATES

381 F.2d 399 (Ct. Claims 1967)

COLLINS, Judge

Plaintiff, a California corporation, brings this action to recover an alleged overpayment in its 1957 income tax. During that year, there was returned to taxpayer two parcels of realty, each of which it had previously donated and claimed as a charitable contribution deduction. The first donation had been made in 1939; the second, in 1940. Under the then applicable corporate tax rates, the deductions claimed ($4,243.49 for 1939 and $4,463.44 for 1940) yielded plaintiff an aggregate tax benefit of $1,877.49.[854]

Each conveyance had been made subject to the condition that the property be used either for a religious or for an educational purpose. In 1957, the donee decided not to use the gifts; they were therefore reconveyed to plaintiff. Upon audit of taxpayer's income tax return, it was found that the recovered property was not reflected in its 1957 gross income. The Commissioner of Internal Revenue disagreed with plaintiff's characterization of the recovery as a nontaxable return of capital. He viewed the transaction as giving rise to taxable income and therefore adjusted plaintiff's income by adding to it $8,706.93 the total of the charitable contribution deductions previously claimed and allowed. This addition to income, taxed at the 1957 corporate tax rate of 52 percent, resulted in a deficiency assessment of $4,527.60. After payment of the deficiency, plaintiff filed a claim for the refund of $2,650.11, asserting this amount as overpayment on the theory that a correct assessment could demand no more than the return of the tax benefit originally enjoyed, *i.e.*, $1,877.49. The claim was disallowed.

This court has had prior occasion to consider the question which the present suit presents. In *Perry v. United States*, 142 Ct. Cl. 7, 160 F. Supp. 270 (1958) (Judges Madden and Laramore dissenting), it was recognized that a return to the donor of a prior charitable contribution gave rise

854 The tax rate in 1939 was 18 percent; in 1940, 24 percent.[Footnote No. 1 in original.]

to income to the extent of the deduction previously allowed. The court's point of division which is likewise the division between the instant parties was whether the "gain" attributable to the recovery was to be taxed at the rate applicable at the time the deduction was first claimed or whether the proper rate was that in effect at the time of recovery. The majority, concluding that the Government should be entitled to recoup no more than that which it lost, held that the tax liability arising upon the return of a charitable gift should equal the tax benefit experienced at time of donation. Taxpayer urges that the *Perry* rationale dictates that a like result be reached in this case.

The Government, of course, assumes the opposite stance. Mindful of the homage due the principle of stare decisis, it bids us first to consider the criteria under which judicial reexamination of an earlier decision is justifiable. We are referred to Judge Davis' concurring opinion in *Mississippi River Fuel Corp. v. United States*, 161 Ct. Cl. 237, 24647, 314 F. 2d 953, 958 (1963), wherein he states that:

> . . . The question is not what we would hold if we now took a fresh look but whether we should take that fresh look. A court should not scrutinize its own prior ruling putting constitutional adjudication, which has its own standards, to one side merely because, as now constituted, it might have reached a different result at the earlier time. Something more is required before a reexamination is to be undertaken: (a) a strong, even if not yet firm, view that the challenged precedent is probably wrong; (b) an inadequate or incomplete presentation in the prior case; (c) an intervening development in the law, or in critical comment, which unlocks new corridors; (d) unforeseen difficulties in the application or reach of the earlier decision; or (e) inconsistencies in the court's own rulings in the field. Where these or like reasons for reopening are lacking, respect for an existing precedent is counseled by all those many facets of stabilitypluseconomy which are embodied in the principle of *stare decisis*. . . .

Judged in light of the abovelisted criteria, reexamination is claimed to be warranted. In expanding its position on this point, the Government begins by recommending consideration of the views of the *Perry* dissent. Stress is placed upon the point therein noted, namely, that the "balancing" technique adopted by the court in *Perry* though equitable was otherwise without legal foundation. The dissent viewed the majority result as going beyond the recognized limits of either statutory or judgemade law. Like expressions of disagreement have been voiced elsewhere. . . .

As additional ground in support of reconsideration, the Government mentions that *Perry* was decided on a ground which neither of its parties had argued and which we, in later decisions, are said to have abandoned. The Government contrasts the principle of taxation adopted in *Perry* with that reflected in such later decisions as *California & Hawaiian Sugar Ref. Corp. v. United States*, 159 Ct. Cl. 561, 311 F. 2d 235 (1962), and *Citizens Fed. Sav. & Loan Ass'n v. United States*, 154

Ct. Cl. 305, 290 F. 2d 932 (1961). These last cited cases are said to contradict *Perry* because they sanction taxation of "recovered" deductions at the tax rate prevailing in the later year, that is, the year of recovery. The foregoing considerations express sufficient reason to relinquish our deference to precedent in order to examine anew the issue which this case presents.

A transaction which returns to a taxpayer his own property cannot be considered as giving rise to "income" at least where that term is confined to its traditional sense of "gain derived from capital, from labor, or from both combined." *Eisner v. Macomber*, 252 U.S. 189, 207 (1920). Yet the principle is well ingrained in our tax law that the return or recovery of property that was once the subject of an income tax deduction must be treated as income in the year of its recovery. *Rothensies v. Electric Storage Battery Co.*, 329 U.S. 296 (1946) . . . . The only limitation upon that principle is the socalled "taxbenefit rule." This rule permits exclusion of the recovered item from income so long as its initial use as a deduction did not provide a tax saving. *California & Hawaiian Sugar Ref. Corp. v. United States, supra* . . . . But where full tax use of a deduction was made and a tax saving thereby obtained, then the extent of saving is considered immaterial. The recovery is viewed as income to the full extent of the deduction previously allowed.[855]

Formerly the exclusive province of judgemade law, the taxbenefit concept now finds expression both in statute and administrative regulations. Section 111 of the Internal Revenue Code of 1954 accords taxbenefit treatment to the recovery of bad debts, prior taxes, and delinquency amounts. Treasury regulations have "broadened" the rule of exclusion by extending similar treatment to "all other losses, expenditures, and accruals made the basis of deductions from gross income for prior taxable years . . . ."

Drawing our attention to the broad language of this regulation, the Government insists that the present recovery must find its place within the scope of the regulation and, as such, should be taxed in a manner consistent with the treatment provided for like items of recovery, *i.e.*, that it be taxed at the rate prevailing in the year of recovery. We are compelled to agree.

Set in historical perspective, it is clear that the cited regulation may not be regarded as an unauthorized extension of the otherwise limited congressional approval given to the taxbenefit concept. . . .

. . .

. . . To insure the vitality of the singleyear concept, it is essential not only that annual income be ascertained without reference to losses experienced in an earlier accounting period, but also that income be taxed without reference to earlier tax rates. And absent specific statutory authority sanctioning a departure from this principle, it may only be said of *Perry* that it achieved a result which was more equitably just than legally correct.

---

855 The rationale which supports the principle, as well as its limitation, is that the property, having once served to offset taxable income (i.e., as a tax deduction) should be treated, upon its recoupment, as the recovery of that which had been previously deducted. See Plumb, The Tax Benefit Rule Today, 57 Harv. L. Rev. 129, 131 n. 10 (1943). [Footnote No. 2 in original.]

Since taxpayer in this case did obtain full tax benefit from its earlier deductions, those deductions were properly classified as income upon recoupment and must be taxed as such. This can mean nothing less than the application of that tax rate which is in effect during the year in which the recovered item is recognized as a factor of income. We therefore sustain the Government's position and grant its motion for summary judgment. *Perry v. United States, supra,* is hereby overruled, and plaintiff's petition is dismissed.

Note on the *Dobson* Doctrine

The *Perry* doctrine was not the only equitable rule to bite the dust. There is also the doctrine from *Dobson v. Commissioner*[856] which ruled that if the prior deduction produced *no* tax benefit, it cannot be taxed. *Dobson* was washed away by §111, although §111 supplies the same rule by statute.

2. The Tax Treatment of "Recoveries" without Receipts, or "What is a Recovery?"

The following case answered a lingering question that needed answering; can a taxable recovery come through something other than cash or property?

BLISS DAIRY v. COMMISSIONER
460 U.S. 370 (1983)

[The taxpayer was a corporation that operated a dairy farm. In the taxable year ending June 30, 1973, the corporation deducted the full cost of the cattle feed it purchased for use in its operations as permitted by §162, but a substantial portion of the feed was still on hand at the end of the taxable year. Two days into the next taxable year, the taxpayer adopted a plan of liquidation and distributed its assets, including the cattle feed, to its shareholders. According to the Court's statement, the distribution was of about $56,000 worth of grain. Under corporate tax law then in effect, the act of distributing the feed would generally be nontaxable to the corporation. However, the cost of the feed had already been deducted. The IRS asserted that the corporation enjoyed a taxable "recovery" in the form of a bookkeeping reversal of the earlier deduction.]

JUSTICE O'CONNOR delivered the opinion of the Court.

These consolidated cases present the question of the applicability of the tax benefit rule to two corporate tax situations: the repayment to the shareholders of taxes for which they were liable but that were originally paid by the corporation; and the distribution of expensed assets in a corporate liquidation. We conclude that, unless a nonrecognition provision of the Internal Revenue Code prevents it, the tax benefit rule ordinarily applies to require the inclusion of

856 320 US 489 (1943).

income when events occur that are fundamentally inconsistent with an earlier deduction. Our examination of the provisions granting the deductions and governing the liquidation in these cases leads us to hold that the rule requires the recognition of income in the case of the liquidation but not in the case of the tax refund.

. . .

II

The Government in each case relies solely on the tax benefit rule a judicially developed principle that allays some of the inflexibilities of the annual accounting system. An annual accounting system is a practical necessity if the federal income tax is to produce revenue ascertainable and payable at regular intervals. *Burnet v. Sanford & Brooks Co.*, 282 U.S. 359, 365 (1931). Nevertheless, strict adherence to an annual accounting system would create transactional inequities. Often an apparently completed transaction will reopen unexpectedly in a subsequent tax year, rendering the initial reporting improper. For instance, if a taxpayer held a note that became apparently uncollectible early in the taxable year, but the debtor made an unexpected financial recovery before the close of the year and paid the debt, the transaction would have no tax consequences for the taxpayer, for the repayment of the principal would be recovery of capital. If, however, the debtor's financial recovery and the resulting repayment took place after the close of the taxable year, the taxpayer would have a deduction for the apparently bad debt in the first year under § 166(a) . . . . Without the tax benefit rule, the repayment in the second year, representing a return of capital, would not be taxable. The second transaction, then, although economically identical to the first, could, because of the differences in accounting, yield drastically different tax consequences. The Government, by allowing a deduction that it could not have known to be improper at the time, would be foreclosed from recouping any of the tax saved because of the improper deduction. Recognizing and seeking to avoid the possible distortions of income, the courts have long required the taxpayer to recognize the repayment in the second year as income. . . .

The taxpayers and the Government in these cases propose different formulations of the tax benefit rule. The taxpayers contend that the rule requires the inclusion of amounts *recovered* in later years, and they do not view the events in these cases as "recoveries." The Government, on the other hand, urges that the tax benefit rule requires the inclusion of amounts previously deducted if later events are inconsistent with the deductions; it insists that no "recovery" is necessary to the application of the rule. Further, it asserts that the events in these cases are inconsistent with the deductions taken by the taxpayers. We are not in complete agreement with either view.

An examination of the purpose and accepted applications of the tax benefit rule reveals that a "recovery" will not always be necessary to invoke the tax benefit rule. The purpose of the rule is not simply to tax "recoveries." On the contrary, it is to approximate the results produced by a tax system based on transactional rather than annual accounting. See . . . Tye, The Tax Benefit Doctrine Reexamined, 3 Tax L. Rev. 329 (1948) (hereinafter Tye). It has long been accepted that a taxpayer using accrual accounting who accrues and deducts an expense in a tax year before it becomes payable and who for some reason eventually does not have to pay the liability must then take into income the amount of the expense earlier deducted. See, *e. g., Mayfair Minerals, Inc. v. Commissioner*, 456 F.2d 622 (CA5 1972) (*per curiam*); . . . . The bookkeeping entry canceling the liability, though it increases the balance sheet net worth of the taxpayer, does not fit within any ordinary definition of "recovery." Thus, the taxpayers' formulation of the rule neither serves the purposes of the rule nor accurately reflects the cases that establish the rule. Further, the taxpayers' proposal would introduce an undesirable formalism into the application of the tax benefit rule. Lower courts have been able to stretch the definition of "recovery" to include a great variety of events. For instance, in cases of corporate liquidations, courts have viewed the corporation's receipt of its own stock as a "recovery," reasoning that, even though the instant that the corporation receives the stock it becomes worthless, the stock has value as it is turned over to the corporation, and that ephemeral value represents a recovery for the corporation. . . . Or, payment to another party may be imputed to the taxpayer, giving rise to a recovery. . . . Imposition of a requirement that there be a recovery would, in many cases, simply require the Government to cast its argument in different and unnatural terminology, without adding anything to the analysis.

The basic purpose of the tax benefit rule is to achieve rough transactional parity in tax, . . . and to protect the Government and the taxpayer from the adverse effects of reporting a transaction on the basis of assumptions that an event in a subsequent year proves to have been erroneous. Such an event, unforeseen at the time of an earlier deduction, may in many cases require the application of the tax benefit rule. We do not, however, agree that this consequence invariably follows. Not every unforeseen event will require the taxpayer to report income in the amount of his earlier deduction. On the contrary, the tax benefit rule will "cancel out" an earlier deduction only when a careful examination shows that the later event is indeed fundamentally inconsistent with the premise on which the deduction was initially based. That is, if that event had occurred within the same taxable year, it would have foreclosed the deduction. In some cases, a subsequent recovery by the taxpayer will be the only event that would be fundamentally inconsistent with the provision granting the deduction. In such a case, only actual recovery by the taxpayer would justify application of the tax benefit rule. For example, if a calendaryear taxpayer made a rental payment on December 15 for a 30day lease deductible in the current year under § 162(a)(3), see Treas. Reg. § 1.4611(a)(1) . . . ; *e. g., Zaninovich v. Commissioner*, 616 F.2d 429 (CA9 1980), the tax benefit rule would not require the recognition of income if the leased premises were destroyed by fire on January 10. The resulting inability of the taxpayer to occupy the building would be an event not fundamentally inconsistent with his prior deduction as an ordinary and necessary business expense under § 162(a). The loss is attributable to the business and therefore is consistent with the deduction of the rental payment as an ordinary and necessary business expense. On the other hand, had the premises not burned and, in January, the taxpayer decided to use them to house his family rather than to continue the operation of his business, he would have converted the leasehold to personal use. This would be an event fundamentally inconsistent with the business use on which the deduction was based. In the case of the fire, only if the lessor by virtue of some provision in the lease had refunded the rental payment would the taxpayer be required under the tax benefit rule to recognize income on the subsequent destruction of the building. In other words, the subsequent recovery of the previously deducted rental payment would be the only event inconsistent with the provision allowing the deduction. It therefore is evident that the tax benefit rule must be applied on a casebycase basis. A court must consider the facts and circumstances of each case in the light of the purpose and function of the provisions granting the deductions.

When the later event takes place in the context of a nonrecognition provision of the Code, there will be an inherent tension between the tax benefit rule and the nonrecognition provision. ... We cannot resolve that tension with a blanket rule that the tax benefit rule will always prevail. Instead, we must focus on the particular provisions of the Code at issue in any case.

The formulation that we endorse today follows clearly from the long development of the tax benefit rule....

.... The failure to mention inconsistent events in §111 no more suggests that they do not trigger the application of the tax benefit rule than the failure to mention the recovery of a capital loss suggests that it does not, see *Dobson, supra.*

...

Bliss paid the assessment on an increase of $60,000 in its taxable income. In the District Court, the parties stipulated that the value of the grain was $56,565, but the record does not show what the original cost of the grain was, or what portion of it remained at the time of liquidation. The proper increase in taxable income is the portion of the cost of the grain attributable to the amount on hand at the time of liquidation. In *Bliss*, then, we remand for a determination of that amount....

[The various dissenting and concurring opinions are omitted. Eds.]

Computing the Reversed Deduction

The Supreme Court issued a companion case, *Hillsboro National Bank v. Commissioner*,[857] the same day as it handed down *Bliss Dairy*. That case described the purpose of the inclusionary

857 460 U.S. 370 (1983).

feature of the tax benefit rule as being to achieve "rough transactional parity" with what would be self-canceling events in a single year, by reversing a prior year's deductions (and thus creating income) when a later event that is fundamentally inconsistent with the prior deduction takes place in a later year. That implies the later reversal of the earlier deduction should be of the same dollar amount as the original deduction. In the case of Bliss Dairy Corporation that means that the income the taxpayer reported when it distributed the leftover feed should be equal to what it cost, not what it was worth. Justice O'Connor correctly remanded the case to determine that figure.

3. The Mechanics of §111

Section 111 provides that recoveries of previously deducted items and certain prior tax credits[858] will not produce gross income or tax credit recapture if and to the extent that the prior deduction or credit did not reduce the taxpayer's previous Federal Income Taxes (the "exclusionary" rule). The regulations use the term *recovery exclusion* to describe the nontaxable portion of a recovery of a prior deduction. The statute no longer uses that terminology, but the term is used here because it is still a useful distillation.

As you saw in *Bliss Dairy*, no actual recovery is required in order to produce gross income to the taxpayer under the inclusionary tax benefit rule. Rather, there can be a so-called "fundamentally inconsistent event," such as the distribution to shareholders of an asset whose cost was previously deducted, indicating that the premise on which the deduction was founded (e.g., that the item would be consumed in the business) was not satisfied.[859] The inclusion of tax credits is triggered when there is a price (or other similar) adjustment to the basis of the property on which the calculation of the credit was based.[860] In a sense, §111 belongs in Chapter Four of the book on exclusions from gross income, but it is easier to grapple with §111 here as a counterpoint to §1341.

The basic goal of §111 is to exclude from gross income the taxable recovery of amounts which were deducted in a prior year if and to the extent such amounts did not reduce taxes in the prior year. This requires the taxpayer to locate the prior year's tax return and evaluate the impact of the event on the prior year's tax return, if any, as if the deduction that was recovered or reversed in the current year was never received in the first place. This is more slippery than it seems. If the taxpayer paid no tax in the prior year because of tax credits, then recoveries from prior years are excluded from gross income.[861] In determining whether the previously deducted item did

858 A recovery includes a reversal of a prior deduction as well as reductions of credits other than those for foreign taxes and investments. See below.

859 460 U.S. 370 (1983).

860 §111(b)(1)(B).

861 Tax Reform Act of 1986, vol. 2, H. Rpt. 99-841 vol. 2, bill number 99 H.R. 3838, at page 846.

reduce taxes, there is a pro-taxpayer presumption that if a deduction was claimed in a prior year, the first dollars handed back to the taxpayer in the later year are the ones that did *not* reduce taxes; as a result, §111 goes out of its way to protect recoveries from being taxed.

> **To illustrate**: Fred paid $10,000 in medical expenses last year, but because of 7.5% of AGI limit on medical expense deductions, he could only deduct $2,500, and $7,500 was rendered non-deductible. This year, the doctor to whom he paid the money refunded $7,600. Of that amount, only $100 is taxed.

Section 111(a) limits the inclusion to the lesser of the amount of the prior deduction or the amount recovered, which seems obvious. Other points about §111 are not so obvious and, unfortunately, the regulations are out of date and so one must often rely on other authorities, especially IRS Publication 525 (2018)

If the recovery related to a deduction did not reduce the prior year's taxes, but was instead part of a loss carryover to the year of recovery, the deduction is deemed to have produced a tax benefit, on the theory that the deduction remains alive and well, embodied in the loss carryforward.[862] If it were not for that rule, loss carryforwards would unjustifiably exempt tax benefit recoveries that would have been taxable if they had simply been deducted in the initial year.

D. ACCOUNTING FOR LONG-TERM CONTRACTS

In 1986 Congress addressed a festering scandal concerning the use of the completed contract method, under which the profit on a contract is not reported until the project is completed. Because of the terms of private contracts with the Defense Department it was possible for some contracts to virtually never end, putting off taxes more or less forever. The legislative reaction was the death of the long-term contract method and its replacement with the percentage-of-completion method under §460, which is now mandatory for most long-term contracts, meaning contracts that are not completed in the taxpayer's current tax year. The basic approach of §460 is to require the contractor to report in its income each year a part of the total contract price in proportion to the amount of total anticipated costs over the life of the contract that were incurred in the current tax year. This tough rule virtually forces contractors to make sure their contracts provide for collecting part of the contract price (and taxable profit) along the way so as to avoid the possibility of not having the cash required to pay their taxes. This description ignores a mountain of limitations and other details.

862 See §111(c).

Problem 10-2:

In year 1 Alexis, a cash method calendar year taxpayer, paid $2,000 in local real estate taxes on her personal residence. She did not itemize her deductions, on her year 1 tax return, so she did not deduct the $2,000. In year 3 she was refunded $1,200 of the $2,000 payment. Assume Alexis was in the 15% bracket in year 1 and the 35% bracket in year 3.

1) Can she amend her year 1 tax return to reduce the $2,000 deduction to $800? See §6511(a).

2) How much of the $1,200, if anything, can Alexis exclude from her year 3 income?

3) Assume she had a large income in year 1 and that her standard deduction that year was $3,000. Assume also that she had no other itemized deductions, and that she had a $7,000 real estate tax payment, all of which was refunded in year 3. In other words, assume she itemized her deductions in year 1, claiming a $7,000 real estate tax deduction in that year.

   a. How much of the $7,000 should be included in her gross income in year 3?

   b. What tax rate applies to the $4,000 received in year 3?

4) Assuming that her itemized deductions in year 1 had been reduced by §§ 67 or 68, should that entitle her to increase the amount that she could exclude under §111?

5) Assume that in year 1 Alexis had claimed a $100 business expense deduction for stamps she bought for use in her business of being an architect, but did not in fact use. In year 2, she used the stamps for her personal mail. When, if ever, must she include the $100 in income? Disregard §111.

6) Texas Industries, Inc. contracts to build the Transatlantic Bridge, which is expected to take 30 years to complete. It is an especially challenging project because the structure is to be made of compacted sand. The total contract price is $300 billion. Assuming an equal amount of costs are incurred each year, how much income must Texas Industries report in gross income each year under the contract?

E. ETHICAL DUTY TO ADVISE THE IRS OF MISTAKES AND THE DUTY OF CONFIDENTIALITY

These inter-year problems raise the question of what one is supposed to do about mistakes by the taxpayer; but what about IRS mistakes? It is lovely to imagine that the IRS might grossly undercalculate your, or a favorite client's, taxes. Does this mean you have to tell the IRS and give back the windfall to the government?

Conversion and the duty to inform the client. First things first. Can the client safely keep the money? No. That would be the crime of conversion.[863] Also, the lawyer must advise the client of the issue, as part of the general duty of care.[864]

Second, if the issue arises in the context of litigation, the lawyer cannot mislead the court.[865] That means the lawyer must disclose the error to the court and does not require consent of the client.[866]

The big tension arises in non-litigation settings (such as settlement negotiation with the IRS) where the government is being victimized, but the lawyer may owe a duty to the client that conflicts with dealing fairly with the government.

The duty of confidentiality to the client. A.B.A. Model Rule of Professional Conduct 1.6 declares that a lawyer must not reveal information relating to a representation of a client or former client without the client's consent, unless the revelation is necessary to prevent the client from "committing a criminal act that the lawyer believes is likely to result in imminent death or substantial bodily harm" or to establish a claim or defense on behalf of the lawyer in a controversy between the lawyer and the client. Some states let a lawyer disclose fraud under limited circumstances.[867]

The duty of confidentiality differs from the attorney-client privilege. The latter is a rule of evidence, not an ethical rule. The attorney-client privilege only applies to a limited class of communications, namely those delivered in confidence in the course of rendering legal advice and which were not disclosed beyond lawyer and client. By contrast, the ethical duty of confidentiality attaches to all information that the client might *wish* to be kept confidential, even if already communicated beyond lawyer and client. But a lawyer who knows that an IRS miscalculation will result in an erroneous refund cannot become an instrumentality in creating the erroneous refund. However, because the potential crime is not likely to result in imminent death or

---

863 See United States v. McRee, 7 F. 3d 976 (11th Cir. 1993 (taxpayer was convicted of converting Government property by cashing an erroneously issued refund, even though the taxpayer did nothing to induce issuance of the refund).

864 See ABA Model Rule of Professional Conduct 2.1.

865 Model Rule 3.3(a)(1).

866 Rule 3.3(b) specifically requires disclosure.

867 See, e.g., GTE Prod. Corp. v. Stewart, 421 Mass. 22, 653 N.E. 2d 161 (1995), discussing Mass. law, esp. SJC Rule 3:07 and DR 4-101(c)(3).

substantial bodily harm, a lawyer cannot generally disclose this client confidence.[868] The general rule in such cases seems to be that a lawyer may not disclose the IRS miscalculation without the client's consent or unless disclosure is impliedly authorized. If the client refuses to consent (and there is no implied authorization to disclose), then Model Rule 1.16(a) says the lawyer must withdraw if the lawyer's continued representation would advance the client's crime or fraud. Otherwise, Model Rule 1.16(b) merely lets the lawyer withdraw if he or she considers the client's course of conduct to be imprudent or repugnant.

Problem 10-3:

Mr. Swindler recently received a windfall because his tax return (prepared by Garfield Peabody, CPA) erroneously calculated a $2,500 deduction as $25,000. As a result, his Federal Income Tax return liability declined by $10,000. He recently visited your office with his tax return because you were going to advise him on an unrelated tax planning idea. You noticed the $22,500 mistake on the return.

1) Must you advise him of the error?

2) Must you advise the IRS of the error?

3) Would your answer to "b)" change if Mr. Swindler were involved in a tax controversy that had reached the litigation stage and the error was based on information you submitted to the IRS under a stipulation you thought was correct at the time but later found to be erroneous?

4) Assuming that statute of limitations on the erroneous return has not run, can Swindler file an amended return to correct the error?

868 ABA Model Rule of Professonal Conduct 1.6(b)(1).

CHAPTER 11 - TAX DEFERRED TRANSACTIONS

A. INTRODUCTION

Section 1001(c) contains a crucial statement that, "except as otherwise provided in this subtitle" (meaning the Internal Revenue Code) all "realized" gains and losses on sales and exchanges of property must be "recognized," (meaning reported on the spot for Federal Income Tax purposes). The *Cottage Savings* case and the accompanying materials in Chapter 3 investigated the question of when a gain or loss is "realized." Because of §1001(c)'s imperious mandatory recognition of all realized gains and losses, it takes a separate Code section to provide the necessary exemption from recognition. This Chapter focuses on three such key exemptions, namely those found in §§ 1033, 1031 and 1091, in that order. At the risk of stating the obvious, a "recognized gain" is a subset of "realized gain," so a recognized gain on the disposition of a particular property can never exceed the realized gain on that property.

The paradigm in this area is to bar immediate recognition, but instead defer the gain or loss by modifying the basis of property so as to assure than an eventual disposition captures any previously untaxed gain or deferred loss. This is completely distinct from the question of whether something is excluded from gross income; that was the subject of Chapter Four. The transactions you are about to review are subject to eventual taxation, and can be thought of in terms of whether the transaction will be taxed "sooner or later," as opposed to being taxed "now or never."

The deep theme is the correspondence between income and basis. If Congress chooses to treat some transactions as not taxable at the time of realization, it must take a corresponding step with respect to basis in order to preserve the chance to tax the gain, or provide a tax benefit for the loss, at a later date.

Here is a simple example of how deferral provisions operate. It involves former §1034, which is still relevant for determining the basis of a huge part of the U.S.'s older residential housing stock. Section 1034 provides a down-to-earth example of how tax-deferred rollovers work:

To illustrate: It is the past and §1034 is still in bloom. Dr. DeSoto, a leading orthodontist, owns a home at the south end of the street in a suburban development. It has an adjusted basis of

$100,000 and a fair market value of $300,000. Dr. DeSoto sells his old home and quickly buys an identical one at the north end of the street. The new house cost him exactly the same amount as the old home was sold for, namely $300,000. Under former § 1034, Dr. DeSoto recognized no gain or loss on the transaction, but his basis in his new home remained $100,000 (his $300,000 cost reduced by the $200,000 of unrecognized gain on the sale of the first house). Thus, he only achieved a deferral of his gain and the deferral was manifested in the form of a continuation in the dollar amount of his basis in the home that was the subject of the transaction. If Dr. DeSoto sold his new home for $300,000 the next day, or in the next decade, he would have recognized the same $200,000 gain as if he had moved out of the neighborhood, sold the old home and moved into a rented apartment. Nowadays, §121 allows Dr. DeSoto to exclude the gain on the sale of the first house and get a cost basis in the new house, as long as he satisfies the various conditions of §121.

As you can see, §1034 was a deferral provision, not an exemption from tax, and it was only available to the extent that sales proceeds were fully reinvested. Thus, if and to the extent the taxpayer paid less for the new home than he sold the old one for, the gain was taxable to the extent of the shortfall.

A common alternative way of expressing the constancy-of-income-and-basis precept is to say that the nonrecognition provisions involve a situation in which the taxpayer's investment in property has remained relatively static, making it inappropriate to impose a tax. To reduce it to simpler terms, another useful way of thinking of it is that "nothing happened," so the gain or loss should be deferred pending a final sale of the recently-obtained property. Keeping basis and holding periods constant as between the old and new property assures that result. Section 1223 rounds out the picture by supplying the holding period rules for the replacement property. Those rules conform to the concept that "nothing happened."

This Chapter looks at two different kinds of nonrecognition transactions. One is an exchange of property "in kind." The other is a so-called "rollover," meaning a transaction in which the taxpayer receives the proceeds of one transaction and reinvests the proceeds in other property so as to achieve a tax deferral. The example of Dr. DeSoto under former §1034 illustrated a "rollover" of cash.

Losses can work the same way as gains; that is, Congress can declare a realized loss unrecognized for the time being. One first needs to distinguish the realized but unrecognized loss from the loss that is recognized but *disallowed* for some reason. The primary source of disallowance is §165(c), which stands as a road block to the recognition of many losses with respect to dealing in property because they are in the nature of personal consumption, as opposed to business, investment or other gain-seeking losses. For example, a consumer who discards a worn-out washing machine gets no tax deduction, whereas §165(c)(1) allows the local Laundromat operator a loss deduction on discarding a similar machine because the event was a feature of his business. Section 165(c) is the property loss analog of §262, which bars deductions for personal expenses, as opposed to business or investment expenses.

B. ROLLOVER OF PROCEEDS OF INVOLUNTARY CONVERSIONS UNDER §1033

Read §1033(a)(1)-(2) (A), (B), (E) and (b)

1. Introduction

Section 1033's lineage goes back to World War I. Its predecessor was enacted in 1921, codifying Regulations issued by the Treasury Department under the Revenue Act of 1918 which softened the blow of taxable war-time gains from governmental requisitioning of ships and other facilities and the insurance proceeds from property destroyed in battle.[869] The theory for the tax relief was that as long as the taxpayer ploughed proceeds back into the same general kind of property, there should be no current tax. This comes at the price of the preservation of the potential gain in the form of frozen basis. Today's §1033(b) assures that result (but with no requirement that there be a war). Nowadays, §1033 most often comes into play with condemnations, casualties, and theft. By the way, despite the concept of "reinvestment," there has never been an actual tracing of funds into the new property. Taxpayers can use other moneys, including borrowed funds, to buy the replacement property.

2. Meaning of "Similar or Related in Service or Use"

Section 1033 only applies if the replacement property is "similar or related in service or use" to the involuntarily converted property. The *Clifton* case is an important precedent with respect to defining that term.

CLIFTON INV. CO. v. COMMISSIONER
312 F.2d 719 (6th Cir. 1963), cert. denied (CA6 1963)

BOYD, Judge.

Petitioner is a real estate investment corporation organized and existing under the laws of the State of Ohio, with headquarters in Cincinnati. In 1956 the petitioner sold to the City of Cincinnati under its threat of exercising its power of eminent domain a sixstory office building,

869 Revenue Act of 1918, 40 Stat. 1057, Cumulative Bulletin No. 1-655 inclusive, Regulation 45, Article 49 at page 67 and Article 50 at page 77 (1919) Government printing office https://www.govinfo.gov/content/pkg/GOVPUB-T22-071599b823b253b057dcbea7a97fefc8/pdf/GOVPUB-T22-071599b823b253b057dcbea7a97fefc8.pdf.

known as the United Bank Building, located in the downtown section of that city, which building was held by petitioner for production of rental income from commercial tenants. The funds realized from the sale of this property to the city were used by the petitioner to purchase eighty percent of the outstanding stock of The Times Square Hotel of New York, Inc., also an Ohio corporation, which had as its sole asset a contract to buy the Times Square Hotel of New York City. The purchase of the hotel was effected by the corporation. The taxpayerpetitioner contends herein that the purchase of the controlling stock in the hotel corporation was an investment in property 'similar or related in service or use' to the office building it had been forced to sell, thus deserving of the nonrecognition of gain provisions of Section 1033(a)(3)(A) . . . . More specifically, the taxpayer contends that since both the properties herein were productive of rental income, the similarity contemplated by the statute aforesaid exists. The Commissioner ruled to the contrary, holding that any gain from the sale of the office building was recognizable and a deficiency was assessed against the taxpayer for the year 1956 in the amount of $19,057.09. The Tax Court agreed with the Commissioner, finding that the properties themselves were not 'similar or related in service or use' as required by the statute. . . . From the decision of the Tax Court this appeal was perfected.

In order to determine whether the requisite similarity existed under the statute between the properties herein, the Tax Court applied the socalled 'functional test' or 'enduse test.' This it seems has been the Tax Court's traditional line of inquiry, when similar cases under the within statute have been considered by it. This approach takes into account only the actual physical end use to which the properties involved are put, whether that use be by the ownertaxpayer or by his tenant; that is, whether the taxpayerowner is the actual user of the property or merely holds it for investment purposes, as in the case of a lessor. We reject the functional test as applied to the holder of investment property, who replaces such property with other investment property, as in the case at bar.

The Tax Court in this case relied in part on its earlier decision in Liant Record, Inc. v. Commissioner, 36 T.C. 224 and chiefly on the decision of the Court of Appeals for the Third Circuit in McCaffrey v. Commissioner, 275 F.2d 27, 1960, cert. denied 363 U.S. 828 . . . the latter case approving and applying the aforesaid functional test in such a case as here presented. However, the Court of Appeals for the Second Circuit has since reversed the Tax Court's decision in Liant, 303 F.2d 326, 1962, and in so doing advanced what we consider to be the soundest approach among the number of decisions on this point. . . .

Congress must have intended that in order for the taxpayer to obtain the tax benefits of Section 1033 he must have continuity of interest as to the original property and its replacement in order that the taxpayer not be given a taxfree alteration of his interest. In short, the properties must be reasonably similar in their relation to the taxpayer. This reasonableness, as noted in the Liant case, is dependent upon a number of factors, all bearing on whether or not the relation of the taxpayer to the property has been changed. The ultimate use to which the properties are put, then, does not control the inquiry, when the taxpayer is not the user of the properties as in the case under consideration. As exemplary of the factors which are relevant the Liant decision mentions the following, after advancement of its 'relation of the properties to the taxpayer' test:

> 'In applying such a test to a lessor, a court must compare, inter alia, the extent and type of the lessor's management activity, the amount and kind of services rendered by him to the tenants, and the nature of his business risks connected with the properties.'

Thus, each case is dependent on its peculiar facts and the factors bearing on the service or use of the properties to the taxpayer must be closely examined. The Tax Court employed an erroneous test in this case, but on examination of the record, the correctness of the result is manifest.

The record before us discloses that the United Bank Building and the Times Square Hotel both produced rental income to the taxpayer. However, examination of what the properties required in the way of services to the tenants, management activity, and commercial tenancy considerations reveals an alteration of the taxpayer's interest. The record herein shows that the taxpayer corporation itself managed the United Bank Building, but deemed it necessary to procure professional management for the Times Square Hotel. There were primarily two employees for the United Bank Building, who afforded elevator and janitorial services to the tenants. In the Times Square Hotel between 130 and 140 employees were necessary to attend the hotel operation and offer services to the commercial tenants and hotel guests. Approximately 96% of the rental income from the hotel was from the guest room facilities and the large number of transients required daily services of varying kinds. Furniture, linens, personal services of every description were furnished the hotel guests, which were not furnished the commercial tenants of the United Bank Building. The hotel guests reside in the hotel rooms and that is obviously the only reason they are tenants. In the office building herein several tenants also used parts of the premises for living quarters, but were clearly not furnished the typical services the hotel guest demands. There was no great limitation placed on the types of commercial tenants to whom space was rented in the United Bank Building, but as the enumeration of commercial tenants of the hotel building reveals, space therein was leased for the most part and primarily with an eye to how such a business operation might fit in with the operation of a hotel, how it relates to the hotel guests. It is common experience that the services offered by a lessee of business premises in a hotel will reflect in the minds of its guests on the service they associate with the hotel itself. If a leased restaurant in a hotel offers good or bad service, there is a tendency to think of the food service at the hotel as good or bad. A number of unique business considerations enter when leasing commercial space in a hotel which do not apply to an office building.

We consider there to be, then, a material variance between the relation of the office building in question and the within hotel operation of the taxpayer, in the light of the relevant inquiry found in the Liant case. It is true that what the taxpayer derived from both properties herein was generally the same, rental income. But what the properties demanded of the taxpayer in the way of management, services, and relations to its tenants materially varied. That which the taxpayers receives from his properties and that which such properties demand of the taxpayer must both be considered in determining whether or not the properties are similar or related in service or use to the taxpayer.[870]

The decision of the Tax Court is affirmed.

SHACKELFORD MILLER, Jr., Circuit Judge (concurring).

I concur in the result reached in the majority opinion.

However, I am not willing to adopt, without some modification thereof, the test adopted and applied in Liant Record, Inc. v. Commissioner, 303 F.2d 326, C.A.2d, upon which the majority opinion relies. I think that the investment character of the properties involved should be given more consideration than what seems to me is given by the ruling in the Liant case, although I do not think that investment basis alone is sufficient to comply with the statute, as Steuart Brothers, Inc. v. Commissioner, 261 F.2d 580, C.A.4th, might be construed as holding. As pointed out in Loco Realty Co. v. Commissioner, 306 F.2d 207, 215, C.A.8th, the statute was not intended to penalize but to protect persons whose property may be taken on condemnation and, accordingly, should be construed liberally. I agree with the standard adopted in the opinion in that case, although for our present purposes I do not think that it results in a reversal of the decision of the Tax Court.

Notes on Rollovers

Section 1033 Rollovers: Rollover or tax-free exchange provisions are typically limited to specific kinds of property. Not so for §1033; nonrecognition under §1033 also depends on how the property was disposed of. Still, there has to be a general similarity between the converted assets and the replacement property. For example, replacing income-producing real estate with income-producing securities has been held not to qualify for tax-deferred rollover treatment.[871] Thus, if a thief stole the family TV set, and the insurance covered the loss, §1033 may be at hand to prevent taxation of any otherwise taxable gain as long as the taxpayer replaces the stolen TV with another property that is similar or related in service or use. Unfortunately for the taxpayers, the replacement property must be "for the purpose of" replacing the converted property. Thus, for example, a video camera cannot replace a TV, for purposes of §1033.

870 Congress has since provided that replacement of property held for productive use in trade or business or for investment purposes with property of 'like kind' satisfies the 'similar or related in service or use' requirement. However, the acquisition of controlling interest in stock of a corporation holding property was specifically excepted from the relaxation of the test. Title 26 U.S.C. Section 1033(g)(1) and (2). (Technical Amendments Act of 1958). [Footnote No. 2 in original.]

871 Rev. Rul. 71-122, 1971-1 C.B. 224.

Notice that there is an option to replace involuntarily converted property with a controlling interest in the stock of a corporation that owns replacement property in §1033(a)(2)(A) and (E). It seems that as long as the corporation owns a proportionately substantial amount of property of the type that was converted, the entire investment in stock qualifies.[872] Acquiring an interest in a partnership cannot qualify for §1033 treatment.

Now for a tax anecdote that may bring §1033 to life. Some years ago Pennzoil entered into negotiations with the Getty Oil interests to get control of Getty Oil stock in order to gain access to some valuable oil fields. After Getty and Pennzoil had entered into an apparently nonbinding understanding that the transaction would go forward, Texaco barged in and sweetened the offer and eventually got the Getty Oil stock. Pennzoil sued in the Texas courts on the theory that Texaco misappropriated its interest in the Getty stock, as a result of which Pennzoil ultimately recovered approximately four billion dollars. Pennzoil was of course delighted with the recovery, but was puzzled by how it should report the transaction, given that it looked like a pure taxable windfall.[873] Pennzoil's lawyers recommended that Pennzoil invest in productive oil fields within the framework of §1033, theorizing that Texaco's snatching of the Getty Oil investments was a form of involuntary conversion, a creative assertion. By the way, Pennzoil sent its legal memo on the issue to the IRS and adhered to the position on its tax return. The IRS audited the issue and settled it on unpublicized terms that Pennzoil reported with undisguised satisfaction.

Miscellaneous dispositions: A relaxation in §1033(f) allows the reinvestment of proceeds of dispositions of environmentally contaminated livestock (cows poisoned by PCBs?) into farm property (sheep fencing?) if there is no feasible way to reinvest those proceeds.

IRA rollovers: The most common rollover of all is probably one in which funds are passed from some other kind of pension plan to an individual retirement arrangement ("IRA"). Here is just one of various examples of how transfers to IRAs can defer taxes.

> **To illustrate:** Buzz has worked for Grabber.Com for some years, and has accumulated more than $500,000 in the company's pension plan. If, as and when he gets the pension money, he will definitely pay taxes on the proceeds as ordinary income. Buzz was fired yesterday and given a check for $500,000 -- the value of his pension rights. If he transfers ("rolls over") the money to an IRA within 60 days of getting the company's check, there will be no tax. Instead, he will be taxed when money comes out of the IRA.[874]

872 See B.Bittker & L.Lokken, FEDERAL TAXATION OF INCOME, ESTATES AND GIFTS, ¶44.3.4 (2019).

873 Dodson, S. (1987, Dec 27). WEEK IN BUSINESS; PENZOIL PONDERS $3 BILLION QUESTION. New York Times. https://www.nytimes.com/1987/12/27/business/week-in-business-penzoil-ponders-3-billion-question.html.

874 §§ 402 (c) (5) (rollover), 408 (d) (1) (tax treatment on distribution).

3. Rulings by the Treasury Department as a Means of Obtaining Certainty

What if you cannot be sure if an important transaction will qualify under §1033? One procedure for those who can afford it is to seek the opinion of a qualified attorney. Failing that, prudent taxpayers who are involved with large transactions seek the shelter of a specially-tailored opinion from the federal government, usually in the form of a Private Letter Ruling or Determination Letter (in the latter case, only if the issue is clear). For the Private Letter Ruling or Determination Letter to be watertight, the taxpayer must be complete and truthful about the facts. There are specific "no ruling areas" as to which the IRS will not opine on the tax results. No ruling areas are specified in Revenue Procedures. Also, the IRS generally will not rule on areas that it considers "inherently factual," nor on various other areas that it is wary of. The following Revenue Procedure explains the government's process for getting an official letter on a §1033 rollover.

Rev. Proc. 2019-1, 2019-1 IRB 1 -- IRC Sec(s). 7121, 12/28/2018

1. What Is The Purpose Of This Revenue Procedure?

This revenue procedure explains how the Service provides advice to taxpayers on issues under the jurisdiction of the Associate Chief Counsel (Corporate), the Associate Chief Counsel (Financial Institutions and Products), the Associate Chief Counsel (Income Tax and Accounting), the Associate Chief Counsel (International), the Associate Chief Counsel (Passthroughs and Special Industries), the Associate Chief Counsel (Procedure and Administration), and the Associate Chief Counsel (Employee Benefits, Exempt Organizations, and Employment Taxes). It explains the forms of advice and the manner in which advice is requested by taxpayers and provided by the Service. A sample format for a letter ruling request is provided in Appendix B. See section 4 of this revenue procedure for information on certain issues outside the scope of this revenue procedure on which advice may be requested under a different revenue procedure.

***

.02. Updated annually

.02. This revenue procedure is updated annually as the first revenue procedure of the year, but it may be modified, amplified or clarified during the year.

***

2. What Are The Forms In Which The Service Provides Advice To Taxpayers?

The Service provides advice in the form of letter rulings, closing agreements, determination letters, information letters, and oral advice.

.01. Letter ruling

.01. A "letter ruling" is a written determination issued to a taxpayer by an Associate office in response to the taxpayer's written inquiry, filed prior to the filing of returns or reports that are required by the tax laws, about its status for tax purposes or the tax effects of its acts or transactions. A letter ruling interprets the tax laws and applies them to the taxpayer's specific set of facts. A letter ruling is issued when appropriate in the interest of sound tax administration. One type of letter ruling is an Associate office's response granting or denying a request for a change in a taxpayer's method of accounting or accounting period.

Once issued, a letter ruling may be revoked or modified for a number of reasons. See section 11 of this revenue procedure. A letter ruling may be issued with a closing agreement, however, and a closing agreement is final unless fraud, malfeasance, or misrepresentation of a material fact can be shown. See section 2.02 of this revenue procedure.

Letter rulings are subject to exchange of information under U.S. tax treaties or tax information exchange agreements in accordance with the terms of such treaties and agreements (including terms regarding relevancy, confidentiality, and the protection of trade secrets.)

.02. Closing agreement

.02. A "closing agreement" is a final agreement between the Service and a taxpayer on a specific issue or liability. It is entered into under the authority in § 7121, and it is final unless fraud, malfeasance, or misrepresentation of a material fact can be shown.

A taxpayer may request a closing agreement with a letter ruling or in lieu of a letter ruling, with respect to a transaction that would be eligible for a letter ruling. In such situations, the Associate Chief Counsel with subject matter jurisdiction signs the closing agreement on behalf of the Service.

A closing agreement may be entered into when it is advantageous to have the matter permanently and conclusively closed or when a taxpayer can show that there are good reasons for an agreement and that making the agreement will not prejudice the interests of the Government. In appropriate cases, a taxpayer may be asked to enter into a closing agreement as a condition for the issuance of a letter ruling.

If, in a single case, a closing agreement is requested for each person or entity in a class of taxpayers, separate agreements are entered into only if the class consists of 25 or fewer taxpayers.

If the issue and holding are identical for the class and there are more than 25 taxpayers in the class, a "mass closing agreement" will be entered into with the taxpayer who is authorized by the others to represent the class.

.03. Determination letter

.03. A "determination letter" is a written determination issued by a Director that applies the principles and precedents previously announced by the Service to a specific set of facts. It is issued only when a determination can be made based on clearly established rules in a statute, a tax treaty, the regulations, a conclusion in a revenue ruling, or an opinion or court decision that represents the position of the Service.

.04. Information letter

.04. An "information letter" is a statement issued by an Associate office or Director that calls attention to a well-established interpretation or principle of tax law (including a tax treaty) without applying it to a specific set of facts. An information letter may be issued if the taxpayer's inquiry indicates a need for general information or if the taxpayer's request does not meet the requirements of this revenue procedure and the Service concludes that general information will help the taxpayer. An information letter is advisory only and has no binding effect on the Service. If the Associate office issues an information letter in response to a request for a letter ruling that does not meet the requirements of this revenue procedure, the information letter is not a substitute for a letter ruling. The taxpayer should provide a daytime telephone number with the taxpayer's request for an information letter.

Information letters that are issued by the Associate offices to members of the public are made available to the public. Information letters that are issued by the Field offices are generally not made available to the public.

Because information letters do not constitute written determinations as defined in § 6110, they are not subject to public inspection under § 6110. The Service makes the information letters available to the public under the Freedom of Information Act (the "FOIA"). Before any information letter is made available to the public, an Associate office will redact any information exempt from disclosure under the FOIA. See, e.g., 5 U.S.C. § 552(b)(6) (exemption for information the disclosure of which would constitute a clearly unwarranted invasion of personal privacy); 5 U.S.C. § 552(b)(3) in conjunction with § 6103 (exemption for returns and return information as defined in § 6103(b)).

***

3. On What Issues May Taxpayers Request Written Advice Under This Revenue Procedure?

Taxpayers may request letter rulings, information letters, and closing agreements under this revenue procedure on issues within the jurisdiction of the Associate offices.

***

6. Under What Circumstances Does The Service Not Issue Letter Rulings Or Determination Letters?

.01. Ordinarily not if the request involves an issue under examination or consideration or in litigation

.01. The Service ordinarily does not issue a letter ruling or a determination letter if, at the time of the request, the identical issue is involved in the taxpayer's return for an earlier period and that issue—

(1) is being examined by a Field office;

(2) is being considered by Appeals;

(3) is pending in litigation in a case involving the taxpayer or a related taxpayer;

(4) has been examined by a Field office or considered by Appeals and the statutory period of limitations on assessment or on filing a claim for refund or credit of tax has not expired; or

(5) has been examined by a Field office or considered by Appeals and a closing agreement covering the issue or liability has not been entered into by a Field office or by Appeals.

If a return dealing with an issue for a particular year is filed while a request for a letter ruling on that issue is pending, an Associate office will issue the letter ruling unless it is notified by the taxpayer or otherwise learns that an examination of that issue or the identical issue on an earlier year's return has been started by a Field office. See section 7.05 of this revenue procedure. In income and gift tax matters, as well as in qualified retirement plan, IRA, and exempt organizations matters, even if an examination has begun, an Associate office ordinarily will issue the letter ruling if the Field office agrees by memorandum to the issuance of the letter ruling.

.02. Ordinarily not in certain areas because of factual nature of the problem or for other reasons

The Service ordinarily does not issue letter rulings or determination letters in certain areas because of the factual nature of the matter involved or for other reasons. Rev. Proc. 2019-3, this Bulletin, and Rev. Proc. 2019-7, this Bulletin, provide a list of these areas. This list is not all-inclusive because the Service may decline to issue a letter ruling or a determination letter when appropriate in the interest of sound tax administration, including due to resource constraints, or on other grounds whenever warranted by the facts or circumstances of a particular case.

Instead of issuing a letter ruling or determination letter, the Service may, when it is considered appropriate and in the interest of sound tax administration, issue an information letter calling attention to well-established principles of tax law.

If the Service determines that it is not in the interest of sound tax administration to issue a letter ruling or determination letter due to resource constraints, it will adopt a consistent approach with respect to taxpayers that request a ruling on the same issue. The Service will also consider adding the issue to the no rule list at the first opportunity. See sections 2.01 and 3.02 of Rev. Proc. 2019-3, this Bulletin.

***

.11. No "comfort" letter rulings

Except with respect to a Covered Transaction within the meaning of Rev. Proc. 2017-52, 2017-41 I.R.B. 283, a letter ruling will not be issued with respect to an issue that is clearly and adequately addressed by statute, regulations, decision of a court, revenue rulings, revenue procedures, notices, or other authority published in the Internal Revenue Bulletin (Comfort Ruling). However, except with respect to issues under § 332, § 351, § 368, or § 1036 and the tax consequences resulting from the application of such Code sections (see generally section 6.03(2) of this revenue procedure), the Associate office may, in its discretion, decide to issue a Comfort Ruling if the Associate office is otherwise issuing a letter ruling to the taxpayer on another issue arising in the same transaction.

.12. Not on alternative plans or hypothetical situations

The Service will not issue a letter ruling or a determination letter on alternative plans of proposed transactions or on hypothetical situations.

7. What Are The General Instructions For Requesting Letter Rulings And Determination Letters?

This section provides the general instructions for requesting letter rulings and determination letters.

***

.01. Documents and information required in all requests

.01. Facts

- Complete statement of facts and other information. Each request for a letter ruling or a determination letter must contain a complete statement of all facts relating to the transaction.

These facts include—

(a) names, addresses, telephone numbers, and taxpayer identification numbers of all interested parties (the term "all interested parties" does not mean all shareholders of a widely held corporation requesting a letter ruling relating to a reorganization or all employees where a large number may be involved);

(b) the annual accounting period, and the overall method of accounting (cash or accrual) for maintaining the accounting books and filing the Federal income tax return, of all interested parties;

(c) a description of the taxpayer's business operations;

(d) a complete statement of the business reasons for the transaction;

(e) a detailed description of the transaction; and

(f) all other facts relating to the transaction or to the taxpayer's requested tax treatment thereof.

***

Notes on Private Rulings, Determination Letters and Closing Agreements

Fees and timing: The IRS charges fees for rulings and most determination letters. The fees are commonly $30,000, but can be as little as $2,800 if the taxpayer has an adjusted gross income of under $250,000. If the taxpayer's income is between $250,00 and $1 million, the fee is $7,600 and a determination letter costs $275.[875]

It usually takes about 90 days to get a private letter ruling, although the National Office normally gives an informal answer within two weeks. Sometimes the ruling can be accelerated if the need is urgent, such as a major business transaction that is conditioned on getting an IRS

875 See IRB 2019-1 for full fee schedule

ruling; business transactions are often conditioned on the receipt of a favorable ruling from the National Office or a favorable determination letter from the District Director. From time to time people seek rulings in order to get a negative answer, perhaps to trip up a competitor.

Closing agreements: Another way to achieve administrative finality is to get a "closing agreement" under §7121. This document is usually used in connection with settling matters that arise on audit. A closing agreement can be used to settle tax liabilities retrospectively, but perhaps its greatest value is that it can settle particular issues prospectively, such as the value of an asset, the basis of stock, and so forth. Closing agreements are generally executed on Forms 866 or 906, and may be required as a condition for seeking a ruling.[876]

Problem 11-1:

Klopman Lines oldest cruise ship, the Vacation Flame, caught fire and sank a few months back. Klopman Lines took the insurance money and used it to acquire the following replacement properties. Which of them can qualify for §1033 tax-deferred rollover treatment?

1) A large ocean-going container ship?

2) All the stock of a corporation whose function is owning and operating an ocean-going liner? How about 79% of the stock? See §1033(a)(2)(A) and (c)

3) A resort hotel?

Problem 11-2:

Barney's Road Kill Café, a sole proprietorship that operates a tavern, was recently condemned by the Health Department for reasons too repulsive to detail. Barney's basis in the tavern was $30,000. The tavern is uninsured. Fourteen months later the state paid him the following amounts, which he invested in a new tavern, that Barney also operates as a sole proprietorship. What if:

1) The state pays $70,000 and Barney reinvests $80,000 12 months later.

    a. How much gain or loss does he realize?

    b. How much does he recognize?

876 See generally, M Saltzman, IRS PRACTICE AND PROCEDURE, ¶9.09(1) (2019).

c. What is his basis and holding period in the new tavern? Assume he makes any necessary elections.

d. If he does not make any election under §1033, does that mean he reports the gain? Assume there is a good reason to report the gain, such as using up a loss carryforward. Review §1033 (a)(2) (A)-(B)

2) The state pays $70,000 and Barney reinvests $60,000 12 months later.

a. How much gain or loss does he realize?

b. How much does he recognize?

c. What is his basis and holding period in the new tavern? Assume he makes any necessary elections.

3) Assume the same facts as under "(1)," but that he uses the proceeds to buy 90% of the stock of a corporation, by value. The corporation's main asset is a comparable tavern. Assume 75% of the corporation's value is its tavern.

a. How much gain or loss does he realize?

b. How much does he recognize?

c. What is his basis and holding period in the stock?

4) If the state paid proceeds less than his adjusted basis in the property, but he reinvested the proceeds, would he be entitled to report a loss?

C. TAX-DEFERRED §1031 EXCHANGES

Read §1031(a)-(d)

1. Introduction

Section 1031 is used to allow for tax-free exchanges of comparable ("like-kind") properties held for business or investment uses. After the Tax Cuts and Jobs Act of 2017, §1031 is limited to exchanges of real property held for productive use or investment that is not held primarily for sale. As you might expect, the theory underlying §1031 is that after the exchange the parties have not changed their economic positions or property holdings in a way that is compelling for income tax purposes (i.e., "nothing happened"), with the predictable result that the taxpayer will wind up with the same basis in the property that she transferred away, a holding period in the new property that is "tacked" (meaning "added") to the holding period of the old property, and the same risk of subsequent taxable gain or loss should she dispose of the new property taxably before she dies.

A key feature of §1031 is that the exchange, and recognition of gain or loss, can be asymmetrical. That is, there may be a like-kind exchange as to one taxpayer and not as to the other. Also, one can transfer away business property and get back investment property (or vice-versa) and still enjoy the protection of §1031. Treas. Reg. §1.1031(a)-1(a).

You will find the basis rules in §1031(d) to be somewhat difficult to parse. It is essentially just one more provision that identifies the amount of deferred gain and uses that amount to link the basis of the "nonrecognition property" which was taken back in the exchange to the basis of the property given up in the exchange. Appropriate adjustments are required for any gain or loss that is recognized due to the presence of "boot" (nonqualifying) property added to the exchange, along with rules for how to apportion basis between the boot and the like-kind property. Some problems later in the book will sort out these technical issues.

2. Meaning of "Exchange"

The following case presents some major questions about §1031: just exactly what is an "exchange"; and, is §1031 mandatory or elective?

CENTURY ELECTRIC CO. v. COMMISSIONER OF INTERNAL REVENUE

192 F.2d 155 (8th Cir. 1951)

[The taxpayer, a manufacturer, sold its foundry to Jewell College for $150,000, then rented the foundry from the college for 95 years. The sales price was unrealistically low, being tied to real estate tax values only. The value of the foundry was really $250,000. The leaseback was tied to the sale, by contract. The taxpayer claimed a major loss, computed as follows:

Amount Realized	$150,000
Adjusted Basis	($531,000)
Loss	($381,000)

The court considered former §112 (the predecessor of §1031) in order to resolve the issue. The IRS countered that the proper characterization of the deal was a like-kind exchange.]

RIDDICK, Judge.

. . .

The questions presented are:

1. Whether the transaction stated was for tax purposes a sale of the foundry property within the meaning of section 112 of the Internal Revenue Code, . . . on which petitioner realized in 1943 a deductible loss of $ 381,710.97 determined under section 111 of the code (the adjusted basis of the foundry property of $ 531,710.97 less $ 150,000) as petitioner contends; or, as the Tax Court held, an exchange of property held for productive use in a trade or business for property of a like kind to be held for productive use in trade or business in which no gain or loss is recognized . . . .

2. Whether if the claimed loss deduction is denied, its amount is deductible as depreciation over the 95year term of the lease as the Tax Court held, or over the remaining life of the improvements on the foundry as the petitioner contends.

On the first question the Tax Court reached the right result. The answer to the question is not to be found by a resort to the dictionary for the meaning of the words 'sales' and 'exchanges' in other contexts, but in the purpose and policy of the revenue act as expressed in section 112. . . . In this section Congress was not defining the words 'sales' and 'exchanges'. It was concerned with the administrative problem involved in the computation of gain or loss in transactions of the character with which the section deals. Subsections 112(b)(1) or 112(e) indicate the controlling policy and purpose of the section, that is, the nonrecognition of gain or loss in transactions where neither is readily measured in terms of money, where in theory the taxpayer may have realized gain or loss but where in fact his economic situation is the same after as it was before the transaction. . . . For tax purposes the question is whether the transaction falls within the category just defined. If it does, it is for tax purposes an exchange and not a sale. So much is indicated by subsection 112(b)(1) with regard to the exchange of securities of readily ascertainable market value measured in terms of money. Gain or loss on exchanges of the excepted securities is recognized. Under subsection 112(e) no loss is recognized on an exchange of property held for productive use in trade or business for like property to be held for the same use, although other property or money is also received by the taxpayer. Compare this subsection with subsection 112(c)(1) where in the same circumstances gain is recognized but only to the extent of the other property or money received in the transaction. The comparison clearly indicates that in the computation of gain or loss on a transfer of property held for productive use in trade or business for property of a like kind to be held for the same use, the market value of the properties of like kind involved in the transfer does not enter into the equation.

The transaction here involved may not be separated into its component parts for tax purposes. Tax consequences must depend on what actually was intended and accomplished rather than on the separate steps taken to reach the desired end. The end of the transaction between the petitioner and the college was that intended by the petitioner at its beginning, namely, the transfer of the fee in the foundry property for the 95year lease on the same property and $ 150,000.

It is undisputed that the foundry property before the transaction was held by petitioner for productive use in petitioner's business. After the transaction the same property was held by the petitioner for the same use in the same business. Both before and after the transaction the property was necessary to the continued operation of petitioner's business. The only change wrought by the transaction was in the estate or interest of petitioner in the foundry property. In Regulations . . . the Treasury has interpreted the words 'like kind' as used in subsection 112(b)(1). Under the Treasury interpretation a lease with 30 years or more to run and real estate are properties of 'like kind.' With the controlling purpose of the applicable section of the revenue code in mind, we can not say that the words 'like kind' are so definite and certain that interpretation is neither required nor permitted. The regulation, in force for many years, has survived successive reenactments of the internal revenue acts and has thus acquired the force of law. . . .

On the second question the Tax Court held that petitioner was not entitled to depreciation on the improvements on the foundry property over their useful life after December 1, 1943. The answer to this question depends upon whether as a result of the transaction under consideration the petitioner has an identifiable capital investment in the improvements on the land covered by the lease. Petitioner contends that the amount of its claimed loss, $ 381,710.97, should be apportioned between the land and improvements in proportion to their respective cost bases as of November 30, 1943. This would result in an allocation of $ 277,076.68 of petitioner's investment in the leasehold to the improvements and $ 104,634.29 to the land. The difficulty with petitioner's position is that it involves assumptions and inferences which find no support in the record. What the petitioner has done is to exchange the foundry property having an adjusted basis of $ 531,710.97 on December 1, 1943, for a leasehold and $ 150,000 in cash. Its capital investment is in the leasehold and not its constituent properties. Accordingly, we agree with the Tax Court that petitioner is entitled to depreciation on the leasehold. The basis for depreciation of the leasehold on December 1, 1943, is, therefore, $ 381,710.97 under section 113(a)(6) of the revenue code, deductible over the term of the lease.

The decision of the Tax Court is affirmed.

REV. RUL. 61-119

19611 C.B. 395

Editor's note: Remember that §1031 once applied to a wide range of real and personal property. The rules discussed here still apply to §1031; but now §1031 only addresses exchanges of real property.

. . .

Advice has been requested whether a transaction of the type described below constitutes a sale of used equipment and the purchase of new equipment or whether it is one integrated transaction constituting an exchange with respect to which section 1031(a) of the Internal Revenue Code of 1954 provides for the nonrecognition of gain or loss.

A taxpayer has equipment used in his trade or business for more than six months for which his adjusted basis is $500. This used equipment has a fair market value of $1,000. Better equipment is now available which the taxpayer desires to acquire. Such equipment has a listed retail price of $10,000 but is regularly sold for $9,000.

Ordinarily, the taxpayer would accomplish the exchange by surrendering the old equipment to the dealer and receiving a tradein allowance to cover part of the cost of the new equipment. Thus, the dealer would bill the taxpayer for $8,000, representing the $9,000 sales price of the new equipment minus the $1,000 tradein allowance for the old equipment. Alternatively, the dealer's invoice might reflect the new equipment at its list price, or $10,000, in which case the tradein allowance would be shown as $2,000, leaving $8,000 as the balance due from the customer. In either case, the transaction would be treated as a nontaxable exchange, in view of section 1031(a) of the Code, which provides, in part, that no gain or loss shall be recognized if property held for productive use in trade or business is exchanged solely for property of a like kind to be held for the same purpose, and in view of section 1.1031(a)1(a) of the Income Tax Regulations, which provides, in part, that a transfer of property meeting the requirements of section 1031(a) may be within the provision of section 1031(a) even though the taxpayer transfers in addition property not meeting the requirements of section 1031(a) or money.

In the above situation, therefore, no gain or loss would be recognized even though the taxpayer was allowed $1,000 in the first instance, or $2,000 in the second instance, for the used equipment for which his basis was $500. The taxpayer's unrecognized gain on the tradein would be applied, in accordance with I.T. 2615, C.B. XI1, 112 (1932), to reduce his basis of the new equipment for depreciation purposes. Thus, the taxpayer's basis for the new equipment would be $8,500, the purchase price less the unrecognized gain on the used equipment.

The question has been raised whether the foregoing authorities will continue to govern the tax consequences of the transaction if, instead of entering into a direct exchange in the manner outlined above, the parties entered into separate contracts, one covering the sale of the old equipment and the other covering the purchase of the new equipment.

The recognition to be accorded a particular transaction for Federal Income Tax purposes depends upon the substance of the transaction rather than the form in which it is cast. The Internal Revenue Service and the courts look to what is actually done rather than to the formalities of the transaction or to the declared purpose of the participants in gauging its tax consequences. . . . The courts have held that a sale is to be disregarded where it is a step in a transaction the purpose of which is to make an exchange, and which results in an exchange. See *Century Electric Co. v. Commissioner*, 192 Fed. (2d) 155, certiorari denied 342 U.S. 954. See also Revenue Ruling 6043, C.B. 19601, 687.

In the instant case the sale of the used equipment and the purchase of the new equipment are reciprocal and mutually dependent transactions. The taxpayer's acquisition of the new equipment from the dealer is contingent upon the dealer taking his used equipment and granting a tradein allowance equal to or in excess of its fair market value. Moreover, the dealer's acceptance of the old equipment is dependent upon the taxpayer's purchase of the new equipment. Under these circumstances, the transfer of the old equipment to the dealer, irrespective of the form or the technique through which the transfer is accomplished, represents but a step in a single integrated transaction.

Accordingly, it is held that the transfer of the old equipment to the dealer and purchase of the new equipment from him is a nontaxable exchange under section 1031 of the Code, even though the purchaser and the seller execute separate contracts and treat the purchase and sale as unrelated transactions for record keeping purposes.

The fact that the purchase and sale are consummated concurrently, or that the sales price of the new equipment and the tradein allowance for the old equipment are in excess of the price at which such items are ordinarily sold, may serve as indication that the purchase and sale were not intended as separate or unrelated transactions. However, the absence of either or both of these factors, standing alone, will not be taken to indicate that separate or unrelated transactions were consummated.

Notes

When is a lease real estate for §1031 purposes? Congress intended that real property that was eligible for nonrecognition before the 2017 tax reform would remain eligible for §1031 treatment.[877] Only a lease with a term of at least 30 years can rise to the level of being "real estate" according to Reg. §1.1031(a)-1(c). Now consider the tax implication; if Century Electric could have leased back the property for only 20 years, would it have been willing to do so as a business matter? That is, what would be the business disadvantage of a shorter-term lease? What if

877 Conference Report 115-466, 115th Congress, 1st Session 394 to 396. See footnote 726.

the property were rented for 20 years with an 11 year renewal option? The answer is that one adds the renewal option to the base lease; the result is a 31-year lease.[878]

How does one separate a sale and long-tem leaseback from a swap of real estate for a lease? According to the Third Circuit in Leslie Co., Inc.[879] it is a sale and a leaseback if the sale price is correct from a market perspective and the leaseback is independent of the sale, even if the leaseback is preplanned. Here are the facts of Leslie in simplified form:

> **To illustrate:** Leslie Co. needed a new factory. It borrowed money from an insurance company (Prudential) to build a new factory at a fixed price. Leslie Co. completed construction and, by prearangement, sold the new factory at a loss to Prudential, which in turn leased the property back to Leslie for 30 years. The transaction was held to be a true sale (preserving Leslie' loss) to the insurer, followed by a true lease to Leslie, because both the sale price and the rental terms were at fair market rates, determined independently of the terms of the purchase. Had Leslie Co. lost, the result would have been a nontaxable exchange as in *Century Electric* in which Leslie Co. exchanged real estate for a lease.Instead Leslie Co. received both an immediate loss on the transfer and rental expense deductions as a tenant.

The IRS evidently still adheres to the idea that integrated sales and leasebacks are really exchanges.[880] For taxpayers holding appreciated property they want to sell and lease back, this has to be good news.

The meaning of "like-kind": The term "like kind" is loosely defined when dealing with real estate, where virtually anything goes; for example, ranches can be swapped tax-free for apartment buildings.

Although §1031 generally assures that basis stays the same, it does not prevent shifting the balance between depreciable and nondepreciable assets. This is the key to some powerful tax planning.

> **To illustrate:** Ms. Oakley owns a ranch with a basis of $100,000 and a value of $500,000, of which 95% of the value is allocable to the land. She swaps it for a city apartment with a value of $500,000, of which 95% of the value is allocable to the building. She has increased her depreciable basis from $5,000 to $95,000.[881] Likewise, she might trade her ranch for a mine, as to which she could claim depletion deductions as the mine is exhausted by excavation.

---

878 Rev. Rul. 78-72, 1978-1 CB 258.

879 Leslie Co. v. Commissioner, 539 F.2d 943 (3d Cir. 1976. See also Jordan Marsh Co. v. Commissioner, 269 F.2d 453 (2d Cir. 1959) (taxpayer sold real estate parcels at a loss followed by promptly leasing the property back from seller. Held: the transaction was a sale and leaseback, not an exchange under § 1031; Tax Court reversed). The IRS explicitly rejects Jordan Marsh, Rev. Rul. 60-43, 1960-1 CB 687.

880 See Rev Rul. 76-301, 1976-2 CB 241.

881 Rev. Rul. 68-36, 1968-1 C.B. 357.

3. The "Holding" Requirement

Section 1031 requires that the taxpayer hold the replacement property for rental or business use. How long must the property be held? There is no answer, but there has to be a period during which there is a bona fide holding, with no preconceived plan to dispose of the property. What if the taxpayer plans to transfer the asset to an entity under the taxpayer's control, say to a partnership in which the partner has significant retained powers? The leading case in the area, *Magneson v. Commissioner*,[882] held that where a party to a like-kind exchange promptly dumped the real estate he received in the exchange into a California general partnership, he still "held" the property indirectly via the partnership interest. The decision is reasonably clear that if he had been a limited partner, the outcome would have differed because a limited partner has so much less control over the partnership's property than a general partner does.

Problem 11-3:

Which of the following can be exchanged tax-free under §1031?

1) A residential building lot held for sale to customers in Florida for a comparable lot in Maine.

2) Assuming the transaction in "(1)" is of qualifying like-kind property, can the exchange be electively rendered taxable?

Problem 11-4:

Marge entered into a tax-deferred §1031 exchange with a neighbor in which they swapped their residential apartment buildings. Marge has held her apartment house for four years and it had a $0 basis in her hands, though it originally cost her $100,000 and is still worth that much. Her neighbor has held his apartment building for over a year.

1) What holding period doeseach taxpayer have in the building they received in their exchange? See §1221.

2) If either building had §1250 recapture potential, will the parties be taxed on the recapture potential? See §1250(d)(4). What if Marge later sold the building she got in the exchange for $80,000?

---

882 753 F.2d 1490 (9th Cir. 1985)

3) Assume the same facts as "(1)" above, except that the exchange is with Marge and a real estate dealer. Would this change your answer in "(1)"?

4) Refer back to problem 11-2 (relating to §1033). Assume the same facts as problem "11-2(1)," except that Barney reinvests the full proceeds in a mini-warehouse. Assume he makes any necessary elections. Will the rollover qualify for tax deferral under §1033? See §1033(g) and Reg. §1.1031(a)-1(b).

4. Deferred Like-Kind Exchanges

Section 1031(a)(3) permits the owner of property to transfer away property at the closing and to defer the receipt of the nonrecognition property to be received in the exchange. In fact, the parties need not even have identified the nonrecognition property to be received, but they must do so on or before 45 days following the closing. Other time limits require that replacement property is received no more than 180 days after the taxpayer transferred the relinquished property. Otherwise, the transaction loses the protection of §1031.

The 180 days rule is supplemented by another rule that says if the property is received after the date the taxpayer's income return for the year in which the exchange occurred is due, then the exchange also fails. The due date of most people's tax returns is April 15, so that means that if the closing occurred on December 31 of year one, for most people the exchange would have to be completed not later than April 15th of year two. The deadline can be extended by filing for an extension of time to file one's tax return under Reg. §1.1031(k)-1(b)(3).

Deferred payment arrangements have given rise to a small, bustling industry based on some safe harbors found in Reg. §1.1031(b)(2) and (k)-1. The regulations produce the concepts of "qualified escrow accounts," "qualified trusts", and "qualified intermediaries" all of which are persons or entities that can take cash and hold it subject to instructions with respect to the transaction. The intermediary can then use cash to buy nonrecognition property to satisfy the owner's directions.

To illustrate: Imagine you owned a farm that you held for investment. One day, Blanche Buyer showed up at your barn and declared she wanted to buy your farm for $200,000. Imagine the price is exceptionally high and you want to go ahead with the sale, but your basis in the farm is small, and you would just buy another farm anyway. Here is what you might do.

- First, you transfer the farm to a qualified intermediary, say, a title company.
- The title company transfers the farm to Blanche right away in exchange for $200,000 that your buyer paid the title company.
- The title company then follows your directions in applying the $200,000 to acquire another farm to complete the "like-kind exchange" as to you.

Incidentally, an attorney can be a qualified intermediary.[883] The major problem is likely your ability to meet the 45/180 day requirements with respect to identifying and closing on the replacement property following your disposal of the farm. Your buyer will not suffer any income tax at all, so she is unlikely to mind accommodating you and your tax problem. Also, notice that this is a "one-size-fits-all" provision that may be fine for small transactions but could be very demanding for larger, more complex deals.

5. Reverse Like-Kind Exchanges

The trouble with the deferred like-kind exchange contemplated by §1031(a)(3) is its pressure to get title to the replacement property within a relatively short period if it is a "big ticket" deal. It may be possible to escape this time limit by doing a "reverse" like-kind exchange. It is reversed in the sense that the replacement property is obtained before the relinquished property is transferred.

> **To illustrate:** A devious law professor at your school owns a property in Maine (known as Profacre) that she holds for investment. One of her neighbors has wanted Profacre for years. This year the neighbor and the professor enter into a contract, pursuant to which the neighbor contracts to buy an investment property that the professor identifies as acceptable. Once the neighbor has the replacement property (Dryacre), the contract obligates the professor and neighbor to enter into a simultaneous exchange in which the professor relinquishes Profacre in exchange for Dryacre. The 45/180 day issue never surfaces because it is formally a simple simultaneous exchange.

The IRS has denounced the practice and has also provided a narrow safe harbor in Rev. Proc. 2000-37, 2004-51, 2004-2 CB 294.

Problem 11-5:

Refer back to Problem 4-22 involving Harold and Edna's interest in selling their Long Island home. Using the same facts, consider the next three questions:

a. Could Harold and Edna engage in some kind of three party transaction so as to sell the Long Island house and buy a summer place in Maine? How would you set it up if you were their tax advisor?

---

883 PLR 9232030 (May 12, 1992).

b. If they do engage in such a transaction, can Harold and Edna buy more than one replacement property? See Reg. §1.1031(k)-(c)(4).

c. Assume that Long Island has recently become infested with huge mutant fire ants that make being outdoors dangerous. As a result, their Long Island property has declined in value. Harold and Edna would like to know if they can sell the Long Island property to the Friendly Bank at its fair market value and then lease it back for 15 year with a 15-year renewal option and still report the loss? They want to know what the IRS view is, and if the courts agree.

D. BOOT IN §1031 EXCHANGES

1. General Rules

An otherwise qualifying exchange is not disqualified merely because the taxpayer also received nonqualifying property ("boot"), but boot will trigger recognition of realized gains to the extent of the boot received.[884] The term comes from the phrase "to boot," meaning "in addition." Transaction costs, such as broker's commissions, reduce boot received,[885] but the receipt of boot cannot trigger a loss if the transaction is otherwise within §1031.[886]

The payment of cash does not trigger recognition of gain by the payor of the cash because American currency that is "legal tender" always has a basis equal to value. If the taxpayer pays with nonqualifying property (say, common stock) as well as qualifying property, the disposition of the stock is treated as if that transfer were a separate taxable sale to a third party. The model assumes the illustrative stock is sold for cash -- resulting in taxable gain or loss-- and that the imaginary cash proceeds are added to the §1031 exchange. More on that later.

The rules for computing the basis of property that one receives in the exchange appear in §1031(d). The easy part concerns boot; the recipient of boot allocates basis in the relinquished property first to the boot, up to its value. This strips the boot out of the like-kind transaction and assures that the boot can be sold at once for a value equal to basis, with no resulting taxable gain or loss.[887]

The remaining basis is allocated to the like-kind property. The basis of the like-kind property one receives will be equal to:

884 §1031(b).

885 See Rev. Rul. 72-456. 1972-2- C.B. 468.

886 §1031(c).

887 See Reg. §1.1031(d)-1(d).

1. The basis of the relinquished property;
2. Minus money one received or the value of non-like-kind property one received (or bothcombined);
3. Plus cash or the value of property one paid out;
4. Plus gain one recognized;
5. Minus the loss one recognized (loss can arise if one pays in part with nonqualified property that has declined in value).

Steps "4" and "5" deserve comment. One adds recognized gain to basis of the nonrecognition property one receives in order to assure no over-taxation when one later sells that nonrecognition property. Again, if one provides non-qualified property (such as appreciated common stock) as added payment, that property is treated as if it were sold.

> **To illustrate:** Assume that in order to facilitate the deal between the professor and the neighbor, the professor has to pay the neighbor an extra $10,000 when the exchange occurs because the parties agree Dryacre is worth $10,000 more than Profacre. If the professor pays the $10,000 in the form of shares of appreciated stock, she is treated as if he sold the stock and transferred the cash proceeds to the neighbor. The professor adds this gain to the basis of the property she receives in the exchange (Dryacre). The neighbor will report the $10,000 worth of stock as "boot," if the neighbor claims a like-kind exchange as to himself. The stock will take a basis of $10,000 in the neighbor's hands. Most likely the neighbor cannot claim the benefits of §1031 because he has not "held" Dryacre for any purpose other than disposing of it, and he does not care anyway because there is no inherent gain in the property he is using to get Profacre.

Likewise, one subtracts losses from basis to prevent duplication of losses.

> **To illustrate:** You own real property used in your business. The property has a basis of $600 and is worth $1,000. You swap it for real property worth $1,500 in a §1031 exchange. To make up the difference, you transfer stock to the owner of the other real property. The stock is worth $500, but has a basis of $750. Result: you have a recognized loss of $250 on the stock. Your basis in the real property is $1,100, as follows:

1. Basis of the like-kind property given up	$600
2. Minus money received or value of non-like-kind property received	0
3. Plus cash, or the basis of "boot" property, paid	750
4. Plus gain recognize	0
5. Minus loss recognized (on the stock, as if sold to a stranger)	(250)[888]
Total	$1,100

Is the result correct? Yes. Had there been no stock transfer, the basis of the property you received would have been $600. The stock sale was taxed just as if it were with an outsider, which makes sense, given that the stock clearly does not qualify for §1031 treatment. Adding a net $500 to the basis of the property you received has to be right, in that you really did pay an extra $500 in value to the transferor to get the property. That certainly would have been true if you in fact sold the stock on the stock exchange and took the $500 in cash and added it to the amount transferred to the other party.

Whenever you work a tax problem that involves deferral of gain or loss, it is a good idea to imagine that you immediately sold the property you received at its fair market value and compare the combined results of the two steps with the result of a single transaction in which you simply sold your property outright. Any gains or losses on the first exchange plus the gains or losses on the subsequent sale should sum to exactly the same amount you would have recognized if you had just sold the original property outright. If the two transactions do not equate to the same number, something is wrong with your computation of the gain or of the basis.

> **To illustrate:** You sell the property you got in the exchange for $1,500 cash. Your taxable gain will be the $1,500 amount realized minus $1,100 basis = $400. Had you simply sold your property, rather than going through the exchange-plus-sale, you would have realized a $400 gain (namely its $1,000 value minus its $600 basis). This test shows the basis and gain computations with respect to the like-kind exchange were correct.

2. Role of Liabilities

America thrives on debt. We are forced to consider its role in like-kind exchanges. The rules are fairly easy. The key concept is that liabilities assumed or taken subject to are treated as boot to the party relieved of the liability. If both the property transferred and the property received are encumbered, the liabilities are netted, and only the difference is treated as boot or (conversely)

888 See Reg. §1.1031(d)-1(e).

further cash consideration paid.[889] If the realized gain is less than the net debt reduction, the recognized gain cannot exceed the realized gain.

To illustrate: Karl owns Karlacre which is worth $100. Karl has a basis of $75 and Karlacre is subject to a $70 debt. Karl swaps Karlacre for Billacre, which was worth $60, but was subject to a $30 debt. Notice that the properties have the same net value of $30, in light of the debts. Nevertheless, Karl must recognize a $25 gain (which is also the realized gain). Here is the impact on Karl.

Value of Billacre:	$60
Less debt on Billacre:	($30)
Net value of Billacre:	$30
Plus mortgage on Karlacre:	$70
Total consideration:	$100 = amount realized
Less basis of Karlacre:	($75)
Realized gain:	$25

Karl must recognize the full $25 gain, because it is less than the $40 net reduction in his debts.

Problem 11-6:

Alvin is single and lives in Atlanta. He owns a mini-warehouse that he runs as a business. The warehouse is worth $100,000 and he has a basis of $60,000. Orville Lampwick, now an over-paid National League pitcher, is willing to pay $100,000 for the warehouse. Alvin wants to get an apartment unit to be held for investment in exchange for his warehouse and he also wants to avoid tax on his $40,000 unrealized gain. Assume Orville owns a fine apartment unit in Flyneck that would please Alvin, but it is worth only $90,000. Orville is willing to pay $10,000 cash along with his apartment unit for the mini-warehouse. Alvin will hold the apartment unit for investment. Assuming the deal goes through:

1) Does the $10,000 disqualify the transactions entirely as to Alvin?

2) What is Alvin's realized gain?

3) What is Alvin's recognized gain?

889 §1031(d). While taxpayers net liabilities, no other netting of boot is permissible; thus, if the taxpayer›s liabilities are released, that release cannot be reduced by boot consisting of other property transferred by the taxpayer. Reg. §1.1031(d)-2 example (2)(c).

4) What is Alvin's basis in the apartment unit?

5) What is Alvin's holding period for the apartment unit?

6) If the mini-warehouse were worth only $50,000 and Lampwick traded an apartment unit worth $50,000 for it, could Alvin recognize the loss?

7) Lampwick does not own an apartment unit, but he is prepared to commit to buying one and transferring it to Alvin in exchange for Alvin's mini-warehouse.

    a. It is June 30 of year 1. Lampwick pays $100,000 (the value of the warehouse) to a bank escrow agent and obtains title to the warehouse from the escrow agent. How long does Alvin have to identify the property he wants the escrow agent to buy on his behalf? See Reg. §1.1031(k)-1(b).

    b. How long can the parties wait until the property is conveyed to Alvin?

    c. If the 180 or 45 day tests are not met, is the transaction taxable, or is §1031(a)(3) just a "safe harbor" rule?

Problem 11-7:

Swindler Enterprises, a sole proprietorship, exchanges business realty with a basis of $6,000 and worth $9,000 for like-kind property worth $7,000, plus stock worth $2,000. The other party to the transaction is Donna D. Developer. Both are cash-method, calendar-year taxpayers. The transactions of both parties to the exchange qualify under §1031.

1) What is Swindler's realized gain?

2) What is Swindler's recognized gain?

3) What is the basis in the stock in Swindler's hands?

4) What if the stock had a basis of $1,000 in Developer's hands? Would she recognize a gain of $1,000 on the transaction even if the exchange were otherwise tax-free to her?

5) What is the basis and holding period of the property that Swindler receives?

6) Is the result as to the basis of the property Swindler received correct from a Federal Income Tax point of view?

7) What is the basis and holding period of the property Developer received in the exchange?

Problem 11-8:

Mrs. Smith transfers her investment real estate, which has a basis and value of $2,000 and is subject to a $1,000 bank debt, to Mrs. Jones, whose investment real estate has a basis of $2,000 and a gross value of $3,000, but is subject to a $2,000 debt. Both are nonrecourse debts.

1) How much boot does Mrs. Smith have?

2) How much boot does Mrs. Jones have?

3) How might you plan to avoid any adverse tax consequences implied by this fact pattern?

E. THE WASH SALES RULE OF §1091

Read §1091(a) and (d)

1. Introduction

Imagine you are a wealthy investor with a big stock portfolio. One of the blocks of stock you own (called "A") has lost value, say $10,000. If you sell it, you can use the losses to offset ("wash out") some capital gains you would like to recognize right now on stock B, because you think the appreciated B stock had topped out. By happenstance, the gain is $10,000. You think the price of the A stock will rise fairly soon. How about this tax planning idea? Sell the A stock and the B stock, offsetting the gain and loss, then quickly repurchase $10,000 worth of A stock and hope for the best. This is the kind of transaction that §1091 is designed to thwart.

Problem 11-9:

Zork owns 100 shares of Deep Space Growth, Inc., a speculative investment that his stockbroker talked him into. He paid $10,000 for the stock two years ago, but he sold it for a mere $2,000 two weeks ago. Last week, sensing that the company was going to recover, he changed his mind and bought another 100 shares of the Deep Space Growth, Inc. for $2,200. Advise him as to the following matters, after reviewing §1091(a) and (d):

1) Can he use the $8,000 loss to reduce his tax base? (Assume the loss is deductible if realized, except perhaps for §1091.)

2) Does it make a difference that he was not trying to avoid taxes when he entered into these transactions?

3) What is Zork's basis in the recently purchased block of 100 shares?

4) Assuming he sells the second block for $2,200 a year later, what will be his recognized gain or loss on the sale?

5) Assume Zork sells the stock to his sister, Zinka, for $2,000, instead of to an unknown buyer on the stock market. Read §267(a)(1).

    a. Assume Zinka later sells the stock for $3,000. How much of the $3,000 is taxed?

    b. What if she sells the stock for $11,000? How much of the $11,000 is taxed?

    c. Reading §267(a)(1) and (d) together, would you characterize them as a disallowance rule, a deferral rule or something else?

    d. As a seller, would you rather be trapped by §267(a)(1) or §1091?

2. Avoidance of §1091

Section 1091 is often more bark than bite. One way to beat it is to sell the old stock (say, General Motors) and reinvest promptly in stock of a different issuer with the same basic characteristics (say, Ford). This works if the reason for your investment was a hunch that the domestic automobile industry was going to flourish. The strategy works because securities of different issuers (GM and Ford) are considered definitely not "substantially identical" under §1091[890]. Another trick is to "double up," meaning buy more of the stock (say GM) and wait for 30 days and sell the block of shares that had lost value. That way, the taxpayer always has a GM investment, so she does not lose out if it rise in value, but gets the loss if the stock's value continues to languish.

890 Rev. Rul. 58-210, 1958-1 C.B. 523.

a) Corporations can consolidate, merge or divide on a tax-deferred basis at the corporate and shareholder levels under §§ 354, 355, 361 and 368, among others. This is of enormous importance to the world of high finance.

b) Life insurance and annuity policies can be exchanged tax-free under §1035 as long as it does not result in shifting property outside the United States.

c) Common stock of one corporation can be swapped for common stock of the same corporation under §1036.

d) Section 1037 allows holders to swap certain old U.S. Savings Bonds for new ones on a tax-deferred basis.

e) Section 1038 gives sellers who repossess property they sold on the installment sale method an election to defer the gain on repossession in exchange for an appropriately reduced basis and a holding period that presumes the property was never sold.

f) Section 1042 allows an owner of a small business who sells at least 30% of the stock to an employee stock ownership plan (or "ESOP") to pay no tax on the sale as long as he has held the business at least three years and plows the proceeds back into other domestic corporate securities and does not sell them during his lifetime. Former Secretary of the Treasury William Simon reportedly did this when he and his partners sold the Avis car rental company to Avis's employees.[891]

g) Section 1045 allows noncorporate taxpayers to reinvest the proceeds from the sale of qualified small business stock to other qualified small business stock in a rollover that has the effect of deferring income taxes until the recently-purchased stock is sold. The taxpayer recognizes gain only to the extent that the amount realized on the sale exceeds amounts reinvested in qualified small business stock during the 60-day period. If the taxpayer sells the stock she reinvested in, then the taxpayer can do a rollover again. In all cases, the taxpayer needs to hold the stock for a minimum

891 Diana B. Henriques and Floyd Norris, "[Special Report] Wealthy, Helped by Wall St., New Find Ways to Escape Tax on Profits," New York Times, Dec. 01, 1996.

of six months (not the usual five years) required to exclude gain under §1202.[892] The rules of §1202 generally supplement the rules of §1045. The taxpayer has to reduce his or her basis in the new stock to reflect the untaxed gain in the stock that was sold.[893] It is a venture capitalist's dream come true.

To illustrate: Moneybags invests $400,000 in stock of Omega.com, Inc. in Year 1, and sells it in Year 6, for $800,000 as qualified small business stock. He immediately reinvests the $800,000 in Alpha.com, Inc., which is also a qualified small business. Moneybags need not hold the Alpha.com stock for 5 years in order to claim the 50 percent exclusion. Moneybags can sell the Alpha.com stock any time after he holds it for six months and claim the 50 percent exclusion.

h) Section 1058 prevents the taxation of "securities lending" transactions where the taxpayers engage in technical sales in the sense that the stock certificates or debt papers merely differ in form.

i) Section 1092 disallows losses on straddle transactions. These deals occur when a taxpayer buys personal properties that vary inversely in value. For example, suppose a taxpayer (who owned no gold) paid for an option to buy an ounce of gold for $300 and also a right to sell an ounce of gold for $300. No matter how the price of gold moves, the "legs" of the straddle will move in opposite directions. Cunning taxpayers used to buy offsetting positions like this and then sell the loss "leg" at the end of the year, while retaining the gain "leg." The core idea of §1092 is to suspend deduction of that loss until the taxpayer disposes of the offsetting (gain) leg. The reverse approach might be to force the taxpayer to engage in a deemed sale of the unsold leg, which is what occurs under the increasingly popular "mark-to-market" approach in which liquid assets are deemed sold and taxed.

892 The replacement stock must generally meet the active-business requirement for the six-month period following the purchase. See H. Rep't No. 105-220, 105th Cong., 1st Sess. 57 (1997).

893 Gain from any sale that is deferred under §1045(a) is applied to reduce (in the order acquired) the basis for determining gain or loss of any qualified small business stock that the taxpayer bought in the 60-day period described in §1045(a). §1045(b)(3). §1045 is inapplicable to gain that is treated as ordinary income. §1045(a).

CHAPTER 12 - IDENTIFICATION OF THE PROPER TAXPAYER

A. INTRODUCTION

The subject of this chapter might be, "honestly now, who ought to pay income taxes on this money?" Section 1 of the Code imposes the Federal Income Tax on "taxpayers", as if it were always obvious who should bear the tax. In fact, it often is not. The problem of identifying the "real taxpayer" often arises in a family setting with a heavily-taxed parent attempting to shift income from property or services to children who are in comparatively low tax brackets or to a closely-held corporation that is in a relatively low bracket. The parent's plan will not reduce the overall amount of taxable income, but it may reduce total taxes on that income.

The tax-avoidance practice of shifting income within families has been partially controlled by the enactment of §1(g), popularly known as the "Kiddie Tax," but the pressure to shift income to lower-bracket relatives (or affiliates) will not stop as long as there is a progressive income tax, and it is not a sufficient reason for ending progressive taxation. We will look at the Kiddie Tax later in connection with computing Federal Income Tax liabilities. The important thing to know about the Kiddie Tax now is that beyond a certain minimum, investment income earned by a child under age 19 (and dependent student-children under age 24) is taxed to the child at the parents' marginal income tax rates for years 1987 through 2017. For tax years 2018 to 2025, §1(j)(4) changes the child's tax rate to the rate for trusts and estates.

The Code does not tax parents on their minor childrens' incomes. This result is the work of §73, which provides that income earned by a minor child is taxed to the minor child and not to the parent, even if local law makes the earnings the property of the parent's and even if the child never received the money.[894] This has occasionally risen up to stun television show Whiz Kids who thought they knew everything. If the Code taxed the parents on their childrens' income, there would be no need for the Kiddie Tax.

Another important issue in this area is the coordination of community property laws with the Federal Income Tax laws. Early on, in *Poe v. Seaborn*,[895] the Supreme Court chose to respect

894 All expenditures attributable to such amounts, whether made by parent or child, are treated as paid or incurred by the child.

895 282 U.S. 101 (1930).

state community property concepts by ruling that each spouse is subject to income tax on one half of the community income, an important result for people living in states that adopted Civil Law property concepts, such as Texas, Louisiana and California. *Poe v. Seaborn* remains good law. However, the decision was a source of unfairness before the time of the joint return because the *Poe v. Seaborn* rule meant that if one spouse had a high income and the other spouse had a low income, the income was effectively split in a community property state and the net tax liability that the couple owed to the IRS was often lower than the tax liability owed by otherwise identical families in non-community property states. The disparity in tax burdens is the result of graduated tax rates.

> **To illustrate:** It is 1939. The Cals live in Los Angeles and the Yorks live in New York. Only one spouse in each family has income, and it is all earned income. California law causes the Cals to share the income, and as a result let's assume their Federal Income Tax is $10,000 each or $20,000 total, thanks to income-splitting. The income-earning York alone pays taxes on his income and incurs a tax of $23,000 because the Yorks cannot split the income between them.

In order to eliminate that disparity, in 1948 Congress gave married taxpayers the opportunity to file a "joint" return, which melds the income and deductions of the two spouses. As a result, in 1949, if the Yorks filed a joint return, they would pay the same Federal Income Tax as the Cals.

This latest zigzag in the course of tax history has left spouses in community property states in peril, because if one of the spouses unscrupulously conceals and fails to report income, the other spouse is deemed to have received one-half of that income and is liable for Federal Income Taxes on it. In a noncommunity property state, the solution for the honest but suspicious spouse is to file a separate return. In a community property state a separate return does not work, because the innocent spouse is still attributed half of the cheater's income. Section 66(b) lets a spouse in this situation off the hook if she files separately and meets certain other tests. Alternative policy solutions include amending the Code to repeal joint and several liability for joint returns or amending state laws concerning community income.

For spouses who file jointly, perhaps because one spouse was intimidated into doing so by the other spouse, there is still a significant problem because the IRS may track down the blameless spouse and try to collect unpaid income taxes generated by the other spouse while they were married. The IRS can impose liability on an innocent spouse based on the rule that joint filing produces joint and several liability in each spouse. If the innocent spouse in either state can meet the standards of §6015(b) she can avoid personal liability for the underpayment, but to prevail she must not know of the omission and it must be fair to let her off the hook. That can be hard to prove and can create hardships, especially among low-paid people with unstable marital lives.[896]

A taxpayer who is divorced, legally separated, widowed or living apart for 12 months from the spouse with whom she filed a joint return can elect separate tax liability under §6015(c), (known as an "innocent spouse election"), as long as some modest conditions are met. The important point is that when a marriage begins to dissolve a taxpayer who filed a joint return has the option of limiting her liability on the joint return to what her liability would have been had she filed a separate return. This should be a matter of great interest to divorce lawyers.

This Chapter falls into distinct categories. The first area involves taxpayers' attempts to gratuitously transfer income from services. The second area involves efforts to gratuitously transfer income from property, and the third area involves *sales* of unearned income. The first two components fall under the general heading of "gratuitous assignment of income" and the last falls under the heading "acceleration of income by sales of carved-out interests." The rest of the Chapter covers the use of entities to shift income, the Kiddie Tax, low-interest loans, and finally the tax aspects of divorce. Divorce is included in here because the effect of alimony is to split the payors income with the payer.

B. GRATUITOUS ASSIGNMENT OF INCOME FROM SERVICES

1. General Rule

The case you are about to read is the bedrock decision with respect to the gratuitous assignment of income from services. Interestingly, the contract that was the subject of the case was executed in a year before enactment of the Federal Income Tax, and was not driven by Federal Income or Federal Estate Tax considerations, though perhaps by estate planning factors. (The Federal Estate Tax was first enacted in 1916.)

LUCAS v. EARL
281 U.S. 111 (1930)

MR. JUSTICE HOLMES delivered the opinion of the Court.

This case presents the question whether the respondent, Earl, could be taxed for the whole of the salary and attorney's fees earned by him in the years 1920 and 1921, or should be taxed for only a half of them in view of a contract with his wife which we shall mention. The Commissioner of Internal Revenue and the Board of Tax Appeals imposed a tax upon the whole,

896 See generally, Beck, *The Innocent Spouse Problem: Joint and Several Liability for Income Taxes Should be Repealed*, 43 Vand. L. Rev. 317 (1990).

but their decision was reversed by the Circuit Court of Appeals, 30 F.2d 898. a writ of certiorari was granted by this Court.

By the contract, made in 1901, Earl and his wife agreed "that any property either of us now has or may hereafter acquire . . . in any way, either by earnings (including salaries, fees, etc.), or any rights by contract or otherwise, during the existence of our marriage, or which we or either of us may receive by gift, bequest, devise, or inheritance, and all the proceeds, issues, and profits of any and all such property shall be treated and considered and hereby is declared to be received, held, taken, and owned by us as joint tenants, and not otherwise, with the right of survivorship." The validity of the contract is not questioned, and we assume it to be unquestionable under the law of the State of California, in which the parties lived. Nevertheless we are of opinion that the Commissioner and Board of Tax Appeals were right.

The Revenue Act of 1918 . . . imposes a tax upon the net income of every individual including "income derived from salaries, wages, or compensation for personal service . . . of whatever kind and in whatever form paid," § 213 (a). The provisions of the Revenue Act of 1921, c. 136, 42 Stat. 227, in sections bearing the same numbers are similar to those of the above. A very forcible argument is presented to the effect that the statute seeks to tax only income beneficially received, and that taking the question more technically the salary and fees became the joint property of Earl and his wife on the very first instant on which they were received. We well might hesitate upon the latter proposition, because however the matter might stand between husband and wife he was the only party to the contracts by which the salary and fees were earned, and it is somewhat hard to say that the last step in the performance of those contracts could be taken by anyone but himself alone. But this case is not to be decided by attenuated subtleties. It turns on the import and reasonable construction of the taxing act. There is no doubt that the statute could tax salaries to those who earned them and provide that the tax could not be escaped by anticipatory arrangements and contracts however skillfully devised to prevent the salary when paid from vesting even for a second in the man who earned it. That seems to us the import of the statute before us and we think that no distinction can be taken according to the motives leading to the arrangement by which the fruits are attributed to a different tree from that on which they grew.

Judgment reversed.

The CHIEF JUSTICE took no part in this case.

Notes

First, some terminology. The "assignment of income doctrine" is a misnomer, because it suggests that income can be assigned. A better name might be the "no assignment of income doctrine."

If the Earls had formed a *bona fide* partnership, they could have succeeded where they failed by their contractual assignment. Their being married would not have prevented the couple from organizing a legitimate partnership, but it is not enough just to pool their salaries; there must be a genuine joint undertaking with a view to earning joint profits, such as a practice of accounting or medicine, for the partnership to be legitimated for tax purposes.[897] Partnerships are dealt with at some length later in the Chapter.

2. Waiver of Income

Taxpayers can reject income they have not yet earned. The following case raises the provocative question of whether a taxpayer can achieve by a renunciation of income, coupled with a direction as to how that income is applied what the taxpayer could not achieve by merely redirecting payment to someone else.

COMMISSIONER v. GIANNINI
129 F.2d 638 (9th Cir. 1942)

STEPHENS, Circuit Judge

[The taxpayer was director and president of Bancitaly Corporation from 1919 to 1925 without compensation. In 1927, it was agreed that the taxpayer be paid 5% of net profits each year, beginning in 1927, with a minimum of $100,000. The taxpayer owed $215,603.76 to the corporation as of November 20, 1927. On that date the taxpayer was credited with $445,704.20, that sum being 5% of the net profits for the period January to July 1927. On learning the amount of profits for that period [the court does not tell us when] the taxpayer informed the corporation he would accept no further compensation for 1927, and suggested the corporation do something worthwhile with the money. The directors of the corporation decided to donate what it estimated would be 5% of the net profits for the remainder of the year to the University of California to establish an agricultural foundation, and thereafter offered a $1,500,000 contribution to the university. The $1.5 million was an estimate of 5% of the net profits for the remainder of the year. The money was to be made in honor of the taxpayer and the foundation named for him. The 5% turned out to be only $1,357,607.40, but the taxpayer made up the difference. The Commissioner assessed a deficiency on the taxpayer because the taxpayer did not report the $1,357,607.40 as income.]

. . .

The Commissioner's argument in support of the claimed deficiency may be summarized as follows: That actual receipt of money or property is not always necessary to constitute taxable

897 See Rev. Rul. 64-90, 1964-1 C.B. 226.

income; that it is the "realization" of taxable income rather than actual receipt which gives rise to the tax; that a taxpayer "realizes" income when he directs the disposition thereof in a manner so that it reaches the object of his bounty; that in the instant case the taxpayer had a right to claim and receive the whole 5% of the corporation profit as compensation for his services; and that his waiver of that right with the suggestion that it be applied to some useful purpose was such a disposition thereof as to render the taxpayer taxable for income "realized" in the tax year in which the suggestion is carried out. In connection with this latter argument the Commissioner states in his opening brief that "For the purposes of income tax it would seem immaterial whether the taxpayer waived his compensation, thus in effect giving it to Bancitaly Corporation, with the suggestion that it be applied to some useful purpose, or whether he failed to waive the right to receive the compensation and directed that it be paid to a donee of his choice." Again it is stated by the Commissioner, "Insofar as the question of taxation is concerned it would not seem to make much difference whether he directed Bancitaly Corporation to pay his compensation to the University of California or whether he merely told his employer to keep it."

Supplemental to the argument as above summarized, the Commissioner urges that the Board's finding that the money paid to the Foundation of Agricultural Economics as above set forth "was the property of Bancitaly and the petitioner [taxpayer] had no right, title or interest therein" is unsupported by the evidence; and that in any event such finding is an "ultimate finding" and therefore reviewable by this court under the rule announced in Commissioner v. Boeing, 9 Cir., 106 F.2d 305 and cases therein cited. We agree that the question of the effect of the taxpayer's unqualified refusal to take the compensation for his services is a question of law subject to review by this court. That question is the sole question presented by this appeal.

The taxpayer, on the other hand, urges that "A person has the right to refuse property proffered to him, and if he does so, absolutely and unconditionally, his refusal amounts to a renunciation of the proffered property, which, legally, is an abandonment of right to the property without a transfer of such right to another. Property which is renounced (i.e. abandoned) cannot be 'diverted' or 'assigned' by the renouncer, and cannot be taxed upon the theory that it was received."

. . .

Now, turning again to the instant case. The findings of the Board, supported by the evidence, are to the effect that the taxpayer did not receive the money, and that he did not direct its disposition. All that he did was to unqualifiedly refuse to accept any further compensation for his services with the suggestion that the money be used for some worthwhile purpose. So far as the taxpayer was concerned, the corporation could have kept the money. All arrangements with the University of California regarding the donation to the Foundation were made by the corporation, the taxpayer participating therein only as an officer of the corporation.

In this circumstance we cannot say as a matter of law that the money was beneficially received by the taxpayer and therefore subject to the income tax provisions of the statute. It should be kept in mind that there is no charge of fraud in this case. It would be impossible to support the Commissioner in his contention that the money was received by the taxpayer without arriving at the conclusion that the taxpayer was acting in less than full and open frankness.[898] The Board rejects this suggestion and we see no occasion for drawing inferences from the evidence contrary to the plain intent of the testimony which is not disputed. To support the Commissioner's argument we should have to hold that only one reasonable inference could be drawn from the evidence, which is that the donation is but a donation of the taxpayer masquerading as a creature of the corporation to save the true donors [taxpayer and his wife] some tax money. The circumstances do not support this contention. In our opinion the inferences drawn by the Board are more reasonable and comport with that presumption of verity that every act of a citizen of good repute should be able to claim and receive.

Affirmed.

[The concurring opinion of Circuit Judge HEALY is omitted. Eds.]

Notes on Waiver, Agencies and Payments Received under a Compulsion to Pay Them Over to Another Person

You may have noticed two important facts of the case:

1. Mr. Giannini did not tell the company to cancel the employment contract. Instead, the company deflected a continuing stream of income away from Giannini in favor of a local exempt-organization. Does this mean one can achieve by waiver and subtle direction of income what one cannot do by an outright assignment?

2. The court was unclear as to when Giannini announced his waiver, a disturbing fact to many readers. A later Second Circuit decision,[899] declared that the only effective waiver is one made before the services are performed and repudiated *Giannini* to the extent it proposed any different rule of law.

898 We say that the Commissioner's argument compels this conclusion for the reason that the claimed deficiency is for the tax year in which the donation was actually made to the Foundation. It should be recalled that the taxpayer's unqualified refusal to take any further compensation for his services in 1927 was made prior to December 31, 1927. If the Commissioner were earnestly taking the position that a waiver of compensation, with nothing more, is such an exercise of dominion over the moneys to be received as to render it taxable, it seems apparent that the deficiency if any would be in the year of the waiver, rather than some subsequent year in which the corporation disposes of the fund in some other manner. [Footnote No. 1 in original.]

899 Hedrick v. Commissioner, 154 F.2d 90, 91 (2d Cir. 1946)

Waiver issues can even affect U.S. Presidents. According to an article in the New York Times on April 14, 1998, Hillary Rodham Clinton made over $1 million in 1996-1997 from her book, "It Takes a Village." She and her husband gave away all the royalties they received. Unfortunately for them, §170's 50%-of-modified-AGI limit allowed them less than a full deduction, so they paid extra taxes of about $185,000. What might they have done differently? For one thing, they might have simply waived the income prospectively, *a laGiannini* and *Hedrick*, perhaps in favor of a short list of favorite charities that the publisher could select among. If the Clintons never got the royalties (and so were never taxed), they would never have to deduct the charitable contribution and the 50% limit would never become a problem. Another possibility is that they might give away their literary property rights to a charity, and have the charity get the income. Would it work? Absolutely, but under §1221(3) a copyright or similar self-produced literary property is not a capital asset. Because it is not a capital asset (even in a donee's hands), the deduction has to be reduced to the basis of the donated property under §170(e)(1)(A). Basis in the manuscript is likely to be minuscule, so the charitable contribution deduction will be trivial.

Agency and compulsion as exceptions to assignment of income: Agency and contractual arrangements can also cause income to be taxed to someone other than the recipient. Specifically, if an agent receives income on behalf of a principal, the income is taxable to the principal.[900] The same is true if a taxpayer receives income subject to a legal obligation to pay it over to someone else. An example might be a law professor who works in a legal aid clinic affiliated with the law school, subject to a contract which obligates the professor to turn over the clients' fees from the clinic to the law school. In such cases, the professor would neither report the income nor an offsetting deduction.[901]

Gifts of property that embody services: Perhaps the easiest way of all to shift income is to make a gift of service-rich property. For example, if a famous artist painted a picture and gave it to her child, the result would be an effective transfer of income from services. The same is true for inventors who give away patents and authors who give away their literary rights.[902] This cannot sit well with people whose sole income is from wages and salaries, but it is the law.

Deflection of income to charities: One of the more interesting stories in this field involved President Franklin Roosevelt's patrician wife, Eleanor. Eleanor was an energetic public speaker who received offers of payment for doing radio broadcasts. She refused the money in advance of her radio speeches in favor of having it paid over to a charity of her choice. She received a ruling from the IRS to the effect that she would not be taxed on the money because she never had any right to it.[903] The IRS later dealt with variations on the Roosevelt situation and concluded that as long as the performer's contract is with the sponsoring charity, and not between the performer

---

900 Rev. Rul. 58-515, 1958-2 C.B. 28.

901 Rev. Rul. 74-581, 1974-2 C.B. 25.

902 See, e.g., Heim v. Fitzpatrick, 262 F.2d 887 (2d Cir. 1959), later in the chapter.

903 See B. Bittker & L. Lokken, FEDERAL TAXATION OF INCOME, ESTATES AND GIFTS at ¶ 75.2 (2019).

and the audience or between the performer and a promoter, the performer is not taxed on the proceeds of the performance.[904] One might wonder "who cares?" given that the performer could have sold the tickets and then donated the proceeds (deductibly) to the charity. The answer is that it often does matter because of the percentage-of-adjusted-gross-income limits that §170 imposes on charitable contributions that you saw in Chapter 5.

Problem 12-1:

As was mentioned earlier, the brother of the "Unabomber" received a large reward for turning in his brother to the authorities. He said he would turn the reward over to the victims of his brother's evil. Could he direct the payor of his reward to pay the victims and thereby avoid personal tax problems?

Problem 12-2:

You are a first-year associate employed by the law firm of Lust, Envy, Greed, Hatred & Sloth, PC. The firm charges $110 per hour for your time. The firm pays you a salary of $50 per hour. A client of the firm pays you in cash for some work you did.

1) Are you taxed on the $110, assuming you receive the funds and then pay them over to the firm? If not, why not?

2) Assume that you earned a healthy salary at the law firm and that it was located in a community property state and that you are married. If you filed a separate return, would your spouse be taxed on half your earnings?

3) You also have an office at home out of which you engage in some private practice (the firm does not mind). A year passed and the law firm failed to pay you a bonus of $1,000 that it promised you. You hired a lawyer (Larry) to represent you. Larry recently sent you a bill for $325 for representing you in a suit against the law firm in which you demand payment of the bonus. You got one of your clients, who owes you $325, to pay Larry the $325 out of what the client owes you. How should this be reported on your tax return? Consider the effects, if any, of §62.

904 See Reg. §1.61-2(c).

Problem 12-3:

Believe it or not, you are an IRS Agent. The taxpayer who you are auditing is a cheapskate famous comedian who has fathered a number of greedy children. One evening at dinner the comedian and the children agreed that the children would sell tickets in the neighborhood for a performance to be held soon at a local auditorium which the children will rent. The father will not be paid. The event turned out to be a roaring success and each child pocketed $4,000. How would you attack this plan? Would you expect to win?

C. GRATUITOUS ASSIGNMENT OF INCOME FROM PROPERTY

1. The Basic Rule

The general rule is that the income from transferred property belongs to the owner. In the usual case, there is simply no problem. For example, if a parent gives stock or land to an adult child, the child will be taxed on the dividends or rents earned after the transfer. A polar opposite example would be a parent/shareholder's promise to give her child the next dividend from stock the parent owns. In the latter case, the parent is clearly just giving away income to the child, and the parents will inevitably be taxed under the "anticipatory assignment of income" doctrine on those dividends, including the dividend "given" to the child. What we will be looking at is the eccentric transactions that lie in the middle of these extremes.

The following case involves "coupon bonds" without explaining what coupon bonds are. Apparently, the Supreme Court did not know it was writing a masterpiece for law students. Be that as it may, a coupon bond is a debt instrument the front of which is a wordy explanation of the rights and duties of the debtor including the principal amount of the debt, and the bottom of which has lots of little interest coupons, dated by month and year, which the owner clips off one-by-one with the passage of time and hands over to a payment agent for the debtor for collection. The agent in turn gives the clipper his or her cash for collection of the current period's interest due and payable. You may have heard of rich people who spend their time clipping coupons. These are the coupons they are referring to.

HELVERING v. HORST

311 U.S. 112 (1940)

MR. JUSTICE STONE delivered the opinion of the Court.

[Mr. Horst owned negotiable bonds, with coupons attached. In 1934 and 1935 he detached some of them and gave them to his son, who cashed them in later years. The IRS sought to tax the father when the son cashed the coupons.]

. . .

Admittedly not all economic gain of the taxpayer is taxable income. From the beginning the revenue laws have been interpreted as defining "realization" of income as the taxable event, rather than the acquisition of the right to receive it. And "realization" is not deemed to occur until the income is paid. But the decisions and regulations have consistently recognized that receipt in cash or property is not the only characteristic of realization of income to a taxpayer on the cash receipts basis. Where the taxpayer does not receive payment of income in money or property realization may occur when the last step is taken by which he obtains the fruition of the economic gain which has already accrued to him. . . .

In the ordinary case the taxpayer who acquires the right to receive income is taxed when he receives it, regardless of the time when his right to receive payment accrued. But the rule that income is not taxable until realized has never been taken to mean that the taxpayer even on the cash receipts basis, who has fully enjoyed the benefit of the economic gain represented by his right to receive income, can escape taxation because he has not himself received payment of it from his obligor. The rule, founded on administrative convenience, is only one of postponement of the tax to the final event of enjoyment of the income, usually the receipt of it by the taxpayer, and not one of exemption from taxation where the enjoyment is consummated by some event other than the taxpayer's personal receipt of money or property. . . . This may occur when he has made such use or disposition of his power to receive or control the income as to procure in its place other satisfactions which are of economic worth. The question here is, whether because one who in fact receives payment for services or interest payments is taxable only on his receipt of the payments, he can escape all tax by giving away his right to income in advance of payment. If the taxpayer procures payment directly to his creditors of the items of interest or earnings due him, . . . or if he sets up a revocable trust with income payable to the objects of his bounty . . . he does not escape taxation because he did not actually receive the money. . . .

Underlying the reasoning in these cases is the thought that income is "realized" by the assignor because he, who owns or controls the source of the income, also controls the disposition of that which he could have received himself and diverts the payment from himself to others as the means of procuring the satisfaction of his wants. The taxpayer has equally enjoyed the fruits of his labor or investment and obtained the satisfaction of his desires whether he collects and uses the income to procure those satisfactions, or whether he disposes of his right to collect it as the means of procuring them. . . .

Although the donor here, by the transfer of the coupons, has precluded any possibility of his collecting them himself, he has nevertheless, by his act, procured payment of the interest as a valuable gift to a member of his family. Such a use of his economic gain, the right to receive income, to procure a satisfaction which can be obtained only by the expenditure of money or property, would seem to be the enjoyment of the income whether the satisfaction is the purchase of goods at the corner grocery, the payment of his debt there, or such nonmaterial satisfactions as may result from the payment of a campaign or community chest contribution, or a gift to his favorite son. Even though he never receives the money, he derives money's worth from the disposition of the coupons which he has used as money or money's worth in the procuring of a satisfaction which is procurable only by the expenditure of money or money's worth. The enjoyment of the economic benefit accruing to him by virtue of his acquisition of the coupons is realized as completely as it would have been if he had collected the interest in dollars and expended them for any of the purposes named. *Burnet v. Wells, supra.*

In a real sense he has enjoyed compensation for money loaned or services rendered, and not any the less so because it is his only reward for them. To say that one who has made a gift thus derived from interest or earnings paid to his donee has never enjoyed or realized the fruits of his investment or labor, because he has assigned them instead of collecting them himself and then paying them over to the donee, is to affront common understanding and to deny the facts of common experience. Common understanding and experience are the touchstones for the interpretation of the revenue laws.

The power to dispose of income is the equivalent of ownership of it. The exercise of that power to procure the payment of income to another is the enjoyment, and hence the realization, of the income by him who exercises it. We have had no difficulty in applying that proposition where the assignment preceded the rendition of the services, *Lucas v. Earl, supra*; *Burnet v. Leininger, supra,* for it was recognized in the *Leininger* case that in such a case the rendition of the service by the assignor was the means by which the income was controlled by the donor and of making his assignment effective. But it is the assignment by which the disposition of income is controlled when the service precedes the assignment, and in both cases it is the exercise of the power of disposition of the interest or compensation, with the resulting payment to the donee, which is the enjoyment by the donor of income derived from them.

. . .

The dominant purpose of the revenue laws is the taxation of income to those who earn or otherwise create the right to receive it and enjoy the benefit of it when paid. See, *Corliss v. Bowers, supra,* 378 . . . . The tax laid by the 1934 Revenue Act upon income "derived from . . . wages, or compensation for personal service, of whatever kind and in whatever form paid . . .; also from interest . . ." therefore cannot fairly be interpreted as not applying to income derived from interest or compensation when he who is entitled to receive it makes use of his power to dispose of it in procuring satisfactions which he would otherwise procure only by the use of the money when received.

It is the statute which taxes the income to the donor although paid to his donee. *Lucas v. Earl, supra; Burnet v. Leininger, supra.* True, in those cases the service which created the right to income followed the assignment, and it was arguable that in point of legal theory the right to the compensation vested instantaneously in the assignor when paid, although he never received it; while here the right of the assignor to receive the income antedated the assignment which transferred the right and thus precluded such an instantaneous vesting. But the statute affords no basis for such "attenuated subtleties." The distinction was explicitly rejected as the basis of decision in *Lucas v. Earl.* It should be rejected here; for no more than in the *Earl* case can the purpose of the statute to tax the income to him who earns, or creates and enjoys it be escaped by "anticipatory arrangements however skillfully devised" to prevent the income from vesting even for a second in the donor.

Nor is it perceived that there is any adequate basis for distinguishing between the gift of interest coupons here and a gift of salary or commissions. The owner of a negotiable bond and of the investment which it represents, if not the lender, stands in the place of the lender. When, by the gift of the coupons, he has separated his right to interest payments from his investment and procured the payment of the interest to his donee, he has enjoyed the economic benefits of the income in the same manner and to the same extent as though the transfer were of earnings, and in both cases the import of the statute is that the fruit is not to be attributed to a different tree from that on which it grew. See *Lucas v. Earl, supra*, 115.

Reversed.

Notes

When is the donor taxed:? The donor is taxed when the donee gets the transferred income. For example, in *Horst*, the father would be taxed when his son redeemed the coupons for cash.[905] If, however, *Horst* rests on a "realization" theory, then the proper time to tax the father would be when he makes the gift! The realization theory seems to have sunk into oblivion. It never made any sense to begin with, because what the Court said about the "realization" of "non-material satisfactions" would be just as true if Mr. Horst had given his son a watch or an acre of land or the bonds plus the coupons.

Gift of "ripe fruit": If at the time of the transfer some of the income has accrued (in the practical sense of having been earned, even if not due and payable), the transferor will be taxed on that income. For example, if a mother gives a child stock as to which a dividend has already been declared and is payable, the mother will be taxed on the dividend when it is paid to the child. The fact that the child has the money from the dividend has to be explained; the right answer is that it is a gift, and that may in turn attract a gift tax. Likewise, if a taxpayer transfers rental

905 See Rev. Rul. 69-102, 1969-1 C.B. 32 (same results as to annuity and life insurance policies).

property, rents that have been earned (in effect, accrued on a daily basis) as of the date of the transfer are taxed to the donor, and the balance is taxed to the donee.

> **To illustrate:** The Braunsteins placed a wager on the Irish Sweepstakes and got lucky. Two days before the running of the race, they received a notice of assignment of a horse. This assignment also notified taxpayers that if their horse lost, they would nevertheless receive a guaranteed small prize ($2,147). The next day they set up trusts for their children to hold portions of "any proceeds which may be obtained from said ticket." The assigned horse, Crepello, thereafter won the race. The court held that the $2,147 was taxable to the parents when it was paid because they had earned the money by then, but the rest of the winnings were taxable to the trust.[906]

2. Meaning of the Term "Property"

BLAIR v. COMMISSIONER
300 U.S. 5 (1937)

MR. CHIEF JUSTICE HUGHES delivered the opinion of the Court.

[Mr. Blair was the life income beneficiary of a trust. He gave away shares in his life estate, stated in dollar amounts per year, to his daughters. The shares lasted as long as his rights in the trust existed and there was no doubt that the assignments to his daughters were legally valid. The IRS asserted that he alone was taxed on the shares he attempted to give away.]

. . .

. . . The question remains whether, treating the assignments as valid, the assignor was still taxable upon the income under the federal income tax act. That is a federal question.

Our decisions in *Lucas v. Earl*, 281 U.S. 111, and *Burnet v. Leininger*, 285 U.S. 136, are cited. In the *Lucas* case the question was whether an attorney was taxable for the whole of his salary and fees earned by him in the tax years or only upon onehalf by reason of an agreement with his wife by which his earnings were to be received and owned by them jointly. We were of the opinion that the case turned upon the construction of the taxing act. We said that "the statute could tax salaries to those who earned them and provide that the tax could not be escaped by anticipatory arrangements and contracts however skillfully devised to prevent the same when paid from vesting even for a second in the man who earned it." That was deemed to be the meaning of the statute as to compensation for personal service, and the one who earned the income was held to be subject to the tax. In *Burnet v. Leininger, supra*, a husband, a member of a firm, assigned future partnership income to his wife. We found that the revenue act dealt explicitly with the liability of partners as such. The wife did not become a member of the firm; the act

906 Braunstein v. Commissioner, 21 T.C.M. 1132 (1962)

specifically taxed the distributive share of each partner in the net income of the firm; and the husband by the fair import of the act remained taxable upon his distributive share. These cases are not in point. The tax here is not upon earnings which are taxed to the one who earns them. Nor is it a case of income attributable to a taxpayer by reason of the application of the income to the discharge of his obligation.... There is here no question of evasion or of giving effect to statutory provisions designed to forestall evasion; or of the taxpayer's retention of control....

In the instant case, the tax is upon income as to which, in the general application of the revenue acts, the tax liability attaches to ownership....

The Government points to the provisions of the revenue acts imposing upon the beneficiary of a trust the liability for the tax upon the income distributable to the beneficiary. But the term is merely descriptive of the one entitled to the beneficial interest. These provisions cannot be taken to preclude valid assignments of the beneficial interest, or to affect the duty of the trustee to distribute income to the owner of the beneficial interest, whether he was such initially or becomes such by valid assignment. The one who is to receive the income as the owner of the beneficial interest is to pay the tax. If under the law governing the trust the beneficial interest is assignable, and if it has been assigned without reservation, the assignee thus becomes the beneficiary and is entitled to rights and remedies accordingly. We find nothing in the revenue acts which denies him that status.

The decision of the Circuit Court of Appeals turned upon the effect to be ascribed to the assignments. The court held that the petitioner had no interest in the corpus of the estate and could not dispose of the income until he received it. Hence it was said that "the income was *his*" and his assignment was merely a direction to pay over to others what was due to himself. The question was considered to involve "the date when the income became transferable." ... The Government refers to the terms of the assignment, that it was of the interest in the income "which the said party of the first part now is, or may hereafter be, entitled to receive during his life from the trustees." From this it is urged that the assignments "dealt only with a right to receive the income" and that "no attempt was made to assign any equitable right, title or interest in the trust itself." This construction seems to us to be a strained one. We think it apparent that the conveyancer was not seeking to limit the assignment so as to make it anything less than a complete transfer of the specified interest of the petitioner as the life beneficiary of the trust, but that with ample caution he was using words to effect such a transfer. That the state court so construed the assignments appears from the final decree which described them as voluntary assignments of interests of the petitioner "in said trust estate," and it was in that aspect that petitioner's right to make the assignments was sustained.

The will creating the trust entitled the petitioner during his life to the net income of the property held in trust. He thus became the owner of an equitable interest in the corpus of the property.... By virtue of that interest he was entitled to enforce the trust, to have a breach of trust enjoined and to obtain redress in case of breach. The interest was present property alienable like any other, in the absence of a valid restraint upon alienation. . . . The beneficiary may thus transfer a part of his interest as well as the whole. . . . The assignment of the beneficial interest is not the assignment of a chose in action but of the "right, title and estate in and to property." . . .

We conclude that the assignments were valid, that the assignees thereby became the owners of the specified beneficial interests in the income, and that as to these interests they and not the petitioner were taxable for the tax years in question. The judgment of the Circuit Court of Appeals is reversed and the cause is remanded with direction to affirm the decision of the Board of Tax Appeals.

Reversed.

Notes on Transfers of Property

Income versus property or something deeper?: At a profound level, the trouble with the assignment of income cases is that the taxpayer is typically at work trying to subvert the progressive income tax by shifting income to lower bracket family members, and yet, as you have seen, this deep concern is not always expressly articulated by the courts. Perhaps judges feel a fear of being reversed if they decide the case on the nontechnical grounds that they really believe in. Whatever the reason, the judicial reaction to the more complicated assignment of income cases has been to deal only with the formal question of whether the taxpayer successfully transferred "property." Acute commentators believe that behind the screen, judges are really expressing their deeper view that if the transfer is of a type the taxpayer can repeat in later years, then they will tend to find no transfer of property. This is the analysis of Professor Chirelstein in his book,[907] among other sources:

> **To illustrate:** If Mother transfers property that includes a producing oil well to her daughter, there is no doubt that the donee-daughter alone will be taxed on future income from the well. If Mother transferred an undivided half interest in the property to her daughter, they would share future income from the well equally. The more difficult case might arise if, for example, Mother gave her daughter a 5% royalty interest in the well, or a share of income from the well for all time. These more complicated cases cannot be solved by a simple "fruit and tree analysis." The courts will frame the question in terms of whether the mother has transferred "property" to her daughter, while in fact worrying about (and silently deciding the case on the basis of) whether the transaction is one that Mother can voluntarily repeat in the future so as to subvert the progressive tax system by leveling family income.

907 Marvin Chirelstein and Lawrence Zelenak, FEDERAL INCOME TAXATION (13th edition) (his discussion of this subject is especially good).

Gifts of carved-out interests: A transfer of income out of a larger estate is often called a transfer of a "carved-out" interest. For example, a landowner who is getting a royalty from a miner working her land under a long-term lease may transfer ("carve out") a few years worth of royalties to her child. Likewise, Mr. Horst may transfer a few bond coupons to his son. Neither of these gifts of carve-outs will succeed in shifting income to the child. If the donor instead sold the "carve-out," it would result in ordinary income to the seller on the theory that the seller sold income, not "property." The cases involving sales of carved-out interests offer useful guidance in trying to evaluate whether a gift of the same kind of carve-out would result in taxation to the donor of a like interest. If the sale does not produce ordinary income to the seller, then a gift of the same interest will succeed in shifting income to the donee. Otherwise, the gift will be denounced as a mere defective attempt to assign income. Likewise, the gratuitous assignment of income cases offer useful guidance in determining if the sale of the same interest will be treated as a property transfer, or merely accelerates the recognition of ordinary income.[908]

Gifts of income-producing property followed by leasebacks to shift income and create deductions: The rule that income follows transfers of property has led to a good deal of intrafamily tax planning. The gift-and-leaseback is an especially popular approach; it offers a double tax advantage in that it can provide the high-bracket donor a rental expense deduction as well as increased income to the lower-bracket donee:

> **To illustrate:** Imagine a dentist who owns her own medical office building. The building basis has been written off to $0. The dentist has several children who she hopes will go to college. Her tax advisor says she should give the building to the children in trust and rent it back from them. The advisor says that if it works she can deduct the rent as a business expense and the income can be shifted to her children who are in lower Federal Income Tax brackets than she is. The IRS has attacked these transactions, with little success as long as the terms are arm's-length.[909]

However, the Fifth Circuit has accepted the questionable theory that the dentist gets no deduction under §162 because the expense is not "necessary" because the transfer to the trust was not necessary.[910] The IRS's implacability in pursuing these cases seems unreasonable, given that the same transactions, if entered into with third parties at arm's-length rates, would be unassailable.[911]

---

908 See Lyon & Eustice, *Fruit and Tree as Irrigated by the P.G. Lake Case,* 17 Tax l. Rev. 293 (1962).

909 See, e.g., Rosenfeld v. Commissioner, 706 F.2d 1277 (2d Cir. 1983).

910 Mathews v. Commissioner, 520 F.2d 323 (5th Cir. 1975), rev'g 61 T.C. 12 (1973), cert. denied (1976).

911 See B. Bittker, FEDERAL TAXATION OF INCOME, ESTATES & GIFTS, ¶75.3.5 (2019).

Problem 12-4:

Mother is a sculptor. She gives her latest work to her daughter.

1) If Daughter sells it some years later, who is taxed on the personal services income from producing the sculpture?

2) Mother also gave Daughter the next three years worth of dividends on stock she owns. Who would be taxed on that income? When?

Problem 12-5:

You represent a famous pulp fiction writer. He wants your advice on how to structure his affairs so that more income can be shifted to his children. Incidentally, any publisher he deals with is sure to demand the copyright as long as the book is selling well. Assume the writer has not completed his manuscript and the publishing company is willing to either hire the author for $200,000 to do the work, or to grant the author a royalty of 20% of gross sales, which it views as equivalent. The publisher does not mind cooperating with the author in tax matters. The parties agree that the author can either get the copyright personally and assign it to the publisher, or the publisher can obtain the copyright for itself. Either way, the publisher gets the manuscript. What would you advise?

Problem 12-6:

Parent owns a bond with a face amount of $1,000 and a basis of $800. The bond pays interest of $100 per year, $50 of which is paid on December 31 and $50 on June 30. Parent contemplates giving the following items to her son at various times of year. Advise Parent on the Federal Income Tax effects of transferring the bond to her son at the following times of year. Assume everyone is a cash method, calendar year taxpayer. Describe the tax results of the following transactions:

1) On March 31 Parent gives her son the bond and all the coupons.

2) On March 31 Parent gives her son a half interest in the bond and coupons.

3) On March 31 Parent gives her son all the coupons.

4) On March 31, Parent gives her son the bond and keeps the coupons.

5) On March 31, Parent gives the coupons to her daughter and the bond to her son.

6) On March 31, Parent gives all but one coupon (out of 30) to her son and keeps the bond and one coupon, being the very last one to be paid.

3. Transfers of Property in Anticipation of Recognizing a Gain on its Disposition

Given a choice, some shrewd high-bracket taxpayers would prefer to transfer property that is about to be sold at a profit to their children and let the children pay the income tax on the sale rather than pay a higher tax themselves. This can be done, as long as the sales contract is not sewn up. To put it another way, as long as the donee can still bargain with the ultimate buyer, the donee and not the donor will be taxed on the gain.[912] There is a large body of case law on the subject. The controversy often involves gifts of corporate stock to children, or to trusts for children, just before the corporation goes through a major event, such as a merger or liquidation.[913] By contrast, if the terms remain open at the time of the gift, the general rule is that the donee is taxed on the gain.

> **To illustrate**: Mrs. Salvatore owned a gas station which a large oil company wanted to buy. After contracting to sell the property, she deeded interests in the gas station to her children. The court held Mrs. Salvatore alone was taxable on the gain on the sale of the gas station. Conversely, if the terms of the contract were not set when the gas station was transferred, then the children would have been taxed on the gain.

Likewise, taxpayers have a tax incentive to transfer claims for payments for personal services, such as commissions that have not quite yet been earned, to others in order to change the identity of the payee. Sometimes it works and sometimes it does not. The next case explores some important threads of judicial authority in the area.

KOCHANSKY v. COMMISSIONER
92 F.3d 957 (9th Cir. 1996)

CANBY, Circuit Judge:

As part of a divorce settlement, Richard Kochansky ("Kochansky") and his wife, Carol, agreed that a portion of the contingent fee which Kochansky earned by representing a client in a medical malpractice suit would be paid to Carol. After the divorce, the malpractice case was settled

912 See, e.g., Salvatore v. Commissioner, 434 F.2d 600 (2d Cir. 1970).

913 See, e.g., Jones v. United States, 531 F.2d 1343 (6th Cir. 1976); Wood Harmon Corp. v. United States, 311 F.2d 918 (2d Cir. 1963); and, Allen v. Commissioner, 66 T.C. 340 (1976).

favorably and the fee paid. Kochansky appeals the Tax Court's decision that the entire amount of the contingent fee is taxable to Kochansky despite the fact that a portion of the contingent fee was distributed to Carol. In addition, Kochansky appeals the Tax Court's judgment upholding the Commissioner's decision to assess against Kochansky a negligence addition to the tax. We affirm the Tax Court with regard to Kochansky's tax liability but we reverse the assessment of the addition to the tax.

BACKGROUND

Kochansky is an attorney who brought a medical malpractice lawsuit on behalf of the McNarys. Kochansky entered an agreement with the McNarys which provided that Kochansky would be paid for his services on a contingent fee basis. After the McNarys' lawsuit was filed, but before the suit settled, Kochansky and Carol divorced. The divorce agreement provided that Kochansky and Carol would split, after deduction of expenses, the contingent fee earned from the McNarys' lawsuit. After the McNarys' lawsuit settled, a portion of the contingent fee was paid to Carol and a portion was paid to Kochansky. Kochansky paid tax on his portion and Carol paid tax on hers. The Commissioner of Internal Revenue and the Tax Court both determined that Kochansky was liable for the tax on the entire amount of the contingent fee, as well as an addition for negligence. Kochansky appeals. . . .

ANALYSIS

I. The Tax Court did not err in holding that the entire contingent fee resulting from the malpractice suit is taxable to Kochansky, despite the fact that Carol's share was paid to her.

Kochansky's case is controlled by ancient precedent. In Lucas v. Earl . . . the Supreme Court held that income is taxable to the person who earns it. The Court held that Earl, the taxpayer, could be taxed for the whole of his salary and attorney's fees earned by him, even though he had executed a contract whereby half of his earnings were to become the property of his wife. Id. at 11415. Justice Holmes wrote:

> This case is not to be decided by attenuated subtleties. It turns on the import and reasonable construction of the taxing act. There is no doubt that the statute could tax salaries to those who earned them and provide that the tax could not be escaped by anticipatory arrangements and contracts however skillfully devised to prevent the salary when paid from vesting even for a second in the man who earned it. That seems to us the import of the statute before us and we think that no distinction can be taken according to the motives leading to the arrangement by which the fruits are attributed to a different tree from that on which they grew.

Id. Subsequently, the Supreme Court held that assignment of income accruing in the future is also taxable to the assignor. Helvering v. Eubank . . . (holding that life insurance agent who assigned future renewal commissions is liable for income tax on those commissions). The contingent fee that Kochansky divided with his former wife was compensation for legal services that he rendered, and thus Kochansky must pay tax on the entire amount of the fee.

Kochansky argues that his case is not governed by Lucas v. Earl and Eubank because the outcome in the medical malpractice suit, and therefore the fee, was "uncertain, doubtful and contingent." Jones v. C.I.R., 306 F.2d 292, 301 (5th Cir. 1962); see also Cold Metal Process Co. v. C.I.R., 247 F.2d 864, 87273 (6th Cir. 1957); Dodge v. United States, 443 F. Supp. 535, 538 (D. Or. 1977). Although Jones contains the language upon which Kochansky relies, it is distinguishable from his case. Jones was a construction subcontractor who had earlier transferred all of his assets to a successor corporation; he then assigned to that corporation a disputed claim for past overages claimed on a government construction contract. The corporation undertook to pay further expenses of the claim litigation. The Fifth Circuit held that, in the circumstances, the claims award, when paid, was taxable to the transferee corporation and not Jones. One reason offered by the Fifth Circuit was the "uncertain, doubtful and contingent" nature of the assigned claim. Jones, 306 F.2d at 301. But the Fifth Circuit also rested its decision on the facts that the assignment contract was conducted at an arm's length, the assignment was for a business purpose, and the assignee undertook to finance the remainder of the litigation. Id. at 302. We need not decide here whether Jones is a proper interpretation of Lucas v. Earl; it is enough that it is very different from Kochansky's case. Jones had transferred his whole business to a corporation that undertook to maintain and finance the litigation of a claim for past construction services. Kochansky transferred nothing but his right to income which, if it arose, was not disputed. He remained in control of his own services, the source or "tree" from which the fruit came.

Cold Metal is even more easily distinguished. There the Sixth Circuit held that Cold Metal did not have to pay tax on royalties from patents it had assigned, in part because collection of the royalties was contingent upon the outcome of a lawsuit in which the government was seeking to cancel the patents.

Cold Metal, 247 F.2d at 866. The court distinguished the Lucas v. Earl incomeassignment cases as follows:

> Those cases involved a gift of income payable in the future, as distinguished from a gift of income producing property where the donor relinquishes to the donee not merely the income which is payable in the future, but also complete ownership and control of the property which produces the income.

Id. at 871. In the present case, Kochansky did not own, and could not transfer, the McNarys' claim that was producing the contingency. Nor did he transfer himself or his law practice. He continued to render and control the personal services that produced the fee. He transferred only the right to receive the income. In terms of the treefruit analogy, "there was no tree other than [the taxpayer] himself." Hall v. United States, 242 F.2d 412, 413 (7th Cir.), cert. denied, 355 U.S. 821, 2 L. Ed. 2d 36, 78 S. Ct. 27 (1957). That Kochansky's fee was contingent upon the successful outcome of the McNary litigation does not change the fact that, when the fee materialized, it was undisputed compensation for Kochansky's personal services. Under Lucas v. Earl and Eubank, it was taxable to Kochansky.

Kochansky further argues that under Idaho's community property law, Idaho Code 32906, Carol had a community property interest in the contingent fee at the time of the divorce. Upon divorce, that interest became her sole and separate property, he argues, and therefore she is solely responsible for paying tax on her portion of the malpractice contingency fee. We decline to consider this argument because Kochansky did not raise it in the Tax Court and because the necessary facts to support the existence of a community property interest have not been developed. See United States v. Kimball, 896 F.2d 1218, 1219 (9th Cir. 1990) ("As a general rule, we will not consider an issue raised for the first time on appeal."), vacated in part on other grounds, 925 F.2d 356 (9th Cir. 1991).

. . .

Notes

As long as the transferee of the property to be sold has room to negotiate the terms of the contract, the transferee alone is taxed on the gain from the later sale of the property. What about the case where the contract has been formed, but it is subject to contingencies? The Tax Court and the Ninth Circuit applied step transaction principles to tax the transferor, despite the contingencies.[914] Here is a simplified synopsis of the case.

> **To illustrate:** The Fergusons owned a large share of a corporation (AHC) whose stock was publicly-traded. On July 28, AHC entered into a merger agreement with an acquiring corporation called CDI. By August 31, over 85 percent of the AHC stock had been offered to CDI, which was more than the minimum required to obligate the CDI to carry out the transaction, subject to some contingencies. The acquisition was completed on October 14. In the midst of the acquisition the Fergusons made a contribution of AHC stock to the Mormon Church, which was completed on September 9. The Mormon church then sold the AHC stock to CDI. The court held that the September 9 date was too late to be effective -- and so the Fergusons were taxed on gain on the church's stock sale -- because completion of the deal was a virtual "sure thing," despite the remote possibility that the shareholders might change their minds and withdraw the stock they

914 Ferguson v. Commissioner, 174 F.3d 997 (1999), aff'g 108 T.C. 244 (1997). The case is criticized by Haimes, *Assignment of Income -- Has Ferguson Hastened the 'Ripening' Process?* 87 Tax Notes 807 (2000).

tendered, and despite the further fact that the Fergusons had no right to the cash from the tender offer until the buyer accepted the tenders, which it had not done by September 9. The moral is that in the view of the Tax Court and the Ninth Circuit, minor contingencies and uncertainties are ignored for purposes for determining whether right to payment is "locked in." When income is locked in, the person who holds the property at that moment is taxable on the disposition of the property. Tax planners need to treat *Ferguson* like nitroglycerin if they plan to rely on transfers of property subject to executory contracts with contingencies.

Problem 12-7:

Suppose a carpenter retires in year 1, but wants to keep active, so he buys a plot of land for $80,000, materials for $64,000 and builds a house. Upon its completion in year 2, he could sell the house and land for $200,000. Instead, in year 2 he gives it to his adult son who, in year 3 sells the house for $248,000.

1) What income tax consequences to father and son?

2) What if the carpenter had found a buyer in year 2 and contracted to sell the house, but then gave the house, subject to the contract of sale, to his son?

3) Same as "(2)," but the price has not been agreed on?

4) Same as "(2)," but the contract is subject to various contingencies, all of which seem likely to be satisfied the way the deal is going.

5) What if the father had given the vacant house to the son and then the son rented it out for $1,250 per month, instead of selling it?

6) What if father gave the right to all rentals from the house for ten years to the son?

7) Father has been engaged in a big lawsuit against a customer for years. Father alleges the customer failed to pay him $100,000 in profits. Father transfers his claim to his son. Is father or son taxed when, to everyone's surprise, the customer has to pay the $100,000?

In the United States, each individual taxpayer has as a kind of birthright to a separate graduated income tax. By contrast, France has taxed the family as a unit for many years.[915]

In the American system, family income splitting is a completely predictable activity. For example, because of the graduated rates on each individual taxpayer's return, a child might be in a zero tax bracket because the standard deduction protects him from tax on whatever small income he has. On the other hand, the child's parent might be at a 40.8% rate on net investment income if the parent is at the top income tax rate of 37% and also subject to the §1411 net investment tax. In this situation, it makes more sense for a prosperous parent to transfer some capital to each child so that the income from that capital taxed in at the child's lower rates than to earn the money, pay the tax and then give away the after-tax earnings to the child.

Congress' counterattack appears in §1(g), also known as the kiddie tax.

From 1986 through 2017, the kiddie tax taxed a dependent child's investment income at his parents' marginal rates if those rates exceeded the child's own marginal tax rates. From 2018 through 2025, the child pays the same rate as a trust or estate.

A dependent child is a child who is either (a) under the age of 19 or (b) a full-time student under the age of 24, whose earned income is less than one-half of his support. Other requirements include that the:

- child is required to file a tax return;
- child does not file a joint return for the tax year;
- child has at least one living parent; and,
- child's investment income is more than $2,200 for 2019 (See Rev. Proc. 2018-57) .

One considers only the custodial parent if the parents are divorced or separated. In the typical case, the first $2,200 (for 2019) of a child's taxable income is exempt from tax. The amount is twice the whittled-down standard deduction provided in §151 for people who can be claimed as a dependent on another person's return.

The Kiddie Tax does not reach children who have income from the sweat of their brows with no investment income to muddy the picture.[916] However, these children are likely subject to Social Security Taxes, unless the parent is the employer and they are under age 18.[917]

915 See H. Ault, COMPARATIVE INCOME TAXATION 41 (Kluwer 1997).

916 §1(g)(4)(A)(i).

917 §3121(b)(3)(A).

1. Computing the Kiddie Tax

The core idea behind the kiddie tax is to tax the child on net unearned income at the same rate as trusts pay. Under the old rule, the parent's rates applied to the child's unearned income. This led to parents having to decide whether they wanted to put income-producing property in trust for a child or give the property directly to the child. The answer would depend on a comparison of the parent's rates to trust rates. Of course, the difference between those rates could change year by year. Now, the rate is the same whether the parent gives the property directly to the child or puts the property in trust for the child. Unfortunately, the trust rate is significantly higher than the individual rate. Nevertheless, this is Congress' idea of simplifying the IRC.

In order to calculate a dependent child's tax liability:

- First, add up the child's earned income and unearned income. This is the child's gross income under §61

    1. Earned income is defined in §911(d)(2). Earned income is most likely wages although the IRC includes some trust income in this definition.

    2. Unearned Income is defined in §1(g)(4) as income that is not earned income under §911(d)(2).

- Second, subtract all above the line deductions related to the earned and unearned income. This is the child's adjusted gross income under §62.

- Third, decide whether the child will deduct Schedule A itemized deductions or take the standard deduction for a single person. After the child takes the itemized or standard deduction, you have the child's taxable income under §63.
    - Section 63(c)(5)(A) limits a dependent child's standard deduction for 2019 to the greater of $1,100 or the sum of the child's earned income plus $350 up to the standard deduction for a single person ($12,200 for 2019).
    - Therefore, a dependent child's standard deduction for 2019 could be as small as $1,100 or as large as $12,200.

- Fourth, determine if the child's unearned income is greater than the reduced standard deduction contained in §63(c)(5)(A) ($1,100) plus the greater of another $1,100 (this amount is also adjusted for inflation each year) or the itemized deductions which are directly connected with the production of the unearned income

- This is the portion of unearned income that exceeds the unearned income threshold for the year

The Kiddie Tax taxes the portion of taxable income that consists of net unearned income at the rates that apply to trusts and estates.

The IRC taxes the portion of taxable income that consists of net earned income at the regular rates for a single taxpayer.

Example:

For 2019, a 16-year-old, dependent child who is subject to the kiddie tax has $6,100 in wages from a part-time job and $10,000 in dividend income. The child has no itemized or above the line deductions.

The child has gross income of $16,100 under §61. Her gross income consists of $6,100 of earned income §911(d)(2) and $10,000 of unearned income §1(g)(4).

The child also has adjusted gross income under §62 of $16,100 because the facts do not supply above the line deductions.

The child has taxable income of $15,000 because the facts do not provide for any itemized deductions and the child's standard deduction is limited by §63(c)(5)(A) to $1,100 (for 2019).

The child's net unearned income is $7,800. The calculation starts with the original $10,000 of unearned income and is reduced by twice the standard deduction allowed by §63(c)(5)(A). A child with itemized deductions related to the unearned income might be able to deduct more but this problem does not contain itemized deductions. §1(g)(4).

The child will pay at trust and estates rates on the $7,800. The child will pay at the rate of a single individual on the remaining $7,200.

Given that each individual taxpayer has as a kind of birthright a separate graduated income tax, family income-splitting is a completely predictable activity. For example, it makes perfect sense for a parent to transfer some capital to each child so as to have the income from that capital taxed in the lower brackets (starting at 10%) enjoyed by the child, as compared to having the prosperous parent earn the money at rates as high as 39.6% and then give away the after-tax earnings to the child. (By contrast, for many years France has taxed the family as a unit.[918])

Congress's counterattack appears in §1(g) which taxes the investment income of a dependent child (under the age of 19 at year-end, and a child who is a full-time student and under the age of 24 at year-end whose earned income is less than one-half of their support), at their parents' marginal rates if higher than the child's own marginal tax rates. One considers only the custodial parent if the parents are divorced or separated. In the typical case, the first $2,000 (representing a whittled-down standard deduction for 2013) of a child's taxable income is exempt from tax. The next $1,000 is taxed at the child's rates, and the child's remaining net unearned income is

918 See H. Ault, COMPARATIVE INCOME TAXATION 41 (Kluwer 1997).

taxed at parents' top marginal rates. The $1,000 is the 2013 inflation-adjusted figure (which was originally $500).[919] The result was that in 2013, a child whose only income was passive paid no tax on the first $1,000 of such income, tax at 10% on the next $1,000, and the balance was taxed at the parents' rates. These computations can get confusing, but the important point is that unearned income of children under 19 at year-end and some children under age 24 at year end is taxed at the parents' rates to the extent the child has more than a modest amount of unearned income.

On top of §1(g), §151(d)(2) provides that a child cannot claim a personal exemption if his parents can claim him as a dependent.[920]

The Kiddie Tax does not reach children who have income from the sweat of their brows and no investment income.[921] They may, however, be subject to Social Security Taxes, unless the parent is the employer and they are under age 18.[922]

Problem 12-8:

Now that socialite Caldwell Murchison has returned from Switzerland and married their daughter, Wanda, Mr. and Mrs. Friendly have only one dependent, their child, Fairlee, who is 12 years old. Mr. and Mrs. Friendly are in the 37 percent bracket. Fairlee has $5,000 of investment income.

1) Of the $5,000, how much is not taxed at all?

2) Of the $5,000, how much is taxed at Fairlee's 10 percent rate?

3) Of the $5,000, how much is taxed at 35 percent?

4) If Fairlee also had $2,000 of income from mowing lawns, how much of that would be taxed?

5) If Fairlee earned $8,000 mowing lawns, at what rate would the last such dollar be taxed?

6) Same as "a)," but assume that Fairlee will be 19 before the end of the year and will earn more than one-half of her support. How much tax will she` pay on her $5,000?

919 §§ 1(g) and 63(c)(4).

920 §151(d)(2).

921 §1(g)(4)(A)(i).

922 §3121(b)(3)(A).

7) How much tax would the parents pay if they earned the $5,000 and then paid over the after-tax proceeds to Fairlee?

8) Assume you were the tax advisor to the family. Might you advise them to pay Fairlee generously to mow the lawns? What about paying her generously to do menial work in their office at home where they have a small mail-order business? How would you characterize an excessive payment to Fairlee?

E. ACCELERATION OF INCOME BY SALES OF CARVED-OUT INTERESTS

You are now in a completely different sphere. The subject is whether a disposition of a carved-out interest *for value* results in immediate taxation of the transferor. The subject was seen before tangentially in the *Hort* case where a landlord was taxed on a payment he received from a tenant who wanted to get out of a lease.[923] This topic does not concern who is the proper taxpayer, but it does complement the assignment of income doctrine, as you will come to see.

Believe it or not, there are times when accelerating income makes sense. For example, imagine a corporation incurred a net operating loss 20 years ago and it was so big that the corporation still has not fully used it up. The corporation might try to accelerate some income into this year -- say by selling an installment obligation -- in order to offset that income with the NOL. The corporation would come out ahead by receiving the tax free money sooner than expected. Using the strategy of accelerating income, it actually eliminated income in later years.

ESTATE OF STRANAHAN v. COMMISSIONER

472 F.2d 867 (6th Cir. 1973)

PECK, Circuit Judge.

[In 1964, in order to generate ordinary income so as to use up interest expenses that would otherwise have been useless on his personal income tax return, Mr. Stranahan purported to sell $122,820 worth of future dividends to his son (Duane) for $115,000 (an appropriate discount if the substance of the transaction was either a loan or a sale of the dividends). Mr. Stranahan did not guarantee the dividends. The father reported ordinary income in that amount of the "sale proceeds." The dividends were paid in a timely manner. The question presented was whether the substance of the transaction was a sale of income, or instead a loan from son to father, as alleged

923 In Hort the tenant paid the landlord to extinguish the lease. The landlord was held to have received a substitute for ordinary income. In this, the analog would be the landlord's sale of the lease to a third party, which will cause the same tax result to the landlord as the lease cancellation income in Hort. 112 F.2d 167 (1940).

by the IRS, in which case the dividend income was taxable to the father, and used as a fund to repay Duane.]

. . .

The Commissioner's view regards the transaction as merely a temporary shift of funds, with an appropriate interest factor, within the family unit. He argues that no change in the beneficial ownership of the stock was effected and no real risks of ownership were assumed by the son. Therefore, the Commissioner concludes, taxable income was realized not on the formal assignment but rather on the actual payment of the dividends.

It is conceded by taxpayer that the sole aim of the assignment was the acceleration of income so as to fully utilize the interest deduction.[924] . . . In the present transaction, however, it appears that both the form and the substance of the agreement assigned the right to receive future income. What was received by the decedent was the present value of that income the son could expect in the future. On the basis of the stock's past performance, the future income could have been (and was) estimated with reasonable accuracy. Essentially, decedent's son paid consideration to receive future income. Of course, the fact of a family transaction does not vitiate the transaction but merely subjects it to special scrutiny. . . .

We recognize the oftstated principle that a taxpayer cannot escape taxation by legally assigning or giving away a portion of the income derived from income producing property retained by the taxpayer. . . . Here, however, the acceleration of income was not designed to avoid or escape recognition of the dividends but rather to reduce taxation by fully utilizing a substantial interest deduction which was available. As stated previously, tax avoidance motives alone will not serve to obviate the tax benefits of a transaction. Further, the fact that this was a transaction for good and sufficient consideration, and not merely gratuitous, distinguishes the instant case from the line of authority beginning with Helvering v. Horst, supra.

The Tax Court in its opinion relied on three cases. In Fred W. Warner, 5 B.T.A. 963 (1926), which involved an assignment by taxpayer to his wife of all dividend income respecting his 12,500 shares of General Motors Corporation stock, it was held the dividends were income to the taxpayer and were not diverted to the wife through the purported assignment. However, this was a mere gratuitous assignment of income since apparently the only consideration for the assignment was ten dollars. Alfred LeBlanc, 7 B.T.A. 256 (1927), involved a shareholderfather assigning dividends to his son for as long as the son remained with the father's corporation. The Court held that in effect the father postdated his assignment to the dates when he was to receive dividends and hence the dividends were income to the father. However, here again it is apparent that at the time of the assignment there was no consideration. In Trousdale v. Commissioner, 219 F.2d 563 (9th Cir. 1955), a taxpayerpartner attempted to convert future ordinary income into

924 No part of the cash received from the sale of the right to future dividends was used to make payment of interest or principal of the tax settlement. [Footnote No. 4 in original.]

capital by selling his partnership interest. The Ninth Circuit determined that the sale of future partnership profits cannot be converted to capital gain but must be considered ordinary income. It is significant to note that the consideration for the assignment was recognized as ordinary income in the year the assignment was executed even though several outstanding accounts were apparently not collected in full until the following year.

Hence the fact that valuable consideration was an integral part of the transaction distinguishes this case from those where the simple expedient of drawing up legal papers and assigning income to others is used. The Tax Court uses the celebrated metaphor of Justice Holmes regarding the "fruit" and the "tree," and concludes there has been no effective separation of the fruit from the tree. Judge Cardozo's comment that "metaphors in law are to be narrowly watched, for starting as devices to liberate thought, they end often by enslaving it" (Berkey v. Third Avenue Railway Co., 244 N.Y. 84, 94, 155 N.E. 58 (1926)) is appropriate here, as the genesis of the metaphor lies in a gratuitous transaction, while the instant situation concerns a transaction for a valuable consideration.

The Commissioner also argues that the possibility of not receiving the dividends was remote, and that since this was particularly known to the parties as shareholders and employees of the corporation, no risks inured to the son. The Commissioner attempts to bolster this argument by pointing out that consideration was computed merely as a discount based on a prevailing interest rate and that the dividends were in fact paid at a rate faster than anticipated.[925] However, it seems clear that risks, however remote, did in fact exist. The fact that the risks did not materialize is irrelevant. Assessment of the risks is a matter of negotiation between the parties and is usually reflected in the terms of the agreement. Since we are not in a position to evaluate those terms, and since we are not aware of any terms which dilute the son's dependence on the dividends alone to return his investment, we cannot say he does not bear the risks of ownership.

Accordingly, we conclude the transaction to be economically realistic, with substance, and therefore should be recognized for tax purposes even though the consequences may be unfavorable to the Commissioner. The facts establish decedent did in fact receive payment. Decedent deposited his son's check for $115,000 to his personal account on December 23, 1964, the day after the agreement was signed. The agreement is unquestionably a complete and valid assignment to decedent's son of all dividends up to $122,820. The son acquired an independent right against the corporation since the latter was notified of the private agreement. Decedent completely divested himself of any interest in the dividends and vested the interest on the day of execution of the agreement with his son.

The Commissioner cites J. A. Martin, 56 T.C. 1255 (1972), aff'd 469 F.2d 1406 (5th Cir. 1972), to show how similar attempts to accelerate income have been rejected by the courts. There taxpayer assigned future rents in return for a stated cash advance. Taxpayer agreed to repay

925 The dividends for the years 1965 through 1967 were, respectively, $2.10, $2.20, and $2.20 per share. [Footnote No. 9 in original.]

the principal advanced plus 7% per annum interest. These facts distinguish this situation from the instant case as there the premises were required to remain open for two years' full rental operation, suggesting a guarantee toward repayment. No such commitment is apparent here.

The judgment is reversed and the cause remanded for further proceedings consistent with this opinion.

Notes

Sales of "carved-out interests": The Supreme Court's decision in *Commissioner v. P. G. Lake, Inc.*[926] is an important landmark. The facts involved a so-called "oil payment," meaning the right to receive in cash or in kind a share of the production from an oil well, limited by time or amount. The Supreme Court held that the producer's sale of some future oil production (known as the sale of a "carved-out oil payment" in the petroleum industry) was an anticipatory sale of ordinary income, as opposed to the sale of a capital asset. The result occurred even though oil payments were interests in land under local law. The case was decided partly on the basis of the judicial preference for seeing capital gains as a narrow exception to be allowed only grudgingly in cases of legal doubt. By contrast, a natural resource royalty interest for all time, such as 5% of gross production as long as a well produces, is viewed as a capital asset, because it is not limited by time or amount; it lasts as long as the well does. For that reason, the tax law allows it to be sold at a long-term capital gain or be given away, with the donee alone taxed on post-transfer income.[927]

Symmetry of acceleration of income and assignment of income: There is an important symmetry between the anticipation of income cases and the assignment of income cases. In *Stranahan*, the taxpayer sold his son, Duane, a right to a limited amount of future dividends, but not the stock. If he had *given* the right to $122,820 of dividends to Duane, you should recognize that the assignment would fail, and that Mr. Stranahan would be taxed as Duane received the dividends because he did not give Duane the stock that was the source of the income. This leads to the conclusion that if an interest is sold and results in acceleration of income, a gift of the same interest would result in a defective assignment of income, and vice versa.

Some comparative tax law: There is no consistent solution to the anticipation of income issue in other countries. In Japan, for example, it is not legally possible to separate income and underlying property. As a result, abusive assignments and accelerations of income problem have apparently been trivialized, and no special tax rules are needed. Other countries have engaged in a wide array of responses. All evidently recognize the problem of rate-splitting by assignments of income.[928]

926 356 U.S. 260 (1958).

927 Rev. Rul. 72-117, 1972-1 C.B. 226, Rev. Rul. 73-428, 1973-2 C.B. 303.

928 See H. Ault, COMPARATIVE INCOME TAXATION, 280-283 (Kluwer 1997).

Problem 12-9:

Using the facts of Problem 12-6, assume the following variations, and determine who is taxed on what, and when:

1) On March 31 Parent sells Son the bond and all the coupons.

2) On March 31 Parent sells Son all the coupons, but keeps the bond.

3) Oilman, owner of a producing well sells his son the next 2,000 barrels of oil from the well, at a price representing the value of the oil, discounted for the fact that it will be extracted and sold over several years, believing the field has 4,500 barrels of production left.

   a. Can Parent claim ordinary income on the sale?

   b. What if Parent sells the next 2,000 barrels, but provides a guarantee of full payment of the full value of the oil in today's dollars?

   c. If Parent gives the right to the next 2,000 barrels to the son, will it be effective to transfer the income from the next 2,000 barrels to the son?

   d. What if instead Parent sold a 40% undivided share of the well (and associate production) to the son?

F. TRUSTS

Read §1(e) and Reg. §301.7701-4(a)

The next subject area involves the use of entities to shift income, either to the entity (which is in a lower bracket than the founder) or to the beneficial owners of the entity -- typically descendants of the founder. The materials begin with trusts because they are the entity that is most commonly used for *inter vivos* estate planning.

1. Background

A trust is an arrangement whereby a person places legal title in property in the hands of another person, to be used and managed for the benefit of one or more third persons known as the beneficiaries. It is a safe and popular way to shift income among family members. The party who transfers the property is known as a "grantor" or "settlor," and the property in the trust is known as the "corpus," "res" or "principal." The duration and terms of trusts are highly flexible and are determined by written documents and controlled by state or foreign law. The usual purpose of a trust is to provide for the needs of younger family members or a surviving spouse after the death or incapacity of the grantor and to avoid the costs of probate. A trust can also serve commercial purposes, such as holding assets of liquidated corporations, or concealing the ownership of slum properties.

A trust is a separate tax-paying entity. Trusts are taxed on income they generate if and to the extent they do not distribute that income currently. Section 1(e) provides the tax rates, which are sharply progressive. If and to the extent a trust *does* make current distributions, its beneficiaries are taxed as if they earned the distributed income directly. To prevent double taxation, the trust gets a corresponding tax deduction.[929] The initial transfer to the trust is not subject to Federal Income Taxes; it is ordinarily a gift. Because the income earned by the trust flows through to the beneficiaries as if they had personally generated the income, the character of the income on which a beneficiary is taxed is not necessarily the same as the income reported as the beneficiary's "accounting income" under state trust law.

Trusts fall into two basic categories: permanent trusts and grantor trusts. Permanent trusts in turn fall into two groupings: simple trusts, which annually distribute all their income, and complex trusts which have the ability to accumulate income, and which often allow the trustee to distribute income at his or her discretion. The trust is taxed as a separate taxpayer on income that it retains. To the extent it distributes income to its beneficiaries it is generally entitled to deduct the distribution, but the beneficiaries are in turn taxed on the distributions as if the beneficiaries had earned the money directly.[930] Permanent trusts cannot flow losses to their beneficiaries.

Grantor trusts are state law trusts as to which a special Federal Income Tax overlay applies, the practical effect of which is to tax people with excessive controls over income or property of the trust as if there were no trust to the extent of the offending retained control.

2. Grantor Trusts

In the early years of tax avoidance in this area, the game was to structure the trust so that the person who funded it could either get those funds back or use the funds to pay bills the grantor would have incurred anyway, while having the income taxed to the trust, its beneficiaries, or

929 §§ 661-662. The core concept is to identify an amount, known as distributable net income, and tax that to the beneficiaries and to allow the trust to deduct it.

930 Sections 641-663.

both combined. The enactment of subchapter J in 1954 fairly well put an end to that tax avoidance by frequently ignoring the trust and taxing trust income directly to the grantor.

Taxpayers' ability to shift future income via trusts is controlled by §§ 671-679, which contain a body of intricate rules, known as the Grantor Trust Rules. The basic concept is that each of the operative Code sections establishes a type of relationship that can result in taxing the grantor of the trust to the extent of the retained control over income or corpus of the trust. These relationships are often thought of as strings running from the grantor to the trust's assets or income. Only if and to the extent each and every string is severed will the grantor avoid being taxed as the true owner of the trust asset or income to which the string is attached. Section 671 and 672 are largely definitional; the important operative strings appear in §§ 673-677.

Now, prepare for a close order drill of the relevant Code sections.

Section 671 states that the sole basis for taxing the grantor is "this subpart." Look at the heading to see what Code sections "this subpart" covers. Note that §§ 671-679 do not displace the assignment of income doctrine nor the rule that the transferor is taxed on income that has economically accrued before the property's transfer.

Section 672 defines some key terms, seeking to sort out who is or is not deemed to be under the grantor's thumb.

Section 673 tells one when a reversionary interest in trust assets held by the grantor will result in taxing the grantor. The five percent interest referred to in this section means that it takes over 32 years of delay in vesting in the grantor before the reversion will *not* cause the grantor to be taxed on the income from the assets subject to the reversion.

Section 674 tells one what administrative powers over the trust the grantor can retain without becoming a deemed owner.

Section 675 contains a list of powers that the trust must not have, relating to the grantor's power to buy from, sell to, or borrow from the trust.

Section 676 describes powers of revocation that the grantor must not retain.

Section 677 describes impermissible use of trust income for the benefit of the grantor (or the benefit of the grantor's spouse).

Section 678 taxes third persons on trust income to the extent they can vest income or corpus in themselves. If §678 and some other grantor trust provision overlap, then the other provision displaces §678. This will be ignored henceforth.

Section 679 taxes U.S. grantors of foreign trusts if there is or can be a U.S. beneficiary. This is primarily for the course in International Taxation.

If the trust's income or property is entirely taxable to the grantor, then under some circumstances the trust does not even file an income tax return.[931]

931 A permanent trust files a tax return on Form 1041. §§6012(a)(4), 6072(a). a pure grantor trust generally does not file. Reg. §1.671-4(b). a hybrid -- one which is only partly taxable to the grantor -- files a tax return with special notations revealing its nature. Reg. §1.671-4(a).

Trusts are often used as tools for saving money for childrens' college education. But what happens if a trust pays for a child's tuition? Is it a nontaxable gift to the child? Does it discharge the parent's duty to pay, thereby causing the parents to be taxed? Where parents who fund the trust commit to paying the bills, but the trust instead steps in and pays the bills, it has understandably been held that the trust is a grantor trust as to those payments under §677(a)(1) resulting in a deemed distribution to the parent because the trust discharged the parent's liability to the payees.[932] What if the parent is clever enough to avoid personally committing to paying for college expenses, but a trust she establishes steps in and pays the bills? Does this discharge some kind of State law duty owned to the children?

BRAUN v. COMMISSIONER

48 T.C.M. 210 (1984)

[Parents established two trusts for their children (three children for each trust). These were short-term trusts whose corpuses would revert to the taxpayers after 10.5 years, which was effective under prior law generally to cause trust income to the be shifted to the children before the reversion. The trusts required that all net income be distributed to the children, but the asset-related transfers were poor. The plan was to put office and residential properties into the trusts and then lease them back, but there were no proper trust documents. The money in the trusts was used for education, some for college and some for secondary education. The court did not have good enough facts to determine whether the taxpayer had committed himself to paying for the education as a matter of contract law. The trustees were petitioner (a doctor) and Torres, a friend. New Jersey law was found to allow "sprinkling" of income from the trusts to its beneficiaries.]

. . .

. . . [W]e prefer to focus on the two trust issues on which petitioners have primarily focused, whether the income of the two trusts was taxable to petitioners under section 674 by reason of the grantors having the power exercisable by them and by a nonadverse party to control the disposition of the income or whether under section 677(b) use of the income for education expenses of the children discharged the support obligation of Dr. Braun. On Each of these issues, we find for respondent.

Respondent assumes that Mr. Torres is not an adverse party. The term "adverse party" is defined in section 672 to mean "any person having a substantial beneficial interest in the trust which would be adversely affected by the exercise or nonexercise of the power which be possesses respecting the trust." a nonadverse party means any party who is not an adverse party. We agree with respondent that Mr. Torres is not an adverse party. Thus, under section 674(a),

932 See Morrill v. United States, 228 F. Supp. 734 (D. Me. 1964).

the issue is whether or not the grantors as trustees, along with Mr. Torres, retained the power to sprinkle the income among the three beneficiaries of each of the two trusts.[933]

The trust instrument does not prescribe the shares of each of the three beneficiaries of each trust in the income. While one might tend to assume that each beneficiary was entitled to an equal share, New Jersey follows the rule that extrinsic evidence may be considered to interpret the terms of a trust which is ambiguous. . . .

. . .

The extrinsic evidence in this case illustrating intent, which under New Jersey law can be looked to, is the contemporaneous action by the parties, that is, the grantortrustees in making distributions from the two trusts. In each trust, during each of the years, one of the beneficiaries was ignored altogether and income which was distributed was utilized in varying amounts for the benefit of the other two beneficiaries without any apparent pattern.[934] This clearly evidences a sprinkling of the income among the beneficiaries. On the basis of the New Jersey cases cited, we conclude that the trust instrument must be construed as permitting such sprinkling. We agree with respondent that this is not a case such as *Bennett v. Commissioner*, 79 T.C. 470, 487 (1982), where the grantortrustees misadministered the express directions of the trust instrument. Based on this interpretation of these trust instruments, we hold that the income of the two trusts is taxable to petitioners under section 674(a). . . .

There is also some interplay between sections 674 and 677(b) in that pursuant to section 674(b)(1), income which may be used to discharge a support obligation is not taxed under section 674(a) except to the extent that it is so used and is thus taxable under section 677. Under section 677(b), the income of a trust is taxable to the grantor to the extent that such income is applied or distributed for the support or maintenance of a beneficiary whom the grantor is legally obligated to support or maintain. Petitioners argue that under New Jersey law the petitioners had no obligation to pay college tuition and room and board expenses of an unmarried child over 18 or to pay private school expense for an unmarried child under 18. Petitioners further argue that this issue has come up in New Jersey only in controversies between divorced parents and that such cases are inapplicable to this situation. We do not agree.

The recent decision of *Newburgh v. Arrigo*, 88 N.J. 529, 443 A.2d 1031 (1982), fully reviews the obligation of parents to continue to provide educational expenses for unmarried children over the age of 18. The Supreme Court of New Jersey held that necessary education is a flexible concept that can vary in different circumstances.

In general, financially capable parents should contribute to the higher education of children who are qualified students. In appropriate circumstances, parental responsibility includes the

933 In later years, Mr. Torres became the sole trustee. [Footnote No. 5 in original.]

934 Dr. Braun testified that bills which had to be paid were paid without reference to the child being benefitted. [Footnote No. 6 in original.]

duty to assure children of a college and even of a postgraduate education such as law school. [*Newburgh v. Arrigo, supra* at 1038.]

In an adversarial situation, courts in New Jersey consider all relevant factors, which include 12 which were enumerated in *Newburgh v. Arrigo, supra.* It is obvious that many of these factors would have no bearing except in a controversy between divorced parents or between a child and a noncustodial parent. But the support rule is not limited to such divorced parent context. *Sakovits v. Sakovits*, 178 N.J. Super. 623, 429 A.2d 1091, 1095 (1981). While many of these factors described by the New Jersey Supreme Court are not directly applicable to the instant facts, the import to our facts is clearly that petitioners retained the obligation to provide their children with a college education. They were both able and willing to do so, a college education was imminently [sic] reasonable in the light of the background, values and goals of the parents as well as the children, and petitioners have brought forward no facts or arguments which would militate against the recognition of this obligation on the part of these particular parents. *Newburgh v. Arrigo, supra.*

With respect to private high school education, the law of New Jersey is less clear. There is dictum in the case of *Rosenthal v. Rosenthal*, 19 N.J. Super. 521, 88 A.2d 655 (1952) to the effect that a father is not required to provide his son with private school, college or professional training, or with any education beyond public schools, but that dictum as to college and professional education is certainly obsolete. *Khalaf v. Khalaf*, 58 N.J. 63, 275 A.2d 132, 137 (1971). . . . While that court's reference to the annotation was with respect to college expenses, the annotation also recognizes the existence of a parental obligation in similar circumstances to provide for private or boarding school education. It would be an anomaly to find a support obligation for college tuition for an emancipated child but none for private high school expense for a younger child in the same family. In view of the recent New Jersey cases cited, we do not think the dictum in *Rosenthal v. Rosenthal, supra*, represents the current view of the New Jersey courts. We believe that private high school education in appropriate cases would be held by the New Jersey courts to be within the scope of parental obligation. Accordingly, we hold that the income of these two trusts, to the extent actually utilized for tuition, room and board for four of the six children of petitioners was used to discharge Dr. Braun's legal support obligations and is therefore taxable to him under section 677(b).

. . .

An appropriate order will be entered.

3. Can Trusts Save Burned-Out Tax Shelters?

In the bad old days, tax shelter promoters peddled shares of tax-shelter limited partnerships to people bent on minimizing their taxes. The partnerships passed their losses through to their partners; but, in time, there was inevitably trouble. Here was the problem: the partnership typically borrowed heavily, on a nonrecourse basis, thereby allowing the partners to increase their bases in their partnership interests. Those bases, in turn, created a foundation for claiming loss deductions, usually by virtue of accelerated depreciation deductions. However, in time, the deductions for interest and depreciation slowed and basis was exhausted. This process gradually reduced the partnership's deductions, and, in time, the partnership would begin to report taxable income; often more income than there was cash to pay the taxes. If a partner tried to sell his interest in the partnership at that time, or even abandon it, the partner had to treat his share of the partnership's debt as an amount realized under §1001, often resulting in large gains (and perhaps recapture of depreciation as ordinary income). To avoid this result, some canny partners put their partnership interests into trusts at the outset. The trust would be salted with a defect, such as free revocability, which meant the losses flowed from the partnership to the trust to the investor, because they were grantor trusts under §§ 671-677. The trusts were designed so that, when taxable profits began, the defect self-destructed and the trust ceased to be a grantor trust. The investor then took the position that he was no longer taxable on the trust's profits, and instead the trust and the beneficiary (his worst enemy?) were. It was a creative trick. Eventually, the IRS wrote a regulation which claimed to pinch off the practice. The Treasury declared the Regulation to be effective retroactively.

First, the Regulation. Reg. § 1.10012(c), example (5), provides:

> In 1975 C, an individual, creates T, an irrevocable trust. Due to certain powers expressly retained by C, T is a 'grantor trust' for purposes of subpart E of part 1 of sub J of the Code and therefore C is treated as the owner of the entire trust. T purchases an interest in P, a partnership. C, as owner of T, deducts the distributive share of partnership losses attributable to the partnership interest held by T. In 1978, when the adjusted basis of the partnership interest held by T is $ 1,200, C renounces the powers previously and expressly retained that initially resulted in T being classified as a grantor trust. Consequently, T ceases to be a grantor trust and C is no longer considered to be the owner of the trust. At the time of the renunciation all of P's liabilities are liabilities on which none of the partners have assumed any personal liability and the proportionate share of which of the interest held by T is $ 11,000. Since prior to the renunciation C was the owner of the entire trust, C was considered the owner of all the trust property for Federal Income Tax purposes, including the partnership interest. Since C was considered to be the owner of the partnership interest, C not T, was considered to be the partner in P during the time T was a 'grantor trust.' However, at the time C renounced the powers that gave rise to T's classification as a grantor trust, T no longer qualified as a grantor trust with the result that C was no longer considered to be the owner of the trust and trust property for Federal Income Tax purposes. Consequently, at that time, C is considered to have transferred ownership of the interest in P to T, now a separate taxable entity, independent of its grantor C. On the transfer, C's share of

partnership liabilities ($ 11,000) is treated as money received. Accordingly, C's amount realized is $ 11,000 and C's gain realized is $ 9,800 ($ 11,000 $ 1,200).

How courts treat Treasury regulations has changed significantly since the IRS first promulgated §1.1001-2(c). As discussed in Chapter 1, *Chevron U.S.A., Inc. v. Natural Resources Defense Counsel, Inc.*, changed how courts view all administrative regulations.[935] Courts just took a little more time before matching *Chevron* to Treasury regulations. As one distinguished professor explains:

> 1984 was a watershed year in administrative law jurisprudence in the United States. That year, the Supreme Court outlined the degree of deference courts must show to agency regulatory interpretations of statutes. The Court concluded in *Chevron, U.S.A., Inc. v. Natural Resources Defense Council, Inc.* that an administering agency's reasonable regulatory interpretation of a statute must prevail over a differing judicial interpretation in two instances: (1) when Congress fails to unambiguously address the issue involved or (2) when the agency's interpretation is consistent with Congress' intentions. In so doing, the Court broke new ground in administrative law by asserting that the judiciary must yield to the reasonable legal and policy determinations of an executive agency. ...
>
> Analysis of several post-Chevron cases indicates that every major Supreme Court case since 1984 involving the validity of a Treasury regulation is consistent with Chevron. Indeed, since 1984 every challenged Treasury regulation interpreting a statute in which Congress failed to address a specific tax issue has been upheld by the Court. In fact, no Supreme Court case since 1984 could be discovered in which the Court invalidated a Treasury regulation on the grounds that it was an unreasonable interpretation of a statute. Several post-Chevron Supreme Court decisions, however, rejected the Treasury's application of a tax regulation to a particular factual situation. Additionally, there have been times when the Court failed to defer to the Treasury's non-regulatory interpretations. However, at least with respect to Treasury regulatory interpretations, the Supreme Court's review of tax cases since 1984 has been consistent with Chevron.[936]

Problem 12-10:

Myra Klopman wants to establish a complicated *inter vivos* trust. She has a cousin in Philadelphia named Vincent Pugugli, who is a prosperous ex-boxer who loves Myra and will do anything for her. He wears small pork pie hats and has a low IQ. The trustee who will be her accountant,

935 467 U.S. 837 (1984)

936 David Brennen, "Treasury Regulations and Judicial Deference in the Post-Chevron Era" 13 Georgia State University Law Review, 387-430, 1997.

Spineless, will also do almost anything for Myra out of fear of losing her business. Myra wants your advice as to which of the following clauses in the trust will cause her to be taxed as if she were the owner:

1) "Grantor can borrow from the trust upon demand, at a rate of 6%, simple interest, as long as she provides adequate security for the loan." See §675.

2) "Grantor can get back the assets of the trust any time after eight years have passed, upon presenting a certified letter to the trustee." See §676.

3) Vincent (or his estate) is the remainderman if there is no reversion. The trust reads: "The assets of the trust shall revert to Grantor after 10 years, unless the remainderman (Vincent), intervenes, blocks the reversion, and demands that the assets go to him on the death of Grantor, in which case, they shall go to him (or to his estate if he predeceases Grantor) on the death of Grantor." See §673.

4) Same as "(3)," except that Myra's retained power is the power to revoke the trust and get back the assets. See §676.

5) "Grantor can, once a year, change the persons who enjoy the income from the trust, but those persons must be lineal descendants of the Grantor or an unaffiliated charity." See §674.

6) In year one Myra transfers a building with a basis and value of $100,000 to the trust. It is subject to a nonrecourse debt. The trust provides that it is revocable at will as to the building. In year 10, the power of revocation lapses. What result if at that time the building has a basis of $95,000 and is subject to a $98,000 nonrecourse debt?

7) Myra is a lawyer. She directs that her salary be paid to the trust. Will this be effective to shift such income to the trust?

8) Myra holds a 40-year bond. She transfers half the coupons to the trust. Who is taxed on the coupons as they are paid, assuming the trust is in no respect a grantor trust? Assume the income in the trust will be accumulated (not paid out) for the next 20 years.

1. Introduction

Partnerships are contractual arrangements that are acknowledged under state law, whereby the parties to the contract agree to join in a business or investment, with each making a contribution of some kind, sharing in the joint profits, losses and distributions as they occur, and each having some sort of voice in the management of the enterprise. Partnerships can arise orally, but limited partnerships, which confine the liability of the limited partners much as if they were shareholders in corporations, must be organized formally, and must generally pay a significant filing fee to the state under whose laws they are formed. There must always be at least one general partner in a limited partnership, so that at least one member has unlimited liability. The general partner is often a corporation formed for that purpose alone, and having only a small interest in the limited partnership; that can eliminate practical liability for the limited partners. All state law partnerships other than limited partnerships are general partnerships.

Partnerships file annual federal tax returns on Form 1065, for the purpose of informing the IRS of how much income or loss each partner must report on his or her own annual tax return. In addition, the partnership distributes a Form K-1 to each partner showing exactly her share of the partnership's results for the year. The partner uses the data on the K-1 in preparing her personal tax return. The results from the K-1 go onto Schedule E of the partner's tax return, and from there fan out to other parts of the Form 1040. Only the partners are taxed, and they are taxed whether or not partnership profits are actually distributed. Their distributive shares of profits and losses are determined by the partnership agreement, which can be amended at will. As with trusts, the character of the income or loss flows through to the partners as if they had generated the income or loss by their own personal efforts.[937] Because partnerships do not pay income taxes, but instead flow their results through to their partners, they are often referred to as "conduits" or "flow-through entities." The same is true of "limited liability companies" (LLCs) and "limited liability partnerships," assuming they elect to be taxed as partnerships rather than as corporations.[938] LLCs are popular because they offer flow-through taxation with no need to make any member personally liable for the entity's obligations.

Limited liability partnerships are partnerships that limit the vicarious liability of the partners' for each others' malpractice. They are popular with lawyers, but have no special tax characteristics.

937 §702.

938 See §701.

2. Validity and Tax Efficacy of Family Partnerships

Read §704(e)

Income-splitting through family partnerships has a long history. Congress has counterattacked with §704(e), which places special limits on the ability to manipulate the flow of income to partners. On the positive side, §704(e) offers a safe harbor for transfers of interests in partnerships that are capital intensive, assuring the tax validity of the partnership.[939] On the negative side, §704(e) requires transferors of partnership interests and those who act as service providers in those partnerships to be attributed enough profits to cover the value of their services before any other profits are allocated. Third, §704(e) limits allocations of profits to donees or buyer-relatives to their proportionate share of partnership capital. The people who are trapped by these two rules are (1) donees and (2) family members, as defined in §704(e), who buy their partnership interests from their relatives. Here is an example of §704(e) at work.

> **To illustrate**: Mom owns an apartment building she manages and that generates $40,000 of net rental income. She gives a one half interest in the building to a trust for her daughter, Sis, who is by definition a related person under 704. Mom's services as a building manager are worth $10,000. The trust for Sis then joins Mom as the second member of the newly-formed Mom-Trust Partnership. Section 704(e) validates the trust as a partner (assuming the transfer of the building is genuine) because it is obviously a capital intensive partnership (in the words of the Code, it is a partnership in which capital is a material income-producing factor). At the same time, the Code limits allocations of profits to the trust in order to prevent tax shenanigans in two ways: (1) the partnership must first allocate enough profits to Mom -- here $10,000 -- to assure that Mom was adequately compensated, and (2) the partnership cannot allocate more than half the remaining profits, namely half of $30,000, i.e., $15,000, to the Trust.

TINKOFF v. COMMISSIONER

120 F.2d 564 (7th Cir. 1941)

WOODWARD, District Judge.

This is a petition to review a decision of the Board of Tax Appeals redetermining deficiencies in income taxes and a penalty of petitioner for the years 1926, 1927, 1928, 1929, 1930 and 1932.

. . .

The petitioner, during the years in question, was a certified public accountant and an attorney at law with offices in Chicago, Illinois. On June 5, 1917, he registered for service in the United States Army and was married June 26, 1917. After his discharge from the army and until 1923 he

939 §704(e)(1).

was employed as a revenue agent, when he resigned and opened an office for himself and conducted the business of accounting in his own name until the latter part of 1925. From January 1, 1926, to November 11, 1929, he operated his business under the name of Paysoff Tinkoff & Company, and from November 11, 1929, to January 1, 1931, under the name of Paysoff Tinkoff Son Co. [sic]. Paysoff Tinkoff & Company was constituted by a formal instrument constituting petitioner and his wife, Ella H. Tinkoff, equal partners in the legal and accounting business of petitioner. On November 11, 1929, a son, Paysoff Tinkoff, Jr., was born to petitioner and his wife. On the same day another formal instrument was executed constituting a partnership in the accounting business, the partnership consisting of petitioner, his wife, Ella H. Tinkoff, and the infant son, Paysoff Tinkoff, Jr., each having a onethird interest in the partnership.

The partnership returns for 1926, 1927 and 1928 and for the period ending November 11, 1929, reflected a distribution of the net income of the business equally between petitioner and his wife. Those for the period November 12 to December 31, 1929, and for the year 1930 reflected a distribution of the net income of the accounting and tax business equally between petitioner, his wife, Ella H. Tinkoff, and infant son, Paysoff Tinkoff, Jr.

Petitioner made an individual income tax return for the year 1932.

While petitioner was in the military service Ella H. Tinkoff acted as a companion. After his discharge she acted purely as a housekeeper. She is not a lawyer, accountant, bookkeeper or stenographer. She never worked in an office. Neither Ella H. Tinkoff nor the infant son, Paysoff Tinkoff, Jr., ever contributed any capital or services to the business of either partnership.

. . .

Upon the facts found by the Board, supported by substantial evidence, the Board found that:

(1) There was no valid partnership for income tax purposes;

. . .

In form petitioner was a member of partnerships from January 1, 1926 to January 1, 1931. But the income tax statutes regard substance rather than form. United States v. Phellis, 257 U.S. 156, 42 S.Ct. 63, 66 L.Ed. 180; Helvering v. Gordon, 8 Cir., 87 F.2d 663 . . . . Tax laws deal with realities and look at the entire transaction. Helvering v. Gordon, supra. Looking at the substance of the partnership transactions and disregarding mere form, it is obvious that the two partnerships had no business functions. Neither the wife nor the infant son contributed either capital, services or anything of value to the partnerships. The partnerships were merely patent devices "to exalt artifice above reality." Gregory v. Helvering, 293 U.S. 465, 470 . . . . The partnerships in this case amounted in essence to no more than an attempt by petitioner to separate his income, for tax purposes, in one partnership, into two parts and in the other partnership into three parts. It is fundamental that income is taxable to the person who earns it. This Court holds with the

Board that there was no valid existing partnership under the income tax laws. The device of a partnership was without legal effect, so far as the income tax law is concerned, and the taxes were properly assessed against petitioner. . . .

. . .

The findings of fact amply support the Board's conclusion.

. . .

Notes on Partnerships

Tinkoff is bad enough, but consider the following testimony from *Redd v. Commissioner.*[940] The testimony is from the wife in a case concerning the La Salle Livestock Company, a family partnership which included children ranging in age from three months to seven years:

> Q: Now, do you participate in the management of the business of the La Salle Livestock Company?
>
> A: Well, I have been producing partners.
>
> Q: Beg pardon?
>
> A: I have been too busy producing partners so far.[941]

Social Security taxes: For general purposes, net income from the operation of a business in partnership form is subject to Social Security Taxation as net income from self-employment.[942] Limited partners and General partners are liable to self employment taxes on guaranteed payments for services they render. Employees of a partnership are subject to Social Security taxation on their wages, like any other employee. Thus, partners in a law firm pay their own self-employment Social Security Taxes. Associates pay their one-half share of Social Security Tax and the law firm pays the other half.

Limited liability companies as partnerships: The Federal Income Tax characterization of an entity is a matter of federal law. For many years there was uncertainty as to whether limited partnerships and limited liability companies ("LLCs") were correctly characterized as partnerships or as corporations for Federal Income Tax purposes, but that has now been resolved in

940 5 T.C.M. 528 (1946).

941 Our thanks to Professors Bittker and Lokken for unearthing this extraordinary tidbit. See B. Bittker & L. Lokken, FEDERAL TAXATION OF INCOME, ESTATES AND GIFTS ¶86.3.1 (2019).

942 Reg. §1.1402(a)-1(a)(2).

favor of letting the LLC elect whether to be treated as a partnership or as a corporation.[943] The practical advantage of LLCs is that *no* owner need be exposed to unlimited liability, unlike limited partnerships where at least one partner must have unlimited liability. Every state now authorizes the formation of LLCs.

Back to the case law: Following the *Tinkoff* case, but before the *Culbertson* decision (below), the Supreme Court at least seemingly revised the definition of a partnership to disregard partners who did not contribute *vital services* or *original capital*, a tough standard.[944]

In 1949, the Supreme Court revisited the issue in *Commissioner v. Culbertson*, 337 U.S. 733, which quietly repudiated the vital services or original capital requirements in favor of a rule that if the partners

> [j]oined together in good faith to conduct a business, having agreed that the services or capital to be contributed presently by each is of such value to the partnership that the contributors should participate in the distribution of profits, that is sufficient [to find a partnership]. . . .[945]

Because the law was still confusing, Congress stepped in and enacted §704(e) to provide some black-letter rules that can validate partnerships whose capital is a material income-producing factor. As a practical matter, §704(c)(1) is of no help at all in evaluating whether a service partnership is valid. Section 703(e) is helpful when the partnership is capital intensive. It recognizes a person as a partner "whether or not such interest was derived by the purchase or gift from any other persons."

> **To illustrate:** Mom gave her daughter a 10% interest in a partnership of which Mom is a member. Mom also sold her husband a 15% interest in the same partnership. If the partnership is capital intensive and the transfers put real control of the partnership interest in the hands of the daughter and the husband, then the daughter and husband are genuine partners for Federal Income Tax purposes. Accordingly, each will report his or her own share of the partnership's profit or loss for the year.

Genuine service partnerships: If someone purports to be a member of a service partnership that is not capital-intensive, but the individual fails to satisfy the *Culbertson* test, then all the partnership's income is taxed to the remaining (genuine) partners. If there is only one genuine service provider, then there is no partnership, just a sole proprietorship. One cannot effectively give or sell a minor child a partnership interest in a law, accounting, medical, or other professional partnership, because those partnerships normally do not depend on capital for

943 Reg. §301.7701-1(a)(1).

944 Commissioner v. Tower, 327 U.S. 280 (1946) and Lusthaus v. Commissioner, 327 U.S. 293 (1946).

945 337 U.S. 733, 734 (1949).

their success.[946] On the other hand, one can effectively admit a family member who will truly contribute services into a service partnership, even though capital is not a material factor. For example, a father and capable 15 year-old child might well operate a TV repair partnership.

Capital-intensive family partnerships: Where the family member who claims to be a partner will not provide genuine services, the partnership must rely on capital and the donee (or related buyer) of the interest must get a capital interest in the partnership if the family member is to be recognized as a partner. This means the business should have substantial inventories, goodwill, or capital such as plant or equipment. There is no fixed rule for determining whether capital is a material income-producing factor; instead there is a tangle of cases from which one may be able to generalize. For example, the Tax Court held an engineering and technical services firm that had a large volume of accounts receivable to be an enterprise requiring capital as a material income-producing factor.[947] Likewise, a husband and wife medical practice was treated as a true (capital intensive) partnership where the enterprise required X-ray equipment and supplies.[948] Notice how the medical practice is a "service partnership" in a loose sense, but it can still be capital intensive, allowing a minor who does not render services to be a partner. Where one relies on the existence of capital as a material income-producing factor, there must be an *effective* transfer of ownership of a capital interest[949] to the donee partner. Failing such a transfer, the alleged transferor will be taxed on the partnership interest on assignment of income principles.

Capital interest in a partnership defined: The term means a claim on partnership assets in the event of liquidation of the entity or withdrawal of the partner.[950] A mere transfer of a right to share in the profits of the partnership (a "profits interest") is not a transfer of a capital interest.

Joint ventures: The partnership need not be long-term. Thus, taxpayers who see a chance to profit on a short-term transaction, such as a land subdivision program, can form a partnership and give capital interests to family members for that purpose alone. Partnerships to accomplish particular projects are often called "joint ventures."

Minors as partners: Minors can be outright partners if they can fend for themselves.[951] If they cannot, prudence dictates putting their partnership interests in trust, in a way that assures that the transfer in favor of the minor is real, the key requirement of which is that the donor not retain excessive controls over the child's partnership interest.[952]

---

946 Reg. §1.704-1(e)(1)(iv).

947 Bennett v. Commissioner, 21 T.C.M. 903 (1962).

948 Nichols v. Commissioner, 32 T.C. 1322 (1959), acq. 1960-2 CB 6.

949 A capital interest is the right to proceeds on liquidation, as opposed to the right to share in profits. Reg. §1.704-1(e)(1)(v).

950 Reg. §1.704-1(e)(1)(v).

951 Reg. §1.704-1(e)(2)(viii).

952 See Reg. §1.704-1(e)(2). A trustee for the benefit of the child can be a partner.

Problem 12-11:

Marge and her adult son, Barnacle Bill, have decided to come ashore. Marge now runs a seafood deli. She sold a one-third interest in the capital of the deli operation to Bill, who is a full-time employee of another company, for $30,000 on January 1 of the present year. They agree to share profits and losses 50:50, as partners in a cash-method, calendar-year partnership. Her services are worth $40,000 per year. The deli earned a net profit of $100,000 this year, before compensation to Marge. She took no compensation for services this year. Bill does not work at the deli.

1) Assume that pursuant to the partnership agreement and State law, Bill was paid $40,000 of this year's profits. Nevertheless, what is Bill's distributive share of partnership profits this year for Federal Income Tax purposes? See §704(e).

2) If there is a disparity between an attempted profit allocation and the one allowed for tax purposes, how do you explain the distribution of any extra amounts of cash (compared to the correct allocation for Federal Income Tax purposes)? Rely on your common sense.

3) Bill is only 7 years old. What would you advise Marge as to how to structure Bill's ownership of his partnership interest?

4) Would you answer to "(3)" differ if Bill were 14? What if the deli used leased equipment and required virtually no capital to operate?

H. CORPORATIONS

Scan §11 and read §482

1. Regular Corporations

Corporations are separate legal persons, organized under state or federal law. The chief characteristics are that they are separate legal entities that offer their owners limited liability, free transferability of their interests, continuity of existence despite the withdrawal of an owner, and centralized management.

Corporations are taxed at a flat rate of 21% under §11. The trouble with corporations from a tax point of view is that corporate earnings are subject to a double tax in the sense that corporations are taxed on their profits and then the shareholders are taxed when the profits are distributed, with no deduction for the corporation for paying the dividend. (Tax-exempt shareholders, such as pension plans, do not suffer taxes on dividends they receive.) Nowadays, dividends are generally taxable as long-term capital gains, and the corporate tax rate is low, so the burden of double taxation has been greatly reduced.

An important tax policy consideration in this area is subject of the incidence of taxes. "Incidence" really means where the tax comes to rest. For example, if there is a tax on cigarettes and all smokers are so addicted that retailers just pass along the tax to their customers, the incidence of the tax is on smokers, a subset of consumers. People who favor repeal of the corporate income tax are fond of saying, "corporations do not pay taxes, people do," implying the tax is a fraud of some sort. Their point is not foolish, however, in that the burden of the corporate income tax is in substance on some combination of shareholders (whose profits may go down if the tax rises), laborers (who have to take a wage "hit" because the tax is eroding the corporation's income), or consumers (who, if the corporation has great market power, may find themselves paying more for the corporation's output to cover the tax). The area is highly controversial and seems unsettled.[953]

In the past at least, professionals and celebrities often formed corporations that were set up to sell their services. The nontax reason might have been to limit personal liability, but often the real reason had to do with taxes. For one thing, for many years (and again today) corporations were in much lower income tax brackets than their shareholders..[954]

In fact, it is now fairly risky to incorporate, for several reasons. First, there is the double tax, discussed above. Second, if the corporation has an owner-employee who works primarily for another entity -- such as a doctor whose corporation contracts to provide the physician's services to a hospital staff -- then §269A empowers the IRS to reallocate corporate income to the physician (or other service provider) alone when the corporation was used for tax avoidance. One of the few remaining tax reasons for incorporation is to manufacture an "employer" so that the employees can cash in on some kind of fringe benefit, such as a health plan that offers tax-free orthodontic work for a child of the founder.

Reallocations under§482: Section 482 allows the IRS to adjust transactions between taxpayers that are under common control (such as two subsidiary corporations that are controlled by a common parent corporation) or between a parent corporation and its controlled subsidiary. (Control here means "practical control"). In fact, the IRS can use §482 as follows:

> In any case of two or more organizations, trades, or businesses (whether or not incorporated, whether or not organized in the United States, and whether or not affiliated) owned or controlled directly or indirectly by the same interests, the Secretary may distribute, apportion, or allocate gross income, deductions, credits, or allowances between or among such organizations,

953 For a comprehensive discussion, see g. Kahn & p. Gann, CORPORATE TAXATION, 1 (1989).

954 Compare §§ 1 with 11.

> trades, or businesses, if he determines that such distribution, apportionment, or allocation is necessary in order to prevent evasion of taxes or clearly to reflect the income of any of such organizations, trades, or businesses.

The only way to beat an IRS attack is to show that the adjustment the IRS proposes is arbitrary and capricious. Section 482 audits are the daily bread of international tax lawyers working for business corporations, but they can arise in humbler settings as well. One legendary case involved the comedian Victor Borge, a Dane who made it big in America.[955] Here is an illustration that offers a synopsis of the case.

> **To illustrate:** Victor Borge was in the business of being a comedian, which earned him a lot of money. He also owned an unincorporated chicken farm (ViBo Farms) in Connecticut that he claimed was a bona fide business. ViBo Farms lost over $50,000/year. Victor Borge incorporated ViBo Farms and contracted to work for its benefit for $50,000 per year. ViBo Farms then hired Victor Borge out to the public for $166,000/year. Using the §482 weapon, the IRS reallocated $75,000 from ViBo to Borge. Borge argued that he was just an employee and not a "trade or business," but the court disagreed, finding that he was a sought-after entertainer in his own right. Moreover, the allocation was reasonable on the facts.

What about obscure people? Borge was a publicly known entertainer whose activities were fairly treated as a separate trade or business, with little question about it. But what if the owner is an everyday figure, unknown to the public? The key case on that point, *Foglesong v. Commissioner* involved a steel tubing salesman who formed a corporation and transferred its preferred stock to his daughters.[956] The preferred stock paid steady, generous dividends and the common stock, which the father got, paid no dividends but held voting control of the enterprise. The IRS failed in asserting that Mr. Foglesong in his capacity as a corporate employee was a separate "trade or business" for §482 purposes, because he was a humdrum person, not a celebrity. As a result, a reallocation of income between the corporation and Mr. Foglesong under §482 was not possible. The *Foglesong* courts also refused to apply the assignment-of-income doctrine because it was considered too crude; that is, it might lopsidedly cause the payor to be further taxed without correspondingly reducing the payee's tax burden, an issue that might arise because, for example, the statute of limitations had run on the payee so that it could not file for a refund as a result of the audit adjustment to the payor.

---

955 Borge v. Commissioner, 405 F.2d 673 (2d Cir. 1968), cert. denied (1969).

956 691 F.2d 848 (7th Cir. 1982).

The IRS has announced its refusal to follow the *Foglesong* doctrine, and the Tax Court is presumably sticking to its position that people like Mr. Foglesong can be "organizations, trades or business."[957]

Problem 12-12:

Caldwell Muchison, Sr. owns an incorporated lead mine business, Murchison Mines, Inc. ("MMI"), whose head office is located in Flyneck, NJ, convenient to the port. More and more of MMI's customers seem to be abroad, so Caldwell, Sr. recently organized a corporation in the Cayman Islands, called MMI, Caymans, to undertake foreign sales. Sam is the 80% owner. Under the new system, employees at MMI locate the overseas customer and then direct the customer to MMI, Caymans to close the deal. Assume in a particular transaction, MMI, Caymans buys the products from MMI, Inc. for $65,000, which is $20,000 less than MMI charges its other customers. Title to the goods changes from MMI, Inc. to MMI, Caymans at sea on the way to the foreign port. The overseas customer calls a telephone number in the Cayman Islands, which rings through on a different phone in the U.S., which is invariably answered by Caldwell, Sr. or one of the staff in Flyneck. MMI, Caymans has a name on an office door in the Cayman Islands, and has a part-time employee who completes the paperwork on these transactions and makes sure that MMI, Caymans is in compliance with Cayman law. Assume there are no taxes in the Cayman Islands.

1) What is Sam up to?

2) If you were an IRS Agent auditing MMI, and you believed that the Cayman Islands corporation was formed for tax avoidance purposes, do you think you could make a successful §482 attack?

3) Assuming the answer to "b)" is "yes," what would be your adjustment under §482?

2. S Corporations

An S corporation is a regular ("C") American corporation whose owners elect to have its owners alone taxed on its profits or losses, pursuant to Subchapter S of the IRC, namely §§ 1361-1379. Subchapter S avoids the corporate income tax and can be an effective income-shifting device. There are numerous detailed requirements that the entity must satisfy to qualify as an S Corporation. The common statement is that an S corporation is a C corporation that elects to be taxed like a partnership. The statement is only a memorable generalization.

957 Rev. Rul. 88-38, 1988-21 I.R.B. 11.

One of the curious features is that inactive investors in S corporations are generally deemed to receive "passive income" from the S corporation, which in theory makes it possible for wealthy taxpayers to vary their portfolios by purchasing stock of profitable S corporations and using the passive activity income of the S corporation to offset passive losses from rental activities and even from traditional syndicated tax shelters.[958] On the other hand, if the S corporation merely flows through investment income, such as interest on bank accounts, that is "portfolio income" and not passive income. Lawyers and accountants, for example, often form professional service corporations under specialized state incorporation statutes and make the S election as to the corporation so as to avoid corporate level Federal Income Taxes while retaining at least some measure of protection from personal liability.

Section 1375 imposes a corporate-level tax on an S corporation's "excess net passive income." Under Section 1362(d)(3), passive investment income means gross receipts from royalties, rents, dividends, interest, and annuities for any tax year in which the Subchapter S corporation has:

- Accumulated earnings and profits (i.e., E&P from a year it was taxed as a C corporation) at the close of the tax year, and
- passive investment income that exceeds 25% of gross receipts

Net passive income is passive investment income reduced by deductions directly connected with the production of that income except for reductions for the net operating loss (NOL) deduction or any of the special corporate deductions (e.g., for dividends received).

Excess net passive income means the amount that bears the same ratio to total net passive income for the year as: (1) the amount by which passive investment income for the tax year exceeds 25% of gross receipts for the year ("excess passive investment income"), bears to (2) total passive investment income for the tax year.

I. BELOW MARKET INTEREST RATE LOANS

Below market loans have been a popular way to allow a borrower to earn income that is not reclaimed by the lender as interest.

> **To illustrate**: Mom lends $20,000 to Sis, who is 15. Mom is in the 37% bracket and Sis is in the 10% bracket. Mom charges no interest. Sis puts the money to work and earns $2,000/year. The $2,000 is taxed at Sis's 10% rate. This saves a lot of money compared to having Mom earn the income, pay income tax at a 37% or even 40.8% rate on it, and then give the balance to Sis.

958 See §469(c).

Aggressive taxpayers have taken a step further by getting a deduction for a loan-back. Here is an example:

> **To illustrate**: Pop is a businessman who wants to fund his children's college education on a tax-favored basis. To do so, he lends $200,000 to a trust for his children, charging no interest. His loan is a "demand loan," meaning he can demand back his loan money at his whim. (The alternative is a "term" loan, meaning one for a fixed period, such as 10 years.) The trust will lend the money back to Pop for an indefinite term at 10 percent for use in his business. The children will be taxed on the interest income that Pop pays the trust. Make sure you understand what Pop achieved from a tax vantage point, compared to earning the money himself on his own $200,000 of capital and then using the after-tax proceeds to pay his childrens' tuition bills.

The gaudy days of big interest-free or low-interest loans seem to have come to an end with the enactment of §7872. By adding §7872 to the Code, Congress prescribed a comprehensive set of rules that determine the income tax consequences of loans with no, or inadequate, interest.

1. Demand Loans and Gift Loansunder §7872

Section 7872 works on a two-step model for demand loans and gift loans that are terms loans. In the first step, there is a reconstruction of the actual interest-free loan from the lender (e.g., father) to the borrower (e.g., child) *as a loan made at full interest rates*, followed by at least one (and maybe more) imputed interest payment back to the lender, with substantial tax consequences for both parties. In the second phase, the lender is deemed to transfer to the borrower (e.g., child) cash equal to interest not actually paid by the borrower, the consequence of which may be a gift from the lender, a dividend if the borrower were instead a shareholder, compensation if the borrower is an employee, or perhaps even raw taxable income to the recipient.

The model, then, is to start with an imaginary arm's-length transaction in which the lender is deemed to make a loan to the borrower, requiring the reporting of interest at one of three market-related statutory interest rates designated by §7872 using the Applicable Federal Rate (A.F.R.) in force at the time. By so characterizing the first step, the borrower is treated as if he or she in fact paid market rate interest on the loan, compounded semi-annually. This imaginary interest is included in the lender's income, and may be deductible by the borrower under §163, depending on how the borrower actually used the money. The second step produces the "real" outcome, such as a gift of the use of capital.

> **To illustrate:** Mother makes a bona fide $100,000 demand loan to Son at four per cent interest so that he can buy a business. She made the loan out of kindness. Son pays interest of $4,000 per

year. The loan is a demand loan under §7872(a)(1). If the appropriate A.F.R. were applied to the loan, he would pay interest of $10,000 per year. What are the results?

Answer: Each year Son is presumed to have made a $10,000 market rate interest payment to Mother. Mother is presumed to have made a transfer to Son of the amount of the *foregone interest* as defined in §7872(e)(2) -- in this case $6,000 -- at the end of each year in which the loan is outstanding. The foregone interest of $6,000 per year is treated as an interest payment from Son to Mother, which will give rise to extra interest income to Mother. The imaginary transfer from Mother to Son of the foregone interest is most likely a gift on the facts, and may be subject to a Federal Gift Tax if it is large enough. The $6,000 of deemed interest that Son pays Mother may give rise to a business interest expense deductions for Son, depending on his use of the loan.

The presumed second-step payment is characterized, depending on the circumstances of the loan. For example, where the loan is to a shareholder, the deemed interest payment is considered a distribution; where the loan is to an employee or independent contractor, the payment is considered compensation, and so on. Compensation-related below-market loans are subject to FICA and FUTA taxes, but not income tax with holding.[959] In the example, it is a $6,000 annual gift to Son.

2. Term Loans that are not Gift Loans under §7872

The worst case scenario takes place with a term loan which is not a gift loan. The lender is deemed to pay *all* the foregone interest to the borrower on the last day of the first calendar year, with the astounding result that *all* the foregone interest payments over the life of the loan are considered to fall into the *borrower's* lap (as a gift, compensation, etc.) in the year the loan is made.[960] The lender's monster payment is compressed into the year the loan is made and may be deductible by the lender, depending on how the money was used. For example, if the borrower is an employee, the lender's total unstated interest might be deductible as compensation. The borrower, however, gets a ratable annual deduction (if any) for hypothetical interest paid over the full term of the loan, and the lender reports an identical amount of annual income over that period. Notice how this shield against tax planning might be turned into a tax planning device if the borrower had an expiring NOL and the lender had a basis for deducting the monster "payment" of interest to the borrower.

959 Deficit Reduction Act of 1984, 13594, H.R. Conf. Rep. 861, 98th Cong., 2d Sess. pages 1011-1024 (1984). See Rev. Proc. 85-46, 1985-2 C.B. 507 for gift tax reporting requirements for low-interest and interest-free demand loans.

960 §7872(e)(2), (a)(2).

Problem 12-13:

Alpha lends Beta $1 million dollars at zero interest for one year. It is a demand loan. Assume the A.F.R. is such that, compounded semi-annually, it produces interest of $100,000. Assuming the transactions might fall into one of the following categories, what is the impact on Alpha and Beta at year's end if:

1) Alpha is a corporation in which Beta is a shareholder.

2) Alpha is Beta's doting parent.

3) Alpha is Beta's employer.

4) Lender has done business with Borrower for many years. Lender made Borrower a 10-year $1 million term loan bearing no interest and not made as a gift. This loan was made June, 7 years ago and the IRS has only now discovered the issue on audit and that Lender and Borrower were unaware that there was a potential tax problem. Assume that the discounted present value of $1 million due in 10 years at the A.F.R. applicable in June, 7 years ago, was $650,000.

   a. How should Lender and Borrower have reported the transaction seven years ago?

   b. Is the tax year 7 years ago open? See §6501.

   c. Assuming it is closed, how should Lender and Borrower report the impact of the loan in the current year?

Problem 12-14:

Burt lent Harry $5,000 dollars at no interest. What exceptions might apply to prevent Burt from having constructive interest under §7872. Focus on §7872(c) and (d).

1. Who is Married?

It can cost more in taxes to be married than to be single and co-habitate if the spouses have comparable incomes, but it can cost less in Federal Income Taxes to be married if the spouses have very different levels of income. This makes it important to know whether one is married, or perhaps even decide whether to marry. According to §7703(a), marriage is a status that is evaluated at year-end and only at year-end.

Does this mean married couples can take a year-end trip to a holiday resort, get divorced there and remarry soon thereafter and pay for the trip with the tax savings? That is what family lawyers in the Dominican Republic liked to say.

BOYTER v. COMMISSIONER
668 F.2d 1382 (4th Cir. 1981)

Winter, J.

[The taxpayers were a married couple who lived in Maryland. They took a year-end vacation in the Dominican Republic, which they combined with a divorce action. They promptly remarried. The divorce was clearly undertaken to avoid the Federal Income Tax burden of being married. The Tax Court sustained the IRS's theory that the divorce was invalid as a matter of Maryland law.]

. . .

II.

We agree with the government's argument that under the Internal Revenue Code a federal court is bound by state law rather than federal law when attempting to construe marital status. Eccles v. Commissioner, 19 T.C. 1049, aff'd, 208 F.2d 796 (4 Cir. 1953). The difficulty with this approach in this case, however, is that the Maryland authorities do not establish beyond peradventure of doubt that the two divorces with which we are concerned are invalid under Maryland law. As the Tax Court stated, "the law in Maryland with regard to the recognition of migratory divorces obtained in a foreign country by Maryland domiciliaries has not been explicitly declared by either the legislature or the highest court of that state," although, as the taxpayers have demonstrated, a number of Maryland trial courts, explicitly and implicitly, have recognized the validity of migratory foreign divorces.[961]

961 This option was not available to the Tax Court because the Maryland statute does not permit a certification from that tribunal. [Footnote No. 3 in original.]

In this ambiguous state of the Maryland law, we would ordinarily be disposed to invoke the certification procedure authorized by Ann.Code of Md., Cts. & Jud.Proc. § 12601 (1980), and ask the Maryland Court of Appeals for a definitive pronouncement on the validity of these bilateral foreign migratory divorces.

But there are other factors which must be considered. The Commissioner has made it clear to us both in his brief and in oral argument that he intends to press the contention . . . that under the sham transaction doctrine taxpayers must be treated as husband and wife in computing their federal income taxes for the years 1975 and 1976 even if Maryland recognizes the validity of their migratory foreign divorces. Of course, if the issue of their validity were certified to the Maryland Court of Appeals and that court ruled them invalid, that decision would decide this case. Significantly, however, if the Maryland Court of Appeals ruled them valid, further proceedings would still be necessary in a federal tribunal and those proceedings might result in an adjudication which would render the certification and the opinion of the Maryland court a futile, academic exercise with respect to final disposition of this case.

We think that certification is inappropriate here. Considerations of comity lead us to conclude that we ought not to request the Maryland Court of Appeals to answer a question of law unless and until it appears that the answer is dispositive of the federal litigation or is a necessary and inescapable ruling in the course of the litigation. . . .

III.

We therefore turn to the question of whether in principle the sham transaction doctrine may be dispositive in this case. Although we hold that the doctrine may be applicable, we do not decide that the divorces in question are in fact shams.

The sham transaction doctrine has its genesis in Gregory v. Helvering, 293 U.S. 465 (1935). [The court's description of the facts of the transaction the taxpayer in Gregory contrived is omitted. Eds.]

The [Gregory] Court conceded that the reorganization was conducted in technical compliance with applicable statutes and that taxpayers are entitled to arrange their affairs so as to decrease their tax liability. It held nonetheless that the "whole undertaking ... was in fact an elaborate and devious form of conveyance masquerading as a corporate reorganization" and should be disregarded for income tax purposes. 293 U.S. at 470. The Court relied on the fact that the transaction had no business or corporate purposethat it was "a mere device which put on the form of a corporate reorganization as a disguise for concealing its real character, ... the sole object of which was the consummation of a preconceived plan, not to reorganize a business, or any part of a business, but to transfer a parcel of corporate shares to (taxpayer)." Id. at 469, 55 S. Ct. at 267. The Court concluded: "The rule which excludes from consideration the motive of tax avoidance is not pertinent to this situation, because the transaction upon its face lies outside the plain intent of the statute. To hold otherwise would be to exalt artifice above reality and to deprive the statutory provision in question of all serious purpose." Id. at 470 . . . .

Gregory has been subsequently invoked by the courts to disregard the form of a variety of business transactions and to apply the tax laws on the basis of the substance or economic reality of the transactions. . . . As the Court stated in Minnesota Tea Co. v. Helvering, "A given result at the end of a straight path is not made a different result because reached by following a devious path." 302 U.S. 609 . . . (1938).

In evaluating the substance of a transaction, the courts take care to examine the transaction as a whole, not as the sum of its component parts. . . .

Although the sham transaction doctrine has been applied primarily with respect to the tax consequences of commercial transactions, personal tax consequences have often served as the motive for those transactions. . . . The principles involved, moreover, are fundamental to the system of income taxation in the United States and should be applicable generally. As Judge Learned Hand, the author of the Gregory opinion in the Court of Appeals, noted:

> The question always is whether the transaction under scrutiny is in fact what it appears to be in form; a marriage may be a joke; a contract may be intended only to deceive others; an agreement may have a collateral defeasance. In such cases the transaction as a whole is different from its appearance. True, it is always the intent that controls; and we need not for this occasion press the difference between intent and purpose. We may assume that purpose may be the touchstone, but the purpose which counts is one which defeats or contradicts the apparent transaction, not the purpose to escape taxation which the apparent, but not the whole, transaction would realize. In Gregory v. Helvering, ..., the incorporators adopted the usual form for creating business corporations; but their intent, or purpose, was merely to draught the papers, in fact not to create corporations as the court understood that word. That was the purpose which defeated their exemption, not the accompanying purpose to escape taxation; that purpose was legally neutral. Had they really meant to conduct a business by means of the two reorganized companies, they would have escaped whatever other aim they might have had, whether to avoid taxes, or to regenerate the world.

Chisholm v. Commissioner, 79 F.2d 14, 15 (2 Cir. 1935) (citation omitted). Thus Revenue Ruling 76255 applies the sham transaction doctrine to the divorce of taxpayers who promptly remarry. The underlying purpose of the transaction, viewed as a whole, is for the taxpayers to remain effectively married while avoiding the marriage penalty in the tax laws. It is the prompt remarriage that defeats the apparent divorce when assessing the taxpayers' liability, just as the prompt reincorporation of a business enterprise in continuous operation defeats the apparent liquidation of the predecessor corporation. Atlas Tool Co., 614 F.2d at 86667. Thus, the sham transaction doctrine may apply in this case if, as the record suggests, the parties intended merely to procure divorce papers rather than actually to effect a real dissolution of their marriage contract.[962]

Having decided in principle that the sham transaction doctrine may apply to the conduct of the parties, we make no finding that the conduct in fact constituted a sham. In our view, the Tax Court as the trier of fact is the only body competent to make that determination in the first instance.

It is generally held that whether a transaction lacks real substance and thus constitutes a sham is a question of fact reviewable only under the clearlyerroneous standard. . . . It is the Tax Court which "has the primary function of finding the facts in tax disputes, weighing the evidence, and choosing from among conflicting inferences and conclusions those which it considers most reasonable." Commissioner v. Scottish American Investment Co., 323 U.S. 119, 12324 (1944). Indeed, Scottish American also admonishes us that we have "no power to change or add to these findings of fact or to reweigh the evidence." Id. at 124.

In summary, we conclude that the correctness of the Tax Court's basis of decision cannot be determined under the present state of Maryland law without certifying the precise question to the Maryland Court of Appeals. Certification should not now be undertaken because there is present and undecided a federal issue which may be dispositive of the litigation, and it is proper that the federal issue be decided before certification is made. The sham transaction doctrine is not inapplicable to this case as a matter of law, but whether the two divorces with the subsequent marriages were shams for income tax purposes are questions of fact which must be determined by the Tax Court and not by us in the first instance.

Accordingly we remand the case to the Tax Court to determine whether the divorces, even if valid under Maryland law, are nonetheless shams and should be disregarded for federal income tax purposes for the years in question.

REMANDED.

[Circuit Judge Widener dissented on the grounds that the taxpayers did not engage in a sham because they literally were divorced at the end of the year, as required by the tax law. Accordingly, he considered there was no sham in the sense of a bogus transaction. He would have asked only that the divorce be evaluated under Maryland law to determine if it was valid.]

962 Relevant to their intention is the evidence suggesting that they may have practiced fraud upon the tribunals granting the divorces. [Footnote No. 7 in original.]

Notes on the "Marriage Penalty" and "Marriage Bonus"

Prior law

It was true that there was a disincentive to marry on the given facts. The so-called marriage penalty was apparent when one compares an unmarried couple with roughly equal earnings to a married couple with the same income as the unmarried couple. For example, using 2019 tax rates and brackets, assume the Marrieds are a two-earner couple each of whom earns taxable income of $50,000 and the Unmarrieds (living together) each earn $50,000. Neither pair has children. The result is that the unmarried couple pays $5,454 more in taxes.

2019 rates Rev. Proc. 2018-57	**Married Couple**	**Unmarried**	**Unmarried**
Total Income	$100,000	$50,000	$50,000
Less standard deduction	($24,400)	($12,200)	($12,200)
Taxable income	$75,600	$37,800	$37,800
10% rate	On $19,400 = $1,940	On $9,700 = $970	On $9,700 = $970
12% rate	On $56,200 = $6,744	On $29,775 = $3,573	On $29,775 = $3,573
24% rate		On $10,525 = $2,526	On $10,525 = $2,526
Total Tax	$8,684	$7,069	$7,069
Difference		Total unmarried is $14,138	Together Unmarried couple pays $5,454 more in tax

What if the Marrieds consisted of one Spouse with taxable income of $100,000 and another with no income and filing a joint return? Their tax bill remains $8,684. If they divorced (and became the Unmarrieds), their taxes would rise; to put it another way, there was (and is) a "marriage bonus" because this time the Unmarrieds would owe a tax of $25,282.

2019 rates Rev. Proc. 2018-57	Married Couple	Unmarried	Unmarried
Total Income	$100,000	$100,000	$0
Less standard deduction	($24,400)	($12,200)	N/A
Taxable income	$75,600	$87,800	$0
10% rate	On $19,400 = $1,940	On $9,700 = $970	
12% rate	On $56,200 = $6,744	On $29,775 = $3,573	

24% rate		On $48,325 = $11,598	
Total Tax	$8,684	$16,141	Together Unmarried couple pays $7,457 more in tax

The marriage bonus here was $7,457, much bigger than the marriage penalty. In both cases, the non-earner partner may have provided imputed income in the form of household services, bargain-hunting and so on, justifying a higher rate for couples which include a non-earner partner.

So, there is a marriage tax penalty when two people with more or less equal incomes married, and a marriage bonus when two people with very different incomes married.

In addition, the portrayal of graduated rates and joint/single filing status suggests that, if one Spouse is earning $100,000 and the other one is a house wife or husband, re-entering the "work force" (market) might be discouraged because the next $50,000 would have been taxed largely at 24% rather than largely at 10% or 12%, as is the first $50,000 of income of the wage-earning Spouse. The same effect of graduated rates might also discourage "moonlighting" by a single or married taxpayer, or discourage taking on a promotion at higher pay, especially if more stress, commuting or expensive clothing result.

2. The Background to Separation and Divorce

Before looking at the tax aspects of divorce it is best to have some understanding of the chronology of a typical divorce. There is a simplifying assumption that this is a "traditional" divorce in which one party bears primary responsibility for financial affairs, there is at least one child, the wage earner leaves the home and the children and the caregiver has less income than the wage earner after the divorce.

In the early stage of a typical divorce, the wage earner moves out of the house and may pay the caregiver enough money to keep the household going. These payments are known as "temporary support." By now, both spouses will have found their own lawyers who will begin the process of trying to evaluate their rights and duties. In general the search is to determine the caregiver's claims stated in monetary terms. If the wage earner refuses to provide enough temporary support to the caregiver, from the local court may provide temporary support.

If the divorce is uncontested, a few months later the spouses will hammer out and sign a written separation agreement, which usually states that it will be incorporated into their divorce decree. Not long thereafter the couple will seek a final decree of divorce, which the court will routinely grant. The decree will typically incorporate the separation agreement. If the payor fails to keep up with payments, the same court that issued the divorce decree will handle a suit for support. If the parties seek to modify the terms of the divorce decree, their right to do so will depend in part upon local law and in part upon the terms of the decree and its incorporated separation agreement.

If the divorce is contested, there will typically be no separation agreement. Instead the rights and duties of the parties will be worked out by means of trials and hearings, and will be incorporated by the final divorce decree.

3. Taxation of Alimony and Separate Maintenance Payments

Read §§ 71(a)-(c) and 215

a. General Rules for divorces entered into after 2018

Before the Tax Cuts and Jobs Act of 2017, alimony and separate maintenance payments were deductible by the payor spouse under §215(a) as above the line deductions. The recipient spouse included the alimony in income under §§ 71(a) and 61(a)(8) .

For any divorce or separation agreement executed after Dec. 31, 2018, or executed before that date but modified after it (if the modification expressly provides that the new amendments apply), alimony and separate maintenance payments are not deductible by the payor spouse and are not included in the income of the payee spouse. Rather, income used for alimony is taxed at the rates applicable to the payor spouse and former code sections 215, 61(a)(8), and 71 are stricken from the IRC.

The new rules do not apply to existing divorces and separations. Instead, §§ 215, 61(a)(8), and 71 continue to apply to already-existing divorces and separations, as well as to divorces and separations that are executed before 2019. To complicate matters further, the new law specifically permits ex-spouses to modify an earlier divorce agreement to adopt the new rule after it goes into effect in 2019

Thus, for many years to come, tax lawyers will have to shift between divorce tax rules depending on when their clients divorced and whether the couple selects to opt into the newer rules that prohibit the deduction for alimony and make the receipt of alimony a tax free event.

b. General Rules for divorces entered into before 2019

Section 71 and its companion, §215, are conceptually stapled together. Section 71 declares what kind of payments from a spouse or former spouse are taxable to the recipient; §215 dovetails neatly with §71 by declaring that the payor can deduct payments which are taxable to the recipient under §71. Perhaps the simplest statement of reasons ever given for this tax pattern was expressed by Representative Disney during the floor debate on the 1942 provisions in which he told the Congress that:

> the amount of a husband's income which goes to the wife as alimony under a court order is in reality not income to him at all since he has no control over it as to the use to which it is to be put.[963]

This helps explain why alimony is an adjustment to gross income under §62 and not an itemized deduction, and why the divorce material often appears in a Chapter on identifying the proper taxpayer. In effect, §71 allows the payor's income to be shifted to the payee, a successful statutory assignment of income with no property transfer.

Section 71 is 'transparent' in the tax policy sense of providing clear rules as to when divorce or separation-related payments are deductible and offering an explicit election to declassify cash payments from being income. Other important elections in this area include the opportunity to classify items as child support or not by negotiation, and an explicit opportunity to treat children as the dependents of either ex-spouse, as they prefer from time to time. This preference for direct electivity answers one of the primary objections to the Internal Revenue Code, namely that it is in fact wiggling with hidden elections that are visible only to people who have the money to hire the necessary legal or accounting talent to ferret them out.

Take a glance at §215(c). Here you will see the Congress's solution to the common problem that, in the past, payors have claimed deductions for transfers to former spouses, which the former spouses have concluded that they need not report as gross income, leaving the government in the worst possible fiscal situation. Section 215(c) is founded on the belief that sunshine is the best disinfectant.

The heart of §71 is the definition of "alimony or separate maintenance payments." There are a few things you must observe. First, the definition does not depend upon local law. Second, a payment qualifies for deduction only if it meets each and every one of the following eight tests. If not, there is no deduction for the payor and apparently no risk of taxation of the payee. Now let us look at the elements:

1. The payment must be in cash, check or money order;
2. The cash must be received under a written "divorce or separation instrument";
3. The cash must be received either directly by the spouse or former spouse or by a third party acting on her behalf;
4. The parties must not designate the payment as *not* alimony in the divorce or separation instrument;
5. If the money is received under a final divorce decree or a separation agreement (but not, for example, a temporary support decree), the payor and the payee

963 88 Cong. Rec. 6377 (1942).

must not be members of the same household (live under the same roof) when the payment is made[964];

6. The divorce or separation agreement must create no obligation to make any payment, after the death of the payee spouse;[965]
7. The payment must not be child support; and,
8. If the spouses are married, they must not file a joint return.

One assembles these requirements by reading together §71(b), (c)(1), and (e).

There are reports that it is theologically possible to be married in the "eyes of God" only, and not in the eyes of man.[966] This means the couple will never know the agonies of legal divorce, but they will not be able to file a joint return. If, however, they hold themselves out as legally married, their relationship may in time become a common law marriage, which would permit them to file joint returns.[967] That depends on state law finding them "married."

c. Front-loading of Alimony for divorces before 2019

One of the major complications of the old system appears in §71(f), the purpose of which is to limit the attraction of paying unduly generous amounts of alimony in early years so as to load up on deductions for the payor in the early years following the divorce or separation. The underlying theory is that a particularly large payment made early is more in the nature of a property settlement than the typical support-related alimony payment. Recapture applies to alimony and separate maintenance payments, but we refer to alimony alone for convenience in the following paragraphs.

When it applies, the sting of §71(f) recapture is that it forces the payor to report extra gross income for the third post-separation year -- thereby partly offsetting his prior deductions -- and (conversely) an equal above-the-line deduction for the payee spouse in that same year -- reversing her prior over-inclusions. It only happens once, in the third post-separation year. The inclusion is referred to as "excess alimony payments."

---

964 In theory this means that the Code does not encourage people who are having a stressful relationship to physically separate for tax reasons.

965 Under Reg. §1.711T(b), Q & A11 if the divorce or separation instrument fails to contain a termination at death contingency, none of the payments, whether made before or after the death of the payee Spouse, would qualify as alimony. Reg. Section 1.711T(b), Q & A12 state that a termination provision under applicable state law is not imputed to an agreement lacking the requisite termination language, but Notice 87-9, 1987-1 C.B. 421 (implementing law enacted in 1982) states that termination of liability to make payments after the death of the payee Spouse need not be stated in the instrument.

966 See Blakesley, *The Putative Marriage Doctrine*, 60 Tulane L. Rev. 1, 28, 46-47 (1985) (reportedly such a marriage may be good enough for State workers' compensation purposes).

967 See Rev. Rul. 58-66, 1958-1 C.B. (if a marriage is valid at State law, it is valid for Federal Income Tax purposes), See also United States v. Windsor 133 S. Ct. 2675 (June 2013) Rev. Rule 2013-17

Procedurally, one first determines the second-year excess under §71(f)(4), and then, the first post-separation year excess under §71(f)(3); this is because the first year recapture can be computed only after determining the amount of the second-year recapture. If the payments in the second year exceed payments in the third year by over $15,000, there is a recapture of the excess in the third year. If the alimony payments in the first year (less the usual $15,000) exceed the average of the payments in the second year and the third year, that excess amount is also recaptured in the third year.

The second year excess alimony is:
(A) the payments in the second year, minus
(B) payments in the third year plus $15,000.

The first year excess alimony payment is:
(A) the payments in the first year less $15,000 minus
(B) half of:
[(i) alimony paid in the second year less
(ii) the excess alimony payment in year two plus
(iii) the payment in the third year]

After the excess alimony payments for both the first and second post-separation years have been determined, one sums the results. This is the income the payor "recaptures" (and the payee deducts) in the third post-separation year. It is independent of how the regular third-year payments are treated. It they would be §71 alimony aside from the recapture rule, they remain §71 alimony.

The recapture rules do not apply to decrees for temporary support,[968] to payments that fluctuate with the payor's income, or to a cessation in payment caused by death or remarriage.[969]

The following is a fairly complex example:

To Illustrate: Assume that a payor makes alimony payments of $50,000 during the first post-separation year, $20,000 during the second post-separation year, and zero during the third post-separation year. All of the payments made during the first, second and third years are deductible by the payor and includable in the income of the payee; no recapture calculation is made until the third post-separation year.

In the third year, the recapture amount with respect to the payments made in the second year is $5,000; this is the amount by which the payments in the second year ($20,000) exceed the payments in the third year (zero) by more than $15,000.

968 §71(f)(5)(B).

969 §71(f)(5).

The recapture amount with respect to the payments made in the first year is $27,500. This is the amount by which (A) the payments in the first year ($50,000) less $15,000 exceed (B) half of [(i) alimony paid in the second year ($20,000) less (ii) the excess payment in year two ($5,000) plus (iii) the payment in the third year ($0)]. In calculating the recapture amount with respect to the first year, only $15,000, rather than $20,000, is treated as paid in the second year. This is to avoid recapturing the same dollars twice; thus, the average of payments made in the second and third years does not include the $5,000 because that has already been found recapturable in the third year. The total amount of recapture income to the payor is therefore $32,500 ($5,000 plus $27,500) and the payee will deduct this amount in the third year.

Problem 12-15:

Wilma and Fred are talking about divorce again. They want your advice as to whether and how the following payments will be taxed if they are included in their separation agreement:

1) Fred will pay Wilma $5,000/year by check for life or until she remarries. Reg. §1.71-1T(b), (Q & A -5).

2) Same, but the first few payments will be in the form of promissory notes, because Fred is low on cash.

3) Instead of paying in cash or notes, Fred will pay with bonds having a basis and value of $5,000.

4) The payments otherwise qualify under §71 as income, but the parties specify in the divorce documentation that for the first two years, they will not be taxable to Wilma.

5) The agreement calls for Fred to pay Wilma $5,000 per year for five years, absolutely. The payments otherwise qualify under §71.

6) Same as "(5)," but local law would release Fred from his duty to pay Wilma's estate if she dies before the payments terminate.

7) Fred will pay Wilma $400/month under the separation agreement until they have legally separated or divorced. During that period, they will live in the same house and will file separate returns. The payments otherwise qualify under §71.

8) Fred and Wilma are married, but Fred recently moved out of the house. He is paying Wilma $250/week so she can take care of herself. There is nothing in writing and no one has gone to court for anything. They file separate returns. Is Wilma taxed on the $250/week?

9) Fred and Wilma have the following alimony payment schedule under a divorce decree, which meets all the requirements of §71(b):

Year 1	$30,000
Year 2	$15,000
Year 3	-0-

a. What does this do to Fred's income? To Wilma's?

b. What if the decree calls for Fred to pay Wilma half the profits from his mine and the payment schedule comes out looking like the one above?

c. What if the decree calls for payments of $30,000 per year, but Fred dies during year one, and the payments end according to the provisions of the decree, leaving the payments for years two and three at $0?

10) Fred and Wilma divorced recently. The divorce decree specified that Fred had to contribute principal of $100,000 to a trust for her benefit, with the income payable to Wilma.

a. Under general tax principles do you think Fred or Wilma should be taxed on the income from the trust?

b. What is the impact of §682 on their alimony trust?

d. Indirect Alimony for divorces before 2019

Payors often promise to pay such things as rental obligations, medical expenses and the like for the benefit of ex-wives. It is often more convenient to have the payor make these payments directly to a provider than to the ex-spouse. Old §71(b) accommodates this spending pattern by including the payments made "on behalf of" the ex-wife as well as "to" her in her income as alimony. But, there are some fringe issues, as the following case reveals.

MARINELLO V. COMMISSIONER

54 T.C. 577 (1970)

SIMPSON, Judge:

OPINION

The respondent determined a deficiency of $ 273 in the petitioner's 1966 income tax. One issue has been settled; the only issue remaining for decision is whether the petitioner is taxable on amounts expended in her behalf for rent and heat by her former husband pursuant to a divorce decree.

All of the facts have been stipulated, and those facts are so found.

The petitioner, Doris B. Marinello, resided in Malden, Mass., at the time the petition was filed in this case. She filed her 1966 Federal income tax return with the district director of internal revenue in Boston, Mass.

The petitioner was divorced from Anthony L. Marinello in 1955. The divorce decree provided that the petitioner have custody of her two minor children and that Mr. Marinello pay $ 15 per week as alimony and $ 25 per week for the support of the children. In addition, the decree provided that Mr. Marinello furnish "free rent and heat" for the petitioner's home.

Pursuant to the decree of divorce, the petitioner resided in one unit of a threefamily dwelling at 55 Cleveland Street, Malden, Mass., from 1955 to 1962. From 1955 to 1960, such dwelling was owned by Mr. Marinello. In 1960, Mr. Marinello transferred the 55 Cleveland Street residence to Anthony Homes, Inc., a corporation wholly owned by him.

In 1962, due to the deteriorated condition of the 55 Cleveland Street residence, the petitioner moved to the secondfloor apartment of premises owned by Mr. Marinello at 96 Cross Street, Malden, Mass., where she continued to reside through 1966. In 1965, Mr. Marinello transferred his interest in 96 Cross Street to Anthony Homes, Inc.

During 1966, Mr. Marinello, pursuant to the decree of divorce, paid $ 600 to Anthony Homes, Inc., as rent for the apartment occupied by the petitioner; he also made payment for fuel in the amount of $ 235.41.

...

The petitioner contends that her receipt, during the taxable year, of free rent and heat was in the nature of a property interest, and was not a periodic payment taxable as alimony under section 71. In support of this position, she relies on the cases of *Pappenheimer v. Allen*, 164 F. 2d 428 (C.A. 5, 1947), and *James Parks Bradley*, 30 T.C. 701 (1958).

In both of these cases, the taxpayers sought to deduct the fair rental value of houses owned by them and occupied rent free by their former wives pursuant to divorce judgments. In each case, the judgment specified the particular house to be occupied by the wife. The courts held that the rentfree occupancy of the houses did not appear to be periodic payments in the ordinary sense, but even if the rental values of the houses were periodic payments taxable to the wives, they were not deductible by the husbands since such payments were not paid out of income taxable to the husbands.

These holdings do not support the petitioner's position. In *Pappenhiemer* and *Bradley*, the courts, in making the tentative finding that there were no periodic payments, heavily relied on the absence of payments made by the husbands for their wives' lodging and on the fact that the wives were given the right under the divorce judgments to occupy specific parcels of realty.

Neither of these facts exists in the present case. The divorce decree did not give the petitioner the right to occupy any specific premises, and it is therefore impossible to view the petitioner's right to free housing and heat as any kind of interest in property. More importantly, during the taxable year, payments were actually made by Mr. Marinello for the petitioner's rent and heat. It is true that the building in which the petitioner lived was owned by Mr. Marinello prior to being transferred by him to his wholly owned corporation, and that the rental payments were made to such corporation. However, corporations are ordinarily accorded separate identity from their shareholders, and there is no suggestion in either the facts of this case or the petitioner's arguments that the transfer of the residence at 96 Cross Street to Anthony Homes, Inc., or the payments made to such corporation by Mr. Marinello, should be ignored for tax purposes. Nor is there any suggestion that the payments made by Mr. Marinello did not equal the value of the occupancy allowed the petitioner.

Because rental and heat payments were actually made for the petitioner by Mr. Marinello, it is not necessary for us to reach the question of whether the bare transfer of occupancy constitutes a periodic payment. Clearly, Mr. Marinello made periodic payments during the taxable year for rent and heat in discharge of a legal obligation imposed on him by the divorce decree. Such payments are taxable to the petitioner under section 71(a)(1).

Decision will be entered for the respondent.

e. Child Support and the Questionable Differentiation from Alimony

Read §71(c)

The child support rules apply to divorces made before and after 2019. The 2017 Tax Act did not affect the rules described below.

Parents are not entitled to deduct payments for the support or other benefit of their children while they are married. Section 71(c) continues the rule against such deductions for periods after the parent's marriage dissolves, either by divorce or legal separation. Child support continues to be nondeductible after the dissolution of marriage.

The current law continues the rule that only amounts fixed as child support can qualify as such, but the Regulations take an objective, realistic view of whether a payment is in substance child support.

> **To illustrate:** The Parents agree to reduce child support when their child, Charley, marries or reaches age 21. The payor might object, preferring to make all the payments alimony, and the payee's tax advisor may agree. So, how about drafting their documents to show only alimony, but have the alimony decline at Charley's marriage or his reaching age 21? Congress is on to this gimmick. The Code flushes out bogus alimony payments by reference to the way payments change when major life events occur to the child. With this in mind re-read §71(c)(2). You will see that the part of the payments to Charley that decline with life events such as marriage are nondeductible child support.

The tax system is designed to induce payors to stay current on their child support payments. Take another look at §71(c)(3) and see how it does not punish the defaulting payor during the period of non-payment, but that when he finally does make his payments, he is punished by being granted the minimum tax deduction under the circumstances by deeming the back payments to be first for delayed child support. This puts tax pressure on payors – who are operating under the old regime where alimony remains deductible – to make their child support payments on time.

From a policy perspective, there is serious doubt as to whether the alimony/child support distinction works. The problem is that child support is received by an ex-wife who can apply the money as she wishes, subject to some legal constraints. For example, if the wife received alimony of $2,000 per month and $500 per month of child support she will virtually never use exactly $500 per month for the benefit of the child. This is an area in which the parties are free to negotiate, but the results are difficult to measure. There is no doubt a tax system that allows an alimony deduction encourages payors to replace child support with alimony.

> **To illustrate:** Assume a payor in the 37% bracket is ordinarily obligated to pay $1,000 per month for alimony and $200 per month for child support. The payor is in a higher tax bracket than the payee (who is in the 10% bracket). The payor offers to pay $1,300 per month, but with the understanding that the entire amount will be treated as alimony. The payee agrees that this is a reasonable deal and accepts it. As a consequence, the Treasury Department is worse off because what use to be a tax-neutral payment of $200 has now become a $300 deduction (saving $111 in taxes) combined with $300 more taxable income to a less wealthy person (attracting taxes of $30). Only the government stands to lose. The payee gains after-tax cash of $100 - $30 = $70. The payor pays an extra $100 in pre-tax cash, but reduces income taxes by $111, or $11 ahead compared to the pre-change situation.

Comparative tax law: Foreign systems face the same problem. For example, Sweden's divorce tax system follows the United States, whereas the Australian system (perhaps wisely) ignores the difference between alimony and child support, and instead treats both like gifts. It uses the tax system to enforce collections.[970] Given that the real recipient of child support is normally an ex-spouse, who may or may not in fact use the money for the child, Australia may have made the right decision to ignore the distinction, but was it right to allow no tax deduction? Consider the hapless man with three ex-wives whose nondeductible alimony might consume most of his taxable income.

f. Property Transfers in Connection with Divorce

Read §1041

You have already seen an allusion to §1041 in connection with the *Farid-es-Sultaneh* case in Chapter 3 and how it treats all interspousal transfers as gifts. Now we will look at that section somewhat more closely. The key concept this time is that any interspousal property transfer made within one year after the date of divorce is conclusively presumed to be in connection with the divorce. The transfer is rebuttably presumed to be on account of divorce if it appears in the divorce or separation instrument and occurs more than one year after, but less than six years after the date the marriage ceases. Thereafter, transfers between the former spouses are rebuttably presumed not to be incident to divorce.

To illustrate: In connection with their divorce, Ron transfers his interest in Rancho del Cal to Nancy. His interest in the ranch is worth $2 million and has a basis of $600,000. There is no income tax to anyone on the transfer and Nancy takes a basis in the interest received from Ron of $600,000. Notice how Ron and his lawyers may have taken advantage of Nancy if, suppose Nancy paid $2 million to Ron for his interest, leaving her with a low basis ranch.

g. Life Insurance

Put yourself in the position of the payee spouse. Assume you were offered a so-so property settlement and a promise of generous alimony. After thinking it over, you might rightly worry about what would happen if the payor died. To prevent trouble, you would likely ask for insurance coverage on the life of the payor. Premiums paid on whole-life insurance contracts are potentially deductible as alimony by the payor if the new policy names the former spouse as beneficiary, or if the payor irrevocably assigns a pre-existing policy to the payee, stripping the payor of all incidents of ownership in the policy, and making the payee the irrevocable

970 H. Ault, COMPARATIVE INCOME TAXATION pp. 276-280 (Kluwer 1997).

beneficiary of the policy, with a right to the proceeds even if the payee predeceases the payor.[971] If the payor is unwilling to purchase a policy, the payor should increase the alimony payments so as to cover the need for life insurance.

By contrast, the transfer of the policy falls under §1041 as a hypothetical gift. It is not a transfer for value for purposes of §101(a)(2) and therefore the payee is not subject to income taxes on the death proceeds.[972]

Problem 12-16:

Assume that the requirements of §71(b) are otherwise satisfied. In which of the following situations can the payor (Fred) claim a §215 deduction?

1) Fred lets Wilma occupy a home he owns, rent-free. The home has a rental value of $1,000 per month.

2) Fred pays Wilma's landlord rent of $1,000. Normally, Wilma would have paid it, as she signed the lease.

3) Fred pays $1,000 to the Friendly Bank on a mortgage of a home that he owns and in which Wilma resides, rent-free.

4) Fred pays $1,000 to the Friendly Bank on a mortgage of a home owned by Wilma and which Wilma occupies.

5) Fred pays the legal expenses of the divorce in the form of paying Wilma's lawyer directly.

6) Fred assigns an insurance contract on his life to Wilma and pays the premiums. The contract names Wilma as the beneficiary, but he retains the right to name his mother as the beneficiary.

h. Antenuptial Arrangements

There is a marked trend in favor of premarital contracts, as reflected by the promulgation in 1983 of the Uniform Premarital Agreements Act. That act reflects an effort to secure similar

971 Reg. §1.71-1T(b), Q&A 6 and, e.g., Rev. Rul. 70-218, 1970-1 C.B. 19 (pre-1984 law but presumably still valid).

972 §101(a)(2)(A).

treatment of antenuptial agreements nationwide.[973] While it is generally against public policy to attempt to make contractual alterations in the basic support duties of a marriage relationship, property transfers may be agreed to as either an inducement to marry or to clarify the parties' rights and duties in the event they divorce.

Section 1041 does not prevent taxation on exchanges of appreciated property between spouses before they marry. Wise planners will take advantage of §1041 for any transfer of appreciated property. This will necessitate waiting until the parties are married before conveying appreciated property, whether in consideration of marriage or of a surrender of dower or similar rights. If property that has declined in value is to be transferred, however, the timing objective will be reversed; the game will be to realize losses between non-spouses outside of §267. Because they are not related (married) when they make their antenuptial transfers, the high road to recognizing losses is wide open.

If an antenuptial agreement provides for separate maintenance or alimony in the event of separation or divorce, the contract under those circumstances becomes a divorce or separation instrument under §71(b)(2) if it is referred to in (and is therefore "incident to") the divorce decree.[974]Section 71 only applies to divorces that take place before 2018.

i. Invalidation of Divorce and Annulment

If a married New Yorker gets an ex parte divorce in Florida, but the divorce is later invalidated by a New York court, do intervening payments lose their deductible character? The IRS, predictably, says "yes." Until 1976, the Second and Third Circuits said "no",[975] the intervening payments did not lose their deductible character until after the divorce was invalidated in Florida.[976] Note that for divorces that took place before 2018, the separation agreement may be an independent basis for §71 and §215 treatment even if the divorce decree is invalid. Tax cases decided in the government's favor concerning the marital deduction for estate tax purposes appear equally applicable to alimony issues.[977]

---

973 See Zabel & Walloch, *From Status to Contract: The 1984 Tax Act and Current Matrimonial Law Trends,* 124 Trusts & Est. No 4, at 14, 15 (Apr. 1985).

974 It fits because of §71(b)(2) which includes "written instruments incident to a [divorce] decree. See Reg. §1.71-1(b)(6). Reg. §1.71-1T, A4 incorporates prior law for this purpose. There is little authority on antenuptial agreements and how they relate to divorces under §§ 71 and 215.

975 Rev. Rul. 67-442, 1967-2 C.B. 65. Borax v Commissioner, 40 T 1001 (1963), rev'd, 349 F2d 666 (2d Cir 1965); Wondsel v. Commissioner, 23 T.C.M. 1278 (1964); Feinberg v. Commissioner, 16 T.C. 1485 (1961); Gersten v. Commissioner, 28 T.C. 756 (1957), aff'd in part, rev'd in part, 267 F.2d 195 (9th Cir. 1959). In Rev. Rul. 67-442, the IRS announced it will not challenge divorces *sua sponte.*

976 Estate of Borax v. Commissioner, 349 F.2d 666 (2d Cir 1965), cert denied, 383 U.S. 935 (1966); Wondsel v. Commissioner, 350 F2d 339 (2d Cir. 1965); Feinberg v. Commissioner, 198 F.2d 260 (3d Cir. 1952).

977 Estate of Goldwater v. Commissioner, 539 F.2d 878 (2d Cir. 1976); Estate of Steffke v. Commissioner, 538 F.2d 730 (7th Cir. 1976).

An annulment differs from a divorce in that the parties are deemed not to have never married. Even so, alimony paid pursuant to an annulment may be treated as alimony or separate maintenance payments under §§ 71 and 215 whether or not the original marriage was void or voidable.[978] Reg. §1.1041-1T, Q & A-8 treats an annulment of a marriage void *ab initio* the same way as a divorce, meaning §1041 applies. Sections 71 and 215 should also apply, given that §1041 complements these sections.

Problem 12-17:

Socialite Caldwell Murchfield and Wanda Friendly married a few months ago, and engaged in the following transaction after the wedding. Please describe the income and basis effects of the transaction to each party:

1) Recently she sold Caldwell 400 shares of stock of Murchfield Lead Co. costing $1,000 and having a value of $10,000. He paid the $10,000 in timely fashion.

2) A few years later, they decided to divorce. What are the tax implications to each party if Caldwell transfers the same stock to Wanda? In each case, the transaction was denominated by a "sale" and was not referred to in the divorce or separation papers. See Reg. §1.1041-1T. They now live in Bermuda.

    a. Nine months following their divorce. Would it matter if the arrangement for the transfer was not in writing?

    b. Two and a half years following their divorce.

    c. More than six years following their divorce.

4) What if he had transferred Murchfield Lead Co. stock with a basis of $60,000 and a value of $100,000 as part of an antenuptial agreement? The transfer occurred before they got married and was absolute.

    a. Does Caldwell have a taxable gain?

    b. Does Wanda have income?

978 Rev. Rul. 59-130, 1959-1 C.B. 61 (where annulment in substance is the same as a divorce); Reisman v. Commissioner, 49 T.C. 570 (1968); Newburger v. Commissioner, 61 T.C. 457 (1974).

c. Would the result differ if the transfer took place after they married?

Problem 12-18:

The Friendlys came over to dinner one night in 2016, concerned about their daughter Fairlee's marriage proposal from Eddie Swindler and a tax planning scheme of his. It seems he owns a building he holds for investment. The building, which is unencumbered, has a basis of $0 and is worth $100,000. He is suggesting that prior to their marriage, he exchange the building (which will offset a large capital loss carryover he has) for a release of her marital rights under an antenuptial agreement.

1) After they are married, Swindler says he and Fairlee can file a joint return and depreciate the building all over again. See §§ 1041 and 1239.

2) Bad news! The marriage took place and now Fairlee (who recently fell in love with Caldwell Murchfield) and Swindler, are talking about divorce. Swindler has hired you as his lawyer. He tells you that some years back while they were married, Fairlee swapped the building (which had a basis of $90,000 at the time and a value of $100,000) for a different property of Swindler's, namely a painting with a basis of $10,000 and a value of $100,000. Assuming that they are about to divorce and that these are the only important assets and that Fairlee will earn more money than Swindler, how should they divide up the building and the painting?

3) Caldwell and Wanda had two children by their marriage, Nigel and Hubert. Wanda got custody of them in the divorce, when Caldwell left her for Fairlee. The separation agreement was incorporated in the divorce decree, and in all respects it seems that the payments it calls for qualify under §71 as gross income to Wanda. As to the children, the separation agreement reads as follows in pertinent part:

   Children: There are two children of the marriage, Nigel (age 6) and Hubert (age 4). It is agreed that Nigel and Hubert shall each receive child support of $400/month, which amount shall decline to $0 when either turns 18, dies or marries. Said $400 shall be delivered by check payable to Wanda, for the childrens' benefit.

   a. Is the $400 per month per child taxable to Wanda?

b. Would the result differ if the agreement did not provide for the children, but did provide that Wanda's alimony would drop by $200/month whenever Nigel or Hubert died, married or turned 18? See Reg. 1.71-1(c), Q & A-16 et seq.

c. Assume Wanda has custody of the children, but a few years later Caldwell agrees to increase his alimony payments somewhat if she will yield the dependency deductions to the children to him, which she justifiably does, under the authority of §152(e). Can she still claim head of household status and get a more favorable tax rate schedule than if she files as a single person? See §2(b).

4) Assume Caldwell transfers absolutely an insurance policy on his life to Wanda and dies a few years later following their divorce.

a. Can Wanda receive the proceeds free of Federal Income Taxes? See §101(a)(2).

b. Would your answer change if the transfer was on account of an annulment based the surprising fact that they were cousins? See Reg. 1.1041-1T(b), Q & A-8.

5) Same as question 4(a), but the transfer of the policy occurred before marriage and in consideration of her release of her marital rights under an antenuptial agreement.

6) How do your answers to questions 1 through 5 change if the events take place today?

CHAPTER 13 - ALTERNATIVE MINIMUM TAX

A. INTRODUCTION

Read §55(a), (b)(1)(A), (b)(2), and (d)(1) and (3)

This curious tax was enacted in 1969 in response to a public outcry following press reports of wealthy taxpayers who were paying no Federal Income Taxes. Reports of high-income individuals and corporations paying no taxes surfaced once again in 1997.[979] Since that time, Congress has shut down syndicated tax shelters for individuals and generally strengthened the alternative minimum tax ("AMT") as to people, but repealed the AMT as to corporations.

The core of the AMT is §55, which imposes a graduated tax of 26% and 28% on a base known as "alternative minimum taxable income" or "AMTI." §55(b)(2). The tax only applies if and to the extent the AMT exceeds regular Federal Income Taxes under §1. AMTI means taxable income *plus* the items of tax preference added to the AMT base by §56 and then *modified* by certain adjustments found in §57.[980]

> **To illustrate:** Igor has a regular Federal Income Tax bill of $40,000 for this year under §1. His AMT calculation reveals a $52,000 liability under §55. He will have to pay a $12,000 AMT and $40,000 in regular Federal Income Tax. Igor may be able to get a $12,000 credit against his regular income in a later year when he is only liable for the regular income tax.

The tax is generally only a problem for people with large gross incomes, because a specified amount of AMTI is "exempt", meaning subject to a zero AMT rate. Section 55(d) provides the "exemption amount," which is $55,850 in 2019 for married filing separately, $71,700 (unmarried or head of household), and $11,700 for married filing a joint return. The exemption amount is phased out by an amount equal to 25 percent of the amount by which the individual's AMTI exceeds (1) $1,020,600 in the case of married individuals filing a joint return and surviving spouses, (2) $510,300 in the case of other unmarried individuals, head of household, married

979 See, e.g., Dallas Morning News, April 18, 1997, *Many Top Earners Had No '93 Taxes; IRS Says Nearly 2,400 making $200,000 Plus Paid Nothing.*

980 There is also a loss-denial provision in §58, but it has been largely superannuated by the passive loss rules of §469.

individuals filing separate returns,and an estate or trust [IRC sec. 55(d)(3)].[981] These amounts are not indexed for inflation.

In form, the final tax imposed consists of the excess of tax on alternative minimum taxable income minus the regular income tax, but the concept is so Byzantine that everyone refers to the AMT as a separate complete tax, not merely a (distasteful) icing on the cake of the Federal Income Tax. The details of the tax can fill a treatise. The easiest way to get a grip on the tax is to scan Form 6521. It shows how one begins with taxable income and then adds back a seemingly endless list of exclusions and deductions.

Taxpayers are obligated to compute a Form 6521 every year to see if there is an AMT liability. One wonders how many taxpayers just throw up their hands and do not bother. One major group that does not have to worry about the problem consists of high-bracket investors who put their money in tax-exempt bonds, other than "specified private activity bonds." Sections 56 through 58 do *not* treat most tax-exempt interest as a tax preference, except for interest on specified private activity bonds, under §57(a)(5). Other key items that could be added to the AMT base, but Congress has chosen to ignore, include qualified dividends, installment sale gains[982] and capital gains.[983] In fact, §55(b)(3) strains to assure that the AMT rate on capital gains is the same as the regular tax rate.

B. EXPLANATION

The following material was prepared by the staff of the Joint Committee on Taxation. It may help to put the AMT into perspective. It will also give you a glimpse into various fairly obscure tax benefits. The materials in brackets were added as part of this book.

DESCRIPTION OF POSSIBLE PROPOSALS RELATING TO THE INDIVIDUAL ALTERNATIVE MINIMUM TAX ("AMT")

June 22, 1998, [JOINT COMMITTEE PRINT]; JCX4898

. . .

981 Rev. Proc. 2018-57.

982 See Staff of the Joint Comm. on Tax'n, GENERAL EXPLANATION OF 1997 TAX LEGISLATION (JCS-23-97), p. 62 (December 17, 1997). This modified prior law and reduced the burden of the AMT.

983 There is a minor capital gains add-back relating to §1202, which is mentioned the following materials.

II. PRESENT LAW AND LEGISLATIVE BACKGROUND

A. Present Law

In general

Present law imposes a minimum tax on an individual to the extent the taxpayer's minimum tax liability exceeds his or her regular tax liability. This alternative minimum tax ("AMT") is imposed upon individuals at rates of (1) 26 percent on the first $175,000 of alternative minimum taxable income in excess of a phasedout exemption amount and (2) 28 percent on the amount in excess of $175,000. Since 1993, the exemptions amounts are $45,000 in the case of married individuals filing a joint return and surviving spouses; $33,750 in the case of other unmarried individuals; and $22,500 in the case of married individuals filing a separate return. These exemption amounts are phasedout by an amount equal to 25 percent of the amount that the individual's alternative minimum taxable income exceeds a threshold amount. These threshold amounts are $150,000 in the case of married individuals filing a joint return and surviving spouses; $112,500 in the case of other unmarried individuals; and $75,000 in the case of married individuals filing a separate return, estates, and trusts. The exemption amounts, the threshold phaseout amounts, and the $175,000 breakpoint amount are not indexed for inflation. The lower capital gains rates applicable to the regular tax also apply for purposes of the AMT.

Alternative minimum taxable income ("AMTI") is the taxpayer's taxable income increased by certain preference items and adjusted by determining the tax treatment of certain items in a manner that negates the deferral of income resulting from the regular tax treatment of those items.

Preference items in computing AMTI

The minimum tax preference items are:

(1) The excess of the deduction for percentage depletion over the adjusted basis of the property at the end of the taxable year. This preference does not apply to percentage depletion allowed with respect to oil and gas properties.

(2) The amount by which excess intangible drilling costs arising in the taxable year exceed 65 percent of the net income from oil, gas, and geothermal properties. . . .

(3) Taxexempt interest income on private activity bonds (other than qualified 501(c)(3) bonds) issued after August 7, 1986.

(4) Accelerated depreciation or amortization on certain property placed in service before January 1, 1987.

(5) Fortytwo percent of the amount excluded from income under section 1202 (relating to gains on the sale of certain small business stock.)

. . .

Adjustments in computing AMTI

The adjustments that all taxpayers (including corporations) must make are:

(1) Depreciation on property placed in service after 1986 and before January 1, 1999, must be computed by using the generally longer class lives prescribed by the alternative depreciation system of section 168(g) and either (a) the straightline method in the case of property subject to the straightline method under the regular tax or (b) the 150percent declining balance method in the case of other property. Depreciation on property placed in service after December 31, 1998, is computed by using the regular tax recovery periods and the AMT methods described in the previous sentence.
(2) Mining exploration and development costs must be capitalized and amortized over a 10year period.
(3) Taxable income from a longterm contract (other than a home construction contract) must be computed using the percentage of completion method of accounting.
(4) The amortization deduction allowed for pollution control facilities placed in service before January 1, 1999 (generally determined using 60month amortization for a portion of the cost of the facility under the regular tax), must be calculated under the alternative depreciation system (generally, using longer class lives and the straightline method). The amortization deduction allowed for pollution control facilities placed in service after December 31, 1998, is calculated using the regular tax recovery periods and the straightline method.

The adjustments applicable only to individuals are:

(1) Miscellaneous itemized deductions are not allowed under the AMT. This limitation is irrelevant for tax years 2018 to 2025 because miscellaneous itemized deductions are suspended during these years;
(2) Deductions for State, local, and foreign real property taxes; State and local personal property taxes; and State, local, and foreign income, war profits, and excess profits taxes are not allowed;
(3) Medical expenses are allowed only to the extent they exceed ten percent of the taxpayer's adjusted gross income;
(4) Standard deductions and personal exemptions are not allowed;
(5) The amount allowable as a deduction for [newspaper and magazine] circulation expenditures must be capitalized and amortized over a 3year period;

(6) The amount allowable as a deduction for research and experimental expenditures must [generally] be capitalized and amortized over a 10year period [as opposed the usual 5-year period under §174(b)]; and

(7) The special regular tax rules relating to incentive stock options do not apply.

Other rules

The combination of the taxpayer's net operating loss carryover and foreign tax credits cannot reduce the taxpayer's AMT liability by more than 90 percent of the amount determined without these items.

The various tax credits (including credits such as the dependent care credit and child tax credit) generally may not reduce the individual's regular tax liability below the tentative minimum tax. . . . [For tax years beginning in 2009, however, non-refundable personal tax credits reduce regular tax and the AMT. Examples of such credits are the child tax credit, the credit for costs of dependent care, and the Hope and Lifetime Learning Credits. Eds.]

If an individual is subject to AMT in any year, the amount of tax exceeding the taxpayer's regular tax liability is allowed as a credit (the "AMT credit") in any subsequent taxable year to the extent the taxpayer's regular tax liability exceeds his or her tentative minimum tax in such subsequent year. For individuals, the AMT credit is allowed only to the extent the taxpayer's AMT liability is a result of adjustments that are timing in nature. The individual AMT adjustments relating to itemized deductions and personal exemptions and are not timing in nature, and no minimum tax credit is allowed with respect to these items. . . .

. . .

. . .

C. COMPUTATION OF AMT AND AMT CREDIT

The following problem is fairly complicated, but it has the advantage of forcing you through a review of a lot of what you have learned so far in the course. Before you try your hand at it, consider the following distillation of the computation of an individual taxpayer's AMT:

Step 1: Taxable income computed under §63
Step 2: Add back into taxable income preferences and adjustments under §§ 56 - 58
Step 3: Subtract the AMT exemption under §55(d)(1)
Alternative minimum taxable income (AMTI) under §55(b)(2)

Step 4: Calculate the AMT owed as: AMTI x 26/28% AMT rate

AMT foreign tax credit and nonrefundable personal credits

Tentative minimum tax [§55(b)(1)]

Step 5: Subtract regular tax liability from the tentative minimum tax

-Regular tax

Alternative Minimum Tax [§55(a)]

There is a nasty catch here. The taxpayer *reduces* regular taxable income by her credits, which *raises* the odds of being subject to the AMT. It used to be that she only reduced her tentative minimum tax by the foreign tax credit and refundable credits,[984] but nowadays nonrefundable credits also reduce the AMT. In turn, the AMT generates its own credit, which is available to offset regular federal income tax liabilities in later years, if and when the AMT does not apply. As a result, for many taxpayers the AMT is just a timing problem that forces them to prepay some taxes. This credit appears in §53, which has to be up near the top of the list of impenetrable Code sections.[985] In effect §53 declares that in any year that the AMT does not apply, the taxpayer can reduce her regular (§1) tax liability by a credit for AMT produced in prior years by her "deferral preferences" (those of a timing nature only), as opposed to "exclusion preferences" that caused an *exemption* from taxation. The accelerated component of accelerated depreciation is an example of a deferral preference, and the preference for tax-exempt interest is an example of an exclusion preference.

To illustrate: Last year Igor had a $12,000 AMT and $40,000 in regular Federal Income Tax. Of his $12,000 AMT bill, $10,000 is attributable to the accelerated portion of his depreciation deductions. The remaining $2,000 is attributable to exclusion preferences. Assume that this year, the AMT does not apply to Igor. Igor can claim a $10,000 credit against his regular income this year because that is the extent to which his AMT bill is attributable to "deferral preferences." Notice that what has really happened is that Igor partly prepaid his regular Federal Income Tax to the extent he claimed deferral preferences.

984 These refundable credits include the §31 tax on income withheld from wages (including over-withheld Social Security taxes), estimated tax payments, the earned income credit of §32, the §33 credit for withholdings on nonresident aliens, and the §34 credit for gasoline and special fuels for off-highway use or public transportation.

985 According to Hall, *Compliance Costs of Alternative Tax Systems*, 71 Tax Notes 1081 (1996), the AMT is the second most complex provision in the Code for taxpayers, after depreciation, and according to a release from the Joint Economic Committee, the cost of compliance with the AMT may exceed the revenues it generates. J.E.C. Release on Flat Tax (Jan. 17, 1996) (Doc. 96-2618).

Corporations are not handicapped this way. They obtain an AMT credit against exclusion preferences also.[986] Their problem is ever getting into a regular tax year.

Closing Thoughts on the AMT

The AMT is a troubling provision. One has to wonder if it is just a political "public relations" expedient that operates as a weak substitute for a broader tax base, which Congress could achieve by repealing the various preferences and exclusions, but which are too well protected politically for Congress to cut back directly. Conversely, might it be better to broaden the AMT base even more so that everyone pays an AMT, or is that too complicated a way to achieve tax reform? In the meantime the AMT is creeping into more and more taxpayers' lives because of the low thresholds. Does this mean the AMT exemption should be "indexed" for inflation to stave it off?

Another approach would be to invest more money in the IRS. According to one authority, for each extra dollar budgeted for the IRS's examination function, there is another $13.72 of revenue.[987] That suggests a large gap between what is rightly owed and what is collected, and a possibility that more vigorous enforcement of the existing tax laws would reduce or eliminate the need for the AMT.

Problem 13-1:

Your client sued a contractor for damages to her business. This year she received a recovery of $50,000. Unfortunately, she also paid $120,000 in legal fees this year in order to get that $50,000 recovery. Your client has no other deductions of any sort. She has regular salary of $100,000 per year in addition to the income from her business. Assume, correctly, that her legal fee is deductible under §62 and that her AGI is $300,000 (which includes the $50,000 recovery).

1) What is her regular taxable income?

2) What is her alternative minimum taxable income under §56(b)(2)? Keep in mind that the standard deduction allowed for §1 purposes is not allowed under the AMT. §56(b)(1)(E).

3) What is her total federal tax bill for the year?

4) Will she get a §53 credit in a subsequent ("regular tax") year?

986 §53(d)(1)(B)(iv).

987 See Dubin, Graetz & Wilde, *The Changing Face of Tax Enforcement*, 43 Tax Lawyer 893, 903 (1990).

5) Assume for a moment that your client is a partner in the Murchfield Lead Company and that the partnership has been claiming percentage depletion on its lead sales because it long ago exhausted its basis in the lead mine.

   a. What is the AMT burden on your client for using percentage depletion? See §57(a)(1).

   b. Assume that you had the power to rewrite the Code. Would you eliminate percentage depletion? What about cost depletion? The AMT preference for depletion in excess of basis? Is there a reasonable way out of this mess without distorting income? Do not calculate the amount of tax due. Simply share your thoughts on the general concepts.

APPENDIX

I. GLOSSARY OF TERMS

A

Accelerated Cost Recovery System (ACRS): A method of computing depreciation deductions for tangible property used in a business or held for the production of income. It assumes zero salvage value income and, in general, declining balances. §168.

Accrual Method: An overall method of accounting under which income is reported in the taxable year when all the events have occurred which fix the taxpayer's right to receive the income, provided the amount is ascertainable and likely to be paid. Deductions arise in the taxable year in which all events have occurred which fix the taxpayer's liability to pay the item, provided the amount is reasonably ascertainable and economic performance has occurred. §451.

Additional Standard Deduction: Extra amounts a taxpayer can claim if he is age 65 before the end of the taxable year, plus an additional claim on account of blindness. The additional amount is generally $600 plus inflation. The additional standard deduction is added to the basic standard deduction in computing taxable income if the taxpayer does not itemize his or her deductions. §63.

Adjusted Basis: The basis of property, as adjusted under §1016 to reflect things such as improvements, depreciation, and other such effects.

Adjusted Gross Income: Gross income (§61) minus adjustments to gross income under §62. This calculation is unique to individuals.

Alternative Minimum Tax: The tax under §55, added to the regular income tax computed under §1, to prevent avoidance of income tax via claims of extensive adjustments and tax preferences.

Amortization Deductions: Deductions to write off basis of intangible property used in a taxpayer's business or held for the production of income. The deductions are generally on the straight-line method. See §167 and specific provisions such as §197.

Amount Realized: Money plus the fair market value of property received from the sale or other disposition of property. See §1001(b). It includes nonrecourse debt to which transferred property is subject and recourse debt the transferee assumes.

Announcement: A public communication by the IRS stating its position, commonly used as early interpretation of a new Code section (or subsection).

Annuity: A contract under which a purchaser buys the right to a stream of income for a fixed period or a period limited to the life of one or more persons.

Assess a Deficiency: A internal administrative action by the IRS by which it renders a potential federal tax liability absolute. The typical case occurs when the taxpayer receives a notice of proposed deficiency, and the taxpayer fails to respond by filing a petition in the Tax Court within 90 days.

Assignment of Income: The attempted transfer of income and the incidence of taxation from one taxpayer (usually in a relatively high tax rate bracket) to another taxpayer (usually in a relatively low tax rate bracket). It is a pejorative term.

Audit: An informal term for an IRS examination of the taxpayer's return.

B

Basic Standard Deduction: A deduction that most taxpayers can subtract from adjusted gross income if they do not have sufficient itemized deductions. The basic standard deduction depends on the taxpayer's filing status. Taxpayers combine the basic standard deduction and the additional standard deduction with then itemized deductions to decide if they wish to elect to itemize their deductions.

Basis: The taxpayer's investment, in property, stated in dollars. Initial basis depends on how the property was obtained. For example, if it was a gift, the donee generally takes the donor's basis.

Bond: A debt obligation, normally issued by a corporation, providing for the periodic payment of interest, with principal deferred until the end of the life of the obligation.

Boot: Money or other property that cannot be received without recognizing gain or loss under a nonrecognition provision in the Internal Revenue Code.

C

Capital Asset: An asset owned by a taxpayer, other than certain types of property listed in §1221, such as inventory.

Carryovers (Carrybacks): Items given effect for tax purposes in a particular taxable year that must be moved to a subsequent (or earlier) taxable year; examples include the net operating loss provisions [§ 172], the deductions for net capital losses [§1212] and excess charitable contributions [§170(d)], and passive loss and credit carryovers [§469(b)]. These provisions generally operate as crude devices to average income.

Cash Method of Accounting: An overall method of accounting under which gross income is reported in the taxable year actually or constructively received, and deductions are reported in the taxable year in which they are actually paid.

Claim of Right Doctrine: A tax law doctrine that forces a taxpayers to report as gross income earnings received in a taxable year as to which the taxpayer claims the amount and its unrestricted use, even though he or she may become obligated to return the amount in a later year.

Constructive Receipt Doctrine: A doctrine which requires persons using the cash method to report gross income amounts that are credited to a taxpayer's account, set apart for the taxpayer, or otherwise made available so that the taxpayer may draw on them at any time.

Cost Basis: The basis of property that was purchased, or that was acquired in a taxable exchange.

Credit: see Tax Credit.

D

Deduction: An amount the taxpayer uses to reduce his or her gross income (or to reduce his or her adjusted gross income).

Deficiency: The amount by which the taxpayer understates his tax liability. It consists of the amount of tax actually due less the amount reported by the taxpayer on his or her return plus any previous assessments less any rebates. §6211(a) and Reg. §301.62111(a).

Dependency Exemption: This is a deduction that allows the taxpayer to deduct the exemption amount for his or her adjusted gross income for each qualifying dependent whose gross income is below the exemption amount, or each of the taxpayer's children who qualify as a dependent and are less than nineteen years old, or if a student, less than twenty four years old. [§151] The dependency exemption and personal exemption amount were originally set at $2,000 and have been indexed for inflation since 1989.

Dependent: An individual described in §152, such as a son or daughter who lives at home and is supported by his or her parents. Section 152 provides standards for determining who qualifies. The existence of a dependent opens the door to a dependency deduction for the provider(s) of support.

Depletion Deductions: Write-offs of natural resources.

Depreciation Deductions: Recovery allowed for the basis of tangible property, excluding natural resources, over the useful life of such property in the taxpayer's hands. The property must be used in connection with a trade or business or held for the production of income, and must be subject to wear and tear, exhaustion, or obsolescence. Most tangible and real property deductions are arrived at using the Accelerated Cost Recovery System (ACRS) under §168; however, §167 rules apply to several categories of property, including intangible personal property. Natural resources are written off under depletion methods. Intangible property write-offs are generally referred to as "amortization."

E

Exchange: A barter of property or services for the property or services of another, as opposed to a sale of property or services.

Exchange Basis: Also known as "substituted basis." Basis in property which is wholly or partially arrived at by looking to the taxpayer's basis or adjusted basis in previously held property. [§7701 (a)(44)]. Such basis arises in like-kind exchanges, for example.

Exclusions: Code Sections which allow the exemption from gross income of items which are encompassed by the definition of gross income. Common exclusions are qualified gifts and inheritances. §102.

F

Face Amount: The stated principal amount of a debt. It is not necessarily the same as the issue price of the debt (what is paid for it when first sold). If it is first sold for a price lower than its face amount, it has original issue discount, defined below.

Fair Market Value: The price for property that a willing buyer will offer and that a willing seller will accept, if neither are under any compulsion, and if both are reasonably aware of the relevant facts.

Filing Status: The nature of the individual when he or she files a tax return, such as married, single, head of household. Filing status affects tax rates.

Fiscal Year: A one year accounting period which concludes on the last day of any month except December. Also, an annual accounting period ranging from fifty-two to fifty-three weeks that specified taxpayers may elect to use. §441(e), (f).

Fringe Benefits: Non-cash employee benefits. Unless specifically excluded by the Code, these benefits are included in gross income. Section 132 lists eight categories of fringe benefits which are non-taxable to the employee and deductible by the employer: (1) no additional cost service; (2) qualified employee discount; (3) working condition fringe benefits; (4)de minimis fringe benefits; (5) qualified transportation fringe; (6) qualified moving expense reimbursement; (7) qualified retirement planning services, or (8) qualified military base realignment and closure fringe. §§ 61(a)(1) and 132(a).

G

Gain: The amount realized in a disposition of property less the adjusted basis of the property disposed of.

Going Concern Value: The value that resides in the fact that a business entity does not end if its ownership is transferred.

Goodwill: An intangible asset held by a trade or business which encompasses such intangibles as consumer loyalty, reputation for quality, etc. The belief is that these intangibles may attach to the trade or business irrespective of the particular management or ownership. If goodwill (or going concern value) is purchased in connection with the acquisition of a trade or business, than amortization deductions may be taken under §197.

Gross Income: All accretions to wealth (over which the taxpayer has dominion (which are not excluded by specific Code sections, judicial determinations, or administrative rules) after deductions have been taken for either the costs of goods sold, or the basis of property which has been transferred. §61.

H

Haig-Simons Definition: An economist's definition of gross income for a period, consisting of changes in wealth plus consumption.

Head of Household: A term used to describe a taxpayer who is usually classified as unmarried (except for a surviving Spouse) and who cares for his or her dependent(s) within the home. §2(b).

Holding Period: The period during which a taxpayer owns property. A taxpayer's holding period begins with the day after acquisition and includes the day of disposal. Rev.Rul. 54-607, 1954-2 C.B. 177.

I

Imputed Income: The monetary value of goods and services produced and consumed within the immediate family unit. Also, the monetary value attached to the use of an immediate family member's property. Problems of administrative manageability usually preclude the inclusion of imputed income in gross income.

Indexing: The process by which certain items are annually adjusted for inflation by referring to the Consumer Price Index. Examples of currently indexed items include the quantity of taxable income effected by the fifteen percent tax rate and the size of the personal exemption.

Individual: A human being (sometimes also a trust or estate).

Installment Method of Accounting: A procedure for arriving at the taxable year in which gain from the sale of property must be reported where a minimum of one payment is to be made in the taxable year after the sale is completed. The installment method allows for the recognition of gain as payments are received, as opposed to when the sale is completed. §453.

Interest: Payments made from a borrower to a lender for the use of money. Interest is included in a lender's gross income and may be deductible by the borrower. §§ 61(a)(4) and 163.

Internal Revenue Code of 1986 (IRC): The codification of federal taxation statutes located at Title 26 of the United States Code, the last major revision being in 1986.

Itemized Deductions: Deductions, for individuals, other than those allowable for computing adjusted gross income and for personal exemptions under §151. Itemized deductions are only allowable to the extent that they collectively exceed two percent of adjusted gross income (two percent floor). §63(d).

J

Joint Return: A single tax return filed by husband and wife jointly. [§6013] The tax rates for joint returns appear in §1(a).

K

"Kiddie Tax:" The tax imposed under §1(g) on the unearned income of a child which is computed as if the income were taxed in the hands of the child's parent, rather than the child, if that results in a higher tax.

L

Legislative History: The body of materials which may be helpful in interpreting a statute that has become law. Legislative history is derived from many sources and can consist of reports of Congressional committees, committee hearing transcripts, and Congressional debates.

Legislative Process: Tax law development. The process usually begins with public hearings, which may lead to a bill's introduction before the House or Senate, and culminates in the President signing an act.

Legislative Regulations: Regulations that are issued pursuant to a broad grant of legislative authority to the Treasury. They are virtually unassailable.

Long-Term Capital Gain (or Loss): Gain or loss from the sale or exchange of a capital asset which has been held for a more than one year, or more than 12 months. §1222(3), (4).

Loss: An amount that reflects the degree by which the adjusted basis of property exceeds the amount realized in a sale or other disposition.

M

Married Taxpayer: A classification which attaches to a taxpayer who is either married at the close of his or her taxable year, or whose Spouse dies within the taxable year. §7703(a). Married persons may file joint or separate returns.

Material Participation: Regular, continuous, and substantial participation in an activity. [§469(h)] This test is relevant in determining whether a taxpayer is engaging in a passive activity, and as a consequence, whether the passive activity loss rules apply to that taxpayer. With the exception of rental activities, material participation in an activity renders that activity non-passive. Objective tests for distinguishing regular, continuous, and substantial participation are provided in the regulations.

Maturity Date: The date on which a debt obligation matures, in the sense that the issuer of the debt pays off the principal.

Miscellaneous Itemized Deductions: Deductions that are not included within the deductions allowable in the computation of gross income, personal exemptions, and the deductions outlined in §67 (b). The computation of taxable income may include the use of miscellaneous itemized deductions only if the taxpayer elects to itemize deductions under §63 (e), and then only to the extent that, when aggregated, they exceed two percent of adjusted gross income (two percent floor) [§67(a)] and are not reduced by §68, which provides a further cutback. Examples of miscellaneous itemized deductions include deductions for unreimbursed employee business expenses otherwise allowable under §162, and hobby deductions otherwise allowable under §212 (a).

N

Net Capital Gain: An amount that reflects the degree by which a taxpayer's net long-term capital gain for a taxable year exceeds his net short-term capital loss for that year. §1222(11).

Non-Recognition Provisions: Statutory provisions which provide that either all or part of gain (sometimes loss) realized from the disposition of property either may not be recognized or must not be recognized. Generally, non-recognition provisions postpone the recognition of gain or loss through the use of substituted basis rules. Generally, the holding period of the disposed property is 'tacked' to the new property.

O

Ordinary and Necessary Expense: An expense which results from either the operation of a trade or business, or the production of income. A necessary expense is appropriate and helpful, and an ordinary expense results from the normal course of regular conduct as reflected in the community. Expenses associated with prolonging a property's useful life by over a year or permanently adding to a property's value are said to be capital expenditures and are added to the property's basis. Reg. §1.162-4.

Ordinary Income: Gross income, including gain from the disposition of property except for long and short-term capital gain. §65.

Ordinary Loss: A loss that results from the disposition of property that is not a capital loss. §65.

Original Issue Discount: The excess of what a debt was issued for (say $900) and its face amount (say $1,000). The difference is gradually reported as interest income by the owner and the issuer generally gets a symmetrical deduction for interest expense. §§ 1272 and 163(e).

P

Passive Activity Losses and Credits: Losses and credits from passive activities. Usually, losses and tax credits that are attributable to passive activities may only be used to offset the income or income taxes that result from those activities. [§469] If these losses and credits are disallowed in one taxable year, they may be carried over to subsequent taxable years.

Penalty: A fine that punishes a failure to comply with the Code. Examples include the penalties for lack of timeliness in either the filing of a return or the payment of tax. §6651.

Personal Exemption: The amount that taxpayers may deduct for themselves (and possibly their spouses) in the computation of taxable income. The personal exemption was $2,000 in 1989 and has been indexed for inflation thereafter.

Progressive Rates: Usually, tax rates that increase as taxable income (the tax base) increases. They are also known as accelerated rates.

R

Realized Gain (or Loss): The gain or loss that results from the sale or disposition of property. If the amount realized exceeds the adjusted basis, then a realized gain results. If the adjusted basis exceeds the amount realized, then a realized loss results. Only recognized gains and losses are reported, but they are asubset of realized gains and losses.

Recapture: The imposition of current tax liability for a taxpayer's use of undue tax benefits in previous taxable years. Usually, recapture for improper deductions takes the form of an addition to the current year's ordinary income; and, recapture for improper tax credits is reflected in an increase in the taxpayer's current tax liability. In addition, when a taxpayer has claimed cost recovery and depreciation deductions that exceed the statutory limit, recapture can be achieved through the recharacterization of capital gains as ordinary income. §§ 71(f), 465(e), 1245(a) and 1250(a).

Recognized Gain (or Loss): A realized gain or loss that does not fall within a non-recognition provision. a recognized gain must be added to gross income; and, a recognized loss may be deductible. §1001(c).

Redeem: Buy back. For example, issues of debt often redeem the debt from holders at opportune moments.

Refund: The amount which a taxpayer is owed in the event of an overpayment of taxes.

Refundable Credit: A tax credit that can exceed tax liability for the year and thus result in a negative tax.

Return: The form that a taxpayer uses to report his or her financial information to the IRS. Unless it is reasonably complete, it is not viewed as having been filed.

Revenue Procedure (Rev. Proc.): An official published administrative statement of the IRS that covers a procedural issue under the Internal Revenue Code.

Revenue Ruling (Rev. Rul.): An official published interpretation of the tax law by the IRS. Usually, revenue rulings are the result of a taxpayer request. Revenue rulings are not a strong authority but they do bind the IRS until revoked.

S

Sale: A disposition of property for money.

Salvage Value: The value of property when its rental or depreciation period ends.

Short-Term Capital Gain (or Loss): A gain or loss that is realized from the sale or exchange of a capital asset that has been held for less than one year and a day. §1222(1), (2).

Single Taxpayer: See "unmarried taxpayer."

Sixteenth Amendment: A Constitutional Amendment which disposes with the requirement of Art. 1 §§ 2, 9 that income taxes be apportioned among the States according to population.

Standard Deduction: The basic standard deduction and the additional standard deduction added together [§63(c)(1)]. The basic standard deduction is dependent on the taxpayer's filing status, and ranges from $1,000 to

$12,200 [§63(c)(2)] plus inflation. A taxpayer who is claimed as a dependent may claim the basic standard deduction but is limited to the greater of $1,000 or earned income. The additional standard deduction may be taken by taxpayers who are blind or who are over sixty five and ranges from $1,200 to $1,500 [§63(f)]. The standard deduction may not be used if the taxpayer has chosen to itemize deductions.

Straight-Line Depreciation: The method by which an asset's cost is written off in equal annual depreciation deductions throughout the asset's useful life.

Substituted Basis: A determination of the basis of property which is made by reference to the basis or adjusted basis of property previously held by the taxpayer. [§1223(1).] Substituted basis can also refer to carryover basis, which defines cases where the basis of property held by a transferee is determined by reference to the basis of that property as it was when held by the transferor. In this scenario, §1223(2) provides for the 'tacking' of the transferor's holding period to the transferee's holding period. A typical use of carryover basis is in a simple gift transfer. §§ 1015, 1016(b).

Surviving Spouse: A taxpayer classification which is used to describe a single taxpayer who provides a home for his or her dependent(s), and whose spouse died within the past two taxable years. §2(a).

T

"Tack": Adding to a holding period of property by including the holding period of a different piece of property, or the same property when held by someone else. For example a donee of property adds ("tacks") the donor's holding period to his or her period of ownership. Section 1223 contains the holding period rules and is the usual source of authority for tacking holding periods.

Tax Accounting: The methods and accounting (timing) rules that are used in arriving at a taxpayer's tax liability.

Tax Credit: An amount that a taxpayer may subtract from the amount of tax liability that would otherwise be owed, in order to arrive at the payments or refunds that must be made.

Tax Rates: The percentage figure which when applied to a taxpayer's tax base (taxable income), will result in a figure that represents the taxpayer's tax liability before the subtraction of any tax credits.

Taxable Income: Taxable income for taxpayers who elect to itemize their deductions is gross income less the sum of all allowable deductions, including personal exemptions. [§ 63 (a)] For those who do not elect to itemize deductions, taxable income is adjusted gross income less the sum of the standard and personal exemption deductions. §63(b).

Taxable Year: The period over which the Federal Income Tax is imposed. A taxable year can be either a standard calendar year, or a twelve month fiscal year which ends on the last day of any month except December or a 52-53 week year. §441(b).

Taxpayer: A person to whom the Internal Revenue Tax applies, even though that person may not pay or be required to pay any tax. §7701(a)(14).

Transferred Basis: Basis in property that is determined in whole or in part by referring back to the basis of the transferor, donor, or grantor of the property.

Treasury Regulations (Regs.): Interpretive and procedural (legislative) regulations that are issued by the IRS with the approval of the Treasury Department, which, if valid, bind both the IRS and taxpayers. Procedural regulations are rarely questioned. However, interpretive regulations are sometimes rejected by the courts. Treasury regulations are located at Title 26 Code of Federal Regulations (C.F.R.).

U

Unmarried Taxpayer: A taxpayer classification used to describe a taxpayer who is both single at the close of the taxable year, and did not have a spouse die during the taxable year. The unmarried classification includes a taxpayer legally separated from his or her spouse by a decree of divorce or separate maintenance. The classification may include married taxpayers who are separated, and provide a home for their dependent children. [§7703] An unmarried taxpayer may not necessarily be classified as such, if they qualify for the surviving spouse or head of household classification.

CPSIA information can be obtained
at www.ICGtesting.com
Printed in the USA
BVHW062143210822
644982BV00002B/5

9 781600 425080